في ذكرى

مارك لينز

ROYAL ASIATIC SOCIETY BOOKS

The Royal Asiatic Society was founded in 1823 'for the investigation of subjects connected with, and for the encouragement of science, literature and the arts in relation to Asia'. Informed by these goals, the policy of the Society's Editorial Board is to make available in appropriate formats the results of original research in the humanities and social sciences having to do with Asia, defined in the broadest geographical and cultural sense and up to the present day.

www.royalasiaticsociety.org

IBRAHIM PASHA OF EGYPT FUND SERIES

The Royal Asiatic Society's Ibrahim Pasha of Egypt Fund, established in 2001 by Princess Fazilé Ibrahim, encourages the growth and development of Ottoman studies internationally by publishing Ottoman documents and manuscripts of historical importance from the classical period up to 1839, with transliteration, full or part translation and scholarly commentaries. The members of the Ibrahim Pasha of Egypt Fund Editorial Board are as follows: Princess Fazilé Ibrahim, Founder, Professor Francis Robinson, CBE, Royal Holloway, University of London (Chair), Dr Evrim Binbaş, Institute of Oriental and Asian Studies, University of Bonn, Professor Erdem Çıpa, University of Michigan, Professor Edhem Eldem, Boğaziçi University, Istanbul, Professor Emine Fetvacı, Boston University, Dr. Kate Fleet, University of Cambridge, Professor Mayte Green-Mercado, Rutgers University- Newark, Dr Colin Heywood, SOAS, University of London, Professor Marinos Sariyannis, Foundation for Research and Technology-Hellas.

Publications in the series include:

Michael Ursinus, *Grievance Administration (şikayet) in an Ottoman Province: The Kaymakam of Rumelia's 'Record Book of Complaints' of 1781–1783*, Routledge, 2005.

Hakan Karateke, *An Ottoman Protocol Register, Containing ceremonies from 1736 to 1808: BEO Sadaret Defterleri 350 in the Prime Ministry Ottoman State Archives, Istanbul*, The Ottoman Bank Archive and Research Centre, 2007.

Robert Dankoff, Nuran Tezcan and Michael Sheridan, *Ottoman Explorations of the Nile: Evliya Çelebi's 'Matchless Pearl These Reports of the Nile' map and his accounts of the Nile and the Horn of Africa in The Book of Travels*, Gingko, 2018.

The Early Ottoman Peloponnese

A study in the Light of an Annotated *editio princeps* of the TT10-1/14662 Ottoman Taxation Cadastre (ca. 1460-1463)

Georgios C. Liakopoulos

GINGKO

First published in 2019 by Gingko
4 Molasses Row
London SW11 3UX

A CIP catalogue record for this book is available from the British Library.

ISBN 978-1-909942-32-5
e-ISBN 978-1-909942-33-2

Typeset in Times New Roman by Adot Publishing Services
Printed in Spain

Published in collaboration with the Royal Asiatic Society as an Ibrahim Pasha of Egypt Fund title.

www.gingko.org.uk
@GingkoLibrary

In memoriam
Julian Chrysostomides

امدی اخوان صفانك شویله معلوم شریفلری اولسونکم آل عثمان دستنده
بویله بر آب و هواسی لطیف و محصوللی جزیره یوقدر

Let my noble and sincere brothers know now that there is no other
more fertile island of finer water and weather in the Ottoman dominion

Evliyā Çelebi

Contents

List of Tables	ix
List of Charts	xi
List of Maps	xiii
Acknowledgements	xv
Introduction	1
1 The Historical Geography of the Peloponnese	11
2 The Demography of the Peloponnese	211
3 The Administrative and Economic Structures of the Peloponnese	229
Conclusion	311
Index of Place Names	313
Principles of Edition	335
Appendix I Editio princeps of TT10	339
Appendix II Editio princeps of 1/14662	455
Bibliography and Abbreviations	507
General Index	537
Facsimiles	
Facsimile of TT10	575
Facsimile of 1/14662	625

List of Tables

Table 1	Pagination of TT10	6
Table 2	Identified and unidentified localities	12
Table 3	List of *mezraʿa*s	14
Table 4	Demographic statistics of the Peloponnese	221
Table 5	Distribution of settlements according to their size	222
Table 6	Distribution of population (families)	223
Table 7	Households-bachelors-widows	224
Table 8	Towns and their quarters	225
Table 9	Average tax paid by Greek and Albanian families (*aḳçe*s p.a.)	226
Table 10	List of timariots	230
Table 11	District of Ḳalavrita (Kalavryta)	250
Table 12	District of Mizis̱re (Mystras)	252
Table 13	District of Miḫlu (Mouhli)	253
Table 14	District of Bejenik (Vlaherna)	254
Table 15	District of Voştiça (Aigio)	255
Table 16	District of Ḫulumiç (Hlemoutsi)	259
Table 17	District of Vumero (Goumero)	262
Table 18	District of Kirvuḳor (Palaiokastro/Koufoplaiiko Kastro)	268
Table 19	District of Arḳadya (Kyparissia)	273

Table 20	District of Londar (Leontari)	274
Table 21	District of Ḳoris̱os (Korinthos)	279
Table 22	District of Balya Badra (Patra)	282
Table 23	District of Ḳalandriça (Halandritsa)	285
Table 24	District of Ṣandamiri (Santomeri)	287
Table 25	District of Girbene (Spartia)	289
Table 26	District of Ayo İlya (Agios Ilias)	294
Table 27	District of Ġardicḳo (Gatsiko)	297
Table 28	Province of Mora (the Peloponnese)	300
Table 29	Wheat and barley	309
Table 30	Tithes	310
Table 31	Viticulture yield (*ḫāṣṣa* vineyards)	310

List of Charts

Chart 1	Distribution of settlements according to their size	222
Chart 2	Distribution of population (families)	223
Chart 3	Households-bachelors-widows	224
Chart 4	Average tax paid by Greek and Albanian families	226
Chart 5	Economic distribution of *tīmār*s	233
Chart 6	District of Ḳalavrita (Kalavryta)	252
Chart 7	District of Mizis̱ra (Mystras)	252
Chart 8	District of Miẖlu (Mouhli)	253
Chart 9	District of Bejenik (Vlaherna)	254
Chart 10	District of Voştiça (Aigio)	258
Chart 11	District of Ḫulumiç (Hlemoutsi)	261
Chart 12	District of Vumero (Goumero)	267
Chart 13	District of Kirvuḳor (Palaiokastro/Koufoplaiiko Kastro)	272
Chart 14	District of Arḳadya (Kyparissia)	272
Chart 15	District of Londar (Leontari)	278
Chart 16	District of Ḳoris̱os (Korinthos)	281
Chart 17	District of Balya Badra (Patra)	284
Chart 18	District of Ḳalandriça (Halandritsa)	286

Chart 19	District of Ṣandamiri (Santomeri)	288
Chart 20	District of Girbene (Spartia)	293
Chart 21	District of Ayo İlya (Agios Ilias)	296
Chart 22	District of Ġardicḳo (Gatsiko)	299
Chart 23	Province of Mora (the Peloponnese)	308

List of Maps

Map 1	Ḳalavrita (Kalavryta), demographic distribution
Map 2	Ḳalavrita (Kalavryta), economic distribution
Map 3	Miziṣra (Mystras), demographic distribution
Map 4	Miziṣra (Mystras), economic distribution
Map 5	Miḫlu (Mouhli), demographic distribution
Map 6	Miḫlu (Mouhli), economic distribution
Map 7	Bejenik (Vlaherna), demographic distribution
Map 8	Bejenik (Vlaherna), economic distribution
Map 9	Voştiça (Aigio), demographic distribution
Map 10	Voştiça (Aigio), economic distribution
Map 11	Ḫulumiç (Hlemoutsi), demographic distribution
Map 12	Ḫulumiç (Hlemoutsi), economic distribution
Map 13	Vumero (Goumero), demographic distribution
Map 14	Vumero (Goumero), economic distribution
Map 15	Kirvuḳor (Palaiokastro), demographic distribution
Map 16	Kirvuḳor (Palaiokastro), economic distribution
Map 17	Arḳadya (Kyparissia), demographic distribution
Map 18	Arḳadya (Kyparissia), economic distribution

Map 19	Londar (Leontari), demographic distribution
Map 20	Londar (Leontari), economic distribution
Map 21	Ḳorisos (Korinthos), demographic distribution
Map 22	Ḳorisos (Korinthos), economic distribution
Map 23	Balya Badra (Patra), demographic distribution
Map 24	Balya Badra (Patra), economic distribution
Map 25	Ḳalandriça (Halandritsa), demographic distribution
Map 26	Ḳalandriça (Halandritsa), economic distribution
Map 27	Ṣandamiri (Santomeri), demographic distribution
Map 28	Ṣandamiri (Santomeri), economic distribution
Map 29	Girbene (Spartia), demographic distribution
Map 30	Girbene (Spartia), economic distribution
Map 31	Ayo İlya (Agios Ilias), demographic distribution
Map 32	Ayo İlya (Agios Ilias), economic distribution
Map 33	Ġardicḳo (Gatsiko), demographic distribution
Map 34	Ġardicḳo (Gatsiko), economic distribution
Map 35	Mora (The Peloponnese), ethnic composition
Map 36	Mora (The Peloponnese), demographic distribution
Map 37	Mora (The Peloponnese), economic distribution
Map 38	Mora (The Peloponnese), demographic/ethnic distribution

Acknowledgements

In writing this book I received much support and encouragement. My deepest gratitude goes to my teacher and supervisor, the late Julian Chrysostomides, for her guidance in the preparation of this study and her most generous help and encouragement. All these years she advised me not only as a true scholar but also as a caring spiritual mother. Her passing away on 18 October 2008 left us with a feeling of irreplaceable loss. Her scholarship, integrity and humanity will always remain a source of inspiration for me. This study is dedicated to her memory. I would also like to thank Dr Kate Fleet and Dr George Dedes for their constructive criticisms, corrections and advice. Particular thanks are due to Dr Charalambos Dendrinos, who read the entire manuscript and generously offered me his advice, expertise and unstinting support.

I would like to express my warmest thanks to Professor Francis Robinson, HH Princess Fazilé Ibrahim and Professor Edhem Eldem for putting their trust and faith in me, by including this study in the Ibrahim Pasha of Egypt series of the Royal Asiatic Society – Gingko Library Publications.

I gratefully acknowledge the financial support I received throughout my doctoral studies from the Bakala Foundation, the Department of History and the Hellenic Institute of Royal Holloway, University of London, the A.G. Leventis Foundation, and the Gibb Memorial Trust. The University of London Central Research Fund and the Royal Historical Society generously funded the research I conducted in the Prime Ministry Archives in Istanbul.

I am also pleased to acknowledge the help I received from the staff of the following libraries and archives where my research was carried out: Sts Cyril and Methodius National Library of Bulgaria (especially Professor Stoyanka Kenderova, Head of the Oriental Department) in Sofia, the Prime Ministry Archives and the İslâm Araştırmaları Merkezi, in Istanbul, the Society for Peloponnesian Studies, the History and the Folklore Libraries of the University of Athens, the Parnassos Literary Society, and the Blegen and Gennadius Libraries of the American School of Classical Studies at Athens, the Albanian State's Archive in Tirana, the British Library, the Founder's and Bedford Libraries of Royal Holloway, University of London, the Libraries of King's College London, School of Oriental and African Studies, School of Slavonic and East European Studies of University College London, Institute of Classical Studies, Warburg Institute, and the Royal Geographical Society in London.

Grateful thanks are due to Dr Maria Pigaki for her invaluable assistance in digital mapping techniques, Dr Dritan Egro, Bishop Astius of Bylisi (Asti Bakallbashi), and Mrs Amalia Rontou who checked the Albanian onomastics, Mr Stamatios Methenitis and Mr Georgios Gerou for suggesting bibliography on the Arvanites, Dr Petros Karatsareas for his notes on linguistics, Dr Maria Litina and Miss Snezhana Georgieva Stoyanova for their help on Bulgarian and Russian articles, and to Mr Uroš Milivojević for his help on Serbo-Croatian onomastics. I owe particular thanks to Professor Evangelia Balta, Dr Metin Berke, Mr Seyit Ali Kahraman, Dr Bora Keskiner, Professor Machiel Kiel, Professor Heath W. Lowry, Professor Oktay Özel, Dr Mohammad Shariat-Panahi, and Professor Fariba Zarinebaf-Shahr for deciphering some obscure words in the MSS. The responsibility for any mistakes is my own. Dr Alison Ohta and Dr Evrim Binbaş did an outstanding job proofreading and correcting the manuscript.

Over the years I have received valuable support and advice from scholars and colleagues, to whom I offer my deep thanks: Dr Angelos Afroudakis, Dr Antonios Anastasopoulos, Mr Vasilis Anastasopoulos, Professor Steven Bowman, Dr Antonios Chatzikyriakou, Dr Stella Chrysochoou, Mrs Hayia Cohen, Professor Nicolas de Lange, Dr Tuba Demirci, Dr Evangelia Eleftheriou, Colonel Panagiotis Farantatos, Professor Jonathan Harris, Professor Athena Kolia-Dermitzaki, Mr Panagiotis Kokkas, Mr Dimitrios Kollintzas, Professor Eleni Kondyli, Professor Barbara Koutava-Delivoria, Professor Pierre A. MacKay, Dr Theodoros G. Palioungas, Dr Foteini Perra, Dr Angeliki Papageorgiou, Professor Ioannis A. Pikoulas, Mr Christos Reppas, Mr Vasilios Siakotos, Dr Leonidas Souhleris, Professor Malcolm Wagstaff, and Dr Diana Gilliland Wright. A number of local Moreote people helped me in identifying abandoned settlements during my field research; to them I would like to offer my deep appreciation.

Among my friends I would like to warmly thank Mr Aristotle G. Sakellariou, Mrs Despoina Sarikou, Mrs Marianthi Smagadou, Miss Maria Zolota, Mr Muzaffer Malkoç, and Mr Cheng Wang for their understanding and unfailing help in taming this journey's *Chimaeras*.

Last but not least, there are no words to express my gratitude to my late father Constantine, my mother Demetra and my sisters Efstathia and Foteini, for their love, for being a constant source of support and for teaching me above all that *πάντων χρημάτων μέτρον ἄνθρωπος*.

Athens, July 2018

Introduction

This publication is a revised version of the doctoral thesis conducted under the supervision of the late Julian Chrysostomides at Royal Holloway, University of London. The study explores geographic, demographic and economic aspects of the Peloponnese in the first years of the Ottoman conquest (beginning 1460), on the basis of an annotated *editio princeps* of the first Ottoman taxation cadastre of the province of the Peloponnese (*Defter-i Livā᾿-ı Mora*), compiled some time between 1460 and 1463. The cadastre was split in the recent past into two parts: the first, TT10, is now preserved in the Prime Ministry Ottoman Archives in Istanbul, while the second part, 1/14662, is in the Sts Cyril and Methodius National Library of Bulgaria in Sofia.

The study comprises two Parts. The first Part contains an Introduction, three Chapters (1–3) and a Conclusion. The Introduction presents the aims, scope and methodology adopted, followed by a survey of previous scholarship conducted on the subject, and a brief historical examination of the late Byzantine Peloponnese and its conquest by the Ottomans. It concludes with a brief codicological and palaeographical description and dating of the cadastre TT10-1/14662.

Chapter 1 presents the Historical Geography of the Peloponnese, listing all the place names mentioned in the sequence they appear in the TT10-1/14662 register accompanied by topographic and linguistic notes. This is complemented by a set of 38 digital maps of the early Ottoman Peloponnese using GIS (Geographical Information Systems).

Chapter 2 discusses the Demography of the Peloponnese, including the settlement patterns, the density of population and its categorisation into urban/rural, sedentary/nomadic, concentrating in particular on the influx and settlement of the second largest ethnic group, after the Greeks, in the peninsula, namely the Albanians.

Chapter 3 explores the administrative and economic structures of the Peloponnese, concentrating on the Ottoman *tīmār* system and taxation. A detailed presentation of the level of agricultural production, types of crops, livestock, fishing, commerce, industrial development, etc. is illustrated with tables and charts.

The Conclusion summarises the findings of the research and attempts to identify areas for possible future investigation.

Part II comprises a diplomatic edition of the transcribed Ottoman text. The study closes with a full bibliography followed by facsimiles of the cadastre.

Half a century ago, Cvetkova was the first to draw attention to the 1/14662 cadastre in her article on the Christian timariots in the Balkans, although she erroneously identified the register with northern and central Greek regions.[1] This was followed by the more meticulous study by Assenova, Stojkov and Kacori. They examined linguistically the toponyms and athroponyms of this document in a paper given at the *XIe Congrès International des Sciences Onomastiques* (Sofia, 1974).[2] Three years later they provided a Bulgarian translation of the register (with a brief summary in French).[3] Their study includes a useful map of Albania giving place names common in Albania and the north-western Peloponnese.

The first scholar to maintain that the MSS TT10 and 1/14662 belong to the same taxation cadastre and complement each other was Alexandropoulos,[4] who dated the cadastre after 1459 and before the Ottoman–Venetian war of 1463, drawing attention to the importance of the cadastre despite its fragmentary nature as a unique source for the late Byzantine Peloponnese. His study is limited to the district of Arḳadya (Kyparissia) and is accompanied by a table of revenues per village, followed by a commentary on economic and fiscal matters with an attempt to identify toponyms. No edition of the text is included.

1 Cvetkova 1958, 188–193.
2 Assenova–Kacori–Stojkov 1974.
3 Assenova–Stojkov–Kacori 1977.
4 Alexandropoulos 1978.

In their seminal article, Beldiceanu and Beldiceanu-Steinherr presented a survey on the economy, society and demography of the fifteenth-century Peloponnese, based on primary Ottoman sources in Paris and Istanbul, including the TT10 cadastre.[5] In a second article, the Beldiceanus examined the economy and demography of Corinthia, mostly on the basis of the TT10 cadastre.[6] The study includes Greek and Albanian anthroponymy and a French translation of the section of TT10 concerning the Corinthian district (with a facsimile).

Subsequently, in his extensive study on the historical demography of the Peloponnese from the thirteenth to eighteenth centuries Panagiotopoulos explored the Venetian documents concerning the censuses the Venetian authorities undertook in the Peloponnese between 1685 and 1715, focusing on the analysis of the Grimani census.[7] Within the context of the *Pax Ottomana* of the sixteenth century, he analysed the 1/14662 register on the basis of the article by Assenova, Stojkov and Kacori,[8] without however using the TT10 counterpart. According to Panagiotopoulos, the Greek population inhabited the fortified towns or large villages mainly along the seashore, while the Albanian settlers resided in small unfortified villages in the hinterland.[9] This study broke fresh ground in the field by using the Venetian sources demographically, though without studying in depth the Ottoman material.

Another study, which attempted to establish a chronology and a scientific methodology for the examination of the transition of the Peloponnese from Byzantine to Ottoman rule tracing aspects of continuity, is the unpublished doctoral thesis by Kayapınar.[10] This work is primarily based on published Greek, Ottoman and Venetian sources. The first and second parts of the study are dedicated to the late Byzantine Peloponnese up to the Ottoman conquest (1204–1460). The third, and last, part is a survey of the Ottoman taxation census system (*taḥrīr*) in the Peloponnese with a brief presentation of the TT10-1/14662 taxation cadastre. The only data extracted from the register are the villages and their total revenues, which are presented in tables without further analysis. Some inconsistencies and errors have been noted in his identification of toponyms and calculation of taxes due to erroneous transcription of the Ottoman text and the misspelling of Greek names – with the result that the transliteration of the majority of the non-Turkish names into Turkish is inaccurate.[11] So far, this thesis remains unpublished with the exception of sections dealing with the demography of Leontari and Dimitsana, which have appeared in a Greek translation at the *1st Panarcadic Internet Conference* (2006).[12]

Among general studies on the evaluation and methodology to be adopted in research of the *taḥrīr defter*s, the article by Lowry deserves special mention, for it was the first to point out the limitations of the evidence derived from them. The enthusiasm with which the Ottomanists welcomed the *taḥrīr defter*s studies after the works of the father of *defterology*, Barkan, signalled the beginning of an extensive use of the cadastres more for quantitative analysis and less for qualitative analysis. The corpus of nearly 1,500 unpublished *taḥrīr defter*s in the Ottoman archives appealed to scholars as a most promising area of research, particularly as the 'Barkan-Braudelian School' emphasised the reliability of the figures recorded therein.[13] A pioneering work in this field was that of İnalcık in 1954, concerning the register of Albania, focusing on the edition and analysis of a single *defter*.[14] A key methodological question posed by Heywood is whether the *defter*s should be treated for editing purposes simply as documents or, more controversially, as texts.[15] In the course of time, it became clear that the data contained in the registers are not verifiable and indeed adequate; hence their previously celebrated quantitative study was criticised as unsatisfactory and insufficient. For the *taḥrīr defter*s simply deal with the timariots, namely the fief-holders, thus excluding from the list all other categories of subjects, and hence no overall complete perspective on toponymy, topography, agricultural production, taxation or population can be adduced. To provide a more accurate view it is necessary that *taḥrīr defter*s are used in conjunction with other contemporary records.[16]

5 Beldiceanu–Beldiceanu-Steinherr 1980.
6 Beldiceanu–Beldiceanu-Steinherr 1986.
7 Panagiotopoulos 1987, 225ff.
8 Assenova–Stojkov–Kacori 1977.
9 Panagiotopoulos 1987, 90–100. See Chapter 2, The Demography of the Peloponnese.
10 Kayapinar 1999.
11 E.g. Kayapinar 1999, 255: for *Piratno: 1214* read *Pratano: 1314*, for *Lugasin: 2272* read *Loġaṣeti: 2372*, for *Helidon: 21994* read *Hiliẓon: 20994*, for *Maji: 148* read *Maji: 78*; 256: for *Lali: 1465* read *Lali: 1461*; 263: for *Aya Yorgi: 31428* read *Aya Yorgi: 31427*, for *Lonkanik: 7220* read *Lonḳanik: 7720*; 272–273: for *Minhalu* read *Miḫlu*; 287: for *İskliva: 1106* read *İsliva: 1102*, etc.
12 Kayapinar 2005a and Kayapinar 2005b.
13 Lowry 1992, 4.
14 İnalcik 1954a.
15 Heywood 1988, 326.
16 Lowry 1992, 8–9, 12–14.

Concerning the debate on the reliability of the TT10-1/14662 cadastre, Alexander maintains that some of the tax amounts, according to his calculations on the tithe of wheat and barley, were mere estimates and did not correspond to the size of the actual crop raised, though he admits that the figures recorded were the total tax on wheat and barley, which had been paid by the Moreotes.[17] Beldiceanu and Beldiceanu-Steinherr, on the other hand, adhere to the economic reliability of this early register and consider that the figures correspond to the actual quantity and value of the crops.[18] In my view, this cadastre should be treated as a reasonably reliable source of the population and their activities whose taxes were accrued as *tīmār* revenue.

Compiled immediately after the Ottoman conquest, the TT10-1/14662 cadastre provides partial but unique information on settlements, including different ethnic groups that settled in the Peloponnese, as well as on demography, economy, trade, produce and revenues. A number of difficulties emerge when studying the cadastre, including the vague definition of size and value units of measurements, and the lack of any evidence that points to the application of a certain coefficient number for members per family. The fragmentary nature of the register resulted in geographical gaps when the settlements mentioned were mapped out. It should be stressed that the demographic study reveals general trends in population and does not calculate the number of people living in the Morea from the number of fiscal units recorded. Similarly, the treatment of the economic figures is at this stage only preliminary, as the main aim of the study is to offer an edition of the TT10-1/14662 taxation cadastre and present its data.

The fact that no similar Byzantine document of the period has survived makes the study of the Ottoman archival material imperative.[19] In the wake of the conquest of a new province it was necessary for the Ottoman government to conduct a survey in order to record the tax-paying population and their produce. In this sense the TT10-1/14662 taxation cadastre depicts the late Byzantine Peloponnese. Thus, this study also offers a unique insight on late Byzantine society and its economy, and how these were incorporated into the Ottoman Empire.

HISTORICAL BACKGROUND

In 1352 the Ottomans established themselves in Europe by conquering the castle of Tzympi in Thrace.[20] Henceforth, their advance in the Balkans was rapid. This was followed by the capture of Thessaloniki (April 1387), which formed a base for their incursions into the Peloponnese, often at the instigation of the local petty *archon*s. Their method of conquest followed two phases: after having extirpated the power of the local governors or rulers, the Ottomans brought the conquered lands under their direct central control by implementing the *tīmār* system, namely granting land in return for military service.[21] Independent warriors, who simply sought booty in an infidel land, were very often the protagonists of this first phase of the conquest.

In 1341–1342 the Peloponnese suffered frequent Turkish attacks conducted by Umūr Beg of Aydın (1334–1348).[22] The first Ottoman raids in the Morea seem to have taken place in 1387–1388 under the command of the warrior Ġāzī Evrenos Beg.[23] In 1387 Theodore I Palaeologus (1384–1407), despot at Mystras, called in Evrenos for help against the Navarrese Military Company, the rulers of the principality of Achaia. This Byzantino–Ottoman co-operation resulted after the capture of Thessaloniki (1387) and the submission of Theodore's brother and later Emperor Manuel II (1391–1425) to Murād I (1362–1389). This was to last until the accession of Bāyezīd I (1389–1402), when relations between the two deteriorated, culminating in the siege of Constantinople, which dragged on until 1402 and came to an end with the battle of Ankara and the death of Bāyezīd. During this period Evrenos gave his support first to the Navarrese and later, in 1395, to Carlo Tocco, duke of Cephalonia, against Theodore.[24] By then the Ottomans had become acquainted with the Peloponnesian politics and geography, a significant advantage for their future incursions;[25] for

17 Alexander 1999, 63.

18 Beldiceanu–Beldiceanu-Steinherr 1980, 24–37; Beldiceanu–Beldiceanu-Steinherr 1986, 39–40.

19 The Byzantine *praktika* and *kodikes* are the registers where the property of the landowners, both laymen and clergy, and the taxes levied upon them, are recorded. Beside the fiscal surveys held in the archives of the Athonite monasteries, the only surviving Byzantine taxation cadastre is the one pertaining to Thebes published by Svoronos: Svoronos 1959.

20 Aktepe 1950.

21 İnalcık 1954b, 103. On the *tīmār* system see Chapter 3, The Administrative and Economic Structures of the Peloponnese.

22 Zachariadou 1983, 42–43.

23 Schreiner 1975, I 244 (no. 33/14); Loenertz 1943, 155; revised in Loenertz 1970, 237.

24 Chrysostomides 1995, 325 (doc. 166).

25 There were eight subsequent Ottoman attacks in the Peloponnese in: 1395, 1397, 1423, 1431, 1446, 1453, 1458 and 1460: Zakythinos 1975, I 124.

the rivalry among the local *archons* and the government of the Despotate brought the Ottomans closer to their target. In 1397 Bāyezīd sent Evrenos Beg and Yaʿḳūb Paşa with 60,000 men to the Peloponnese. They demolished the Hexamilion wall and were then divided into two groups.[26] Yaʿḳūb Paşa captured Argos and deported, according to a Venetian document, up to 14,000 – 3,000, according to Chalcocondyles – of its inhabitants to Asia Minor.[27] The second group, led by Evrenos, plundered the lands of the Despotate as far as Modon and Coron and withdrew to Thessaly.[28] On 21 June the same year the troops of Theodore were defeated at Leontari.[29]

The Ottoman interregnum (1402–1413) allowed the Byzantines a breathing space. In 1407 Theodore I died and was succeeded in the Despotate of Mystras by his nephew Theodore II Palaeologus (1407–1443), first under his father Manuel II's guidance. In 1415 Manuel revisited the Morea and rebuilt the Hexamilion wall.[30] In 1422 the new Ottoman Sultan, Murād II (1421–1451), attacked Constantinople, in response to the release from captivity of Murād's brother and pretender to the succession Muṣṭafā and his ally Cüneyd by Manuel in 1421. In 1423 Turaḫan Beg marched against Hexamilion, which was once more destroyed, and pillaged Mystras, Leontari, Gardiki and Tavia.[31] Following his retreat, the Christian rulers of the Peloponnese failed to act in concert. Constantine Palaeologus, based in Hlemoutsi, Thomas in Kalavryta and Theodore in Mystras were constantly fighting against one another. In 1430 Thomas married Catherine, the daughter of the prince of Achaia, Centurione Zaccaria (1404–1432). Though this marriage alliance in essence proved ineffectual, nevertheless with the death of Centurione in 1432 the Frankish Principality of Achaia became part of the Byzantine possessions.[32] At the time the Despotate of Mystras was under the joint rule of Thomas and Constantine. In 1444 Constantine repaired the Hexamilion wall and attacked the Duchy of Athens, then under Ottoman protection.[33] Consequently, Murād II marched towards the Peloponnese in 1446 and after unsuccessful negotiations he invaded the peninsula. He destroyed the Hexamilion and took more than 60,000 hostages, forcing Constantine and Thomas to pay an annual tribute to the Sultan.[34] After John VIII Palaeologus's death in 1448, Constantine succeeded to the imperial throne thus leaving the rule of the province to his brothers, Thomas and Demetrius. Continuing their rivalry, Demetrius turned to the Ottomans and Thomas to the Latins, for help, since by then with the fall of Constantinople in 1453 the Byzantine Empire had ceased to exist. In that year ʿÖmer Beg, son of Turaḫan Beg, was sent to quash the Albanian rebellion in the Peloponnese. In 1454, after his successful campaign, the revolutionaries recognised the authority of the Byzantine Despots, who agreed to pay the Sultan 12,000 golden coins annually.

Three years later, Meḥmed II (1444–1446, 1451–1481), having not yet received the annual tribute from the Peloponnese, decided to lead his troops to southern Greece in person. On 15 May 1458 he camped outside Corinth.[35] The town surrendered four months later under Matthew Asan.[36] According to the treaty, the Corinthians secured their property; the conquered lands (a triangle in the northern Peloponnese, roughly one third of it) passed to the Ottoman Empire; and the remaining castles were left to the possession of Thomas and Demetrius, who were each to pay 3,000 golden coins annually. In return, the Sultan undertook to assist the Despots in the event of any external attack.[37] In the same year (1458) Meḥmed II established the *sancaḳ* of the Morea and appointed ʿÖmer Beg as its first *sancaḳbegi*.[38] In the following year Thomas, despite his undertaking to the Sultan, did not keep his word and formed a common front with Peloponnesian lords and the Albanians, primarily against Demetrius but also against the Ottomans. Matthew Asan and Zaġanos Paşa joined Demetrius. Meḥmed II decided to lead the final campaign against the Despots in

26 The Hexamilion wall took its name from the length of the Isthmus, which was six miles. It was 24 *stadia* long, and was enforced by one castle on each side and one in the middle. It had 153 fortified towers in total and a deep moat. In Turkish sources it is called Germeḥiṣār: Bees, *Mora*, 419.

27 Chrysostomides 1995, 392 (doc. 197); Chalcocondyles 1922, I $92_{13\text{-}14}$.

28 Palaeologus 1985, $157_{14\text{-}19}$. The Ottoman anonymous chronicles, ʿĀşıḳpaşazāde and Oruc mentioned this incursion without giving either the exact date or the name of the military leaders: Anonymous–Giese 1922, I 28_{29}; Anonymous–İKK, 42_{16}; Anonymous–BNF, 42_{13}; Anonymous–Öztürk 2000, $19a_{19}$, 35; ʿĀşıḳpaşazāde 1929, 62_{14}; ʿĀşıḳpaşazāde 1913, 62; Oruc 1925, 98_{21}.

29 Zakythinos 1975, I 157.

30 Zakythinos 1975, I 166–168.

31 Schreiner 1975, I 235 (no. 32/37), 249 (nos 33/34, 33/35), 292 (no. 36/15) and 555 (no. 72/5). In Tavia/Davia Turaḫan Beg slaughtered 800 resisting Albanians: Chalcocondyles 1923, II 16_{21}-17_{7}.

32 Zakythinos 1975, I 209.

33 Schreiner 1975, I 251 (no. 33/49).

34 Ducas 1834, $223_{10\text{-}14}$; ʿĀşıḳpaşazāde 1929, 115_{16}–117_{15}.

35 Sphrantzes 1990, $148_{17\text{-}23}$.

36 Chalcocondyles 1923, II 209_{22}–211_{2}.

37 Uzunçarşılı 1949, II 23–24.

38 Sphrantzes 1990, $150_{19\text{-}22}$.

1460.[39] On 30 May of that year Demetrius surrendered Mystras to the Ottomans[40] and under the protection of the Sultan he moved to Ainos (Enez) in Thrace, receiving an annual sum of 700,000 *aḳçes* (Ottoman silver coin) from the mint of Adrianople and the revenues of Ainos and the islands of Imbros, Lemnos, Thasos and Samothrace.[41] In the meantime, his brother, Thomas, sought asylum in Rome.[42]

With the exception of the Venetian colonies of Modon, Coron, Argos and Nauplion, the Peloponnese became an integral part of the Ottoman Empire. In less than a century the Ottomans completed the conquest with Argos being captured in 1463,[43] Modon and Coron in 1500, and Nauplion and Monemvasia in 1540.

CODICOLOGICAL DESCRIPTION OF THE TT10 AND THE 1/14662

Among the *taḥrīr defter*s of the Peloponnese (either solely of this province or contained in broader surveys of the Balkans) preserved in the Prime Ministry Ottoman Archives of Istanbul, the earliest extant one is the Tapu Tahrir Defteri no. 10 (hereafter TT10). According to the handwritten Turkish note on its front flyleaf verso, the register was repaginated on 9 January 1990; the underlined Arabic numerals refer to the new pagination. I consulted the microfilm obtained by Julian Chrysostomides in the late 1970s, which is more readable than the scanned copy I acquired in a CD ROM (TIF format) in 2005. Thus, I follow the pre-1990 pagination of the manuscript; the new and old sequence is provided in Table 1. Complying with the conservation regulations of the Prime Ministry Archives, I have been unable to examine the original document *in situ* and, hence, I was compelled to rely partially on the following codicological description by other scholars.

This mutilated register numbers 188 pages, five of which are blank: pp. 27, 41, 75, 103 and 177. It measures, according to the Beldiceanus 37x14.5cm,[44] according to Kayapınar, 36x13.5cm,[45] and according to the Prime Ministry Archives, 37x14cm. It is bound with black thick carton decorated with oval-shaped floral patterns. High levels of humidity have caused the ink to bleed on some pages, with the result that some characters are unreadable.[46] In other cases, ink traces from one page appear to have migrated to the opposite one, causing difficulties in the decipherment.

The second part of the MS, Цг. Дефтерхане Фонд 1/Арх. Ед. 14662 (hereafter 1/14662) is kept in the Oriental Collections Department of the Sts Cyril and Methodius National Library of Bulgaria in Sofia. It was acquired by the Bulgarian authorities together with several other Ottoman documents by chance, when in the early 1930s the nascent Turkish Republic ordered the old state archives of the Ministry of Finance, Istanbul Treasury Office (*Maliye Vekâleti*, *İstanbul Evrak Hazinesi*) to dispose of documents not considered valuable. Two paper factories in Knjaževo and Kostenec purchased at the price of 3 *kuruş*es and 12 *para*s per *okka* more than 34 tons of these as wastepaper for recycling and brought them to Bulgaria. On 13 May 1931, the columnist İbrahim Hakkı (Koyalı) revealed in the *Son Posta* newspaper the loading of the material at the Sirkeci railway station.[47] Turkish intellectual Muallim Cevdet (İnançalp) was moved and sent repeated telegrams and reports to Prime Minister İsmet İnönü, which eventually resulted in halting the sale of the manuscripts as scrap paper.[48] Following the publicity attracted by the issue, the consul general of Bulgaria in Istanbul informed the Bulgarian authorities of this transaction, noting that the archival material might contain important documents. The Bulgarian government bought the greatest part of the paper from the two factories; unfortunately, five tons of it had already been destroyed. The Ottoman documents were then deposited in the Oriental Department of the National Library of Bulgaria (est. 1878).[49]

---

39 Meḥmed's first decision was to send Uzun Ḥasan, leader of Aḳḳoyunlu, but he changed his mind; he took command of the campaign and let Uzun Ḥasan plunder the area: Uzunçarşılı 1949, II 25.

40 The itinerary that Meḥmed followed was: Corinth, Argos, Mystras, Kastritsi, Gardiki, Leontari, Pylos, Hlemoutsi, Santameri, Salmeniko: Vakalopoulos 1974, I 345–348. This campaign is presented in detail by Chalcocondyles and Critobulus: Chalcocondyles 1923, II 227_4–237_2; Critobulus 1983, 142_{16}–150_{28}; ʿĀşıḳpaşazāde 1929, 141–144. See also Kordosis 1984.

41 Critobulus 1983, $150_{1\text{-}24}$.

42 Setton 1978, II 228.

43 In 1463 the inhabitants of Argos agreed to surrender their city to the besieging Ottoman troops of Meḥmed II and were deported to Istanbul: Critobulus 1983, $183_{12\text{-}23}$. The sources remain silent on the status of the city until 1479, when the Ottoman–Venetian treaty ratified Ottoman rule: Panagiotopoulos 1987, 108–109; IEE 1974, X 274–275.

44 Beldiceanu–Beldiceanu-Steinherr 1980, 19.

45 Kayapinar 1999, 231.

46 Kayapinar 1999, 232.

47 Altay 2017, 35.

48 Aktaş–Kahraman 1994, 3–13.

49 Parveva 2001, 1–2; Wittek 1938, 692–693.

Table 1. *Pagination of TT10.*

new	**old**	50	86	98	134	146	182
1	39	51	87	99	135	147	183
2	40	52	88	100	136	148	184
3	41	53	89	101	137	149	185
4	42	54	90	102	138	150	186
5	43	55	91	103	139	151	187
6	44	56	92	104	140	152	188
7	45	57	93	105	141	153	-
8	46	58	94	106	142	154	38
9	47	59	95	107	143	155	1
10	48	60	96	108	144	156	2
11	49	61	97	109	145	157	3
12	50	62	98	110	146	158	4
13	51	63	99	111	147	159	5
14	52	64	100	112	148	160	6
15	53	65	101	113	149	161	7
16	54	66	102	114	150	162	8
17	55	67	103	115	151	163	9
18	56	68	104	116	152	164	10
19	57	69	105	117	153	165	11
20	58	70	106	118	154	166	12
21	59	71	107	119	155	167	13
22	60	72	108	120	156	168	14
23	61	73	109	121	157	169	15
24	62	74	110	122	158	170	16
25	63	75	111	123	159	171	17
26	64	76	112	124	160	172	18
27	65	77	113	125	161	173	19
28	66	78	114	126	162	174	20
29	69	79	115	127	163	175	21
30	70	80	116	128	164	176	22
31	67	81	117	129	165	177	23
32	68	82	118	130	166	178	24
33	71	83	119	131	167	179	25
34	72	84	120	132	168	180	26
35	73	85	121	133	169	181	27
36	74	86	122	134	170	182	28
37	75	87	123	135	171	183	29
40	76	88	124	136	172	184	30
41	77	89	125	137	173	185	31
42	78	90	126	138	174	186	32
43	79	91	127	139	175	187	33
44	80	92	128	140	176	188	34
45	81	93	129	141	177	189	35
46	82	94	130	142	178	190	36
47	83	95	131	143	179	191	37
48	84	96	132	144	180		
49	85	97	133	145	181		

The 1/14662 numbers 96 pages, nine of which are blank: pp. 1, 2, 3, 12, 13, 20, 65, 82 and 83. The register's incipit and desinit are mutilated. Page 40 has been numbered twice as 40/42. It measures 35x14cm. The paper of many of the pages is totally or partially yellowed and the ink in places has faded. This, however, did not affect its readability.[50] Dr Stoyanka Kenderova, director of the Oriental Collections Department in Sofia, kindly provided me with a microfilm copy of this MS. In this case too I have not been able to examine the original.

The text in both the TT10 and the 1/14662 is written in the *tevḳīʿ* script, while, when the numbers are written down in letters, preference has been given to the encoded *siyāḳat* script.[51] The use of the *tevḳīʿ* script was customary in the fifteenth-century Ottoman cadastres. It belongs to the *s̱ülüs̱* family of scripts and its letter strokes are narrower than the *s̱ülüs̱* and *riḳʿa* and wider than the *nesiḫ* one. This is the first element that dates the manuscript to the fifteenth century. A second one is the figures used in both manuscripts for numbers zero and five:

Arabic	Indian	manuscript
0	٠	
5	٥	

These figures occur also in the cadastres of Albania[52] and Trikala,[53] dated in 1431 and 1454/5 respectively, and on early Ottoman coins.[54] The watermark on the paper depicts a pair of scissors measuring 7x3cm, identified by Kayapınar as denoting Florentine (1459–1460) or Neapolitan (1457) provenance.[55]

As mentioned, above the first scholar to note that the two MSS belonged to the same document was Alexandropoulos in 1977,[56] supported by the Beldiceanus in 1986.[57] The striking similarity of the script, the same orthography, the dimensions of the folios, the watermark and, above all, the fact that the contents in both sections do not overlap constitute incontestable evidence that both parts belonged to the original document before it was split into two.[58] Moreover, Kayapınar pointed out that Nikifor Ḳavasila, a Christian timariot who, according to the 1/14662,[59] had been granted the revenues of Aya Baraskevi village (today's Agia Paraskevi uninhabited location in the NW of Asfalakto, Elis), should be identical with TT10's Nikifor Ḳavasila,[60] after whom a quarter in Ḫulumiç (Hlemoutsi) was named.[61]

DATE OF THE *DEFTER*'S COMPILATION

The missing first page of the TT10 must have given, as was the convention, the compilation date and the scribe's name. The register records that the governor of the Peloponnese (*mīrlivāʾ-ı vilāyet-i Mora*) at the time was Sinān Beg bin Elvān Beg,[62] who, according to Ottoman chronicles, held this post between 1460 and 1463. The document, therefore, should be attributed with a high degree of certainty to those years. As stated

50 Assenova–Stojkov–Kacori 1977, 213.
51 TT10, 26, 45, 52, 63, 69, 73–74, 76, 79, 130, 132, 160, 166, 168, 182; 1/14662, 84, 97. On the *tevḳīʿ* script see Yazır 1974, 120–122. On the *siyāḳat* script see Öztürk 1996.
52 İnalcık 1954a, xii-xiii.
53 Delilbaşı –Arikan 2001, *passim.*
54 Eldem 1916, I ج.
55 Kayapınar 1999, 232–233; Briquet 1968, I 237, III no. 3685.
56 Alexandropoulos 1978, 398–399.
57 Beldiceanu–Beldiceanu-Steinherr 1986, 37.
58 Kayapınar 1999, 232–234.
59 1/14662, 49.
60 TT10, 76.
61 Kayapınar 1999, 234.
62 TT10, 76.

above, the first governor of the Morea was ʿÖmer Beg, who probably ruled until the revolt of 1459, when, according to Chalcocondyles, he joined the rebellion of Thomas Palaeologus; as a result he was removed from the governorship of Thessaly by Meḥmed II.[63] He was succeeded by Zaġanoz Beg, the *hyparch* of Gallipoli, who held the governorship of Thessaly and the Peloponnese.[64] However, being cruel towards the populace of Santameri and having failed to protect their persons and property, despite the agreement he had entered upon when the Santameriotes surrendered their town, he too was removed from his post by Meḥmed.[65] The new governor of the Morea, Ḥamza Beg, held this post for a very brief period.[66] Acting as greedily as Zaġanos and against Islamic law, which protects those who surrender, Ḥamza Beg arrested the inhabitants of Santameri who were fleeing to the Venetians. On receiving the Santameriotes' letters of complaint, Meḥmed reappointed Zaġanos to the provincial administration.[67] Indeed, our document confirms that Zaġanos Beg preceded Sinān Beg in the governorship of the Peloponnese, since he is mentioned as the former *mīrlivāʾ-ı vilāyet-i Mora.*[68] This raises important administrative questions, of whether Zaġanos was once more replaced in his old post either as a result of his being found not guilty or whether in fact lack of individuals with the adequate qualities necessitated his replacement. No answer can be given at this stage before further research. The Ottoman chronographer ʿĀşıḳpaşazāde, when giving a detailed account of the Ottoman campaign in Corinthia in AH 864 (AD 1460), refers to Elvān Beg-oġlı Sinān Beg as the *sancaḳbegi* of the Peloponnese:

> Maḥmūd Paşa proceeded in the vicinity of Hexamilion; at that time Elvān Beg-oġlı Sinān Beg was the governor of the *sancaḳ* of the Peloponnese.[69]

Narrating the same events, subsequent writers, including Neşrī (his work was probably completed between 1487 and 1493),[70] İbn Kemāl (the first eight volumes of his work were completed in 1510–1511),[71] and Ḥadīdī (his verse-chronicle was completed in 1523–1524),[72] follow or agree with ʿĀşıḳpaşazāde. Ṭursun Beg confirms, in his history, that Sinān Beg still held the post in 1463 during the Ottoman–Venetian war,[73] and İbn Kemāl gives a detailed account of the governor's deeds against the Venetians in Corinth.[74] However, when describing the same events, Critobulus erroneously mentions ʿÖmer Beg (Ἀμάρης) son of Turaḫan, as the governor of the Peloponnese – information adopted by Uzunçarşılı.[75] About the ancestors of Sinān, İbn Kemāl, following the Ottoman anonymous chronicles, sheds light on the life of Sinān's father, Elvān Beg, who was the chief butler (*çāşnīgīrbaşı*) of Sultan Meḥmed I (1413–1421), dedicated to the war against the infidels.[76]

63 Chalcocondyles 1923, II 214$_{7\text{-}17}$.

64 Chalcocondyles 1923, II 226$_{6\text{-}10,\ 14\text{-}15}$: 'ξυνηνέχθη δὲ καὶ μετὰ Ὀμάρεω τοῦ Θετταλίας ὑπάρχου, στασιάσαντος διὰ διαφοράν, ἀφικόμενον ἀναβῆναί τε παρὰ βασιλέα, καὶ οὐ πολλὰς ὕστερον ἡμέρας Ὀμάρην βασιλέα ἀφελόμενον τὴν ἀρχὴν ἐπιτρέψαι Ζαγάνῳ τῷ τότε Καλλιουπόλεως ὑπάρχῳ. (...) οὗτος μὲν οὖν ὡς παρέλαβε τὴν Θετταλίαν καὶ Πελοπόννησον ὑπὸ βασιλέως, εἰσέβαλεν ἐς τὴν Ἀχαΐαν...'

65 Chalcocondyles 1923, II 232$_{4\text{-}17}$.

66 Chalcocondyles 1923, II 235$_{14\text{-}19}$.

67 Chalcocondyles 1923, II 235$_{20}$–236$_{8}$.

68 Zaġanos Beg – recorded as Zaġanoz Beg in the document – possessed one rice mill in Vumero (Goumero) and two watermills in Londar (Leontari): TT10, 86, 139.

69 ʿĀşıḳpaşazāde 1929, 144$_{1\text{-}3}$: 'Maḥmūd daḫi bu ṭarafda yüridi Germe ḥiṣārına yaḳın vardı, ol zamānda Mora'nıñ sancaġı begi Elvān Beg-oġlı Sinān Begdi'; ʿĀşıḳpaşazāde 1913, 151–152: 'Maḥmūd Paşa yüridi Germe ḥiṣārına yaḳın vardı, ol zamānda Mora'nıñ sancaġı begi Elvān Beg-oġlı Sinān Beg idi.'

70 Neşrī 1995, II 734-735: 'Maḥmūd Paşa daḫi Germe ḥiṣārına yaḳın varıcaḳ ol zamānda Mora sancaġı begi Elvān Beg-oġlı Sinān Begidi.' Neşrī was to a large extent based on the chronicle of ʿĀşıḳpaşazāde: Ménage 1964, 7–8; Kalicin 1983, 65–66.

71 İbn Kemāl 1954–7, I 166$_{15}$, II 162: 'Elvān Beg-oġlı Sinān Beg'iñ ki Mora sancaġı aña vėrilmişdi.'

72 Ḥadīdī 1991, 248$_{3548}$: 'Sinân Beg Mora'da Körfüz içinde // Mora sancağı begiyidi o hînde.'

73 Ṭursun Beg 1977, 131, Ṭursun Beg 1978, 113b$_{1\text{-}2}$: 'Elvān Beg-oġlı Sinān Beg ki sancaġ-ı Mora anuñ taḫt-ı yedinde idi.' Müneccimbaşı dates the campaign of Maḥmūd Paşa against the Venetians at Hexamilion to spring AH 869 (AD 1465): Müneccimbaşı 1995, 269.

74 İbn Kemāl 1954–7, I 256$_{2}$–258$_{9}$, II 245–247. He even composed a verse (*naẓm*) praising Sinān's heroism: ibid., I 258$_{8\text{-}9}$, II 247:
'Eline alan ḫūn-ı şimşīrdi öñünce sinān çāşnīgīrdi
Yiyen ḫancer-i künd-i nā-peykeri ṭoyub ḫūna göñli gözi sīrdi.'
The first encounter of this war took place in the outskirts of Corinth on 6 Ṣafer 868 (20 October 1463): Danişmend 1947, I 303.

75 Critobulus 1983, 177$_{25}$; Uzunçarşılı 1949, II 25–27.

76 In a marginalia note İbn Kemāl added the following piece of information: İbn Kemāl 1954-7, I 258, II 247: 'meẕkūr Sinān Beg ki atası, sulṭān Meḥmed bin Bāyezīd Ḫān'a çāşnīgīrbaşıydı, iş görmiş baş geçürmiş kişiydi, ġāzīlerüñ āb-rūyı şuyı ve ḫūn-ı ġazā işiydi'; Anonymous–Giese 1922, I 55$_{20,\ 23}$. For an overview of the information on Sinān Beg obtained from the Ottoman chronicles see Kayapinar 1999, 237–239. The 'Elvan Bey' entry in Meḥmed S̱üreyyā's prosopographic lexicon is rather short, merely stating his position: Meḥmed S̱üreyyā 1996, II 447.

In the course of the sixteen-year Ottoman–Venetian war, launched in 1463, a number of Peloponnesian castles changed hands. According to Stefano Magno's enumeration, published by Hopf,[77] the following castles, which are mentioned in our register, were occupied by the Venetians in 1463:

Stefano Magno	**TT10-1/14662**	**Modern Greek**
Arulia	Arula (1/14662, 28)	Arla
Astrizi	Astriçi (TT10, 21)	Astros
Astro	Astro (TT10, 21)	Agios Ioannis/Kastro Orias
Avolanizza	Añloniça (1/14662, 40/42)	Epitalio
Belveder	Pondiḳo (1/14662, 97)	Katakolo
Bocenico	Bejenik (TT10, 28)	Vlaherna
Calaurata vel Calavita	Ḳalavrita (TT10, 1, 38)	Kalavryta
Calendrizzo	Ḳalandriça (1/14662, 4)	Halandritsa
Camenizza vel Camomenizza	Ḳamaniça (TT10, 181)	Kamenitsa
Camero Castro vel Cumero Castro	Ḳurnaroḳastro (TT10, 186)	Pournarokastro
Chilidoni vel Clidoni	Hilizon (TT10, 92)	Helidoni
Dimizana vel Dimiza	Ẕimiçana (TT10, 157)	Dimitsana
Elena vel Alona	Olana (1/14662, 94)	Oleni
Focena vel Phonea	Fostana (1/14662, 30)	Fostaina
Francavilla	Franḳa Vila (1/14662, 62)	Frangavilas Monastery
Gardisco vel Cradici	Ġardicḳo, (1/14662, 66)	Gatsiko
Graveno vel Guevano	Girbene (1/14662, 21)	Spartia
Gribani vel Grebani	Ġırebini (TT10, 131)	Kato Melpeia
Gurenes	Ġurenas (TT10, 145)	Agoriani
Lastrana vel Listrenu	Listirna (TT10, 50)	Listraina/Listrena/Listrina
Lendari	Londar (TT10, 137)	Leontari
Longonico	Lonḳanik (TT10, 144)	Longanikos
Mondrusa vel Mondrizza	Mundriza (TT10, 125)	Gryllos
Montepoli	Mitepoli (1/14662, 35)	Mitopoli
Paleo Castro vel Paolo Castro	Pavloḳastro (TT10, 179)	Pavlokastro
Porsos vel Pertes	Porta (1/14662, 15)	Portes
Ruolio vel Ruolo	İryolo (1/14662, 60)	Riolos
S. Zorzi de Scorta	Aya Yorgi (TT10, 140)	Lykosoura
Santameri vel Santomari	Ṣandamiri (1/14662, 14)	Santomeri
Seravali	Ṣaravali (TT10, 39)	Saravali
Sidero Castro	Siẕereḳastro (TT10, 178)	Sidirokastro
Stamero vel Stamiro	İstamiro (1/14662, 75)	Hatzi
Tripotama vel Trisetenia	Trestena (TT10, 123)	Melissopetra
Vasilica sivè Valica	Vaşılıḳa (TT10, 167)	Sikyona
Vostizza vel Vistizza	Voştiça (TT10, 42)	Aigio
Vumeri	Vumero (TT10, 82)	Goumero
Vunengo vel Vunango	Vunarġo (1/14662, 59)	Vounargo
Zoia	Coya (1/14662, 91)	Prasino

77 Hopf 1873, 202.

According to the evidence contained in the TT10-1/14662, the Ottomans levied taxes on the inhabitants of these areas assigned as *tīmār*s by autumn 1463, which constitutes the *terminus ante quem* for the compilation of the cadastre. In addition, the cadastre gives glimpses of the peaceful relations between the Ottomans and the Venetians which existed prior to the outbreak of hostilities (1463).[78] Of these, the first is the case of *mezraʿa* Plaşa, then in 'Frankish' (= Venetian) hands, which was given to the villagers of Raḫova for cultivation, on account of their poverty;[79] and the second case, the revenue of the fishery at Ẕiġanato, was farmed jointly ¼ by the governor of the Morea and ¾ by Venice.[80] If future archaeological evidence corroborates our proposed identification of the latter with the mediaeval settlement on the north-eastern Venetiko/Tigani Island, this will be a significant case of Turco–Venetian dialogue and agreement on the exploitation of an area in the immediate vicinity of Venetian Coron.[81]

On the basis of Sinān's dated governorship in the Morea and the conquest of the above-mentioned castles by the Venetians in 1463, it is clear that the TT10-1/14662 cadastre recorded the data of a survey taken sometime between 1460 and 1463, without being able to ascertain an exact date of its compilation.

78 One of Venice's most important goals, throughout her history, was to trade peacefully: 'far la marchadantia pacifichamente', as Venetian diarist Antonio, son of Marco Morosini, noted, Nanetti 2011, 13.
79 TT10, 26.
80 TT10, 130.
81 See Chapter 1, The Historical Geography of the Peloponnese, 126, no. 367. For the boundaries of the Venetian colonies Modon and Coron see Bon 1967; Thiriet 1976–78.

1

The Historical Geography of the Peloponnese

The TT10-1/14662 taxation cadastre offers, in terms of historical geography – among other things – a unique cross-section of the late mediaeval Peloponnese, as it was compiled immediately after the Ottoman conquest. The 667 place names listed in the document not only furnish the historian with a tool for an in-depth examination of this region's toponymy, but also provide him/her with a solid basis for the social and economic reconstruction of the fifteenth-century Peloponnese, though partial, because of the nature of the documentation, namely the *taḥrīr defter*s.[1] For, though the register was compiled for the years 1460–1463, it casts light on the pre-Ottoman, namely the Byzantine, period, thus providing evidence for elements of continuity and change.

So far, the reading of place names in the TT10-1/14662 taxation cadastre and their localisation have been the most difficult part of the work. The anonymous scribe of the register seems to have attempted to render as closely as possible the late mediaeval pronunciation of the place names and the anthroponyms.[2] For the most part he used the diacritical dots in the text and, in some cases, even the *ḥarakāt* (signs used to represent short vowel sounds). However, the fact that he had to adjust the Ottoman alphabet to the phonetic rules of Greek, Albanian, Slavic, Italian and Frankish causes some uncertainties in our transcription.[3] The use by the scribe of the following Arabic letters to denote dental phonemes in Greek and Albanian, which do not exist in Turkish, is a sign of his literacy:

Arabic	Greek	Albanian	Phonetic Alphabet	Ottoman Transcription
ذ	δ	dh	/ð/	ẕ
ث	θ	th	/θ/	s̱

In the case of an initial consonant cluster, something that Turkish and Arabic phonetics do not permit, an i /i /, ı /ɯ / or u /u/ is added, e.g. اشپاته (İşpata < shpatë)[4], اولاخو (İvlaẖo< Βλάχος)[5], اصقوری (Işḳuri < Σκουρής)[6], اوستروزه (Ustruza<Στρούζα).[7] The same holds true when a Greek word starting with letter ξ /ks/ or ψ /ps/ appears, e.g. اكسانيه [İksanya < Ξένια (=Ξένιες)],[8] اپساری (İpsari < Ψάρι).[9]

1 For an evaluation of the land registers as sources for place onomastics see in general İnalcik 1956. For the problem of the partial evidence of the Ottoman cadastres see Lowry 1992, 8–9.
2 It should be noted that throughout the manuscript he recorded the family names that in Standard Modern Greek typically end in *-(ó)πουλος* opting for the spelling پلو(س)- [-plo(s)], hence providing an early attestation of the well-known deletion of unstressed /u/ that still characterises the Peloponnesian dialects of Greek. For the phenomenon of unstressed vowel deletion in Peloponnesian see Pantelidis 2001a, 553–554; Pantelidis 2001b. Respective entries of family names in the MM10 taxation cadastre of Trikala, Thessaly 1454/5, are given with the spelling پولو(س)- [-pulo(s)]: Delilbaşi–Arikan 2001, II *passim*.
3 For the adoption of Byzantine place names in Turkish language see Wittek 1935.
4 TT10, 97.
5 1/14662, 71.
6 TT10, 56.
7 TT10, 157.
8 1/14662, 18.
9 1/14662, 46.

The register records the districts (*nāḥiyyet-i x*) (*x* standing for the toponym), the local centres (*nefs-i x*), the villages (*ḳarye-i x*) and the arable or cultivated lands with no settlements on them (*mezraʿa-ı x*). Fiscal units belonging to one particular *tīmār*, *zeʿāmet* or *ḫāṣṣ* are listed consecutively under the heading *tīmār-ı x*, *zeʿāmet-i x* or *ḫāṣṣhā-ı x* (*x* standing for the name of the timariot), respectively. No term is used to indicate which settlements were considered as towns. The use of the word *nefs* (*Ar. n.* soul; itself; identical) is applied to the administrative centres of each district, after which the district was named, e.g. *nefs-i Voştiça* refers to the actual/proper town of Voştiça. Moreover, the size of the settlement and its subdivision into neighbourhoods (*maḥalle*) underline a central economic and administrative function. The villages, irrespective of their size, form the vast majority of the entries. Entries for both district capitals and villages are introduced with the term *nefs* and *ḳarye*, written in extended form across the whole page with the name of the town/village continuing to the line below. When an Albanian settlement is recorded, the phrase 'of the Albanian community' (*ez cemāʿat-i Arnavudān*) is noted. At the end of the same line the name of the timariot appears, usually replaced by *meẕkūr*, *mezbūr*, *masṭūr*, *mesfūr* (*Ar. adj.* aforementioned) or *o* (*ū*) (*Pers. pers. prn.* he) in the subsequent entries belonging to the same timariot. In cases where a village is listed under the name of a certain timariot, though belonging to a different district, the note 'dependent on/belonging to *x*' (*tābiʿ-i x*) (*x* standing for the name of district) is added. In a single case, the toponym is accompanied by a second name: 'village of Ayo Vaṣıl *alias* Çağıl Ḥiṣārı' (*ḳarye-i Ayo Vaṣıl ve nām-ı dīğer Çağıl Ḥiṣārı*).[10] The *mezraʿa*s were arable lands with no sign of permanent settlement, dispersed along the surrounding area of the villages, yet set apart from the main fields. The word *mezraʿa* is written in an elongated form, but this time covering only half of the page width, followed by the place name and the phrase 'in the vicinity of village *x*' (*nezd-i ḳarye-i x*) (*x* standing for the name of the village) in the line below.

The identification of place names has been hindered by the fact that many of the settlements are now abandoned and others have been renamed, particularly the toponyms of non-Greek etymology, i.e., Albanian, Slavic or Turkish. Following the independence of Greece from the Ottoman Empire and the foundation of the Modern Greek State (1830) a large number of these toponyms were renamed with their ancient names. At the beginning of the twentieth century, a special Commission for the Toponyms of Greece (*Ἐπιτροπεία τῶν τοπωνυμίων τῆς Ἑλλάδος*) under the presidency of Nikolaos Politis undertook the task to find appropriate Greek place names for the foreign ones.[11] The local population, however, often continued to use the old place names, without paying much attention to the new road signs – a somewhat confusing situation for the modern scholar

Table 2. *Identified and Unidentified Localities.*

District	total number of localities	identified	unidentified	percent identified
Ḳalavrita	62	36	26	58.0%
Miziṣra	2	2	0	100.0%
Miḫlu	13	8	5	61.5%
Bejenik	22	19	3	86.4%
Voştiça	73	61	12	83.6%
Ḫulumiç	45	25	20	55.5%
Vumero	78	44	34	56.4%
Kirvuḳor	69	59	10	85.5%
Arḳadya	17	13	4	76.5%
Londar	61	40	21	65.6%
Ḳoriṣos	28	18	10	64.3%
Balya Badra	39	27	12	69.2%
Ḳalandriça	14	11	3	78.6%
Ṣandamiri	14	8	6	57.1%
Girbene	56	33	23	58.9%
Ayo İlya	33	21	12	63.6%
Ġardicḳo	40	23	17	57.5%
Salmenik	1	1	0	100.0%
total	667	449	218	67.3%

10 TT10, 168.

11 Politis 1920a; Politis 1912–13; Politis 1915; Politis 1920b; Kyriakidis 1926.

who conducts field research. The results of the identification are shown in Table 2. This is an ongoing process that requires detailed topographic research; we hope researchers will continue the identification of localities and correct possible errors in the present study.

Most of the Albanian settlements in the cadastre were named after the original settler or the clan leader.[12] In almost every Albanian entry the first name of the head of a household listed is the same as that of the village. Sometimes the place name is formed by both the personal and the family name of the settler, e.g. 'the village of Marti Helmi' (*ḳarye-i Marti Helmi*), followed by the name of the first inhabitant 'the aforementioned Marti' (*Marti el-mezkūr*), a clear indication that Marti Helmi was the chieftain.[13] With the passage of time, although the first name of the settler was omitted and thus forgotten, his surname survived as the place name, often appearing in the genitive or locative case, e.g. *σ/του Σπάτα*, *σ/του Μπούγα*, *σ/του Μπαρδικώστα*, etc.

In other cases, the Albanian settlers seem to have opted to name their settlement after the local flora, e.g. Vola[14] < volë (*Al. n.* mountain ash, *Sorbus*), Dardesi[15] < dardhë (*Al. n.* pear), dardhëz (*Al. n.* kind of wild pear, *Pyrus sativa*), etc. The equivalents of the Albanian place names in the Peloponnese, which are found in modern Albania, indicate either the same process of *onomatopoeia* or a possible link to the original place of the clans, e.g. Muriki:[16] place name Muriq in Shkodër, Ḳonbi S̱eḳra:[17] place name Këmbëthekër in Korçë.

The Slavic linguistic stratum is apparent in the Peloponnesian toponymy. The Slavic toponyms could be categorised into: (a) those which refer to the migration of Slavic nomadic groups in the Morea in the seventh and eighth centuries AD; and (b) those which were introduced by the Albanians who acquired them when crossing the Slavic lands in their southward migration in the thirteenth and fourteenth centuries.[18] The second category becomes evident when the Slavic surname of the Albanian settler is the same as the name of the village he resides in. The studies by Vasmer and Koder proved most helpful in the identification of the Slavic place names.[19] According to Kordosis, who mapped out the toponyms in the Peloponnese listed by Vasmer and Koder, most of the Slavs lived inland in lush mountainous areas in close proximity to fertile valleys mainly in Achaia, western and central Arcadia, south-western Elis and on Mt Taygetus.[20] On the other hand, the Albanians settled all over the Peloponnese regardless of the geomorphology (map 35) and, in contrast to the Slavs, they were not entirely linguistically hellenised.[21]

So far, identifying the *mezraʿa*s has not been very fruitful. The very nature of these locations that lack a permanent settlement increased their vulnerability in the course of the centuries.[22] Very occasionally some of them did evolve to the status of a village retaining the same name. In most cases their names were forgotten and their mention in secondary literature varies from minimal to non-existent. In fact, it is considered fortunate if one succeeds in tracing their microtoponymy, if this is still preserved in the local oral history among the elderly. So far, I have been able to identify 25 of the 77 *mezraʿa*s that appear in the register or 32.5%, fourteen of which evolved into villages at a later stage, six remain uninhabited, four are locations of chapels or monasteries, and one is the location of castle ruins (Table 3). The connection of each *mezraʿa* to a village proved very helpful in its localisation, as it pointed to a broader geographical area in which one could search for it.

In the process of identification of the place names I have been aided by the *Gazetteer of the Greek Toponyms* of the Hellenic Military Geographical Service;[23] the exhaustive geographical dictionary of the Peloponnese by Pikoulas;[24] the geographical dictionary of Greece by

12 Lambros was the first to notice the anthroponymic origin of the Albanian place names in Greece: Lambros 1896, 184, followed by the observation of Beldiceanu and Beldiceanu-Steinherr in Corinthia: Beldiceanu–Beldiceanu-Steinherr 1986, 42–43, and supported by Balta: Balta 1990–91, 60–62. On the other hand, Fourikis had erroneously considered the connection between the settler and the toponym loose: Fourikis 1929, 124. For a general survey on the Albanian toponymy of Greece see Vagiakakos 1962, 344–348; for the Albanian anthroponymy see Vagiakakos 1963–64, 248–252. A list of the Arvanitic-speaking villages in Greece has been compiled by Bellusci: Bellusci 1994, 29–42.

13 TT10, 146.

14 TT10, 180.

15 TT10, 179.

16 TT10, 15.

17 1/14662, 34.

18 Kordosis 1981a, 386. See also Malingoudis 1983.

19 Vasmer 1941; Koder 1978. See also Zakythinos 1944, Georgacas 1941 and Malingoudis 1981.

20 Kordosis 1981a, 425–426.

21 Georgacas 1956, 405; Philippson 1890.

22 For the dispersed arable lands in the Venetian period see Malliaris 2008, 137–138.

23 Glet 1998.

24 Pikoulas 2001a.

Table 3. *List of mezraʿas.*

no.	*mezraʿa*	dependent on	district	evolved into a village	uninhabited
10.	Petrovuni	Amuri	Ḳalavrita		+
27.	Ḳaratula-ı dīğer	Ḳaçana	Ḳalavrita		+
33.	Puloti	Dara	Ḳalavrita		+
40.	İskliva	Niḳola Manesi	Ḳalavrita		+
54.	İvlaḫo Ḳalanas	Ṣavanus	Ḳalavrita	+	
55.	İvlaḫo Yalya	Ṣavanus	Ḳalavrita		+
62.	Liḳuresi	Sumaki	Ḳalavrita	+	
67.	Astro	Astriçi	Miḫlu		+[1]
68.	Duşa Dara	Astriçi	Miḫlu		+
69.	Luvari	Astriçi	Miḫlu		+
70.	Plaşa	Astriçi	Miḫlu		+
77.	Plaşa	Raḫova	Miḫlu		+
78.	Vuzyas	Bejenik	Bejenik		+
80.	Plaşa	Bejenik	Bejenik	+	
99.	İvlaḫo Filito	Ustruza/ İstruza Potamya	Bejenik		+
130.	Ḳapareli	Maji	Voştiça		+
167.	Ḳumaniçi Luzi	Zepandi	Voştiça	+	
169.	Pelyura	Ṣoḫyana	Voştiça		+
170.	Mayira	Ṣoḫyana	Voştiça		+
175.	Potamya Ṣarandinu	Ġastuni	Ḫulumiç	+[2]	
176.	Kiḫomiro	Ġastuni	Ḫulumiç		+
178.	İskliva	Ṣavalya	Ḫulumiç		+
180.	Sinasi	Kelavi	Ḫulumiç		+
196.	Potamya Ṣarandinu	Ḳoḳla Marġariti	Ḫulumiç		+
201.	Foloḳobuva	Andraviza	Ḫulumiç		+
205.	Ḳanbiziya	Marḳoplu	Ḫulumiç		+
210.	Pendani	İpsari	Ḫulumiç	+	

[1] Ruins of the castle are still visible.
[2] In 1700 it was listed in the Grimani census as a village named Sarandino, the exact location of which remains unknown today: PANAGIOTOPOULOS 1987, 273, 304.

Stamatelatos and Vamva-Stamatelatou;[25] the study on the south-western Peloponnesian toponymy by Georgacas and McDonald;[26] the list of Greek municipalities between 1833 and 1912 by Skiadas;[27] and the statistical surveys on Greek geography, administration and demography by Houliarakis, Drakakis and Koundouros, Nouhakis, and, especially for the year 1837, the *Almanach* of Klados.[28] Concerning the castles and fortresses of the Morea, I have consulted the monograph of Sfikopoulos.[29] In addition, the Venetian Grimani census of 1700 published by Panagiotopoulos,[30] the inventories of the Venetians published by Pier' Antonio Pacifico,[31] the travelogues of William Martin Leake[32] and

25 STAMATELATOS–VAMVA-STAMATELATOU 2001.
26 GEORGACAS–MCDONALD 1968.
27 SKIADAS 1993.
28 HOULIARAKIS 1973; HOULIARAKIS 1974; DRAKAKIS–KOUNDOUROS 1939–40; NOUHAKIS 1901; KLADOS 1837.
29 SFIKOPOULOS 1987.
30 PANAGIOTOPOULOS 1987, 231–311. This census, conducted by the Venetian *provveditor* Francesco Grimani, is held in Venice, Archivio di Stato, Archivio Grimani dai Servi B. 54, no. 158 and has been partially published (f. 11^{v}) by Dokos: DOKOS 1975, 206–210. See also PANAGIOTOPOULOS 1976–78; LAMBROS 1924; and ANTONIADI 1966. The census contains the following administrative divisions (*territorii*): Territorio di [Napoli di] Romania, Città [di Napoli] di Romania, Territorio di Corinto, Territorio di Tripolizza, Territorio d'Argos, Territorio di S. Pietro di Zacugna, Giurisdizione di Porto Porro, Giurisdizione di Termis, Territorio d'Arcadia, Territorio di Fanari, Territorio di Calamata, Territorio di Leondari, Territorio d'Andrussa, Territorio di Caritena, Territorio di Navarino, Territorio di Coron, Territorio di Modon, Territorio di Callavritta, Territorio di Gastugni, Territorio di Patrasso, Territorio di Vostizza, Territorio di Malvasia, Territorio di Crisaffa, Territorio di Mistra, Territorio d'Eleos, Territorio d'Alta Maina, Territorio della Bassa Maina. For the Venetian reports on the Peloponnese see TSELIKAS 1982–4; TSELIKAS 1987–88; TSELIKAS 1995; TSELIKAS 1996–97.
31 PACIFICO 1700; PACIFICO 1704, 117–135 (the second edition is a more reliable source for toponymy); SAUERWEIN 1969.
32 LEAKE 1830; LEAKE 1846.

Table 3. *List of mezraʿas.*

no.	*mezraʿa*	dependent on	district	evolved into a village	uninhabited
211.	Lonci	İpsari	Ḫulumiç		+
212.	Başta	İpsari	Ḫulumiç	+	
213.	Tunba	İpsari	Ḫulumiç		+
214.	Ḳapaleto	İpsari	Ḫulumiç	+	
231.	Ayo Ḳostandino	Ẕervini	Vumero		+
246.	Purdanu	Maḳri Poẕi	Vumero	+	
247.	Matranḳa	İşpata	Vumero		+
269.	İspani-i dīğer	İspani	Vumero		+
270.	Persena	İspani	Vumero	+	
278.	Velizi	Coya	Vumero		+
376.	Meğaliç		Arḳadya		+
379.	Ḳozomuli		Arḳadya		+
437.	İvrato Ḳuçi Ḳonbi S̱eḳra	Çarnuḫlu	Londar		+
440.	Veliğosti	Londar	Londar		+
441.	Aya Niḳola	Amuri	Londar		+
445.	Ḳuvara	Vaşılıḳa	Ḳoris̱os		+
447.	Petro Ḫayḳal	Ayo Vaşıl/Çağıl Ḥiṣārı	Ḳoris̱os		+
448.	Manesi	Ayo Vaşıl/Çağıl Ḥiṣārı	Ḳoris̱os		+
449.	Sermorini	Ayo Vaşıl/Çağıl Ḥiṣārı	Ḳoris̱os		+
450.	Ḳalo İstemati	Ayo Vaşıl/Çağıl Ḥiṣārı	Ḳoris̱os		+
452.	Piça	Pulimeno Ḳondostavlo	Ḳoris̱os		+
457.	İksaroḳastalya	Ayonori	Ḳoris̱os		+

François C.H.L. Pouqueville,[33] and the memoirs of Theodore Kolokotronis[34] have been most useful in my research. Finally, for the modern place names I have consulted the series of maps (scale 1:100,000) pertaining to the Peloponnese produced by the Hellenic Military Geographical Service,[35] the British maps of the Geographical Section, General Staff (scale 1:100,000)[36] and the German *Heereskarte* produced by the Generalstab der Luftwaffe (scale 1:200,000).[37] For the early nineteenth-century toponymy I have used the detailed map of the French Expédition scientifique de Morée (scale 1:200,000), accompanied by a list of place names.[38] Other works on the historical geography of the Peloponnese are cited in the relevant entries.[39]

The list of the place names below follows the sequence of the TT10-1/14662 register. I opted for this format in order to remain as faithful as possible to the geographical image of the source. No decisive rule determines the order in which the fiscal units appear in the register, except for

33 Pouqueville 1826–27.

34 Kolokotronis 1981.

35 HMGS 1977–79: Aíyion (1978), Filiatrá (1978), Kalamáta (1979), Kórinthos (1978), Leonídhion (1978), Levadhiá (1977), Mégara (1978), Mesolóngion (1977), Neápolis (1978), Pátrai (1979), Pílos (1978), Pírgos (1978), Spétsai (1978), Trípolis (1978), Trópaia (1978), Xirokámbion (1978), and Yíthion (1978).

36 GSGS 1944: Aiyina, Dhimitsana, Idhra, Kalámai, Kiparissia, Kíthira, Korinthos, Koróni, Leonídhion, Levádhia, Mesolóngion, Molaoí, Pátrai, Pílos, Pirgos, Spárti, Tainaron, Trípolis, Xilókastron, and Yíthion.

37 Luftwaffe 1943: Südost-Europa: Athen, Kalame, Kithira, Leonidion, Patras, Pilos, and Tripolis.

38 Expédition 1832; Bory de Saint-Vincent 1834, 64–95. In case of a discrepancy between the map and the list, both of the forms are noted. I would like hereby to express my deep gratitude to Julian Chrysostomides, for allowing me to examine her copy of the map.

39 For an overview of mediaeval and modern maps of the Peloponnese see Kourelis 2003, 426–445 and Melas 2006, 77–179. The meticulous study of the seventeenth/eighteenth-century Venetian maps of the Peloponnese edited by Professor Olga Katsiardi-Hering was published just before the final revision of the present work and, unfortunately, its findings were not incorporated (Katsiardi-Hering 2018).

Table 3. *List of mezraʿas.*

no.	*mezraʿa*	dependent on	district	evolved into a village	uninhabited
483.	Patura	Pavloḳastro	Balya Badra		+
491.	Meliġala	Ḳamaniça	Balya Badra		+
492.	Liḳuresi	Ḳamaniça	Balya Badra		+
493.	Draġoti	Ḳamaniça	Balya Badra		+
494.	İksenozoẖiyo	Ḳamaniça	Balya Badra		+
495.	Ḳomi	Ḳamaniça	Balya Badra	+	
502.	Çernota	Buryalisa	Balya Badra		+
505.	Zastupa	Ḳurnaroḳastro	Balya Badra	+	
531.	Orfano	Porta	Şandamiri	+[3]	
534.	Lukişta	Puliça	Şandamiri		+
535.	Gin Floḳa	Puliça	Şandamiri	+	
536.	Mariçi	Puliça	Şandamiri	+	
552.	Viriça	Divye	Girbene		+
562.	Besulḳa	Lenḳoni	Girbene	+	
563.	Ayo Yorgi	Lenḳoni	Girbene		+
569.	Serḳofayi	Petrovişta	Girbene		+
570.	Şurbi	Petrovişta	Girbene		+
616.	Ayiya	İryolo	Ayo İlya		+
617.	Fenaromeni	İryolo	Ayo İlya	+	
618.	Şamuna	Vunarġo	Ayo İlya		+
621.	Rado	Rovyata	Ayo İlya		+
622.	Barçi	Rovyata	Ayo İlya		+
647.	Rozinotiẖo	Ġardicḳo	Ġardicḳo		+
648.	Ḳomi	Ġardicḳo	Ġardicḳo	+	
649.	İsliva-ı dīğer	Ġardicḳo	Ġardicḳo		+
658.	Ranesi	Liḳuresi	Ġardicḳo		+
666.	Kiziḳuma		Ġardicḳo		+

[3] In 1700 it was listed in the Grimani census as a village named Arfano, the exact location of which remains unknown today: PANAGIOTOPOULOS 1987, 278, 306.

their grouping according to the districts (*nāḥiyyet*). Each entry refers to one place name; every toponym is given in both Romanised and Arabic alphabet, followed by the manuscript name and page number. GR stands for Greek settlements, AL for Albanian, and M for settlements of mixed population. The coordinates, X/Y in metres, of the located toponyms are noted in GGRS87 (*Greek Geodetic Reference System 1987*).[40] In cases where place names are identified with certainty, the Modern Greek equivalent is given in vernacular Greek (*dēmotikē*) as it is pronounced today, with the Greek alphabet version in parentheses, followed by the definite article. In case of renamed place names, the old toponym and the date of the change are noted. The modern administrative division, to which the settlement pertains, is also given according to the regional unit (*περιφερειακή ενότητα*) (in English), the municipality (*δήμος*) and the municipal unit (*δημοτική ενότητα*).[41] Each entry closes with a short list of bibliography on the geographical position, and the references to the place name in primary sources, followed by notes on the topographical identification and the ethnic origin of the toponym. In the process of identification through linking the toponyms to a special local feature (geographical, geological, botanical, zoological, etc.), an attempt has been made to trace the meaning and etymology of the non-Greek place names; however, an in-depth etymological analysis is beyond the scope of this study.

40 Fundamental point: Dionysos. Latitude 38°04’33.8”N, longitude 23°55’51.0”E of Greenwich; geoid height 7.0m.

41 The administrative division refers to the current situation after the 3852/2010 ‘Kallikratis’ Law.

This chapter is accompanied by a set of 38 maps, which illustrate the data. These maps have been processed in the ArcGIS 9 ArcMap™ by ESRI™ software package using GIS (Geographical Information Systems) technology.[42] The economic and demographic distribution and the ethnic composition of the early Ottoman Peloponnese based on the data obtained from the TT10-1/14662 cadastre in relation to geographical factors (each district and settlement/*mezraʿa* entry) fall under the category of the *geographical phenomenon*, according to Atsuyuki.[43] The primary attribute data (number of households, annual revenue, kind of taxes, ethnicity, etc.) were combined with the modern geographical data of the digitalised maps (scale 1:50,000) of the Peloponnese, acquired from the National Technical University of Athens. Perhaps one of the most helpful features of these maps for the identification of deserted villages and *mezraʿa*s is the layer on which the uninhabited localities are grouped.[44] The locations (dots) and the sea- and land-elevation (polygons), whose coordinates are checked via satellite, functioned as the background, on which the middle-fifteenth-century toponyms were placed. For each one of the seventeen districts a separate database has been created where each place name (dot) put on the map is given a unique number – identical with the one given in the list below, e.g. Ḳalavrita: 1 – followed by the toponym as it appears in the cadastre in Romanised alphabet, the ethnicity of the inhabitants, the population and revenue figures, and the modern name. With reference to this *relational database*[45] the software automatically presents the economic, demographic or ethnic values using dots of different sizes or colours, which results in two thematic maps per district respectively.[46] In this manner both the geographical and the attribute data for a specific region in a particular time cross-section can be visualised, and hence provide a useful tool for the historian.

1. District of Ḳalavrita (Kalavryta) (Maps 1–2)

1. Ḳalavrita, nefs-i (قلاورته), TT10, 1, 38. GR

Coordinates:	X: 334019.053 Y: 4210783.876
Modern Greek:	Kalavryta (Καλάβρυτα, τα)
Regional Unit:	Achaia
Municipality:	Kalavryta
Municipal Unit:	Kalavryta
Bibliography:	Pikoulas 2001a, 166.1290; Panagiotopoulos 1987, 268, 302.15: Territorio di Callavritta, Calavrita; Pacifico 1704, 122: Territorio di Calaurita, La Terra di Calaurita; Bory de Saint-Vincent 1834, 73: Éparchie de Kalavrita, Kalavrita; Leake 1846, map: Kalavryta (Cynætha); Sfikopoulos 1987, 198–200; Triantafyllou 1974, 61–62; Triantafyllou 1995, I 922–925; Hopf 1873, 202: Calaurata vel Calavita, 205: Calavita; Bon 1969, 468–469.

2. Manastır-ı Meġaspilyo Aya Ḳori (مناستر مغاسپليو ايا قورى), TT10, 1. GR

Coordinates:	X: 340571.697 Y: 4217304.390
Modern Greek:	Megalou Spilaiou Monastery (I.M. Μεγάλου Σπηλαίου, η)

42 Among the standard GIS textbooks see Burrough–McDonnell 1998; Star–Estes 1990; Bailey–Gatrell 1995; for an introduction to ArcView see Androulakakis 2000.

43 Atsuyuki 2004, 1.

44 It is worth noting that most of those localities have retained their old name.

45 Atsuyuki 2004, 8.

46 In the mapping process Hütteroth's, Abdulfattah's and Göyünç's pioneering studies on the historical geography of the Ottoman lands and their elaborate maps have been a source of inspiration: Hütteroth 1968; Hütteroth–Abdulfattah 1977; Göyünç–Hütteroth 1997.

Regional Unit:	Achaia
Municipality:	Kalavryta
Municipal Unit:	Kalavryta
Bibliography:	PIKOULAS 2001a, 312.2697; BORY DE SAINT-VINCENT 1834, 75: Éparchie de Kalavrita, Mon[re] Mégaspiléon; ZAKYTHINOS 1953, 305–306.

3. **İvraḫni (اوراخنى), TT10, 1. GR**

Coordinates:	X: 339736.509 Y: 4211255.798
Modern Greek:	Vrahni (Βράχνι, το)
Regional Unit:	Achaia
Municipality:	Kalavryta
Municipal Unit:	Kalavryta
Bibliography:	PIKOULAS 2001a, 109.751; PANAGIOTOPOULOS 1987, 269, 302.58: Territorio di Callavritta, Vracni; PACIFICO 1704, 122: Territorio di Calaurita, Vracnì; BORY DE SAINT-VINCENT 1834, 73: Éparchie de Kalavrita, Vrakhni; LEAKE 1846, map: Vrakhni.
Notes:	In ruins. According to Symeonidis, < **βραχνί* < **βλαχνί* (*Gr. n. dim.* of βλάχνον, *anc. Gr. n.* fern, *Pteridium aquilinum*): SYMEONIDIS 2010, I 386. According to Vasmer, < vrechnij (*Ru. adj.* upper): VASMER 1941, 132.

4. **Sudana (سودانه), TT10, 2. GR**

Coordinates:	X: 336574.741 Y: 4207359.798
Modern Greek:	Ano & Kato Loussoi (Άνω & Κάτω Λουσοί, οι)
Old Toponym:	Until 1928: Soudena Theotokou (Σουδενά Θεοτόκου, τα), Soudena/Agios Vasileios (Σουδενά, τα/Άγιος Βασίλειος, ο)
Regional Unit:	Achaia
Municipality:	Kalavryta
Municipal Unit:	Kalavryta
Bibliography:	PIKOULAS 2001a, 262.2213, 2214; PANAGIOTOPOULOS 1987, 268, 302.17: Territorio di Callavritta, Sudena, Cassagli di sopra, 302.18: Sudena, Cassagli di sotto; PACIFICO 1704, 122: Territorio di Calaurita, Sudenà; BORY DE SAINT-VINCENT 1834, 74: Éparchie de Kalavrita, Soudéna, Péra Soudéna; KOLOKOTRONIS 1981, 268; LEAKE 1830, II 108, III 180: Sudhenà; LEAKE 1846, map: Sudhena (Lusi); SKIADAS 1993, 243; STAMATELATOS–VAMVA-STAMATELATOU 2001, 84.
Notes:	According to Symeonidis, < **Studena* < *studenъ* (*Slav. adj.* cold): SYMEONIDIS 2010, II 1294. Cf. place name Studena in Bulgaria, Studena Voda in North Macedonia, Studena in Slovenia, Studená in Slovakia and the Czech Republic. According to Vasmer, < sǫdьnъ (*old Slav. n.* dish): VASMER 1941, 51.

5. Beluşi (بلوشى), TT10, 3. AL

Notes: Unidentified.
Vasmer and Symeonides argued that it derives from a Slavic **Bělušь* (*Slav. adj.* white): VASMER 1941, 148; SYMEONIDIS I, 982–983; belush (*Al. n.* white/red whortleberry, *Vaccinium myrtillus*). Belushi (*Al. sn.*). Also, possibly from Bello (*Al. pn.* or *adj.* denoting the inhabitant of Bellova in Dibër, Albania): KOLLEKA 1987, 87. Place name Belushi in Fier and Vlorë, Albania. Μπελούσης is a well-attested Arvanitic anthroponym: BIRIS 1998, 198; GEORGACAS–MCDONALD 1968, 296.

6. Ḫamaḳu (خاماقو), TT10, 3. AL

Coordinates:	X: 334770.591 Y: 4203652.590
Modern Greek:	Lousiko (Λουσικό, το)
Old Toponym:	Until 1928: Hamakou (Χαμάκου, του)
Regional Unit:	Achaia
Municipality:	Kalavryta
Municipal Unit:	Kalavryta
Bibliography:	PIKOULAS 2001a, 262.2211; PANAGIOTOPOULOS 1987, 269, 302.65: Territorio di Callavritta, Camacus; PACIFICO 1704, 122: Territorio di Calaurita, Camacus; BORY DE SAINT-VINCENT 1834, 74: Éparchie de Kalavrita, Khamakou; LEAKE 1846, map: Khamaku; SKIADAS 1993, 243; STAMATELATOS–VAMVA-STAMATELATOU 2001, 440.

7. Şiġuni (شيغونى), TT10, 3. AL

Coordinates:	X: 333414.603 Y: 4200781.325
Modern Greek:	Sigouni (Σιγούνι, το)
Regional Unit:	Achaia
Municipality:	Kalavryta
Municipal Unit:	Kalavryta
Bibliography:	PIKOULAS 2001a, 420.3744; PANAGIOTOPOULOS 1987, 269, 302.67: Territorio di Callavritta, Seguni; PACIFICO 1704, 122: Territorio di Calaurita, Sigugni; BORY DE SAINT-VINCENT 1834, 74: Éparchie de Kalavrita, Sigouni; LEAKE 1846, map: Siguni.
Notes:	Shguni (*Al. sn.* woman's close-fitting woollen dress) > σιγκούνα or σεγκούνα (*Gr. n.* woman's close-fitting woollen dress): BAMBINIOTIS 2002, 1590.

8. Zuġra (زوغره), TT10, 3. AL

Modern Greek:	Zougras (Ζούγρας, ο)
Regional Unit:	Achaia

Municipality:	Kalavryta
Municipal Unit:	Kalavryta
Bibliography:	Papandreou 2011, 282.
Notes:	Unidentified. Hydronym Zougras tou Karnesiou (Ζούγρας του Καρνεσίου, ο) to the south of Lefki (Λεύκη, η); its exact location is unknown.

9. Amuri (آموری), TT10, 4. AL

Modern Greek:	Amouri (Αμούρι, το)
Regional Unit:	Achaia
Municipality:	Kalavryta
Municipal Unit:	Kalavryta
Bibliography:	Pikoulas 2001a, 69.369; Panagiotopoulos 1987, 270, 303.103: Territorio di Callavritta, Amuri; Pacifico 1704, 122: Territorio di Calaurita, Amuri.
Notes:	Unidentified. Microtoponym in the surroundings of Soudena Theotokou (no. 4): Papandreou 2011, 279–280; its exact location is unknown. Amur (*Al. pn*); Amor (*Al. pn.*) < amë + orë: Zoto 2005, 31.

10. Petrovuni (پتروووونی), *mezraʿa* in the vicinity of Amuri, TT10, 4.

Notes:	Unidentified.

11. Zuġra-ı dīğer (زوغره دیکر), TT10, 4. AL

Notes:	Unidentified. See no. 8.

12. Ḫaraḳtinu (خراقتنو), TT10, 4. AL

Coordinates:	X: 331575.062 Y: 4204053.958
Modern Greek:	Haraktinou (Χαρακτινού, του)
Regional Unit:	Achaia
Municipality:	Kalavryta
Municipal Unit:	Kalavryta
Bibliography:	GLET 1998, III 438: Χαρακτινός; Pikoulas 2001a, 481.4345; Bory de Saint-Vincent 1834, 74: Éparchie de Kalavrita, K(h)araktinou; Papandreou 2011, 281: Χαρακτηνοῦ; Skiadas 1993, 243.

13. Ḫoloropoẕi (خولوروپوذى), TT10, 4. GR

Notes:	Unidentified. Cf. microtoponym Hloropoti (Χλωροπότι, το) in the surroundings of Hrysanthi (no. 152) and Ambelokipoi (no. 158): Fotopoulos 1982, II 259.

14. Dima Plaşa (ديمه پلاشه), TT10, 5. AL

Notes:	Unidentified. Δήμας (*Gr. pn., sn.*) > Dhima (*Al. pn. dim.* of Dhimitër). According to Vasmer, < Pleš (*Slav. n.* bold spot): Vasmer 1941, 127. According to Georgacas, < Pleshë, Plesha: Georgacas 1965, 161. Πλέσας (*Gr. sn.*). Place name Pleshë in Shkodër and Dibër, Albania. See also Kolleka 1983, 26, and Symeonidis 2010, II 1161.

15. Epano Ḳurnofita (اپانو قورنوفته), TT10, 5. GR

Coordinates:	X: 338844.688 Y: 4192611.457
Modern Greek:	Krinofyta (Κρινόφυτα, τα)
Regional Unit:	Achaia
Municipality:	Kalavryta
Municipal Unit:	Kleitoria
Bibliography:	Pikoulas 2001a, 198.1598; Panagiotopoulos 1987, 270, 303.89: Territorio di Callavritta, Castria; Pacifico 1704, 122: Territorio di Calaurita, Castria; Bory de Saint-Vincent 1834, 74: Éparchie de Kalavrita, Kastria; Leake 1846, map: Kastria.

16. Ḳastriya (قاستريه), TT10, 5. GR

Coordinates:	X: 335882.534 Y: 4201188.927
Modern Greek:	Kastria [Καστρία, τα (= Καστριά)]
Regional Unit:	Achaia
Municipality:	Kalavryta
Municipal Unit:	Kleitoria
Bibliography:	Pikoulas 2001a, 198.1598; Panagiotopoulos 1987, 270, 303.89: Territorio di Callavritta, Castria; Pacifico 1704, 122: Territorio di Calaurita, Castria; Bory De Saint-Vincent 1834, 74: Éparchie de Kalavrita, Kastria; Leake 1846, map: Kastria.

17. Vorstena (وورستنه), TT10, 6. AL

Coordinates:	X: 335690.616 Y: 4199010.588
Modern Greek:	Glastra (Γλάστρα, η)

Old Toponym:	Until 1940: Vrosthaina (Βρώσθαινα, η); until 1961: Vrostena (Βρόστενα, η)
Regional Unit:	Achaia
Municipality:	Kalavryta
Municipal Unit:	Kleitoria
Bibliography:	Pikoulas 2001a, 123.880; Panagiotopoulos 1987, 268, 302.22: Territorio di Callavritta, Vrostena; Pacifico 1704, 122: Territorio di Calaurita, Vrostena; Bory de Saint-Vincent 1834, 74: Éparchie de Kalavrita, Vrosténa; Leake 1846, map: Vrostena; Skiadas 1993, 237; Stamatelatos–Vamva-Stamatelatou 2001, 166.
Notes:	According to Symeonidis, < **broshtinë* (*Al. n.* place where smoketree or smoke bush, *Tinus coggygria*, *Rhus cotinus* is found in abundance): Symeonidis 2010, I 390. See also Vasmer 1941, 132: < broštь (*Slav. n.* madder, *Rubia tinctorum*); perhaps linked to vresht or vreshtë (*Al. n.* vineyard): Georgacas–McDonald 1968, 360.

18. Taşi (تاشى), TT10, 6. AL

Notes:	Unidentified. Τάσης, Τάσος (*Gr. pn. dim.* of Αναστάσιος) > Tasi, Tasho (*Al. pn. dim.* of Anastas): Zoto 2005, 33.

19. Velimiri (ولیمیرى), TT10, 6. AL

Coordinates:	X: 341539.779 Y: 4195945.784
Modern Greek:	Velimiri (Βελιμίρι, το)
Regional Unit:	Achaia
Municipality:	Kalavryta
Municipal Unit:	Kleitoria
Bibliography:	GLET 1998, I 273.
Notes:	Uninhabited location to the east of Agios Nikolaos (Άγιος Νικόλαος, ο). Velimir (*Scr. pn.*).

20. Ḳani (قانى), TT10, 6. GR

Coordinates:	X: 334130.350 Y: 4197313.116
Modern Greek:	Kallithea (Καλλιθέα, η)
Old Toponym:	Until 1971: Kani (Κάνι, το)
Regional Unit:	Achaia
Municipality:	Kalavryta
Municipal Unit:	Kleitoria

Bibliography: Pikoulas 2001a, 171.1335; Panagiotopoulos 1987, 270, 303.81: Territorio di Callavritta, Cani; Pacifico 1704, 122: Territorio di Calaurita, Cauni; Bory de Saint-Vincent 1834, 74: Éparchie de Kalavrita, Kanni; Leake 1830, II 262: Stukáni; Leake 1846, map: Kani; Skiadas 1993, 237; Stamatelatos–Vamva-Stamatelatou 2001, 286.

Notes: For a folk etymology of the toponym see Papandreou 2011, 326.

21. Marti Plaşa (مارتی پلاشه), TT10, 7. AL

Unidentified.

Notes: Marti is a variant of Martin (*Al. pn.*) < Martinus (*Lat. pn.*): Zoto 2005, 266. For Plaşa see no. 14. Place name Martin in Fier, Albania.

22. Todoro Manesi (تودرو مانسی), TT10, 7. AL

Unidentified.

Notes: Θεόδωρος or Θόδωρος (*Gr. pn.* Theodore) > Teodor (*Al. pn.*). Manesi (*Arb. sn.*), Manësi (*Al. sn.*), Μάνεσης (*Arv. sn.*) < mënes (*Arb. adv.* late); mënesëm (*Arb. adj.* slow, late-comer, indolent, lazy, sluggish); mënesë (*Al. n.* tardiness, lateness, delay): Biris 1998, 197; Georgacas–McDonald 1968, 331. Place name Manës in Durrës, Albania.

23. Barçi (بارچی), TT10, 7. AL

Bibliography: Pacifico 1704, 123: Territorio di Calaurita, Barzi.

Unidentified.

Notes: Μπάρτσης (*Arv. sn.* attested in Markopoulo, Attica) < barxhë (*Al. n.* goat with mottled white and black coat): Biris 1998, 198, attested as barxë in Argolis and Messenia: Jochalas 2011, II 634, 669. See also Symeonidis 2010, I 978. Place name Barç in Berat, Durrës and Korçë, Albania.

24. Todoroplu (تودروپلو), TT10, 8. AL

Unidentified.

Notes: Θεοδωρόπουλος (*Gr. sn.*) < Θεόδωρος (*Gr. pn.* Theodore) + -όπουλος (*Gr. end.* son of).

25. Petros Ḳaratula (پتروس قراتولا), TT10, 8. AL

Unidentified.

Notes: Πέτρος (*Gr. pn.* Peter). Καρατούλας, Καράτολας (*Arv. sn.*): Biris 1998, 194.

26. Ḳaçana including the community of İştopanşi (قاچانه مع جماعت اشتوپانشی), TT10, 8. GR

Bibliography: Sakellariou 1939, 103.

Notes:	Unidentified. Katsanes (Κατσάνες, οι) was one of the subdivisions of the Kalavryta district (*vilāyet*) during the second phase of the Ottoman rule (1715–1821), which, according to the *Expédition*, comprised the following villages: Klitouras, Apano/Kato-Kovoli, Kastéli, Mamalouka, Mostitsi, Planitérou, Khamakou, Kastria, Vrosténa, Kanni, Péra-Soudena, Hagios-Vasilios, Soudéna, Kokova, Mazi, Arbouna and Krinophyta: Bory de Saint-Vincent 1834, 74. Leake mentioned the Katzána valley and river by Mazeítika Kalyvia area: Leake 1830, II 262: 'which probably once contained a village of that name.' Ruins of an abandoned settlement are still visible today on the banks of the Katsanas/Aroanios River (Κατσάνας/Αροάνιος, ο). Microtoponym Stoupathi Spring (Στουπάθι, το) in the surroundings of Agios Nikolaos (Άγιος Νικόλαος, ο) in Kalavryta, Achaia: Papandreou 2011, 327; its exact location is unknown. Στουπάθης (*Arv. sn.*); Shtopani (*Al. sn.*); stopaneshë or stopan (*Al. n.* herdsman in a camp of dairy animals, dairyman).

27. Ḳaratula-ı dīğer (قراتولاء دیکر), *mezraʿa* in the vicinity of Ḳaçana, TT10, 9.

Notes:	Unidentified. See no. 25.

28. Lapata (لاپاته), TT10, 9. GR

Coordinates:	X: 322856.692 Y: 4211967.992
Modern Greek:	Lapatheia (Λαπάθεια, η)
Old Toponym:	Until 1955: Lapata (Λαπάτα, η)
Regional Unit:	Achaia
Municipality:	Kalavryta
Municipal Unit:	Kalavryta
Bibliography:	Pikoulas 2001a, 248.2077; Panagiotopoulos 1987, 269, 302.71: Territorio di Callavritta, Lapata; Pacifico 1704, 123: Territorio di Calaurita, Lapata; Bory de Saint-Vincent 1834, 73: Éparchie de Kalavrita, Lapata; Leake 1846, map: Lapata; Kolokotronis 1981, 201: Λάπατες; Skiadas 1993, 239; Stamatelatos–Vamva-Stamatelatou 2001, 414.

29. Ḳato Ḳurnofita (قاتو قورنوفته), TT10, 9. GR

Coordinates:	X: 338585.699 Y: 4192957.168
Modern Greek:	Krinofyta (Κρινόφυτα, τα)
Regional Unit:	Achaia
Municipality:	Kalavryta
Municipal Unit:	Kleitoria

Bibliography:	Pikoulas 2001a, 235.1958; Panagiotopoulos 1987, 270, 303.114: Territorio di Callavritta, Cernofita di Sotto; Pacifico 1704, 122: Territorio di Calaurita, Crinofita; Bory de Saint-Vincent 1834, 74: Éparchie de Kalavrita, Krinophyta; Leake 1846, map: Krinofyta.

30. Ġolemi (غولمی), TT10, 10. AL

Coordinates:	X: 317064.472 Y: 4222949.757
Modern Greek:	Golemi (Γολέμι, το)
Regional Unit:	Achaia
Municipality:	Erymanthos
Municipal Unit:	Leontio
Bibliography:	Pikoulas 2001a, 124.891; Panagiotopoulos 1987, 270, 303.118: Territorio di Callavritta, Golemo; Pacifico 1704, 123: Territorio di Calaurita, Golemi.
Notes:	According to Biris, Γκολέμης (*Arv. sn.*) < golem (*Arv. adj.* glutton, voracious, edacious), an etymology I was unable to confirm: Biris 1998, 193. He is probably linking it to golë (*Arv. n.* mouth; modern *Al.* gojë). Place name Golem in Fier, Shkodër, Durrës, Tiranë and Gjirokastër, Albania. Golemi (*Al. sn.*): Georgacas–McDonald 1968, 304. Vasmer connected it to golěmь (*Slav. adj.* big, large): Vasmer 1941, 161. Symeonidis 2010, I 439.

31. Maḳriyeni Çamanda (ماقری ینی چاماندا), TT10, 10. AL

Coordinates:	X: 326407.012 Y: 4210520.383
Modern Greek:	Tsamanta (Τσαμαντά, του)
Regional Unit:	Achaia
Municipality:	Kalavryta
Municipal Unit:	Kalavryta
Bibliography:	GLET 1998, III 373.
Notes:	Uninhabited location to the south-east of Flamboura (no. 38). Μακρυγένης (*Gr. sn.* long-bearded). Τσαμαντάς (*Arv. sn.*). According to Biris, it derives from an *Al. phr.* meaning go closer, something I was unable to confirm: Biris 1998, 202. Symeonidis connected Tsamanta in Thesprotia to the ancient Greek place name Θύαμις: Symeonidis 2010, II 1373. See also çamandalj (*Arv. n.* men's vest): Jochalas 2011, II 683.

32. Dara (دآره), TT10, 10. AL

Coordinates:	X: 341555.790 Y: 4185757.134
Modern Greek:	Daras [Δάρας, ο (= Ντάρα, του)]
Regional Unit:	Arcadia

Municipality: Tripoli

Municipal Unit: Levidi

Bibliography: Pikoulas 2001a, 129.942; Panagiotopoulos 1987, 243, 293.22: Territorio di Tripolizza, Darra; Pacifico 1704, 119: Territorio di Tripolizza, Dara; Bory de Saint-Vincent 1834, 92: Éparchie de Tripolitsa, Dara; Leake 1846, map: Tara or Dara; Papantoniou 1964, 20.

Notes: Ruins of the initial settlement are located in Paliohori (Παλιοχώρι, το) and Mouria (Μούρια).
Dara (*Arb., Al. sn.*), Δάρας or Ντάρας (*Arv. sn.*): Georgacas–McDonald 1968, 298–299; possibly from darë (*Al. n.* pincers, tongs) or dare (*Al. n.* tare).

33. Puloti (پولوتی), *mezraʿa* in the vicinity of Dara, TT10, 10.

Notes: Unidentified.

34. Peryale (پریاله), TT10, 11. AL

Notes: Unidentified.

35. Zepandi (زپاندی), TT10, 11. AL

Notes: Unidentified.
Ζαπάντης (*Arv. sn.*): Biris 1998, 193. According to Vasmer, < zapadь (*Slav. n.* occident, sunset): Vasmer 1941, 71; zapād (*Scr. n.* shadowy place). See also zapat (*Al. adj.* very cold, low temperature): Symeonidis 2010, II 538–539.

36. Ḳrastiki (قراستکی), TT10, 11. GR

Coordinates: X: 330553.241 Y: 4205899.661

Modern Greek: Krastikoi (Κραστικοί, οι)

Regional Unit: Achaia

Municipality: Kalavryta

Municipal Unit: Kalavryta

Bibliography: Pikoulas 2001a, 234.1943; Panagiotopoulos 1987, 270, 303.85: Territorio di Callavritta, Craticus; Pacifico 1704, 122: Territorio di Calaurita, Crasticus; Bory de Saint-Vincent 1834, 74: Éparchie de Kalavrita, Krastiki; Leake 1846, map: Krastiki; Bon 1969, 469–470.

37. Suli (سولی), TT10, 12. AL

Notes: Unidentified.
According to Fourikis and Sarigiannis, Σούλι < sul (*Al. n.* column, pillar, pole; observation post): Fourikis 1922; Sarigiannis 1981, 21–24. According to Biris, < **suli* (*Arv. adj.* tall, upstanding man): Biris 1998, 201; sul (*Al. n.* tree trunk hollowed out to make a boat, dugout); Suli (*Arb. sn.*): Georgacas–McDonald 1968, 353.

38. İflamurari (افلاموراری), TT10, 12. AL

Coordinates:	X: 324090.520 Y: 4211872.855
Modern Greek:	Flamboura (Φλάμπουρα, τα)
Regional Unit:	Achaia
Municipality:	Kalavryta
Municipal Unit:	Kalavryta
Bibliography:	PIKOULAS 2001a, 471.4246. BORY DE SAINT-VINCENT 1834, 73: Éparchie de Kalavrita, Phlamboura; LEAKE 1846, map: Flambura; BON 1969, 469.
Notes:	flamurar (*Arb. n.* ensign, standard bearer); flamurtar (*Al. n.* standard-bearer, flag-bearer). Cf. microtoponym Flambouriari (Φλαμπουριάρη, του) near Seires (Σειρές, οι) in Kalavryta, Achaia: PAPANDREOU 2011, 347.

39. Niķola Manesi (نیقولا مانسی), TT10, 12. AL

Coordinates:	X: 320961.621 Y: 4209463.958
Modern Greek:	Manesi (Μάνεσι, το)
Regional Unit:	Achaia
Municipality:	Kalavryta
Municipal Unit:	Kalavryta
Bibliography:	PIKOULAS 2001a, 273.2316; PANAGIOTOPOULOS 1987, 270, 303.112: Territorio di Callavritta, Manesi; PACIFICO 1704, 123: Territorio di Calaurita, Manessi; BORY DE SAINT-VINCENT 1834, 73: Éparchie de Kalavrita, Manési; LEAKE 1846, map: Mancsi.
Notes:	Νικόλας or Νικόλαος (*Gr. pn.* Nicholas) > Nikollë (*Al. pn.* Nicholas). For Manesi see no. 22.

40. İskliva (اسکلیوه), *mez̧raʿa* in the vicinity of Niķola Manesi, TT10, 12.

Notes:	Unidentified. According to Vasmer, < sliva (*Slav. n.* plum, *Prunus domestica*): VASMER 1941, 145; SYMEONIDIS 2010, II 1281. Σκλήβας (*Gr. sn.*). See also no. 144.

41. Fila (فیله), TT10, 12. AL

Coordinates:	X: 333972.074 Y: 4190878.688
Modern Greek:	Filia [Φίλια, τα (= του)]
Regional Unit:	Achaia
Municipality:	Kalavryta

Municipal Unit: Kleitoria

Bibliography: Pikoulas 2001a, 470.4238; Panagiotopoulos 1987, 269, 302.56, Territorio di Callavritta, Figlia; Pacifico 1704, 122: Territorio di Calaurita, Figlià, *olim Phlius*; Bory de Saint-Vincent 1834, 74: Éparchie de Kalavrita, Philia; Leake 1846, map: Filia.

Notes: According to Symeonidis, < Filiati (*Al. sn.*) < Φίλης, Φίλιος (*Gr. sn.*): Symeonidis 2010, II 1404.

42. **Tireẖlista (ترخلسته), TT10, 13. GR**

Coordinates: X: 322125.884 Y: 4211181.580

Modern Greek: Trehlo (Τρεχλό, το)

Old Toponym: Until 1955: Treklistra (Τρεκλίστρα, η)

Regional Unit: Achaia

Municipality: Kalavryta

Municipal Unit: Kalavryta

Bibliography: Pikoulas 2001a, 456.4099; Panagiotopoulos 1987, 270, 303.83, Territorio di Callavritta, Treclistra; Pacifico 1704, 123: Territorio di Calaurita, Triclisora; Bory de Saint-Vincent 1834, 73: Éparchie de Kalavrita, Triklistra; Leake 1846, map: Triklistra; Skiadas 1993, 239; Stamatelatos–Vamva-Stamatelatou 2001, 745.

43. **Palunbi Ranesi (پالونبی رانسی), TT10, 13. AL**

Notes: Unidentified.
Pëllumb (*Al. pn.* pigeon, dove, *Columbidae*), pallumb (*Arb. n.* pigeon) < palumbus (*Lat. n.* pigeon). Ρένεσης (*Arv. sn.*) < rrenës (*Al. n. colloq.* liar): Biris 1998, 200–201; Georgacas–McDonald 1968, 344. See also rrënjës (*Al. n.*, original inhabitant). According to Symeonidis, < rrënjësi (*Al. n.* place with English oaks, *Quercus robur*): Symeonidis 2010, II 1213.

44. **Ayo İvlaşi (آیو اولاشی), TT10, 14. GR**

Coordinates: X: 316267.227 Y: 4207440.655

Modern Greek: Agios Vlasios (Άγιος Βλάσιος, ο)

Regional Unit: Achaia

Municipality: Kalavryta

Municipal Unit: Kleitoria

Bibliography: Pikoulas 2001a, 44.127; Panagiotopoulos 1987, 269, 302.45: Territorio di Callavritta, S. Vlasi; Pacifico 1704, 122: Territorio di Calaurita, San Biasio; Bory de Saint-Vincent 1834, 74: Éparchie de Kalavrita, Apano/Kato Hagios-Vlasis; Leake 1846, map: A. Vlasios; Sfikopoulos 1987, 196.

45. Ġurġa (غورغه), TT10, 14. AL

Notes:	Unidentified. Cf. microtoponym Gourgia (Γουργιά, του) in the surroundings of Kato Potamia (Κάτω Ποταμιά, η) in Aigialeia, Achaia, Fotopoulos 1982, II 250; Gourga (Γούργα, η) and Gourgou [Γουργού (= στη λάκκα του)] in Messenia: Georgacas–McDonald 1968, 128.

46. Muriki (موریکی), TT10, 15. AL

Coordinates:	X: 317551.752 Y: 4213283.986
Modern Greek:	Mouriki (Μουρίκι, το)
Regional Unit:	Achaia
Municipality:	Kalavryta
Municipal Unit:	Kalavryta
Bibliography:	Pikoulas 2001a, 323.2807; Panagiotopoulos 1987, 270, 303.99: Territorio di Callavritta, Murichi; Pacifico 1704, 122: Territorio di Calaurita, Murichi; Bory de Saint-Vincent 1834, 74: Éparchie de Kalavrita, Mouriki; Leake 1846, map: Muriki.
Notes:	Muriqi (*Al. pn.*), name of an Albanian clan: Georgacas–McDonald 1968, 334. Place name Muriq in Shkodër, Albania.

47. Debrani (دبرانی), TT10, 15. AL

Bibliography:	Pacifico 1704, 122: Territorio di Calaurita, Dembreni.
Notes:	Unidentified. Microtoponym Tembreni Spring (Τεμπρένι, το) in the surroundings of Agios Vlasios (no. 44): Papandreou 2011, 296; its exact location is unknown. Dibran (*Al. n.* of/from Dibër, Albania or neighbouring Debar, North Macedonia; bricklayer, mason). See also no. 609.

48. İştin Bondaya (اشتین بوندایه), TT10, 15. AL

Coordinates:	X: 320397.857 Y: 4215122.620
Modern Greek:	Megas Pontias (Μέγας Ποντιάς, ο)
Regional Unit:	Achaia
Municipality:	Kalavryta
Municipal Unit:	Kalavryta
Bibliography:	Pikoulas 2001a, 282.2409; Panagiotopoulos 1987, 270, 303.115: Territorio di Callavritta, Bodia apano; Pacifico 1704, 122: Territorio di Calaurita, Bodia; Bory de Saint-Vincent 1834, 74: Éparchie de Kalavrita, Bontiadès; Leake 1846, map: Bondia.
Notes:	Στίνης (*Arv. sn.*) < shtyj, shtinj or shtynj (*Al. v.* to push): Biris 1998, 202. Shtini (*Al. sn.*). For Bondaya see no. 86.

49. Ṣavanus (صاوانوس), TT10, 16. GR

Coordinates:	X: 325535.958 Y: 4201949.940
Modern Greek:	Kallifoni (Καλλιφώνι, το)
Old Toponym:	Until 1928: Savanoi (Σαβανοί, οι), Savanous (Σαβανούς, τους)
Regional Unit:	Achaia
Municipality:	Kalavryta
Municipal Unit:	Kalavryta
Bibliography:	Pikoulas 2001a, 172.1341; Panagiotopoulos 1987, 270, 303.111: Territorio di Callavritta, Savanus; Pacifico 1704, 122: Territorio di Calaurita, Sauanus; Bory de Saint-Vincent 1834, 74: Éparchie de Kalavrita, Savani; Leake 1846, map: Savani; Bon 1969, 467, 479; Stamatelatos–Vamva-Stamatelatou 2001, 287.

50. Anastasova (اناستاسوه), TT10, 16. GR

Coordinates:	X: 324704.795 Y: 4197416.321
Modern Greek:	Anastasi (Ανάσταση, η)
Old Toponym:	Until 1953: Anastasova (Αναστάσοβα, η)
Regional Unit:	Achaia
Municipality:	Kalavryta
Municipal Unit:	Aroania
Bibliography:	Pikoulas 2001a, 74.415; Panagiotopoulos 1987, 270, 303.119: Territorio di Callavritta, Anastasova; Pacifico 1704, 122: Territorio di Calaurita, Anastasoua; Bory de Saint-Vincent 1834, 74: Éparchie de Kalavrita, Anastasova; Leake 1846, map: Anastasova; Stamatelatos–Vamva-Stamatelatou 2001, 72.
Notes:	< ανάσταση (*Gr. n.* resurrection) + -ova (*Slav. end.*): Vasmer 1941, 128; Symeonidis 2010, I 249.

51. Droġolavoş (دروغولاوش), TT10, 17. GR

Coordinates:	X: 321480.888 Y: 4200640.228
Modern Greek:	Drovolovo (Δροβολοβό, το)
Regional Unit:	Achaia
Municipality:	Kalavryta
Municipal Unit:	Aroania
Bibliography:	Pikoulas 2001a, 142.1064; Bory de Saint-Vincent 1834, 74: Éparchie de Kalavrita, Drogolovos; Leake 1846, map: Drovoloi.

Notes:	According to Vasmer and Symeonidis, < **Dragalevo(s)*: Vasmer 1941, 133, 153, 166; Symeonidis 2010, I 500. Dragalj (*Scr. pn.*); Place name Dragaljevac Gornji in Bosnia & Herzegovina, Dragaljevina in Montenegro and Dragalevci in Bulgaria; cf. microtoponym Tragaletsi Spring (Τραγαλέτσι, το) in the surroundings of Drymos (no. 539): Papandreou 2011, 332.

52. Seliça (سليچه), TT10, 17. GR

Coordinates:	X: 336139.588 Y: 4227161.895
Modern Greek:	Kato Pteri (Κάτω Πτέρη, η)
Old Toponym:	Until 1971: Selitsa (Σέλιτσα, η)
Regional Unit:	Achaia
Municipality:	Aigialeia
Municipal Unit:	Aigio
Bibliography:	Pikoulas 2001a, 399.3542, 418.3728; Bory de Saint-Vincent 1834, 93: Éparchie de Vostitsa, Ptéri; Leake 1846, map: Fiteri; Stamatelatos–Vamva-Stamatelatou 2001, 332; Dokos–Panagopoulos 1993, 27–28, 333–353: Fter(r)i.
Notes:	According to Vasmer, < **selьce* (*Slav. n. dim.* of selo, village, settlement): Vasmer 1941, 84, 138. Cf. selishtë (*Al. n.* kitchen garden) and selište (*Mac. n.* garden plot near the house), Symeonidis 2010, II 1255.

53. Mavromati (ماوروماتى), TT10, 17. AL

Notes:	Unidentified. Μαυρομάτης (*Gr. sn.* black-eyed).

54. İvlaḫo Ḳalanas (اولاخو قالناس), *mezra'a* in the vicinity of Ṣavanus, TT10, 18.

Coordinates:	X: 311884.729 Y: 4213409.919
Modern Greek:	Kalanos (Κάλανος, ο)
Regional Unit:	Achaia
Municipality:	Erymanthos
Municipal Unit:	Farres
Bibliography:	Pikoulas 2001a, 169.1314; Panagiotopoulos 1987, 268, 302.1: Territorio di Callavritta, Calanos di Nexerò; Bory de Saint-Vincent 1834, 73: Éparchie de Kalavrita, Kalanos; Leake 1846, map: Kalano.
Notes:	Βλάχος (*Gr. n.* Vlach); Vllah (*Al. n.* Vlach). Κάλανος < **κάναλος* (*Gr. n.* big and deep irrigation canal): Symeonidis 2010, I 594.

55. İvlaẖo Yalya (اولاخو یالیا), *mezraʿa* in the vicinity of Şavanus, TT10, 18.

Notes:	Unidentified. The inhabitants of the mountain villages in eastern Achaia use to call the region between Aigeira (Αιγείρα, η) and the Krathis River (Κράθις, ο) Gialos (Γιαλός, ο): Papadopoulos-Papargyriadis 1986, 158. İvlaẖo Yalya, however, does not refer to Gialos, since the latter is located in north-eastern Achaia, on the Corinthian Gulf shore. For İvlaẖo see no. 54. γιαλός < αἰγιαλός (*anc. Gr. n.* seaside).

56. Ḳastel (قاستل), TT10, 18. GR

Coordinates:	X: 328356.876 Y: 4197063.706
Modern Greek:	Kastelli (Καστέλλι, το)
Regional Unit:	Achaia
Municipality:	Kalavryta
Municipal Unit:	Kleitoria
Bibliography:	Pikoulas 2001a, 197.1590; Panagiotopoulos 1987, 270, 303.93: Territorio di Callavritta, Castel Apano e Catù; Pacifico 1704, 122: Territorio di Calaurita, Costeglia; Bory de Saint-Vincent 1834, 74: Éparchie de Kalavrita, Kastéli; Leake 1846, map: Kastelio; Sfikopoulos 1987, 207–208.

57. Ḳazneş (قازنش), TT10, 19. AL

Coordinates:	X: 331429.662 Y: 4196862.212
Modern Greek:	Ano Kleitoria (Άνω Κλειτορία, η)
Old Toponym:	Until 1928: Karnesi (Καρνέσι, το)
Regional Unit:	Achaia
Municipality:	Kalavryta
Municipal Unit:	Kleitoria
Bibliography:	Pikoulas 2001a, 210.1715; Panagiotopoulos 1987, 270, 303.96: Territorio di Callavritta, Carnesi; Pacifico 1704, 122: Territorio di Calaurita, Carnesi; Bory de Saint-Vincent 1834, 74: Éparchie de Kalavrita, Karnési; Leake 1846, map: Karnesi; Skiadas 1993, 237; Stamatelatos–Vamva-Stamatelatou 2001, 83.
Notes:	kasnec (*Al. n.* herald, town-crier, announcer) < kaznьсь (*Slav. n.* announcer): Orel 1998, 173; Jochalas 2011, I 35. Κασνέσης (*Arv. sn.*): Biris 1998, 194. Place name Kasnec in Shkodër, Albania. Symeonidis proposed a possible connection to qazhnësi [*Al. n.* place where coarse homespun white flannels (qazhnë) are made]: Symeonidis 2010, I 583.

58. İstrazova (استرازوه), TT10, 20. GR

Coordinates:	X: 325888.573 Y: 4186006.715

Modern Greek:	Dafni (Δάφνη, η)
Old Toponym:	Until 1928: Strezova (Στρέζοβα, η)
Regional Unit:	Achaia
Municipality:	Kalavryta
Municipal Unit:	Païoi
Bibliography:	Pikoulas 2001a, 130.952; Panagiotopoulos 1987, 268, 302.28: Territorio di Callavrita, Stresova; Pacifico 1704, 122: Territorio di Calaurita, Stressoua; Bory de Saint-Vincent 1834, 74: Éparchie de Kalavrita, Strézova; Kolokotronis 1981, 156; Leake 1830, II 106–107, 240, 249: Strézova; Leake 1846, map: Strezova; Skiadas 1993, 242; Stamatelatos–Vamva-Stamatelatou 2001, 179; Sfikopoulos 1987, 206.
Notes:	Vasmer linked it to place name Strežovo and Strezovce in North Macedonia: Vasmer 1941, 139. According to Symeonidis, the etymology of the word is **strъžь* (*Slav. n.* the deepest part of a river, talweg): Symeonidis 2010, II 1321; cf. hydronym Strežna Reka in Bulgaria.

59. Vesini (وسينى), 1/14662, 25. GR

Coordinates:	X: 321455.701 Y: 4188374.271
Modern Greek:	Vesini (Βεσίνι, το)
Regional Unit:	Achaia
Municipality:	Kalavryta
Municipal Unit:	Païoi
Bibliography:	Pikoulas 2001a, 102.680; Panagiotopoulos 1987, 268, 302.35: Territorio di Callavritta, Vesigni; Pacifico 1704, 122: Territorio di Calaurita, Vessini; Bory de Saint-Vincent 1834, 74: Éparchie de Kalavrita, Vésini; Leake 1846, map: Vesini; Sfikopoulos 1987, 206–207.

60. Ḳaratula (قراتولا), 1/14662, 25. AL

Coordinates:	X: 335887.720 Y: 4185729.660
Modern Greek:	Karatoula (Καράτουλα, του)
Regional Unit:	Arcadia
Municipality:	Gortynia
Municipal Unit:	Kleitoras
Bibliography:	GLET 1998, II 25.
Notes:	Uninhabited location to the north-east of Theoktisto (Θεόκτιστο, το). See no. 25.

61. Sumaki (سوماکی), 1/14662, 25. AL

Notes:	Unidentified. Σουμάκης (*Arv. sn.*): Biris 1998, 201; sumak or shqeme (*Al. n.* Sicilian sumac, *Rhus coraria*).

62. Liḳuresi (ليقورسى), *mezraʿa* in the vicinity of Sumaki, 1/4662, 25.

Coordinates:	X: 342662.961 Y: 4191648.551
Modern Greek:	Lykouria [Λυκουρία, η (= Λυκούρι, Λυκούρια)]
Regional Unit:	Achaia
Municipality:	Kalavryta
Municipal Unit:	Kleitoria
Bibliography:	Pikoulas 2001a, 266.2250; Panagiotopoulos 1987, 268, 302.23: Territorio di Callavritta, Licuria; Pacifico 1704, 122: Territorio di Calaurita, Licuria; Bory de Saint-Vincent 1834, 74: Éparchie de Kalavrita, Lykouria; Leake 1846, map: Lykuria.
Notes:	Λικούρεσης (*Arv. sn.*) < lëkurë (*Al. n.* skin, leather): Biris 1998, 196; lëkurës or lëkurërrjepës (*Al. n.* flayer of hides, skinner). See also Georgacas–McDonald 1968, 326–327. The schwa ë /ə/ occasionally turned into i /i/ in Arvanitic: Botsaris 1993, 75; Fourikis 1933, 143; cf. likurë and lëkurë in Arbërisht.

2. District of Mizis̱ra(Mystras) (Maps 3–4)

63. Mizis̱ra (ميزثره), TT10, 18.

Coordinates:	X: 355530.509 Y: 4103482.625
Modern Greek:	Mystras (Μυστράς, ο). *Byz. Gr.* Myzithras (Μυζηθράς, ο)
Regional Unit:	Laconia
Municipality:	Sparti
Municipal Unit:	Mystras
Bibliography:	Pikoulas 2001a, 336.2932; Panagiotopoulos 1987, 285, 309.78, 79, 81: Territorio di Mistra, Borgo di Missocori, P° Recinto della Città, Recinto Superior della Città (Mistra); Pacifico 1704, 132: Territorio di Mistrà, Mistrà Città; Hopf 1873, 206: Misitra; Bory de Saint-Vincent 1834, 80: Éparchie de Mistra, Mistra; Leake 1830, I 126–130: Mistrá; Leake 1846, map: Mistra; Bon 1969, 639–642; Zakythinos 1953, 90–91, 169–172; Andrews 2006, 159–182.
Notes:	The capital town of the Mizis̱ra District (*nefs-i Mizis̱ra*) is mentioned in TT10-1/14662 only referring to Priniḳos village (no. 64).

64. Priniḳos (پرنيقوس), TT10, 18. GR

Coordinates:	X: 386411.221 Y: 4077001.121
Modern Greek:	Asteri (Αστέρι, το)

Old Toponym:	Until 1928: Vriniko (Βρίνικο, το)
Regional Unit:	Laconia
Municipality:	Evrotas
Municipal Unit:	Elos
Bibliography:	Pikoulas 2001a, 88.543; Panagiotopoulos 1987, 286, 309.8: Territorio d'Eleos, Duragli Brignico e Baba; Bory de Saint-Vincent 1834, 81: Éparchie de Mistra, Birniko; Leake 1830, I 195–197: Príniko; Skiadas 1993, 391; Stamatelatos–Vamva-Stamatelatou 2001, 108.
Notes:	< **Brъnьnikъ* < brъnьje (*old Bg. n.* mud, slime, sediment): Vasmer 1941, 166; Symeonidis 2010, I 387. Place name Bъrnik in Bulgaria.

3. District of Miḫlu (Mouhli) (Maps 5–6)

65. Miḫlu (میخلو), TT10, 21.

Coordinates:	X: 361852.986 Y: 4148964.273
Modern Greek:	Mouhli (Μούχλι/Μουχλί, το)
Regional Unit:	Arcadia
Municipality:	Tripoli
Municipal Unit:	Mantineia
Bibliography:	Hopf 1873, 205: Mucli; Pacifico 1704, 119: Territorio di Tripolizza, Steno Muclì; Expédition 1832: Palæo Moukhli; Leake 1830, II 335–337: Mukhla (τὰ Παλαιὰ Μούχλα), Mokhlí (ἡ Παλαιὰ Μοχλή); Leake 1846, map: P. Mukhli; Nezeritis 1998, 291–293; Sfikopoulos 1987, 132–136; Kordosis 1986c; Vasilikopoulou 1990; Bon 1969, 523–524; Konti 1985, 112–114; Zakythinos 1953, 157–158; Dragoumis 1921, 84–93, 101–118; Eleftheriou 2004, 8–25.
Notes:	The Miḫlu entry in the TT10 does not include the town of Miḫlu, (*nefs-i Miḫlu*), as expected. According to the Aragon chronicle, Nikli was destroyed in 1296 by a Byzantine general who defeated the Franks, on the grounds that as it was situated on the plain it was not strategically important: Fatio 1885, 106, §485. The fortresses of Mouhli and Tsipiana (no. 74) were constructed in its place on the overlooking moutains.

66. Astriçi (آستریچی), TT10, 21.

Coordinates:	X: 386608.691 Y: 4140409.946
Modern Greek:	Astros (Άστρος, το)
Old Toponym:	Agiannitika Kalyvia (Αγιαννίτικα Καλύβια, τα)
Regional Unit:	Arcadia
Municipality:	Voreia Kynouria
Municipal Unit:	Voreia Kynouria

Bibliography:	PIKOULAS 2001a, 89.547; HOPF 1873, 202, 206: Astrizi; BORY DE SAINT-VINCENT 1834, 72: Éparchie d'Hagios Petros, (Kalyvia d') Hagios Joannis; LEAKE 1846, map: Kal. A.I.; KOLOKOTRONIS 1981, 125; CARILE 1970, 403; MARKL 1966, 22; BON 1969, 515–516, *planche* 6.
Notes:	Astriçi village is mentioned in the TT10 only referring to its *mezraʿa*s: Astro (no. 67), Duşa Dara (no. 68), Luvari (no. 69) and Plaşa (no. 70). According to Sfikopoulos, the ruins of Pyrgos (Πύργος, ο) and the later Kastro (Κάστρο, το) near Astros could possibly belong to Astriçi: SFIKOPOULOS 1987, 212. Bees suggested that it should be located in Kastraki/Kastritsi (Καστράκι/Καστρίτσι, το) or Astritsi (tower-house next to the chapel of Agios Petros, dependency of Agia Triada) near Thyrea (Θυρέα, η): BEES 1908, 98–99. In Venetian documents it is mentioned as Astrizi, identified with Astros by Zakythinos and supported by Ballas: ZAKYTHINOS 1975, 164; BALLAS 2001–2, 208–209.

67. Astro (آسترو), *mezraʿa* in the vicinity of Astriçi, TT10, 21.

Coordinates:	X: 378080.286 Y: 4134059.006
Modern Greek:	Agios Ioannis/Kastro Orias (Άγιος Ιωάννης, ο/Κάστρο Ωριάς, το)
Regional Unit:	Arcadia
Municipality:	Voreia Kynouria
Municipal Unit:	Voreia Kynouria
Bibliography:	PIKOULAS 2001a, 51.194; HOPF 1873, 202, 206: Astro; EXPÉDITION 1832: Kastro tis Orias; LEAKE 1830, II 486; SFIKOPOULOS 1987, 213–215; BON 1969, 515–516, *planche* 6; BALLAS 2001–2, 209–210; BEES 1908, 100–101.
Notes:	It is identified as the castle 'La Estella' of the Aragon Chronicle and Κάστρον της Ωριάς: FATIO 1885, 49, §214. Its ruins are still visible on a hilltop opposite Agios Ioannis village.

68. Duşa Dara (دوشه دآره), *mezraʿa* in the vicinity of Astriçi, TT10, 21.

Notes:	Unidentified. Dusha (*Arv. pn. dim.* of Diamantis): BIRIS 1998, 87, n. 4; KOLLEKA 1987, 88. Place name Dusha in Elbasan, Albania. For Dara see no. 32.

69. Luvari (لووارى), *mezraʿa* in the vicinity of Astriçi, TT10, 21.

Notes:	Unidentified. Possibly from luvari (*Al. n.* laurel, *Laurus nobilis L.*). Λουβιάρης (*Gr. sn.*): GEORGACAS–MCDONALD 1968, 182. See also lluver (*Ȧrv. adj.* bitter): JOCHALAS 2011, II 781.

70. Plaşa (پلاشه), *mezraʿa* in the vicinity of Astriçi, TT10, 21.

Notes:	Unidentified. See no. 14.

71. Pikerni (پكرنى), TT10, 21. AL

Coordinates:	X: 360893.864 Y: 4167783.794

Modern Greek:	Pikernis [Πικέρνης, ο (= Πικέρνη, του)]
Regional Unit:	Arcadia
Municipality:	Tripoli
Municipal Unit:	Mantineia
Bibliography:	Pikoulas 2001a, 382.3380; Panagiotopoulos 1987, 244, 293.54: Territorio di Tripolizza, Picherni e Sanga; Pacifico 1704, 119: Territorio di Tripolizza, Pichierni; Bory de Saint-Vincent 1834, 92: Éparchie de Tripolitsa, Pikerni; Leake 1846, map: Pikerni.
Notes:	Πικέρνης (*Byz. Gr., Arv. sn.*): Biris 1998, 200. Place name Piqeras in Vlorë, Albania. As Ginosatis informs, the Arvanites inhabitants of Spata (Σπάτα, τα) in Attica, used to call Pikermi (Πικέρμι, το) as Pikera (Πικερά), something that supports the link to the place name Piqeras: Ginosatis 1988, 130; Ginosatis 1994; Kallivretakis 2003, 224–225. According to Lambros, the word originates from ἐπικέρνης or πιγκέρνης (*Byz. Gr. n.* cup-bearer) < pincerna (*Lat. n.* butler, chief wine-attendant): Lambros 1896, 158; Symeonidis 2010, II 1145.

72. Naşi (ناشی), TT10, 22. AL

Coordinates:	X: 361282.697 Y: 4170557.469
Modern Greek:	Nasia (Νάσια, η)
Regional Unit:	Arcadia
Municipality:	Tripoli
Municipal Unit:	Mantineia
Bibliography:	GLET 1998, II 435.
Notes:	Ununhabited location to the west of Sangas (no. 73).

73. Brasna Sanḳa (براسنه سانقه), TT10, 23. AL

Coordinates:	X: 363926.762 Y: 4170090.870
Modern Greek:	Sangas [Σάγκας, ο (= Σάγκα, του)]
Regional Unit:	Arcadia
Municipality:	Tripoli
Municipal Unit:	Mantineia
Bibliography:	Pikoulas 2001a, 412.3672; Panagiotopoulos 1987, 244, 293.54: Territorio di Tripolizza, Picherni e Sanga; Pacifico 1704, 119: Territorio di Tripolizza, Sanga; Expédition 1832: Sanga; Bory de Saint-Vincent 1834, 92: Éparchie de Tripolitsa, Zanga; Leake 1846, map: Sanga.
Notes:	Σάγκας (*Al. sn.*): Symeonidis 2010, II 1234.

74. Çipyana (چیپانه), TT10, 23. GR

Coordinates:	X: 364341.517 Y: 4163817.696
Modern Greek:	Nestani (Νεστάνη, η)
Old Toponym:	Until 1927: Tsipiana (Τσιπιανά, τα)
Regional Unit:	Arcadia
Municipality:	Tripoli
Municipal Unit:	Mantineia
Bibliography:	Pikoulas 2001a, 342.2995; Panagiotopoulos 1987, 244, 293.55, Territorio di Tripolizza, Zipiana; Pacifico 1704, 119: Territorio di Tripolizza, Sipianà; Hopf 1873, 205: Zipiana; Bory de Saint-Vincent 1834, 92: Éparchie de Tripolitsa, Tsipiana; Leake 1830, I 101, 109, III 95: Tzipianá; Leake 1846, 377, map: Tzipiana; Sfikopoulos 1987, 223–224; Bon 1969, 524; Konti 1985, 112; Dragoumis 1921, 101–118.
Notes:	It was constructed in 1296 after the demolition of the Nikli fortress (see no. 65). According to Dragoumis, < **Κηπιανά* < **κήπια* (*Byz. Gr. n.* gardens), Dragoumis 1921, 104. Place name Banja Čepino in Bulgaria and Čeplje in Slovenia: Vasmer 1941, 145, 159.

75. Perişori (پریشوری), TT10, 24. GR

Coordinates:	X: 361464.153 Y: 4155574.435
Modern Greek:	Parori (?) (Παρόρι, το)
Regional Unit:	Arcadia
Municipality:	Tripoli
Municipal Unit:	Korythio
Bibliography:	Pikoulas 2001a, 370.3267; Bory de Saint-Vincent 1834, 93: Éparchie de Tripolitsa, Parori; Leake 1846, map: Parori.

76. Raḫova (راخوه), TT10, 25. AL

Notes:	Unidentified. The settlement should be sought in the vicinity of Mouhli (no. 65). Orěchovo, orěchь (*old Slav. n.* walnut, walnut tree, *Juglans L.*; place with nut trees): Vasmer 1941, 21; Symeonidis 2010, II 1210.

77. Plaşa (پلاشه), *mezraʿa* in the vicinity of Raḫova, TT10, 26.

Notes:	Unidentified. See no. 14.

4. District of Bejenik (Vlaherna) (Maps 7–8)

78. Bejenik, nefs-i (بژنيك), TT10, 28. GR

Coordinates:	X: 345627.151 Y: 4175480.097
Modern Greek:	Vlaherna (Βλαχέρνα, η)
Old Toponym:	Until 1928: Bezeniko (Μπεζενίκο, το)
Regional Unit:	Arcadia
Municipality:	Tripoli
Municipal Unit:	Levidi
Bibliography:	PIKOULAS 2001a, 105.705; PANAGIOTOPOULOS 1987, 244, 293.59: Territorio di Tripolizza, Besegnicò; PACIFICO 1704, 119: Territorio di Tripolizza, Bessenico; BORY DE SAINT-VINCENT 1834, 92: Éparchie de Tripolitsa, Bézéniko; HOPF 1873, 202: Bocenico, 206: Posenichi; LEAKE 1830, II 275, III 103, 118, 120: Bazeníko; SKIADAS 1993, 304; STAMATELATOS–VAMVA-STAMATELATOU 2001, 136; SFIKOPOULOS 1987, 224–225; BALLAS 1995, 151; BON 1969, 404.
Notes:	According to Vasmer, < **bъzьnikъ*, bъzъ (*Slav. n.* elder, *Sambucus nigra*): VASMER 1941, 156; SYMEONIDIS 2010, I 980. Place name Bezník in the Czech Republic and Beźnik in Poland.

79. Vuzyas (ووزياس), *mezraʿa* in the vicinity of Bejenik, TT10, 28.

Notes:	Unidentified.

80. Plaşa (پلاشه), *mezraʿa* in the vicinity of Bejenik, TT10, 28.

Coordinates:	X: 347808.795 Y: 4177978.431
Modern Greek:	Ples(i)a [Πλέσ(ι)α, του]
Regional Unit:	Arcadia
Municipality:	Tripoli
Municipal Unit:	Levidi
Bibliography:	PIKOULAS 2001a, 389.3441; LEAKE 1846, map: Plesia; SKIADAS 1993, 304.
Notes:	See no. 14.

81. Levizi (لويذى), TT10, 29. GR

Coordinates:	X: 349708.936 Y: 4171785.378
Modern Greek:	Levidi (Λεβίδι, το)
Regional Unit:	Arcadia
Municipality:	Tripoli

Municipal Unit:	Levidi
Bibliography:	Pikoulas 2001a, 250.2096; Panagiotopoulos 1987, 243, 292.3: Territorio di Tripolizza, Levidi; Pacifico 1704, 119: Territorio di Tripolizza, Levidi; Bory de Saint-Vincent 1834, 92: Éparchie de Tripolitsa, Lévidi; Leake 1846, map: Levidhi (Elymia).

82. Ḳameniça (قامنيچه), TT10, 29. GR

Coordinates:	X: 340454.544 Y: 4176957.985
Modern Greek:	Kamenitsa (Καμενίτσα, η)
Regional Unit:	Arcadia
Municipality:	Gortynia
Municipal Unit:	Vytina
Bibliography:	Pikoulas 2001a, 182.1443; Panagiotopoulos 1987, 243, 293.21: Territorio di Tripolizza, Caminizza; Pacifico 1704, 119: Territorio di Tripolizza, Caminizza; Bory de Saint-Vincent 1834, 92: Éparchie de Tripolitsa, Kaminitsa; Leake 1846, map: Kaminitza; Sfikopoulos 1987, 226; Bon 1969, 403–404.
Notes:	According to Vasmer, < kamenica (*Slav. n.* rocky place or river): Vasmer 1941, 135; Symeonidis 2010, I 615–616. Place name Kamenica in Kosovo, Serbia. Hydronym Kamenica in Russia and Kamenyća in Ukraine.

83. Lopesi (لوپسی), TT10, 30. AL

Coordinates:	X: 348336.612 Y: 4182060.217
Modern Greek:	Lopesi [Λόπεσι, το (= Λόπεση, του)]
Regional Unit:	Arcadia
Municipality:	Tripoli
Municipal Unit:	Levidi
Notes:	Uninhabited location to the south of Limni (Λίμνη, η), where the ruins of an abandoned village are used as sheep-folds by the locals. According to Sarris, < lopë (*Al. n.* cow): Sarris 1928, 146. Place name Lopsi Martalosit in Gjirokastër and Mt Lopes in Tepelenë, Albania: Hahn 1854, I 239. According to Lambros, Fourikis, and Biris, it should not be linked to the Albanian word for cow: Lambros 1896, 188; Fourikis 1929, 124–128; Biris 1998, 196. Symeonidis, on the other hand, connected it to lopësi (*Al. n.* cowshed, cowhouse): Symeonidis 2010, I 833. The toponym most probably derives from an Albanian surname of uncertified meaning, Λόπεσης (*Arv. sn.*). See also llopës [*Al. n.* light-coloured September-ripening (fig) with very large sweet fruit]; llopës or llupës (*Al. adj.* voracious).

84. Aġali (آغالی), TT10, 30. AL

Coordinates:	X: 348477.363 Y: 4184875.241
Modern Greek:	Elatos (Έλατος, ο)

Old Toponym:	Until 1940: Ano Agali (Άνω Άγαλη, η); until 1955: Ano Agalis (Άνω Άγαλης, ο)
Regional Unit:	Arcadia
Municipality:	Tripoli
Municipal Unit:	Levidi
Bibliography:	Pikoulas 2001a, 147.1114; Panagiotopoulos 1987, 243, 292.15: Territorio di Tripolizza, Agagli e Pungachi; Pacifico 1704, 119: Territorio di Tripolizza, Aguli; Expédition 1832: Apano/Kato Agali; Bory de Saint-Vincent 1834, 92: Éparchie de Tripolitsa, Apano Agali; Leake 1846, map: Ap./K. Agali; Skiadas 1993, 303; Stamatelatos–Vamva-Stamatelatou 2001, 210.

85. Bendeni/Pendeni (بندنی/پندنی), TT10, 30. AL

Coordinates:	X: 351785.017 Y: 4183010.287
Modern Greek:	Diakopi (Διακόπι, το)
Old Toponym:	Until 1928: Benteni (Μπεντένι, το)
Regional Unit:	Arcadia
Municipality:	Tripoli
Municipal Unit:	Levidi
Bibliography:	Pikoulas 2001a, 135.1000; Panagiotopoulos 1987, 244, 293.38: Territorio di Tripolizza, Bedegnico; Pacifico 1704, 119: Territorio di Tripolizza, Micro-Bedegni; Bory de Saint-Vincent 1834, 92: Éparchie de Tripolitsa, Bédéni; Leake 1830, III 103: Bedéni; Skiadas 1993, 304; Stamatelatos–Vamva-Stamatelatou 2001, 187.
Notes:	Μπεντένης (*Arv. sn.*): Biris 1998, 198.

86. Bondaya (بوندایه), TT10, 31. AL

Coordinates:	X: 354037.036 Y: 4174811.529
Modern Greek:	Palaiopyrgos (Παλαιόπυργος, ο)
Old Toponym:	Until 1928: Bontia (Μποντιά, του)
Regional Unit:	Arcadia
Municipality:	Tripoli
Municipal Unit:	Levidi
Bibliography:	Pikoulas 2001a, 356.3128; Panagiotopoulos 1987, 244, 293.40: Territorio di Tripolizza, Bondia; Pacifico 1704, 119: Territorio di Tripolizza, Bodea; Bory de Saint-Vincent 1834, 92: Éparchie de Tripolitsa, Botia; Leake 1830, II 277: Bútia; Leake 1846, map: Butia; Skiadas 1993, 304; Stamatelatos–Vamva-Stamatelatou 2001, 575.

Notes:	The locals call it Bontia (Μποντιά, η). According to Stavropoulos, the place name Bontia (Μποντιά, η), modern Malthi (Μάλθη, η) in Trifylia, Messenia, derives from Ποντιάς < Ποντέας < Ποντεύς (*anc. Gr. pn.*): Stavropoulos 1988, 542–544. He noted, however, that Bontia in Arcadia derives from botinë (*Al. n.* swamp, marsh); cf. botë (*Al. n.* light-gray clay): Symeonidis 2010, I 992.

87. Sina (سينه), TT10, 31. AL

Coordinates:	X: 354037.036 Y: 4171855.754
Modern Greek:	Sinas (Σίνας, ο)
Regional Unit:	Arcadia
Municipality:	Tripoli
Municipal Unit:	Levidi
Bibliography:	GLET 1998, III 250.
Notes:	Uninhabited location 4km east of Levidi. Σίνας (*Gr., Al. sn.*). Place name Sina e Epërme and Sina e Poshtme in Dibër, Albania: Symeonidis 2010, II 1267.

88. Çarnota (چارنوته/چارنوتا), TT10, 31. AL

Coordinates:	X: 333909.613 Y: 4192123.928
Modern Greek:	Lefkasio (Λευκάσιο, το)
Old Toponym:	Until 1928: Tsorota (Τσορωτά, τα)
Regional Unit:	Achaia
Municipality:	Kalavryta
Municipal Unit:	Kleitoria
Bibliography:	Pikoulas 2001a, 252.2119; Panagiotopoulos 1987, 270, 303.102: Territorio di Callavritta, Cernotà; Pacifico 1704, 122: Territorio di Calaurita, Cernotà; Bory de Saint-Vincent 1834, 74: Éparchie de Kalavrita, Tsérota; Leake 1830, II 268: Tzernotá; Leake 1846, 226: Tzernota; Skiadas 1993, 240.
Notes:	< černota (*Ru. adj.* black), (*Bg. n.* blackness). It is a commonly used prefix in Russian surnames: Benson 1992, 136. Τσερνοτάς, Τσερωτάς, Τσερνετόπουλος (*Gr. sn.*): Vertsetis 1991, 120–124.

89. Ḳandila (قانديله), TT10, 32. GR

Coordinates:	X: 357027.999 Y: 4181673.151
Modern Greek:	Kandila (Κανδήλα, η)
Regional Unit:	Arcadia
Municipality:	Tripoli
Municipal Unit:	Levidi

Bibliography:	Pikoulas 2001a, 185.1468; Panagiotopoulos 1987, 243, 293.20: Territorio di Tripolizza, Candilla; Pacifico 1704, 119: Territorio di Tripolizza, Candilla; Leake 1830, III 103: Kandíla; Hopf 1873, 206: Candela Catafigo; Bory de Saint-Vincent 1834, 92: Éparchie de Tripolitsa, Kandila; Sfikopoulos 1987, 137–138; Carile 1970, 401.

90. Doşkesi (دوشكسى), TT10, 33. AL

Coordinates:	X: 354318.538 Y: 4181356.461
Modern Greek:	Toskesi/Doskesi [Τόσκεσι/Ντόσκεσι, το (= Τόσκεση/Ντόσκεση του)]
Regional Unit:	Arcadia
Municipality:	Tripoli
Municipal Unit:	Levidi
Bibliography:	Vagenas 1986, 108–109.
Notes:	Uninhabited location to the south-west of Kandila (no. 89), where ruins are traced. Toshk or tosk (*Arb. n.* Tosk, inhabitant of Toskëri region in southern Albania); toskë (*Al. n.* Tosk; *adj.* pertaining to Toskëri). Τόσκεσης (*Arv. sn.*): Biris 1998, 202. Place name Toshkes in Gjirokastër and Fier, Albania.

91. Ḫayḳal (خايقال), TT10, 33. AL

Notes:	Unidentified. The local oral history refers to a deserted village named Haikali (Χαϊκάλι, το) in the vicinity of Kandila (no. 89). Its exact location is unknown. According to Biris, Χαϊκάλης (*Arv. sn.*) < kalë (*Al. n.* horse): Biris 1998, 202–203. According to Symeonidis, < haj e kalit (*Al. phr.* stud-farm): Symeonidis 2010, II 1423. Place name Hekal in Fier, Vlorë and Tiranë, and Hekalë in Tiranë, Albania: Gelasius 1942a, 269; Kolleka 1983, 30. Hekal (*Al. sn.*). See also Georgacas–McDonald 1968, 278.

92. Ḳoraḳovuni (قورهقوووني), TT10, 34. GR

Coordinates:	X: 389870.356 Y: 4128698.808
Modern Greek:	Oreino Korakovouni (Ορεινό Κορακοβούνι, το)
Regional Unit:	Arcadia
Municipality:	Voreia Kynouria
Municipal Unit:	Voreia Kynouria
Bibliography:	Pikoulas 2001a, 352.3088; Panagiotopoulos 1987, 246, 294.11: Territorio di S. Pietro di Zacugna, Coracovugni; Pacifico 1704, 120: Territorio di S.Pietro di Zaccognà, Caracomegni; Bory de Saint-Vincent 1834, 72: Éparchie d'Hagios Petros, Karakovouni; Leake 1846, map: Korako vuni.

93. Perṯor (پرثور), TT10, 34. GR

Coordinates:	X: 353820.548 Y: 4155845.238

Modern Greek:	Perthori (Περθώρι, το)
Regional Unit:	Arcadia
Municipality:	Tripoli
Municipal Unit:	Tripoli
Bibliography:	Pikoulas 2001a, 375.3306; Panagiotopoulos 1987, 243, 292.12: Territorio di Tripolizza, Peritori; Pacifico 1704, 119: Territorio di Tripolizza, Perthori; Bory de Saint-Vincent 1834, 93: Éparchie de Tripolitsa, Perthori; Leake 1846, map: Perthori; Konti 1985, 115–116.

94. Açiḫolos (آچيخولوس), TT10, 35. GR

Coordinates:	X: 325631.285 Y: 4155064.175
Modern Greek:	Atsiholos (Ατσίχολος, ο)
Regional Unit:	Arcadia
Municipality:	Megalopoli
Municipal Unit:	Gortyna
Bibliography:	Pikoulas 2001a, 89.550; Panagiotopoulos 1987, 259, 299.46: Territorio di Caritena, Acigolos; Pacifico 1704, 129: Territorio di Caritena, Accigolas; Bory de Saint-Vincent 1834, 76: Éparchie de Karytæne Atsikholo; Leake 1846, map: Atzikolo; Konti 1985, 101; Gritsopoulos 1987–88, 455.

95. İskiliç (اسكليج), TT10, 36. AL

Coordinates:	X: 333370.907 Y: 4150803.833
Modern Greek:	Skyliki (?) (Σκυλίκη, του)
Regional Unit:	Arcadia
Municipality:	Gortynia
Municipal Unit:	Trikolona
Bibliography:	Dokos 1977–84, 313.
Notes:	In the Grimani Archive (1696–1700) a church of St George is mentioned in Skyliki in the vicinity of Palamari (Παλαμάρι, το); its exact location is unknown. Σκυλίτζης (*Gr. sn.*).

96. Mujaki (موژاكى), TT10, 36. AL

Coordinates:	X: 357299.828 Y: 4147324.554
Modern Greek:	Perpataris (?) (Περπατάρης, ο)
Old Toponym:	Until 1928: Mouzaki (Μουζάκι, το); until 1940: Perpatari (Περπατάρι, το)

Regional Unit:	Arcadia
Municipality:	Tripoli
Municipal Unit:	Tripoli
Bibliography:	Pikoulas 2001a, 376.3322; Panagiotopoulos 1987, 243, 292.10: Territorio di Tripolizza, Musachi; Pacifico 1704, 119: Territorio di Tripolizza, Mosachi; Bory de Saint-Vincent 1834, 93: Éparchie de Tripolitsa, Mouzaki; Leake 1846, map: Muzaki; Skiadas 1993, 297; Stamatelatos–Vamva-Stamatelatou 2001, 613.
Notes:	Muzhak (*Al. pn.*). The inhabitants of Myzeqe region in central Albania were named by their ancestor and chieftain, Lalë Muzhaqi (see no. 410). Place name Muzhak in Berat, Albania. See also no. 380.

97. Kerbova (كربووه), TT10, 36. AL

Coordinates:	X: 324637.205 Y: 4142638.177
Modern Greek:	Kastanohori (?) (Καστανοχώρι, το)
Old Toponym:	Until 1928: Krambovos (Κραμποβός, ο)
Regional Unit:	Arcadia
Municipality:	Megalopoli
Municipal Unit:	Megalopoli
Bibliography:	Pikoulas 2001a, 197.1588; Panagiotopoulos 1987, 255, 297.1: Territorio di Leondari, Grambobo; Pacifico 1704, 128: Territorio di Leondari, Grambobò; Bory de Saint-Vincent 1834, 79: Éparchie de Léondari, Krambovos; Leake 1846, map: Krabovo; Skiadas 1993, 333; Stamatelatos–Vamva-Stamatelatou 2001, 316.
Notes:	Cf. Krambovikos Spring (Κραμποβίκος, ο) by the deserted village Agridaki (Αγριδάκι, το) in the vicinity of Kamenitsa (no. 82). < grabъ (*Slav. n.* hornbeam, *Carpinus betulus*): Vasmer 1941, 155; Symeonidis 2010, I 766. Place name Grabovo, Grabovac and Grabovica in Serbia, Croatia, Bosnia & Herzegovina and Grabovec in Slovenia.

98. Ustruza/İstruza Potamya (اوستروزه/استروزه پوتامیه), TT10, 36. AL

Coordinates:	X: 335146.049 Y: 4129253.603
Modern Greek:	Potamia (?) (Ποταμιά, η)
Regional Unit:	Arcadia
Municipality:	Megalopoli
Municipal Unit:	Falaisia
Bibliography:	Pikoulas 2001a, 393.3486; Bory de Saint-Vincent 1834, 79: Éparchie de Léondari, Potamia; Leake 1846, map: Potamia.
Notes:	< **stružьja* < struga (*Slav. n.* wave): Vasmer 1941, 97, 117, 158; Symeonidis 2010, II 1323–1324; strúga (*Slov. n.* rill, riverbed, creek). ποταμιά (*Gr. n.* river-basin, riverside).

99. İvlaẖo Filito (اولاخو فليتو), *mezraʿa* in the vicinity of İstruza Potamya, TT10, 37.

Notes:	Unidentified. For İvlaẖo see no. 54.

5. District of Voştiça (Aigio) (Maps 9–10)

100. Voştiça, nefs-i (ووشتيچه), TT10, 42. GR

Coordinates:	X: 332412.875 Y: 4235059.712
Modern Greek:	Aigio (Αίγιο, το)
Old Toponym:	Vostitsa (Βοστίτσα, η)
Regional Unit:	Achaia
Municipality:	Aigialeia
Municipal Unit:	Aigio
Bibliography:	Pikoulas 2001a, 62.301; Panagiotopoulos 1987, 279, 307.33: Territorio di Vostizza, Vostizza; Pacifico 1704, 121: Territorio di Vostizza, Vostizza Terra; Bory de Saint-Vincent 1834, 93: Éparchie de Vostitsa, Vostitsa; Kolokotronis 1981, 66, 82, 109ff.; Leake 1830, II 111, III 178, 184–192: Vostítza; Leake 1846, 408, map: Vostitza (Ægium); Skiadas 1993, 228; Sfikopoulos 1987, 147–149; Wagstaff–Sloane–Chrysochoou 2002; Hopf 1873, 202, 205: Vostizza vel Vistizza; Longnon–Topping 1969, 254–255; Bon 1969, 463–466; Dokos–Panagopoulos 1993, 7–8: Vostizza.
Notes:	< **Ovoštica* (*Slav. n.* place with orchards) < ovoštь (*Slav. n.* fruit): Vasmer 1941, 131–132; Symeonidis 2010, I 373.

101. Manastır-ı Yirondos der Taḳsiyarẖi (مناستر يروندوس در تاقسيارخى), TT10, 44. GR

Coordinates:	X: 328197.836 Y: 4226706.974
Modern Greek:	Gerontos Osiou Leontiou Monastery (I.M. Γέροντος Οσίου Λεοντίου, η), Palaiomonastiro (Παλαιομονάστηρο, το)
Regional Unit:	Achaia
Municipality:	Aigialeia
Municipal Unit:	Aigio
Bibliography:	Pikoulas 2001a, 314.2717; Panitsas–Papatheodorou 2003, 21, 31; Tsiknakis 1995, 54–56; Bory de Saint-Vincent 1834, 94: Éparchie de Vostitsa, Mon[re] Taxiarkhi; Zakythinos 1953, 306; Dokos–Panagopoulos 1993, 9, 23–25, 295–297: Monastero di S. Michel Archangelo/S. Michiel Arcangello.
Notes:	The monastery was founded by Osios Leontios (ca. 1377–1452) on a steep cliff of Mt Klokos (Κλωκός, ο), 15km south of Aigio (no. 100) in 1415–1420. After a devastating fire in 1621–1638, the monastery was deserted and its monks built the Taxiarhon monastery on a nearby plateau of lower altitude (the above bibliography refers to the Taxiarhon monastery). The ruins of Palaiomonastiro are still visible today.

102. Manastır-ı S̱otoḳos (مناستر ثوتوقوس), TT10, 44. GR

Coordinates:	X: 326032.311 Y: 4227055.005
Modern Greek:	Panagias Pepelenitsis Monastery (I.M. Παναγίας Πεπελενίτσης, η)
Old Toponym:	Elpis ton Apilpismenon Monastery (I.M. Ελπίς των Απηλπισμένων, η)
Regional Unit:	Achaia
Municipality:	Aigialeia
Municipal Unit:	Aigio
Bibliography:	Pikoulas 2001a, 316.2745; Panitsas–Papatheodorou 2003, 18; Bory de Saint-Vincent 1834, 94: Éparchie de Vostitsa, Mon[re] Pépélenitsa; Zakythinos 1953, 306; Dokos–Panagopoulos 1993, 23–24, 292–294: Monaster(i)o Madonna Pepeligniza/Madona Pepeglinizza.
Notes:	The monastery was founded by Theodora Mamona, mother of Osios Leontios (see no. 101). It is located across the Selinountas River (Σελινούντας, ο) opposite the Gerontos Monastery (no. 101).

103. Buḫuşta (بوخوشته), TT10, 46. GR

Coordinates:	X: 333514.972 Y: 4225237.511
Modern Greek:	Boufouskia/Bofonokia (Μπουφούσκια/Μποφονόκια, η)
Regional Unit:	Achaia
Municipality:	Aigialeia
Municipal Unit:	Aigio
Bibliography:	Pikoulas 2001a, 332.2900; Panagiotopoulos 1987, 279, 306.2: Territorio di Vostizza, Seg[o] Pucustia, 306.3: Territorio di Vostizza, Apano Bucusta; Pacifico 1704, 121: Territorio di Vostizza, Buguschia; Expédition 1832: Riv. Bouphouskia; Skiadas 1993, 228; Dokos–Panagopoulos 1993, 34–35, 391–401: Bucuschia Cattù/Panù.

104. Ġardena (غاردنه), TT10, 46. AL

Coordinates:	X: 335351.801 Y: 4229607.230
Modern Greek:	Keryneia (Κερύνεια, η)
Old Toponym:	Until 1928: Gardena (Γαρδενά, η)
Regional Unit:	Achaia
Municipality:	Aigialeia
Municipal Unit:	Diakopto
Bibliography:	Pikoulas 2001a, 207.1682; Expédition 1832: Cerynia; Leake 1846, map: Cerynia; Skiadas 1993, 228; Stamatelatos–Vamva-Stamatelatou 2001, 343; Dokos–Panagopoulos 1993, 387–390: Gardena/Gardenà.

Notes:	< **Gordьno* < gradь (*Slav. n.* town, castle): Vasmer 1941, 132; Symeonidis 2010, I 407.

105. Ayo Yani (آيو يانى), TT10, 47. AL

Coordinates:	X: 334269.039 Y: 4230399.967
Modern Greek:	Agios Ioannis (Άγιος Ιωάννης, ο)
Regional Unit:	Achaia
Municipality:	Aigialeia
Municipal Unit:	Diakopto
Bibliography:	Pikoulas 2001a, 50.189; Panagiotopoulos 1987, 279, 307.22: Territorio di Vostizza, Seg^{o} S. Zuane; Pacifico 1704, 121: Territorio di Vostizza, San Zuanne; Bory de Saint-Vincent 1834, 94: Éparchie de Vostitsa, Hagiannis; Leake 1846, map: Agiannis; Dokos–Panagopoulos 1993, 28–29, 354–359: S. Zuan(n)e.
Notes:	Άγιος Ιωάννης (*Gr. hag.* St John).

106. Ḳroḳova (قروقوه), TT10, 47. AL

Coordinates:	X: 333460.605 Y: 4231870.216
Modern Greek:	Selinountas (Σελινούντας, ο)
Old Toponym:	Until 1955: Krokova (Κρόκοβα, η)
Regional Unit:	Achaia
Municipality:	Aigialeia
Municipal Unit:	Aigio
Bibliography:	Pikoulas 2001a, 418.3727; Panagiotopoulos 1987, 279, 307.32: Territorio di Vostizza, Mett^{o} Procova; Pacifico 1704, 121: Territorio di Vostizza, Procoua; Expédition 1832: Krokova Kalyvia; Leake 1846, map: Krokova; Skiadas 1993, 228; Stamatelatos–Vamva-Stamatelatou 2001, 683; Dokos–Panagopoulos 1993, 29–30, 360–364: Crocoua e Palio Crocoua.
Notes:	According to Vasmer, < **Krokovo*: Vasmer 1941, 135. Symeonidis suggested an etymology from kroqe (*Al. n.* spoon, bucket) + -ova denoting the concave landform of the area: Symeonidis 2010, I 776.

107. Roẕa (روذه), TT10, 47. AL

Coordinates:	X: 338495.954 Y: 4230049.744
Modern Greek:	Rodia (Ροδιά, η)
Regional Unit:	Achaia
Municipality:	Aigialeia

Municipal Unit:	Diakopto
Bibliography:	Pikoulas 2001a, 409.3639.

108. Luḳa İfrati (لوقه افراتى), TT10, 47. AL

Coordinates:	X: 327740.965 Y: 4231444.148
Modern Greek:	Palioloukas (Παλιολουκάς, ο)
Regional Unit:	Achaia
Municipality:	Aigialeia
Municipal Unit:	Aigio
Bibliography:	Pikoulas 2001a, 261.2201; Panagiotopoulos 1987, 279, 307.9: Territorio di Vostizza, Seg° Luca; Pacifico 1704, 121: Territorio di Vostizza, Luccà; Hatzisotiriou 1988, 628–630; Dokos–Panagopoulos 1993, lxxviii, 22–23, 289–291: Lucha Zeogolatio.
Notes:	Uninhabited location, which, according to the *Catastico Ordinario* of Vostizza of the year 1700, bordered Dafnes (no. 112) to the west and Paraskevi (no. 111) to the north: Dokos–Panagopoulos 1993, 22–23; Sauerwein located Pacifico's Luccà in Lakka (Λάκκα, η): Sauerwein 1969, *Ortsverzeichnis*, Territorio di Vostizza, 26. However, Lakka's old name was Ahouria (Αχούρια, τα). Λουκάς (*Gr. pn.* Lucas) > Lukë (*Al. pn.* Lucas). frat (*Al. n.* brother in a monastic order, Franciscan monk, friar) < frater (*Lat. n.* brother).

109. Ẕiyaleş Tunba (ذيالش تونبه), TT10, 48. AL

Coordinates:	X: 323970.908 Y: 4233419.554
Modern Greek:	Toumba (Τούμπα, η)
Regional Unit:	Achaia
Municipality:	Aigialeia
Municipal Unit:	Sympoliteia
Bibliography:	Pikoulas 2001a, 453.4077; Panagiotopoulos 1987, 279, 307.27: Territorio di Vostizza, Tumba; Pacifico 1704, 121: Territorio di Vostizza, Tumba; Bory de Saint-Vincent 1834, 93: Éparchie de Vostitsa, Toumba; Leake 1846, map: Tumba; Dokos–Panagopoulos 1993, 142–155: Tumba.
Notes:	djaloç, djalosh (*Al. n.* boy, lad, youth); djallush (*Al. n.* little devil). τούμπα (*Gr. n.* peak, treeless hilltop, bare mountain top) < tumba (*Lat. n.* mound).

110. Ḳondorafti (قوندورافتى), TT10, 48. AL

Notes:	Unidentified. < κοντός (*Gr. adj.* short) + ράφτης (*Gr. n.* tailor).

111. Ayo Paraskevi (آیو پراسکوی), TT10, 48. GR

Coordinates:	X: 323596.485 Y: 4228138.893
Modern Greek:	Paraskevi (Παρασκευή, η)
Regional Unit:	Achaia
Municipality:	Aigialeia
Municipal Unit:	Aigio
Bibliography:	Pikoulas 2001a, 369.3257; Pacifico 1704, 121: Territorio di Vostizza, Paraschieui; Bory de Saint-Vincent 1834, 93: Éparchie de Vostitsa, Paraskévi; Leake 1846, map: Paraskevi; Dokos–Panagopoulos 1993, 20, 232–270: Paraschieuà/Paraschieui.

112. Ḳaḳoḫoryo (قاقوخوریو), TT10, 48. GR

Coordinates:	X: 324435.710 Y: 4230243.411
Modern Greek:	Dafnes (Δάφνες, οι)
Old Toponym:	Until 1928: Kakohori (Κακοχώρι, το)
Regional Unit:	Achaia
Municipality:	Aigialeia
Municipal Unit:	Aigio
Bibliography:	Pikoulas 2001a, 129.946; Panagiotopoulos 1987, 279, 307.25: Territorio di Vostizza, Cacocori; Pacifico 1704, 121: Territorio di Vostizza, Cacò Coriò; Bory de Saint-Vincent 1834, 93: Éparchie de Vostitsa, Kakokhorio; Leake 1846, map: Kakokhorio; Skiadas 1993, 228; Stamatelatos–Vamva-Stamatelatou 2001, 179; Dokos–Panagopoulos 1993, 21, 271–286: Caco Corio.

113. Lopesi (لویسی), TT10, 48. AL

Coordinates:	X: 321065.899 Y: 4226550.822
Modern Greek:	Lopesi (Λόπεσι, το)
Regional Unit:	Achaia
Municipality:	Aigialeia
Municipal Unit:	Sympoliteia
Bibliography:	Dokos–Panagopoulos 1993, 17–18, 195–197: Lopes(s)i.
Notes:	Name of a mountain to the south of Krini (Κρήνη, η). See no. 83.

114. Franḳo (فرانقو), TT10, 49. AL

Coordinates:	X: 319981.363 Y: 4224962.750
Modern Greek:	Ano Franga (Άνω Φράγκα, η)
Regional Unit:	Achaia
Municipality:	Erymanthos
Municipal Unit:	Leontio
Bibliography:	Anavasi 2009, map 10; Panagiotopoulos 1987, 279, 307.12: Territorio di Vostizza, Franga; Pacifico 1704, 121: Territorio di Vostizza, Franga; Expédition 1832: Franka; Leake 1846, map: Franka; Bon 1969, 457; Dokos–Panagopoulos 1993, 16–17, 192–195: Franca.
Notes:	Modern holiday settlement to the north of Rakita (Ρακίτα, η) in the place of the Franga village abandoned in the mid-19th c. Its inhabitants established Franga/Kato Franga (Φράγκα/Κάτω Φράγκα, η) in the western Achaian plain: Triantafyllou 1995, II 2191–2192. Franco (*It. pn.* Frank).

115. İvlanduşa (اولاندوشه), TT10, 49. AL

Coordinates:	X: 373588.463 Y: 4206616.004
Modern Greek:	Stylia (Στύλια, τα)
Old Toponym:	Until 1928: Vlantous(i)a [Βλαντούσ(ι)α, η]
Regional Unit:	Corinthia
Municipality:	Xylokastro-Evrostini
Municipal Unit:	Xylokastro
Bibliography:	Pikoulas 2001a, 443.3972; Panagiotopoulos 1987, 242, 292.97: Territorio di Corinto, Viladusa; Pacifico 1704, 116: Territorio di Corintho, Valandussa; Bory de Saint-Vincent 1834, 68: Éparchie de Corinthe, Vlandousa; Skiadas 1993, 287; Stamatelatos–Vamva-Stamatelatou 2001, 723.
Notes:	Vladuša (*Scr. pn.* wanderer) attested in Croatia in 1667–1700; Vladušić (*Scr. sn.* in Croatia and Bosnia & Herzegovina): RHSJ 1973, XXI 166. Place name Vladoš in Slovenia: Vasmer 1941, 124. Vladush (*Al. sn.*) < Vladi, Vlado < Vladimir (*Scr. pn.*): Kolleka 1987, 84.

116. Petro Tunba (پترو تونبه), TT10, 49. AL

Notes:	Unidentified. For Petro see no. 25, and for Tunba see no. 109.

117. Ḳlaẕi (قلاذى), TT10, 49. AL

	Unidentified.
Notes:	According to Vasmer, < **klada* (*Slav. n.* block of wood; balk): VASMER 1941, 168. According to Georgacas, the place name Klada (Κλαδά, του) in Laconia derives from Κλαδάς (*Byz. Gr. sn.*) < κλαδίον (*Gr. n.* branch): GEORGACAS 1938, 72.

118. Aya İğliġori (آيه اكليغورى), TT10, 50. AL

Coordinates:	X: 323751.419 Y: 4232373.751
Modern Greek:	Grigoris (Γρηγόρης, ο)
Old Toponym:	Until 1940: Gligouri/Grigori (Γληγούρι/Γρηγόρι, το)
Regional Unit:	Achaia
Municipality:	Aigialeia
Municipal Unit:	Sympoliteia
Bibliography:	PIKOULAS 2001a, 127.922; PANAGIOTOPOULOS 1987, 279, 307.26: Territorio di Vostizza, Gligori; PACIFICO 1704, 121: Territorio di Vostizza, Gligori; BORY DE SAINT-VINCENT 1834, 93: Éparchie de Vostitsa, Gligori; LEAKE 1846, map: Gigori; SKIADAS 1993, 228; STAMATELATOS–VAMVA-STAMATELATOU 2001, 173; DOKOS–PANAGOPOULOS 1993, 13–14, 155–165: Eftapites e Gligori.
Notes:	Άγιος Γρηγόριος (*Gr. hag.* St Gregory).

119. Listirna (لسترنه), TT10, 50. AL

Coordinates:	X: 322060.058 Y: 4230888.968
Modern Greek:	Listraina/Listrena/Listrina (Λίστραινα/Λίστρενα/Λίστρινα, η)
Regional Unit:	Achaia
Municipality:	Aigialeia
Municipal Unit:	Sympoliteia
Bibliography:	SFIKOPOULOS 1987, 150–151; BON 1969, 454, 466; SATHAS 1885, VI 31; HOPF 1873, 202: Lastrana vel Listrenu, 205: Listrena.
Notes:	Byzantine fortress east of Graikas (no. 120). In 1463, the already Ottoman fortress was conquered by the Venetian lord Marco Vegia. It is reported dilapidated in 1467. Its ruins are still visible today. Carile connected it to Drestena (no. 509) and Vrestaina (= Vrosthaina, no. 17): CARILE 1970, 396–397, neither of which are in the vicinity, though.

120. Graḳa (كراقه), TT10, 50. AL

Coordinates:	X: 321078.811 Y: 4230863.146
Modern Greek:	Graikas (Γκραίκας, ο)

Regional Unit:	Achaia
Municipality:	Aigialeia
Municipal Unit:	Sympoliteia
Bibliography:	Pikoulas 2001a, 122.878; Bory de Saint-Vincent 1834, 93: Éparchie de Vostitsa, Gréka; Leake 1846, map: Greka; Dokos–Panagopoulos 1993, 14–15, 165–175: Greca Panù/Catù.
Notes:	Grek (*Al. n.* Greek) < Græcus (*Lat. n.* Greek). Γκρέκας (*Gr. sn.*).

121. Martina der Noḳastro (مارتنه در نوقاسترو), TT10, 50. M

Coordinates:	X: 325830.114 Y: 4217706.683
Modern Greek:	Martina (Μαρτίνα, η)
Regional Unit:	Achaia
Municipality:	Kalavryta
Municipal Unit:	Kalavryta
Bibliography:	Pikoulas 2001a, 277.2360; Panagiotopoulos 1987, 271, 303.120: Territorio di Callavritta, Martina; Pacifico 1704, 123: Territorio di Calaurita, Martina; Expédition 1832: Martina; Leake 1846, map: Martina.

122. Epanolaġo (اپانولاغو), TT10, 51. GR

Coordinates:	X: 322111.703 Y: 4219849.934
Modern Greek:	Lapanagoi (Λαπαναγοί, οι)
Regional Unit:	Achaia
Municipality:	Kalavryta
Municipal Unit:	Kalavryta
Bibliography:	Pikoulas 2001a, 248.2078; 270, 303.84: Territorio di Callavritta, Apano Lagus; Pacifico 1704, 122: Territorio di Calaurita, Lagus apano; Bory de Saint-Vincent 1834, 74: Éparchie de Kalavrita, Lapanagous; Leake 1846, map: Lapanagus.

123. Valḳu (والقو), TT10, 51. AL

Coordinates:	X: 353560.681 Y: 4222187.630
Modern Greek:	Ambelos (Άμπελος, η)
Old Toponym:	Until 1955: Valkouvina (Βαλκουβίνα, η)
Regional Unit:	Achaia
Municipality:	Aigialeia

Municipal Unit:	Akrata
Bibliography:	PIKOULAS 2001a, 70.383; SKIADAS 1993, 230; STAMATELATOS–VAMVA-STAMATELATOU 2001, 67.
Notes:	< **Vlkovina* (*Slav. n.* place of wolves): VASMER 1941, 129; SYMEONIDIS 2010, I 326. Place name Vukova in Serbia and Vъlkovo in Bulgaria.

124. Sotira (سوتيره), TT10, 51. AL

Coordinates:	X: 328479.368 Y: 4233345.224
Modern Greek:	Sotiras (Σωτήρας, ο)
Regional Unit:	Achaia
Municipality:	Aigialeia
Municipal Unit:	Aigio
Bibliography:	PIKOULAS 2001a, 447.4011.
Notes:	σωτήρας (*Gr. n.* saviour). Σωτήριος or Σωτήρης (*Gr. pn.*).

125. Burlaşa (بورلاشه), TT10, 51. AL

Modern Greek:	Bourlesia (Μπουρλέσια)
Regional Unit:	Achaia
Municipality:	Kalavryta
Municipal Unit:	Kalavryta
Bibliography:	PACIFICO 1704, 122: Territorio di Calaurita, Brolessa.
Notes:	Unidentified. Microtoponym Bourlesia Spring in the surroundings of Petsakoi (no. 126): PAPANDREOU 2011, 291; its exact location is unknown. < **Borolěsъ* (*Slav. n.* pine forest): VASMER 1941, 43.

126. Beçaḳus (بچاقوس), TT10, 51. GR

Coordinates:	X: 327867.628 Y: 4218091.636
Modern Greek:	Petsakoi (Πετσάκοι, οι)
Regional Unit:	Achaia
Municipality:	Kalavryta
Municipal Unit:	Kalavryta
Bibliography:	PIKOULAS 2001a, 380.3354; PANAGIOTOPOULOS 1987, 269, 302.49: Territorio di Callavritta, Pezacus; PACIFICO 1704, 123: Pezacus; Territorio di Calaurita, BORY DE SAINT-VINCENT 1834, 74: Éparchie de Kalavrita, Pétzaki; LEAKE 1846, map: Petzaki.

Notes: Possibly linked to **pesъkъ* (*Slav. n.* sand, sandy ground): Symeonidis 2010, II 1138.

127. Kiriçova (كريچوه), TT10, 52. GR

Coordinates: X: 326976.617 Y: 4217213.923

Modern Greek: Korfes (Κορφές, οι)

Old Toponym: Until 1928: Kyritsova (Κυρίτσοβα, η)

Regional Unit: Achaia

Municipality: Kalavryta

Municipal Unit: Kalavryta

Bibliography: Pikoulas 2001a, 220.1808; Panagiotopoulos 1987, 270, 303.107: Territorio di Callavritta, Chirizova; Pacifico 1704, 123: Territorio di Calaurita, Clirizoua; Bory de Saint-Vincent 1834, 73: Éparchie de Kalavrita, Kyritsova; Leake 1846, map: Kyritzova; Skiadas 1993, 235; Stamatelatos–Vamva-Stamatelatou 2001, 372.

Notes: According to Vasmer, < Κυρίτσης (*Gr. sn.*) + -ova (*Slav. end.*): Vasmer 1941, 135.

128. Ġumaniça (غومانيچه), TT10, 52. GR

Coordinates: X: 327521.863 Y: 4214740.369

Modern Greek: Drosato (Δροσάτο, το), Goumenissa (Γουμένισσα, η)

Old Toponym: Until 1955 Drosato was called Pano Goumenitsa (Πάνω Γουμένιτσα, η); until 1955 Goumenissa was called Kato Goumenitsa (Κάτω Γουμένιτσα, η) and until 1991 Vrysari (Βρυσάρι, το).

Regional Unit: Achaia

Municipality: Kalavryta

Municipal Unit: Kalavryta

Bibliography: Pikoulas 2001a, 142.1066, 111.767; Panagiotopoulos 1987, 269, 302.50: Territorio di Callavritta, Gumenizza; Pacifico 1704, 123: Territorio di Calaurita, Gumenizza; Bory de Saint-Vincent 1834, 74: Éparchie de Kalavrita, Apano/Kato Gouménitsa; Leake 1846, map: Gumenitza; Skiadas 1993, 239; Bon 1969, 469; Stamatelatos–Vamva-Stamatelatou 2001, 170, 200.

Notes: < **Gumьnьnica* or gumьnьce (*old. Slav.*) < gumьno (*Slav. n.* germination/threshing/barn floor): Vasmer 1941, 132–133; Symeonidis 2010, I 442. Place name Gumnište and Gumьništa in Serbia.

129. Maji (ماژى), TT10, 52. AL

Coordinates: X: 340448.181 Y: 4200657.065

Modern Greek: Elatofyto (Ελατόφυτο, το)

Old Toponym: Until 1971: Mazi (Μάζι, το)

Regional Unit:	Achaia
Municipality:	Kalavryta
Municipal Unit:	Kleitoria
Bibliography:	Pikoulas 2001a, 148.1115; Panagiotopoulos 1987, 270, 303.98: Territorio di Callavritta, Masi; Pacifico 1704, 122: Territorio di Calaurita, Masi; Bory de Saint-Vincent 1834, 74: Éparchie de Kalavrita, Mazi; Leake 1846, map: Mazi; Skiadas 1993, 237; Stamatelatos–Vamva-Stamatelatou 2001, 210.
Notes:	Mazhi (*Al. sn.*). According to Fourikis and Georgacas–McDonald, < mazi (*Al. n.* flat field; ploughed earth ready for sowing): Fourikis 1929, 134; Georgacas–McDonald 1968, 332–333. According to Biris, Μάζης (*Arv. sn.*) < majë (*Al. n.* top, peak): Biris 1998, 197. According to Sarris, < magje (*Al. n.* basin, dell): Sarris 1928, 139. Jochalas proposed an etymology of the surname Μάζης from mazë (*Al. n.* cream): Jochalas 1976, 317. Finally, according to Symeonidis, < maz or mëz (*Al. n.* foal): Symeonidis 2010, I 860.

130. Ḳapareli (قپارلی), *mezraʿa* in the vicinity of Maji, TT10, 52.

Notes:	Unidentified. Καπαρέλης (*Arv. sn.*): Biris 1998, 194. According to Symeonidis, καπαρέλλι < κάπαρο (*Gr. n.* black and dark rock) + -έλλι (*Gr. dim. end.*): Symeonidis 2010, I 624.

131. Rayḳu (رايقو), TT10, 53. AL

Coordinates:	X: 327974.018 Y: 4210976.842
Modern Greek:	Raïko [Ράικο, το (= Ράικου, του)]
Regional Unit:	Achaia
Municipality:	Kalavryta
Municipal Unit:	Kalavryta
Bibliography:	GLET 1998, III 202; Pikoulas 2001a, 403.3579; Panagiotopoulos 1987, 268, 302.26: Territorio di Callavritta, Raicos; Pacifico 1704, 122: Territorio di Calaurita, Raicu; Bory de Saint-Vincent 1834, 73: Éparchie de Kalavrita, Rhaïkou.
Notes:	Uninhabited location to the south-west of Skepasto (no. 132). Rajko (*Scr. pn.*) < raj (*Slav. n.* paradise).

132. Visoḳa (ويسوقه), TT10, 53. AL

Coordinates:	X: 330899.728 Y: 4211987.542
Modern Greek:	Skepasto (Σκεπαστό, το)
Old Toponym:	Until 1928: Visoka (Βισοκά, η)
Regional Unit:	Achaia
Municipality:	Kalavryta

Municipal Unit:	Kalavryta
Bibliography:	Pikoulas 2001a, 423.3783; Panagiotopoulos 1987, 268, 302.25: Territorio di Callavritta, Visoca; Pacifico 1704, 122: Territorio di Calaurita, Vissocà; Bory de Saint-Vincent 1834, 74: Éparchie de Kalavrita, Visoka; Leake 1830, II 109, 113–114: Visocá; Skiadas 1993, 233; Stamatelatos–Vamva-Stamatelatou 2001, 695.
Notes:	< visok, *f.* visoka (*Scr. adj.* high): Vasmer 1941, 130–131; Symeonidis 2010, I 360. The place name perhaps denotes the settlement's altitude (800m). It is commonly used in Yugoslav and Bulgarian toponymy: RHSJ 1971–72, XX 950–951; NSID 1917, 299, 507.

133. **Kerpini (كرپنى), TT10, 53. GR**

Coordinates:	X: 333891.931 Y: 4216096.834
Modern Greek:	Kerpini (Κερπινή, η)
Regional Unit:	Achaia
Municipality:	Kalavryta
Municipal Unit:	Kalavryta
Bibliography:	Pikoulas 2001a, 206.1678; Panagiotopoulos 1987, 268, 302.13: Territorio di Callavritta, Chierpini; Pacifico 1704, 122: Territorio di Calaurita, Chierpenì; Bory de Saint-Vincent 1834, 74: Éparchie de Kalavrita, Kerpini; Leake 1846, map: Kerpini; Bon 1969, 464, 467, 479.
Notes:	Symeonidis proposed an etymology from Čerepjane (*Slav. n. pl.* inhabitants of a place with potteries): Symeonidis 2010, I 688.

134. **Zaḫlori (زاخلورى), TT10, 54. GR**

Coordinates:	X: 338812.443 Y: 4217719.273
Modern Greek:	Ano & Kato Zahlorou (Άνω & Κάτω Ζαχλωρού, η)
Regional Unit:	Achaia
Municipality:	Kalavryta
Municipal Unit:	Kalavryta
Bibliography:	Pikoulas 2001a, 155.1180–1181; Panagiotopoulos 1987, 268, 302.13: Territorio di Callavritta, Zaclorù; Pacifico 1704, 123: Territorio di Calaurita, Zaclorù; Bory de Saint-Vincent 1834, 74: Éparchie de Kalavrita, Zakhlorou; Leake 1846, map: Zakhloru; Bon 1969, 467, 469.

135. **Tumena (تومنا), TT10, 55. GR**

Coordinates:	X: 336538.368 Y: 4218889.557
Modern Greek:	Doumena (Δουμενά, τα)
Regional Unit:	Achaia

Municipality:	Kalavryta
Municipal Unit:	Kalavryta
Bibliography:	Pikoulas 2001a, 140.1045; Panagiotopoulos 1987, 270, 303.90: Territorio di Callavritta, Dumena; Pacifico 1704, 123: Territorio di Calaurita, Dumena; Bory de Saint-Vincent 1834, 73: Éparchie de Kalavrita, Douména; Leake 1846, map: Dumena.
Notes:	< dymъ (*Slav. n.* smoke) or **Dǫbьna* < dǫbъ (*Slav. n.* oak, oak tree, *Quercus*): Vasmer 1941, 133; Symeonidis 2010, I 489.

136. Ẕilivina (ذيليوينه), TT10, 55. GR

Coordinates:	X: 334157.905 Y: 4221083.840
Modern Greek:	Vilivina (Βιλιβίνα, η)
Regional Unit:	Achaia
Municipality:	Kalavryta
Municipal Unit:	Kalavryta
Bibliography:	Pikoulas 2001a, 103.692; Panagiotopoulos 1987, 268, 302.14: Territorio di Callavritta, Vellivina; Pacifico 1704, 123: Territorio di Calaurita, Veliuina; Bory de Saint-Vincent 1834, 74: Éparchie de Kalavrita, Vilivina; Leake 1846, map: Vilivina.
Notes:	According to Vasmer, < Beljevina < bělъ (*Slav. adj.* white): Vasmer 1941, 129. According to Symeonidis, < **Βέλβινα* (*anc. Gr. pln.*): Symeonidis 2010, I 359.

137. Rolo (رولو), TT10, 56. GR

Coordinates:	X: 336126.109 Y: 4215990.445
Modern Greek:	Rogoi (?) (Ρογοί, οι)
Regional Unit:	Achaia
Municipality:	Kalavryta
Municipal Unit:	Kalavryta
Bibliography:	Pikoulas 2001a, 409.3635; Panagiotopoulos 1987, 269, 302.39: Territorio di Callavritta, Rogus; Pacifico 1704, 122: Territorio di Calaurita, Rogus; Bory de Saint-Vincent 1834, 74: Éparchie de Kalavrita, Rhogi; Leake 1846, map: Rogus.

138. Ḳılapaçuna (قلاپاچونه), TT10, 56. GR

Coordinates:	X: 332269.492 Y: 4219448.102
Modern Greek:	Plataniotissa (Πλατανιώτισσα, η)

Old Toponym:	Until 1915: Klapatsouna (Κλαπατσούνα, η)
Regional Unit:	Achaia
Municipality:	Kalavryta
Municipal Unit:	Kalavryta
Bibliography:	Pikoulas 2001a, 387.3421; Panagiotopoulos 1987, 269, 302.48: Territorio di Callavritta: Clazozuna; Pacifico 1704, 123: Territorio di Calaurita, Clapazuna; Bory de Saint-Vincent 1834, 74: Éparchie de Kalavrita, Klapatsouna; Leake 1846, map: Klapatzouna; Skiadas 1993, 235; Politis 1915, 267.

139. Namuni (نامونی), TT10, 57. GR

Notes:	Unidentified. Cf. microtoponym Amonia (Αμόνια, τα) near Aigio (no. 100): Fotopoulos 1982, II 248.

140. Yaḳoḫto (یاقوختو), TT10, 57. GR

Coordinates:	X: 344584.071 Y: 4222200.929
Modern Greek:	Ano Diakopto/Diakofto (Άνω Διακοπτό/Διακοφτό, το)
Old Toponym:	Until 1940: Pera Mahalas (Πέρα Μαχαλάς, ο)
Regional Unit:	Achaia
Municipality:	Aigialeia
Municipal Unit:	Diakopto
Bibliography:	Pikoulas 2001a, 135.1001; Panagiotopoulos 1987, 279, 306.4: Territorio di Vostizza, Diacoftò; Pacifico 1704, 121: Territorio di Vostizza, Diacoftò; Bory de Saint-Vincent 1834, 93: Éparchie de Vostitsa, Diakopto; Leake 1846, map: Dhiakofto; Stamatelatos–Vamva-Stamatelatou 2001, 81; Skiadas 1993, 231; Dokos–Panagopoulos 1993, 36–38, 414–595: Diacoftò; Bees 1956, 446; Papageorgiou 1975, 70–71.

141. İstavriya/İstavrina (استاوریه/استاورینه), TT10, 59. AL

Coordinates:	X: 338373.586 Y: 4223810.069
Modern Greek:	Stavria (Σταυριά, η)
Regional Unit:	Achaia
Municipality:	Aigialeia
Municipal Unit:	Diakopto
Bibliography:	Pikoulas 2001a, 437.3920; Dokos–Panagopoulos 1993, 33–34, 387, 391: Stiuiria/Stiniria.

142. Potamya (پوتامیه), TT10, 59. GR

Coordinates:	X: 343645.702 Y: 4216108.590
Modern Greek:	Ano & Kato Potamia (Άνω & Κάτω Ποταμιά, η)
Regional Unit:	Achaia
Municipality:	Aigialeia
Municipal Unit:	Akrata
Bibliography:	Pikoulas 2001a, 393.3481, 3487; Panagiotopoulos 1987, 270, 303.86: Territorio di Callavritta, Potamia di Sopra, 269, 302.41: Potamia di Sotto; Pacifico 1704, 123: Territorio di Calaurita, Potamia; Bory de Saint-Vincent 1834, 74: Éparchie de Kalavrita, Apano/Kato Potamia; Leake 1846, map: Ap./K. Potamiá; Dokos–Panagopoulos 1993, 38–39: Potamia di Calaurita.

143. Çimlo (چیملو), TT10, 60. GR

Coordinates:	X: 344519.433 Y: 4215183.029
Modern Greek:	Tsivlos (Τσιβλός, ο)
Regional Unit:	Achaia
Municipality:	Aigialeia
Municipal Unit:	Akrata
Bibliography:	Pikoulas 2001a, 463.4169; Panagiotopoulos 1987, 269, 302.68: Territorio di Callavritta, Civlò; Bory de Saint-Vincent 1834, 73: Éparchie de Kalavrita, Tsivlos; Leake 1846, map: Tzivlo; Stamatelatos–Vamva-Stamatelatou 2001, 755.
Notes:	In 1913 a landslide on the northern slope of Mt Helmos (Χελμός, ο) destroyed the villages of Tsivlos and Sylivaina (no. 144) and formed the Tsivlou Lake of the Krathis River. Tsivlos was refounded on the south bank of the lake.

144. İstilivena (استلیونه), TT10, 60. GR

Coordinates:	X: 345055.019 Y: 4215378.724
Modern Greek:	Sylivaina (Συλίβαινα, η)
Regional Unit:	Achaia
Municipality:	Aigialeia
Municipal Unit:	Akrata
Bibliography:	Pikoulas 2001a, 444.3980; Panagiotopoulos 1987, 269, 302.52: Territorio di Callavritta: Sillivena; Pacifico 1704, 123: Territorio di Calaurita, Siliuena; Bory de Saint-Vincent 1834, 73: Éparchie de Kalavrita, Sylivéna; Leake 1830, III 174: Silívena; Leake 1846, map: Sylivena; Stamatelatos–Vamva-Stamatelatou 2001, 755.

Notes: After the landslide of 1913 (see no. 143), the inhabitants of devastated Sylivaina moved to Sylivainiotika (Συλιβαινιώτικα, τα) on the southern shore of the Corinthian Gulf.
According to Vasmer, < **Slivьno* < **Slivьna* < sliva (*Slav. n.* plum, *Prunus domestica*): Vasmer 1941, 139. The locals call *Prunus pseudoarmeniaca* σιλιβιά: Fotopoulos 1982, II 283, n. 282.

145. Ḳulukina (قلوكينه/قلوكنه), TT10, 61. GR

Coordinates: X: 346393.985 Y: 4211124.933

Modern Greek: Kloukines/Kloukinohoria (Κλουκίνες, οι/Κλουκινοχώρια, τα)

Regional Unit: Achaia

Municipality: Aigialeia

Municipal Unit: Akrata

Bibliography: Pacifico 1700, 126: Territorio di Calaurita: Cuchilnis; Leake 1830, III 159–160: Klukínes; Leake 1846, map: Klukines; Bon 1969, 467; Skiadas 1993, 241; Stamatelatos–Vamva-Stamatelatou 2001, 354; Fotopoulos 1982, II 273–275, n. 130.

Notes: Kloukines refers to a group of villages in southern Akrata, namely Agia Varvara (Αγία Βαρβάρα, η), Zarouhla (Ζαρούχλα, η), Agridi (Αγρίδι, το), Solos (Σόλος, ο), Peristera (Περιστέρα, η) and Mesorrougi (Μεσορρούγι, το). According to Pouqueville, the 'Kloukinais' valley overlooks the river of Akrata (Acratho-Potamos or Crathis River), situated on the slope descending from Zarouhla: Pouqueville 1826, IV 422–423. The *Expédition* listed under the name 'Kloukinæs': Hagia-Varvara, Zaroukla, Agridi, Vounaki, Vrakhni, Tsivlos, Souvardo, Péristéra, Gounarianika (partie supérieure de Mésorougi), Mésorougi, Solos and Sylivéna: Bory de Saint-Vincent 1834, 73. The Royal Verdict of 8/20 April 1835 established the Municipality of Nonakris, which pertained to Kloukines and consisted of Nonakris (Zarouhla), Agridi, Vounaki, Varvara, Halkianika, Solos, Mesorougia and Peristeri (Peristera). The exact location of a certain Kloukina village remains unknown.

146. Ẕaruḫla (ذآروخله), TT10, 63. GR

Coordinates: X: 348402.687 Y: 4205180.790

Modern Greek: Zarouhla (Ζαρούχλα, η)

Regional Unit: Achaia

Municipality: Aigialeia

Municipal Unit: Akrata

Bibliography: Pikoulas 2001a, 154.1171; Panagiotopoulos 1987, 268, 302.9: Territorio di Callavritta, Zarucla; Pacifico 1704, 122: Territorio di Calaurita, Sarucla; Expédition 1832: Zaroukhla; Bory de Saint-Vincent 1834, 73: Éparchie de Kalavrita, Zaroukla; Leake 1846, map: Zarukhla; Bon 1969, 467.

Notes: < za Ruchla (*Slav. phr.* behind Ruhla): Vasmer 1941, 133–134; Symeonidis 2010, I 541; rúchvam (*Bg. v.* to fall, decline, overthrow), rušitьsa (*Ru. v.* to fall, decline, overthrow). Perhaps it denoted a ruined settlement.

147. Siyiniski (سینسکی), TT10, 64. GR

Coordinates: X: 347707.855 Y: 4217904.904

Modern Greek: Siginiskes (Σιγίνισκες, οι)

Regional Unit: Achaia

Municipality: Aigialeia

Municipal Unit: Akrata

Bibliography: Pikoulas 2001a, 419.3743; Pacifico 1704, 123: Territorio di Calaurita, Clinischies; Skiadas 1993, 238; Fotopoulos 1982, II 283, n. 280.

Notes: Relics of the initial settlement in Gyros (Γύρος, ο): Papandreou 2011, 310.

148. Valimi (والیمی), TT10, 64. GR

Coordinates: X: 349010.665 Y: 4217253.499

Modern Greek: Valimi (Βαλιμή, η)

Regional Unit: Achaia

Municipality: Aigialeia

Municipal Unit: Akrata

Bibliography: Pikoulas 2001a, 92.583; Panagiotopoulos 1987, 268, 302.34: Territorio di Callavritta, Valimi; Pacifico 1704, 123: Territorio di Calaurita, Valimus; Bory de Saint-Vincent 1834, 74: Éparchie de Kalavrita, Valimi; Leake 1846, map: Valimi.

149. Ayo Yorgi (آیو یورکی), TT10, 64. GR

Coordinates: X: 349672.927 Y: 4218360.888

Modern Greek: Agios Georgios (Άγιος Γεώργιος, ο)

Regional Unit: Achaia

Municipality: Aigialeia

Municipal Unit: Akrata

Bibliography: Panagiotopoulos 1987, 271, 303: Territorio di Callavrita, S. Zorzi; Hopf 1873, 205: S. Zorzi Tropico.

Notes: A chapel of Agios Georgios to the north-east of Valimi (no. 148) is noted on the British map: GSGS 1944, Xilókastron.

150. Ḫotoġosti (خوتوغوستی), TT10, 65. GR

Notes: Unidentified.

151. Lovoḳa (لوووقه), TT10, 65. GR

Coordinates:	X: 356165.265 Y: 4218176.323
Modern Greek:	Aiges (Αιγές, οι)
Old Toponym:	Until 1928: Vlovoka (Βλωβοκά, η)
Regional Unit:	Achaia
Municipality:	Aigialeia
Municipal Unit:	Aigeira
Bibliography:	Pikoulas 2001a, 61.297; Panagiotopoulos 1987, 269, 302.47: Territorio di Callavritta, Vlovocà; Pacifico 1704, 123: Territorio di Calaurita, Vlouoca; Bory de Saint-Vincent 1834, 74: Éparchie de Kalavrita, Vlogoka; Leake 1830, III 141, 391: Vlogoká; Bon 1969, 398–399; Skiadas 1993, 229: Βλοχοκά; Stamatelatos–Vamva-Stamatelatou 2001, 49–50.
Notes:	According to Vasmer, < **glъbokъ* or **dlbokъ* (*old Slav. adj.* deep): Vasmer 1941, 131.

152. Virastova (وراستوه), TT10, 65. GR

Coordinates:	X: 352995.093 Y: 4218295.747
Modern Greek:	Hrysanthi (Χρυσάνθι, το)
Old Toponym:	Until 1961: Versova (Βερσοβά, η)
Regional Unit:	Achaia
Municipality:	Aigialeia
Municipal Unit:	Aigeira
Bibliography:	Pikoulas 2001a, 488.4413; Panagiotopoulos 1987, 269, 302.70: Territorio di Callavritta, Vesovà; Pacifico 1704, 123: Territorio di Calaurita, Versouà; Bory de Saint-Vincent 1834, 74: Éparchie de Kalavrita, Versova; Leake 1846, map: Versova; Skiadas 1993, 229; Stamatelatos–Vamva-Stamatelatou 2001, 800.
Notes:	< **Versovo* < **versъ* (*Slav. n.* heather, *Calluna vulgaris*): Vasmer 1941, 130; Symeonidis 2010, I 355.

153. Cilardi (جلاردى), TT10, 66. GR

Coordinates:	X: 352169.980 Y: 4216569.523
Modern Greek:	Tsilardi (Τσιλάρδι/Τσιλαρδί, το)
Regional Unit:	Achaia
Municipality:	Aigialeia
Municipal Unit:	Aigeira

Bibliography:	Pikoulas 2001a, 463.4174; Panagiotopoulos 1987, 269, 302.38: Territorio di Callavritta, Zilardi; Pacifico 1704, 123: Territorio di Calaurita, Cilardi; Bory de Saint-Vincent 1834, 74: Éparchie de Kalavrita, Tsilardi; Leake 1846, map: Tzilara; Fotopoulos 1982, II 285–286, n. 325.
Notes:	Settlement noted on the maps of the *Expédition* and Leake. The uninhabited village was probably in the vicinity of Agiou Vasileiou Monastery (I.M. Αγίου Βασιλείου, η).

154. Vela (ولا), TT10, 66. GR

Coordinates:	X: 352083.126 Y: 4214626.165
Modern Greek:	Vela (Βελά, η)
Regional Unit:	Achaia
Municipality:	Aigialeia
Municipal Unit:	Aigeira
Bibliography:	Pikoulas 2001a, 98.638; Panagiotopoulos 1987, 269, 303.78: Territorio di Callavritta, Vellà; Pacifico 1704, 123: Territorio di Calaurita, Vella; Bory de Saint-Vincent 1834, 74: Éparchie de Kalavrita, Véla; Leake 1846, map: Vela.
Notes:	According to Vasmer, < *slav.* Běla; Βελάς (*Byz. Gr. sn.*): Vasmer 1941, 130.

155. Sinoviro (سينوويرو), TT10, 66. GR

Coordinates:	X: 354145.909 Y: 4214105.041
Modern Greek:	Sinevro (Σινεβρό, το)
Regional Unit:	Achaia
Municipality:	Aigialeia
Municipal Unit:	Aigeira
Bibliography:	Pikoulas 2001a, 421.3758; Panagiotopoulos 1987, 270, 303.106: Territorio di Callavritta, Svirù e Screvenò; Pacifico 1704, 123: Territorio di Calaurita, Sineurò; Bory de Saint-Vincent 1834, 74: Éparchie de Kalavrita, Sinévro; Leake 1846, map: Sinovro.

156. Plaşa (پلاشه), TT10, 67. AL

Coordinates:	X: 350378.616 Y: 4219413.993
Modern Greek:	Plessa (Πλέσσα, του)
Regional Unit:	Achaia
Municipality:	Aigialeia
Municipal Unit:	Akrata

Bibliography:	PIKOULAS 2001a, 389.3444; PANAGIOTOPOULOS 1987, 279, 307.19: Territorio di Vostizza, Seg° Plessa; DOKOS–PANAGOPOULOS 1993, 39–40, 635–669: Plessa.
Notes:	Uninhabited location to the south-east of Pyrgos (Πύργος, ο). The settlement must have been deserted by 1821: DOKOS–PANAGOPOULOS 1993, lxxiii, n. 174, lxxx, lxxxii. See no. 14.

157. Maneşi (مانشى), TT10, 67. AL

Notes:	Unidentified. See no. 22.

158. Arfara (آرفارا), TT10, 67. AL

Coordinates:	X: 352354.545 Y: 4217742.053
Modern Greek:	Ambelokipoi (Αμπελόκηποι, οι)
Old Toponym:	Until 1928: Arfara (Αρφαρά, τα)
Regional Unit:	Achaia
Municipality:	Aigialeia
Municipal Unit:	Aigeira
Bibliography:	PIKOULAS 2001a, 70.382; PANAGIOTOPOULOS 1987, 269, 302.54: Territorio di Callavritta, Arfarà; PACIFICO 1704, 123: Territorio di Calaurita, Arfarà; BORY DE SAINT-VINCENT 1834, 74: Éparchie de Kalavrita, Arphara; LEAKE 1846, map: Arfara; SKIADAS 1993, 229; STAMATELATOS–VAMVA-STAMATELATOU 2001, 67; FOTOPOULOS 1982, II 264, n. 24.
Notes:	αρφαράς or αλφαράς (*Gr. n.* plumb-maker) < αλφάδι (*Gr. n.* plumb): GEORGACAS 1938–48, 62–65.

159. Verġuviça (ورغوويچه), TT10, 67. GR

Coordinates:	X: 355622.427 Y: 4215451.278
Modern Greek:	Monastiri (Μοναστήρι, το)
Old Toponym:	Until 1940: Vergovitsa (Βεργοβίτσα, η); until 1955: Vergouvitsa (Βεργουβίτσα, η)
Regional Unit:	Achaia
Municipality:	Aigialeia
Municipal Unit:	Aigeira
Bibliography:	PIKOULAS 2001a, 296.2545; PANAGIOTOPOULOS 1987, 269, 302.44: Territorio di Callavritta, Verguvizza; PACIFICO 1704, 123: Territorio di Calaurita, Vergouizza; BORY DE SAINT-VINCENT 1834, 74: Éparchie de Kalavrita, Vergovitsa; LEAKE 1846, map: Vergovitza; SKIADAS 1993, 244; STAMATELATOS–VAMVA-STAMATELATOU 2001, 506.
Notes:	< *Bergovica < *brgъ (*Slav. n.* bank, coast): VASMER 1941, 130; SYMEONIDIS 2010, I 353. Place name Bregovo in Bulgaria.

160. Selyana (سليانه), TT10, 68. GR

Coordinates:	X: 355622.427 Y: 4215451.278
Modern Greek:	Seliana (Σελιάνα, η)
Regional Unit:	Achaia
Municipality:	Aigialeia
Municipal Unit:	Aigeira
Bibliography:	Pikoulas 2001a, 417.3723; Panagiotopoulos 1987, 269, 302.42: Territorio di Callavritta, Selliana; Pacifico 1704, 122: Territorio di Calaurita, Seliana; Bory de Saint-Vincent 1834, 74: Éparchie de Kalavrita, Séliana; Leake 1846, map: Seliana; Bon 1969, 479.
Notes:	< **Seljane*, **Seljani* (*Slav. n. pl.* newcomers): Symeonidis 2010, II 1254. Place name Seljane in Serbia and Seljani in Montenegro: Vasmer 1941, 138.

161. Peris̲ori (پريثورى), TT10, 68. GR

Coordinates:	X: 354102.482 Y: 4210131.469
Modern Greek:	Perithori (Περιθώρι, το)
Regional Unit:	Achaia
Municipality:	Aigialeia
Municipal Unit:	Aigeira
Bibliography:	Pikoulas 2001a, 376.3316; Panagiotopoulos 1987, 268, 302.20: Territorio di Callavritta, Pertori; Pacifico 1704, 122: Territorio di Calaurita, Perthori; Bory de Saint-Vincent 1834, 74: Éparchie de Kalavrita, Perthori; Leake 1846, map: Perthori.
Notes:	Also pronounced as Perthori (Περθώρι, το): Papandreou 2011, 307.

162. İvlah̲o (اولاخو), TT10, 69. AL

Notes:	Unidentified. Cf. microtoponym Vlahos (Βλάχος, ο) and Vlahou (Βλάχου, του) in the surroundings of Hrysanthi (no. 152): Fotopoulos 1982, II 249. See no. 54.

163. Rah̲ova (راخوه), TT10, 69. GR

Coordinates:	X: 352256.834 Y: 4212226.822
Modern Greek:	Exohi (Εξοχή, η)
Old Toponym:	Until 1940: (A)Rahova [(A)Ράχωβα, η]; until 1955: Arahova Felloïs (Αράχοβα Φελλόης, η)
Regional Unit:	Achaia

Municipality:	Aigialeia
Municipal Unit:	Aigeira
Bibliography:	Pikoulas 2001a, 150.1135; Panagiotopoulos 1987, 269, 302.46: Territorio di Callavritta, Aragova; Pacifico 1704, 123: Territorio di Calaurita, Aracoua; Bory de Saint-Vincent 1834, 74: Éparchie de Kalavrita, Arakhova; Leake 1846, map: Arakhova; Skiadas 1993, 244; Stamatelatos–Vamva-Stamatelatou 2001, 219.
Notes:	See no. 76.

164. Zaẖoli (زاخولی), TT10, 71. GR

Coordinates:	X: 359107.445 Y: 4214387.316
Modern Greek:	Evrostina (Εβροστίνα, η)
Old Toponym:	Until 1928: Zaholi/Kounianika (Ζάχολη, η/Κουνιάνικα, τα); until 1940 Evrostini (Ευρωστινή, η)
Regional Unit:	Corinthia
Municipality:	Xylokastro-Evrostini
Municipal Unit:	Evrostini
Bibliography:	Pikoulas 2001a, 145.1091; Pacifico 1704, 118: Territorio di Corintho, Zaccali; Leake 1830, III 141: Zákuli, 386: Zákhuli; Leake 1846, map: Zakhuli (Phelloe); Bory de Saint-Vincent 1834, 68: Éparchie de Corinthe, Zakholi; Skiadas 1993, 284; Stamatelatos–Vamva-Stamatelatou 2001, 206; Politis 1915, 534–535.
Notes:	< za (*Slav. prep.* behind) + unknown second component: Vasmer 1941, 124.

165. Yelini (یلینی), TT10, 72. GR

Coordinates:	X: 364828.953 Y: 4211477.707
Modern Greek:	Gelini (Γελήνη, η/Γελήνι, το)
Regional Unit:	Corinthia
Municipality:	Xylokastro-Evrostini
Municipal Unit:	Xylokastro
Bibliography:	Pikoulas 2001a, 116.817; Panagiotopoulos 1987, 242, 292.60: Territorio di Corinto: Gelini; Pacifico 1704, 118: Territorio di Corintho, Gielinì; Bory de Saint-Vincent 1834, 93: Éparchie de Vostitsa, Guélini; Leake 1846, map: Gelini; Skiadas 1993, 292; Miliarakis 1886, 121.
Notes:	In the early 19th c. the inhabitants of Gelini moved northwards to a lower altitude seeking winter quarters for their flocks and employment in the agricultural sector, where they established Geliniatika (Γεληνιάτικα/Γελινιάτικα, τα) on the southern shore of the Corinthian Gulf. The original settlement, which was gradually abandoned, was located to the north-west of Sofiana (no. 168). Possibly linked to jelenъ (*old Slov.* deer) or jelinъ (*old Slov.* idolater) < Ἕλλην (*Gr. n.* Greek, Hellene): Symeonidis 2010, I 409–410.

166. Zepandi (زپاندی), TT10, 72. AL

Bibliography:	Pacifico 1704, 119: Territorio di Corintho, Sapandi; Kordosis 1981b, 292; Miliarakis 1886, 111.
Notes:	Unidentified. A certain Zapanti (Ζαπάντι, το) is identified with modern Soulinari (Σουληνάρι, το) in Corinthia, which is not in the vicinity, though. See no. 35.

167. Ḳumaniçi Luzi (قومانیچی لوزی), *mezraʿa* in the vicinity of Zepandi, TT10, 72.

Coordinates:	X: 367347.720 Y: 4217818.050
Modern Greek:	Elliniko (Ελληνικό, το)
Old Toponym:	Until 1928: Louzi, (Λούζι, το); until 1940: Ellinika (Ελληνικά, τα)
Regional Unit:	Corinthia
Municipality:	Xylokastro-Evrostini
Municipal Unit:	Evrostini
Bibliography:	Pikoulas 2001a, 148.1122; Pacifico 1704, 118: Territorio di Corintho, Lussi; Bory de Saint-Vincent 1834, 68: Éparchie de Corinthe, Louzi; Leake 1846, map: Luzi; Stamatelatos–Vamva-Stamatelatou 2001, 217; Skiadas 1993, 284; Kordosis 1981b, 309–310; Miliarakis 1886, 130.
Notes:	Luzi (*Al. sn.*). Vasmer attempted an etymology from **luža* (*Slav. n.* puddle) and mentioned the place names Luža and Luže in Slovenia: Vasmer 1941, 125. Place name Luzi i Madh and Luzi i Vogël in Kavajë, Albania.

168. Ṣoḫyana (صوخیانه), TT10, 73. AL

Coordinates:	X: 365762.634 Y: 4210544.026
Modern Greek:	Sofiana (Σοφιανά, τα)
Regional Unit:	Corinthia
Municipality:	Xylokastro-Evrostini
Municipal Unit:	Xylokastro
Bibliography:	Pikoulas 2001a, 431.3860; Panagiotopoulos 1987, 241, 292.53: Territorio di Corinto, Sofianà; Pacifico 1704, 118: Territorio di Corintho, Soffiana; Expédition 1832: Sophiana; Leake 1846, map: Sofiana; Bon 1969, 455–456.
Notes:	Cf. Bon's Souchiana (no. 499).

169. Pelyura (پلیوره), *mezraʿa* in the vicinity of Ṣoḫyana, TT10, 73.

Notes:	Unidentified. According to Georgacas–McDonald, < pilurë (*Al. n.* kind of spiny shrub, *Genista acanthoclada*): Georgacas–McDonald 1968, 337. According to Katsouleas, < παλιούρα (*Gr. n. Paliurus aculeatus*): Katsouleas 1979, 93. Πυλιόρας (*Arv. sn.*): Biris 1998, 200.

170. Mayira (مییره), *mezraʿa* in the vicinity of Ṣoẖyana, TT10, 73.

Notes: Unidentified. Cf. microtoponym Magerou (Μαγέρου, του), where a dependency of Koimiseos tis Theotokou Monastery (I.M. Κοιμήσεως της Θεοτόκου, η) is mentioned in the Grimani Archive (1696–1700): Dokos 1971–74, 122; its exact location is unknown. If it is located on Magerou peak, to the north-east of Elatofyto (no. 129), it cannot be taken into consideration, as it is not in the vicinity of Sofiana (no. 168).
μάγειρας or μάγειρος (*Gr. n.* cook).

171. Revaniça (روانیچه), TT10, 73. GR

Coordinates: X: 322824.178 Y: 4236502.521

Modern Greek: Arravonitsa (Αρραβωνίτσα, η)

Regional Unit: Achaia

Municipality: Aigialeia

Municipal Unit: Erineos

Bibliography: Pikoulas 2001a, 84.505; Panagiotopoulos 1987, 278, 306.90: Territorio di Patrasso, Aravonizza; Pacifico 1704, 121: Territorio di Patrasso, Arauonizza; Bory de Saint-Vincent 1834, 86: Éparchie de Patras, Aravonitsa; Leake 1846, map: Aravonitza.

Notes: According to Vasmer, < **Rovъnica* < rovъ (*Slav. n.* ditch, trench, fosse): Vasmer 1941, 60; ravan (*Scr. adj.* straight, direct, unbroken): RHSJ 1953, XIII 406–414. Place name Ravanica River in Serbia, Rovnice in Bosnia & Herzegovina and Rovelitsis Monastery (I.M. Ροβελίτσης, η) in Arta. Symeonidis (Symeonidis 2010, I 294) proposed an etymology from **Arbënicë* (*Al. n.* Albanian settlement), which is not based in historical facts, as this is a Greek village.

172. Poroviça (پروویچه), TT10, 73. GR

Coordinates: X: 351849.441 Y: 4221922.203

Modern Greek: Porovitsa (Ποροβίτσα, η)

Regional Unit: Achaia

Municipality: Aigialeia

Municipal Unit: Akrata

Bibliography: Pikoulas 2001a, 392.3470; Panagiotopoulos 1987, 279, 306.7: Territorio di Vostizza, Porovizza; Pacifico 1704, 121: Territorio di Vostizza, Porouizza; Bory de Saint-Vincent 1834, 93: Éparchie de Vostitsa, Porovitsa; Leake 1846, map: Morovitza; Dokos–Panagopoulos 1993, 39–40, 609–634: Porouiz(z)a.

Notes: < borъ (*m. Bg. n.* spruce, spruce forest, *Picea*): Vasmer 1941, 137; Symeonidis 2010, II 1174; bor (*Scr. n.* pine, *Pinus silvestris*); bor (*Bg. n.* pine, fir). Place name Borovica and Borovec in Bulgaria, Borovica and Borovac in Bosnia & Herzegovina.

6. District of Ḫulumiç (Hlemoutsi) (Maps 11–12)

173. Ḫulumiç, nefs-i (خلومچ), TT10, 76. GR

Coordinates:	X: 248117.581 Y: 4197352.306
Modern Greek:	Hlemoutsi/Kastro (Χλεμούτσι/Κάστρο, το)
Regional Unit:	Elis
Municipality:	Andravida-Kyllini
Municipal Unit:	Kastro-Kyllini
Bibliography:	Pikoulas 2001a, 199.1610; Panagiotopoulos 1987, 275, 305.162: Territorio di Gastugni, Borgo Castel Torneze; Pacifico 1704, 124: Territorio di Gastugni, Castel Tornese; Hopf 1873, 206: Chiaramonte; Expédition 1832: Khlémoutsi; Leake 1846, map: Khlemutzi or Kastro (Kastel Tornese); Sfikopoulos 1987, 271–282: Χλεμοῦτσι or Χλουμοῦτσι; Bon 1969, 608-629; Iliopoulos 1948, 160–162; Andrews 2006, 146–158.
Notes:	It was built by Geoffroy II de Villehardouin in 1220–1223 and was called Clermont. Vasmer proposed two etymologies: < **χλωμός* (*Gr.*) < **chl̥mъ* (*Slav.*) + -ούτσι (*Gr. end.*) or < **Chl̥mьсь* (*Slav.*): Vasmer 1941, 145. However, χλωμός or χλομός (*Gr. adj.* pale, wan) < φλομός (*Byz. Gr. adj.* poisonous plant): Bambiniotis 2002, 1891, 1954.

174. Ġastuni (غاستنی), TT10, 78. GR

Coordinates:	X: 258101.999 Y: 4192635.258
Modern Greek:	Gastouni (Γαστούνη, η)
Regional Unit:	Elis
Municipality:	Pineios
Municipal Unit:	Gastouni
Bibliography:	Pikoulas 2001a, 116.813. Panagiotopoulos 1987, 275, 305.161: Territorio di Gastugni, Terra di Gastugni; Pacifico 1704, 123: Territorio di Gastugni, Città di Gastugna; Bory de Saint-Vincent 1834, 70: Éparchie de Gastouni, Gastouni; Leake 1846, map: Gastuni; Sfikopoulos 1987, 322; Hopf 1873, 229: Gastogne; Longnon–Topping 1969, 236; Bon 1969, 335; Iliopoulos 1948, 170–171; Tsamboukou 1988.
Notes:	< Gaston (*Fr. pn.*): Vasmer 1941, 140–141; Symeonidis 2010, I 409.

175. Potamya Ṣarandinu (پوتامیه صراندنو), *mezraʿa* in the vicinity of Ġastuni, TT10, 79.

Modern Greek:	Sarantinou (?) (Σαραντινού, του)
Regional Unit:	Elis
Municipality:	Pineios

Municipal Unit:	Gastouni (?)
Bibliography:	Pikoulas 2001a, 416.3706; Panagiotopoulos 1987, 273, 304.79: Territorio di Gastugni, Sarandino; Pacifico 1704, 124: Territorio di Gastugni, Sarandinù.
Notes:	Unidentified.

176. Kiḫomiro (كخوميرو), *mezra'a* in the vicinity of Ġastuni, TT10, 79.

Notes:	Unidentified.

177. Ṣavalya (صوآليه), TT10, 79. GR

Coordinates:	X: 261816.673 Y: 4189097.473
Modern Greek:	Savalia (Σαβάλια, τα)
Regional Unit:	Elis
Municipality:	Ilida
Municipal Unit:	Amaliada
Bibliography:	Pikoulas 2001a, 412.3669; Panagiotopoulos 1987, 273, 304.85: Territorio di Gastugni, Savaglia; Pacifico 1704, 124: Territorio di Gastugni, Sauaglia; Bory de Saint-Vincent 1834, 70: Éparchie de Gastouni, Savalia; Leake 1846, map: Savalia; Bon 1969, 360; Iliopoulos 1948, 212.
Notes:	Vasmer considered doubtful the etymology from **Sobolьja* < sobolь (*Ru. n.* sable, *Mustella zibellina*), whereas Symeonidis proposed a link to shavarinë (*Al. n.* reed-bed): Vasmer 1941, 144–145; Symeonidis 2010, II 1234.

178. İskliva (اسكليوه), *mezra'a* in the vicinity of Ṣavalya, TT10, 79.

Notes:	Unidentified. See no. 40.

179. Kelavi (كلاوى), TT10, 79. GR

Coordinates:	X: 261973.908 Y: 4193657.285
Modern Greek:	Koroivos (Κόροιβος, ο)
Old Toponym:	Until 1955: Kelevi (Κελεβή, του)
Regional Unit:	Elis
Municipality:	Pineios
Municipal Unit:	Gastouni
Bibliography:	Pikoulas 2001a, 219.1804; Panagiotopoulos 1987, 275, 305.158: Territorio di Gastugni, Celevi; Bory de Saint-Vincent 1834, 70: Éparchie de Gastouni, Kélévi; Leake 1846, map: Kelevi; Skiadas 1993, 250; Stamatelatos–Vamva-Stamatelatou 2001, 370–371.

180. Sinasi (سیناسی), *mezraʿa* in the vicinity of Kelavi, TT10, 79.

Notes:	Unidentified.

181. Girḳa Ḳumani (كرقه قومانى), TT10, 79. AL

	Unidentified.
Notes:	Gërq or Gërk (*Al. n.* Greek) < Græcus (*Lat. n.* Greek): MANN 1948, 126; qerkë (*Al. n.* handcart, barrow). Κουμάνος (*Byz. Gr. sn.* Cuman): LAIOU-THOMADAKIS 1977, 120; Kumani (*Al. sn.*).

182. Çavuşi (چاوشى), TT10, 80. AL

Coordinates:	X: 275103.024 Y: 4197175.417
Modern Greek:	Kentro (Κέντρο, το)
Old Toponym:	Until 1928: Imam Tsaousi (Ιμάμ Τσαούση, του)
Regional Unit:	Elis
Municipality:	Ilida
Municipal Unit:	Amaliada
Bibliography:	PIKOULAS 2001a, 205.1664; PANAGIOTOPOULOS 1987, 274, 305.127: Territorio di Gastugni, Mamù Zausi; PACIFICO 1704, 123: Territorio di Gastugni, Mamut Zaussi; BORY DE SAINT-VINCENT 1834, 70: Éparchie de Gastouni, Imam Tchaouchi; LEAKE 1846, map: Imam Tchaus; SKIADAS 1993, 254; STAMATELATOS–VAMVA-STAMATELATOU 2001, 338; ILIOPOULOS 1948, 181; ZAKYTHINOS 1953, 92.
Notes:	τζαούσιος (*Byz. Gr. n.* executor of imperial orders; *anc.* mandator) < çavuş (*Tr. n.* sergeant; herald; messenger), KAZHDAN 1991, III 2135–2136.

183. Ḳoḳla (قوقله), TT10, 80. AL

Coordinates:	X: 270661.138 Y: 4198511.913
Modern Greek:	Pigadi (Πηγάδι, το)
Old Toponym:	Until 1928: Kokla (Κόκλα, του)
Regional Unit:	Elis
Municipality:	Pineios
Municipal Unit:	Tragano
Bibliography:	PIKOULAS 2001a, 381.3370; BORY DE SAINT-VINCENT 1834, 70: Éparchie de Gastouni, Kokla; LEAKE 1846, map: Kokla; SKIADAS 1993, 248; STAMATELATOS–VAMVA-STAMATELATOU 2001, 619.
Notes:	Κόκλας (*Arv. sn.*) < kokël (*Al. n.* lump, clump; knot, tangled knot; pit of a fruit): BIRIS 1998, 194–195; GEORGACAS–McDONALD 1968, 314. See also qokël (*Al. n.* large walnut).

184. Dramşa (درامشه), TT10, 80. AL

Modern Greek: Dramesi (?) (Δράμεσι, το/Δράμεση, του)

Regional Unit: Elis

Municipality: Pineios

Municipal Unit: Gastouni (?)

Bibliography: Pikoulas 2001a, 141.1055; Panagiotopoulos 1987, 271, 303.2: Territorio di Gastugni, Dramesi; Pacifico 1704, 124: Territorio di Gastugni, Dramessi.

Notes: Unidentified.
< Dramësi (*Al. n.* fold, pen, stockyard) < dremit (*Al. v.* to feel sleepy); or < **Dërmësi* (*Al. n.* place on a slope where rocks stopped after a landslide) < dërrmoj (*Al. v.* to break, to crush, to squash). It is also plausible to propose an etymology from **Dremishtë* (*Al. n.*) < **Drjamišta* or **Drĕmišče* (*Slav. n.* fold, pen, stockyard): Symeonidis 2010, I 495–496.

185. Poleşka (پولسقه), TT10, 80. AL

Notes: Unidentified.
poleskë or aguliçe (*Al. n.* primrose, cowslip, *Primula vulgaris*). Place name Poloskë/Poleskë in Korçë, Albania.

186. Ķuçi (قوچی), TT10, 81. AL

Notes: Unidentified.
Κούτσης (*Arv. sn.*) < kuç (*Al. n. colloq.* puppy, doggie): Biris 1998, 195; kucë (*Arb. n.* puppy). According to Sarris, < kuci (*Al. n.* place of high altitude, summit), and, according to Fourikis, < kuci (*Al. n.* steep high rock), which I was unable to confirm: Sarris 1928, 134; Fourikis 1929, 119. According to Georgacas–McDonald, Kuç (*Al. sn.*) < place name Kuç in Shkodër, Tiranë, Berat, Vlorë and Korçë, Albania: Georgacas–McDonald 1968, 319. Symeonidis suggested an etymology from i kuq (*Al. adj.* red): Symeonidis 2010, I 761.

187. Bavasi (باواسی), TT10, 81. AL

Notes: Unidentified.
Bua (*Al. sn.*). Μπούας (*Arv. sn.* name of an eminent mediaeval Albanian clan): Biris 1998, 199; Kolleka 1982, 31. According to Symeonidis, Bua < buall (*Al. n.* buffalo) or bujar (*Al. n.* boyar, nobleman): Symeonidis 2010, I 995.

188. Şarakin (صراكن), TT10, 81. AL

Coordinates: X: 264627.248 Y: 4189863.993

Modern Greek: Sarakina (Σαρακίνα, η)

Regional Unit: Elis

Municipality: Ilida

Municipal Unit: Amaliada

Bibliography:	GLET 1998, III 237; Palla-Hronopoulou 2003, 268.
Notes:	Uninhabited location to the north-east of Savalia (no. 177). Σαρακηνός (*Gr. n.* Saracen) > Saraqin (*Al. n.* Saracen): Thanopoulos 1988.

189. Zenbeş (زنبش), TT10, 81. AL

Notes:	Unidentified. < Ζενεμπίσης (*Arv. sn.*): Kolleka 1983, 16; İnalcik 1951, 126; İnalcik 1954a, xiv–xv.

190. Orfano (اورفانو), TT10, 81. AL

Notes:	Unidentified. Ορφανός (*Gr. sn.* orphan).

191. Ḳoromiẕi (قورومیذی), TT10, 82. AL

Coordinates:	X: 271899.363 Y: 4205233.706
Modern Greek:	Kremmydi (Κρεμμύδι, το)
Regional Unit:	Elis
Municipality:	Andravida-Kyllini
Municipal Unit:	Vouprasia
Bibliography:	Pikoulas 2001a, 234.1947.
Notes:	κρομμύδι or κρεμμύδι (*Gr. n.* onion, *Allium cepa*).

192. Ḳarẕiyoḳafti (قارذیوقافتی), 1/14662, 40/42. AL

Coordinates:	X: 257197.898 Y: 4195268.943
Modern Greek:	Kardiakafti (Καρδιακαύτι, το)
Regional Unit:	Elis
Municipality:	Pineios
Municipal Unit:	Gastouni
Bibliography:	Pikoulas 2001a, 190.1527; Panagiotopoulos 1987, 273, 304.97: Territorio di Gastugni, Cardhiocafti; Pacifico 1704, 124: Territorio di Gastugni, Cardiocafti; Bory de Saint-Vincent 1834, 69: Éparchie de Gastouni, Kardiakafti; Leake 1846, map: Kardhiakafti.
Notes:	καρδιοκαύτης (*Gr. n.* heartbreaker) < καρδιά (*Gr. n.* heart) + καίω (*Gr. v.* to burn).

193. Jujli Palamiẕi (ژوژلی پالامیذی), 1/14662, 40/42. GR

	Unidentified.
Notes:	According to Vasmer and Symeonidis, the place name Zouzouli (Ζούζουλη, η) in Kastoria derives from žuželь (*old. Slav.* beetle): Vasmer 1941, 192; Symeonidis 2010, I 551. παλαμίδι (*Gr. n. Ononis antiquorum*): Oikonomou 1988, 283–284. Παλαμήδης, Παλαμίδης (*Gr. sn.*). Cf. microtoponym Stou Palamidi ston Diago (στου Παλαμήδη στον Διαγό) in Gortynia, Arcadia: Gritsopoulos 1987–88, 442; Palamidi (Παλαμίδι, το) in Nafplio (Ναύπλιο, το), Trifylia and Olympia, Palamidia (Παλαμίδια, τα) in Trifylia, Messenia: Georgacas–McDonald 1968, 220.

194. Ḫavaro Protopapa (خاوارو پرتوپاپا), 1/14662, 40/42. AL

Coordinates:	X: 270641.483 Y: 4193165.926
Modern Greek:	Synoikismos Havariou/Palaio Havari (Συνοικισμός Χαβαρίου, ο/Παλαιό Χάβαρι, το)
Regional Unit:	Elis
Municipality:	Ilida
Municipal Unit:	Amaliada
Bibliography:	Pikoulas 2001a, 476.4299; Panagiotopoulos 1987, 275, 305.155: Territorio di Gastugni, Ghavaria; Bory de Saint-Vincent 1834, 70: Éparchie de Gastouni, Khavari; Leake 1846, map: Khavari; Nouhakis 1901, II 584: Χάβαρη.
Notes:	Χάβαρος (*Gr. sn.*) < χάβρος, φάβρος < favro (*Ven.* ironsmith): Symeonidis 2010, II 1423. Cf. χάβαρο (*Gr. n.* sea-shell) attested in Elis and Zakynthos. πρωτόπαπας (*Gr. n.* head priest).

195. Ḳoḳla Marġariti (قوقلا مرغارتی), 1/14662, 40/42. AL

Coordinates:	X: 269619.456 Y: 4189647.795
Modern Greek:	Koklaki (Κοκλάκι, το)
Regional Unit:	Elis
Municipality:	Ilida
Municipal Unit:	Amaliada
Bibliography:	Pikoulas 2001a, 215.1757; Bory de Saint-Vincent 1834, 70: Éparchie de Gastouni, Koklaki; Leake 1846, map: Koklaki; Skiadas 1993, 254.
Notes:	For Ḳoḳla see no. 183. Μαργαρίτης (*Gr. sn.*).

196. Potamya Ṣarandinu (پوتامیه صراندنو), *mezraʿa* in the vicinity of Ḳoḳla Marġariti, 1/14662, 40/42.

Notes:	Unidentified. Different from no. 175.

197. Niḫor (نیخور), 1/14662, 43. GR

Coordinates:	X: 253974.582 Y: 4198983.618

Modern Greek:	Neohori (Νεοχώρι, το)
Regional Unit:	Elis
Municipality:	Andravida-Kyllini
Municipal Unit:	Kastro-Kyllini
Bibliography:	Pikoulas 2001a, 339.2967; Panagiotopoulos 1987, 273, 62: Territorio di Gastugni, Nioghori S. Elia; Pacifico 1704, 124: Territorio di Gastugni, Niocori; Bory de Saint-Vincent 1834, 70: Éparchie de Gastouni, Néokhori; Leake 1846, map: Neokhori; Iliopoulos 1948, 207.

198. Ṣuli (صولی), 1/14662, 43. AL

Coordinates:	X: 277382.930 Y: 4197195.071
Modern Greek:	Souli (Σούλι, το)
Regional Unit:	Elis
Municipality:	Ilida
Municipal Unit:	Pineia
Bibliography:	Pikoulas 2001a, 430.3847; Panagiotopoulos 1987, 273, 304.100: Territorio di Gastugni, Sulli; Pacifico 1704, 124: Territorio di Gastugni, Sulli Musachi; Bory de Saint-Vincent 1834, 70: Éparchie de Gastouni, Souli; Leake 1846, map: Suli; Stamatelatos–Vamva-Stamatelatou 2001, 704; Iliopoulos 1948, 179.
Notes:	Souli, like Xenies (no. 527), was covered by the lake formed by the dam in the Pineios River (Πηνειός, ο) in the 1960s. It reappeared on the south bank of the lake in 1991. See no. 37.

199. Manesi (مانسی), 1/14662, 43. AL

Bibliography:	Panagiotopoulos 1987, 271, 303.7: Territorio di Gastugni, Manesi.
Notes:	Unidentified. See no. 22.

200. Andraviza (اندراویزه), 1/14662, 44. GR

Coordinates:	X: 259811.928 Y: 4198669.148
Modern Greek:	Andravida (Ανδραβίδα, η)
Regional Unit:	Elis
Municipality:	Andravida-Kyllini
Municipal Unit:	Andravida
Bibliography:	Pikoulas 2001a, 75.420; Panagiotopoulos 1987, 271, 303: Territorio di Gastugni, Andravida; Pacifico 1704, 124: Territorio di Gastugni, Andravida, *olim Cillenes*; Bory de Saint-Vincent 1834, 70: Éparchie de Gastouni, Andravida; Leake 1846, map: Andravidha; Longnon–Topping 1969, 234; Bon 1969, 318–320; Iliopoulos 1948, 152–153.

201. Foloḳobuva (فولوقوبووه), *mezraʿa* in the vicinity of Andraviza, 1/14662, 44.

Unidentified.

Notes: Perhaps from Floka + Bua. Φλόκας or Φλώκας (*Gr. sn.*) < flok (*Al. n.* hair) or floqe, flokje, floke (*Al. n.* woollen blanket): KOLLEKA 1983, 29–30. Place name Floq in Fier, Elbasan, Berat and Korçë, Albania. For Buva see no. 187.

202. İzlatḳa (ازلاتقه), 1/14662, 44. AL

Coordinates: X: 269462.221 Y: 4208850.109

Modern Greek: Neromylos (Νερόμυλος, ο)

Old Toponym: Until 1928: Zoulatika (Ζουλάτικα, τα)

Regional Unit: Elis

Municipality: Andravida-Kyllini

Municipal Unit: Vouprasia

Bibliography: PIKOULAS 2001a, 342.2992; PANAGIOTOPOULOS 1987, 274, 304.105: Territorio di Gastugni, Slatica; BORY DE SAINT-VINCENT 1834, 70: Éparchie de Gastouni, Zonga Zoulatika; LEAKE 1846, map: Zulatika; SKIADAS 1993, 371; STAMATELATOS–VAMVA-STAMATELATOU 2001, 545.

Notes: Pikoulas noted an old water mill known as Zoulatika.
Zlatka (*Scr. pn. dim.* of Zlatija; golden) < zlato (*Scr. n.* gold): RHSJ 1975, XXII 900–901.

203. Ḳanḳaẕi (قانقاذى), 1/14662, 45. AL

Coordinates: X: 275869.544 Y: 4213233.033

Modern Greek: Kangadi (Καγκάδι, το)

Regional Unit: Achaia

Municipality: Dytiki Ahaïa

Municipal Unit: Larissos

Bibliography: PIKOULAS 2001a, 164.1268; PANAGIOTOPOULOS 1987, 274, 304.104, Territorio di Gastugni, Cangadhi; PACIFICO 1704, 124: Territorio di Gastugni, Cangadi; BORY DE SAINT-VINCENT 1834, 70: Éparchie de Gastouni, Kangadi; LEAKE 1846, map: Kangadhi.

Notes: Καγκάδης (*Arv. sn.*) < **këngëdhi* (*Arv. adj.* singsong) < këngë or kângë (*Al. n.* song): BIRIS 1998, 193; kângëz (*Al. n.* canto).

204. Marḳoplu (مارقوپلو), 1/14662, 45. AL

Coordinates: X: 265157.916 Y: 4197568.504

Modern Greek: Markopoulo (Μαρκόπουλο, το)

Regional Unit: Elis

Municipality: Pineios

Municipal Unit: Tragano

Bibliography: Pikoulas 2001a, 276.2350; Panagiotopoulos 1987, 274, 304.103, Territorio di Gastugni, Marcopulo; Pacifico 1704, 124: Territorio di Gastugni, Marcopulo e Mauria; Bory de Saint-Vincent 1834, 70: Éparchie de Gastouni, Markoplou; Leake 1846, map: Markoplu; Iliopoulos 1948, 212.

Notes: Μαρκόπουλος (*Gr. sn.*) < Μάρκος (*Gr. pn.* Mark) + -όπουλος (*Gr. end.* son of).

205. Ḳanbiziya (قانبیزیه), *mezraʿa* in the vicinity of Marḳoplu, 1/14662, 46.

Notes: Unidentified.
< καμπίσια (*Gr. adj. f.* lowland, pertaining to flat or level land).

206. İvlanduşa (اولاندوشه), 1/14662, 46. AL

Notes: Unidentified.
See no. 115.

207. Ḳavasila (قواسله), 1/14662, 46. AL

Coordinates: X: 259399.187 Y: 4195426.178

Modern Greek: Kavasilas [Καβάσιλας, ο (= τα)]

Regional Unit: Elis

Municipality: Pineios

Municipal Unit: Gastouni

Bibliography: Pikoulas 2001a, 163.1259; Panagiotopoulos 1987, 273, 304.82-83: Territorio di Gastugni, Cavasilla alto, Cavassila basso; Pacifico 1704, 124: Territorio di Gastugni, Carassilla Cato, Carassila apano; Bory de Saint-Vincent 1834, 70: Éparchie de Gastouni, Apano/Kato Kavasila; Leake 1846, map: Ap./K. Kavasula; Bon 1969, 332; Iliopoulos 1948, 155, 212.

Notes: Καβάσιλας (*Gr., Arv. sn.*) < **Καλοβάσιλας* (*Byz. sn.*): Biris 1998, 193; Symeonidis 2010, I 579.

208. Lihyana (لهيانه), 1/14662, 47. GR

Coordinates: X: 259202.643 Y: 4202187.280

Modern Greek: Lehaina (Λεχαινά, τα)

Regional Unit: Elis

Municipality: Andravida-Kyllini

Municipal Unit: Lehaina

Bibliography: Pikoulas 2001a, 254.2132; Panagiotopoulos 1987, 271, 303.13: Territorio di Gastugni, Lechiena; Pacifico 1704, 124: Territorio di Gastugni, Lechienà; Expédition 1832: Lékhæna; Bory de Saint-Vincent 1834, 70: Éparchie de Gastouni, Lekhæna; Leake 1846, map: Lekhená; Longnon–Topping 1969, 236; Bon 1969, 339–340; Iliopoulos 1948, 156, 212.

Notes: < **lechina* (*Slav. n.* place with kitchen gardens): Symeonidis 2010, I 819.

209. İpsari (اپساری), 1/14662, 48. AL

Coordinates: X: 270621.829 Y: 4211169.324

Modern Greek: Psari (Ψάρι, το)

Regional Unit: Elis

Municipality: Andravida-Kyllini

Municipal Unit: Vouprasia

Bibliography: Pikoulas 2001a, 493.4458; Panagiotopoulos 1987, 274, 304.108: Territorio di Gastugni, Psaria; Bory de Saint-Vincent 1834, 70: Éparchie de Gastouni, Psari; Leake 1846, map: Psari; Iliopoulos 1948, 207.

Notes: ψάρι (*Gr. n.* fish) < (ὁ)ψάριν (*Byz. Gr.*): Koukoules 1948, 36. Place name Psar in Gjirokastër and Korçë, and Psar i Zi in Korçë, Albania: Georgacas–McDonald 1968, 340. See also Symeonidis 2010, II 1460.

210. Pendani (پندانی), *mezraʿa* in the vicinity of İpsari, 1/14662, 48.

Coordinates: X: 272980.353 Y: 4210717.274

Modern Greek: Neapoli (Νεάπολη, η)

Old Toponym: Until 1955: Benteni (Μπεντένι, το)

Regional Unit: Elis

Municipality: Andravida-Kyllini

Municipal Unit: Vouprasia

Bibliography: Pikoulas 2001a, 336.2940; Panagiotopoulos 1987, 274, 305.139: Territorio di Gastugni, Bendegni; Pacifico 1704, 124: Territorio di Gastugni, Bedegni; Bory de Saint-Vincent 1834, 70: Éparchie de Gastouni, Bédéni; Leake 1846, map: Bedenia; Skiadas 1993, 248; Stamatelatos–Vamva-Stamatelatou 2001, 537.

Notes: See no. 85.

211. Lonci (لونجی), *mezraʿa* in the vicinity of İpsari, 1/14662, 48.

Notes: Unidentified.
Perhaps linked to lonxho (*Al. n.* shameless person; laughing stock); Lunxhëri (*Al. n.* ethnographic region in southern Albania).

212. Başta (باشته), *mezraʿa* in the vicinity of İpsari, 1/14662, 48.

Coordinates: X: 265118.607 Y: 4202934.145

Modern Greek: Agioi Theodoroi (Άγιοι Θεόδωροι, οι)

Old Toponym: Until 1961: Bastas (Μπάστας, ο)

Regional Unit:	Elis
Municipality:	Andravida-Kyllini
Municipal Unit:	Lehaina
Bibliography:	Pikoulas 2001a, 40.94; Expédition 1832: Basta; Leake 1846, map: Basta; Stamatelatos–Vamva-Stamatelatou 2001, 15; Iliopoulos 1948, 178.
Notes:	Μπάστας (*Arv. sn.*): Biris 1998, 198; bashtë (*Al. n.* garden, orchard): Georgacas–McDonald 1968, 295.

213. Tunba (تونبه), *mezraʿa* in the vicinity of İpsari, 1/14662, 48.

Notes:	Unidentified. See no. 109.

214. Ḳapaleto (قپالتو), *mezraʿa* in the vicinity of İpsari, 1/14662, 48.

Coordinates:	X: 269049.480 Y: 4208280.133
Modern Greek:	Kapaleto (Καπαλέτο, το)
Regional Unit:	Elis
Municipality:	Andravida-Kyllini
Municipal Unit:	Vouprasia
Bibliography:	Pikoulas 2001a, 185.1477; Panagiotopoulos 1987, 274, 304.107: Territorio di Gastugni, Capelesù; Pacifico 1704, 124: Territorio di Gastugni, Capeletù; Bory de Saint-Vincent 1834, 70: Éparchie de Gastouni, Kapéléti; Leake 1846, map: Kapeleto; Iliopoulos 1948, 173.
Notes:	Capeletti (*It. sn.*).

215. Aya Baraskevi (آيه براسكوى), 1/14662, 49. GR

Coordinates:	X: 272803.463 Y: 4201283.179
Modern Greek:	Agia Paraskevi (Αγία Παρασκευή, η)
Regional Unit:	Elis
Municipality:	Andravida-Kyllini
Municipal Unit:	Lehaina
Bibliography:	GLET 1998, I 22.
Notes:	Uninhabited place to the east of Agios Halarambos (Άγιος Χαράλαμπος, ο), where a chapel of Agia Paraskevi is located.

1 Nāḥiyyet-i Ḳalavrita (Kalavryta)

Demographic Distribution

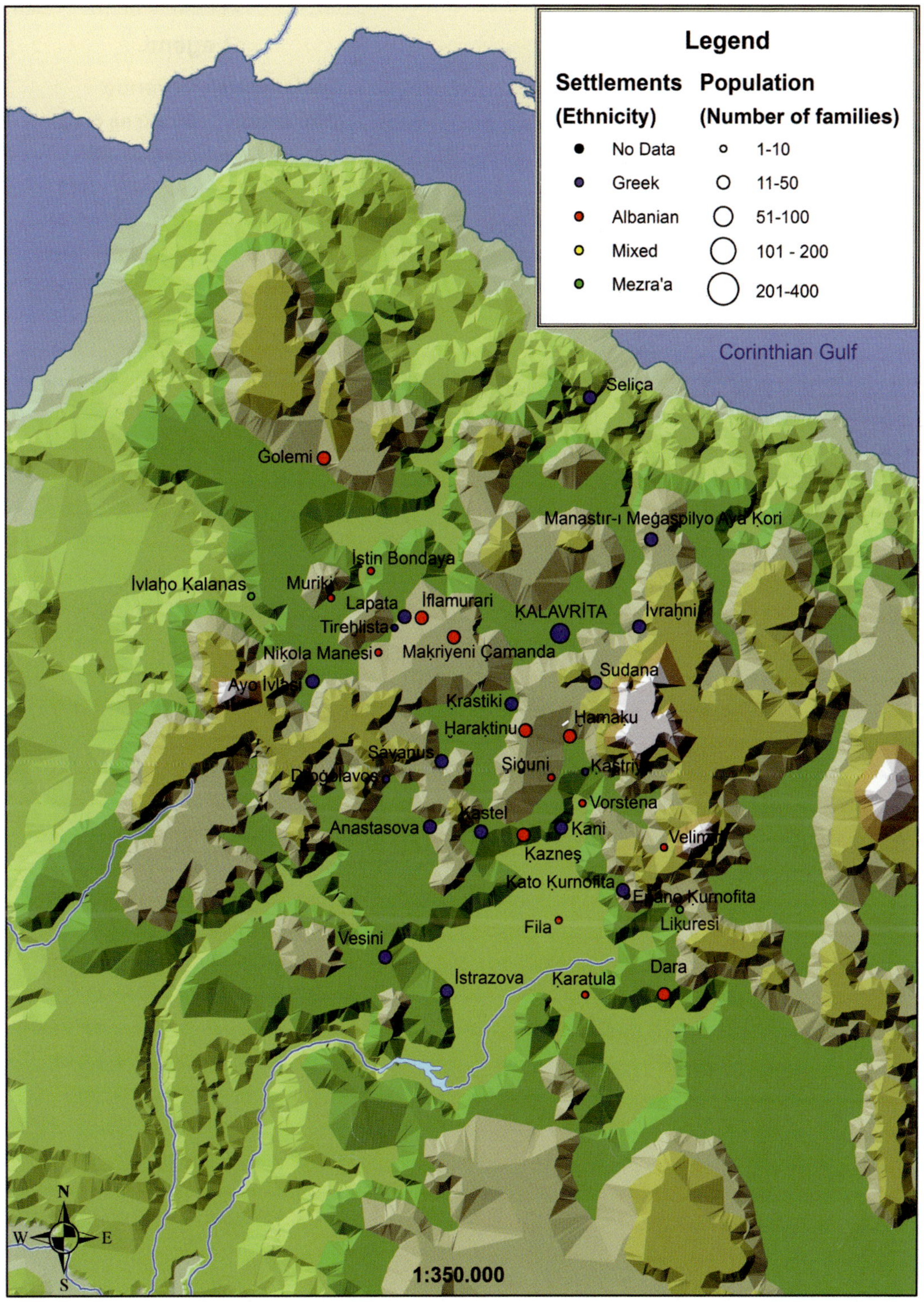

Designed by G.C. Liakopoulos

2 Nāḥiyyet-i Ḳalavrita (Kalavryta)

Economic Distribution

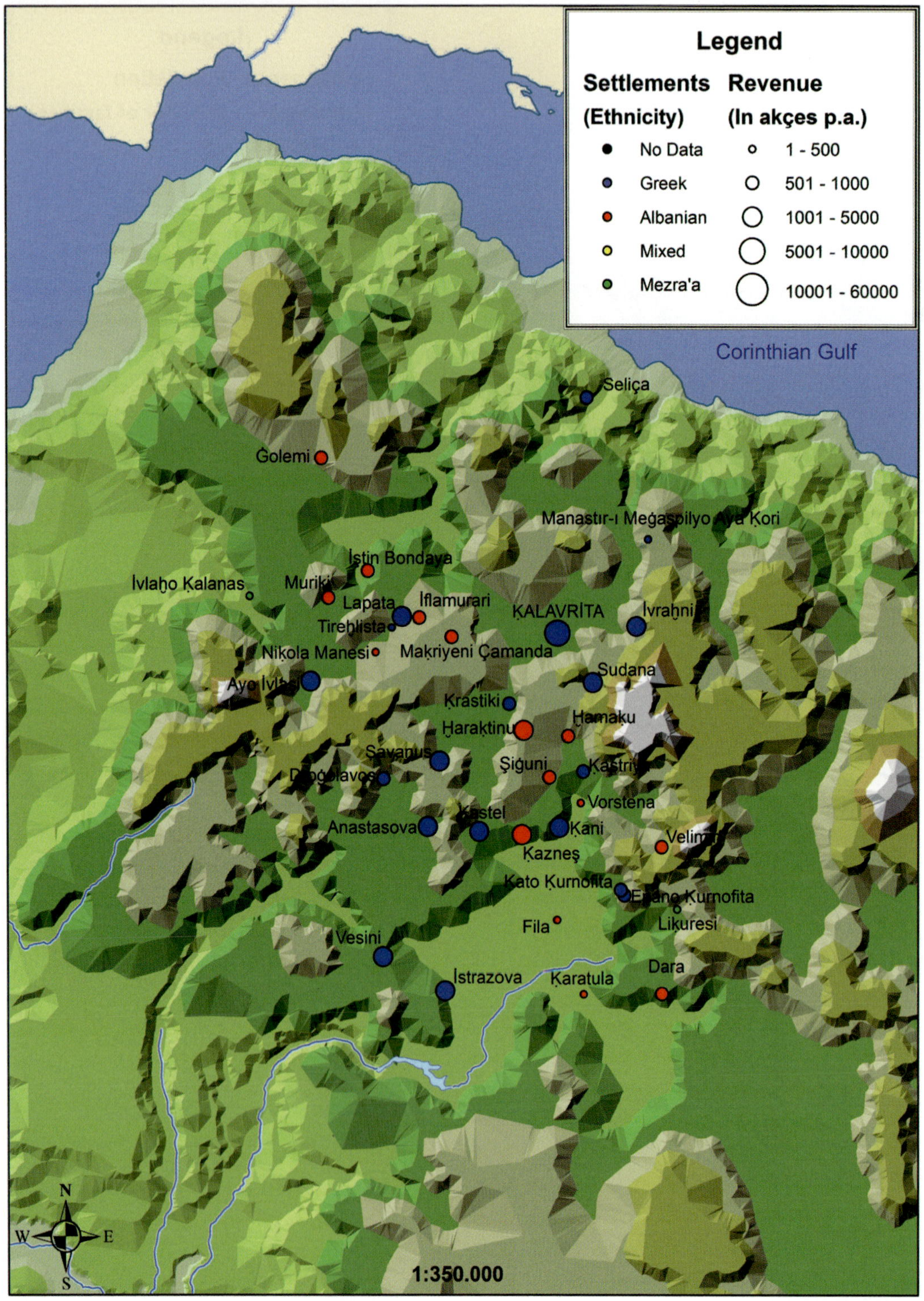

Designed by G.C. Liakopoulos

3 Nāḥiyyet-i Mizişra (Mystras)
Demographic Distribution

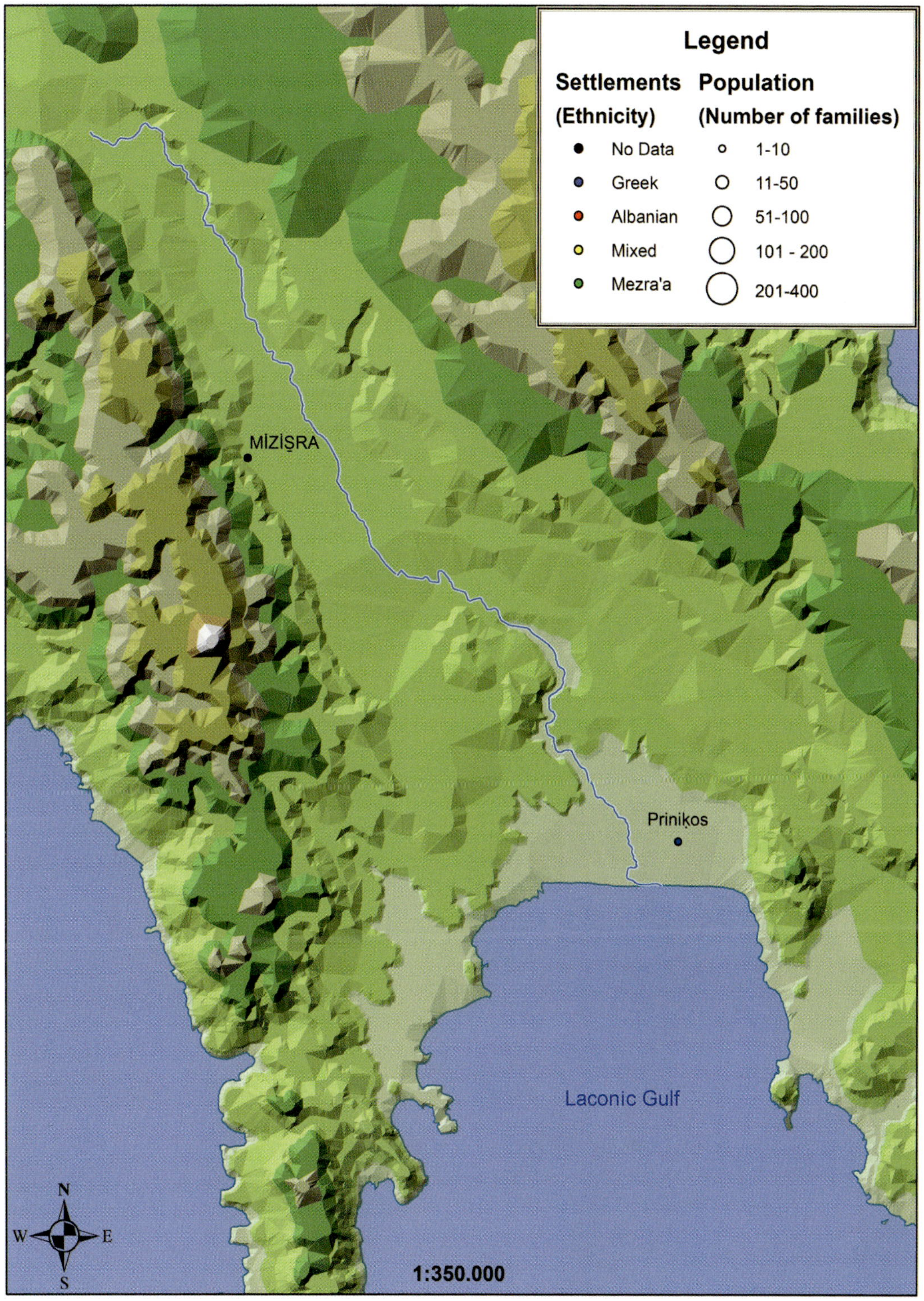

Designed by G.C. Liakopoulos

4 Nāḥiyyet-i Miziṣra (Mystras)
Economic Distribution

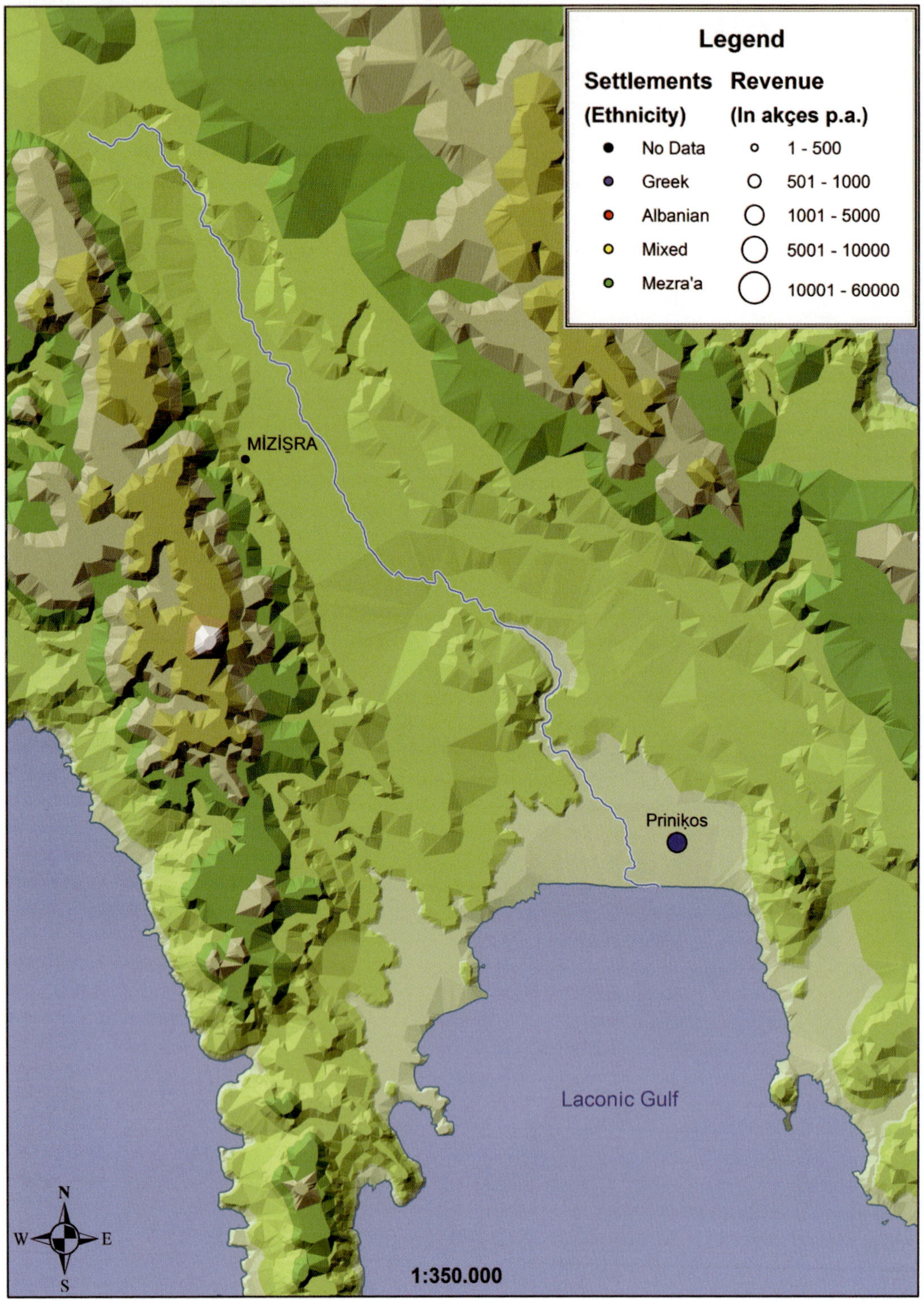

Designed by G.C. Liakopoulos

5 Nāḥiyyet-i Miḫlu (Mouhli)
Demographic Distribution

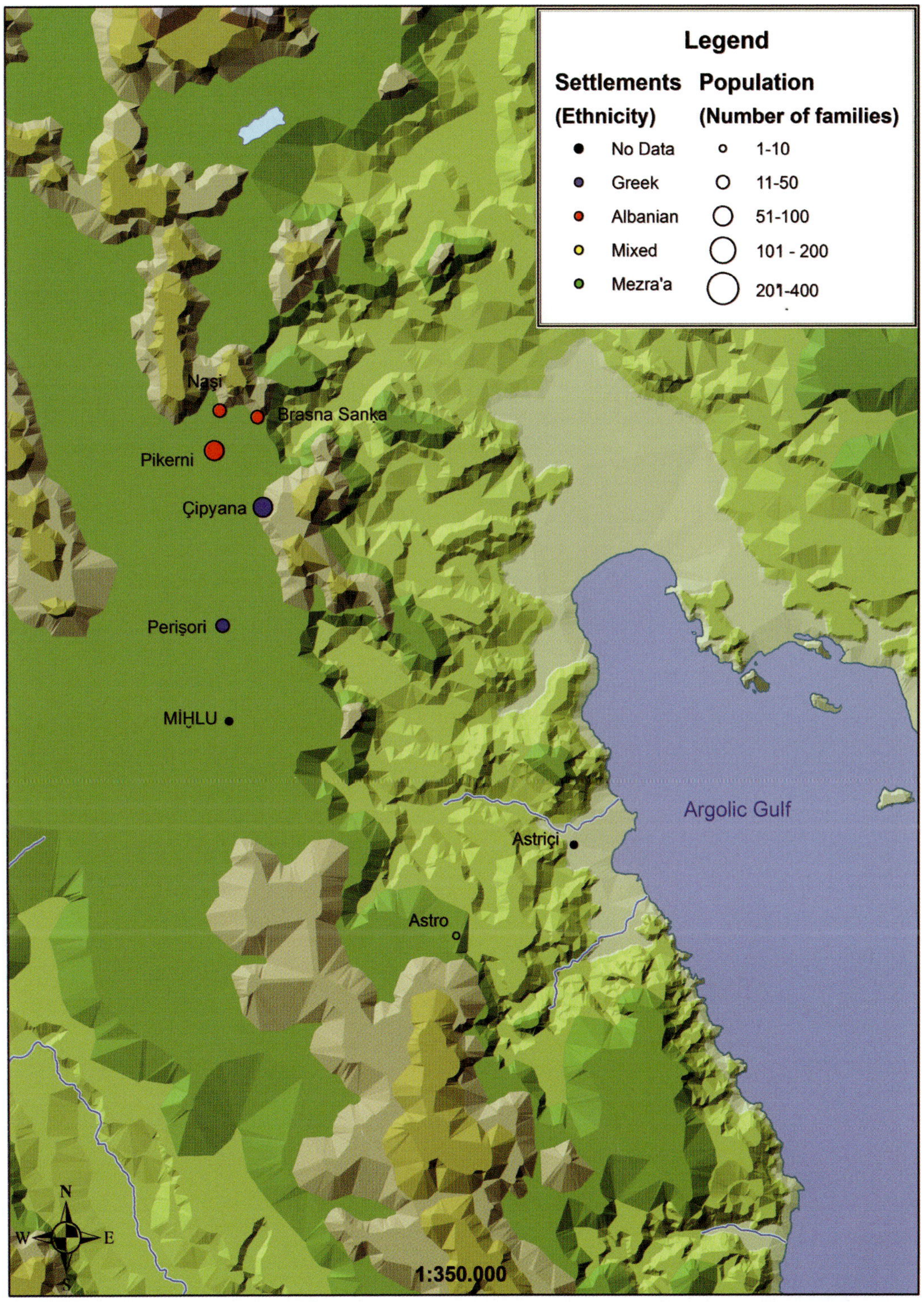

Designed by G.C. Liakopoulos

6 Nāḫiyyet-i Miḫlu (Mouhli)

Economic Distribution

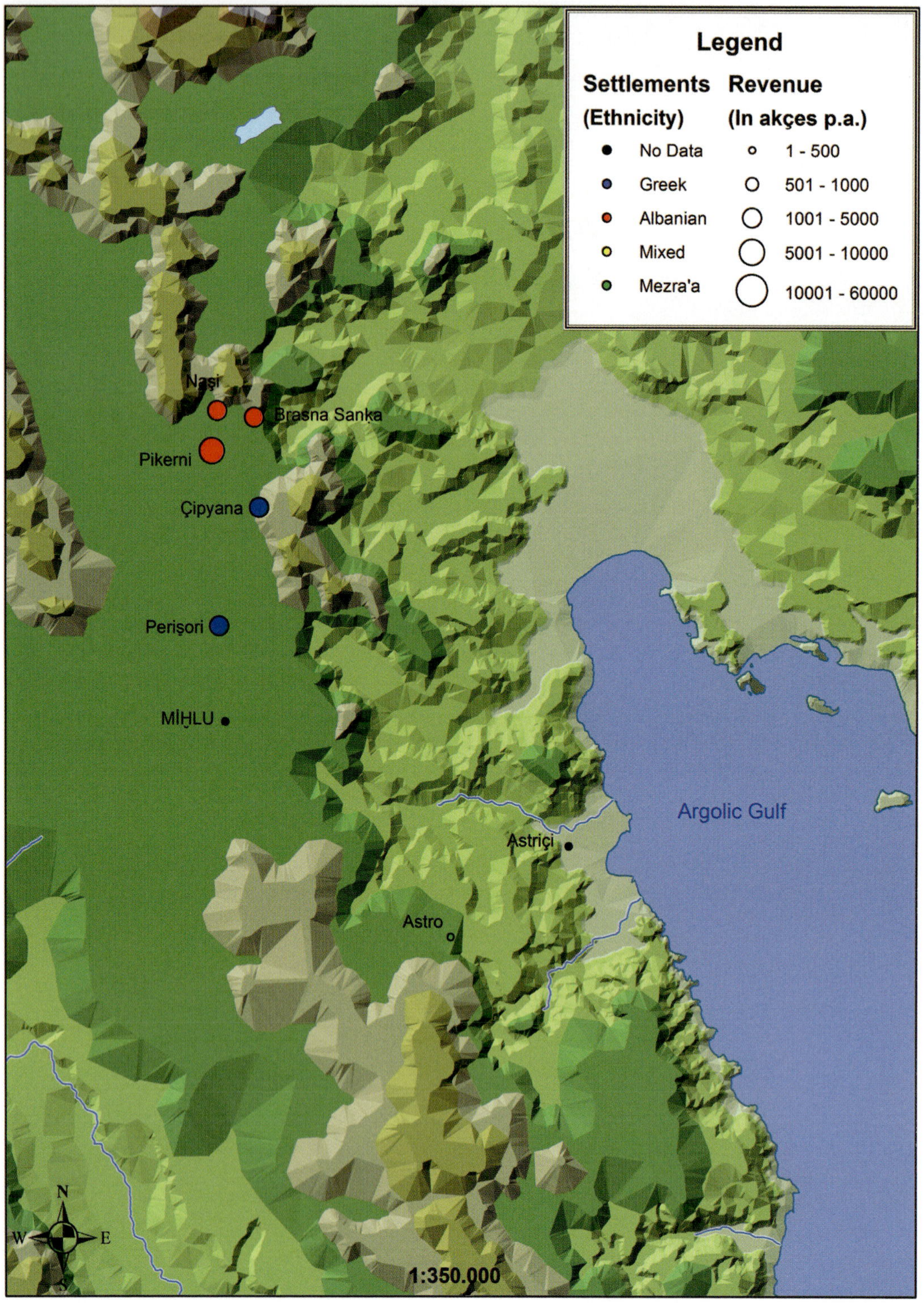

Designed by G.C. Liakopoulos

7 Nāḥiyyet-i Bejenik (Vlaherna)
Demographic Distribution

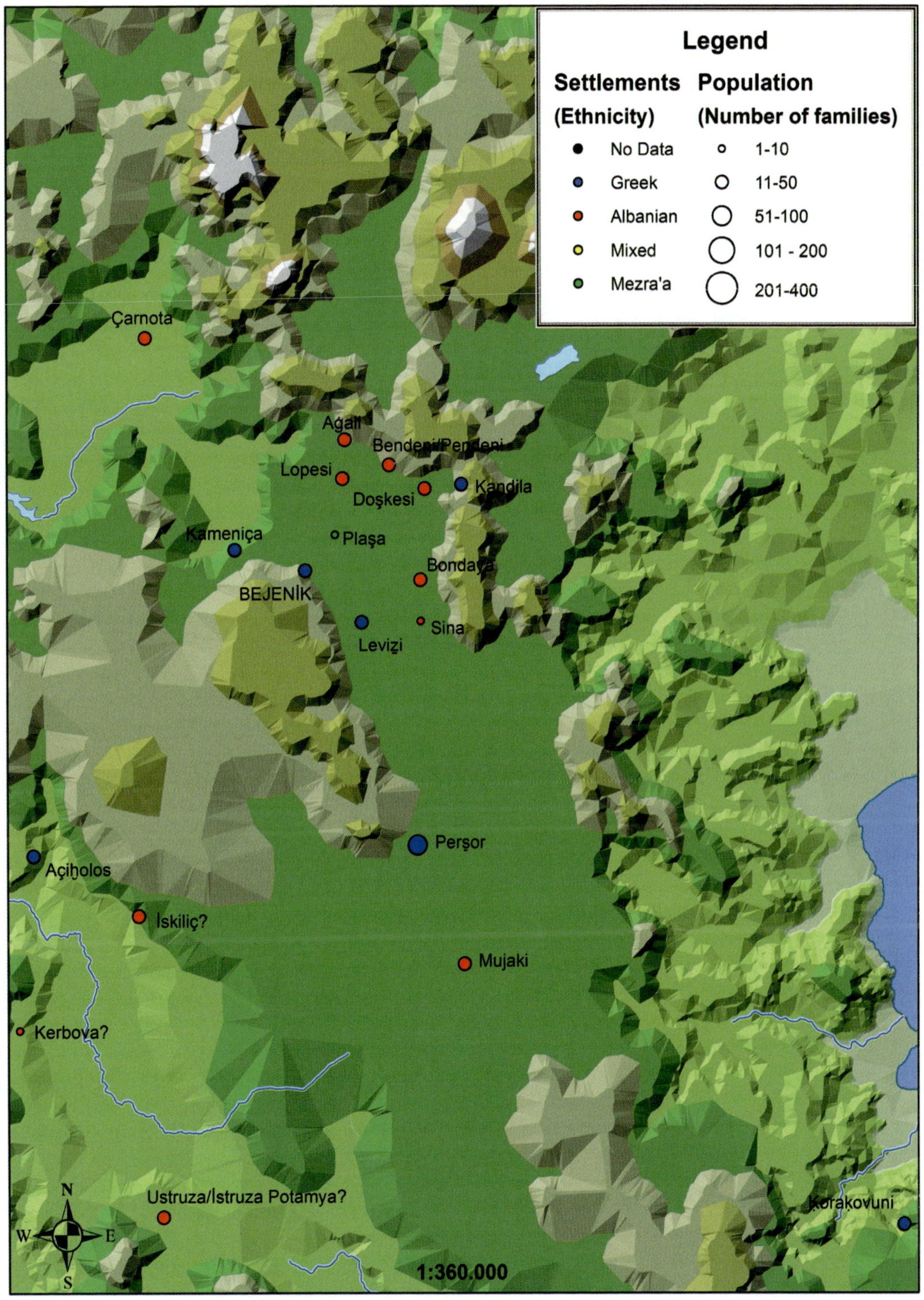

Designed by G.C. Liakopoulos

8 Nāḫiyyet-i Bejenik (Vlaherna)
Economic Distribution

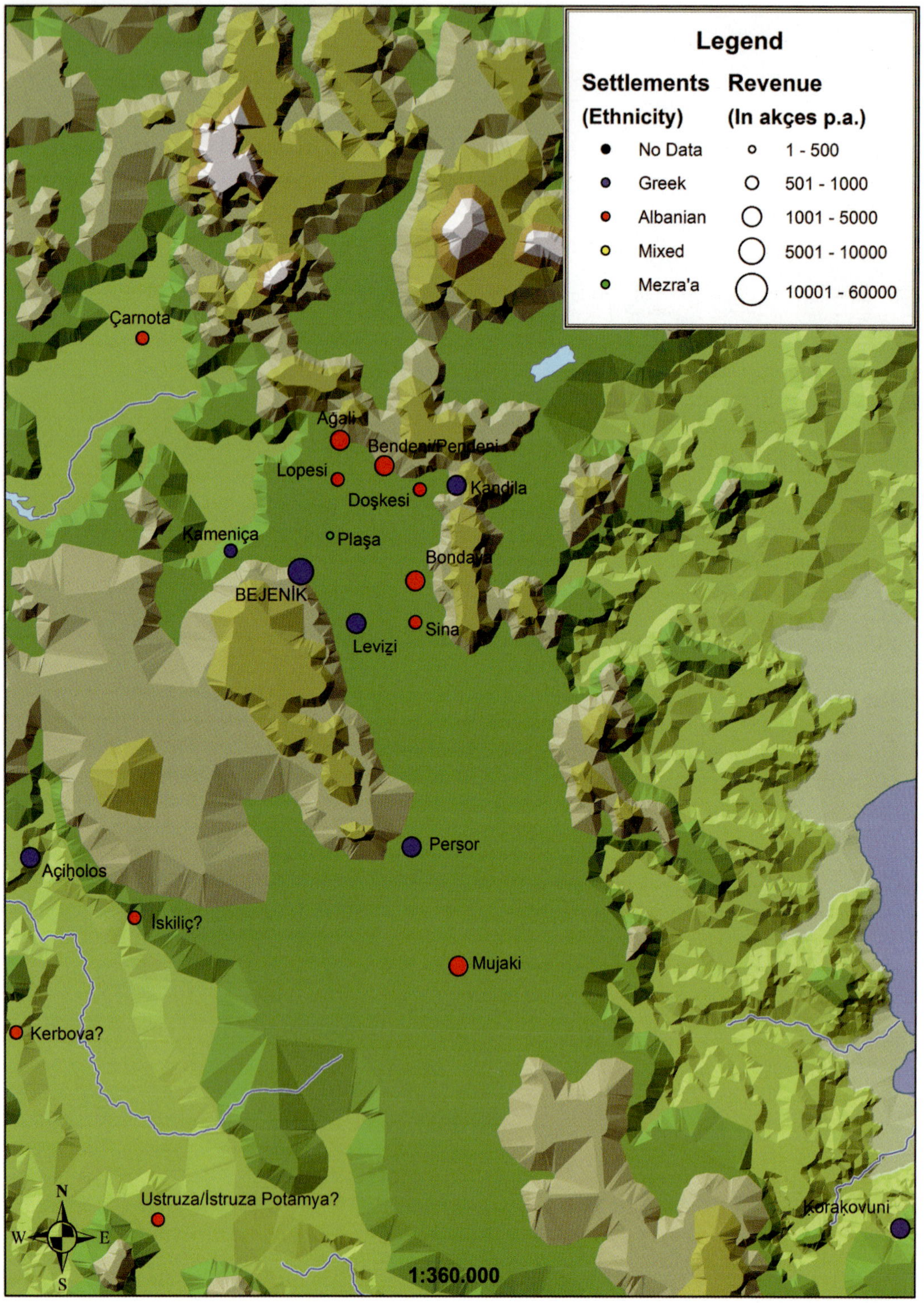

Designed by G.C. Liakopoulos

9 Nāḫiyyet-i Voştiça (Aigio)

Demographic Distribution

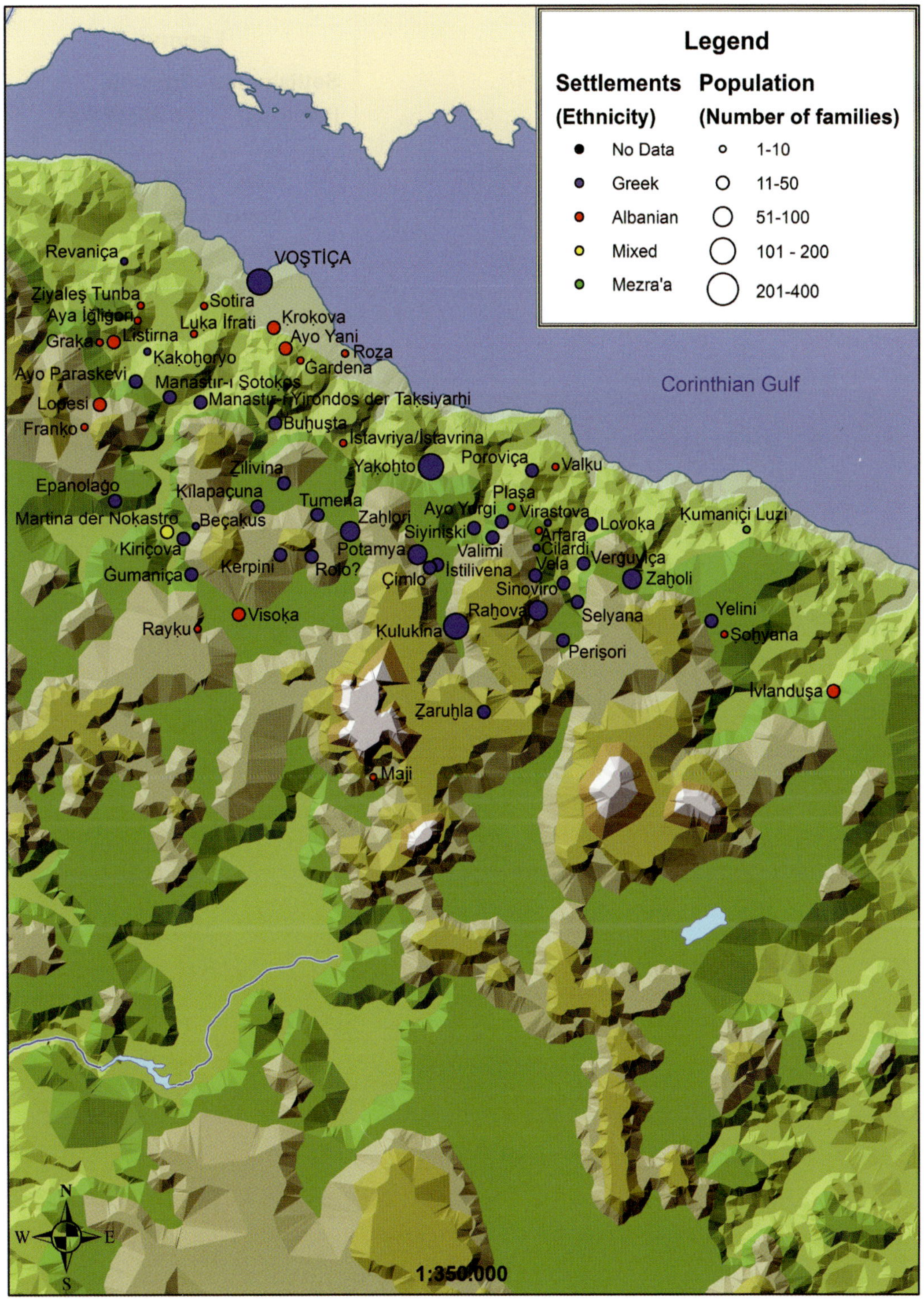

Designed by G.C. Liakopoulos

10 Nāḥiyyet-i Voştiça (Aigio)
Economic Distribution

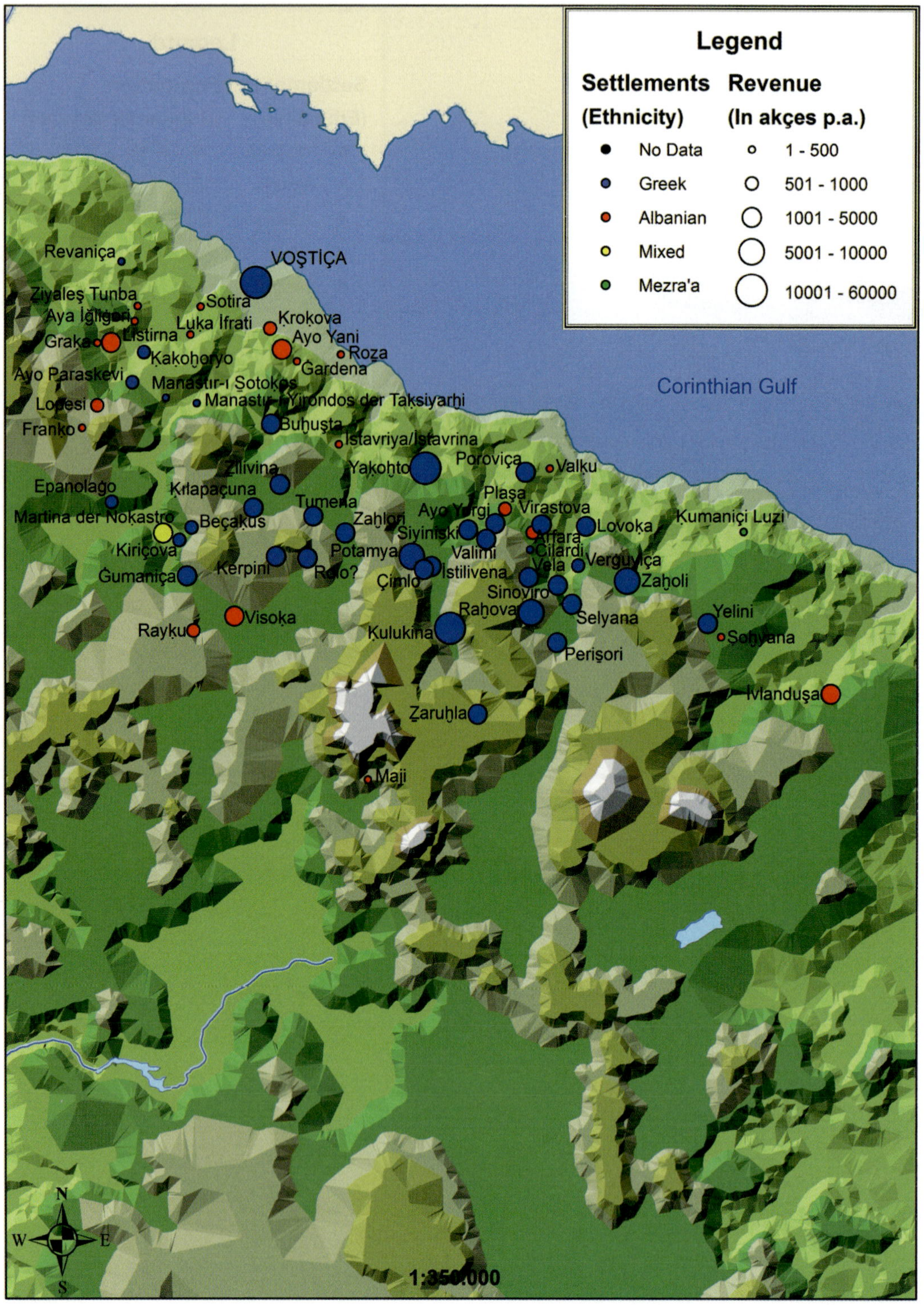

Designed by G.C. Liakopoulos

11 Nāḥiyyet-i Ḫulumiç (Hlemoutsi)
Demographic Distribution

Designed by G.C. Liakopoulos

12 Nāḫiyyet-i Ḫulumiç (Hlemoutsi)
Economic Distribution

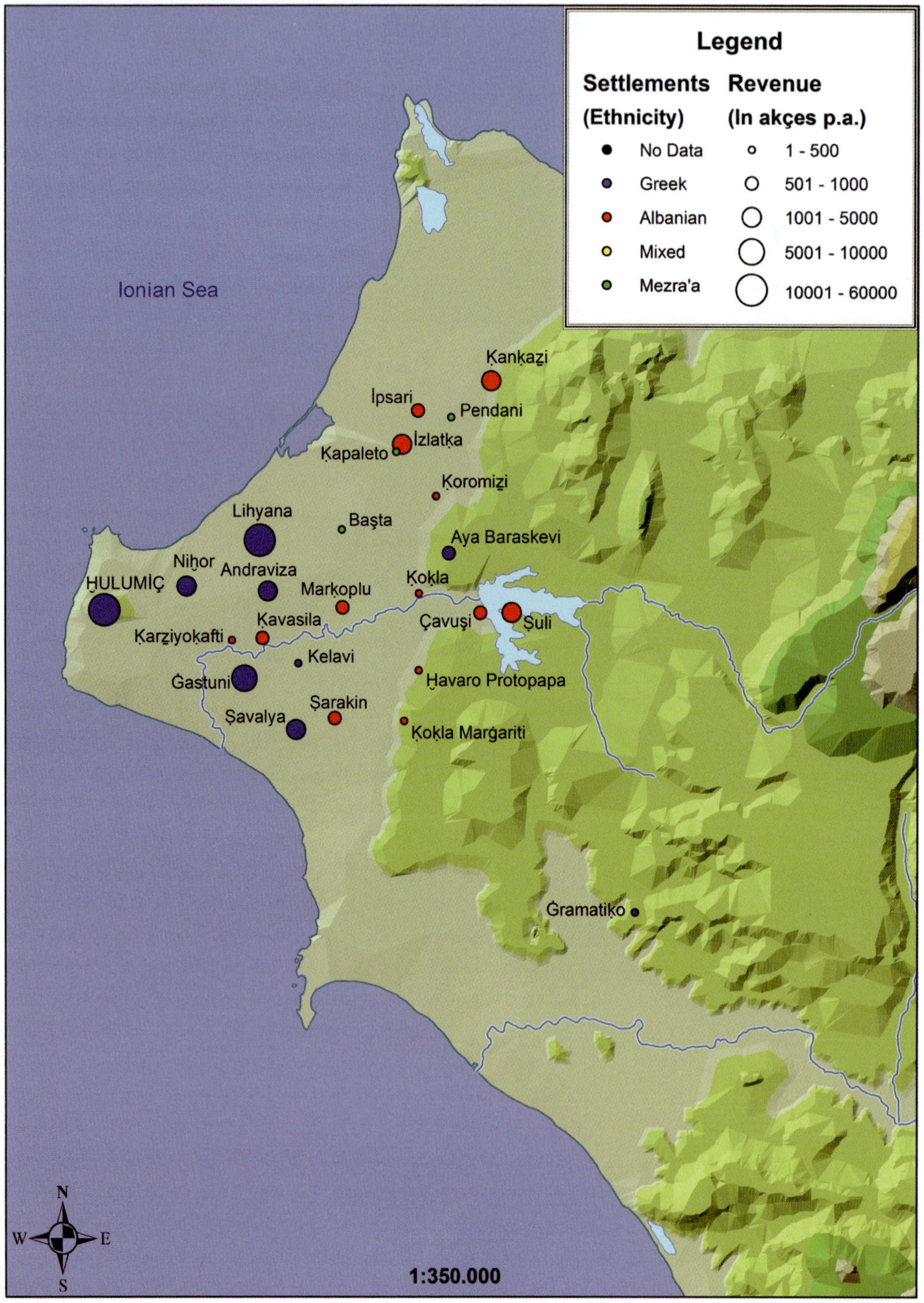

Designed by G.C. Liakopoulos

13 Nāḥiyyet-i Vumero (Goumero)

Demographic Distribution

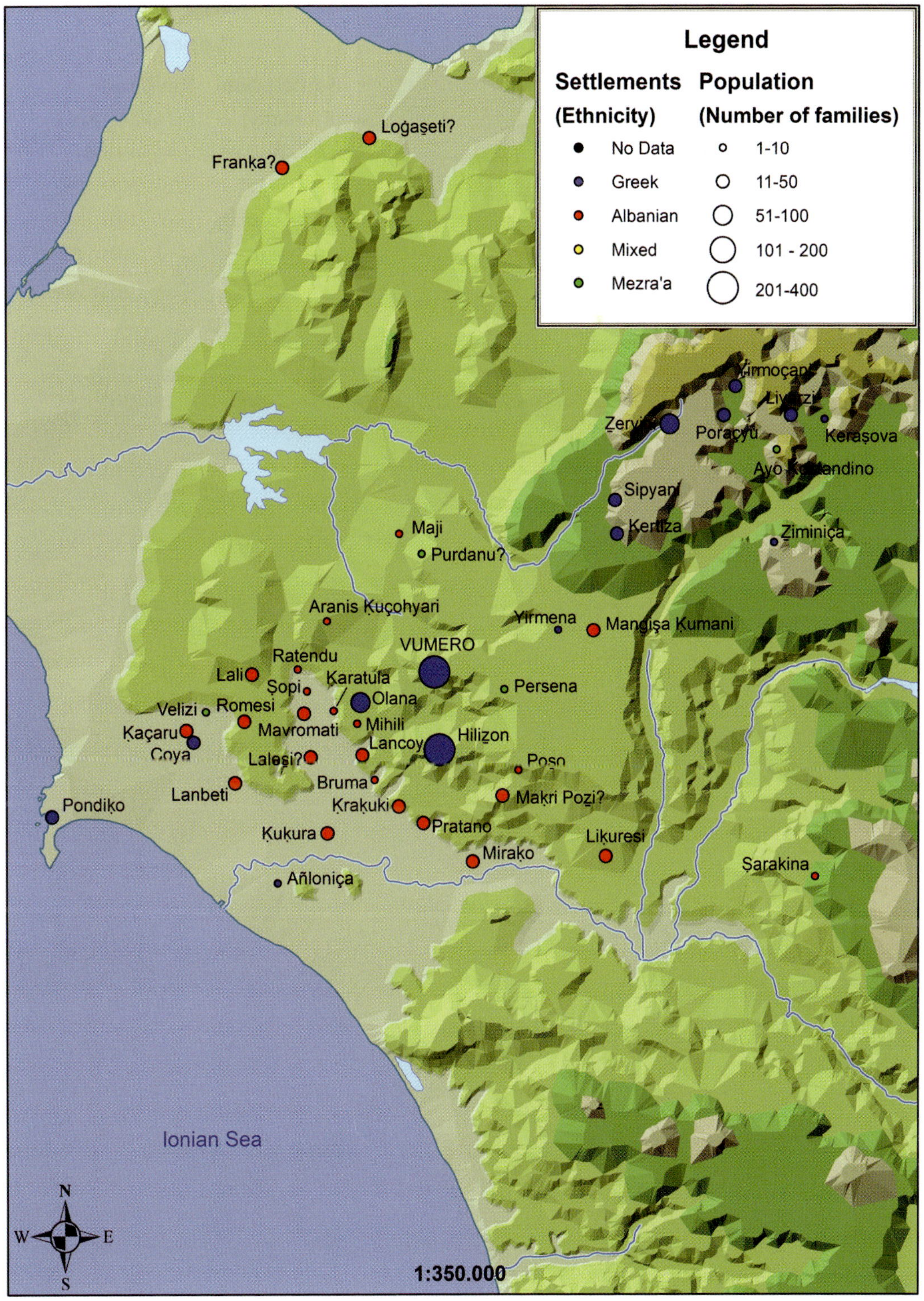

Designed by G.C. Liakopoulos

14 Nāḫiyyet-i Vumero (Goumero)
Economic Distribution

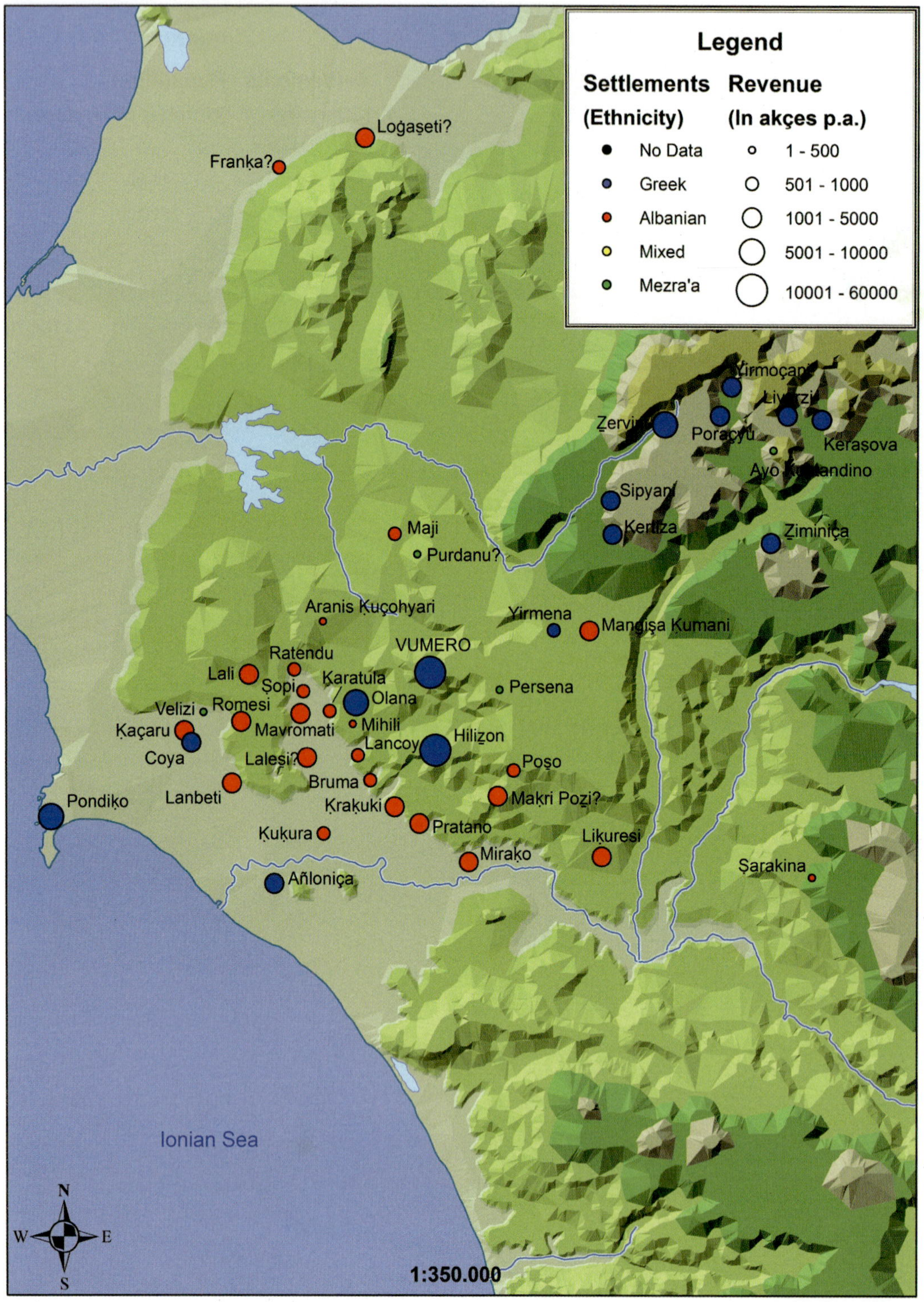

Designed by G.C. Liakopoulos

15 Nāḥiyyet-i Kirvuḳor (Palaiokastro/Koufoplaiiko Kastro)
Demographic Distribution

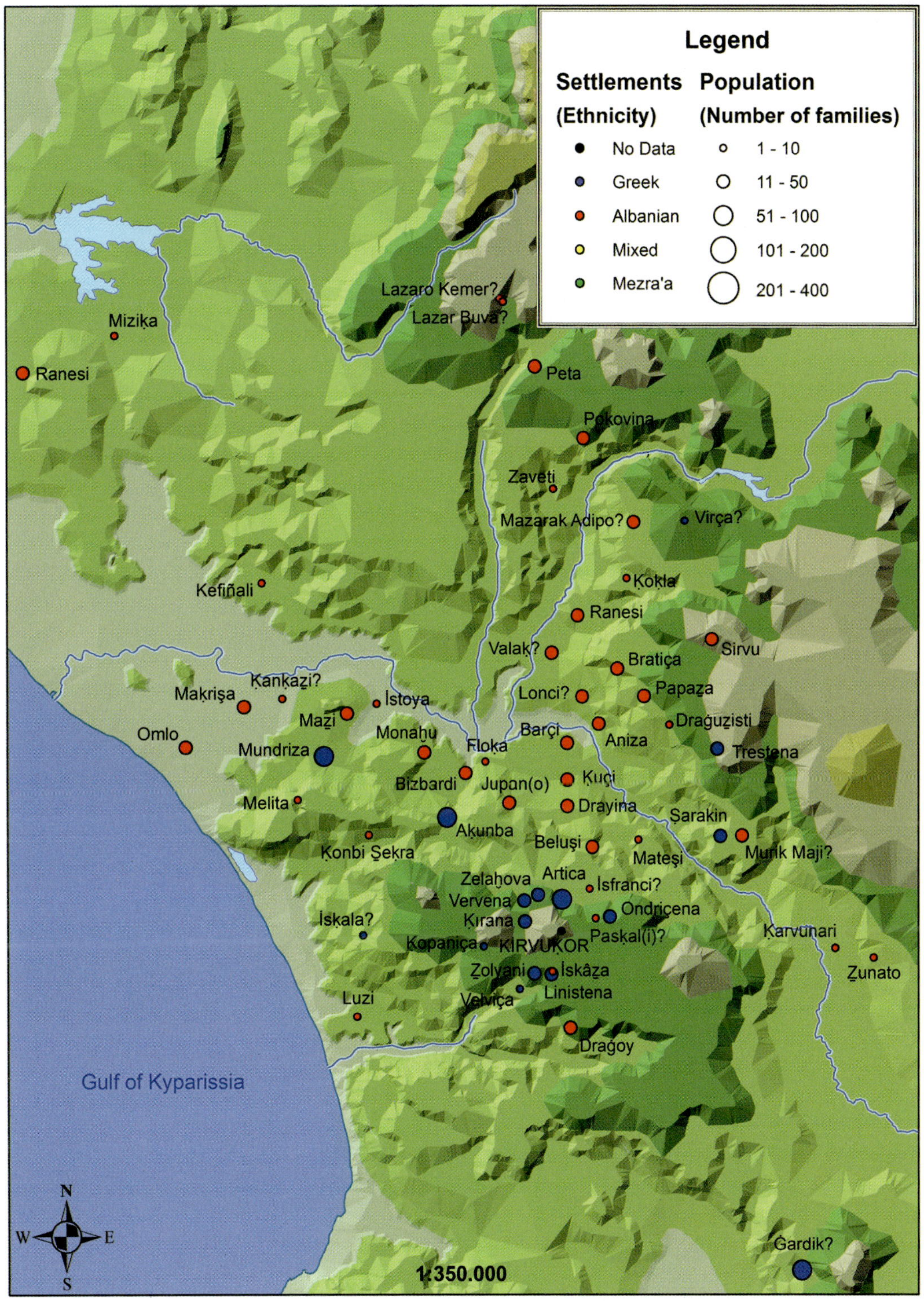

Designed by G.C. Liakopoulos

216. Ġramatiḳo (غراميقو), 1/14662, 49. GR

Coordinates:	X: 286188.086 Y: 4176400.753
Modern Greek:	Grammatikos (Γραμματικός, ο)
Regional Unit:	Elis
Municipality:	Pyrgos
Municipal Unit:	Oleni
Bibliography:	PIKOULAS 2001a, 126.917; ILIOPOULOS 1948, 166.

217. Murji (مورژى), 1/14662, 85. GR

Notes:	Unidentified. Cf. microtoponym Mourzi (Μούρζη, του), where a dependency of Eleousas Monastery (I.M. Ελεούσας, η) is mentioned in the Grimani Archive (1696–1700): DOKOS 1971–74, 96; its exact location is unknown. < murriz (*Al. n.* hawthorn, *Crataegus*): GEORGACAS–MCDONALD 1968, 334; OIKONOMOU 1988, 282. Microtoponym Murrizi Kuq in Damës, Tepelenë, Albania: DAKA 1988, 254.

7. District of Vumero (Goumero) (Maps 13–14)

218. Vumero, nefs-i (وومرو), TT10, 82. GR

Coordinates:	X: 289952.370 Y: 4181815.279
Modern Greek:	Goumero (Γούμερο, το)
Regional Unit:	Elis
Municipality:	Pyrgos
Municipal Unit:	Oleni
Bibliography:	PIKOULAS 2001a, 125.906; PANAGIOTOPOULOS 1987, 274, 305.140: Territorio di Gastugni, Gumero; PACIFICO 1704, 123: Territorio di Gastugni, Gumero; BORY DE SAINT-VINCENT 1834, 71: Éparchie de Gastouni, Gouméron; LEAKE 1846, map: Gumero; SFIKOPOULOS 1987, 288–290; HOPF 1873, 202: Vumeri, 206: Vumero; BON 1969, 331, 344.
Notes:	< γήμορο < γημόριον (*anc. Gr. n.* rent of arable land paid in kind by the tenant to his landlord): SYMEONIDIS 2010, I 443. The proposed etymologies by Vasmer, < gumьno (see no. 128), and Iliopoulos, < **Βρωμερόν* < βρώμη (*Gr. n.* oats, *Avena sativa*) seem doubtful: VASMER 1941, 141; ILIOPOULOS 1948, 154–155.

219. Ḳonbi S̱eḳra (قنبى ثقره), TT10, 87. AL

Notes:	Unidentified. < **këmbëthekër* (*Al. n.* leggy, rangy; καλαμοπόδης in the Peloponnesian dialects) < këmbë (*Al. n.* leg, foot) + thekër (*Al. n.* rye, *Secale cereale*): ASSENOVA–STOJKOV–KACORI 1977, 243; SYMEONIDIS 2010, I 721. According to Biris, Κομποθέκρας (*Arv. sn.*) derives from **kombothekër* (*Al. n.* rye sheaf) < komb (*Al. n.* knot) < κόμπος (*Gr. n.* knot, node, knob, gurl) + thekër (*Al. n.* rye): BIRIS 1998, 195; MEYER 1982, 196. Place name Këmbëthekër in Korçë, Albania.

220. Nasa (ناسه), TT10, 87. AL

Modern Greek: Nasa (Νάσα)

Regional Unit: Elis

Bibliography: Pikoulas 2001a, 336.2935; Panagiotopoulos 1987, 274, 305.129: Territorio di Gastugni, Nasa; Pacifico 1704, 124: Territorio di Gastugni, Nassa.

Notes: Unidentified.
Νάσος (*Gr. pn. dim.* of Αθανάσιος).

221. Ḳaḳusi (قاقوسی), TT10, 87. AL

Notes: Unidentified.
Κακόσης (*Arv. sn.*) < kokosh (*Al. n.* rooster, cock) < kokošь (*old Bg.* chicken, hen): Biris 1998, 194; Symeonidis 2010, I 587. According to Kolleka, Kaqush or Kakush (*Al. sn.*) < Kako, Kaqo < Qiriako/Qirjiako < Κυριάκος (*Gr. pn.*): Kolleka 1987, 85. Place name Kakousi (Κακούση, του) in Messenia: Georgacas–McDonald 1968, 141, 308.

222. Ġurdesi (غوردسی), TT10, 87. AL

Notes: Unidentified.
Cf. microtoponym Gardesi (Γάρδεσι, το), where a dependency of Notenon Monastery (I.M. Νοτενών, η) is mentioned in the Grimani Archive (1696–1700): Dokos 1971–74, 95; its exact location is unknown. Cf. Gourdisi [Γουρδίση, του (= η λάκκα του)] by Makistos (Μάκιστος, η) area in Elis: Georgacas–McDonald 1968, 128.

223. Branca (برانجا), TT10, 87. AL

Notes: Unidentified.
Brančе (*Scr. pn.*) < Branko or Branka.

224. Şurbi (شوربی), TT10, 87. AL

Notes: Unidentified.
Shurbi (*Al. sn.*); shurbë (*Al. n.* service tree, *Sorbus domestica*). Σούρπης (*Arv. sn.*) < surb (*Al. v.* to sip, to slurp): Biris 1998, 201.

225. Lancoy (لانجوی), TT10, 88. AL

Coordinates: X: 284774.098 Y: 4176023.286

Modern Greek: Latzoï (Λατζόι, το)

Regional Unit: Elis

Municipality: Pyrgos

Municipal Unit: Oleni

Bibliography:	Pikoulas 2001a, 249.2086; Panagiotopoulos 1987, 272, 304.49: Territorio di Gastugni, Lanzoi; Pacifico 1704, 124: Territorio di Gastugni, Lanzoi; Bory de Saint-Vincent 1834, 71: Éparchie de Gastouni, Lantsoï; Leake 1846, map: Landzoi.
Notes:	Perhaps from llonxhë (*Al. n.* large rain puddle, pond; burrow, den, foxhole): Symeonidis 2010, I 806.

226. **Pratano (پراتنو), TT10, 88. AL**

Coordinates:	X: 289166.040 Y: 4171343.662
Modern Greek:	Platanos (Πλάτανος, ο)
Regional Unit:	Elis
Municipality:	Arhaia Olympia
Municipal Unit:	Arhaia Olympia
Bibliography:	Pikoulas 2001a, 387.3425; Panagiotopoulos 1987, 272, 304.42: Territorio di Gastugni, Platano; Pacifico 1704, 124: Territorio di Gastugni, Platano; Bory de Saint-Vincent 1834, 71: Éparchie de Gastouni, Platanos; Leake 1846, map: Platano.

227. **Kertiza (كرتيزه), TT10, 88. GR**

Coordinates:	X: 303095.194 Y: 4191416.040
Modern Greek:	Agia Kyriaki (Αγία Κυριακή, η)
Old Toponym:	Until 1955: Kertiza (Κέρτιζα, η)
Regional Unit:	Elis
Municipality:	Arhaia Olympia
Municipal Unit:	Lasionas
Bibliography:	Pikoulas 2001a, 35.46; Panagiotopoulos 1987, 272, 303.23: Territorio di Gastugni, Carthizza; Pacifico 1704, 123: Territorio di Gastugni, Chiertizza; Expédition 1832: Kertéza; Bory de Saint-Vincent 1834, 71: Éparchie de Gastouni, Kertiza; Leake 1846, map: Kertiza; Skiadas 1993, 251; Stamatelatos–Vamva-Stamatelatou 2001, 6.
Notes:	< **Κέρθιζα* < kërthizë (*Al. n.* navel, belly button; centre, middle): Symeonidis 2010, I 688.

228. **Loġaṣeti (لوغاثتى), TT10, 89. AL**

Coordinates:	X: 285287.290 Y: 4218884.570
Modern Greek:	Logothetis (?) (Λογοθέτης, ο)
Regional Unit:	Achaia
Municipality:	Dytiki Ahaïa
Municipal Unit:	Dymi

Bibliography:	Pikoulas 2001a, 260.2193.
Notes:	Λογοθέτης (*Gr. sn.* logothete).

229. Laleşi (لالشی), TT10, 89. AL

Coordinates:	X: 281119.377 Y: 4175915.374
Modern Greek:	Lanthi (?) (Λάνθι, το)
Regional Unit:	Elis
Municipality:	Pyrgos
Municipal Unit:	Oleni
Bibliography:	Pikoulas 2001a, 246.2065, 247:2075; Panagiotopoulos 1987, 272, 304.52: Territorio di Gastugni, Lalti; Pacifico 1704, 124: Territorio di Gastugni, Lalathi; Bory de Saint-Vincent 1834, 71: Éparchie de Gastouni, Lanthi; Leake 1846, map: Lanthi.
Notes:	Same as Lalush or Lalosh (*Al. pn.*) < Lalë (see nos 410, 522): Zoto 2005, 231; lalush (*Al. n.* darling, sweethart) < lalush (*Al. v.* to fondle, caress); lalë (*Al. n.* elder brother) + -thi (*Al. dim. end.*). See also Kolleka 1987, 85 and Symeonidis 2010, I 802.

230. Ẕervini (ذروینی), TT10, 90. GR

Coordinates:	X: 306893.957 Y: 4199030.257
Modern Greek:	Kryovrysi (Κρυόβρυση, η)
Old Toponym:	Until 1928: Verveni (Βερβενή, η)
Regional Unit:	Elis
Municipality:	Arhaia Olympia
Municipal Unit:	Lasionas
Bibliography:	Pikoulas 2001a, 236.1970; Expédition 1832: Vervini; Leake 1846, map: Verveni; Skiadas 1993, 251. Stamatelatos–Vamva-Stamatelatou 2001, 393; Giannakopoulos 1994 1994, 381: Δερβινή-Βερβενή; GSGS 1944, Dhimitsána: Dhervini.
Notes:	According to Vasmer, < Vьrbьna (*Slav. n.* pastureland): Vasmer 1941, 140, with which Symeonidis disagreed: Symeonidis 2010, I 352. Tsopanakis, on the other hand, attempted a connection of the place name Vervena (Βέρβενα, τα) in Kynouria, Arcadia, to the ancient Arcadian clan Vervenioi (Βερβένιοι) mentioned by Hesychius: Tsopanakis 1958–59.

231. Ayo Ḳostandino (آیو قستندینو), *mezraʿa* in the vicinity of Ẕervini, TT10, 91.

Coordinates:	X: 314594.672 Y: 4197244.009
Modern Greek:	Agios Konstantinos (Άγιος Κωνσταντίνος, ο)

Regional Unit: Achaia

Municipality: Kalavryta

Municipal Unit: Aroania

Bibliography: GLET 1998, I 96.

Notes: Uninhabited location to the west of Livadi (Λιβάδι, το).

232. **Yirmoçani (ييرموچانى), TT10, 91. GR**

Coordinates: X: 311617.591 Y: 4201650.088

Modern Greek: Platanitsa (Πλατανίτσα, η)

Old Toponym: Until 1928: Germotzani (Γερμοτζάνη, η)

Regional Unit: Achaia

Municipality: Kalavryta

Municipal Unit: Aroania

Bibliography: Pikoulas 2001a, 386.3420; Panagiotopoulos 1987, 272, 303.22: Territorio di Gastugni, Germonzani; Bory de Saint-Vincent 1834, 71: Éparchie de Gastouni, Germoutsani; Leake 1830, II 121, 235, 240, Leake 1846, 206: Ghermotzáni; Skiadas 1993, 251; Stamatelatos–Vamva-Stamatelatou 2001, 629.

Notes: Vasmer proposed an etymology from **Jarьmъčane* [*Slav. adj.* of/from **Jarьmьno*, possibly Giarmena (no. 272)]: Vasmer 1941, 141. According to Symeonidis, the toponym denotes the inhabitants of a place with hot springs < gjermë or gjirmë (*Al. n.* firepit in a fireplace): Symeonidis 2010, I 414–415. The connection to the Albanian language stratum is not convincing though.

233. **Poraçyu (پوراچيو), TT10, 92. GR**

Coordinates: X: 310764.162 Y: 4199665.368

Modern Greek: Agrambela (Αγράμπελα, τα)

Old Toponym: Until 1928: Poretzou/Poretzo (Πορετζού, η/Πορετζό, το)

Regional Unit: Achaia

Municipality: Kalavryta

Municipal Unit: Aroania

Bibliography: Pikoulas 2001a, 57.259; Panagiotopoulos 1987, 272, 304.24: Territorio di Gastugni, Porichio; Pacifico 1704, 123: Territorio di Gastugni, Porizo; Bory de Saint-Vincent 1834, 71: Éparchie de Gastouni, Poretso; Leake 1830, II 240: Poretjó; Stamatelatos–Vamva-Stamatelatou 2001, 41; Politis 1915, 266–267.

Notes: According to Vasmer, < porěčьje (*Slav. n.* river area) < rěka (*Slav. n.* river): Vasmer 1941, 144.

234. Hiliz̲on (هليذون), TT10, 92. GR

Coordinates:	X: 290341.389 Y: 4176404.445
Modern Greek:	Helidoni (Χελιδόνι, το)
Regional Unit:	Elis
Municipality:	Arhaia Olympia
Municipal Unit:	Arhaia Olympia
Bibliography:	Pikoulas 2001a, 484.4376; Panagiotopoulos 1987, 272, 304.39: Territorio di Gastugni, Ghelidoni; Pacifico 1704, 123: Territorio di Gastugni, Chielidoni; Bory de Saint-Vincent 1834, 71: Éparchie de Gastouni, Khélidoni; Leake 1846, map: Khelidhoni; Sfikopoulos 1987, 291; Hopf 1873, 202, 206: Chilidoni vel Clidoni; Bon 1969, 344, 356; Iliopoulos 1948, 159–160.

235. Ṣuli (صولى), TT10, 95. AL

Notes:	Unidentified. See no. 37.

236. Ḳuḳura (قوقوره), TT10, 95. AL

Coordinates:	X: 282287.072 Y: 4170633.306
Modern Greek:	Salmoni (Σαλμώνη, η)
Old Toponym:	Until 1928: Koukoura (Κούκουρα, του)
Regional Unit:	Elis
Municipality:	Pyrgos
Municipal Unit:	Pyrgos
Bibliography:	Pikoulas 2001a, 413.3683; Panagiotopoulos 1987, 272, 304.56: Territorio di Gastugni, Cucura; Pacifico 1704, 124: Territorio di Gastugni, Cuccura; Bory de Saint-Vincent 1834, 70: Éparchie de Gastouni, Koukoura; Leake 1846, map: Kukura; Bon 1969, 341; Skiadas 1993, 247; Stamatelatos–Vamva-Stamatelatou 2001, 674; Politis 1912–13, 582.
Notes:	kukurë (*Al. n.* quiver for arrows).

237. Küraleş (كورالش), TT10, 96. AL

Bibliography:	GLET 1998, I 344.
Notes:	Unidentified. gur leshi (*Al. n.* asbestos) < gur or gjur (*Al. n.* stone); guralec (*Al. n.* pebble, gravel). Place name Kurvelesh in Vlorë, Albania. Cf. torrent Kourlesas/Gourlesas [(Γ)Κουρλέσας, ο] in Elis, which rises east of Gastouni (no. 174) and discharges south-west of it: Palla-Hronopoulou 2003, 258–259, 268. According to Papandreou, Gourlesia/Pourleska (Γκουρλέσια/Πουρλέσκα, η) is the modern name of ancient Elison (Ἐλισών, ὁ): Papandreou 1924, 16.

238. Ḳraḳuki (قراقوکی), TT10, 96. AL

Coordinates:	X: 287412.749 Y: 4172481.121
Modern Greek:	Pelopio (Πελόπιο, το)
Old Toponym:	Until 1928: Kriekouki (Κριεκούκι, το)
Regional Unit:	Elis
Municipality:	Arhaia Olympia
Municipal Unit:	Arhaia Olympia
Bibliography:	PIKOULAS 2001a, 373.3290; PANAGIOTOPOULOS 1987, 272, 304.43: Territorio di Gastugni, Crecuchi; PACIFICO 1704, 124: Territorio di Gastugni, Crecuchi; BORY DE SAINT-VINCENT 1834, 71: Éparchie de Gastouni, Krékouki; LEAKE 1846, map: Krekuki (Salmone); SKIADAS 1993, 253; STAMATELATOS–VAMVA-STAMATELATOU 2001, 603.
Notes:	Leake connected Krekuki to Salmone. krahëkuq (*Al. adj.* red-armed). Κριεκούκης (*Arv. sn.*) < kryekuq (*Al. adj.* red-headed, red-haired): BIRIS 1998, 195; kriekuq (*Arv. n.* goldfinch, *Carduelis carduelis balcanica*) attested in Messenia: JOCHALAS 2011, II 642.

239. Sitara (ستاره), TT10, 96. AL

Notes:	Unidentified. σιτάρι or σίτος (*Gr. n.* wheat). Cf. microtoponym Sitaria/Sitaries (Σιταριά, η/Σιταριές, οι) in Elis and Messenia, Sitarithra (Σιταρίθρα, η) by Latzoï (no. 225): GEORGACAS–MCDONALD 1968, 250; ILIOPOULOS 1948, 206; and Stara/Sitara (Σταρά/Σιταρά, η) in Messenia: VAGIAKAKOS 1991, 503.

240. Miraḳo (میراقو), TT10, 96. AL

Coordinates:	X: 292764.413 Y: 4168636.727
Modern Greek:	Arhaia Pisa (Αρχαία Πίσα, η), Miraka (Μιράκα, η)
Old Toponym:	Until 1940: Mirakia/Moirakia (Μιράκια/Μοιράκια, τα); until 2010: Miraka (Μιράκα, η)
Regional Unit:	Elis
Municipality:	Arhaia Olympia
Municipal Unit:	Arhaia Olympia
Bibliography:	PIKOULAS 2001a, 294.2525; PANAGIOTOPOULOS 1987, 272, 304.40: Territorio di Gastugni, Miraca; PACIFICO 1704, 124: Territorio di Gastugni, Miraca; BORY DE SAINT-VINCENT 1834, 71: Éparchie de Gastouni, Miraka; LEAKE 1830, I 25, 32, LEAKE 1846, 218: Miráka (Harpinna); SKIADAS 1993, 253; STAMATELATOS–VAMVA-STAMATELATOU 2001, 503.
Notes:	Mirak or Miraka [*Scr. pn. dim.* of Miros(l)av]: RHSJ 1904–10, VI 734. Mirak (*Al. pn.* variant of Mira): ZOTO 2005, 281. Mirak and Miranka are well-attested names in the taxation cadastre of Shkodër (1485): PULAHA 1974, 4, 38, 184, 192: Mirak, 103: Miranka. Place name Mirakë in Elbasan, Albania.

241. İşpata (اشپاته), TT10, 97. AL

	Unidentified.
Notes:	Σπάτας (*Arv. sn.*) < shpatë (*Al. n.* sword) < spata (*Lat. n.* sword) < σπάθη (*Gr. n.* sword): Biris 1998, 201–202; Orel 1998, 428; Georgacas–McDonald 1968, 351; Kolleka 1982, 31.

242. Bruma (بروما), TT10, 97. AL

Coordinates:	X: 285659.157 Y: 4174323.941
Modern Greek:	Irakleia (Ηράκλεια, η)
Old Toponym:	Until 1928: Brouma (Μπρούμα, του)
Regional Unit:	Elis
Municipality:	Arhaia Olympia
Municipal Unit:	Arhaia Olympia
Bibliography:	Pikoulas 2001a, 159.1221; Panagiotopoulos 1987, 272, 304.48: Territorio di Gastugni, Brumma; Pacifico 1704, 124: Territorio di Gastugni, Bruma; Bory de Saint-Vincent 1834, 71: Éparchie de Gastouni, Brouma; Leake 1830, I 24: Bruma; Skiadas 1993, 253; Stamatelatos–Vamva-Stamatelatou 2001, 246; Politis 1912–13, 582.
Notes:	brumë (*Al. n.* dough); brymë (*Al. n.* frost, hoarfrost).

243. Ḳazani (قزانی), TT10, 97. AL

	Unidentified.
Notes:	kazan (*Al. n.* cauldron, kettle, boiler) < kazan (*Tr. n.* boiler). Cf. microtoponym Kazania (Καζάνια, τα) in Messenia: Georgacas–McDonald 1968, 139.

244. Toşkesi (توشکسی), TT10, 98. AL

Notes:	Unidentified. See no. 90.

245. Maḳri Poẕi (ماقری پوذی), TT10, 98. AL

Coordinates:	X: 294880.266 Y: 4173232.098
Modern Greek:	Makrypodi (?) (Μακρυπόδι, το)
Regional Unit:	Elis
Municipality:	Arhaia Olympia
Municipal Unit:	Arhaia Olympia
Bibliography:	GLET 1998, II 288.

Notes:	Hydronym to the north of Pefkes (no. 432). Its appellation probably echoes the name of a deserted village. The identification remains under question, if its *mezraʿa*, Purdanu (no. 246), is located in Vouliagmeni. Μακρυπόδης (*Gr. sn.* long-legged).

246. Purdanu (پوردانو), *mezraʿa* in the vicinity of Maḳri Poẕi, TT10, 98.

Coordinates:	X: 289065.576 Y: 4189975.599
Modern Greek:	Vouliagmeni (?) (Βουλιαγμένη, η)
Old Toponym:	Until 1928: Bourdanou (Μπουρδάνου, του); until 1940: Milies (Μηλιές, οι)
Regional Unit:	Elis
Municipality:	Ilida
Municipal Unit:	Pineia
Bibliography:	Pikoulas 2001a, 107.726; Panagiotopoulos 1987, 271, 303.1: Territorio di Gastugni, Burdanno; Pacifico 1704, 124: Territorio di Gastugni, Burdanu; Bory de Saint-Vincent 1834, 71: Éparchie de Gastouni, Bourdanou; Leake 1846, map: Burdanu; Skiadas 1993, 254; Stamatelatos–Vamva-Stamatelatou 2001, 142.
Notes:	< *Burdhanë (*Al. n. pl.* sack makers) < burdhë (*Al. n.* sackcloth, sack) +-anë: Symeonidis 2010, I 1000.

247. Matranḳa (مترانقه), *mezraʿa* in the vicinity of İşpata, TT10, 98.

Notes:	Unidentified. Matranga or Matrenga (*Al. sn.*) < matrangë or matrakë (*Al. n.* club, life-preserver): Mann 1948, 266. Mataranga (*Arb. sn.*) is the name of an Albanian clan. Ματαράγκας and Ματράγκας (*Gr. sn.*). Place name Mataranga (Ματαράγκα, του/το/η) in Messenia: Georgacas–McDonald 1968, 332.

248. Poẕo (پوثو), TT10, 98. AL

Coordinates:	X: 296024.228 Y: 4175012.363
Modern Greek:	Pothos (Πόθος, ο)
Regional Unit:	Elis
Municipality:	Arhaia Olympia
Municipal Unit:	Foloï
Bibliography:	Pikoulas 2001a, 390.3452; Bory de Saint-Vincent 1834, 71: Éparchie de Gastouni, Pothou; Leake 1846, map: Pothou.
Notes:	πόθος (*Gr. n.* desire, lust).

249. Maji (ماژى), TT10, 99. AL

Notes:	Unidentified. See no. 129.

250. Sela (سله), TT10, 99. AL

Notes: Unidentified.
According to Vasmer, < **Sela* (*Slav. pln. pl.* villages): Vasmer 1941, 84, 149; sella (*It. n.* saddle) > selë (*Arb. n.* saddle). Σελάς (*Gr. sn.* saddler). See also Georgacas–McDonald 1968, 248.

251. Ẕiminiça (ذيمنيچه), TT10, 99. GR

Coordinates: X: 314424.098 Y: 4190829.421

Modern Greek: Tripotama (Τριπόταμα, τα), Kastro (Κάστρο, το)

Old Toponym: Diminitsa (?) (Διμίνιτσα, η)

Regional Unit: Achaia

Municipality: Kalavryta

Municipal Unit: Aroania

Bibliography: Pikoulas 2001a, 137.1018, 457.4109; Panagiotopoulos 1987, 270, 303.94: Territorio di Callavritta, Diminizza; Pacifico 1704, 122: Territorio di Calaurita, Diminizza, *olim Psophis*; Hopf 1873, 206: Diminiza.

Notes: According to Sfikopoulos, the ruins of a citadel on a 300m-high hill in Tripotama could be attributed to Diminizza: Sfikopoulos 1987, 203. To the south of Tripotama the microtoponym Kastro (Κάστρο, το) (*Gr. n.* castle, citadel) has survived. Carile noted that in G. Alberghetti's register it is recorded as Diminizza olim Psophis: Carile 1970, 398–399; ancient Psophis is located to the north of Tripotama.
Vasmer connected Diminitsa (Δημηνίτσα, η) in Grevena to a Slavic place name **Dymьnica*, which may denote a settlement/village or a kind of cereal: Vasmer 1941, 181; Symeonidis 2010, I 472. Place name Dimenica in Bulgaria < dumъ (*old. Slav. n.* smoke).

252. Ḫayḳal (خايقال), TT10, 99. AL

Notes: Unidentified.
See no. 91.

253. Ṣarakina (صراكنه), TT10, 99. AL

Coordinates: X: 317391.036 Y: 4167606.462

Modern Greek: Sarakini (Σαρακίνι, το)

Regional Unit: Arcadia

Municipality: Gortynia

Municipal Unit: Iraia

Bibliography: Pikoulas 2001a, 415.3703; Pacifico 1704, 129: Territorio di Caritena, Sarachini; Bory de Saint-Vincent 1834, 76: Éparchie de Karytæne, Sarakini; Leake 1846, map: Sarakini; Thanopoulos 1988.

Notes: See no. 188.

254. Plaşa (پلاشه), TT10, 99. AL

Notes:	Unidentified. See no. 14.

255. Ḳondari (قوندارى), TT10, 100. AL

Notes:	Unidentified. Κονταρής (*Gr. sn.*); κοντάρι (*Gr. n.* pole).

256. Franḳa (فرانقه), TT10, 100. AL

Coordinates:	X: 279125.197 Y: 4216823.088
Modern Greek:	Franga (?) (Φράγκα, η)
Regional Unit:	Achaia
Municipality:	Dytiki Ahaïa
Municipal Unit:	Movri
Bibliography:	Pikoulas 2001a, 475.4285.
Notes:	Franca (*It. pn.*).

257. Lazaro Buva (لازارو بوه), TT10, 100. AL

Modern Greek:	Lazaro-Bouga (?) (Λαζαρο-Μπούγα, του)
Bibliography:	Pikoulas 2001a, 245.2049; Panagiotopoulos 1987, 273, 304.70: Territorio di Gastugni, Lazar Buga; Pacifico 1704, 124: Territorio di Gastugni, Lazarobua.
Notes:	Unidentified. Λάζαρος (*Gr. pn.* Eleazar) > Llazar (*Al. pn.*). For Buva see no. 187.

258. Liḳuresi (ليقورسى), TT10, 101. AL

Coordinates:	X: 302315.934 Y: 4169032.416
Modern Greek:	Vasilaki (Βασιλάκι, το)
Old Toponym:	Until 1928: Lykouresi (Λυκούρεσι, το)
Regional Unit:	Elis
Municipality:	Arhaia Olympia
Municipal Unit:	Arhaia Olympia

Bibliography: Pikoulas 2001a, 96.619; Panagiotopoulos 1987, 260, 299.78: Territorio di Caritena, Licuresi Capuzzi; Pacifico 1704, 123: Territorio di Gastugni, Licuressi; Bory de Saint-Vincent 1834, 77: Éparchie de Karytæne, Lykourési; Leake 1846, map: Lykuresi; Bon 1969, 341; Skiadas 1993, 253; Stamatelatos–Vamva-Stamatelatou 2001, 125; Iliopoulos 1948, 177.

Notes: See no. 62.

259. Aranis Ḳuçohyari (ارانس قوچوهیاری), TT10, 101. AL

Coordinates: X: 282275.030 Y: 4185346.384

Modern Greek: Koutsohera (Κουτσοχέρα, η)

Regional Unit: Elis

Municipality: Pyrgos

Municipal Unit: Oleni

Bibliography: Pikoulas 2001a, 233.1933; Bory de Saint-Vincent 1834, 71: Éparchie de Gastouni, Koutsokéra; Leake 1846, map: Xilokera; Iliopoulos 1948, 211.

Notes: Κουτσοχέρης (*Gr. sn.* one-armed, one-handed; armless, handless).

260. Aranis Ḳavalari (ارانس قوالاری), TT10, 101. AL

Notes: Unidentified.
καβαλάρης (*Gr. n.* horseback rider, horseman).

261. Romesi (رومسی), TT10, 101. AL

Coordinates: X: 276377.448 Y: 4178400.292

Modern Greek: Ambelonas (Αμπελώνας, ο)

Old Toponym: Until 1961: Romesi (Ρόμεσι, το)

Regional Unit: Elis

Municipality: Pyrgos

Municipal Unit: Pyrgos

Bibliography: Pikoulas 2001a, 71.386; Panagiotopoulos 1987, 273, 304.63: Territorio di Gastugni, Romesi; Pacifico 1704, 124: Territorio di Gastugni, Romessi; Bory de Saint-Vincent 1834, 70: Éparchie de Gastouni, Rhomési; Leake 1846, map: Romesi; Skiadas 1993, 247; Stamatelatos–Vamva-Stamatelatou 2001, 68.

Notes: Romësi (*Al. n.* place of Greeks): Symeonidis 2010, II 1226. Place name Rromanat in Durrës, Albania.

262. Vaşıloplos (واصلوپلوس), TT10, 102. AL

Notes: Unidentified.
Βασιλόπουλος (*Gr. sn.*) < Βασίλης (*Gr. pn.* Basil) + -όπουλος (*Gr. end.* son of).

263. Maji (ماژی), TT10, 102. AL

Coordinates:	X: 287433.796 Y: 4191410.662
Modern Greek:	Mazi (Μάζι, το)
Regional Unit:	Elis
Municipality:	Ilida
Municipal Unit:	Pineia
Bibliography:	GLET 1998, II 281.
Notes:	Uninhabited location between Simopoulo (no. 640) and Skliva (no. 642). See no. 129.

264. Añloniça (اكلونيچه), 1/14662, 40/42. GR

Coordinates:	X: 278743.352 Y: 4167142.876
Modern Greek:	Epitalio (Επιτάλιο, το)
Old Toponym:	Until 1928: Agoulinitsa (Αγουλινίτσα, η)
Regional Unit:	Elis
Municipality:	Pyrgos
Municipal Unit:	Volakas
Bibliography:	Pikoulas 2001a, 151.1147; Panagiotopoulos 1987, 253, 296.48: Teritorrio di Fanari, Agulinizza; Pacifico 1704, 130: Territorio di Fanari, Agulinizza; Leake 1830, I 65: Agulenítza (Epitalium); Leake 1846, map: Agulinitza; Expédition 1832: Agoulinitsa; Bory de Saint-Vincent 1834, 89: Éparchie de Pyrgos, Agoulinitza; Hopf 1873, 202: Avolanizza; Georgacas–McDonald 1968, 96; Longnon–Topping 1969, 238–239; Bon 1969, 348–349; Skiadas 1993, 369; Stamatelatos–Vamva-Stamatelatou 2001, 223.
Notes:	According to Vasmer, < **Ogulinьcь* (*Slav.*): Vasmer 1941, 145. According to Georgacas, < γλινίτσα *dim.* of γλίνα (*Gr. n.* fat; dirt; river sediment): Georgacas 1938–48, 177–178. Symeonidis agreed with Georgacas on an etymology from **Glinica* < glina (*old. Slav. n.* mud, grime, sludge) and proposed another one from jegulja/jagulja (*Scr. n.* eel) < anguilla (*Lat. n.* European eel, *Anguilla anguilla*), as the Agoulinitsa Lake, before its artificial drainage, was famous for its eel production: Symeonidis 2010, I 206.

265. Mihili (مهلی), 1/14662, 77. AL

Coordinates:	X: 284400.000 Y: 4178234.155
Modern Greek:	Mihalos (Μίχαλος, ο)
Regional Unit:	Elis
Municipality:	Pyrgos

Municipal Unit:	Oleni
Notes:	Uninhabited location to the east of Magoula (Μαγούλα, η), where Papandreou mentioned ancient ruins: Papandreou 1924, 174. Mëhill or Mihill (*Al. sn.* Michael): Zoto 2005, 279.

266. Sipyani (سپیانی), 1/14662, 86. GR

Coordinates:	X: 302964.676 Y: 4193740.095
Modern Greek:	Tsipiana (Τσιπιανά, τα)
Regional Unit:	Elis
Municipality:	Arhaia Olympia
Municipal Unit:	Lasionas
Bibliography:	Pikoulas 2001a, 464.4182; Panagiotopoulos 1987, 272, 303.17: Territorio di Gastugni, Cipiena; Pacifico 1704, 123: Territorio di Gastugni, Cipiana; Expédition 1832: Tsipiana; Leake 1846, map: Tzipiana; Iliopoulos 1948, 212.
Notes:	See no. 74.

267. Mangişa Ḳumani (مانکشه قومانی), 1/14662, 86. AL

Coordinates:	X: 301438.608 Y: 4184701.228
Modern Greek:	Koumanis (Κουμάνης, ο)
Regional Unit:	Elis
Municipality:	Arhaia Olympia
Municipal Unit:	Foloï
Bibliography:	Pikoulas 2001a, 225.1862; Panagiotopoulos 1987, 272, 304.29: Territorio di Gastugni, Nexocumeni; Pacifico 1704, 123: Territorio di Gastugni, Cumani; Expédition 1832: Koumani; Leake 1846, map: Kumani.
Notes:	mëngash, mëngjash, mêngash or mëngjarash (*Al. adj.* left-handed). For Ḳumani see no. 181.

268. İspani (اسپانی), 1/14662, 87. AL

Notes:	Unidentified. Σπανός (*Gr. sn.* beardless) > spanoj (*Al. adj.* beardless).

269. İspani-i dīğer (اسپانی دیکر), *mezraʿa* in the vicinity of İspani, 1/14662, 87.

Notes:	Unidentified. See no. 268.

270. Persena (پرسنه), *mezraʿa* in the vicinity of İspani, 1/14662, 87.

Coordinates:	X: 294999.526 Y: 4180611.159
Modern Greek:	Persaina (Πέρσαινα, η)
Regional Unit:	Elis
Municipality:	Arhaia Olympia
Municipal Unit:	Foloï
Bibliography:	Pikoulas 2001a, 377.3323; Panagiotopoulos 1987, 272, 304.28: Territorio di Gastugni, Persenna; Pacifico 1704, 124: Territorio di Gastugni, Persina; Expédition 1832: Pérséna; Bory de Saint-Vincent 1834, 71: Éparchie de Gastouni, Perséna; Leake 1846, map: Persena.

271. Ḳuçi (قوچى), 1/14662, 88. AL

Notes:	Unidentified. See no. 186.

272. Yirmena (ييرمنه), 1/14662, 88. GR

Coordinates:	X: 298866.736 Y: 4184734.635
Modern Greek:	Foloï (Φολόη, η)
Old Toponym:	Until 1928: Giarmena (Γιάρμενα, η)
Regional Unit:	Elis
Municipality:	Arhaia Olympia
Municipal Unit:	Foloï
Bibliography:	Pikoulas 2001a, 473.4268; Panagiotopoulos 1987, 272, 303.20: Territorio di Gastugni, Germena; Pacifico 1704, 124: Territorio di Gastugni, Germanu; Expédition 1832: Giarména; Bory de Saint-Vincent 1834, 71: Éparchie de Gastouni, Giaména; Leake 1846, map: Ghiarmena; Skiadas 1993, 251: Κάρμενα, η; Stamatelatos–Vamva-Stamatelatou 2001, 774; Iliopoulos 1948, 211.
Notes:	Sauerwein erroneously connected Pacifico's Germanu to Germotzani (no. 232): Sauerwein 1969, *Ortsverzeichnis*, Territorio di Gastugni, 136. < **Jarьmьno* < jarьmъ (*old Bg. n.* yoke): Vasmer 1941, 141; Symeonidis 2010, I 423.

273. Ḳaçaru (قچارو), 1/14662, 88. AL

Coordinates:	X: 272281.404 Y: 4177769.733
Modern Greek:	Katsaros [Κατσαρός, ο (= Κατσαρού, του)]
Regional Unit:	Elis

281. Ḳondomiḫal (قوندوميخال), 1/14662, 93. AL

Notes:	Unidentified. Κοντομιχάλης (*Gr. sn.*) < κοντός (*Gr. adj.* short) + Μιχάλης (*Gr. pn.* Michael).

282. Ratendu (راتندو), 1/14662, 93. AL

Coordinates:	X: 280199.696 Y: 4182002.635
Modern Greek:	Heimadio (Χειμαδιό, το)
Old Toponym:	Until 1928: Retentou (Ρετεντού, του)
Regional Unit:	Elis
Municipality:	Pyrgos
Municipal Unit:	Oleni
Bibliography:	Pikoulas 2001a, 484.4373; Panagiotopoulos 1987, 272, 304.50: Territorio di Gastugni, Retendù; Pacifico 1704, 124: Territorio di Gastugni, Retendu; Bory de Saint-Vincent 1834, 71: Éparchie de Gastouni, Rhétendou; Leake 1846, map: Retendu; Sfikopoulos 1987, 286; Bon 1969, 337: Renta; Skiadas 1993, 255; Stamatelatos–Vamva-Stamatelatou 2001, 792; Iliopoulos 1948, 158–159.
Notes:	< *Ρεντιτού < rendita (*It. n.* revenue) denoting a wealthy village: Symeonidis 2010, II 1215.

283. Ḳosta Lanca (قوسته لانجه), 1/14662, 93. AL

Notes:	Unidentified. Κώστας (*Gr. pn. dim.* of Κωνσταντίνος, Constantine) > Kosta (*Al. pn. dim.* of Kostandin). Possibly from laxhë (*Al. n.* goblin, gnome). See also no. 225.

284. Nikifor (نيكفور), 1/14662, 94. AL

Notes:	Unidentified. Νικηφόρος (*Gr. pn.* Nicephorus).

285. Olana (اولانه), 1/14662, 94. GR

Coordinates:	X: 284648.155 Y: 4179701.212
Modern Greek:	Oleni (Ωλένη, η), Paliolena (Παλιόλενα, η)
Old Toponym:	Olena (Ωλενα, η)
Regional Unit:	Elis
Municipality:	Pyrgos

Municipal Unit:	Oleni
Bibliography:	Pikoulas 2001a, 495.4479; Panagiotopoulos 1987, 274, 304.33: Territorio di Gastugni, Ollena; Pacifico 1704, 124: Territorio di Gastugni, Elena; Hopf 1873, 202: Elena vel Alona, 206: Olena; Bory de Saint-Vincent 1834, 71: Éparchie de Gastouni, Oléna; Leake 1846, map: Olena; Sfikopoulos 1987, 287–288; Longnon–Topping 1969, 239; Bon 1969, 344–345; Iliopoulos 1948, 162–163; Zakythinos 1953, 150.
Notes:	The ruins of the Episcopal church of Metamorfosis tou Sotiros (Μεταμόρφωσις του Σωτήρος, η) are found on a 300m-high hill near the Paliolena area, on the north-eastern outskirts of today's Oleni village. This was probably the cathedral of mediaeval Olena. The inhabitants were deported to modern-day Oleni at the beginning of the 19th c.: Papandreou 1924, 174–177, 182–184.

286. **Iğlava (اغلاوه), 1/14662, 95. AL**

Notes:	Unidentified. glava (*Scr. n.* head). Γλαβάς (*Byz. Gr. sn.*); Place name Gllavë in Tepelenë, Albania: Kolleka 1983, 13.

287. **Şopi (صوپى), 1/14662, 95. AL**

Coordinates:	X: 280846.753 Y: 4180491.234
Modern Greek:	Sopi (Σόπι, το)
Regional Unit:	Elis
Municipality:	Pyrgos
Municipal Unit:	Oleni
Bibliography:	Pikoulas 2001a, 428.3828; Panagiotopoulos 1987, 272, 304.50: Territorio di Gastugni, Soppi; Pacifico 1704, 124: Territorio di Gastugni, Sopos; Bory de Saint-Vincent 1834, 71: Éparchie de Gastouni, Sopi; Leake 1846, map: Sopi.
Notes:	sop or sopë (*Al. n.* hummock; ridge).

288. **Dorza (دورزه), 1/14662, 96. AL**

Modern Greek:	Doriza (?) (Δόριζα, η)
Regional Unit:	Arcadia
Municipality:	Gortynia (?)
Bibliography:	Panagiotopoulos 1987, 346, 365; Bory de Saint-Vincent 1834, 77: Éparchie de Karytæne, Doriza.
Notes:	Unidentified; possibly located in northern Gortynia. It is not mentioned on the map of the *Expédition* and in its list it appears deserted. Δόριζας, Δώριζας or Ντόριζας (*Gr. sn.*) < dorezë, dorëz (*Al. n.* glove; handle) < dorë (*Al. n.* hand, arm): Kolleka 1983, 15. Ντόριζας (*Arv. sn.* person having small hands): Biris 1998, 200. Place name Dorzë in Gjirokastër and Elbasan, Albania.

289. Ḳonbi S̱eḳra (قنبی ثقره), 1/14662, 96. AL

Notes: Unidentified.
See no. 219.

290. Ḳoḳla (قوقلا), 1/14662, 96. AL

Notes: Unidentified.
See no. 183.

291. Ḳaratula (قراتولا), 1/14662, 96. AL

Coordinates: X: 282747.413 Y: 4179127.203

Modern Greek: Karatoulas [Καράτουλας, ο (= Καράτουλα, του)]

Regional Unit: Elis

Municipality: Pyrgos

Municipal Unit: Oleni

Bibliography: Pikoulas 2001a, 188.1506; Panagiotopoulos 1987, 272, 304.51: Territorio di Gastugni, Caratulla; Pacifico 1704, 124: Territorio di Gastugni, Caratulla; Bory de Saint-Vincent 1834, 71: Éparchie de Gastouni, Karatoula; Leake 1846, map: Karatola.

Notes: See no. 25.

292. Pondiḳo (پوندقو), 1/14662, 97. GR

Coordinates: X: 262719.473 Y: 4171784.143

Modern Greek: Katakolo (Κατάκολο, το)

Regional Unit: Elis

Municipality: Pyrgos

Municipal Unit: Pyrgos

Bibliography: Pikoulas 2001a, 199.1614; Expédition 1832: Fort Katakolo, *Pondiko Kastron*; Leake 1830, I 22: Pondikó-kastro, II 191: Pondikókastro; Leake 1846, map: Pondiko Kastro (Pheia); Sfikopoulos 1987, 292–294; Bon 1969, 328–330, 663, 665, *planche* 2; Markl 1966, 23; Carile 1970, 399; Hopf 1873, 202, 206: Belveder; Iliopoulos 1948, 166–167; Dragoumis 1921, 13.

Notes: Fortress Pontiko (Ποντικό, το) is situated on the Katakolo Cape (ancient Ichthys) between the Katakolo and Tigani (Τηγάνι, το) bays. It was renamed by the Franks as Beauvoir or Belveder.

293. Mavromati (ماوروماتی), 1/14662, 97. AL

Coordinates: X: 280631.687 Y: 4178950.500

Modern Greek:	Mavromati (Μαυρομάτη, του)
Regional Unit:	Elis
Municipality:	Pyrgos
Municipal Unit:	Oleni
Bibliography:	Pikoulas 2001a, 280.2390.
Notes:	See no. 53.

294. **Livarzi (لوارزی), 1/14662, 98. GR**

Coordinates:	X: 315614.195 Y: 4199630.075
Modern Greek:	Livartzi (Λιβάρτζι, το)
Regional Unit:	Achaia
Municipality:	Kalavryta
Municipal Unit:	Aroania
Bibliography:	Pikoulas 2001a, 255.2149; Pacifico 1704, 122: Territorio di Calaurita, Liuarzi; Bory de Saint-Vincent 1834, 74: Éparchie de Kalavrita, Apano/Kato Livartzi; Leake 1846, map: Livarzi.

295. **Keraşova (كراصوه), 1/14662, 98. GR**

Coordinates:	X: 318026.809 Y: 4199357.683
Modern Greek:	Kerasia (Κερασιά, η)
Old Toponym:	Until 1928: Keresova (Κερέσοβα, η)
Regional Unit:	Achaia
Municipality:	Kalavryra
Municipal Unit:	Aroania
Bibliography:	Pikoulas 2001a, 205.1668; Panagiotopoulos 1987, 269, 302.69: Territorio di Callavritta, Geresova; Pacifico 1704, 122: Territorio di Calaurita, Chieressoua; Bory de Saint-Vincent 1834, 74: Éparchie de Kalavrita, Kérésova; Leake 1846, map: Keritzova; Skiadas 1993, 245.
Notes:	< κέρασος (*Gr. n.* cherry, *Prunus*) + -ova (*Slav. end.*): Vasmer 1941, 37, 135.

8. District of Kirvuķor (Palaiokastro/Koufoplaiiko Kastro) (Maps 15–16)

296. **Kirvuķor (كيرووقور), TT10, 104.**

Coordinates:	X: 311023.434 Y: 4149254.801

Modern Greek:	Palaiokastro/Koufoplaiiko Kastro (Παλαιόκαστρο/Κουφοπλαίικο Κάστρο, το)
Regional Unit:	Elis
Municipality:	Andritsaina-Krestena
Municipal Unit:	Andritsaina
Bibliography:	Hopf 1873, 202: Crivocori, 206: Crivo Cori; Bon 1969, 379, 388, *planche* 3; Markl 1966, 28; Georgacas–McDonald 1968, 171, 222; Kordosis 1992–93, 9–10.
Notes:	The capital town of the Kirvuḳor District (*nefs-i Kirvuḳor*) is not mentioned in either the TT10 or the 1/14662. The local centre and largest town is Artica (no. 297). Sfikopoulos identified it with the Frankish fortress Crèvecœur on the top of Mt Minthi (Μίνθη, η) (1342m) in the vicinity of Linistaina (no. 303) and Koufopoulo (Κουφόπουλο, το): Sfikopoulos 1987, 315–316.

297. Artica (ارتيجه), TT10, 104. GR

Coordinates:	X: 311065.423 Y: 4151455.098
Modern Greek:	Fanari (Φανάρι, το)
Old Toponym:	Artitza (Αρτίτζα, η)
Regional Unit:	Elis
Municipality:	Andritsaina-Krestena
Municipal Unit:	Andritsaina
Bibliography:	Pikoulas 2001a, 85.511, 468.4220; Panagiotopoulos 1987, 253, 296.51: Territorio di Fanari, Artizza; Pacifico 1704, 130: Territorio di Fanari, Artizza; Dokos 1977–84, 295, 315: Ἀρτίτζα.
Notes:	Sarris located it in Fanari: Sarris 1934–35, Table 1. In the census of Rigas Palamidis and his team in 1828 the Fanari entry reads: Φανάρι, ὀνομαζόμενον Ἀρτιόζα: Gritsopoulos 1971, 433. Pikoulas suggested it should be sought in Messenia, whereas in Panagiotopoulos's enumeration it remained unidentified.

298. Zelaḫova (زلاخووه), TT10, 105. GR

Coordinates:	X: 309348.559 Y: 4151765.507
Modern Greek:	Amygdalies (Αμυγδαλιές, οι)
Old Toponym:	Until 1928: Zelehova (Ζελέχοβα, η)
Regional Unit:	Elis
Municipality:	Andritsaina-Krestena
Municipal Unit:	Alifeira

Bibliography: PIKOULAS 2001a, 72.392; PANAGIOTOPOULOS 1987, 252, 296.17: Territorio di Fanari, Zelecova; PACIFICO 1704, 130: Territorio di Fanari, Zelogoua; BORY DE SAINT-VINCENT 1834, 88: Éparchie de Phanari, Tzélékhova; LEAKE 1846, map: Tzelekhova; GEORGACAS–MCDONALD 1968, 136; BON 1969, 387; SKIADAS 1993, 367; STAMATELATOS–VAMVA-STAMATELATOU 2001, 68–69.

Notes: Vasmer proposed a connection to place name Żelechów and Żelechowo in Poland, yet he could not find any parallel in south Slavic: VASMER 1941, 147. Symeonidis agreed and added its meaning: grassland, meadow < zele (*Bg. n.* sorrel, *Rumex acetosa*): SYMEONIDIS 2010, I 543.

299. Vervena (وروِنه), TT10, 105. GR

Coordinates: X: 308375.730 Y: 4151350.434

Modern Greek: Vervena (Βέρβενα, τα)

Regional Unit: Elis

Municipality: Andritsaina-Krestena

Municipal Unit: Alifeira

Bibliography: PANAGIOTOPOULOS 1987, 252, 295.3: Territorio di Fanari, Vervena; PACIFICO 1704, 130: Territorio di Fanari, Veruena; TSOPANAKIS 1958–59; ROMAIOS 1957, 18.

Notes: Uninhabited location situated, according to Sarris, between Myronia (Μυρώνια, τα) and Amygdalies (no. 298): SARRIS 1934–35, 78–80, Table 1. Ruins of its houses were still visible in 1935 in the Palatia (Παλάτια, τα) area. It should not be mistaken for the homonymous settlement in Voreia Kynouria, Arcadia. See no. 230.

300. Ḳırana (قرانه), TT10, 106. GR

Coordinates: X: 308414.643 Y: 4149904.162

Modern Greek: Krana (Κράνα, η)

Regional Unit: Elis

Municipality: Andritsaina-Krestena

Municipal Unit: Alifeira

Bibliography: PIKOULAS 2001a, 233.1940; PANAGIOTOPOULOS 1987, 253, 296.32: Territorio di Fanari, Crana; BORY DE SAINT-VINCENT 1834, 88: Éparchie de Phanari, Krana; LEAKE 1846, map: Kraia; GEORGACAS–MCDONALD 1968, 171.

301. Ḳopaniça (قوپانيچه), TT10, 106. GR

Coordinates: X: 305441.586 Y: 4148188.881

Modern Greek: Kryoneri (Κρυονέρι, το)

Old Toponym: Until 1955: Ano Kopanitsa (Άνω Κοπάνιτσα, η)

Regional Unit: Elis

Municipality:	Zaharo
Municipal Unit:	Figaleia
Bibliography:	Pikoulas 2001a, 237.1973; Panagiotopoulos 1987, 252, 296.19: Territorio di Fanari, Copanizza; Pacifico 1704, 130: Territorio di Fanari, Copanizza; Bory de Saint-Vincent 1834, 88: Éparchie de Phanari, Kopanitsa; Leake 1846, map: Kopanitza; Georgacas–McDonald 1968, 162; Bon 1969, 358; Skiadas 1993, 371; Stamatelatos–Vamva-Stamatelatou 2001, 394.
Notes:	< *dim.* of kopáňa (*Bg. n.* trough, hollowed wooden trough), kopánja (*Slov. n.* trough, hollowed wooden trough), копань (*Ru. n.* water pit): Vasmer 1941, 147; Symeonidis 2010, I 726. Place name Kopanica in Bulgaria, Croatia and Slovakia.

302. Velviça (ولويچه), TT10, 107. GR

Coordinates:	X: 308050.488 Y: 4145246.146
Modern Greek:	Petralona (Πετράλωνα, τα)
Old Toponym:	Until 1928: Vervitsa (Βερβίτσα, η)
Regional Unit:	Elis
Municipality:	Zaharo
Municipal Unit:	Figaleia
Bibliography:	Pikoulas 2001a, 378.3335; Expédition 1832: Vervitza; Bory de Saint-Vincent 1834, 76: Éparchie de Karytæne, Vervitsa; Leake 1830, I 400, II 15: Vervítza; Skiadas 1993, 371; Stamatelatos–Vamva-Stamatelatou 2001, 615; Georgacas–McDonald 1968, 113.
Notes:	< **vъrbьca* (*old Slav. n.* willow, *Salix*): Vasmer 1941, 146; Symeonidis 2010, I 352. Place name Vъrbica in Yugoslav and Bulgarian toponymy, and Wierzbica in Poland.

303. Linistena (لينستنه), TT10, 107. GR

Coordinates:	X: 310300.965 Y: 4146257.887
Modern Greek:	Linistaina (Λινίσταινα, η)
Old Toponym:	Lykistena (Λυκίστενα, η)
Regional Unit:	Elis
Municipality:	Andritsaina-Krestena
Municipal Unit:	Andritsaina
Bibliography:	Pikoulas 2001a, 258.2175; Panagiotopoulos 1987, 252, 296.11: Territorio di Fanari, Linistena; Pacifico 1704, 130: Territorio di Fanari, Leuistena; Bory de Saint-Vincent 1834, 88: Éparchie de Phanari, Linistæna; Leake 1830, II 15: Linístena; Smyrnis 1989, 179–180; Georgacas–McDonald 1968, 181; Bon 1969, 380–381.

Notes:	< **Leništane* (*Slav. n. pl.* inhabitants of flax place) < **Lenište* or **Lenišče* (*Slav. n.* flax place): Symeonidis 2010, I 832. Place name Leništa in North Macedonia and Lenište in Bulgaria. See also Georgacas 1938, 15.

304. Ondriçena (اوندريچنه), TT10, 107. GR

Coordinates:	X: 314552.091 Y: 4150252.072
Modern Greek:	Andritsaina (Ανδρίτσαινα, η)
Regional Unit:	Elis
Municipality:	Andritsaina-Krestena
Municipal Unit:	Andritsaina
Bibliography:	Pikoulas 2001a, 75.424; Panagiotopoulos 1987, 252, 295.1: Territorio di Fanari, Andrizzena; Pacifico 1704, 130: Territorio di Fanari, Andrizena; Expédition 1832: Andritsena; Bory de Saint-Vincent 1834, 87: Éparchie de Phanari, Andritséna; Leake 1830, II 16: Andrítzena; Georgacas–McDonald 1968, 103; Bon 1969, 380–381.
Notes:	According to Georgacas, < Ανδρίτσος, -αινα (*Gr. pn.*): Georgacas 1938, 22–25. Symeonidis found this etymology superficial and proposed **drěničen* < drěnъ (*old. Bg. n.* cornel, cornel-tree, *Cornus mas*): Symeonidis 2010, I 251–252.

305. Z̲olyani (ذوليانى), TT10, 108. GR

Coordinates:	X: 309082.630 Y: 4146342.260
Modern Greek:	Kokkaliara (Κοκκαλιάρα, η)
Old Toponym:	Doliana (Δολιανά, τα)
Regional Unit:	Elis
Municipality:	Andritsaina-Krestena
Municipal Unit:	Andritsaina
Notes:	According to Smyrnis, a teacher from Linistaina, there was a village called Doliana in Kokkaliara, a location to the west of Linistaina (no. 303): Smyrnis 1989, 181. **doljane* (*old Slav. n.* valley inhabitant) < dolь (*Slav. n.* valley): Vasmer 1941, 31; Symeonidis 2010, I 484. Place name Doljane in Montenegro, Doljani in Serbia, Dolene in Bulgaria and Dolany in the Czech Republic.

306. Drȧgoy (دراغوى), TT10, 108. AL

Coordinates:	X: 311653.593 Y: 4142534.567
Modern Greek:	Dragogi (Δραγώγι, το)
Regional Unit:	Elis
Municipality:	Andritsaina-Krestena

Municipal Unit: Andritsaina

Bibliography: Pikoulas 2001a, 140.1050; Panagiotopoulos 1987, 253, 296.69: Territorio di Fanari, Dragoi; Pacifico 1704, 130: Territorio di Fanari, Dragoi; Bory de Saint-Vincent 1834, 88: Éparchie de Phanari, Dragogi; Leake 1830, I 488–489, 501: Tragóï; Georgacas–McDonald 1968, 133.

Notes: < dragoi, *pl.* of dragua (*Al. n.* dragon). Vasmer and Symeonidis argued that it derives from Dragoje (*Slav. pn.* place/village of the beloved, dear), whereas Georgacas and Komborozos supported an etymology from ὑδραγώγιον (*anc. Gr.* aqueduct): Vasmer 1941, 147; Symeonidis 2010, I 493; Georgacas 1938–48, 65–67; Komborozos 1962, 343. However, the fact that Draġoy is a well-attested surname in the register supports the link to dragoi. See also Hahn 1854, I 163.

307. İskâẕa (اسكاذه), TT10, 109. AL

Coordinates: X: 310392.238 Y: 4146473.870

Modern Greek: Skiadas (Σκιαδάς, ο)

Regional Unit: Elis

Municipality: Andritsaina-Krestena

Municipal Unit: Andritsaina

Notes: A quarter of Linistaina (no. 303). Smyrnis informs that Skiadas was a well-attested surname in the area: Smyrnis 1989, 182.
Σκιαδάς (*Byz. Gr. sn.* tent- or hatmaker) > Schiada (*Arb. sn.*), Shqadha (*Al. sn.*). Place name Skiadas (Σκιαδάς, ο) in Preveza is rendered as Shqadhë in Albanian: Georgacas–McDonald 1968, 344.

308. Mazarak (مزراك), TT10, 109. AL

Notes: Unidentified.
Mazarak (*Al. sn.*). Μαζαράκης (*Arv. sn.*): Biris 1998, 196–197. Ginosatis suggested an etymology from mazi (*Al. n.* ploughed earth ready for sowing) or the Mazarak clan, whereas, according to Lambros, Politis and Jochalas, < mazërak (*Al. n.* inhabitant of Mazi village): Ginosatis 1988, 129; Lambros 1896, 187; Politis 1915, 270; Jochalas 1976, 317. See also Symeonidis 2010, I 859–860.

309. Mateşi (ماتشى), TT10, 110. AL

Coordinates: X: 316598.011 Y: 4155608.867

Modern Greek: Matesi (Μάτεσι, το)

Regional Unit: Elis

Municipality: Andritsaina-Krestena

Municipal Unit: Andritsaina

Bibliography:	Pikoulas 2001a, 278.2371; Panagiotopoulos 1987, 252, 296.15, Territorio di Fanari, Mattesi; Pacifico 1704, 130: Territorio di Fanari, Metesi; Bory de Saint-Vincent 1834, 88: Éparchie de Phanari, Matési; Leake 1846, map: Matesi; Skiadas 1993, 366: Δ. Ανδριτσαίνης; Georgacas–McDonald 1968, 190, 332.
Notes:	According to Symeonidis, < **matësi* (*Al. n.* place in the vicinity of a spring or a river bank) < mat (*Al. n.* sea coast, river bank): Symeonidis 2010, I 886; matës (*Al. n.* measurer, metre; teller). Mates (*Arb. sn.*). Place name and hydronym Mat in northern Albania.

310. İsfranci (اسفرانجی), TT10, 110. AL

Coordinates:	X: 313067.738 Y: 4152186.575
Modern Greek:	Agia Paraskevi (?) (Αγία Παρασκευή, η)
Regional Unit:	Elis
Municipality:	Andritsaina-Krestena
Municipal Unit:	Andritsaina
Bibliography:	GLET 1998, I 19; Dokos 1977–84, 292: Φραγγὴ (= εἰς τὸ σύνορον τοῦ).
Notes:	Uninhabited location. Dokos mentions the church of Agia Paraskevi in Franggi (Φραγγή, τοῦ), which is probably identical to the chapel of Agia Paraskevi located to the south of Myloi (Μύλοι, οι). (Σ)Φρα(ν)τζής (*Gr. sn.*). Cf. microtoponym Frantzi (Φραντζή, του) in the surroundings of Agionori (no. 456): Oikonomou 1988, 286.

311. Mizotoro (میزوتورو), TT10, 110. AL

Notes:	Unidentified. Μειζότερος (*Byz. Gr. sn. comp.* of μείζων; greater, higher, mightier): Kriaras 1988, X 11–12.

312. Beluşi (بلوشی), TT10, 111. AL

Coordinates:	X: 313282.134 Y: 4155109.106
Modern Greek:	Sykies (Συκιές, οι)
Old Toponym:	Until 1928: Belousi (Μπελούσι, το)
Regional Unit:	Elis
Municipality:	Andritsaina-Krestena
Municipal Unit:	Andritsaina
Bibliography:	Pikoulas 2001a, 443.3978; Panagiotopoulos 1987, 252, 296.23: Territorio di Fanari, Belusi; Pacifico 1704, 130: Territorio di Fanari, Belussi; Bory de Saint-Vincent 1834, 88: Éparchie de Phanari, Bélousi; Leake 1846, map: Belusi; Skiadas 1993, 366; Stamatelatos–Vamva-Stamatelatou 2001, 725; Georgacas–McDonald 1968, 204.
Notes:	See no. 5.

313. Mujak (مژاك), TT10, 111. AL

Notes:	Unidentified. See no. 96.

314. Ḳanḳaẕi (قانقاذى), TT10, 111. AL

Coordinates:	X: 291009.911 Y: 4165392.681
Modern Greek:	Kangadi (?) (Καγκάδι, το)
Regional Unit:	Elis
Municipality:	Andritsaina-Krestena
Municipal Unit:	Skillountas
Bibliography:	Georgacas–McDonald 1968, 139.
Notes:	Microtoponym in Bambes (Μπάμπες, οι); its exact location is unknown. See no. 203.

315. Mazarak Adipo (مزراك آديپو), TT10, 112. AL

Coordinates:	X: 316250.011 Y: 4177649.396
Modern Greek:	Mazaraki (?) (Μαζαράκι, το)
Regional Unit:	Arcadia
Municipality:	Gortynia
Municipal Unit:	Tropaia
Bibliography:	GLET 1998, II 281.
Notes:	Uninhabited location to the west of Tropaia (no. 364). For Mazarak see no. 308. Αντύπας (*Gr. sn.*).

316. Floḳa (فلوقه), TT10, 112. AL

Coordinates:	X: 305590.818 Y: 4161030.473
Modern Greek:	Flokas [Φλόκας, ο (= Φλόκα, του)]
Regional Unit:	Elis
Municipality:	Andritsaina-Krestena
Municipal Unit:	Skillountas
Bibliography:	GLET 1998, III 410.

Notes:	Uninhabited location to the north-east of Trypiti (no. 339). Cf. microtoponym Floka (Φλόκα, του) to the north-west of Melissopetra (no. 353), Gritsopoulos 1972, 241. See no. 201.

317. Jupan/Jupano (ژوپان/ژوپانو), TT10, 112. AL

Coordinates:	X: 307331.778 Y: 4158159.759
Modern Greek:	Zioupani (Ζιουπάνη, του)
Regional Unit:	Elis
Municipality:	Andritsaina-Krestena
Municipal Unit:	Alifeira
Bibliography:	Anavasi 2009, map 70: Ζουπάνι; Georgacas–McDonald 1968, 137.
Notes:	Hydronym to the north-east of Kallithea (Καλλιθέα, η). župan (*Scr. n.* head of tribal state): Vasmer 1941, 35; RHSJ 1975, XXIII 509. Zhupani (*Al. sn.*).

318. Aniza (آنیزه), TT10, 113. AL

Coordinates:	X: 313751.950 Y: 4163664.702
Modern Greek:	Anaziri (Αναζήρι, το)
Regional Unit:	Arcadia
Municipality:	Gortynia
Municipal Unit:	Iraia
Bibliography:	Pikoulas 2001a, 73.406; Panagiotopoulos 1987, 261, 300.118: Territorio di Caritena, Anasiri; Pacifico 1704, 129: Territorio di Caritena, Anasiri; Bory de Saint-Vincent 1834, 76: Éparchie de Karytæne, Anaziri; Leake 1846, map: Anaziri; Skiadas 1993, 312.
Notes:	Cf. microtoponym Anneza (Αννεζά, η) in the surroundings of Kalyvia Xenion (Καλύβια Ξενιών, τα) in Elis that derives from Ανέζα, Ανεζίνα (*Gr. pn.*) < Agnès or Agnese (*Fr. pn.*): Iliopoulos 1948, 172; Krekoukias 1955, 28.

319. Lonci (لونجی), TT10, 113. AL

Coordinates:	X: 312539.334 Y: 4165528.781
Modern Greek:	Lotis (?) [Λώτης, ο (= Λότι, το)]
Regional Unit:	Arcadia
Municipality:	Gortynia
Municipal Unit:	Iraia

Bibliography:	Pikoulas 2001a, 267.2256; Panagiotopoulos 1987, 261, 299.92: Territorio di Caritena, Lotti; Pacifico 1704, 129: Territorio di Caritena, Lotti; Bory de Saint-Vincent 1834, 76: Éparchie de Karytæne, Loti; Leake 1846, map: Loti.
Notes:	See no. 211.

320. Sirvu (سيروو), TT10, 114. AL

Coordinates:	X: 321890.910 Y: 4169513.765
Modern Greek:	Servos [Σέρβος, ο (= Σέρβου, του)]
Regional Unit:	Arcadia
Municipality:	Gortynia
Municipal Unit:	Iraia
Bibliography:	Pikoulas 2001a, 419.3736; Panagiotopoulos 1987, 259, 299.34: Territorio di Caritena, Servù; Pacifico 1704, 129: Territorio di Caritena, Xeruò; Bory de Saint-Vincent 1834, 76: Éparchie de Karytæne, Servou; Leake 1846, map: Servu; Bon 1969, 355.
Notes:	Σέρβος (*Gr. n.* Serbian).

321. Ranesi (رانسى), TT10, 114. AL

Coordinates:	X: 312224.164 Y: 4171159.970
Modern Greek:	Kastraki (Καστράκι, το)
Old Toponym:	Until 1928: Renesi (Ρένεσι, το)
Regional Unit:	Arcadia
Municipality:	Gortynia
Municipal Unit:	Tropaia
Bibliography:	Pikoulas 2001a, 198.1596; Panagiotopoulos 1987, 345.133: Territorio di Caritena, Renési; Pacifico 1704, 129: Territorio di Caritena, Renesi; Bory de Saint-Vincent 1834, 76: Éparchie de Karytæne, Rhénési; Leake 1830, II 95: Renési; Skiadas 1993, 319; Stamatelatos–Vamva-Stamatelatou 2001, 318; Iliopoulos 1948, 179.
Notes:	See no. 43.

322. Valaḳ (والاق), TT10, 114. AL

Coordinates:	X: 310332.585 Y: 4168564.523
Modern Greek:	Hrysohori (?) (Χρυσοχώρι, το)
Old Toponym:	Until 1961: Vlahos/Vlahoi (Βλάχος, ο/Βλάχοι, οι)
Regional Unit:	Arcadia

Municipality:	Gortynia
Municipal Unit:	Iraia
Bibliography:	Pikoulas 2001a, 489.4426; Panagiotopoulos 1987, 346.188 Territorio di Caritena, Βλάχοι; Bory de Saint-Vincent 1834, 76: Éparchie de Karytæne, Vlakhi; Leake 1846, map: Vlakhi; Georgacas–McDonald 1968, 114; Bon 1969, 398: Valaques; Skiadas 1993, 312; Stamatelatos–Vamva-Stamatelatou 2001, 802; Nouhakis 1901, II 581: Βάλακας.
Notes:	Cf. microtoponym Valaka (Βαλάκα) in the Loti (no. 319) area mentioned as a location of a field in April 1709, Gritsopoulos 1960, 145_9; Tsotsoros 1986, 47, 67–68; its exact location is unknown. See no. 54. vëllako or vëllaçko (*Al. n.* brother). Place name Vlaka in Croatia and Bosnia & Herzegovina. Vasmer suggested an etymology from vólok (*Ru. n.* isthmus between two rivers) or βλάκας (*Gr. adj.* stupid, silly): Vasmer 1941, 146; also, possibly from Βλάχος (*Gr. n.* Vlach), Vllah (*Al. n.* Vlach): Georgacas 1938, 72.

323. Ḳraḳuki (قراقوكى), TT10, 115. AL

Notes:	Unidentified. See no. 238.

324. Peta (پته), TT10, 115. AL

Coordinates:	X: 309139.644 Y: 4188446.953
Modern Greek:	Petas (Πέτας, ο)
Regional Unit:	Arcadia
Municipality:	Gortynia
Municipal Unit:	Kontovazaina
Bibliography:	Pikoulas 2001a, 377.3329; Panagiotopoulos 1987, 272, 304.30 Territorio di Gastugni, Petta; Bory de Saint-Vincent 1834, 71: Éparchie de Gastouni, Péta; Leake 1846, map: Peta.
Notes:	Cf. microtoponym Peta (Πέτα, του) to the west of Rizospilia (no. 433). petë (*Al. n.* layer of dough; pitta; pasty; *Arb. n.* wedding cake; shield; thin plate, lamina); Peta (*Al. pn.*); Πέτας (*Arv. sn.*): Biris 1998, 200. Place name Petë in Vlorë, Albania.

325. Draġuẕisti (دراغوذستى), TT10, 115. AL

Coordinates:	X: 318829.410 Y: 4163572.219
Modern Greek:	Tragoudisti (Τραγουδιστή, του)
Regional Unit:	Arcadia
Municipality:	Gortynia
Municipal Unit:	Iraia

Notes:	Uninhabited location to the north-west of Raptis (Ράπτης, ο), where ruins of an abandoned settlement and cemetery are still visible today. τραγουδιστής (*Gr. n.* singer, vocalist).

326. Drayina (درايينه), TT10, 115. AL

Coordinates:	X: 311457.374 Y: 4157930.050
Modern Greek:	Pefki (Πευκί, το)
Old Toponym:	Until 1928: Draïna/Drena (Δραΐνα/Δρένα, η)
Regional Unit:	Elis
Municipality:	Andritsaina-Krestena
Municipal Unit:	Alifeira
Bibliography:	Pikoulas 2001a, 380.3360; Panagiotopoulos 1987, 258, 298.67: Territorio d'Andrussa, Draina; Pacifico 1704, 127: Territorio di Andrusa, Draina; Bory de Saint-Vincent 1834, 88: Éparchie de Phanari, Draïna; Leake 1846, map: Draina; Skiadas 1993, 367; Stamatelatos–Vamva-Stamatelatou 2001, 618; Georgacas–McDonald 1968, 133; Gritsopoulos 1987–88, 450–451.
Notes:	Possibly linked to drenjë (*Al. n.* quail, *Coturnix coturnix*; woodlark, *Lullula arborea*; doe); drënjë (*Al. n.* dark-coloured she-goat), attested as drenja in Argolis: Jochalas 2011, II 695; trainë (*Arb. n.* load; dragging; truck). See also Symeonidis 2010, I 494.

327. Ḳonbi S̱eḳra (قنبی ثقره), TT10, 116. AL

Coordinates:	X: 297130.320 Y: 4155931.197
Modern Greek:	Artemida (Αρτέμιδα, η)
Old Toponym:	Until 1997: Koumouthekras (Κουμουθέκρας, ο)
Regional Unit:	Elis
Municipality:	Zaharo
Municipal Unit:	Zaharo
Bibliography:	Pikoulas 2001a, 226.1869; Panagiotopoulos 1987, 252, 296.18: Territorio di Fanari, Combotecra; Pacifico 1704, 130: Territorio di Fanari, Cambothecra; Bory de Saint-Vincent 1834, 88: Éparchie de Phanari, Kombothékla; Leake 1846, map: Komothekra; Bon 1969, 372; Skiadas 1993, 368; Georgacas–McDonald 1968, 167.
Notes:	See no. 219.

328. İstoya (استويه), TT10, 116. AL

Coordinates:	X: 297686.694 Y: 4165045.205
Modern Greek:	Ploutohori (Πλουτοχώρι, το)

Old Toponym:	Until 1928: Togia (Τόγια, του)
Regional Unit:	Elis
Municipality:	Andritsaina-Krestena
Municipal Unit:	Skillountas
Bibliography:	Pikoulas 2001a, 390.3450; Panagiotopoulos 1987, 253, 296.27: Territorio di Fanari, Togia; Skiadas 1993, 370; Stamatelatos–Vamva-Stamatelatou 2001, 639.
Notes:	Stoja (*Scr. pn.*) < Stojan; Stoja (*Scr. sn.* in Istra): RHSJ 1956–58, XVI 601.

329. Lazar Buva (لازار بووه), TT10, 116. AL

Coordinates:	X: 306864.757 Y: 4192952.814
Modern Greek:	Lazarades/Gynaikohori (?) (Λαζαράδες, οι/Γυναικοχώρι, το)
Regional Unit:	Elis
Municipality:	Arhaia Olympia
Municipal Unit:	Lambeia
Bibliography:	Pikoulas 2001a, 244.2046; Iliopoulos 1948, 212; Giannakopoulos 1994, 381; Georgacas–McDonald 1968, 155; Antonios 1961, 37.
Notes:	Different from no. 257. Pikoulas noted that it was one of the seven neighbourhoods of Divri-Lambeia (no. 609). The plural of the modern Greek toponym, Lazarades, might imply that two adjacent settlements under the name Lazaros (Λάζαρος, ο), i.e. Lazar Buva and Lazaro Kemer (no. 330), may have expanded and merged to form a polyfocal settlement.

330. Lazaro Kemer (لازارو كمر), TT10, 116. AL

Coordinates:	X: 306659.636 Y: 4193153.118
Modern Greek:	Lazarades/Gynaikohori (?) (Λαζαράδες, οι/Γυναικοχώρι, το)
Regional Unit:	Elis
Municipality:	Arhaia Olympia
Municipal Unit:	Lambeia
Bibliography:	Pikoulas 2001a, 244.2046; Iliopoulos 1948, 212; Giannakopoulos 1994, 381; Georgacas–McDonald 1968, 155; Antonios 1961, 37.
Notes:	See no 329. Cf. microtoponym Kemera [Κεμερά, η (= στην)] by Graika (no. 597). For Lazaro see no. 257. καμάρα (*Gr. n.* arch) and kemer (*Tr. n.* arch) > qemer (*Al. n.* archway, arch).

331. Ẕunato (ذوناتو), TT10, 117. AL

Coordinates:	X: 333537.109 Y: 4147420.600
Modern Greek:	Zoni (Ζώνη, η)
Old Toponym:	Until 1928: Zounati (Ζουνάτι, το)
Regional Unit:	Arcadia
Municipality:	Megalopoli
Municipal Unit:	Gortyna
Bibliography:	Pikoulas 2001a, 158.1212; Panagiotopoulos 1987, 345.155; Pacifico 1704, 128: Territorio di Leondari, Xonaiti; Bory de Saint-Vincent 1834, 76: Éparchie de Karytæne, Zounati; Leake 1846, map: Zunati; Skiadas 1993, 310; Stamatelatos–Vamva-Stamatelatou 2001, 242.
Notes:	Cf. microtoponym Zounatou (Ζουνάτου, του) by Diasella (Διάσελλα, τα) area in Elis: Georgacas–McDonald 1968, 137. Donat (*Al. pn.* St Donat †387, Buthrotum) < Donatus (*Lat. pn.*): Zoto 2005, 108–109. According to Symeonidis, possibly from zonja (*Al. adj. f.* capable, skillful) +-ati: Symeonidis 2010, I 551.

332. Ḳarvunari (قاروونارى), TT10, 117. AL

Coordinates:	X: 330788.362 Y: 4148077.899
Modern Greek:	Karvounaris (Καρβουνάρης, ο)
Regional Unit:	Arcadia
Municipality:	Megalopoli
Municipal Unit:	Gortyna
Bibliography:	Pikoulas 2001a, 189.1517; Panagiotopoulos 1987, 259, 298.18: Territorio di Caritena, Carvunari; Pacifico 1704, 129: Territorio di Caritena, Caruunari; Leake 1846, map: Karvunaria; Bory de Saint-Vincent 1834, 76: Éparchie de Karytæne, Karvounaria.
Notes:	καρβουν(ι)άρης (*Gr. n.* coal worker; coal merchant).

333. Murik Maji (موريك ماژى), TT10, 117. AL

Coordinates:	X: 324078.427 Y: 4155888.991
Modern Greek:	Mouriki (?) (Μουρίκι, το)
Regional Unit:	Arcadia
Municipality:	Megalopoli

Municipal Unit:	Gortyna
Bibliography:	GLET 1998, II 402.
Notes:	Uninhabited location to the north of Vlahorraptis (Βλαχορράπτης, ο). For Murik see no. 46, and for Maji see no. 129.

334. Mizịka (مزيقه), TT10, 117. AL

Coordinates:	X: 279199.616 Y: 4190604.709
Modern Greek:	Dafniotissa (Δαφνιώτισσα, η)
Old Toponym:	Until 1928: Mouzika (Μουζίκα, η)
Regional Unit:	Elis
Municipality:	Ilida
Municipal Unit:	Amaliada
Bibliography:	Pikoulas 2001a, 131.959; Panagiotopoulos 1987, 274, 305.126: Territorio di Gastougni, Dafniotisa; Pacifico 1704, 123: Territorio di Gastuni, Musica; Leake 1846, map: Muzika; Bory de Saint-Vincent 1834, 70: Éparchie de Gastouni, Mouzika; Skiadas 1993, 254; Stamatelatos–Vamva-Stamatelatou 2001, 180.
Notes:	The *Expédition* and Skiadas listed two distinct settlements: Daphniotisa and Mouzika, Δαφνιώτισσα and Μουζίκα respectively. The microtoponym Mouzakia (Μουζακιά, η) has survived to the south-east of Dafniotissa. According to Symeonidis < muzhik (*Al. adj.* Russian Muzhik, peasant, boorish): Symeonidis 2010, I 961.

335. Ḳuçi (قوچى), TT10, 118. AL

Coordinates:	X: 311460.561 Y: 4159754.527
Modern Greek:	Helidoni (Χελιδόνι, το)
Old Toponym:	Until 1955: Koutsi (Κούτσι, το)
Regional Unit:	Elis
Municipality:	Andritsaina-Krestena
Municipal Unit:	Andritsaina
Bibliography:	Pikoulas 2001a, 484.4377; Panagiotopoulos 1987, 253, 296.34: Territorio di Fanari, Cuzi; Pacifico 1704, 130: Territorio di Fanari, Cuzzi; Expédition 1832: Koutsi; Leake 1846, map: Kutzi; Stamatelatos–Vamva-Stamatelatou 2001, 792; Georgacas–McDonald 1968, 169.
Notes:	See no. 186.

336. Ranesi (رانسى), TT10, 118. AL

Coordinates:	X: 272661.533 Y: 4188047.320
Modern Greek:	Renesi (Ρένεσι, το)
Regional Unit:	Elis
Municipality:	Ilida
Municipal Unit:	Amaliada
Bibliography:	Pikoulas 2001a, 406.3607; Bory de Saint-Vincent 1834, 70: Éparchie de Gastouni, Lopési et Rhénési; Giannakopoulos 1994, 372: Ρένεσι-Ἀνάληψις (κ. Κρυονέρου, νῦν Γερακίου); Gritsopoulos 1971, 452: Ρενεσάκι; Palla-Hronopoulou 2003, 257.
Notes:	In the 1828 census it is reported deserted. Pikoulas sought it by Kryoneri (no. 301) area. See no. 43.

337. Maḳriṣa (ماقريشه), TT10, 119. AL

Coordinates:	X: 288290.855 Y: 4164830.474
Modern Greek:	Makrisia (Μακρίσια, τα)
Regional Unit:	Elis
Municipality:	Andritsaina-Krestena
Municipal Unit:	Skillountas
Bibliography:	Pikoulas 2001a, 269.2285; Pacifico 1704, 130: Territorio di Fanari, Catu Macrisa, Apanu Macrisia; Bory de Saint-Vincent 1834, 88: Éparchie de Phanari, Apano/Kato Makrysia; Leake 1846, map: Makrysia; Georgacas–McDonald 1968, 186.
Notes:	Vasmer and Symeonidis connected it to **Mokrešь* < mokrъ (*Slav. adj.* humid, moist): Vasmer 1941, 117; Symeonidis 2010, I 865. Place name Makreš in Serbia and Mokreš in Bulgaria: RHSJ 1904–10, VI 404.

338. Omlo (اوملو), TT10, 119. AL

Coordinates:	X: 284162.925 Y: 4162014.729
Modern Greek:	Ombras (Ομπράς, ο)
Old Toponym:	Omblos (Ομπλός, ο)
Regional Unit:	Elis
Municipality:	Andritsaina-Krestena
Municipal Unit:	Skillountas

Bibliography:	GLET 1998, III 4: Ομπρός; Dragoumis 1921, 126; Georgacas–McDonald 1968, 219; Bon 1969, 352–353.
Notes:	Dragoumis mentioned it as a ford on the Alfeios River (Αλφειός, ο) between Krestena (Κρέστενα, τα) and Ancient Olympia. Modern Ombras is an uninhabited location to the south-west of Rahes (Ράχες, οι). < **ǫblъ* (*Slav. n.* source, spring): Vasmer 1941, 136; Symeonidis 2010, I 951–952. According to Georgacas, the name of Mt Omblos (Ομπλός, ο) in Achaia derives from πηλός (*Gr. n.* clay): Georgacas 1938, 51–58.

339. **Bizbardi (بزباردى), TT10, 119. AL**

Coordinates:	X: 304141.741 Y: 4160232.823
Modern Greek:	Trypiti (Τρυπητή, η)
Old Toponym:	Until 1928: Bitsibardi/Bitzibardi (Μπιτσιμπάρδι/Μπιτζιμπάρδι, το)
Regional Unit:	Elis
Municipality:	Andritsaina-Krestena
Municipal Unit:	Skillountas
Bibliography:	Pikoulas 2001a, 459.4130; Panagiotopoulos 1987, 252, 295.8: Territorio di Fanari, Bisbardi; Pacifico 1704, 130: Territorio di Fanari, Bisbardi; Expédition 1832: Bisbardi; Bory de Saint-Vincent 1834, 87: Éparchie de Phanari, Bizbardi; Leake 1830, II 90: Bisbárdhi; Skiadas 1993, 367; Bon 1969, 352–353; Stamatelatos–Vamva-Stamatelatou 2001, 752.
Notes:	In a list of the Karytaina-Fanari settlements and local administrators dated 8 October 1830, it is recorded as Bizibardi (Μπιζιμπάρδι, το): Kotsonis 1990, 307. buzëbardhë (*Al. adj.* white-lipped, white-muzzled). Buzbardh (*Al. pn.*): Zoto 2005, 82. Georgacas–McDonald proposed an etymology from bishtbardhë (*Al. adj.* white-tailed): Georgacas–McDonald 1968, 206, 297.

340. **Monaḫu (موناخو), TT10, 120. AL**

Coordinates:	X: 301171.755 Y: 4161668.165
Modern Greek:	Monahou (Μοναχού, του)
Regional Unit:	Elis
Municipality:	Andritsaina-Krestena
Municipal Unit:	Skillountas
Bibliography:	GLET 1998, II 382; Georgacas–McDonald 1968, 197–198.
Notes:	Uninhabited location Monahosykia (Μοναχοσυκιά, η) to the north-east of Diasella (Διάσελλα, τα). μοναχός (*Gr. n.* monk).

341. Ḳoḳla (قوقله), TT10, 120. AL

Coordinates:	X: 315751.949 Y: 4173740.036
Modern Greek:	Kokla (Κόκλα, του)
Regional Unit:	Arcadia
Municipality:	Gortynia
Municipal Unit:	Tropaia
Bibliography:	Pikoulas 2001a, 214.1755; Bory de Saint-Vincent 1834, 76: Éparchie de Karytæne, Kokla; Leake 1830, II 96: Kokhla; Leake 1846, map: Kokla; Skiadas 1993, 319: Δ. Τροπαίων.
Notes:	See no. 183.

342. Kefiñali (كفيكالى), TT10, 120. AL

Coordinates:	X: 289548.858 Y: 4173417.219
Modern Greek:	Kafkonia (Καυκωνία, η)
Old Toponym:	Until 1940: Kafkania (Καυκανιά, η)
Regional Unit:	Elis
Municipality:	Arhaia Olympia
Municipal Unit:	Arhaia Olympia
Bibliography:	Pikoulas 2001a, 203.1650; Bory de Saint-Vincent 1834, 71: Éparchie de Gastouni, Kafkania; Leake 1846, map: Kafkania; Skiadas 1993, 253; Stamatelatos–Vamva-Stamatelatou 2001, 335.
Notes:	Cf. microtoponym Kafkoula (Καυκούλα, η) in the surroundings of Pefki (no. 326), and Kafkoules (Καυκούλες, οι) near Maniaki (Μανιάκι, το) in Messenia: Georgacas–McDonald 1968, 155. Perhaps linked to καύκαλο (*Gr. n.* cranium, skull) > kafkall (*Arb. n.* jaw).

343. Ḳopiça (قوپيچه), TT10, 121. AL

Notes:	Unidentified. According to Meyer, Kovitsa (Κόβιτσα, η) was the name of Graikas's (no. 597) rivulet that Papandreou identified with ancient Acheron (Αχέρων, ο): Meyer 1957, 42–43; Papandreou 1924, 13. Cf. microtoponym Kopitsa (Κόπιτσα, η) in the surroundings of Sitohori (Σιτοχώρι, το) in Messenia: Georgacas–McDonald 1968, 162. kopicë (*Al. n.* moth, *Microlepidoptera*).

344. Barçi (بارچى), TT10, 121. AL

Coordinates:	X: 311435.406 Y: 4162311.033
Modern Greek:	Dafnoula (Δαφνούλα, η)

Old Toponym:	Until 1928: Bartzi/Roggouzi (Μπάρτζι, το/Ρογγούζη, η)
Regional Unit:	Elis
Municipality:	Andritsaina-Krestena
Municipal Unit:	Andritsaina
Bibliography:	Pikoulas 2001a, 131.961; Panagiotopoulos 1987, 253, 296.29: Territorio di Fanari, Barzi; Pacifico 1704, 130: Territorio di Fanari, Barzi; Bory de Saint-Vincent 1834, 87: Éparchie de Phanari, Bartzi; Leake 1846, map: Bartzi; Skiadas 1993, 367; Stamatelatos–Vamva-Stamatelatou 2001, 180; Georgacas–McDonald 1968, 203.
Notes:	See no. 23.

345. Maẕi (ماذى), TT10, 121. AL

Notes:	Unidentified. i madh (*Al. adj.* big, large). Madhi (*Al. sn.*).

346. Pasḳali/Pasḳal (پسقالى/پسقال), TT10, 121. AL

Coordinates:	X: 313507.722 Y: 4150143.445
Modern Greek:	Paschalinou t' aloni (?) [Πασχαλινού τ' αλώνι, το (= Paschalinos's threshing floor)]
Regional Unit:	Elis
Municipality:	Andritsaina-Krestena
Municipal Unit:	Andritsaina
Bibliography:	Georgacas–McDonald 1968, 229.
Notes:	Microtoponym in Koufopoulo (Κουφόπουλο, το) in Elis; its exact location is unknown. Πασχάλης (*Gr. pn.*) > Paskal (*Al. pn.*).

347. Ḳukesi (قوكسى), TT10, 122. AL

Notes:	Unidentified. Kuqësi < i kuq (*Al. adj.* red): Symeonidis 2010, I 742–743). Place name Kukës in the homonymous region of Albania and Qukës in Librazhd: Kolleka 1983, 19.

348. Melita (مليتا), TT10, 122. AL

Coordinates:	X: 292112.554 Y: 4158357.475
Modern Greek:	Melita (Μελιτά, του)
Regional Unit:	Elis
Municipality:	Zaharo

Municipal Unit: Zaharo

Bibliography: GLET 1998, II 348; Georgacas–McDonald 1968, 194.

Notes: Uninhabited location to the north-east of Smerna (Σμέρνα, η).
Μελιτάς (*Gr. sn.*); Malita (*Al. sn.*).

349. Maji (ماژی), TT10, 122. AL

Bibliography: Dokos 1977–84, 299: Μάζη.

Notes: Unidentified.
See no. 129.

350. Luzi (لوزی), TT10, 122. AL

Coordinates: X: 296299.197 Y: 4143307.825

Modern Greek: Trani Louza (Τρανή Λούζα, η)

Regional Unit: Elis

Municipality: Zaharo

Municipal Unit: Zaharo

Bibliography: GLET 1998, III 352.

Notes: Uninhabited location to the west of Agios Ilias (Άγιος Ηλίας, ο).
See no. 167.

351. İsḳala (اسقاله), TT10, 122. GR

Coordinates: X: 296299.197 Y: 4143307.825

Modern Greek: Skala (?) (Σκάλα, η)

Regional Unit: Elis

Municipality: Zaharo

Municipal Unit: Zaharo

Bibliography: Georgacas–McDonald 1968, 250.

Notes: Microtoponym in Kalidona (Καλίδονα, η); its exact location is unknown, however it should have been by the seaside as it had fish-farms.
σκάλα (*Gr. n.* ladder, staircase, pier) < scalae (*Lat. n.* stairs).

352. Ṣarakin (صراکن), TT10, 123. GR

Coordinates: X: 322493.399 Y: 4155858.093

Modern Greek:	Sarakini (Σαρακίνι, το)
Regional Unit:	Arcadia
Municipality:	Megalopoli
Municipal Unit:	Gortyna
Bibliography:	PIKOULAS 2001a, 415.3702; BORY DE SAINT-VINCENT 1834, 76: Éparchie de Karytæne, Zoula Sarakini; LEAKE 1846, map: Zula Sarakini; THANOPOULOS 1988.
Notes:	See no. 188.

353. Trestena (ترستنه), TT10, 123. GR

Coordinates:	X: 322277.366 Y: 4161912.444
Modern Greek:	Melissopetra (Μελισσόπετρα, η)
Old Toponym:	Until 1928: Trestena (Τρεστενά, η)
Regional Unit:	Arcadia
Municipality:	Gortynia
Municipal Unit:	Dimitsana
Bibliography:	PIKOULAS 2001a, 284.2427; PANAGIOTOPOULOS 1987, 260, 299.55: Territorio di Caritena, Tristena; PACIFICO 1704, 129: Territorio di Caritena, Tristene; LEAKE 1846, map: Trestena; HOPF 1873, 202: Tripotama vel Trisetenia, 205: Trisotenia; BORY DE SAINT-VINCENT 1834, 76: Éparchie de Karytæne, Tristéna; SKIADAS 1993, 308; STAMATELATOS–VAMVA-STAMATELATOU 2001, 482–483.
Notes:	< trъstěna < trъstь (*old Slav. n.* duct, reed place). VASMER 1941, 159; SYMEONIDIS 2010, II 1360. Place name Trstená in Slovakia, Trstena in Serbia and Trsteno in Croatia.

354. Aḳunba (آقونبه), TT10, 123. GR

Coordinates:	X: 302807.591 Y: 4157144.991
Modern Greek:	Paliakoumba Platianas (Παλιάκουμπα Πλατιάνας, η)
Regional Unit:	Elis
Municipality:	Andritsaina-Krestena
Municipal Unit:	Skillountas
Bibliography:	PIKOULAS 2001a, 388.3435; HOPF 1873, 206: Acumba; SFIKOPOULOS 1987, 304–308; BON 1969, 391.
Notes:	The ruins of the Frankish fortress Accomba, Acumba or Cumba (la Combe) were located by Meyer in Paliakoumba, over Roupaki (Ρουπάκι, το), across the bridge of Diagon/Tsemberoula (Διάγων, ο/Τσεμπερούλα, η), south-west of Platiana: MEYER 1957, 36–39, plan III.

355. Maẕi (ماذى), TT10, 125. AL

Coordinates:	X: 295618.662 Y: 4164360.930
Modern Greek:	Skillountia (Σκιλλουντία, η)
Old Toponym:	Until 1928: Mazi (Μάζι, το)
Regional Unit:	Elis
Municipality:	Andritsaina-Krestena
Municipal Unit:	Skillountas
Bibliography:	Pikoulas 2001a, 424.3787; Panagiotopoulos 1987, 253, 296.39: Territorio di Fanari, Basso Masi; Pacifico 1704, 130: Territorio di Fanari, Masi; Bory de Saint-Vincent 1834, 88: Éparchie de Phanari, Mazi; Leake 1846, map: Mazi; Skiadas 1993, 370; Stamatelatos–Vamva-Stamatelatou 2001, 696; Politis 1915, 286–287.
Notes:	See no. 345.

356. Manḳa (مانقه), TT10, 125. AL

Notes:	Unidentified. mangë (*Al. n.* hobo, bum; sly person) > μάγκας (*Gr. n.* sly person). Μάγκας (*Gr. sn.*).

357. Ketesi (كتسى), TT10, 125. AL

Notes:	Unidentified. As an anthroponym it is possibly linked to qetës [*Al. adj.* sneaky (person)]. See also qetësi (*Al. n.* quietness, calmness, tranquillity); këtejsë or këtejshëm (*Al. adv.* from here, local).

358. Mundriza (موندريزه), TT10, 125. GR

Coordinates:	X: 293972.627 Y: 4161395.302
Modern Greek:	Gryllos (Γρύλλος, ο)
Old Toponym:	Until 1928: Moundraza (Μουνδράζα, η)
Regional Unit:	Elis
Municipality:	Andritsaina-Krestena
Municipal Unit:	Skillountas
Bibliography:	Pikoulas 2001a, 127.924; Panagiotopoulos 1987, 253, 296.43: Territorio di Fanari, Mundrisa; Pacifico 1704, 130: Territorio di Fanari, Mandrissa; Bory de Saint-Vincent 1834, 88: Éparchie de Phanari, Moundritsa; Leake 1846, map: Mundritza; Hopf 1873, 202: Mondrusa vel Mondrizza, 206: Mondriza; Georgacas–McDonald 1968, 199; Bon 1969, 349, 358; Skiadas 1993, 370; Stamatelatos–Vamva-Stamatelatou 2001, 174; Dragoumis 1921, 264.

Notes:	Sfikopoulos traced no ruins of the fortress on Mikro Kastro (Μικρό Κάστρο, το) sand-hill: Sfikopoulos 1987, 318. According to Symeonidis, < mëndrëzë (*Al. n.* little wall, stockyard): Symeonidis 2010, I 963. See also mendërz (*Al. n.* peppermint, *Mentha piperita L.*). Vasmer suggested it derives from mǫdrъ (*Slav. adj.* prudent, sage, wise) + -zë (*Al. dim. end.*): Vasmer 1941, 148. Place name Mъdrec and Mъdrica in Bulgaria.

359. Bratiça (براتيچه), TT10, 126. AL

Coordinates:	X: 315081.698 Y: 4167457.034
Modern Greek:	Parnassos (Παρνασσός, ο)
Old Toponym:	Until 1928: Bratitsa (Μπρατίτσα, η)
Regional Unit:	Arcadia
Municipality:	Gortynia
Municipal Unit:	Iraia
Bibliography:	Pikoulas 2001a, 370.3264; Panagiotopoulos 1987, 346.169: Territorio di Caritena, Bastitza (Bartitza); Bory de Saint-Vincent 1834, 76: Éparchie de Karytæne, Bratitsa; Skiadas 1993, 312; Stamatelatos–Vamva-Stamatelatou 2001, 593.
Notes:	Μπρατίτσας (*Arv. sn.*): Biris 1998, 199. bratъ (*Slav. n.* brother). Bratica, Bratić or Brati (*Scr. pn. dim.* of Bratoslav). Place name Bratići in Serbia and Bosnia & Herzegovina: Vasmer 1941, 156; RHSJ 1880–82, I 601–602.

360. Papaẕa (پاپاذا), TT10, 127. AL

Coordinates:	X: 317017.289 Y: 4165568.733
Modern Greek:	Pappadas [Παππαδάς, ο (= Παππαδού)]
Regional Unit:	Arcadia
Municipality:	Gortynia
Municipal Unit:	Iraia
Bibliography:	Pikoulas 2001a, 365.3217; Panagiotopoulos 1987, 260, 299.58: Territorio di Caritena. Papadà; Pacifico 1704, 129: Territorio di Caritena, Papà dà; Bory de Saint-Vincent 1834, 76: Éparchie de Karytæne, Papadæs; Leake 1846, map: Papadha.
Notes:	παπαδάς, ο or παπαδού, η (*Gr. n.* place where priests live): Symeonidis 2010, II 1101.

361. Ġardik (غارديك), TT10, 127. GR

Coordinates:	X: 328351.001 Y: 4125705.839
Modern Greek:	Gardiki-Amfeia (?) (Γαρδίκι, το - Άμφεια, η)
Regional Unit:	Arcadia

Municipality:	Megalopoli
Municipal Unit:	Megalopoli
Bibliography:	ANAVASI 2009, map 106; PANAGIOTOPOULOS 1987, 255, 297.18: Territorio di Leondari, Gardichi; PACIFICO 1704, 128: Territorio di Leondari, Gardichi, *olim Clitor*; HOPF 1873, 206: Gordichi salo; LEAKE 1830, I 80: castle of Xuriá; LEAKE 1846, map: Ampheia; LONGNON–TOPPING 1969, 244; BON 1969, 422–425; DRAGOUMIS 1921, 181–196.
Notes:	Uninhabited location in Kokkala (Κόκκαλα, τα), to the south-west of Hirades (Χιράδες, οι), where ruins of the Byzantine fortress Gardikion (Γαρδίκιον, το) and the ancient Greek settlement of Ampheia (Ἄμφεια, ἡ) are traced: PIKOULAS 1988, 240–241. Cf. microtoponym Gardiki (Γαρδίκι, το) to the north of Kafkonia (no. 342) and Gardiki (Γαρδίκι, το) [today's Anavryto village (Αναβρυτό, το)] in Falaisia, Arcadia. < **gordьkъ* (*old Slav.* small fort, castle): VASMER 1941, 103; SYMEONIDIS 2010, I 407; cf. gardhiqe (*Al. n.* small wicker fence). Place name Kardhiq in Gjirokastër, and Kardhikaq or Gardhikaq in Vlorë, Albania.

362. Poḳovina (پوقووینه/پوقوینه), TT10, 128. AL

Coordinates:	X: 312633.475 Y: 4183473.206
Modern Greek:	Peleki (Πελέκι, το)
Old Toponym:	Until 1928: Bo(u)kovina [Μπο(υ)κοβίνα, η]
Regional Unit:	Arcadia
Municipality:	Gortynia
Municipal Unit:	Kontovazaina
Bibliography:	PIKOULAS 2001a, 372.3285; PANAGIOTOPOULOS 1987, 261, 299.97: Territorio di Caritena, Bocovina; PACIFICO 1704, 129: Territorio di Caritena, Boccorina; BORY DE SAINT-VINCENT 1834, 71: Éparchie de Gastouni, Bokovina; LEAKE 1846, map: Bokovina; SKIADAS 1993, 311; STAMATELATOS–VAMVA-STAMATELATOU 2001, 602; POLITIS 1915, 269–270.
Notes:	< bukva (*Scr. n.* beech, *Fagus sylvatica*): VASMER 1941, 143–144; SYMEONIDIS 2010, I 997. Place name Bukowina in Poland, Bukovina in the Czech Republic and Slovakia; Bukovina region split between Romania and Ukraine.

363. Zaveti (زاوتی), TT10, 129. AL

Coordinates:	X: 310440.071 Y: 4179955.510
Modern Greek:	Zaveti (Ζάβετη, η)
Regional Unit:	Arcadia
Municipality:	Gortynia
Municipal Unit:	Tropaia
Bibliography:	GLET 1998, I 426.
Notes:	Uninhabited location to the west of Kato Spatharis (Κάτω Σπαθάρης, ο). Ζαβάτοσης (*Arv. sn.* cuirassier): BIRIS 1998, 193.

364. Virça (ویرچه), TT10, 129. GR

Coordinates:	X: 319910.220 Y: 4177727.322
Modern Greek:	Tropaia (?) (Τρόπαια, τα)
Old Toponym:	Vervitsa (Βερβίτσα, η)
Regional Unit:	Arcadia
Municipality:	Gortynia
Municipal Unit:	Tropaia
Bibliography:	Pikoulas 2001a, 458.4119; Panagiotopoulos 1987, 260, 299.67: Territorio di Caritena, Vervizza; Pacifico 1704, 129: Territorio di Caritena, Veruizza; Bory de Saint-Vincent 1834, 76: Éparchie de Karytæne, Vervitsa; Leake 1830, II 96, 104: Vervítza; Bon 1969, 355, 395; Skiadas 1993, 319; Stamatelatos–Vamva-Stamatelatou 2001, 751.
Notes:	See no. 302.

9. District of Arḳadya (Kyparissia) (Maps 17–18)

365. Arḳadya (ارقادیه), TT10, 130.

Coordinates:	X: 293362.035 Y: 4124957.783
Modern Greek:	Kyparissia (Κυπαρισσία, η)
Old Toponym:	Until 1834: Arkadia (Αρκαδιά, η)
Regional Unit:	Messenia
Municipality:	Trifylia
Municipal Unit:	Kyparissia
Bibliography:	Pikoulas 2001a, 240.2000; Panagiotopoulos 1987, 252, 295.92: Territorio d'Arcadia, Città di Arcadia; Pacifico 1704, 130: Territorio d'Arcadia, Arcadia Città, *olim Cyparissia*; Bory de Saint-Vincent 1834, 66: Éparchie d'Arkadia, Arkadia (*Cyparissia*); Leake 1830, I 68–69, 372, 484: Arkadhía (Cyparissiæ); Stamatelatos–Vamva-Stamatelatou 2001, 400; Sfikopoulos 1987, 329–331; Vagiakakos 1987, 270, 278–279; Georgacas–McDonald 1968, 107, 173; Longnon–Topping 1969, 240–241; Bon 1969, 412–414; Andrews 2006, 84–89.
Notes:	Its ancient name, Kyparissēeis (Κυπαρισσήεις, ὁ) (Homer, *Iliad*, B 593) changed to Arkadia, which was mentioned for the first time in 1097. King of Greece, Otto I, renamed it to Kyparissia. The TT10-1/14662 does not mention the capital of the district (*nefs-i Arḳadya*).

366. Provanda Aya Yorgi (پروانده آیه یورکی), TT10, 130. GR

Coordinates:	X: 308875.318 Y: 4131381.477
Modern Greek:	Agios Georgios (Άγιος Γεώργιος, ο)

Regional Unit:	Messenia
Municipality:	Oihalia
Municipal Unit:	Dorio
Bibliography:	Pikoulas 2001a, 46.147; Alexandropoulos 1978, 405; Georgacas–McDonald 1968, 94.
Notes:	The name possibly denotes an ecclesiastic endowment (St George). praebenda, prevenda or provenda (*med. Lat. n.* estates granted to a religious community for its maintenance): Niermeyer–van de Kieft 2002, II 1071–1073.

367. Ẕiġanato (ذغاناتو), TT10, 130. GR

Coordinates:	X: 311044.890 Y: 4063843.660
Modern Greek:	Venetiko/Tigani Island (?) (Νήσος Βενέτικο/Τηγάνι, η)
Regional Unit:	Messenia
Municipality:	Pylos-Nestoras
Municipal Unit:	Koroni
Bibliography:	Nanetti 2011, 131–132, 252–257.
Notes:	The fact that, according to the cadastre entry, its fishery was jointly farmed by the Ottomans and the Venetians indicates a place in the vicinity of the Venetian territories of southern Messenia. From the place-onomastics point of view, the Ottoman rendering of the toponym, Ẕiġanato < **Δηγανάτο* < **Θηγανάτο*, reveals a link to Venetiko/Tigani Island (Νήσος Βενέτικο/Τηγάνι, η), ancient Thēganoussa (Θηγανοῦσσα, ἡ, Pausanias 1983, II, IV.34.12), off the shore of Cape Tainaro (Ακρωτήριο Ταίναρο, το). The archaeological relics of a settlement on its north-eastern side are dated to the Byzantine period, with later phases from the 17th–18th centuries: Kavvadia-Spondyli 2002, 224, 228. In 1418, the Lord of Caumont, while sailing in the Messenian Gulf, observed high on a peak a church inhabited by a few hermits (Greek Orthodox monks); this was most probably the church of St Nicholas, after which the island was named and commonly known during the 15th and 16th c.: Nanetti 2011, 131–132: 'du chief de Maynes al Venetigui: xl milles; ylle déserte mes hy demeurent iiij hermittes en une églize haulte sur ung puy.' Evidence of salt-pans is also found. A small landlocked water basin in the northern part of the island may have been used as the salt-pan and fish-farm recorded in the register. The archaeological research, which will cast light on the mediaeval settlement of the island, is a *desideratum*. Tigani (Τηγάνι, το) is a common Greek toponym pertaining to salt-pans: Pikoulas 2001b, 299–300.

368. Vurçanos (وورچانوس), TT10, 130. GR

Coordinates:	X: 315555.870 Y: 4116380.983
Modern Greek:	Mavrommati (Μαυρομμάτι, το)
Old Toponym:	Vourkanon/Voulkanon (Βουρκάνον/Βουλκάνον, το)
Regional Unit:	Messenia

Municipality:	Messini
Municipal Unit:	Ithomi
Bibliography:	Pikoulas 2001a, 281.2392; Panagiotopoulos 1987, 257, 298.42: Territorio d'Andrussa, Mavromatti Micrò; Longnon–Topping 1969, 245; Pacifico 1704, 126–127: Territorio d'Andrussa, Monte Itome/Vulcano (Monastero di Caloieri, Mauromati Micrò); Bory de Saint-Vincent 1834, 64: Éparchie d'Androusa, Apano Mavromati; Leake 1846, map: Vurkano (Ithome), Mavromati; Sfikopoulos 1987, 337–338; Komborozos 1967, 363; Georgacas–McDonald 1968, 197; Bon 1969, 417–418; Zakythinos 1953, 301.
Notes:	Voulkanon is the mediaeval name of ancient Messene; the toponym survived as the name of the mountain and the monastery on the top of it. Possibly linked to volcano (*It. n.* volcano): Katsouleas 1978, 350–351.

369. Ġırebini (غربنى), TT10, 131. M

Coordinates:	X: 316680.446 Y: 4132913.752
Modern Greek:	Kato Melpeia (Κάτω Μέλπεια, η)
Old Toponym:	Until 1928: Kato Garantza (Κάτω Γαράντζα, η)
Regional Unit:	Messenia
Municipality:	Oihalia
Municipal Unit:	Andania
Bibliography:	Pikoulas 2001a, 285.2430, 122.879; Panagiotopoulos 1987, 257, 298.21: Territorio d'Andrussa, Grenbeni; Pacifico 1704, 127: Territorio d'Andrussa, Garanza; Expédition 1832: Garenza; Bory de Saint-Vincent 1834, 64: Éparchie d'Androusa, Garantsa; Hopf 1873, 202: Gribani vel Grebani; Sfikopoulos 1987, 333; Georgacas–McDonald 1968, 120; Bon 1969, 440–441; Dokos 1971–74, 132: Κρεμπενί; Skiadas 1993, 344; Stamatelatos–Vamva-Stamatelatou 2001, 330.
Notes:	Longnon and Topping mentioned a mediaeval fortress to the south-west of Ano Melpeia and a hill named Krembeni (Κρεμπενή, η) in the vicinity of Kato Melpeia that could be identified as the Grebeni fortress: Longnon–Topping 1969, 244–245. Panagiotopoulos argued that the ruined fortress of Grembeni (Γκρεμπενή, η) is located within the boundaries of Kato Melpeia: Panagiotopoulos 1987, 195. According to Vasmer, < **grebenь* (*Slav. n.* ridge): Vasmer 1941, 162.

370. Arḫangeli (ارخانكلى), TT10, 133. M

Coordinates:	X: 316694.281 Y: 4129868.966
Modern Greek:	Polihni (Πολίχνη, η)
Regional Unit:	Messenia
Municipality:	Oihalia
Municipal Unit:	Meligala

Bibliography:	Pikoulas 2001a, 390.3459; Longnon–Topping 1969, 242–243; Sfikopoulos 1987, 333; Bon 1969, 429.
Notes:	The name refers to the church of Agios Taxiarhis/Agioi Taxiarhes (Άγιος Ταξιάρχης, ο/Άγιοι Ταξιάρχες, οι) situated within a small fortress – Kastraki (Καστράκι, το) – 500m to the north-east of Polihni.

371. Loyi (لويي), TT10, 133. GR

Coordinates:	X: 310036.284 Y: 4105340.295
Modern Greek:	Diodia (Διόδια, τα)
Old Toponym:	Until 1928: Loï (Λόι, το)
Regional Unit:	Messenia
Municipality:	Messini
Municipal Unit:	Aristomenis
Bibliography:	Pikoulas 2001a, 137.1019; Panagiotopoulos 1987, 263, 300.25: Territorio di Coron, Loi; Pacifico 1704, 126: Territorio di Coron, Lay; Hopf 1873, 205: Loi; Bory de Saint-Vincent 1834, 64: Éparchie d'Androusa, Logi; Leake 1846, map: Loghi; Sfikopoulos 1987, 333–334; Skiadas 1993, 345; Stamatelatos–Vamva-Stamatelatou 2001, 190.
Notes:	< *Λοΐς (*Gr. pn.*): Symeonidis 2010, I 839. Georgacas–McDonald noted that its correct pronunciation is Λοΐ (το Λοΐ, του Λοΐ) instead of Λόι, something that I confirmed with the locals: Georgacas–McDonald 1968, 182.

372. Platana (پلاتنه), TT10, 134. GR

Coordinates:	X: 297639.353 Y: 4098572.767
Modern Greek:	Platanos (Πλάτανος, ο)
Regional Unit:	Messenia
Municipality:	Pylos-Nestoras
Municipal Unit:	Pylos
Bibliography:	Pikoulas 2001a, 387.3428; Panagiotopoulos 1987, 262, 300.10: Territorio di Navarino, Plutano; Pacifico 1704, 125: Territorio di Navarin Novo, Platano; Bory de Saint-Vincent 1834, 85: Éparchie de Navarin, Platanos; Leake 1846, map: Platano; Alexandropoulos 1978, 405; Bon 1969, 431–432; Georgacas–McDonald 1968, 236; Dragoumis 1921, 246.

373. Mili Ḳalivya (ميلى قاليويه), TT10, 135. GR

Coordinates:	X: 296890.439 Y: 4098191.245
Modern Greek:	Palaiopyrgos (Παλαιόπυργος, ο)
Regional Unit:	Messenia
Municipality:	Pylos-Nestoras

Municipal Unit:	Pylos
Bibliography:	Georgacas–McDonald 1968, 224; Bon 1969, 435-436.
Notes:	Alexandropoulos suggested a possible connection to Longnon and Topping's Molini/Molina to the north-east of Pylos (Πύλος, η), which should be located to the north of Iklaina (Ίκλαινα, η): Alexandropoulos 1978, 405; Longnon–Topping 1969, 248–249. The microtoponym Palaiopyrgos in the area probably refers to this settlement.

374. Palari (پالاری), TT10, 135. AL

Coordinates:	X: 326838.426 Y: 4124824.778
Modern Greek:	Paliarovouni (?) (Παλιαροβούνι, το)
Regional Unit:	Messenia
Municipality:	Oihalia
Municipal Unit:	Oihalia
Bibliography:	GLET 1998, III 26.
Notes:	Uninhabited location to the east of Oihalia (Οιχαλία, η). Perhaps linked to pelar (*Al. n.* stableman, horse wrangler).

375. Platoḳomati (پلاتوقوماتی), TT10, 135. GR

Bibliography:	Alexandropoulos 1978, 406.
Notes:	Unidentified.

376. Meġaliç (مغالچ), *mezraʿa*, TT10, 136.

Bibliography:	Alexandropoulos 1978, 404.
Notes:	Unidentified.

377. Malena (مالنه), TT10, 136. GR

Coordinates:	X: 293817.109 Y: 4121706.732
Modern Greek:	Xirokambos (?) (Ξηρόκαμπος, ο)
Old Toponym:	Until 1928: Maleniti (Μαλενίτι, το)
Regional Unit:	Messenia
Municipality:	Trifylia
Municipal Unit:	Kyparissia

Bibliography:	Pikoulas 2001a, 349.3054; Panagiotopoulos 1987, 250, 295.33: Territorio d'Arcadia, Malogniti; Pacifico 1704, 130: Territorio d'Arcadia, Melagniti; Bory de Saint-Vincent 1834, 66: Éparchie d'Arkadia, Maléniti; Leake 1846, map: Maleniti; Skiadas 1993, 357; Stamatelatos–Vamva-Stamatelatou 2001, 555; Georgacas–McDonald 1968, 187.
Notes:	Alexandropoulos proposed an identification with Bon's Saint-Élie, if the A[y]lya, i.e. Aï Lias (Αϊ-Λιας, ο), reading is accepted: Alexandropoulos 1978, 404; Bon 1969, 290–291, 429, 432, 435. < mëllenjë or mëllënjë (*Al. n.* blackbird, *Turdus merula*): Symeonidis 2010, I 867–868.

378. Ḳalazoni (قالازونى), TT10, 136. GR

Coordinates:	X: 288713.853 Y: 4117972.642
Modern Greek:	Halazoni (Χαλαζόνι, το)
Regional Unit:	Messenia
Municipality:	Trifylia
Municipal Unit:	Filiatra
Bibliography:	Pikoulas 2001a, 476.4301; Panagiotopoulos 1987, 250, 294.2: Territorio d'Arcadia, Calossoni; Pacifico 1704, 130: Territorio d'Arcadia, Calasogni; Bory de Saint-Vincent 1834, 66: Éparchie d'Arkadia, Khalazonia; Leake 1846, map: Khalazoni; Georgacas–McDonald 1968, 278.

379. Ḳozomuli (قوزومولى), *mezraʿa*, TT10, 136.

Notes:	Unidentified.

380. Muzak Mengişa (مزاك منكشه), 1/14662, 47. AL

Coordinates:	X: 297053.621 Y: 4107669.319
Modern Greek:	Mouzaki (Μουζάκι, το)
Regional Unit:	Messenia
Municipality:	Trifylia
Municipal Unit:	Gargalianoi
Bibliography:	Pikoulas 2001a, 321.2794; Panagiotopoulos 1987, 250, 294.12: Territorio d'Arcadia, Musachi; Pacifico 1704, 131: Territorio d'Arcadia, Musachi; Bory de Saint-Vincent 1834, 66: Éparchie d'Arkadia, Muzaki; Leake 1846, map: Mūzaki; Biris 1998, 197; Georgacas–McDonald 1968, 335.
Notes:	Muzaka was an eminent mediaeval Albanian clan; muzeqar (*Al. adj.* of/from Myzeqe region in Albania). Μουζάκης (*Arv. sn.*), Muzaqi (*Al. sn.*) < muzaqi (*Al. n.* calf, steer). See also Kolleka 1983, 23. For Mengişa see no. 267.

381. Gerbesi (كربسى), 1/14662, 47. AL

Notes: Unidentified. Assenova, Stojkov and Kacori mentioned village Krypsa (Κρύψα, η) in Trifylia citing Georgacas–McDonald 1968, 173.3727: Assenova–Stojkov–Kacori 1977, 227.
According to Biris, Γκέρμπεσης (*Arv. sn.*) < Γερβάσιος (*Gr. pn.*): Biris 1998, 192–193. Cf. place name Gjerbës (Γκέρμπεσι, το), today's Midea (Μιδέα, η), in Argolis: Jochalas 2011, I 139, and in Mallakastër and Berat, Albania: Gelasius 1942a, 43; Kolleka 1983, 13. Vasmer and Symeonidis argued that it derives from **gъrbъ* (*Slav. n.* hump, heightening): Vasmer 1941, 126; Symeonidis 2010, I 427. Place name Grbši in Mostar, Bosnia & Herzegovina.

10. District of Londar (Leontari) (Maps 19–20)

382. Londar, nefs-i (لوندار), TT10, 137. GR

Coordinates: X: 335465.505 Y: 4131907.677

Modern Greek: Leontari (Λεοντάρι, το)

Regional Unit: Arcadia

Municipality: Megalopoli

Municipal Unit: Falaisia

Bibliography: Pikoulas 2001a, 251.2106; Panagiotopoulos 1987, 256, 297.56: Territorio di Leondari, Leondari; Pacifico 1704, 128: Territorio di Leondari, Leondari Fortezza; Bory de Saint-Vincent 1834, 79: Éparchie de Léondari, Léondari; Leake 1830, I 81, 115, 346, 354, 372, 485: Londári; Sfikopoulos 1987, 257; Katrivanos 1960, 347–349; Hopf 1873, 202, 205: Lendari; Bon 1969, 520–521.

Notes: Often pronounced as Lontari (Λοντάρι, το).

383. Maji (ماژى), TT10, 140. AL

Notes: Unidentified.
See no. 129.

384. Aya Yorgi (آيه يوركى), TT10, 140. GR

Coordinates: X: 325731.479 Y: 4140370.359

Modern Greek: Lykosoura (Λυκόσουρα, η)

Regional Unit: Arcadia

Municipality: Megalopoli

Municipal Unit: Megalopoli

Bibliography:	Pikoulas 2001a, 265.2245; Expédition 1832: Ch[lle] Hagios Géorgios; Leake 1846, map: (Lycosura); Sfikopoulos 1987, 245-249; Romaios 1957, 4; Hopf 1873, 202, 205: S. Zorzi de Scorta; Bon 1969, 377–387; Sarris 1934–35, 73–84; Dragoumis 1921, 204–212.
Notes:	The remnants of Agios Georgios Skorton (Άγιος Γεώργιος Σκορτών, ο) are found to the west of Megalopoli near Karyes village (Καρυές, οι) near the ruins of ancient Lykosoura.

385. Lonḳanik (لونقانيك), TT10, 144. GR

Coordinates:	X: 344642.436 Y: 4121860.814
Modern Greek:	Longanikos (Λογκανίκος, ο)
Regional Unit:	Laconia
Municipality:	Sparti
Municipal Unit:	Pellana
Bibliography:	Pikoulas 2001a, 260.2192; Panagiotopoulos 1987, 285, 309.72: Territorio di Mistra, Longanigo; Pacifico 1704, 132: Territorio di Mistrà, Longanigo; Hopf 1873, 202: Longonico, 206: Longanico; Bory de Saint-Vincent 1834, 81: Éparchie de Mistra, Longaniko; Leake 1846, map: Longanikos; Sfikopoulos 1987, 386–387; Bon 1969, 512; Souhleris 2001–2.
Notes:	< **Lǫgovnik* (*Slav. n.* place in lush and dense forest) < lǫgъ (*Slav. n.* forest): Symeonidis 2010, I 838.

386. Ġurenas (غورناس), TT10, 145. GR

Coordinates:	X: 346409.063 Y: 4118847.773
Modern Greek:	Agoriani (Αγόριανη, η)
Regional Unit:	Laconia
Municipality:	Sparti
Municipal Unit:	Pellana
Bibliography:	Pikoulas 2001a, 57.258; Panagiotopoulos 1987, 284, 308.20: Territorio di Mistra, Agoriani; Pacifico 1704, 132: Territorio di Mistrà, Apriani; Hopf 1873, 202: Gurenes; Bory de Saint-Vincent 1834, 81: Éparchie de Mistra, Agoriani; Leake 1846, map: Agoriani, 165.
Notes:	Cf. Bon's Gueraines, which should be sought though in the region of Kalavryta (no. 1), Bon 1969, 396. < **(O)gorjane* (*Slav. n. pl.* residents of a mountainous area): Vasmer 1941, 102–103. Place name Gorjani in Serbia and Croatia, Gorjane in Slovenia, Gorany, Gorzany and Zagorzany in Poland: Symeonidis 2010, I 206.

387. Ḳoçiça (قوچيچه), TT10, 145. GR

Coordinates:	X: 345221.482 Y: 4119911.163
Modern Greek:	Kotitsa (Κοτίτσα, η)

Regional Unit:	Laconia
Municipality:	Sparti
Municipal Unit:	Pellana
Bibliography:	PIKOULAS 2001a, 221.1823; PANAGIOTOPOULOS 1987, 283, 308.12: Territorio di Mistra, Cotizza; PACIFICO 1704, 132: Territorio di Mistrà, Cotizza; EXPÉDITION 1832: Palæo Kotitsa; SKIADAS 1993, 382: Κόνιτσα, η; SOUHLERIS 2000.
Notes:	Sauerwein erroneously identified Pacifico's Cotizza with Goritsa (Γκοριτσά, η): SAUERWEIN 1969, *Ortsverzeichnis*, Territorio di Mistrà, 8. According to Vasmer, < kotьcь (*old Slav. n.* dwelling, cabin): VASMER 1941, 169.

388. İksifya (اکسفیه), TT10, 146. AL

Notes:	Unidentified. Ξιφίας (*Byz. sn.*). Cf. Xifias (Ξιφιάς, ο) in south-eastern Laconia.

389. Yani Ẕyavoliçi (یانی ذیاوولیچی), TT10, 146. AL

Coordinates:	X: 319588.807 Y: 4129820.375
Modern Greek:	Diavolitsi (Διαβολίτσι, το)
Regional Unit:	Messenia
Municipality:	Oihalia
Municipal Unit:	Andania
Bibliography:	PIKOULAS 2001a, 135.999; PANAGIOTOPOULOS 1987, 258, 298.62: Territorio d'Andrussa, Diavoglici; PACIFICO 1704, 127: Territorio d'Andrussa, Diauolizzi; BORY DE SAINT-VINCENT 1834, 69: Éparchie d'Emblakika, Diavolitsi; LEAKE 1846, map: Dhiavolitzi; GEORGACAS–MCDONALD 1968, 131.
Notes:	Γιάννης < Ιωάννης (*Gr. pn.* John). Διαβολίτζης (*Byz. Gr. sn.*).

390. Marti Helmi (مارتی هلمی), TT10, 146. AL

Notes:	Unidentified. Cf. Helmos (Χελμός, ο) peak to the south-east of Skortsinos [Σκορτσινός, ο (= Σκορτσινού, του)] in Arcadia. For Marti see no. 21. Χέλμης (*Arv. sn.*) < helm (*Al. n.* poison): BIRIS 1998, 203.

391. Yani Evzenati (یانی اوزناتی), TT10, 147. AL

Notes:	Unidentified. Cf. microtoponym Evgeni (Ευγένη, του) to the south-east of Stemnitsa (Στεμνίτσα, η) in Arcadia. For Yani see no. 389.

392. Aleksi Manesi (الکسی مانسی), TT10, 147. AL

Coordinates:	X: 364224.868 Y: 4142753.442

Modern Greek:	Psili Vrysi (?) (Ψηλή Βρύση, η)
Old Toponym:	Until 1927: Manesi (Μάνεσι, το)
Regional Unit:	Arcadia
Municipality:	Tripoli
Municipal Unit:	Tegea
Bibliography:	Pikoulas 2001a, 493.4464; Panagiotopoulos 1987, 244, 293.39: Territorio di Tripolizza, Manessi; Pacifico 1704, 120: Territorio di Tripolizza, Manessi; Bory de Saint-Vincent 1834, 93: Éparchie de Tripolitsa, Manési; Leake 1846, map: Manesi; Skiadas 1993, 305.
Notes:	Αλέξης or Αλέξιος (*Gr. pn.* Alex). For Manesi see no. 22.

393. Yorgi Maji (یورکی ماژی), TT10, 147. AL

Notes:	Unidentified. Γιώργης, Γιωργής or Γιώργος < Γεώργιος (*Gr. pn.* George). For Maji see no. 129.

394. Yani Lata (یانی لاته), TT10, 148. AL

Notes:	Unidentified. For Yani see no. 389. latë (*Al. n.* hatchet).

395. Niḳola Maḳrişa (نیقولا ماقریشه), TT10, 148. AL

Coordinates:	X: 337644.047 Y: 4141584.474
Modern Greek:	Kato Makrysi (?) (Κάτω Μακρύσι, το)
Regional Unit:	Arcadia
Municipality:	Megalopoli
Municipal Unit:	Megalopoli
Bibliography:	Pikoulas 2001a, 270.2290.
Notes:	Different from Makrysi (Μακρύσι, το), whose old name was Sialesi (Σιάλεσι, το). Its exact location is unknown. For Niḳola see no. 39, and for Maḳrişa see no. 337.

396. Marti Plaşa (مارتی پلاشه), TT10, 148. AL

Notes:	Unidentified. For Marti see no. 21, and for Plaşa see no. 14.

397. Domaniḳa Beluşi (دومانیقه بلوشی), TT10, 149. AL

Coordinates:	X: 346482.898 Y: 4146707.763

Modern Greek:	Belousia (?) (Μπελούσια, τα)
Regional Unit:	Arcadia
Municipality:	Tripoli
Municipal Unit:	Valtetsi
Bibliography:	Pikoulas 1988, 53.
Notes:	Uninhabited location to the north-west of Dorizas (no. 409). Domenika (*Al. pn.*) < Domenico (*It. pn.*). For Beluşi see no. 5.

398. Dimitri Maçuki (دیمتری ماچوکی), TT10, 149. AL

Notes:	Unidentified. Δημήτριος (*Gr. pn.* Demetrius) > Dhimitër or Dimitri (*Al. pn.*). Possibly from macukë (*Al. n.* shepherd's staff); ματσούκι (*Gr. n.* stick, baton) < mazzoca (*Ven. n.* stick): Bambiniotis 2002, 1057; Ματσούκης or Ματσούκας (*Gr. sn.*). See also maçok (*Al. n.* male cat, tomcat; sly and untrustworthy person).

399. Duḳa Plaşa (دوقه پلاشه), TT10, 149. AL

Notes:	Unidentified. < dukë (*Al. n.* duke) < δούκας (*Gr. n.* duke) or duca (*It. n.* duke): Meyer 1982, 77. For Plaşa see no. 14.

400. Miḫal Manesi (میخال مانسی), TT10, 149. AL

Coordinates:	X: 343060.044 Y: 4114942.574
Modern Greek:	Manesi (?) (Μάνεσι, το)
Regional Unit:	Arcadia
Municipality:	Megalopoli
Municipal Unit:	Falaisia
Bibliography:	GLET 1998, II 297; Leake 1846, map: Manesi.
Notes:	Uninhabited location to the south of Neohori (Νεοχώρι, το). Μιχάλης < Μιχαήλ (*Gr. pn.* Michael); Mihal (*Al. pn.* Michael). For Manesi see no. 22.

401. Miḫal Zora (میخال زوره), TT10, 149. AL

Coordinates:	X: 318807.616 Y: 4145826.198
Modern Greek:	Zoria (?) (Ζοριά, τα)
Regional Unit:	Messenia
Municipality:	Oihalia

Municipal Unit:	Eira
Bibliography:	Georgacas–McDonald 1968, 137.
Notes:	Microtoponym in Agios Sostis (Άγιος Σώστης, ο); its exact location is unknown. For Mih̯al see no. 400. Perhaps from zorrë (*Al. n.* intestine, bowel, hose).

402. Pavlo Doçi (پاولو دوچی), TT10, 150. AL

Notes:	Unidentified. The Τότσης surname occurs in Katsoura/Katzoura (Κατσούρα/Κατζούρα, του) today's Ano Vasiliko (Άνω Βασιλικό, το), Maliki (Μαλίκι, το) today's Polythea (Πολυθέα, η), and in minor villages to the north of Dorio (Δώριο, το) in Messenia. Παύλος (*Gr. pn.* Paul) > Pavllo (*Al. pn.*). doç or dobiç (*Al. n.* illegitimate child); Ndoçi (*Al. sn.*).

403. Mangişa Burlaşa (مانکشه بورلاشه), TT10, 150. AL

Notes:	Unidentified. For Mangişa see no. 267, and for Burlaşa see no. 125.

404. Yorgi Muzaki (یورکی مزاکی), TT10, 150. AL

Notes:	Unidentified. For Yorgi see no. 393, and for Muzaki see no. 380.

405. Ġulyamu Argiroplu (غولیامو ارکیروپلو), TT10, 150. AL

Notes:	Unidentified. The Αργυρόπουλος surname occurs in Konstantinoi (Κωνσταντίνοι, οι) in Messenia. Guliem (*Al. pn.* William). Αργυρόπουλος (*Gr. sn.*) < Αργύρης (*Gr. pn.* silver) + -όπουλος (*Gr. end.* son of).

406. Todoro Zupata (تودرو زوپاته), TT10, 151. AL

Coordinates:	X: 312594.318 Y: 4133110.561
Modern Greek:	Zoumbata (?) (Ζουμπάτα, του)
Regional Unit:	Messenia
Municipality:	Oihalia
Municipal Unit:	Dorio
Bibliography:	Georgacas–McDonald 1968, 361; Jochalas 2011, I 97.
Notes:	Microtoponym in Psari (Ψάρι, το); its exact location is unknown. For Todoro see no. 22. zhubetë (*Al. n.* wasteland, scrubland): Mann 1948, 588. Georgacas–McDonald proposed an etymology from zumbatë (*Arv. n.* axe) perhaps relating it to sopatë: Georgacas–McDonald 1968, 361. Finally, according to Vasmer, < zǫbatъ < zǫbъ (*Slav. n.* tooth, jag): Vasmer 1941, 134.

407. İlya Maji (الیا ماژی), TT10, 151. AL

Notes:	Unidentified. Ηλίας (*Gr. pn.* Elias, Elijah) > Ilia (*Al. pn.*). For Maji see no. 129.

408. Lazaro Zupata (لازآرو زوپاته), TT10, 151. AL

Coordinates:	X: 309273.405 Y: 4134193.374
Modern Greek:	Zoumbatiza (?) (Ζουμπάτιζα, η)
Regional Unit:	Messenia
Municipality:	Oihalia
Municipal Unit:	Dorio
Bibliography:	Georgacas–McDonald 1968, 361; Dokos 1977–84, 289: Ζηοπάτηζα.
Notes:	Microtoponym in Ano Dorio (Άνω Δώριο, το), perhaps related to Zoumbata (no. 406); its exact location is unknown. For Lazaro see no. 257. According to Georgacas–McDonald, zumbatëzë (*Arv. n.* little axe) < zumbatë + -zë (*Al. dim. end.*) (see no. 406): Georgacas–McDonald 1968, 361.

409. Petro Dorza (پترو دورزه), TT10, 151. AL

Coordinates:	X: 348888.051 Y: 4144497.108
Modern Greek:	Dorizas [Δόριζας, ο (= Ντόριζα, η)]
Regional Unit:	Arcadia
Municipality:	Tripoli
Municipal Unit:	Valtetsi
Bibliography:	Pikoulas 2001a, 139.1034; Panagiotopoulos 1987, 256, 297.45: Territorio di Leondari, Dorisa; Pacifico 1704, 128: Territorio di Leondari, Dorissa; Bory de Saint-Vincent 1834, 79: Éparchie de Léondari, Doriza; Leake 1846, map: Doriza.
Notes:	For Petro see no. 25, and for Dorza see no. 288.

410. Lala Z̲yavoliçi (لاله ذیاوولیچی), TT10, 151. AL

Notes:	Unidentified. Cf. Diavolitzi village (Διαβολίτζι, το) mentioned in the Methoni region in an enumeration of Messenian settlements dated 2 March 1829 and signed by the interim Commander of the Messenian Fortresses, F.K. Mavros: Reppas 2008–9, 522. Lalë (*Al. n.* brother; name of ancient inhabitants of Myzeqe; derisive term of address for poor Myzeqe villagers; according to the tradition, the inhabitants of this area were named by their ancestor and chieftain Lalë Muzhaqi; *colloq.* young father, daddy; elder brother; paternal uncle). Lala (*Al. sn.*); lala (*Arv. n.* uncle) attested in Argolis: Jochalas 2011, II 769. For Z̲yavoliçi see no. 389.

411. Ẕupano Buryalişa (ذوپانو بوريالشه), TT10, 152. AL

Notes:	Unidentified. For Ẕupano see no. 317, and for Buryalişa see no. 125.

412. Yani Jura (يانى ژوره), TT10, 152. AL

Notes:	Unidentified. For Yani see no. 389. Perhaps from zhurrë (*Al. n.* gravel, grit, coarse, sand, shingle) or zorrë (*Al. n.* intestine). Zhura is the Arbërisht name of Ginestra in Potenza, Italy. See also žura (*Scr. adj.* slim, short man). Žura (*Scr. sn.*) attested in Bribir, Croatia in the 17th c.: RHSJ 1975–76, XXIII 516.

413. Todoro Doşkesi (تودرو دوشكسى), TT10, 152. AL

Coordinates:	X: 322715.316 Y: 4124072.667
Modern Greek:	Toskesi (Τόσκεσι, το)
Regional Unit:	Messenia
Municipality:	Oihalia
Municipal Unit:	Oihalia
Bibliography:	Pikoulas 2001a, 453.4073; Panagiotopoulos 1987, 255, 297.17: Territorio di Leondari, Toschelli; Pacifico 1704, 128: Territorio di Leondari, Toschiesi; Bory de Saint-Vincent 1834, 79: Éparchie de Léondari, Toskesi; Leake 1846, map: Toskesi; Skiadas 1993, 348; Klados 1837, 247: Διοίκησις Μεσσηνίας, Ὑποδιοίκησις Μεσσήνης, Δῆμος Οἰχαλίας, Τόσκεσι; Politis 1915, 280–281.
Notes:	For Todoro see no. 22, and for Doşkesi see no. 90.

414. İstoya Volomiri (استويه ولوميرى), TT10, 152. AL

Coordinates:	X: 309396.884 Y: 4142372.801
Modern Greek:	Voliria/Voliries (?) (Βολιριά, η/Βολιριές, οι)
Regional Unit:	Elis
Municipality:	Zaharo
Municipal Unit:	Figaleia
Bibliography:	Georgacas–McDonald 1968, 115; Giannaropoulou 1979, 124–125.
Notes:	Microtoponym in Perivolia (Περιβόλια, τα); its exact location is unknown. Cf. place name Volymiri [today's microtoponym Volimiria (Βολιμίρια, τα) to the south-east of Agios Adrianos (Άγιος Αδριανός, ο) in Argolis] that the *Expédition* listed in Éparchie de Nauplie: Bory de Saint-Vincent 1834, 85. For İstoya see no. 328. Volomiri or Volimiri < Volimir (*Slav. pn.* peaceful will). valamir (*Arb. n.* producer of good quality oil).

415. Yani Mazaraki (یانی مزراکی), TT10, 152. AL

Coordinates:	X: 338132.198 Y: 4162327.430
Modern Greek:	Mazaraki (?) (Μαζαράκι, το)
Regional Unit:	Arcadia
Municipality:	Gortynia
Municipal Unit:	Vytina
Bibliography:	GLET 1998, II 281.
Notes:	Uninhabited location to the south-east of Elati (Ελάτη, η). For Yani see no. 389, and for Mazaraki see no. 308.

416. Niḳola Sirgi (نیقولا سرکی), TT10, 153. AL

Coordinates:	X: 314890.606 Y: 4137683.669
Modern Greek:	Syrrizo (Σύρριζο, το)
Old Toponym:	Until 1941: Sirtzi (Σίρτζι, το)
Regional Unit:	Messenia
Municipality:	Oihalia
Municipal Unit:	Eira
Bibliography:	Pikoulas 2001a, 445.3995; Panagiotopoulos 1987, 251, 295.65: Territorio d'Arcadia, Sirgi; Pacifico 1704, 131: Territorio d'Arcadia, Sirgi; Bory de Saint-Vincent 1834, 66: Éparchie d'Arkadia, Sirki; Leake 1830, I 485: Djirdje; Skiadas 1993, 360; Stamatelatos–Vamva-Stamatelatou 2001, 727; Georgacas–McDonald 1968, 250: Σίρτζι (Σίργκι).
Notes:	The locals called it Sirki (Σίρκι, το) until the 1960s. For Niḳola see no. 39.

417. Lazar Palunbi (لازار پالونبی), TT10, 153. AL

Coordinates:	X: 318660.671 Y: 4165401.729
Modern Greek:	Paloumba [Παλούμπα, η (= του)]
Regional Unit:	Arcadia
Municipality:	Gortynia
Municipal Unit:	Iraia
Bibliography:	Pikoulas 2001a, 360.3164; Panagiotopoulos 1987, 260, 299.60: Territorio di Caritena, Paluba; Pacifico 1704, 129: Territorio di Caritena, Palumba; Bory de Saint-Vincent 1834, 76: Éparchie de Karytæne Paloumba; Leake 1846, map: Palumba.

Notes:	For Lazar see no. 257, and for Palunbi see no. 43.

418. Yorgi Mujaki (یورکی مژاکی), TT10, 153. AL

Notes:	Unidentified. For Yorgi see no. 393, and for Mujaki see no. 96.

419. Andriya Pupuḳa (اندریه پوپوقه), TT10, 153. AL

Coordinates:	X: 311600.134 Y: 4092180.428
Modern Greek:	Boumboukas (?) (Μπούμπουκας, ο)
Regional Unit:	Messenia
Municipality:	Messini
Municipal Unit:	Petalidi
Bibliography:	Pikoulas 2001a, 331.2889; Skiadas 1993, 355; Georgacas–McDonald 1968, 208.
Notes:	Ανδρέας (*Gr. pn.* Andrew) > Andrea, Andrija or Andreja (*Al. pn.*). bubuqe or bubuk (*Arb. n.* bud). Place name Bubuq in Korçë, Albania. Meyer noted that bubuqe derives from pupak (*Slav. n.* bud) and not from **μπουμπουκιά* (*Gr.*), as the latter comes from βομβύκιον, βόμβυξ (*Gr. n.* silkworm): Meyer 1982, 50. Bambiniotis, on the other hand, supported the etymology from βόμβυξ: Bambiniotis 2002, 1147.

420. Yani Ḳanḳaẕi (یانی قنقاذی), TT10, 154. AL

Coordinates:	X: 305986.833 Y: 4087478.343
Modern Greek:	Kangadi (?) (Καγκάδη, του)
Regional Unit:	Messenia
Municipality:	Messini
Municipal Unit:	Petalidi
Bibliography:	Georgacas–McDonald 1968, 139; Pacifico 1704, 125: Territorio di Modon, Cangadi; Bory de Saint-Vincent 1834, 82: Éparchie de Modon, Kangandi.
Notes:	Microtoponym in Kokkino (Κόκκινο, το); its exact location is unknown. For Yani see no. 389, and for Ḳanḳaẕi see no. 203.

421. Lazaro Klesura (لازارو كلسوره), TT10, 154. AL

Coordinates:	X: 311940.847 Y: 4129856.573
Modern Greek:	Amfithea (Αμφιθέα, η)
Old Toponym:	Until 1940: Klesoura [Κλέσουρα, το (= του)]; until 1959: Kliesoura [Κλιέσουρα, το (= του)]

Regional Unit:	Messenia
Municipality:	Oihalia
Municipal Unit:	Dorio
Bibliography:	Pikoulas 2001a, 73.401; Panagiotopoulos 1987, 251, 295.60: Territorio d'Arcadia, Clessura; Pacifico 1704, 131: Territorio d'Arcadia, Clissura; Bory de Saint-Vincent 1834, 66: Éparchie d'Arkadia, Klisoura; Leake 1830, I 387, 484: Klisúra; Skiadas 1993, 360; Georgacas–McDonald 1968, 157, 313; Longnon–Topping 1969, 241.
Notes:	For Lazaro see no. 257. κλεισούρα (*Gr. n.* narrow mountainous pass). Procopius in *Περὶ Κτισμάτων* defined it as such: Procopius 1838, IV, 2, $271_{21\text{-}24}$: 'ὄρη δύο ἐπὶ μακρότατον ἀλλήλοιν ὡς ἀγχοτάτω ξυνίασι, στενωπὸν ἐν βραχεῖ ἀπεργαζόμενα τὴν μεταξὺ χώραν (Κλεισούρας νενομίκασι τὰ τοιαῦτα καλεῖν)'; > klysyrë and klisyrë (*Al. n.* mountain pass, gorge). Place name Klisurë and Këlcyrë in Gjirokastër, Albania.

422. Marti Çaşi (مارتی چاشی), TT10, 154. AL

Coordinates:	X: 320191.959 Y: 4140876.464
Modern Greek:	Tsasi (?) (Τσάση, του)
Regional Unit:	Arcadia
Municipality:	Megalopoli
Municipal Unit:	Megalopoli
Bibliography:	GLET 1998, III 375.
Notes:	Hydronym to the north-west of Lykosoura (Λυκόσουρα, η). Cf. microtoponym Tsasi (Τσάση, του) in the surroundings of Agnanti (Αγνάντι, το) in Messenia: Georgacas–McDonald 1968, 270; microtoponym Tzasi t' ambeli (Τζάση τ' αμπέλι, του) in Messenia: Vagiakakos 1991, 505. For Marti see no. 21. Τζάσις (*Byz. Gr. sn.* title similar to τζαούσιος) attested in an inscription (AD 1331–1332) of Agios Georgios ton Stefanopoulon (Άγιος Γεώργιος των Στεφανοπούλων) church in Oitylo (Οίτυλο, το), Laconia: Avramea 1974.

423. Ḳokino Marti (قوكنو مارتی), TT10, 154. AL

Coordinates:	X: 322290.105 Y: 4137090.249
Modern Greek:	Kokkino Diaselo (?) (Κόκκινο Διάσελο, το)
Regional Unit:	Arcadia
Municipality:	Megalopoli
Municipal Unit:	Megalopoli
Bibliography:	GLET 1998, II 107.

Notes:	Uninhabited location to the north-east of Vastas (Βάστας, ο). Cf. microtoponym Kokkinia (Κοκκινιά, η) to the south-east of Diavolitsi (no. 389). Κόκκινος (*Gr. sn.* red). For Marti see no. 21.

424. Barbuçi (بربوچی), TT10, 155. AL

Coordinates:	X: 348708.808 Y: 4138622.294
Modern Greek:	Ambelaki (?) (Αμπελάκι, το)
Old Toponym:	Until 1928: Barbitsa (Μπαρμπίτσα, η)
Regional Unit:	Arcadia
Municipality:	Tripoli
Municipal Unit:	Valtetsi
Bibliography:	Pikoulas 2001a, 70.376; Bory de Saint-Vincent 1834, 81: Éparchie de Mistra, Barbitsa; Leake 1830, III 24, 31, 33, 40, 43: Barbítza (Eutæa); Skiadas 1993, 298; Stamatelatos–Vamva-Stamatelatou 2001, 66.
Notes:	Perhaps from bar buçi (*Al. n.* snake-grass, *Ceterach officinarum*). See also barbuzza (*It. n.* kind of casque).

425. Ḫırisoviryi Ḳozma (خرسوويريي قزما), TT10, 155. AL

Coordinates:	X: 318113.726 Y: 4163318.192
Modern Greek:	Kosma (Κοσμά, σ/του)
Regional Unit:	Arcadia
Municipality:	Gortynia
Municipal Unit:	Iraia
Notes:	Uninhabited location to the south of Paloumba (no. 417). The locals reported scattered ceramics in the place. Χρυσοβέργης [*Gr. sn.* (person) holding a golden baguette, stick]. Κοσμάς (*Gr. pn.*) > Kozma (*Al. pn.*).

426. Trima İşpata (ترما اشپاته), TT10, 155. AL

Notes:	Unidentified. trim (*Al. n.* armed guard, warrior; *adj.* brave, heroic). For İşpata see no. 241. trima të shpatës (*Al. phr.* brave swordmen, *sing.* trim i shpatës).

427. Ẕima Rala (ذيمه رآله), TT10, 155. AL

Coordinates:	X: 303832.349 Y: 4135807.122
Modern Greek:	Ralia (?) (Ράλια, του)
Regional Unit:	Messenia

Municipality:	Trifylia
Municipal Unit:	Avlonas
Bibliography:	GEORGACAS–MCDONALD 1968, 241.
Notes:	Microtoponym between Avlonas (Αυλώνας, ο) and Sidirokastro (Σιδηρόκαστρο, το); its exact location is unknown. For Z̲ima see no. 14. Perhaps linked to i rrallë (*Al. adj.* sparse, sporadic). Ράλλης (*Gr. sn.*).

428. Yani Dara (یانی دآره), TT10, 155. AL

Coordinates:	X: 299590.085 Y: 4121654.765
Modern Greek:	Daras (Δάρας, ο)
Regional Unit:	Messenia
Municipality:	Trifylia
Municipal Unit:	Tripyla
Bibliography:	PIKOULAS 2001a, 129.941; PANAGIOTOPOULOS 1987, 250, 295.35: Territorio d'Arcadia, Darra; BORY DE SAINT-VINCENT 1834, 66: Éparchie d'Arkadia, Dara.
Notes:	For Yani see no. 389, and for Dara see no. 32.

429. Yorgi Manesi (یورکی مانسی), TT10, 156. AL

Notes:	Unidentified. For Yorgi see no. 393, and for Manesi see no. 22.

430. Gin Ḳondostavlo Manesi (کین قوندستاولو مانسی), TT10, 156. AL

Coordinates:	X: 313019.028 Y: 4106091.830
Modern Greek:	Manesis (?) (Μάνεσης, ο)
Regional Unit:	Messenia
Municipality:	Messini
Municipal Unit:	Aristomenis
Bibliography:	PIKOULAS 2001a, 272.2314; BORY DE SAINT-VINCENT 1834, 78: Éparchie de Koron, Manési; LEAKE 1846, map: Manesi; REPPAS 2008–9, 524.
Notes:	Gjin (*Al. pn.* John). Γκίνης (*Arv. sn.*): BIRIS 1998, 193. κοντόσταβλος, κοντοστάβλος, κοντοστάβλης, κονοστάβλος, or κονοσταῦλος (*Byz. Gr. n.* military leader; high dignitary, chamberlain; officer third in military rank after *protostrator* and *megas stratopedarches*) < comes stabuli (*Lat. phr.* count of the stable): KRIARAS 1982, VIII 253–254, 266; KAZHDAN 1991, II 1147. In the hierarchy of the Latin Empire of Constantinople the title was recorded as constabularies: HENDRICKX 1970, 110–111. For Manesi see no. 22.

431. Lazaro Ḳuveli (لآزارو قوولی), TT10, 156. AL

Coordinates:	X: 312072.408 Y: 4138265.187
Modern Greek:	Kouvelas [Κούβελας, ο (= Κούβελα/Κουβέλα, του)]
Regional Unit:	Messenia
Municipality:	Oihalia
Municipal Unit:	Dorio
Bibliography:	PIKOULAS 2001a, 223.1840; PANAGIOTOPOULOS 1987, 227, 251, 295.66: Territorio d'Arcadia, Cuvel(l)a; PACIFICO 1704, 131: Territorio d'Arcadia, Cuuelia; BORY DE SAINT-VINCENT 1834, 66: Éparchie d'Arkadia, Kouvéla; LEAKE 1846, map: Kuvela; SKIADAS 1993, 360; GEORGACAS–MCDONALD 1968, 165.
Notes:	For Lazaro see no. 257. kuvellë (*Arv. n.* weight appr. 3kg): MANN 1948, 232; kuvele (*Arb. n.* hollow, lair, den, hole). According to Iliopoulos, < κουβέλ(λ)ι (*Gr. n.* beehive; unit of measurement for grain of appr. 50 *oḳḳa*s) < κυβέλλι(ον): ILIOPOULOS 1948, 200. Κούβελας (*Gr. sn.* beehive maker, apiarist): SYMEONIDIS 2010, I 741.

432. Velize (ولیزه), TT10, 156. AL

Coordinates:	X: 295962.574 Y: 4171942.988
Modern Greek:	Pefkes (?) (Πεύκες, οι)
Old Toponym:	Until 1928: Vyliza/Velitsa (Βύλιζα/Βέλιτσα, η)
Regional Unit:	Elis
Municipality:	Arhaia Olympia
Municipal Unit:	Arhaia Olympia
Bibliography:	PIKOULAS 2001a, 380.3356; BORY DE SAINT-VINCENT 1834, 71: Éparchie de Gastouni, Viliza; LEAKE 1846, map: Vilizá; LONGNON–TOPPING 1969, 239; BON 1969, 341; SKIADAS 1993, 253; STAMATELATOS–VAMVA-STAMATELATOU 2001, 618; ILIOPOULOS 1948, 176.
Notes:	According to Vasmer, Velitsa derives from **Bělica* < bělъ (*Slav. adj.* white); however, the ending -za should be Albanian: -zë: VASMER 1941, 314. Symeonidis proposed an etymology from **Veliča* < **velikъ* (*Slav. adj.* big, large): SYMEONIDIS 2010, I 348; place name Wieliczka in Poland. The place name Velitsa belongs to the Slavic toponymic stratum, which preceded the Albanian one in the Peloponnese.

433. Maḳrisa Ustruza (ماقریسه اوستروزه), TT10, 157. AL

Coordinates:	X: 318997.942 Y: 4159403.137
Modern Greek:	Rizospilia (Ριζοσπηλιά, η)
Old Toponym:	Until 1928: Strouza (Στρούζα, η)
Regional Unit:	Arcadia

Municipality:	Gortynia
Municipal Unit:	Dimitsana
Bibliography:	Pikoulas 2001a, 407.3622; Panagiotopoulos 1987, 346.177: Strousa; Bory de Saint-Vincent 1834, 77: Éparchie de Karytæne, Apano/Kato Strouza; Leake 1846, map: Strouza; Skiadas 1993, 308: Στρούζαις; Stamatelatos–Vamva-Stamatelatou 2001, 665.
Notes:	For Maḳrisa see no. 337, and for Ustruza see no. 98.

434. Ẕimiçana (ذيميچانه), TT10, 157. GR

Coordinates:	X: 326765.028 Y: 4162520.442
Modern Greek:	Dimitsana (Δημητσάνα, η)
Regional Unit:	Arcadia
Municipality:	Gortynia
Municipal Unit:	Dimitsana
Bibliography:	Pikoulas 2001a, 135.996; Panagiotopoulos 1987, 260, 299.70: Territorio di Caritena, Dimizana; Pacifico 1704, 128: Territorio di Caritena, Dimizana; Bory de Saint-Vincent 1834, 75: Éparchie de Karytæne, Dimitsana; Leake 1830, I 82, II 19, 22, 60, 63, III 125: Dhimitzána; Hopf 1873, 202: Dimizana vel Dimiza, 205: Limisana; Sfikopoulos 1987, 236; Gritsopoulos 1987–88; Konti 1985, 105–106.

435. Ḳoḳova (قوقوه), TT10, 159. GR

Coordinates:	X: 329969.696 Y: 4191308.338
Modern Greek:	Skotani (Σκοτάνη, η)
Old Toponym:	Until 1928: Kokova (Κόκοβα, η)
Regional Unit:	Achaia
Municipality:	Kalavryta
Municipal Unit:	Païoi
Bibliography:	Pikoulas 2001a, 425.3800; Panagiotopoulos 1987, 270, 303.97: Territorio di Callavritta, Cocova; Pacifico 1704, 122: Territorio di Calaurita, Cocora; Bory de Saint-Vincent 1834, 74: Éparchie de Kalavrita, Kokova; Leake 1846, map: Kokova; Bon 1969, 394, 396; Skiadas 1993, 240; Stamatelatos–Vamva-Stamatelatou 2001, 699.
Notes:	According to Vasmer, < Κοκός (*Gr. pn. dim.* of Νικόλαος) + -ova (*Slav. end.*): Vasmer 1941, 135.

436. Çarnuḫlu (چارنوخلو), TT10, 160. GR

Coordinates:	X: 327438.075 Y: 4192105.578
Modern Greek:	Pefko (Πεύκο, το)
Old Toponym:	Until 1955: Tsarouhli (Τσαρούχλι, το)

Regional Unit:	Achaia
Municipality:	Kalavryta
Municipal Unit:	Païoi
Bibliography:	PIKOULAS 2001a, 381.3363; PANAGIOTOPOULOS 1987, 269, 302.57: Territorio di Callavritta, Zarugli; PACIFICO 1704, 122: Territorio di Calaurita, Zarucli; BORY DE SAINT-VINCENT 1834, 74: Éparchie de Kalavrita, Tsaroukhli; LEAKE 1830, II 107: Tjarnalí/Τζαρναλί; LEAKE 1846, map: Tzarnali; SFIKOPOULOS 1987, 207; STAMATELATOS–VAMVA-STAMATELATOU 2001, 618.

437. İvrato Ḳuçi Ḳonbi S̱eḳra (اوراتو قوچی قنبی ثقره), *mezraʿa* in the vicinity of Çarnuḫlu, TT10, 160.

Notes:	Unidentified. Ευρετός, Βρετός (*Gr. n.* foundling: name commonly given by the Byzantines to a child when the latter was left by its parents in the streets to be found – and consequently baptised – by a stranger): KOUKOULES 1952, V Suppl. 39; LAIOU-THOMADAKIS 1977, 120; Βρετ(τ)ός (*Gr. sn.*). See also no. 451. For Ḳuçi see no. 186 and for Ḳonbi S̱eḳra see no. 219.

438. Ṭarpun (طرپون), 1/14662, 84. GR

Coordinates:	X: 323028.707 Y: 4142369.260
Modern Greek:	Lykaio (Λύκαιο, το)
Old Toponym:	Until 1928: Derbouni (Ντερμπούνι/Δερμπούνι, το)
Regional Unit:	Arcadia
Municipality:	Megalopoli
Municipal Unit:	Megalopoli
Bibliography:	PIKOULAS 2001a, 265.2239; PANAGIOTOPOULOS 1987, 255, 297.3: Territorio di Leondari, Derbugni; PACIFICO 1704, 128: Territorio di Leondari, Derbuni; BORY DE SAINT-VINCENT 1834, 79: Éparchie de Léondari, Terbouni; LEAKE 1846, map: Terbuni; SKIADAS 1993, 333; STAMATELATOS–VAMVA-STAMATELATOU 2001, 444.
Notes:	< **terbyni* (*Slav. n.* cleared land): SYMEONIDIS 2010, I 470. Place name Trebinje in Bosnia & Herzegovina, Třebíč in the Czech Republic.

439. Amuri (آموری), 1/14662, 84. GR

Coordinates:	X: 342114.511 Y: 4136117.713
Modern Greek:	Anemodouri (?) (Ανεμοδούρι, το)
Regional Unit:	Arcadia
Municipality:	Megalopoli
Municipal Unit:	Falaisia

Bibliography:	Pikoulas 2001a, 76.428; Pacifico 1704, 133: Territorio di Mistrà, Anemoduri; Bory de Saint-Vincent 1834, 76: Éparchie de Karytæne, Anémodouri; Leake 1846, map: Anemodhuri; Bon 1969, 423–425; Velissariou 1984.
Notes:	Cf. microtoponym Ammouri (Αμμούρι, το) in Halazoni (no. 378) and Mouzaki (no. 380): Georgacas–McDonald 1968, 101.

440. Veliġosti (وليغوستى), ***mezraʿa*** **in the vicinity of Londar, 1/14662, 84.**

Coordinates:	X: 333401.120 Y: 4132307.835
Modern Greek:	Veligosti (Βελιγοστή, η)
Old Toponym:	Until 1940: Samara (Σαμαρά, του)
Regional Unit:	Arcadia
Municipality:	Megalopoli
Municipal Unit:	Falaisia
Bibliography:	Pikoulas 2001a, 99.651; Panagiotopoulos 1987, 255, 297.39: Territorio di Leondari, Samarà; Bory de Saint-Vincent 1834, 79: Éparchie de Léondari, Samara; Pacifico 1704, 128: Territorio di Leondari, Samarà; Leake 1830, II 44, 297, 235: Samará; Leake 1846, 150: Veligósti, map: Samara (Cromi); Sfikopoulos 1987, 254–256; Velissariou 1984; Katrivanos 1960, 344–347; Bon 1969, 518–521; Zakythinos 1953, 157–158; Dragoumis 1921, 69–84; Kordosis 1986a, 107–108; Dokos 1977–84, 304: Βελήγοστη; Skiadas 1993, 334; Stamatelatos–Vamva-Stamatelatou 2001, 129.
Notes:	The inhabitants of Veligosti moved to Leontari (no. 382) at the end of the 13th / beginning of the 14th c., for the Greek Chronicle informs: Kalonaros 1989, 86_{2025}: 'εἰς χαμοβοῦνι ἐκοίτετον τὸ κάστρο ἐκεῖνο ἐτότε'. Its exact location is unknown; it should be sought in the vicinity of modern Samaras, where the Veligosti torrent flows into the Xerilas River (Ξερίλας, ο). < velii (*Slav. adj.* big, large) + gostь: Vasmer 1941, 150; Symeonidis 2010, I 347. Place name Velgošte in North Macedonia.

441. Aya Niḳola (آيه نيقولا), ***mezraʿa*** **in the vicinity of Amuri, 1/14662, 84.**

Coordinates:	X: 342221.461 Y: 4135171.859
Modern Greek:	Agios Nikolaos (Άγιος Νικόλαος, ο)
Regional Unit:	Arcadia
Municipality:	Megalopoli
Municipal Unit:	Falaisia
Bibliography:	GLET 1998, I 110; Pikoulas 1988, 102–103.
Notes:	A chapel of St Nicholas is located to the south of Anemodouri (no. 439).

442. Pavla (پاولا), 1/14662, 85. GR

Coordinates:	X: 335453.441 Y: 4150505.089
Modern Greek:	Pavlia (Παύλια, η)
Regional Unit:	Arcadia
Municipality:	Gortynia
Municipal Unit:	Trikolona
Bibliography:	Pikoulas 2001a, 371.3277; Panagiotopoulos 1987, 259, 298.19, Territorio di Caritena, Pavlia; Pacifico 1704, 129: Territorio di Caritena, Paulia; Bory de Saint-Vincent 1834, 77: Éparchie de Karytæne, Pavlia; Leake 1846, map: Pavlia.

11. District of Ḳoris̱os (Korinthos) (Maps 21–22)

443. Ḳoris̱os, nefs-i (قوريثوس), TT10, 161. GR

Coordinates:	X: 405755.210 Y: 4199145.017
Modern Greek:	Korinthos (Κόρινθος, η)
Regional Unit:	Corinthia
Municipality:	Korinthos
Municipal Unit:	Korinthos
Bibliography:	Pikoulas 2001a, 219.1800; Panagiotopoulos 1987, 242, 291.100: Territorio di Corinto, Fortezza di Corinto; Pacifico 1704, 118: Territorio di Corintho, Corintho città; Hopf 1873, 205: Coranto; Bory de Saint-Vincent 1834, 67: Éparchie de Corinthe, Corinthe; Leake 1830, III 229–284: Corinth; Leake 1846, map: Korintho; Kordosis 1981b, 228–239; Sfikopoulos 1987, 67–75; Kordosis 1986b, 49–54; Longnon–Topping 1969, 255–256; Bon 1969, 473–478; Vagiakakos 1975, 76–80; Andrews 2006, 135–145.

444. Vaṣılıḳa (وآصلقه), TT10, 167. GR

Coordinates:	X: 387744.801 Y: 4204230.514
Modern Greek:	Sikyona (Σικυώνα, η)
Old Toponym:	Until 1928: Vasiliko (Βασιλικό, το)
Regional Unit:	Corinthia
Municipality:	Sikyona
Municipal Unit:	Sikyona

Bibliography:	Pikoulas 2001a, 420.3748; Pacifico 1704, 118: Territorio di Corintho, Vassilicò *olim Sicyon*; Kolokotronis 1981, 81, 105, 114, 118: Βασιλικά; Bory de Saint-Vincent 1834, 67: Éparchie de Corinthe, Vasilika; Leake 1830, III 226, 356: Vasiliká; Leake 1846, map: Vasilikó; Kordosis 1981b, 196–203; Sfikopoulos 1987, 80; Hopf 1873, 202, 205: Vasilica sivè Valica; Longnon–Topping 1969, 256; Bon 1969, 481–482; Skiadas 1993, 289; Stamatelatos–Vamva-Stamatelatou 2001, 689; Politis 1915, 532.

445. Ḳuvara (قوواره), *mezraʿa* in the vicinity of Vaşıliḳa, TT10, 168.

Bibliography:	Kordosis 1981b, 240; Lambros 1896, 163.
Notes:	Unidentified.

446. Ayo Vaşıl/Çağıl Ḥiṣārı (آيو وآصل/چاغل حصارى), TT10, 168. GR

Coordinates:	X: 394216.042 Y: 4183428.947
Modern Greek:	Agios Vasileios (Άγιος Βασίλειος, ο)
Regional Unit:	Corinthia
Municipality:	Korinthos
Municipal Unit:	Tenea
Bibliography:	Pikoulas 2001a, 43.117; Panagiotopoulos 1987, 242, 292.85: Territorio di Corinto, S. Basillis; Pacifico 1704, 118: Territorio di Corintho, San Vassili; Bory de Saint-Vincent 1834, 67: Éparchie de Corinthe, Hagios Vasilios; Leake 1846, map: A. Vasilios; Hopf 1873, 205: S. Vassili; Kordosis 1981b, 173–176; Sfikopoulos 1987, 81–83; Longnon–Topping 1969, 257; Bon 1969, 483–484, 635–637.
Notes:	This is the only place name in the TT10-1/14662 mentioned in Turkish. Çağıl Hisarı (*Tr. phr.* citadel where the babbling sound of running water is heard): Kadrî 1928, II 384. The ruins of an aqueduct nearby justify the appellation. Rangavis mentioned a stream: Rangavis 1853, II 380: ῥύαξ μικρός, χρήσιμος' by the settlement. Place name Çağıl in Çorum and Gümüşhane, Çağılardı in Çorum, Çağılcaveran in Sivas, Çağıllar in Manisa and Çağıllı in Sivas, Turkey: TMYK 1946, I 219; Gülensoy 1995, 10. According to the *Yeni Tarama Sözlüğü*, çağıl could also be a variant of çakıl (*Tr. n.* pebble, small stone): Dilgîn 1983, 48; in that case, the toponym may refer to the castle's stonework.

447. Petro Ḫayḳal (پترو خايقال), *mezraʿa* in the vicinity of Ayo Vaşıl, TT10, 170.

Bibliography:	Kordosis 1981b, 251.
Notes:	Unidentified. For Petro see no. 25, and for Ḫayḳal see no. 91.

448. Manesi (مانسى), *mezraʿa* in the vicinity of Ayo Vaşıl, TT10, 170.

Bibliography:	Kordosis 1981b, 244.
Notes:	Unidentified. See no. 22.

449. Sermorini (سرمورينى), *mezraʿa* in the vicinity of Ayo Vaşıl, TT10, 170.

Bibliography: KORDOSIS 1981b, 260.

Notes: Unidentified.
Place name Sermarinovo/Tsarmarinovo (Σερμαρίνοβο/Τσαρμαρίνοβο, το) [today's Marina (Μαρίνα, η)] in Pella: VASMER 1941, 201; SYMEONIDIS 2010, II 1260.

450. Ḳalo İstemati (قالو استماتى), *mezraʿa* in the vicinity of Ayo Vaşıl, TT10, 170.

Bibliography: KORDOSIS 1981b, 215.

Notes: Unidentified.

451. Pulimeno Ḳondostavlo (پوليمنو قوندستاولو), TT10, 170. AL

Coordinates: X: 389777.308 Y: 4186526.831

Modern Greek: Arhaies Kleones (Αρχαίες Κλεωνές, οι)

Old Toponym: Until 1971: Kontostavlos (Κοντόσταβλος, ο)

Regional Unit: Corinthia

Municipality: Nemea

Municipal Unit: Nemea

Bibliography: PIKOULAS 2001a, 86.523; EXPÉDITION 1832: Kondo Stavlo; BORY DE SAINT-VINCENT 1834, 68: Éparchie de Corinthe, Kondostavlo; LEAKE 1846, map: Kondostavlo; SKIADAS 1993, 285; STAMATELATOS–VAMVA-STAMATELATOU 2001, 103; MILIARAKIS 1886, 169; KORDOSIS 1999; KORDOSIS 1981b, 227–228; VAGIAKAKOS 1975, 86.

Notes: πουλημένος (*Byz. Gr. pn.* sold). According to a Byzantine tradition, in case a family suffered from infant mortality, when a child was born, his parents would go in the streets crying: 'πουλῶ ἕνα παιδί/ἀρνάκι' (I am selling a child/sappy); the first person whom they met, 'bought' the baby and became his godfather naming him Ποῦλος, Πουλημένος, Ἀγοραστὸς or Βρετός: KOUKOULES 1952, V Suppl., 38–39; VAGIAKAKOS 1991, 501. For Ḳondostavlo see no. 430.

452. Piça (پيچا), *mezraʿa* in the vicinity of Pulimeno Ḳondostavlo, TT10, 170.

Notes: Unidentified. Different from Ano/Kato Pitsa (Ἄνω/Κάτω Πιτσά, τα), mentioned as Kalyvia tou Bitsa/Kato Bitsa (Καλύβια του Μπιτσά, τα/Κάτω Μπιτσά, του) by Miliarakis, in the Municipality of Xylokastro (Ξυλόκαστρο, το): MILIARAKIS 1886, 130.
Perhaps from **πιτσί* < **πιτύον* < πίτυς (*anc. Gr.* pine tree, *Pinus L.*): SYMEONIDIS 2010, II 1149–1150. Cf. Pitsa (Πιτσά, του/το), today's Sitohori (Σιτοχώρι, το) in Messenia: GEORGACAS–MCDONALD 1968, 234. picë (*Al. n.* little girl); pica (*Al. n.* pony, nag).

453. Buzbardi (بزباردى), TT10, 170. AL

Coordinates:	X: 391539.819 Y: 4188990.189
Modern Greek:	Velanidies (Βελανιδιές, οι)
Old Toponym:	Until 1927: Bouz(ou)bardi [Μπουζ(ου)μπάρδι, το]
Regional Unit:	Corinthia
Municipality:	Nemea
Municipal Unit:	Nemea
Bibliography:	GLET 1998, II 421; Pikoulas 2001a, 99.646; Bory de Saint-Vincent 1834, 67: Éparchie de Corinthe, Bousbardi; Kordosis 1981b, 245–246.
Notes:	Uninhabited location to the north-east of Arhaies Kleones (no. 451). See no. 339.

454. Ḫarkâ (خركا), TT10, 171. AL

Coordinates:	X: 387969.248 Y: 4193191.836
Modern Greek:	Halkeio (Χαλκείο, το)
Regional Unit:	Corinthia
Municipality:	Velo-Voha
Municipal Unit:	Voha
Bibliography:	Pikoulas 2001a, 477.4306; Pacifico 1704, 118: Territorio di Corintho, Calchi; Bory de Saint-Vincent 1834, 67: Éparchie de Corinthe, Khalki; Kordosis 1981b, 268–269.
Notes:	χαρκιός < χαλκοῦς (*anc. Gr. adj.* copper, made of copper); χαλκιάς < χαλκεὺς (*anc. Gr.* coppersmith): Symeonidis 2010, II 1427, 1433.

455. Ḳutala (قوتالا), TT10, 171. AL

Coordinates:	X: 398182.609 Y: 4187146.812
Modern Greek:	Koutalas [Κουταλάς, ο (= Κουταλά, του)]
Regional Unit:	Corinthia
Municipality:	Korinthos
Municipal Unit:	Tenea
Bibliography:	Pikoulas 2001a, 230.1908; Expédition 1832: Koutala; Miliarakis 1886, 168; Kordosis 1981b, 240.
Notes:	Κουταλάς (*Gr. sn.* spoon, ladle, scoop maker or merchant).

456. Ayonori (آيونورى), TT10, 171. GR

Coordinates:	X: 401022.056 Y: 4178746.371
Modern Greek:	Agionori (Αγιονόρι, το)
Regional Unit:	Corinthia
Municipality:	Korinthos
Municipal Unit:	Tenea
Bibliography:	Pikoulas 2001a, 41.98; Panagiotopoulos 1987, 242, 292.93: Territorio di Corinto, Agionori; Pacifico 1704, 118: Territorio di Corintho, Agio Nori; Bory de Saint-Vincent 1834, 67: Éparchie de Corinthe, Hagionori; Leake 1846, map: Aionori; Miliarakis 1886, 168; Kordosis 1988; Kordosis 1981b, 141–172; Oikonomou 1988, 271–272; Katsaros 2014; Longnon–Topping 1969, 257; Bon 1969, 483–484, 658–660.

457. İksarokastalya (اكساروقاستاليه), *mezra'a* in the vicinity of Ayonori, TT10, 172.

Coordinates:	X: 401696.390 Y: 4179473.206
Modern Greek:	Xerokastellia (Ξεροκαστελλιά, η)
Regional Unit:	Corinthia
Municipality:	Korinthos
Municipal Unit:	Tenea
Bibliography:	Kordosis 1981b, 143, 247; Oikonomou 1988, 277.
Notes:	Probably the name of a fortress – Kastraki (Καστράκι, το) – in the entrance of the Agionori mountainous pass. It is different from Xerokastelli (Ξεροκαστέλλι, το) fortress located 15km west of Nafplio in Argolis, mentioned as Sero Castelia in Hopf 1873, 205, and Sorcastella in Longnon–Topping 1969, 258; Bon 1969, 479, 485, 662; Buchon 1843a, 376–377; Sfikopoulos 1987, 116–117; Konti 1983, 195.

458. Likuresi (ليقورسى), TT10, 172. AL

Bibliography:	Kordosis 1981b, 244.
Notes:	Unidentified. Kordosis read Lykovrysi (Λυκόβρυση, η) and did not locate it. See no. 62.

459. Ḳlimandi (قليماندى), TT10, 172. AL

Coordinates:	X: 373658.336 Y: 4202032.781
Modern Greek:	Klimenti (Κλημέντι, το)

Regional Unit: Corinthia

Municipality: Sikyona

Municipal Unit: Sikyona

Bibliography: Pikoulas 2001a, 211.1723; Panagiotopoulos 1987, 242, 292.98: Territorio di Corinto, Climendi; Pacifico 1704, 118: Territorio di Corintho, Clemendi; Bory de Saint-Vincent 1834, 68: Éparchie de Corinthe, Klimendi; Leake 1846, map: Klimendi; Miliarakis 1886, 159; Kordosis 1981b, 226–227.

Notes: Κλημέντης (*Arv. sn.*): Biris 1998, 194; Kelmendi (*Al. sn.*) < Κλήμης (*Gr. pn.*) < Clemens (*Lat. pn.*). Kelmend (*Al. pln.* mountainous ethnographic region in north-western Albania).

460. Pulimeno Soyḳa (پولیمنو سویقه), TT10, 172. AL

Coordinates: X: 401981.147 Y: 4183160.337

Modern Greek: Soïka/Skopia (Σόικα/Σκοπιά, η)

Regional Unit: Corinthia

Municipality: Korinthos

Municipal Unit: Tenea

Bibliography: GLET 1998, III 265; Dokos 1971–74, 116: Σοηκα; Miliarakis 1886, 169; Kordosis 1981b, 262–263.

Notes: A dependency (*metochi*) of the Faneromenis/Koimiseos tis Theotokou Monastery (I.M. Φανερωμένης/Κοιμήσεως της Θεοτόκου, η), on an altitude of 385m between Hiliomodi (Χιλιομόδι, το) and Mt Agios Dimitrios Reitou (Όρος Αγίου Δημητρίου Ρειτού, το) – modern-day Mt Metohi (Βουνό Μετοχίου, το). The place is uninhabited today. For Pulimeno see no. 451. sojkë or sojak (*Al. n.* pocket-knife).

461. Fenari (فناری), TT10, 173. GR

Coordinates: X: 431466.435 Y: 4158841.662

Modern Greek: Ano Fanari (Άνω Φανάρι, το); Kato Fanari/Dryopi (Κάτω Φανάρι, το/Δρυόπη, η)

Old Toponym: Until 1928 Dryopi was called Kato Fanari and during 1928–1940, Ortholithi (Ορθολίθι, το).

Regional Unit: Piraeus (Nisoi)

Municipality: Troizinia

Municipal Unit: Troizina

Bibliography: Pikoulas 2001a, 468.4219, 144.1084; Panagiotopoulos 1987, 247, 294.12: Giurisdizione di Porto Porro, Fanari; Pacifico 1704, 119: Territorio di Corintho, Fanari; Bory de Saint-Vincent 1834, 67: Éparchie de Corinthe, Phanari Apano/Kato; Leake 1846, map: Ap./K. Fanari; Kordosis 1981b, 266; Stamatelatos–Vamva-Stamatelatou 2001, 202; Sfikopoulos 1987, 126–127; Bon 1969, 490.

462. Bardi (باردى), TT10, 173. AL

Coordinates:	X: 408600.474 Y: 4181057.625
Modern Greek:	Agios Ioannis (Άγιος Ιωάννης, ο)
Regional Unit:	Corinthia
Municipality:	Korinthos
Municipal Unit:	Saronikos
Bibliography:	Pikoulas 2001a, 50.184; Kordosis 1981b, 244–245.
Notes:	Settlement in the vicinity of Agios Ioannis. Cf. village Bardi (Μπάρδι, το) in Argolis. Bardhi (*Al. sn.*), Bardh (*Al. pn.*) < i bardhë (*Al. adj.* white). Μπάρδης (*Arv. sn.*): Biris 1998, 198.

463. Ḳunbaki (قونباكى), TT10, 173. AL

Bibliography:	Kordosis 1981b, 240.
Notes:	Unidentified.

464. Biçi (بچى), TT10, 174. AL

Notes:	Unidentified. Bici (*Al. sn.*); bic (*Al. n.* piglet; dog or other animal with a small body; *adj.* chubby, robust).

465. Ṣarakin (صراكن), TT10, 174. AL

Coordinates:	X: 409927.957 X: 4184544.781
Modern Greek:	Sarakinia (Σαρακηνιά, η)
Regional Unit:	Corinthia
Municipality:	Korinthos
Municipal Unit:	Saronikos
Bibliography:	GLET 1998, III 237; Kordosis 1981b, 259.
Notes:	Uninhabited location to the south-west of Ryto (Ρυτό, το). See no. 188.

466. Luḳa (لوقه), TT10, 174. AL

Coordinates:	X: 402750.540 Y: 4190708.213
Modern Greek:	Lefka (Λεύκα, η)
Regional Unit:	Corinthia

Municipality: Korinthos

Municipal Unit: Korinthos

Bibliography: Pikoulas 2001a, 252.2113; Pacifico 1704, 119: Territorio di Corintho, Lefco; Kordosis 1981b, 308; Skiadas 1993, 283.

Notes: See no. 108.

467. Laluḳa (لالوقه), TT10, 174. AL

Coordinates: X: 392536.964 Y: 4165007.893

Modern Greek: Laloukas (?) [Λάλουκας, ο (= Λάλουκα, του)]

Regional Unit: Argolis

Municipality: Argos-Mykines

Municipal Unit: Argos

Bibliography: Pikoulas 2001a, 246.2064; Pacifico 1704, 118: Territorio di Argo, Lalucca piccolo, Lalucca grande; Bory de Saint-Vincent 1834, 84: Éparchie de Nauplie, Lalouka; Leake 1846, map: Laluka; Miliarakis 1886, 41; Kordosis 1981b, 241.

Notes: Kordosis did not locate it.
Lalukë (*Al. pn.*) < Lalë (see no. 410): Zoto 2005, 231. According to Symeonidis, Lalko (*Al. pn. dim.* of Lala): Symeonidis 2010, I 800. According to Biris, Λαλούκας (*Arv. sn.*) < Λιας (*Gr. pn. dim.* of Ηλίας) + Λουκάς (*Gr. pn.* Lucas): Biris 1998, 196.

468. Frati (فراتی), TT10, 174. AL

Bibliography: Kordosis 1981b, 268.

Notes: Unidentified.
See no. 108.

469. Pisratu (پسراتو), TT10, 175. AL

Coordinates: X: 397207.371 Y: 4184715.042

Modern Greek: Pistratou (Πιστρατού, του)

Regional Unit: Corinthia

Municipality: Korinthos

Municipal Unit: Tenea

Bibliography: GLET 1998, III 121; Kordosis 1981b, 269.

Notes: Uninhabited location to the north-east of Agios Vasileios (no. 446).
Probably from επίστρατος [*Gr. n.* mobilised, reservist (army)].

470. Frosina (فرسينه), TT10, 175. AL

Coordinates:	X: 361166.977 Y: 4174666.942
Modern Greek:	Frousiouna [Φρουσιούνα, η (= Φρουσίνα)]
Regional Unit:	Argolis
Municipality:	Argos-Mykines
Municipal Unit:	Alea
Bibliography:	Pikoulas 2001a, 475.4292; Panagiotopoulos 1987, 242, 292.81: Territorio di Corinto, Frissina; Pacifico 1704, 118: Territorio di Corintho, Frissina; Expédition 1832: Phrosyna; Bory de Saint-Vincent 1834, 68: Éparchie de Corinthe, Phrosina; Leake 1846, map: Frosyna; Skiadas 1993, 266; Miliarakis 1886, 52; Kordosis 1981b, 268.
Notes:	Φροσύνας (*Arv. sn.*) < Ευφροσύνη (*Gr. pn.*): Biris 1998, 202. Frosina (*Al. pn.*). See also Symeonidis 2010, II 1417.

12. District of Balya Badra (Patra) (Maps 23–24)

471. Balya Badra (باليه بادره), TT10, 178.

Coordinates:	X: 301296.847 Y: 4234990.232
Modern Greek:	Patra (Πάτρα, η)
Regional Unit:	Achaia
Municipality:	Patra
Municipal Unit:	Patra
Bibliography:	Pikoulas 2001a, 371.3271; Panagiotopoulos 1987, 278, 306.100: Territorio di Patrasso, Città e Borgo [di Patrasso]; Pacifico 1704, 120: Territorio di Patrasso, Patrasso Città; Hopf 1873, 205: Patras; Bory de Saint-Vincent 1834, 86: Éparchie de Patras, Patras; Leake 1830, II 123–147: Patra (Patræ); Longnon–Topping 1969, 254; Bon 1969, 449–453, 670–674; Moutzali 1994; Andrews 2006, 116–129.
Notes:	The Balya Badra entry in the TT10-1/14662 does not include the town of Balya Badra (*nefs-i Balya Badra*) as expected.

472. Ṣaravali (صآرەوالى), TT10, 39. GR

Coordinates:	X: 303636.110 Y: 4229047.828
Modern Greek:	Saravali (Σαραβάλι, το)
Regional Unit:	Achaia
Municipality:	Patra
Municipal Unit:	Messatida

Bibliography:	Pikoulas 2001a, 415.3700; Panagiotopoulos 1987, 276, 305.20: Territorio di Patrasso, Saravali; Pacifico 1704, 120: Territorio di Patrasso, Saravali; Bory de Saint-Vincent 1834, 86: Éparchie de Patras, Saravali; Leake 1846, map: Saravali; Sfikopoulos 1987, 173–174; Hopf 1873, 202: Seravali, 205: Saravali; Bon 1969, 453–454.
Notes:	Saravalle (*It. sn.*): Symeonidis 2010, II 1243.

473. Lala Vizi (لاله ویزی), TT10, 178. AL

Coordinates:	X: 316551.269 Y: 4228251.112
Modern Greek:	Kalyvia Laliokosta (Καλύβια Λαλιοκώστα, τα)
Regional Unit:	Achaia
Municipality:	Aigialeia
Municipal Unit:	Erineos
Bibliography:	Pikoulas 2001a, 177.1395; Panagiotopoulos 1987, 276, 305.8: Territorio di Patrasso, Lalucosta; Pacifico 1704, 121: Territorio di Patrasso, Lalucosta; Bory de Saint-Vincent 1834, 86: Éparchie de Patras, Lalikosta; Leake 1846, map: Lalikosta; Triantafyllou 1995, I 1112.
Notes:	Probably Lala Vizi merged with Ḳoşta Ḫāṣṣ (no. 474) into Lalikosta. For Lala see no. 410. Possibly from vizi (*Arb. n.* poor crop); vizi (*Al. n.* kingfisher).

474. Ḳoşta Ḫāṣṣ (قوشته خاص), TT10, 178. AL

Coordinates:	X: 316649.525 Y: 4228257.451
Modern Greek:	Kalyvia Laliokosta (Καλύβια Λαλιοκώστα, τα)
Regional Unit:	Achaia
Municipality:	Aigialeia
Municipal Unit:	Erineos
Bibliography:	See no. 473.
Notes:	See no. 473. For Ḳoşta see no. 283. خاصّ (ḫāṣṣ) (*Ar. adj.* special; private; fief of high revenue).

475. Ranesi (رانسی), TT10, 178. AL

Notes:	Unidentified. See no. 43.

476. Si̱zereḳastro (سیذرەقاسترو/سیذەرەقاسترو), TT10, 178. GR

Coordinates:	X: 306878.307 Y: 4227084.120
Modern Greek:	Sidirokastro (Σιδηρόκαστρο, το)

Regional Unit:	Achaia
Municipality:	Patra
Municipal Unit:	Messatida
Bibliography:	Sfikopoulos 1987, 175–176; Expédition 1832: Sidero Kastron; Hopf 1873, 202: Sidero Castro, 205: Sidro Castro; Leake 1846, map: Sidhero K°; Bon 1969, 453–454.
Notes:	The ruins of the fortress are still visible today opposite Omblou Monastery (I.M. Ομπλού, η) across the Xeropotama River (Ξεροπόταμα, τα). The mountain of 697m is called Siderokastro.

477. Petro Ḳarava Klesura (پترو قراوه کلسوره), TT10, 179. AL

Coordinates:	X: 325931.006 Y: 4216214.726
Modern Greek:	Karava rahi (?) [Καραβά ράχη, η (= Karavas's ridge)]
Regional Unit:	Achaia
Municipality:	Kalavryta
Municipal Unit:	Kalavryta
Bibliography:	GLET 1998, II 20; Dokos 1971–74, 93: Καράβω.
Notes:	Uninhabited location to the south-east of Bosi (Μπόσι, το). The word Klesura indicates a mountainous pass. For Petro see no. 25. καραβάς (*Gr. n.* roadstead, anchorage; *sn.* skipper, shipowner) < καράβι (*Gr. n.* ship, boat) > karavë, karav (*Al. n.* ship, boat): Symeonidis 2010, I 629. For Klesura see no. 421.

478. Ayo Ẕimitri Liḳo Anbali (آیو ذیمتری لیقو انبالی), TT10, 179. AL

Notes:	Unidentified. Cf. Kalyvia Lykos (Καλύβια Λύκος, τα), which is listed among the villages of Patra in 1699, possibly identical to Kalyvia Porton (Καλύβια Πορτών, τα): Triantafyllou 1995, I 946. Άγιος Δημήτρης/Δημήτριος (*Gr. hag.* St Demetrius). λύκος (*Gr. n.* wolf, *Canis lupus*). αμπέλι (*Gr. n.* vineyard).

479. Dardesi (داردسی), TT10, 179. AL

Coordinates:	X: 297102.814 Y: 4221504.402
Modern Greek:	Agrapidokambos (?) (Αγραπιδόκαμπος, ο)
Regional Unit:	Achaia
Municipality:	Erymanthos
Municipal Unit:	Farres
Bibliography:	GLET 1998, I 132.

Notes:	Perhaps related to Agrapidokambos (Αγραπιδόκαμπος, ο) to the south of Stefani (Στεφάνη, η), since Albanian *dardhëz* is translated as *(αγρ)απιδιά* in Greek. dardhë (*Al. n.* pear); dardhëz (*Al. n.* kind of wild pear, *Pyrus sativa*). Place name Dardhë in Korçë, Dardhas in Fier and Korçë and Dardhëz(ë) in Elbasan, Albania.

480. Klesura (كلسوره), TT10, 179. AL

Notes:	Unidentified. See no. 421.

481. Pavloḳastro (پاولوقاسترو), TT10, 179. GR

Coordinates:	X: 299100.175 Y: 4226178.777
Modern Greek:	Pavlokastro (Παυλόκαστρο, το)
Regional Unit:	Achaia
Municipality:	Patra
Municipal Unit:	Messatida
Bibliography:	Pikoulas 2001a, 371.3278; Panagiotopoulos 1987, 277, 306.63: Territorio di Patrasso, Pavlo Castro; Pacifico 1704, 120: Territorio di Patrasso, Paulo Castro; Expédition 1832: Pavlo Kastron; Bory de Saint-Vincent 1834, 87: Éparchie de Patras, Pavlokastron; Leake 1846, map: Pavlo Kastro; Hopf 1873, 202: Paleo Castro vel Paolo Castro, 205: Paulo Castro; Sfikopoulos 1987, 177; Bon 1969, 453–454; Koumousi 2007.

482. Vola (وولا), TT10, 180. AL

Coordinates:	X: 299431.062 Y: 4223136.732
Modern Greek:	Vola (Βόλα, η)
Regional Unit:	Achaia
Municipality:	Patra
Municipal Unit:	Messatida
Bibliography:	Pikoulas 2001a, 106.716; Panagiotopoulos 1987, 277, 306.65: Territorio di Patrasso, Volla; Pacifico 1704, 120: Territorio di Patrasso, Volla; Bory de Saint-Vincent 1834, 87: Éparchie de Patras, Vola; Leake 1846, map: Vola; Skiadas 1993, 222.
Notes:	volë (*Al. n.* mountain ash, *Sorbus*).

483. Patura (پاتوره), *mezraʿa* in the vicinity of Pavloḳastro, TT10, 180.

Notes:	Unidentified.

484. İstefano Mazaraki (استفانو مزراکی), TT10, 181. AL

Notes:	Unidentified. Στέφανος (*Gr. pn.* Stephen) > Stefan (*Al. pn.*). For Mazaraki see no. 308.

485. Ḳamaniça (قمانیچه), TT10, 181. GR

Coordinates:	X: 289974.520 Y: 4222844.578
Modern Greek:	Kamenitsa (Καμενίτσα, η)
Regional Unit:	Achaia
Municipality:	Dytiki Ahaïa
Municipal Unit:	Dymi
Bibliography:	PIKOULAS 2001a, 182.1442; PANAGIOTOPOULOS 1987, 277, 306.51: Territorio di Patrasso, Caminizza; PACIFICO 1704, 121: Territorio di Patrasso, Caminizza; HOPF 1873, 202: Camenizza vel Camomenizza, 205: Camemonia; BORY DE SAINT-VINCENT 1834, 86: Éparchie de Patras, Kaménitsa; LEAKE 1846, map: Kamenitza; SFIKOPOULOS 1987, 178; BON 1969, 454; TRIANTAFYLLOU 1995, I 949.
Notes:	See no. 82.

486. S̱eryanu (ثریانو), TT10, 182. AL

Coordinates:	X: 292143.825 Y: 4223494.854
Modern Greek:	Theriano (Θεριανό, το)
Regional Unit:	Achaia
Municipality:	Patra
Municipal Unit:	Vrahnaiika
Bibliography:	PIKOULAS 2001a, 160.1232; PANAGIOTOPOULOS 1987, 277, 306.51: Territorio di Patrasso, Terianù; PACIFICO 1704, 120: Territorio di Patrasso, Terianù; BORY DE SAINT-VINCENT 1834, 87: Éparchie de Patras, Thérianou; LEAKE 1846, map: Therianu; TRIANTAFYLLOU 1995, I 866–867: Θερειανοῦ, τοῦ.

487. Runbaḳa (رونباقه), TT10, 182. AL

Coordinates:	X: 294229.032 Y: 4221072.700
Modern Greek:	Roumbieka (?) (Ρουμπιέκα, η)
Regional Unit:	Achaia
Municipality:	Dytiki Ahaïa
Municipal Unit:	Olenia

Bibliography:	Triantafyllou 1995, II 1784; Dokos 1971–74, 96: Ρουμπιἕκα.
Notes:	Microtoponym in the vicinity of Palaia Peristera (Παλαιά Περιστέρα, η); its exact location is unknown. Perhaps from rrupaq (*Arb. n.* small oak tree, tangle of trees) < ρουπάκι < ῥώπαξ (*anc. Gr. n.* small acorn tree, *Quercus*): Katsouleas 1978, 355; Katsouleas 1979, 94. See also no. 656.

488. İzlatḳa (ازلاتقه), TT10, 182. AL

Notes:	Unidentified. See no. 202.

489. Çuḳala (چوقاله), TT10, 183. GR

Coordinates:	X: 294118.607 Y: 4223599.417
Modern Greek:	Tsoukala (Τσουκαλά, του)
Regional Unit:	Achaia
Municipality:	Patra
Municipal Unit:	Vrahnaiika
Bibliography:	Pikoulas 2001a, 465.4191; Panagiotopoulos 1987, 277, 306.76: Territorio di Patrasso, Zucalla; Pacifico 1704, 121: Territorio di Patrasso, Zucalà; Bory de Saint-Vincent 1834, 87: Éparchie de Patras, Tsoukala; Leake 1846, map: Tzokala; Expédition 1832: Tsoukala; Triantafyllou 1995, II 2127–2128; Skiadas 1993, 222.
Notes:	The old village was gradually abandoned in the second half of the 19th c. Its ruins are still visible in Paliohori/Tsoukala (Παλιοχώρι, το/Τσουκαλά, του).

490. Ribesi (ريبسى), TT10, 183. AL

Notes:	Unidentified. rrip (*Al. n.* belt, strap); rripë (*Al. n.* precipice, ravine; *adj.* very steep, precipitous). According to Sarris, Rimbes (Ρίμπες, name of a torrent on Mt Parnes, Attica) derives from rim (*Al. n.* rill): Sarris 1928, 137; the same, according to Fourikis, is a derivative form of remb or rëmb (*Al. n.* rill; creek): Fourikis 1929, 156. Cf. Ripesi (Ρίπεσι, το < Rripësi), today's Kefalovrysi (Κεφαλόβρυση, η) in Messenia: Jochalas 2011, I 96; cf. microtoponym Repesi [Ρέπεσι, το (= Ρέπεση, του)] in the surroundings of Ano Psari (Άνω Ψάρι, το) and Avlona (Αυλώνα, η) in Messenia, that derives from rrap (*Al. n.* oriental plane tree, *Platanus orientalis*): Georgacas–McDonald 1968, 344.

491. Meliġala (مليغاله), *mezraʿa* in the vicinity of Ḳamaniça, TT10, 183.

Notes:	Unidentified. Μελιγαλάς (*Byz. Gr. sn.*) < μελίγαλον or μελίγαλα (*Byz. Gr. n.* refreshment made with milk and honey): Vertsetis 1991, 113–117.

492. Liḳuresi (ليقورسى), *mezraʿa* in the vicinity of Ḳamaniça, TT10, 183.

Notes:	Unidentified. See no. 62.

493. Draġoti (دراغوتی), *mezraʿa* in the vicinity of Ḳamaniça, TT10, 183.

	Unidentified.
Notes:	Δαριγκότης (*Arv. sn.* lost tare): Biris 1998, 193; dragat (*Al. n.* field watchman); dragotës (*Al. n.* variety of fig). Place name Dragot in Elbasan and Gjirokastër, Albania: Kolleka 1983, 16. See also Dragota (*Scr. pn.*) < dragost (*Scr. n.* dearness, cuteness, affection, love): RHSJ 1884–86, II 753–755. Δραγώτης (*Gr. sn.*). Cf. microtoponym Drougouti (Δρουγούτι, το) to the east of Hiona (Χιόνα, η) in Achaia.

494. İksenoẕoḫiyo (اكسنوذوخيو), *mezraʿa* in the vicinity of Ḳamaniça, TT10, 183.

Coordinates:	X: 282274.525 Y: 4225740.061
Modern Greek:	Paralia Niforaiikon (Παραλία Νιφοραϊικων, η)
Regional Unit:	Achaia
Municipality:	Dytiki Ahaïa
Municipal Unit:	Dymi
Bibliography:	Pikoulas 2001a, 368.3246; Expédition 1832: Khani; Gell 1817, 24: Khan; Dodwell 1819, II 309–310: Khan of Palaio Achaia; Pouqueville 1826, IV 377–378: khan de Cato-Achaïa; Triantafyllou 1995, I 561.
Notes:	Uninhabited location to the south of Paralia Niforaiikon. The Greek toponym Xenodoheio (Ξενοδοχείο, το) refers to an inn or hotel that several travellers mentioned as *khan* (< ḫān, *Pers. n.* inn, caravansary) to the west of Palaia/Palaio Achaia, today's Kato Ahaïa (Κάτω Αχαΐα, η). Leake's travelogue reads: Leake 1830, II 159: 'From the village of Lower Akhaía there is an interval of 8 minutes to the khan of Seid Agá, which stands in the direct road at a small distance from the sea-side. It was lately built by the proprietor of the two Akhaíes to save the inhabitants from the expense of the Konáks'; Asvesta 2012, 305–307. The *Expédition* map locates it on the west bank of the Rethi Rivulet (Ρέθι, το), 3.3km to the north-west of Kato Akhaïa.

495. Ḳomi (قومی), *mezraʿa* in the vicinity of Ḳamaniça, TT10, 183.

Coordinates:	X: 294445.770 Y: 4214168.185
Modern Greek:	Komi (Κώμη, η)
Regional Unit:	Achaia
Municipality:	Dytiki Ahaïa
Municipal Unit:	Olenia
Bibliography:	Pikoulas 2001a, 241.2016; Panagiotopoulos 1987, 277, 306.48: Territorio di Patrasso, Comni; Pacifico 1704, 121: Territorio di Patrasso, Comi; Bory de Saint-Vincent 1834, 86: Éparchie de Patras, Komi; Leake 1846, map: Komi; Skiadas 1993, 225; Triantafyllou 1995, I 1033–1034.
Notes:	κώμη (*Gr. n.* town, township).

496. Ḳastriçi (قاستریچی), TT10, 183. GR

Coordinates:	X: 310436.098 Y: 4237901.053
Modern Greek:	Ano Kastritsi (Άνω Καστρίτσι, το)
Regional Unit:	Achaia
Municipality:	Patra
Municipal Unit:	Rio
Bibliography:	PIKOULAS 2001a, 198.1603; PANAGIOTOPOULOS 1987, 278, 306.84: Territorio di Patrasso, Castrici; PACIFICO 1704, 121: Territorio di Patrasso, Castrici; HOPF 1873, 205: Castrizzi; EXPÉDITION 1832: Kastritsa; BORY DE SAINT-VINCENT 1834, 86: Éparchie de Patras, Kastritsi; LEAKE 1846, map: Kastritza; BON 1969, 455; SKIADAS 1993, 222: Κάτω Καστρίτσι; TRIANTAFYLLOU 1995, I 999–1001.

497. Lihyana including the community of İpsari (لهیانه مع جماعت اپساری), TT10, 184. GR

Coordinates:	X: 308818.629 Y: 4239159.391
Modern Greek:	Lehaina (Λεχαινά, τα)
Old Toponym:	Lihina (Λιχινά, τα)
Regional Unit:	Achaia
Municipality:	Patra
Municipal Unit:	Rio
Bibliography:	TRIANTAFYLLOU 1995, I 1138.
Notes:	According to the documents published by Buchon, La Lichina and La Mandria were the two fiefs that the Acciaiuoli House had acquired in Achaia in 1324: BUCHON 1843b, II 33. Gerland identified Lichina with Lehen near Syhaina (no. 499): GERLAND 1903, 28, 277. According to Thomopoulos, Lihina (Λιχινά, τα) – pronounced as Lehaina (Λεχαινά, τα) in his times – formed a large allotment ½ hour uphill the Rio (Ρίο, το) railway towards the old road to Kastritsi (no. 496): THOMOPOULOS 1950, 316, note 1. See no. 208.

498. Vundeni (ووندنی), TT10, 184. GR

Coordinates:	X: 306302.424 Y: 4236410.132
Modern Greek:	Skioessa (Σκιόεσσα, η)
Old Toponym:	Until 1955: Vounteni (Βούντενη, η)
Regional Unit:	Achaia
Municipality:	Patra

Municipal Unit:	Patra
Bibliography:	Pikoulas 2001a, 424.3790; Panagiotopoulos 1987, 278, 306.99: Territorio di Patrasso, Vudeni; Pacifico 1704, 121: Territorio di Patrasso, Vodeni; Bory de Saint-Vincent 1834, 86: Éparchie de Patras, Voundéli; Leake 1846, map: Vundeli; Skiadas 1993, 222; Stamatelatos–Vamva-Stamatelatou 2001, 697; Triantafyllou 1995, I 344–345.
Notes:	< voden (*Slav. adj.* water, watery): Symeonidis 2010, I 378.

499. Ṣofyana (صوفيانه), TT10, 185. M

Coordinates:	X: 304754.335 Y: 4236569.094
Modern Greek:	Syhaina (Συχαινά, τα)
Regional Unit:	Achaia
Municipality:	Patra
Municipal Unit:	Patra
Bibliography:	Pikoulas 2001a, 445.3996; Panagiotopoulos 1987, 278, 306.95: Territorio di Patrasso, Sichena; Pacifico 1704, 121: Territorio di Patrasso, Sichienà; Bon 1969, 455–456: Souchiana; Bory de Saint-Vincent 1834, 86: Éparchie de Patras, Apano/Kato Skhéna; Leake 1830, III 209: Apáno/Kato Sykená; Skiadas 1993, 222: Επάνω/Κάτω Σχοινιά; Triantafyllou 1995, II 1965–1967.

500. Raḫova (راخوه), TT10, 185. GR

Coordinates:	X: 321061.180 Y: 4228531.314
Modern Greek:	Krini (Κρήνη, η)
Old Toponym:	Until 1940: Rahova (Ράχωβα, η); until 1955: Arahova Aigieon (Αράχωβα Αιγιέων, η)
Regional Unit:	Achaia
Municipality:	Aigialeia
Municipal Unit:	Sympoliteia
Bibliography:	Pikoulas 2001a, 235.1952; Panagiotopoulos 1987, 279, 307.29: Territorio di Vostizza, Aracova; Pacifico 1704, 121: Territorio di Patrasso, Aracoua; Bory de Saint-Vincent 1834, 93: Éparchie de Vostitsa, Arakhova; Leake 1846, map: Arákhova; Skiadas 1993, 228; Stamatelatos–Vamva-Stamatelatou 2001, 389; Dokos–Panagopoulos 1993, 15–16, 176–188: Aracoua.
Notes:	See also Arahova (Αράχοβα, η) to the south-east of Patra (no. 471), a village of 15 households and 54 inhabitants in 1851: Rangavis 1853, II 85. According to Triantafyllou, this village appeared in a Venetian enumeration of Patra's settlements as Ciracova; unfortunately, he did not cite his source: Triantafyllou 1995, I 236–237. See no. 76.

501. Buryalisa (بوريالسه), TT10, 186. AL

Notes:	Unidentified. See no. 125.

502. Çernota (چرنوتا), *mezra'a* in the vicinity of Buryalisa, TT10, 186.

Notes:	Unidentified. See no. 88.

503. İsḳura (اسقوره), TT10, 186. AL

Coordinates:	X: 302033.246 Y: 4227021.993
Modern Greek:	Skoura (Σκούρα, του)
Regional Unit:	Achaia
Municipality:	Patra
Municipal Unit:	Messatida
Bibliography:	PANAGIOTOPOULOS 1987, 276, 306.30: Territorio di Patrasso, Scura; PACIFICO 1704, 121: Territorio di Patrasso, Scura; BORY DE SAINT-VINCENT 1834, 86: Éparchie de Patras, Skoura; LEAKE 1846, map: Skoura; TRIANTAFYLLOU 1995, II 1864–1865.
Notes:	Settlement located on the *Expédition* map and Leake's map to the north-west of Gaïdouriari (Γαϊδουριάρη, του), modern Ano Kallithea (Άνω Καλλιθέα, η). The place is uninhabited today. According to the *Expédition*, the village numbered two families. Skoura (Σκούρα, η) in Tritaia was established in Ioannis Kapodistrias's times (1827–1831). Σκούρας (*Arv. sn.*): BIRIS 1998, 201. Skura and Skuraj (*Al. sn.*). Place name Skuraj in Lezhë, Albania.

504. Ḳurnaroḳastro (قورناروقاسترو), TT10, 186. GR

Coordinates:	X: 308348.297 Y: 4230852.266
Modern Greek:	Pournarokastro (Πουρναρόκαστρο, το)
Regional Unit:	Achaia
Municipality:	Patra
Municipal Unit:	Patra
Bibliography:	PIKOULAS 2001a, 395.3500; PANAGIOTOPOULOS 1987, 276, 305.19: Territorio di Patrasso, Cunaro Castro; PACIFICO 1704, 121: Territorio di Patrasso, Cuunaro-Castro; EXPÉDITION 1832: Pournaro Kastron; BORY DE SAINT-VINCENT 1834, 86: Éparchie de Patras, Pournarokastro; LEAKE 1846, map: Purnaro Kastro; SFIKOPOULOS 1987, 171–172; HOPF 1873, 202: Camero Castro vel Cumero Castro, 205: Curnaro Castro; BON 1969, 455; TRIANTAFYLLOU 1995, II 1705–1706.

505. Zastupا (زاستوپه), *mezraʿa* in the vicinity of Ḳurnaroḳastro, TT10, 187.

Coordinates:	X: 309057.264 Y: 4232276.652
Modern Greek:	Zastova (Ζάστοβα, η)
Regional Unit:	Achaia
Municipality:	Patra
Municipal Unit:	Patra
Bibliography:	Pikoulas 2001a, 154.1173; Bory de Saint-Vincent 1834, 87: Éparchie de Patras, Zastova; Skiadas 1993, 222; Triantafyllou 1995, I 813–814.
Notes:	Possibly from zastọръ (*old Slav. n.* protection, help). Place name Zastup in Serbia: RHSJ 1975, XXII 440–441.

506. Suli (سولی), TT10, 187. AL

Coordinates:	X: 308602.989 Y: 4227762.955
Modern Greek:	Souli (Σούλι, το)
Regional Unit:	Achaia
Municipality:	Patra
Municipal Unit:	Patra
Bibliography:	Pikoulas 2001a, 430.3848; Panagiotopoulos 1987, 276, 305.10: Territorio di Patrasso, Sulli; Pacifico 1704, 120: Territorio di Patrasso, Sulli; Bory de Saint-Vincent 1834, 86: Éparchie de Patras, Souli; Leake 1846, map: Suli; Skiadas 1993, 222; Triantafyllou 1995, II 1897–1898.
Notes:	Possibly the Castello dell Torre de Bosco refers to Souli: Sfikopoulos 1987, 174. See no. 37.

507. Topolova (توپولوه), TT10, 187. AL

Coordinates:	X: 309827.588 Y: 4222662.073
Modern Greek:	Agia Paraskevi (Αγία Παρασκευή, η)
Old Toponym:	Until 1955: Topolova (Τοπόλοβα, η)
Regional Unit:	Achaia
Municipality:	Patra
Municipal Unit:	Messatida
Bibliography:	Pikoulas 2001a, 37.60; Panagiotopoulos 1987, 276, 305.6: Territorio di Patrasso, Topolova; Pacifico 1704, 121: Territorio di Patrasso, Topolara; Expédition 1832: Topolova; Leake 1846, map: Topolova; Skiadas 1993, 222; Stamatelatos–Vamva-Stamatelatou 2001, 8; Triantafyllou 1995, II 2065–2066.

Notes:	< **Topolova* < topolov (*Scr. n.* poplar, *Populus*): Vasmer 1941, 139; Symeonidis 2010, II 1352. Place name Topolovo in Bulgaria, Topolovac in Serbia and Croatia and Topolovec in Slovenia.

508. Bardoḳosta (باردوقوسته), TT10, 187. AL

Coordinates:	X: 306770.266 Y: 4223847.861
Modern Greek:	Krystallovrysi (Κρυσταλλόβρυση, η)
Old Toponym:	Until 1940: Bardikosta (Μπαρδικώστα, του); until 1955: Bardikostas (Μπαρδικώστας, ο)
Regional Unit:	Achaia
Municipality:	Patra
Municipal Unit:	Messatida
Bibliography:	Pikoulas 2001a, 238.1983; Panagiotopoulos 1987, 276, 305.3: Territorio di Patrasso, Bardicosta; Pacifico 1704, 121: Territorio di Patrasso, Barducosta; Bory de Saint-Vincent 1834, 86: Éparchie de Patras, Bardikosta; Leake 1846, map: Bardikosta; Skiadas 1993, 226; Stamatelatos–Vamva-Stamatelatou 2001, 394; Triantafyllou 1995, II 1323–1324.
Notes:	< i bardhë (*Al. adj.* white) + Κώστας (*Gr. pn.*); Bardi (*Al. sn.*).

509. Tiristena (تيرستنه), 1/14662, 36. GR

Coordinates:	X: 295939.222 Y: 4223749.818
Modern Greek:	Stavros (Σταυρός, ο)
Old Toponym:	Until 1955: Drestena/Dresthena (Δρεστενά/Δρεσθενά, τα)
Regional Unit:	Achaia
Municipality:	Patra
Municipal Unit:	Vrahnaiika
Bibliography:	Pikoulas 2001a, 438.3928; Panagiotopoulos 1987, 277, 306.57: Territorio di Patrasso, Tristena; Pacifico 1704, 121: Territorio di Patrasso, Tristena; Bory de Saint-Vincent 1834, 87: Éparchie de Patras, Dresténa; Leake 1846, map: Drestena; Skiadas 1993, 222; Triantafyllou 1995, I 545–546.
Notes:	See no. 353.

13. District of Ḳalandriça (Halandritsa) (Maps 25–26)

510. Ḳalandriça, nefs-i (قلاندريجه), 1/14662, 4. GR

Coordinates:	X: 305556.850 Y: 4219705.427
Modern Greek:	Halandritsa (Χαλανδρίτσα, η)

Regional Unit:	Achaia
Municipality:	Erymanthos
Municipal Unit:	Farres
Bibliography:	PIKOULAS 2001a, 476.4302; PANAGIOTOPOULOS 1987, 277, 306.41: Territorio di Patrasso, Calandrizza; PACIFICO 1704, 120: Territorio di Patrasso, Callandrizza; BORY DE SAINT-VINCENT 1834, 86: Éparchie de Patras, Khalandritsa; LEAKE 1846, map: Khalandritza; SFIKOPOULOS 1987, 195; HOPF 1873, 202: Calendrizzo, 205: Calandrezza; LONGNON–TOPPING 1969, 255; BON 1969, 460–461; TRIANTAFYLLOU 1995, II 2223–2230.

511. Ḳazneş (قازنش), 1/14662, 7. AL

Coordinates:	X: 314789.418 Y: 4220962.492
Modern Greek:	Katsaïtaiika (Κατσαϊταίικα, τα)
Old Toponym:	Kaznesi/Kasnesi (Καζνέσι/Κασνέσι, το)
Regional Unit:	Achaia
Municipality:	Erymanthos
Municipal Unit:	Leontio
Bibliography:	PIKOULAS 2001a, 164.1270, 201.1627; PANAGIOTOPOULOS 1987, 276, 305.7: Territorio di Patrasso, Casenensi Trano; BORY DE SAINT-VINCENT 1834, 86: Éparchie de Patras, Kasnési; LEAKE 1846, map: Kasnesi; SKIADAS 1993, 226.
Notes:	Triantafyllou identified it with modern Katsaïtaiika: TRIANTAFYLLOU 1995, I 998. Panagiotopoulos's attempt to identify it with Katarraktis (no. 632) seems erroneous: PANAGIOTOPOULOS 1987, 305.7. See no. 57.

512. Ḳuçi (قوچی), 1/14662, 7. AL

Notes:	Unidentified. See no. 186.

513. Maji (ماژی), 1/14662, 7. AL

Coordinates:	X: 313967.022 Y: 4226353.580
Modern Greek:	Ereipia Maziou [Ερείπια Μαζίου, τα (= Mazi's ruins)]
Regional Unit:	Achaia
Municipality:	Patra
Municipal Unit:	Patra
Bibliography:	GLET 1998, II 282; TRIANTAFYLLOU 1995, II 1208.

Notes:	On the HMGS 1978, Pátrai map it is noted as an uninhabited location to the south-east of Souli (no. 506) downhill Makrya Lakka (Μακρυά Λάκκα, η) and Ovryokastro (Οβρυόκαστρο, το). The British map of 1944 and the German one of 1943 named it Mazi and Masi respectively, so it must have been a proper village then: GSGS 1944, Pátrai; Luftwaffe 1943, Tripolis. See no. 129.

514. Ġolemi (غولمی), 1/14662, 7. AL

Coordinates:	X: 295553.531 Y: 4207634.338
Modern Greek:	Golemi (Γολέμι, το)
Regional Unit:	Achaia
Municipality:	Erymanthos
Municipal Unit:	Tritaia
Bibliography:	Pikoulas 2001a, 124.892; Pacifico 1704, 121: Territorio di Patrasso, Golemi; Bory de Saint-Vincent 1834, 86: Éparchie de Patras, Golémi; Leake 1846, map: Vulemi; Triantafyllou 1995, I 443–444.
Notes:	See no. 30.

515. Rapsomati (راپسوماتی), 1/14662, 7. AL

Notes:	Unidentified. According to Symeonidis, < rrapësi (*Al. n.* place with plane trees, *Platanus orientalis*) + mat (*Al. n.* seacoast, river bank): Symeonidis 2010, II 1211–1212. See no. 309.

516. Lisarya (لساریه), 1/14662, 8. AL

Coordinates:	X: 301253.584 Y: 4221273.743
Modern Greek:	Kydonies (Κυδωνίες, οι)
Old Toponym:	Lyssaria (Λυσσαριά, η)
Regional Unit:	Achaia
Municipality:	Erymanthos
Municipal Unit:	Farres
Bibliography:	Pikoulas 2001a, 239.1989; Panagiotopoulos 1987, 276, 305.26: Territorio di Patrasso, Lisaria; Pacifico 1704, 120: Territorio di Patrasso, Lissaria; Bory de Saint-Vincent 1834, 86: Éparchie de Patras, Lysaria; Leake 1846, map: Lysaria; Bon 1969, 462–463; Dragoumis 1921, 242–243; Triantafyllou 1995, I 1197.
Notes:	< lisare (*Al. n.* oak grove) < lis (*Al. n.* oak, *Quercus*): Jochalas 1976, 319; Symeonidis 2010, I 854.

517. Bala (باله), 1/14662, 8. AL

Coordinates:	X: 307301.922 Y: 4236009.295
Modern Greek:	Balas (Μπάλας, ο)
Regional Unit:	Achaia
Municipality:	Patra
Municipal Unit:	Patra
Bibliography:	Pikoulas 2001a, 324.2822; Panagiotopoulos 1987, 278, 306.40: Territorio di Patrasso, Balla; Pacifico 1704, 121: Territorio di Patrasso, Balla; Bory de Saint-Vincent 1834, 86: Éparchie de Patras, Bala; Leake 1846, map: Bala; Triantafyllou 1995, II 1318.
Notes:	Μπάλας (*Arv. sn.*) < ballë (*Al. n.* forehead): Ginosatis 1988, 129; Bala (*Al. sn.*). Place name Bala in Kukës, Albania. According to Vasmer, an etymology from a *Slav.* Běla < bělъ (*Slav. adj.* white) cannot be proved with certainty: Vasmer 1941, 122, 136.

518. İş Ari (ایش اری), 1/14662, 9. AL

Coordinates:	X: 297728.182 Y: 4219117.777
Modern Greek:	Isoma (Ίσωμα, το)
Old Toponym:	Until 1928: Isari (Ίσαρι, το)
Regional Unit:	Achaia
Municipality:	Erymanthos
Municipal Unit:	Farres
Bibliography:	Pikoulas 2001a, 163.1256; Panagiotopoulos 1987, 277, 306.42: Territorio di Patrasso, Isari; Pacifico 1704, 121: Territorio di Patrasso, Issari; Bory de Saint-Vincent 1834, 86: Éparchie de Patras, Isari; Leake 1846, map: Ysari; Skiadas 1993, 226; Triantafyllou 1995, I 896–897.
Notes:	Possibly from ishari (*Al. n.* a fatal disease); ish *pl.* -ra (*Arb. n.* worm, woodworm that grows in wood or wheat).

519. Mazaraki (مزراکی), 1/14662, 9. AL

Coordinates:	X: 293738.748 Y: 4215969.834
Modern Greek:	Kato Mazaraki (Κάτω Μαζαράκι, το)
Regional Unit:	Achaia
Municipality:	Dytiki Ahaïa
Municipal Unit:	Olenia
Bibliography:	Pikoulas 2001a, 268.2272; Pacifico 1704, 121: Territorio di Patrasso, Massarachi.

Notes:	See no. 308.

520. Ḳral (قرال), 1/14662, 10. AL

Coordinates:	X: 290036.801 Y: 4218964.928
Modern Greek:	Agios Nikolaos (Άγιος Νικόλαος, ο)
Old Toponym:	Until 1940: Krali (Κράλη, του); until 1955: Krali (Κράλι, το)
Regional Unit:	Achaia
Municipality:	Dytiki Ahaïa
Municipal Unit:	Olenia
Bibliography:	Pikoulas 2001a, 54.230; Panagiotopoulos 1987, 277, 306.60: Territorio di Patrasso, Cragli; Pacifico 1704, 121: Territorio di Patrasso, Cralì; Bory de Saint-Vincent 1834, 87: Éparchie de Patras, Krali; Leake 1846, map: Krali; Skiadas 1993, 223; Stamatelatos–Vamva-Stamatelatou 2001, 29; Triantafyllou 1995, I 1069.
Notes:	< kraljь (*Slav. n.* king): Vasmer 1941, 135; Symeonidis 2010, I 766. Place name Kralje in Montenegro, Kralji in Serbia and Slovenia, Kralevo and Kraljovo in Bulgaria. According to Zoto, Kral (*Al. pn.*) < krale or kralë (*Al. n.* chicory, *Cichorium intybus L.*): Zoto 2005, 226.

521. Zoġa (زوغه), 1/14662, 10. AL

Coordinates:	X: 302230.265 Y: 4214674.824
Modern Greek:	Zogas (Ζώγας, ο)
Regional Unit:	Achaia
Municipality:	Erymanthos
Municipal Unit:	Farres
Bibliography:	Pikoulas 2001a, 158.1211; Panagiotopoulos 1987, 276, 305.12: Territorio di Patrasso, Zoga; Pacifico 1704, 121: Territorio di Patrasso, Cozza; Bory de Saint-Vincent 1834, 86: Éparchie de Patras, Zoga; Leake 1846, map: Zoga; Triantafyllou 1995, I 822.
Notes:	Zoga (*Al. sn.*); zog (*Al. n.* bird); zoge and zogë (*Arb. n.* bird, fowl).

522. Laluş (لالوش), 1/14662, 10. AL

Coordinates:	X: 302606.305 Y: 4214052.507
Modern Greek:	Ano Starohori (Άνω Σταροχώρι, το)
Old Toponym:	Until 1928: Lalousi (Λάλουσι, το); until 1940: Starohori (Σταροχώρι, το)
Regional Unit:	Achaia
Municipality:	Erymanthos

Municipal Unit:	Farres
Bibliography:	Pikoulas 2001a, 437.3914; Panagiotopoulos 1987, 276, 305.27: Territorio di Patrasso, Lallusi; Pacifico 1704, 121: Territorio di Patrasso, Lalussi; Bory de Saint-Vincent 1834, 86: Éparchie de Patras, Lalousi; Leake 1830, II 122: Lálusi/Lalúsia; Skiadas 1993, 226; Stamatelatos–Vamva-Stamatelatou 2001, 86; Triantafyllou 1995, I 1112–1113.
Notes:	Lalush or Lalosh (*Al. pn.*) < Lalë: Zoto 2005, 231. See nos 229, 410.

523. Virzaḫo (ورزاخو), 1/14662, 10. AL

Notes:	Unidentified.

14. District of Ṣandamiri (Santomeri) (Maps 27–28)

524. Ṣandamiri, nefs-i (صاندهمیری), 1/14662, 14. GR

Coordinates:	X: 286712.555 Y: 4206871.009
Modern Greek:	Santomeri [Σαντομέρι, το (= Σανταμέρι)]
Regional Unit:	Achaia
Municipality:	Dytiki Ahaïa
Municipal Unit:	Olenia
Bibliography:	Pikoulas 2001a, 415.3695; Panagiotopoulos 1987, 277, 306.66: Territorio di Patrasso, Sandamesi; Pacifico 1704, 120: Territorio di Patrasso, Sandameri; Expédition 1832: Santaméri; Bory de Saint-Vincent 1834, 86: Éparchie de Patras, Santa-Méri; Leake 1830, II 230–231: Sandaméri; Sfikopoulos 1987, 187–189; Hopf 1873, 202: Santameri vel Santomari, 205: S. Dameri; Longnon–Topping 1969, 236; Bon 1969, 646–648; Skiadas 1993, 225: Δ. Τριταίας; Triantafyllou 1995, II 1862–1864.
Notes:	According to Symeonidis, the etymology from *Fr.* anthroponym Saint-Omer may be based on a preceding Slavic toponym. Place name Sandomierz in Poland and Sudoměř in the Czech Republic < **Sǫdoměrъ*: Symeonidis 2010, II 1242. Vasmer had rejected this theory: Vasmer 1941, 138.

525. Porta (پورتا), 1/14662, 15. GR

Coordinates:	X: 286279.718 Y: 4201586.821
Modern Greek:	Portes (Πόρτες, οι)
Regional Unit:	Achaia
Municipality:	Dytiki Ahaïa
Municipal Unit:	Olenia

Bibliography:	Pikoulas 2001a, 392.3471; Panagiotopoulos 1987, 277, 306.46: Territorio di Patrasso, Portes; Pacifico 1704, 120: Territorio di Patrasso, Portes; Expédition 1832: Porta; Bory de Saint-Vincent 1834, 86: Éparchie de Patras, Portès; Leake 1846, map: Portes (Thalamæ?); Sfikopoulos 1987, 189; Hopf 1873, 202, 205: Porsos vel Pertes; Bon 1969, 343; Triantafyllou 1995, II 1699–1700.

526. Maẕiñik (ماذيكك/ماذكك), 1/14662, 16. AL

Bibliography:	Pacifico 1704, 120: Territorio di Patrasso, Meidanus.
Notes:	Unidentified. Possibly from mednik or međnik (*Scr. n.* frontier between two men's land property); mednik or mednika (*Scr. n.* species of pear). Place name Mednik in Serbia; medenik or medenika (*Scr. n.* something bordered or sweetened with honey); medenika (*Scr. n. Melitis melissophyllum*; species of pear): RHSJ 1904–10, VI 558–559, 561–562.

527. İksanya (اكسانيه), 1/14662, 17. AL

Coordinates:	X: 279617.267 Y: 4198336.828
Modern Greek:	Xenies (Ξενιές, οι)
Regional Unit:	Elis
Municipality:	Ilida
Municipal Unit:	Pineia
Bibliography:	Pikoulas 2001a, 347.3041; Panagiotopoulos 1987, 274, 305.130: Territorio di Gastugni, Xegnia; Bory de Saint-Vincent 1834, 70: Éparchie de Gastouni, Apano/Kato Xénia; Leake 1846, map: Ap./K. Xenies; Skiadas 1993, 248; Stamatelatos–Vamva-Stamatelatou 2001, 553.
Notes:	Its inhabitants were forced to abandon their village in the 1960s as the lake formed by the dam in the Pineios River covered Xenies. Many of them moved to neighbouring Varda (Βάρδα, η). In 1991 it was mentioned under the same name in a different location hosting 95 inhabitants.

528. Mirati (ميراتى), 1/14662, 18. AL

Coordinates:	X: 286692.540 Y: 4210492.737
Modern Greek:	Polylofo (Πολύλοφο, το)
Old Toponym:	Until 1928: Brati (Μπράτι, το); until 1956: Agia Marina (Αγία Μαρίνα, η)
Regional Unit:	Achaia
Municipality:	Dytiki Ahaïa
Municipal Unit:	Olenia
Bibliography:	Pikoulas 2001a, 391.3466; Pacifico 1704, 120: Territorio di Patrasso, Brati; Bory de Saint-Vincent 1834, 86: Éparchie de Patras, Brati; Leake 1846, map: Brati; Skiadas 1993, 223; Gritsopoulos 1971, 451: Μπιράτι; Triantafyllou 1995, II 1343.

Notes: Mira (*Al. pn.*) < i mirë (*Al. adj.* good): Zoto 2005, 281–282; Mirat (*Al. pn.*) < Mirat, të Mirat [*Al. n.* three feminine mythological figures that fly on butterfly wings to visit the nurslings on their third day and predetermine their fate; similar to the Greek folk tradition of μοίρες. See attestation in an Arvanitic fairy tale of Messenia: 'çë gjegj miratë': Jochalas 2011, I 102–103 (57)].

529. Platistomo (پلاتستمو), 1/14662, 18. AL

Notes: Unidentified.
πλατύστομος (*Gr. adj.* wide-mouthed).

530. Valmi (وآلمی), 1/14662, 18. AL

Coordinates: X: 284945.828 Y: 4197904.369

Modern Greek: Valmi (Βάλμη, η)

Regional Unit: Elis

Municipality: Ilida

Municipal Unit: Pineia

Bibliography: Pikoulas 2001a, 93.586; Bory de Saint-Vincent 1834, 71: Éparchie de Gastouni, Valmi; Leake 1846, map: Valmi.

Notes: < Βαλάμης (*Arv. sn.*) < vllam, vllamë or vëllamë (*Al. n.* blood-brother, adopted brother; fraternisation): Biris 1998, 192; Symeonidis 2010, I 326.

531. Orfano (اورفانو), *mezra'a* in the vicinity of Porta, 1/14662, 18.

Modern Greek: Orfano (?) (Ορφανό, το)

Regional Unit: Achaia

Bibliography: Pikoulas 2001a, 85.513; Panagiotopoulos 1987, 278, 306.89: Territorio di Patrasso, Arfano.

Notes: Unidentified.
See no. 190.

532. Ġarnaze (غارنازه), 1/14662, 18. AL

Notes: Unidentified. As noted in the register, it was in the vicinity of Şandamiri (no. 524).

533. Puliça (پولیچه), 1/14662, 19. AL

Notes: Unidentified.
Cf. microtoponym Poulitsa (Πουλίτσα, η < Pulicë, *Arv. pln.*) near Lambokambos (Λαμπόκαμπος, ο) in Laconia: Jochalas 2011, I 52.

534. Lukişta (لوكشته), *mezraʿa* in the vicinity of Puliça, 1/14662, 19.

Coordinates:	X: 287979.766 Y: 4206705.159
Modern Greek:	Loukistra (Λουκίστρα, η)
Regional Unit:	Achaia
Municipality:	Dytiki Ahaïa
Municipal Unit:	Olenia
Bibliography:	Triantafyllou 1995, I 1189.
Notes:	This settlement of the Patra District is listed as Luchistra in the Venetian survey of 1699. In 1713 it belonged to the same parish with neighbouring Hatzouri (Χατζούρι, το), modern Haravgi (Χαραυγή, η). Its exact location is unknown. According to Vasmer, < lukъ (*old Slav. n.* leek, *Allium ampeloprasum*): Vasmer 1941, 142–143. Place name Lukavica in Bulgaria and Serbia.

535. Gin Floḳa (كين فلوقه), *mezraʿa* in the vicinity of Puliça, 1/14662, 19.

Coordinates:	X: 292453.569 Y: 4211450.946
Modern Greek:	Flokas (Φλόκας, ο)
Regional Unit:	Achaia
Municipality:	Dytiki Ahaïa
Municipal Unit:	Olenia
Bibliography:	Pikoulas 2001a, 472.4260; Panagiotopoulos 1987, 277, 306.49: Territorio di Patrasso, Flocca; Pacifico 1704, 121: Territorio di Patrasso, Flocca; Bory de Saint-Vincent 1834, 86: Éparchie de Patras, Phloka; Leake 1846, map: Floka; Triantafyllou 1995, II 2184.
Notes:	For Gin see no. 430, and for Floḳa see no. 201.

536. Mariçi (ماريچى), *mezraʿa* in the vicinity of Puliça, 1/14662, 19.

Coordinates:	X: 285460.487 Y: 4211566.437
Modern Greek:	Agias Marinis Maritsis Monastery (I.M. Αγίας Μαρίνης Μαρίτσης, η)
Regional Unit:	Achaia
Municipality:	Dytiki Ahaïa
Municipal Unit:	Olenia
Bibliography:	Pikoulas 2001a, 297.2556; Bory de Saint-Vincent 1834, 87: Éparchie de Patras, Mon^{re} de Maritsa; Leake 1846, map: Maritza; Triantafyllou 1995, II 1228–1230.

537. **Ẕervini (ذروینی), 1/14662, 19. AL**

Modern Greek:	Dervini (?) (Δερβίνι, το)
Regional Unit:	Elis
Municipality:	Ilida
Bibliography:	Pikoulas 2001a, 133.978; Panagiotopoulos 1987, 272, 304.26: Territorio di Gastugni, Deruvini.
Notes:	Unidentified. Different from no. 230.

15. District of Girbene (Spartia) (Maps 29–30)

538. **Girbene (کیربنه), 1/14662, 21.**

Coordinates:	X: 305792.860 Y: 4205597.148
Modern Greek:	Spartia (Σπαρτιά, η)
Old Toponym:	Until 1940: Grevena (Γρεβενά, τα); until 1961: Greveno (Γρεβενό, το)
Regional Unit:	Achaia
Municipality:	Erymanthos
Municipal Unit:	Tritaia
Bibliography:	Pikoulas 2001a, 433.3878; Panagiotopoulos 1987, 276, 306.34: Territorio di Patrasso, Gervano; Pacifico 1704, 121: Territorio di Patrasso, Greuenò; Bory de Saint-Vincent 1834, 86: Éparchie de Patras, Grévéno; Leake 1846, map: Greveno; Sfikopoulos 1987, 192; Hopf 1873, 202: Graveno vel Guevano, 205: Greban; Bon 1969, 343; Skiadas 1993, 225; Stamatelatos–Vamva-Stamatelatou 2001, 709; Triantafyllou 1995, I 453–454.
Notes:	The Girbene entry in the 1/14662 does not include the town of Girbene (*nefs-i Girbene*), as expected. See no. 369.

539. **Motista (موتسته), 1/14662, 21. GR**

Coordinates:	X: 326814.110 Y: 4196916.525
Modern Greek:	Drymos (Δρυμός, ο)
Old Toponym:	Until 1957: Mostitsi (Μοστίτσι, το)
Regional Unit:	Achaia
Municipality:	Kalavryta
Municipal Unit:	Kleitoria

Bibliography: Pikoulas 2001a, 144.1083; Panagiotopoulos 1987, 270, 303.108: Territorio di Callavritta, Mostizzi; Bory de Saint-Vincent 1834, 74: Éparchie de Kalavrita, Mostitsi; Leake 1830, II 255–256: Mostítza; Bon 1969, 344; Skiadas 1993, 237.

Notes: < mostьсь < mostъ (*Slav. n.* bridge): Vasmer 1941, 136; Symeonidis 2010, I 959. Place name Mostec in Slovenia and the Czech Republic.

540. Gin Manesi (كين مانسى), 1/14662, 21. AL

Coordinates: X: 295496.549 Y: 4205962.239

Modern Greek: Manesi (Μάνεσι, το)

Regional Unit: Achaia

Municipality: Erymanthos

Municipal Unit: Tritaia

Bibliography: Pikoulas 2001a, 273.2315; Pacifico 1704, 125: Territorio di Gastugni, Manesi; Bory de Saint-Vincent 1834, 86: Éparchie de Patras, Manési; Leake 1846, map: Manesi; Triantafyllou 1995, II 1221–1222.

Notes: For Gin see no. 430, and for Manesi see no. 22.

541. İsfardina (اسفاردنه), 1/14662, 22. GR

Coordinates: X: 331543.006 Y: 4220036.493

Modern Greek: Spartinou (?) [Σπαρτινού, η (= του)]

Regional Unit: Achaia

Municipality: Kalavryta

Municipal Unit: Kalavryta

Bibliography: Pikoulas 2001a, 433.3881; Papandreou 2011, 290.

542. Avrami (آورامى), 1/14662, 22. AL

Coordinates: X: 296958.512 Y: 4207660.473

Modern Greek: Avrami (Αβράμι, το)

Regional Unit: Achaia

Municipality: Erymanthos

Municipal Unit: Kalentzi

Bibliography: Pikoulas 2001a, 31.4; Triantafyllou 1995, I 28-29.

Notes: Avram (*Al. pn.*) < Αβράμης (*Gr. pn.*) < Αβραάμ (*Gr. pn.* Abraham): Zoto 2005, 189.

543. Lazaryo (لازاريو), 1/14662, 23. AL

Coordinates:	X: 297724.899 Y: 4203782.489
Modern Greek:	Lazargio/Bantsaiika (Λαζαργιό, το/Μπαντσαίικα, τα)
Regional Unit:	Achaia
Municipality:	Erymanthos
Municipal Unit:	Kalentzi
Bibliography:	Pikoulas 2001a, 245.2047; Bory de Saint-Vincent 1834, 86: Éparchie de Patras, Lazario; Skiadas 1993, 225; Triantafyllou 1995, I 1109.
Notes:	Settlement in the vicinity of Koumberi (Κουμπέρι, το) and Kalentzi (no. 641). See no. 257.

544. Papaẕato (پاپاذاتو), 1/14662, 23. AL

Notes:	Unidentified. See no. 360.

545. Ḳavalari Trusa (قوآلارى تروسا), 1/14662, 24. AL

Coordinates:	X: 302725.076 Y: 4212007.716
Modern Greek:	Trousas (Τρούσας, ο)
Regional Unit:	Achaia
Municipality:	Erymanthos
Municipal Unit:	Farres
Bibliography:	Pikoulas 2001a, 459.4125; Pacifico 1704, 121: Territorio di Patrasso, Trussa; Bory de Saint-Vincent 1834, 86: Éparchie de Patras, Trousa; Leake 1846, map: Trusa; Gritsopoulos 1971, 450: Καβὰλ Τροῦσα; Triantafyllou 1995, II 2108–2109.
Notes:	Place name Trush in Shkodër and Trushaj in Fier, Albania. Symeonidis suggested an etymology from trushkyej (*Al. v.* to plunder, to steal from a holy place): Symeonidis 2010, II 1368. For Ḳavalari see no. 260.

546. Bardi Zuġra (باردى زوغره), 1/14662, 24. AL

Notes:	Unidentified. For Bardi see no. 462.

547. Ayo Yani (ايو يانى), 1/14662, 24. AL

Coordinates:	X: 316547.102 Y: 4220242.552

Modern Greek:	Agios Ioannis (Άγιος Ιωάννης, ο)
Regional Unit:	Achaia
Municipality:	Erymanthos
Municipal Unit:	Leontio
Bibliography:	ANAVASI 2009, map 10; LEAKE 1846, map: A. Ianni (Leontium); EXPÉDITION 1832: Khani d'Hagiannis; TRIANTAFYLLOU 1995, I 1131–1132.
Notes:	Leake noted on his map a certain A. Ianni south-west of Guzumistra (no. 587), in the vicinity of which the ruins of ancient Leontium are located. On the *Expédition* map the same location is named as Khani d'Hagiannis. Today the settlement is uninhabited. Cf. Agiou Ioanni Monastery (I.M. Αγίου Ιωάννη, η) in Greveno (no. 538), reported abandoned in 1835. Its dependencies are mentioned in documents of the Grimani Archive (1696–1700): DOKOS 1971–74, 93. See no. 105.

548. Ḳavalari (قوالارى), 1/14662, 26. AL

Coordinates:	X: 298174.410 X: 4207532.462
Modern Greek:	Kavalari (Καβαλάρη, του)
Regional Unit:	Achaia
Municipality:	Erymanthos
Municipal Unit:	Kalentzi
Bibliography:	GLET 1998, I 454; KOSTOPOULOS 1989, 185.
Notes:	Uninhabited location to the east of Avrami (no. 542). See no. 260.

549. Asfalaḫto (اسفلاختو), 1/14662, 26. GR

Coordinates:	X: 267851.068 Y: 4180176.347
Modern Greek:	Asfalakto (Ασφάλακτο, το)
Regional Unit:	Elis
Municipality:	Pyrgos
Municipal Unit:	Iardanos
Bibliography:	PIKOULAS 2001a, 89.548; PALLA-HRONOPOULOU 2003, 264.

550. [---]şta ([---]شته), 1/14662, 27. AL

Notes:	Unidentified.

551. Divye (دویه), 1/14662, 27. AL

Notes:	Unidentified.

552. Viriça (ویریچه), *mezraʿa* in the vicinity of Divye, 1/14662, 27.

Notes:	Unidentified.

553. Arula (آرولا), 1/14662, 28. GR

Coordinates:	X: 289091.616 Y: 4214625.746
Modern Greek:	Arla (Άρλα, η)
Regional Unit:	Achaia
Municipality:	Dytiki Ahaïa
Municipal Unit:	Olenia
Bibliography:	PIKOULAS 2001a, 83.495; PANAGIOTOPOULOS 1987, 277, 306.56: Territorio di Patrasso, Arrulla; PACIFICO 1704, 121: Territorio di Patrasso, Arula; BORY DE SAINT-VINCENT 1834, 87: Éparchie de Patras, Arla; LEAKE 1846, map: Arula; SFIKOPOULOS 1987, 183; HOPF 1873, 202: Arulia; BON 1969, 461; TRIANTAFYLLOU 1995, I 250–251.
Notes:	According to Vasmer, < **orьlъ* (*old Slav. n.* eagle): VASMER 1941, 129. Symeonidis suggested an etymology from arula (*Lat. n. dim.* of ara, small altar): SYMEONIDIS 2010, I 289. Place name Gornja Orlja in Montenegro, Orlovica in Serbia, and Orela in Bulgaria.

554. Trahya Manesi (تراخیا/تراخیه مانسی), 1/14662, 29. AL

Notes:	Unidentified. τραχύς (*Gr. adj.* rough); trahua (*Arb. n.* whetstone). For Manesi see no. 22.

555. Trusa (تروسه), 1/14662, 30. AL

Coordinates:	X: 304109.811 Y: 4212718.504
Modern Greek:	Trousaki (Τρουσάκι, το)
Regional Unit:	Achaia
Municipality:	Erymanthos
Municipal Unit:	Farres
Bibliography:	PIKOULAS 2001a, 458.4124; TRIANTAFYLLOU 1995, II 2108–2109.
Notes:	Settlement to the south-east of Ano Starohori (no. 522). See no. 545.

556. Fostana (فوستانه), 1/14662, 30. GR

Coordinates:	X: 288557.638 Y: 4217309.589
Modern Greek:	Fostaina (Φώσταινα, η)
Regional Unit:	Achaia
Municipality:	Dytiki Ahaïa
Municipal Unit:	Olenia
Bibliography:	Pikoulas 2001a, 476.4297; Panagiotopoulos 1987, 277, 306.58: Territorio di Patrasso, Fostena; Pacifico 1704, 121: Territorio di Patrasso, Fostena; Expédition 1832: Phosténa; Bory de Saint-Vincent 1834, 87: Éparchie de Patras, Phostæna; Leake 1846, map: Fostena; Hopf 1873, 202: Focena vel Phonea, 205: Chestena; Sfikopoulos 1987, 182; Bon 1969, 458; Triantafyllou 1995, II 2207–2208.
Notes:	The exact position of the castle or tower of Fostaina was located after field research by Papagiannopoulos in Xeropigado (Ξεροπήγαδο, το): Panitsas–Papagiannopoulos 2012, 67. According to Symeonidis, the toponym is also pronounced as Hosmina (Χόσμηνα, η) < **Chvostьna* < hvost (*Scr. n.* forest) or chvostъ (*Ru. n.* tail, river island). Hydronyms Chvoščña and Chvošña are common in Russia: Symeonidis 2010, II 1420. Vasmer had rejected this theory, because he could not find any parallel in south Slavic: Vasmer 1941, 140; however, cf. place name Hvostno (also spelled as Hvosno, Fostno and Fosno) in Serbia.

557. Ayo Niḳolas (آيو نيقولاس), 1/14662, 31. AL

Coordinates:	X: 303001.266 Y: 4214300.254
Modern Greek:	Agios Nikolaos (Άγιος Νικόλαος, ο)
Regional Unit:	Achaia
Municipality:	Erymanthos
Municipal Unit:	Farres
Bibliography:	Bory de Saint-Vincent 1834, 86: Éparchie de Patras, Hagios-Nikolaos; Leake 1846, map: A. Nikolaos; Triantafyllou 1995, I 135.
Notes:	Settlement in the vicinity of Ano Starohori (no. 522) on an altitude of 350m, formerly known as Laliotaiika (Λαλιωταίικα, τα). Άγιος Νικόλας/Νικόλαος (*Gr. hag.* St Nicholas).

558. Oṣiya Mariya (اوصيه مريه), 1/14662, 31. AL

Notes:	Unidentified. Οσία Μαρία (*Gr. hag.* St Mary of Egypt).

559. Ayo Lisyo (آيو لسيو), 1/14662, 31. AL

Coordinates:	X: 289496.380 Y: 4223657.727

Modern Greek:	Profitis Elissaios (Προφήτης Ελισσαίος, ο)
Regional Unit:	Achaia
Municipality:	Dytiki Ahaïa
Municipal Unit:	Dymi
Bibliography:	Pikoulas 2001a, 398.3528; Triantafyllou 1995, I 612.
Notes:	Άγιος Ελισσαίος (*Gr. hag.* St Eliseus/Elisha).

560. Venetiḳa (ونتقه), 1/14662, 31. AL

Notes:	Unidentified. Cf. Dokos 1971–74, 92, 98: Βενετιά. βενετικός (*Gr. adj.* Venetian).

561. Lenḳoni (لنقونى), 1/14662, 32. AL

Notes:	Unidentified.

562. Besulḳa (بسولقه), *mezraʿa* in the vicinity of Lenḳoni, 1/14662, 32.

Coordinates:	X: 284693.855 Y: 4215391.388
Modern Greek:	Vythoulkas (Βυθούλκας, ο)
Old Toponym:	Until 1940: Bethoulka (Μπεθούλκα, του)
Regional Unit:	Achaia
Municipality:	Dytiki Ahaïa
Municipal Unit:	Dymi
Bibliography:	Pikoulas 2001a, 113.782; Panagiotopoulos 1987, 277, 306.73: Territorio di Patrasso, Beltulca; Pacifico 1704, 120: Territorio di Patrasso, Bitulea; Bory de Saint-Vincent 1834, 87: Éparchie de Patras, Béthulka; Leake 1846, map: Vythurka; Skiadas 1993, 223: Βυθούλκα; Triantafyllou 1995, I 357.
Notes:	Perhaps from bathulku or bathë ulku (*Arb. n.* green herb): Kamsi 2000, 29. According to Symeonidis, < bërthokël (*Al. n.* squill, sea onion, *Scilla maritima*): Symeonidis 2010, I 394.

563. Ayo Yorgi (آيو يوركى), *mezraʿa* in the vicinity of Lenḳoni, 1/14662, 32.

Coordinates:	X: 287612.269 Y: 4212305.985
Modern Greek:	Agios Georgios (Άγιος Γεώργιος, ο)
Regional Unit:	Achaia

Municipality:	Dytiki Ahaïa
Municipal Unit:	Olenia
Bibliography:	GLET 1998, I 61.
Notes:	A chapel is noted to the north-west of Pigadia (Πηγάδια, τα).

564. **Balçi (بالچی), 1/14662, 32. AL**

Coordinates:	X: 269693.704 Y: 4208139.542
Modern Greek:	Baltzes (?) (Μπάλτζες, οι)
Regional Unit:	Elis
Municipality:	Andravida-Kyllini
Municipal Unit:	Vouprasia
Bibliography:	Iliopoulos 1948, 178.
Notes:	Microtoponym in the surroundings of Kapaleto (no. 214); its exact location is unknown. According to Vasmer, the place name Baltsi (Μπαλτσί, το) in Larissa should be connected to baltë (*Al. n.* mud, soil; muddy place) + -si (*Al. end.*) like mal > malësi: Vasmer 1941, 101. Indeed, in Arbërisht a baltësi is attested (*Arb. n.* wetland, sludge): Giordano 1963, 23. In our case, though, it should have been rendered as بالتسی (Baltesi). I am inclined to suggest an etymology from balç (*Al. n.* common St John's wort, Klamath weed, *Hypericum perforatum*).

565. **Sirveliça (سرولچه), 1/14662, 32. AL**

Notes:	Unidentified.

566. **Palopirġo (پالوپرغو), 1/14662, 32. AL**

Coordinates:	X: 284217.035 Y: 4216938.477
Modern Greek:	Pyrgaki (?) (Πυργάκι, το)
Regional Unit:	Achaia
Municipality:	Dytiki Ahaïa
Municipal Unit:	Dymi
Bibliography:	GLET 1998, III 193.
Notes:	Uninhabited location to the south of Petrohori (Πετροχώρι, το). παλαιόπυργος (*Gr. n.* old tower).

567. Yirano (يرانو), 1/14662, 32. AL

Notes:	Unidentified. γερανός [*Gr. n.* crane (machine); crane, *Grus grus*].

568. Petrovişta (پتروووشته), 1/14662, 32. AL

Coordinates:	X: 283217.950 Y: 4205038.424
Modern Greek:	Petrovithia (?) (Πετροβίθια, τα)
Regional Unit:	Achaia
Municipality:	Dytiki Ahaïa
Municipal Unit:	Larissos
Bibliography:	GLET 1998, III 104.
Notes:	Uninhabited location to the west of Mihoïo (no. 571). < **Petrovьcь* (*Slav. pln.* Peter's village) < Petъr (*Slav. pn.* Peter): Vasmer 1941, 46; Symeonidis 2010, II 1135. Place name Petrovica and Petrovice in Bosnia & Herzegovina: RHSJ 1924–27, IX 828.

569. Serḳofayi (سرقوفايى), *mezraʿa* in the vicinity of Petrovişta, 1/14662, 33.

Notes:	Unidentified. σαρκοφάγος (*Gr. n.* sarcophagus).

570. Şurbi (شوربى), *mezraʿa* in the vicinity of Petrovişta, 1/14662, 33.

Notes:	Unidentified. See no. 224.

571. Miḫoy (ميخوى), 1/14662, 33. AL

Coordinates:	X: 281037.667 Y: 4205308.167
Modern Greek:	Mihoïo (Μιχόιο, το)
Old Toponym:	Until 1940: Mihoï/Mihi (Μιχόι/Μιχί, το)
Regional Unit:	Achaia
Municipality:	Dytiki Ahaïa
Municipal Unit:	Larissos
Bibliography:	Pikoulas 2001a, 295.2535; Panagiotopoulos 1987, 277, 306.64: Territorio di Patrasso, Michoi; Expédition 1832: Mikhoï; Bory de Saint-Vincent 1834, 87: Éparchie de Patras, Mykhoï; Leake 1846, map: Mikhoi; Skiadas 1993, 223; Stamatelatos–Vamva-Stamatelatou 2001, 504; Triantafyllou 1995, II 1285.

Notes:	Vasmer attempted to link it to place name Mihovo in Bulgaria: Vasmer 1941, 136. I would not rule out a possible etymology from Miho < Mihal (*Al. pn.* Michael): Zoto 2005, 278–279, for the register lists first a certain Niḳola Miẖoy. See also Symeonidis 2010, I 936.

572. Ḳazneş (قازنش), 1/14662, 33. AL

Coordinates:	X: 276289.537 Y: 4203356.409
Modern Greek:	Agia Marina (Αγία Μαρίνα, η)
Old Toponym:	Until 1928: Kasnesi (Κασνέσι, το); until 1940: Marina (Μαρίνα, η)
Regional Unit:	Elis
Municipality:	Andravida-Kyllini
Municipal Unit:	Vouprasia
Bibliography:	Pikoulas 2001a, 36.48; Bory de Saint-Vincent 1834, 87: Éparchie de Patras, Kasnésaki; Leake 1846, map: Kasnesaki; Skiadas 1993, 248; Stamatelatos–Vamva-Stamatelatou 2001, 7.
Notes:	See no. 57.

573. Maliki (ماليكى), 1/14662, 34. AL

Coordinates:	X: 273338.317 Y: 4206864.373
Modern Greek:	Nisi (Νησί, το)
Old Toponym:	Until 1955: Maliki (Μαλίκι, το)
Regional Unit:	Elis
Municipality:	Andravida-Kyllini
Municipal Unit:	Vouprasia
Bibliography:	Pikoulas 2001a, 343.2999; Panagiotopoulos 1987, 274, 304.106: Territorio di Gastugni, Maluchi; Pacifico 1704, 124: Territorio di Gastugni, Malichi; Bory de Saint-Vincent 1834, 70: Éparchie de Gastouni, Maliki; Leake 1846, map: Maliki; Skiadas 1993, 248; Stamatelatos–Vamva-Stamatelatou 2001, 546; Iliopoulos 1948, 181.
Notes:	Maliqi (*Al. sn., pn.*). Place name Maliq in Durrës and Korçë, Albania.

574. Ḳonbi Ṣeḳra (قونبى ثقره), 1/14662, 34. AL

Coordinates:	X: 277908.598 Y: 4201983.727
Modern Greek:	Dafni (Δάφνη, η)
Old Toponym:	Until 1940: Koumouthekra (Κουμουθέκρα, του); until 1955: Kombothekra (Κομποθέκρα, του)
Regional Unit:	Elis

Municipality:	Andravida-Kyllini
Municipal Unit:	Vouprasia
Bibliography:	Pikoulas 2001a, 130.953; Panagiotopoulos 1987, 277, 306.67: Territorio di Patrasso, Combotecra; Pacifico 1704, 120: Territorio di Patrasso, Combothecra; Bory de Saint-Vincent 1834, 87: Éparchie de Patras, Kombothékra; Leake 1846, map: Komofekra; Skiadas 1993, 248: Κουμουθέκλα, η; Stamatelatos–Vamva-Stamatelatou 2001, 179; Triantafyllou 1995, I 1035–1036.
Notes:	See no. 219.

575. Gerbesi (كربسى), 1/14662, 34. AL

Coordinates:	X: 315623.143 Y: 4214161.706
Modern Greek:	Profitis Ilias (Προφήτης Ηλίας, ο)
Old Toponym:	Until 1928: Gerbesi (Γκέρμπεσι, το)
Regional Unit:	Achaia
Municipality:	Kalavryta
Municipal Unit:	Kalavryta
Bibliography:	Pikoulas 2001a, 399.3535; Panagiotopoulos 1987, 268, 302.29: Territorio di Callavritta, Chierpeno; Pacifico 1704, 122: Territorio di Calaurita, Gerbesi; Bory de Saint-Vincent 1834, 74: Éparchie de Kalavrita, Guerbési; Leake 1846, map: Gerbesi; Skiadas 1993, 239.
Notes:	See no. 381.

576. Mitepoli (ميتەپولى), 1/14662, 35. GR

Coordinates:	X: 296303.762 Y: 4214666.307
Modern Greek:	Mitopoli (Μιτόπολη, η)
Regional Unit:	Achaia
Municipality:	Dytiki Ahaïa
Municipal Unit:	Olenia
Bibliography:	Pikoulas 2001a, 295.2531; Panagiotopoulos 1987, 277, 306.47: Territorio di Patrasso, Mitopogli; Pacifico 1704, 121: Territorio di Patrasso, Mitopoli; Bory de Saint-Vincent 1834, 86: Éparchie de Patras, Mitopolis; Leake 1846, map: Mitopoli; Hopf 1873, 202: Montepoli; Sfikopoulos 1987, 186–187; Bon 1969, 461–462; Triantafyllou 1995, II 1279–1280.

577. Yatopa (ياتوپا), 1/14662, 35. AL

Notes:	Unidentified.

578. **Melitena (ملیتنه), 1/14662, 35. AL**

	Unidentified.
Notes:	Possibly from Μελίταινα (*Gr. pln.* place that produces honey) < Μελίτης < μέλι (*Gr. n.* honey): Symeonidis 2010, I 908. Cf. Melitaina (Μελίταινα, η) in Rodopi and Meliti (Μελίτη, η) in Florina.

579. **Malesina (مالسنه), 1/14662, 36. AL**

	Unidentified.
Notes:	According to Vasmer, < malësinë *acc. sing.* of malësi (*Al. n.* mountainous region): Vasmer 1941, 106. According to Symeonidis, < **malësinë* < malësi + -inë (*Al. end.* denoting place): Symeonidis 2010, I 868. Place name Malesina (Μαλεσίνα, η) in Phthiotis.

580. **Eksoriya (اکسوریه), 1/14662, 36. AL**

	Unidentified.
Notes:	εξορία (*Gr. n.* exile).

581. **Şalesi (شالسی), 1/14662, 36. AL**

	Unidentified.
Notes:	< shalë (*Al. n.* saddle, col, pass): Fourikis 1929, 157; Symeonidis 2010, II 1237. shalës (*Al. n.* wooden trough used in beating flax), shalësinë (*Al. n.* infertile soil). Shalësi (*Al. sn.*). Place name Shalësi in Vlorë, Elbasan, Gjirokastër and Korçë, Albania. See also Georgacas–McDonald 1968, 347.

582. **Mazarak (مزراك), 1/14662, 37. AL**

Coordinates:	X: 322641.454 Y: 4222743.860
Modern Greek:	Ano Mazaraki (Άνω Μαζαράκι, το)
Regional Unit:	Achaia
Municipality:	Erymanthos
Municipal Unit:	Leontio
Bibliography:	Pikoulas 2001a, 268.2271; Bory de Saint-Vincent 1834, 86: Éparchie de Patras, Mazaraki; Leake 1846, map: Mazaraki; Politis 1915, 269–270; Triantafyllou 1995, II 1207–1208.
Notes:	See no. 308.

583. **Junbata (ژونبته), 1/14662, 37. AL**

Coordinates:	X: 313315.569 Y: 4224020.101
Modern Greek:	Pigi (Πηγή, η)
Old Toponym:	Until 1940: Tsimbata (Τσιμπάτα, τα); until 1971: Zoumbata (Ζουμπάτα, τα)

Regional Unit:	Achaia
Municipality:	Patra
Municipal Unit:	Patra
Bibliography:	PIKOULAS 2001a, 158.1210, 382.3376; PANAGIOTOPOULOS 1987, 276, 305.17: Territorio di Patrasso, Zumbata; BORY DE SAINT-VINCENT 1834, 86: Éparchie de Patras, Zoumbata; LEAKE 1846, map: Zubata; KOLOKOTRONIS 1981, 270; SKIADAS 1993, 226; STAMATELATOS–VAMVA-STAMATELATOU 2001, 621; TRIANTAFYLLOU 1995, I 820–821.
Notes:	See no. 406.

584. Milyas (ملياس), 1/14662, 37. AL

Coordinates:	X: 312011.915 Y: 4224602.712
Modern Greek:	Moira (Μοίρα, η)
Regional Unit:	Achaia
Municipality:	Patra
Municipal Unit:	Patra
Bibliography:	PIKOULAS 2001a, 292.2536; PACIFICO 1704, 120: Territorio di Patrasso, Mira; BORY DE SAINT-VINCENT 1834, 86: Éparchie de Patras, Apano/Kato Mira; LEAKE 1846, map: Ap./K. Mira.

585. Frati (فراتى), 1/14662, 37. AL

Coordinates:	X: 314278.080 Y: 4219640.674
Modern Greek:	Frati (Φράτι, το)
Regional Unit:	Achaia
Municipality:	Erymanthos
Municipal Unit:	Leontio
Bibliography:	GLET 1998, III 418; PACIFICO 1704, 120: Territorio di Patrasso, Fratti; BORY DE SAINT-VINCENT 1834, 86: Éparchie de Patras, Phrati; TRIANTAFYLLOU 1995, II 2199.
Notes:	Uninhabited location to the north-west of Demestiha [Δεμέστιχα, τα (= η)]. See no. 108.

586. İstoyan (استويان), 1/14662, 38. AL

Notes:	Unidentified. See no. 328.

587. Ġurzumişa (غرزمشه), 1/14662, 38. AL

Coordinates:	X: 318432.999 Y: 4220920.674
Modern Greek:	Leontio (Λεόντιο, το)
Old Toponym:	Until 1923: Gourzoumisa (Γουρζούμισα, η)
Regional Unit:	Achaia
Municipality:	Erymanthos
Municipal Unit:	Leontio
Bibliography:	Pikoulas 2001a, 251.2108; Bory de Saint-Vincent 1834, 86: Éparchie de Patras, Gouzoumistra; Leake 1830, III 420: Guzúmistra; Skiadas 1993, 226; Triantafyllou 1995, I 1131–1135.
Notes:	The initial settlement was located in Palaiogourzoumisa (Παλαιογουρζούμισα, η), an uninhabited place between Vetaiika (Βεταίικα, τα) and Thomaïka (Θωμάικα, τα). Today's Leontio/Gourzoumisa was populated in 1821. According to Biris, Γριζούμψας (*Arv. sn.* carrion, crow): Biris 1998, 193. According to Symeonidis, the toponym is a compound word: gur (*Al. n.* stone) + unknown second component: Symeonidis 2010, I 444.

588. Buza (بوزه), 1/14662, 38. AL

Modern Greek:	Bouzia (Μπούζια, η)
Regional Unit:	Elis
Municipality:	Ilida
Bibliography:	Pikoulas 2001a, 330.2876; Skiadas 1993, 366.
Notes:	Unidentified. Μπούζας or Μπούζης (*Arv. sn.*) < buzë (*Al. n.* lip): Biris 1998, 199. Buza (*Al. sn.*). Place name Buza e Madhe (*Arv. pln.* big mouth) and Buza Vaje in Euboea: Jochalas 2002, 36.

589. Duḳati (دوقه‌تی), 1/14662, 39. AL

Notes:	Unidentified. Cf. Doukas (Δούκας, ο) in Foloï (no. 272). According to Pouqueville, Doukas was founded by the Ducatès from the Acroceraunian Mountains (Mali Kanalit) of south-western Albania: Pouqueville 1827, V 441. Place name Dukat in Vlorë, Albania.

590. Gin Bodya (كين بوديه), 1/14662, 39. AL

Coordinates:	X: 319104.351 Y: 4215093.825
Modern Greek:	Mikros Pontias (Μικρός Ποντιάς, ο)
Regional Unit:	Achaia
Municipality:	Kalavryta
Municipal Unit:	Kalavryta

Bibliography:	Pikoulas 2001a, 293.2516. Panagiotopoulos 1987, 270, 303.92: Territorio di Callavritta, Bodia Catù; Bory de Saint-Vincent 1834, 74: Éparchie de Kalavrita, Bontiadès.
Notes:	For Gin see no. 430, and for Bodya see no. 86.

591. Şergi (شرکی), 1/14662, 39. AL

Notes:	Unidentified. Possibly from sherqi (*Al. n.* watermelon). See also no. 416.

592. İsḳlaviça (اسقلاویچه), 1/14662, 89. GR

Coordinates:	X: 284068.459 Y: 4218665.480
Modern Greek:	Sklavoutsa (Σκλάβουτσα, η)
Regional Unit:	Achaia
Municipality:	Dytiki Ahaïa
Municipal Unit:	Dymi
Bibliography:	Bon 1969, 292.
Notes:	Carile suggested a localisation by Riolos (no. 612), Santomeri (no. 524) and Portes (no. 525) area: Carile 1970, 397. It should be in the vicinity of Saravali (no. 472) and Riolos, as Constantine Palaeologus conquered those three fortresses of western Achaia on 5 May 1429. Triantafyllou informs us that the mountain peak between Petrohori (Πετροχώρι, το) and Bada (Μπάδα) is called Sklavoutsa, on which the ruins of a fortress are visible: Triantafyllou 1995, II 1860–1861. Kordosis located it south-east of Gomosto (no. 630) on a map of mid-15th c. Albanian settlements of the north-western Peloponnese: Kordosis 1981a, map 9. According to the 1/14662 however, it was inhabited by Greeks. See also Panitsas–Papagiannopoulos 2012, 68. Cf. microtoponym Sklavoutsou (Σκλαβούτσου, του) to the west of Thelika (Θελίκα, η) in Achaia. Slavica (*Scr. pn.*). Place name Slavica in Croatia: RHSJ 1956, XV 465.

593. Marḳoplu (مارقوپلو), TT10, 20. AL

Notes:	Unidentified. See no. 204.

16. District of Ayo İlya (Agios Ilias) (Maps 31–32)

594. Ayo İlya, nefs-i (آیو الیا), 1/14662, 50. GR

Coordinates:	X: 276031.041 Y: 4195816.178
Modern Greek:	Agios Ilias (Άγιος Ηλίας, ο)
Regional Unit:	Elis

Municipality:	Ilida
Municipal Unit:	Amaliada
Bibliography:	Pikoulas 2001a, 49.175; Panagiotopoulos 1987, 274, 305.117: Territorio di Gastugni, S. Elia; Pacifico 1704, 123: Territorio di Gastugni, Sant'Elia; Bory de Saint-Vincent 1834, 70: Éparchie de Gastouni, Hagios Ilias; Leake 1846, map: Ailiadhes.
Notes:	According to Longnon and Topping, Santu Lya in Nicolas de Boiano's report is possibly identical to *Expédition*'s Hagios Ilias in the vicinity of Palaiopolis and Kolokyntha: Longnon–Topping 1969, 153, 237. Bon's château de Saint-Élie should be sought further south in the Alfeios valley, Bon 1969, 238, 276, 691, *planche* 2. Considering the proximity of the settlements listed in the 1/14662 under the *nāḥiyyet-i Ayo İlya* heading, Santu Lya/Hagios Ilias emerges as the district's geographical centre.

595. **Muzak (موزاك), 1/14662, 52. AL**

Coordinates:	X: 284958.980 Y: 4184395.722
Modern Greek:	Mouzaki (Μουζάκι, το)
Regional Unit:	Elis
Municipality:	Pyrgos
Municipal Unit:	Oleni
Bibliography:	Pikoulas 2001a, 321.2795; Pacifico 1704, 124: Territorio di Gastugni, Musachi; Bory de Saint-Vincent 1834, 71: Éparchie de Gastouni, Mouzaki; Leake 1846, map: Muzaki; Bon 1969, 341; Iliopoulos 1948, 178.
Notes:	See no. 380.

596. **İşpata (اشپاته), 1/14662, 52. AL**

Coordinates:	X: 281454.135 Y: 4209154.392
Modern Greek:	Agios Nikolaos (Άγιος Νικόλαος, ο)
Old Toponym:	Until 1957: Spata (Σπάτα, τα)
Regional Unit:	Achaia
Municipality:	Dytiki Ahaïa
Municipal Unit:	Larissos
Bibliography:	Pikoulas 2001a, 52.211; Bory de Saint-Vincent 1834, 70: Éparchie de Gastouni, Spata; Pacifico 1704, 123: Territorio di Gastugni, Spataria; Leake 1846, map: Spata; Bon 1969, 360; Skiadas 1993, 248; Iliopoulos 1948, 179; Triantafyllou 1995, II 1903.
Notes:	See no. 241.

597. Ḳozma Greḳa (قوزمه كرقه), 1/14662, 52. AL

Coordinates:	X: 296539.864 Y: 4159529.074
Modern Greek:	Graikas (?) [Γραίκας, ο (= του Γκρέκα)]
Regional Unit:	Elis
Municipality:	Andritsaina-Krestena
Municipal Unit:	Skillountas
Bibliography:	Pikoulas 2001a, 126.915; Pacifico 1704, 130: Territorio di Fanari, Grica; Bory de Saint-Vincent 1834, 87: Éparchie de Phanari, Gréka; Leake 1846, map: Kreka; Skiadas 1993, 370.
Notes:	For Ḳozma see no. 425, and for Greḳa see no. 120.

598. Simiza (سيميزه), 1/14662, 52. AL

Coordinates:	X: 270878.806 Y: 4200129.131
Modern Greek:	Simiza (Σιμίζα, η)
Regional Unit:	Elis
Municipality:	Andravida-Kyllini
Municipal Unit:	Lehaina
Bibliography:	Pikoulas 2001a, 420.3751; Pacifico 1704, 124: Territorio di Gastugni, Dimisa; Bory de Saint-Vincent 1834, 70: Éparchie de Gastouni, Simiza.
Notes:	symizë (*Al. adj.* having small dark eyes) < sy (*Al. n.* eye) + mizë (*Al. n.* fly). For the transformation of y /y/ to i /i/ in Arvanitic and Arbërisht see Botsaris 1993, 75.

599. Ayo Vaṣıl (آيو وآصيل), 1/14662, 53. AL

Modern Greek:	Agios Vasileios (Άγιος Βασίλειος, ο)
Regional Unit:	Elis
Municipality:	Arhaia Olympia
Bibliography:	Pikoulas 2001a, 43.116; Skiadas 1993, 370.
Notes:	Unidentified. Άγιος Βασίλειος (*Gr. hag.* St Basil).

600. Romyo (روميو), 1/14662, 53. AL

Notes:	Unidentified. Ρωμιός (*Gr. n.* Greek).

601. İştopanşi Lopesi (اشتوپانشی لوپسی), 1/14662, 53. AL

Coordinates:	X: 274146.399 Y: 4190463.638
Modern Greek:	Kryonero (Κρυόνερο, το)
Old Toponym:	Until 1928: Lopesi (Λόπεσι, το)
Regional Unit:	Elis
Municipality:	Ilida
Municipal Unit:	Amaliada
Bibliography:	Pikoulas 2001a, 238.1980; Panagiotopoulos 1987, 275, 305.153: Territorio di Gastugni, Lopessi; Pacifico 1704, 124: Territorio di Gastugni, Lopesi; Bory de Saint-Vincent 1834, 70: Éparchie de Gastouni, Lopési; Leake 1846, map: Lopesi; Skiadas 1993, 254; Iliopoulos 1948, 177.
Notes:	For İştopanşi see no. 26, and for Lopesi no. 83.

602. Ġolomi (غلومی), 1/14662, 53. AL

Coordinates:	X: 274146.399 Y: 4190463.638
Modern Greek:	Rodina (Ροδινά, τα)
Old Toponym:	Until 1928: Golemi (Γολέμι, το)
Regional Unit:	Elis
Municipality:	Zaharo
Municipal Unit:	Zaharo
Bibliography:	Pikoulas 2001a, 409.3641; Pacifico 1704, 131: Territorio d'Arcadia, Golemi; Bory de Saint-Vincent 1834, 66: Éparchie d'Arkadia, Golémi; Leake 1846, map: Golemi; Skiadas 1993, 368; Stamatelatos–Vamva-Stamatelatou 2001, 667.
Notes:	See no. 30.

603. Arvano Ḳastro (آروانو قاسترو), 1/14662, 54. GR

Coordinates:	X: 303559.458 Y: 4151736.746
Modern Greek:	Arvanokastro (Αρβανόκαστρο, το)
Regional Unit:	Elis
Municipality:	Zaharo
Municipal Unit:	Zaharo

Bibliography:	Pikoulas 2001a, 81.473; Panagiotopoulos 1987, 275, 305.147: Territorio di Gastugni, Arvanocastro; Hopf 1873, 206: Arvano Castro; Georgacas–McDonald 1968, 99; Giannakopoulos 1994, 384; Meyer 1957, 55.
Notes:	Uninhabited location to the south-east of Minthi (Μίνθη, η) on Mt Vounouka (Όρος Βουνούκα, το). Sarris identified it with the Alvaina fortress: Sarris 1934–35, 65, 66, Table 1. Kordosis, on the other hand, argued that the Alvaina fortress should be Araklovo (Bucelet): Kordosis 1986c, 98–99; Kordosis 1989, 71–86; Kordosis 1992–93.

604. Sirvu (سروو), 1/14662, 55. AL

Notes:	Unidentified. See no. 320.

605. Bavasi (باواسى), 1/14662, 55. AL

Notes:	Unidentified. See no. 187.

606. Ḳastel İksovuni (قاستل اكسوونى), 1/14662, 55. GR

Coordinates:	X: 299886.152 Y: 4193293.301
Modern Greek:	Xyvouni/Xivouni (Ξυβούνι/Ξίβουνι, το)
Regional Unit:	Elis
Municipality:	Arhaia Olympia
Municipal Unit:	Lasionas
Bibliography:	Pikoulas 2001a, 349.3061; Panagiotopoulos 1987, 272, 304.27: Territorio di Gastugni, Xivugni.
Notes:	Perhaps linked to Carile's Chosivuni or Cerovugni: Carile 1970, 398.

607. Poliça (پوليچه), 1/14662, 57. GR

Coordinates:	X: 300913.626 Y: 4190359.547
Modern Greek:	Politsa (Πολίτσα, η)
Regional Unit:	Elis
Municipality:	Arhaia Olympia
Municipal Unit:	Lasionas
Bibliography:	GLET 1998, III 144.
Notes:	Place name Polica in Montenegro and Croatia, Police in Croatia: Vasmer 1941, 125

608. Zorila (زوريله), 1/14662, 57. AL

Coordinates:	X: 287272.160 Y: 4193491.171
Modern Greek:	Zorlia (Ζορλιά, η)
Regional Unit:	Elis
Municipality:	Ilida
Municipal Unit:	Pineia
Bibliography:	GLET 1998, I 433.
Notes:	Uninhabited location to the north-east of Simopoulo (no. 640).

609. Miġali Ẕivri (مغالى ذورى), 1/14662, 58. GR

Coordinates:	X: 306834.869 Y: 4192190.904
Modern Greek:	Lambeia (Λάμπεια, η)
Old Toponym:	Until 1928: Divri/Prinofyto (Δίβρη, η/Πρινόφυτο, το)
Regional Unit:	Elis
Municipality:	Arhaia Olympia
Municipal Unit:	Lambeia
Bibliography:	Pikoulas 2001a, 247.2068; Panagiotopoulos 1987, 272, 303.19: Territorio di Gastugni, Divri; Pacifico 1704, 123: Territorio di Gastugni, Diuri; Bory de Saint-Vincent 1834, 71: Éparchie de Gastouni, Divri; Kolokotronis 1981, 205; Leake 1830, II 116, 229, 236–239: Dhívri; Skiadas 1993, 251; Stamatelatos–Vamva-Stamatelatou 2001, 413; Antonios 1961; Anastopoulos 1994.
Notes:	< dьbrь (*Slav. n.* canyon): Vasmer 1941, 142; Symeonidis 2010, I 476. Place name Dibër in Albania, Debar in North Macedonia, and Gornji Dabar in Bosnia & Herzegovina.

610. Vunarġo (وونارغو), 1/14662, 59. GR

Coordinates:	X: 271477.145 Y: 4179614.466
Modern Greek:	Vounargo (Βούναργο, το)
Regional Unit:	Elis
Municipality:	Pyrgos
Municipal Unit:	Iardanos

Bibliography:	PIKOULAS 2001a, 107.728; PANAGIOTOPOULOS 1987, 273, 304.71: Territorio di Gastugni, Gunargo; PACIFICO 1704, 124: Territorio di Gastugni, Guneruo; HOPF 1873, 202: Vunengo vel Vunango, 206: Vunargo; BORY DE SAINT-VINCENT 1834, 70: Éparchie de Gastouni, Vounargo; LEAKE 1846, map: Vunargo; SFIKOPOULOS 1987, 286; BON 1969, 337; ILIOPOULOS 1948, 153–154.

611. Mihili (مهيلى), 1/14662, 60. AL

Notes:	Unidentified. Different from no. 265.

612. İryolo (اريولو), 1/14662, 60. GR

Coordinates:	X: 277135.249 Y: 4215006.409
Modern Greek:	Riolos (Ρίολος, ο)
Regional Unit:	Achaia
Municipality:	Dytiki Ahaïa
Municipal Unit:	Larissos
Bibliography:	PIKOULAS 2001a, 408.3628; PANAGIOTOPOULOS 1987, 274, 305.13: Territorio di Gastugni, Riolo; PACIFICO 1704, 124: Territorio di Gastugni, Riolo; BORY DE SAINT-VINCENT 1834, 70: Éparchie de Gastouni, Rhiolo; LEAKE 1846, map: Oriolo; SFIKOPOULOS 1987, 181; HOPF 1873, 202: Ruolio vel Ruolo, 205: Riolo; BON 1969, 333; TRIANTAFYLLOU 1995, II 1762–1763.
Notes:	< rivulus (*Lat. n. dim.* of rivus, rivulet, small brook): VASMER 1941, 129; SYMEONIDIS 2010, II 1220. Place name Rrjoll in Shkodër, Albania that derives from the same Latin word.

613. Prifti (پرفتى), 1/14662, 60. AL

Notes:	Unidentified. Πρίφτης (*Arv. sn.*) < prift (*Al. n.* priest): BIRIS 1998, 200.

614. Ḳartazori (قارتازورى), 1/14662, 61. AL

Notes:	Unidentified. Perhaps from kërthizor (*Al. adj.* umbilical; shaped like an umbilical cord).

615. Mayira (مايره), 1/14662, 61. AL

Coordinates:	X: 286463.516 Y: 4214750.306
Modern Greek:	Magera (Μάγερα, του)
Regional Unit:	Achaia
Municipality:	Dytiki Ahaïa
Municipal Unit:	Olenia

Bibliography:	Triantafyllou 1995, II 1206.
Notes:	Anamangra (Αναμαγκρά) height near Arla (no. 553) is still called Μάγερα by the locals. See no. 170.

616. Ayiya (آييه), *mezraʿa* in the vicinity of İryolo, 1/14662, 61.

Notes:	Unidentified. Cf. Cape Agia (Αγιά, η) to the north-west of Syhaina (no. 499).

617. Fenaromeni (فنارومنى), *mezraʿa* in the vicinity of İryolo, 1/14662, 61.

Coordinates:	X: 280541.818 Y: 4214244.211
Modern Greek:	Panagias Filokaliotissas Monastery (?) (I.M. Παναγίας Φιλοκαλιώτισσας, η)
Regional Unit:	Achaia
Municipality:	Dytiki Ahaïa
Municipal Unit:	Larissos
Bibliography:	Pikoulas 2001a, 320.2779; Bory de Saint-Vincent 1834, 87: Éparchie de Patras, Mon[re] de Philokali; Leake 1846, map: Filokali.

618. Ṣamuna (صامونا), *mezraʿa* in the vicinity of Vunarġo, 1/14662, 61.

Notes:	Unidentified.

619. Franḳa Vila (فرانقا ويله), 1/14662, 62. GR

Coordinates:	X: 267697.799 Y: 4184422.084
Modern Greek:	Frangavilas Monastery (I.M. Φραγκαβίλας, η)
Regional Unit:	Elis
Municipality:	Ilida
Municipal Unit:	Amaliada
Bibliography:	Pikoulas 2001a, 320.2780; Panagiotopoulos 1987, 273, 304.80: Territorio di Gastugni, Fr. Vill[a], Gerachi e Pagliof[anaro]; Pacifico 1704, 123: Territorio di Gastugni, Franca Villa; Expédition 1832: Mon[re] de Francavilla; Sfikopoulos 1987, 322; Hopf 1873, 202: Francavilla; Papandreou 1924, 197–199; Palla-Hronopoulou 2003, 252; Bon 1969, 359–360; Iliopoulos 1948, 174.

620. Rovyata including the communities of Niḳola Buva and Plaşa (روویاتا مع جماعت نیقولا بووه و پلاشه), 1/14662, 62. AL

Coordinates:	X: 262263.055 Y: 4188220.006
Modern Greek:	Roviata (Ροβιάτα, η)

Regional Unit:	Elis
Municipality:	Ilida
Municipal Unit:	Amaliada
Bibliography:	Pikoulas 2001a, 408.3632; Panagiotopoulos 1987, 273, 304.77: Territorio di Gastugni, Roviata; Pacifico 1704, 124: Territorio di Gastugni, Rouita; Bory de Saint-Vincent 1834, 70: Éparchie de Gastouni, Rhoviata; Leake 1846, map: Ruviati; Bon 1969, 332–333; Iliopoulos 1948, 159.
Notes:	Symeonidis did not embrace the Slavic etymology from **rovja* < rovъ (*Slav. n.* moat) proposed by Vasmer and Assenova, Stojkov and Kacori, and, based on the toponym's *end.* -άτα, put forward an Albanian etymology of a **Rrobjat* or **Rrojbat* < rrojbë or rrolbë (*Al. n.* safflower, *Carthamus tinctorius*): Symeonidis 2010, II 1221; Vasmer 1941, 149; Assenova–Stojkov–Kacori 1977, 233. However, this should be a pre-Albanian name as it was already mentioned in 1304 (Ruuiata) in the Aragon Chronicle: Fatio 1885, 80, §362. For Niḳola see no. 39, for Buva see no. 187, and for Plaşa see no. 14.

621. Rado (رادو), *mezraʿa* in the vicinity of Rovyata, 1/14662, 63.

Notes:	Unidentified. According to Vasmer, < Rado (*Scr. pn.*): Vasmer 1941, 157–158. Ράδος (*Gr. sn.*). Place name Radë in Durrës, Albania: Georgacas 1965, 161.

622. Barçi (بارچی), *mezraʿa* in the vicinity of Rovyata, 1/14662, 63.

Notes:	Unidentified. See no. 23.

623. Ḳrapeşi (قراپشی), 1/14662, 63. AL

Notes:	Unidentified. krep or krap (*Arb. n.* rock, crag; precipice; mountainside). Krapje (*Al. n.* black cherry). Place name Krapthi (Κράπθι, το) in Attica, and Krapës in Fier, Albania.

624. Androniḳa (اندرونقه), 1/14662, 63. AL

Coordinates:	X: 269402.884 Y: 4195219.071
Modern Greek:	Andronika (Ανδρόνικα, η)
Regional Unit:	Elis
Municipality:	Ilida
Municipal Unit:	Amaliada
Bibliography:	GLET 1998, I 185.
Notes:	Uninhabited location to the south of Ilida (Ήλιδα, η). Ανδρόνικος (*Gr. pn.*).

625. Niḳola Ḳumi (نيقولا قومى), 1/14662, 64. AL

Coordinates:	X: 270370.208 Y: 4212222.124
Modern Greek:	Komi (Κώμη, η)
Regional Unit:	Elis
Municipality:	Andravida-Kyllini
Municipal Unit:	Vouprasia
Bibliography:	Pikoulas 2001a, 242.2017; Pacifico 1704, 123: Territorio di Gastugni, Comi.
Notes:	For Niḳola see no. 39. kumi (*Al. n.* kiln for baking tiles); kumi or kuminë (*Al. n.* chimney); Kumi (*Al. sn.*). See also no. 495.

626. Pendeni including the community of Palunbi Ipṣari (پندنى مع جماعت پالونبى ايصارى), 1/14662, 64. AL

Coordinates:	X: 293468.028 Y: 4183130.189
Modern Greek:	Pefki (Πεύκη, η)
Old Toponym:	Until 1928: Benteni (Μπεντένι, το)
Regional Unit:	Elis
Municipality:	Pyrgos
Municipal Unit:	Oleni
Bibliography:	Pikoulas 2001a, 380.3359; Pacifico 1704, 123: Territorio di Gastugni, Bendegni; Bory de Saint-Vincent 1834, 71: Éparchie de Gastouni, Bédéni; Leake 1846, map: Bedenia; Skiadas 1993, 251; Stamatelatos–Vamva-Stamatelatou 2001, 618.
Notes:	For Pendeni see no. 85, for Palunbi see no. 43, and for Ipṣari see no. 209.

17. District of Ġardicḳo (Gatsiko) (Maps 33–34)

627. Ġardicḳo, nefs-i (غارديجقو), 1/14662, 66. GR

Coordinates:	X: 294864.713 Y: 4193510.143
Modern Greek:	Gatsiko (Γάτσικο, το)
Regional Unit:	Achaia
Municipality:	Erymanthos
Municipal Unit:	Tritaia
Bibliography:	Sfikopoulos 1987, 190-191. Hopf 1873, 202: Gardisco vel Cradici, 206: Gardizi; Triantafyllou 1974, 557.

Notes:	Ruins of a fortress and a settlement are visible on a 544m-high hill in Gatsiko, south-west of Skiadas (Σκιαδάς, ο), which the locals call Kastro tis Ohias [Κάστρο της Οχιάς, το (= Viper's Castle)]: Papandreou 1924, 180–181. See no. 361.

628. İvlanduşa (اولاندوشه), 1/14662, 68. AL

Notes:	Unidentified. See no. 115.

629. Ranesi (رانسی), 1/14662, 68. AL

Coordinates:	X: 296891.460 Y: 4200255.199
Modern Greek:	Xirohori (Ξηροχώρι, το)
Old Toponym:	Until 1928: Renesi (Ρένεσι, το)
Regional Unit:	Achaia
Municipality:	Erymanthos
Municipal Unit:	Tritaia
Bibliography:	Pikoulas 2001a, 349.3058; Panagiotopoulos 1987, 271, 303.3: Territorio di Gastugni, Renesi; Pacifico 1704, 124: Territorio di Gastuni, Renesi; Bory de Saint-Vincent 1834, 71: Éparchie de Gastouni, Rhénesi; Leake 1846, map: Renesi; Skiadas 1993, 225; Stamatelatos–Vamva-Stamatelatou 2001, 556; Triantafyllou 1995, II 1740–1741.
Notes:	See no. 43.

630. Ġomosto (غومستو), 1/14662, 69. AL

Coordinates:	X: 280982.673 Y: 4221897.772
Modern Greek:	Gomosto (Γομοστό, το)
Regional Unit:	Achaia
Municipality:	Dytiki Ahaïa
Municipal Unit:	Movri
Bibliography:	Pikoulas 2001a, 124.893; Panagiotopoulos 1987, 277, 306.54: Territorio di Patrasso, Gomosto; Pacifico 1704, 120: Territorio di Patrasso, Gomostò; Bory de Saint-Vincent 1834, 87: Éparchie de Gastouni, Gomosto; Leake 1846, map: Gomosto; Triantafyllou 1995, I 443–444.
Notes:	γιομοστός, γιομιστός or γεμιστός (*Gr. adj.* stuffed). Γεμιστός (*Gr. sn.*).

631. Ṣuli (صولی), 1/14662, 70. AL

Coordinates:	X: 311732.195 Y: 4225894.163
Modern Greek:	Ano Souli (Άνω Σούλι, το)

Regional Unit:	Achaia
Municipality:	Patra
Municipal Unit:	Patra
Bibliography:	Pikoulas 2001a, 430.3849; Triantafyllou 1995, II 1897–1898.
Notes:	See no. 37.

632. Gön Lopesi (كون لوپسى), 1/14662, 70. AL

Coordinates:	X: 310072.867 Y: 4218643.953
Modern Greek:	Katarraktis (Καταρράκτης, ο)
Old Toponym:	Until 1928: Lopesi (Λόπεσι, το)
Regional Unit:	Achaia
Municipality:	Erymanthos
Municipal Unit:	Farres
Bibliography:	Pikoulas 2001a, 200.1616; Panagiotopoulos 1987, 268, 302.7: Territorio di Callavritta, Lepessi; Pacifico 1704, 122: Territorio di Calaurita, Lopessi; Bory de Saint-Vincent 1834, 73: Éparchie de Kalavrita, Lopési; Leake 1830, II 121: Lópesi; Skiadas 1993, 226; Stamatelatos–Vamva-Stamatelatou 2001, 321; Triantafyllou 1995, I 1184–1186.
Notes:	Gjon (*Al. pn.* John). For Lopesi see no. 83.

633. Çapoġa (چاپوغه), 1/14662, 70. AL

Coordinates:	X: 299273.522 Y: 4197942.956
Modern Greek:	Pteri (Πτέρη, η)
Old Toponym:	Until 1955: Tsapoga (Τσαπόγα, η); until 1971: Mavrohori (Μαυροχώρι, το)
Regional Unit:	Achaia
Municipality:	Erymanthos
Municipal Unit:	Tritaia
Bibliography:	Pikoulas 2001a, 399.3541; Panagiotopoulos 1987, 271, 303.8: Territorio di Gastugni, Zapoga; Pacifico 1704, 124: Territorio di Gastugni, Zapogna; Bory de Saint-Vincent 1834, 71: Éparchie de Gastouni, Tsapoga; Leake 1846, map: Tzapova; Skiadas 1993, 225; Stamatelatos–Vamva-Stamatelatou 2001, 652; Triantafyllou 1995, II 2114.
Notes:	According to Biris, Τσαπόγας (*Arv. sn.* long-legged): Biris 1998, 202; possibly from çapok (*Al. n.* hipbone, haunch).

634. İvlaḫo (اولاخو), 1/14662, 71. AL

Coordinates:	X: 313269.750 Y: 4209062.872

Modern Greek:	Vlahoi (?) (Βλάχοι, οι)
Regional Unit:	Achaia
Municipality:	Erymanthos
Municipal Unit:	Farres
Bibliography:	GLET 1998, I 284.
Notes:	Uninhabited location to the south-west of Mihas (Μίχας, ο). See no. 54.

635. Maji (ماژی), 1/14662, 71. AL

Coordinates:	X: 264348.430 Y: 4206357.576
Modern Greek:	Ano Kourtesi/Kourtesis (?) (Άνω Κούρτεσι, το/Κουρτέσης, ο)
Old Toponym:	Until 1928: Mazi (Μάζι, το)
Regional Unit:	Elis
Municipality:	Andravida-Kyllini
Municipal Unit:	Vouprasia
Bibliography:	PIKOULAS 2001a, 229.1902; BORY DE SAINT-VINCENT 1834, 70: Éparchie de Gastouni, Mazi; LEAKE 1830, II 168–169: Mazi; SKIADAS 1993, 248; STAMATELATOS–VAMVA-STAMATELATOU 2001, 83; ILIOPOULOS 1948, 173.
Notes:	See no. 129.

636. Mastro Andoni (ماسترو اندونی), 1/14662, 71. AL

Coordinates:	X: 294648.498 Y: 4204400.792
Modern Greek:	Mastrantonis (Μαστραντώνης, ο)
Regional Unit:	Achaia
Municipality:	Erymanthos
Municipal Unit:	Tritaia
Bibliography:	PIKOULAS 2001a, 278.2366; PANAGIOTOPOULOS 1987, 271, 303.6: Territorio di Gastugni, Mastrodogni; PACIFICO 1704, 124: Territorio di Gastugni, Nastrandagni; BORY DE SAINT-VINCENT 1834, 71: Éparchie de Gastouni, Mastrandoni; LEAKE 1846, map: Mastrandoni; TRIANTAFYLLOU 1995, II 1235.
Notes:	Μαστραντώνης (*Gr. sn.*).

637. Barbuc (باربوج), 1/14662, 72. AL

Notes:	Unidentified. See no. 424.

638. S̱opiya (ثوپیه), 1/14662, 72. AL

Notes:	Unidentified. Thopia or Topia (*Al. sn.*): Kolleka 1982, 31–32.

639. Lopesi (لوپسی), 1/14662, 72. AL

Coordinates:	X: 317375.178 Y: 4193485.735
Modern Greek:	Agioi Theodoroi (Άγιοι Θεόδωροι, οι)
Old Toponym:	Until 1940: Lopesi (Λόπεσι, το); until 1953: Lopesion (Λοπέσιον, το)
Regional Unit:	Achaia
Municipality:	Kalavryta
Municipal Unit:	Aroania
Bibliography:	Pikoulas 2001a, 40.92; Panagiotopoulos 1987, 261, 300.116: Territorio di Caritena, Lopesi; Pacifico 1704, 129: Territorio di Caritena, Lopesi; Bory de Saint-Vincent 1834, 76: Éparchie de Karytæne, Lopési; Leake 1846, map: Lopesi; Skiadas 1993, 245; Stamatelatos–Vamva-Stamatelatou 2001, 16.
Notes:	See no. 83.

640. Simoplu (سیموپلو), 1/14662, 73. AL

Coordinates:	X: 286102.528 Y: 4191564.456
Modern Greek:	Simopoulo (Σιμόπουλο, το)
Regional Unit:	Elis
Municipality:	Ilida
Municipal Unit:	Pineia
Bibliography:	Pikoulas 2001a, 420.3752; Panagiotopoulos 1987, 274, 304.102: Territorio di Gastugni, Simopollo; Pacifico 1704, 124: Territorio di Gastugni, Simopulo; Bory de Saint-Vincent 1834, 71: Éparchie de Gastouni, Simoplu; Leake 1846, map: Simoplu.
Notes:	Σιμόπουλος (*Gr. sn.*) < Σίμος (*Gr. pn. colloq.* Simeon) + -όπουλος (*Gr. end.* son of): Seremetakis–Dimitriou 2005, 218–219.

641. Ḳalanci (قالانجی), 1/14662, 73. AL

Coordinates:	X: 303082.675 Y: 4202259.867
Modern Greek:	Kalentzi (Καλέντζι, το)
Regional Unit:	Achaia
Municipality:	Erymanthos
Municipal Unit:	Kalentzi
Bibliography:	Pikoulas 2001a, 169.1319; Panagiotopoulos 1987, 276, 305.15: Territorio di Patrasso, Callenzi; Pacifico 1704, 121: Territorio di Patrasso, Calenzi; Bory de Saint-Vincent 1834, 86: Éparchie de Patras, Kalendzi; Leake 1846, map: Kalendzi; Triantafyllou 1995, I 936–937.
Notes:	Καλέντζης (*Gr., Arv. sn.*): Biris 1998, 194. Kalanxhi and Galanxhi (*Al. sn.*). According to Vasmer, < **Kalenьcь* (*old Slav. dim.* small mudflat) < kalъ (*old Slav. n.* potter's clay, mortar, puddle): Vasmer 1941, 111–112, 163. See also Symeonidis 2010, I 595.

642. İsliva (اسلیوه), 1/14662, 73. AL

Coordinates:	X: 289216.149 Y: 4191606.130
Modern Greek:	Skliva (Σκλίβα, η)
Regional Unit:	Elis
Municipality:	Ilida
Municipal Unit:	Pineia
Bibliography:	Pikoulas 2001a, 425.3796; Panagiotopoulos 1987, 271, 303.4: Territorio di Gastugni, Scliva; Pacifico 1704, 124: Territorio di Gastugni, Seliua; Bory de Saint-Vincent 1834, 71: Éparchie de Gastouni, Skliva; Leake 1846, map: Skliva.
Notes:	See no. 40.

643. Şaleşi (شالشی), 1/14662, 73. AL

Notes:	Unidentified. See no. 581.

644. Lala (لالا), 1/14662, 74. AL

Coordinates:	X: 298709.341 Y: 4175806.744
Modern Greek:	Lalas (Λάλας, ο)
Regional Unit:	Elis
Municipality:	Arhaia Olympia

Municipal Unit:	Foloï
Bibliography:	Pikoulas 2001a, 246.2059; Pacifico 1704, 123: Territorio di Gastugni, Lalla; Bory de Saint-Vincent 1834, 71: Éparchie de Gastouni, Lala; Leake 1846, map: Lala (Lasion); Iliopoulos 1948, 177.
Notes:	See no. 410.

645. Gerbeşi (كربشى), 1/14662, 74. AL

Coordinates:	X: 270914.585 Y: 4229661.643
Modern Greek:	Paralimni (Παραλίμνη, η)
Old Toponym:	Until 1955: (Mesa) Gerbesi [(Μέσα) Γκέρμπεσι, το]; until 1991: Mavron Oros (Μαύρον Όρος, το)
Regional Unit:	Achaia
Municipality:	Dytiki Ahaïa
Municipal Unit:	Larissos
Bibliography:	Pikoulas 2001a, 281.2394; Skiadas 1993, 223; Stamatelatos–Vamva-Stamatelatou 2001, 591.
Notes:	See no. 381.

646. İsturġova (استورغوه), 1/14662, 74. GR

Notes:	Unidentified. struga (*Scr. n.* riverbed). Place name Strugovi in Montenegro: RHSJ 1956–58, XVI 778. See also no. 98.

647. Ro̱zinotiẖo (روذينوتيخو), *mezra'a* dependent on Ġardicḳo, 1/14662, 74.

Notes:	Unidentified.

648. Ḳomi (قومى), *mezra'a* dependent on Ġardicḳo, 1/14662, 74.

Coordinates:	X: 325553.732 Y: 4220349.602
Modern Greek:	Komi (Κώμη, η)
Regional Unit:	Achaia
Municipality:	Kalavryta
Municipal Unit:	Kalavryta
Bibliography:	Pikoulas 2001a, 241.2014; Panagiotopoulos 1987, 269, 303.79: Territorio di Callavritta, Comi; Pacifico 1704, 122: Territorio di Calaurita, Comi; Bory de Saint-Vincent 1834, 74: Éparchie de Kalavrita, Komi.
Notes:	See no. 495.

649. İsliva-ı dīğer (اسليوه ديكر), *mezraʿa* dependent on Ġardicḳo, 1/14662, 74.

Notes:	Unidentified. See no. 40.

650. İstamiro (استاميرو), 1/14662, 75. GR

Coordinates:	X: 282925.586 Y: 4192268.104
Modern Greek:	Hatzi [Χατζί, το (= Χατζή, του)]
Regional Unit:	Elis
Municipality:	Ilida
Municipal Unit:	Pineia
Bibliography:	Pikoulas 2001a, 484.4372; Pacifico 1704, 124: Territorio di Gastugni, Stamerò Canzides; Expédition 1832: Hadjidès; Bory de Saint-Vincent 1834, 71: Éparchie de Gastouni, Hadgidès; Leake 1846, map: Atzides; Dragoumis 1921, 257–258; Hopf 1873, 202, 206: Stamero vel Stamiro; Bon 1969, 336–337.
Notes:	Papandreou mentioned ruins of Frankish fortifications in Hatzi, to the west of Simopoulo (no. 640), which, according to Sfikopoulos, are connected to the fortress of Stamiro: Papandreou 1924, 101; Sfikopoulos 1987, 285–286. Markl's identification with Santameri (no. 524) seems erroneous: Markl 1966, 60. Stamer (*Scr. sn.*) attested in the 9th c.; Stamir (*Scr. pn.*): RHSJ 1956–58, XVI 361.

651. Mazarak including the community of Ḳuçi (مزراك مع جماعت قوچى), 1/14662, 76. AL

Coordinates:	X: 287737.614 Y: 4194868.649
Modern Greek:	Mazaraki (Μαζαράκι, το)
Regional Unit:	Elis
Municipality:	Ilida
Municipal Unit:	Pineia
Bibliography:	Pikoulas 2001a, 268.2273; Expédition 1832: Mazaraki; Leake 1846, map: Mazaraki; Iliopoulos 1948, 178.
Notes:	For Mazarak see no. 308, and for Ḳuçi see no. 186.

652. Manesi (مانسى), 1/14662, 76. AL

Notes:	Unidentified. See no. 22.

653. Ẕirmi (ذيرمى), 1/14662, 76. AL

Notes:	Unidentified. Place name Dhërmi in Vlorë, Albania.

654. Ḫarkâ (خركا), 1/14662, 77. AL

Notes:	Unidentified. See no. 454.

655. Maẕiñik (ماذكك), 1/14662, 77. AL

Notes:	Unidentified. See no. 526.

656. Ranbiyaḳa (رانبياقه), 1/14662, 78. AL

Coordinates:	X: 284131.433 Y: 4187143.432
Modern Greek:	Roumbieka (Ρουμπιέκα, η)
Regional Unit:	Elis
Municipality:	Pyrgos
Municipal Unit:	Oleni
Bibliography:	GLET 1998, III 224.
Notes:	Uninhabited location to the north-east of Koutsohera (no. 259). Place name Rubjekë in Durrës, Albania: Georgacas–McDonald 1968, 346. Ρεμπέκας (*Arv. sn.* branched) < rremb (*Al. n.* branch): Biris 1998, 200. See also no. 487.

657. Liḳuresi including the community of Bura (ليقورسى مع جماعت بوره), 1/14662, 78. AL

Coordinates:	X: 322235.865 Y: 4167852.637
Modern Greek:	Lykouresis [Λυκούρεσης, ο (= Λυκούρεσι, το)]
Regional Unit:	Arcadia
Municipality:	Gortynia
Municipal Unit:	Iraia
Bibliography:	Pikoulas 2001a, 266.2249; Panagiotopoulos 1987, 260, 299.66: Territorio di Caritena, Licuresi Bodia; Pacifico 1704, 129: Territorio di Caritena, Ricurissipodia; Bory de Saint-Vincent 1834, 75: Éparchie de Karytæne, Lykourési; Leake 1846, map: Lykuresi; Skiadas 1993, 312.
Notes:	For Liḳuresi see no. 62. burrë (*Al. n.* male person, man); Μπούρας (*Gr. sn*). Cf. microtoponym Boura Tzeleva (Μπούρα Τζελέβα, σ/του) in the surroundings of Zygovisti (Ζυγοβίστι, το) in Arcadia.

658. Ranesi (رانسى), *mezraʿa* in the vicinity of Liḳuresi, 1/14662, 78.

Notes:	Unidentified. See no. 43.

659. Fil Adrofinos including the community of Muzak (فل ادرفنوس مع جماعت مزاك), 1/14662, 79. AL

Notes:	Unidentified. Φιλανθρωπινός (*Byz. Gr. sn.* philanthrope). For Muzak see no. 380.

660. Malaḳas (مالاقاس), 1/14662, 79. AL

Coordinates:	X: 276538.303 Y: 4180244.845
Modern Greek:	Elaionas (Ελαιώνας, ο)
Old Toponym:	Until 1928: Malakasi (Μαλακάσι, το)
Regional Unit:	Elis
Municipality:	Pyrgos
Municipal Unit:	Pyrgos
Bibliography:	Pikoulas 2001a, 147.111; Bory de Saint-Vincent 1834, 70: Éparchie de Gastouni, Malapasi; Leake 1846, map: Malapasi; Skiadas 1993, 247; Stamatelatos–Vamva-Stamatelatou 2001, 209; Giannakopoulos 1994, 372; Iliopoulos 1948, 178: Malapasi (Μαλαπάση, σ/του) seldom called Malakasi (Μαλακάση, σ/του); Rangavis 1853, II 182: Μαλαπάσι.
Notes:	Μαλακάσας (*Arv. sn.*): Biris 1998, 197. Place name Mallakastër in Dibër, Albania. According to Kolleka, from mallëkesë (*Al. n.* curse): Kolleka 1982, 30. According to Hahn, the word must have a Vlach etymology: mala (*Vl. adv.* much) + kasch (*Vl. n.* cheese): Hahn 1854, I 341, n. 176. See also Symeonidis 2010, I 866.

661. Andon (اندون), 1/14662, 79. AL

Modern Greek:	Antoni (?) (Αντώνη, του)
Regional Unit:	Arcadia (?)
Municipality:	Megalopoli (?)
Municipal Unit:	Gortyna (?)
Bibliography:	Pikoulas 2001a, 77.443; Panagiotopoulos 1987, 261, 300.114, 358: Territorio di Caritena, Andoni; Pacifico 1704, 129: Territorio di Caritena, Andoni; Bory de Saint-Vincent 1834, 76: Éparchie de Karytæne, Andoni.
Notes:	Unidentified. The *Expédition* listed this deserted village next to Zounati (no. 331), Katsimbali and Karvounaria (no. 332), without locating it on the map. Panagiotopoulos suggested it was probably located by Panagia (Παναγιά, η) area in Dimitsana (no. 434): Panagiotopoulos 1987, 358. Αντώνιος (*Gr. pn.* Anthony) > Anton, Andon (*Al. pn.*).

662. Manesi (مانسی), 1/14662, 80. AL

Notes:	Unidentified. See no. 22.

663. Murik Buva (موريك بووه), 1/14662, 80. AL

Coordinates:	X: 309250.747 Y: 4216884.361
Modern Greek:	Rodia (Ροδιά, η)
Old Toponym:	Until 1955: Bouga (Μπούγα, του)
Regional Unit:	Achaia

Municipality:	Erymanthos
Municipal Unit:	Farres
Bibliography:	Pikoulas 2001a, 409.3640; Expédition 1832: Bouga; Leake 1846, map: Buga; Skiadas 1993, 226; Stamatelatos–Vamva-Stamatelatou 2001, 667; Triantafyllou 1995, II 1336–1337.
Notes:	For Murik see no. 46, and for Buva see no. 187.

664. Niķola Buva (نيقولا بووه), 1/14662, 80. AL

Coordinates:	X: 317118.709 Y: 4171940.109
Modern Greek:	Kokkinorrahi (?) (Κοκκινορράχη, η)
Old Toponym:	Until 1928: Bouga (Μπούγα, του)
Regional Unit:	Arcadia
Municipality:	Gortynia
Municipal Unit:	Tropaia
Bibliography:	Pikoulas 2001a, 214.1752; Panagiotopoulos 1987, 347: Territorio di Caritena: Bouza/Bouga; Bory de Saint-Vincent 1834, 76: Éparchie de Karytæne, Bouza; Leake 1846, map: Buza; Skiadas 1993, 312; Stamatelatos–Vamva-Stamatelatou 2001, 360.
Notes:	For Niķola see no. 39, and for Buva see no. 187.

665. Duranķorgi (دورانقوركى), 1/14662, 80. AL

Notes:	Unidentified.

666. Kiẕiķuma (كيذقمه), *mezraʿa*, 1/14662, 81.

Notes:	Unidentified. Cf. microtoponym Kidikima/Kidikoma/Kidikouma/Ikdikima/Kidikma (Κιδίκιμα/Κιδίκωμα/Κιδίκουμα/Ικδίκημα/Κηδίκμα, η) in the surroundings of Skliros (Σκληρός, ο) in Messenia: Georgacas–McDonald 1968, 157; Dokos 1977–84, 296. **Kedhikuma* (*Arv. sn.*) perhaps linked to kedh or keth (*Al. n.* child, kid) + kum (*Al. n.* godfather): Mann 1948, 190, 225.

18. District of Salmenik (Salmeniko) (see maps 25–26)

667. Salmenik (سلمنيك), TT10, 184.

Coordinates:	X: 317142.795 Y: 4233414.121
Modern Greek:	Ano Salmeniko (Άνω Σαλμενίκο, το)
Regional Unit:	Achaia
Municipality:	Aigialeia

Municipal Unit:	Erineos
Bibliography:	Pikoulas 2001a, 413.3681; Panagiotopoulos 1987, 278, 306.86: Territorio di Patrasso, Salmenico; Pacifico 1704, 121: Territorio di Patrasso, Salmenico, *olim Salmeniaca*; Expédition 1832: Salméniko; Leake 1830, III 193, 418: Salmeníko; Hopf 1873, 205: Selmenico; Sfikopoulos 1987, 152–154; TT80, 551–552, 1101, 1104, 1111–1112; Triantafyllou 1995, II 1816–1818.
Notes:	The castle of Salmeniko is mentioned in the TT10 with reference to its warden, timariot Ayas. In the TT80 cadastre (1514/5), Salmenik formed a distinct district. < **Solmьnikъ* or **slamenьnikь* < slama (*old Slav. n.* straw): Vasmer 1941, 138; Symeonidis 2010, II 1237. Place name Slamniki in Slovenia, Słomnik and Słomniczki in Poland.

2

The Demography of the Peloponnese

The function of the Ottoman *taḥrīr*s, like the Byzantine cadastres, was primarily to register landholdings for tax purposes. Nevertheless, they also indirectly provide us with details which cast light on demographic elements and structures, in our case, of the late Byzantine and early Ottoman Peloponnese.[1]

The Ottoman State put remarkable effort into recording as accurately as possible the tax-paying units in its domains. The TT10-1/14662 cadastre registers the non-Muslim units encumbered with the *ispence*. The basic fiscal unit was the family, namely the household or hearth (*ḫāne*), headed by an adult male. The *ispence* in this instance amounted to 25 *aḳçe*s annually. The single adult men, recorded as *mücerred*, also paid 25 *aḳçes*. On the other hand, the widows (*bīve*) in charge of a household paid only 6 *aḳçes*. By virtue of paying the *ispence*, widows were included in the register, while the rest of the female population, under-age males, or male adults who were physically disabled or mentally ill, were not registered and therefore not obliged to pay the *ispence*.

Each individual was recorded in different ways on the basis of the existing information: (a) forename followed by family name, e.g. *Yorgi Ḳaçari*;[2] (b) when the family name was unknown, the individual was identified on the basis of family relationships: son, brother, son-in-law, nephew, stepson or relative of a person, e.g. *Yani veled-i Pavlos*,[3] *Miḫal birāder-i Todoros Ḳaloyiroplos*,[4] *İstemad dāmād-ı Yorgi Damyano*,[5] *Niḳola anebsosti Niḳola Livan*,[6] *Todoros proġonostu Andra*,[7] *Todo ḫīş-i Gergi Zepandi*;[8] (c) if no family connections could be ascertained, the individual was identified by virtue of whose neighbour he was, e.g. *Reçi ki nezd-i Aresti mī-şeved*;[9] or (d) whose lodger he was, e.g. *mücerred Yani besleme-i Evorondino*.[10] When two entries in the same settlement refer to namesakes, the word *dīğer* (other) is used to distinguish one from another, e.g. *Aleksi Muzaki* and *Aleksi-i dīğer Muzaki*.[11]

The scribe in some cases added special features or characteristics of certain inhabitants in order to provide the Ottoman administration with significant attributes and capacities of the taxpayers and hence avoid misidentification, namely: janissary (*yeñiçeri*),[12] soldier (*ʿazab*),[13] paid cavalryman (*ʿulūfeci*),[14] apostate (*mürted*),[15] lame (*aʿrec*),[16] monk (*keşīş*),[17] young boy (*küçük oġlan*),[18] elderly man [*yiros* < γέρος (*Gr.*)],[19] of/from Mystras (*Mizis̱raʾi*).[20]

1 Lowry 1992, 12.
2 1/14662, 67. This was the custom in the registers compiled immediately after the Ottoman conquest of an ex-Byzantine province, whereas in later registers the relevant entries were usually in the form of forename-patronym, e.g. *Aleksi veled-i Ḳosta*. In this aspect the Ottoman registers constitute a thesaurus for late Byzantine family names, see Lowry 1992, 13.
3 TT10, 56. In a single case the Arabic term *veled* (offspring, child, son) was replaced by *bin* (son): TT10, 3.
4 1/14662, 54. The term *birāder* is also rendered in its Middle Persian form: *birāẕer*.
5 TT10, 91.
6 The Ottoman scribe used the Greek phrase *anebsosti* < ἀνεψιός του (his nephew) to record this relationship; it appears three times: 1/14662, 69.
7 The Greek term *proġonostu* < προγονός του (his stepson) was used four times in the register: 1/14662, 70, 71, 74.
8 TT10, 22.
9 Mentioned once: 1/14662, 67.
10 Mentioned once: 1/14662, 67.
11 1/14662, 79.
12 Manol in İvraḫni (Vrahni): TT10, 1; Miḫal in Rolo (Rogoi?): TT10, 56; İstefano in Ḳulukina (Kloukines/Kloukinohoria): TT10, 62; Yorgi and Manol in Vumero (Goumero): TT10, 83–84.
13 Manol in Ayo İvlaşi (Agios Vlasios): TT10, 14; widow Mariya, wife of an ʿ*azab* in Vunarġo (Vounargo): 1/14662, 59. For the term ʿ*azab* see Pakalin 1946, 'Azab', I 123–131.
14 Yani in Londar (Leontari): TT10, 137.
15 Yani in Ġardik (Gardriki-Amfeia?): TT10, 128; Petros and Niḳola in Ḳalandriça (Halandritsa): 1/14662, 4; Todoros in Maẕiñik: 1/14662, 16.
16 Niḳola Manṣo Ġramatiḳo in Ḳalavrita (Kalavryta): TT10, 38.
17 Papamarti in Lapata (Lapatheia): TT10, 9; Todoros in Pratano (Platanos): TT10, 88; Asani in Ayo Vaşıl: 1/14662, 53; Nofitos Ḳaloyiros in Ġardicḳo (Gatsiko): 1/14662, 67.
18 Yorgi Monoḫo from Patras (*Blaya Badraʾi*) in Ṣaravali (Saravali): TT10, 40.
19 Dimitri Ġatro in Ayo İlya (Agios Ilias): 1/14662, 50.
20 Yadriḳo in Ġardicḳo (Gatsiko): 1/14662, 67.

Due to the persisting wars and the plague, the Peloponnesian population had suffered losses.[55] These losses were counterbalanced to some degree by the invitation and settlement of Albanian nomadic clans, who formed populous groups consisting of families, or tribes.[56] They came to the Peloponnese carrying their animals and movable goods and offered military service in return for being allowed to settle, and enjoy free movement and tax exemption.[57] In the first stage of their arrival, in the space of ten to thirty years they were probably in search of appropriate land for animal husbandry. As portrayed on map 35, drawn in the light of the evidence contained in the TT10-1/14662 register, by the early 1460s the Albanians had established their settlements throughout the Peloponnese in areas of low, middle and high altitude.

As mentioned above, the main reason for placing them in a different category in the cadastre is the 20% reduction on the *ispence* encumbrance (20 *aḳçe*s instead of the 25 the Greeks paid). This most probably mirrors a late Byzantine and Venetian practice that the Ottomans adopted to control the intractable Albanians and should be examined within the context of the 'continuity for stability' policy. In the contemporary Ottoman cadastres of Trikala 1454/5[58] and Euboea (1474)[59] such a reduction is not attested. Within half a century, the favourable taxation terms granted to the Albanians had ceased to exist. The TT80 register of the Peloponnese, compiled in the reign of Selīm I (1514/5), recorded the same amount of *ispence* (25 *aḳçe*s annually) levied on both Greeks and Albanians and, for this reason, did not earmark the Albanian villages.[60] This shows that by the early sixteenth century Ottoman rule in the peninsula was consolidated. In the law codes (*ḳānūnnāme*s) of the mid-sixteenth century concerning the regions of Thebes and Livadeia the taxes levied on the productive activities of the Albanians are explicitly mentioned, without revealing any reduction though.[61] The TT10-1/14662, on the other hand, clearly noted the Albanian villages with the heading: 'of the Albanian community' (*ez cemāʿat-i Arnavudān*). Besides the villages marked as Albanian, there were inhabitants of Albanian origin in Greek villages and towns, as their names indicate (see list below).[62] These, however, like the rest were due to pay a 25-*aḳçe ispence*:

Ḳalavrita (Kalavryta) District. İvraḫni (Vrahni): Vorila bin Vorila;[63] Ḳalavrita: Yani Petrobuva.[64]

Bejenik (Vlaherna) District. Bejenik: Mangişa Mazaraki and bachelor Andriya Mazaraki;[65] Perso̱r (Perthori): Vaṣıl Praski and his brother S̱otoki.[66]

Balya Badra (Patra) Disrict. Ṣaravali (Saravali): Gin Peta.[67]

Voştiça (Aigio) District. Voştiça: Gin Muzaki and Cani Buva;[68] Ayo Paraskevi (Paraskevi): Andriya Dorza and his brother Yani;[69] Epanolaġo (Lapanagoi): Bardi son of Andriya Kiniġos, Gin Kiniġos, Yorgi Prifti, and Ḳozma Barçi;[70] Ġumaniça (Drosato, Goumenissa): Mangişa Rusi;[71] Ẕilivina (Vilivina): Muriki İvlaḫo;[72] Rolo (Rogoi?): Trimas İksanos;[73] Ḳılapaçuna (Plataniotissa): Yorgi Ḳaratula;[74] Namuni: Ẕyaleşi Ḳalimani;[75]

55 For the depopulation of the Peloponnese see Zakythinos 1949a, 9–10. The 'Black Death' struck the Peloponnese in autumn 1347 with later outbreaks in 1361, 1372–1374, 1388, 1422, and 1431: Panagiotopoulos 1987, 61–68; Detorakis 1976–78, 15–16.

56 The Albanian term *farë* (*literary* seed, sperm, progeny) denotes this tribal social structure; see Alexakis 1994, 170–171.

57 Panagiotopoulos 1987, 60. See also Braudel 1972, I 48–49. Two Byzantine documents dated 1451 that cast light on the Despots' practice of recruiting Albanian horsemen by offering them tax exemption are published by Vranoussi: Vranoussi 1998. See also Vranoussis 1967, 689–690.

58 Delilbaşi–Arikan 2001, *passim*.

59 Balta 1989, *passim*.

60 TT80, *passim*.

61 Oğuz–Balta 1998, 30, 4b§3–5, 4b§7, 34, 6b§4–5; repr. Oğuz–Balta 1999, 162, 165.

62 This list contains dwellers whose forename and/or family name is of Albanian etymology; due to lack of further evidence, it does not include Slavic names that may have been acquired by Albanians during their migration to Greek lands through Slavic-speaking territories. In any case, the names correspond to the anthroponymy of the settlements, which were noted by the scribe as Albanian.

63 TT10, 2.

64 TT10, 39.

65 TT10, 28.

66 TT10, 34.

67 TT10, 40.

68 TT10, 42.

69 TT10, 48.

70 TT10, 51.

71 TT10, 52.

72 TT10, 55.

73 TT10, 56.

74 TT10, 56.

75 TT10, 57.

Yaḳoḫto (Ano Diakopto/Diakofto): İvrato Peta, Yorgi Peta, Yorgi Muzaki, Dimitri Rali, bachelor Todoros Peta, bachelor Aleksi Muzaki, and bachelor Yani Rali;[76] Potamya (Ano & Kato Potamia): Gin Zenbeş, Gön son-in-law of Nomiḳo;[77] Çimlo (Tsivlos): Manḳola Suḫina;[78] Ḳulukina (Kloukines/Kloukinohoria): Gin Ġunari;[79] Ḫotoġosti: İstanişa Mazaraki;[80] Sinoviro (Sinevro): İstini Çarḫoplo;[81] Perisori (Perithori): Dima Beluşi;[82] Revaniça (Arravonitsa): Dimitri Suli, Mangişa Suli, and Leḳa Nikita.[83]

Ḫulumiç (Hlemoutsi) District. Ḫulumiç: Ḳuvara Mazaraki, bachelor Manḳolas Ronberto, Petro Mazaraki, Leḳa İşpata, and Petro Manesi;[84] Ġastuni (Gastouni): Muriki Platistomo, Dimitri Mangişa, and Gin Aleksi;[85] Şavalya (Savalia): Petro Beluşi and Miḫal Bezulḳa;[86] Kelavi (Koroivos): Miḫal Girḳa, bachelor Yani Pikerna, and widow Skâva spouse of Pikerna;[87] Andraviza (Andravida): Gin Ḳaluzi, Muriki Floḳa, Ḳosta Manesi, Gön Artiki, and Peta Ḳazneş;[88] Lihyana (Lehaina): İştin Buḳomad, Niḳa Ḳunḳuli, Leḳa Ḳunḳuli, Marti İskliva, Dima Ḳunḳuli, Yani Ḳaḳuri, and bachelor Petro Ḳaḳuri;[89] Aya Baraskevi (Agia Paraskevi): Muriki Leoplos;[90] the entire Ġramatiḳo (Grammatikos) village: Murik Franḳuli, Uzġos Yani, and Gön Siraḳ;[91] Murji: Mangişa Murji, Marti Klasira, Leḳa Prifti, Petro Lata, Gön brother of Marti Kiriçi, and widow Todora wife of Toskesina (judging from her andronym, her late husband must have been Albanian).[92]

Vumero (Goumero) District. Vumero: Papas Manḳola and Praski Liyoroviti;[93] Zervini (Kryovrysi): Praski Floḳuni;[94] Yirmoçani (Platanitsa): Sotoki Ḳuḳa;[95] Zelaḫova (Amygdalies): Petros Praski and Niḳola Buva[96] Vervena: Muriki Ḳufoplo,[97] Yani Vari, and Dimitri İstralica;[98] Şarakin (Sarakini): Vasi Şarakin, Gin Ḳulami, Muriki Şarakin, Gin İsḳarpi, Gön Şarakin, and Gin Şarakin;[99] Dumeña: Yani Mazarak and Yani Ḳalapüs;[100] Ḳariza: Gin Ḳarida;[101] Olana (Oleni, Paliolena): Petro Lata;[102] Pondiḳo (Katakolo): Yorgi İskliva, Niḳola Klasira, and Lazaro Klaşira.[103]

Kirvuḳor (Palaiokastro/Koufoplaiiko Kastro) District. Mundriza (Gryllos): Yani Bardi.[104]

Arḳadya (Kyparissia) District. Loyi (Diodia): Leo Ḳruya and Miḫal Lalesi.[105]

Londar (Leontari) District. Londar: Miḫal Marti, Dimitri Prapa, Niḳola İstraliça, Dimitri Rondaki, Vasi Lala, and Yani Rondaki;[106] Aya Yorgi (Lykosoura): Dimitri Ḳurti, Yani Ḳurti, Yorgi Iḳraḳuki, Yorgi Malesini, Niḳola Beluçi, Papas Marti, Gin Ḳayi, Dimitri Ḳayi, Yorgi Ḳayi, Sotoki Ḳurtesi, İstemati Ḳurtesi, Andon Manesi, Mangişa Manesi, Pavlos Arvaniti, bachelor İstemati Ḳurtesi, bachelor Yani Marti, and widow

76 TT10, 58.
77 TT10, 59.
78 TT10, 60.
79 TT10, 62.
80 TT10, 65.
81 TT10, 66.
82 TT10, 68.
83 TT10, 73.
84 TT10, 76–77.
85 TT10, 78.
86 TT10, 79.
87 TT10, 79.
88 1/14662, 44.
89 1/14662, 47.
90 1/14662, 49.
91 1/14662, 49.
92 1/14662, 85.
93 TT10, 83, 85.
94 TT10, 90.
95 TT10, 91.
96 TT10, 105.
97 TT10, 105.
98 TT10, 108.
99 TT10, 123.
100 1/14662, 89.
101 1/14662, 90.
102 1/14662, 94.
103 1/14662, 97.
104 TT10, 126.
105 TT10, 133–134.
106 TT10, 137–139.

Ḳurtasina;[107] Lonḳanik (Longanikos): S̱otoki Ḳurtesi and Ḳosta Ḳurtesi;[108] Ẕimiçana (Dimitsana): Manol Praski, Ḳondostavla Manesi, and Yani Manesi;[109] Çarnuẖlu (Pefko): Andriya Buva, Mangişa Traẖya, Petros Bezulḳa, Duşa Sirvos, Gin Ḫayḳal, bachelor Dima Bezulḳa, and bachelor Leḳa Sirvos.[110]

Ḳoris̱os (Korinthos) District. Ḳoris̱os: Niḳola Praski, Niḳola Ḳurtesi, Yorgi Dara, Yani Ḳuḳas, Andriya son-in-law of Gin (we cannot determine whether Andriya was of Albanian origin, like his father-in-law), Marti Zepandi, Vas̱i Ranesi, Yorgi Şurbi, Niḳola Manḳola, Pavlos Ranbaḳa, Dimitri Praski, Gin Plaşa, Ranesi son-in-law of Mastromiẖal Cingene, and bachelor Todoros Praski;[111] Vaṣılıḳa (Sikyona): Ḳonda Dara, S̱odoro Dara, and Niḳola Ḳurtesa;[112] Ayo Vaṣıl/Çağıl Ḥiṣārı (Agios Vasileios): Gin Şalesi.[113]

Balya Badra (Patra) District. Siẕereḳastro (Sidirokastro): Dima Maji;[114] Ḳamaniça (Kamenitsa): Yani Gerbesi, Gin Orfano, Ḳondaki Muzaki, Gön İştranbi and his namesake, Gin İştranbi, Gön Muzaki, Gin Ḫayḳal, and bachelor Gön Mavrongele;[115] Ḳastriçi (Ano Kastritsi): Yorgi Mazaraki;[116] Ḳurnaroḳastro (Pournarokastro): Miẖal Ḳoḳla, Bojik İstratiri, Todoro Bojik, Ḳurnos Mazarak, and bachelor Gin son of Nikifor.[117]

Ḳalandriça (Halandritsa) District. Ḳalandriça: Yani Gegiẕi, Petros Mazaraki, Todoros Bojik, Gin Gerḳas and his brother Gön, bachelor Dimitri Pojik, and bachelor Todoros Gerḳas.[118]

Ṣandamiri (Santomeri) District. Ṣandamiri: Yani Duşa, Gin Floḳa, Mirşekle Buva, Dima Arvaniti, Ḳozma Ḳuri, İvretos Miẖoys, and Lazari Miẖoys;[119] Porta (Portes): Yorgi Ḳuri, Yani Çani, and Miẖal Ġolemi;[120] Platistomo: Gin Ḳastamoniti.[121]

Girbene (Spartia) District. Motista (Drymos): widow Dyala wife of Ḳovondi;[122] Arula (Arla): Gön Ḫruso;[123] Mitepoli (Mitopoli): Runcari Durfis and Ḳonstandin Runcari.[124]

Ayo İlya (Agios Ilias) District. Ayo İlya: Pavlos Ġulami, İştin Ṣuli, Gin Mayiro, and Ḳosta Poleṣḳa;[125] Arvano Ḳastro (Arvanokastro): Pavlo Ḳuçi, Niḳola Ḳuçi, Gön Zenbeş, and Lal İskeliti;[126] Miġali Ẕivri (Lambeia): Ḳosta Ṣulima and his bother Niḳola, and Vaṣıl Ṣulima;[127] İryolo (Riolos): Gin Maẕiñik, Todoro Maẕiñik, Peta Mazaraki, Andriya Ḳonbi S̱eḳra, Yorgi Dramesi, Gin Ḫarma, Yorgi Piça, Petro Çimri, and Ḫarma Drameşi;[128] Franḳa Vila (Frangavilas Monastery): Pavlo Ḳurtik, Yani Ḳurtik, widow Pelañrin wife of Ḳurtik, and Miẖal İsḳutari.[129]

Ġardicḳo (Gatsiko) District. İsturġova: bachelor Palunbi Ġaralanbo;[130] İstamiro (Hatzi), where the best part of the rice cultivators – if not all – belongs to the Albanian community: Muriki Kiẕiḳuma, Ḳosta Marti and his son Yani, Gön Vaṣıl, Niḳola Vari, Dimitri Varipongi and his son İstefano.[131]

The Slavic element is traced with reference to the ethnic names of the Slavs in general, the Serbians and the Bulgarians.

107 TT10, 141–143.
108 TT10, 144.
109 TT10, 157.
110 TT10, 160. For Duşa Sirvos and bachelor Leḳa Sirvos see below 217, n. 149.
111 TT10, 161–163, 165.
112 TT10, 167.
113 TT10, 169.
114 TT10, 178.
115 TT10, 181.
116 TT10, 184.
117 TT10, 186.
118 1/14662, 4–5.
119 1/14662, 14.
120 1/14662, 15–16.
121 1/14662, 18.
122 1/14662, 21.
123 1/14662, 28.
124 1/14662, 35.
125 1/14662, 50–51.
126 1/14662, 54.
127 1/14662, 58.
128 1/14662, 60.
129 1/14662, 62.
130 1/14662, 74.
131 1/14662, 75.

Slavs: Yani İslavoplo, Miḫal, Yani and Niḳola İsḳlavoplo, widow wife of Foros İsḳlavoplos, and widow wife of Yorgi İsḳlavoplo in Ḳoraḳovuni (Oreino Korakovouni);[132] İstematiḳo İslaviçi in Ġardicḳo (Gatsiko);[133] Işlav Yani in Porta (Portes).[134]

Serbians: Yani Sirvo and his bachelor brother in Marti Plaşa;[135] bachelor Servoplo Hilyasti in Çipyana (Nestani);[136] Niḳola Servos in Voştiça (Aigio);[137] Rayḳo Servo and his brother Niḳola in Rayḳu (Raïko);[138] İstoyan Servos and his sons Yorgo and Yani in Zepandi;[139] Dobro Sirvos in Ḫulumiç (Hlemoutsi);[140] widow S̱etaḳo, whose late husband was Sirvo in Artica (Fanari);[141] Sirvo brother of Yorgi Suḳula in Aniza (Anaziri);[142] Yorgi Sirvo and his namesake, Lazaro Sirvo and his brother Gin, Sirvo Velyano, Sirvo son of Yorgi Manolato, and Sirvo brother of Yorgi Manolato in Sirvu (Servos);[143] bachelor Sirvo brother of Todoros S̱ana in Ranesi (Kastraki);[144] Niḳola Sirvo and his son Dimitri in Ḳarvunari (Karvounaris);[145] Sirvo brother of Andriya Ranesi in Ranesi (Renesi);[146] Andriya Sirvo and his son Gin in Monaḫu (Monahou);[147] İstayḳo Sirvo in Londar (Leontari);[148] Duşa Sirvos and bachelor Leḳa Sirvos in Çarnuḫlu (Pefko);[149] Martin Servo and Yani Servoplo in Ḳamaniça (Kamenitsa);[150] Yorgi Sirvo in Raḫova (Krini);[151] Yuvan Servo in Ayo İlya (Agios Ilias);[152] Dima Sirvos in Ayo Vaşıl;[153] Yani Sirvo and his brothers Todoros and Yani in Sirvu;[154] Yorgi Servo in Franḳa Vila (Frangavilas Monastery);[155] Sirvo Rafti in Ġardicḳo (Gatsiko).[156]

Bulgarians: Petros, Miḫal, Manol, Leḳa Vurġari, Petros son-in-law of Vurġari, Todoros son-in-law of Vurġari, and bachelors Dimitri and Yorgi Vurġari in Ayo Yani (Agios Ioannis);[157] İstematiḳo Vurġari in Yaḳoḫto (Ano Diakopto/Diakofto);[158] İvrato Vurġari, his brother Yani, and widow Ḫırisi wife of Vurġari in Loġas̱eti (Logothetis?);[159] Dimitri Vurġari and widow İstemata wife of Vurġari in Ḳavasila (Kavasilas).[160]

The Muslim/Turkish element appears in the document mainly with reference to the timariots, some of whom were of Balkan origin and had recently converted to Islam.[161] The group of the Balkan timariots consists of Evrenos son of Yaʿḳūb Beg bin İştin,[162] of Albanian descent as his grandfather's name denotes;[163] İbrāhīm son of ʿĪsā Beg bin Pavlo Kurtik[164] from the mediaeval Albanian family of the Kurtiks; Zaġanos Arnavud

132 TT10, 34. Several İsḳlavos/İsḳlava/İsḳlavina entries are not included in this ethnic group, as their surname may also derive from σκλάβος (*Gr.* slave) and not necessarily denote Slavic origin in the fifteenth century: TT10, 35, 61, 76, 109, 113, 132, 138, 161. It should also be noted that inhabitants with Slavic names of Albanian villages are more likely to have been Albanians that had acquired a Slavic name when migrating through the south-western Balkans; see Chapter 1, The Historical Geography of the Peloponnese.
133 1/14662, 67.
134 1/14662, 15.
135 TT10, 7.
136 TT10, 24.
137 TT10, 42.
138 TT10, 53.
139 TT10, 72.
140 TT10, 76.
141 TT10, 104.
142 TT10, 113.
143 TT10, 114.
144 TT10, 114.
145 TT10, 117.
146 TT10, 118.
147 TT10, 120.
148 TT10, 138.
149 TT10, 160. See above 216, n. 110.
150 TT10, 181.
151 TT10, 185.
152 1/14662, 50.
153 1/14662, 53.
154 1/14662, 55.
155 1/14662, 62.
156 1/14662, 66.
157 TT10, 47.
158 TT10, 58.
159 TT10, 89.
160 1/14662, 46.
161 See Chapter 3, The Administrative and Economic Structures of the Peloponnese, 230-235.
162 1/14662, 4.
163 See Chapter 1, The Historical Geography of the Peloponnese, 29, no. 48.
164 1/14662, 14. ʿĪsā Beg, son of Pavlo Kurtik, had been granted in 1431 an 81,306-*aḳçe*-worth *tīmār* in Albania, which comprised, among others, the district of Pavlo Kurtik (*vilāyet-i Pavlo*

Timurḫiṣārī[165] from today's Demir Hisar, North Macedonia; Ḳaragöz Arnavud brother of Çāşnīgīr İsḥāḳ Paşa,[166] apparently an Albanian; Meḥmed son of Ḥāccī Bāyezīd Yeñisehirī[167] possibly from Yeñişehir-i Fenār, that is Larissa, Greece; Ḫıżır son of Ṣavcı Sirozī[168] from Serres, Greece; Muḥyi'd-dīn Yanina'i and his son Ḳāsım[169] from Ioannina, Greece; Yūsuf Arnavud[170] clearly an Albanian; Mūsā Siyāh Livadya'i[171] from Livadeia, Greece; Balaban Yanina'i[172] also from Ioannina, Greece; Ḫalīl Siyāh Tırḫala'i[173] from Trikala, Greece; Paşa Yiğit son of Ḳaragöz Beg bin Yuvan[174] of Albanian or Slavic descent; Tırḫallü Timur Ḫanoġlı Muḥammed[175] also from Trikala, Greece; İbrāhīm Engürüs[176] possibly of Hungarian origin; ʿAlī Ṣūfī İzdinī[177] from Lamia, Greece; and Fīrūz son of ʿĪsā Ḳaraviryevī[178] from Veroia, Greece. The patronymics of the above-mentioned timariots show the geographical expansion of the Ottomans in the Balkans. Furthermore, eleven timariots were recorded as *ġarīb yiğit*,[179] a term employed for soldiers of Arabic, Persian, Kurdish or non-Muslim origin who later embraced Islam (new Muslims) and voluntarily contributed on the battlefield.[180]

During this preliminary phase, the Muslim population consisted of the Turkish authorities and the garrisons in the peninsula's administrative centres. A Turkish group of artisans, necessary for the support of the political, military and religious authorities, joined the conquerors in the Peloponnese.[181] A number of private property holders, some of whom had attained administrative posts, belong to this group, namely: Serrāc Pīr in Meġaspilyo Aya Ḳori (Megalou Spilaiou Monastery);[182] cavalrymen timariots Yūsuf and his brother Yaʿḳūb in Pikerni (Pikernis);[183] new Muslim Ḳāsım in Ḳandila (Kandila);[184] İbrāhīm son of Süle Beg former police superintendent (*subaşı*) of Balya Badra (Patra), and Ḫāccī Ḳaragöz man of İbrāhīm Beg in Ṣaravali (Saravali);[185] Yūsuf warden of Ḫulumiç (Hlemoutsi) castle, and Yūsuf son of Şāhīn Dirāz from the men of the same castle;[186] Zaġanos Beg, former governor of the Peloponnese, in Vumero (Goumero) and Londar (Leontari);[187] new Muslim Yūnus in Vumero;[188] ʿAbdu'l-lāh warden of Londar castle, and timariot Muṣṭafā Fenarī in Londar;[189] Ḫāccī Ḳaraca warden of Ḳoriṣos (Korinthos) castle;[190] Yūsuf son of İsmāʿīl man of İbrāhīm, in Ḳamaniça (Kamenitsa);[191] İbrāhīm Beg former cavalryman (*sipāhī*) of Balya Badra (Patra), in Ṣofyana (Syhaina);[192] and timariot Ḳāsım İzdinī in Porta (Portes).[193]

Kurtik), named after his father: İnalcık 1954a, 85-89. İbrāhīm and his brother, Yūsuf, were recorded in the MM10 cadastre of Trikala (1454/5) as the holders of a 42,399-*aḳçe*-worth *tīmār* in Thessaly: Delilbaşı–Arikan 2001, I, 132–140, II, 212a–221a. On the family of Pavlo Kurtik, see İnalcık 1951, 124–126.

165 1/14662, 21.
166 1/14662, 22.
167 1/14662, 24.
168 1/14662, 26.
169 1/14662, 28, 29.
170 1/14662, 29.
171 1/14662, 33.
172 1/14662, 44.
173 1/14662, 44.
174 1/14662, 50.
175 1/14662, 80.
176 1/14662, 84.
177 1/14662, 87.
178 1/14662, 90.
179 Namely İbrāhīm Zerd: 1/14662, 7; Ḥāccī Kürd: 1/14662, 8; Seyyidī ʿAlī: 1/14662, 10; Burhān Aġa: 1/14662, 17; Kürd Şeyḫ Ḥasan: 1/14662, 26; Elvānoġlı Maḥmūd: 1/14662, 43; Aḥmed Simġārī and Ḳaraca Aġa: 1/14662, 75; Ṭāhir son of Seyf: 1/14662, 76; Meḥmed son of Alagöz: 1/14662, 77; and Umūr son of Devlet Paşa: 1/14662, 79.
180 Pakalin 1946, 'Gureba', I 680; Uzunçarşili 1988, II 152–154, 190.
181 Asdrachas 2003b, 223.
182 TT10, 1.
183 TT10, 22.
184 TT10, 32.
185 TT10, 40.
186 TT10, 77.
187 TT10, 86, 139.
188 TT10, 86.
189 TT10, 139.
190 TT10, 166.
191 TT10, 182.
192 TT10, 185.
193 1/14662, 16.

The two mosques mentioned, one in Londar (Leontari)[194] and the other in Ḳoris̱os (Korinthos),[195] imply the existence of a rather confined Muslim community.[196] Finally, on the basis of their onomatology, one can establish a connection between a small number of Christian inhabitants and the Muslim/Turkish element, i.e. Todoros İbrayimis in Ġastuni (Gastouni);[197] İstas̱i Yaḫşi and Dimitri Turḳo in Ḳoris̱os;[198] Miḫal Turḳos, bachelor Niḳola Turḳos, and his brother bachelor Yorgi in Andraviza (Andravida);[199] Petro Turḳoplo in Arvano Ḳastro (Arvanokastro).[200] Çavuş Majis in Çavuşi (Kentro)[201] and Çavuşi, brother of Pavlos Barça, in Barçi (Dafnoula)[202] should not be included in this list, as their names probably echo the Byzantine military title *tzaousios* (τζαούσιος), which derives from Turkish *çavuş*.[203]

A distinctive Jewish community (*cemāʿat-i Yahūd*) was recorded in Corinth. The Romaniote community of Corinth was first mentioned in Agrippa's memorandum to Gaius in the first century AD.[204] The populous and thriving community of 300 Jews engaged in the silk industry described by Benjamin of Tudela in the twelfth century seems to have considerably shrunk,[205] though its existence and the activities of its inhabitants as businessmen, bankers and pawnbrokers at the time of Neri Acciaiuoli and shortly after his death are attested by the documentation.[206] Their number, however, was reduced to three households in the TT10.[207] The register renders them with the Arabic form of their names: Abraham Pepanos/Pipano (*İbrāhīm Pepano*), Joseph son of Moses (*Yūsuf veled-i Mūsā*), Elijah Petos (*İlyaḫu Peto*).[208]

No other ethnic group is distinguished in the TT10-1/14662 cadastre. Based on the anthroponymy, we presume that a small number of Gypsies dwelled in the Peloponnese; nine families are recorded followed by the epithet *Çingene/Cingene*.[209] Probably of Catalan origin was the late husband of a certain widow named Tomasa, the wife of Catalan (*Tomasa zen-i Ḳatalan*)[210] in Ḫulumiç (Hlemoutsi), and George the Catalan (*Yorgi Ḳatalani*)[211] residing in the Albanian village of Pendeni (Pefki). Other names linked to, mainly, the Latin West are: Marco Giovanelli (*Marḳo Covaneli*) and Giovanello (*Covanelo*) son of Dimitri Graḳoplo in Todoroplu;[212] Yani and Miḫal Engürüs, possibly of Hungarian ancestry, in Naşi (Nasia);[213] Giacomi (*Caḳomi*) Lulamireniti and bachelor John Giacomi (*Yani Çaḳomi*) in Leviẕi (Levidi);[214] bachelors Bernardo Clara (*Bernardo Ḳlara*) and Paul Bernardo (*Pavlos Bernardo*) in Voştiça (Aigio);[215] Theodore Lombardi (*Todoros Lonbardi*) in Ḳulukina (Kloukines/Kloukinohoria);[216] bachelor Manḳolas Roberto (*Ronberto*) and Ḳosta Giovanelli (*Covanali*) in Ḫulumiç (Hlemoutsi);[217] Dimitri Signori (*Sinori*), Nestor Bernardo (*Nestora Pernardo*), Theodore Bernardo (*Todoros Pernardo*), bachelor Dimitri Signorina (*Sinorina*) and widow Theodora wife

194 TT10, 139.
195 TT10, 166.
196 See Chapter 3, The Administrative and Economic Structures of the Peloponnese, 244.
197 TT10, 78.
198 TT10, 161.
199 1/14662, 44.
200 1/14662, 54.
201 TT10, 80.
202 TT10, 121.
203 Guilland 1967, I 512, 596-600; Hendrickx 1992, 211–212.
204 Philo Alexandrinus 1970, 125_{15-22}.
205 Benjamin of Tudela 1907, 10; Benjamin of Tudela 1995, 119. For the archaeological evidence of the Corinthian Jewry see Lambropoulou 1995, 49–50; Lambropoulou 1999, 36–37; Stavroulakis–DeVinney 1992, 228–229.
206 Chrysostomides 1995, 414 (doc. 212), 420 (doc. 216), 450, n. 38 (doc. 225).
207 For the Jewish community of Byzantine Corinth see Bowman 1985, 64–65, 84–85, 285–286 (doc. 89), 313–314 (doc. 136); Sharf 1971, 137, 142, 145. Venetian documents of the late fourteenth and the early fifteenth centuries presented a quite well-to-do Jewish community, which enjoyed a peaceful symbiosis with the Greek and the Italian elements: Chrysostomides 1992–93, 122–124.
208 TT10, 166.
209 Two households were headed by a *Çingene* in Plaşa: TT10, 100; three in Mazarak Adipo (Mazaraki?): TT10, 112; two in Ḳoris̱os (Korinthos): TT10, 165; one in Lihyana (Lehaina): 1/14662, 47; and one in Vunarġo (Vounargo): 1/14662, 59. Moreover, two gypsy bachelors were listed in Drayina (Pefki): TT10, 115. For the Gypsies in the Peloponnese see Zakythinos 1949b, 131–132.
210 TT10, 77.
211 1/14662, 64.
212 TT10, 8.
213 TT10, 22.
214 TT10, 29.
215 TT10, 43.
216 TT10, 61.
217 TT10, 76–77.

of Signorina (*Sinorina*) in Ġastuni (Gastouni);[218] Francesco Emiliano (*Franceșko Milyano*) and his son Thomas (*S̱omas*) in Mundriza (Gryllos);[219] George the Englishman (*Yorgi Eglazo*) in Londar (Leontari);[220] Dimitri son of Lombard (*Lonbardoplo*) and Miẖal son of Lombard (*Lanbardoplo*) in Ẕimiçana (Dimitsana);[221] John Famoso (*Yani Famozo*) and John Raimondo (*Yani Remondo*) in Vaşılıḳa (Sikyona);[222] widow Giovanella (*Covanela*) wife of Mavromati in Ayo İlya (Agios Ilias);[223] John Lombard (*Yani Lonbardo*), Theotokis Lombard (*S̱otoki Lonberdo*), John Lombard (*Yani Lonberdo*), bachelor Ḳosta Lombard (*Lonbardo*), and bachelor George Lombard (*Yorgi Lonbardo*) in Ḳastel İksovuni (Xyvouni/Xivouni);[224] Dimitri, Miẖal and Niḳola Giovanni (*Covani*) in Ġardicḳo (Gatsiko).[225]

The register also renders the ethnic names of Alemanni and Cumans as surnames: bachelor Manol[226] and Todoro Ḳumaniti[227] in Ḳalavrita (Kalavryta); Ḫayḳal and Dima Ḳumani in Bondaya (Palaiopyrgos);[228] Andriya son-in-law of Alaman and Niḳola Alamanos in Listirna (Listraina/Listrena/Listrina);[229] Dimitri, Miẖal, Miẖal and Yani Ḳumaniçi in Beçaḳus (Petsakoi);[230] Yani, Ḳosta and bachelor Yorgi Alamano, Yorgi Ḳumani, and Miẖal Ḳumanis in Kerpini;[231] Tavulari, Todoros, bachelor Yani and bachelor İstemad Ḳumanos, and Papas Yorgi Ḳumeno in Ḳulukina (Kloukines/Kloukinohoria);[232] Gin and bachelor Yorgi Ḳumani and Muriki Ḳumano in Girḳa Ḳumani;[233] Ḳumani Zuġra in Ẕunato (Zoni);[234] Yani Ḳumaniçi in Londar (Leontari);[235] bachelor Ḳumani Ḫayḳal and widow Ḳumaniya in Yani Dara (Daras);[236] Todoros Alaman and Miẖal Ḳumani in İzlatḳa;[237] Mengişa Alaman in Marḳoplu (Markopoulo);[238] Gin Ḳumani, Miẖal Ḳumano, Ḳumani brother of Mangişa Ḳaratula, Manḳola Ḳumani, bachelor Andriya Ḳumano, and bachelor Andriya Ḳumani in Mangişa Ḳumani (Koumanis).[239] Finally, seven people are recorded with the surname Miliġos[240] or Milengit,[241] descendants of the *Melingoi/Milingoi* Slavic tribe that had immigrated into the Peloponnese in the eighth century and settled at the western foot of Mt Taygetus.[242]

Despite the fragmentary state of the cadastre, the evidence contained therein enables us to establish a firm base for projecting our estimates for demographic figures. The 580 inhabited locations registered in the TT10-1/14662 are divided into 169 Greek villages, 407 Albanian, and four villages of mixed population (Table 4). This overwhelmingly Albanian image changes when one examines the households recorded in each one of them (maps 35–36). Table 5 and Chart 1 demonstrate that the Albanian villages were less densely populated. The majority of the Albanian settlements, 233 (57.24%), consisted of 1–20 households, whereas the Greeks tended to reside in larger towns. The regional capitals were inhabited by Greeks only; the Jewish presence in Corinth constitutes the only exception to this rule. The average number of families residing in Greek villages is 41.29 and the Albanian counterpart is 11.86; hence, the average Greek village was approximately three and a half

218 TT10, 78.
219 TT10, 126.
220 TT10, 137.
221 TT10, 158.
222 TT10, 167.
223 1/14662, 51.
224 1/14662, 56.
225 1/14662, 66–67.
226 TT10, 1.
227 TT10, 38.
228 TT10, 31.
229 TT10, 50.
230 TT10, 51–52. Cf. *mezra'a* Ḳumaniçi Luzi (Elliniko) near Zepandi: TT10, 72.
231 TT10, 53–54.
232 TT10, 62–63.
233 TT10, 79.
234 TT10, 117.
235 TT10, 138.
236 TT10, 155.
237 TT10, 182.
238 1/14662, 45.
239 1/14662, 86–87.
240 Ḫartofilaḳa, S̱otoki, Dimitri, Niḳola, Niḳola, and Anastas Miliġos in Lonḳanik (Longanikos): TT10, 144.
241 Milengi[t] C[---] in Londar (Leontari): TT10, 138.
242 Zerlentos 1922, 9; Kyriakidis 1947, 19–20.

Table 4. *Demographic statistics of the Peloponnese.*

District	Greek villages	Albanian villages	mixed villages	Greek households	Albanian households	households total	Greek bachelors	Albanian bachelors	bachelors total	Greek widows	Albanian widows	widows total	villages total	Greek families	Albanian families	families total
Ḳalavrita	20	34	-	428	420	848	52	45	97	23	12	35	54	451	432	883
Mizişra	1	-	-	9	-	9	1	-	1	-	-	-	1	9	-	9
Miḫlu	2	4	-	77	186	263	11	24	35	5	11	16	6	82	197	279
Bejenik	7	12	-	222	189	411	43	50	93	15	11	26	19	237	200	437
Voştiça	38	28	1	1287	242	1529	255	10	265	84	7	91	67	1371	249	1620
Ḫulumiç	11	22	-	281	189	470	29	14	43	24	18	42	33	305	207	512
Vumero	17	55	-	755	617	1372	89	71	160	51	23	74	72	806	640	1446
Kirvuḳor	16	52	-	467	725	1192	38	93	131	42	17	59	68	509	742	1251
Arḳadya	9	3	2	229	57	286	30	7	37	15	3	18	14	244	60	304
Londar	11	47	-	728	435	1163	95	58	153	60	48	108	58	788	483	1271
Ḳorişos	5	16	-	553	154	707	71	12	83	82	2	84	21	635	156	791
Balya Badra	11	18	1	439	177	616	48	15	63	64	4	68	30	503	181	684
Ḳalandriça	1	13	-	116	116	232	22	12	34	15	5	20	14	131	121	252
Şandamiri	2	8	-	146	95	241	14	3	17	12	4	16	10	158	99	257
Girbene	7	43	-	162	425	587	13	18	31	21	18	39	50	183	443	626
Ayo İlya	8	20	-	446	187	633	75	22	97	34	12	46	28	480	199	679
Ġardicḳo	3	32	-	197	467	664	22	10	32	14	24	38	35	211	491	702
total	169	407	4	6551	4672	11223	909	463	1372	562	218	780	580	7103	4900	12003

times larger than the Albanian one. The average Peloponnesian village, when we count Greek, Albanian and mixed settlements, hosted 20.69 families.

As stated above, family reconstruction from the nominal listings of household heads, bachelors and widows is a thorny procedure with often arbitrary results. A rather 'Ottoman' method of counting families has been adopted, that is the total number given by the households headed by males (*ḫāne*) plus the ones headed by widows (*bīve*). The bachelors are not included in this number, as they probably lived with their parents. As can be seen in Table 6 and Chart 2, the Albanian families residing in villages of 1–20 households, 3,142 in number, constitute 65.09% of the total Albanian population. The picture of the distribution of Greek families is the exact opposite: 5,093 (72.99%) families dwelled in settlements of over 40 households. All the villages of 1–2 families were inhabited by Albanians, whereas, in contrast, all towns of over 151 families were inhabited by Greeks (Chart 2). In this respect the Ottoman register confirms the tendency of the pre-Ottoman Moreote authorities to confine the Albanians to the countryside.[243] This small Albanian settlement is better conveyed by the term *katund*, which refers to a temporary settlement, named after the chieftain, of one or more families belonging to the same clan.[244] Many of these settlements – a product of the semi-nomadic/nomadic tribal

243 In 1397 the Venetians settled Albanians in Argos and its territory, yet did not allow them into the Argive acropolis of Larissa: Topping 1980, 261; in 1425 the Venetian senate ordered the settlement of 300 Albanians in Euboea without permitting them to reside in any fortresses: ibid., 264. According to an early fifteenth-century source, the Albanians preferred to settle in the mountains, wintering in the plains, yet never residing in villages or towns: Lambros 1926, $194_{25\text{-}29}$: 'καὶ τανῦν ᾤκισται σποράδην ἐκείνη καὶ κατὰ μικρὸν ὑπ' Ἀλβανῶν, γένους ἰλλυρικοῦ ξύμπασα καὶ κωμηδόν· νομαδικὸν γὰρ τὸ γένος καὶ λυπρόβιον, οὐ πόλεσιν, οὐ φρουρίοις, οὐ κώμαις, οὐκ ἀγροῖς, οὐκ ἀμπελῶσιν, ἀλλ' ὄρεσι χαῖρον καὶ πεδιάσιν. Αἱ δὲ πόλεις καθαρὸν ἔτι σώζουσι τὸ ἑλληνικὸν γένος.' Mercati has shown that this oration was composed by Isidore of Kiev solely on John VIII Palaeologus: Mercati 1926, 6–7.

244 The term *katund*, perhaps of Thraco-Illyrian origin, is a mediaeval word attested in a number of languages: *κατούνα* in Greek (tent, military camp, residence) > *κατουνεύω* (to reside, to camp), *katun* in Serbo-Croatian, *cătun* in Romanian, *canto*, *cantone* in Italian, *canton* in French. While in the Middle Ages it denoted 'an organised group of people who engaged in both animal breeding and agriculture', today in the ex-Yugoslav lands it means a temporary pastoral settlement: Vucinich 1975, 13, 23–35, 149–150, n. 1; Du Cange 1688, I 623; Kriaras 1982, VIII 106; Lambros 1880, 37_{875}, 52_{1228}, 345. In northern Albania, by the end of the fifteenth century the pastoral *katund*s had transformed into settlements of mixed stock-rearing and agricultural economy: Pulaha 1976, 174.

Table 5. *Distribution of settlements according to their size.*

families per village	Greek villages number	Greek villages percentage	Albanian villages number	Albanian villages percentage	mixed villages number	mixed villages percentage
1-2	0	0%	16	3.93%	0	0%
3-4	8	4.73%	46	11.30%	0	0%
5-10	33	19.53%	171	42.01%	0	0%
11-20	42	24.85%	118	28.99%	1	25.00%
21-40	34	20.12%	51	12.54%	2	50.00%
41-80	30	17.75%	5	1.23%	0	0%
81-100	6	3.55%	0	0%	0	0%
101-150	6	3.55%	0	0%	1	25.00%
151-200	5	2.96%	0	0%	0	0%
201+	5	2.96%	0	0%	0	0%
total	169	100%	407	100%	4	100%

Chart 1. *Distribution of settlements according to their size.*

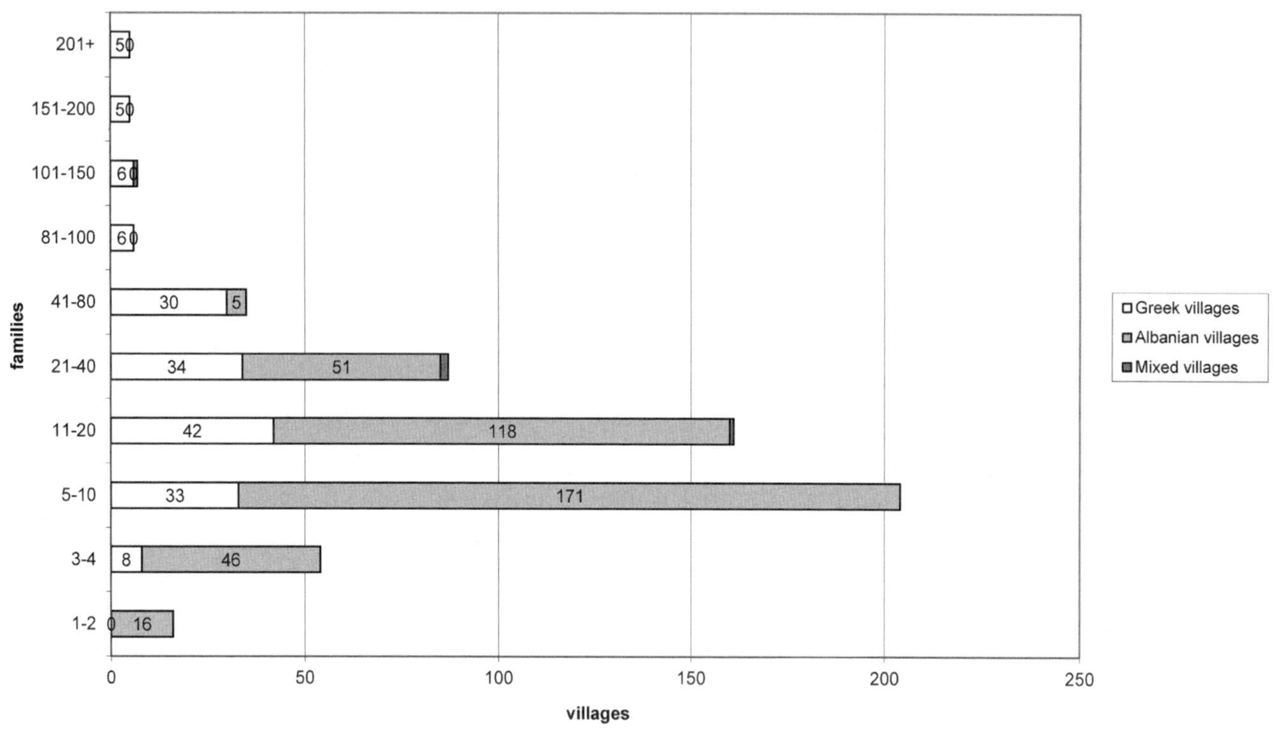

structure of late mediaeval Albanian society – were in later stages abandoned without leaving any traces.[245] In our register 71.6% of the unidentified localities refer to Albanian settlements (156).

245 The houses made of mud-brick and wood were sensitive to weathering. In some cases the dwellings are better described as huts; Leake's record of Aï Giannis and Anemodouri villages in Arcadia reads: Leake 1830, II 91: 'in each hamlet there is one stone house; the remaining habitations are thatched huts shaped like a great oval tent; – a large post in the middle supports the roof, which slopes to within three or four feet of the ground, where a wall of that height, made of pliant wicker branches interwoven with upright sticks, forms the rest of the structure'. For the demographic and economic pressures that resulted in the abandonment of villages see Antoniadis-Bibicou 1965; Wagstaff 1978. In Arvanitic, the term employed to describe such villages is *katundi shtje*: Jochalas 2011, I 93.

Table 6. *Distribution of population (families).*

families per village	Greek families number	Greek families percentage	Albanian families number	Albanian families percentage	families in mixed villages number	families in mixed villages percentage
1-2	0	0%	26	0.54%	0	0%
3-4	26	0.37%	164	3.40%	0	0%
5-10	268	3.84%	1260	26.10%	0	0%
11-20	630	9.03%	1692	35.05%	18	9.09%
21-40	961	13.77%	1404	29.09%	63	31.81%
41-80	1716	24.59%	281	5.82%	0	0%
81-100	532	7.62%	0	0%	0	0%
101-150	736	10.55%	0	0%	117	59.10%
151-200	827	11.85%	0	0%	0	0%
201+	1282	18.38%	0	0%	0	0%
total	6978	100%	4827	100%	198	100%

Chart 2. *Distribution of population (families).*

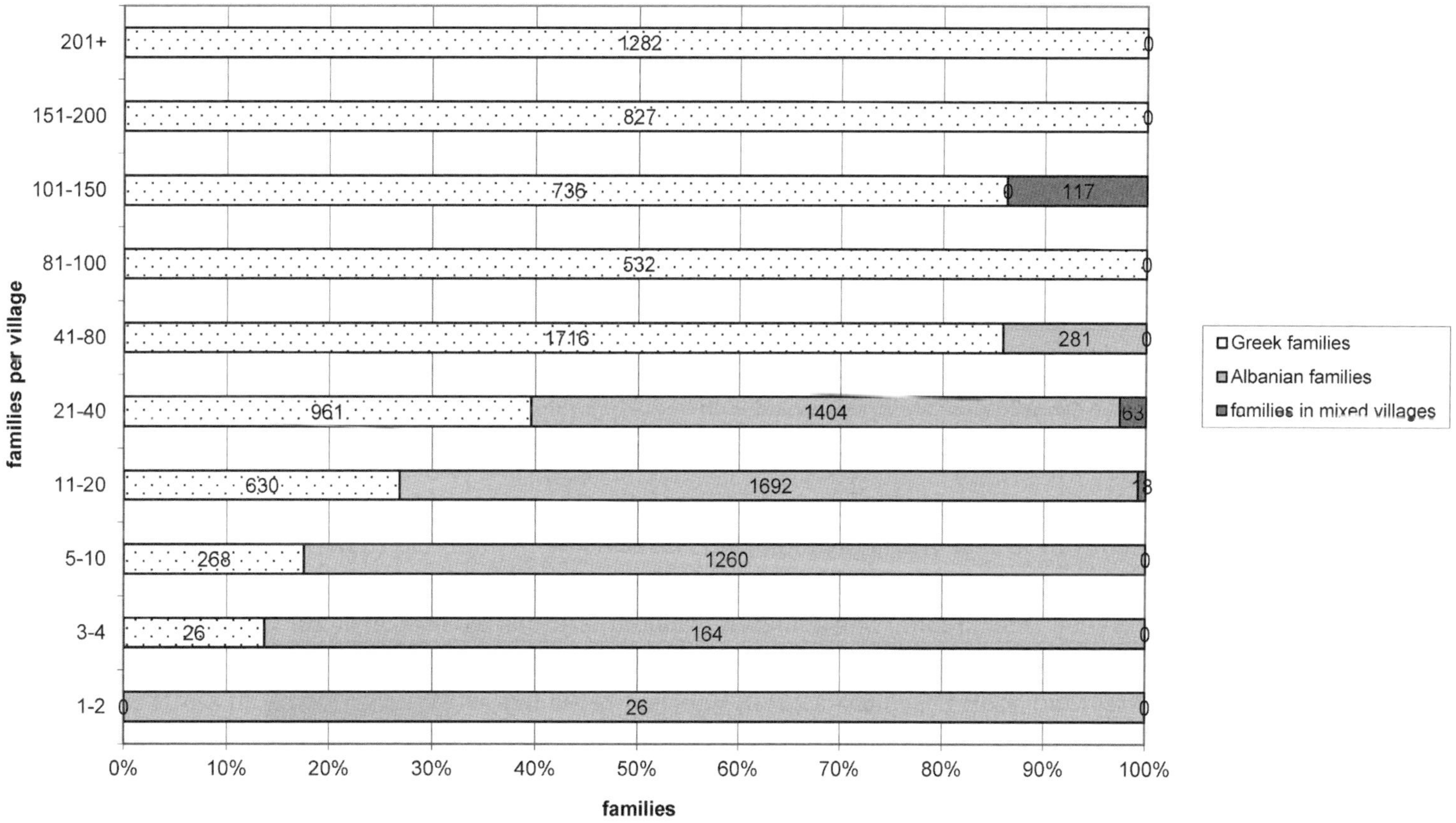

The division of the population into households, bachelors and widows provides the basis for a demographic analysis of the family relations within the two ethnic groups. Table 7 gives the figures and percentages of these demographic units and Chart 3 illustrates the difference in the composition of the Greek and the Albanian family. While the Greek bachelors constitute 11.34% of the Greek population, the Albanian bachelors reach 8.65% of the Albanian one. The same comparison between the Greek and the Albanian widows shows a similar difference of 7% and 4.07% respectively. This may be attributed to different marital customs, i.e. the Albanians may marry at a younger age and widows remarry soon after

Table 9. *Average tax paid by Greek and Albanian families (aķçes p.a.).*

Districts	Greek	Albanian
Ķalavrita	92.32	65.17
Mizişra	189.33	-
Miḫlu	89.79	56.06
Bejenik	104.46	62.06
Voştiça	122.85	63.58
Ḫulumiç	150.88	68.71
Vumero	160.13	75.24
Kirvuķor	101.33	69.52
Arķadya	147.85	65.92
Londar	118.65	51.52
Ķorişos	83.01	64.81
Balya Badra	126.9	80.36
Ķalandriça	140.75	65
Şandamiri	131.65	57.85
Girbene	120.09	68.66
Ayo İlya	128.27	72.12
Ġardicķo	131.6	58.3
average	122.9	65.69
average (without the *ispence*)	96.89	44.46

Chart 4. *Average tax paid by Greek and Albanian families.*

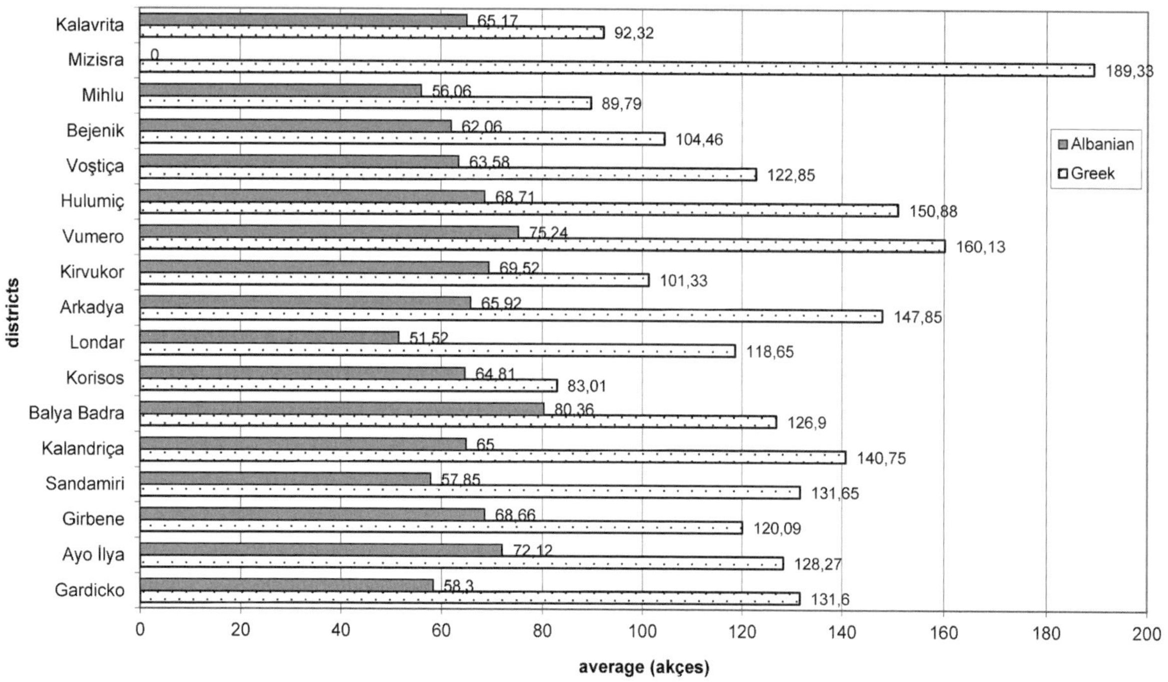

475–476. Indeed, most taxes levied on livestock were intended for the Sultan's treasury.

This relative poverty of the Albanian population is attested even two and a half centuries later, when in 1708 Angelo Emo, the Venetian general *provveditor*, described the Albanians as 'gente miserabile concentrata con le famiglie nei recessi de monti in povere Cappanne vivendo de i frutti delle mandre, di cui sono essi da per tutto i Custodi'.[252]

To conclude, the main settlement pattern of the mid-fifteenth-century Peloponnese was the fortified large village or town dating back to the Franco-Byzantine era (thirteenth to fifteenth centuries). The multiplication of fortifications in that period should be examined in the light of the enemy's ability to appear anywhere and to dispute or challenge one's suzerainty;[253] the enemy could have been Frankish, Venetian or Byzantine.[254] The largest *tīmār*s were established around such a fortified centre, which functioned as the local administrative capital and market.[255] The Albanian newcomers altered this image by adding a significant number of small satellite settlements, some of which were temporary. The TT10-1/14662 cadastre seems to be in agreement with the picture given by the contemporary sources – namely, the existence of Greek towns *vis-à-vis* remote Albanian villages.[256]

252 Lambros 1900, 647.

253 Panagiotopoulos 1987, 46. In the Frankish Morea, the construction, control and demolition of castles were considered 'affairs of state': Topping 1949, 29 (Assize 19), 57 (Assize 94), 115.

254 For the topic of the relations between the conquerors and the local population and its historical problematic see Jacoby 1973; Topping 1976; Ilieva 1991, 171–190.

255 For the relations among the fortified and unfortified settlements of the late Middle Ages in the Peloponnese see Panagiotopoulos 2007, 44–49.

256 The tough character of the mountainous Albanian populace in contrast with the urban Greeks is described in the satirical dialogue of Mazaris composed in 1414–1415: Mazaris 1975, $78_{18\text{-}21}$.

3

The Administrative and Economic Structures of the Peloponnese

In the wake of the conquest it was necessary for the Ottoman government to conduct a survey of each province to record the tax-paying population, their produce and revenues.[1] Such surveys were then repeated at regular intervals of twenty to thirty years or at the enthronement of a new Sultan.[2] The results of the survey were compiled in two types of registers, known as *mufaṣṣal* (detailed) and *icmāl* (abridged) *taḥrīr defteri* (*defter-i ḫaḳanī*). All land belonged to the Sultan, 'God's shadow on earth' (*ẓıllu'l-lāhi fi'l-arż*) and consequently to the Muslim community.[3] In his introduction to the registers of Budin in the mid-sixteenth century, the Ottoman jurist Meḥmed Ebū's-suʿūd presented the following interpretation of the Ottoman landholding:

> The fields, however, are not considered as freehold property in the manner of their other possessions. As elsewhere in the well-protected territories [of the Ottoman Sultans] they are rather considered as *memleke* lands, also known as *mīrī*. On these lands the *dominium eminens* (*raḳabe*) belongs to the public treasury (*beytü'l-māl*) of the Islamic community. The fields are considered to be in possession of the *reʿāyā* on a lease (*ʿāriyye*, *ʿāriyyet*); the *reʿāyā* may sow grain or other crops as they choose, and must render the *ḫarāc-ı muḳāseme* under the name of the tithe (*ʿöşr*) and other taxes.[4]

The *tīmār* holder was not granted the land *per se*, but the right to collect a fixed amount of state revenue from the people in a defined area. Such revenue grants had to be renewed by every succeeding Sultan. The revenues assigned to the members of the military or religious elite (*ʿaskerī* class) were collected by them directly from the inhabitants *in lieu* of salary. As Imber emphasised, 'it is this – in effect, an entitlement to collect taxes, and an exemption from paying them – that was perhaps the most important marker of legal status in the Ottoman Empire'.[5] The smallest unit of land granted to a cavalryman (*tīmārlı sipāhī*), providing an annual revenue of no more than 20,000 *aḳçe*s, was called *tīmār*. A *zeʿāmet* was a larger fief, annually yielding up to 100,000 *aḳçe*s. If its value surpassed 100,000 *aḳçe*s, it was called *ḫāṣṣ*. These fiefs consisted of a registered indivisible nucleus (*ḳılıç*), to which further incomes (*ḥiṣṣe*) could be added in the course of time. Farms, vineyards, orchards and other sources of revenue brought under the direct control of the timariot, called *ḫāṣṣa*, were also included in the *tīmār*. In the later sixteenth century, the *tīmār* holder gradually lost his right to such a demesne (*ḳılıç yeri*, *ḫāṣṣa çiftliği*), which was given in its entirety to the peasants.[6]

In return, the *tīmār* holder had to participate in the Sultan's expeditions with a certain number of auxiliary soldiers, servants, tents, etc., depending on the size of his *tīmār* income. He was also responsible for law and order in his *tīmār*. The *sipāhī* usually lived in the village, the source of his income, or, if his fief comprised more than one village, then he resided in the local economic centre and largest market, where he could easily collect the tithe, a levy on harvests paid by farmers in kind due to coinage shortage. Thus, in the words of İnalcık, 'in a way, the soldier replaced

1 According to Cvetkova, the surveyors were the first Ottoman officials to arrive in a newly conquered or annexed territory: Cvetkova 1983, 134.
2 By 1540, it had been standardised to conduct such a survey every thirty years: Luṭfī Paşa 1910, 33, 41; Káldy-Nagy 1968, 185, n. 15.
3 İnalcık 1994, I 103–110.
4 İnalcık 1992, 102.
5 Imber 1997, 115–116.
6 McGowan 1981, 55–56; İnalcık 1997, 110.

Table 10. *List of timariots.*

timariot	villages	households	bachelors	widows	*mezra'as*	*aḳçes*
İbrāhīm Beg police superintendent of Ḳalavrita	38	586	71	21	4	45970
Müstaḳdim sword-bearer of the commander-in-chief of Ḳalavrita	5	65	10	5	-	6987
'Alī son of Cāyim	6	100	11	4	-	9790
Meḥmed new Muslim	3	70	4	6	-	5556
Ḥamza new Muslim and his brother, Yūsuf	1	18	2	-	-	2080
Yūsuf new Muslim and his brother, Ya'ḳūb new Muslim	5	206	31	16	-	16849
Mübārek lord's servant of the warden of Miḫlu castle	1	57	4	-	1	1558
'Ömer Beg son of Ezmir police superintendent of Bejenik	19	411	93	26	3	37170
Ḥażret-i Maḥmūd Paşa	67	1529	265	91	4	161494
Sinān Beg bin Elvān Beg governor of the Morea	214	4538	502	334	17	448610
Murād Beg son of Timurtaş police superintendent of Balya Badra	28	459	54	46	8	50150
Evrenos son of Ya'ḳūb Beg bin İştin	1	116	22	15	-	18439
İbrāhīm Zerd from the foreign adventurers	6	37	4	1	-	2348
Ḥāccī Kürd from the foreign adventurers	3	32	4	3	-	2476
Seyyidī 'Alī from the foreign adventurers	4	47	4	1	-	3042
İbrāhīm son of 'Īsā Beg bin Pavlo Kurtik police superintendent Ṣandamir	3	182	14	15	-	22952
Burhān Āġā from the foreign adventurers	7	59	3	1	4	3576
Zaġanos Arnavud Timurḥiṣārī	2	40	1	4	-	2872
Ḳaragöz Arnavud brother of Çāşnīgīr İsḥāḳ Paşa	2	44	-	-	-	2861

Ḥamza Derbendci lord's servant	2	38	-	5	-	3604
Meḥmed son of Ḥāccī Bāyezīd Yeñişehirī	6	72	1	1	1	4118
Ḫıżır son of Ṣavcı Sirozī	1	39	2	-	-	3416
Kürd Şeyḫ Ḥasan from the foreign adventurers	1	3	1	-	-	3355
Rus Ormanı	2	15	4	1	1	1266
Muḥyi'd-dīn Yanina'i	½	37	3	4	-	4842
Ḳāsım son of the aforementioned Muḥyi'd-dīn Yanina'i	½	17	5	3	-	2538
Yūsuf Arnavud	2	32	3	4	-	2554
ʿAlī son of Ḳulaġuz, and his son İskender	11	47	4	1	4	5944
Mūsā Siyāh Livadya'i	5	35	-	3	-	2103
Mevlānā ʿAbdu'l-lāh judge of Balya Badra	7	67	3	4	-	5019
Ḫoca ʿAlī	10	110	4	2	-	7360
Ḫıżır commander-in-chief of Ḫulumiç and Ayo İlya and Ġardicḳo	5	19	-	1	1	6017
Elvānoġlı Maḥmūd from the foreign adventurers	3	26	4	1	-	2222
Balaban Yanina'i	1	32	2	2	1	3085
Ḫalīl Siyāh Tırḫala'i	2	34	6	2	-	2039
ʿĪsā brother of İlyās Siyāh	3	37	2	4	1	2473
Ḳasṭamonlu Pīr Ḥasanoġlı Aḥmed	3	55	7	4	-	4040
Manol Mahtar	1	12	-	2	5	994
Nikifor Ḳavasila	1	8	-	-	-	739
Leḳa İzmolda	1	3	-	-	-	378
Paşa Yiğit son of Ḳaragöz Beg bin Yuvan	22	554	95	45	2	66415[1]
İbrāhīm Dīvāne lord's servant who had been from the men of the Balya Badra castle	2	48	2	1	2	6683

ʿAlī Tekkelü	3	26	-	-	-	2539
Andriya Fenārī and his brother, Yorgi	1	5	-	-	-	283
Sinān Ġaşır Beg son of Süleymān Beg bin Ẕū'l-ḳādir	20	457	27	27	3	41039
Aḥmed Simġārī and Ḳaraca Āġā from the foreign adventurers	1	40	2	2	-	5172
Ṭāhir son of Seyf from the foreign adventurers	5	67	2	5	-	4010
Meḥmed son of Alagöz from the foreign adventurers	3	38	1	2	1	2358
Umūr son of Devlet Paşa from the foreign adventurers	3	37	1	1	-	2131
Tırḫallü Timur Ḫānoġlı Muḥammed	4	31	1	1	-	2137
İbrāhīm Engürüs from the Janissary regiment of the tent-pitchers of the commander-in-chief of Vumero and Kirvuḳor	4	45	13	2	2	6092
Ḥamza lord's servant who had been from the men of the Balya Badra castle	2	58	13	3	-	5420
ʿAlī Ṣūfī İzdinī man of Balaban Āġā	4	28	5	3	2	2881
Ḳāsım lord's servant who had been from the men of the Balya Badra castle	2	45	9	5	-	6957
Fīrūz son of ʿĪsā Ḳaraviryevī	2	25	2	-	-	2015
İlyās lord's servant who had been from the men of the Miḫlu castle	3	48	11	15	1	5117
Ġarb brother of Süleymān	4	32	13	2	-	2979
Nuṣret son of Celāl Ḳasṭamonī and his son, İlyās	7	93	5	7	-	8828
Süleymān brother of Ġarb	2	29	5	1	-	2885
Mezīd new Muslim	2	31	7	-	-	3615
total	579	11071	1364	755	68	1092442

[1] The register erroneously gives a total of 66,411 *aḳçe*s.

Chart 5. *Economic distribution of tīmārs*.

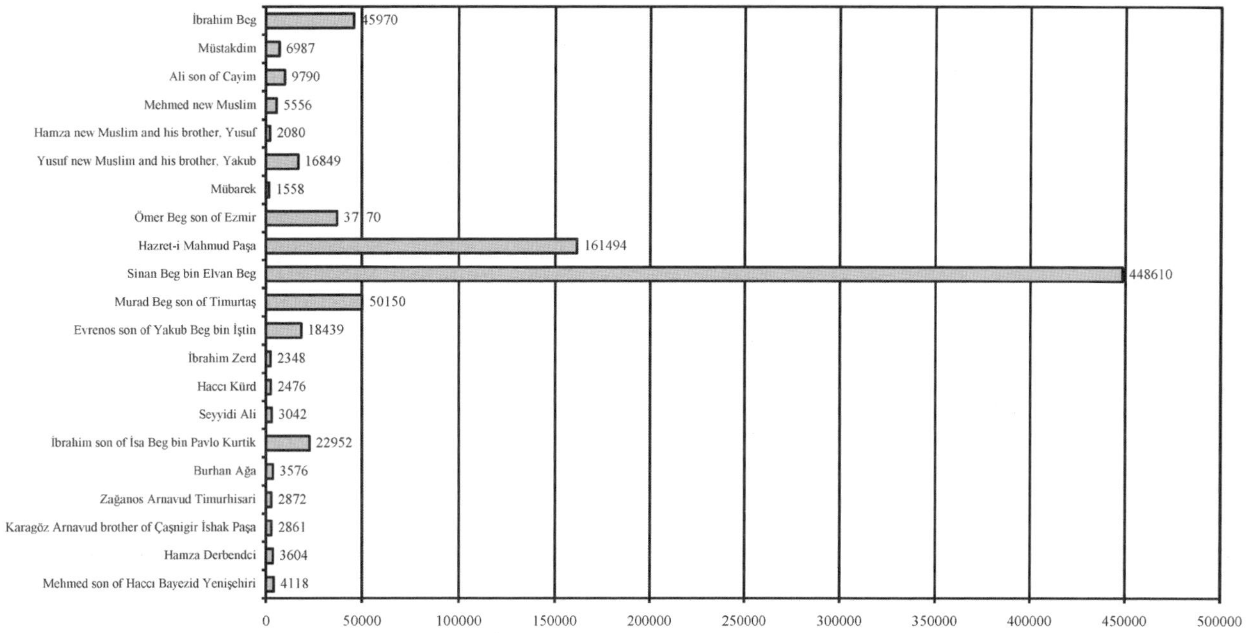

Chart 5. *Economic distribution of tīmārs*.

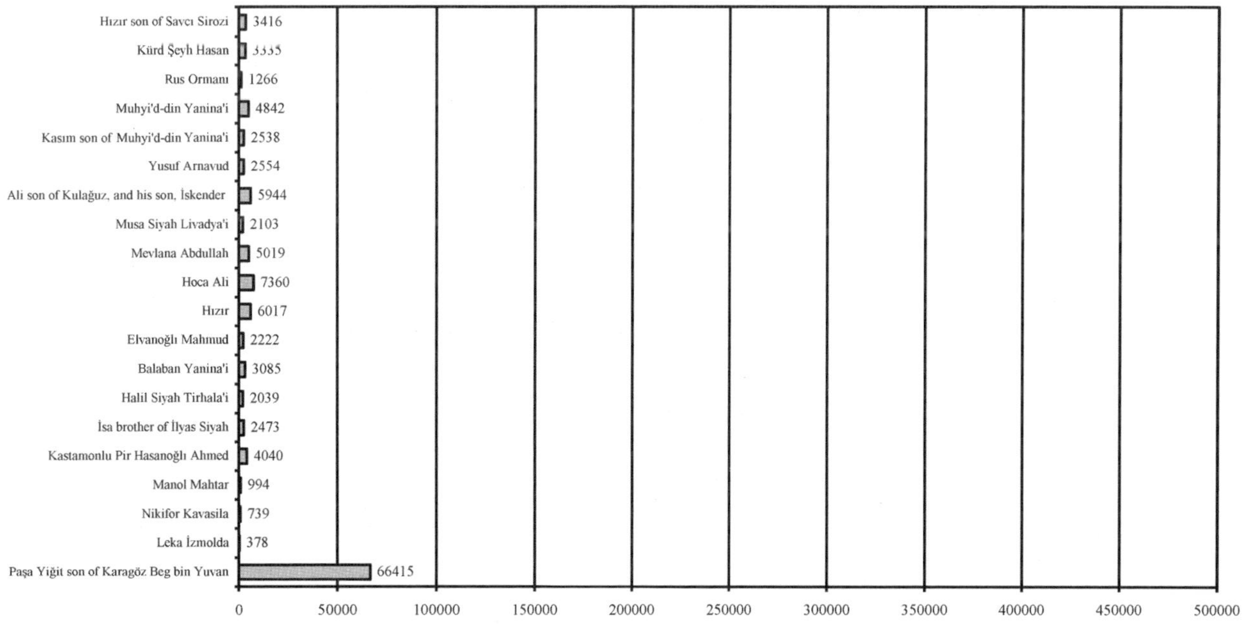

Chart 5. *Economic distribution of tīmārs.*

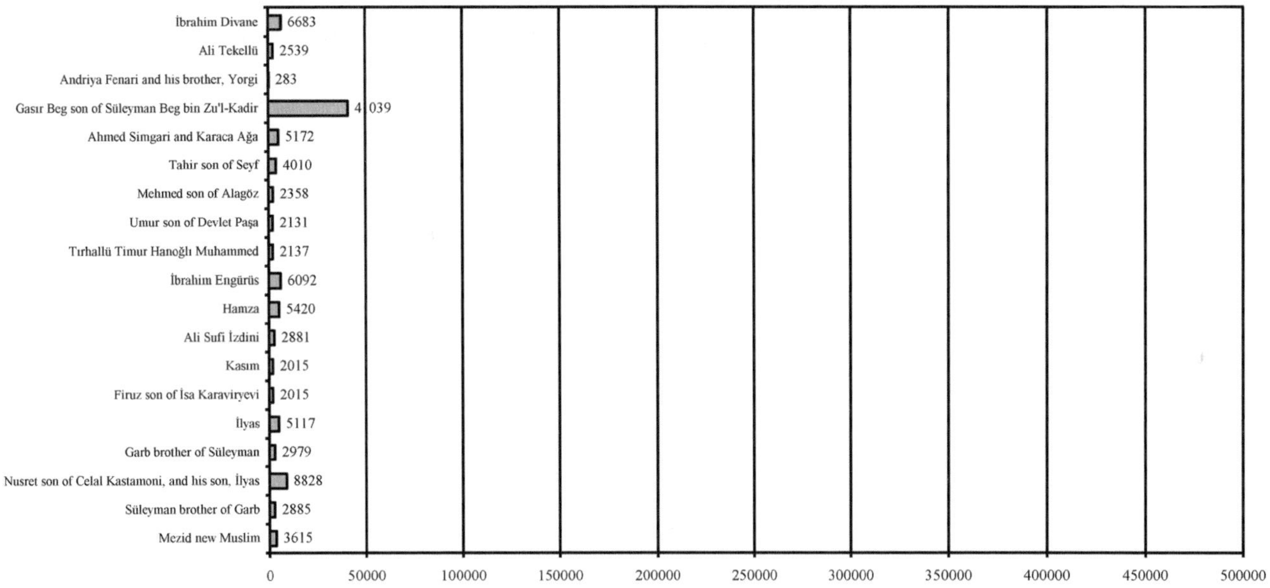

the tax collector, and on him fell the responsibility of converting the tithe into cash'.[7] The implementation of the *tīmār* system is considered a key feature of the establishment of Ottoman rule. In the Balkans and Asia Minor it replaced both the Byzantine *pronoia* (*πρόνοια*) and the Seljuk *iḳṭāʿ*.[8]

When the Sultan decided to conduct a census of a certain region, he appointed the local dignitary (*emīn*) and a scribe (*kātib*) and ordered the region's *tīmār* holders to gather and present all the legal documents in their possession. It was of particular importance for the financial administration to ensure that the data was collected on the spot.[9] The *tīmār* holder brought all the adults in his *tīmār* before the *emīn* who recorded them with their fathers' name. Under the name of the district (*nāḥiyyet*), the village (*ḳarye*) and the timariot, every married adult male (*müzevvec*) was designated as a household (*ḫāne*), regarded as the fiscal unit. Then came the single adult males (*mücerred*) followed by the widows (*bīve*) as heads of households. The total sum of the village tax revenue was then calculated and followed by a detailed record of each crop's tax.[10]

The TT10-1/14662 cadastre lists 66 timariots, who shared the revenue of the Peloponnesian districts. Three of them were allotted a *ḫāṣṣ*, six a *zeʿāmet* and the remaining 57 a *tīmār* (Table 10). The governor of the Morea (*mīrlivāʾ-ı vilāyet-i Mora*), Sinān Beg, took the lion's share as his annual income of 448,610 *aḳçe*s forms 41.06% of the total revenue (Chart 5). There are five Christian timariots mentioned, namely Manol Mahtar,[11] Nikifor Ḳavasila,[12] Leḳa İzmolda,[13] Andriya Fenarī, and his brother Yorgi.[14] Moreover, a Christian former timariot is recorded only with his title, Meġa Ẕuḳa (*Byz. Μέγας Δούξ*),[15] as a mill owner in Frosina (Frousiouna).[16] As İnalcık has shown, it was customary for the early Ottoman administration to grant a number of fiefs of recently conquered lands to magnates or soldiers of the local population.[17] The Christian timariots in

7 İNALCIK 1997, 107. See also İNALCIK, *Tīmār* and BARKAN, *Timar*.

8 For the discussion on whether the *tīmār* system had been based on the strikingly similar *pronoia* and *iḳṭāʿ* see VRYONIS 1969–70, 273–275; KÖPRÜLÜZADE 1931, 219–240. For *pronoia* see MANIATI-KOKKINI 1990; CHEYNET 2006, 28–30; HALDON 1999, 94. For the *iḳṭāʿ* see CAHEN, *Iḳṭāʿ*; CAHEN 1953.

9 BELDICEANU-STEINHERR–BELDICEANU 1978, 18; İNALCIK 1954b, 110–111.

10 For the *tīmār* registration see the *Ṣūret-i ḳānūnnāme-i kitābet-i vilāyet ki nişān-ı hümāyūn yazılur* in AKGÜNDÜZ 1990, I 368–377; İNALCIK 1954a, xviii–xxiv; BARKAN 1953; FEKETE 1955, 75–84, 101–110; KÁLDY-NAGY 1968, 189–212. For the stages of a petition to the palace (*ʿarż*) for the grant of a *tīmār* see İNALCIK 1980b.

11 1/14662, 48.

12 1/14662, 49.

13 Ibid.

14 1/14662, 64.

15 GUILLAND 1967, I 542–551.

16 TT10, 175.

17 İNALCIK 1953, 214–233; İNALCIK 1951, 118–138; İNALCIK 1954b, 113–117. For the Christian *tīmārlı sipāhī*s see also CVETKOVA 1958, 184–197; LOWRY 1990, 265–266; BELDICEANU 1985; DELİLBAŞI 2005.

the Peloponnese constituted 7.57% and their revenue of 2,394 *aḳçe*s formed 0.22% of the total. Five of the timariots bore the epithet 'new Muslim' (*nev müslümān*), a clear indication that they had recently converted to Islam.[18]

The auxiliary soldiers that each timariot was obliged to lead into battle during an imperial campaign were as follows:

Bürüme: breastplated soldier; it only appears in the phrase *kendü bürüme*[19] (he campaigns on his own behalf, wearing a coat of mail).[20]

Cebelü:[21] armoured soldier; likewise, *kendü cebelü*[22] denotes that the timariot campaigns on his own behalf, wearing armour (*cebe*).[23]

Ġulām:[24] military servant of rural origin recruited among the timariot's offspring.[25]

Oğlan:[26] same as *ġulām*.[27]

High ranking timariots were responsible for maintaining and supplying certain accessories and military tents to the campaign such as:

Geçim:[28] armour for a soldier and his horse.[29]

Çadır:[30] tent brought by a timariot whose *tīmār* was worth 9,000–15,000 *aḳçe*s.[31]

Tenktür:[32] tent brought by a timariot whose *tīmār* was worth 4,000–9,000 *aḳçe*s.[33]

Günlük:[34] tent which protected against the rays of the sun.[35]

Çadır maʿa soḳaḳ ve ābrīz:[36] probably a tent with curtains fitted out to allow one a basic wash or dressing.[37]

Other tents served as:

Ḫazīne:[38] treasury.[39]

Kilar:[40] provisions.[41]

Maṭbaḫ:[42] kitchen.[43]

Serrāc̱ḫāne:[44] saddlery.[45]

When crosschecking the timariots' responsibilities for supplying the army on campaign as recorded in the TT10-1/14662 with Meḥmed II's list[46] promulgated between 1477 and 1481, certain discrepancies come to light. Twenty-four out of the 57 *tīmār* holders appear to have different military obligations, according to their revenue, than the ones defined in the mentioned list; namely, new Muslim Meḥmed (5,556 *aḳçe*s)[47] sustained

18 Meḥmed: TT10, 18; Ḥamza: TT10, 20; Yūsuf and his brother Yaʿḳūb: TT10, 21; Mezīd: 1/14662, 98.
19 TT10, 14, 16, 18, 20, 21, 28, 38, 76, 178; 1/14662, 4, 10, 14, 17, 21, 22, 23, 24, 26, 28, 30, 35, 37, 40/42, 44, 47, 50, 62, 66, 75, 76, 84, 86, 87, 89, 91, 93, 94, 97, 98.
20 Beldiceanu 1980, 83–85.
21 TT10, 14, 16, 17, 20, 21, 28, 38, 42, 76, 178; 1/14662, 4, 7, 8, 10, 14, 17, 21, 22, 23, 24, 26, 28, 30, 35, 37, 40/42, 44, 47, 50, 62, 66, 76, 84, 86, 87, 89, 91, 93, 94, 97, 98.
22 1/14662, 27, 29, 43, 44, 45, 48, 63, 77, 79, 80, 90.
23 Beldiceanu 1980, 85.
24 TT10, 14, 16, 28, 38; 1/14662, 8, 17, 24, 28, 35, 37, 43, 44, 45, 47, 62, 63, 75, 76, 77, 79, 80, 89, 90, 91.
25 Beldiceanu 1980, 87–89.
26 1/14662, 7, 29.
27 Beldiceanu 1980, 87.
28 TT10, 28, 38, 42, 76, 178; 1/14662, 50, 66.
29 Beldiceanu 1980, 86–87.
30 TT10, 14, 16, 18, 21, 28, 38, 178; 1/14662, 4, 14, 30, 37, 40/42, 50, 62, 66, 84, 86, 89, 94.
31 Beldiceanu 1980, 89–90.
32 TT10, 20, 28, 38, 178; 1/14662, 4, 10, 14, 17, 21, 22, 23, 24, 26, 28, 35, 44, 47, 50, 66, 75, 76, 87, 91, 93, 97, 98.
33 Beldiceanu 1980, 89–90.
34 TT10, 76, 178; 1/14662, 50.
35 Beldiceanu 1980, 90–91.
36 TT10, 76.
37 Beldiceanu 1980, 92.
38 TT10, 76.
39 Beldiceanu 1980, 92.
40 TT10, 76.
41 Beldiceanu 1980, 92.
42 TT10, 76.
43 Beldiceanu 1980, 92.
44 TT10, 76.
45 Beldiceanu 1980, 92.
46 Beldiceanu 1967, 9v–10r.
47 TT10, 18.

one *bürüme*, two *cebelü*s and one *çadır* instead of one *bürüme*, two *cebelü*s and one *tenktür*; new Muslims Ḥamza and his brother Yūsuf (2,080 *aḳçe*s)[48] sustained one *bürüme* each, one *cebelü* and one *tenktür* instead of campaigning on their own behalf wearing armour (*cebe*) and bringing one *ġulām*; Seyyidī ʿAlī (3,042 *aḳçe*s)[49] sustained one *bürüme*, one *cebelü* and one *tenktür* instead of one *bürüme* and one *ġulām*; Zaġanos Arnavud Timurḥiṣārī (2,872 *aḳçe*s)[50] sustained one *bürüme*, one *cebelü* and one *tenktür* instead of one *bürüme* and one *ġulām*; similarly Ḳaragöz Arnavud brother of Çāşnīgīr İsḥāḳ Paşa (2,861 *aḳçe*s)[51] sustained one *bürüme*, one *cebelü* and one *tenktür* instead of one *bürüme* and one *ġulām*; Ḥamza Derbendci (3,604 *aḳçe*s)[52] sustained one *bürüme*, one *cebelü* and one *tenktür* instead of one *bürüme* and one *ġulām*; similarly H̱ıżır son of Ṣavcı Sirozī (3,416 *aḳçe*s)[53] sustained one *bürüme*, one *cebelü* and one *tenktür* instead of one *bürüme* and one *ġulām*; similarly Kürd Şeyḫ Ḥasan (3,355 *aḳçe*s)[54] sustained one *bürüme*, one *cebelü* and one *tenktür* instead of a *bürüme* and a *ġulām*; ʿAlī son of Ḳulaġuz, and his son İskender (5,944 *aḳçe*s)[55] sustained one *bürüme* each, two *cebelü*s and one *çadır* instead of one *bürüme* each, two *cebelü*s and one *tenktür*; H̱oca ʿAlī (7,360 *aḳçe*s)[56] sustained one *bürüme*, two *cebelü*s, one *ġulām* and one *çadır* instead of one *bürüme*, two *cebelü*s, one *ġulām* and one *tenktür*; H̱ıżır commander-in-chief (*serʿasker*) of H̱ulumiç (Hlemoutsi), Ayo İlya (Agios Ilias) and Ġardicḳo (Gatsiko) (6,017 *aḳçe*s)[57] sustained one *bürüme*, two *cebelü*s and one *çadır* instead of one *bürüme*, two *cebelü*s and one *tenktür*; Balaban Yaninaʾi (3,085 *aḳçe*s)[58] sustained one *bürüme*, one *cebelü* and one *tenktür* instead of one *bürüme* and one *ġulām*; İbrāhīm Dīvāne (6,683 *aḳçe*s)[59] sustained one *bürüme*, two *cebelü*s, one *ġulām* and one *çadır* instead of one *bürüme*, two *cebelü*s, one *ġulām* and one *tenktür*; Aḥmed Simġārī and Ḳaraca Aġa (5,172 *aḳçe*s)[60] sustained one *bürüme* each, one *ġulām* and one *tenktür* instead of one *bürüme* each, one *cebelü*, one *ġulām* and one *tenktür*; İbrāhīm Engürüs (6,092 *aḳçe*s)[61] sustained one *bürüme*, two *cebelü*s and one *çadır* instead of one *bürüme*, two *cebelü*s and one *tenktür*; similarly Ḥamza (5,420 *aḳçe*s)[62] sustained one *bürüme*, two *cebelü*s and one *çadır* instead of one *bürüme*, two *cebelü*s and one *tenktür*; ʿAlī Ṣūfī İzdinī (2,881 *aḳçe*s)[63] sustained one *bürüme*, one *cebelü* and one *tenktür* instead of one *bürüme* and one *ġulām*; Ḳāsım (6,957 *aḳçe*s)[64] sustained one *bürüme*, two *cebelü*s, one *ġulām* and one *çadır* instead of one *bürüme*, two *cebelü*s, one *ġulām* and one *tenktür*; Ġarb (2,979 *aḳçe*s)[65] sustained one *bürüme*, one *cebelü* and one *tenktür* instead of one *bürüme* and one *ġulām*; similarly, his brother Süleymān (2,885 *aḳçe*s)[66] sustained one *bürüme*, one *cebelü* and one *tenktür* instead of one *bürüme* and one *ġulām*; finally new Muslim Mezīd (3,615 *aḳçe*s)[67] sustained one *bürüme*, one *cebelü* and one *tenktür* instead of one *bürüme*, one *cebelü*, one *ġulām* and one *tenktür*. All these possibly point either to a hitherto unknown, more detailed, categorisation of the military obligations or to the fluidity of the *tīmār* system at this early stage.

Certain inaccuracies of the *termini technici* used in the *defter* are further demonstrated by the following cases. The fief of Evrenos son of Yaʿḳūb Beg bin İştin is called *zeʿāmet* even though the accrued revenue is only 18,439 *aḳçe*s.[68] If we assume that there is no *lacuna* in the document, we may well have a discrepancy, as this should be a *tīmār* instead. İbrāhīm Beg, police superintendent (*subaşı*) of Ḳalavrita (Kalavrita), held a 45,970-*aḳçe*

48 TT10, 20.
49 1/14662, 10.
50 1/14662, 21.
51 1/14662, 22.
52 1/14662, 23.
53 1/14662, 26.
54 1/14662, 26.
55 1/14662, 30.
56 1/14662, 37.
57 1/14662, 40/42.
58 1/14662, 44.
59 1/14662, 62.
60 1/14662, 75.
61 1/14662, 84.
62 1/14662, 86.
63 1/14662, 87.
64 1/14662, 89.
65 1/14662, 93.
66 1/14662, 97.
67 1/14662, 98.
68 1/14662, 4–6.

fief, which is erroneously recorded as *ḫāṣṣ*.[69] The fiefs of ʿÖmer Beg son of Ezmir, police superintendent of Bejenik (Vlaherna), (37,170 *aḳçe*s),[70] Paşa Yiğit son of Ḳaragöz Beg bin Yuvan (66,415 *aḳçe*s),[71] and Sinān Ġaṣır Beg son of Süleymān Beg bin Ẕū'l-Ḳā-dir (41,039 *aḳçe*s)[72] are recorded firstly as *zeʿāmet* and then as *ḫāṣṣ*. The fief of İbrāhīm son of ʿĪsā Beg bin Pavlo Kurtik, police superintendent of Şandamir (Santomeri), (22,952 *aḳçe*s), is in the first place correctly recorded as a *zeʿāmet*, but then as a *tīmār*.[73]

The taxes mentioned in the TT10-1/14662 register can be categorised as follows:

A. Taxes *per capita*
  I. İspence
  II Niyābet
  III. Resm-i ʿarūsī

B. Taxes on crops
  I. Tithe on cereals
  II. Tithe on viticulture
  III. Other tithes and taxes on agricultural produce

C. Taxes on stock-rearing
  I. Tax on swine
  II. Tax on sheep

D. Taxes on private property (*mülk*)
  I. Taxes on water-powered gristmills
  II. Taxes on fulling mills

E. Revenue from personal holdings (*ḫāṣṣa*)

F. *Muḳāṭaʿ*as
  I. Imperial demesne
  II. Part of a *tīmār*

G. Other taxes

A. TAXES *PER CAPITA*

İspence: this is an *ʿörfī per capita* tax levied on all the non-Muslim adult males, married or unmarried, which appears for the first time in the cadastre of Albania (1431).[74] In the TT10-1/14662 the term *ispence* is preceded by the letter ʿayn (ع), which abbreviates the Arabic preposition *ʿan* (from, on account of, about). The origin of this tax is still under examination.[75] It is considered the equivalent of the Muslims' *resm-i çift* [tax on

69 TT10, 1, 38.
70 TT10, 28, 37.
71 1/14662, 50, 61.
72 1/14662, 66, 74.
73 1/14662, 14, 17.
74 İnalcık 1954a, 5, 88, 103.
75 Alexander noted the possible etymological connection with Serbian *spenza* (*la Spenza*), as rendered in Theodoro Spandugnino's *Partitio Constantinopolitano, de la origine deli imperatori ottomani, ordini de la corte, forma del guerreggiare loro, religione, rito, et costumi de la natione*: Sathas 1890, IX 224_{43}, $225_{7, 14, 41}$, and suggested it is related to Serbian *soće* and Byzantine *telos* (*τέλος*); however he emphasised that these pre-Ottoman taxes were collected per household: Alexander 1985, 423–426. Wittek, on the other hand, suggested a derivation from *župan* (i.e., local lord), **župan-ja*: Wittek 1955, 273, n. 1. Hammer-Purgstall attempted an etymology from *pencik* (i.e., booty fifth): Hammer-Purgstall 1815, I 213, accepted by Beldiceanu: Beldiceanu 1960, I 163. İnalcık denied both *spenza* and *pencik* as possible etymologies and argued that it was probably a poll-tax paid in Stefan Dušan's Empire, later maintained by the Ottomans: İnalcık, *Ispendje*. See also Bojanić-Lukač 1976.

farmland tilled by a pair (*çift*) of oxen].[76] Alexander argues that the *ispence* and the *resm-i çift* were 'seemingly separate but parallel systems of personal taxation', since the Ottoman jurists considered the two as identical.[77] The non-Muslim *reʿāyā* paid this head tax in place of providing corvée (*anġarya*), which was an illegal imposition enforced in exceptional conditions. In the law code of Meḥmed II[78] the *ispence* was set at 25 *aḳçe*s, which was enforced on every Greek and Jewish male adult in our document; widows who were head of households were encumbered with 6 *aḳçe*s per annum.[79] The Albanians, on the other hand, as stated in our cadastre, had to pay only 20 *aḳçe*s. This was a privilege most probably deriving from a late Byzantine reduction of taxes to the Albanians for services rendered to the state.[80] It is for this reason that the cadastre clearly distinguishes every Albanian settlement – or ethnically distinguishes the community in mixed villages – by noting the existence 'of the Albanian community' (*ez cemāʿat-i Arnavudān*). An administration otherwise indifferent towards the ethnic origin of its subjects followed the local fiscal practice as the safest way of assimilating the conquered areas.[81]

Resm-i niyābet: tax levied on criminals and offenders of the law. It was later called *niyābet-i cürm ve cināyet*.[82]

Resm-i ʿarūsī: tax on marriage.[83]

B. TAXES ON CROPS

I. Tithe on cereals

The tithe constituted the basic tax on harvests calculated usually at one tenth of the production, which varied according to the time and yield of the crop. The TT10-1/14662 does not record the *sālāriyye*,[84] a surtax on the tithe on cereals of approximately one fourth of the tithe, as is the case in the register of 1474 pertaining to the island of Euboea.[85] Perhaps one should consider that in our cadastre the *sālāriyye* had already been included in the tithe paid.

ʿÖşr-i ḥınṭa, ʿöşr-i gendüm:[86] tithe on wheat (one eighth of the production).[87]
ʿÖşr-i cev, ʿöşr-i şaʿīr:[88] tithe on barley (one eighth of the production).[89]

II. Tithe on viticulture

ʿÖşr-i bāġāt, ʿöşr-i bāġ: tithe on vineyards. In two entries the tithe on vineyards is further divided into grape-must (*ʿan şīre*) and dry raisins (*ʿan istafide*).[90]

76 Alexander 1985, 418–419. In some places in Thrace and western Anatolia non-Muslims paid the *resm-i çift* instead of the *ispence*: İnalcik 1959, 606. For the *resm-i çift* see İnalcik, *Čift-Resmi*, 32, and Alexander 1985, 394–404. The term *çift* (pair) denoted the land which may be cultivated with a pair of oxen, similar to the Byzantine *zeugarion* (*ζευγάριον*); for the *zeugarion* see Laiou-Thomadakis 1977, 163–173. It is attested that in Ohrid in 1613 the Muslims who had the use and disposal (*taṣarruf*) of Christians' farms (*baştina*) were obliged to pay the *ispence*: Çağatay 1947, 508.

77 Alexander 1985, 421–422.

78 İnalcik 1959, 602. See the *Ḳānūn-ı cebelüyān bā ḳānūn-ı müzevvec-i gebrān* in Akgündüz 1990, I 355.

79 See the *Ḳānūn-ı livāʾ-ı Tırḫala* in Alexander 1985, 92_{6-7}.

80 The reduction and even exemption of taxes offered by the Byzantines and the Venetians to attract the Albanians is well documented in contemporary sources; see Chapter 2, The Demography of the Peloponnese, 213, n. 45, 214, n. 57.

81 For the Byzantine influence on Ottoman practice see Köprülüzade 1931, 165–313 and especially for the taxation system 215–219; Cvetkova 1962; İnalcik 1960.

82 İnalcik 1954a, xxvii.

83 According to the *ḳānūnnāme* of the Morea in the TT367 abridged register (AD 1530), 30 *aḳçe*s were imposed on infidel virgin women and 15 on widows who remarried; Muslim women paid double the amounts for the same tax: Özkiliç–Coşkun–Sivridağ–Yüzbaşioğlu 2007, II 112; Balta 1993, 44; see also the *ʿArūsāne ḳānūnı* in Barkan 1943, I 301, §16.

84 For the *sālāriyye* or *sālārlıḳ* see Alexander 1985, 490–494; Beldiceanu 1980, 61.

85 Balta 1989, 19.

86 *ʿÖşr-i gendüm* is mentioned once in Raḫova: TT10, 26.

87 Beldiceanu–Beldiceanu-Steinherr 1980, 24.

88 *ʿÖşr-i şaʿīr* is mentioned once in Raḫova: TT10, 26.

89 Beldiceanu–Beldiceanu-Steinherr 1980, 24.

90 Mentioned twice, in Ayo Vaşıl/Çağıl Ḥiṣārı (Agios Vasileios) and Ayonori (Agionori): TT10, 170, 172. For *istafide* or *istafidiye* < σταφίδα (*Gr. n.* raisin, currant) see Balta 1993, 35.

III. Other tithes and taxes on agricultural produce

ʿÖşr-i āsiyāb (?): tithe on water-powered gristmills.[91] This unique entry is a problematic one, since, to my knowledge, such a tithe is not attested in Ottoman documents. In some cases, the *resm-i āsiyāb* (see *infra*) was collected in kind.[92] However, it is possible that in this case a Byzantine precedent may have been followed.

ʿÖşr-i bostān, ʿöşr-i besātīn:[93] tithe on kitchen gardens (one eighth of the production).[94]

ʿÖşr-i çam saḳızı: tithe on resin[95] (one tenth of the production).[96]

ʿÖşr-i ḳazz: tithe on raw silk (one tenth of the production).[97]

ʿÖşr-i kettān: tithe on flax (one tenth of the production).[98]

ʿÖşr-i meyve: tithe on fruit (one tenth of the production).[99]

ʿÖşr-i penbe: tithe on cotton (one tenth of the production).[100]

ʿÖşr-i ṭut: tithe on mulberries[101] (one tenth of the production).[102]

ʿÖşr-i zeyt: tithe on olive oil (one tenth of the production).[103]

ʿÖşr-i ʿasel: tithe on honey (one tenth of the production).[104]

Resm-i ḫamr: tax on wine (one tenth of the production).[105]

C. TAXES ON STOCK-REARING

Resm-i aġnām: tax on sheep.[106] During the reign of Meḥmed II the tax on sheep was set at 1 *aḳçe* per 3 heads;[107] however, we are not in a position to confirm that this is also the case in our document.[108] In the *ḳānūnnāme* of the Morea issued in the period of Bayezid II (1481–1512) it is noted that the tax on sheep (*ʿādet-i aġnām*) was 1 *aḳçe* per 3 heads, since the sheep in certain districts of this province lambed twice a year.[109]

Resm-i ḫanāzīr, resm-i ḫınzīr: tax on swine (1 *aḳçe* per head for home-bred animals and 1 *aḳçe* per 2 heads for herded animals).[110]

91 Mentioned once in Namuni: TT10, 57.
92 Kraelitz-Greifenhorst 1921–2, 25, §24.
93 *ʿÖşr-i besātīn* is mentioned once in Ḳoriṣos (Korinthos): TT10, 166.
94 Beldiceanu–Beldiceanu-Steinherr 1980, 25.
95 Mentioned twice in Hiliẓon (Helidoni) and Sela: TT10, 95, 99.
96 Beldiceanu–Beldiceanu-Steinherr 1980, 25.
97 Ibid.
98 Beldiceanu–Beldiceanu-Steinherr 1980, 24–25.
99 Ibid.
100 Ibid.
101 Mentioned once in Ḳastriçi (Ano Kastritsi): TT10, 184.
102 Beldiceanu–Beldiceanu-Steinherr 1980, 25.
103 Ibid. In 1716, according to the Ottoman taxation system, the annual fruit yield of one olive tree was estimated at 20 *oḳḳa*s (3 *oḳḳa*s of olive oil) on average; the price was set at 12 *aḳçe*s per *oḳḳa* of olive oil: Parveva 2003, 95.
104 Beldiceanu–Beldiceanu-Steinherr 1980, 24–25.
105 Ibid.
106 Mentioned only in the Voştiça (Aigio) district: TT10, 42–74.
107 *Ḳānūn-ı cebelüyān bā ḳānūn-ı müzevvec-i gebrān* in Akgündüz 1990, I 356; Beldiceanu–Beldiceanu-Steinherr 1980, 25. This tax was generally collected in April: Alexander 1985, 475; Beldiceanu 1964, II 300–301.
108 See below, district of Voştiça, 245, 255-258.
109 *Ḳānūnnāme-i memlaḥa-ı Mora ve resm-i aġnām ve dalyan ve ġayrihi* in Alexander 1985, $178_{11\text{-}14}$, 354; Balta 1993, 32.
110 Beldiceanu–Beldiceanu-Steinherr 1980, 25; Alexander 1985, 486; see also the *Ḳānūn-ı cebelüyān bā ḳānūn-ı müzevvec-i gebrān* in Akgündüz 1990, I 355.

D. TAXES ON PRIVATE PROPERTY (*MÜLK*)

The *emlāk* (*pl.* of *mülk*) constituted private property, whose owner had full proprietorial rights over them; he could sell, lease, donate, endow (as a *vaḳf*), or bequeath them, but always in accordance with the Islamic law (*şerīʿat*). Our register lists only mills under this heading.

Āsiyāb, āsiyāb-ı ġalle: tax on watermills grinding grain into flour (water-powered gristmills).[111] In Bursa the custom was to impose a levy of 5 *aḳçe*s per month on the watermills and for the rest of the empire 60 *aḳçe*s per annum on mills that were in service throughout the year, 30 *aḳçe*s on those operating for six months and 15 *aḳçe*s on those working for three months.[112] Different levies were imposed on mills equipped with multiple grinding stones (*göz*).[113]

Āsiyāb-ı peşmīne: tax on woollen cloth fulling mills. These mills, found throughout the Balkan Peninsula, are known in Greece by two different names: *nerotrivi* (νεροτριβή) and *dristela* (ντριστέλα).[114] They were used to treat the newly woven woollen cloth so as to mat its fibres, to tighten its weave and thus make it warmer, fluffier, firmer and more durable. The cloth was put in a flat-bottomed funnel-shaped wooden vat where fast running water diverted through a pipe washed it and gave its finish.[115] In many places the fulling mill was constructed on a slope underneath a water-powered gristmill so as to benefit from the same source of hydropower. The much later *ḳānūnāme* of Süleymān I (1520–1566), pertaining to the Peloponnese, ordered a tax of 15 *aḳçe*s per annum for the fulling mills (*kebe değirmenleri*).[116] This tax assessment was already in force in the majority of cases in the TT10-1/14662, which, according to the register, was always lower than the one levied on gristmills.[117]

E. REVENUE FROM PERSONAL HOLDINGS (*ḪĀṢṢA*)

The *tīmār* comprised two parts: (a) the tax revenue of the *reʿāyā* in a defined allotment granted to the timariot and (b) *ḫāṣṣa* revenue from resources, which were under the direct control and exploitation of the timariot as his personal reserve.[118] Our register recorded the following *ḫāṣṣa* revenues:

Āsiyāb-ı ḫāṣṣa: water-powered gristmills. In the register the watermills recorded as *ḫāṣṣa* were generally more profitable than the ones registered as the private property of the *reʿāyā*.

Āsiyāb-ı peşmīne-i ḫāṣṣa: fulling mills.

Bāġāt-ı ḫāṣṣa: vineyards. The vineyards were measured in *dönüm*s (1 *dönüm* = 919.3m^2).[119]

Bāġçe-i or *bāġçehā-yı türünc-i ḫāṣṣa*:[120] bitter orange groves.

Bāġçe-i ḫāṣṣa: gardens.

Bostān-ı ḫāṣṣa: kitchen gardens.

Eşcār-ı balamutlu-yı[121] *ḫāṣṣa*: oak trees.[122] All kinds of trees were counted in units (*ʿaded*).

Eşcār-ı cevz-i ḫāṣṣa: walnut trees.

Eşcār-ı emrūd-ı ḫāṣṣa: pear trees.[123]

Eşcār-ı enār-ı ḫāṣṣa: pomegranate trees.[124]

Eşcār-ı meyve-i ḫāṣṣa: fruit trees.

---

111 For a general survey on watermills in Greece see Nomikos 1997a; Nomikos 1997b; Nomikos 1999.

112 Alexander 1985, 193$_{4\text{-}6}$, 370; Balta 1993, 44; Akgündüz 1990, I 189.

113 Murphey 1988, 235.

114 *Ντριστέλα* is a loanword from Albanian *dërstilë* (fulling mill): Oikonomou 1999, 95.

115 Oikonomidou–Skambalis 2006, 18–19.

116 Alexander 1985, 193$_7$, 370; Balta 1993, 44.

117 Mr Dimitris Mihas, an old gentleman whom I met in Raftopoulo village, Messenia, showed me the old watermill, which today houses the only taverna in the village, and the fulling mill further downhill, and informed me that they both operated until World War II. According to Mr Mihas, the price for cloth fulling was half the one for wheat grinding.

118 On no account were the *ḫāṣṣa* resources considered as private property of the timariot: Moutafchieva 1988, 55–60. See also İnalcik 1994, 117–118.

119 İnalcik 1983, 340.

120 Mentioned twice, in Ḫulumiç (Hlemoutsi) and Vaşıliḳa (Sikyona): TT10, 77, 168.

121 Should read *palamutlu*.

122 Mentioned once in Buryalisa: TT10, 186.

123 Mentioned once in Porta (Portes): 1/14662, 16.

124 Mentioned once in Priniḳos (Asteri): TT10, 18.

Eşcār-ı saḳız-ı çam-ı ḫāṣṣa: resin trees.

Eşcār-ı ṭut-ı ḫāṣṣa: mulberry trees.

Eşcār-ı zeyt-i ḫāṣṣa: olive trees.

Ḳısṭ-ı ṭalyan-ı ḫāṣṣa: fish-farms. In the case of a state-owned fishery the imperial appointee (*ʿāmil*) was ordered to collect half of the fish caught for the state.[125]

Ṭāḥūne-i zeyt-i ḫāṣṣa: oil presses.[126] According to the *ḳānūnnāme* of the Morea dated in the reign of Süleymān I, the tax on oil presses (*zeyt yaġı değirmenleri*) was set at 20 *aḳçe*s yearly plus a cup (*bardaḳ*) of olive oil.[127]

Ṭalyan-ı ḫāṣṣa: fish-farms.[128]

F. *MUḲĀṬAʿAS*

*Muḳāṭaʿa*s were 'state revenue sources divided into portions to be distributed in return for a mutually agreed price'.[129] For the most part there were three kinds of *muḳāṭaʿa*s: (a) those farmed out to private contractors (*ber vech-i iltizām*); (b) those under the direct control of the central treasury collected by a salaried governmental agent (*emīn* or *mübāşir*); and (c) those awarded as part of a *tīmār*.[130] In the register under examination one encounters *muḳāṭaʿa*s belonging to the second and third category and deriving from land (rice fields, orchards), sea (fish-farms), state monopolies (salt-pans) and other taxable activities (customs dues, market tax, *niyābet*, etc.).[131] It is to be noted that the revenue of the *muḳāṭaʿa*s which constituted imperial demesne (second category) was not counted in the timariot's income.[132] Their value was estimated in a lump sum (*ber vech-i maḳṭūʿ*).[133] The TT10-1/14662 records the following *muḳāṭaʿa* revenues:

I. Imperial demesne

Muḳāṭaʿa-ı çeltük: tax on rice fields.[134]

Muḳāṭaʿa-ı memlaḥa: tax on salt-pans.[135]

II. Part of a tīmār

Muḳāṭaʿa-ı bāġçe-i türünc-i ḫāṣṣa: tax on bitter orange groves.

Muḳāṭaʿa-ı bāzār: market tax assessed according to the amount of goods sold.[136]

Muḳāṭaʿa-ı gümrük: customs dues.

Muḳāṭaʿa-ı maʿber: transit duty, tax on the traffic of commodities, which in other sources is called *resm-i geçüd/geçid*. The duty differed

125 Alexander 1985, 180_{13}, $188_{3\text{-}4}$, 356, 364; Balta 1993, 33, 40.

126 The types of oil presses in operation during the late mediaeval and early modern period in the Peloponnese were: (a) hand-operated (small-scale or domestic use), (b) animal-powered (most commonly used), and (c) water-powered: Giannopoulou 2007, 107–114.

127 Alexander 1985, $193_{8\text{-}9}$, 370; Balta 1993, 44. For *bardaḳ* see İnalcik 1983, 327.

128 For the unique feature of the fish-farm in Ẓiġanato (Venetiko/Tigani Island?): TT10, 130, see Introduction, 10.

129 Darling 1996, 123. See also Gerber, *Muḳāṭaʿa*; İnalcik 1994, 64–66.

130 For the *muḳāṭaʿa* practice in the fifteenth century see Gökbilgin 1952, 87–159; Akdağ 1999, II 231–247.

131 The state monopolies (*appalti*) under the Venetian system were on: salt (*sale*), which was the most important one in effect throughout the Peloponnese, gunpowder (*polvere*), bread (*pane à cornetti e tondo*), oil (*oglio*), soap (*sapone*), candles (*candelle di cera e sevo*), sherbet (*serbetto*), coffee (*café*), tobacco (*tabacco*), spirits (*acqua vita*), pork (*luganega*), pasta (*minestre di pasta*), hostelries (*hostarie*), hiring of horses (*sedie e cavalli a nolo*), and playing-cards (*carti da gioco d'ogni sorte*): Davies 1996, 161–194; Dokos–Panagopoulos 1993, xiv, n. 6.

132 TT10, 86, 132: 'ḥāṣıl ġayr ez çeltük'; TT10, 18, 45, 73, 74, 130, 134, 135, 166, 168, 182, 1/14662, 47, 97: 'ḥāṣıl ġayr ez memlaḥa'.

133 İnalcik 1954a, xxxv.

134 See Beldiceanu–Beldiceanu-Steinherr 1978; İnalcik 1982.

135 For the taxation on salt as defined in the Peloponnesian *ḳānūnnāme*s see Alexander 1985, $178_{1\text{-}11}$, $187_{1\text{-}13}$, 354, 363–364; Balta 1993, 31–32, 38, 40. For the salt production in the Peloponnese under the Venetian rule see Panopoulou 1987–88.

136 It was called *ḳısṭ-ı bāzār* in the 1431 land register of Albania and *bāc-ı bāzār* in later registers: İnalcik 1954a, xxvii. For the different prices of this tax see Alexander 1985, $190_{1\text{-}16}$, 366-367; Balta 1993, 42. In our cadastre it is always calculated with reference to *resm-i niyābet* or *gümrük ve maʿber* and only once it is recorded as *ḳısṭ-ı bāzār ve niyābet* in Vumero (Goumero): TT10, 86.

according to the nature of the goods.[137]

Muḳāṭaʿa-ı niyābet: tax levied on criminals and offenders of the law.

Muḳāṭaʿa-ı ṭāḥūne-i zeyt-i ḫāṣṣa: tax on oil presses.

Muḳāṭaʿa-ı ṭalyan: tax on fish-farms.

G. OTHER TAXES

Resm-i ıġrıb-ı māhī gīrān: tax on drag seine fishing.[138] According to the much later *ḳānūnnāme* of Aḥmed III (1703–1730) dated in 1716, one fourth of the fish caught by nets and *ıġrıb* was to be collected by the state.[139]

Resm-i gümrük: see *muḳāṭaʿa-ı gümrük*.

Resm-i maʿber: see *muḳāṭaʿa-ı maʿber.*

Resm-i bāzār: see *muḳāṭaʿa-ı bāzār.*

The figures given in the registers seem to be estimates calculated before or after the harvest. It is, therefore, very difficult to assess exactly the actual revenue from each crop, as the specific register does not provide a correlation between the value (*bahā*) of a crop and the unit of measurement (*keyl/kile*, *ḥıml*, *lidre*, etc.).[140] Even if such a connection were attested, the actual sum ought to be calculated with caution, since the average sum given is a mere approximation based on previous crops. The sum of the crops from the three previous years was divided by three and the average deduced was recorded in the cadastre.[141] The only case where the crop's value is estimated on the basis of a unit of measurement is in Raḫova, where an Adrianople *müdd* (*müdd-i Edrene*)[142] of wheat cost 80 *aḳçe*s and a bushel (*keyl*)[143] 4 *aḳçe*s; an Adrianople *müdd* of barley cost 60 *aḳçe*s and a bushel 3 *aḳçe*s.[144] It should be noted that the TT10 specifically mentions that the Adrianople *müdd* was checked by the official assayers (*keylciyān*).[145] An attempt to calculate the actual production of wheat and barley will be made on the basis of this correlation.

The currency used for all calculations was the Ottoman silver coin, *aḳçe*, what the Greeks called *aspron* (*ἄσπρον*) and the Westerners *asper*.[146] It is probable that our document refers to the *aḳçe*s minted in 1460–1461, perhaps in Serres, with an official weight of 0.952gr.[147] In 1462 the exchange rate was 42–43 *aḳçe*s for one Venetian ducat.[148]

A number of cases of tax exemption are recorded in the TT10-1/14662:

(a) Individuals exempt (*müsellem*) from the *ispence*: Ḳosta Ḫırisoḫoplo, inhabitant of Ḳalavrita (Kalavryta), for having worked as a builder (*bennāʾ*) and carpenter (*neccār*) at the castle of Ḳalavrita;[149] Milengi[t] C[---] (his surname is unreadable), inhabitant of Londar (Leontari), for

137 See the *Ḳānūnnāme-i İskele-i Budun ve Estergon* in Barkan 1943, 302–303, §38.

138 Mentioned once in the town of Ḫulumiç (Hlemoutsi): TT10, 77. ıġrıb < *Gr.* γρίπος: Kahane–Tietze 1958, 503–504, and Koukoules 1948, 29, 37 published in revised form in Koukoules 1952, V 331–343 (for γρίπος see 332, 340). For a detailed description of this manner of fishing in Kotyhi and Mourgia, Elis, see Papandreou 1924, 49–50.

139 See the *Ḳānūnnāme-i vilāyet-i Mora* in Barkan 1943, 329, §20; Balta 1993, 55.

140 Corresponding entries in other registers read e.g.: Kołodziejczyk 2004, I 102: 'ʿöşr-i ḥınṭa: keyl 48, bahā 1140' (Kolubayofçi village, Podolia, Ukraine); Delilbaşı–Arikan 2001, I 146: 'ḥınṭa: 35 kile, fī kile 8, yekūn 280' (Nostimo village, Evrytania, Greece).

141 Beldiceanu-Steinherr–Beldiceanu 1978, 6–7, 19, §4; Kołodziejczyk 2004, I 39–40.

142 The *müdd* used in Adrianople weighed 20 bushels (*keyl*, *kile* or *keylçe/kilece*), as its equivalent used in Istanbul, see Hinz 1955, 47; İnalcik 1983, 324–325. *Müdd* is a loanword from Greek *modios* (μόδιος) (*Lat.* modius; *It.* moggio); for the Byzantine *modios* see Schilbach 1970, 95–100, 103–108.

143 For fixed prices of crops per *kile* or *yük* see İnalcik 1983, 332, 334.

144 TT10, 26. One *müdd* of wheat weighed 513.12kg and one *müdd* of barley 445kg: Hinz 1955, 47. As Beldiceanu and Beldiceanu-Steinherr pointed out, this price corresponds to the one given by Barkan for the years 1463–1500: 1 *kile* wheat = 3.5–5.5 *aḳçe*s: Beldiceanu–Beldiceanu-Steinherr 1980, 57; Barkan 1964, 258.

145 TT10, 26: 'be-müdd-i Edrene-i keylciyān'. The assayer (*kileci* or *keylci*) and the stamper (*tamġacı*), who had their office in Çardak pier, Istanbul, tested and certified the units of measurement: İnalcik 1983, 335–336.

146 Liata 1996, 95–114; Aykut 2002, 823–833.

147 Beldiceanu–Beldiceanu-Steinherr 1980, 21; Beldiceanu 1960, I 173. See also Srećković 2000, II 27–28, 61 (nos 97–99); Jem Sultan 1977, I 78–79 (nos 713–721), II plate 58. For the Ottoman mint at Serres see Kokkas 1996.

148 Pamuk 2000, 46. For the evolution of the *aḳçe* see Pamuk 2004, 954–956. Specifically, for the reign of Meḥmed II see Beldiceanu 1965, 27–39.

149 TT10, 38.

having worked as blacksmith (*āhenger*) at the castle of Londar;[150] Yani Mikâli, inhabitant of Ḳoris̱os (Korinthos), for having worked as builder at the castle of Ḳoris̱os;[151] İstemati H̱ırisinos, inhabitant of Ḳoris̱os, for having worked as carpenter at the castle of Ḳoris̱os;[152] Mastrotoma Cingene, inhabitant of Ḳoris̱os, for having worked as blacksmith at the castle of Ḳoris̱os.[153] All these individuals enjoyed tax exemption in return for services rendered in the castle building and/or maintenance. This practice is linked to the term castle-building (*ḥiṣār yapması*) attested in the *ḳānūnnāme* of the TT424 pertaining to the inhabitants of Kitros and Libanovo (today's Aiginio, Pieria, Greece)[154] and to the Byzantine *kastroktisia* (*καστροκτισία*).[155]

(b) Groups exempt (*mu'āf ve müsellem*) from the *ispence* included monastic foundations. The monastic community of the Manastır-ı Yirondos der Taḳsiyarẖi (Gerontos Osiou Leontiou Monastery) was exempt from both the *ispence* and the capitation (*ḫarāc*). These fiscal privileges were granted to them in the past by the Byzantine authorities – privileges that the Ottoman authorities acknowledged after having examined the documentation that the monks provided to the surveyor for his inspection. According to that decree (*ḥükm*), the monastic land registered as private property was to be left intact; the term used to describe this property is *laftero* (لافترو).[156] The entry reads:

> The community of Gerontos in Taxiarhon Monastery, in the vicinity of the aforementioned town of Aigio: the priests of the aforesaid monastery have been granted a decree in the infidels' language, in accordance with which, no one should interfere with the private properties the monastery had previously acquired; they should be exempt from the *ispence* and the capitation and their private properties have been registered as *laftero*.[157]

Similarly, the Manastır-ı S̱otoḳos (Panagias Pepelenitsis Monastery) was exempt; the respective entry in the TT10 reads:

> The community of Theotokou Monastery, in the vicinity of the aforementioned Gerontos Monastery: in accordance with the decrees in the infidels' language these priests too, like the ones mentioned above, should be understood to be exempt from the *ispence* and the capitation and that their private properties to be *laftero*.[158]

The *ḫarāc* is the poll-tax paid by non-Muslim subjects, different from the *ispence*, and used in the place of the term *cizye* by the sixteenth century.[159] In this case it should be distinguished from the two classical forms of the tax incumbent on land, namely the *ḫarāc-ı muḳāseme* (proportional levy) and the *ḫarāc-ı muvaẓẓaf* (fixed levy). As a *şer'ī* tax it belonged to the *beytü'l-māli'l-müslimīn* and was collected directly for the Sultan's treasury under the supervision of the *ḳāḍīs*. Only in exceptional cases did the Sultan grant *cizye*/*ḫarāc* revenues as *tīmār* or *mülk*.[160] The population subject to *cizye* was recorded in a special register called *defter-i cizye-i gebrān*. It is possible that the word *ḫarāc* derives from the Greek *χορηγία* or *χορηγεῖον*.[161]

---

150 TT10, 138.
151 TT10, 165.
152 Ibid.
153 Ibid.
154 Alexander 1985, 67_2, 238, 471–472.
155 Trojanos 1969.
156 λεύτερο < ἐλεύθερον (*Gr. adj.* free). The term *ἐλεύθερον* was used in Byzantine documents to denote a tax exempt allotment or private property, Act of Protokynegos John Vatatzes (1341): Oikonomidès 1984, $155_{1\text{-}3}$: 'Ἐπεὶ εὗρον τὴν κατὰ τὸ ἅγι(ον) ὄρος τοῦ Ἄθω διακειμένην σεβασμί(αν) βασιλικὴν μονὴν, τὴν εἰς ὄνομα τιμωμένην τῶν τιμίων ταξιαρχῶν τῶν ἄνω δυνάμεων (καὶ) ἐπικεκλημένην τοῦ Δοχειαρίου κατέχουσαν κτήμ(α)τα γον(ικ)ὰ διὰ θείων και σεπτῶν χρυσοβούλλων, προσκυνητῶν τε προσταγμάτων καὶ λοιπῶν διαφόρων παλαιγενῶν δικαιωμάτ(ων) ἐλεύθερα καὶ ἐκτὸς τέλους (καὶ) βάρ(ους) τινός.' Act of the three census takers (1418): ibid., 289_1–290_4; *Praktikon* of Andronicus Sphrantzes Sebastopoulos (1430): Oikonomidès 1968, $151_{134\text{-}135}$; *Horismos* of Despot Demetrius Palaeologus (1430): ibid., $154_{1\text{-}4}$. The same term, *ἐλεύθερος*, was used in the Byzantine records to define poor peasants not inscribed at a certain moment on any *praktikon*: Laiou-Thomadakis 1977, 34, 160.
157 TT10, 44. In April 2007 I visited the Taxiarhon Monastery in quest of this Byzantine decree. Unfortunately, the archive does not contain documents dating before the beginning of the eighteenth century, as a fire in 1621–1638 devastated the old monastery; see Chapter 1, The Historical Geography of the Peloponnese, 46, no. 101.
158 TT10, 44. As the nun Sister Filothei informed me in April 2007, the Panagias Pepelenitsis Monastery does not own any Byzantine documents. My communication with her was over the telephone, as the road leading to the monastery had been blocked after a landslide.
159 Cahen–İnalcik–Hardy, D̲jizya, 562.
160 Ibid; the law codes of Avlonya (Vlorë), Erzurum and Silistre read 'cizye-i şāhī ve ispence-i sipāhī': İnalcik 1959, 604–605.
161 Schwarz 1916. On the basis of a Byzantine *prostagma* dated in December 1408, Oikonomides proposed an etymology from *χορηγεῖον*: Oikonomides 1969, 684–685: 'ἐπεὶ δὲ εὐεργετήσαμεν πρὸς αὐτοὺς ἀπὸ τοῦ χορηγείου αὐτῶν, ὅπερ ἐχάρισεν ἰδίως πρὸς ἡμᾶς ὁ μέγας ἀμηρᾶς, ἵνα ἔχωσι τὸ δίμοιρον, συνέβη δὲ εἴς τινα, ὅτι ἐδίδουν τὸ ἥμισυ χορηγεῖον, ἀφ' οὗ μέρους ἐκράτουν, διοριζόμεθα ἵνα διδῶσιν ἀπὸ τούτου τὸ τρίτον, ὡσὰν ἐξ ἀρχῆς ἀπεφηνάμεθα καὶ ὡρίσαμεν.'

The inhabitants of the city of Corinth were exempt from the capitation, the *ispence*, and the extraordinary taxes levied in emergency situations (*ʿavārıż*), including the customary impositions (*tekālif-i dīvāniyye*),[162] as they were obliged to guard the castle, whenever the warden of the castle (*dizdār*) commanded them to do so. The TT10 mentions the warden's name, Ḫāccī Ḳaraca, when recording his watermill.[163] The entry reads:

> According to the decrees in the hands of the aforementioned community of Corinth, they (the Corinthians) should be exempt from the capitation and the *ispence* and all the extraordinary taxes and customary impositions, and they should stand guard at the castle, when the warden of the castle demands it. However, when the register was submitted [to the Sublime Porte], they were immediately exempted from the *ispence*, but not from their capitation and other [taxes].[164]

The final group to benefit from a tax reduction were the inhabitants of Raḫova village, by virtue of their service as guardians of the mountainous pass (*derbend*) of Miḫlu (Mouhli).[165] As a result, each household and bachelor had to pay 10 *aḳçe*s instead of 25. The *derbend* was similar to the Byzantine system of *kleisourai* (*κλεισοῦραι*).[166] The entry reads:

> The village of Raḫova guards the mountainous pass of Mouhli, but according to the decrees in the hands of the aforementioned villagers, it has been recorded that whoever is appointed as the warden of the castle of Mouhli becomes the guard [of the pass] as well.[167]

Part of the taxes collected was meant to be used for the needs of the Muslim religious authorities in the Peloponnese. The Ottomans put much effort into founding Islamic religious establishments in the conquered lands; the key role of mosques, theological schools, public kitchens for the poor, etc. in the process of Ottomanisation is well attested. However, according to the evidence in the TT10-1/14662, at this early stage immediately after the conquest this process had hardly begun, or it is better documented in other sources, like the *vaḳf defter*s. In our register only two mosques are recorded, one in Londar (Leontari) and the other in Corinth with special reference to the provisions for the religious ministers and functionaries. In Londar, the judge of the district (*ḳāḍī*), Our Lord (*Mevlānā*) Muḥyi'd-dīn, a prayer leader (*imām*) at the mosque of the Muslim community (previously a monastery) in the town, was to receive 5 *aḳçe*s per day.[168] The mosque in Corinth enjoyed a more detailed entry: the judge of the district (*ḳāḍī*), *Mevlānā* Muḥyi'd-dīn, the *imām* who delivered the sermon after the Friday prayer at the mosque (*ḫutbe*), received 6 *aḳçe*s per day, ʿAlī, the muezzin (*müʾeẕẕin*) 2 *aḳçe*s per day, and the caretaker of the mosque (*ḳayyım*) another 2. Moreover, 1 *aḳçe* per day was to be collected for the oil of the lamps (*pīh*) and for the mats (*ḥaṣīr*) of the mosque. A portion of the revenue of the town of Corinth (375 *aḳçe*s: 360 *aḳçe*s from the vineyards and 15 *aḳçe*s from 15 fruit trees, plus a deserted *mezraʿa*) was allotted to the *ḳāḍī* as it had been ceded in the past to the church now converted to a mosque.[169] The *ḳāḍī* of Londar and Corinth is likely to have been the same person, but given the greater award he received in Corinth it may be assumed that the town had a larger Muslim population.

The wealth of these details concerning taxation casts light on the economic conditions of the districts of the Peloponnese. In the following section an attempt will be made to present the economic image of each district briefly together with a table and a chart, which display in detail the tax revenues yielded from each settlement (town, village) or *mezraʿa*.

162 Alexander 1985, 461–464. The local population often bargained with the Ottoman government on the amount of *ʿavārıż* taxes to be levied on them: İnalcik 1980a, 315.
163 TT10, 166.
164 Ibid.
165 The *derbend* villages enjoyed exemptions from all taxes with the exception of the tithe: Orhonlu 1990, 45. For the service of the Albanians as defile guards in the Peloponnese see Topping 1980, 271, n. 28, where he comments on the phrase 'expenso custodia Seraley': Sathas 1880, I 118_{17}.
166 Glykatzi-Ahrweiler 1960, 81–82; Ferluga 1975; Grigoriou-Ioannidou 1989.
167 TT10, 25. The warden of the castle of Miḫlu at the time was a certain Mübārek.
168 TT10, 139.
169 TT10, 166.

District of Ḳalavrita (Kalavryta) (Table 11; Chart 6)[170]

The sum of the tax revenue from the district of Ḳalavrita was 69,792 *aḳçe*s, 29,310 (41.99%) of which derived from wheat, 21,620 (30.98%) from the *ispence*; 8,223 (11.78%) from viticulture and 4,541 (6.51%) from barley. The remaining revenue derived from crops and taxable activities amounting to less than 1%. The timariots' *ḫāṣṣa* revenues amounted to 4,705 *aḳçe*s (6.74%).

District of Miziṯra (Mystras) (Table 12; Chart 7)

Because of the missing pages, the only village mentioned in the register belonging to the district of Miziṯra is Priniḳos (Asteri), which was ceded to ʿAlī son of Cāyim, whose allotment was in Ḳalavrita; hence, it was conscribed within the Ḳalavrita district. The entry of the Miziṯra district unfortunately is missing from our register. Priniḳos yielded annually 1,704 *aḳçe*s: 380 (22.30%) of these derived from viticulture; 250 (14.67%) from the *ispence*, and 200 (11.74%) from wheat. The timariot's *ḫāṣṣa* revenues amounted to 1,110 *aḳçe*s (65.14%) Its fish-farms were estimated at 800 *aḳçe*s per year, or 46.95% of the total revenue. The salt-pan's revenue had been registered in the Miziṯra district and is thus unknown.[171]

District of Miḫlu (Mouhli) (Table 13; Chart 8)

The district of Miḫlu yielded annually 18,407 *aḳçe*s, of which 7,956 *aḳçe*s (43.22%) derived from wheat; 5,886 *aḳçe*s (31.98%) from the *ispence* and 1,976 *aḳçe*s (10.73%) from viticulture. The timariots' *ḫāṣṣa* revenues ran to 1,530 *aḳçe*s (8.31%).

District of Bejenik (Vlaherna) (Table 14; Chart 9)

The district of Bejenik's annual tax revenue was estimated at 37,170 *aḳçe*s, of which 13,050 *aḳçe*s (35.11%) came from the tithe on wheat; 11,561 *aḳçe*s (31.10%) from the *ispence* and 7,076 *aḳçe*s (19.04%) from viticulture. The timariot's *ḫāṣṣa* revenues totalled 2,850 *aḳçe*s (7.67%).

District of Voştiça (Aigio) (Table 15; Chart 10)

The total sum of the taxes levied on the district of Voştiça is, according to the register, 161,494 *aḳçe*s, whereas our calculations give the actual amount of 161,694 *aḳçe*s. This should be attributed to a scribal error. After adding the imperial *muḳāṭaʿa*s from the salt-pans, 20,564 *aḳçe*s (11.28%), the total sum works out at 182,258 *aḳçe*s. Of these, 44,250 *aḳçe*s (24.28%) derived from the cultivation of wheat; 43,426 *aḳçe*s (23.82%) from the *ispence* and 22,766 *aḳçe*s (12.49%) from viticulture. The district of Voştiça presents the highest amount of tax obtained from the silk industry: 22,762 *aḳçe*s (12.49%). A unique feature was the imposition on sheep, according to which 1,035 *aḳçe*s (0.57%) were levied on 6,402 heads. The timariot's *ḫāṣṣa* revenues amounted to 11,265 *aḳçe*s (6.18%).

District of Ḫulumiç (Hlemoutsi) (Table 16; Chart 11)

The total amount of the taxes levied on the district of Ḫulumiç was 60,241 *aḳçe*s, of which 18,050 *aḳçe*s (29.96%) derived from wheat; 12,144 *aḳçe*s (20.16%) from viticulture, and 12,047 *aḳçe*s (20%) from the *ispence*. The timariots' *ḫāṣṣa* revenues amounted to 1,890 *aḳçe*s (3.14%). The governor of the Peloponnese, Sinān Beg, was granted the tax assessed on the fish-farms in the town of Ḫulumiç as a *muḳāṭaʿa* of 750 *aḳçe*s (1.24%). The imperial *muḳāṭaʿa* of salt-pans in Lihyana (Lehaina) was estimated at 9,000 *aḳçe*s (14.94%).[172]

170 The economic tables and charts are drawn up according to the presentation of the taxes in the *defter*.

171 TT10, 18.

172 The exact location of the salt-pans remains unknown; however, they could be linked to the salt-pans in Sperone (*alias* l'Espero), which produced in 1379 1,700 *modii* of salt: Longnon Topping 1969, $200_{12,\ 21\text{-}24}$ (doc. xi). The place name Sperone has not survived, but should be sought in the coastal area of Manolada and Kotyhi: Longnon–Topping 1969, 235–236; Longnon 1949, 321; Bon 1969, 340–341; Panopoulou 2003, 161–162. The Kotyhi lagoon, where salt-pans were recorded in the seventeenth century: Panopoulou 1987–8, 309, n. 29, is in any case in the vicinity of Lihyana.

District of Vumero (Goumero) (Table 17; Chart 12)

The district of Vumero yielded annually 177,218 *aḳçe*s, of which 48,700 *aḳçe*s (27.48%) derived from wheat; 35,344 *aḳçe*s (19.94%) from the *ispence*, and 30,299 *aḳçe*s (17.10%) from viticulture. The timariots' *ḫāṣṣa* revenues amounted to 13,065 *aḳçe*s (7.37%). The *muḳāṭaʿa* ceded as part of the *tīmār* was on the fish-farms and the transit duty, which amounted to 4,500 *aḳçe*s (2.54%). Finally, the imperial *muḳāṭaʿa*s of rice fields and salt-pans worked out at 35,500 *aḳçe*s (20.03%).

District of Kirvuḳor (Palaiokastro/Koufoplaiiko Kastro) (Table 18; Chart 13)

The district of Kirvuḳor's annual tax revenue was estimated at 103,161 *aḳçe*s, of which 44,100 *aḳçe*s (42.75%) derived from wheat; 29,289 *aḳçe*s (28.39%) from the *ispence*, and 14,048 *aḳçe*s (13.62%) from viticulture. The timariot's *ḫāṣṣa* revenues totalled 4,266 *aḳçe*s (4.13%). The only *muḳāṭaʿa* mentioned was on fish-farms that was estimated at 250 *aḳçe*s (0.24%).

District of Arḳadya (Kyparissia) (Table 19; Chart 14)

The total amount of taxation levied on the district of Arḳadya was 40,032 *aḳçe*s, the largest portion of which, 15,720 *aḳçe*s (39.27%), derived from viticulture, followed by 8,543 (21.34%) from the cultivation of wheat, and 7,863 (19.64%) from the *ispence*. Viticulture's domination over grain production is attested in the town of Arḳadya as late as 1716 when the TT880 register was compiled.[173] The timariots' *ḫāṣṣa* revenues amounted to 13,760 *aḳçe*s (34.37%). The imperial *muḳāṭaʿa*s on salt-pans and rice fields were estimated at 1,000 *aḳçe*s (2.5%).

District of Londar (Leontari) (Table 20; Chart 15)

The district of Londar yielded annually 118,382 *aḳçe*s, one third of which, 40,182 *aḳçe*s (33.94%), derived from viticulture. The *ispence* encumbrance was calculated at 31,158 *aḳçe*s (26.32%). Furthermore, 28,550 *aḳçe*s (24.12%) were raised from the cultivation of wheat. The timariots' *ḫāṣṣa* revenues amounted to 13,840 *aḳçe*s (11.69%). The market tax and the *niyābet* were estimated in the manner of *muḳāṭaʿa* at 3,500 *aḳçe*s (2.96%). The TT10 register erroneously gives a total of 113,647 *aḳçe*s, which should be corrected to 113,657 *aḳçe*s.

District of Ḳoriṯos (Korinthos) (Table 21; Chart 16)

The total amount of the taxes levied on the district of Corinth was 62,826 *aḳçe*s, of which 24,450 *aḳçe*s (38.92%) derived from the tithe on wheat; 13,793 *aḳçe*s (21.95%) from viticulture and 9,715 *aḳçe*s (15.46%) from the *ispence*. The timariot's *ḫāṣṣa* revenues amounted to 2,350 *aḳçe*s (3.74%). The *muḳāṭaʿa*s covering market tax, customs dues, transit duty and bitter orange groves were allotted as part of the *tīmār* of an estimated sum of 3,450 *aḳçe*s (5.49%). The imperial *muḳāṭaʿa* on salt-pans was estimated at 320 *aḳçe*s (0.51%). According to a recent study, the sixteenth-century registers show a reduction in cereal production in Corinthia. A probable explanation may be that the lands devoted to the cultivation of wheat and barley were partially used for growing millet, oat, broad, beans, walnuts, figs, onions, garlic, black millet, lentils and vetch to meet the nutritional needs of the inhabitants.[174]

District of Balya Badra (Patra) (Table 22; Chart 17)

The district of Balya Badra's annual tax revenue was estimated at 78,378 *aḳçe*s, of which 19,112 *aḳçe*s (24.38%) derived from viticulture; 16,423 *aḳçe*s (20.95%) from the *ispence*, followed by the tithe on wheat of 16,331 *aḳçe*s (20.84%). The timariots' *ḫāṣṣa* revenues ran to 10,611 *aḳçe*s (13.54%). The governor of the Peloponnese, Sinān Beg, had agreed on an amount of 250 *aḳçe*s (0.32%) as a *muḳāṭaʿa* on the oil presses. The imperial *muḳāṭaʿa* of salt-pans at Ḳamaniça (Kamenitsa) was estimated at 7,000 *aḳçe*s (8.93%).[175]

173 Parveva 2003, 96, 98–99.
174 Shariat-Panahi 2015, 55.
175 Even though the contemporary primary sources remain silent, one assumes that the salt-pans in Ḳamaniça were in use before the fifteenth century: Panopoulou 2003, 162. The Venetian

District of Ḳalandriça (Halandritsa) (Table 23; Chart 18)

The district of Ḳalandriça yielded annually 26,305 *aḳçe*s, of which 7,740 *aḳçe*s (30.59%) was the tithe on wheat; 6,130 *aḳçe*s (23.30%) constituted the *ispence* encumbrance, and 5,281 *aḳçe*s (20.08%) derived from viticulture. The timariots' *ḫāṣṣa* revenues totalled 4,503 *aḳçe*s (17.12%).

District of Ṣandamiri (Santomeri) (Table 24; Chart 19)

The total amount of the taxes levied on the district of Ṣandamiri was 26,528 *aḳçe*s, of which 8,154 *aḳçe*s (30.74%) derived from viticulture; 7,700 *aḳçe*s (29.03%) from wheat and 6,056 *aḳçe*s (22.83%) from the *ispence*. The timariots' *ḫāṣṣa* revenues amounted to 5,106 *aḳçe*s (19.25%). There were no *muḳāṭaʿa*s recorded in this district.

District of Girbene (Spartia) (Table 25; Chart 20)

The district of Girbene's annual tax revenue was estimated at 52,395 *aḳçe*s, more than one third of which (20,850 *aḳçe*s (39.79%) constituted the tithe on wheat. The *per capita* tax of the *ispence* accounted for 13,469 *aḳçe*s (25.71%) and 7,976 *aḳçe*s (15.22%) derived from viticulture. The timariots' *ḫāṣṣa* revenues amounted to 4,544 *aḳçe*s (8.67%). The only *muḳāṭaʿa* mentioned is a fish-farm granted as part of the *tīmār*, which yielded annually 2,500 *aḳçe*s (4.77%).

District of Ayo İlya (Agios Ilias) (Table 26; Chart 21)

The total amount of the taxes levied on the district of Ayo İlya was 75,920 *aḳçe*s; because of an accounting error the register gives a total of 75,916 *aḳçe*s. Almost one third of the total taxes, 24,639 *aḳçe*s (32.45%), derived from viticulture, followed by the tithe on wheat, amounting to 20,600 *aḳçe*s (27.13%). The *ispence* tax reached 17,525 *aḳçe*s (23.08%). The timariots' *ḫāṣṣa* revenues amounted to 21,393 *aḳçe*s (28.19%). No *muḳāṭaʿa*s were recorded in this district.

District of Ġardicḳo (Gatsiko) (Table 27; Chart 22)

The district of Ġardicḳo yielded annually 56,395 *aḳçe*s, of these, 22,159 *aḳçe*s (39.28%) referred to the tithe on wheat; 15,229 *aḳçe*s (27%) constituted the *ispence* and 11,717 *aḳçe*s (20.78%) were levied on viticulture. The *ḫāṣṣa* revenues of the timariots reached 6,380 *aḳçe*s (11.31%). No *muḳāṭaʿa*s were recorded in this district.

Province of Mora (the Peloponnese) (Table 28; Chart 23)

The total amount of the taxes assessed on the districts of the Peloponnese recorded in the TT10-1/14662 taxation cadastre ran at 1,187,112 *aḳçe*s or approximately 27,932 golden ducats. Nearly one third of this, 362,530 *aḳçe*s (30.54%), constituted the tithe on wheat, which, when calculated on the basis of the correlation recorded in Raḫova (1 Adrianople *müdd* of wheat cost 80 *aḳçe*s), amounts to an actual value of 2,900,240 *aḳçe*s for 36,253 *müdd*s, or approximately 18,602,139.36kg (Table 29).

The second most widely cultivated cereal after wheat was barley, whose tithe gave 56,084 *aḳçe*s (4.72%). Again, based on the Raḫova correlation (1 Adrianople *müdd* of barley cost 60 *aḳçe*s), this crop's value runs to 448,672 *aḳçe*s for 7,477.87 *müdd*s or approximately 3,837,042.94kg (Table 29). This clearly shows that the Peloponnesian economy was oriented towards the cultivation of cereals, which tallies with the general tendency of the Ottomans to support these crops.[176] At this stage it is difficult to calculate the surplus of grain that the cultivators traded/exported, which would

sources of the *Regno di Morea* (1688–1715) give a more detailed account: in land surveyor Marin Michiel's words (1691): Lambros 1884, 200: 'in questa provintia vi sono le saline dette di Caminizza in qualche parte deteriorate;' according to *provveditor* Francesco Grimani's report (1698), they produced salt in large quantities, but of poor quality, as it contained sand: Panopoulou 2012, 270–271. The *Breve descrittione del Regno di Morea* (1704), written by Giust' Emilio Alberghetti on the basis of a Venetian census carried out between 1702–1703, reads: Dokos 1993, 123: 'quattr' hore di camino da Patrasso distante, si vede il Fiume Caminizza; vicino alla sua bocca vi sono le Saline.' Today's Alykes village, located 2km north-west of Kato Ahaïa, was named after the salt-pans, whose traces were still visible in the early twentieth century.

176 Güçer 1964.

have generated a cash income, intended for paying the *per capita* taxes, since it is impossible to estimate the exact population of the Peloponnese. Asdrachas suggested that 200kg of cereals would have been required per individual per year as a subsistence minimum, in addition to 59kg for seed and 36kg for tax – a total of 295kg.[177] The fact that the cultivation of wheat and barley left negligible space for other cereals demonstrates that the basic nutrition consisted of the two; barley in particular consisted of two categories, a high quality for people and a low one for horses, as a much later source states.[178]

The second highest imposition was the *ispence* whose 282,991 *akçe*s averaged 23.84% of the total taxes. Viticulture – from both *ḫāṣṣa* and *reʿāyā* vineyards – was placed in the third position with a total of 243,486 *akçe*s (20.51%). A tax of 80,359 *akçe*s was levied on the vine produced in the *ḫāṣṣa* vineyards occupying 831 *dönüm*s (= 763,938.3m^2). According to the Beldiceanus, this tax should have been encumbered on the *reʿāyā* who cultivated the timariots' vineyards.[179] If we apply the 75% of the vine production received by the *reʿāyā* cultivators, as set in the law code of the Morea compiled during the reign of Bāyezīd II (1481–1512),[180] the actual production of the *ḫāṣṣa* vineyards should amount to 321,436 *akçe*s. The *reʿāyā* vineyards yielded 1,631,270 *akçe*s annually (Table 30). Thus, we assume that the total vineyard production of the Peloponnese totalled 1,952,706 *akçe*s. In an attempt to examine the productivity of viticulture in each district we divided the production in *akçe*s by the *dönüm*s. This was applied to the *ḫāṣṣa* vineyards without taking into account the different varieties of vine and the soil fertility. As illustrated in Table 31, the districts of Ġardicḳo (Gatsiko), Vumero (Goumero) and Ayo İlya (Agios Ilias) located in the Elis plain present a high ratio of 684.57, 589.86 and 531.36 *akçe*s per *dönüm* respectively. On the other hand, the mainly mountainous districts of Ḳalandriça (Halandritsa), Şandamiri (Santomeri) and Londar (Leontari) give 300, 308 and 330.88 *akçes/dönüm* respectively.[181] Special mention should be made of the dry raisins (*μαύρη* or *κορινθιακή σταφίδα*), which are recorded only in Ayo Vaşıl/Çağıl Ḥiṣārı (Agios Vasileios) and Ayonori (Agionori) village in Corinthia. The trade of raisins or currants (its *etymon* is Corinth), which flourished in the late eighteenth and nineteenth century, is not attested in our document.[182]

The 2,108 *ḫāṣṣa* fruit trees held as a personal reserve of the timariots were taxed with 4,212 *akçe*s or approximately 0.5 *akçe*s/tree. Following the calculation employed on the *ḫāṣṣa* vineyards, this impost should tally with a total of 16,848 *akçe*s or approximately 8 *akçe*s/tree. When adding the actual value of the *reʿāyā* orchards, namely 24,350 *akçe*s, the total fruit production of the Peloponnese runs at 41,198 *akçe*s.

The silk industry, whose taxation amounted to 27,548 *akçe*s (2.32%), seems rather poor with the noteworthy exception of the Voştiça (Aigio) district, as mentioned above, which contributed by 22,762 *akçe*s (82.63%) to the entire raw silk production. The word *ḳazz* refers to the cocoons and not the silk fabric. The total silk production worth 275,480 *akçe*s ranks fourth in the tithes list, at 4.98%. The TT10-1/4662 does not record any silk manufactory, nor does it imply any further taxation on the silk-making process. Connected with silk is the cultivation of mulberry trees in *ḫāṣṣa* orchards [the register records a tithe of 13 *akçe*s on a *reʿāyā* mulberry orchard only in Ḳastriçi (Ano Kastritsi) in Achaia].[183] The tax on 4,566 *ḫāṣṣa* trees amounts to 13,858 *akçe*s, which points to an actual production worth 55,432 *akçe*s, or 55,562 *akçe*s after adding the value of the Ḳastriçi production. It was the Greeks who were mostly engaged in the silk industry (99.1%) with a negligible number of Albanians (0.9%).

The picture of the fabric industry would not be complete without an examination of flax and cotton production. Flax was produced throughout the peninsula and the value of the total crop was 154,170 *akçe*s. On the other hand, cotton seems to have been confined to the plains, since its cultivation requires good irrigation and a warm climate; hence, no cotton is recorded in the mountainous districts of Ḳalavrita (Kalavryta), Miḫlu (Mouhli), Bejenik (Vlaherna) and Londar (Leontari). Its total value runs at 61,950 *akçe*s. Cotton was cultivated by the Greeks at a rate of 81.8% and by Albanians at 18.2%. Again, the register does not include any evidence of a fabric industry that supposedly surpassed the level of domestic consumption.

The olive trees are divided into those held as the personal reserve of the timariots and those of the *reʿāyā*. 4,554 *akçe*s were levied on 3,635 *ḫāṣṣa* olive trees, which raise the value of the olive oil produced at 18,216 *akçe*s, if we accept that the tax recorded forms the 25% of the actual

177 Asdrachas 1999, 90. The same figure, 200kg/person annually, is also employed as a subsistence minimum by the World Food Organisation: Kiel 2007, 41.

178 Pouqueville 1827, VI 235: 'L'orge qui est dans la catégorie des herbacées pivotantes est de deux espèces appelées γυμνοκριθὶ, *orge sans balle*, ἀλογοκριθὶ, *orge de cheval*. Le premier est le plus estimé, qui sert à faire du pain, est particulièrement cultivé dans la Phocide et dans l'Achaïe. Quant à la seconde qualité on la trouve partout et on ne s'en sert guères que pour la nourriture des chevaux auxquels on en donne en guise d'avoine.'

179 Beldiceanu–Beldiceanu-Steinherr 1980, 31.

180 Paris, Bibliothèque Nationale, fonds turc anc. MS. 35, fol. 42^v, cited in Beldiceanu–Beldiceanu-Steinherr 1980, 31.

181 Liakopoulos 2009, 203–204, 214–215 (maps 3–4).

182 For the raisin trade of the Peloponnese see Wright et al. 1990, 599–600; for the process of drying the raisins see Veis 1957.

183 TT10, 184.

production.[184] The tithe on oil produced from the *reʿāyā* olive groves was 2,180 *aḳçe*s (total value: 21,800 *aḳçe*s). Certainly, the number of olive trees recorded in the TT10-1/14662 is only a small fraction of the trees cultivated in the twentieth-century Peloponnese.[185] A rather confined olive cultivation for the district of Pylos is attested in the TT880 register, too.[186] The number of oil presses recorded is disproportionate to the overall olive cultivation, as only three are mentioned, located in Ṣaravali (Saravali), Provanda Aya Yorgi (Agios Georgios), and Lọyi (Diodia).[187] Balya Badra's (Patra) total production of olive oil (*ḫāṣṣa* and *reʿāyā* olive groves) ranks first with 16,520 *aḳçe*s with Arḳadya (Kyparissia) second with 6,648 *aḳçe*s. We can only assume that oil presses existed in other districts as well, but they were not recorded in the register as their tax was intended to meet needs other than the timariots' earnings.

Apiculture did not play a large role in the Moreote economy as its tithe contributed 943 *aḳçe*s (0.08%) to the taxes assessed on the Peloponnese. The value of the honey produced is estimated at 9,430 *aḳçe*s. If we apply the price of 3 *aḳçe*s per *oḳḳa* of honey in Adrianople in 1463,[188] the total production amounts to 3,143.33 *oḳḳa*s or 4,032.26kg.[189]

The tax on wine production yielded 16,283 *aḳçe*s (1.37%). The taxes deriving from other agricultural production, livestock and taxable activities (marketing, manufacturing, etc.) averaged less than 1%. The *ḫāṣṣa* revenues of the timariots who were granted allotments in the Peloponnese add up to 123,538 *aḳçe*s (10.41%). The *muḳāṭaʿa*s ceded as part of the *tīmār*s were estimated at 17,200 *aḳçe*s (1.45%). On the other hand, the *muḳāṭaʿa*s held in the imperial demesne were estimated at 73,384 *aḳçe*s (6.18%), of which 44,384 *aḳçe*s derived from salt-pans and 29,000 *aḳçe*s from rice fields.

The tithe on flax, vineyards, wheat, barley, olive oil, fruits, cotton, honey, silk, resin, mulberries, watermills and kitchen gardens totalled 636,822 *aḳçe*s (53.64%) (Table 30). From the breakdown of the tithes and the actual value of the crops on which they were levied we deduce that Braudel's 'eternal trinity' of wheat, olives and vines does not apply precisely in the mid-fifteenth-century Peloponnese.[190] The cultivation of wheat obviously dominates the agricultural sector (52.44% of the tithes), followed by an impressive 29.50% accounted for by viticulture. On the other hand, olive oil appears with a humble 0.40%. It is probable that a part of the wine and the dry raisins produced was exported to the West, as was the case in the late Byzantine period. The commercialisation of the most profitable crop surpluses, in our case cereals and vines, was obligatory for the sustainability of households encumbered with the *ispence* and the capitation. This constitutes a key characteristic of pre-industrial economies, namely the complementarity of agrarian production.[191] The underexploitation of the earth necessitated the engagement of the population in other activities. As Asdrachas has shown, the image of a mainly agricultural economy given by the register does not tally with the reality of a mixed agricultural and stock-breeding economy, mainly because the stock-breeding is very poorly attested in the *defter*.[192]

184 Beldiceanu–Beldiceanu-Steinherr 1980, 33.
185 Balta 2007, 91; Moutoulas 2007, 148–149.
186 Zarinebaf–Bennet–Davis 2005, 185–186.
187 TT10, 40, 130, 134 respectively. Cf. 112½ oil presses recorded throughout the Peloponnese in Marin Michiel's survey (1691): Panopoulou 2007, 85.
188 Barkan 1964, 258, cited in Beldiceanu–Beldiceanu-Steinherr 1980, 33.
189 1 *oḳḳa* = 1.2828kg: Hinz 1955, 24.
190 Braudel 1972, I 236.
191 Asdrachas 1999, 221–222; Asdrachas 1988, 15–17.
192 Asdrachas 2003a, 336–337.

Table 11. *District of Ḳalavrita (Kalavryta).*

			Ḳalavrita[i]	İvrahni	Sudana	Beluşi	Ḥamaku	Şiġuni	Zuġra	Amuri[ii]	Zuġra-ı diğer	Ḥaraktinu	Ḥoloropozi	Dima Plaşa	Epano Ḳurnofita	Ḳastriya	Vorstena	Taşi
inhabitants		households	83	29	41	13	13	8	5	10	8	20	3	31	7	9	7	8
		bachelors	21	2	7	4	1	1	-	-	-	-	-	1	1	-	-	1
		widows	5	1	2	-	-	-	-	-	-	2	-	-	-	-	-	-
taxes *per capita*		ispence	2605	781	1412	340	280	180	100	200	160	412	60	640	200	225	140	180
		ʿarūsī	-	-	-	-	-	-	-	-	-	-	-	-	-	-	-	-
		niyābet	1000	-	-	-	-	-	-	-	-	-	-	-	-	-	-	-
ḫāṣṣa	vineyards	dönüm	-	1	2	-	-	-	-	-	-	-	-	-	-	-	-	-
		aḳçe	-	120	240	-	-	-	-	-	-	-	-	-	-	-	-	-
	fruit trees	trees	-	-	-	-	-	-	-	-	-	-	-	-	-	-	-	-
		aḳçe	-	-	-	-	-	-	-	-	-	-	-	-	-	-	-	-
	mulberry trees	trees	-	30	30	-	-	-	-	-	-	35	-	-	-	-	-	-
		aḳçe	-	50	60	-	-	-	-	-	-	65	-	-	-	-	-	-
	watermills	number	-	-	-	-	-	-	-	-	-	-	-	-	-	-	-	-
		aḳçe	-	-	-	-	-	-	-	-	-	-	-	-	-	-	-	-
tithe (in aḳçes)		flax	100	20	40	10	-	-	-	10	-	20	-	-	10	10	-	-
		vineyards	1345	288	336	-	-	-	32	8	8	-	-	-	54	54	16	24
		wheat	3050	1000	1500	700	600	300	150	300	200	600	100	1100	250	350	200	400
		barley	475	155	231	109	96	47	24	48	31	95	16	172	38	53	31	46
		olive oil	8	-	-	-	-	-	-	-	-	-	-	-	-	-	-	-
		fruits	18	8	3	-	-	-	3	-	-	-	-	-	-	-	-	-
		honey	-	-	-	-	-	-	-	-	-	-	-	-	-	-	-	-
		silk	197	144	76	-	-	-	3	-	-	-	-	-	12	18	-	-
units (in aḳçes)		wine	150	45	40	-	-	-	-	-	-	-	-	-	-	-	-	-
		swine	-	-	7	12	13	25	-	-	2	3	8	-	-	5	5	5
watermills (mülk)		number	4	2	-	1	-	-	-	-	-	-	-	-	2	-	-	-
		aḳçe	160	80	-	40	-	-	-	-	-	-	-	-	80	-	-	-
fulling mills (mülk)		number	1	-	-	-	-	-	-	-	-	-	-	-	-	-	-	-
		aḳçe	15	-	-	-	-	-	-	-	-	-	-	-	-	-	-	-
		total	9123	2691	3945	1211	989	552	312	566	401	1195	184	1912	644	715	392	655

			Velimiri	Ḳani	Marti Plaşa	Todoro Manesi	Barçi	Todoroplu	Petros Ḳaratula	Ḳaçana[iii]	Lapata	Kato Ḳurnofita	Ġolemi	Maḳriyeni Çamanda	Dara[iv]	Peryale	Zepandi	Ḳrastiki
inhabitants		households	6	13	15	23	24	16	7	24	21	11	12	11	10	12	27	13
		bachelors	1	1	3	2	8	-	1	2	2	-	-	2	1	2	4	-
		widows	-	1	-	-	-	-	-	1	-	-	-	1	1	2	1	1
taxes *per capita*		ispence	140	356	360	500	640	320	160	656	575	275	240	266	226	292	626	331
		ʿarūsī	-	-	-	-	-	-	-	-	-	-	-	-	-	-	-	-
		niyābet	-	-	-	-	-	-	-	-	-	-	-	-	-	-	-	-
ḫāṣṣa	vineyards	dönüm	-	3	-	-	-	-	-	-	-	-	-	-	-	-	-	-
		aḳçe	-	360	-	-	-	-	-	-	-	-	-	-	-	-	-	-
	fruit trees	trees	-	-	-	-	-	-	-	-	-	-	-	-	-	-	-	-
		aḳçe	-	-	-	-	-	-	-	-	-	-	-	-	-	-	-	-
	mulberry trees	trees	-	5	-	-	-	-	-	-	-	-	-	-	-	-	-	-
		aḳçe	-	10	-	-	-	-	-	-	-	-	-	-	-	-	-	-
	watermills	number	-	-	-	-	-	-	-	-	-	-	-	-	-	-	-	-
		aḳçe	-	-	-	-	-	-	-	-	-	-	-	-	-	-	-	-
tithe (in aḳçes)		flax	-	-	-	10	-	-	-	-	20	-	-	-	-	-	-	-
		vineyards	-	80	-	96	112	16	-	176	160	-	80	-	24	8	80	88
		wheat	300	450	500	800	950	500	200	450	800	400	500	450	400	400	1050	250
		barley	46	72	76	125	148	78	31	70	124	63	80	68	61	64	161	38
		olive oil	-	-	-	-	-	-	-	-	-	-	-	-	-	-	-	-
		fruits	-	4	-	3	3	-	-	9	-	-	-	-	-	-	-	-
		honey	-	-	-	-	-	-	-	-	-	-	-	-	-	-	-	-
		silk	-	9	-	-	3	-	-	51	-	-	-	-	-	-	3	21
units (in aḳçes)		wine	-	8	-	36	-	-	-	25	-	-	-	-	-	-	-	-
		swine	18	-	-	-	35	-	20	11	8	5	19	13	16	29	5	-
watermills (mülk)		number	-	-	-	1	-	-	-	-	-	-	1	-	-	-	1	-
		aḳçe	-	-	-	40	-	-	-	-	-	-	40	-	-	-	40	-
fulling mills (mülk)		number	-	-	-	-	-	-	-	-	-	-	2	-	-	-	-	-
		aḳçe	-	-	-	-	-	-	-	-	-	-	30	-	-	-	-	-
		total	504	1349	936	1610	1891	914	411	1478	1687	743	959	797	727	793	1965	728

Table 11. *District of Ķalavrita (Kalavryta).*

			Suli	İflamurari	Niķola Manesi[v]	Fila	Tireḫlista	Palunbi Ranesi	Ayo İvlaşi	Ġurġa	Muriki	Debrani	İştin Bondaya	Şavanus[vi]	Anastasova	Droġolavoş	Seliça	Mavromati
inhabitants		households	11	13	8	5	3	6	37	8	7	5	8	33	13	6	13	26
		bachelors	1	1	1	-	-	-	7	1	-	-	2	3	1	1	1	4
		widows	2	-	-	-	-	1	3	-	1	-	1	2	1	-	1	-
taxes *per capita*		ispence	252	280	100	100	75	126	1118	180	146	100	206	912	356	175	356	600
		ʿarūsī	-	-	-	-	-	10	40	10	-	-	10	30	10	-	10	20
		niyābet	-	-	-	-	-	-	-	-	-	-	-	-	-	-	-	-
ḫāṣṣa	vineyards	dönüm	-	-	-	-	2	-	5	-	-	-	-	1	3	2	-	-
		aķçe	-	-	-	-	120	-	600	-	-	-	-	120	360	240	-	-
	fruit trees	trees	-	-	-	-	6	-	5	-	-	-	-	-	3	-	11	-
		aķçe	-	-	-	-	10	-	10	-	-	-	-	-	10	-	20	-
	mulberry trees	trees	-	-	-	-	6	-	30	-	-	-	-	20	30	40	50	-
		aķçe	-	-	-	-	15	-	90	-	-	-	-	30	50	60	75	-
	watermills	number	-	-	-	-	-	-	1	-	-	-	-	-	-	-	-	-
		aķçe	-	-	-	-	-	-	500	-	-	-	-	-	-	-	-	-
tithe (in aķçes)		flax	-	-	-	-	-	-	-	-	-	-	-	30	-	10	-	-
		vineyards	16	-	-	40	80	-	496	-	-	-	-	240	272	57	32	57
		wheat	350	600	250	100	-	210	1600	350	350	200	350	1300	400	100	300	950
		barley	55	92	40	16	-	34	250	55	56	32	56	196	60	15	47	142
		olive oil	-	-	-	-	-	-	-	-	-	-	-	-	-	-	-	-
		fruits	2	-	2	-	4	-	-	-	-	-	-	21	18	5	2	-
		honey	-	-	-	-	-	-	-	-	-	-	-	5	-	-	-	-
		silk	-	-	-	-	7	-	99	-	-	-	-	65	82	27	14	-
units (in aķçes)		wine	-	-	-	-	-	-	60	-	-	-	-	40	40	-	-	-
		swine	5	-	-	-	-	-	-	5	10	-	8	-	-	-	2	3
watermills (mülk)		number	-	-	-	-	-	-	-	-	-	-	-	1	1	1	-	-
		aķçe	-	-	-	-	-	-	-	-	-	-	-	40	40	40	-	-
fulling mills (mülk)		number	-	-	-	-	-	-	-	-	-	-	-	-	-	-	-	-
		aķçe	-	-	-	-	-	-	-	-	-	-	-	-	-	-	-	-
		total	680	972	392	256	311	380	4863	600	562	332	630	3029	1698	729	858	1772

			Ķastel	Ķazneş	İstrazova	Vesini	Ķaratula	Sumaki[vii]	total
inhabitants		households	38	23	18	13	8	6	848
		bachelors	1	3	2	-	-	-	97
		widows	5	-	-	-	-	-	35
taxes *per capita*		ispence	1005	520	500	355	160	120	21620
		ʿarūsī	35	25	20	15	10	10	255
		niyābet	-	-	-	-	-	-	1000
ḫāṣṣa	vineyards	dönüm	4	-	3	-	-	-	23
		aķçe	480	-	360	-	-	-	3000
	fruit trees	trees	-	-	-	-	-	-	25
		aķçe	-	-	-	-	-	-	50
	mulberry trees	trees	30	-	-	-	-	-	306
		aķçe	50	-	-	-	-	-	555
	watermills	number	1	-	1	-	-	-	3
		aķçe	200	-	400	-	-	-	1100
tithe (in aķçes)		flax	30	40	-	20	20	-	400
		vineyards	448	-	272	128	-	-	5223
		wheat	1050	500	400	400	200	150	29310
		barley	165	75	63	64	32	24	4541
		olive oil	-	-	-	-	-	-	8
		fruits	7	-	-	4	-	-	116
		honey	-	-	-	-	-	-	5
		silk	71	-	-	36	-	-	938
units (in aķçes)		wine	40	-	35	20	-	-	539
		swine	-	-	-	-	-	-	297
watermills (mülk)		number	3	-	1	-	-	-	19
		aķçe	160	-	30	-	-	-	790
fulling mills (mülk)		number	-	-	-	-	-	-	3
		aķçe	-	-	-	-	-	-	45
		total	3741	1160	2080	1042	422	304	69792

[i] Including the Manastır-ı Meġaspilyo Aya Ķori.
[ii] The deserted (*ḫāliyye*) *mezraʿa* of Petrovuni belonged to this village.
[iii] Including the community of İştopanşi. The deserted (*ḫāliyye*) *mezraʿa* of Ķaratula-ı dīğer belonged to this village.
[iv] The deserted (*ḫāliyye*) *mezraʿa* of Puloti belonged to this village.
[v] The deserted (*ḫāliyye*) *mezraʿa* of İskliva belonged to this village.
[vi] The deserted (*ḫāliyye*) *mezraʿas* of İvlaḫo Ķalanas and İvlaḫo Yalya belonged to this village.
[vii] The deserted (*ḫāliyye*) *mezraʿa* of Liķuresi belonged to this village.

Chart 6. *District of Ḳalavrita (Kalavryta).*

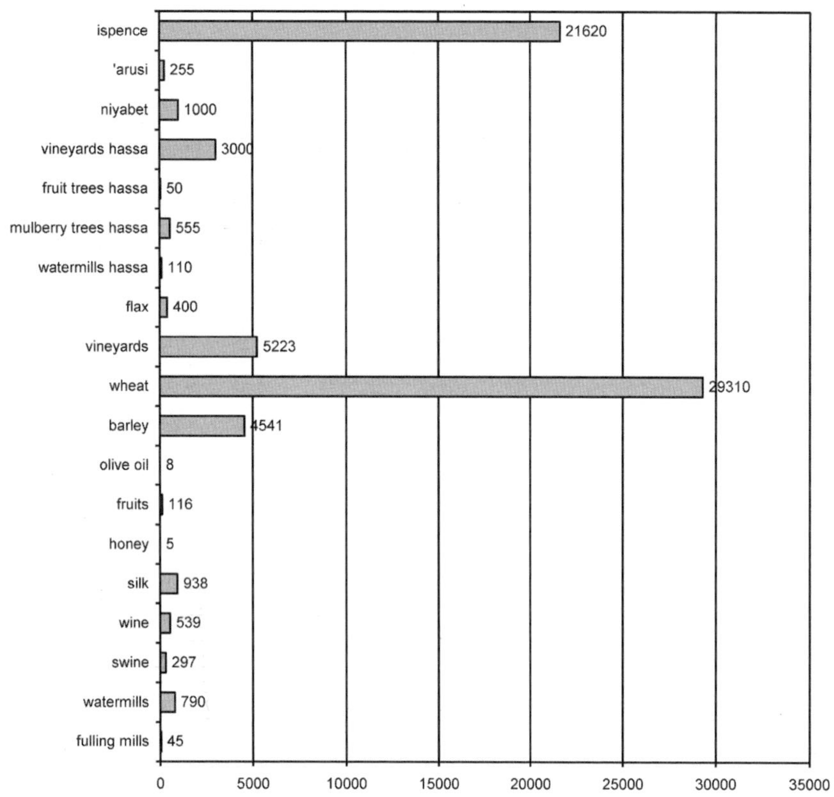

Table 12. *District of Mizis̱ra (Mystras).*

			Prinikos
inhabitants		households	9
		bachelors	1
		widows	-
taxes *per capita*		ispence	250
		ʿarūsī	10
ḫāṣṣa	vineyards	dönüm	5
		aḳçe	300
	olive trees	trees	5
		aḳçe	5
	pomegranate trees	trees	2
		aḳçe	5
	fish-farms	aḳçe	800
tithe (in aḳçes)		flax	20
		vineyards	80
		wheat	200
		barley	31
		fruits	3
		total	1704

Chart 7. *District of Mizis̱ra (Mystras).*

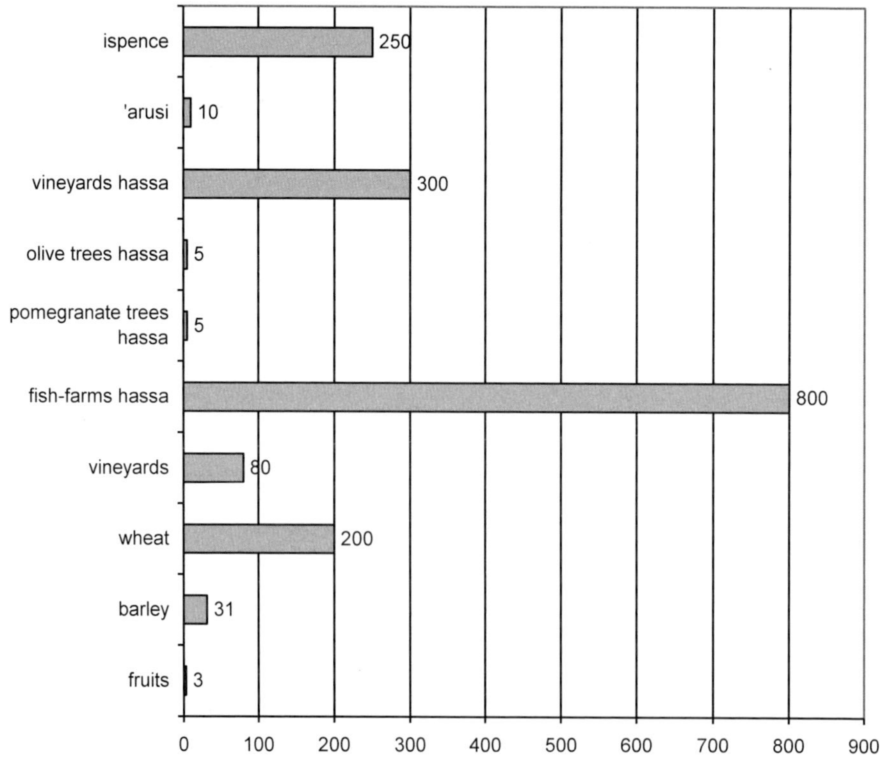

Table 13. *District of Miḫlu (Mouhli).*

		Astro	Duşa Dara	Luvari	Plaşa[i]	Pikerni	Naşi	Brasna Sanka	Çipyana	Perişori	Raḫova[ii]	total
inhabitants	households	-	-	-	-	73	18	38	60	17	57	263
	bachelors	-	-	-	-	10	5	5	10	1	4	35
	widows	-	-	-	-	5	3	3	5	-	-	16
taxes *per capita*	ispence	-	-	-	-	1690	478	878	1780	450	610	5886
	ʿarūsī	-	-	-	-	80	20	40	60	20	150	370
ḫāṣṣa: vineyards	dönüm	-	-	-	-	-	-	-	6	5	-	11
	akçe	-	-	-	-	-	-	-	720	600	-	1320
ḫāṣṣa: fruit trees	trees	-	-	-	-	-	-	-	-	6	-	6
	akçe	-	-	-	-	-	-	-	-	10	-	10
ḫāṣṣa: mulberry trees	trees	-	-	-	-	30	-	-	-	10	-	40
	akçe	-	-	-	-	150	-	-	-	50	-	200
tithe (in akçes)	flax	-	-	-	-	-	-	-	100	20	-	120
	vineyards	-	-	-	-	-	-	-	480	176	-	656
	wheat	-	-	-	-	3000	600	1500	1900	500	456	7956
	barley	-	-	-	-	453	94	233	296	78	342	1496
	fruits	-	-	-	-	-	-	-	-	10	-	10
	silk	-	-	-	-	-	-	-	-	1	-	1
units (in akçes)	wine	-	-	-	-	-	-	-	60	20	-	80
	swine	-	-	-	-	79	21	140	2	-	-	242
watermills (mülk)	number	-	-	-	-	1	-	-	1	-	-	2
	akçe	-	-	-	-	30	-	-	30	-	-	60
	total	-	-	-	-	5482	1213	2791	5428	1935	1558	18407

[i] These four deserted (*ḫāliyye*) *mezraʿas*, namely Astro, Duşa Dara, Luvari and Plaşa belonged to the village Astriçi that is missing in the register.
[ii] The *mezraʿa* of Plaşa, which was under Frankish rule, was granted to the inhabitants of Raḫova.

Chart 8. *District of Miḫlu (Mouhli).*

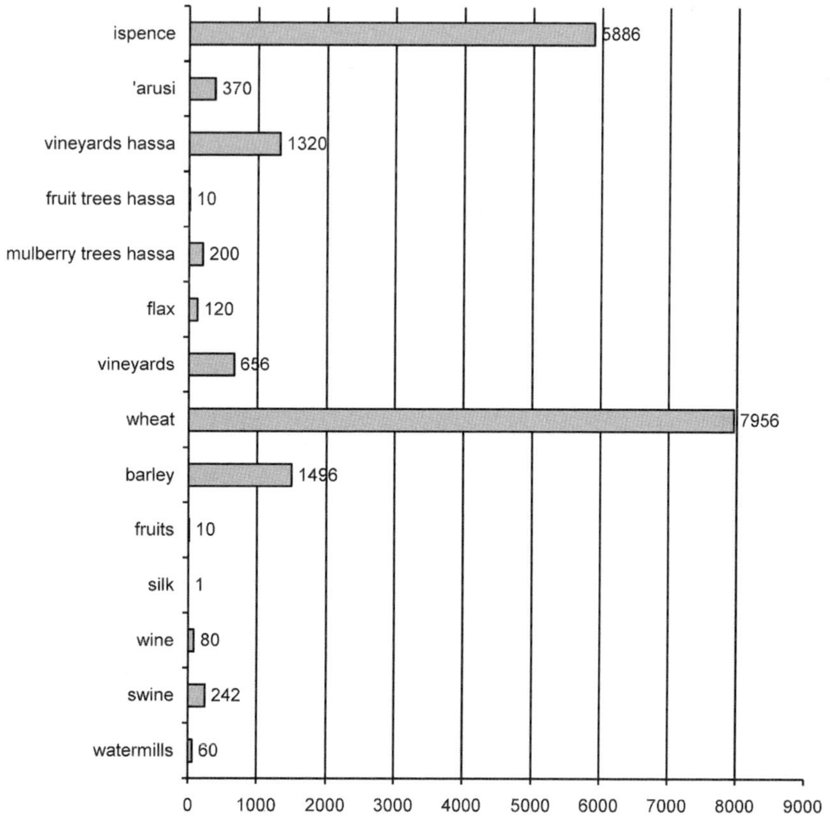

Table 14. *Distirct of Bejenik (Vlaherna).*

			Bejenik[i]	Levizi	Ḳameniça	Lopesi	Aġali	Bendeni/ Pendeni	Bondaya	Sina	Çarnota	Ḳandila	Doşkesi	Ḥayḳal	Ḳoraḳovuni	Perşor	Açiḥolos
inhabitants		households	49	27	10	11	21	28	16	10	13	28	15	26	30	57	21
		bachelors	6	11	-	3	8	4	7	2	4	18	8	8	5	-	3
		widows	1	2	2	-	1	2	-	-	1	3	1	4	4	2	1
taxes *per capita*		ispence	1381	962	262	280	586	652	460	240	346	1168	466	704	899	1437	606
		ʿarūsī	-	30	10	10	20	30	20	10	15	30	15	30	30	60	20
		niyābet	250	-	-	-	-	-	-	-	-	-	-	-	-	-	-
ḫāṣṣa	vineyards	dönüm	11	-	-	-	-	-	-	-	-	7	-	-	-	2	2
		akçe	1020	-	-	-	-	-	-	-	-	840	-	-	-	240	240
	fruit trees	trees	30	-	-	-	-	-	-	-	-	-	-	-	-	-	-
		akçe	100	-	-	-	-	-	-	-	-	-	-	-	-	-	-
	mulberry trees	trees	46	-	-	-	-	-	-	-	-	8	-	-	-	8	-
		akçe	200	-	-	-	-	-	-	-	-	40	-	-	-	20	-
	watermills	number	-	-	-	-	-	-	-	-	-	0.5	-	-	-	-	-
		akçe	-	-	-	-	-	-	-	-	-	150	-	-	-	-	-
tithe (in akçes)		flax	150	100	30	40	50	80	50	20	30	150	40	-	-	80	25
		vineyards	1448	1040	240	-	-	-	-	-	-	1336	-	-	248	272	152
		wheat	1600	1000	300	350	900	600	550	250	400	400	400	850	1250	1900	700
		barley	245	155	47	56	144	96	86	39	64	64	75	134	189	295	109
		olive oil	-	-	-	-	-	-	-	-	-	-	-	-	3	-	-
		fruits	11	20	7	-	-	-	-	-	-	14	-	-	15	-	-
		silk	55	21	2	-	-	-	-	-	-	69	-	-	-	20	-
		honey	-	-	-	-	-	-	-	-	-	-	-	-	43	-	-
units (in akçes)		wine	180	120	30	-	-	-	-	-	-	180	-	-	30	40	20
		swine	-	-	-	10	29	8	4	3	26	-	-	19	-	3	5
watermills (mülk)		number	-	-	-	-	-	-	-	-	-	4	-	-	-	-	1
		akçe	-	-	-	-	-	-	-	-	-	320	-	-	-	-	30
		total	6640	3448	928	746	1729	1466	1170	562	881	4761	996	1737	2707	4367	1907

Table 14. *Distirct of Bejenik (Vlaherna).*

			İskiliç	Mujaki	Kerbova	Ustruza/ İstruza Potamya[ii]	total
inhabitants		households	11	21	6	11	411
		bachelors	2	-	4	-	93
		widows	1	-	-	1	26
taxes *per capita*		ispence	266	420	200	226	11561
		ʿarūsī	15	25	10	10	390
		niyābet	-	-	-	-	250
ḫāṣṣa	vineyards	dönüm	-	-	-	-	22
		akçe	-	-	-	-	2340
	fruit trees	trees	-	-	-	-	30
		akçe	-	-	-	-	100
	mulberry trees	trees	-	-	-	-	62
		akçe	-	-	-	-	260
	watermills	number	-	-	-	-	0.5
		akçe	-	-	-	-	150
tithe (in akçes)		flax	15	30	-	20	910
		vineyards	-	-	-	-	4736
		wheat	450	500	300	350	13050
		barley	69	80	48	56	2051
		olive oil	-	-	-	-	3
		fruits	-	-	-	-	67
		silk	-	-	-	-	167
		honey	-	-	-	-	43
units (in akçes)		wine	-	-	-	-	600
		swine	17	-	11	7	142
watermills (mülk)		number	-	-	-	-	5
		akçe	-	-	-	-	350
		total	832	1055	569	669	37170

[i] The deserted (*ḫāliyye*) *mezraʿas* of Vuzyas and Plaşa belonged to this village.
[ii] The deserted (*ḫāliyye*) *mezraʿa* of İvlaḫo Filito belonged to this village.

Chart 9. *Distirct of Bejenik (Vlaherna).*

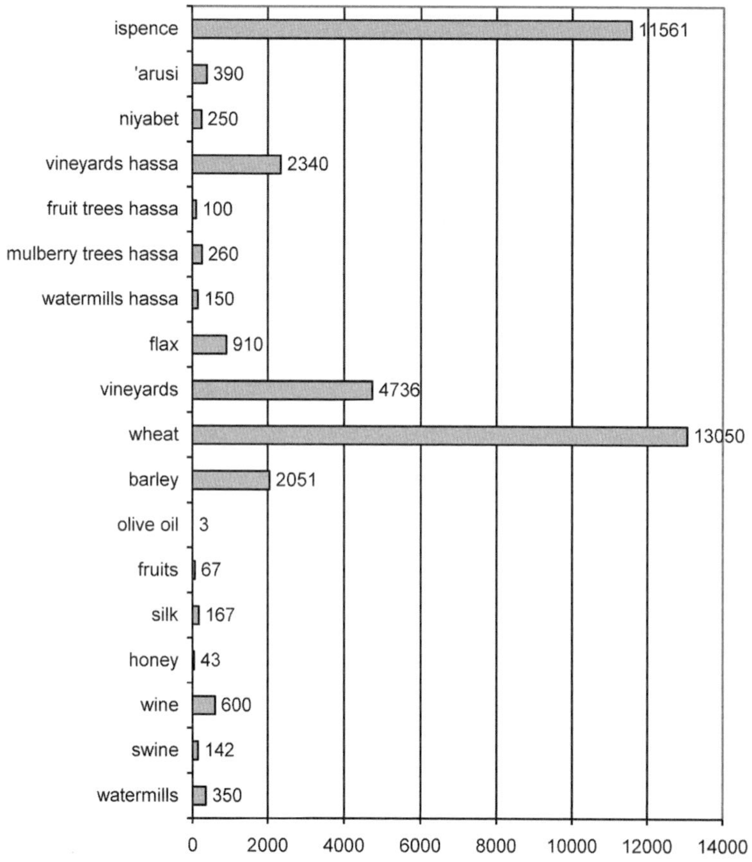

Table 15. *District of Voştiça (Aigio).*

			Voştiça[i]	Buḫuşta	Ġardena	Ayo Yani	Ḳroḳova	Roẓa	Luḳa İfrati	Ẓiyaleş Tunba	Ḳondorafti	Ayo Paraskevi	Ḳaḳoḫoryo	Lopesi	Franḳo	İvlanduşa	Petro Tunba	Ḳlaẓi
inhabitants		households	159	39	5	16	11	8	8	2	3	14	8	14	8	30	3	5
		bachelors	64	6	-	3	1	1	-	-	-	-	-	-	-	-	-	-
		widows	26	5	-	-	-	-	1	-	-	-	-	-	1	-	-	-
taxes *per capita*		ispence	5021	1155	100	380	240	180	166	40	60	350	200	280	166	600	60	100
ḫāṣṣa	vineyards	dönüm	37	-	-	-	-	-	-	-	-	-	-	-	-	-	-	-
		aḳçe	3942	-	-	-	-	-	-	-	-	-	-	-	-	-	-	-
	olive trees	trees	85	-	-	-	-	-	-	-	-	-	-	-	-	-	-	-
		aḳçe	78	-	-	-	-	-	-	-	-	-	-	-	-	-	-	-
	fruit trees	trees	200	105	-	-	-	-	-	-	-	-	-	-	-	-	-	-
		aḳçe	500	660	-	-	-	-	-	-	-	-	-	-	-	-	-	-
	mulberry trees	trees	557	-	-	5	-	-	-	-	-	-	-	-	-	-	-	-
		aḳçe	1590	-	-	40	-	-	-	-	-	-	-	-	-	-	-	-
	watermills	number	-	1	-	-	-	-	-	-	-	-	-	-	-	-	-	-
		aḳçe	-	600	-	-	-	-	-	-	-	-	-	-	-	-	-	-
	fulling mills	number	-	-	-	-	-	-	-	-	-	-	-	-	-	-	-	-
		aḳçe	-	-	-	-	-	-	-	-	-	-	-	-	-	-	-	-
watermills held in common		number	1	-	-	-	-	-	-	-	-	-	-	-	-	-	-	-
		aḳçe	90[ii]	-	-	-	-	-	-	-	-	-	-	-	-	-	-	-
tithe (in aḳçes)		flax	200	50	-	15	-	10	10	-	-	15	10	15	10	20	-	-
		vineyards	4725	471	-	60	-	-	-	-	-	212	285	-	-	-	-	-
		wheat	2300	1200	150	700	400	150	200	-	-	200	100	300	200	850	100	100
		barley	367	185	24	110	64	24	32	-	-	32	16	48	32	135	16	16
		olive oil	16	-	-	-	-	-	-	-	-	-	-	-	-	-	-	-
		fruits	124	-	-	-	-	-	-	-	-	-	-	-	-	-	-	-
		cotton	100	30	-	-	-	-	-	-	-	-	-	-	-	-	-	-
		silk	630	127	-	-	-	-	-	-	-	57	66	-	-	-	-	6
		watermills	-	-	-	-	-	-	-	-	-	-	-	-	-	-	-	-
units (in aḳçes)		wine	600	60	-	-	-	-	-	-	-	-	-	-	-	-	-	-
		swine	-	2	5	-	-	4	-	-	-	-	-	-	-	-	-	-
		sheep[iii]	-	141	50	630	225	50	96	-	-	-	-	205	60	333	85	40
watermills (mülk)		number	-	-	-	-	-	-	-	-	-	1	-	-	-	-	-	-
		aḳçe	-	-	-	-	-	-	-	-	-	30	-	-	-	-	-	-
transit duty			6000	-	-	-	-	-	-	-	-	-	-	-	-	-	-	-
		total	28283[iv]	4540	279	1305	704	368	408	40	60	896	677	643	408	1605	176	222
muḳāṭaʿa (imperial)		salt-pans	4500	-	-	-	-	-	-	-	-	-	-	-	-	-	-	-
muḳāṭaʿa (tīmār)		niyābet	2000	-	-	-	-	-	-	-	-	-	-	-	-	-	-	-

[i] The following monasteries that belonged to Voştiça town were exempt from *ispence*: Manastır-ı Yirondos der Taḳsiyarḫi (bachelors: 25) and its Christian community (*cemāʿat-i gebrān*) (households: 15), the Manastır-ı Şotoḳos (bachelor: 1, widows: 10) and its Christian community (*cemāʿat-i gebrān*) (households: 12, bachelor: 1).
[ii] 70 (⅓) of which were *ḫāṣṣa* and 20 (⅔) belonged to the *reʿāyā*.
[iii] The figure stands for the number of livestock and not the tax on sheep (*resm-i aġnām*).
[iv] Not including the 4,500 *aḳçes* deriving from the salt-pan revenue.

Table 15. *District of Voştiça (Aigio).*

			Aya İġliġori	Listirna	Graḳa	Martina der Noḳastro	Epanolaġo	Valḳu	Sotira	Burlaşa	Beçaḳus	Kiriçova	Ġumaniça	Maji[v]	Rayḳu	Visoḳa	Kerpini	Zaḫlori
inhabitants		households	6	14	4	14	15	4	5	9	10	10	19	4	7	23	42	53
		bachelors	-	-	-	2	-	-	1	2	3	1	-	-	-	-	5	3
		widows	-	2	-	4	-	-	-	1	-	1	1	-	-	-	2	2
taxes *per capita*		ispence	120	292	80	404	375	80	120	226	325	281	481	80	140	460	1187	1412
ḫāṣṣa	vineyards	dönüm	-	-	-	-	-	-	-	-	-	-	-	-	-	-	2	-
		aḳçe	-	-	-	-	-	-	-	-	-	-	-	-	-	-	240	-
	olive trees	trees	-	-	-	-	-	-	-	-	-	-	-	-	-	-	-	-
		aḳçe	-	-	-	-	-	-	-	-	-	-	-	-	-	-	-	-
	fruit trees	trees	-	-	-	-	-	-	-	-	-	-	-	-	-	-	-	-
		aḳçe	-	-	-	-	-	-	-	-	-	-	-	-	-	-	-	-
	mulberry trees	trees	-	-	-	-	-	-	-	-	-	-	128	-	-	150	310	-
		aḳçe	-	-	-	-	-	-	-	-	-	-	180	-	-	100	960	-
	watermills	number	-	-	-	-	-	-	-	-	-	-	-	-	-	-	-	-
		aḳçe	-	-	-	-	-	-	-	-	-	-	-	-	-	-	-	-
	fulling mills	number	-	-	-	-	-	-	-	-	-	-	2	-	-	-	-	-
		aḳçe	-	-	-	-	-	-	-	-	-	-	70	-	-	-	-	-
watermills held in common		number	-	-	-	-	-	-	-	-	-	-	1	-	-	-	-	-
		aḳçe	-	-	-	-	-	-	-	-	-	-	120[vi]	-	-	-	-	-
tithe (in aḳçes)		flax	10	15	-	15	15	-	-	-	10	10	20	-	10	20	40	40
		vineyards	-	544	128	152	56	8	16	15	72	72	120	-	24	-	288	448
		wheat	100	200	150	350	200	150	150	300	300	250	400	200	250	1200	900	1200
		barley	16	30	24	56	32	24	24	47	48	38	64	31	40	188	142	185
		olive oil	-	-	-	-	-	-	-	-	-	-	-	-	-	-	-	-
		fruits	-	6	-	-	-	-	-	-	-	-	1	-	-	-	8	3
		cotton	-	-	-	-	-	-	-	-	-	-	-	-	-	-	-	-
		silk	-	41	24	57	6	-	12	-	156	165	72	-	39	27	762	798
		watermills	-	-	-	-	-	-	-	-	-	-	-	-	-	-	-	-
units (in aḳçes)		wine	-	-	-	-	-	-	-	-	-	-	-	-	-	-	30	70
		swine	-	-	-	-	3	-	-	-	-	-	-	-	-	2	5	-
		sheep	155	-	30	104	56	47	90	106	55	24	30	23	90	1046	91	103
watermills (mülk)		number	-	-	-	-	-	-	-	-	-	-	-	-	-	-	-	-
		aḳçe	-	-	-	-	-	-	-	-	-	-	-	-	-	-	-	-
transit duty			-	-	-	-	-	-	-	-	-	-	-	-	-	-	-	-
		total	246	1128	406	1034	687	262	322	588	911	816	1528	311	503	1997	4562	4156
muḳāṭaʿa (imperial)		salt-pans	-	-	-	-	-	-	-	-	-	-	-	-	-	-	-	-
muḳāṭaʿa (tīmār)		niyābet	-	-	-	-	-	-	-	-	-	-	-	-	-	-	-	-

[v] The deserted (*ḫāliyye*) *mezraʿa* of Ḳapareli belonged to this village.
[vi] 100 (⅓) of which were *ḫāṣṣa* and 20 (⅔) belonged to the *reʿāyā*.

Table 15. *District of Voştiça (Aigio).*

			Lovoḳa	Virastova	Cilardi	Vela	Sinoviro	Plaşa	Maneşi	Arfara	Verġuviça	Selyana	Perişori	İvlaḫo	Raḫova	Zaḫoli	Yelini	Zepandi[vii]
inhabitants		households	25	10	5	24	9	10	4	8	12	27	47	9	62	91	15	9
		bachelors	4	4	2	6	-	-	-	1	-	2	10	1	35	8	-	-
		widows	-	-	1	2	2	-	-	-	1	2	2	1	11	5	-	-
taxes *per capita*		ispence	725	350	181	762	237	200	80	180	306	737	1437	206	2491	2505	375	180
ḫāṣṣa	vineyards	dönüm	-	-	-	-	-	-	-	-	-	-	-	-	-	-	-	-
		aḳçe	-	-	-	-	-	-	-	-	-	-	-	-	-	-	-	-
	olive trees	trees	-	-	-	-	-	-	-	-	-	-	-	-	-	-	-	-
		aḳçe	-	-	-	-	-	-	-	-	-	-	-	-	-	-	-	-
	fruit trees	trees	-	-	-	-	-	-	-	-	-	-	-	-	-	-	-	-
		aḳçe	-	-	-	-	-	-	-	-	-	-	-	-	-	-	-	-
	mulberry trees	trees	-	180	-	-	-	-	-	-	-	-	-	-	-	-	-	-
		aḳçe	-	300	-	-	-	-	-	-	-	-	-	-	-	-	-	-
	watermills	number	1	-	-	-	-	-	-	-	-	-	-	-	-	-	-	-
		aḳçe	200	-	-	-	-	-	-	-	-	-	-	-	-	-	-	-
	fulling mills	number	-	-	-	-	-	-	-	-	-	-	-	-	-	-	-	-
		aḳçe	-	-	-	-	-	-	-	-	-	-	-	-	-	-	-	-
watermills held in common		number	-	-	-	-	-	-	-	-	-	-	-	-	-	-	-	-
		aḳçe	-	-	-	-	-	-	-	-	-	-	-	-	-	-	-	-
tithe (in aḳçes)		flax	-	-	-	-	-	-	-	-	-	-	-	10	-	-	-	-
		vineyards	272	128	32	304	208	-	-	-	136	256	432	-	944	1408	192	-
		wheat	600	200	100	1500	300	350	100	300	300	900	1500	200	3600	2300	300	350
		barley	93	32	16	226	48	55	16	46	48	139	230	31	546	347	48	53
		olive oil	-	-	-	-	10	-	-	-	-	-	-	-	-	4	-	-
		fruits	-	8	2	5	6	-	-	-	3	8	3	-	8	4	-	-
		cotton	-	-	-	-	-	-	-	-	-	-	-	-	-	-	-	-
		silk	561	360	60	66	279	3	-	-	108	738	663	-	1827	2052	180	-
		watermills	-	-	-	-	-	-	-	-	-	-	-	-	-	-	-	-
units (in aḳçes)		wine	40	10	-	40	30	-	-	-	10	40	60	-	140	150	25	-
		swine	-	-	-	3	2	-	-	-	-	-	-	2	-	-	-	-
		sheep	67	30	16	111	6	17	35	118	-	26	40	79	32	86	-	200
watermills (mülk)		number	-	-	-	-	-	-	-	-	-	1	-	-	1	3	3	-
		aḳçe	-	-	-	-	-	-		-	-	40	-	-	40	200	240	-
transit duty			-	-	-	-	-	-	-	-	-	-	-	-	-	-	-	-
		total	2491	1388	391	2906	1120	608	196	526	911	2858	4325	449	9596	8970	1360	583
muḳāṭaʿa (imperial)		salt-pans	-	-	-	-	-	-	-	-	-	-	-	-	-	-	-	-
muḳāṭaʿa (tīmār)		niyābet	-	-	-	-	-	-	-	-	-	-	-	-	-	-	-	-

[vii] The deserted (*ḫāliyye*) *mezraʿa* of Ḳumaniçi Luzi belonged to this village.

Chart 10. *District of Voştiça (Aigio).*

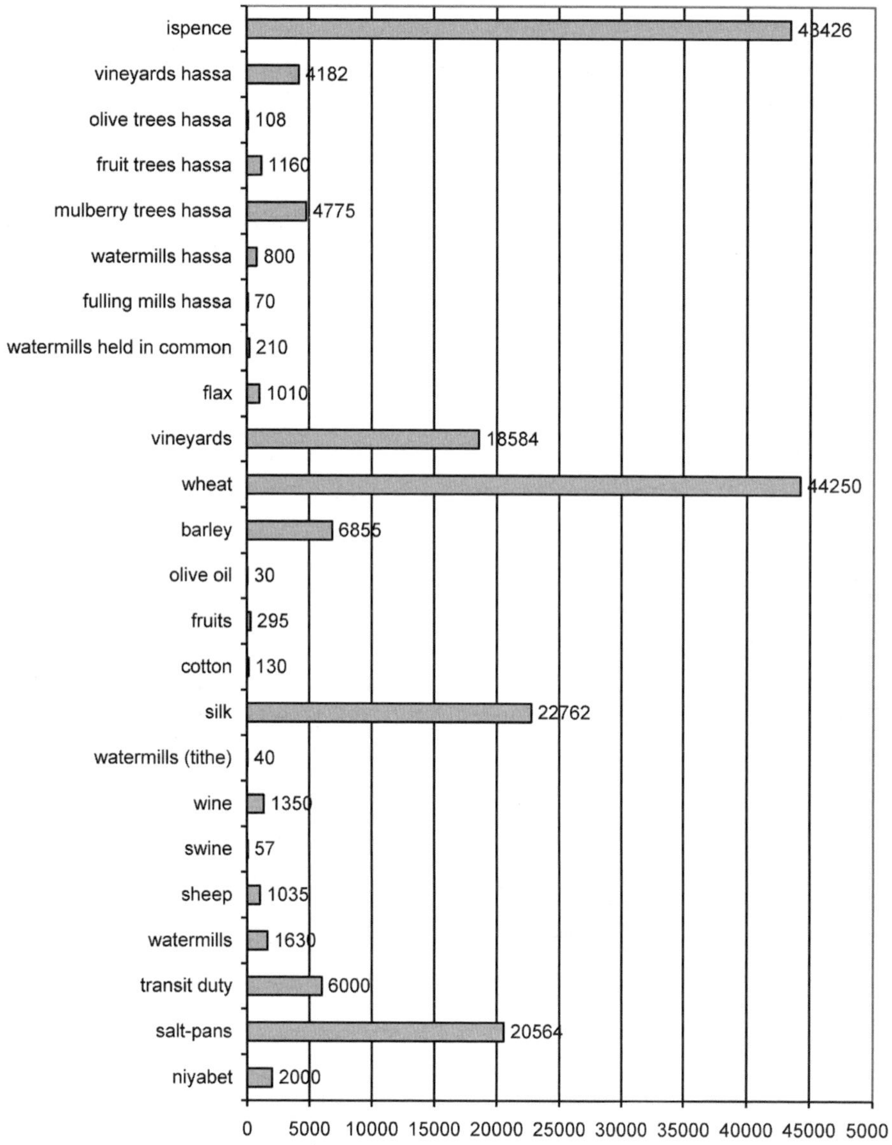

Table 16. *District of Ḫulumiç (Hlemoutsi).*

			Ḫulumiç	Ġastuni[i]	Ṣavalya[ii]	Kelavi[iii]	Girḳa Ḳumani	Çavuşi	Ḳoḳla	Dramşa	Poleşḳa	Ḳuçi	Bavasi	Şarakin	Zenbeş	Orfano	Ḳoromiẓi	Ḳarẓiyoḳafti	Jujli Palamiẓi
inhabitants		households	101	64	10	4	7	7	7	20	6	4	4	8	9	5	3	5	3
		bachelors	11	10	1	1	3	-	-	-	2	-	-	-	-	-	-	-	-
		widows	12	4	3	1	-	1	-	-	1	-	1	1	3	1	-	-	-
taxes *per capita*		ispence	2872	1874	293	131	200	146	140	400	166	80	86	166	198	106	60	100	60
		ʿarūsī	-	-	-	-	-	-	-	-	-	-	-	-	-	-	-	-	-
ḫāṣṣa	vineyards	dönüm	-	6	6	-	-	-	-	-	-	-	-	-	-	-	-	-	-
		akçe	-	720	720	-	-	-	-	-	-	-	-	-	-	-	-	-	-
	bitter orange groves	groves	3	-	-	-	-	-	-	-	-	-	-	-	-	-	-	-	-
		akçe	450	-	-	-	-	-	-	-	-	-	-	-	-	-	-	-	-
tithe (in akçes)		flax	200	200	40	-	-	-	-	30	-	-	-	14	20	20	10	-	-
		vineyards	9350	32	-	-	-	-	-	-	-	-	-	-	-	-	-	32	-
		wheat	2000	3000	700	100	200	500	200	600	500	300	200	400	500	300	150	200	100
		barley	323	465	109	16	31	73	32	96	76	46	32	63	79	48	24	32	16
		fruits	95	-	-	-	-	-	-	-	-	-	-	-	-	-	-	-	-
		olive oil	6	-	-	-	-	-	-	-	-	-	-	-	-	-	-	-	-
		cotton	200	100	30	-	-	-	-	50	-	-	-	25	25	25	13	-	-
		honey	-	7	-	-	-	-	-	-	-	-	-	-	-	-	-	-	-
units (in akçes)		wine	650	-	-	-	-	-	-	-	-	-	-	-	-	-	-	-	-
		swine	28	25	14	2	65	40	24	17	-	-	-	-	-	-	-	-	-
watermills (mülk)		number	3	-	-	-	-	-	-	-	-	-	-	-	-	-	-	-	-
		akçe	130	-	-	-	-	-	-	-	-	-	-	-	-	-	-	-	-
market tax and niyābet			700	-	-	-	-	-	-	-	-	-	-	-	-	-	-	-	-
custom dues			1200	-	-	-	-	-	-	-	-	-	-	-	-	-	-	-	-
drag seine fishing			450	-	-	-	-	-	-	-	-	-	-	-	-	-	-	-	-
		total	19404	6423	1906	249	496	759	396	1193	742	426	318	668	822	499	257	364	176
muḳāṭaʿa (imperial)		salt-pans	-	-	-	-	-	-	-	-	-	-	-	-	-	-	-	-	-
muḳāṭaʿa (tīmār)		fish-farms	750	-	-	-	-	-	-	-	-	-	-	-	-	-	-	-	-

[i] The deserted (*ḫāliyye*) *mezraʿa*s of Potamya Şarandinu and Kiḫomiro belonged to this village.
[ii] The deserted (*ḫāliyye*) *mezraʿa* of İskliva belonged to this village.
[iii] The deserted (*ḫāliyye*) *mezraʿa* of Sinasi belonged to this village.

Table 16. *District of Ḫulumiç (Hlemoutsi).*

		Ḫavaro Protopapa	Ḳoḳla Marġariti[iv]	Niḫor	Şuli	Manesi	Andraviza[v]	İzlatḳa	Ḳanḳaẕi	Marḳoplu[vi]	İvlanduşa	Ḳavasila	Lihyana	İpsari[vii]	Aya Baraskevi	Ġramatiḳo	Murji	total
inhabitants	households	5	3	13	10	3	32	15	19	16	9	12	25	12	8	3	18	470
	bachelors	-	-	3	1	-	2	5	1	-	2	-	1	-	-	-	-	43
	widows	1	-	-	1	-	2	1	1	1	1	2	1	2	-	-	1	42
taxes *per capita*	ispence	106	60	400	226	60	862	406	406	326	226	252	656	252	200	75	456	12047
	ʿarūsī	-	-	10	10	-	30	15	20	15	10	15	25	10	10	-	-	170
ḫāṣṣa vineyards	dönüm	-	-	-	-	-	-	-	-	-	-	-	-	-	-	-	-	12
	aḳçe	-	-	-	-	-	-	-	-	-	-	-	-	-	-	-	-	1440
ḫāṣṣa bitter orange groves	groves	-	-	-	-	-	-	-	-	-	-	-	-	-	-	-	-	3
	aḳçe	-	-	-	-	-	-	-	-	-	-	-	-	-	-	-	-	450
tithe (in aḳçes)	flax	-	-	-	-	-	-	-	-	-	-	-	-	-	50	10	20	614
	vineyards	96	-	224	-	-	-	-	-	-	-	-	784	-	186	-	-	10704
	wheat	250	100	400	500	200	1900	500	500	500	450	400	600	600	250	250	700	18050
	barley	40	15	63	79	30	293	79	80	80	69	63	77	94	39	38	109	2809
	fruits	-	-	2	-	-	-	-	-	-	-	-	-	-	-	-	-	97
	olive oil	-	-	-	-	-	-	-	-	-	-	-	-	-	-	-	-	6
	cotton	-	-	-	-	-	-	-	-	-	-	-	-	-	-	-	30	498
	honey	-	-	-	-	-	-	-	-	-	-	-	-	-	-	-	-	7
units (in aḳçes)	wine	-	-	16	-	-	-	-	-	-	-	-	32	-	-	-	-	698
	swine	5	-	2	-	-	-	8	5	4	9	4	-	8	4	5	52	321
watermills (mülk)	number	-	-	-	-	-	-	1	-	1	-	-	-	1	-	-	-	6
	aḳçe	-	-	-	-	-	-	20	-	50	-	-	-	30	-	-	-	230
market tax and niyābet		-	-	-	-	-	-	-	-	-	-	-	-	-	-	-	-	700
custom dues		-	-	-	-	-	-	-	-	-	-	-	-	-	-	-	-	1200
drag seine fishing		-	-	-	-	-	-	-	-	-	-	-	-	-	-	-	-	450
	total	497	175	1117	815	290	3085	1028	1011	975	764	734	2174[viii]	994	739	378	1367	51241[ix]
muḳāṭaʿa (imperial)	salt-pans	-	-	-	-	-	-	-	-	-	-	-	9000	-	-	-	-	9000
muḳāṭaʿa (tīmār)	fish-farms	-	-	-	-	-	-	-	-	-	-	-	-	-	-	-	-	750

[iv] The deserted (*ḫāliyye*) *mezraʿa* of Potamya Şarandinu belonged to this village.
[v] The deserted (*ḫāliyye*) *mezraʿa* of Foloḳobuva belonged to this village.
[vi] The deserted (*ḫāliyye*) *mezraʿa* of Ḳanbiziya belonged to this village.
[vii] The deserted (*ḫāliyye*) *mezraʿa*s of Pendani, Lonci, Başta, Tunba, and Ḳapaleto belonged to this village.
[viii] Not including the revenue of the salt-pans.
[ix] The total revenue of the district of Ḫulumiç, including the salt-pans, ran at 60,241 *aḳçes*.

Chart 11. *District of Ḫulumiç (Hlemoutsi).*

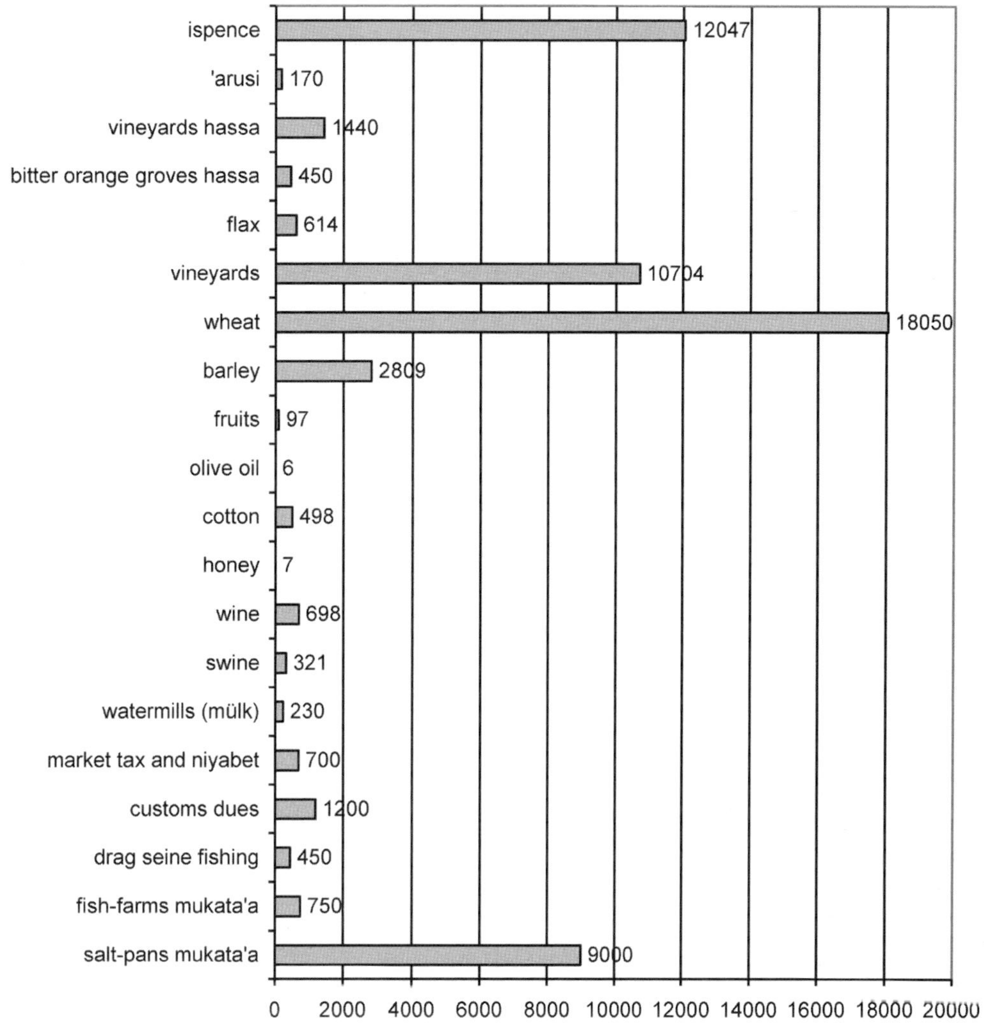

Table 17. *District of Vumero (Goumero).*

			Vumero	Ķonbi Şeķra	Nasa	Ķaķusi	Ġurdesi	Branca	Şurbi	Lancoy	Pratano	Kertiza	Loġaşeti	Laleşi	Zervini[i]	Yirmoçani	Poraçyu
inhabitants		households	236	6	8	3	3	2	23	11	14	27	33	17	70	33	19
		bachelors	35	-	-	-	-	-	1	2	1	-	2	-	11	1	-
		widows	6	-	-	-	-	-	-	-	-	1	3	-	4	5	-
taxes *per capita*		ispence	6811	120	160	60	60	40	480	260	300	681	718	340	2049	880	475
		ʿarūsī	-	-	-	-	-	-	-	-	-	-	-	-	70	30	40
ḫāṣṣa	vineyards	dönüm	24	-	-	-	-	-	-	-	-	3	-	-	0.5	-	-
		aķçe	2880	-	-	-	-	-	-	-	-	720	-	-	84	-	-
	gardens	number	-	-	-	-	-	-	-	-	-	-	-	-	-	-	-
		aķçe	-	-	-	-	-	-	-	-	-	-	-	-	-	-	-
	fruit trees	trees	200	-	-	-	-	-	-	-	-	5	-	-	5	-	-
		aķçe	500	-	-	-	-	-	-	-	-	15	-	-	15	-	-
	mulberry trees	trees	-	-	-	-	-	-	-	-	-	30	-	-	30	-	-
		aķçe	-	-	-	-	-	-	-	-	-	150	-	-	120	-	-
	olive trees	trees	-	-	-	-	-	-	-	-	-	-	-	-	-	-	-
		aķçe	-	-	-	-	-	-	-	-	-	-	-	-	-	-	-
	resin trees	trees	-	-	-	-	-	-	-	-	-	-	-	-	-	-	-
		aķçe	-	-	-	-	-	-	-	-	-	-	-	-	-	-	-
	watermills	number	2	-	-	-	-	-	1	-	-	-	-	-	-	-	-
		aķçe	500	-	-	-	-	-	200	-	-	-	-	-	-	-	-
tithe (in aķçes)		flax	300	-	-	-	-	-	30	55	40	100	100	40	100	-	-
		vineyards	7548	-	-	-	-	-	32	-	320	384	-	-	800	248	315
		wheat	6500	200	350	200	200	100	800	400	500	800	1300	800	2100	1200	500
		barley	963	32	53	31	30	15	126	63	76	124	198	126	323	188	78
		silk	-	-	-	-	-	-	-	-	-	119	-	-	264	65	46
		cotton	250	-	-	-	-	-	-	50	30	-	-	-	-	-	-
		fruits	53	-	-	-	-	-	-	-	5	3	-	-	36	23	6
		olive oil	57	-	-	-	-	-	-	-	-	-	-	-	-	-	-
		honey	-	-	-	-	-	-	-	-	-	-	-	-	10	-	-
		resin	-	-	-	-	-	-	-	-	-	-	-	-	-	-	-
units (in aķçes)		wine	640	-	-	-	-	-	-	-	25	30	-	-	65	30	40
		swine	2	15	8	13	3	-	-	13	18	5	16	-	4	9	-
watermills (mülk)		number	3	-	-	-	-	-	-	-	-	1	2	-	-	-	-
		aķçe	160	-	-	-	-	-	-	-	-	20	40	-	-	-	-
fulling mills (mülk)		number	1	-	-	-	-	-	-	-	-	-	-	-	-	-	-
		aķçe	15	-	-	-	-	-	-	-	-	-	-	-	-	-	-
market tax and niyābet			2500	-	-	-	-	-	-	-	-	-	-	-	-	-	-
		total	29679[ii]	367	571	304	293	155	1668	841	1314	3151	2372	1306	6040	2673	1500
muķāṭaʿa (imperial)		rice fields	28500	-	-	-	-	-	-	-	-	-	-	-	-	-	-
		salt-pans	-	-	-	-	-	-	-	-	-	-	-	-	-	-	-
muķāṭaʿa (tīmār)		fish-farms and transit duty	-	-	-	-	-	-	-	-	-	-	-	-	-	-	-

[i] The deserted (*ḫāliyye*) *mezraʿa* of Ayo Ķostandino belonged to this village.
[ii] Not including the revenue of the rice fields.

Table 17. *District of Vumero (Goumero).*

			Hilizon	Şuli	Kuḳura	Küraleş	Kraḳuki	Sitara	Miraḳo	İşpata[iii]	Bruma	Ḳazani	Toşkesi	Maḳri Pozi[iv]	Poşo	Maji	Sela
inhabitants		households	185	16	16	9	16	9	21	11	7	16	15	17	9	1	4
		bachelors	8	-	-	-	-	-	-	-	1	-	3	2	1	-	-
		widows	17	-	-	-	-	-	1	-	-	-	-	-	-	-	-
taxes *per capita*		ispence	4927	320	320	180	360	180	426	220	160	320	360	380	200	20	80
		ʿarūsī	-	-	-	-	-	-	-	-	-	-	-	-	-	-	-
ḫāṣṣa	vineyards	dönüm	9	-	-	-	-	-	-	-	-	-	-	-	-	-	-
		akçe	2160	-	-	-	-	-	-	-	-	-	-	-	-	-	-
	gardens	number	-	-	-	-	-	-	-	-	-	-	-	-	-	-	-
		akçe	-	-	-	-	-	-	-	-	-	-	-	-	-	-	-
	fruit trees	trees	9	-	-	-	-	-	-	-	-	-	-	-	-	-	-
		akçe	20	-	-	-	-	-	-	-	-	-	-	-	-	-	-
	mulberry trees	trees	7	-	-	-	-	-	-	-	-	-	-	-	-	-	-
		akçe	25	-	-	-	-	-	-	-	-	-	-	-	-	-	-
	olive trees	trees	10	-	-	-	-	-	-	-	-	-	-	-	-	-	-
		akçe	13	-	-	-	-	-	-	-	-	-	-	-	-	-	-
	resin trees	trees	-	-	-	-	-	-	-	-	-	-	-	-	-	-	-
		akçe	-	-	-	-	-	-	-	-	-	-	-	-	-	-	-
	watermills	number	1.5	-	-	-	-	-	-	-	-	-	-	-	-	-	-
		akçe	300	-	-	-	-	-	-	-	-	-	-	-	-	-	-
tithe (in akçes)		flax	320	50	30	20	40	15	50	40	30	40	30	50	15	-	20
		vineyards	5248	64	-	-	-	-	-	-	-	-	112	224	-	-	-
		wheat	6100	600	500	400	700	200	700	400	400	500	700	1000	450	50	200
		barley	936	90	76	61	106	32	106	62	60	76	107	152	68	8	31
		silk	25	-	-	-	-	-	-	-	-	-	-	-	-	-	-
		cotton	120	50	30	20	40	-	40	30	-	-	-	20	-	-	-
		fruits	154	-	-	-	-	-	-	-	-	-	-	-	-	-	-
		olive oil	34	-	-	-	-	-	-	-	-	-	-	-	-	-	-
		honey	16	-	-	-	5	-	-	-	-	-	-	-	13	-	-
		resin	10	-	-	-	-	-	-	-	-	-	-	-	-	-	1
units (in akçes)		wine	420	-	-	-	12	-	-	-	-	-	-	-	-	-	-
		swine	16	5	19	14	-	2	4	3	13	-	5	9	14	-	8
watermills (mülk)		number	3	1	-	-	1	-	-	-	-	1	-	-	-	-	-
		akçe	105	50	-	-	25	-	-	-	-	25	-	-	-	-	-
fulling mills (mülk)		number	3	-	-	-	-	-	-	-	-	-	-	-	-	-	-
		akçe	45	-	-	-	-	-	-	-	-	-	-	-	-	-	-
market tax and niyābet			-	-	-	-	-	-	-	-	-	-	-	-	-	-	-
		total	20994	1229	975	695	1288	429	1326	755	663	961	1314	1835	760	78	340
muḳāṭaʿa (imperial)		rice fields	-	-	-	-	-	-		-	-	-	-	-	-	-	-
		salt-pans	-	-	-	-	-	-	-	-	-	-	-	-	-	-	-
muḳāṭaʿa (tīmār)		fish farms and transit duty	-	-	-	-	-	-	-	-	-	-	-	-	-	-	-

[iii] The deserted (*ḫāliyye*) *mezraʿa* of Matranḳa belonged to this village.
[iv] The deserted (*ḫāliyye*) *mezraʿa* of Purdanu belonged to this village.

Table 17. *District of Vumero (Goumero).*

			Ziminiça	Ḫayḳal	Şarakina	Plaşa	Ḳondari	Franḳa	Lazaro Buva	Liḳuresi	Aranis Ḳuçohyari	Aranis Ḳavalari	Romesi	Vaşıloplos	Maji	Añloniça
inhabitants		households	8	12	3	17	10	11	6	12	7	16	16	6	7	3
		bachelors	-	1	1	5	3	2	-	1	-	1	5	-	1	-
		widows	2	-	-	1	-	-	-	-	-	1	-	-	-	-
taxes *per capita*		ispence	212	260	80	446	260	260	120	260	140	346	420	120	160	75
		ʿarūsī	-	-	-	-	-	-	-	-	-	-	20	10	10	-
ḫāṣṣa	vineyards	dönüm	5	-	-	-	-	-	-	-	-	-	-	-	-	-
		aḳçe	600	-	-	-	-	-	-	-	-	-	-	-	-	-
	gardens	number	-	-	-	-	-	-	-	-	-	-	-	-	-	-
		aḳçe	-	-	-	-	-	-	-	-	-	-	-	-	-	-
	fruit trees	trees	-	-	-	-	-	-	-	-	-	-	-	-	-	-
		aḳçe	-	-	-	-	-	-	-	-	-	-	-	-	-	-
	mulberry trees	trees	-	-	-	-	-	-	-	-	-	-	-	-	-	-
		aḳçe	-	-	-	-	-	-	-	-	-	-	-	-	-	-
	olive trees	trees	-	-	-	-	-	-	-	-	-	-	-	-	-	-
		aḳçe	-	-	-	-	-	-	-	-	-	-	-	-	-	-
	resin trees	trees	-	-	-	-	-	-	-	-	-	-	-	-	-	-
		aḳçe	-	-	-	-	-	-	-	-	-	-	-	-	-	-
	watermills	number	1	-	-	-	-	-	-	-	-	-	-	-	-	-
		aḳçe	1000	-	-	-	-	-	-	-	-	-	-	-	-	-
tithe (in aḳçes)		flax	10	30	-	40	30	20	-	30	10	50	30	30	30	-
		vineyards	112	-	128	-	-	-	-	-	-	-	-	60	-	-
		wheat	200	450	100	900	400	350	250	600	200	900	500	200	250	200
		barley	32	68	15	137	61	55	40	91	31	136	77	32	40	30
		silk	-	-	-	-	-	-	-	-	-	-	-	-	-	-
		cotton	-	-	-	40	20	20	-	20	-	30	20	20	20	-
		fruits	-	-	-	-	-	-	-	-	-	-	-	-	-	-
		olive oil	-	-	-	-	-	-	-	-	-	-	-	4	-	-
		honey	-	-	-	26	-	-	6	-	-	-	-	-	-	-
		resin	-	-	-	-	-	-	-	-	-	-	-	-	-	-
units (in aḳçes)		wine	10	-	-	-	-	-	-	-	-	-	-	-	-	-
		swine	5	2	-	26	35	50	18	20	8	29	6	2	-	-
watermills (mülk)		number	-	-	1	-	-	-	-	-	-	-	-	-	-	-
		aḳçe	-	-	80	-	-	-	-	-	-	-	-	-	-	-
fulling mills (mülk)		number	-	-	-	-	-	-	-	-	-	-	-	-	-	-
		aḳçe	-	-	-	-	-	-	-	-	-	-	-	-	-	-
market tax and niyābet			-	-	-	-	-	-	-	-	-	-	-	-	-	-
		total	2181	810	403	1615	806	755	434	1021	389	1491	1073	478	510	4805
muḳāṭaʿa (imperial)		rice fields	-	-	-	-	-	-	-	-	-	-	-	-	-	-
		salt-pans	-	-	-	-	-	-	-	-	-	-	-	-	-	-
muḳāṭaʿa (tīmār)		fish farms and transit duty	-	-	-	-	-	-	-	-	-	-	-	-	-	4500

Table 17. *District of Vumero (Goumero).*

			Mihili	Sipyani	Mangişa Ḳumani	İspani[v]	Ḳuçi	Yirmena	Ḳaçaru	Dumeña	Ḳariza	Lali	Coya[vi]	Lanbeti	Ḳuçi	Ḳondomiḫal
inhabitants		households	6	28	30	6	5	5	12	31	6	19	7	25	16	10
		bachelors	2	7	6	2	-	-	3	9	2	-	3	3	5	5
		widows	-	1	2	2	1	-	-	2	-	-	9	3	3	2
taxes *per capita*		ispence	160	881	732	172	106	125	300	1012	200	380	304	578	438	312
		ʿarūsī	10	30	30	10	-	10	15	35	10	20	10	25	20	10
ḫāṣṣa	vineyards	dönüm	-	-	-	-	-	-	-	8	-	-	3	-	-	-
		akçe	-	-	-	-	-	-	-	880	-	-	720	-	-	-
	gardens	number	-	-	-	-	-	-	-	-	-	-	1	-	-	-
		akçe	-	-	-	-	-	-	-	-	-	-	100	-	-	-
	fruit trees	trees	-	-	-	-	-	-	-	4	-	-	20	-	-	-
		akçe	-	-	-	-	-	-	-	10	-	-	52	-	-	-
	mulberry trees	trees	-	-	-	-	-	-	-	-	-	-	-	-	-	-
		akçe	-	-	-	-	-	-	-	-	-	-	-	-	-	-
	olive trees	trees	-	-	-	-	-	-	-	-	-	-	-	-	-	-
		akçe	-	-	-	-	-	-	-	-	-	-	-	-	-	-
	resin trees	trees	-	-	-	-	-	-	-	-	-	-	-	-	-	-
		akçe	-	-	-	-	-	-	-	-	-	-	-	-	-	-
	watermills	number	-	-	-	-	-	1	-	-	-	-	-	-	-	-
		akçe	-	-	-	-	-	300	-	-	-	-	-	-	-	-
tithe (in akçes)		flax	30	-	-	20	-	-	-	50	20	138	40	40	30	50
		vineyards	-	512	128	-	-	90	75	1320	90	-	360	60	240	60
		wheat	200	1250	1200	250	250	200	650	1200	200	900	300	700	700	400
		barley	32	193	188	42	40	25	102	188	32	-	48	108	108	64
		silk	-	164	-	-	-	-	-	-	-	-	-	-	-	-
		cotton	20	-	-	-	-	-	-	-	-	-	30	30	30	40
		fruits	-	18	-	-	-	5	-	10	-	-	5	-	-	-
		olive oil	-	-	-	-	-	-	-	-	-	-	-	-	-	-
		honey	-	-	-	-	-	-	-	-	-	-	-	-	-	-
		resin	-	-	-	-	-	-	-	-	-	-	-	-	-	-
units (in akçes)		wine	-	-	-	-	-	-	-	120	-	-	30	-	-	-
		swine	-	7	62	3	4	-	42	4	2	23	-	3	8	12
watermills (mülk)		number	-	1	-	-	-	-	1	1	-	-	-	-	-	-
		akçe	-	25	-	-	-	-	30	50	-	-	-	-	-	-
fulling mills (mülk)		number	-	-	-	-	1	-	-	-	-	-	-	-	-	-
		akçe	-	-	-	-	15	-	-	-	-	-	-	-	-	-
market tax and niyābet			-	-	-	-	-	-	-	-	-	-	-	-	-	-
		total	452	3080	2340	497	415	755	1214	4879	554	1461	1999	1544	1574	948
muḳāṭaʿa (imperial)		rice fields	-	-	-	-	-	-	-	-	-	-	-	-	-	-
		salt-pans	-	-	-	-	-	-	-	-	-	-	-	-	-	-
muḳāṭaʿa (tīmār)		fish-farms and transit duty	-	-	-	-	-	-	-	-	-	-	-	-	-	-

[v] The deserted (*ḫāliyye*) *mezraʿa* s of İspani-i dīğer and Persena belonged to this village.
[vi] The deserted (*ḫāliyye*) *mezraʿa* of Velizi belonged to this village.

Table 17. *District of Vumero (Goumero).*

		Ratendu	Ḳosta Lanca	Nikifor	Olana	Iğlava	Ṣopi	Dorza	Ḳonbi Şeḳra	Ḳoḳla	Ḳaratula	Pondiḳo	Mavromati	Livarzi	Keraṣova	total
inhabitants	households	8	11	3	51	12	9	2	6	5	8	15	14	24	7	1372
	bachelors	2	6	-	4	-	-	-	-	-	1	2	3	4	3	160
	widows	-	-	-	3	2	1	1	-	-	-	1	-	-	-	74
taxes *per capita*	ispence	200	340	60	1393	252	186	46	120	100	180	431	340	700	250	35344
	ʿarūsī	10	10	-	50	15	10	-	10	-	10	15	15	25	10	595
ḫāṣṣa – vineyards	dönüm	-	-	-	5	-	-	-	-	-	-	6	-	-	-	63.5
	aḳçe	-	-	-	600	-	-	-	-	-	-	720	-	-	-	9364
ḫāṣṣa – gardens	number	-	-	-	-	-	-	-	-	-	-	-	-	-	-	1
	aḳçe	-	-	-	-	-	-	-	-	-	-	-	-	-	-	100
ḫāṣṣa – fruit trees	trees	-	-	-	-	-	-	-	-	-	-	9	-	-	-	252
	aḳçe	-	-	-	-	-	-	-	-	-	-	15	-	-	-	627
ḫāṣṣa – mulberry trees	trees	-	-	-	-	-	-	-	-	-	-	-	-	-	-	67
	aḳçe	-	-	-	-	-	-	-	-	-	-	-	-	-	-	295
ḫāṣṣa – olive trees	trees	-	-	-	20	-	-	-	-	-	-	10	-	-	-	40
	aḳçe	-	-	-	22	-	-	-	-	-	-	14	-	-	-	49
ḫāṣṣa – resin trees	number	-	-	-	300	-	-	-	-	-	-	-	-	-	-	300
	aḳçe	-	-	-	80	-	-	-	-	-	-	-	-	-	-	80
ḫāṣṣa – watermills	number	-	-	-	1	-	-	-	-	-	-	-	-	-	-	7.5
	aḳçe	-	-	-	250	-	-	-	-	-	-	-	-	-	-	2550
tithe (in aḳçes)	flax	40	40	-	100	40	30	20	20	20	20	50	50	-	-	2673
	vineyards	60	135	-	1080	150	-	-	-	-	80	-	-	480	420	20935
	wheat	300	500	100	1600	300	400	100	200	100	250	500	500	800	300	48700
	barley	47	78	16	250	48	64	16	32	16	40	74	77	124	48	7342
	silk	-	-	-	-	-	-	-	-	-	-	-	-	172	68	923
	cotton	30	30	-	200	30	20	15	15	10	-	30	40	-	-	1440
	fruits	-	-	-	50	-	-	-	-	-	-	-	-	14	7	389
	olive oil	-	-	-	10	-	-	-	-	-	-	-	-	-	-	105
	honey	-	-	-	10	-	-	-	-	-	-	-	-	-	-	86
	resin	-	-	-	-	-	-	-	-	-	-	-	-	-	-	11
units (in aḳçes)	wine	-	-	-	100	-	-	-	-	-	-	-	-	40	35	1597
	swine	-	5	-	12	10	10	3	-	3	-	4	10	2	-	648
watermills (mülk)	number	-	1	-	-	-	-	-	1	-	-	-	-	2	1	21
	aḳçe	-	30	-	-	-	-	-	30	-	-	-	-	90	30	790
fulling mills (mülk)	number	-	-	-	-	-	-	-	-	-	-	-	-	-	-	5
	aḳçe	-	-	-	-	-	-	-	-	-	-	-	-	-	-	75
market tax and niyābet		-	-	-	-	-	-	-	-	-	-	-	-	-	-	2500
	total	687	1168	176	5807	845	720	200	427	249	580	1853[vii]	1032	2447	1168	141718[viii]
muḳāṭaʿa (imperial)	rice fields	-	-	-	-	-	-	-	-	-	-	-	-	-	-	28500
	salt-pans	-	-	-	-	-	-	-	-	-	-	7000	-	-	-	7000
muḳāṭaʿa (tīmār)	fish-farms and transit duty	-	-	-	-	-	-	-	-	-	-	-	-	-	-	4500

[vii] Not including the imperial *muḳāṭaʿa* of salt-pans.
[viii] Not including the imperial *muḳāṭaʿa*s of rice fields and salt-pans.

Chart 12. *District of Vumero (Goumero).*

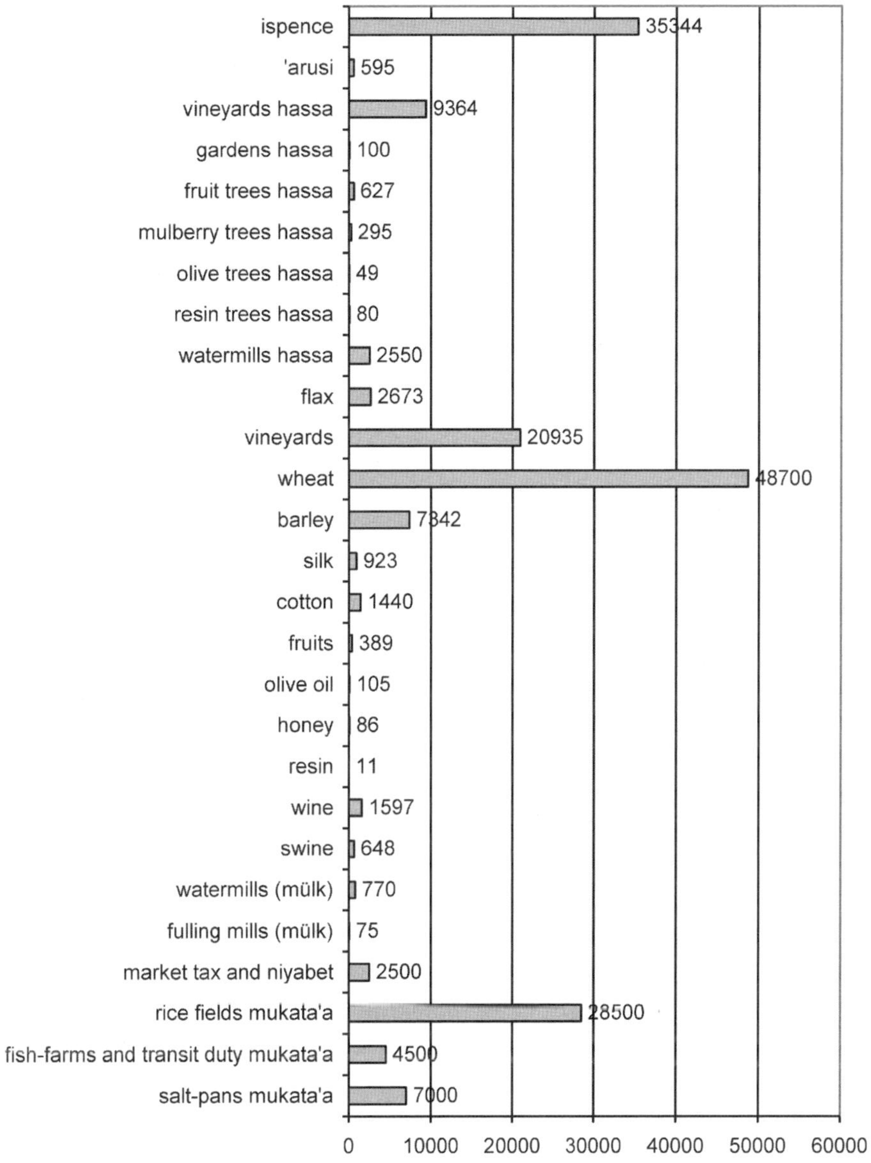
ispence
35344
'arusi
595
vineyards hassa
9364
gardens hassa
100
fruit trees hassa
627
mulberry trees hassa
295
olive trees hassa
49
resin trees hassa
80
watermills hassa
2550
flax
2673
vineyards
20935
wheat
48700
barley
7842
silk
923
cotton
1440
fruits
389
olive oil
105
honey
86
resin
11
wine
1597
swine
648
watermills (mülk)
770
fulling mills (mülk)
75
market tax and niyabet
2500
rice fields mukata'a
28500
fish-farms and transit duty mukata'a
4500
salt-pans mukata'a
7000
0
10000
20000
30000
40000
50000
60000

Table 18. *District of Kirvuḳor (Palaiokastro/Koufoplaiiko Kastro).*

			Artica	Zelaḫova	Vervena	Ḳırana	Ḳopaniça	Velviça	Linistena	Ondriçena	Ẓolyani	Draġoy	İskâẓa	Mazarak	Mateşi	İsfranci	Mizotoro	Beluşi
inhabitants		households	62	20	27	29	6	10	13	42	17	34	10	34	10	6	5	17
		bachelors	10	1	1	4	-	-	1	5	2	5	4	4	1	1	-	4
		widows	9	2	5	3	-	-	4	7	-	2	-	-	-	-	1	-
taxes *per capita*		ispence	1854	537	680	843	150	250	374	1217	475	792	280	760	220	140	106	420
		ʿarūsī	70	20	30	30	10	10	15	40	20	30	10	30	10	5	-	15
ḫāṣṣa	vineyards	dönüm	1?	-	10?	-	-	-	-	-	-	-	-	-	-	-	-	-
		aḳçe	168	-	1174	-	-	-	-	-	-	-	-	-	-	-	-	-
	olive trees	trees	-	-	-	-	-	-	-	-	-	-	-	-	-	-	-	-
		aḳçe	-	-	-	-	-	-	-	-	-	-	-	-	-	-	-	-
	fruit trees	trees	-	-	-	-	-	-	-	-	-	-	-	-	-	-	-	-
		aḳçe	-	-	-	-	-	-	-	-	-	-	-	-	-	-	-	-
	mulberry trees	trees	-	10	-	-	-	-	-	-	-	-	-	-	-	-	-	-
		aḳçe	-	40	-	-	-	-	-	-	-	-	-	-	-	-	-	-
	resin trees	trees	-	-	-	-	-	-	-	-	-	-	-	-	-	-	-	-
		aḳçe	-	-	-	-	-	-	-	-	-	-	-	-	-	-	-	-
	oak trees	trees	-	-	-	-	-	-	-	-	-	-	-	-	-	-	-	-
		aḳçe	-	-	-	-	-	-	-	-	-	-	-	-	-	-	-	-
	kitchen gardens	number	-	-	-	-	-	-	-	-	-	-	-	-	-	-	-	-
		aḳçe	-	-	-	-	-	-	-	-	-	-	-	-	-	-	-	-
	watermills	number	-	-	-	-	-	-	-	-	-	-	-	-	-	-	-	-
		aḳçe	-	-	-	-	-	-	-	-	-	-	-	-	-	-	-	-
tithe (in aḳçes)		flax	100	20	30	30	10	15	15	40	20	30	15	45	15	10	-	20
		vineyards	2250	866	956	743	158	248	428	945	551	-	-	-	-	45	-	-
		wheat	3100	700	1000	1150	100?	500	550	1500	800	1200	400	1200	450	200	350	500
		barley	468	108	194	172	16	76	85	230	122	185	62	185	69	31	54	78
		cotton	-	-	-	-	-	-	-	-	-	-	-	-	-	-	-	-
		olive oil	5	-	-	-	-	-	-	-	-	-	-	-	-	-	-	-
		fruits	11	7	26	-	1	3	6	15	4	-	-	17	-	-	-	-
		honey	-	-	8	-	-	-	-	-	-	59	-	-	-	-	6	-
		silk	204	69	64	86	9?	-	28	94	37	-	-	-	-	-	-	-
units (in aḳçes)		wine	250	100	100	80	15	30	50	100	60	-	-	-	-	-	-	-
		swine	50	5	17	14	1?	7	3	6	1	28	29	46	15	8	4	15
watermills (mülk)		number	2	-	1	-	-	-	1	-	-	-	-	-	-	-	-	-
		aḳçe	120	-	40	-	-	-	40	-	-	-	-	-	-	-	-	-
		total	8650	2472	4319	3148	470	1139	1594	4187	2090	2324	796	2283	779	439	520	1048
muḳāṭaʿa (tīmār)		fish-farms	-	-	-	-	-	-	-	-	-	-	-	-	-	-	-	-

Table 18. *District of Kirvuḳor (Palaiokastro/Koufoplaiiko Kastro).*

		Mujak	Ḳanḳaẓi	Mazarak Adipo	Floḳa	Jupan/ Jupano	Aniza	Lonci	Sirvu	Ranesi	Valaḳ	Ḳraḳuki	Peta	Draġuẓisti	Drayina	Ḳonbi Ṣeḳra	İstoya
inhabitants	households	10	10	39	10	23	15	27	27	15	9	8	10	2	12	7	5
	bachelors	1	1	4	-	1	3	3	3	1	2	-	-	-	7	-	2
	widows	-	-	3	-	-	-	-	-	-	2	1	1	-	-	-	1
taxes *per capita*	ispence	220	220	878	200	480	360	600	600	320	232	166	206	40	380	140	146
	ʿarūsī	10	10	40	10	20	15	20	25	15	10	10	10	-	10	10	10
ḫāṣṣa – vineyards	dönüm	-	-	-	-	-	-	-	-	-	-	-	-	-	-	-	-
	aḳçe	-	-	-	-	-	-	-	-	-	-	-	-	-	-	-	-
ḫāṣṣa – olive trees	trees	-	-	-	-	-	-	-	-	-	-	-	-	-	-	-	-
	aḳçe	-	-	-	-	-	-	-	-	-	-	-	-	-	-	-	-
ḫāṣṣa – fruit trees	trees	-	-	-	-	-	-	-	-	-	-	-	-	-	-	-	-
	aḳçe	-	-	-	-	-	-	-	-	-	-	-	-	-	-	-	-
ḫāṣṣa – mulberry trees	trees	-	-	-	-	-	-	-	-	-	-	-	-	-	-	-	-
	aḳçe	-	-	-	-	-	-	-	-	-	-	-	-	-	-	-	-
ḫāṣṣa – resin trees	trees	-	-	-	-	-	-	-	-	-	-	-	-	-	-	-	-
	aḳçe	-	-	-	-	-	-	-	-	-	-	-	-	-	-	-	-
ḫāṣṣa – oak trees	trees	-	-	-	-	-	-	-	-	-	-	-	-	-	-	-	-
	aḳçe	-	-	-	-	-	-	-	-	-	-	-	-	-	-	-	-
ḫāṣṣa – kitchen gardens	number	-	-	-	-	-	-	-	-	-	-	-	-	-	-	-	-
	aḳçe	-	-	-	-	-	-	-	-	-	-	-	-	-	-	-	-
ḫāṣṣa – watermills	number	-	-	-	-	-	-	-	-	-	-	-	-	-	-	-	-
	aḳçe	-	-	-	-	-	-	-	-	-	-	-	-	-	-	-	-
tithe (in aḳçes)	flax	15	15	100	15	60	15	30	100	80	40	10	40	-	15	15	20
	vineyards	-	-	-	-	-	-	-	-	-	-	-	-	22	-	-	22
	wheat	450	500	2050	550	800	400	800	900	600	300	450	250	100	750	300	200
	barley	68	76	309	83	120	64	123	138	91	48	69	40	16	109	46	31
	cotton	-	-	-	-	-	-	-	-	-	-	-	-	-	-	-	-
	olive oil	-	-	-	-	-	-	-	-	-	-	-	-	-	-	-	-
	fruits	-	-	-	-	-	-	-	-	-	-	-	-	2	-	-	-
	honey	2	-	23	-	18	-	-	-	-	-	-	-	-	-	-	-
	silk	-	-	-	-	-	-	-	-	-	-	-	-	-	-	-	-
units (in aḳçes)	wine	-	-	-	-	-	-	-	-	-	-	-	-	-	-	-	-
	swine	30	33	107	23	44	52	51	72	15	23	22	28	-	25	11	5
watermills (mülk)	number	-	-	-	-	-	-	1	-	1	-	-	-	-	2	-	-
	aḳçe	-	-	-	-	-	-	80	-	40	-	-	-	-	160	-	-
	total	795	854	3507	881	1542	906	1704	1835	1161	653	727	574	180	1449	522	434
muḳāṭaʿa (tīmār)	fish-farms	-	-	-	-	-	-	-	-	-	-	-	-	-	-	-	-

Table 18. *District of Kirvuḳor (Palaiokastro/Koufoplaiiko Kastro).*

			Lazar Buva	Lazaro Kemer	Ẕunato	Ḳarvunari	Murik Maji	Miziḳa	Ḳuçi	Ranesi	Maḳrişa	Omlo	Bizbardi	Monaḫu	Ḳoḳla	Kefiñali	Ḳopiça	Barçi
inhabitants		households	8	6	5	10	14	5	11	34	26	10	18	15	6	6	9	28
		bachelors	-	-	-	-	1	-	-	6	4	6	4	1	2	-	-	1
		widows	1	-	-	-	-	-	-	-	-	2	-	-	-	-	-	-
taxes *per capita*		ispence	166	120	100	200	300	100	220	800	600	332	440	320	160	120	180	580
		ʿarūsī	10	-	-	10	15	-	10	35	25	15	20	15	-	-	10	25
ḫāṣṣa	vineyards	dönüm	-	-	-	-	-	-	-	-	-	-	-	-	-	-	-	-
		aḳçe	-	-	-	-	-	-	-	-	-	-	-	-	-	-	-	-
	olive trees	trees	-	-	-	-	-	-	-	-	-	-	-	-	-	-	-	-
		aḳçe	-	-	-	-	-	-	-	-	-	-	-	-	-	-	-	-
	fruit trees	trees	-	-	-	-	-	-	-	-	-	-	-	-	-	-	-	-
		aḳçe	-	-	-	-	-	-	-	-	-	-	-	-	-	-	-	-
	mulberry trees	trees	-	-	-	-	-	-	-	-	-	-	-	-	-	-	-	-
		aḳçe	-	-	-	-	-	-	-	-	-	-	-	-	-	-	-	-
	resin trees	trees	-	-	-	-	-	-	-	-	-	-	-	-	-	-	-	-
		aḳçe	-	-	-	-	-	-	-	-	-	-	-	-	-	-	-	-
	oak trees	trees	-	-	-	-	-	-	-	-	-	-	-	-	-	-	-	-
		aḳçe	-	-	-	-	-	-	-	-	-	-	-	-	-	-	-	-
	kitchen gardens	number	-	-	-	-	-	-	-	-	-	-	-	-	-	-	-	-
		aḳçe	-	-	-	-	-	-	-	-	-	-	-	-	-	-	-	-
	watermills	number	-	-	-	-	-	-	-	-	-	-	-	-	-	-	-	-
		aḳçe	-	-	-	-	-	-	-	-	-	-	-	-	-	-	-	-
tithe (in aḳçes)		flax	20	10	20	15	20	15	25	100	60	20	30	30	10	10	20	80
		vineyards	22	44	-	22	22	-	56	67	78	-	-	-	-	-	-	-
		wheat	350	300	200	200	300	200	300	1350	700	300	600	400	200	200	300	900
		barley	54	45	31	30	47	30	48	215	108	45	91	62	31	30	46	138
		cotton	-	-	-	-	-	-	-	-	-	-	-	-	-	-	-	-
		olive oil	-	-	-	-	-	-	-	-	-	-	-	-	-	-	-	-
		fruits	-	-	-	-	-	-	-	2	-	-	-	-	-	-	-	-
		honey	-	-	-	-	-	-	-	-	-	-	-	-	10	-	14	8
		silk	-	-	-	-	-	-	-	-	-	-	-	-	-	-	-	-
units (in aḳçe)		wine	-	-	-	-	-	-	-	-	-	-	-	-	-	-	-	-
		swine	8	15	5	2	57	6	18	77	63	22	6	59	2	3	23	79
watermills (mülk)		number	1	-	-	-	1	-	-	1	1	-	-	-	-	-	-	-
		aḳçe	30	-	-	-	30	-	-	60	50	-	-	-	-	-	-	-
		total	660	534	356	479	791	351	677	2706	1684	734	1187	886	413	363	593	1810
muḳāṭaʿa (tīmār)		fish-farms	-	-	-	-	-	-	-	-	-	-	-	-	-	-	-	-

Table 18. *District of Kirvuḳor (Palaiokastro/Koufoplaiiko Kastro).*

			Maẓi	Pasḳali/ Pasḳal	Ḳukesi	Melita	Maji	Luzi	İsḳala	Ṣarakin	Trestena	Aḳunba	Maẓi	Manḳa	Ketesi	Mundriza	Bratiça	Papaẓa
inhabitants		households	5	6	6	4	9	4	5	23	19	72	16	15	9	56	38	39
		bachelors	-	-	1	-	1	3	-	-	-	4	-	2	-	6	5	8
		widows	-	-	1	-	-	-	-	2	1	5	-	-	-	-	1	1
taxes *per capita*		ispence	100	120	146	80	200	140	125	587	481	1930	320	340	180	1550	866	946
		ʿarūsī	-	10	-	-	10	-	-	25	20	80	20	15	10	60	40	40
ḫāṣṣa	vineyards	dönüm	-	-	-	-	-	-	-	-	-	10	-	-	-	5	-	-
		akçe	-	-	-	-	-	-	-	-	-	1260	-	-	-	588	-	-
	olive trees	trees	-	-	-	-	-	-	6	-	-	-	-	-	-	-	-	-
		akçe	-	-	-	-	-	-	7	-	-	-	-	-	-	-	-	-
	fruit trees	trees	-	-	-	-	-	-	32	-	-	-	-	-	-	-	-	-
		akçe	-	-	-	-	-	-	60	-	-	-	-	-	-	-	-	-
	mulberry trees	trees	-	-	-	-	-	-	-	-	-	-	-	-	-	-	-	-
		akçe	-	-	-	-	-	-	-	-	-	-	-	-	-	-	-	-
	resin trees	trees	-	-	-	-	-	-	500	-	-	-	-	-	-	-	-	-
		akçe	-	-	-	-	-	-	90	-	-	-	-	-	-	-	-	-
	oak trees	trees	-	-	-	-	-	-	200	-	-	-	-	-	-	-	-	-
		akçe	-	-	-	-	-	-	50	-	-	-	-	-	-	-	-	-
	kitchen gardens	number	-	-	-	-	-	-	-	-	-	-	-	-	-	-	-	-
		akçe	-	-	-	-	-	-	-	-	-	-	-	-	-	-	-	-
	watermills	number	-	-	-	-	-	-	-	-	-	-	-	-	-	-	-	-
		akçe	-	-	-	-	-	-	-	-	-	-	-	-	-	-	-	-
tithe (in akçes)		flax	15	10	15	10	20	15	15	50	30	100	30	50	30	100	60	60
		vineyards	-	-	-	-	-	-	-	-	170	717	-	-	-	1057	-	-
		wheat	150	150	250	100	350	200	200	500	600	2600	500	500	250	2000	1300	1500
		barley	23	24	53	16	54	31	30	80	95	395	75	76	38	308	198	232
		cotton	-	-	-	-	-	-	-	-	-	50	20	30	-	50	-	-
		olive oil	-	-	-	-	-	-	-	-	-	-	-	-	-	6	-	-
		fruits	-	-	-	-	-	-	-	-	-	13	-	-	-	5	-	-
		honey	-	-	-	-	-	-	-	-	-	-	-	-	-	36	-	18
		silk	-	-	-	-	-	-	-	-	13	-	-	-	-	-	-	-
units (in akçes)		wine	-	-	-	-	-	-	-	-	20	60	-	-	-	120	-	-
		swine	-	-	15	10	20	10	-	15	3	10	15	6	3	40	79	45
watermills (mülk)		number	1	-	-	-	-	-	-	-	-	1	1	-	-	-	-	-
		akçe	40	-	-	-	-		-	-	-	30	40	-	-	-	-	-
		total	328	314	479	216	654	396	827	1257	1432	7245	1020	1017	511	5920	2543	2841
muḳāṭaʿa (tīmār)		fish-farms	-	-	-	-	-	-	250	-	-	-	-	-	-	-	-	-

Chart 13. *District of Kirvuķor (Palaiokastro/Koufoplaiiko Kastro).*

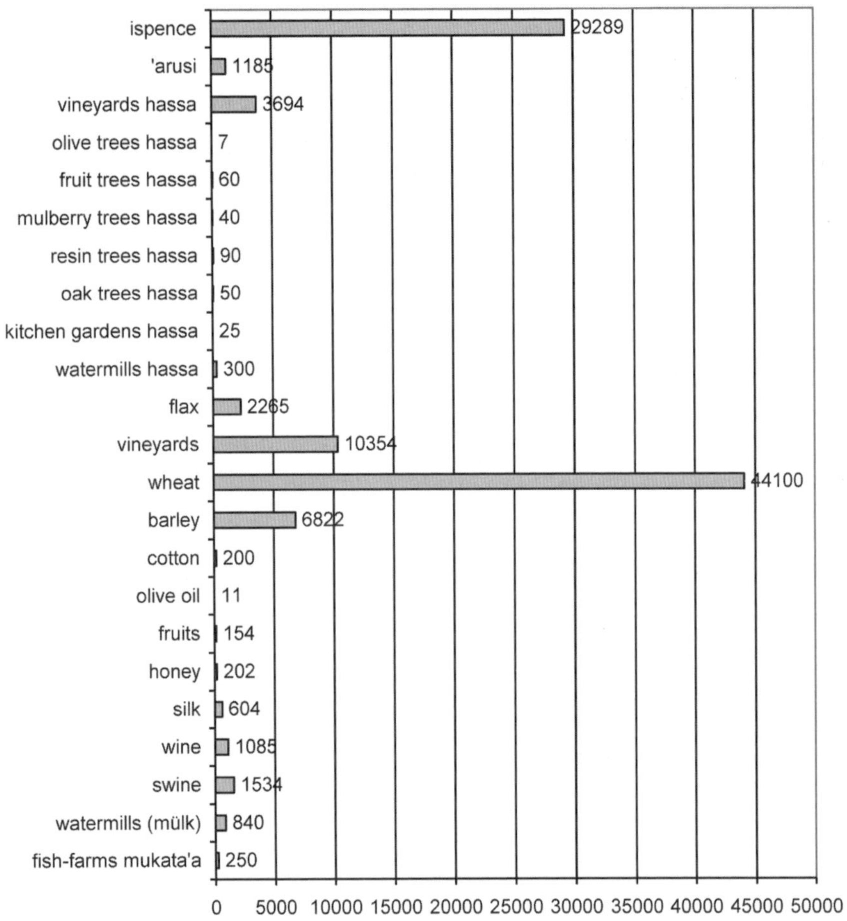

Chart 14. *District of Arķadya (Kyparissia).*

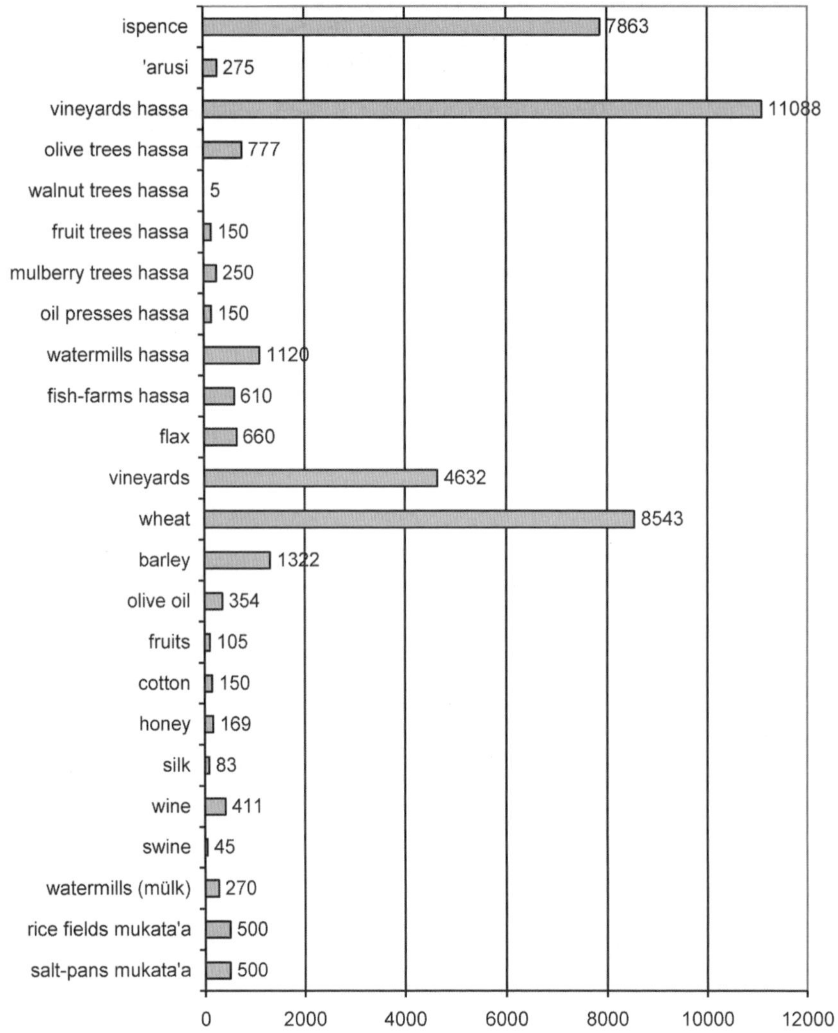

16 Nāḥiyyet-i Kirvuḳor (Palaiokastro/Koufoplaiiko Kastro)
Economic Distribution

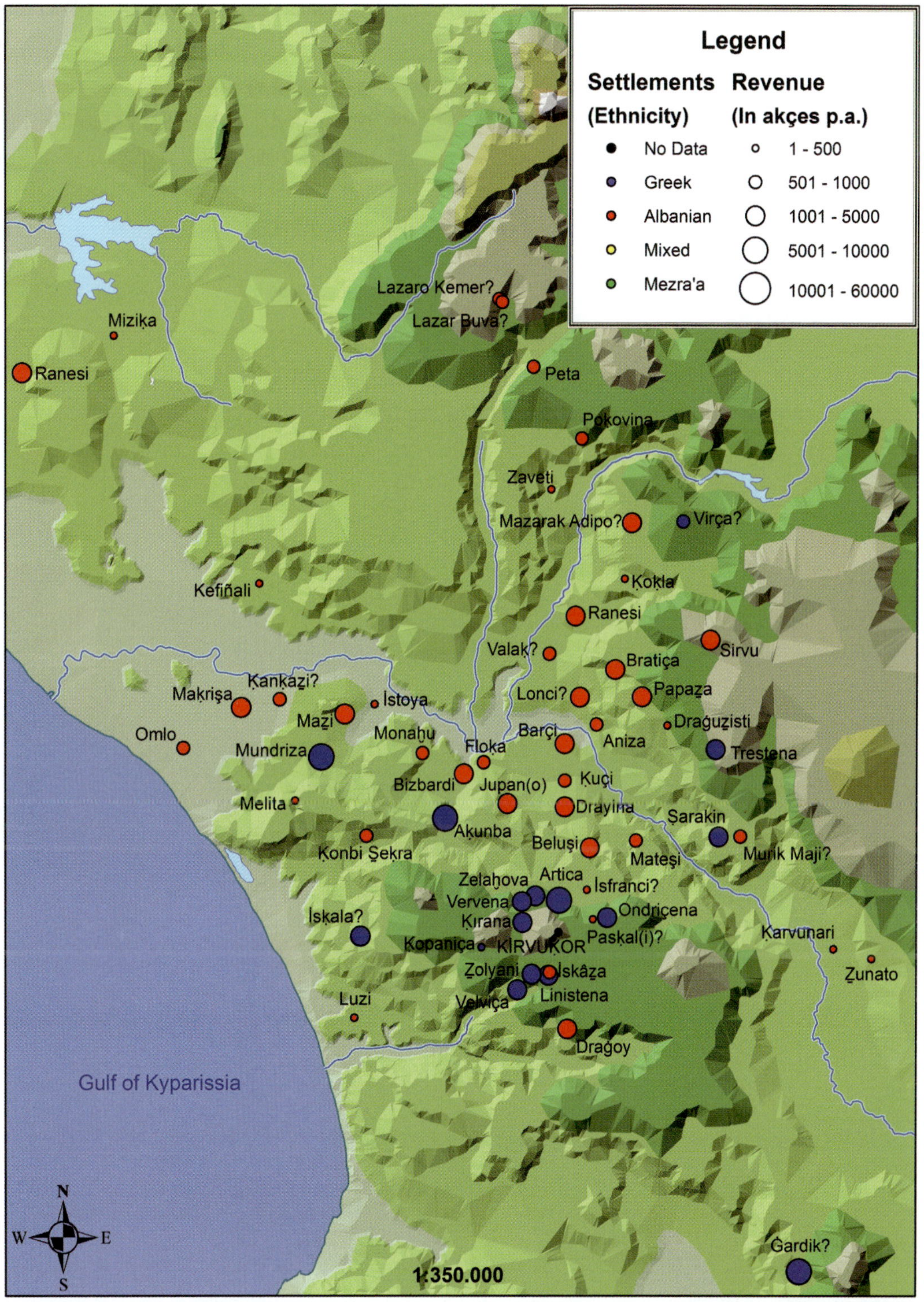

Designed by G.C. Liakopoulos

17 Nāḥiyyet-i Arḳadya (Kyparissia)
Demographic Distribution

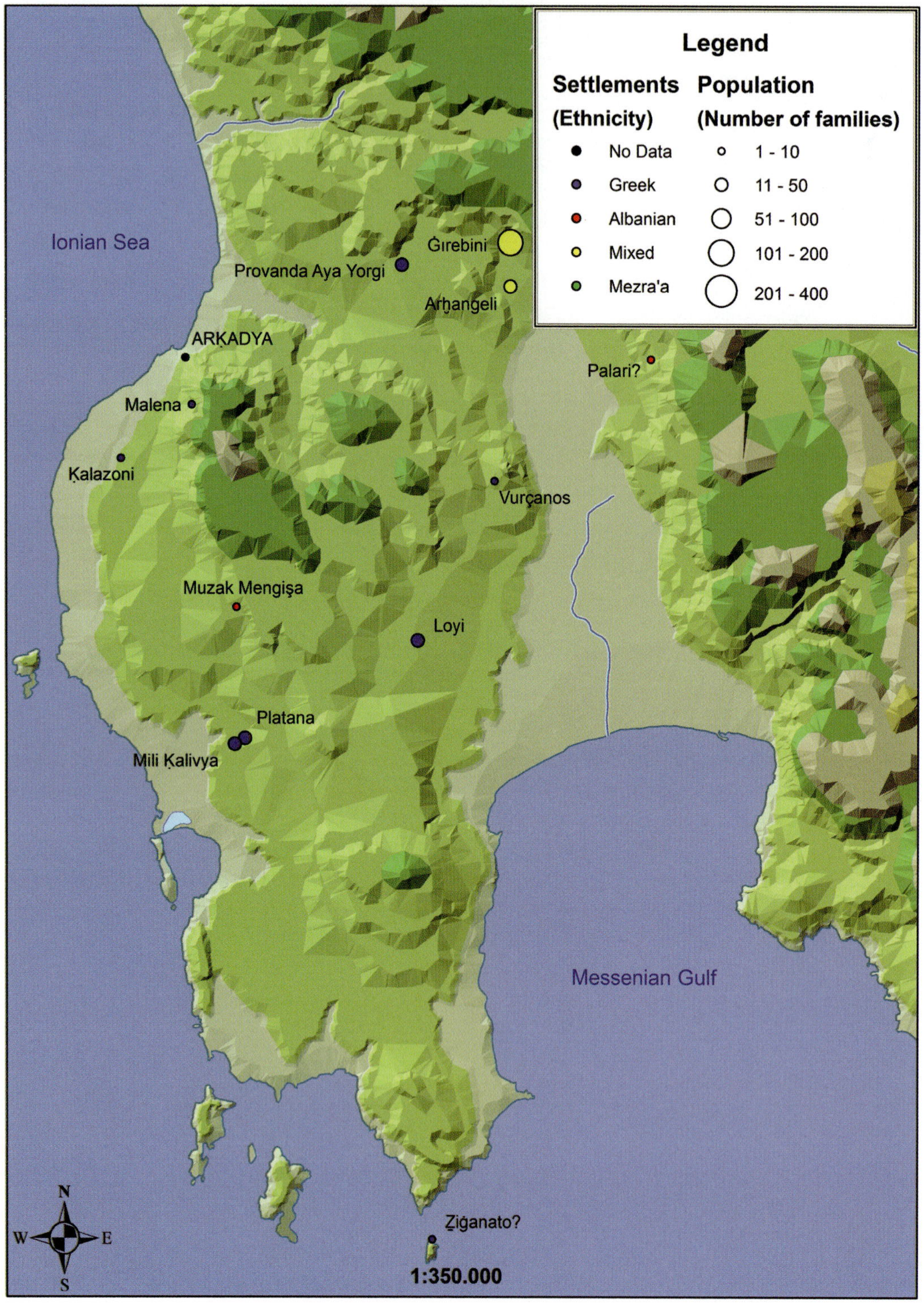

Designed by G.C. Liakopoulos

18 Nāḥiyyet-i Arḳadya (Kyparissia)
Economic Distribution

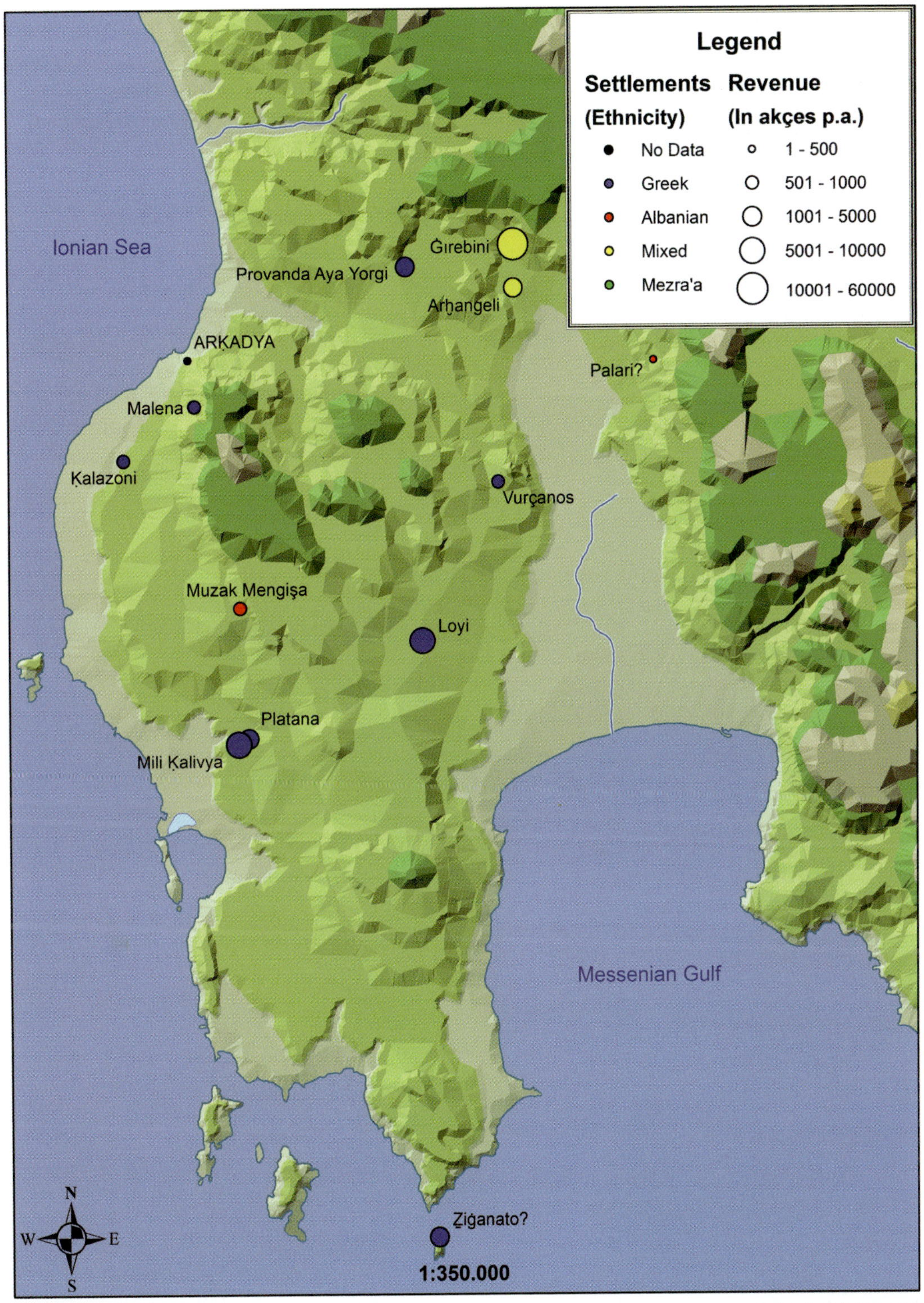

Designed by G.C. Liakopoulos

19 Nāḥiyyet-i Londar (Leontari)
Demographic Distribution

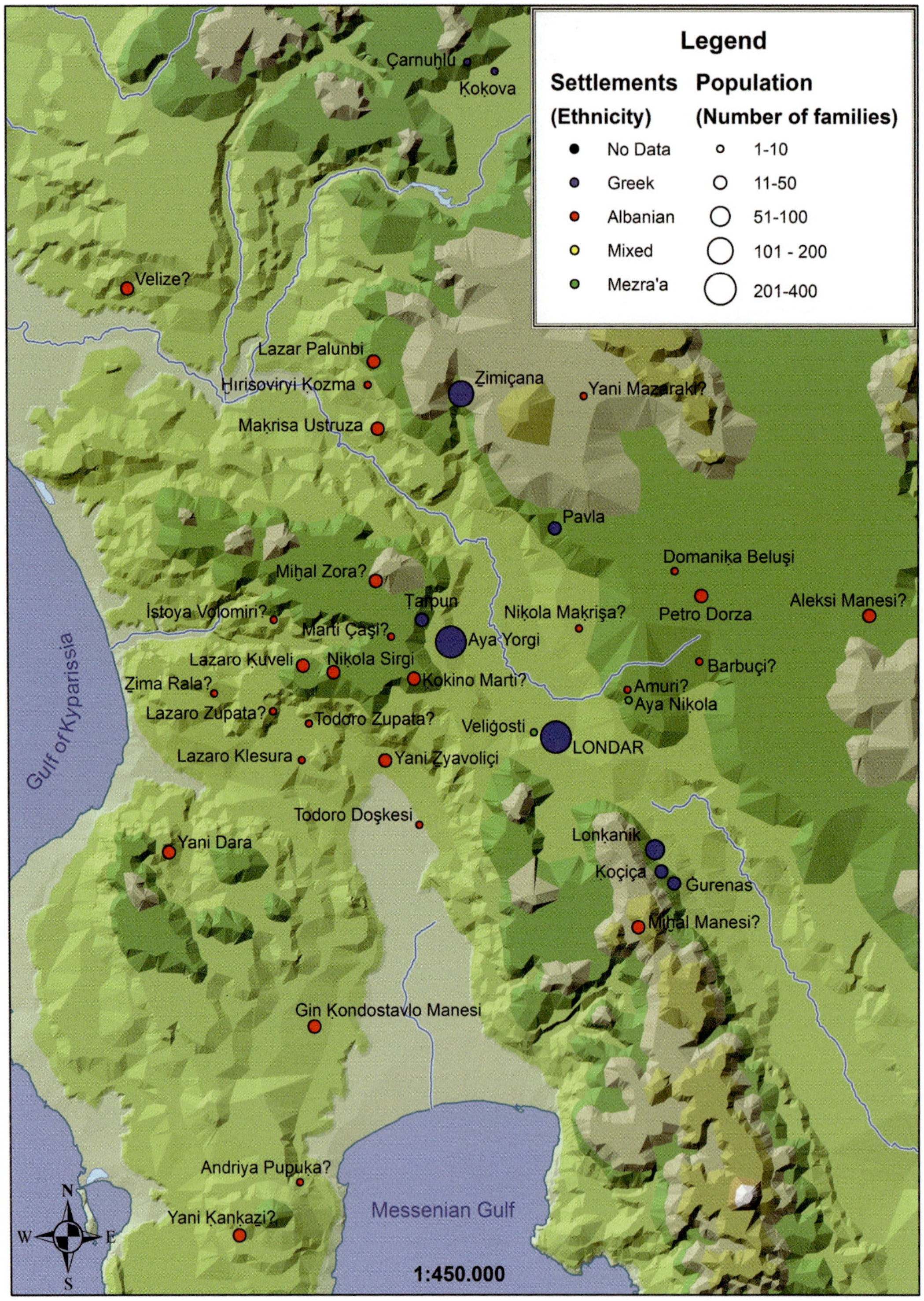

Designed by G.C. Liakopoulos

20 Nāḥiyyet-i Londar (Leontari)
Economic Distribution

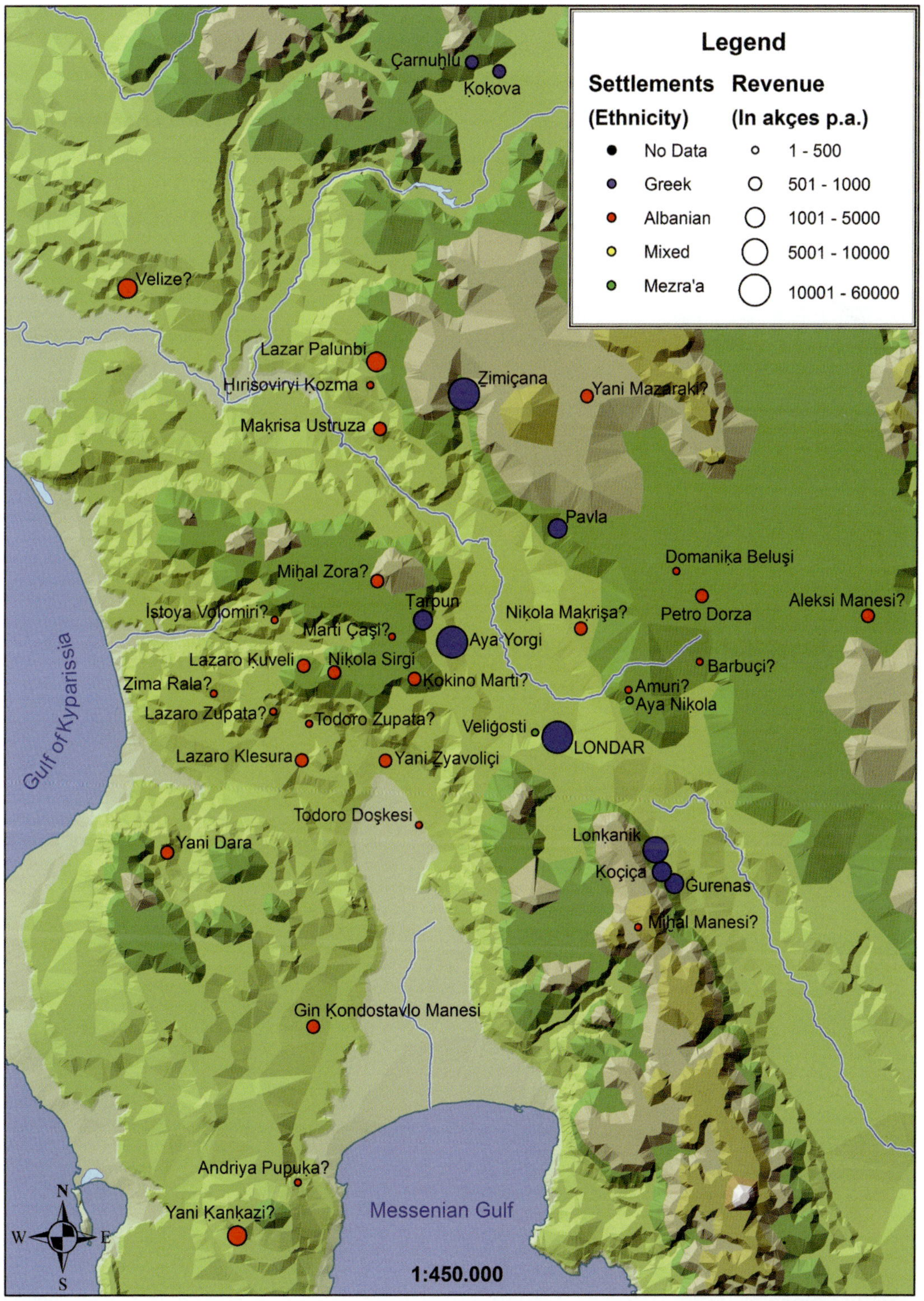

Designed by G.C. Liakopoulos

21 Nāḥiyyet-i Ḳorişos (Korinthos)
Demographic Distribution

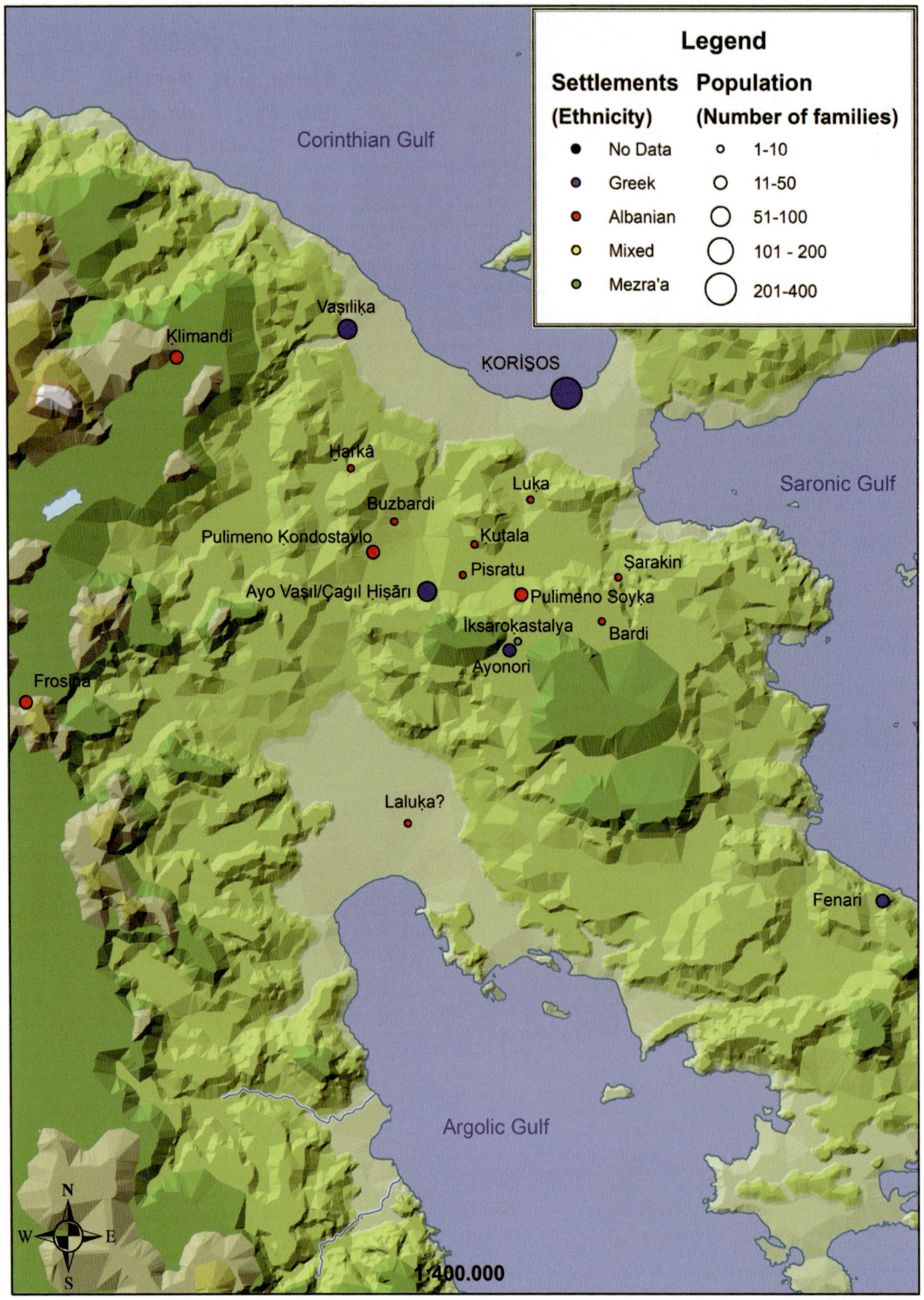

Designed by G.C. Liakopoulos

22 Nāḫiyyet-i Ḳoriṣos (Korinthos)
Economic Distribution

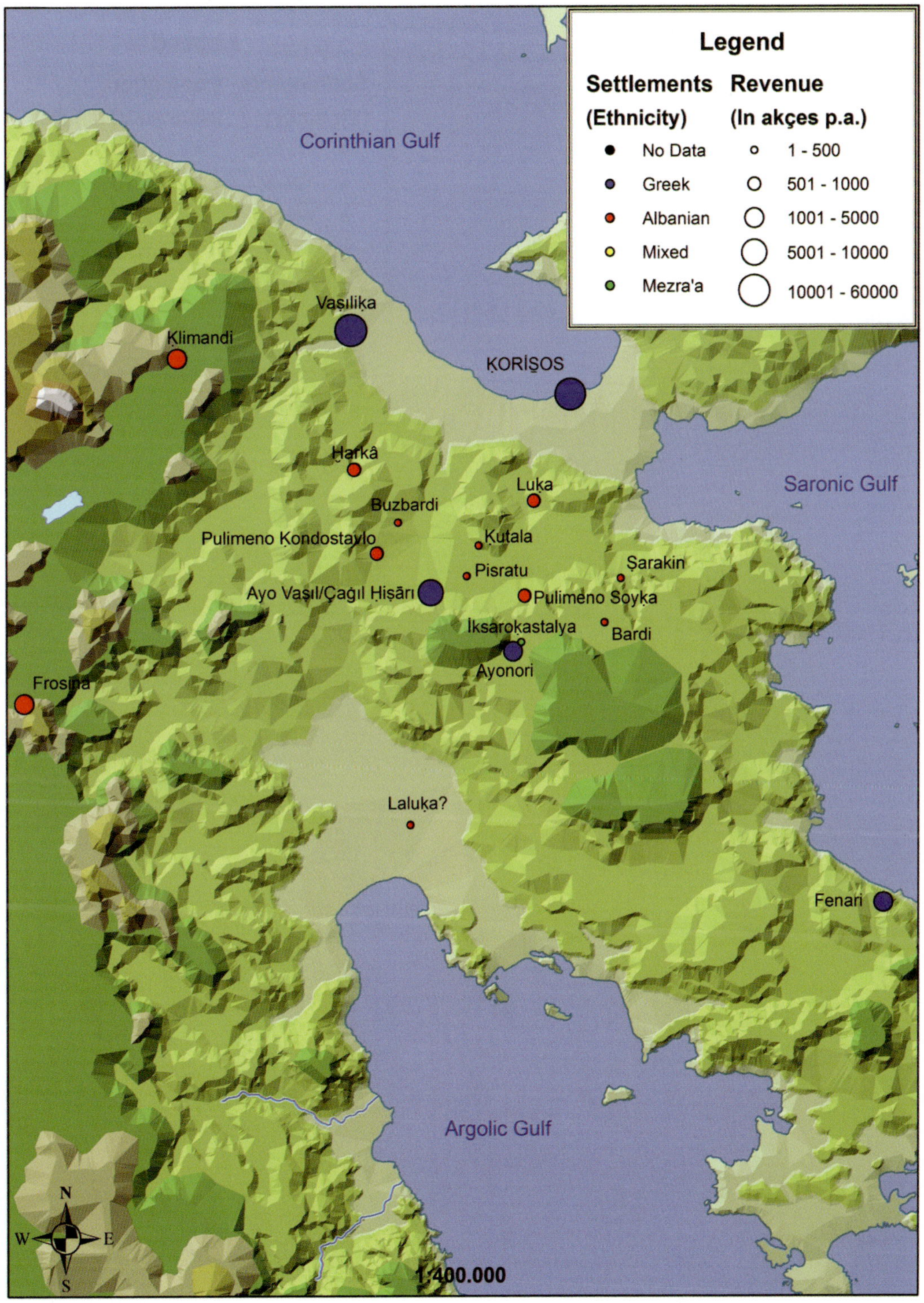

Designed by G.C. Liakopoulos

23 Nāḫiyyet-i Balya Badra (Patra) Demographic Distribution

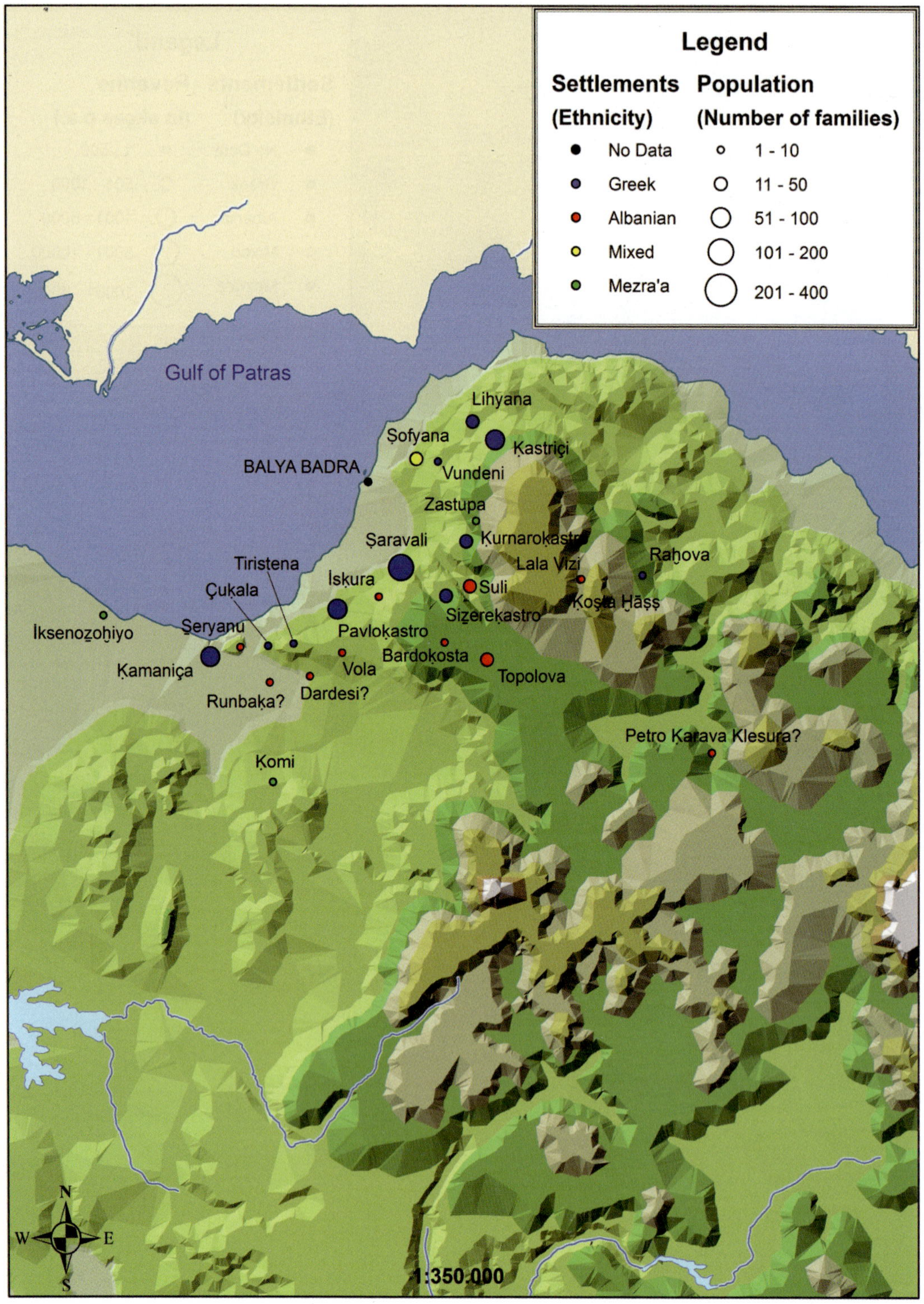

Designed by G.C. Liakopoulos

Table 19. *District of Arḳadya (Kyparissia)*[i].

			Provanda Aya Yorgi	Ẓiğanato	Vurçanos	Ġırebini	Arḫangeli	Loyi	Platana	Mili Ḳalivya	Palari	Platoḳomati	Meġaliç[ii]	Malena	Ḳalazoni	Ḳozomuli[iii]	Muzak Mengişa	Gerbesi	total
inhabitants		households	13	10	5	113[iv]	27[v]	42	13	15	2	4	-	5	7	-	9	21	286
		bachelors	-	-	2	5	1	19	4	-	-	-	-	-	-	-	3	3	37
		widows	2	-	-	4	-	5	-	2	-	-	-	-	2	-	-	3	18
taxes *per capita*		ispence	337	250	175	2939	605	1555	425	387	40	100	-	125	187	-	240	498	7863
		ʿarūsī	15	10	-	120	30	50	15	15	-	-	-	10	10	-	-	-	275
ḫāṣṣa	vineyards	dönüm	35	10	2	8	-	7	14	42	-	1	2	1.5	3	3	-	-	128.5
		akçe	2588	750	325	1200	-	1050	1050	3150	-	150	150	225	225	225	-	-	11088
	olive trees	trees	301	152	55	-	-	153	375	183	-	10	20	40	20	30	-	-	1339
		akçe	142	86	32	-	-	90	225	124	-	7	18	23	12	18	-	-	777
	walnut trees	trees	-	-	-	-	-	3	-	-	-	-	-	-	-	-	-	-	3
		akçe	-	-	-	-	-	5	-	-	-	-	-	-	-	-	-	-	5
	fruit trees	trees	-	9	4	32	-	-	-	22	-	-	-	4	-	-	-	-	71
		akçe	-	20	10	60	-	-	-	50	-	-	-	10	-	-	-	-	150
	mulberry trees	trees	-	-	-	50	-	-	-	-	-	-	-	-	-	-	-	-	50
		akçe	-	-	-	250	-	-	-	-	-	-	-	-	-	-	-	-	250
	oil presses	number	1	-	-	-	-	1	-	-	-	-	-	-	-	-	-	-	2
		akçe	100	-	-	-	-	50	-	-	-	-	-	-	-	-	-	-	150
	watermills	number	-	-	-	-	-	1	-	4	-	-	-	1	-	-	-	-	6
		akçe	-	-	-	-	-	-	-	900	-	-	-	100	-	-	-	-	1000
	fish-farms	number	-	1	-	-	-	-	1	-	-	-	-	-	-	-	-	-	2
		akçe	-	90[vi] [360]	-	-	-	-	250	-	-	-	-	-	-	-	-	-	340 [610]
watermills held in common		number	-	-	-	-	-	1	-	-	-	-	-	-	-	-	-	-	1
		akçe	-	-	-	-	-	120[vii]	-	-	-	-	-	-	-	-	-	-	120
tithe (in akçes)		flax	20	30	20	300	60	100	-	50	20	-	-	-	-	20	-	40	660
		vineyards	1090	220	50	1110	80	780	820	180	-	120	-	80	102	-	-	-	4632
		wheat	250	300	150	3200	950	1400	400	300	100	100	100	150	143	100	300	600	8543
		barley	65	46	23	489	145	221	64	48	15	15	-	23	24	-	48	96	1322
		olive oil	23	32	33	-	-	60	178	-	-	8	-	15	5	-	-	-	354
		fruits	-	14	-	-	-	-	79	2	-	8	-	2	-	-	-	-	105
		cotton	-	20	-	100	-	-	-	-	-	-	-	-	-	-	-	30	150
		honey	-	-	-	121	13	35	-	-	-	-	-	-	-	-	-	-	169
		silk	-	-	-	77	-	-	6	-	-	-	-	-	-	-	-	-	83
units (in akçes)		wine	-	56	5	150	-	100	100	-	-	-	-	-	-	-	-	-	411
		swine	-	-	-	9	18	4	-	-	-	-	-	-	-	-	-	14	45
watermills (mülk)		number	-	-	-	3	-	1	1	-	-	-	-	-	-	-	-	-	5
		akçe	-	-	-	190	-	50	30	-	-	-	-	-	-	-	-	-	270
		total	4630	1924[viii]	823	10315[ix]	1901	5670	3642[x]	5206[xi]	175	508	268	763	708	363	588	1278	38762[xii]
muḳāṭaʿa (imperial)		salt-pans	-	100	-	-	-	-	200	200	-	-	-	-	-	-	-	-	500
		rice fields	-	-	-	500	-	-	-	-	-	-	-	-	-	-	-	-	500

[i] A similar table has been published by Alexandropoulos 1978.
[ii] This *mezraʿa* is mentioned as deserted (*ḫāliyye*), cultivated by outsiders.
[iii] This *mezraʿa* is mentioned as deserted (*ḫāliyye*), cultivated by outsiders.
[iv] 106 of them were Greek and 7 Albanian.
[v] 9 of them were Greek and the remaining 18 households and 1 bachelor belonged to the Albanian community.
[vi] ¼ of its revenue was collected by the Ottoman governor of the Peloponnese and ¾ by Venice, its total amounting to 360 *akçes*.
[vii] 100 (½) of which were *ḫāṣṣa* and 20 (½) belonged to Papaandriya Rondaki.
[viii] Not including the sultan's *muḳāṭaʿa* of the salt-pan, estimated at 100 *akçes*/year.
[ix] Not including the sultan's *muḳāṭaʿa* of the rice field, estimated at 500 *akçes*/year.
[x] Not including the sultan's *muḳāṭaʿa* of the salt-pan, estimated at 200 *akçes*/year.
[xi] Not including the sultan's *muḳāṭaʿa* of the salt-pan, estimated at 200 *akçes*/year.
[xii] The total revenue of Arḳadya was 40,032 *akçes*, of which 1,000 *akçes* were held in imperial demesne and 270 *akçes* were farmed by Venice.

Table 20. *District of Londar (Leontari).*

			Londar	Maji	Aya Yorgi	Lonḳanik	Ġurenas	Ḳoçiça	İksifya	Yani Zyavoliçi	Marti Helmi	Yani Evzenati	Aleksi Manesi	Yorgi Maji	Yani Lata	Niḳola Maḳrişa	Marti Plaşa
inhabitants		households	186[i]	9	226	78	29	21	10	10	11	7	17	10	24	10	8
		bachelors	1	-	41	4	-	2	-	3	1	2	1	3	10	1	-
		widows	18	-	16	6	2	3	4	2	1	2	1	1	5	-	1
taxes *per capita*		ispence	4758	180	6771	2086	737	593	224	272	246	192	366	266	710	220	166
		ʿarūsī	-	-	-	-	-	-	-	-	-	-	-	-	-	-	-
ḫāṣṣa	vineyards	dönüm	40	-	68	3	6	4	-	-	-	-	-	-	-	-	-
		akçe	3600	-	5280	360	540	480	-	-	-	-	-	-	-	-	-
	fruit trees	trees	-	-	8	-	-	-	-	-	-	-	-	-	-	-	-
		akçe	-	-	15	-	-	-	-	-	-	-	-	-	-	-	-
	mulberry trees	trees	-	-	217	10	50	20	-	-	-	-	-	-	-	-	-
		akçe	-	-	1050	50	250	100	-	-	-	-	-	-	-	-	-
	olive trees	trees	-	-	8	12	60	10	-	-	-	-	-	-	-	-	-
		akçe	-	-	9	6	34	6	-	-	-	-	-	-	-	-	-
	walnut trees	trees	-	-	-	-	11	-	-	-	-	-	-	-	-	-	-
		akçe	-	-	-	-	20	-	-	-	-	-	-	-	-	-	-
	watermills	number	-	-	2	-	-	-	-	-	-	-	-	-	-	-	-
		akçe	-	-	800	-	-	-	-	-	-	-	-	-	-	-	-
tithe (in akçes)		flax	325	15	200	150	80	50	50	20	50	15	30	20	40	15	10
		vineyards	14768	-	7680	2672	832	752	-	-	-	-	-	-	-	-	-
		wheat	2600	300	6900	1600	500	500	200	300	200	200	400	300	550	250	200
		barley	393	45	1035	240	75	75	32	48	32	31	61	45	85	40	32
		silk	-	-	178	26	37	61	-	-	-	-	-	-	-	-	-
		fruits	-	-	14	-	9	-	-	-	-	-	-	-	-	-	-
		olive oil	-	-	-	21	8	10	-	-	-	-	-	-	-	-	-
		honey	-	-	52	-	-	-	-	-	-	-	-	-	-	-	-
		kitchen gardens	-	-	-	-	-	-	-	-	-	-	-	-	-	-	-
units (in akçes)		wine	1200	-	960	330	100	90	-	-	-	-	-	-	-	-	-
		swine	18	85	73	29	-	-	-	-	-	20	-	60	33	9	20
watermills (mülk)		number	8	-	10	3	-	1	-	-	-	-	-	-	-	-	-
		akçe	380	-	410	150	-	30	-	-	-	-	-	-	-	-	-
		total	31542	625	31427	7720	3222	2747	506	640	528	458	857	691	1418	534	428
muḳāṭaʿa (tīmār)		niyābet and market tax	3500	-	-	-	-	-	-	-	-	-	-	-	-	-	-

[i] Including one tax exempt household (*müsellem*).

Table 20. *District of Londar (Leontari).*

			Domanịka Beluşi	Dimitri Maçuki	Duḳa Plaşa	Miḫal Manesi	Miḫal Zora	Pavlo Doçi	Mangişa Burlaşa	Yorgi Muzaki	Ġulyamu Argiroplu	Todoro Zupata	İlya Maji	Lazaro Zupata	Petro Dorza	Lala Ẕyavoliçi	Ẕupano Buryalişa
inhabitants		households	5	5	4	11	10	4	11	7	12	7	4	7	19	7	8
		bachelors	2	1	1	-	1	-	1	-	1	-	-	-	-	2	-
		widows	1	1	1	-	1	1	1	-	1	1	1	-	2	1	-
taxes *per capita*		ispence	146	126	106	220	226	86	246	140	266	146	86	140	392	186	160
		ʿarūsī	-	-	-	-	-	-	-	-	-	-	-	-	-	-	-
ḫāṣṣa	vineyards	dönüm	-	-	-	-	-	-	-	-	-	-	-	-	-	-	-
		akçe	-	-	-	-	-	-	-	-	-	-	-	-	-	-	-
	fruit trees	trees	-	-	-	-	-	-	-	-	-	-	-	-	-	-	-
		akçe	-	-	-	-	-	-	-	-	-	-	-	-	-	-	-
	mulberry trees	trees	-	-	-	-	-	-	-	-	-	-	-	-	-	-	-
		akçe	-	-	-	-	-	-	-	-	-	-	-	-	-	-	-
	olive trees	trees	-	-	-	-	-	-	-	-	-	-	-	-	-	-	-
		akçe	-	-	-	-	-	-	-	-	-	-	-	-	-	-	-
	walnut trees	trees	-	-	-	-	-	-	-	-	-	-	-	-	-	-	-
		akçe	-	-	-	-	-	-	-	-	-	-	-	-	-	-	-
	watermills	number	-	-	-	-	-	-	-	-	-	-	-	-	-	-	-
		akçe	-	-	-	-	-	-	-	-	-	-	-	-	-	-	-
tithe (in akçes)		flax	10	15	10	20	20	20	20	15	20	20	10	20	30	20	10
		vineyards	-	-	-	-	-	-	-	-	-	-	-	-	-	-	-
		wheat	100	100	100	200	200	100	200	100	300	150	100	150	300	300	300
		barley	16	15	16	32	32	16	32	16	48	24	16	24	48	46	46
		silk	-	-	-	-	-	-	-	-	-	-	-	-	-	-	-
		fruits	-	-	-	-	-	-	-	-	-	-	-	-	-	-	-
		olive oil	-	-	-	-	-	-	-	-	-	-	-	-	-	-	-
		honey	-	-	-	-	-	-	-	-	-	-	-	-	-	-	-
		kitchen gardens	-	-	-	-	-	-	-	-	-	-	-	-	-	-	-
units (in akçes)		wine	-	-	-	-	-	-	-	-	-	-	-	-	-	-	-
		swine	12	-	8	3	45	16	30	13	24	-	2	-	-	25	42
watermills (mülk)		number	-	-	-	-	-	-	-	-	-	-	-	-	-	-	-
		akçe	-	-	-	-	-	-	-	-	-	-	-	-	-	-	-
		total	284	256	240	475	523	238	528	284	658	340	214	334	770	577	558
muḳāṭaʿa (tīmār)		niyābet and market tax	-	-	-	-	-	-	-	-	-	-	-	-	-	-	-

Table 20. *District of Londar (Leontari).*

			Yani Jura	Todoro Doşkesi	İstoya Volomiri	Yani Mazaraki	Niḳola Sirgi	Lazar Palunbi	Yorgi Mujaki	Andriya Pupuḳa	Yani Ḳanḳazi	Lazaro Klesura	Marti Çaşi	Ḳokino Marti	Barbuçi	Ḫrisoviryi Ḳozma	Trima İşpata
inhabitants		hâne	5	3	3	8	13	17	7	4	14	6	8	15	4	4	9
		mücerred	-	-	-	1	5	4	-	-	-	14	-	-	-	1	-
		bîve	-	-	-	-	-	3	2	-	-	1	2	4	-	-	-
taxes *per capita*		ispence	100	60	60	180	380	438	152	80	280	406	172	324	80	100	180
		ʻarûsî	-	-	-	-	-	-	-	-	-	-	-	-	-	-	-
ḫāṣṣa	vineyards	dönüm	-	-	-	-	-	-	-	-	-	-	-	-	-	-	-
		aḳçe	-	-	-	-	-	-	-	-	-	-	-	-	-	-	-
	fruit trees	trees	-	-	-	-	-	-	-	-	-	-	-	-	-	-	-
		aḳçe	-	-	-	-	-	-	-	-	-	-	-	-	-	-	-
	mulberry trees	trees	-	-	-	-	-	-	-	-	-	-	-	-	-	-	-
		aḳçe	-	-	-	-	-	-	-	-	-	-	-	-	-	-	-
	olive trees	trees	-	-	-	-	-	-	-	-	-	-	-	-	-	-	-
		aḳçe	-	-	-	-	-	-	-	-	-	-	-	-	-	-	-
	walnut trees	trees	-	-	-	-	-	-	-	-	-	-	-	-	-	-	-
		aḳçe	-	-	-	-	-	-	-	-	-	-	-	-	-	-	-
	watermills	number	-	-	-	-	-	-	-	-	-	-	-	-	-	-	-
		aḳçe	-	-	-	-	-	-	-	-	-	-	-	-	-	-	-
tithe (in aḳçes)		flax	10	10	-	20	30	50	20	10	60	50	20	30	10	10	20
		vineyards	-	-	-	-	-	-	-	-	-	-	-	-	-	-	-
		wheat	100	100	100	200	300	500	200	100	800	200	150	300	100	100	200
		barley	16	16	15	31	48	80	31	16	120	31	24	47	15	16	31
		silk	-	-	-	-	-	-	-	-	-	-	-	-	-	-	-
		fruits	-	-	-	-	-	-	-	-	-	-	-	-	-	-	-
		olive oil	-	-	-	-	-	-	-	-	-	-	-	-	-	-	-
		honey	-	-	-	-	-	-	-	-	-	-	-	-	-	-	-
		kitchen gardens	-	-	-	-	-	-	-	-	-	-	-	-	-	-	-
units (in aḳçes)		wine	-	-	-	-	-	-	-	-	-	-	-	-	-	-	-
		swine	-	-	-	80	96	19	9	11	10	20	5	16	11	8	8
watermills (mülk)		number	-	-	-	-	-	-	-	-	-	-	-	-	-	-	-
		aḳçe	-	-	-	-	-	-	-	-	-	-	-	-	-	-	-
		total	226	186	175	511	854	1087	412	217	1270	707	371	717	216	234	439
muḳāṭaʻa (tīmār)		niyābet and market tax	-	-	-	-	-	-	-	-	-	-	-	-	-	-	-

Table 20. *District of Londar (Leontari).*

		Ẕima Rala	Yani Dara	Yorgi Manesi	Gin Ḳondostavlo Manesi	Lazaro Ḳuveli	Velize	Maḳrisa Ustruza	Ẕimiçana	Ḳoḳova	Çarnuḫlu[ii]	Ṭarpun	Amuri[iii]	Veliġosti[iv]	Pavla	total
inhabitants	households	3	12	2	13	12	20	16	142	9	10	13	3	-	11	1163
	bachelors	-	3	-	-	-	-	-	31	-	3	3	1	-	9	153
	widows	-	2	3	-	1	1	-	13	1	-	1	-	-	-	108
taxes *per capita*	ispence	60	312	58	260	246	406	320	4528	186	325	406	100	-	500	31158
	ʿarūsī	-	-	-	-	-	-	-	-	-	10	15	-	-	10	35
ḫāṣṣa: vineyards	dönüm	-	-	-	-	-	-	-	-	1	-	3	-	-	11	136
	aḳçe	-	-	-	-	-	-	-	-	150	-	180	-	-	660	11250
ḫāṣṣa: fruit trees	trees	-	-	-	-	-	-	-	-	-	-	-	-	-	100	108
	aḳçe	-	-	-	-	-	-	-	-	-	-	-	-	-	200	215
ḫāṣṣa: mulberry trees	trees	-	-	-	-	-	-	-	-	-	4	6	-	-	-	307
	aḳçe	-	-	-	-	-	-	-	-	-	20	30	-	-	-	1500
ḫāṣṣa: olive trees	trees	-	-	-	-	-	-	-	-	-	-	-	-	-	-	90
	aḳçe	-	-	-	-	-	-	-	-	-	-	-	-	-	-	55
ḫāṣṣa: walnut trees	trees	-	-	-	-	-	-	-	-	-	-	-	-	-	-	11
	aḳçe	-	-	-	-	-	-	-	-	-	-	-	-	-	-	20
ḫāṣṣa: watermills	number	-	-	-	-	-	-	-	-	-	-	-	-	-	-	2
	aḳçe	-	-	-	-	-	-	-	-	-	-	-	-	-	-	800
tithe (in aḳçes)	flax	-	30	10	50	30	50	30	200	20	15	-	-	-	20	2135
	vineyards	-	-	-	-	-	-	-	1120	100	56	224	144	-	584	28932
	wheat	100	250	50	450	350	500	300	3500	350	300	500	100	200	450	28550
	barley	16	40	8	72	54	80	48	548	53	48	75	15	30	70	4390
	silk	-	-	-	-	-	-	-	82	-	7	17	-	-	-	408
	fruits	-	-	-	-	-	-	-	15	2	6	-	-	-	40	86
	olive oil	-	-	-	-	-	-	-	-	-	-	-	-	-	-	39
	honey	-	-	-	-	-	-	-	-	-	-	-	-	-	-	52
	kitchen gardens	-	-	-	-	-	-	-	-	-	-	-	-	50	-	50
units (in aḳçes)	wine	-	-	-	-	-	-	-	150	10	-	30	-	-	70	2940
	swine	20	55	-	4	3	29	7	4	10	-	-	-	-	5	997
watermills (mülk)	number	-	-	-	-	-	-	-	6	-	-	-	-	-	-	28
	aḳçe	-	-	-	-	-	-	-	300	-	-	-	-	-	-	1270
	total	196	687	126	836	683	1065	705	10447	881	787	1477	359	280	2609	118382[v]
muḳāṭaʿa (tīmār)	niyābet and market tax	-	-	-	-	-	-	-	-	-	-	-	-	-	-	3500

[ii] The deserted (*ḫāliyye*) *mezraʿa* of İvrato Ḳuçi Ḳonbi Şeḳra belonged to this village.
[iii] The deserted (*ḫāliyye*) *mezraʿa* of Aya Niḳola belonged to this village.
[iv] This *mezraʿa* that belonged to the town of Londar was recorded as deserted (*ḫāliyye*), cultivated by outsiders.
[v] The TT10 register gives a total of 113,647 *aḳçe*s; this amount should be corrected to 113,657 *aḳçe*s.

Chart 15. *District of Londar (Leontari).*

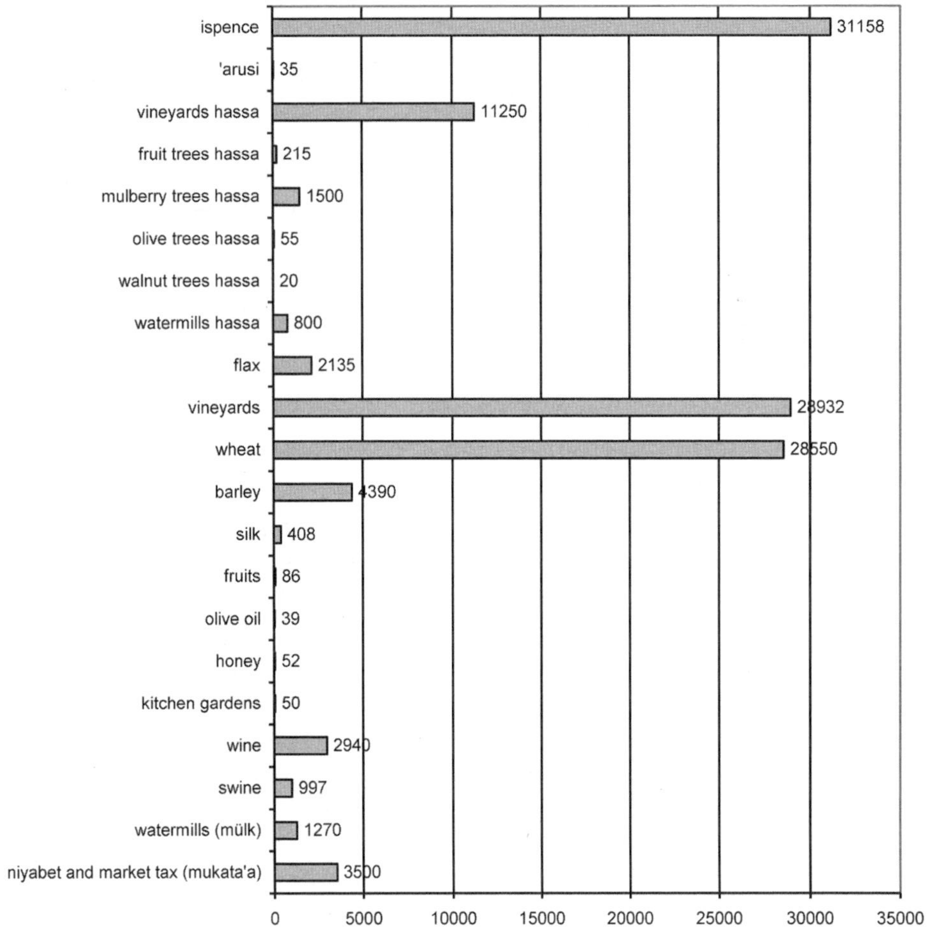

Table 21. *District of Ḳorişos (Corinth).*

			Ḳorişos	Vaşlıḳa[i]	Ayo Vaşıl/ Çağıl Ḥiṣārı[ii]	Pulimeno Ḳondostavlo[iii]	Buzbardi	Ḫarkā	Ḳutala	Ayonori[iv]	Liḳuresi	Ḳlimandi	Pulimeno Soyḳa	Fenari	Bardi	Ḳunbaki	Biçi
inhabitants		households	328	83	80	15	7	9	1	40	7	13	14	22	9	12	5
		bachelors	45	7	12	1	1	-	-	7	-	-	-	-	1	2	-
		widows	64	10	4	-	-	1	-	4	-	-	-	-	-	-	-
taxes *per capita*		ispence	-	2310	2324	320	160	186	20	1199	140	260	280	550	200	280	100
		ʿarūsī	-	100	100	15	10	10	-	-	-	-	-	-	-	-	-
		niyābet	2000	-	-	-	-	-	-	-	-	-	-	-	-	-	-
ḫāṣṣa	vineyards	dönüm	12	3	4	-	-	-	-	-	-	2	-	-	-	-	-
		aḳçe	720	360	480	-	-	-	-	-	-	240	-	-	-	-	-
	fruit trees	trees	-	-	23	-	-	-	-	-	-	-	-	-	-	-	-
		aḳçe	-	-	50	-	-	-	-	-	-	-	-	-	-	-	-
	resin trees	trees	1000[v]	-	-	-	-	-	-	-	-	-	-	-	-	-	-
		aḳçe	500	-	-	-	-	-	-	-	-	-	-	-	-	-	-
tithe (in aḳçes)		flax	380	100	200	20	-	-	-	150	20	20	20	50	15	20	10
		vineyards	7191	1888	2014[vi]	16	-	-	-	676[vii]	-	112	-	96	-	-	-
		kitchen gardens	200	-	-	-	-	-	-	-	-	-	-	-	-	-	-
		wheat	10400	4000	2500	400	200	400	50	1700	100	300	500	800	200	400	200
		barley	1592	620	387	64	32	62	8	267	16	48	80	127	32	64	32
		silk	-	-	-	-	-	-	-	-	-	15	-	-	-	-	-
		fruits		339	91	-	-	-	-	15	-	3	-	7	-	-	-
		cotton	200	200	50	-	-	-	-	-	-	-	-	-	-	-	-
		honey	28	22	60	-	-	-	-	25	-	-	-	139	35	15	3
units (in aḳçes)		wine	740	240	200	-	-	-	-	100	-	15	-	10	-	-	-
		swine	-	-	8	-	-	-	-	-	-	-	-	-	8	6	1
watermills (mülk)		number	3	2	2	-	-	-	-	-	-	-	-	1	-	-	-
		aḳçe	200	120	80	-	-	-	-	-	-	-	-	40	-	-	
		total	27151[viii]	10749[ix]	8544	835	402	658	78	4132	276	1013	880	1819	490	785	346
muḳāṭaʿa (imperial)		salt-pans	120	200	-	-	-	-	-	-	-	-	-	-	-	-	-
muḳāṭaʿa (tīmār)		market tax,	3000	-	-	-	-	-	-	-	-	-	-	-	-	-	-
		custom dues and transit duty															
		bitter orange groves	-	450	-	-	-	-	-	-	-	-	-	-	-	-	-

[i] The deserted (*ḫāliyye*) *mezraʿa* of Ḳuvara belonged to this village.
[ii] The deserted (*ḫāliyye*) *mezraʿa*s of Petro Ḫayḳal, Manesi, Sermorini and Ḳalo İstemati belonged to this village.
[iii] The deserted (*ḫāliyye*) *mezraʿa* of Piça belonged to this village.
[iv] The deserted (*ḫāliyye*) *mezraʿa* of İksaroḳastalya belonged to this village.
[v] Approximately.
[vi] Of which 550 *aḳçe*s derived from dry raisins and 1,464 *aḳçe*s from grape-must.
[vii] Of which 20 *aḳçe*s derived from dry raisins and 656 *aḳçe*s from grape-must.
[viii] Not including the *ispence*, the tax exempt inhabitants (*muʿāf ve müsellem*) and the salt-pan revenues.
[ix] Not including the salt-pan revenues.

Table 21. *District of Ḳoris̱os (Corinth).*

			Ṣarakin	Luḳa	Laluḳa	Frati	Pisratu	Frosina	total
inhabitants		households	6	10	5	4	5	32	707
		bachelors	1	-	-	-	1	5	83
		widows	1	-	-	-	-	-	84
taxes *per capita*		ispence	146	200	100	80	120	740	9715
		ʿarūsī	-	-	-	-	-	35	270
		niyābet	-	-	-	-	-	-	2000
ḫāṣṣa	vineyards	dönüm	-	-	-	-	-	-	21
		aḳçe	-	-	-	-	-	-	1800
	fruit trees	trees	-	-	-	-	-	-	23
		aḳçe	-	-	-	-	-	-	50
	resin trees	trees	-	-	-	-	-	-	1000
		aḳçe	-	-	-	-	-	-	500
tithe (in aḳçes)		flax	10	20	10	-	10	-	1055
		vineyards	-	-	-	-	-	-	11993
		kitchen gardens	-	-	-	-	-	-	200
		wheat	250	250	250	100	150	1300	24450
		barley	40	40	40	16	24	203	3794
		silk	-	-	-	-	-	-	15
		fruits	-	-	-	-	-	-	455
		cotton	-	-	-	-	-	-	450
		honey	6	-	-	-	-	-	333
units (in aḳçes)		wine	-	-	-	-	-	-	1305
		swine	3	1	7	22	3	22	81
watermills (mülk)		number	-	-	-	-	-	3	11
		aḳçe	-	-	-	-	-	150	590
		total	455	511	407	218	307	2450	62506[x]
muḳāṭaʿa (imperial)		salt-pans	-	-	-	-	-	-	320
muḳāṭaʿa (tīmār)		market tax, custom dues and transit duty	-	-	-	-	-	-	3000
		bitter orange groves	-	-	-	-	-	-	450

[x] The total revenue of the district of Ḳoris̱os, including the salt-pans amounted to 62,826 *aḳçes*.

Chart 16. *District of Ḳoriṯos (Corinth).*

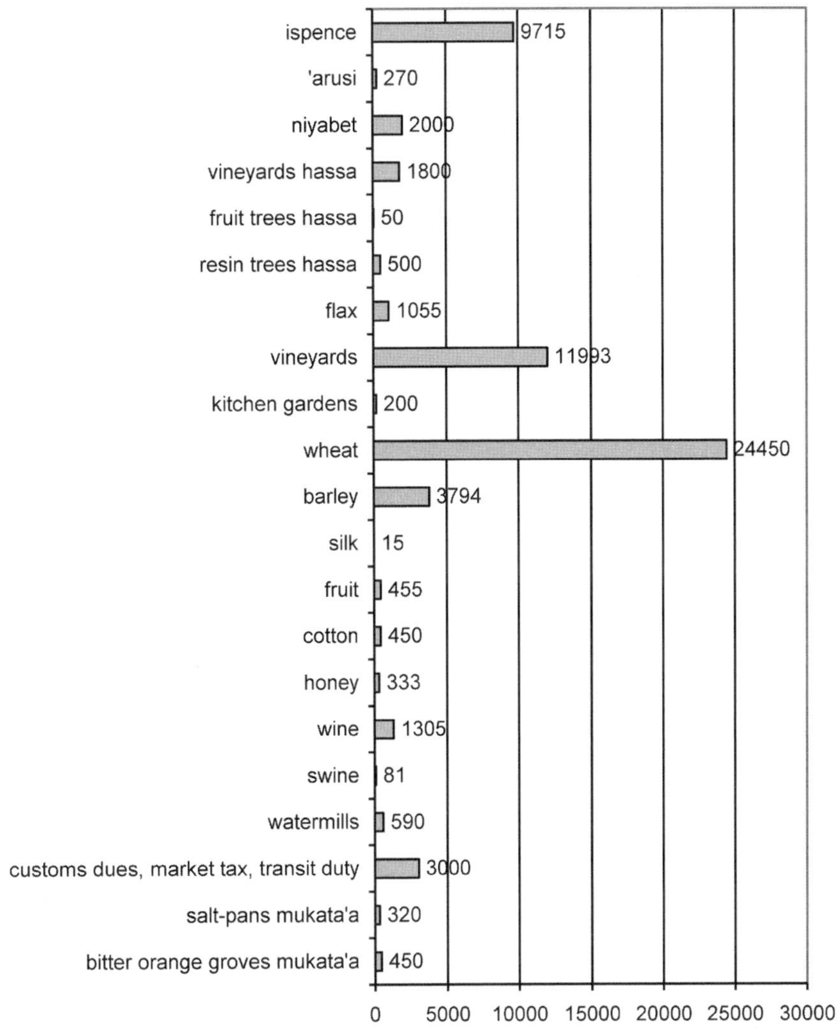

Table 22. *District of Balya Badra (Patra).*

			Şaravali	Lala Vizi	Ḳoşta Ḫāṣṣ	Ranesi	Sizereḳastro	Petro Ḳarava Klesura	Ayo Ẓimitri Liḳo Anbali	Dardesi	Klesura	Pavloḳastro[i]	Vola	İstefano Mazaraki	Ḳamaniça[ii]	Şeryanu	Runbaḳa	İzlatḳa
inhabitants		households	151	9	4	1	45	3	4	2	12	50	9	9	65	9	2	23
		bachelors	9	-	-	2	8	-	-	-	-	8	-	2	5	1	1	1
		widows	22	-	-	-	1	-	-	-	-	10	-	-	13	-	-	1
taxes *per capita*		ispence	4132	180	80	60	1331	60	80	40	240	1510	180	220	1828	200	60	486
		ʿarūsī	-	-	-	-	-	-	-	-	15	-	-	-	-	-	-	-
ḫāṣṣa	vineyards	dönüm	-	-	-	-	-	-	-	-	-	-	-	-	3	-	-	-
		aḳçe	-	-	-	-	-	-	-	-	-	-	-	-	508	-	-	-
	olive trees	trees	900	-	-	-	102	-	-	-	-	296	-	-	25	-	-	-
		aḳçe	1125	-	-	-	135	-	-	-	-	338	-	-	90	-	-	-
	fruit trees	trees	414	-	-	-	140	-	-	-	-	136	-	-	20	-	-	-
		aḳçe	550	-	-	-	70	-	-	-	-	45	-	-	20	-	-	-
	mulberry trees	trees	315	-	-	-	170	-	-	-	-	3	-	-	-	-	-	-
		aḳçe	1700	-	-	-	375	-	-	-	-	4	-	-	-	-	-	-
	oak trees	trees	-	-	-	-	-	-	-	-	-	-	-	-	-	-	-	-
		aḳçe	-	-	-	-	-	-	-	-	-	-	-	-	-	-	-	-
	kitchen gardens	number	1	-	-	-	-	-	-	-	-	1	-	-	-	-	-	-
		aḳçe	450	-	-	-	-	-	-	-	-	20	-	-	-	-	-	-
	watermills	number	-	-	-	-	-	-	-	-	-	-	-	-	-	-	-	-
		aḳçe	-	-	-	-	-	-	-	-	-	-	-	-	-	-	-	-
	fulling mills	number	2	-	-	-	-	-	-	-	-	-	-	-	-	-	-	-
		aḳçe	100	-	-	-	-	-	-	-	-	-	-	-	-	-	-	-
tithe (in aḳçes)		flax	50	-	-	-	-	-	-	-	20	200	-	15	200	-	-	-
		vineyards	8056	21	-	-	1823	90	-	-	-	2633	90	-	1812	45	33	-
		wheat	1395	325	200	100	1300	100	200	-	450	725	350	400	2225	400	100	918
		barley	195	50	31	15	195	15	32	-	72	110	50	60	338	60	15	110
		cotton	400	-	-	-	50	-	-	-	-	125	-	30	600	-	-	-
		olive oil	713	-	-	-	43	-	-	-	-	87	-	-	29	-	-	-
		fruits	133	-	-	-	9	-	-	-	-	6	-	-	26	-	-	-
		silk	153	5	-	-	3	-	-	-	-	-	-	-	-	-	-	-
		mulberries	-	-	-	-	-	-	-	-	-	-	-	-	-	-	-	-
		kitchen	39	-	-	-	-	-	-	-	-	10	-	-	-	-	-	-
		gardens																
units (in aḳçes)		wine	1125	-	-	-	194	-	-	-	-	336	-	-	270	-	-	-
		swine	-	-	-	-	-	-	-	-	-	-	-	8	19	-	-	11
watermills (mülk)		number	3	-	-	-	-	-	-	-	-	-	-	1	2	-	-	-
		aḳçe	240	-	-	-	-	-	-	-	-	-	-	80	160	-	-	-
		total	20806	581	311	175	5528	265	312	40	797	6149	670	813	8125[iii]	705	208	1525
muḳāṭaʿa (imperial)		salt-pans	-	-	-	-	-	-	-	-	-	-	-	-	7000	-	-	-
muḳāṭaʿa (tīmār)		oil presses	250	-	-	-	-	-	-	-	-	-	-	-	-	-	-	-

[i] The deserted (*ḫāliyye*) *mezraʿa* of Patura belonged to this village.
[ii] The deserted (*ḫāliyye*) *mezraʿa*s of Meliġala, Liḳuresi, Draġoti, İksenoẓoḫiyo and Ḳomi belonged to this village.
[iii] Not including the salt-pan revenue.

Table 22. *District of Balya Badra (Patra).*

			Çuḳala	Ribesi	Ḳastriçi	Lihyana[iv]	Vundeni	Şofyana	Raḫova	Buryalisa[v]	İsḳura	Ḳurnaroḳastro[vi]	Suli	Topolova	Bardoḳosta	Tiristena	total
inhabitants		households	7	2	44	16	5	33	9	3	6	31	14	32	10	6	616
		bachelors	-	-	6	1	-	6	1	-	-	9	1	2	-	-	63
		widows	-	2	7	2	1	3	1	-	-	4	-	1	-	-	68
taxes *per capita*		ispence	175	52	1292	437	131	853	256	60	120	1024	300	686	200	150	16423
		ʿarūsī	-	-	-	-	-	-	-	-	-	30	10	35	10	-	100
ḫāṣṣa	vineyards	dönüm	-	-	-	-	-	-	-	-	-	12	-	-	-	-	15
		aḳçe	-	-	-	-	-	-	-	-	-	900	-	-	-	-	1408
	olive trees	trees	-	-	-	-	5	40	-	-	-	-	-	-	-	-	1368
		aḳçe	-	-	-	-	9	63	-	-	-	-	-	-	-	-	1760
	fruit trees	trees	-	-	50	30	7	30	10	-	-	-	-	-	-	20	857
		aḳçe	-	-	100	10	15	60	20	-	-	-	-	-	-	40	930
	mulberry trees	trees	-	-	70	50	15	21	48	-	-	150	-	-	-	-	842
		aḳçe	-	-	250	210	40	44	170	-	-	200	-	-	-	-	2993
	oak trees	trees	-	-	-	-	-	-	-	1500[vii]	-	-	-	-	-	-	1500
		aḳçe	-	-	-	-	-	-	-	1000	-	-	-	-	-	-	1000
	kitchen gardens	number	-	-	-	-	-	-	-	-	-	-	-	-	-	-	2
		aḳçe	-	-	-	-	-	-	-	-	-	-	-	-	-	-	470
	watermills	number	-	-	1	-	-	0.5	-	-	1	1	-	-	-	-	3.5
		aḳçe	-	-	300	-	-	800	-	-	300	450	-	-	-	-	1850
	fulling mills	number	-	-	-	-	-	-	-	-	-	2	-	-	-	-	4
		aḳçe	-	-	-	-	-	-	-	-	-	100	-	-	-	-	200
tithe (in aḳçes)		flax	-	-	15	40	-	30	10	-	-	64	-	50	20	-	714
		vineyards	68	-	1238	293	90	529	293	-	-	590	-	-	-	-	17704
		wheat	250	65	1510	750	-	1033	400	-	350	685	400	1200	300	200	16331
		barley	40	30	230	113	-	158	60	-	50	100	60	188	48	32	2457
		cotton	-	-	50	100	-	100	40	-	-	100	-	-	-	-	1595
		olive oil	-	-	28	26	3	11	8	-	-	-	-	-	-	-	948
		fruits	-	-	41	8	4	22	8	-	-	18	-	-	-	-	275
		silk	-	-	164	23	12	15	14	-	-	15	-	-	-	-	404
		mulberries	-	-	13	-	-	-	-	-	-	-	-	-	-	-	13
		kitchen gardens	-	-	-	-	-	-	-	-	-	-	-	-	-	-	49
units (in aḳçe)		wine	-	-	160	194	12	215	36	-	-	64	-	-	-	-	2606
		swine	-	-	-	-	-	-	-	2		-	3	15	-	-	58
watermills (mulk)		number	-	-	1	-	-	2	1	-	-	1	-	-	-	-	11
		aḳçe	-	-	80	-	-	120	80	-	-	80	-	-	-	-	840
		total	533	147	5471	2204	316	4053	1395	1062	820	4420	773	2174	578	422	71378[viii]
muḳāṭaʿa (imperial)		salt-pans	-	-	-	-	-	-	-	-	-	-	-	-	-	-	7000
muḳāṭaʿa (tīmār)		oil presses	-	-	-	-	-	-	-	-	-	-	-	-	-	-	250

[iv] Including the community of İpsari.
[v] The deserted (*ḫāliyye*) *mezraʿa* of Çernota belonged to this village.
[vi] The deserted (*ḫāliyye*) *mezraʿa* of Zastupa belonged to this village.
[vii] Approximately.
[viii] The total revenue of Balya Badra amounted to 78,378 *aḳçe*s, 7,000 of which were held in imperial demesne.

Chart 17. *District of Balya Badra (Patra).*

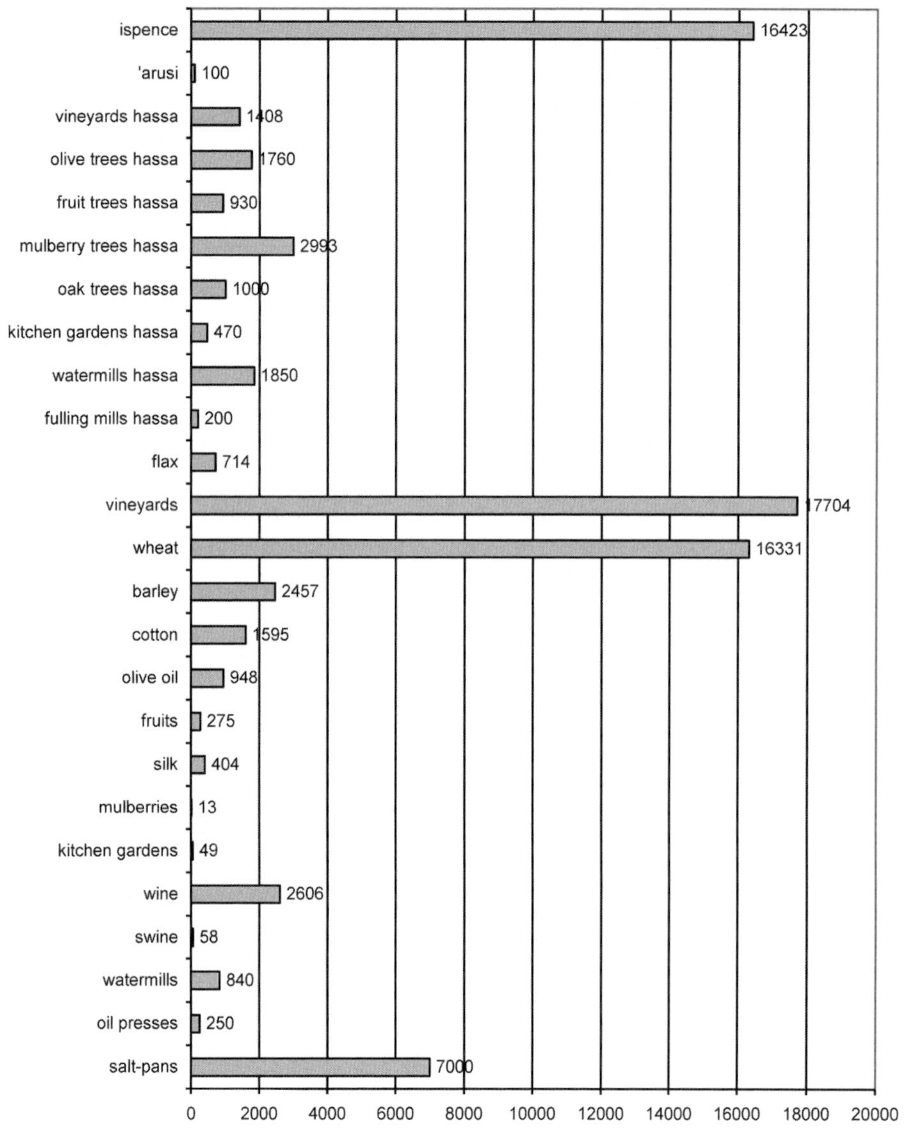

Table 23. *District of Ḳalandriça (Halandritsa).*

			Ḳalandriça	Ḳazneş	Ḳuçi	Maji	Ġolemi	Rapsomati	Lisarya	Bala	İş Ari	Mazaraki	Ḳral	Zoġa	Laluş	Virzaho	total
	inhabitants	households	116	8	3	3	2	7	14	6	18	8	14	6	14	13	232
		bachelors	22	1	-	-	-	-	3	-	4	-	-	-	-	4	34
		widows	15	-	-	-	-	-	1	1	1	1	-	-	1	-	20
taxes *per capita*		ispence	3540	180	60	60	40	140	346	126	446	166	280	120	286	340	6130
ḫāṣṣa	vineyards	dönüm	20	-	-	-	-	-	-	-	-	-	-	-	-	-	20
		aḳçe	1500	-	-	-	-	-	-	-	-	-	-	-	-	-	1500
	kitchen gardens	number	1	-	-	-	-	-	-	-	-	-	-	-	-	-	1
		aḳçe	180	-	-	-	-	-	-	-	-	-	-	-	-	-	180
	olive trees	trees	15	-	-	-	-	-	-	-	-	-	-	-	-	-	15
		aḳçe	563	-	-	-	-	-	-	-	-	-	-	-	-	-	563
	fruit trees	trees	56	-	-	-	-	-	-	-	-	-	-	-	-	-	56
		aḳçe	100	-	-	-	-	-	-	-	-	-	-	-	-	-	100
	mulberry trees	trees	410	-	-	-	-	-	-	-	-	-	-	-	-	-	410
		aḳçe	2000	-	-	-	-	-	-	-	-	-	-	-	-	-	2000
	watermills	number	1	-	-	-	-	-	-	-	-	-	-	-	-	-	1
		aḳçe	160	-	-	-	-	-	-	-	-	-	-	-	-	-	160
tithe (in aḳçes)		flax	150	-	-	-	-	-	-	-	-	-	-	-	-	-	150
		vineyards	3668	-	-	-	-	-	-	-	-	-	-	-	113	-	3781
		wheat	3390	300	50	100	100	250	500	350	800	300	250	350	500	500	7740
		barley	476	45	8	16	16	40	79	53	124	47	39	55	79	76	1153
		olive oil	335	-	-	-	-	-	-	-	-	-	-	-	-	-	335
		fruits	72	-	-	-	-	-	-	-	-	-	-	-	-	-	72
		cotton	750	-	-	-	-	-	-	-	-	-	-	-	-	-	750
		silk	359	-	-	-	-	-	-	-	-	-	-	-	-	-	359
units (in aḳçes)		wine	456	-	-	-	-	-	-	-	-	-	-	-	-	-	456
		swine	-	-	-	-	-	-	18	-	24	-	7	-	10	37	96
watermills (mülk)		number	3	-	-	-	-	-	-	-	-	1	-	-	-	-	4
		aḳçe	240	-	-	-	-	-	-	-	-	40	-	-	-	-	280
market tax and niyābet			500	-	-	-	-	-	-	-	-	-	-	-	-	-	500
		total	18439	525	118	176	156	430	943	529	1394	553	576	525	988	953	26305

Chart 18. *District of Ḳalandriça (Halandritsa).*

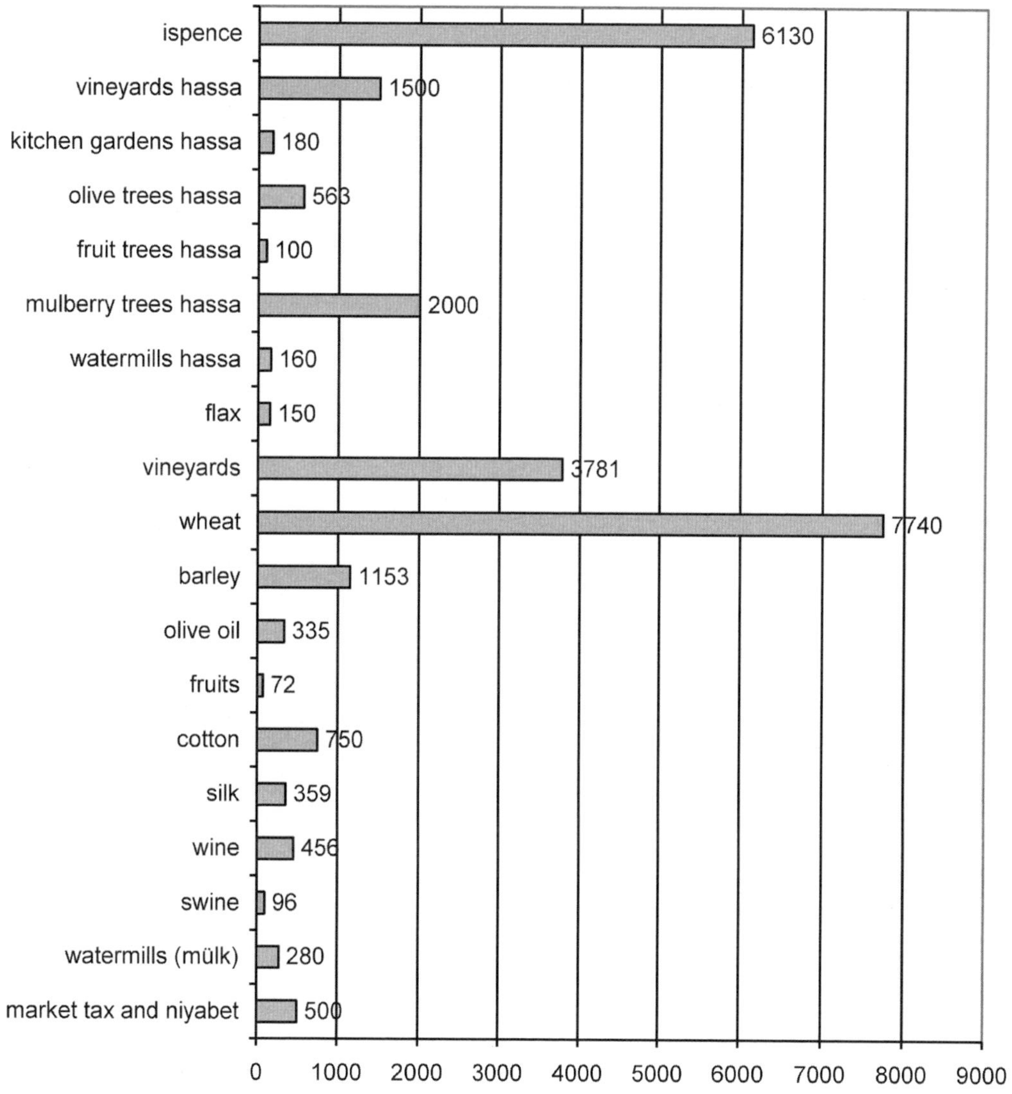

Table 24. *District of Şandamiri (Santomeri).*

			Şandamiri	Porta[i]	Maẕiñik	İksanya	Mirati	Platistomo	Valmi	Ġarnaze	Puliça[ii]	Ẕervini	total
inhabitants		households	80	66	36	20	10	14	4	4	2	5	241
		bachelors	3	11	-	2	-	1	-	-	-	-	17
		widows	7	5	3	1	-	-	-	-	-	-	16
taxes *per capita*		ispence	2117	1955	738	446	200	300	80	80	40	100	6056
		ʿarūsī	80	60	30	20	10	15	-	-	-	-	215
		niyābet	200	-	-	-	-	-	-	-	-	-	200
ḫāṣṣa	vineyards	dönüm	42	4	-	-	-	-	-	-	-	-	46
		aḳçe	2912	630	-	-	-	-	-	-	-	-	3542
	pear trees	number	-	2	-	-	-	-	-	-	-	-	2
		aḳçe	-	5	-	-	-	-	-	-	-	-	5
	olive trees	trees	100	15	-	-	-	-	-	-	-	-	115
		aḳçe	225	34	-	-	-	-	-	-	-	-	259
	fruit trees	trees	43	-	-	-	-	-	-	-	-	-	43
		aḳçe	100	-	-	-	-	-	-	-	-	-	100
	watermills	number	-	2	-	-	-	-	-	-	-	-	2
		aḳçe	-	1200	-	-	-	-	-	-	-	-	1200
tithe (in aḳçes)		flax	-	100	100	50	25	38	10	-	-	-	323
		vineyards	3510	1102	-	-	-	-	-	-	-	-	4612
		wheat	2500	2200	1150	500	200	550	200	200	100	100	7700
		barley	500	336	124	80	32	85	31	31	15	16	1250
		olive oil	84	34	-	-	-	-	-	-	-	-	118
		fruits	29	8	-	-	-	-	-	-	-	-	37
		cotton	-	50	-	-	-	-	-	-	-	-	50
units (in aḳçes)		wine	350	110	-	-	-	-	-	-	-	-	460
		swine	8	2	9	12	-	8	2	-	-	-	41
watermills (mülk)		number	1	4	-	-	-	-	-	-	-	-	5
		aḳçe	40	320	-	-	-	-	-	-	-	-	360
		total	12655	8146	2151	1108	467	996	323	311	155	216	26528

[i] The deserted (*ḫāliyye*) *mezraʿa* of Orfano belonged to this village.
[ii] The deserted (*ḫāliyye*) *mezraʿa*s of Lukişta, Gin Floḳa and Mariçi belonged to this village.

Chart 19. *District of Şandamiri (Santomeri).*

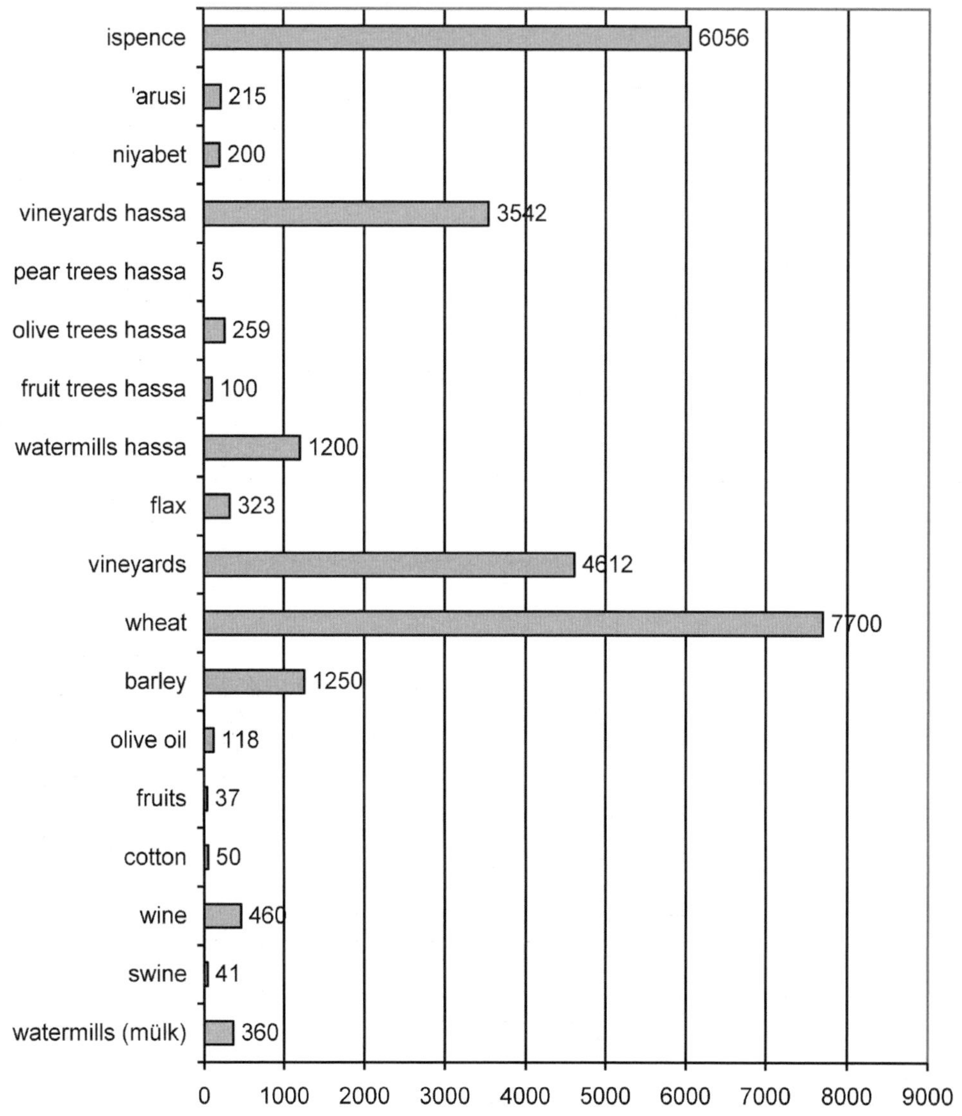

Table 25. *District of Girbene (Spartia).*

		Motista	Gin Manesi	İsfardina	Avrami	Lazaryo	Papazato	Ḳavalari Trusa	Bardi Zuġra	Ayo Yani	Ḳavalari	Asfalaḫto	[---]ṣta	Divye[i]	Arula	
inhabitants	households	28	12	25	19	32	6	23	7	15	39	4	6	9	37	17
	bachelors	1	-	-	-	-	-	1	-	-	2	1	3	1	3	5
	widows	3	1	-	-	3	2	1	-	-	-	-	-	1	4	3
taxes *per capita*	ispence	743	246	625	380	658	132	486	140	300	820	125	180	206	1024	568
	ʿarūsī	-	-	20	20	-	-	-	-	-	-	-	-	-	40	20
ḫāṣṣa – vineyards	dönüm	-	-	-	-	-	-	-	-	-	-	5	-	-	6	-
	akçe	-	-	-	-	-	-	-	-	-	-	394	-	-	868	-
ḫāṣṣa – kitchen gardens	number	-	-	-	-	-	-	-	-	-	-	-	-	-	1	-
	akçe	-	-	-	-	-	-	-	-	-	-	-	-	-	100	-
ḫāṣṣa – gardens	number	-	-	-	-	-	-	-	-	-	-	-	-	-	-	-
	akçe	-	-	-	-	-	-	-	-	-	-	-	-	-	-	-
ḫāṣṣa – olive trees	trees	-	-	-	-	-	-	-	-	-	-	-	-	-	-	-
	akçe	-	-	-	-	-	-	-	-	-	-	-	-	-	-	-
ḫāṣṣa – fruit trees	trees	-	-	-	-	-	-	-	-	-	-	-	-	-	8	-
	akçe	-	-	-	-	-	-	-	-	-	-	-	-	-	20	-
ḫāṣṣa – mulberry trees	trees	-	-	-	-	-	-	-	-	-	-	-	-	-	-	-
	akçe	-	-	-	-	-	-	-	-	-	-	-	-	-	-	-
ḫāṣṣa – watermills	number	-	-	-	-	-	-	-	-	-	-	-	-	-	-	1
	akçe	-	-	-	-	-	-	-	-	-	-	-	-	-	-	200
tithe (in akçes)	flax	-	-	-	-	-	-	-	-	-	-	-	15	20	80	50
	vineyards	12	68	224	23	338	12	-	57	-	360	220	22	-	1125	585
	wheat	850	700	750	550	1650	400	550	250	350	1850	100	300	400	1150	850
	barley	130	106	94	95	257	63	86	38	56	288	16	46	62	182	132
	olive oil	-	-	15	-	2	-	-	-	-	-	-	-	-	21	13
	fruits	1	-	3	-	1	-	-	-	-	-	-	-	-	-	-
	cotton	-	-	-	-	-	-	-	-	-	-	-	-	-	150	50
	silk	-	-	10	-	-	-	-	-	-	-	-	-	-	-	-
units (in akçes)	wine	-	9	35	-	45	-	-	5	-	45	-	-	-	80	70
	swine	-	7	17	-	15	1	18	5	9	13	-	7	8	2	-
watermills (mülk)	number	-	-	-	-	1	-	-	-	-	1	-	-	-	-	-
	akçe	-	-	-	-	30	-	-	-	-	40	-	-	-	-	-
fulling mills (mülk)	number	-	-	-	-	-	-	-	-	-	-	-	-	-	-	-
	akçe	-	-	-	-	-	-	-	-	-	-	-	-	-	-	-
	total	1736	1136	1793	1068	2996	608	1140	495	715	3416	3355	570	696	4842 [ii]	2538[iii]
muḳāṭaʿa (tīmār)	fish-farms	-	-	-	-	-	-	-	-	-	-	2500	-	-	-	-

[i] The deserted (*ḫāliyye*) *mezraʿa* of Viriça belonged to this village.
[ii] This is the share (*ḥiṣṣe*) of Muḥyi'd-dīn Yaninaʾi.
[iii] This is the share (*ḥiṣṣe*) of Ḳāsım veled-i Muḥyi'd-dīn Yaninaʾi.

Table 25. *District of Girbene (Spartia).*

			Traḫya Manesi	Trusa	Fostana	Ayo Niḳolas	Oşiya Mariya	Ayo Lisyo	Venetiḳa	Lenḳoni[iv]	Balçi	Sirveliça	Palopirgo	Yirano	Petrovişta[v]	Miḫoy	Ḳazneş
inhabitants		households	21	11	13	7	1	1	5	3	4	4	4	3	2	6	6
		bachelors	-	3	-	1	-	-	-	-	-	1	-	1	1	-	-
		widows	2	2	4[vi]	-	-	-	-	-	-	-	-	-	-	-	-
taxes *per capita*		ispence	432	292	349	160	20	20	100	60	80	100	80	80	60	120	120
		ʿarūsī	-	-	10	10	-	-	-	-	-	-	-	-	-	-	6
ḫāṣṣa	vineyards	dönüm	-	-	6	-	-	-	-	-	-	-	-	-	-	-	-
		aḳçe	-	-	472	-	-	-	-	-	-	-	-	-	-	-	-
	kitchen gardens	number	-	-	1	-	-	-	-	-	-	-	-	-	-	-	-
		aḳçe	-	-	200	-	-	-	-	-	-	-	-	-	-	-	-
	gardens	number	-	-	-	1	-	-	-	-	-	-	-	-	-	-	-
		aḳçe	-	-	-	50	-	-	-	-	-	-	-	-	-	-	-
	olive trees	trees	-	-	10	-	-	-	-	30	-	-	-	-	-	-	-
		aḳçe	-	-	45	-	-	-	-	67	-	-	-	-	-	-	-
	fruit trees	trees	-	-	6	-	-	-	-	44	-	-	-	-	-	-	-
		aḳçe	-	-	15	-	-	-	-	100	-	-	-	-	-	-	-
	mulberry trees	trees	-	-	-	-	-	-	-	-	-	-	-	-	-	-	-
		aḳçe	-	-	-	-	-	-	-	-	-	-	-	-	-	-	-
	watermills	number	-	-	1	-	-	-	-	-	-	-	-	-	-	-	-
		aḳçe	-	-	500	-	-	-	-	-	-	-	-	-	-	-	-
tithe (in aḳçes)		flax	-	-	60	10	-	-	10	-	10	10	10	-	-	-	10
		vineyards	45	-	450	135	67	45	45	-	67	22	67	22	22	-	-
		wheat	950	550	600	200	50	50	300	100	100	100	100	100	100	200	200
		barley	148	86	93	32	8	8	46	15	16	15	15	16	15	32	30
		olive oil	-	-	12	8	2	-	-	-	5	1	2	-	-	-	-
		fruits	-	-	5	-	3	1	-	-	-	1	1	-	-	-	-
		cotton	-	-	150	-	-	-	-	-	-	-	-	-	-	-	-
		silk	-	-	-	-	-	-	-	-	-	-	-	-	-	-	-
units (in aḳçes)		wine	6	-	30	-	-	-	-	-	-	-	-	-	-	-	-
		swine	1	4	-	-	-	-	14	-	-	-	-	-	-	-	-
watermills (mülk)		number	1	-	-	-	-	-	-	-	-	-	-	-	-	-	-
		aḳçe	40	-	-	-	-	-	-	-	-	-	-	-	-	-	-
fulling mills (mülk)		number	-	-	-	-	-	-	-	-	-	-	-	-	-	-	-
		aḳçe	-	-	-	-	-	-	-	-	-	-	-	-	-	-	-
		total	1622	932	2991	605	150	124	515	342	278	249	275	218	197	352	366
muḳāṭaʿa (tīmār)		fish fields	-	-	-	-	-	-	-	-	-	-	-	-	-	-	-

[iv] The deserted (*ḫāliyye*) *mezraʿa*s of Besulḳa and Ayo Yorgi belonged to this village.

[v] The deserted (*ḫāliyye*) *mezraʿa*s of Serḳofayi and Şurbi belonged to this village.

[vi] The number of widows given in the entry of this village is 4. However, when the scribe sums up the number of widows in the *tīmār*s of ʿAlī veled-i Ḳulaġuz and his son İskender, gives only 1.

Table 25. *District of Girbene (Spartia).*

			Maliki	Ḳonbi Şeḳra	Gerbesi	Mitepoli	Yatopa	Melitena	Malesina	Eksoriya	Şalesi	Mazarak	Junbata	Milyas	Frati	İstoyan	Ġurzumişa
inhabitants		households	11	11	1	24	6	12	9	4	6	19	4	4	6	11	20
		bachelors	-	-	-	3	-	-	-	-	-	-	-	-	-	-	-
		widows	1	2	-	4	-	-	-	-	-	2	-	-	-	-	-
taxes *per capita*		ispence	226	232	20	699	120	240	180	80	120	392	80	80	120	220	400
		ʿarūsī	10	-	-	-	-	-	-	-	-	20	-	-	-	15	20
ḫāṣṣa	vineyards	dönüm	-	-	-	6	-	-	-	-	-	-	-	-	-	-	-
		aḳçe	-	-	-	472	-	-	-	-	-	-	-	-	-	-	-
	kitchen gardens	number	-	-	-	-	-	-	-	-	-	-	-	-	-	-	-
		aḳçe	-	-	-	-	-	-	-	-	-	-	-	-	-	-	-
	gardens	number	-	-	-	-	-	-	-	-	-	-	-	-	-	-	-
		aḳçe	-	-	-	-	-	-	-	-	-	-	-	-	-	-	-
	olive trees	trees	-	-	15	40	-	-	-	-	-	-	-	-	-	-	-
		aḳçe	-	-	33	45	-	-	-	-	-	-	-	-	-	-	-
	fruit trees	trees	-	-	-	-	-	-	-	-	-	-	-	-	-	-	-
		aḳçe	-	-	-	-	-	-	-	-	-	-	-	-	-	-	-
	mulberry trees	trees	-	-	-	30	-	-	-	-	-	-	-	-	-	-	-
		aḳçe	-	-	-	160	-	-	-	-	-	-	-	-	-	-	-
	watermills	number	-	-	-	-	-	-	-	-	-	-	-	-	-	-	-
		aḳçe	-	-	-	-	-	-	-	-	-	-	-	-	-	-	-
tithe (in aḳçes)		flax	15	15	-	50	-	-	-	-	-	-	-	-	10	-	20
		vineyards	-	-	-	563	-	42	-	21	-	-	-	-	22.	77	-
		wheat	350	300	-	350	150	250	150	200	150	800	100	150	200	350	750
		barley	54	48	-	56	23	40	24	31	24	124	16	23	32	56	119
		olive oil	-	-	-	36	-	-	-	-	-	-	-	-	-	-	-
		fruits	-	-	-	-	-	-	-	-	-	-	4	-	-	9	-
		cotton	-	-	-	50	-	-	-	-	-	-	-	-	-	-	-
		silk	-	-	-	56	-	-	-	4	-	2	-	-	-	2	-
units (in aḳçes)		wine	-	-	-	61	-	-	-	-	-	-	-	-	-	-	-
		swine	-	2	-	5	5	3	-	-	2	23	-	-	-	16	-
watermills (mülk)		number	1	-	1	1	1	-	-	-	-	-	1	-	-	1	1
		aḳçe	40	-	40	40	80	-	-	-	-	-	30	-	-	40	40
fulling mills (mülk)		number	-	-	-	-	1	-	-	-	-	-	-	-	-	1	-
		aḳçe	-	-	-	-	15	-	-	-	-	-	-	-	-	15	-
		total	695	597	93	2643	393	575	354	336	296	1361	230	253	384	800	1349
muḳāṭaʿa (tīmār)		fish fields	-	-	-	-	-	-	-	-	-	-	-	-	-	-	-

Table 25. *District of Girbene (Spartia).*

			Buza	Duḳati	Gin Bodya	Şergi	İsḳlaviça	Marḳoplu	total
inhabitants		households	11	20	5	10	14	9	587
		bachelors	1	-	1	2	-	-	31
		widows	-	-	-	-	3	1	39
taxes *per capita*		ispence	240	400	120	240	368	186	13469
		ʿarūsī	-	20	-	10	15	-	236
ḫāṣṣa	vineyards	dönüm	-	-	-	-	5	-	28
		aḳçe	-	-	-	-	528	-	2734
	kitchen gardens	number	-	-	-	-	-	-	2
		aḳçe	-	-	-	-	-	-	300
	gardens	number	-	-	-	-	-	-	1
		aḳçe	-	-	-	-	-	-	50
	olive trees	trees	4	-	-	-	100	-	199
		aḳçe	10	-	-	-	225	-	425
	fruit trees	trees	-	-	-	-	17	-	76
		aḳçe	-	-	-	-	40	-	175
	mulberry trees	trees	-	-	-	-	-	-	30
		aḳçe	-	-	-	-	-	-	160
	watermills	number	-	-	-	-	-	-	2
		aḳçe	-	-	-	-	-	-	700
tithe (in aḳçes)		flax	15	-	-	-	20	-	430
		vineyards	-	-	-	113	371	-	5242
		wheat	500	600	200	200	300	400	20850
		barley	79	96	32	31	48	61	3243
		olive oil	-	-	-	-	30	-	147
		fruits	-	-	-	-	18	-	47
		cotton	-	-	-	-	-	-	400
		silk	-	-	-	-	-	-	74
units (in aḳçes)		wine	-	-	-	-	35	-	421
		swine	4	5	5	23	-	8	222
watermills (mülk)		number	-	-	1	-	2	-	13
		aḳçe	-	-	40	-	80	-	540
fulling mills (mülk)		number	-	-	-	-	-	-	2
		aḳçe	-	-	-	-	-	-	30
		total	848	1121	397	617	2078	655	52395
muḳāṭaʿa (tīmār)		fish fields	-	-	-	-	-	-	2500

Chart 20. *District of Girbene (Spartia).*

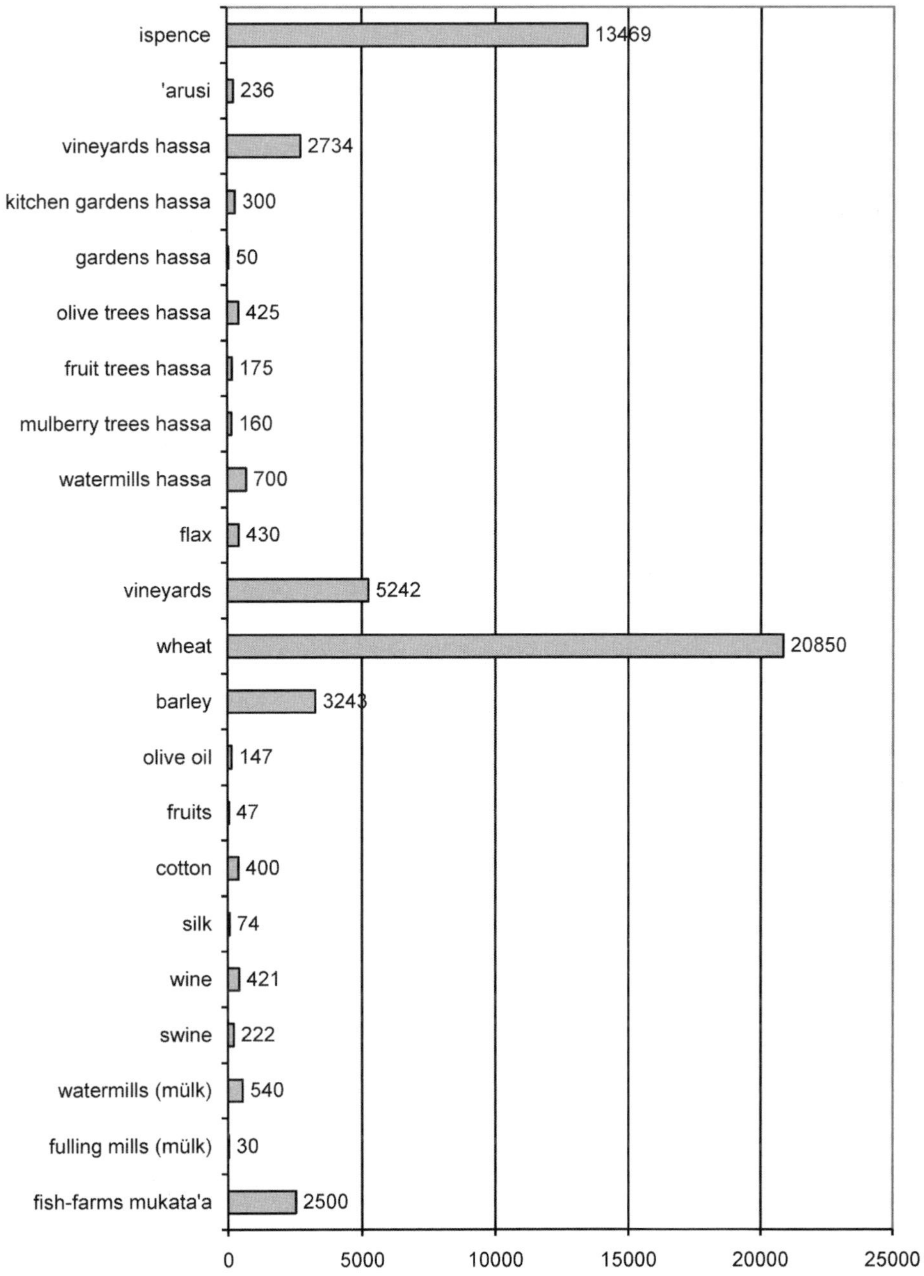

Table 26. *District of Ayo İlya (Agios Ilias).*

			Ayo İlya	Muzak	İşpata	Ḳozma Greḳa	Simiza	Ayo Vaşıl	Romyo	İştopanşi Lopesi	Ġolomi	Arvano Ḳastro	Sirvu	Bavasi	Ḳastel İksovuni	Poliça	Zorila	Miġali Ẓivri
inhabitants		households	114	15	5	8	5	7	9	9	13	51	2	3	127	14	21	101
		bachelors	16	1	1	2	-	-	-	3	4	5	1	-	30	2	3	18
		widows	9	5	2	1	1	-	-	-	-	4	-	1	15	-	2	2
taxes *per capita*		ispence	3304	350	132	206	150	140	180	240	340	1424	60	66	4015	400	492	2987
		ʿarūsī	150	20	10	10	10	10	10	10	20	50	-	-	150	15	25	100
		niyābet	500	-	-	-	-	-	-	-	-	-	-	-	-	-	-	-
ḫāṣṣa	vineyards	dönüm	53	-	-	-	-	-	-	-	-	4	-	-	5	-	-	3
		akçe	7200	-	-	-	-	-	-	-	-	720	-	-	1125	-	-	720
	kitchen gardens	number	1	-	-	-	-	-	-	-	-	-	-	-	-	-	-	-
		akçe	80	-	-	-	-	-	-	-	-	-	-	-	-	-	-	-
	gardens	number	-	-	-	-	-	-	-	-	-	-	-	-	-	-	-	-
		akçe	-	-	-	-	-	-	-	-	-	-	-	-	-	-	-	-
	olive trees	trees	9	-	-	-	-	-	-	-	-	6	-	-	-	-	-	-
		akçe	23	-	-	-	-	-	-	-	-	13	-	-	-	-	-	-
	fruit trees	trees	42	-	-	-	-	-	-	-	-	10	-	-	-	-	-	15
		akçe	100	-	-	-	-	-	-	-	-	20	-	-	-	-	-	30
	mulberry trees	trees	-	-	-	-	-	-	-	-	-	-	-	-	14	-	-	115
		akçe	-	-	-	-	-	-	-	-	-	-	-	-	60	-	-	350
	resin trees	number	-	-	-	-	-	-	-	-	-	300	-	-	-	-	-	-
		akçe	-	-	-	-	-	-	-	-	-	50	-	-	-	-	-	-
	watermills	number	4	-	-	-	-	-	-	-	-	1	-	-	1	-	-	-
		akçe	1800	-	-	-	-	-	-	-	-	100	-	-	250	-	-	-
	fish-farms		-	-	-	-	-	-	-	-	-	-	-	-	-	-	-	-
tithe (in akçes)		flax	250	50	20	30	20	20	25	10	30	200	-	-	200	30	20	200
		vineyards	2656	-	-	-	-	-	-	-	-	910	-	-	1200	210	-	1980
		wheat	3500	700	300	650	150	100	200	200	500	1300	100	200	3650	450	700	3000
		barley	545	108	46	100	23	16	31	31	77	200	15	30	450	72	108	458
		olive oil	-	-	-	-	-	-	-	-	-	19	-	-	-	-	-	-
		fruits	50	-	-	-	-	-	-	-	-	8	-	-	-	2	-	58
		honey	6	-	-	-	-	-	-	11	7	22	-	-	-	-	-	-
		cotton	200	-	-	-	-	-	-	-	-	30	-	-	-	-	-	-
		silk	-	-	-	-	-	-	-	-	-	-	-	-	6	-	-	644
units (in akçes)		wine	250	-	-	-	-	-	-	-	-	120	-	-	120	10	-	170
		swine	15	25	14	4	-	-	2	7	6	4	-	3	-	10	23	-
watermills (mülk)		number	1	-	-	-	-	-	-	-	-	-	-	-	2	1	-	3
		akçe	30	-	-	-	-	-	-	-	-	-	-	-	60	30	-	90
fulling mills (mülk)		number	-	-	-	-	-	-	-	-	-	-	-	-	1	-	-	-
		akçe	-	-	-	-	-	-	-	-	-	-	-	-	15	-	-	-
		total	20659	1253	522	1000	353	286	448	509	980	5190	175	299	11301	1229	1368	10787

Table 26. *District of Ayo İlya (Agios Ilias).*

			Vunargo[i]	Mihili	İryolo[ii]	Prifti	Ḳartazori	Mayira	Franḳa Vila	Rovyata[iii]	Ḳrapeşi	Androniḳa	Niḳola Ḳumi	Pendeni[iv]	total
inhabitants		households	7	6	18	7	8	4	14	34	6	12	8	5	633
		bachelors	4	4	-	1	-	-	-	2	-	-	-	-	97
		widows	1	-	2	-	-	-	1	-	-	-	-	-	46
taxes *per capita*		ispence	281	200	462	160	160	80	356	720	120	240	160	100	17525
		ʿarūsī	10	10	20	8	8	-	15	40	10	15	10	10	746
		niyābet	-	-	-	-	-	-	-	-	-	-	-	-	500
ḫāṣṣa	vineyards	dönüm	20	-	20	-	-	-	19	-	-	1	-	-	125
		aḳçe	2400	-	1920	-	-	-	2280	-	-	240	-	-	16605
	kitchen gardens	number	-	-	-	-	-	-	-	-	-	-	-	-	1
		aḳçe	-	-	-	-	-	-	-	-	-	-	-	-	80
	gardens	number	-	-	-	-	-	-	1	-	-	-	-	-	1
		aḳçe	-	-	-	-	-	-	150	-	-	-	-	-	150
	olive trees	trees	100	-	200	-	-	-	6	-	-	-	-	-	321
		aḳçe	203	-	270	-	-	-	14	-	-	-	-	-	523
	fruit trees	trees	46	-	31	-	-	-	15	-	-	-	-	-	144
		aḳçe	100	-	50	-	-	-	15	-	-	-	-	-	315
	mulberry trees	trees	-	-	-	-	-	-	-	-	-	-	-	-	129
		aḳçe	-	-	-	-	-	-	-	-	-	-	-	-	410
	resin trees	number	-	-	-	-	-	-	-	-	-	-	-	-	300
		aḳçe	-	-	-	-	-	-	-	-	-	-	-	-	50
	watermills	number	-	-	1	-	-	-	2	-	-	-	-	-	9
		aḳçe	-	-	250	-	-	-	700	-	-	-	-	-	3100
	fish-farms		-	-	160	-	-	-	-	-	-	-	-	-	160
tithe (in aḳçes)		flax	40	40	48	-	-	-	60	80	20	40	30	-	1463
		vineyards	210	-	660	-	-	-	144	-	-	64	-	-	8034
		wheat	300	250	500	400	300	100	400	1200	200	500	600	150	20600
		barley	48	40	77	63	47	15	63	186	48	79	91	23	3090
		olive oil	7	-	4	-	-	-	-	-	-	-	-	-	30
		fruits	-	-	4	-	-	-	-	-	-	-	-	-	122
		honey	-	-	-	-	-	-	-	-	-	-	-	-	46
		cotton	30	20	62	-	-	-	25	125	-	-	-	-	492
		silk	-	-	-	-	-	-	-	-	-	-	-	-	650
units (in aḳçes)		wine	-	-	30	-	-	-	-	-		-	-	-	700
		swine	-	-	-	5	4	-	34	76	8	19	45	-	304
watermills (mülk)		number	-	-	-	-	-	-	-	-	-	-	-	-	7
		aḳçe	-	-	-	-	-	-	-	-	-	-	-	-	210
fulling mills (mülk)		number	-	-	-	-	-	-	-	-	-	-	-	-	1
		aḳçe	-	-	-	-	-	-	-	-	-	-	-	-	15
		total	3629	560	4517	636	519	195	4256	2427	406	1197	936	283	75920[v]

[i] The deserted (*ḫāliyye*) *mezraʿa* of Ṣamuna belonged to this village.
[ii] The deserted (*ḫāliyye*) *mezraʿa*s of Ayiya and Fenaromeni belonged to this village.
[iii] Including the communities of Niḳola Buva and Plaşa. The deserted (*ḫāliyye*) *mezraʿa*s of Rado and Barçi belonged to this village.
[iv] Including the community of Palunbi Ipşari.

Chart 21. *District of Ayo İlya (Agios Ilias).*

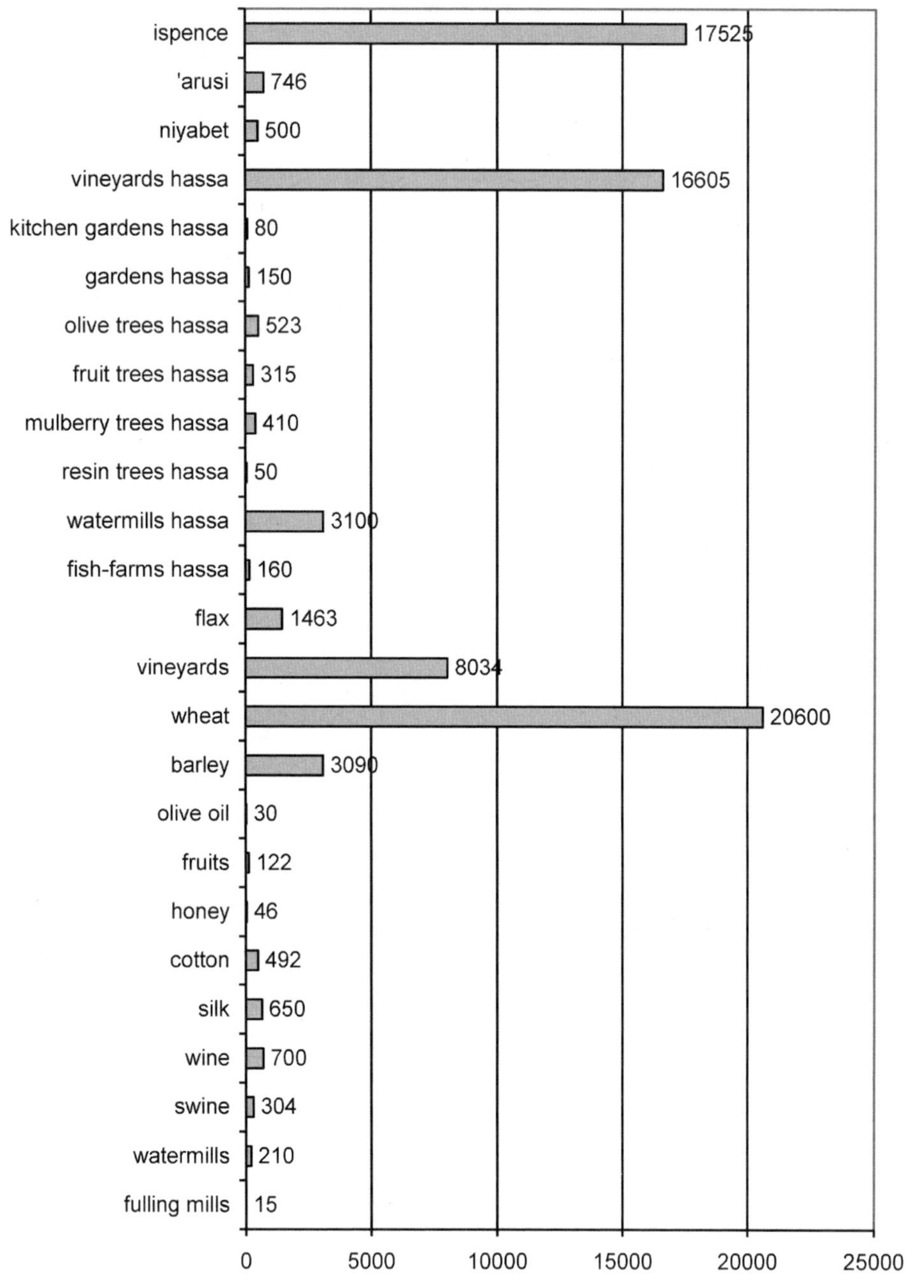

Table 27. *District of Ġardicḳo (Gatsiko).*

			Ġardicḳo[i]	İvlanduşa	Ranesi	Ġomosto	Şuli	Gön Lopesi	Çapoġa	İvlaḫo	Maji	Mastro Andoni	Barbuc	Şopiya	Lopesi	Simoplu	Ḳalanci	İsliva
inhabitants		households	151	5	59	17	10	10	27	15	24	20	32	8	14	12	7	17
		bachelors	18	-	2	-	2	-	1	-	-	-	1	-	1	-	-	-
		widows	12	-	4	-	-	-	2	-	-	1	1	1	1	4	-	1
taxes *per capita*		ispence	4297	100	1244	340	240	200	572	300	480	406	666	166	306	264	140	346
		ʿarūsī	-	10	55	20	10	10	30	15	25	24	40	8	15	15	10	20
		niyābet	220	-	-	-	-	-	-	-	-	-	-	-	-	-	-	-
ḫāṣṣa	vineyards	dönüm	21	-	-	-	-	-	-	-	-	-	-	-	-	-	-	-
		aḳçe	3960	-	-	-	-	-	-	-	-	-	-	-	-	-	-	-
	kitchen gardens	number	-	-	-	-	-	-	-	-	-	-	-	-	-	-	-	-
		aḳçe	-	-	-	-	-	-	-	-	-	-	-	-	-	-	-	-
	olive trees	trees	-	-	-	-	-	-	-	-	-	-	-	-	-	-	-	-
		aḳçe	-	-	-	-	-	-	-	-	-	-	-	-	-	-	-	-
	fruit trees	trees	36	-	-	-	-	-	-	-	-	-	-	-	-	-	-	-
		aḳçe	70	-	-	-	-	-	-	-	-	-	-	-	-	-	-	-
	mulberry trees	trees	125	-	-	-	-	-	-	-	-	-	-	-	-	-	-	-
		aḳçe	300	-	-	-	-	-	-	-	-	-	-	-	-	-	-	-
	watermills	number	1	-	-	-	-	-	-	-	-	-	-	-	-	-	-	-
		aḳçe	300	-	-	-	-	-	-	-	-	-	-	-	-	-	-	-
tithe (in aḳçes)		flax	-	-	100	30	-	-	50	30	30	-	50	-	20	20	-	25
		vineyards	5376	-	192	32	-	-	160	-	160	128	-	-	-	-	-	-
		wheat	6000	150	1600	500	400	300	800	450	750	550	1000	250	500	400	250	600
		barley	918	24	248	77	63	48	128	71	115	84	155	38	80	64	40	94
		olive oil	8	-	-	-	-	-	-	-	-	-	-	-	-	-	-	-
		fruits	40	-	-	-	-	-	-	-	-	-	-	-	-	-	-	-
		cotton	-	-	-	-	-	-	-	-	-	-	-	-	-	-	-	-
		silk	97	-	-	-	-	-	-	-	-	-	-	-	-	-	-	-
units (in aḳçes)		wine	-	-	-	-	-	-	-	-	-	-	-	-	-	-	-	-
		swine	32	-	9	-	10	3	26	-	-	-	-	-	8	3	2	17
watermills (mülk)		number	2	-	-	-	-	-	1	-	1	-	-	-	-	-	-	-
		aḳçe	160	-	-	-	-	-	40	-	40	-	-	-	-	-	-	-
fulling mills (mülk)		number	3	-	-	-	-	-	-	-	-	-	-	-	-	-	-	-
		aḳçe	50	-	-	-	-	-	-	-	-	-	-	-	-	-	-	-
		total	21828	284	3448	999	723	561	1806	866	1600	1192	1911	462	929	766	442	1102

[i] The deserted (*ḫāliyye*) *mezraʿa*s of Roẕinotiḫo, Ḳomi and İsliva-ı dīğer belonged to this village.

Table 27. *District of Ġardicḳo (Gatsiko).*

			Şaleşi	Lala	Gerbeşi	İsturġova	İstamiro	Mazarak[ii]	Manesi	Ẕirmi	Ḫarkâ	Maẕiñik	Ranbiyaḳa	Liḳuresi[iii]	Fil Adrofinos[iv]	Malaḳas	Andon	Manesi
inhabitants		households	6	8	9	6	40[v]	20	19	13	9	11[vi]	9	18	20	7	10	7
		bachelors	-	-	-	2	2	-	-	-	-	1	-	-	1	-	-	-
		widows	-	-	-	-	2	4	-	1	-	1	1	-	1	-	-	-
taxes *per capita*		ispence	120	160	180	200	1062	424	380	266	180	246	186	360	426	140	200	140
		ʿarūsī	10	-	10	-	50	15	20	15	10	10	10	15	20	10	10	10
		niyābet	-	-	-	-	-	-	-	-	-	-	-	-	-	-	-	-
ḫāṣṣa	vineyards	dönüm	-	-	-	1	6	-	-	-	-	-	-	-	-	-	-	-
		aḳçe	-	-	-	112	720	-	-	-	-	-	-	-	-	-	-	-
	kitchen gardens	number	-	-	-	-	1	-	-	-	-	-	-	-	-	-	-	-
		aḳçe	-	-	-	-	100	-	-	-	-	-	-	-	-	-	-	-
	olive trees	trees	-	-	-	-	12	-	-	-	-	-	-	-	-	-	-	-
		aḳçe	-	-	-	-	23	-	-	-	-	-	-	-	-	-	-	-
	fruit trees	trees	-	-	-	44	-	-	-	-	-	-	-	-	-	-	-	-
		aḳçe	-	-	-	100	-	-	-	-	-	-	-	-	-	-	-	-
	mulberry trees	trees	-	-	-	81	-	-	-	-	-	-	-	-	-	-	-	-
		aḳçe	-	-	-	120	-	-	-	-	-	-	-	-	-	-	-	-
	watermills	number	-	-	-	-	1.5	-	-	-	-	-	-	-	-	-	-	0.5
		aḳçe	-	-	-	-	375	-	-	-	-	-	-	-	-	-	-	200
tithe (in aḳçes)		flax	-	-	-	-	100	-	-	-	-	-	-	-	-	-	-	20
		vineyards	-	-	-	-	778	-	-	-	-	-	-	35	-	-	-	-
		wheat	200	250	300	100	1550	600	600	450	250	300	400	550	600	300	200	200
		barley	31	43	48	15	236	94	92	70	40	48	63	83	93	45	31	32
		olive oil	-	-	-	-	33	-	-	-	-	-	-	-	-	-	-	-
		fruits	-	-	-	58	5	-	-	-	-	-	-	-	-	-	-	-
		cotton	-	-	-	-	40	-	-	-	-	-	-	-	-	-	-	-
		silk	-	-	-	63	-	-	-	-	-	-	-	-	-	-	-	-
units (in aḳçes)		wine	-	-	-	-	100	-	-	-	-	-	-	-	-	-	-	-
		swine	-	-	-	-	-	2	-	10	-	-	2	10	16	-	-	-
watermills (mülk)		number	-	-	-	-	-	-	-	1	-	-	1	-	1	-	-	-
		aḳçe	-	-	-	-	-	-	-	40	-	-	40	-	40	-	-	-
fulling mills (mülk)		number	-	-	-	-	-	-	-	-	-	-	-	-	-	-	-	-
		aḳçe	-	-	-	-	-	-	-	-	-	-	-	-	-	-	-	-
		total	361	453	538	768	5172	1135	1092	851	480	604	701	1053	1195	495	441	602

[ii] Including the community of Ḳuçi.
[iii] Including the community of Bura. The deserted (*ḫāliyye*) *mezraʿa* of Ranesi belonged to this village.
[iv] Including the community of Muzak.
[v] Of which 15 households belonged to rice cultivators (*çeltükciyān*).
[vi] Of which 4 households belonged to rice cultivators (*çeltükciyān*).

Table 27. *District of Ġardicḳo (Gatsiko).*

			Murik Buva	Niḳola Buva	Duranḳorgi	total
inhabitants		households	12[vii]	9	3	664
		bachelors	-	-	1	32
		widows	1	-	-	38
taxes *per capita*		ispence	246	180	66	15229
		ʿarūsī	15	10	-	547
		niyābet	-	-	-	220
ḫāṣṣa	vineyards	dönüm	-	-	-	28
		aḳçe	-	-	-	4792
	kitchen gardens	number	-	-	-	1
		aḳçe	-	-	-	100
	olive trees	trees	-	-	-	12
		aḳçe	-	-	-	23
	fruit trees	trees	-	-	-	80
		aḳçe	-	-	-	170
	mulberry trees	trees	-	-	-	206
		aḳçe	-	-	-	420
	watermills	number	-	-	-	3
		aḳçe	-	-	-	875
tithe (in aḳçes)		flax	-	-	-	475
		vineyards	64	-	-	6925
		wheat	400	300	100	22150
		barley	64	47	16	3438
		olive oil	5	-	-	46
		fruits	2	-	-	105
		cotton	-	-	-	40
		silk	-	-	-	160
units (in aḳçes)		wine	-	-	-	100
		swine	13	5	2	170
watermills (mülk)		number	-	-	-	7
		aḳçe	-	-	-	360
fulling mills (mülk)		number	-	-	-	3
		aḳçe	-	-	-	50
		total	809	542	184	56395

[vii] Of which 1 household belonged to a rice cultivator (*çeltükci*).

Chart 22. *District of Ġardicḳo (Gatsiko).*

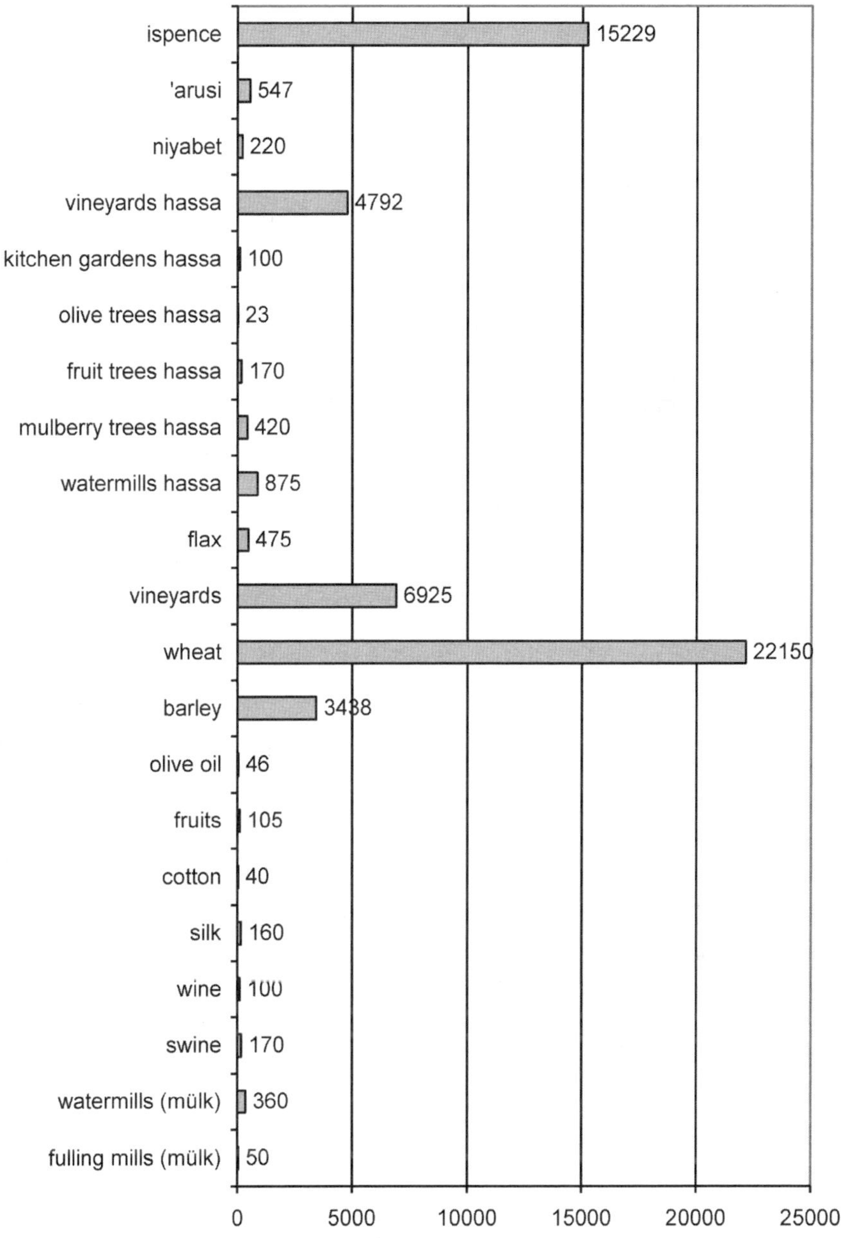

Table 28. *Livā'-ı Mora (the Peloponnese).*

			Ḳalavrita	Mizıṣra	Mıḫlu	Bejenik
inhabitants		households	848	9	263	411
		bachelors	97	1	35	93
		widows	35	-	16	26
taxes *per capita*		ispence	21620	250	5886	11561
		'arūsī	255	10	370	390
		niyābet	1000	-	-	250
ḫāṣṣa	vineyards	dönüm	23	5	11	22
		aḳçe	3000	300	1320	2340
	fruit trees	trees	25	-	6	30
		aḳçe	50	-	10	100
	olive trees	trees	-	5	-	-
		aḳçe	-	5	-	-
	mulberry trees	trees	306	-	40	62
		aḳçe	555	-	200	260
	pomegranate trees	trees	-	2	-	-
		aḳçe	-	5	-	-
	resin trees	trees	-	-	-	-
		aḳçe	-	-	-	-
	oak trees	trees	-	-	-	-
		aḳçe	-	-	-	-
	walnut trees	trees	-	-	-	-
		aḳçe	-	-	-	-
	pear trees	trees	-	-	-	-
		aḳçe	-	-	-	-
	bitter orange groves	groves	-	-	-	-
		aḳçe	-	-	-	-
	gardens	number	-	-	-	-
		aḳçe	-	-	-	-
	kitchen gardens	number	-	-	-	-
		aḳçe	-	-	-	-
	fish-farms	number	-	1	-	-
		aḳçe	-	800	-	-
	watermills	number	3	-	-	0.5
		aḳçe	1100	-	-	150
	fulling mills	number	-	-	-	-
		aḳçe	-	-	-	-
	oil presses	number	-	-	-	-
		aḳçe	-	-	-	-

Table 28. *Livā᾽-ı Mora (the Peloponnese).*

			Voştiça	Ḫulumiç	Vumero	Kirvuḳor	Arḳadya
inhabitants		households	1529	470	1372	1192	286
		bachelors	265	43	160	131	37
		widows	91	42	74	59	18
taxes *per capita*		ispence	43426	12047	35344	29289	7863
		ʿarūsī	-	170	595	1185	275
		niyābet	-	-	-	-	-
ḫāṣṣa	vineyards	dönüm	39	12	63.5	28	128.5
		akçe	4182	1440	9364	3694	11088
	fruit trees	trees	305	-	252	32	71
		akçe	1160	-	627	60	150
	olive trees	trees	125	-	40	6	1339
		akçe	108	-	49	7	777
	mulberry trees	trees	2107	-	67	10	50
		akçe	4775	-	295	40	250
	pomegranate trees	trees	-	-	-	-	-
		akçe	-	-	-	-	-
	resin trees	trees	-	-	300	500	-
		akçe	-	-	80	90	-
	oak trees	trees	-	-	-	200	-
		akçe	-	-	-	50	-
	walnut trees	trees	-	-	-	-	3
		akçe	-	-	-	-	5
	pear trees	trees	-	-	-	-	-
		akçe	-	-	-	-	-
	bitter orange groves	groves	-	3	-	-	-
		akçe	-	450	-	-	-
	gardens	number	-	-	1	-	-
		akçe	-	-	100	-	-
	kitchen gardens	number	-	-	-	1	-
		akçe	-	-	-	25	-
	fish-farms	number	-	-	-	-	2
		akçe	-	-	-	-	610
	watermills	number	2	-	7.5	1	6
		akçe	800	-	2550	300	1000
	fulling mills	number	2	-	-	-	-
		akçe	70	-	-	-	-
	oil presses	number	-	-	-	-	2
		akçe	-	-	-	-	150

Table 28. *Livā'-ı Mora (the Peloponnese).*

			Londar	Ḳorişos	Balya Badra	Ḳalandriça
inhabitants		households	1163	707	616	232
		bachelors	153	83	63	34
		widows	108	84	68	20
taxes *per capita*		ispence	31158	9715	16423	6130
		ʿarūsī	35	270	100	-
		niyābet	-	2000	-	-
ḫāṣṣa	vineyards	dönüm	136	21	15	20
		akçe	11250	1800	1408	1500
	fruit trees	trees	108	23	857	56
		akçe	215	50	930	100
	olive trees	trees	90	-	1368	15
		akçe	55	-	1760	563
	mulberry trees	trees	307	-	842	410
		akçe	1500	-	2993	2000
	pomegranate trees	trees	-	-	-	-
		akçe	-	-	-	-
	resin trees	trees	-	1000	-	-
		akçe	-	500	-	-
	oak trees	trees	-	-	1500	-
		akçe	-	-	1000	-
	walnut trees	trees	11	-	-	-
		akçe	20	-	-	-
	pear trees	trees	-	-	-	-
		akçe	-	-	-	-
	bitter orange groves	groves	-	-	-	-
		akçe	-	-	-	-
	gardens	number	-	-	-	-
		akçe	-	-	-	-
	kitchen gardens	number	-	-	2	1
		akçe	-	-	470	180
	fish-farms	number	-	-	-	-
		akçe	-	-	-	-
	watermills	number	2	-	3.5	1
		akçe	800	-	1850	160
	fulling mills	number	-	-	4	-
		akçe	-	-	200	-
	oil presses	number	-	-	-	-
		akçe	-	-	-	-

Table 28. *Livā'-ı Mora (the Peloponnese).*

			Ṣandamiri	Girbene	Ayo İlya	Ġardiçḳo	total
inhabitants		households	241	587	633	664	11223
		bachelors	17	31	97	32	1372
		widows	16	39	46	38	780
taxes *per capita*		ispence	6056	13469	17525	15229	282991
		ʿarūsī	215	236	746	547	5399
		niyābet	200	-	500	220	4170
ḫāṣṣa	vineyards	dönüm	46	28	125	28	751
		akçe	3542	2734	16605	4792	80359
	fruit trees	trees	43	76	144	80	2108
		akçe	100	175	315	170	4212
	olive trees	trees	115	199	321	12	3635
		akçe	259	425	523	23	4554
	mulberry trees	trees	-	30	129	206	4566
		akçe	-	160	410	420	13858
	pomegranate trees	trees	-	-	-	-	2
		akçe	-	-	-	-	5
	resin trees	trees	-	-	300	-	2100
		akçe	-	-	50	-	720
	oak trees	trees	-	-	-	-	1700
		akçe	-	-	-	-	1050
	walnut trees	trees	-	-	-	-	14
		akçe	-	-	-	-	25
	pear trees	trees	2	-	-	-	2
		akçe	5	-	-	-	5
	bitter orange groves	groves	-	-	-	-	3
		akçe	-	-	-	-	450
	gardens	number	-	1	1	-	3
		akçe	-	50	150	-	300
	kitchen gardens	number	-	2	1	1	8
		akçe	-	300	80	100	1155
	fish-farms	number	-	-	1	-	4
		akçe	-	-	160	-	1570
	watermills	number	2	2	9	3	42.5
		akçe	1200	700	3100	875	14585
	fulling mills	number	-	-	-	-	6
		akçe	-	-	-	-	270
	oil presses	number	-	-	-	-	2
		akçe	-	-	-	-	150

Table 28. *Livā'-ı Mora (the Peloponnese).*

		Ḳalavrita	Mizisra	Mihlu	Bejenik
watermills held in common	number	-	-	-	-
	akçe	-	-	-	-
tithe (in akçes)	flax	400	20	120	910
	vineyards	5223	80	656	4736
	wheat	29310	200	7956	13050
	barley	4541	31	1496	2051
	olive oil	8	-	-	3
	fruits	116	3	10	67
	cotton	-	-	-	-
	honey	5	-	-	43
	silk	938	-	1	167
	resin	-	-	-	-
	mulberries	-	-	-	-
	watermills	-	-	-	-
	kitchen gardens	-	-	-	-
units (in akçes)	wine	539	-	80	600
	swine	297	-	242	142
	sheep	-	-	-	-
watermills (mülk)	number	19	-	2	5
	akçe	790	-	60	350
fulling mills (mülk)	number	3	-	-	-
	akçe	45	-	-	-
transit duty		-	-	-	-
market tax and niyābet		-	-	-	-
custom dues		-	-	-	-
drag seine fishing		-	-	-	-
	total	69792	1704	18407	37170
muḳāṭaʿa (imperial)	salt-pans	-	-	-	-
	rice fields	-	-	-	-
muḳāṭaʿa (tīmār)	niyābet	-	-	-	-
	niyābet and market tax	-	-	-	-
	fish-farms	-	-	-	-
	fish-farms and transit duty	-	-	-	-
	market tax, custom dues and transit duty	-	-	-	-
	bitter orange groves	-	-	-	-
	oil presses	-	-	-	-

Table 28. *Livā'-ı Mora (the Peloponnese).*

		Voştiça	Ḫulumiç	Vumero	Kirvuḳor	Arḳadya
watermills held in common	number	2	-	-	-	1
	akçe	210	-	-	-	120
tithe (in akçes)	flax	1010	614	2673	2265	660
	vineyards	18584	10704	20935	10354	4632
	wheat	44250	18050	48700	44100	8543
	barley	6855	2809	7342	6822	1322
	olive oil	30	6	105	11	354
	fruits	295	97	389	154	105
	cotton	130	498	1440	200	150
	honey	-	7	86	202	169
	silk	22762	-	923	604	83
	resin	-	-	11	-	-
	mulberries	-	-	-	-	-
	watermills	40	-	-	-	-
	kitchen gardens	-	-	-	-	-
units (in akçes)	wine	2285	698	1597	1085	411
	swine	57	321	648	1534	45
	sheep	1035	-	-	-	-
watermills (mülk)	number	25	6	21	17	5
	akçe	1630	230	790	840	270
fulling mills (mülk)	number	-	-	5	-	-
	akçe	-	-	75	-	-
transit duty		6000	-	-	-	-
market tax and niyābet		-	700	2500	-	-
custom dues		-	1200	-	-	-
drag seine fishing		-	450	-	-	-
	total	182258	60241	177218	103161	40032
muḳāṭa'a (imperial)	salt-pans	20564	9000	7000	-	500
	rice fields	-	-	28500	-	500
muḳāṭa'a (tīmār)	niyābet	2000	-	-	-	-
	niyābet and market tax	-	-	-	-	-
	fish-farms	-	750	-	250	-
	fish-farms and transit duty	-	-	4500	-	-
	market tax, custom dues and transit duty	-	-	-	-	-
	bitter orange groves	-	-	-	-	-
	oil presses	-	-	-	-	-

Table 28. *Livā'-ı Mora (the Peloponnese).*

		Londar	Ḳoriṣos	Balya Badra	Ḳalandriça
watermills held in common	number	-	-	-	-
	akçe	-	-	-	-
tithe (in akçes)	flax	2135	1055	714	150
	vineyards	28932	11993	17704	3781
	wheat	28550	24450	16331	7740
	barley	4390	3794	2457	1153
	olive oil	39	-	948	335
	fruits	86	455	275	72
	cotton	-	450	1595	750
	honey	52	333	-	-
	silk	408	15	404	359
	resin	-	-	-	-
	mulberries	-	-	13	-
	watermills	-	-	-	-
	kitchen gardens	50	200	49	-
units (in akçes)	wine	2940	1305	2606	456
	swine	997	81	58	96
	sheep	-	-	-	-
watermills (mülk)	number	28	11	11	4
	akçe	1270	590	840	280
fulling mills (mülk)	number	-	-	-	-
	akçe	-	-	-	-
transit duty		-	-	-	-
market tax and niyābet		-	-	-	500
custom dues		-	-	-	-
drag seine fishing		-	-	-	-
	total	118382	62826	78378	26305
muḳāṭa'a (imperial)	salt-pans	-	320	7000	-
	rice fields	-	-	-	-
muḳāṭa'a (tīmār)	niyābet	-	-	-	-
	niyābet and market tax	3500	-	-	-
	fish-farms	-	-	-	-
	fish-farms and transit duty	-	-	-	-
	market tax, custom dues and transit duty	-	3000	-	-
	bitter orange groves	-	450	-	-
	oil presses	-	-	250	-

Table 28. *Livā'-ı Mora (the Peloponnese).*

		Şandamiri	Girbene	Ayo Ilya	Ġardicko	total
watermills held in common	number	-	-	-	-	3
	akçe	-	-	-	-	330
tithe (in akçes)	flax	323	430	1463	475	15417
	vineyards	4612	5242	8034	6925	163127
	wheat	7700	20850	20600	22150	362530
	barley	1250	3243	3090	3438	56084
	olive oil	118	147	30	46	2180
	fruits	37	47	122	105	2435
	cotton	50	400	492	40	6195
	honey	-	-	46	-	943
	silk	-	74	650	160	27548
	resin	-	-	-	-	11
	mulberries	-	-	-	-	13
	watermills	-	-	-	-	40
	kitchen gardens	-	-	-	-	299
units (in akçes)	wine	460	421	700	100	16283
	swine	41	222	304	170	5255
	sheep	-	-	-	-	1035
watermills (mülk)	number	5	13	7	7	186
	akçe	360	540	210	360	9410
fulling mills (mülk)	number	-	2	1	3	14
	akçe	-	30	15	50	215
transit duty		-	-	-	-	6000
market tax and niyābet		-	-	-	-	3700
custom dues		-	-	-	-	1200
drag seine fishing		-	-	-	-	450
	total	26528	52395	75920	56395	1187112
muḳāṭa'a (imperial)	salt-pans	-	-	-	-	44384
	rice fields	-	-	-	-	29000
muḳāṭa'a (tīmār)	niyābet	-	-	-	-	2000
	niyābet and market tax	-	-	-	-	3500
	fish-farms	-	2500	-	-	3500
	fish-farms and transit duty	-	-	-	-	4500
	market tax, custom dues and transit duty	-	-	-	-	3000
	bitter orange groves	-	-	-	-	450
	oil presses	-	-	-	-	250

Chart 23. *Mora* (*The Peloponnese*).

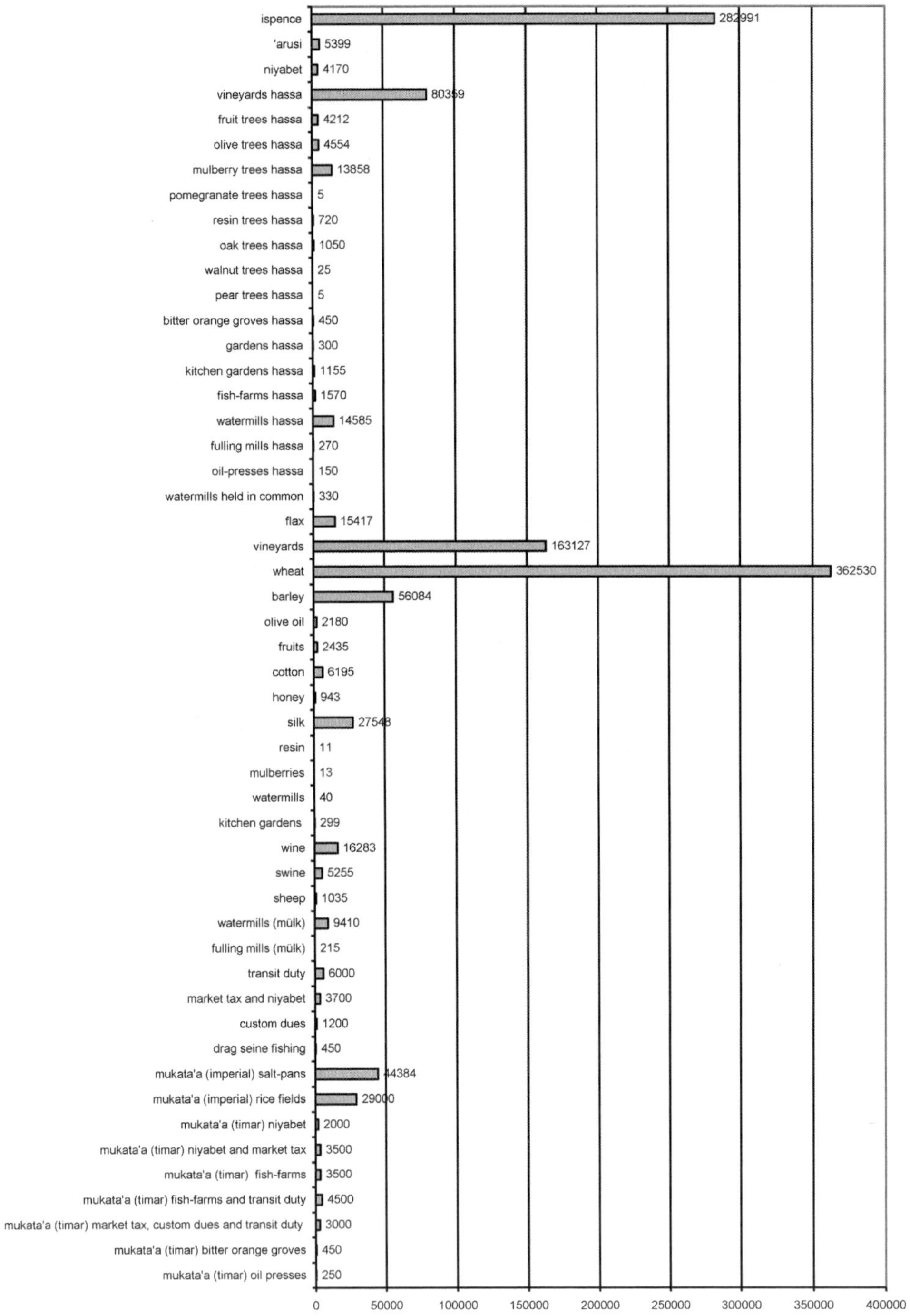

Table 29. *Wheat and barley.*

District		wheat	barley
Ḳalavrita	tithe (*aḳçe*)	29,310	4541
	crop's value (*aḳçe*)	234,480	36,328
	weight *müdd* (kg)	2,931 (= 1,503,954.72kg)	605.47 (= 310,677.06kg)
Mizişra	tithe (*aḳçe*)	200	31
	crop's value (*aḳçe*)	1,600	248
	weight *müdd* (kg)	20 (= 10,262.4kg)	4.13 (= 2,120.9kg)
Miḫlu	tithe (*aḳçe*)	7,956	1,496
	crop's value (*aḳçe*)	63,648	11,968
	weight *müdd* (kg)	795.6 (= 408,238.27kg)	199.47 (= 102,350.37kg)
Bejenik	tithe (*aḳçe*)	13,050	2,051
	crop's value (*aḳçe*)	104,400	16,408
	weight *müdd* (kg)	1,305 (= 669,621.6kg)	273.47 (= 140,321.22kg)
Voştiça	tithe (*aḳçe*)	44,250	6,855
	crop's value (*aḳçe*)	354,000	54,840
	weight *müdd* (kg)	4,425 (= 2,270,556kg)	914 (= 468,991.68kg)
Ḫulumiç	tithe (*aḳçe*)	18,050	2,809
	crop's value (*aḳçe*)	144,400	22,472
	weight *müdd* (kg)	1,805 (= 926,181.6kg)	374.53 (= 192,180.54kg)
Vumero	tithe (*aḳçe*)	48,700	7,342
	crop's value (*aḳçe*)	389,600	58,736
	weight *müdd* (kg)	4,870 (= 2,498,894.4kg)	978.73 (= 502,310.27kg)
Kirvuḳor	tithe (*aḳçe*)	44,100	6,822
	crop's value (*aḳçe*)	352,800	54,576
	weight *müdd* (kg)	4,410 (= 2,262,859.2kg)	909.6 (= 466,733.95kg)
Arḳadya	tithe (*aḳçe*)	8,543	1,322
	crop's value (*aḳçe*)	68,344	10,576
	weight *müdd* (kg)	854.3 (= 438,358.42kg)	176.27 (= 90,445.95kg)
Londar	tithe (*aḳçe*)	28,550	4,390
	crop's value (*aḳçe*)	228,400	35,120
	weight *müdd* (kg)	2,855 (= 1,464,957.6kg)	585.33 (= 300,346.24kg)
Ḳorişos	tithe (*aḳçe*)	24,450	3,794
	crop's value (*aḳçe*)	195,600	30,352
	weight *müdd* (kg)	2,445 (= 1,254,578.4kg)	505.87 (= 259,570.3kg)
Balya Badra	tithe (*aḳçe*)	16,331	2,457
	crop's value (*aḳçe*)	130,648	19,656
	weight *müdd* (kg)	1,633.1 (= 837,976.27kg)	327.6 (= 168,098.11kg)
Ḳalandriça	tithe (*aḳçe*)	7,740	1,153
	crop's value (*aḳçe*)	61,920	9,224
	weight *müdd* (kg)	774 (= 397,154.88kg)	153.73 (= 78,883.65kg)
Şandamiri	tithe (*aḳçe*)	7,700	1,250
	crop's value (*aḳçe*)	61,600	10,000
	weight *müdd* (kg)	770 (= 395,102.4kg)	166.67 (= 85,520kg)
Girbene	tithe (*aḳçe*)	20,850	3,243
	crop's value (*aḳçe*)	166,800	25,944
	weight *müdd* (kg)	2,085 (= 1,069,855.2kg)	432.4 (= 221,873.09kg)
Ayo İlya	tithe (*aḳçe*)	20,600	3,090
	crop's value (*aḳçe*)	164,800	24,720
	weight *müdd* (kg)	2,060 (= 1,057,027.2kg)	412 (= 211,405.44kg)
Ġardicḳo	tithe (*aḳçe*)	22,150	3,438
	crop's value (*aḳçe*)	177,200	27,504
	weight *müdd* (kg)	2,215 (= 1,136,560.8kg)	458.4 (= 235,214.21kg)
Total	tithe (*aḳçe*)	362,530	56,084
	crop's value (*aḳçe*)	2,900,240	448,672
	weight *müdd* (kg)	36,253 (= 18,602,139.36kg)	7,477.87 (= 3,837,042.94kg)

Table 30. *Tithes*.

	tithe	value	percentage
flax	15417	154170	2.79%
vineyards	163127	1631270	29.50%
wheat	362530	2900240	52.44%
barley	56084	448672	8.11%
olive oil	2180	21800	0.40%
fruits	2435	24350	0.44%
cotton	6195	61950	1.12%
honey	943	9430	0.17%
silk	27548	275480	4.98%
resin	11	110	0.001%
mulberries	13	130	0.002%
watermills	40	?	-
kitchen gardens	299	2392	0.04%
total	636822	5529994	100%

Table 31. *Viticulture yield (ḫāṣṣa vineyards).*

District	tax	actual value	*dönüms*	*aḳçe*s per *dönüm*
Ḳalavrita	3000	12000	23	521.74
Mizis̱ra	300	1200	5	240
Miḫlu	1320	5280	11	480
Bejenik	2340	9360	22	425.45
Voştiça	4182	16728	39	428.92
Ḫulumiç	1440	5760	12	480
Vumero	9364	37456	63.5	589.86
Kirvuḳor	3694	14776	28	527.71
Arḳadya	11088	44352	128.5	345.15
Londar	11250	45000	136	330.88
Ḳoris̱os	1800	7200	21	342.86
Balya Badra	1408	5632	15	375.47
Ḳalandriça	1500	6000	20	300
Ṣandamiri	3542	14168	46	308
Girbene	2734	10936	28	390.57
Ayo İlya	16605	66420	125	531.36
Ġardicḳo	4792	19168	28	684.57
total	80359	321436	831	386.81

Conclusion

This study explored the early Ottoman Peloponnese on the basis of an annotated edition of the TT10-1/14662 Ottoman taxation cadastre dated some time between 1460 and 1463 shedding light on the historical geography, demography and economy of Greece's southernmost peninsula immediately after the Ottoman conquest (1460).

Being the earliest extant cadastre for the Peloponnese, the TT10-1/14662 register offers a unique cross-section of this region as it systematically recorded the Moreote population inhabiting land that had been granted as *tīmār*s to certain individuals and their taxable obligations. Despite its fragmentary state, it is invaluable for it casts light also on the late Byzantine period, which lacks similar primary sources.

The examination of the 667 toponyms mentioned in the register resulted in the identification of 449 localities (67.3%). The unidentified 218 place names have been effaced in the course of time, leaving no trace. The identified localities were digitally mapped out in a set of 38 maps with the help of GIS technology. The ArcGIS 9 ArcMap™ software used provides the researcher with interactive mapping tools that can create different thematic maps according to the figures selected from the database (revenues, population and ethnicity). As portrayed in map 35, the surviving part of the register covers adequately the north-western Peloponnese (modern-day regional units of Achaia and Elis) while leaving parts of Argolis, Arcadia, Messenia and, almost in its entirety, Laconia blank. At this stage, before collating the geographical data of our register with the ones of the TT80, we can attribute this image only to the fragmentary state of the TT10-1/14662. In many cases the delineation of the districts appears vague or complex.

Map 35 gives a *prima facie* impression that the Peloponnese in 1460–1463 was mainly inhabited by Albanians, and this would have been sharper if we keep in mind that 71.6% of the unidentified localities are Albanian settlements. This image is strengthened further when we count the families recorded in the register (*ḫāne* + *bīve*): 7,103 (59.18%) Greek families and 4,900 (40.82%) Albanian ones (map 36). The percentage of the Greek and the Albanian population in each district is illustrated in the charts of map 38. The distribution of the Moreote population is based on the following pattern: a large Greek village or town *vis-à-vis* remote(r), smaller and financially weaker Albanian settlements (maps 36–37).

The *tīmār* system was fully implemented in the Peloponnese, as in the other core lands of the Ottoman Empire. As was the custom for early Ottoman rule in the Balkans, a number of revenues were accrued to Christian timariots, which in our case constituted 0.22% of the total. The taxes levied on the Peloponnesians amounted to 1,187,112 *akçe*s or approximately 27,932 golden ducats. Nearly one third of this amount (30.54%) constituted the tithe on wheat followed by the *ispence* (23.84%) and viticulture (20.51%). It should be noted that only wheat, barley and rice are registered among the grains that were conceivably cultivated in the Peloponnese; the absence of legumes is also worth mentioning. The missing crops appear in the posterior TT80.[1] We may assume that small-scale legume cultivation was employed in the gardens (*bostān*, *bāġçe*). Some almost insignificant discrepancies in the totals given in the *defter* should be attributed to accounting errors and certainly do not constitute a major defect. One has to judge the scribe with charity bearing in mind that there were no pocket calculators in the fifteenth-century Peloponnese. On the other hand, the inaccuracies of the terms of the fiefs and the military obligations of the timariots indicate the fluidity in the implementation of the *tīmār* system at this early stage.

Despite this wealth of information, the *taḥrīr defter*s, though a unique source, provide only a partial view, for they refer only to a specific class, namely timariots, excluding any other category. As has been pointed out by Lowry: 'the *tahrir defter*s alone do not provide the basis for any kind of quantitative study, be it toponymy, topography, taxation, agricultural production or population. In order to obtain an overall perspective in any of these areas the *tahrir*s must be used in conjunction with other surviving contemporary records, in particular, with the surviving *vakıf defter*s.'[2]

1 Alexander 1999, 58.
2 Lowry 1992, 8. For the discussion on the credibility of the Ottoman registers as sources of demography and economy see Kolovos 2012, 69–72.

Further research on the first Ottoman period in the Peloponnese (1460–1685) in the light of the TT10-1/14662 cadastre should include an examination of a selection of specific areas of the province, provided the *taḥrīr defter*s show thirty years of continuity or as near as possible between each other, and a collation of these with other extant Ottoman documentation. This would not only help us attest with greater accuracy the revenue paid to the timariots, but it would also cast light on the more extensive Ottoman administration and taxes paid directly to the Sultan or Muslim pious endowments. This collation will also entail the rest of the population, the free landowners (Byzantine *πάροικοι*; Venetian *villani*), the villains bound to the soil (Byzantine *δουλοπάροικοι*; Venetian *villani serve conditionis*), the villains (Greek *δημοσιάριοι πάροικοι, κληροπάροικοι*; Venetian *villani communis, villani ecclesie*) who were granted parcels of land by the state or the Church (Greek *στάσεις*; Venetian *stasia*), which were inalienable and hereditary.[3] This research would also provide information on the legal status of merchants and solicitors, which would in turn necessitate the exploration both of the Venetian-Byzantine and Ottoman documentation in order to identify elements of continuity or change that had occurred from the Byzantine to the Ottoman period. Such a comparative approach may answer the important question posed by scholars on whether the fiscal figures in TT10-1/14662 represent an accurate account or a mere estimate.

Given the scope of the present study, namely to present the data obtained from the TT10-1/14662 register, certain important areas await further investigation. These include: (a) the identification of the abandoned settlements through field research in quest of the microtoponymy; (b) the analysis of the Peloponnesian micro- and macro-economy; and (c) the comparison of the examined register with the one following, namely the TT80 (1514/5), which will present the demographic and economic changes the Peloponnese underwent in a period of half a century, focusing on selected districts to be examined throughout the first Ottoman period (1460–1685).

The much-questioned field of *defterology* has appealed to historians of the Ottoman period from the early 1940s. The initial enthusiasm gradually faded and, as was the case in quantitative history, the study of registers failed to live up to its expectations.[4] In recent years however, the rejuvenating winds of environmental history and geohistory, have started to sweep through this field.[5] The assessment of the plethora of quantitative data contained in the registers, when collated with geological and climatological findings, can lay the foundation for constituting quantifiable historical problems and become a tool to increase historical and environmental understanding in the *longue durée*.

3 Chrysostomides 2003, 158. See also Hodgetts 1983; Oikonomidès 1996, 174–176; Lemerle 1979, 246–247.

4 Faroqhi 1999, 95; Jarausch–Hardy 1991, 3.

5 Tabak 2008, 117–133; White 2011, 57-58; İnal 2011; Kolovos–Kotzageorgis 2015; Kotzageorgis 2018.

Index of Place Names Contained in the TT10-1/14662

Ottoman		Modern Greek	no.
[---]şta	شته [---]		550
Açiḫolos	آچیخولوس	Atsiholos (Ατσίχολος)	94
Aġali	آغالی	Elatos (Έλατος)	84
Aḳunba	آقونبه	Paliakoumba Platianas (Παλιάκουμπα Πλατιάνας)	354
Aleksi Manesi	الکسی مانسی	Psili Vrysi (?) (Ψηλή Βρύση)	392
Amuri	آموری	Amouri (?) (Αμούρι)	9
Amuri	آموری	Anemodouri (?) (Ανεμοδούρι)	439
Anastasova	اناستاسوه	Anastasi (Ανάσταση)	50
Andon	اندون	Antoni (?) (Αντώνη)	661
Andraviza	اندراویزه	Andravida (Ανδραβίδα)	200
Andriya Pupuḳa	اندریه پوپوقه	Boumboukas (?) (Μπούμπουκας)	419
Androniḳa	اندرونقه	Andronika (Ανδρόνικα)	624
Aniza	آنیزه	Anaziri (Αναζήρι)	318
Añloniça	اکلونیچه	Epitalio (Επιτάλιο)	264
Aranis Ḳavalari	ارانس قوالاری		260
Aranis Ḳuçohyari	ارانس قوچوهیاری	Koutsohera (Κουτσοχέρα)	259
Arfara	آرفارا	Ambelokipoi (Αμπελόκηποι)	158
Arḫangeli	ارخانکلی	Polihni (Πολίχνη)	370
Arḳadya	ارقادیه	Kyparissia (Κυπαρισσία)	365
Artica	ارتیجه	Fanari (Φανάρι)	297
Arula	آرولا	Arla (Άρλα)	553
Arvano Ḳastro	آروانو قاسترو	Arvanokastro (Αρβανόκαστρο)	603
Asfalaḫto	اسفلاختو	Asfalakto (Ασφάλακτο)	549
Astriçi	آستریچی	Astros (Άστρος)	66

Astro	آسترو	Agios Ioannis/Kastro Orias (Άγιος Ιωάννης/ Κάστρο Ωριάς)	67
Avrami	آورامی	Avrami (Αβράμι)	542
Aya Baraskevi	آیه براسکوی	Agia Paraskevi (Αγία Παρασκευή)	215
Aya İğliğori	آیه اکلیغوری	Grigoris (Γρηγόρης)	118
Aya Niḳola	آیه نیقولا	Agios Nikolaos (Άγιος Νικόλαος)	441
Aya Yorgi	آیه یورکی	Lykosoura (Λυκόσουρα)	384
Ayiya	آییه		616
Ayo İlya	آیو الیا	Agios Ilias (Άγιος Ηλίας)	594
Ayo İvlaşi	آیو اولاشی	Agios Vlasios (Άγιος Βλάσιος)	44
Ayo Ḳostandino	آیو قستندینو	Agios Konstantinos (Άγιος Κωνσταντίνος)	231
Ayo Lisyo	آیو لسیو	Profitis Elissaios (Προφήτης Ελισσαίος)	559
Ayo Niḳolas	آیو نیقولاس	Agios Nikolaos (Άγιος Νικόλαος)	557
Ayo Paraskevi	آیو پراسکوی	Paraskevi (Παρασκευή)	111
Ayo Vaṣıl	آیو وآصیل	Agios Vasileios (Άγιος Βασίλειος)	599
Ayo Vaṣıl/Çağıl Ḥiṣārı	آیو وآصل/چاغل حصاری	Agios Vasileios (Άγιος Βασίλειος)	446
Ayo Yani	آیو یانی	Agios Ioannis (Άγιος Ιωάννης)	105
Ayo Yani	ایو یانی	Agios Ioannis (Άγιος Ιωάννης)	547
Ayo Yorgi	آیو یورکی	Agios Georgios (Άγιος Γεώργιος)	149
Ayo Yorgi	آیو یورکی	Agios Georgios (Άγιος Γεώργιος)	563
Ayo Ẕimitri Liḳo Anbali	آیو ذیمتری لیقو انبالی		478
Ayonori	آیونوری	Agionori (Αγιονόρι)	456
Bala	باله	Balas (Μπάλας)	517
Balçi	بالچی	Baltzes (?) (Μπάλτζες)	564
Balya Badra	بالیه بادره	Patra (Πάτρα)	471
Barbuc	باربوج		637
Barbuçi	باربوچی	Ambelaki (?) (Αμπελάκι)	424
Barçi	بارچی		23
Barçi	بارچی	Dafnoula (Δαφνούλα)	344
Barçi	بارچی		622
Bardi	باردی	Agios Ioannis (Άγιος Ιωάννης)	462
Bardi Zuġra	باردی زوغره		546
Bardoḳosta	باردوقوسته	Krystallovrysi (Κρυσταλλόβρυση)	508

Başta	باشته	Agioi Theodoroi (Άγιοι Θεόδωροι)	212
Bavasi	باواسی		187
Bavasi	باواسی		605
Beçaḳus	بچاقوس	Petsakoi (Πετσάκοι)	126
Bejenik	بژنیك	Vlaherna (Βλαχέρνα)	78
Beluşi	بلوشی		5
Beluşi	بلوشی	Sykies (Συκιές)	312
Bendeni/Pendeni	بندنی/پندنی	Diakopi (Διακόπι)	85
Besulḳa	بسولقه	Vythoulkas (Βυθούλκας)	562
Biçi	بچی		464
Bizbardi	بزباردی	Trypiti (Τρυπητή)	339
Bondaya	بوندایه	Palaiopyrgos (Παλαιόπυργος)	86
Branca	برانجا		223
Brasna Sanḳa	براسنه سانقه	Sangas (Σάγκας)	73
Bratiça	براتیچه	Parnassos (Παρνασσός)	359
Bruma	بروما	Irakleia (Ηράκλεια)	242
Buḫuşta	بوخوشته	Boufouskia/Bofonokia (Μπουφούσκια/ Μποφονόκια)	103
Bura	بوره	Lykouresis (Λυκούρεσης)	657
Burlaşa	بورلاشه	Bourlesia (Μπουρλέσια)	125
Buryalisa	بوریالسه		501
Buza	بوزه	Bouzia (Μπούζια)	588
Buzbardi	بزباردی	Velanidies (Βελανιδιές)	453
Cilardi	جلاردی	Tsilardi (Τσιλάρδι/Τσιλαρδί)	153
Coya	جویا	Prasino (Πράσινο)	277
Çapoġa	چاپوغه	Pteri (Πτέρη)	633
Çarnota	چارنوته/چارنوتا	Lefkasio (Λευκάσιο)	88
Çarnuḫlu	چارنوخلو	Pefko (Πεύκο)	436
Çavuşi	چاوشی	Kentro (Κέντρο)	182
Çernota	چرنوتا		502
Çimlo	چیملو	Tsivlos (Τσιβλός)	143
Çipyana	چپیانه	Nestani (Νεστάνη)	74
Çuḳala	چوقاله	Tsoukala (Τσουκαλά)	489

Dara	دآره	Daras (Δάρας)	32
Dardesi	داردسی	Agrapidokambos (?) (Αγραπιδόκαμπος)	479
Debrani	دبرانی		47
Dima Plaşa	دیمه پلاشه		14
Dimitri Maçuki	دیمتری ماچوکی		398
Divye	دویه		551
Domanịka Beluşi	دومانیقه بلوشی	Belousia (?) (Μπελούσια)	397
Dorza	دورزه	Doriza (?) (Δόριζα)	288
Doşkesi	دوشکسی	Toskesi/Doskesi (Τόσκεσι/Ντόσκεσι)	90
Draġoti	دراغوتی		493
Draġoy	دراغوی	Dragogi (Δραγώγι)	306
Draġuẕisti	دراغوذستی	Tragoudisti (Τραγουδιστή)	325
Dramşa	درامشه	Dramesi (?) (Δράμεσι)	184
Drayina	دراینه	Pefki (Πευκί)	326
Droġolavoş	دروغولاوش	Drovolovo (Δροβολοβό)	51
Duḳa Plaşa	دوقه پلاشه		399
Duḳati	دوقه‌تی		589
Dumeña	دومکه		274
Duranḳorgi	دورانقورکی		665
Duşa Dara	دوشه دآره		68
Eksoriya	اکسوریه		580
Epano Ḳurnofita	اپانو قورنوفته	Krinofyta (Κρινόφυτα)	15
Epanolaġo	اپانولاغو	Lapanagoi (Λαπαναγοί)	122
Fenari	فناری	Ano Fanari (Άνω Φανάρι); Kato Fanari/ Dryopi (Κάτω Φανάρι/Δρυόπη)	461
Fenaromeni	فنارومنی	Panagias Filokaliotissas Monastery (?) (I.M. Παναγίας Φιλοκαλιώτισσας)	617
Fil Adrofinos	فل ادرفنوس		659
Fila	فیله	Filia (Φίλια)	41
Floḳa	فلوقه	Flokas (Φλόκας)	316
Foloḳobuva	فولوقوبووه		201
Fostana	فوستانه	Fostaina (Φώσταινα)	556
Franḳa	فرانقه	Franga (?) (Φράγκα)	256

Franḳa Vila	فرانقا ویله	Frangavilas Monastery (I.M. Φραγκαβίλας)	619
Franḳo	فرانقو	Ano Franga (Άνω Φράγκα)	114
Frati	فراتی		468
Frati	فراتی	Frati (Φράτι)	585
Frosina	فرسینه	Frousiouna (Φρουσιούνα)	470
Ġardena	غاردنه	Keryneia (Κερύνεια)	104
Ġardicḳo	غاردیجقو	Gatsiko (Γάτσικο)	627
Ġardik	غاردیك	Gardiki-Amfeia (?) (Γαρδίκι-Άμφεια)	361
Ġarnaze	غارنازه		532
Ġastuni	غاستنی	Gastouni (Γαστούνη)	174
Gerbesi	کربسی		381
Gerbesi	کربسی	Profitis Ilias (Προφήτης Ηλίας)	575
Gerbeşi	کربشی	Paralimni (Παραλίμνη)	645
Ġırebini	غربنی	Kato Melpeia (Κάτω Μέλπεια)	369
Gin Bodya	کین بودیه	Mikros Pontias (Μικρός Ποντιάς)	590
Gin Floḳa	کین فلوقه	Flokas (Φλόκας)	535
Gin Ḳondostavlo Manesi	کین قوندستاولو مانسی	Manesis (?) (Μάνεσης)	430
Gin Manesi	کین مانسی	Manesi (Μάνεσι)	540
Girbene	کیربنه	Spartia (Σπαρτιά)	538
Girḳa Ḳumani	کرقه قومانی		181
Ġolemi	غوملی	Golemi (Γολέμι)	30
Ġolemi	غوملی	Golemi (Γολέμι)	514
Ġolomi	غلومی	Rodina (Ροδινά)	602
Ġomosto	غومستو	Gomosto (Γομοστό)	630
Ġurdesi	غوردسی		222
Gön Lopesi	کون لوپسی	Katarraktis (Καταρράκτης)	632
Graḳa	کراقه	Graikas (Γκραίκας)	120
Ġramatiḳo	غرامتیقو	Grammatikos (Γραμματικός)	216
Ġulyamu Argiroplu	غولیامو ارکیروپلو		405
Ġumaniça	غومانیچه	Drosato (Δροσάτο), Goumenissa (Γουμένισσα)	128
Ġurenas	غورناس	Agoriani (Αγόριανη)	386
Ġurġa	غورغه		45

Ġurzumişa	غرزمشه	Leontio (Λεόντιο)	587
Ḫamaḳu	خاماقو	Lousiko (Λουσικό)	6
Ḫaraḳtinu	خراقتنو	Haraktinou (Χαρακτινού)	12
Ḫarkâ	خركا	Halkeio (Χαλκείο)	454
Ḫarkâ	خركا		654
Ḫavaro Protopapa	خاوارو پرتوپاپا	Synoikismos Havariou/Palaio Havari (Συνοικισμός Χαβαρίου/Παλαιό Χάβαρι)	194
Ḫayḳal	خايقال		91
Ḫayḳal	خايقال		252
Ḫırisoviryi Ḳozma	خرسوويريي قزما	Kosma (Κοσμά)	425
Hiliẕon	هليذون	Helidoni (Χελιδόνι)	234
Ḫoloropoẕi	خولوروپوذى		13
Ḫotoġosti	خوتوغوستى		150
Ḫulumiç	خلومچ	Hlemoutsi/Kastro (Χλεμούτσι/Κάστρο)	173
Iġlava	اغلاوه		286
İflamurari	افلامورارى	Flamboura (Φλάμπουρα)	38
İksanya	اكسانيه	Xenies (Ξενιές)	527
İksaroḳastalya	اكساروقاستاليه	Xerokastellia (Ξεροκαστελλιά)	457
İksenoẕoḫiyo	اكسنوذوخيو	Paralia Niforaiikon (Παραλία Νιφοραίικων)	494
İksifya	اكسفيه		388
İlya Maji	اليا ماژى		407
İpsari	اپسارى	Psari (Ψάρι)	209
İpsari	اپسارى	Lehaina (Λεχαινά)	497
İryolo	اريولو	Riolos (Ρίολος)	612
İsfardina	اسفاردنه	Spartinou (?) (Σπαρτινού)	541
İsfranci	اسفرانجى	Agia Paraskevi (?) (Αγία Παρασκευή)	310
İsḳala	اسقاله	Skala (?) (Σκάλα)	351
İskâẕa	اسكاذه	Skiadas (Σκιαδάς)	307
İskiliç	اسكليچ	Skyliki (?) (Σκυλίκη)	95
İsḳlaviça	اسقلاويچه	Sklavoutsa (Σκλάβουτσα)	592
İskliva	اسكليوه		40
İskliva	اسكليوه		178
İsḳura	اسقوره	Skoura (Σκούρα)	503

İsliva	اسليوه	Skliva (Σκλίβα)	642
İsliva-ı dīğer	اسليوه ديكر		649
İspani	اسپانى		268
İspani-i dīğer	اسپانى ديكر		269
İstamiro	استاميرو	Hatzi (Χατζί)	650
İstavriya/İstavrina	استاورييه/استاورينه	Stavria (Σταυριά)	141
İstefano Mazaraki	استفانو مزراكى		484
İstilivena	استليونه	Sylivaina (Συλίβαινα)	144
İstoya	استويه	Ploutohori (Πλουτοχώρι)	328
İstoya Volomiri	استويه ولوميرى	Voliria/Volíries (?) (Βολιριά/Βολιριές)	414
İstoyan	استويان		586
İstrazova	استرازوه	Dafni (Δάφνη)	58
İsturġova	استورغوه		646
İş Ari	ايش ارى	Isoma (Ἴσωμα)	518
İşpata	اشپاته		241
İşpata	اشپاته	Agios Nikolaos (Άγιος Νικόλαος)	596
İştin Bondaya	اشتين بونديه	Megas Pontias (Μέγας Ποντιάς)	48
İştopanṣi	اشتوپانثى		26
İştopanṣi Lopesi	اشتوپانثى لوپسى	Kryonero (Κρυόνερο)	601
İvlaḫo	اولاخو		162
İvlaḫo	اولاخو	Vlahoi (?) (Βλάχοι)	634
İvlaḫo Filito	اولاخو فليتو		99
İvlaḫo Ḳalanas	اولاخو قالناس	Kalanos (Κάλανος)	54
İvlaḫo Yalya	اولاخو ياليا		55
İvlanduşa	اولاندوشه	Stylia (Στύλια)	115
İvlanduşa	اولاندوشه		206
İvlanduşa	اولاندوشه		628
İvraḫni	اوراخنى	Vrahni (Βράχνι)	3
İvrato Ḳuçi Ḳonbi Ṣeḳra	اوراتو قوچى قنبى ثقره		437
İzlatḳa	ازلاتقه	Neromylos (Νερόμυλος)	202
İzlatḳa	ازلاتقه		488
Jujli Palamiẕi	ژوژلى پالاميذى		193

Junbata	ژونبته	Pigi (Πηγή)	583
Jupan/Jupano	ژوپان/ژوپانو	Zioupani (Ζιουπάνη)	317
Ḳaçana	قاچانه		26
Ḳaçaru	قچارو	Katsaros (Κατσαρός)	273
Ḳaḳoḫoryo	قاقوخوريو	Dafnes (Δάφνες)	112
Ḳaḳusi	قاقوسی		221
Ḳalanci	قالانجی	Kalentzi (Καλέντζι)	641
Ḳalandriça	قلاندريچه	Halandritsa (Χαλανδρίτσα)	510
Ḳalavrita	قلاورته	Kalavryta (Καλάβρυτα)	1
Ḳalazoni	قالازونی	Halazoni (Χαλαζόνι)	378
Ḳalo İstemati	قالو استماتی		450
Ḳamaniça	قمانيچه	Kamenitsa (Καμενίτσα)	485
Ḳameniça	قامنيچه	Kamenitsa (Καμενίτσα)	82
Ḳanbiziya	قانبيزييه		205
Ḳandila	قانديله	Kandila (Κανδήλα)	89
Ḳani	قانی	Kallithea (Καλλιθέα)	20
Ḳanḳaẕi	قانقاذی	Kangadi (Καγκάδι)	203
Ḳanḳaẕi	قانقاذی	Kangadi (?) (Καγκάδι)	314
Ḳapaleto	قپالتو	Kapaleto (Καπαλέτο)	214
Ḳapareli	قپارلی		130
Ḳaratula	قراتولا	Karatoula (Καράτουλα)	60
Ḳaratula	قراتولا	Karatoulas (Καράτουλας)	291
Ḳaratula-ı dīğer	قراتولاء ديكر		27
Ḳariza	قريزه		275
Ḳartazori	قارتازوری		614
Ḳarvunari	قاروونارى	Karvounaris (Καρβουνάρης)	332
Ḳarẕiyoḳafti	قارذيوقافتی	Kardiakafti (Καρδιακαύτι)	192
Ḳastel	قاستل	Kastelli (Καστέλλι)	56
Ḳastel İksovuni	قاستل اكسوونی	Xyvouni/Xivouni (Ξυβούνι/Ξίβουνι)	606
Ḳastriçi	قاستريچی	Ano Kastritsi (Άνω Καστρίτσι)	496
Ḳastriya	قاستريه	Kastria (Καστρία)	16
Ḳato Ḳurnofita	قاتو قورنوفته	Krinofyta (Κρινόφυτα)	29

Ḳavalari	قوالاری	Kavalari (Καβαλάρη)	548
Ḳavalari Trusa	قوآلاری تروسا	Trousas (Τρούσας)	545
Ḳavasila	قواسله	Kavasilas (Καβάσιλας)	207
Ḳazani	قزانی		243
Ḳazneş	قازنش	Ano Kleitoria (Άνω Κλειτορία)	57
Ḳazneş	قازنش	Katsaïtaiika (Κατσαϊταίικα)	511
Ḳazneş	قازنش	Agia Marina (Αγία Μαρίνα)	572
Kefiñali	کفیکالی	Kafkonia (Καυκωνία)	342
Kelavi	کلاوی	Koroivos (Κόροιβος)	179
Keraṣova	کراصوه	Kerasia (Κερασιά)	295
Kerbova	کربووه	Kastanohori (?) (Καστανοχώρι)	97
Kerpini	کرپنی	Kerpini (Κερπινή)	133
Kertiza	کرتیزه	Agia Kyriaki (Αγία Κυριακή)	227
Ketesi	کتسی		357
Ḳılapaçuna	قلاپاچونه	Plataniotissa (Πλατανιώτισσα)	138
Ḳırana	قرانه	Krana (Κράνα)	300
Kiḫomiro	کخومیرو		176
Kiriçova	کریچوه	Korfes (Κορφές)	127
Kirvuḳor	کیرووقور	Palaiokastro/Koufoplaiiko Kastro (Παλαιόκαστρο/Κουφοπλαίικο Κάστρο)	296
Kiẕiḳuma	کیذقمه		666
Ḳlaẕi	قلاذی		117
Klesura	کلسوره		480
Ḳlimandi	قلیماندی	Klimenti (Κλημέντι)	459
Ḳoçiça	قوچیچه	Kotitsa (Κοτίτσα)	387
Ḳokino Marti	قوکنو مارتی	Kokkino Diaselo (?) (Κόκκινο Διάσελο)	423
Ḳoḳla	قوقله	Pigadi (Πηγάδι)	183
Ḳoḳla	قوقلا		290
Ḳoḳla	قوقله	Kokla (Κόκλα)	341
Ḳoḳla Marġariti	قوقلا مرغارتی	Koklaki (Κοκλάκι)	195
Ḳoḳova	قوقوه	Skotani (Σκοτάνη)	435
Ḳomi	قومی	Komi (Κώμη)	495
Ḳomi	قومی	Komi (Κώμη)	648

Ḳonbi S̱eḳra	قنبی ثقره		219
Ḳonbi S̱eḳra	قنبی ثقره		289
Ḳonbi S̱eḳra	قنبی ثقره	Artemida (Αρτέμιδα)	327
Ḳonbi S̱eḳra	قونبی ثقره	Dafni (Δάφνη)	574
Ḳondari	قونداری		255
Ḳondomiḫal	قوندومیخال		281
Ḳondorafti	قوندورافتی		110
Ḳopaniça	قوپانیچه	Kryoneri (Κρυονέρι)	301
Ḳopiça	قوپیچه		343
Ḳoraḳovuni	قورهقووونی	Oreino Korakovouni (Ορεινό Κορακοβούνι)	92
Ḳoris̱os	قوریثوس	Korinthos (Κόρινθος)	443
Ḳoromiẕi	قورومیذی	Kremmydi (Κρεμμύδι)	191
Ḳosta Lanca	قوسته لانجه		283
Ḳoşta Ḫāṣṣ	قوشته خاص	Kalyvia Laliokosta (Καλύβια Λαλιοκώστα)	474
Ḳozma Greḳa	قوزمه کرقه	Graikas (?) (Γραίκας)	597
Ḳozomuli	قوزومولی		379
Ḳraḳuki	قراقوکی	Pelopio (Πελόπιο)	238
Ḳraḳuki	قراقوکی		323
Ḳral	قرال	Agios Nikolaos (Άγιος Νικόλαος)	520
Ḳrapeşi	قراپشی		623
Ḳrastiki	قراستکی	Krastikoi (Κραστικοί)	36
Ḳroḳova	قروقوه	Selinountas (Σελινούντας)	106
Ḳuçi	قوچی		186
Ḳuçi	قوچی		271
Ḳuçi	قوچی		280
Ḳuçi	قوچی	Helidoni (Χελιδόνι)	335
Ḳuçi	قوچی		512
Ḳuçi	قوچی	Mazaraki (Μαζαράκι)	651
Ḳukesi	قوکسی		347
Ḳuḳura	قوقوره	Salmoni (Σαλμώνη)	236
Ḳulukina	قلوکینه/قلوکنه	Kloukines/Kloukinohoria (Κλουκίνες/Κλουκινοχώρια)	145

Ḳumaniçi Luzi	قومانيچى لوزى	Elliniko (Ελληνικό)	167
Ḳunbaki	قونباكى		463
Ḳurnaroḳastro	قورناروقاسترو	Pournarokastro (Πουρναρόκαστρο)	504
Ḳutala	قوتالا	Koutalas (Κουταλάς)	455
Ḳuvara	قوواره		445
Küraleş	كورالش		237
Lala	لالا	Lalas (Λάλας)	644
Lala Vizi	لاله ويزى	Kalyvia Laliokosta (Καλύβια Λαλιοκώστα)	473
Lala Ẕyavoliçi	لاله ذياووليچى		410
Lales̱i	لالثى	Lanthi (?) (Λάνθι)	229
Lali	لالى	Laloi (Λαλοί)	276
Laluḳa	لالوقه	Laloukas (?) (Λάλουκας)	467
Laluş	لالوش	Ano Starohori (Άνω Σταροχώρι)	522
Lanbeti	لانبتى	Lambeti/Anthopyrgos (Λαμπέτη/ Ανθόπυργος)	279
Lancoy	لانجوى	Latzoï (Λατζόι)	225
Lapata	لاپاته	Lapatheia (Λαπάθεια)	28
Lazar Buva	لازار بووه	Lazarades/Gynaikohori (?) (Λαζαράδες/ Γυναικοχώρι)	329
Lazar Palunbi	لازار پالونبى	Paloumba (Παλούμπα)	417
Lazaro Buva	لازارو بوه	Lazaro-Bouga (?) (Λαζαρο-Μπούγα)	257
Lazaro Kemer	لازارو كمر	Lazarades/Gynaikohori (?) (Λαζαράδες/ Γυναικοχώρι)	330
Lazaro Klesura	لازارو كلسوره	Amfithea (Αμφιθέα)	421
Lazaro Ḳuveli	لآزارو قوولى	Kouvelas (Κούβελας)	431
Lazaro Zupata	لازآرو زوپاته	Zoumbatiza (?) (Ζουμπάτιζα)	408
Lazaryo	لازاريو	Lazargio/Bantsaiika (Λαζαργιό/ Μπαντσαίικα)	543
Lenḳoni	لنقونى		561
Leviẕi	لويذى	Levidi (Λεβίδι)	81
Lihyana	لهيانه	Lehaina (Λεχαινά)	208
Lihyana	لهيانه	Lehaina (Λεχαινά)	497
Liḳuresi	ليقورسى	Lykouria (Λυκουρία)	62
Liḳuresi	ليقورسى	Vasilaki (Βασιλάκι)	258

Liḳuresi	ليقورسى		458
Liḳuresi	ليقورسى		492
Liḳuresi	ليقورسى	Lykouresis (Λυκούρεσης)	657
Linistena	لينستنه	Linistaina (Λινίσταινα)	303
Lisarya	لساريه	Kydonies (Κυδωνίες)	516
Listirna	لسترنه	Listraina/Listrena/Listrina (Λίστραινα/Λίστρενα/Λίστρινα)	119
Livarzi	لوارزى	Livartzi (Λιβάρτζι)	294
Loġaṯeti	لوغاثتى	Logothetis (?) (Λογοθέτης)	228
Lonci	لونجى		211
Lonci	لونجى	Lotis (?) (Λώτης)	319
Londar	لوندار	Leontari (Λεοντάρι)	382
Lonḳanik	لونقانيك	Longanikos (Λογκανίκος)	385
Lopesi	لوپسى	Lopesi (Λόπεσι)	83
Lopesi	لوپسى	Lopesi (Λόπεσι)	113
Lopesi	لوپسى	Agioi Theodoroi (Άγιοι Θεόδωροι)	639
Lovoḳa	لووقه	Aiges (Αιγές)	151
Loyi	لويي	Diodia (Διόδια)	371
Luḳa	لوقه	Lefka (Λεύκα)	466
Luḳa İfrati	لوقه افراتى	Palioloukas (Παλιολουκάς)	108
Lukişta	لوكشته	Loukistra (Λουκίστρα)	534
Luvari	لووارى		69
Luzi	لوزى	Trani Louza (Τρανή Λούζα)	350
Maji	ماژى	Elatofyto (Ελατόφυτο)	129
Maji	ماژى		249
Maji	ماژى	Mazi (Μάζι)	263
Maji	ماژى		349
Maji	ماژى		383
Maji	ماژى	Ereipia Maziou (Ερείπια Μαζίου)	513
Maji	ماژى	Ano Kourtesi/Kourtesis (?) (Άνω Κούρτεσι/Κουρτέσης)	635
Maḳri Poẕi	ماقرى پوذى	Makrypodi (?) (Μακρυπόδι)	245
Maḳrisa Ustruza	ماقريسه اوستروزه	Rizospilia (Ριζοσπηλιά)	433

Maḳrişa	ماقريشه	Makrisia (Μακρίσια)	337
Maḳriyeni Çamanda	ماقرى ينى چاماندا	Tsamanta (Τσαμαντά)	31
Malaḳas	مالاقاس	Elaionas (Ελαιώνας)	660
Malena	مالنه	Xirokambos (?) (Ξηρόκαμπος)	377
Malesina	مالسنه		579
Maliki	ماليكى	Nisi (Νησί)	573
Manastır-ı Meġaspilyo Aya Ḳori	مناستر مغاسپليو ايا قورى	Megalou Spilaiou Monastery (I.M. Μεγάλου Σπηλαίου)	2
Manastır-ı S̱otoḳos	مناستر ثوتوقوس	Panagias Pepelenitsis Monastery (I.M. Παναγίας Πεπελενίτσης)	102
Manastır-ı Yirondos der Taḳsiyarḫi	مناستر ييروندوس در تاقسيارخى	Gerontos Osiou Leontiou Monastery (I.M. Γέροντος Οσίου Λεοντίου), Palaiomonastiro (Παλαιομονάστηρο)	101
Manesi	مانسى		199
Manesi	مانسى		448
Manesi	مانسى		652
Manesi	مانسى		662
Maneşi	مانشى		157
Mangişa Burlaşa	مانكشه بورلاشه		403
Mangişa Ḳumani	مانكشه قومانى	Koumanis (Κουμάνης)	267
Manḳa	مانقه		356
Mariçi	ماريچى	Agias Marinis Maritsis Monastery (I.M. Αγίας Μαρίνης Μαρίτσης)	536
Marḳoplu	مارقوپلو	Markopoulo (Μαρκόπουλο)	204
Marḳoplu	مارقوپلو		593
Marti Çaşi	مارتى چاشى	Tsasi (?) (Τσάση)	422
Marti Helmi	مارتى هلمى		390
Marti Plaşa	مارتى پلاشه		21
Marti Plaşa	مارتى پلاشه		396
Martina der Noḳastro	مارتنه در نوقاسترو	Martina (Μαρτίνα)	121
Mastro Andoni	ماسترو اندونى	Mastrantonis (Μαστραντώνης)	636
Mateşi	ماتشى	Matesi (Μάτεσι)	309
Matranḳa	مترانقه		247
Mavromati	ماوروماتى		53

Mavromati	ماوروماتی	Mavromati (Μαυρομάτη)	293
Mayira	مايیره		170
Mayira	مايیره	Magera (Μάγερα)	615
Mazarak	مزراك		308
Mazarak	مزراك	Ano Mazaraki (Άνω Μαζαράκι)	582
Mazarak	مزراك	Mazaraki (Μαζαράκι)	651
Mazarak Adipo	مزراك آدیپو	Mazaraki (?) (Μαζαράκι)	315
Mazaraki	مزراکی	Kato Mazaraki (Κάτω Μαζαράκι)	519
Maẕi	ماذی		345
Maẕi	ماذی	Skillountia (Σκιλλουντία)	355
Maẕiñik	ماذیکك/ماذکك		526
Maẕiñik	ماذکك		655
Meġaliç	مغالچ		376
Meliġala	مليغاله		491
Melita	مليتا	Melita (Μελιτά)	348
Melitena	مليتنه		578
Miġali Ẕivri	مغالی ذوری	Lambeia (Λάμπεια)	609
Miḫal Manesi	میخال مانسی	Manesi (?) (Μάνεσι)	400
Miḫal Zora	میخال زوره	Zoria (?) (Ζοριά)	401
Mihili	مهلی	Mihalos (Μίχαλος)	265
Mihili	مهیلی		611
Miḫlu	میخلو	Mouhli (Μούχλι/Μουχλί)	65
Miḫoy	میخوی	Mihoïo (Μιχόιο)	571
Mili Ḳalivya	میلی قاليويه	Palaiopyrgos (Παλαιόπυργος)	373
Milyas	ملياس	Moira (Μοίρα)	584
Miraḳo	میراقو	Arhaia Pisa (Αρχαία Πίσα)	240
Mirati	میراتی	Polylofo (Πολύλοφο)	528
Mitepoli	میته‌پولی	Mitopoli (Μιτόπολη)	576
Miziḳa	مزيقه	Dafniotissa (Δαφνιώτισσα)	334
Mizis̱ra	میزثره	Mystras (Μυστράς)	63
Mizotoro	میزوتورو		311
Monaḫu	موناخو	Monahou (Μοναχού)	340

Motista	موتسته	Drymos (Δρυμός)	539
Mujak	مژاك		313
Mujaki	موژاكی	Perpataris (?) (Περπατάρης)	96
Mundriza	موندریزه	Gryllos (Γρύλλος)	358
Murik Buva	موریك بووه	Rodia (Ροδιά)	663
Murik Maji	موریك ماژی	Mouriki (?) (Μουρίκι)	333
Muriki	موریكی	Mouriki (Μουρίκι)	46
Murji	مورژی		217
Muzak	موزاك	Mouzaki (Μουζάκι)	595
Muzak	مزاك		659
Muzak Mengişa	مزاك منكشه	Mouzaki (Μουζάκι)	380
Namuni	نامونی		139
Nasa	ناسه	Nasa (Νάσα)	220
Naşi	ناشی	Nasia (Νάσια)	72
Niḫor	نیخور	Neohori (Νεοχώρι)	197
Nikifor	نیكفور		284
Niḳola Buva	نیقولا بووه	Roviata (Ροβιάτα)	620
Niḳola Buva	نیقولا بووه	Kokkinorrahi (?) (Κοκκινορράχη)	664
Niḳola Ḳumi	نیقولا قومی	Komi (Κώμη)	625
Niḳola Maḳrişa	نیقولا ماقریشه	Kato Makrysi (?) (Κάτω Μακρύσι)	395
Niḳola Manesi	نیقولا مانسی	Manesi (Μάνεσι)	39
Niḳola Sirgi	نیقولا سركی	Syrrizo (Σύρριζο)	416
Olana	اولانه	Oleni (Ωλένη), Paliolena (Παλιόλενα)	285
Omlo	اوملو	Ombras (Ομπράς)	338
Ondriçena	اوندریچنه	Andritsaina (Ανδρίτσαινα)	304
Orfano	اورفانو		190
Orfano	اورفانو	Orfano (?) (Ορφανό)	531
Oṣiya Mariya	اوصیه مریه		558
Palari	پالاری	Paliarovouni (?) (Παλιαροβούνι)	374
Palopirġo	پالوپیرغو	Pyrgaki (?) (Πυργάκι)	566
Palunbi Ipṣari	پالونبی ایصاری	Pefki (Πεύκη)	626
Palunbi Ranesi	پالونبی رانسی		43

Papaẕa	پاپاذا	Pappadas (Παππαδάς)	360
Papaẕato	پاپاذاتو		544
Pasḳali/Pasḳal	پسقالی/پسقال	Paschalinou t' aloni (?) (Πασχαλινού τ' αλώνι)	346
Patura	پاتوره		483
Pavla	پاولا	Pavlia (Παύλια)	442
Pavlo Doçi	پاولو دوچی		402
Pavloḳastro	پاولوقاسترو	Pavlokastro (Παυλόκαστρο)	481
Pelyura	پلیوره		169
Pendani	پندانی	Neapoli (Νεάπολη)	210
Pendeni	پندنی	Pefki (Πεύκη)	626
Perisori	پریثوری	Parori (?) (Παρόρι)	75
Perisori	پریثوری	Perithori (Περιθώρι)	161
Persena	پرسنه	Persaina (Πέρσαινα)	270
Persor	پرثور	Perthori (Περθώρι)	93
Peryale	پریاله		34
Peta	پته	Petas (Πέτας)	324
Petro Dorza	پترو دورزه	Dorizas (Δόριζας)	409
Petro Ḫayḳal	پترو خایقال		447
Petro Ḳarava Klesura	پترو قراوه کلسوره	Karava rahi (?) (Καραβά ράχη)	477
Petro Tunba	پترو تونبه		116
Petros Ḳaratula	پتروس قراتولا		25
Petrovişta	پترووشته	Petrovithia (?) (Πετροβίθια)	568
Petrovuni	پترووونی		10
Piça	پیچا		452
Pikerni	پکرنی	Pikernis (Πικέρνης)	71
Pisratu	پسراتو	Pistratou (Πιστρατού)	469
Plaşa	پلاشه		70
Plaşa	پلاشه		77
Plaşa	پلاشه	Ples(i)a [Πλέσ(ι)α]	80
Plaşa	پلاشه	Plessa (Πλέσσα)	156
Plaşa	پلاشه		254
Plaşa	پلاشه	Roviata (Ροβιάτα)	620

Platana	پلاتنه	Platanos (Πλάτανος)	372
Platistomo	پلاتستمو		529
Platoḳomati	پلاتوقوماتی		375
Poḳovina	پوقووینه/پوقوینه	Peleki (Πελέκι)	362
Polesḳa	پولسقه		185
Poliça	پولیچه	Politsa (Πολίτσα)	607
Pondiḳo	پوندقو	Katakolo (Κατάκολο)	292
Poraçyu	پوراچیو	Agrambela (Αγράμπελα)	233
Poroviça	پروویچه	Porovitsa (Ποροβίτσα)	172
Porta	پورتا	Portes (Πόρτες)	525
Po<u>s</u>o	پوثو	Pothos (Πόθος)	248
Potamya	پوتامیه	Ano & Kato Potamia (Άνω & Κάτω Ποταμιά)	142
Potamya Ṣarandinu	پوتامیه صراندنو	Sarantinou (?) (Σαραντινού)	175
Potamya Ṣarandinu	پوتامیه صراندنو		196
Pratano	پراتنو	Platanos (Πλάτανος)	226
Prifti	پرفتی		613
Priniḳos	پرنیقوس	Asteri (Αστέρι)	64
Provanda Aya Yorgi	پرواندە آیه یورکی	Agios Georgios (Άγιος Γεώργιος)	366
Puliça	پولیچه		533
Pulimeno Ḳondostavlo	پولیمنو قوندستاولو	Arhaies Kleones (Αρχαίες Κλεωνές)	451
Pulimeno Soyḳa	پولیمنو سویقه	Soïka/Skopia (Σόικα/Σκοπιά)	460
Puloti	پولوتی		33
Purdanu	پوردانو	Vouliagmeni (?) (Βουλιαγμένη)	246
Rado	رادو		621
Raẖova	راخوه		76
Raẖova	راخوه	Exohi (Εξοχή)	163
Raẖova	راخوه	Krini (Κρήνη)	500
Ranbiyaḳa	رانبیاقه	Roumbieka (Ρουμπιέκα)	656
Ranesi	رانسی	Kastraki (Καστράκι)	321
Ranesi	رانسی	Renesi (Ρένεσι)	336
Ranesi	رانسی		475
Ranesi	رانسی	Xirohori (Ξηροχώρι)	629

Ranesi	رانسی		658
Rapsomati	راپسوماتی		515
Ratendu	راتندو	Heimadio (Χειμαδιό)	282
Rayḳu	رايقو	Raïko (Ράικο)	131
Revaniça	روانيچه	Arravonitsa (Αρραβωνίτσα)	171
Ribesi	ريبسی		490
Rolo	رولو	Rogoi (?) (Ρογοί)	137
Romesi	رومسی	Ambelonas (Αμπελώνας)	261
Romyo	روميو		600
Rovyata	رووياتا	Roviata (Ροβιάτα)	620
Roẕa	روذه	Rodia (Ροδιά)	107
Roẕinotiḫo	روذينوتيخو		647
Runbaḳa	رونباقه	Roumbieka (?) (Ρουμπιέκα)	487
Salmenik	سلمنيك	Ano Salmeniko (Άνω Σαλμενίκο)	667
Ṣamuna	صامونا		618
Ṣandamiri	صاندهميرى	Santomeri (Σαντομέρι)	524
Ṣarakin	صراكن	Sarakina (Σαρακίνα)	188
Ṣarakin	صراكن	Sarakini (Σαρακίνι)	352
Ṣarakin	صراكن	Sarakinia (Σαρακηνιά)	465
Ṣarakina	صراكنه	Sarakini (Σαρακίνι)	253
Ṣaravali	صآرهوالى	Saravali (Σαραβάλι)	472
Ṣavalya	صوآليه	Savalia (Σαβάλια)	177
Ṣavanus	صاوانوس	Kallifoni (Καλλιφώνι)	49
Sela	سله		250
Seliça	سليچه	Kato Pteri (Κάτω Πτέρη)	52
Selyana	سليانه	Seliana (Σελιάνα)	160
Serḳofayi	سرقوفايى		569
Sermorini	سرمورينى		449
S̱eryanu	ثريانو	Theriano (Θεριανό)	486
Simiza	سيميزه	Simiza (Σιμίζα)	598
Simoplu	سيموپلو	Simopoulo (Σιμόπουλο)	640
Sina	سينه	Sinas (Σίνας)	87

Sinasi	سيناسى		180
Sinoviro	سينوويرو	Sinevro (Σινεβρό)	155
Sipyani	سپيانى	Tsipiana (Τσιπιανά)	266
Sirveliça	سرولچه		565
Sirvu	سروو		604
Sirvu	سيروو	Servos (Σέρβος)	320
Sitara	ستاره		239
Siyiniski	سينسكى	Siginiskes (Σιγίνισκες)	147
Siẕereḳastro	سيذرهقاسترو/سيذهرهقاسترو	Sidirokastro (Σιδηρόκαστρο)	476
Ṣofyana	صوفيانه	Syhaina (Συχαινά)	499
Ṣoḫyana	صوخيانه	Sofiana (Σοφιανά)	168
Ṣopi	صوپى	Sopi (Σόπι)	287
S̱opiya	ثوپيه		638
Sotira	سوتيره	Sotiras (Σωτήρας)	124
Sudana	سودانه	Ano & Kato Loussoi (Άνω & Κάτω Λούσσοι)	4
Suli	سولى		37
Suli	سولى	Souli (Σούλι)	506
Ṣuli	صولى	Souli (Σούλι)	198
Ṣuli	صولى		235
Ṣuli	صولى	Ano Souli (Άνω Σούλι)	631
Sumaki	سوماكى		61
Şalesi	شالسى		581
Şaleşi	شالشى		643
Şergi	شركى		591
Şiğuni	شيغونى	Sigouni (Σιγούνι)	7
Şurbi	شوربى		224
Şurbi	شوربى		570
Ṭarpun	طرپون	Lykaio (Λύκαιο)	438
Taşi	تاشى		18
Tireḫlista	ترخلسته	Trehlo (Τρεχλό)	42
Tiristena	تيرستنه	Stavros (Σταυρός)	509
Todoro Doşkesi	تودرو دوشكسى	Toskesi (Τόσκεσι)	413

Todoro Manesi	تودرو مانسی		22
Todoro Zupata	تودرو زوپاته	Zoumbata (?) (Ζουμπάτα)	406
Todoroplu	تودروپلو		24
Topolova	توپولوه	Agia Paraskevi (Αγία Παρασκευή)	507
Toşkesi	توشکسی		244
Traḫya Manesi	تراخیا/تراخیه مانسی		554
Trestena	ترستنه	Melissopetra (Μελισσόπετρα)	353
Trima İşpata	ترما اشپاته		426
Trusa	تروسه	Trousaki (Τρουσάκι)	555
Tumena	تومنا	Doumena (Δουμενά)	135
Tunba	تونبه		213
Ustruza/İstruza Potamya	اوستروزه/استروزه پوتامیه	Potamia (?) (Ποταμιά)	98
Valaḳ	والاق	Hrysohori (?) (Χρυσοχώρι)	322
Valimi	والیمی	Valimi (Βαλιμή)	148
Valḳu	والقو	Ambelos (Άμπελος)	123
Valmi	وآلمی	Valmi (Βάλμη)	530
Vaṣılıḳa	وآصلقه	Sikyona (Σικυώνα)	444
Vaṣıloplos	واصلوپلوس		262
Vela	ولا	Vela (Βελά)	154
Veliġosti	ولیغوستی	Veligosti (Βελιγοστή)	440
Velimiri	ولیمیری	Velimiri (Βελιμίρι)	19
Velize	ولیزه	Pefkes (?) (Πεύκες)	432
Velizi	ولیزی	Baliza (Μπάλιζα)	278
Velviça	ولویچه	Petralona (Πετράλωνα)	302
Venetiḳa	ونتقه		560
Verġuviça	ورغوویچه	Monastiri (Μοναστήρι)	159
Vervena	ورونه	Vervena (Βέρβενα)	299
Vesini	وسینی	Vesini (Βεσίνι)	59
Virastova	وراستوه	Hrysanthi (Χρυσάνθι)	152
Virça	ویرچه	Tropaia (?) (Τρόπαια)	364
Viriça	ویریچه		552
Virzaḫo	ورزاخو		523

Visoḳa	ویسوقه	Skepasto (Σκεπαστό)	132
Vola	وولا	Vola (Βόλα)	482
Vorstena	وورستنه	Glastra (Γλάστρα)	17
Voştiça	ووشتیچه	Aigio (Αίγιο)	100
Vumero	وومرو	Goumero (Γούμερο)	218
Vunarġo	وونارغو	Vounargo (Βούναργο)	610
Vundeni	ووندنی	Skioessa (Σκιόεσσα)	498
Vurçanos	وورچانوس	Mavrommati (Μαυρομμάτι)	368
Vuzyas	ووزیاس		79
Yaḳoẖto	یاقوختو	Ano Diakopto/Diakofto (Άνω Διακοπτό/ Διακοφτό)	140
Yani Dara	یانی دآره	Daras (Δάρας)	428
Yani Evzenati	یانی اوزناتی		391
Yani Jura	یانی ژوره		412
Yani Ḳanḳaẕi	یانی قنقاذی	Kangadi (?) (Καγκάδη)	420
Yani Lata	یانی لاته		394
Yani Mazaraki	یانی مزراکی	Mazaraki (?) (Μαζαράκι)	415
Yani Ẕyavoliçi	یانی ذیاوولیچی	Diavolitsi (Διαβολίτσι)	389
Yatopa	یاتوپا		577
Yelini	یلینی	Gelini (Γελήνη/Γελήνι)	165
Yirano	یرانو		567
Yirmena	ییرمنه	Foloï (Φολόη)	272
Yirmoçani	ییرموچانی	Platanitsa (Πλατανίτσα)	232
Yorgi Maji	یورکی ماژی		393
Yorgi Manesi	یورکی مانسی		429
Yorgi Mujaki	یورکی مژاکی		418
Yorgi Muzaki	یورکی مزاکی		404
Zaẖlori	زاخلوری	Ano & Kato Zahlorou (Άνω & Κάτω Ζαχλωρού)	134
Zaẖoli	زاخولی	Evrostina (Εβροστίνα)	164
Ẕaruẖla	ذآروخله	Zarouhla (Ζαρούχλα)	146
Zastupa	زاستوپه	Zastova (Ζάστοβα)	505
Zaveti	زاوتی	Zaveti (Ζάβετη)	363

Zelaḫova	زلاخووه	Amygdalies (Αμυγδαλιές)	298
Zenbeş	زنبش		189
Zepandi	زپاندی		35
Zepandi	زپاندی		166
Ẕervini	ذروینی	Kryovrysi (Κρυόβρυση)	230
Ẕervini	ذروینی	Dervini (?) (Δερβίνι)	537
Ẕiġanato	ذغاناتو	Venetiko/Tigani Island (?) (Νήσος Βενέτικο/Τηγάνι)	367
Ẕilivina	ذیلیوینه	Vilivina (Βιλιβίνα)	136
Ẕima Rala	ذیمه رآله	Ralia (?) (Ράλια)	427
Ẕimiçana	ذیمیچانه	Dimitsana (Δημητσάνα)	434
Ẕiminiça	ذیمنیچه	Tripotama (Τριπόταμα), Kastro (Κάστρο)	251
Ẕirmi	ذیرمی		653
Ẕiyaleş Tunba	ذیالش تونبه	Toumba (Τούμπα)	109
Zoġa	زوغه	Zogas (Ζώγας)	521
Ẕolyani	ذولیانی	Kokkaliara (Κοκκαλιάρα)	305
Zorila	زوریله	Zorlia (Ζορλιά)	608
Zuġra	زوغره	Zougras (Ζούγρας)	8
Zuġra-ı dīğer	زوغره دیکر		11
Ẕunato	ذوناتو	Zoni (Ζώνη)	331
Ẕupano Buryalişa	ذوپانو بوریالشه		411

Principles of Edition

Appendix I and Appendix II comprise the transcription of the Mss TT10 and 1/14662. The transcription of the Ottoman text follows the transliteration system of the *İslâm Ansiklopedisi*. The toponyms and anthroponyms are transcribed according to their rendering in the document and not according to their proper orthography and pronunciation in Greek or Albanian.

TRANSLITERATION OF OTTOMAN[1]

ا	ā, a, e, ı, i, o, ö, u, ü	ض	ż, ḍ
ب	b	ط	ṭ
پ	p	ظ	ẓ
ت	t	ع	‘
ث	s̱	غ	ġ
ج	c	ف	f
چ	ç	ق	ḳ
ح	ḥ	ك	k, g, ğ, ñ, y
خ	ḫ	ل	l
د	d	م	m
ذ	ẕ	ن	n
ر	r	ه	h
ز	z	و	ū, o, ö, u, ü, v
ژ	j	ي	ī, ı, i, y
س	s	ى	ā, ī, ı, i, y
ش	ş	ء	’
ص	ṣ		

TRANSLITERATION OF MODERN GREEK

α	a	τ	t
β	v	υ	y

1 The system of *İslâm Ansiklopedisi* has been followed.

γ	g	φ	f
δ	d	χ	h
ε	e	ψ	ps
ζ	z	ω	o
η	i	αι	ai
θ	th	ει	ei
ι	i	οι	oi
κ	k	αυ	af/av
λ	l	ευ	ef/ev
μ	m	ου	ou
ν	n	μπ	b (initial), mb (medial)
ξ	x	γγ	ng, gg
ο	o	γκ	ng
π	p	τσ	ts
ρ	r	ντ	d (initial), nt (medial)
σ, ς	s	τζ	tz

SIGLA

[ab] letters restored by the editor now missing.

<ab> letters added by the editor, which the scribe has either omitted or for which he has by error inscribed other letters.

[..⁴..] lost or illegible letters equal to the number of dots for which no restoration is proposed.

[---] lost or illegible letters of an uncertain number.

BIBLIOGRAPHIC REFERENCES

Bibliographic references are given in footnotes (chapters) and endnotes (tables and appendices) as follows: author's surname, year of publication, volume number in Roman numerals (if applicable), page number(s) in Arabic numerals, line(s) in subscript (primary sources, in cases); n. stands for note, no. for number, and nos for numbers.

ABBREVIATIONS

acc.	accusative
adj.	adjective
adv.	adverb
Al.	Albanian
anc. Gr.	Ancient Greek
Ar.	Arabic
Arb.	Arbërisht (Albanian spoken in Italy)
Arv.	Arvanitic (Albanian spoken in Greece)
Bg.	Bulgarian
Byz. Gr.	Byzantine Greek
colloq.	colloquial
comp.	comparative
corr.	correxit
dim.	diminutive
end.	ending
f.	feminine
Fr.	French
Gr.	Greek
hag.	hagionym
It.	Italian
Lat.	Latin
m. Bg.	Middle Bulgarian
Mac.	Macedonian
med. Lat.	Mediaeval Latin
n.	noun
old Bg.	Old Bulgarian
old Slav.	Old Slavic
old Slov.	Old Slovenian
Pers.	Persian
pers. prn.	personal pronoun
phr.	phrase
pl.	plural
pln.	place name
pn.	personal name
prep.	preposition
Ru.	Russian
sing.	singular
Slav.	Slavic
Slov.	Slovenian
sn.	surname
Scr.	Serbo-Croatian
Tr.	Turkish
v.	verb
Ven.	Venetian
Vl.	Vlach

Appendix I

***Editio Princeps* of TT10**

(Prime Ministry Ottoman Archives, Istanbul)

1

tetimme-i nefs-i Ḳalavrita el-meẕk[ū]r ḫ[āṣṣ]a-ı zaʿīm

mücerred Dimitri [Fo]ziḫos | mücerred Andon Ḳaḳomali | mücerred Ḳosta İsḳonco | mücerred Yani veled-i Papas Buçyato | mücerred Manol Manoloplos

mücerred Yani Ḳozmos | mücerred Manol Ḳumaniti | mücerred Yani Tomas | bīve Ḳalime Tomata | bīve Faḫripe

bīve Turnare | bīve Plariya | bīve mana Lavrancina

cemāʿat-i manastır-ı Meġaspilyo Aya Ḳori

mücerred Papas [Ma]nṣos Ġumano | mücerred Papas Menasi | mücerred Papas Nilos | mücerred Papas Todoros | mücerred Maḳaryos Ḳaloyeros

mücerred Antifandros Ḳaloyer[o]s | mücerred Maḳaryos Ġunaros | mücerred Nofitos Ḳaloyeros | mücerred Yonas Ḳaloyeros | mücerred Simyos Ḳaloyeros

mücerred İġliġori Ḳaloyeros | ḫāne maʿa müsellem 83 | mücerred maʿa cemāʿat-i manastır 21 | bīve 5

ḥāṣıl ġayr ez müsellem 9123

ʿa(n) ispence	resm-i niyābet	ʿöşr-i bāġāt	ʿöşr-i ḥınṭa	ʿöşr-i cev	ʿöşr-i ḳazz
2605	1000	1345	3050	475	197

ʿöşr-i meyve	ʿöşr-i zeyt	resm-i ḫamr	ʿöşr-i kettān
18	8	150	100

mülk-i Serrāc Pīr

āsiyāb-ı ġalle 2 resm 40 | āsiyāb-ı peşmīne 1 resm 15

mülk-i Balaban dizdār-ı ḳalʿa-ı Ḳalavrita el-meẕkūr āsiyāb 1 resm 80

mülk-i manastır-ı Meġaspilyo el-mezbūr āsiyāb 1 resm 40

nāḥiyyet-i Ḳalavrita

ḳarye-i İvraḫni ḫāṣṣa-ı zaʿīm

Papas Maḳrini | Yani veled-i o | Yorgi Maḳrini | İstemad Maḳrini | Andriya Aṣprini

İstemad Suḳare | Ḳosta Suḳare | Yorgi Suḳare | Manol yeñiçeri | İstemad Rufa

2

tetimme-i ḳarye-i İvraḫni el-meẕkūr ḫāṣṣa-ı zaʿīm

Aleksi Miḫalic | Papas Fagris | Yorgi veled-i o | Yorgi Fratiḳos | Yani veled-i o

Niḳola Malaḫiya | Dimitri veled-i o | Aṣpor Yani Aporiḫto | Yani Ḫarkâplos | Miḫal Ḫarkâplos

Niḳola Landiniya | Yorgi birāder-i o | Niḳola-<yı> dīğer Landiniya | Vorila bin Vorila | Manol Andriyanos

Ḳosta İsḳanbris | Yani Ḳoratura | İvrato Radomiro | Yani Ḳuza | mücerred Yani İsḳanbris

mücerred İstemad Radomiro | bīve Dimitra Frangina | ḫāne 29 | mücerred 2 | bīve 1

ḥāṣıl 2691

ʿa(n) ispence	bāġāt-ı ḫāṣṣa dönüm 1	eşcār-ı ṭut-ı ḫāṣṣa ʿaded 30	ʿöşr-i kettān	ʿöşr-i bāġāt	ʿöşr-i ḳazz
781	[resm] 120	[resm] 50	20	288	144

ʿöşr-i ḥınṭa	ʿöşr-i cev	ʿöşr-i meyve	resm-i ḫamr
1000	155	8	45

mülk-i Yorgi Fratiḳos der ḳarye-i meẕkūr āsiyāb 1 resm 40

mülk-i Andriya Aṣprini der ḳarye-i meẕkūr āsiyāb 1 resm 40

ḳarye-i Sudana ḫāṣṣa-ı zaʿīm

Ḳosta Piroplos	Yani veled-i o	Petros Papaẕoplos	Dimitri Mavroplos	Yani veled-i o
Yorgi Saçilos	Aleksi Ḳozma	Yorgi birāder-i o	Niḳola Ḳulurẕa	Niḳola Liḳoturi
Dimitri Duvos	Dimitri Ḳondos	Aleksi veled-i o	Yorgi Ḳondo	Yani veled-i o
Ḳondo Pulimeno	Yani Ḳondo	Niḳola veled-i o	İstilyano İstranca	Manol Ḳaçivas
Niḳola birāder-i o	Yani Papaẕaplo	Yani Mavriyani	Yorgi Romano	Manol Romanos
Ḳosta Liḳosti	Miḫal Plastara	Dimitri Mavriyani	Yorgi Piroplo	Manol Roğatora
Dimitri veled-i o	Niḳola Mandi	Miḫal Romanos	Papaistemati Romano	Yani Piroplo
Andriya Piroplo	Ḳosta Ḫirisoḳoplo	Niḳola Romanos	Yorgi Romanos	Niḳola Yerasimo

Aleksi Papaẕaplo	mücerred Niḳola Saçilos	mücerred Dimitri Romano	mücerred Niḳola Romanos	Ḳosta Ṣemeli	mücerred Yani Romanos
mücerred Yorgi birāder-i o	mücerred Ḳosta Romanos	bīve Ḳolondo	bīve Ḳaçivu	ḫāne 41	mücerred 7
				bīve 2	

3

ḥāṣıl-ı ḳarye-i Sudana el-meẕkūr 3945

ʿa(n) ispence	bāğāt-ı ḫāṣṣa	eşcār-ı ṭut-ı ḫāṣṣa	ʿöşr-i kettān	ʿöşr-i bāğāt	ʿöşr-i ḥınṭa
1412	dönüm 2 [resm] 240	ʿaded 30 [resm] 60	40	336	1500

ʿöşr-i cev	ʿöşr-i ḳazz	ʿöşr-i meyve	resm-i ḫanāzīr	resm-i ḫamr
231	76	3	7	40

ḳarye-i Beluşi ez cemāʿat-i Arnavudān ḫāṣṣa-ı zaʿīm

Marti Beluşi	Yorgi veled-i o	Duḳa Beluşi	Yorgi Doḳuza	Yorgi-i dīğer Doḳuza
Ḳozma Plaçi	Gin Beluşi	Manḳola Beluşi	Ḳozma Periyalis	Cani Ḳa[p]areli
Ṣoma Tiḫoni	Duḳa birāder-i o	Domeniḳa Ḳoḳla	mücerred Gin Beluşi	mücerred Todoros Doḳuza

mücerred Lazari Periyalis	mücerred Marti Ḳapareli	ḫāne 13	mücerred 4

ḥāṣıl 1211

ʿa(n) ispence	ʿöşr-i ḥınṭa	ʿöşr-i cev	resm-i ḫanāzīr	ʿöşr-i kettān	mülk-i Marti Beluşi der ḳarye-i meẕkūr āsiyāb 1
340	700	109	12	10	resm 40

[ḳ]arye-i Ḫamaḳu ez cemāʿat-i Arnavudān ḫāṣṣa-ı zaʿīm

Lazaro Ḫamaḳo	Yorgi birāder-i o	Emirali Ḫamaḳo	İvrato Zağoriti	Yani veled-i o	
Yorgi veled-i o	Gin Beṣulḳa	Ağali Dramesi	Aleksi Dramesi	Yorgi Beṣulḳa	
Niḳola Kefalinos	Gin birāder-i o	İlya Kefalino	mücerred Mire Ḫamaḳo	ḫāne 13	mücerred 1

ḥāṣıl 989

ʿa(n) ispence	ʿöşr-i ḥınṭa	ʿöşr-i cev	resm-i ḫanāzīr
280	600	96	13

ḳarye-i Şiğuni ez cemāʿat-i Arnavudān ḫāṣṣa-ı zaʿīm

Marti Siğuni[1]	Aleksi biraẕer-i[2] o	Marti Roğire	İstilyano Papaya-noplo	Vağali Ḫarabtino	
Franci veled-i o	Şarakin Ḳuçi	Dima Ḳuçi	mücerred Lazaro veled-i o	ḫāne 8	mücerred 1

ḥāṣıl 552

ʿa(n) ispence	ʿöşr-i ḥınṭa	ʿöşr-i cev	resm-i ḫanāzīr
180	300	47	25

ḳarye-i Zuğra ez cemāʿat-i Arnavudān ḫāṣṣa-ı zaʿīm

Duşa Zuğra	Yorgi Buva	Yorgi Helmisi	İştin Ḳayça	Aleksi Lura
		ḫāne 5		

ḥāṣıl 312

ʿa(n) ispence	ʿöşr-i bāġāt	ʿöşr-i ḥınṭa	ʿöşr-i cev	ʿöşr-i ḳazz	ʿöşr-i meyve
100	32	150	24	3	3

4

tetimme-i nāḥiyyet-i Ḳalavrita

ḳarye-i Amuri ez cemāʿat-i Arnavudān [ḫāṣṣa-ı] zaʿīm

[Gi]n Amuri	[G]in Ḫartoplo	Niḳola Panipari	Andriya Amuri	Petros Am[ur]i
Yorgi birāder-i o	Niḳola Ḫırisoḳoplo	Yani Ḫırisoḳoplo	Miḫal Ḫırisoḳoplo	Andriya Ġolyoplo
		ḫāne 10		

ḥāṣıl 566

ʿa(n) ispence	ʿöşr-i ḥınṭa	ʿöşr-i cev	ʿöşr-i bāġāt	ʿöşr-i kettān
200	300	48	8	10

mezraʿa-ı Petrovuni nezd-i ḳarye-i Amuri el-mezḳūr

ḫāṣṣa-ı zaʿīm ḫāliyye

ḳarye-i Zuġra-ı dīğer ez cemāʿat-i Arnavudān ḫāṣṣa-ı zaʿīm

Vasi Zuġra	Yorgi Maji	Gin Zuġra	Yorgi Ḳayça	Marti Fonya
Petro Zuġra	Niḳola Zuġra	Lazaro Fonayti	ḫāne 8	

ḥāṣıl 401

ʿa(n) ispence	ʿöşr-i bāġāt	ʿöşr-i ḥınṭa	ʿöşr-i cev	resm-i ḫanāzīr
160	8	200	31	2

ḳarye-i Ḫaraḳtinu ez cemāʿat-i Arnavudān ḫāṣṣa-ı zaʿīm

Aleksi Ḫaraḳtino	Petros Ḫaraḳtinos	Gin Bardi	Andriya veled-i o	İlya Gönaçi
Yorgi Gönaçi	Niḳola Zapandi[3]	Dimitri birāder-i o	Yorgi Ḫaraḳtino	Gin veled-i o
İvrato Ḫaraḳtino	Dimitri Plaşa	Niḳola Plaşa	Gin Plaşa	Todoros veled-i o
İvlaşi Muzaki	Dimitri birāder-i o	Andriya Ḫaraḳtino	Lazaro Şurbi	Yorgi Zuġra

bīve İstefaniya Ḫaraḳtini	bīve Muzakina	ḫāne 20	bīve 2

ḥāṣıl 1195

ʿa(n) ispence	eşcār-ı ṭut-ı ḫāṣṣa	ʿöşr-i kettān	ʿöşr-i ḥınṭa	ʿöşr-i cev	resm-i ḫanāzīr
412	ʿaded 35 [resm] 65	20	600	95	3

ḳarye-i Ḫoloropozi ḫāṣṣa-ı zaʿīm

İvrato Ḳursari	Niḳola Ḳursari	Ḳozma Mazarak	ḫāne 3

ḥāṣıl 184

ʿa(n) ispence	ʿöşr-i ḥınṭa	ʿöşr-i cev	resm-i ḫanāzīr
60	100	16	8

5

tetimme-i nāḥiyyet-i Ḳalavrita

ḳarye-i Dima Plaşa ez cemāʿat-i Arnavud[ān] [ḫā]ṣṣa-ı zaʿīm

Dima Plaşa	[To]doros veled-i o	Yorgi veled-i o	İlya Laġatora	Gin [birā]d[er-i o]
Dima Ripi	Marti Laliza	Yani birāẕer-i o	Yorgi Laliza	Petros Laliza
Gin veled-i o	Dimitri Ḳatavati	Dimitri Miḫa	Todoros birāẕer-i o	Yani Mazaraki
Gin Zenbeş	Lazari birāder-i o	Todoros Plaşa	Gön Çornota	İlya Plaşa
Niḳola Çornota	Yorgi Miḫa	Gön Tateza	İstefano Asanas	Gön Maḳrimiḫal
Gön Çarnota	Dimitri Çarnota	Niḳola Çarnota	İlya Çarnota	Gön Dorza
Marti Laleza	mücerred Aleksi Ripi		ḫāne 31	mücerred 1

ḥāṣıl 1912

ʿa(n) ispence	ʿöşr-i ḥınṭa	ʿöşr-i cev
640	1100	172

ḳarye-i Epano Ḳurnofita — ḫāṣṣa-ı zaʿīm

Yani Ḳurnofitinos	İstemad veled-i o	Ḳosta Ḳurnofitino	Miḫal Ḳurnofitino	Dimitri Pisḳopoplo
Manol Ḳumyoti	Dimitri Darvos	mücerred Niḳola Ḳurnofitino	ḫāne 7	mücerred 1

ḥāṣıl 644

ʿa(n) ispence	ʿöşr-i ḥınṭa	ʿöşr-i cev	ʿöşr-i bāġāt	ʿöşr-i ḳazz	ʿöşr-i kettān
200	250	38	54	12	10

mülk-i Miḫal Ḳurnofitino der ḳarye-i mezḳūr āsiyāb 1 resm 40	mülk-i Manol Ḳumyoti der ḳarye-i mezḳūr āsiyāb 1 resm 40

ḳarye-i Ḳastriya — ḫāṣṣa-ı zaʿīm

Papas Dimitri Aḳatiki	Ḳosta birāder-i o	Petros Aḳatiki	Ḳosta Mavroplo	Todoros Liḳoservi
[Y]ani birāder-i o	Aleksi Liḳoservi	Ḳosta Plastara	Angelos Mavroplos	ḫāne 9

ḥāṣıl 715

ʿa(n) ispence	ʿöşr-i ḥınṭa	ʿöşr-i cev	ʿöşr-i bāġāt	resm-i ḫanāzīr	ʿöşr-i ḳazz	ʿöşr-i kettān
225	350	53	54	5	18	10

6
tetimme-i nāḥiyyet-i Ḳalavrita

ḳarye-i Vorstena ez cemāʿat-i Arnavudān — ḫāṣṣa-ı zaʿīm

Niḳola Rusi	Miḫal birāder-i o	Lazaro Rusi	Duḳa Luzi	Lazaro Ġuzeno
Niḳola birāder-i o	[Ma]zaraki İksano		ḫāne 7	

ḥāṣıl 392

ʿa(n) ispence	ʿöşr-i ḥınṭa	ʿöşr-i cev	resm-i ḫanāzīr	ʿöşr-i bāġāt
140	200	31	5	16

ḳarye-i Taşi ez cemāʿat-i Arnavudān — ḫāṣṣa-ı zaʿīm

Gin Ḳaznesi	Ḳaznesi veled-i o	Pavlos Ḳaznesi	Andriya Manesi	Andriya Manesi-i dīġer	
Ḳosta Barçi	Pavlos Manesi	Gin Manesi	mücerred Yorgi Ḳaznesi	ḫāne 8	mücerred 1

ḥāṣıl 655

ʿa(n) ispence	ʿöşr-i ḥınṭa	ʿöşr-i cev	ʿöşr-i bāġāt	resm-i ḫanāzīr
180	400	46	24	5

ḳarye-i Velimiri ez cemāʿat-i Arnavudān — ḫāṣṣa-ı zaʿīm

Domaniḳa Velimiri	Görgi Velimiri	Ḳosta Velimiri	Yanuço Velimiri	Gin İpsari
Vuvani Yorgi	mücerred Rado veled-i o		ḫāne 6	mücerred 1

ḥāṣıl 504

ʿa(n) ispence	ʿöşr-i ḥınṭa	ʿöşr-i cev	resm-i ḫanāzīr
140	300	46	18

ḳarye-i Ḳani — ḫāṣṣa-ı zaʿīm

Yorgi Platindro	Gin Manesi	Ḳozma Manesi	Niḳola Manesi	İlya Manesi
Domaniḳa Nikiforos	Domeniḳa Nikifor-ı dīġer	Papas Panoġromiti	Niḳola Lupo	Andriya birāder-i o
Aleksi Panoġromiti	Andriya Panoġromiti	Niḳola Nikiforo	mücerred Yani Panoġromiti	bīve Gönina
	ḫāne 13	mücerred 1	bīve 1	

ḥāṣıl 1349

ʿa(n) ispence	bāġāt-ı ḫāṣṣa dönüm 3	eşcār-ı ṭut-ı ḫāṣṣa ʿaded 5	ʿöşr-i bāġāt	ʿöşr-i ḥınṭa	ʿöşr-i cev
356	[resm] 360	[resm] 10	80	450	72

ʿöşr-i ḳazz	ʿöşr-i meyve	resm-i ḫamr
9	4	8

7

tetimme-i nāḫiyyet-i Ḳalavrita

ḳarye-i Marti Plaşa ez cemāʿat-i Arnavudān — ḫāṣṣa-ı zaʿīm

[Ma]rti el-mez̲kūr	Gin Plaşa	Marti veled-i o	Lazaro [Pla]şa	Andriya Plaşa
Gin Ḳaznesi	Todoros birāder-i o	Miḫal Çeresi	Mart[i] [Ḳ]oḳla	Duḳa birāder-i o
Todoros Mayira	birāder-i mez̲kūr	Niḳa Mayira	Niḳola Ranesi	Yani Sirvo
mücerred birāz̲er-i o	mücerred Petros Plaşa	mücerred İstefano Çerasi	ḫāne 15	mücerred 3

ḥāṣıl 936

ʿa(n) ispence 360	ʿöşr-i ḥınṭa 500	ʿöşr-i cev 76

ḳarye-i Todoro Manesi ez cemāʿat-i Arnavudān — ḫāṣṣa-ı zaʿīm

Todoros Manesi	Niḳola veled-i o	Ḳuvaras Baḳrati	Leḳa veled-i o	Manḳola Maniki
Aleksi veled-i o	Leḳa Manesi	Yorgi veled-i o	Luzi Manesi	İvlati Manesi
Todoros veled-i o	Manḳola Vaviloni	Yorgi birāz̲er-i o	Manḳola Maliki	Gin veled-i o
Yorgi Manesi	Niḳola Tanuşi	Aleksi veled-i o	Lazaro Ġrabsa	Yorgi Marḳo
Todoros Maji	İvlaşi Meliki	Dimitri Perdiḳari	mücerred Aleksi Manesi	mücerred Gin Meliki

ḫāne 23 — mücerred 2

ḥāṣıl 1610

ʿa(n) ispence 500	ʿöşr-i ḥınṭa 800	ʿöşr-i cev 125	resm-i ḫanāzīr 36	ʿöşr-i bāġāt 96	ʿöşr-i meyve 3	ʿöşr-i kettān 10

mülk-i
Todoros Manesi der ḳarye-i
mez̲kūr
āsiyāb 1 resm 40

ḳarye-i Barçi ez cemāʿat-i Arnavudān — ḫāṣṣa-ı zaʿīm

Leḳa Barçi	İvrato veled-i o	Gin Barçi	Daçi birāder-i o	İvlaş birāder-i o
Leḳa birāz̲er-i o	Todoros Barçi	Gin Suli	Domeniḳa Mara	S̲omas Meliti
S̲omas İvlaḫo	Araçi Ḳataranba	Yani İvlaḫo	Ḳozma Barçi	İstefano Ḳaluşi

8

tetimme-i [ḳar]ye-i Barç[i] el-mez̲kūr — ḫā[ṣṣ]a-ı zaʿīm

[Ni]ḳola Aravula	[Ma]ngişa [A]murino	Gin Bafi	Domeniḳa [Ze]re	Gin Ḳra[pesi]
Miḫ[al] birāder-i o	G[in] [Zere]	A[nd]riya [ve]led-i o	[Tru]şa Yiro	mücerred Gin Barçi
[mü]cerred [Ma]rti Suli	mücerred Palus̲i Mara	mücerred Niḳola Meliti	mücerred Marti İvlaḫo	mücerred Gin Ḳataranya
mücerred Gin Ḳaluşi	mücerred Gin Zere-i dīğer		ḫāne 24	mücerred 8

ḥāṣıl 1891

ʿa(n) ispence 640	ʿöşr-i ḥınṭa 950	ʿöşr-i cev 148	ʿöşr-i bāġāt 112	ʿöşr-i meyve 3	resm-i ḫanāzīr 35	ʿöşr-i ḳazz 3

ḳarye-i Todoroplu ez cemāʿat-i Arnavudān — ḫāṣṣa-ı zaʿīm

Dimitri Todoroplo	Yorgi birāder-i o	İstrati Ḳraḳoplo	Miḫal Ḳraḳo[pl]o	Dimitri birāder-i o
Yani Laġatora	İstemad Ḳraḳoplo	Niḳola Yanaḳoplo	İstemad Plaşa	Marḳo Covaneli
Gin Malaḳas	Todoros Ḳraḳoplo	Marti Zuġra	Ḳosta Perdiḳari	Dimitri Graḳoplo
Covanelo veled-i o		ḫāne 16		

ḥāṣıl 914

ʿa(n) ispence 320	ʿöşr-i ḥınṭa 500	ʿöşr-i cev 78	ʿöşr-i bāġāt 16

ḳarye-i Petros Ḳaratula ez cemāʿat-i Arnavudān — ḫāṣṣa-ı zaʿīm

Petros Ḳaratula	Mangişa Ḳaratula	Gin Ḳoloveloni	Miḫal Ḳastani	Manḳola birāder-i o
İlya Zyavoliçi	Petros birāẕer-i o	mücerred Andriya Ḳaratula	ḫāne 7	mücerred 1

ḥāṣıl 411

ʿa(n) ispence 160	ʿöşr-i ḥınṭa 200	ʿöşr-i cev 31	resm-i ḫanāzīr 20

ḳarye-i Ḳaçana maʿa cemāʿat-i İştopanṣi — ḫāṣṣa-ı zaʿīm

Petros el-meẕkūr	Dima Ḳaratula	Ḳalenci birāẕer-i o	Niḳola Zoġa	Andriya İstayḳo
Ḳalanci Ḳaratula	Aleksi Barçi	Todoros Samandi	Dimitri Ġalino	Aleksi birāẕer-i o

9

tetimme-i ḳarye-i Ḳaçana el-meẕkūr — ḫāṣṣa-ı zaʿīm

Yorgi Ḫayḳ[a]l	Gin veled-i o	Petros Buryaşa	Ḳozma birāder-i o	Niḳola [İştopa]nṣi
Ġolyas	Duḳa Luzi	Yorgi Ḳaḳoprozo[- tiya]	A[ndr]iya Ḳa[ḳo]pr[ozotiya]	Miḫal dāmād-ı [o]
Yani İstaḫtiya	Lazaro İlya	Todoros İstaḫtiya	Duḳa İstaḫ- tiya	mücerred Miḫal Ḳa[ḳo]perzotiya
mücerred Todoros İstaḫtiya	bīve Mariya	ḫāne 24	mücerred 2	bīve 1

ḥāṣıl 1478

ʿa(n) ispence 656	ʿöşr-i bāġāt 176	ʿöşr-i meyve [9]	ʿöşr-i ḳazz 51	resm-i ḫanāzīr 11	ʿöşr-i ḥınṭa 450	ʿöşr-i cev 70

resm-i ḫamr 25	mülk-i Dima Ḳara[tu]la der ḳarye-i meẕkūr āsiyāb-ı peşmīne 1 resm 15	mülk-i Yorgi Ḳaḳoperzotiya der ḳarye-i meẕkūr āsiyāb-ı peşmīne 1 resm 15

mezraʿa-ı Ḳaratula-<yı> dīğer nezd-i ḳarye-i Ḳaçana el-meẕkūr

ḫāṣṣa-ı zaʿīm — ḫāliyye

ḳarye-i Lapata — ḫāṣṣa-ı zaʿīm

Niḳola İstefanoplo	Dimitri İstefanoplo	Miḫal Ḫalḳomata	Niḳola Ḳuzuni	Papas Miḫal
Dimitri Ḳondo	Yorgi Ḫalḳomata	Niḳola Perdiḳari	Miḫal birāẕer-i o	Andron Ḳoroni
Yorgi birāder-i o	Yorgi Filibos[4]	Andriya veled-i o	Yorgi Ḫarḳomata	Yani Draġuli
İstemad Muḫuri	Domeniḳa Ġurzumeş	keşiş[5] Papamarti	Yorgi İpsaro	Andriya Filipoplo
Yani Ḳondo	mücerred Todoros İstefanoplo	mücerred Manol İpsaro	ḫāne 21	mücerred 2

ḥāṣıl 1687

ʿa(n) ispence 575	ʿöşr-i ḥınṭa 800	ʿöşr-i cev 124	resm-i ḫanāzīr 8	ʿöşr-i bāġāt 160	ʿöşr-i kettān 20

ḳarye-i Ḳato Ḳurnofita — ḫāṣṣa-ı zaʿīm

Yorgi Orfano	Yani Arayiri	Niḳola veled-i o	Miḫal veled-i o	Yani Orfano
Dimitri Virgi	Yorgi Vizomati	Yani Ḳorvoluni	Pavlos Andoni	Yani Virgi
Miḫal Zaġoriti		ḫāne 11		

10

ḥāṣıl-ı ḳarye-i Ḳato Ḳurnofita el-meẕkūr 743

ʿa(n) ispence 275	ʿöşr-i ḥınṭa 400	ʿö[şr-i] [cev] 63	resm-i ḫanāzīr 5

ḳarye-i Ġolemi ez cemāʿat-i Arnavudān — ḫāṣṣa-ı zaʿīm

Yorgi Ġolemi	Ḳo[z]ma veled-i o	Pavlos Ġolemi	Ḳozma veled-i o	Niḳola veled-i o
Dimit[ri] Ġolemi	Dimitri Ġolemi-i dīğer	Petros Ġolemi	Vaṣi Ġolemi	Pavlos birāder-i o
Marti Ġolemi	Gin Ġolemi		ḫāne 12	

ḥāṣıl 959

ʿa(n) ispence	ʿöşr-i bāġāt	ʿöşr-i ḥınṭa	ʿöşr-i cev	resm-i ḫanāzīr	mülk-i Dimitri Ġolemi der ḳarye-i mezḳūr āsiyāb 1 resm 40
240	80	500	80	19	

ḳarye-i Maḳriyeni Çamanda ez cemāʿat-i Arnavudān ḫāṣṣa-ı zaʿīm

Andriya Maḳriyeni	Yani veled-i o	Ḳosta Çamanda	Yorgi Anḳarḫo	Yani veled-i o
Yorgi Buvasi	Palunbi Ranesi	Ḳosta Maḳriyeni	Ḳostandin Çamanda	Yorgi Maḳriyeni
Petro Buvasi	bīve Buza	mücerred Yani Çamanda	mücerred Yorgi Çamanda	ḫāne 11 mücerred 2 bīve 1

ḥāṣıl 797

ʿa(n) ispence	ʿöşr-i ḥınṭa	ʿöşr-i cev	resm-i ḫanāzīr
266	450	68	13

ḳarye-i Dara ez cemāʿat-i Arnavudān ḫāṣṣa-ı zaʿīm

Niḳola Dara	Gin Lata	Marti Lata	Niḳola Supaki	İstefano Melyoti
Gin birāder-i o	Todoros Rusi	Yani veled-i o	Miḫal Ḫalköplos	İvrato Metaḳsa
mücerred Pelañrin Supaki	bīve Beliye	ḫāne 10	mücerred 1	bīve 1

ḥāṣıl 727

ʿa(n) ispence	ʿöşr-i ḥınṭa	ʿöşr-i cev	resm-i ḫanāzīr	ʿöşr-i bāġāt
226	400	61	16	24

mezraʿa-ı Puloti nezd-i ḳarye-i Dara el-mezḳūr

ḫāṣṣa-ı zaʿīm ḫāliyye

11

tetimme-i nāḥiyyet-i Ḳalavrita

ḳarye-i Peryale ez cemāʿat-i Arnavu[dā]n ḫāṣṣa-ı zaʿīm

İvlaşi Punbuḳ[a]	Miḫal Poẓaras	Dimitri veled-i o	Gin Punbuḳa	Yorgi Ḳuḳa
Domeniḳa Ḳuḳa	Ḳosta Bunbuḳa	Soki veled-i o	Niḳola Peryale	Ḳuçi Bunbuḳa
Leḳa Bubuḳa	İştin Ḳuḳa	mücerred Gin Bunbuḳa	mücerred Lala Bunbuḳa	[bī]ve Ḳuke
bīve Buza		ḫāne 12	mücerred 2	bīve 2

ḥāṣıl 793

ʿa(n) ispence	ʿöşr-i bāġāt	ʿöşr-i ḥınṭa	ʿöşr-i cev	resm-i ḫanāzīr
292	8	400	64	29

ḳarye-i Zepandi[6] ez cemāʿat-i Arnavudān ḫāṣṣa-ı zaʿīm

Mangişa Zepandi	Marti veled-i o	Varda veled-i o	Varda Repandi[7]	Yorgi birāẓer-i o
Marti Zepandi	Lala birāẓer-i o	Mangişa veled-i o	Mangişa Yeminos	Marti Zepandi
Gin Malaḳas	Gin Zepandi	Lazari veled-i o	Mangişa Zepandi	Marti Ẓramesi
Todoros Platimas	Muriki Manesi	Mangişa Buza	Andriya birāder-i o	Andriya Graḳa
Marti Graḳa	Zapandi veled-i o	Marti Zepandi	Varda veled-i o	Niḳola Bondaya
İvrato Platimas	İstefano Graḳa	mücerred Yorgi Zepandi	mücerred Miḫal birāder-i o	mücerred Niḳola Malaḳas
mücerred Proġono birāẓer-i o	bīve Ḳozmo	ḫāne 27	mücerred 4	bīve 1

ḥāṣıl 1965

ʿa(n) ispence	ʿöşr-i bāġāt	ʿöşr-i ḥınṭa	ʿöşr-i cev	resm-i ḫanāzīr	ʿöşr-i ḳazz
626	80	1050	161	5	3

mülk-i Mangişa Zepandi der ḳarye-i mezḳūr āsiyāb 1 resm 40

ḳarye-i Ḳrastiki — ḫāṣṣa-ı zaʿīm

Yani Platindro	Pavlos Ḳavasila	Pavlos Papaẕas	Dima Draġoti	Yorgi Platindro	
Petro Bafi	Pelañri[8] Zarza	Todoros Meṣoẕoplos	Yorgi Ḳavasila	Yorgi Draġoti	
Niḳola Draġoti	Niḳola Dorza	İvlarunci İksano	bīve Papavya[9]	ḫāne 13	bīve 1

12

ḥāṣıl-ı ḳarye-i Ḳrastiki el-meẕkūr 728

ʿa(n) ispence	ʿöşr-i bāġāt	ʿöşr-i ḳazz	ʿöşr-i ḥınṭa	ʿöşr-i cev
331	88	21	250	38

ḳarye-i [Su]li ez cemāʿat-i Arnavudān — ḫāṣṣa-ı zaʿīm

Suli el-meẕkūr	Gin [Suli]	Vaṣi veled-i o	Gin Ḳapareli	Varda Suli	
Petro Suli	Petro Pilura	Gin veled-i o	Gin Seryapo	Varda Pilura	
Domeniḳa Graḳa	mücerred Lazaro Suli	bīve Todora	bīve Çamina	ḫāne 11	mücerred 1; bīve 2

ḥāṣıl 680

ʿa(n) ispence	resm-i ḫanāzīr	ʿöşr-i ḥınṭa	ʿöşr-i cev	ʿöşr-i bāġāt	ʿöşr-i meyve
252	5	350	55	16	2

ḳarye-i İflamurari ez cemāʿat-i Arnavudān — ḫāṣṣa-ı zaʿīm

Andriya İflamurari	Varda Benaşi	Dimitri veled-i o	Duşa Ḳraçi	Franḳa Zepandi	
Yorgi birāder-i o	Gin Mutuza	İstefano Baza	Duḳa veled-i o	Varda Ftaranbo	
İstefano Bazi	İlya Bazi	Marti Zepandi	mücerred Niḳola Benaşi	ḫāne 13	mücerred 1

ḥāṣıl 972

ʿa(n) ispence	ʿöşr-i ḥınṭa	ʿöşr-i cev
280	600	92

ḳarye-i Niḳola Manesi ez cemāʿat-i Arnavudān — ḫāṣṣa-ı zaʿīm

Niḳola Manesi	Pavlo ḫīş-i o	İş Ari Cani	Gin Cani	Andriya Mazi	
Niḳola Marḳo	Leḳa Ġusati	Yorgi Pondaya	mücerred Petros Cani	ḫāne 8	mücerred 1

ḥāṣıl 392

ʿa(n) ispence	ʿöşr-i ḥınṭa	ʿöşr-i cev	ʿöşr-i meyve
100	250	40	2

mezraʿa-ı İskliva nezd-i ḳarye-i meẕkūr — ḫāṣṣa-ı zaʿīm

ḫāliyye

ḳarye-i Fila ez cemāʿat-i Arnavudān — ḫāṣṣa-ı zaʿīm

Ḳlaşire İvlanduşa	Gin Fila	Gin Beṣulḳa	Yorgi Randi	İsḳarpo Praski

ḫāne 5

ḥāṣıl 256

ʿa(n) ispence	ʿöşr-i bāġāt	ʿöşr-i ḥınṭa	ʿöşr-i cev
100	40	100	16

13

tetimme-i nāḥiyyet-i Ḳalavri[ta]

ḳarye-i Tireḫlista — ḫāṣṣa-ı zaʿīm

Miḫal [Ḳuz]uni	Ḳosta [Ḳ]uzuni	Andriya Torḳari	ḫāne 3

ḥāṣıl [3]1[1]

ʿa(n) ispence 75	bāġāt-ı ḫ[ā]ṣṣa dönüm 2 [resm] 120	eşcār-ı tut-ı ḫāṣṣa ʿaded 6 [resm] 15	eş[c]ār-ı me[yve-i] [ḫā]ṣṣa ʿaded 6 [resm] 10	ʿöşr-i bāġā[t] 80
	ʿöşr-i ḳazz 7		ʿöşr-i meyve 4	

ḳarye-i Palunbi Ranesi ez cemāʿat-i Arnavudān ḫāṣṣa-ı zaʿīm

Yani Opuşi	Niḳola Ḳarnasi	İştin Buşi	Mangişa Traḫya	Gön Traḫya
Ḳostandin Sermorin	bīve Pusina		ḫāne 6	bīve 1

ḥāṣıl 380

ʿa(n) ispence	ʿöşr-i ḥınṭa	ʿöşr-i cev	resm-i ʿarūsī
126	210	34	10

cemʿan ḫāṣṣhā-<yı> subaşı-ı Ḳalavrita

ḳurā maʿa nefs-i Ḳalavrita	mezāriʿ-i ḫāliyye	ḫāne	mücerred	bīve
38	4	586	71	21

ḥāṣıl 45970

14
tetimme-i nāḥiyyet-i Ḳalavrita

kendü bürüme	cebelü	ġulām	çadır
	2	1	1

tīmār-ı Müstaḳdim silāḥdār-ı serʿasker-i Ḳalavrita

ḳarye-i Ayo İvlaşi tīmār-ı o

Niḳola Damali	Todoros Damali	Andriya Damali	Miḫal Serano	Todoros veled-i o
Yorgi İvrana	Dimitri birāder-i o	Yani Platiḳo	Andriya Ḫarkâ	Dimitri birāẕer-i o
Andriya Ḫarkâ-<yı> dīğer	Niḳola Sirgi	Todoros Biçinyos	Dimitri Papaandroplo	Yani Meradis
Yorgi Laġos	Niḳola Liḳoşuri	Yorgi İvlaşi	Yani Ḫıristoforo	Manol Ḳaçuli
Petros veled-i o	Miḫal Ḳaçuli	Todoros Arfonoyani	Yorgi İspiri	Yorgi İskâli
Dimitri Papaandroplo	Yani Ḳaloyanoplo	Miḫal Foti	Niḳola Lardo	Niḳola Ḳalodiki
Dimitri Aleksandroplo	Yani Mavroyini	Manol ʿazab	Yorgi Ḫarkâ	İstilyano Ḳaloyoros
Leḳa Petroplo	Miḫal Petroplos	mücerred Yani Damali	mücerred Manol Laġos	mücerred Miḫal İspiri
mücerred Niḳola İskâli	mücerred Dimitri Lardo	mücerred Aleksi Ḳaloyiryati	mücerred Yani İvlaḫina	bīve İvlaḫina
bīve Varzaniya	bīve Ẕuraḫiya	ḫāne 37	mücerred 7	bīve 3

ḥāṣıl 4863

ʿa(n) ispence 1118	bāġāt-ı ḫāṣṣa dönüm 5 [resm] 600	eşcār-ı ṭut-ı ḫāṣṣa ʿaded 30 [resm] 90	eşcār-ı meyve-i ḫāṣṣa ʿaded 5 [resm] 10	āsiyāb-ı ḫāṣṣa 1 [resm] 500

ʿöşr-i bāġāt	ʿöşr-i ḥınṭa	ʿöşr-i cev	ʿöşr-i ḳazz	resm-i ḫamr	resm-i ʿarūsī
496	1600	250	99	60	40

ḳarye-i Ġurġa ez cemāʿat-i Arnavudān tīmār-ı o

Görgi Ġurġa	Petros Ḳalifonis	Ḳuġa Ḳalifoni	Ḳozma Ḳalifoni	Gin Buzi	
Gin Buzi-i dīğer	İş Ari Buzi	Petros Buzi	mücerred İştin Ġurġa	ḫāne 8	mücerred 1

ḥāṣıl 600

ʿa(n) ispence	ʿöşr-i ḥınṭa	ʿöşr-i cev	resm-i ḫanāzīr	resm-i ʿarūsī
180	350	55	5	10

15
tetimme-i nāḥiyyet-i Ḳalavrita

ḳarye-i Muriki ez cemāʿat-i Arnavudān tīmār-ı o

Andriya Muriki	Niḳola Vilasi	Gin Muriki	İvlaş Muriki	İştin Misepoliti
Filibos[10] İvlaḫos	Niḳola Misepoliti	bīve Bilye	ḫāne 7	bīve 1

ḥāṣıl 562

ʿa(n) ispence	ʿöşr-i ḥınṭa	ʿöşr-i cev	resm-i ḫanāzīr
146	350	56	10

ḳarye-i Debrani ez cemāʿat-i Arnavudān — tīmār-ı o

Lazaro Debrani	Leḳa Dramesi	Andriya Ḳondostavlo	Niḳola birāder-i o	Andriya Maḳriyeni

ḫāne
5

ḥāṣıl 332

ʿa(n) ispence 100	ʿöşr-i ḥınṭa 200	ʿöşr-i cev 32

ḳarye-i İştin Bondaya ez cemāʿat-i Arnavudān — tīmār-ı o

İştin el-mezḳūr	Miḫal Bondaya	Gin Ranesi	Niḳola Bardi	Gin Manesi
Domeniḳa Biçi	Yorgi Biçi	İlya Biçi	mücerred Gin Ranesi	mücerred Ḳozma Manesi
bīve Mariya		ḫāne 8	mücerred 2	bīve 1

ḥāṣıl 630

ʿa(n) ispence 206	ʿöşr-i ḥınṭa 350	ʿöşr-i cev 56	resm-i ḫanāzīr 8	resm-i ʿarūsī 10

cemʿan tīmār-ı serʿasker el-mezḳūr

ḳurā 5	ḫāne 65	mücerred 10	bīve 5

ḥāṣıl 6987

16
tetimme-i nāḥiyyet-i Ḳalavrita

kendü bürüme	cebelü 3	ġulām 1	[ç]ad[ır] [1]

tīmār-ı ʿAlī veled-i Cāyim

ḳarye-i Şavanus — tīmār-ı o

Miḫal Ḳrokiẓa	Yani Ḳrokiẓa	Aleksi Ḳrokiẓa	[Ya]ni Melaẓino	Todoros Mela[zino]s
Petros Mela[zi]nos	Yorgi Ḳuli	Ḳosta Ḳuli	Niḳola Ḳuli	Yani Ḳrapiçi
Todoros Ḳrapiçi	Papatodoros Maliḫorino	Niḳola Sava	Yani Sava	Todoros Kevotos
Niḳola Kevotos	Andron Kivotos	Yorgi Kivoto	Niḳola Bordo	Yorgi Pahiyeni
Yorgi Yanuloplo	Manol Papaistefano- plo	Pavlos Papaistefano- plos	İstfano Yala	Niḳola Yala
Yani Zavraẓino	Franḳoplo İksano	Dimitri Zavraẓino	Petros Filis	Dimitri Filis
Yani Zavraẓino	Dimitri Ḳrokiẓa	Niḳola Zavraẓino	mücerred Dimitri Ḳuli	mücerred Dimitri Sava

mücerred Andon Tirmari	bīve Saviya	bīve Tirmarina	ḫāne 33	mücerred 3	bīve 2

ḥāṣıl 3029

ʿa(n) ispence 912	bāġāt-ı ḫāṣṣa dönüm 1 [resm] 120	eşcār-ı ṭut-ı ḫāṣṣa ʿaded 20 [resm] 30	ʿöşr-i bāġāt 240	ʿöşr-i ḥınṭa 1300	ʿöşr-i cev [1]96

ʿöşr-i ḳazz 65	ʿöşr-i meyve 21	ʿöşr-i ʿasel 5	resm-i ʿarūsī 30	resm-i ḫamr 40	ʿöşr-i kettān 30	mülk-i Miḫal Ḳrokiẓa der ḳarye-i mezḳūr āsiyāb 1 resm 40

ḳarye-i Anastasova — tīmār-ı o

Yani Yanoplo	Yani Ḳosoliva	Dimitri Malyaro	Yorgi Sava	Yorgi Eksarḫoplo
Dimitri Papaan- droplo	Yorgi Papaandroplo	Dimitri Todoroplo	Niḳola Ḳaliġoplo	Ḳondo Traḫya
Yorgi Papayan- oplo	Yorgi Ruso	Niḳola Ḳrokiẓa	mücerred Niḳola Anastasoviti	bīve Luzina
	ḫāne 13	mücerred 1	bīve 1	

ḥāṣıl 1698

ʿa(n) ispence 356	bāġāt-ı ḫāṣṣa dönüm 3 [resm] 360	eşcār-ı ṭut-ı ḫāṣṣa ʿaded 30 [resm] 50	eşcār-ı meyve-i ḫāṣṣa ʿaded 3 [resm] 10	ʿöşr-i bāġāt 272	ʿöşr-i ḥınṭa 400

ʿöşr-i cev 60	ʿöşr-i ḳazz 82	ʿöşr-i meyve 18	resm-i ḫamr 40	resm-i ʿarūsī 10	mülk-i Yani Yanoplo der ḳarye-i mezḳūr āsiyāb 1 resm 40

17

tetimme-i nāḥiyyet-i Ḳalavrita

ḳarye-i Droġola[voş] tīmār-ı o

Yorgi Draġoy	Niḳola Yanoplo	Manol Foti	İstefano Lancunato	Andriya Foti
Yani Papavaşıloplo	mücerred Miḫal [Dra]ġoy		ḫāne 6	mücerred 1

ḥāṣıl 729

ʿa(n) ispence 175	bāġāt-ı ḫāṣṣa dönüm 2 [resm] 240	eşcār-ı ṭut-ı ḫāṣṣa ʿaded 40 [resm] 60	ʿöşr-i bāġāt 57	ʿöşr-i ḥınṭa 100	ʿöşr-i [cev] 15

ʿöşr-i ḳazz 27	ʿöşr-i meyve 5	ʿöşr-i kettān 10	mülk-i Andriya Foti der ḳarye-i mezḳūr āsiyāb 1 resm 40

ḳarye-i Seliça tīmār-ı o

Yani Proḳopi	Todoros Proḳopi	Niḳola Ḳalanesi	Leḳa Ḳalanesi	İş Ari Ḳalanesi
Dimitri Ḳalanesi	Yorgi Ḳalanesi	Miḫal Ḳalanesi	Yorgi İpsari	Ḳozma Taçi
Dimitri Sivasto	Miḫa Vulasi	Gin İflamura	mücerred Yorgi İşpata	bīve Playatina
	ḫāne 13	mücerred 1	bīve 1	

ḥāṣıl 858

ʿa(n) ispence 356	eşcār-ı ṭut-ı ḫāṣṣa ʿaded 50 [resm] 75	eşcār-ı meyve-i ḫāṣṣa ʿaded 11 [resm] 20	ʿöşr-i bāġāt 32	ʿöşr-i ḥınṭa 300	ʿöşr-i cev 47

ʿöşr-i ḳazz 14	ʿöşr-i meyve 2	resm-i ḫanāzīr 2	resm-i ʿarūsī 10

ḳarye-i Mavromati ez cemāʿat-i Arnavudān tīmār-ı o

Ġulyamo Mavromati	Gön Ḳrati	Andriya Ḳrati	İstefano Ḳrati	Niḳola Çapoġa
Lazaro Çapoġa	Vaşıl Çapoġa	Dima Biçi	Gön Burasi	Gin Zepandi
Yorgi Biçi	Gön Pikerni	Petros Zapandi	Niḳola Mavromati	Ḳozma Tiryarḫi
Gön Çapoġa	Ḳosta Buba	Vaṣi Şameri	Todoros Biçi	Petro Çapoġa
Yorgi Ḳrati	Gin İspalata	Andriya Burasi	Petros İşpata	Dima Zapandi

18

tetimme-i ḳarye-i Mavromati el-mezḳūr

[Yo]rgi Lukişa	mücerred Yorgi Mavromati	mücerred Gön Aḫyoti	mücerred Andriya Buba	mücerred Manḳola Ḳrati
	ḫāne 26		mücerred 4	

ḥāṣıl 1772

ʿa(n) ispence 60[0]	ʿöşr-i ḥınṭa [9]50	ʿöşr-i cev 142	ʿöşr-i bāġāt 57	resm-i ḫanāzīr 3	resm-i ʿarūsī 20

ḳarye-i Priniḳos tābiʿ-i Mizisra tīmār-ı o

Todoros İlyaẓi	Yorgi Pliça	Dimitri Suvanduḳo	Yani birāder-i o	Yani İvlaḫo
İstemad Mandilovraki	Lazaro Voẓelyo	Dimitri Perẓefti	Andon Pliyostomo	mücerred Yorgi Ḳoçanbo
	ḫāne 9		mücerred 1	

bu köyde olan ṭuzla Mizişra nāḥiyyetinde yazılmışdır

ḥāṣıl ġayr ez memlaḥa 1704

ʿa(n) ispence 250	ḳısṭ-ı ṭalyan-ı ḫāṣṣa 1 [resm] 800	bāġāt-ı ḫāṣṣa dönüm 5 [resm] 300	eşcār-ı zeyt-i ḫāṣṣa ʿaded 5 [resm] 5	eşcār-ı enār-ı ḫāṣṣa ʿadedān [resm] 5	
ʿöşr-i kettān 20	ʿöşr-i ḥınṭa 200	ʿöşr-i cev 31	ʿöşr-i bāġāt 80	ʿöşr-i meyve 3	resm-i ʿarūsī 10

cemʿan tīmār-ı ʿAlī el-mezḳūr

ḳurā 6	ḫāne 100	mücerred 11	bīve 4

ḥāṣıl 9790

mevḳūf

mezraʿa-ı İvlaḫo Ḳalanas nezd-i ḳarye-i Şavanus el-mezḳūr ḫāliyye

mevḳūf

mezraʿa-ı İvlaḫo Yalya nezd-i ḳarye-i o ḫāliyye

kendü bürüme	cebelü 2	çadır 1

tīmār-ı Meḥmed nev müslümān

ḳarye-i Ḳastel tīmār-ı o

Dimitri Eksarḫo	Niḳola Peliḳanos	Yani veled-i o	Dimitri Peleḳanos	Dimitri Nomiḳos
Leo Kefala	Niḳola Eksarḫoplo	Miḫal Boḫali	Yani İġliġoroplo	Petros İġliġoroplo

19

tetimme-i ḳarye-i Ḳastel el-mezḳūr

Yani Miḫaloplo	Miḫal Protopapazaplo	Yorgi birāder-i o	Yorgi Zefterevoplo	Todoros Mastroyanoplo
Yorgi Ḳalovuni	Todoros Papayorġoplo	Yorgi Zoġrafo	Todoros Argiri	Yorgi Lefteroplo
Yani Lisuta	Dimitri ḫīş-i o	Todoros Romanos	D[imi]tri Duraci	Niḳola Zozoġli

Yani Zozoġli	Todoros Zozoġli	Manol Zozoġli	Pavlos Zozoġli	[And]riya Ermeni		
Yani Ḳrokiza	Niḳola İflamuri	Miḫal Siryani	Ḳaluti Luzi	Yorgi Ḳaçaros		
Yani birāder-i o	Yani Vulesi	Gin Marḳoplos	mücerred Petros Peliḳanos	bīve Kefalu		
bīve Buzariya	bīve İstema-tina	bīve Palyopolisa	bīve Ḳrokiza	ḫāne 38	mücerred 1	bīve 5

ḥāṣıl 3741

ʿa(n) ispence 1005	bāġāt-ı ḫāṣṣa dönüm 4 [resm] 480	eşcār-ı ṭut-ı ḫāṣṣa ʿaded 30 [resm] 50	āsiyāb-ı ḫāṣṣa 1 [resm] 200	ʿöşr-i bāġāt 448	ʿöşr-i ḥınṭa 1050
ʿöşr-i cev 165	ʿöşr-i ḳazz 71	ʿöşr-i meyve 7	resm-i ḫamr 40	resm-i ʿarūsī 35	ʿöşr-i kettān 30

mülk-i Ḳarkür Arnavud ki p<ī>ş ez <ī>n tīmār eri būd der ḳarye-i mezḳūr āsiyāb 2 resm 120

mülk-i Niḳola Zozoġli der ḳarye-i mezḳūr āsiyāb 1 resm 40

ḳarye-i Ḳazneş ez cemāʿat-i Arnavudān tīmār-ı o

Gin Manesi	Miḫal birāder-i o	Aleksi İzlatḳo	Pavlos Ḫayḳal	Manso Franḳos
İstemad Rayḳos	Leḳa Zoġrafo	Andriya Evlavis	Gin Milyoti	Todoros Ḳaçaros
Todoros Ḫarara	Besulḳa İskâza	Yani Bufara	Papazimitri Zoraci	Milandinos Orfanos
Görgi Floḳa	Duḳa Bureşi	Gön Ḫaraḳtinos	Görgi veled-i o	Duḳa veled-i o
Lazaro Floḳa	Gin Franḳo	Vine Franḳo	mücerred Petros Ḳaçaros	mücerred Pavlos Floḳa
mücerred Miḫo Ḫaraḳtinos	ḫāne 23	mücerred 3		

ḥāṣıl 1160

ʿa(n) ispence 520	ʿöşr-i ḥınṭa 500	ʿöşr-i cev 75	ʿöşr-i kettān 40	resm-i ʿarūsī 25

20
tetimme-i nāḥiyyet-i Ḳalavrita

ḳarye-i Marḳoplu ez cemāʿat-i Arnavudān tābiʿ-i Girbene — tīmār-ı o

Yorgi Mazarak	Bardi Mazarak	Manos Mazarak	Dimo Longer	Martin Ḳramastos
Leḳa Helmesi	S̱omas Mazarakis	Niḳola Mazarakis	Dimitri [Ḳram]astos	bīve Lüke zen-i Helmesi

ḫāne	bīve
9	1

ḥāṣıl 655

ʿa(n) ispence	ʿöşr-i ḥınṭa	ʿöşr-i cev	resm-i ḫanāzīr
186	400	61	8

cemʿan tīmār-ı Meḥmed el-meẕkūr

ḳurā	ḫāne	mücerred	bīve
3	70	4	6

ḥāṣıl 5556

kendü bürüme	cebelü	tenktür
	1	1

tīmār-ı Ḥamza nev müslümān bā birāẕereş Yūsuf müşterek be-nevbet dāde şüd

ḳarye-i İstrazova — tīmār-ı meẕkūrān

Yorgi Zirvo	Niḳola İzliḳa[11]	Papas Yani Cinovina	Ḳosta birāder-i o	Andriya Cinovina
Yorgi birāder-i o	Yorgi Nebrovaẓi	Dimitri İvlaşi	Niḳola İvlaşi	Yani İvlaşi
Andon İvlaşi	Todoros Ḳomninos	Dimitri İvlaşi-i dīğer	Yorgi Beli	Dimitri Vaşıloplos
Yani Liḳa	Leo Maḳri	Yorgi Viçyoti	mücerred Miḫal Nebrovaẓi	mücerred Yani Ḳomninos

ḫāne	mücerred
18	2

ḥāṣıl 2080

ʿa(n) ispence	bāğāt-ı ḫāṣṣa	āsiyāb-ı ḫāṣṣa 1	ʿöşr-i bāğāt	ʿöşr-i ḥınṭa	ʿöşr-i cev	resm-i ʿarūsī	resm-i ḫamr	mülk-i Niḳola İzletiḳo der ḳarye-i meẕkūr
500	dönüm 3 [resm] 360	[resm] 400	272	400	63	20	35	āsiyāb 1 resm 30

21
tetimme-i nāḥiyyet-i Miḫlu

mevḳūf
mezraʿa-ı Astro nezd-i ḳarye-i Astriçi el-meẕkūr ḫāliyye

mevḳūf
mezraʿa-ı Duşa Dara nezd-i ḳarye-i meẕkūr ḫāliyye

mevḳūf
mezraʿa-ı Luvari nezd-i ḳarye-i meẕkūr ḫāliyye

mevḳūf
mezraʿa-ı Plaşa nezd-i ḳarye-i o ḫāliyye

kendüler bürüme	cebelü	çadır
	5	1

tīmār-ı Yūsuf nev müslümān ki ḳardaşı Yaʿḳūb nev müslümānla müşterek yėrler ve ikisi bile eşerler

ḳarye-i Pikerni ez cemāʿat-i Arnavudān — tīmār-ı o

Niḳola Başi	Gön veled-i o	Todo Başi	Gön Başi	Niḳola birāder-i o
Andriya birāder-i o	Todo Loçi	Miḫal Ġuresi	Dede birāder-i o	S̱oma Miḫal Ġuresi
Gin Ḳurtesi	Gön veled-i o	Gin veled-i o	Luş Ḳumi	Niḳola birāder-i o
Gön Ḳumi	Seni birāẕer-i o	Gerg Ḳrozmesi	Gerg Zepandi	Gin Sümiza
Duşa birāẕer-i o	Lazar Gin Sümiza	Marti Zepandi	Ḳozma Ḳozomise	Gönime
Mujak veled-i o	Gön Ḳumi	Miḫa birāẕer-i o	Petro Manḳaki	Leḳa birāẕer-i o
Todoro Manḳaki	Petro veled-i o	Lumi Maniḳal	Yorgi İspas̱ari	Lazari İspas̱ari

22

tetimme-i ḳarye-i Pikerni el-meẕkūr — tīmār-ı mezbūrān

S̱o[to]ki birāder-i o	[A]ndriya İsḳura	Gerg Ḳalusi	[Ḳo]z[ma] birāder-i o	Gin Ḳ[al]usi
Mila Ḳalusi	Andriya Ḳrapesi	Pulunbi[12] Ḳoriri	[Dome]niḳa veled-i o	Merti[13] veled-i o
Ḳozma Buzi	Yorgi Manḳaki	Gön birāder-i o	Tanuşi Maliki	Gin veled-i o
Gön veled-i o	Piyatr veled-i o	Petro Maji	Ḳoşta[14] Ḳarvunari	Gin veled-i o
Aleksi Ḳarvunari	Tonda Ḳarvunari	Todoro Ḫaramtino[15]	Gin Ḳaḳusi	Yani Ḳuçi
Yorgi Ḳuçi	Piyatr birāẕer-i o	Gön Biçi	Gin Peta	Man[ol] Do[bri]
İvlaş Dobri	Yani birāder-i o	Gön Zoryani	Gön Loçi	Andriya Loçi
Andron Ḳaluṣi	Gin Lokeşi	Petros Latas	mücerred Duşi Başi	mücerred Todo ḫīş-i Gergi Zepand[i]
mücerred Seni veled-i Gönima	mücerred Andriya birāder-i o	mücerred Leo Manḳak	mücerred Şirmi İspaMari	mücerred Niḳola İsḳura
mücerred Yani Niḳolayti	mücerred Niḳola birāder-i o	mücerred Dede Zoryana	bīve Güre zen-i Niḳolayti	bīve Neje zen-i Ḳuçi

bīve İrine zen-i Peta	bīve Zoryana	bīve Mariya zen-i Zoryana	ḫāne 73	mücerred 10	bīve 5

ḥāṣıl 5482

ʿa(n) ispence 1690	eşcār-ı tut-ı ḫāṣṣa ʿaded 30 [resm] 150	ʿöşr-i ḥınṭa 3000	ʿöşr-i cev 453	resm-i ḫanāzīr 79	resm-i ʿarūsī 80

mülk-i
Yūsuf ve Yaʿḳūb süvāriyān-ı meẕkūrān
āsiyāb 1 resm 30

ḳarye-i Naşi ez cemāʿat-i Arnavudān — tīmār-ı meẕkūrān

İvrato Manesi	Bardi birāder-i o	Bardi Manesi	Gön Manesi	İvrato Mayiri
Yorgi birāder-i o	Todoro Mayiri	Ḳosta Mayiri	Yani Engürüs	Miḫal Engürüs
İştin Ḳorviziya	Pasḳo Musura	Todoro birāẕer-i o	Dima Musura	Yorgi Toskesi
Yorgi Musura	Ḳozma Buva	Ḳandriva Ḳazneşi	mücerred Gön Manesi	mücerred Yani Babevaṣi

23

tetimme-i ḳarye-i Naşi el-meẕkūr

mücerred Ḳral Mayiri	mücerred Ba[r]di Ḫararviziya (?)	[B]ardi Manesi	bīve Bamerva [---]	bīve Mar[a] [ze]n-i Ma[yiri]
bīve Man[ḳ]a zen-i Manḳola		ḫāne 18	mücerred 5	bīve 3

ḥāṣıl 1213

ʿa(n) ispence 478	ʿöşr-i ḥınṭa 600	ʿöşr-i cev 94	resm-i ḫanāzīr 21	resm-i ʿarūsī 20

ḳarye-i Brasna Sanḳa ez cemāʿat-i Arnavudān — tīmār-ı meẕkūrān

G[ö]n Br[a]sna	Niḳola birāder-i o	Yorgi Gön Brasna	Gön Brasna	Andriya Brasna
[Yor]gi-i [d]īğer Brasna	Gürḳa Brasna	Yorgi birāẕer-i o	Dima Brasna	Petros Brasna
Vaṣi Brasna	Pavlos Brasna	Pal Brasna	Domeniḳa İvlandi	Mesḳa birāder-i o
Gin Marḳoplo	Lazaro Ḳuçi	Mesḳa birāẕer-i o	Yorgi Ḳuçi	Yorgi Lata
Yani Ḳanbra	Ḳozma Senḳa	Ḳosta veled-i o	Petro Sanḳa	Dima Sanḳa
Gin birāder-i o	Aleksi veled-i Dima Sanḳa	Gin Sanḳa	Ḳozma-ı dīğer Sanḳa	Mesḳa birāẕer-i o
Yorgi Ḳuçi	Niḳola İspanci	Domeniḳa veled-i o	Niḳola Sanḳa	Gin Sanḳa
Aleksi veled-i o	Gön Ḳoçomaẕi	Ḳumi birāder-i o	mücerred Merti[16] Brasna	mücerred Gin İvlandi

mücerred Lazaro birāder-i o	mücerred Gön Brasna-ı dīğer	mücerred Gön Sanḳa	bīve Niḳola Brasna	bīve Elana zen-i Aleksi
bīve Gön Sanḳa		ḫāne 38	mücerred 5	bīve 3

ḥāṣıl 2791

ʿa(n) ispence 878	ʿöşr-i ḥınṭa 1500	ʿöşr-i cev 233	resm-i ḫanāzīr 140	resm-i ʿarūsī 40

ḳarye-i Çipyana tīmār-ı meẕkūrān

Todoros Milatis	Todoro Hilyasto	Yorgi Ḳofina	Yani Ḳofina	Yorgi Zirvo
Miḫal Todoroplo	Sirġuna İstavrano	Todoros Ḳumnato	Papas Ḳofinas	Yani Ġuralo
Yorgi İfterna	Niḳola Vlayi	Miḫal Geluḳri	İspilyoti Ḳaluḳri	Niḳola Ḳavalari

24

tetimme-i ḳarye-i Çipyana el- meẕkūr

Miḫal Ḳamilafki	Dimitri [Ḳ]amilafki	Yani Plata[ni]ti	Yani Spiri	S̱otoki İstra[ġ]ari
Yani Pavlyoti	Miḫal İftarna	Yorgi Servuna	Yani veled-i o	Yani Ḳaliḳomno
İlya birāder-i o	Manol Malaviti	Ḳalenci Yorġoplo	S̱otoki Çeravastino	Miḫal veled-i o
Yani Çeravastino	Niḳola Plisiça	Ḳarteli birāder-i o	Yani Pavlyoti	Todoro İsklaro
Yani birāder-i o	Niḳola Ḫalyastos	S̱otoki Maloviti	Niḳola Maleviti	Kiryaḳos Ḳuveli
Miḫal Plataniti	S̱otoki Plataniti	Franḳo Dimitri	S̱otoki Pami	Yorgi Meleti
Aleksi İftarniya	Yorgi birāder-i o	Yorgi Meleti	Yorgi Ḳondofeloni	Miḫal Ḳondofeloni
Yani Apoya	Yani Sirġuna	Lumi İftarna	Papadimitri Zirvo	Papas İsḳurçi
Yani Ġavra	S̱otoki Papazirvos	Dimitri Sirġuna	Yorgi Sirġuna	Apostolos Sirġuna

mücerred Niḳola İftarna	mücerred Petro Yorġoplo	mücerred Pavlo birāder-i o	mücerred Yorgi Çeravastino	mücerred Miḫal Malaviti
mücerred Servoplo Hilyasti	mücerred Pavlos Ḳondofeloni	mücerred Miḫal Apoya	mücerred Miḫal Sirġuna	mücerred S̱otoki İsḳuriçi
bīve Ḳaloḳarya	bīve Zoi	bīve Grana zen-i Melitu	bīve Hilyasti	bīve Sirvuno
	ḫāne 60	mücerred 10	bīve 5	

ḥāṣıl 5428

ʿa(n) ispence 1780	bāġāt-ı ḫāṣṣa dönüm 6 [resm] 720	ʿöşr-i bāġāt 480	ʿöşr-i ḥınṭa 1900	ʿöşr-i cev 296	resm-i ḫanāzīr 2	resm-i ḫāmr 60
resm-i ʿarūsī 60	ʿöşr-i kettān 100	mülk-i Kiryaḳos Ḳuveli der ḳarye-i meẕkūr āsiyāb 1 resm 30				

ḳarye-i Periso̱ri tīmār-ı meẕkūrān

Yani Ṣapuna	S̱otoki Ṣapuna	Yorgi veled-i o	Dimitri veled-i o	Niḳola Sotirḫo
Yorgi Ġavra	S̱otoki Arnaḳori	Yani Arnaḳori	Andriya birāẕer-i o	Dimitri Ḳaçuli
Todoro Ḳaçulya	Niḳola Ḳuvara	İstemad veled-i o	Niḳola Zaġoryo	Miḫal birāder-i o

25

tetimme-i ḳarye-i Periso̱ri el- meẕkūr

Niḳola Draġoplo	Ḳosta Vunyati	mücerred Dimitri birāder-i o	ḫāne 17	mücerred 1	manastır-ı [ḫā]ṣṣa 1

ḥāṣıl 193[5]

ʿa(n) ispence 450	bāġāt-ı ḫāṣṣa dönüm 5 [resm] 600	eşcār-ı meyve-i ḫāṣṣa ʿaded 6 [resm] 10	eşcār-ı ṭut-ı ḫāṣṣa ʿaded 10 [resm] 50	ʿöşr-i bāġāt 176

ʿöşr-i ḥınṭa	ʿöşr-i cev	ʿöşr-i meyve	ʿöşr-i ḳazz	resm-i ḫāmr	resm-i ʿarūsī	ʿöşr-i k[ettān]
500	78	10	1	20	20	20

cemʿan tīmār-ı mezkūrān

ḳurā	ḫāne	mücerred	bīve
5	206	31	16

ḥāṣıl 16849

tīmār-ı Mübārek ġulām-ı mīr dizdār-ı ḳalʿa-ı Miḫlu

ḳarye-i Raḫova ki Miḫlu derbendin beklerler ammā mezkūr köylünüñ ellerinde ḥükümleri vardır her ki Miḫlu ḳalʿasına dizdār olursa nāẓır ola deyü ḳayd olunmuşdur

Miḫal Dramesi	Pavlos Dramesi	Petros Dramesi	Domeniḳa Dramesi	Yani Dramesi
Gön Dramesi	Yani Dramesi-i dīğer	Gön Dramesi-i dīğer	Miḫal Helmi	Gin Ḳayça
Gin Ḳayça-ı dīğer	Lanḳa Ḳalanci	İstefano Rusaki	Yorgi Rusaki	Ġolemi Rusaki
Duḳa Brasna	Lazaro Brasna	Ḳosta İstavri	İlya Buzi	Yorgi Şalesi
Pavlos [Z]apandi	Ḳosta Plaşa	Gin Plaşa	Niḳola Vorila	Bardi Mazi

26

tetimme-i ḳarye-i Raḫova el-mezkūr

Draye Malaḳas	İlya Ḫayḳal	Todoro Lopesi	Yorgi Doroḳrik	Duşa Doroḳrik
Yorgi Doroḳrik-i dīğer	Duşa Doroḳrik	Murik Çapoġa	Todoro Ḳoḳla	Ḳosta Marḳo
Yani Marḳo	Yorgi Marḳo	Yani Ġavrili	Yorgi Çaşi	İştin Çaşi
Mataranḳa Maji	Zotli Mazi	Pavlo Ḳalusi	Gin Ḳaluşi	Pavlo Ḳaluşi
Marti Sula	Dimitri Lavza	Pavlo Barçi	Andriya Ḳarvunari	Bardi Ḳarvunari
Yorgi Ḳarvunari	Yani Zenbeş	Niḳola Zenbeş	Yorgi Biçi	Niḳa Ġavril
		mücerred	mücerred	mücerred
Yorgi Toşkesi	Yani Lavda	Yani İstavri	Gön Buzi	Yorgi-i dīğer Doroḳrik

mücerred	ḫāne	mücerred
Mataranḳa Ḳalusi	57	4

ḥāṣıl be-cihe[t]-i resm-i neẓāret

her nefer

naḳd	gendüm	şaʿīr
ʿaşere	be-müdd-i Edrene-i keylciyān	be-müdd-i Edrene-i keylciyān

ʿa(n) ispence	el-ḥınṭa	eş-şaʿīr
610	müdd 5 keyl 14 her müdd fī s̱emānīn 456	müdd 5 keyl 14 her müdd fī sittīn 342

resm-i ʿarūsī
150

yekūn 1558

mezraʿa-ı Plaşa ki aṣılda Frenk elinde imiş ammā mezkūr köylünüñ żarūret olduġıyçün anlara ekinlik vėrildi

27 *blank*

28

kendü bürüme	geçim	cebelü	çadır	tenktür	ġulām
	1	9	1	1	1

zeʿāmet-i Bejenik zaʿīmeş ʿÖmer Beg veled-i Ezmir

nefs-i Bejenik

ḫāṣṣa-ı zaʿīm

Yo[rgi] İlyoplos	Niḳola Aġriḳuḳa	Dimitri Pleṣaki	Dimitri Ḫalke	Dimitri Mavruli
Miḫal Mavruli	N[iḳo]la Pendaki	Yorgi İzviro	Ḳosta Ḫondomiti	Petros Viro
Papas Viro	Manol İzviro	Miḫal Pendaki	Dimitri Pendaki	Miḫal Anamolyo
Manol Ḳokinomati	Todoro Porondo	Sotoki Traġanisti	Andriya Traġanisti	Niḳola Traġanisti

Dimitri Traġanisti	Yani Ḫalke	Niḳola Ḫalke	Yani Ḳonomu	Yani Barbiri
Niḳola Barbiri	Yorgi Ḳa[p]lano	As̱anas Ples̱aki	Papas Ḳalamatyanos	Yani Ḳalamatyano
Papas Simbyasi	Dimitri Simbyasi	Yorgi S̱oma	Yorgi S̱oma-<yı> dīger	Noẕimyoti İpsomalisa[r]o
Miḫal Ḫavari	Yani Ḫavari	Niḳola Ḫondomiti	Yorgi Ḳalamatyano	Niḳola S̱o[m]a
Niḳola Saḳuli	Yani Saḳuli	İspilyoti Ples̱aki	Niḳola Ḳoris̱o	Mangişa Mazaraki
Yani Kiniġo	Dimitri Ḳonomu	Petros Kiniġos	Dimitri Ḫondomiti	mücerred Yani Ples̱aki
mücerred Yorgi Pendaki	mücerred Niḳola İlyoplo	mücerred Todoros Ḳoris̱o	mücerred Andriya Mazaraki	mücerred Ḳosta Ḳonomu
bīve İrini zen-i İpsomalisari	ḫāne 49	mücerred 6	bīve 1	mevżiʿ-i āsiyāb-ı ḫāṣṣa 1

ḫāṣıl 6640

ʿa(n) ispence 1381	bāġāt-ı ḫāṣṣa dönüm 11 [resm] 1020	eşcār-ı ṭut-ı ḫāṣṣa ʿaded 46 [resm] 200	eşcār-ı meyve-i müteferriḳa-ı ḫāṣṣa ʿaded 30 [resm] 100	resm-i niyābet 250

ʿöşr-i kettān 150	ʿöşr-i bāġāt 1448	ʿöşr-i ḫınṭa 1600	ʿöşr-i cev 245	ʿöşr-i meyve 11	ʿöşr-i ḳazz 55	resm-i ḫāmr 180

mezraʿa-ı Vuzyas nezd-i nefs-i Bejenik
ḫāṣṣa-ı zaʿīm ḫāliyye

mezraʿa-ı Plaşa nezd-i nefs-i Bejenik
el-mezkūr ḫāṣṣa-ı zaʿīm
ḫāliyye

29
nāḫiyyet-i Bejenik

ḳarye-i Leviẕi ḫāṣṣa-ı zaʿīm

Yani Ḳohiti	Caḳomi Lulamireniti	Dimitri Ġulyostomo	Yani Niḳo	Dimitri Per[diḳari]
Yani Mavro- miḫalo	Niḳola Maḳri	Yani Perdiḳari	Yorgi Ḳohiti	Niḳola Travlo
Yani Travlo	Yani Ḳohiti	Yani Pulyostomo	Yani Ḳohiti	Yani Las̱ra
Dimitri Perdiḳari	S̱otoki Ḳohiti	Petro Ḳohiti	Manol Zeraḫani	Andon Zeraḫani
Dimitri Mavruli	Niḳola Mavruli	Andriya Mavromiḫalo	Yani Ḳohiti	Papas İsḳortinos
Yani İsḳortinos	Andriya Zeraḫani	mücerred Todoros Ḳohiti	mücerred Todoros Ḳohiti-i dīger	mücerred Yani Çaḳomi
mücerred Dimitri Ḳohiti	mücerred Niḳola Luḳa	mücerred Yorgi Luḳa	mücerred Niḳola Perdiḳari	mücerred Yani Mavromiḫalo
mücerred Niḳola Travlo	mücerred Miḫal Travlo	mücerred Niḳola Perdiḳari	bīve Mariya Ḳohita	bīve İstemato İsḳufo
	ḫāne 27	mücerred 11	bīve 2	

ḫāṣıl 3448

ʿa(n) ispence 962	ʿöşr-i kettān 100	ʿöşr-i bāġāt 1040	ʿöşr-i ḫınṭa 1000	ʿöşr-i cev 155	ʿöşr-i meyve 20	ʿöşr-i ḳazz 21
		resm-i ʿarūsī 30		resm-i ḫāmr 120		

ḳarye-i Ḳameniça ḫāṣṣa-ı zaʿīm

Yorgi Ḳalvi	Yani Ḳoḳorovi	Niḳola Tirifona	S̱otoki Ḳoḳorovi	Dimitri Tirifona
Yorgi Tirifona	Yorgi Ḫarköplo	Dimitri Ḫarköplo	S̱otoki Ḫarköplo	Yorgi Ḫarköplo-<yı> dīger
bīve Ḳostina	bīve Todora zen-i Ḳoris̱o		ḫāne 10	bīve 2

ḫāṣıl 928

ʿa(n) ispence 262	ʿöşr-i kettān 30	ʿöşr-i bāġāt 240	ʿöşr-i ḫınṭa 300	ʿöşr-i cev 47	ʿöşr-i meyve 7	ʿöşr-i ḳazz 2
	resm-i ʿarūsī 10			resm-i ḫāmr 30		

30
tetimme-i nāḫiyyet-i Bejenik

ḳarye-i Lopesi ez cemāʿat-i Arnavudān — ḫāṣṣa-ı zaʿīm

Todoro L[o]pesi	Gin Ḳro[nt]esi	Yorgi Lopesi	Niḳola İstovaḫti	Lazaro Lopesi	
Niḳola Lopesi	Gin Ḳalusi	Duḳa Ḳalusi	Gin Ḳalusi	Andriya İ[s]tov[a]ḫti	
Ḳozma İstovaḫti	mücerred Andriya Lopesi	mücerred Yorgi İstovaḫti	mücerred Yorgi Ḳrali	ḫāne 11	mücerred 3

ḥāṣıl 746

ʿa(n) ispence	ʿöşr-i kettān	ʿöşr-i ḥınṭa	ʿöşr-i cev	resm-i ḫanāzīr	resm-i ʿarūsī
280	40	350	56	10	10

ḳarye-i Aġali ez cemāʿat-i Arnavudān — ḫāṣṣa-ı zaʿīm

Şarakin Aġali	Aleksi Palunbi	Gin Ḳuki	Yorgi Ḳanaẓe	Andriya Lukise
Andriya Ġruzumse	Andriya Ḳalanci	Dayça Bonaẓo	Gin Buzi	Lazaro Plaşa
Leḳa Liḳuresi	Andriya Ḳaratula	Petros Dayça	İvrato Palunbi	Gin Ḳuçi
Sina Draġriki	Gön Draġriki	Gerḳa Liḳuresi	Miḫal Ḳarḳala	Dimitri Ḳarḳala
Barçi Ḳuçimire	mücerred Aleksi Ḳanaẓe	mücerred Gin Ḳanaẓe	mücerred Ḳuvara Plaşa	mücerred Yorgi Ḳarḳala
mücerred Niḳola Ġruzumse	mücerred Domeniḳa Liḳuresi	mücerred Ḳuvara Buri	mücerred Gin Şarakin	bīve Arḫondo Ḳarḳalu
	ḫāne 21	mücerred 8	bīve 1	

ḥāṣıl 1729

ʿa(n) ispence	ʿöşr-i kettān	ʿöşr-i ḥınṭa	ʿöşr-i cev	resm-i ḫanāzīr	resm-i ʿarūsī
586	50	900	144	29	20

ḳarye-i Bendeni ez cemāʿat-i Arnavudān — ḫāṣṣa-ı zaʿīm

Domeniḳa Bendeni	Petros Dayça	Domeniḳa Dayça	Pavlo Dayça	İştin Dayça
Todoro Dayça	Leḳa Dayça	Todoro Peta	Miḫa Peta	Petros Peta
Ḳosta Peta	Yorgi Mamoni	Niḳola Mamoni	Gin Alaġatora	Gin-i dīğer Alaġatora
Mangişa Mamoni	Andriya Prondano	Ḳosta Brulişe	Mano Brulişe	Domeniḳa Rondaki

31
tetimme-i ḳarye-i Pendeni el-meẕkūr — ḫāṣṣa-ı zaʿīm

Andriya İksife	Ḳosta Ḳuki	Mangişa İpsari	Gin İpsari	Ḳozma Pendeni	
Muriki Pendeni	Pavlos Pendeni	Yorgi Peta	mücerred Aleksi Pendeni	mücerred Andriya İpsari	
mücerred Andriya İp[s]ari	mücerred Naki Alaġatora	bīve Mariya Zepandi	bīve Giru Pendeni	ḫāne 28	mücerred 4 bīve 2

ḥāṣıl 1466

ʿa(n) ispence	ʿöşr-i kettān	ʿöşr-i ḥınṭa	ʿöşr-i cev	resm-i ḫanāzīr	resm-i ʿarūsī
652	80	600	96	8	30

ḳarye-i Bondaya ez cemāʿat-i Arnavudān — ḫāṣṣa-ı zaʿīm

Yani Bondaya	Mangişa Bondaya	Gin Bondaya	Margin Nikiforo	Mangişa Nikifor
Gön Palunbi	Lazaro Şalesi	Todoro Fraġna	Niḳa Şalesi	Vaṣi Şalesi
Yorgi Trandafilo	Dima Trandafilo	Mataranḳa Şalesi	Ḳumani Ḫayḳal	Gön Plaşa
[D]ima Ḳumani	mücerred Niḳola Trandafilo	mücerred Jupano Nikiforo	mücerred Gön Trandafilo	mücerred Manol Trandafilo
mücerred Beluşi Palunbi	mücerred Palunbi birāder-i o	mücerred Petro Fraġra	ḫāne 16	mücerred 7

ḥāṣıl 1170

ʿa(n) ispence	ʿöşr-i kettān	ʿöşr-i ḥınṭa	ʿöşr-i cev	resm-i ḫanāzīr	resm-i ʿarūsī
460	50	550	86	4	20

ḳarye-i Sina ez cemāʿat-i Arnavudān ḫāṣṣa-ı zaʿīm

Ḳaḳusi Sina	Yorgi Ḳaḳusi	Niḳola Biçi	Niḳola Ḳarvuni	Miḫal Ḳarvuni
Niḳola Zunbato	Sina Triyarhi	Yorgi Ḳarvuni	Gin İşpata	Domeniḳa İşpata
mücerred Manḳola Jupata	mücerred Todoro Ḳarvuni		ḫāne 10	mücerred 2

ḥāṣıl 562

ʿa(n) ispence 240	ʿöşr-i kettān 20	ʿöşr-i ḥınṭa 250	ʿöşr-i cev 39	resm-i ḫanāzīr 3	resm-i ʿarūsī 10

ḳarye-i Çarnota ez cemāʿat-i Arnavudān ḫāṣṣa-ı zaʿīm

Mataranḳa Çarnota	Ḳosta Çarnota	Yorgi Lonḳa	Leḳa Lonḳa	Marti Ġulami
Niḳa Ġulami	Tonda Ḳumi	Petros Rusi	Pavlos Rusi	Gön Rusi

32

tetimme-i ḳarye-i Çarnota el-meẕkūr ḫāṣṣa-ı zaʿīm

Gi[n] Rusi	Pavlo Rusi	Miḫal Damizes	mücerred Gi[n] Ruşi	mücerred Yorgi Ruşi
mücerred Gin Malaḳas	mücerred Gön Lonḳa	bīve Zane zen-i Plaşa	ḫāne 13	mücerred 4
			[bī]ve 1	

ḥāṣıl 881

ʿa(n) ispence 346	ʿöşr-i kettān 30	ʿöşr-i ḥınṭa 400	ʿöşr-i cev 64	resm-i ḫanāzīr 26	resm-i ʿarūsī 15

ḳarye-i Ḳandila ḫāṣṣa-ı zaʿīm

Yani Raneri	Niḳola Tulpano	Yani Çanḳaroplo	Aleksi Mağni	İstemad Varvari
Miḫal İspanoplo	Yani S̲oẕosi	Dimitri Foḳa	Yani Hilopita	Yani-i dīğer Hilopita
Yani Ḳamyano	Miḫal Hilopita	Yorgi Ḳalaki	Niḳola Ḳalaki	Yani Hilopita
Yorgi Hilopita	Niḳola Hilopita	Yorgi Maḳrona	Todoro Plataniti	Lanbrino Maḳrona
Miḫal Plataniti	Yorgi Plataniti	Miḫal Ġramatiḳoplo	Yorgi Tulpano	Todoro Hilopita
Yorgi Varvari	Niḳola Mağni	Yorgi Mağni	mücerred Niḳola Ḳalaki-i dīğer	mücerred Todoro Ġramatiḳoplo
mücerred İstefano Ġramatiḳoplo	mücerred Dimitri Varvari	mücerred Vaşıl Varvari	mücerred Miḫal Foḳa	mücerred Yorgi Hilopita
mücerred S̲otoki Foḳa	mücerred Yorgi Damyano	mücerred Todoro Foḳa	mücerred Andriya Plataniti	mücerred Yani Plataniti
mücerred Dimitri Hilopita	mücerred Ḳosta Plataniti	mücerred Yani Hilopita	mücerred Miḫal Tulpano	mücerred Yorgi Tulpano
mücerred Dimitri-i dīğer Hilopita	bīve Todora zen-i Verzaniti	bīve Mariya Ḳoris̲o	bīve Kiryaki zen-i Miḫalu	
ḫāne 28	mücerred 18	bīve 3		
	mevżiʿ-i āsiyāb-ı ḫāṣṣa 4			

ḥāṣıl 4761

ʿa(n) ispence 1168	bāġāt-ı ḫāṣṣa dönüm 7 [resm] 840	eşcār-ı ṭut-ı ḫāṣṣa ʿaded 8 [resm] 40	nıṣf-ı āsiyāb-ı ḫāṣṣa 1 [resm] 150	ʿöşr-i kettān 150	ʿöşr-i bāġāt 1336
ʿöşr-i ḥınṭa 400	ʿöşr-i cev 64	ʿöşr-i ḳazz 69	ʿöşr-i meyve 14	resm-i ʿarūsī 30	resm-i ḫamr 180

mülk-i Yani Hilopita der ḳarye-i meẕkūr āsiyāb 1 resm 80	mülk-i Miḫal Ġramatiḳoplo der ḳarye-i meẕkūr āsiyāb 1 resm 80	mülk-i Yorgi Varvari der ḳarye-i meẕkūr āsiyāb 1 resm 80
	mülk-i Ḳāsım nev müslümān āsiyāb 1 resm 80	

33

tetimme-i nāḥiyyet-i Bejenik

ḳarye-i Doşkesi ez cemāʿat-i Arnavudān ḫāṣṣa-ı [zaʿīm]

Ḳozma D[o]şkesi	Gin Muzaki	Avriyoni Muzaki	Luzi Orfano	Ḳosta Ḳalimani

Ḳosta Siküti	İştin Lata	Ḳozma Doskesi	İştin Seküti	Niḳola Seküti
Mi̱hal Po̱sito	Ḳosta Ma̱ziñik	Niḳola Rondaki	Ḳuvara Doskesi	Leḳa Ḳalimani
mücerred Gin Seküti	mücerred Petros Ḳaluman	mücerred Mi̱ha Lata	mücerred Yorgi Lata	mücerred Pondini Lata
mücerred Petros Muzaki	mücerred Yorgi Toskesi	bīve Ḳalimanina	mücerred Gin Muzaki	ḫāne 15 · mücerred 8 · bīve 1

ḥāṣıl 996

ʿa(n) ispence 466	ʿöşr-i kettān 40	ʿöşr-i ḥınṭa 400	ʿöşr-i cev 75	resm-i ʿarūsī 15

ḳarye-i Ḫayḳal ez cemāʿat-i Arnavudān — ḫāṣṣa-ı zaʿīm

Todoro Ḫayḳal	Yorgi Ḫayḳal	Leḳa Ḫayḳal	Petro Ḫayḳal	Yorgi Daçi
Leḳa Ḫayḳal-i dīğer	Tonda Daçi	Proġono İskliva	Gin Buva	Yani Raneri
Lazaro Ḫayḳal	Lazaro Ṣaloniki	İlya Yorgiçi	Leḳa Varponbi	Yorgi Ḫayḳal
Dima İşpata	İvrato Vursa	Gin Daçi	Yorgi Ḫayḳal	Lazaro Liḳuresi
Ḳozma Taçi	Gin Çaşi	Aleksi Çaşi	Lazaro Buva	Petro Taçi
Leḳa Ḫayḳal	mücerred Ḳozma Taçi	mücerred Mangişa Ṣaloniki	mücerred Yorgi Mi̱ha	mücerred Andriya Mi̱ha
mücerred Yorgi Varponbi	mücerred Gin Çerġuni	mücerred Yorgi Ṣaloniki	mücerred Taşe Ṣaloniki	bīve Gegle Çaşe
bīve Manḳa zen-i Çerġuna	bīve Todora zen-i Mi̱ha	bīve Ṣalonike	ḫāne 26 · mücerred 8	bīve 4

ḥāṣıl 1737

ʿa(n) ispence 704	ʿöşr-i ḥınṭa 850	ʿöşr-i cev 134	resm-i ḫanāzīr 19	resm-i ʿarūsī 30

34

tetimme-i nāḥiyyet-i Bejenik

ḳarye-i Ḳora[ḳo]vuni — ḫāṣṣa-ı zaʿīm

Yani Ḳalipso	Dimitri [Mela]s̱riyoti	Ḳosta Laviro	Fora Senberḳo	Yani İslavoplo
Fo[ros] Mi[ḫa]	Yorgi Ḳalosuḳa	Yani Melas̱riyoti	Yorgi Ze[r]zalino	Yorgi Izġuro
Dimi[tri] Mela[s̱riyoti]	Yani Tavlaroplo	Mi̱hal İsḳlavoplo	Niḳola Senberḳo	Yani Ḳokinos
Mi̱hal Zerzalino	Yani Zerzalino	Yani İsḳlavoplo	Yani-i dīğer Zerzalinos	Dimitri Ṣayiti
Niḳola Ṣayiti	Yorgi Zerzalino	Foros Zerzalinos	Leo Senberḳo	Yorgi Zinḳuri
Ḳosta Melas̱riyoti	Dimitri Mas̱i	Rondaki Zinḳuri	Niḳola İsḳlavoplos	Niḳola Senberḳo
mücerred Yorgi Zakeranas	mücerred Mi̱hal Aloġato	mücerred Dimitri Ḳolosuḳa	mücerred Yorgi Ḳokinos	mücerred Ḫoros Senberḳos
bīve zen-i Foros İsḳlavoplos	bīve zen-i Yorgi İsḳlavoplo	bīve İzvirna	bīve Demo-nasya	ḫāne 30 · mücerred 5 · bīve 4

ḥāṣıl 2707

ʿa(n) ispence 899	ʿöşr-i bāġāt 248	ʿöşr-i ḥınṭa 1250	ʿöşr-i cev 189	ʿöşr-i ʿasel 43	ʿöşr-i meyve 15
	ʿöşr-i zeyt 3	resm-i ḫamr 30	resm-i ʿarūsī 30		

ḳarye-i Pers̱or — ḫāṣṣa-ı zaʿīm

Niḳola Eksarḫoplo	Mi̱hal birāder-i o	Ḳosta Ḳozi	Draḳos Lazaros	S̱otoki birāder-i o
Leo Mesimari	Todoro Aṣpriayos	Niḳola birāder-i o	Vaṣıl Praski	S̱otoki birāder-i o
S̱otoki Papaẕa	Niḳola birāder-i o	Niḳola Paskal	Dimitri birāder-i o	Niḳola Apelaẕe
Yorgi birāder-i o	Yorgi Ṣolomo	Papayani dāmād-ı o	Andriya Petruso	Niḳola Aṣpriyani
Niḳola Ġalviça	Yorgi Ḳaliḳa	Manol birāder-i o	Yani veled-i Yorgi el-mezbūr	Papa Vaṣıl Ḳuvara
Yani veled-i o	Yani Ġarviya	Petros Ḳaḳaletri	Yorgi İmeri	İstemad Paskal

35

tetimme-i ḳarye-i Pers̲[o]r el-[m]ez̲kūr — ḫāṣṣa-ı zaʿīm

Niḳ[o]la Ḳayi	Todoro[s] birā[d]er-i o	Niḳola Suvli	S̲otoki vele[d-i] o	Yani veled-i o	
Manol veled-i o	Todoros Aḳratis	İstemati Aḳrati	Dimitri veled-i o	[Miḫ]al [Ro]kindi	
Yani birāder-i o	İstemad veled-i Miḫal el-mezbūr	Yorgi Ḳaliḳotovi	Yorgi Ḫotara	[Pe]t[ro]s [---]	
Ḳozma Litra	Niḳola Malaki	İstemad İsḳlavo	Niḳola İstavri	[Yor]gi Aḳrati	
Yani Ḳardaki	Yorgi Ḫaluḳotovi	Yani Plato	Niḳola İsḳolari	S̲otoki İsḳolari	
Vaṣıl Vari	Todoros Ḳondostavloplo	bīve S̲otoḳu	bīve Yanu	ḫāne 57	bīve 2

ḥāṣıl 4367

ʿa(n) ispence 1437	bāġāt-ı ḫāṣṣa dönüm 2 [resm] 240	eşcār-ı ṭut-ı ḫāṣṣa ʿaded 8 [resm] 20	ʿöşr-i bāġāt 272	ʿöşr-i ḥınṭa 1900	ʿöşr-i cev 295
ʿöşr-i ḳazz 20	resm-i ḫanāzīr 3	resm-i ʿarūsī 60	ʿöşr-i kettān 80	resm-i ḫamr 40	

ḳarye-i Açiḫolos — ḫāṣṣa-ı zaʿīm

Niḳola İpṣomeri	S̲otoki İpṣomeri	Yorgi birāder-i o	Yani İpṣomeri	Dimitri veled-i o
Yorgi veled-i o	Yani Ḳovakâniti	Yorgi dāmād-ı o	Papas Yani Lepsuta	Dimitri dāmād-ı o
Yorgi Çuvalo	Yani birāder-i o	S̲otoki Çuvalo	Todoros birāder-i o	Vaṣıl Çuvalo
Papas Yani Viñliḳomo	S̲otoki veled-i o	Petros İpsomuri	Pavlos İstrati	Miḫal Ḳalusi
Yorgi veled-i o	mücerred Miḫal İpṣomeri	mücerred Niḳola Çuvalo	mücerred Dimitri Viñliḳomo	bīve Paraskevi
ḫāne 21	mücerred 3	bīve 1	mevżiʿ-i āsiyāb-ı ḫāṣṣa 1	

ḥāṣıl 1907

ʿa(n) ispence 606	bāġāt-ı ḫāṣṣa dönüm 2 [resm] 240	ʿöşr-i bāġāt 152	ʿöşr-i ḥınṭa 700	ʿöşr-i cev 109	resm-i ḫanāzīr 5
resm-i ḫamr 20	resm-i ʿarūsī 20	ʿöşr-i kettān 25			

mülk-i Niḳola İpṣomeri
der ḳarye-i mez̲kūr
āsiyāb 1 resm 30

36

tetimme-i nāḥiyyet-i Bejenik

ḳarye-i İskiliç ez cemāʿat-i Arnavudān — ḫāṣṣa-ı zaʿīm

Vas̲i İskiliçi	Mangişa İskiliçi	Yani veled-i o	Arḫondiçi Miḫal	[N]i[ḳol]a veled-i o	
Yorgi Rusaki	Dimitri Ḳaratula	Yani Zula	Yorgi Plaşi	Petros Polimeti	
Martin birāder-i o	mücerred Duḳa Rusaki	mücerred Domaniḳa Z̲üke	bīve Mariya zen-i Z̲üke el-mez̲kūr	ḫāne 11	mücerred 2 bīve 1

ḥāṣıl 832

ʿa(n) ispence 266	ʿöşr-i ḥınṭa 450	ʿöşr-i cev 69	resm-i ḫanāzīr 17	resm-i ʿarūsī 15	ʿöşr-i kettān 15

ḳarye-i Mujaki ez cemāʿat-i Arnavudān — ḫāṣṣa-ı zaʿīm

Proġono Mujaki	Gin veled-i o	Yani Muzaki	Todoros veled-i o	Ḳozma veled-i o
Gin Ḳanḳaz̲i	İş Ari Manesi	Todoros birāz̲er-i o	Niḳola Iġlava	Iġlava birāder-i o
İştin birāz̲er-i o	Gin birāder-i o	Vaṣıl İskliro	Martin İskliro	Yorgi veled-i o
Martin Uzġur	Yorgi birāder-i o	Miḫal birāder-i o	Proġonos Iġlava	Andriya İskliro
	Yani birāder-i o		ḫāne 21	

ḥāṣıl 1055

ʿa(n) ispence 420	ʿöşr-i ḥınṭa 500	ʿöşr-i cev 80	resm-i ʿarūsī 25	ʿöşr-i kettān 30

ḳarye-i Kerbova ez cemāʿat-i Arnavudān ẖāṣṣa-ı zaʿīm

Yorgi Buva	Petro Pasḳaloplo	Leḳa İşpani	Muriki İşpani	Pavlo İspani
Martin İspani	mücerred Yovan Buva	mücerred Mangişa Pasḳaloplo	mücerred Andriya İşpani	mücerred Yorgi Meġalyanos

ẖāne 6	mücerred 4

ḥāṣıl 569

ʿa(n) ispence 200	ʿöşr-i ḥınṭa 300	ʿöşr-i cev 48	resm-i ẖanāzīr 11	resm-i ʿarūsī 10

ḳarye-i Ustruza Potamya ez cemāʿat-i Arnavudān ẖāṣṣa-ı zaʿīm

İstefano Ustruza	Bardi İstruza	Petro Zuġra	Yorgi Maji	Yorgi Peta
Lumi Lukise	Mangişa Lukise	İlya İstruza	Niḳola İstruza	İştin İstaz̲iyo

37

tetimme-i ḳarye-i İstruza el-mez̲kūr

Gin [---]	bīve Manḳa zen-i İstruza	ẖāne 11	b[īve] 1

ḥāṣıl 669

ʿa(n) ispence [22]6	ʿöşr-i ḥınṭa 350	ʿöşr-i cev 56	resm-i ẖanāzīr 7	resm-i ʿarūsī 10	ʿöşr-i kettān [20]

mezraʿa-ı İvlaẖo Filito nezd-i ḳarye-i İstruza el-mez̲kūr

ẖāṣṣa-ı zaʿīm ẖāliyye

cemʿan ẖāṣṣhā-<yı> subaşı-ı Bejenik

ḳurā maʿa nefs-i Bejenik 19	mezāriʿ-i ẖāliyye 3	ẖāne 411	mücerred 93	bīve 26

ḥāṣıl 37170

38

kendü [bürüm]e	geçim 1	cebelü 11	ġulām 1	çadır 1	tenktür 1

ẖāṣṣhā-<yı> İbrahīm[17] Beg subaşı-ı Ḳalavrita

nefs-i Ḳalavrita ẖāṣṣa-ı zaʿīm

Yani Ḳrupa	Ḳosta [.².]l[.².]	Miẖal Papatriḳarde	Dimitri Suḳara	Yani veled-i [o]
İstefano Suḳara	Yorgi Suḳara	Mavrolyo	Ḳomnino Kipro	Dimitri Lavranca
Yorgi Mardari	Papayani veled-i o	Filipos veled-i o	Andriya Tartari	Ḳosta Ḳaz̲yasi
Yorgi Miratino	Niḳola Papaaḳsana	Todoros Niḳolos	Manol Papaḳsana	Yorgi Evrami
Yorgi Ṣameno	Yani Klida	Dimitri Ḳufyo	Dimitri H̱aẖlaḳa	Niḳola veled-i o
Yani Çanḳari	İstilyano Ḳuvara	Miẖal Ḳuvara	Dimitri İksanuli	Aleksi İksavro
Yani Vaveniti	Manol Mamonas	Yorgi birāder-i o	Papapetros Ḳaḳomali	Yani İksavriyo
Manol Pisḳopoplos	Vaṣıl Plamenos	Aleksi Aṣpiyoti	Miẖal Lavranco	Yani Kipro
Manol Papalyoplos	Papas Ḳutruli	Yani Ḳardiyasi	Dimitri Tetraz̲i	Yani İsḳonco
Yorgi İsḳoncos	Papas Buçyato	Miẖal birāder-i o	Yorgi Çervelos	Yorgi H̱arköplos
Manol Tomasi	Todoros Planiḳös	Yani veled-i o	Miẖal Manoloplos	Petros Tetraz̲i
Yani Turnari	Yorgi Manoloplos	Manol Sina	Yani Sina	Papas Ḳozoẖos
Papas Siḳaliḳas	Manol birāder-i o	Manol Pahiyeni	Petros Roz̲os	Ḳosta Hırisoẖoplo müsellem zīrā bennā[18] ve neccār-ı ḳalʿa-ı Ḳalavrita şüd
Dimitri Romo	Niḳola Fras̲yo	Dimitri Turḳari	Niḳola Averlaġos	Yani Suḳara
Aleksi Ḳratura	Todoro Ḳumaniti	Dimitri Kleftaki	Yani Fras̲yos	Yorgi Eksavriyos
Yorgi Tomas	Todoros Tomas	Yorgi Lavranco	Niḳola Manoloplo	Dimitri Azva

Andon Ḳaḳomali	Ẕasḳalo veled-i o	Niḳola Mans̱o Ġrama-tiḳo aʿrec	mücerred Manol H̱aẖlaḳa	mücerred Yorgi Vaveniti

39

tetimme-i maḥalle-i Yani Ḳaḳosimani el-meẕkūr

Ḳosta Taflos	Dimitri Ḳaliġoplo	Todoros Niḳli	İstefanos Ḳomiçi	Papas Yani Ḳozaniti
Yani Ḳaḳoraki	Niḳola Ḳaḳoraki	Ḳosta Paliḳanos	Yorgi Ḳlapsavuġa	Yorgi Ḳapsali
İstefanos veled-i Yanos	Yorgi Varsame	Ḳostandin Mavruçi	İstilyano Paydo	Yani Maḳrini
mücerred Niḳola Dolaniḳa	mücerred Manol Kiryaḳoplo	mücerred Yorgi Klisuri	mücerred Niḳola Damali	mücerred Miẖal Yenaḳuri
bīve Marġarita zen-i Dolaniḳa	bīve Mariya zen-i Mesrase	bīve İstilyanu zen-i Manoloplo	bīve Anuẕa zen-i Triyano	bīve Mariya zen-i Çenbele
	ẖāne 40	mücerred 5	bīve 5	

maḥalle-i İstilyano Ḳuẕuni

İstilyano el-meẕkūr	Yorgi veled-i o	Niḳola Vidoplavri	Yorgi Fiyaliti	Niḳola Rusoplo
İstas̱i Çaġrapa	Niḳola Petroyuni	S̱omas Riminoplo	Petro Eksanosto-mati	Yani birāder-i o
Todoros Ṣavaplos	Vaṣıl Penaplo	Andriya veled-i o	Dimitri Ḳondovaṣıla	İstilyano Ḳondovaṣıla
Niḳola Anemoyanis	Petros Aẖamoluris	Ġulyamo Rominiti	Papatodoros S̱iyoġanosos	Kiryaki Lanḳas
Yani Romiti	Papas Yani Mavra	Papaniḳolas Trofyas	Yorgi veled-i o	Miẖal Politi
Miẖal Ḳalanis	Niḳola Papafilipoplo	Ḳosta Ḳurteş	Andriya Ḳornavla	Ḳosta Ḳanavuçi
Ġulumi İsḳumuçi	İstilyanos Mulanḳas	Yani Ṣolomo	Niḳola Virviri	Yani Petrobuva
Manol İsḳano	Yorgi Ṣolomo	Miẖal Ḳoḳali	Niḳola Luluẕi	Ḳalyoro Lavandino
Yorgi Malato	Niḳola veled-i o	Miẖal Tomeri	Andriya Ṣava	mücerred Niḳola Aẖamoluris
mücerred Dimitri Lova[rd]i	bīve İstematiki zen-i Ṣavaplos	bīve Mariya zen-i İstovaẖtina	bīve Anuda zen-i Alavrica	bīve İstematiki zen-i İspano
	ẖāne 44	mücerred 2	bīve 4	

40

tetimme-i ḳarye-i Ṣaravali el-meẕkūr — ẖāṣṣa ẖullide mülkühu

maḥalle-i Yorgi Peliḳanos

Yorgi el-meẕkūr	Yani veled-i o	Yaḳumelos Tiselanis	Papayani Ḳaḳosimani	Miẖal Lavandino
Yorgi Monaẖo	Yani veled-i o	Manol H̱ırisoviloni	Dimitri H̱ırisoviloni	Ḳozma Ḳonoplo
Yorgi İksilo-prezovite	Andriya İstroni	Ġulyamo Mavruçi	Dimitri Ḳlapsavuġa	Andriya Liġzomaniti
Petro Kerine	Dimitri İsḳomiçi	İstefanos Çanḳuri	Yorgi H̱arkâ	Papaandon Peniki
Gin Peta	Lazaro Pilura	Aleksi Voyẕomati	Yiro Yani	Miẖal Ḳolono
Yorgi Liḳuẕasi	Yorgi Melaçi	Miẖal Melaçi	Andriya Ḳondodi-mitre	Todoro Melaçi
mücerred Petros Ḳonoplos	bīve Anuda duẖter-i Zuġaro	ẖāne 30	mücerred 1	bīve 1

yekūn-ı ḳarye-i Ṣaravali el-meẕkūr

ẖāne 151	mücerred 9	bīve 22	mevżiʿ-i āsiyāb-ı ẖāṣṣa 1

ḥāṣıl 20806

ʿa(n) ispence 4132	eşcār-ı zeyt-i ẖāṣṣa ʿaded 900 [resm] 1125	eşcār-ı ṭut-ı ẖāṣṣa ʿaded 315 [resm] 1700	eşcār-ı meyve-i ẖāṣṣa ʿaded 414 [resm] 550	bostān-ı ẖāṣṣa maʿa eşcārihi'l-müs̱mire [resm] 450
āsiyāb-ı peşmīne-i ẖāṣṣa 2 [resm] 100	muḳāṭaʿa-ı ṭāḥūne-i zeyt-i ẖāṣṣa 1 [resm] 250	ʿöşr-i penbe 400	ʿöşr-i kettān 50	ʿöşr-i bāġāt 8056

resm-i ḫamr 1125	ʿöşr-i zeyt 713	ʿöşr-i ḫınṭa 1395	ʿöşr-i cev 195	ʿöşr-i meyve 133

ʿöşr-i ḳazz 153	ʿöşr-i bostān 39

mülk-i
İbrahīm[19] Beg bin
Süle Beg ki p<ī>ş
ez <ī>n
subaşı-ı Balya Badra
būd
āsiyāb 1 resm 80

mülk-i
Ḥāccī Ḳar<a>göz merdüm-i
İbrahīm[20] Beg
el-meẕkūr
āsiyāb 1 resm 80

mülk-i
Yorgi Monoḫo Blaya Badraʾi
āsiyāb 1 resm 80
meẕkūr Yorgi küçük oğlandır
ispenceye yaramaduğı sebebden
deftere yazılmadı

41 blank

42

geçim 2	cebelü 16

ḫāṣṣhā-<yı> Ḥażret-i Ma[ḥm]ūd Paşa dāme ʿalāhu

nāḥiyyet-i Voştiça ḫāṣṣa-ı Paşa

Todoros Blas	Franḳo Ḳuki	Yani Voşticano	Niḳola Kiryaz[iti]	Todoros Ḳotolenci
Yorgi Ḳaçovini	Vaşıl Ḳaçovini	Yani Çiçiḳa	Yorg[i] İsḳari[y]o	Ḳosta Yorgiçi
Todoros Yorgiçi	Dimitri Kisifinyoti	Petros Ḫartulari	Papas Treḫati	Papas İstemati
Gin Muzaki	Niḳola Tomas	Miḫal Papaiğliġori	Niḳola Mano[l]	Yorgi Kiryaki
Todoros Kiryaki	Papas Ḫarkâplos	Yorgi Ḫarkâplos	Todoros Ḫarkâplos	Miḫal Ḫarkâplos
Ḳosta Mavro	Niḳola Yorgiçi	Yani Ġordori	Todoros Ḳuluri	İvratos İksanos
Yani Çuḳala	İstemad Fafala	Todoros İsḳase	Yorgila Ḳurtiḳo	Yani Ḳrusula
Yorgi Voẕesi	Todoros Ḳatis	Dimitri Ruveli	Dimitri Ḳutupi	Yorgi Ḳutupi
Miḫayili Virinça	Masi Malaḳaza	Yani İstrati	İstefano Markesi	Ḳosta İstriyoti
Niḳola Ġasra	Yani Markesi	Yani Voẕila	Arardos Plandis	Yani İstriyoti
Niḳola Miroloy	Nikifor Ẕiplopita	Yani Ḳaḳuri	Yorgi Mavro	Yani Poẕaro

Yorgi İstrava-poẕi	Miḫal Ḳalamanuẕi	Yorgi Yimoste	[Ya]ni Yimoste	Yani İspar[ti]
Yani Papadamyano	Niḳola Belyo	Petros Amiralis	Ḳosta Soropi	Niḳola Ḳalafati
Miḫal Piroplo	Petros Ḳalafatis	Todoros Damlaġos	Dimitri İskiloḳosta	Dimitri Serimali
Niḳola Servos	Yani Ḳondo	Cani Buva	Veledyanos Çanḳari	[Yorgi] Ḳalafati
Ḳosta Ḳutala	Niḳola Ḳaḳuri	Yani İstavre	Yani İsklalis	Ya[ni] Ḳarmiri
Niḳola Şalyari	Andriya Ḳalarya	Andon Ḳalarya	Yorgi Roẕi	İstilyanos Peryotoris

43

tetimme-i nefs-i Voştiça el-meẕkūr ḫāṣṣa-ı Paşa

Franḳos Ḳalaryas	Yani İsḳafiẕa	Yorgi Voriva	Andriya Voriva	Pavlos Kiklopa
Niḳola Ġulumi	Petros Vaşıl	Yorgi Arasti	Yorgi Ḳar-namorari	Yanul Fakiẕi
Niḳola Argiti	Miḫal Mamoni	Niḳola Dramesi	Yani Mazamya	Andriya Vira
Petro Niḳola Laḫana	Yorgi Ḳaçi	Andon Ġalatari	Ḳosta Ḳarçaḳli	Niḳola Marta
Manol Protopapa	Ḳosta Protopapa	Yani Eksandaḫtilo	Yani Saḳuli	Manol Ḳafiri
Papas Metaḳsas	Yani Mamuẕi	Ḳosta Şaloniti	Yani Poşuli	Todoros Araḫoviti
Dimitri Ḳorvariẕi	Yorgi Vari	Venduras Vuḳolos	Masi Mamuẕi	Aleksi Eksavros
Yani Riços	Aleksi Ḳalusi	Niḳola İsḳuri	Dimitri İsḳarmiköti	Manol İsḳarmiköti
Benos Ḳuluya	Çenderyo veled-i o	Yani Ġramatiḳo	Andron veled-i o	Ḳalos Ḳofyati
Pirḳos Rulya	Niḳola Simiẕali	mücerred Yani Amiralis	mücerred Miḫal Roẕi	mücerred Yani birāder-i o
mücerred Niḳola Ḳuvala	mücerred Yani birāder-i o	mücerred Andriya Ḳuki	mücerred Manol Ḳaçi	mücerred Yani İsḳarso
mücerred Sarakinoplos İstavralis	mücerred Todoros Morayti	mücerred İstefano Bonatos	mücerred Draġos Melitas	mücerred Niḳola Plaḳoti

mücerred Ḳosta Ḳalamapo[z̠]i	mücerred Niḳola Ḳatuli	mücerred Todoros Ḳalafati	mücerred Yani Franḳo	mücerred Bernardo Ḳlara
mücerred Rencari Selanikö	mücerred Andon Ḳaloḫitri	mücerred Yorgi Ḳaloḫitri	mücerred Miḫal Vurvas	mücerred Dimitri Ḳaḳari
mücerred Andon Selaniḳös	mücerred Yani Ḳaçi	mücerred Pavlos Bernardo	mücerred Yorgi Ġalyari	mücerred Manol İstilyano
mücerred Pavlos [---]k[---]	mücerred Andriya Duruyi	mücerred Yani Panaz̠ato	mücerred Ḳostandin Petali	mücerred Simo Labendari
mücerred Yorgi Ḳu[mani]	mücerred Dimitri Meramis̠e	mücerred Manol Tomas̠i	mücerred Yani Dimitreplo	bīve Tirvolina
bīve Varpina	bīve Narenco	bīve İskiloḳostiya	bīve Tetraz̠ina	bīve Ḳulosto- malina

44

tetimme-i nefs-i Voştiça el-mez̠kūr ḫāṣṣa-ı Paşa

bīve Eks̠orsoto	bīve Papamanoliya	bīve Niḳola Ḳura Şula	bīve Ḳorokinz̠o	bīve Ġramatikina
bīve İksavoriya	bīve Yani Varsame	bīve Todora	bīve İştasini	bīve İvlase Buzarina

müsellem ez ispence

cemāʿat-i manastır-ı Yirondos der Taḳsiyarḫi nezd-i nefs-i Voştiça el-mez̠kūr ammā z̠ikr olan manastırıñ papaslarına kāfirce ḫükm vèrilmiş ki evvelden manastır içün dutageldikleri emlākına kimesne daḫl etmeye ḫarācdan ve ispenceden muʿāf ve müsellem olalar ve emlākları laftero deyü ḳayd olunmuşdur

mücerred Yirondos Ġumenos	mücerred Papas Maḳariyos	mücerred İğnatiyos Pnamatiḳos	mücerred Papas Palaz̠iyos	mücerred Papas Kirilos
mücerred Z̠yaḳos Yiramiyas	mücerred Z̠yaḳos Yase	mücerred Ḳaliniḳos Ḳaliros[21]	mücerred İğnatiyos Ḳalyoros	mücerred Sindros Ḳalyoros
mücerred Yasif Ḳalyoros	mücerred Kipriyanos Ḳalyoros	mücerred Şafroniyos Ḳalyoros	mücerred Simiyon Ḳalyoros	mücerred İğnatiyos-ı dīğer Ḳaliros[22]
mücerred Poliḳarpos Ḳaliros[23]	mücerred Yirovaşiyos Ḳaliros[24]	mücerred Z̠iyonisiyos Ḳaliros[25]	mücerred Kirilos Ḳaliros[26]	mücerred S̠odoriḳos Ḳaliros[27]
mücerred Niḳoz̠imos Ḳaliros[28]	mücerred Yosif Ḳaliros[29]	mücerred Şayiya Ḳaliros[30]	mücerred As̠anas Ḳaliros[31]	mücerred Nilos Ḳaliros[32]

yekūn 25 neferen

cemāʿat-i gebrān-ı manastır el-mez̠kūr

Ḳondo- yani	Vastilica	Kerani	Yorgi Boḫa	Dimitri İlyoplo
Ḳosta Sotiriyati	Andriya Bolemas	Dimitri İksanoplos	Niḳola Dimulas	Ḳozma Puçite
Niḳola Nikita	Yani Boḫa	Todoros veled-i o	Andriya İlyoplos	Nikita İstefano

ḫāne 15

müsellem ez ispence

cemāʿat-i manastır-ı S̠otoḳos nezd-i manastır-ı Yirondos el-mez̠kūr ammā bunlar daḫi yuḳaru z̠ikr-olan manastır babaslarınıñ[33] kāfirce olan ḫükümlerine bile añlamışlardır ki ḫarācdan ve ispenceden muʿāf ve müsellem olalar ve emlākları laftero ola deyü

mücerred Yovakim Ḳaliros[34]	bīve Lanbiya Monahi	bīve Anastasiya	bīve Poloni	bīve Evis̠iya
bīve Ḳaliniki	bīve Ḳalisteni	bīve Mağz̠alini	bīve Aḳas̠asti	bīve Zinoviya
bīve Sotiriyani		mücerred 1	bīve 10	

45

tetimmme-i nefs-i Voştiça el-mez̠kūr ḫāṣṣa-ı Paşa

cemāʿat-i gebrān-ı manastır-ı S̠otoḳos el-mez̠kūr

Ḳosta Petroplo	Dimitri Petroplo	Andriya Ġatros	Yani Petroplo	Yani Petroplo-<yı> dīğer
Yorgi Çefaresti	Dimitri Aleksoplo	Leḳa Ḫarara	Yani As̠anasoplo	mücerred Todoros As̠anasoplo
İstemad Ġatros	Yani Ḳondoḫyiri	Yorgi Papaz̠ato	ḫāne 12	mücerred 1

yekūn-ı nefs-i Voştiça el-mez̠kūr

ḫāne maʿa gebrān-ı manastır 159	mücerred maʿa gebr-i manastır ve cemāʿat-i babasān[35] 64	bīve maʿa cemāʿat-i manastır 26

ḫāṣıl ġayr ez memlaḫa ve cemāʿat-i papasān ve bīve-i manastır
28283

ʿa(n) ispence 5021	bāġāt-ı ḫāṣṣa dönüm 37 [resm] 3942	eşcār-ı ṭut-ı ḫāṣṣa ʿaded 557 [resm] 1590	eşcār-ı meyve-i ḫāṣṣa ʿaded 200 [resm] 500	eşcār-ı zeyt-i ḫāṣṣa ʿaded 85 [resm] 78
āsiyāb 1 [resm] 90 minhā	mevżiʿ-i āsiyāb-ı ḫāṣṣa 1	muḳāṭaʿa-ı niyābet 2000	ʿöşr-i penbe 100	ʿöşr-i kettān 200
ḥiṣṣe-i ḫāṣṣa sülṣ 70	ḥiṣṣe-i reʿāyā sülṣān 20			
ʿöşr-i bāġāt 4725	ʿöşr-i ḥınṭa 2300	ʿöşr-i cev 367	ʿöşr-i ḳazz 630	ʿöşr-i meyve 124
	resm-i maʿber 6000	ʿöşr-i zeyt 16	resm-i ḫamr 600	

muḳāṭaʿa-ı memlaḫa der nefs-i Voştiça el-mezḳūr ki ḫāṣṣa ḫullide mülkühu şüd

fī sene erbaʿa ālāf ve ḫamsemiʾe

46
nāḥiyyet-i Voştiça

ḳarye-i Buḫuşta ḫāṣṣa-ı Paşa

Papas Yani Ḫiyondari	Niḳola birāẕer-i o	Miḫal Zaġranbi	Yani Ḳaçina	Andon veled-i o
Dimitri veled-i o	Niḳola Ḫamanbiẕi	Yorgi Ḫamanbiẕi	Yani Luluẕyoti	Yani Proços
Ḳosta Çenberis	Dimitri Varuḫa	Todoros Varuḫa	Dimitri Pandoġavli	Todoros İs[p]avliya
Leo Niḳos	Ḳosta Maraveli	Niḳola İvlaşi	Yorgi Ḳutalo	Niḳola Aṣanas
Niḳola Ḳroḳa	Yani Ḫamapiẕi	Andriya veled-i o	Manol Andonoplo	Ḳozma Ruso
Andriya Ruso	Niḳola Ruso	Dimitri Ḳıloçi	Miḫal Tamisi	Ḳosta Taneşi
İstemad Taneşi	Yorgi Ruso	Todoros Ḫarara	Ḳosta Andonoplo	Andon Tiḫiti
Niḳola Draġuli	Yani Ḳıloçi	Vaşıl Aḫiyondari	Todoros Ḳutuna	mücerred Andriya Zaġranbi
mücerred Miḫal Ḫamanbiẕi	mücerred Niḳola Luluẕyoti	mücerred Pavlos Maraveli	mücerred Yani İksalorina	mücerred Yani Varuḫas
bīve Rusina	bīve Ḳroḳu	bīve İksalona	bīve Andoniya	bīve Mantarina
	ḫāne 39	mücerred 6	bīve 5	aġnām 141

ḥāṣıl 4540

ʿa(n) ispence 1155	eşcār-ı ṭut-ı ḫāṣṣa ʿaded 105 [resm] 660	āsiyāb-ı ḫāṣṣa 1 [resm] 600	ʿöşr-i penbe 30	ʿöşr-i kettān 50	ʿöşr-i bāġāt 471
ʿöşr-i ḥınṭa 1200	ʿöşr-i cev 185	ʿöşr-i ḳazz 127	resm-i ḫanāzīr 2	resm-i ḫamr 60	

ḳarye-i Ġardena ez cemāʿat-i Arnavudān ḫāṣṣa-ı Paşa

Niḳa Dramesi	Gin Dramesi	Yani Zenbeş	Gön Bala	Leḳa Bala
		ḫāne 5	aġnām 50	

ḥāṣıl 279

ʿa(n) ispence 100	ʿöşr-i ḥınṭa 150	ʿöşr-i cev 24	resm-i ḫanāzīr 5

47
tetimme-i nāḥiyyet-i Voştiça

ḳarye-i Ayo Yani ez cemāʿat-i Arnavudān ḫāṣṣa-ı Paşa

Dimitri Paskali	Yani veled-i Papas	Nikifor veled-i Babas	Andriya veled-i Babas	Petros Ġavalas
Petros Vurġari	Miḫal Vurġari	Manol Vurġari	Petros dāmād-ı Vurġari	Todoros dāmād-ı Vurġari
İ[st]ayko İsḳoviri	Niḳola veled-i o	Miḫal İstayḳos	Leḳa Vurġari	Miḫal Vlayiti

Niḳola veled-i o	mücerred Dimitri Vurġari	mücerred Yorgi Mağnaẕa	mücerred Yorgi Vurġari	ḫāne 16	mücerred 3
				ağnām 630	

ḥāṣıl 1305

ʿa(n) ispence 380	eşcār-ı ṭut-ı ḫāṣṣa ʿaded 5 [resm] 40	ʿöşr-i bāġāt 60	ʿöşr-i ḥınṭa 700	ʿöşr-i cev 110	ʿöşr-i kettān 15

ḳarye-i Ḳroḳova ez cemāʿat-i Arnavudān ḫāṣṣa-ı Paşa

Yani Manesi	Andriya Manesi	Andriya Mursi	Yorgi Marḳuça	Yorgi Ḫarkâ
Aleksi Ḫarkâ	Yani Ḫarkâ	Raneri Manesi	Yorgi Manesi	Lala Manesi
Niḳola Manḳola	mücerred Niḳola Ḫarkâ	ḫāne 11	mücerred 1	ağnām 225

ḥāṣıl 704

ʿa(n) ispence 240	ʿöşr-i ḥınṭa 400	ʿöşr-i cev 64

ḳarye-i Roẕa ez cemāʿat-i Arnavudān ḫāṣṣa-ı Paşa

Yorgi Pahimari	Ḳosta Pahimari	Yani Murẕuli	Petros Murẕuli	Domeniḳa İlyoplo	
Bardi Leoplo	İstefano Mursi	Dimitri İskâẕa	mücerred Niḳola İlyoplo	ḫāne 8	mücerred 1
				ağnām 50	

ḥāṣıl 368

ʿa(n) ispence 180	ʿöşr-i ḥınṭa 150	ʿöşr-i cev 24	resm-i ḫanāzīr 4	ʿöşr-i kettān 10

ḳarye-i Luḳa İfrati ez cemāʿat-i Arnavudān ḫāṣṣa-ı Paşa

Luḳa el-meẕkūr	Seni veled-i o	Miḫal Anastas	Niḳola Mursi	Dima Beẕulḳa	
Ḳosta Anastas	Petros Melanos	Yani Melanos	bīve İvratu	ḫāne 8	bīve 1
				ağnām 96	

ḥāṣıl 408

ʿa(n) ispence 166	ʿöşr-i ḥınṭa 200	ʿöşr-i cev 32	ʿöşr-i kettān 10

48
tetimme-i nāḥiyyet-i Voşṭiça

ḳarye-i Ẕiyaleş Tunba ez cemāʿat-i Arnavudān ḫāṣṣa-ı Paşa

Pavlos Tunba	Niḳola Mavrişi	ḫāne 2

ḥāṣıl
ʿa(n) ispence
40

ḳarye-i Ḳondorafti ez cemāʿat-i Arnavudān ḫāṣṣa-ı Paşa

Ġulumi Rafti	Yorgi Ḳaçaro	Todoros Ḳalokiri	[ḫāne] [3]

ḥāṣıl
ʿa(n) ispence
60

ḳarye-i Ayo Paraskevi ḫāṣṣa-ı Paşa

Papas Aṣpra	Dimitri Vaşıloplo	Niḳola Boli	Andriya [D]orza	Yani birāẕer-i o
Niḳola Şurafi	Dimitri Boğdano	Yaḳumi Tartari	Ḳ[o]sta İksanuli	Yorgi Zoğrafo
Niḳola Lavazo	İstefano Mavrota	Niḳola İvlaḫo	İstemad İvlaḫo	ḫāne 14

ḥāṣıl 896

ʿa(n) ispence 350	ʿöşr-i bāġāt 212	ʿöşr-i ḳazz 57	ʿöşr-i ḥınṭa 200	ʿöşr-i cev 32	ʿöşr-i ke[tt]ān 15	mülk-i Dimitri Boğdano der ḳarye-i meẕkūr āsiyāb 1 resm 30

ḳarye-i Ḳaḳoḫoryo ḫāṣṣa-ı Paşa

Ḳosta Pramadefti	Dimitri Nomiḳos	Todoros Varpati	Dimitri Mamesyoni	Duḳa Dumuniça

Yorgi Ḳarvunas	Yani Ḳalokiri	Pavlos Atali	ḫāne 8

ḥāṣıl 677

ʿa(n) ispence	ʿöşr-i ḥınṭa	ʿöşr-i cev	ʿöşr-i bāġāt	ʿöşr-i ḳazz	ʿöşr-i kettān
200	100	16	285	66	10

ḳarye-i Lopesi ez cemāʿat-i Arnavudān ḫāṣṣa-ı Paşa

Andriya Lopesi	Lasḳari birāẕer-i o	Gön birāder-i o	Manol Lopesi	Gön Lopesi
Todoros Lopesi	Andriya Lopesi	Ḳosta Muzaki	Todoros Dorza	Marti Peta
Niḳola Boğdano	Leḳa Boğdano	Gin Lopesi	Niḳola Pondiya	ḫāne 14 aġnām 205

ḥāṣıl 643

ʿa(n) ispence	ʿöşr-i ḥınṭa	ʿöşr-i cev	ʿöşr-i kettān
280	300	48	15

49
tetimme-i nāḥiyyet-i Voştiça el-meẕkūr

ḳarye-i Fran[ḳo] ez [ce]māʿat-ı Arnavudān ḫāṣṣa-ı Paşa

Andriya F[ra]nḳo	Gön Fran[k]os	Bardi birāder-i o	Pulimenos Franḳos	Ḳosta birāẕer-i o
Dimitri İksilirġo	Petros Muzaki	Leḳa İpsari	bīve Muzakina	ḫāne 8 bīve 1 aġnām 60

ḥāṣıl 408

ʿa(n) ispence	ʿöşr-i ḥınṭa	ʿöşr-i cev	ʿöşr-i kettān
166	200	32	10

ḳarye-i İvlanduşa ez cemāʿat-i Arnavudān ḫāṣṣa-ı Paşa

Loyzos İvlandusa	Domaniḳa İvlandusa	Todoros İvlandusa	Yorgi Ḳlaẕi	Gin Milaşi
Domaniḳa Pilura	Leḳa Beleşi	Leḳa Milesi	Gin Milesi	Dima Ḫarḳomata
Todoros birāder-i o	Yorgi Ḫarḳomata	Niḳola Floḳa	Ḳosta birāder-i o	Yorgi birāder-i o

Todoros Maḳrimali	Lazaro Burdano	Niḳola Burdano	Ḳosta Burdano	Gön birāẕer-i o
Gön Beluşi	Duḳa Burdano	Leḳa Mazi	Yorgi Burdano	Gin Burẕano
Yorgi Buvaşi	Yorgi Maḳrimali	Lazaro Floḳa	Gin Beleşi	Yorgi Burdano
		ḫāne 30	aġnām 333	

ḥāṣıl 1605

ʿa(n) ispence	ʿöşr-i ḥınṭa	ʿöşr-i cev	ʿöşr-i kettān
600	850	135	20

ḳarye-i Petro Tunba ez cemāʿat-i Arnavudān ḫāṣṣa-ı Paşa

Petro el-meẕkūr	Yorgi Maḳruni	Yorgi Buzbardi	ḫāne 3	aġnām 85

ḥāṣıl 176

ʿa(n) ispence	ʿöşr-i ḥınṭa	ʿöşr-i cev
60	100	16

ḳarye-i Ḳlaẕi [ez cemā]ʿat-i Arnavudān ḫāṣṣa-ı Paşa

Dyalcşi Ḳlaẕi	Petros Mazi	Todoros Ḳlaẕis	Gin Maji	Dima birāẕer-i o
		ḫāne 5	aġnām 40	

ḥāṣıl 222

ʿa(n) ispence	ʿöşr-i ḥınṭa	ʿöşr-i cev	ʿöşr-i ḳazz
100	100	16	6

50
tetimme-i nāḥiyyet-i Voştiça

ḳarye-i Aya İğligori ez cemāʿat-i Arnavudān ḫāṣṣa-ı Paşa

Ḳosta Manos	Ẕyaleşi Mano	Yorgi Franḳo	Marti Mazaraki	Miḫos birāder-i o

Ḳosta Franḳo	ḫāne 6	aġnām 155

ḥāṣıl 246

ʿa(n) ispence 120	ʿöşr-i ḥınṭa 100	ʿöşr-i cev 16	ʿöşr-i kettān 10

ḳarye-i Listirna ez cemāʿat-i Arnavudān — ḫāṣṣa-ı Paşa

Dimitri Mavra	Todoros Pejaniḳos	S̱omas İpsaruli	Todoros Priçiġari	Yorgi İstaṣi
Yani Varlamo	Manol Ṣavoya	Andriya dāmād-i Alaman	İstasinos Lavazos	Ẕyaḳos Maḳris
Aleksi Anena	Yani Mavromati	Niḳola Alamanos	Yani Laḳasa	bīve Lordina
bīve Buzena		ḫāne 14	bīve 2	

ḥāṣıl 1128

ʿa(n) ispence 292	ʿöşr-i bāġāt 544	ʿöşr-i ḳazz 41	ʿöşr-i ḥınṭa 200	ʿöşr-i cev 30	ʿöşr-i meyve 6	ʿöşr-i kettān 15

ḳarye-i Graḳa ez cemāʿat-i Arnavudān — ḫāṣṣa-ı Paşa

Andriya Graḳa	Marti Graḳa	İvrato Platimesi	Gön Ḳaparali	ḫāne 4 aġnām 30

ḥāṣıl 406

ʿa(n) ispence 80	ʿöşr-i ḥınṭa 150	ʿöşr-i cev 24	ʿöşr-i bāġāt 128	ʿöşr-i ḳazz 24

ḳarye-i Martina der Noḳastro — ḫāṣṣa-ı Paşa

İstemadis İsḳandelari	Todoros Ḳondos	Yani birāẕer-i o	Yani Lukâri	Petros birāẕer-i o
İvrat[o] Carçi	Yorgi birāder-i o	Dimitri [Varṣalemos]	Yani Rali	Papas Dimitri
mücerred Manol Franci	mücerred Pavlos Famaliti	bīve Lorencina	bīve Ḳavasilina	bīve Varṣalomusa

cemāʿat-i Arnavudān der ḳarye-i meẕkūr

Gön Bardi	Gin Pilura	Leḳa Bardi	Yani Ḳavasila	bīve Ḳurtesina

ḫāne 14	mücerred 2	bīve 4	aġnām 104

ḥāṣıl 1034

ʿa(n) ispence 404	ʿöşr-i bāġāt 152	ʿöşr-i ḥınṭa 350	ʿöşr-i cev 56	ʿöşr-i ḳazz 57	ʿöşr-i kettān 15

51

tetimme-i nāḥiyyet-i Voştiça

ḳarye-i Epanolaġo — ḫāṣṣa-ı Paşa

Ḳosta Panḳa	Yorgi Yanaḳoplo	Niḳola Marḳo	Dimitri Marḳo	Niḳola Ḳarava
İstemati Voşticano	Yorgi Ḫolorino	Andriya Kiniġos	Bardi veled-i o	Petros veled-i o
Gin Kiniġos	Yorgi Prifti	Yorgi Kiniġos	Ḳozma Barçi	İvlaş Kiniġos
		ḫāne 15	aġnām 56	

ḥāṣıl 687

ʿa(n) ispence 375	ʿöşr-i bāġāt 56	ʿöşr-i ḥınṭa 200	ʿöşr-i cev 32	resm-i ḫanāzīr 3	ʿöşr-i kettān 15	ʿöşr-i ḳazz 6

ḳarye-i Valḳo ez cemāʿat-i Arnavudān — ḫāṣṣa-ı Paşa

Yani Busi	İstini[36] Busi	Petros Busi	Todoros Mayiras	ḫāne 4 aġnām 47

ḥāṣıl 262

ʿa(n) ispence 80	ʿöşr-i ḥınṭa 150	ʿöşr-i cev 24	ʿöşr-i bāġāt 8

ḳarye-i Sotira ez cemāʿat-i Arnavudān — ḫāṣṣa-ı Paşa

Yorgi Zaġoriti	Dimitri Buḳarinos	Todoros Sotiriyati	İstefano Zaġoriti	Yani Marmaryoti
mücerred Niḳola Buḳarinos		ḫāne 5	mücerred 1	aġnām 90

ḥāṣıl 322

ʿa(n) ispence 120	ʿöşr-i bāġāt 16	ʿöşr-i ḥınṭa 150	ʿöşr-i cev 24	ʿöşr-i ḳazz 12

ḳarye-i Burlaşa ez cemāʿat-i Arnavudān — ḫāṣṣ[a-ı] Paşa

Pa[v]l[o]s B[u]rlaşa	Yorgi Zupano	Gön birāẕer-i o	Yorgi [---]	İvrato Şuliçi
Todoros Draġos	Ḳozma Ḳumi	İstefano Daçi	Ḳosta birāẕer-i o	mücerred Ḳosta Draġos
mücerred Andriya Daçi	bīve Martina	ḫāne 9	mücerred 2	bīve 1 aġnām 106

ḥāṣıl 588

ʿa(n) ispence 226	ʿöşr-i ḥınṭa 300	ʿöşr-i cev 47	ʿöşr-i ḳazz 15

ḳarye-i Beçaḳus — ḫāṣṣa-ı Paşa

Papas Niḳola Dimula	Ya[ni] veled-i o	Niḳola Ḳostalari	İstematiḳo Miḫaloplos	Dimitri Ḳumaniçi
Miḫal Ḳumaniçi	Niḳola veled-i o	Niḳolas Ḫarkemas	İstaṣi Valaryoti	Todoros birāder-i o

52

tetimme-i ḳarye-i Beçaḳus el-meẕkūr — ḫāṣṣa-ı Paşa

mücerred Yorgi Ḳostalari	mücerred Miḫal Ḳumaniçi	mücerred Yani Ḳumaniçi	ḫāne 10	mücerred 3 aġnām 55

ḥāṣıl 911

ʿa(n) ispence 325	ʿöşr-i bāġāt 72	ʿöşr-i ḥınṭa 300	ʿöşr-i cev 48	ʿöşr-i ḳazz 156	ʿöşr-i kettān 10

ḳarye-i Kiriçova — ḫāṣṣa-ı Paşa

Yani Maḳri	Miḫal Maḳri	Dimitri Maḳri	İstefano Fratos	İvrato Pandoġavli
İstilyano Pandoġavli	Yani Ḳafiri	Ḳosta Ḫanci	Niḳola veled-i o	Miḫ[al] Pandoġavli

mücerred Manol Ḫanci	bīve Ḫarköpulina	ḫāne 10	mücerred 1	bīve 1 aġnām 24

ḥāṣıl 816

ʿa(n) ispence 281	ʿöşr-i ḥınṭa 250	ʿöşr-i cev 38	ʿöşr-i bāġāt 72	ʿöşr-i ḳazz 165	ʿöşr-i kettān 10

ḳarye-i Ġumaniça — ḫāṣṣa-ı Paşa

Yorgi Pengi	Ḫıristoforos Liẕiyos	Niḳola veled-i o	İstemati Ḫıristoforos	Niḳola Ḳutupo
Dimitri Pavloplos	Ḳosta Plaġasi	Todoros Vaşıloplos	Yorgi Ḳafiri	Miḫal Ḳafiri
Yani Letirġo	Dimitri birāẕer-i o	Ḳosta Dimitroplo	Mangişa Rusi	Miḫal Ġrusis
Papaniḳola Ḫıristofor	Andon İstrofila	Gön Franḳo	Yorgi Ġurzumise	bīve Pengina
	ḫāne 19	bīve 1	aġnām 30	

ḥāṣıl 1528

ʿa(n) ispence 481	āsiyāb 1 [resm] 120 minhā: ḥiṣṣe-i ḫāṣṣa süls 100; ḥiṣṣe-i raʿiyyet sülṣān 20	ẕikrolan köyde Yorgi Pengi'nindir	āsiyāb-ı peş-mīne-i ḫāṣṣa 2 [resm] 70	eşcār-ı ṭut-ı ḫāṣṣa ʿaded 128 [resm] 180	ʿöşr-i bāġāt 120	ʿöşr-i ḥınṭa 400

ʿöşr-i cev 64	ʿöşr-i ḳazz 72	ʿöşr-i meyve 1	ʿöşr-i kettān 20

ḳarye-i Maji ez cemāʿat-i Arnavudān — ḫāṣṣa-ı Paşa

Lazaro Maji	Yorgi Size	Andriya Beluşi	Pavlos Ḳapareli	ḫāne 4 aġnām 23

ḥāṣıl 311

ʿa(n) ispence 80	ʿöşr-i ḫınṭa 200	ʿöşr-i cev 31

mezraʿa-ı Ḳapareli nezd-i ḳarye-i Maji el-meẕkūr

ḫāṣṣa-ı Paşa ḫāliyye

53

tetimme-i nāḥiyyet-i Voştiça

ḳarye-i Rayḳu ez cemāʿat-i Arnavudān ḫāṣṣa-ı Paşa

Rayḳo Servo	Niḳola birāẕer-i o	Şarandi Ġorġoyiri	Papas Ḳondos	Yani Ḳondopistino
Yani Ḫarara	Ḳosta Pravata		ḫāne 7	aġnām 90

ḥāṣıl 503

ʿa(n) ispence 140	ʿöşr-i ḫınṭa 250	ʿöşr-i cev 40	ʿöşr-i bāġāt 24	ʿöşr-i kettān 10	ʿöşr-i ḳazz 39

ḳarye-i Vi[s]oḳa ez cemāʿat-i Arnavudān ḫāṣṣa-ı Paşa

Duḳa Papaẕato	Todoros Niḳokiris	Dimitri Mazli	Niḳola İskitiḳa	Dimitri İskitiḳa
Yani Çuraki	İstefano Ġorġaloġato	Yani birāder-i o	Yorgi Panḳalo	Miḫal İvlaḫo
Todoros Pos̱ito	Yorgi Poniros	Manḳola Veluşi	Şuzi Veluşi	Yorgi Carci
Yorgi Niḳokiri	Dimitri Meryas	Yani Turyas	Yorgi Turyas	Niḳola Papaẕato
Lazaro Vorila	Yani Turya	Andon Maroni	ḫāne 23	aġnām 1046

ḥāṣıl 1997

ʿa(n) ispence 460	eşcār-ı ṭut-ı ḫāṣṣa ʿaded 150 [resm] 100	ʿöşr-i ḫınṭa 1200	ʿöşr-i cev 188	resm-i ḫanāzīr 2	ʿöşr-i ḳazz 27	ʿöşr-i kettān 20

ıssuz yėrde olduġıyçün ziyāde ḥāṣıl olmaz

ḳarye-i Kerpini ḫāṣṣa-ı Paşa

Yorgi Rimoḫori	Manol Meğaris	Yani Meğari	İstemati Papayanoplo	Yani Aploraẕi
İvratos birāder-i o	Yani Alamano	Ḳosta Alamano	Ḳosta İvrana	Todoros Lanġas
Niḳola Lepsuta	Manol Ġarçuni	İstefano As̱anasoplo	Ḳosta As̱anasoplo	Papas İstemati
Niḳola As̱anasoplo	Yani birāẕer-i o	Yani As̱anasoplo	Ḳosta Burġaki	Aleksi A[l]amano
Yani Lepsuta	İstrati Mastroyanoplo	Manol Mastroyanoplo	Yorgi Ḳumani	Yani İvrana
Miḫal Ḳumanis	Todoros birāẕer-i o	Yani Mastroyanoplo	İstasinos İvranas	Manol Andrito
Yani veled-i o	Miḫal Danili	İstrati Ẕanili	Yani Ẕanili	Niḳola Ḳafiris

54

tetimme-i ḳarye-i Kerpini el-meẕkūr ḫāṣṣa-ı Paşa

Yorgi Ḳros Gina	Yani [Ara]ryas	Mans̱os S̱omas	Miḫal Papaẕaplo	Yorgi Tetr[a]ẕi
Yorgi İstavraki	Papas [Ḳ]aḳuçi	mücerred Yor[gi] Alamano	mücerred Todoros İvrana	mücerred [A]ndron [Le]psuta
mücerred [Ni]ḳ[o]la Mastroyano-plo	mücerred Miḫal Mastroyano-plo	bīve La[l]atina	b[ī]ve Franḳo-pulina	ḫāne 42 bīve 2 / mücerred 5 aġnām 91

ḥāṣıl 45[6]2

ʿa(n) ispence 1187	eşcār-ı ṭut-ı ḫāṣṣa ʿaded 310 [resm] 960	bāġāt-ı ḫāṣṣa dönüm 2 [resm] 240	ʿöşr-i [bā]ġāt 288	ʿöşr-i ḳazz 762	ʿöşr-i meyve 8
ʿöşr-i ḫınṭa 900	ʿöşr-i cev 142	resm-i ḫanāzīr 5	ʿö[ş]r-i kettān 40	resm-i ḫamr 30	

ḳarye-i Zaḫlori ḫāṣṣa-ı Paşa

İstefano Ḳrasato	Dimitri İsḳorila	Yorgi İsḳorila	Ġala[ty]anos Yiros	Yani veled-i o
Todoros Ġalatyanos	Todoros İsḳorilas	Yorgi Ġalatyanos	Dimitri Şavulos	Aporḫitos İsḳorilas

Yani İskâẕa	Niḳola İpsaros	Ḳosta Angele	Dimitri Poloṣiri	Yani veled-i o
Papas Yani	Yorgi Poloṣiri	Miḫal İpsaro	Yorgi Perdiḫyano	Niḳola Perdiḫyanos
Yani veled-i o	Andriya veled-i o	Dimitri Fundomeno	Yorgi Ḳuziya	Yorgi Angelaro
Niḳola Ḳrokiẕa	Yani Ḳondomenos	Ḳosta veled-i o	Yani Angele	Dimitri Angelos
Miḫal Ḳuspari	İstemad birāẕer-i o	Zaẕya Ḳuspari	Ġunari Dimitri	İstemati Ḳaruzo
Miḫal Orandos	Niḳola veled-i o	Yorgi Polyanifuro	Niḳola birāẕer-i o	Miḫal Ẕyavati
Yani Poliṣiri	Niḳola Poloṣiri	Dimitri birāder-i o	Yani Danili	Miḫal veled-i o
Todoro Loveçyano	Dimitri Ḫarkâ	Yani dāmād-ı o	İstemad İpsaros	Dimitri Ṣeryano
Yorgi Platis	Ḳosta Todoros	Niḳola İsḳorilya	mücerred Dimitri Ġalatyanos	mücerred Todoros Platena
mücerred Ḳosta İsḳorila	bīve Platena	bīve Risḳondo	ḫāne 53 / mücerred 3	bīve 2 / aġnām 103

ḥāṣıl 4156

ʿa(n) ispence 1412	ʿöşr-i bāġāt 448	ʿöşr-i ḳazz 798	ʿöşr i ḥınṭa 1200	ʿöşr i cev 185	ʿöşr-i meyve 3	resm-i ḫamr 70
			ʿöşr-i kettān 40			

55
tetimme-i nāḥiyyet-i Voştiça

ḳarye-i Tumena ḫāṣṣa-ı Paşa

Todoros Ḳalapaçun-yoti	Niḳola Lanḳaẕyoti	Ḳosta Melaḫrino	Andriya Ḳolokiṣi	İstefano birāẕer-i o
[İ]stilyano birāder-i o	Yani Aştriḳardo	Yani Pandoluġari	İstemati İḫy[o]na	Yani Ḫalḳomata
Lazaro birāder-i o	Yorgi Ḳonduri	Ḳosta Ḳalimarḫo	Pavlos Fandoluġari	Niḳola birāder-i o
Todoros Flivaris	İstemad birāẕer-i o	Todoros Ḳutupos	Yani Ḳutupo	İstemati Ḳunduri
Todoros Meliġorda	Aleksi Ġavrili	Andriya Platanyotisa	mücerred Yani Lanḳaẕyoti	mücerred Miḫal Pandoluġari
mücerred Niḳola İḫyona	mücerred Ṣotoki Fandoluġari	ḫāne 23	mücerred 4	aġnām 114

ḥāṣıl 2543

ʿa(n) ispence 675	eşcār-ı ṭut-ı ḫāṣṣa ʿaded 18 [resm] 45	ʿöşr-i bāġāt 248	ʿöşr-i ḳazz 456	ʿöşr-i ḥınṭa 900	ʿöşr-i cev 138	ʿöşr-i meyve 16
		resm-i ḫamr 40	ʿöşr-i kettān 25			

ḳarye-i Ẕilivina ḫāṣṣa-ı Paşa

Todoros Ḳalokiri	Papas İstemati	Todoros Ġuneri	İvrato Ḫaleli	Andriya birāder-i o
Yani Vavuli	Ḳosta Kirḳalos	Muriki İvlaḫo	Yani Kiri	Dimitri Velayiti
Niḳola Siboliti	Ṣotoki Ḫaleli	Yorgi Arḳuçi	Yani Arḳuçi	Todoros Falyaros
Vaṣıl U[z]ġuros	Yani veled-i o	Yorgi ḫīş-i o	İstasinos Falyaro	Vaṣıl veled-i o
Todoros Nomiḳos	Miḫal Nomiḳos	Ḳosta Varala	Yorgi Orfano	Dimitri Orfano
Yani Androplo	Niḳola Larda	Yani Nomiḳos	Pavlos dāmād-ı İstasino	Niḳola Arasa
Ḳosta Rasya	Yani Varipati	Todoros R[a]sya	İstemati Rasya	Pavlos dāmād-ı o
Miḫal Rasya	Kiryaki Varipati	İstemati Mamesyoti	Yani Rasya	Miḫal Mamesyoti

56
tetimme-i ḳarye-i Ẕilivina el-meẕkūr ḫāṣṣa-ı Paşa

Manol veled-i o	Yani Mamesyoti	Todoros Mamesyoti	Yani Ḫuvaẕari	mücerred Yani Ḳalokiri

mücerred Yani Nomiḳos	mücerred Niḳola Varala	mücerred Niḳola Orfano	mücerred Yani veled-i Pavlos	mücerred İstefano Varipati
mücerred Yorgi Mamesyoti	mücerred Miḫal Ḫuvaẕari	mücerred Dimitri Ḫaleli	mücerred Dimitri Arasa	bīve Pramaẕeftu
	ḫāne 44	mücerred 10	bīve 1	aġnām 180

ḥāṣıl 4090

ʿa(n) ispence 1356	eşcār-ı ṭut-ı ḫāṣṣa ʿaded 27 [resm] 60	ʿöşr-i ḥınṭa 1900	ʿöşr-i cev 295	ʿöşr-i bāġāt 160	ʿöşr-i ḳazz 243	ʿöşr-i meyve 1
		resm-i ḫamr 25	ʿöşr-i kettān 50			

ḳarye-i Rolo ḫāṣṣa-ı Paşa

Yorgi İsḳurya	Niḳola İsḳurya	Petros veled-i o	Dimitri Lukâri	Yani birāẕer-i o
Miḫal yeñiçeri	Niḳola Ḳariyeni	Yorgi birāder-i o	Yani İspartino	Yorgi Ḳuvaki
Andriya Ḳuvaki	Trimas İksanos	Yorgi İsḳura	mücerred Yani İsḳurya	mücerred S̱oma Ḳuvaki
	ḫāne 13	mücerred 2	aġnām 25	

ḥāṣıl 1356

ʿa(n) ispence 375	eşcār-ı ṭut-ı ḫāṣṣa ʿaded 20 [resm] 60	ʿöşr-i ḥınṭa 400	ʿöşr-i cev 62	ʿöşr-i bāġāt 144	resm-i ḫanāzīr 14	ʿöşr-i kettān 15
		ʿöşr-i ḳazz 186	resm-i ḫamr 20	mülk-i Niḳola İsḳuri Voştiçaʾi āsiyāb 1 resm 80		

ḳarye-i Ḳılapaçuna ḫāṣṣa-ı Paşa

Niḳola Miliġurda	Yorgi Loyizo	İstemad Loyizo	Niḳola İsḳuri	Manol birāder-i o	
Dimitri İsḳuri	Manol Işḳuri	Yorgi Ḳoloçi	Leḳa Miliġurda	İstemati Çanḳaruli	
Yorgi Çanḳaruli	Yani birāder-i o	Miḫal Veronikyoti	Yorgi birāder-i o	Yorgi Ḳaratula	
Niḳola İspartino	Manol İspartino	Dimitri İspartino	Petros İspartino	Todoros Liġuroplos	
mücerred Petros Loyizo	mücerred Yani İsḳuri	bīve Ḳapandritiça	bīve Marula	ḫāne 20 aġnām 66	mücerred 2 bīve 2

57

ḥāṣıl-ı ḳarye-i Ḳılapaçuna el-meẕkūr 2087

ʿa(n) ispence 562	ʿöşr-i ḥınṭa 800	ʿöşr-i cev 122	ʿöşr-i bāġāt 120	ʿöşr-i ḳazz 267	ʿöşr-i meyve 14	resm-i ḫanāzīr 2
resm-i ḫamr 20	ʿöşr-i kettān 20	mülk-i İstemad Loyizo der ḳarye-i meẕkūr āsiyāb 1 resm 80	mülk-i Niḳola İsḳuri der ḳarye-i meẕkūr āsiyāb 1 resm 80			

ḳarye-i Namuni ḫāṣṣa-ı Paşa

Yani Brati	Niḳola birāder-i o	Ẕyaleşi Ḳalimani	Yani Seftari	Manol Lazaroplos
Manol Milona	Yani Ġramatiḳo		ḫāne 7	aġnām 35

ḥāṣıl 595

ʿa(n) ispence 175	ʿöşr-i ḥınṭa 250	ʿöşr-i cev 40	ʿöşr-i bāġāt 48	ʿöşr-i āsiyāb 40	ʿöşr-i ḳazz 30	ʿöşr-i kettān 10	ʿöşr-i meyve 2

ḳarye-i Yaḳoḫto ḫāṣṣa-ı Paşa

Andriya Piri	Aleksi Piris	Dimitri birāder-i o	Yorgi Yiroplos	İstemad Yiroplos
Niḳola Yiroplos	Andon birāder-i o	Yani Argiti	Vaşıl Fakimos	Ḳosta veled-i o

Niḳola Mayiros	Yani Fakimos	Dimitri Pisḳoplos	Niḳola Pisḳoplos	Todoros Pisḳoplos
Ḳosta Ḫarköplos	Dimitri Ḫarköplos	Dimitri Pisḳoplos	Todoros Ḫarkâs	Yorgi veled-i o
Yiros Lestriniti	Lazaro veled-i o	Dimitri veled-i o	Ḳosta Niḫti	Andriya Ḳaçina
Niḳola Bili	Ḳosta Ḳaçina	Yorgi birāder-i o	Yani Çimi	Niḳola veled-i o
Ġulyamo Çimi	Ḳosta Çimi	Pavlos Çimi	Pavlos Papayorġoplos	Niḳola Zastopiti
Dimitri Mavriyano	Todoros Meliẕon	Niḳola Marinos	İstefano Zaḫya	Dimitri Çiyotya
Yani Ġramatiḳo	Dimitri birāder-i o	Yorgi birāder-i o	Petros birāder-i o	İstefano Ḳuḳuçi
İstemad Ḳuḳuçi	Andriya Ḳaçina	İstemad Pronoyti	Niḳola Ḳatelo	Yorgi Pronoyti
Ḳosta Ẕraḳulyo	Yorgi Ẕraḳulyo	Todoros veled-i o	Miḫal Draḳulyo	Niḳola veled-i o
Andriya Draḳulyo	Ḳosta Ḳondovaşılı	Yorgi Ayoparaskeviti	Yani İğliġoroplo	Yorgi Çimi

58

tetimme-i ḳarye-i Yaḳoḫto el-mezḳūr — ḫāṣṣa-ı Paşa

Yani Platanyoti	Ḳosta birāder-i o	Yani Melandoni	Dimitri birāder-i o	Todoros Zaminaḳo
Aleksi Filibo[37]	Petros Zaminaḳos	Miḫal Argiti	Yorgi Ḫaralanbi	Yani Ḫaralanbi
Yani Pronoyti	Pavlos Kefalinos	Aleksi Veryoti	Todoros Ġramatiḳoplos	Ḳosta Yalomati
Dimitri Papayorġoplo	Niḳola Maẕya	Yorgi Lanḳaẕyoti	Yani Ġramatiḳoplo	Niḳola Maẕya
İstemati Ḳusuya	Andriya Mayiros	Dimitri Vavalaris	Niḳola İğliġoroplo	Dimitri Maẕya
Yorgi birāder-i o	Todoros Maẕyas	Todoro Mayiro	İstilyano Çimi	Yani Çimi
Yorgi Traḳardo	Todoros Ṣandameryano	Yani Ġurmi	Yani Ḳapandriti	Ḳosta Poçita
Niḳola Argiti	Todoros Melinẕon	Yorgi Pahiyeni	İstemati Vake	Yaḳumo dāmād-ı Melinẕon
Miḫal Ḳalamati	Yorgi Ẓiẓya	Yani Ṣofyano	İvrato Pet[a]	Yorgi Peta

Yorgi Muzaki	İstematiḳo Vurġari	Yorgi Revandino	Niḳola Ḳaçina	Yani Meliẕoni
İstefano Morfono	Petros Valaris	Niḳola Pronoyti	Yorgi Ḳaçina	Papaniḳolas Ḳaçanas
Niḳola Morfonos	Miḫal Ḳaçanos	Dimitri Rali	mücerred İstemad Argiti	mücerred Ḫıristiyano Marinos
mücerred Niḳola Ḳondovaşılı	mücerred Yorgi İğliġoroplo	mücerred Manol Filibo[38]	mücerred Yani Zaminaḳos	mücerred Yani Ġramatiḳoplos
mücerred İğliġori Lanḳaẕyoti	mücerred İğliġori İğliġoroplo	mücerred Aleksi Melinẕon	mücerred İstefano Pahiyeni	mücerred Todoros Peta
mücerred Aleksi Muzaki	mücerred Yani Dimitroplo	mücerred Yani Rali	bīve Arfeklisifa Petratu	bīve [Fa]rlanina

bīve Ḳalovelono	bīve Aleksiya Platandriya	bīve İste- matinu	bīve Paloloyelina	ḫāne 118 bīve 6	mücerred 15 aġnām 466

ḥāṣıl 12099

ʿa(n) ispence 3361	eşcār-ı ṭut-ı ḫāṣṣa ʿaded 380 [resm] 840	eşcār-ı zeyt-i ḫāṣṣa ʿaded 40 [resm] 30	ʿöşr-i bāġāt 1136	ʿöşr-i ḳazz 1890	ʿöşr-i ḥınṭa 3800	ʿöşr-i cev 585

ʿöşr-i meyve 27	resm-i ḫamr 170	ʿöşr-i kettān 100	mülk-i Dimitri birāder-i Aleksi der ḳarye-i mezḳūr āsiyāb 1 resm 80	mülk-i Todoros Ġramatiḳoplos der ḳarye-i mezḳūr āsiyāb 1 resm 40	mülk-i Dimitri birāẕer-i Yani Ġramatiḳo der ḳarye-i mezḳūr āsiyāb 1 resm 40

ḳarye-i İstavrina

59

tetimme-i nāḥiyyet-i Voştiça

ḳarye-i İstavriya ez cemāʿat-i Arnavudān — ḫāṣṣa-ı Paşa

Leḳa Dorza	Gin Praski	Yorgi Praski	İvlaş Ḳoḳla	Ḳosta Çanḳaroplo

ḫāne	ağnām
5	46

ḥāṣıl 281

ʿa(n) ispence	ʿöşr-i ḥınṭa	ʿöşr-i cev	resm-i ḫanāzīr
100	150	23	8

ḳarye-i Potamya ḫāṣṣa-ı Paşa

Todoros İftoḫos	Todoros Nikiforoplos	Niḳola Ġramyoti	Manol Draġovi	Miḫal veled-i o
Miḫal İsḳoliẕi	Dimitri Ġavrili	Dimitri İsḳoliẕi	Yani İsḳoliẕi	Niḳola veled-i o
Dimitri Franḳoyani	Ḳosta Paraskeviti	Gin Zenbeş	Yani Selanikö	Todoros Selanikö
Dimitri Selanikö	İstemati İvrana	Yani Ġranciyoti	Miḫal Nikiforoplo	Niḳola Nikiforoplo
Yani Ḳalafati	Aleksi birāẕer-i o	Aleksi Ayaparaskeviti	Miḫal Ḳalafati	Yorgi İstefanoplos
Yani birāder-i o	Domaniḳa Paraskevop- loş	Yani Longiti	Marḳo Longiti	Dimitri Ḳaḳomenos
Yani veled-i o	Dimitri Ḳaḳomenos	Maruli Niḳolas	Dimitri veled-i o	Todoros Sarakinoplos
Miḫal Maḳriyeni	Miḫal Raḳoti	Yorgi birāder-i o	Niḳola Randoni	Yani Randoni
Yorgi İftoḫos	Yani İsḳoliẕi	Yorgi Çaḳoni	Mi[ḫa]l Mavriköti	İstilyano Mavriköti
Protopapas Randoni	İstilyano veled-i o	Ẕyaḳo Randoni	Gön dāmād-ı Nomiḳo	Todoros Nomiḳos
Nomiḳos Randonis	Miḫal veled-i o	Aleksi Ḳa[na]ris	Yani Ḳaloyanoplo	Miḫal Mançoyani
Yorgi Damizali	Yani Potamiti	Yani Niḳolaki	Miḫal birāder-i o	Todoros R[a]ndonis
[Ya]ni [veled-i] o	Niḳola İsfaziya[39]	Miḫal İsfaze[40]	Yani birāder-i o	Todoros Ḳaḳomenos
Todoros Çaḳona	Todoros Metaḳsa	Yani Çaḳona	Dimitri veled-i o	Niḳola Çaḳona

60

tetimme-i ḳarye-i Potamya el-meẕkūr ḫāṣṣa-ı Paşa

Miḫal Çaḳona	Niḳola İsḳoliẕi	Ḳosta veled-i o	Yani [vel]ed-i o	Dimitri Randoni
Ḳosta Franḳoyani	İstefano İftoḫos	mücerred Yorgi Nikiforoplos	mücerred Ḳozma	mücerred Andriya Ġavril[i]
mücerred Yorgi İsḳoliẕi	mücerred Vaşıl İsḳoliẕi	mücerred Todoros Papayorgi	mücerred Yorgi Paraskeviti	mücerred Yani Selanikö
mücerred Yorgi Ḳalafati	mücerred Aleksi Longiti	mücerred Proġoni Ḳaḳomenos	mücerred Ḳosta Randonis	mücerred Niḳola İsḳaza
mücerred Yorgi İsḳoliẕi	mücerred Yorgi Nikiforoplo	bīve Mancoyanu	bīve Ḳaḳomeni	

ḫāne	mücerred
77	15
bīve	ağnām
2	143

ḥāṣıl 8576

ʿa(n) ispence	ʿöşr-i bāġāt	ʿöşr-i ḥınṭa	ʿöşr-i cev	ʿöşr-i ḳazz	ʿöşr-i meyve	resm-i ḫamr
2312	1072	2700	417	1728	7	160

ʿöşr-i kettān	mülk-i bīve Mancoyanu der ḳarye-i meẕkūr	mülk-i Yani Niḳolaki der ḳarye-i meẕkūr
100	āsiyāb 1 resm 40	āsiyāb 1 resm 40

ḳarye-i Çimlo ḫāṣṣa-ı Paşa

Todoros Mamesyoti	Yani Suḫina	İstemati birāẕer-i o	Papaḳosta Ḳlukinyoti	Papas Ḫartofilaḳa
Andriya veled-i o	Todoros Suḫina	Andriya Ġurya	Yani Ṣemeli	Dimitri İsḳonço
Yani Mematino	İstemati birāẕer-i o	Dimitri Ḳavasila	Niḳola Suḫina	Yani Rupakyoti
Manḳola Suḫina	İstilyano Suḫina	Todoros Suḫina	Yorgi Ḫarara	mücerred İstilyano Suḫina
mücerred İstemad birāder-i o	mücerred Niḳola Ġurya	mücerred Yani birāder-i o	mücerred Petros Suḫina	mücerred Panḳalo Rupakyoti

ḫāne	mücerred	ağnām
19	6	51

ḥāṣıl 2240

ʿa(n) ispence	ʿöşr-i bāğāt	ʿöşr-i ḳazz	ʿöşr-i ḥınṭa	ʿöşr-i cev	ʿöşr-i meyve	resm-i ḫamr
625	144	561	700	108	2	20

mülk-i
Papas ḪartofilaAa der ḳarye-i
mezḳūr
āsiyāb 1 resm 80

ḳarye-i İstilivena ḫāṣṣa-ı Paşa

Miḫal Alupoklizi	[S]otiri Alupoklizi	Andriya Alupoklizi	Yani Alupoklizi	Yani Larzas

61

tetimme-i ḳarye-i İstilivena el-mezḳūr ḫāṣṣa-ı Paşa

Todoros Ḳoryalos	İstilyano Lanbiri	Yorgi Larzas	Miḫal Rafti	Papas Larzas
Miḫal Ḳayafa	Yani Marḳos	Todoros veled-i o	Papas Ḫarköplos	Niḳola Miğaloyeni
Todoros Tristali	Miḫal Tristali	Rados İvlaḫos	Todoros Mandruvi	Todoros Ḳanavos
Miḫal Miğaloyani	Androni Ḳayafas	Andriya Mermigi	mücerred Yorgi Marḳos	mücerred Yani Miğaloyeni
mücerred Miḫal Ḳanavos	mücerred Niḳola Ḫarköplo	ḫāne 23	mücerred 1	ağnām 74

ḥāṣıl 2406

ʿa(n) ispence	ʿöşr-i bāğāt	ʿöşr-i ḥınṭa	ʿöşr-i cev	ʿöşr-i ḳazz	resm-i ḫamr
675	176	700	108	717	30

ḳarye-i Ḳulukina ḫāṣṣa-ı Paşa

Ḳostandin Draḳulyo	Yorgi veled-i o	Ḳosta veled-i o	Manol Ḳartilas	Papas Ḳartilas
Yani birāder-i o	Yorgi Ḳartila	Yorgi İsḳlavo	Todoros Rizali	Yani Nemayis
Dimitri birāẕer-i o	Yani Rizali	Niḳola birāẕer-i o	Niḳola Ġoloziti	Yani İvlaşi
Andriya İvlaşi	İstilyano Peliḳano	Dimitri Peliḳano	Dimitri veled-i o	İstemati Peliḳano
Manol veled-i o	Todoros veled-i o	Pavlos İstefanoplo	[P]apas İstemad veled-i o	Andriya veled-i o
Ḳosta İstefanoplo	Dimitri İstefanoplo	Andriya Farferi	Yani Turtuli	Papamiḫal Çerina
Andriya veled-i o	Yani Çerina	Todoros Lonbardi	Niḳola Martaniḳo	Yani birāder-i o
Miḫal birāder-i o	Andriya Martaniḳo	İvrato İstefanoplo	Dimitri Trağanisti	Miḫal Ġavril
Yorgi veled-i o	Yorgi Mancaniti	Todoros Larẓomeno	Yorgi <Ḳ>lo[k]inyoti	Lazaro birāder-i o
İstefano birāder-i o	Papas Franḳoyani	Miḫal veled-i o	Aleksi Ḳatrivili	Yani Ḳartilas
Papas Yorgi	Dimitri veled-i o	Todoros veled-i o	Andriya Ḳartelya	Yani Ḫaralanbi

62

tetimme-i ḳarye-i Ḳulukina el-mezḳūr [ḫ]āṣṣa-ı Paşa

İvrato Zemenaḳo	Miḫal Zemenaḳo	Niḳola veled-i o	Yorgi Salivara	Di[m]itri birāder-i o
Miḫal birāder-i o	Protopapas Ḫaralanbi	Todoros Ḫarkâs	Yani birāder-i o	Andriya birāder-i o
Yani Larẓameno	Adnriya İstefanoplo	Yani İsfoniḳoplo	Papamiḫal birāẕer-i o	Dimitri [dāmā]d-ı o
Miḫal Ḳuzuḫo	Nikiforo Ḳuzuḫo	Niḳola Ḳuzuḫo	T[o]doros birāder-i o	To[do]ros Sa[va]llyos
Niḳola Saḫniḳa	Yani veled-i o	Dimitri Tartari	İstemad [Ta]rtari	Yani Çanḳari
İstefano Ḫarköplos	Yani Pozariça	Miḫal Ḫarköplos	İstemati birāẕer-i o	Yani Ḫarköplos
Ḳosta dāmād-ı o	Todoros Pozariça	Yani birāder-i o	Miḫal ḫīş-i o	Yani Ḳostoplo
Niḳola birāder-i o	Dimitri İksanoplo	Aleksi birāẕer-i o	Miḫal Ġunari	Gin Ġunari
Yorgi Ġunari	Miḫal veled-i o	Yani Ḳasuro	Yorg[i] Ġunari	Yani birāder-i o
İstilyano Ġunari	Lazaro Ġunari	Argiti Damoniça	Ṣot[o]ki [R]ofi[ya]	Andriya Turtuli
Papas Dimitri Ḳonco	Yorgi veled-i o	Tavulari Ḳumanos	İstef[a]no birāẕer-i o	Miḫal Romanos
Yani Papaniḳola	Todoros Tremulas	Niḳolas birāder-i o	Dimitr[i] birāẕer-i o	Dimit[r]i İstaḫtiya

Andriya dāmād-ı o	Ḳosta Maḳris	Todoros Ḳumanos	Todoros Rukunas	İvratos Pisyanos
Pulimenos Pisyanos	İstilyano Pisyanos	Niḳola İsḳonco	[Yor]gi Ḳuvari	Todoros Ġavrili
Todoros Ġavrili-i dīğer	Manol Ḳuzuḫo	Niḳola Laġopati	Yani Ġ[uz]inos	Sotoki Zan[be]li
İstefano birāder-i o	Yorgi Zanbeli	Yorgi Yiromiḫalo	[Yor]gi Çuḳala	Yorgi Liḳovuni
İstemati Baltiniḳo	Yorgi Sanbati	Niḳola Saḫniḳa	İstefano yeñiçeri	Ḳosta Pozariçi
İstilyano Ḳostoplo	Yorgi Ḳostoplo	Yani Ḳoncos	Papa[s] Ġol[oz]iti	Dimitri Rofiya

63

tetimme-i [ḳa]rye-i [Ḳu]lukina el-mezḳūr — ḫāṣṣa-ı Paşa

Papas Yorg[i] Ḳumen[o]	Todoros Selato	İstemad İvlaşi	mücerred Manol İvlaşi	mücerred İstilyano İvlaşi
mücerred Va[şı]l Peliḳan[o]	mücerred [Ya]ni İstefanoplo	mücerred Niḳola Çerina	mücerred Andriya Traġanisti	mücerred Niḳola Mancaniti
mücerred And-roniḳo Fra[nḳo]-yani	mücerred Niḳola veled-i Papayorgi	mücerred İstefano İsfoniḳoplo	mücerred İstemad Ḳuzuḫo	mücerred Aleksi Ḳ[u]zuḫo
mücerred Asanas Ḳuzuḫo	mücerred Yani [S]azinos	mücerred Yorgi Saḫniḳo	mücerred Todoros veled-i Ḳosta	mücerred Dimitri Ḳostoplo
mücerred Andriya veled-i Papadimitri Ḳonco	mücerred Yani Ḳumanos	mücerred İstemad Ḳumanos	mücerred Yani Tremulas	mücerred İvratos Ḳondos
mücerred Yani Pisyanos	mücerred Manol Ḳuvari	mücerred İstefano Laġopati	mücerred Dimitri Ġuzinos	mücerred İstemad Zanbali
mücerred [P]avlos İsfoniḳoplos	mücerred İstilyano Ḳartilas	bīve Ḳariḳotepina	bīve Niforya	bīve İstefano-pulina

ḫāne	mücerred	bīve	aġnām
148	29	3	95

ḥāṣıl 16382

ʿa(n) ispence	eşcār-ı ṭut-ı ḫāṣṣa ʿaded 202 [resm] 450	ʿöşr-i bāġāt	ʿöşr-i ḳazz	ʿöşr-i ḥınṭa	ʿöşr-i cev
444[3]		2224	4752	3200	486

ʿöşr-i meyve	resm-i ḫamr	ʿöşr-i kettān	mülk-i Papas Ḳartilas der ḳarye-i mezḳūr āsiyāb 1 resm 80	mülk-i Yani Çanḳari der ḳarye-i mezḳūr āsiyāb 1 resm 80
17	350	100		

mülk-i mezḳūreyn āsiyāb 1 resm 80 minhā

mülk-i Yani Ḳostoplo der ḳarye-i mezḳūr āsiyāb 1 resm 80

mülk-i Dimitri Peliḳano der ḳarye-i mezḳūr āsiyāb 1 resm 40

ḥiṣṣe-i Ḳostandin Draḳouly[o] der ḳarye-i mezḳūr ṣülṣ 27

ḥiṣṣe-i İstefano Ḫarköplos der ḳarye-i mezḳūr ṣülṣān 53

ḳarye-i [Z]aruḫla — ḫāṣṣa-ı Paşa

İstemad Andriça	Yorgi Andriça	Dimitri veled-i o	Yorgi İsḳonco	Todoros Ḳoncos
Yani Simoplos	Todoros birāder-i o	İstemad Ḳoçilos	Yorgi birāder-i o	Yorgi Zaġaços
İste[m]ad [Pa]vloplos	mücerred Aleksi Andriça	mücerred Niḳola Simoplos	mücerred Todoros Ḳoçilos	mücerred Dimitri Ḳoçilos
mücerred Yani Pavloplos	bīve Miḫalina nifitu			

ḫāne	mücerred	bīve	aġnām
11	5	1	9

ḥāṣıl 1[7]08

ʿa(n) ispence	eşcār-ı ṭut-ı ḫāṣṣa ʿaded 130 [resm] 15[0]	ʿöşr-i bāġāt	ʿöşr-i ḥınṭa	ʿöşr-i cev	ʿöşr-i ḳazz	resm-i ḫanāzīr	ʿöşr-i meyve
406		200	400	[6]0	440	5	7

resm-i ḫamr	ʿöşr-i kettān
30	10

64
tetimme-i nāḥiyyet-i Voştiça

ḳarye-i Siyiniski ḫāṣṣa-ı Paşa

Dimitri Apostoloplos	Niḳola Melisa	Apostoli Apostoloplo	Yorgi Apostoloplo	Yani Apostoloplo
Papas Apostoloplo	Niḳola veled-i o	Yani Ḳoyaveli	Petros Ḳoyaveli	Yani A[me]triyoni
	İstaṣi	ḫāne 11	aġnām 16	

ḥāṣıl 1240

ʿa(n) ispence	ʿöşr-i bāġāt	ʿöşr-i ḥınṭa	ʿöşr-i cev	ʿöşr-i ḳazz	ʿöşr-i meyve	resm-i ḫamr	ʿöşr-i kettān
275	136	300	48	288	3	20	10

mülk-i Dimitri Apostoloplo der ḳarye-i mezḳūr āsiyāb 1 resm 80

mülk-i Papas Apostoloplo der ḳarye-i mezḳūr āsiyāb 1 resm 80

ḳarye-i Valimi ḫāṣṣa-ı Paşa

Yani Misriyos	Yorgi Misriyos	Todoros veled-i o	İstemad Misriyos	Ẓyaḳumis Seftaris
Dimitri Ḳutropahi	Nikifori Seftari	Pavlos veled-i o	Dimitri Ḫali	Todoros İst<a>rġari
Nikiforos birāder-i o	Papas Portari	Panḳal veled-i o	Yorgi Ḳanata	Todoros Ḫarköplos
Yani Melisa	Miḫal birāder-i o	Yani Portari	Yorgi birāder-i o	Todoros birāder-i o
Todoros Dabejyo	Miḫal birāder-i o	İstefanos İksanos	Niḳola Vurkiẓa	Ḳosta İstaroni
Niḳola Perniḳavlos	mücerred Yani İstarġari	mücerred Todoros Portari	mücerred Todoros Ḳanata	bīve İst<a>rġaru
	ḫāne 26	mücerred 3	bīve 1	

ḥāṣıl 2594

ʿa(n) ispence	ʿöşr-i bāġāt	ʿöşr-i ḥınṭa	ʿöşr-i cev	ʿöşr-i ḳazz	ʿöşr-i meyve	resm-i ḫamr
731	320	800	125	573	5	40

ḳarye-i Ayo Yorgi ḫāṣṣa-ı Paşa

Todoros Ayoyorgiti	Andriya Ayoyorgiti	Petros Ḫotemelos (?)	Miḫal Kipyoti	Ḫıristyano Kipyoti	
Niḳola Evstaroni	Ḳosta Ayoyorgiti	Apostolos birāder-i o	Papas Yorgi	Yani birāder-i o	
mücerred Yani Ayoyorgiti	mücerred Manol birāder-i Papas Yorgi	bīve Kipyotisa	bīve Pelyanina	ḫāne 10 bīve 2	mücerred 2 aġnām 40

ḥāṣıl 1090

ʿa(n) ispence	ʿöşr-i bāġāt	ʿöşr-i ḳazz	ʿöşr-i ḥınṭa	ʿöşr-i cev	resm-i ḫamr	ʿöşr-i meyve
312	96	315	300	48	15	4

65
tetimme-i nāḥiyyet-i Voştiça

ḳarye-i Ḫotoġosti ḫāṣṣa-ı Paşa

Angelos İsra[t]i	Niḳola İstefanoplo	Dimitri Ḳalamati	Andron birāder-i o	Ḳosta Pavloplo
Yani birā[d]er-i o	Todo[r]os Pavloplos	Yorgi Niḳoloġo	Yani İstefanoplos	İstaniṣa Mazaraki
mücerred Miḫal veled-i o	mücerred Andon Ḳalamati	mücerred Todoros Niḳoloġo	ḫāne 10	mücerred 3 aġnām 39

ḥāṣıl 1096

ʿa(n) ispence	ʿöşr-i bāġāt	ʿöşr-i ḥınṭa	ʿöşr-i cev	ʿöşr-i ḳazz	ʿöşr-i meyve	resm-i ḫamr
325	152	250	40	308	1	20

ḳarye-i Lovoḳa ḫāṣṣa-ı Paşa

Niḳola Papaẓaplo	Todoros birāẓer-i o	Papas Papaẓaplo	Yorgi veled-i o	Yani veled-i o
Yani Papaẓaplo	Aleksi Papaẓaplo	İstemad Papaẓaplo	Aleksi Ḫarköplos	Manol Zatuniti
Yani veled-i o	Yorgi veled-i o	Niḳola veled-i o	Yani Ḳasiḳura	Niḳola birāder-i o
Ṣomas Ḳasiḳura	Yani birāder-i o	Dimitri Rovoplo	Todoros birāder-i o	İstemad Piroplo
Yorgi Ḳolovari	Yani veled-i o	Dimitri veled-i o	Niḳola veled-i o	Niḳola Ḳolovari

mücerred Niḳola Papaẕaplo	mücerred Niḳola-<yı> dīğer Papaẕaplo	mücerred Ḳosta Zatuniti	mücerred Yani Rovoplo	ḫāne [2]5	mücerred 4 aġnām 67

ḥāṣıl 2491

ʿa(n) ispence 725	nıṣf-ı āsiyāb-ı ḫāṣṣa 2 [resm] 200	ʿöşr-i bāġāt 272	ʿöşr-i ḥınṭa 600	ʿöşr-i cev 93	ʿöşr-i ḳazz 561	resm-i ḫamr 40

ḳarye-i Virastova ḫāṣṣa-ı Paşa

Manol Maruli	Yani Ḳalyoris	Yorgi Mastroḳosta	Papas Miḫal	İstefano Mastroḳosta	
Yorgi Politi	Niḳola Ḫarköplos	Yani Mavroplo	Ḳosta Ḳ[ondo]- stemati	İstemati Andonoplo	
mücerred Ḳosta Maruli	mücerred Todo[ro]s birāder-i [Yani] Ḳalyoris	mücerred Yani Soropi	mücerred Ḳosta [Ma]vroplo	ḫāne 10	mücerred 4 aġnām 30

ḥāṣıl 1388

ʿa(n) ispence 350	eşcār-ı ṭut-ı ḫāṣṣa ʿaded 180 [resm] 300	ʿöşr-i bāġāt 128	ʿöşr-i ḳazz 360	ʿöşr-i ḥınṭa 200	ʿöşr-i cev 32	ʿöşr-i meyve 8
			resm-i ḫamr 10			

66

tetimme-i nāḥiyyet-i Voştiça

ḳarye-i Cilardi ḫāṣṣa-ı Paşa

Todoros Cilardi	Yani Mastrolyo	Yorgi Mas[t]rolyo	Todoros Mas[t]rolyo	Dimitri [S]erya[n]o	
mücerred Dimitri Cilardi	mücerred Todoros Seryanos	bīve Cilardu	[ḫ]āne 5	mücerred 2 aġnām 16	bīve 1

ḥāṣıl 391

ʿa(n) ispence 181	ʿöşr-i ḥınṭa 100	ʿöşr-i cev 16	ʿöşr-i ḳazz 60	ʿöşr-i bāġāt 32	ʿöşr-i [me]yve 2

ḳarye-i Vela ḫāṣṣa-ı Paşa

İstemad Laḳasa	Yani birāder-i o	İstefanos Ḫarköplos	Niḳola Foti	Yani İpsasino
Ḳosta Ṣoma	Papas Ḫarköplos	Yorgi Papaẕoplo	Niḳola birāẕer-i o	Papas Suḫina
Ḳosta Maḳris	Manol Maḳris	Yorgi Turḫa	Aleksi Turḫa	Niḳola Corḫo
Yani Rodoḳsla- vos[41]	Miḫal Ṣomas	Niḳola Ṣomas	İstemati Ṣoma	Yani Prosopa
Yorgi Vaşılas	Yani Vaşılas	İstemad birāẕer-i o	Yorgi birāder-i o	mücerred Yani Çorḫo
mücerred Dimitri Papaẕaplo	mücerred Miḫal Façi	mücerred Yani Ṣomas	mücerred Todoros Ṣomas	mücerred Niḳola Vaşılas
bīve Laḳasu	bīve Çorḫu	ḫāne 24	mücerred 6 aġnām 111	bīve 2

ḥāṣıl 2906

ʿa(n) ispence 762	ʿöşr-i ḥınṭa 1500	ʿöşr-i cev 226	ʿöşr-i bāġāt 304	ʿöşr-i ḳazz 66	ʿöşr-i meyve 5	resm-i ḫanāzīr [3]
			resm-i ḫamr 40			

ḳarye-i Sinoviro ḫāṣṣa-ı Paşa

Niḳola İlyoplo	Dimitri İlyoplo	İstini[42] Çarḫoplo	Yani Bala[n]iḳo	Niḳola Ḳaçanos
Miḫal Samula	Ṣotoki Samula	Dimitri Ḳoraḳa	Yani Pastriḳo	bīve [zen-i] Yorgi Ṣamula
bīve Mastroyana		ḫāne 9	bīve 2	aġnām 6

ḥāṣıl 1120

ʿa(n) ispence 237	ʿöşr-i ḥınṭa 300	ʿöşr-i cev 48	ʿöşr-i bāġāt 208	ʿöşr-i ḳazz 279	ʿöşr-i meyve [6]	ʿöşr-i zeyt 10

resm-i ḫanāzīr	resm-i ḫamr
2	30

67
tetimme-i nāḫiyyet-i Voştiça

ḳarye-i Pla[şa ez] cemāʿat-i Arnavudān ḫāṣṣa-ı Paşa

Gön Plaşa	Miḫal Plaş[a]	Yorgi Plaşa	İvrato Plaşa	Pranci Ḳalanci
Yorgi veled-i o	Andriya veled-i o	Lazaro Ḳalanci	Bardi Ḳalanci	Gön Ḳalanci
		ḫāne 10	aġnām 17	

ḥāṣıl 608

ʿa(n) ispence	ʿöşr-i ḥınṭa	ʿöşr-i cev	ʿöşr-i ḳazz
200	350	55	3

ḳarye-i Maneşi ez cemāʿat-i Arnavudān ḫāṣṣa-ı Paşa

Gön Manesi	Yorgi Aġali	Gin Arfa	Dima Arfa	ḫāne 4 aġnām 35

ḥāṣıl 196

ʿa(n) ispence	ʿöşr-i ḥınṭa	ʿöşr-i cev
80	100	16

ḳarye-i Arfara ez cemāʿat-i Arnavudān ḫāṣṣa-ı Paşa

Gin Arfara	Todoros Arfara	Bardi Arfara	Niḳola Arfara	Gin Laluza
Niḳola Mavrasi	Ḳosta Mavrasi	İstoyḳa Mavrasi	mücerred Yorgi Arfara	ḫāne 8 mücerred 1 aġnām 118

ḥāṣıl 526

ʿa(n) ispence	ʿöşr-i ḥınṭa	ʿöşr-i cev
180	300	46

ḳarye-i Verġuviça ḫāṣṣa-ı Paşa

Yani Kilari	Niḳola İzviroplo	Todoros birāder-i o	Aleksi Aryo	[Ya]ni İsḳano
Miḫal Ḳavalariçi	Yorgi birāder-i o	Yorgi Aryo	Niḳolas Aryo	Yani birāẕer-i o
Ḳosta Suruline	Yorgi Leftari	bīve Pelarina	ḫāne 12	bīve 1

ḥāṣıl 911

ʿa(n) ispence	ʿöşr-i ḥınṭa	ʿöşr-i cev	ʿöşr-i meyve	ʿöşr-i bāġāt	ʿöşr-i ḳazz	resm-i ḫamr
306	300	48	3	136	108	10

68
tetimme-i nāḫiyyet-i Voştiça

ḳarye-i Selyana ḫāṣṣa-ı Paşa

Yorgi Ġularmo	Simos dāmād-ı o	Niḳola Vunari	Papas Aleksi	Yani Ġurnari dāmād-ı o
Androni Franḳuli	Todoros birāder-i o	Dimitri Ḳolokiṣa	Ṣotoki Ḳaponoloġo	Yani birāẕer-i o
Ṣotoki Maḳris	İstemad Ḳoçilo	Ḳosta Alifoyeni	Todoros Varis	Yorgi Ḳolokiṣa
Miḫal birāẕer-i o	Dimitri Afrati	Ṣotoki Afrati	Yorgi Ġunari	Miḫal birāẕer-i o
Aleksi Kolokiṣa	Yorgi birāder-i o	Yani Ḳalapoẕi	Miḫal veled-i o	Todoros Niḳoloġos
Andriya veled-i o	İvrano Andruşi	mücerred Yani Vunari	mücerred Miḫal Ḳolokiṣa	bīve Ḳolokiṣu
bīve [zen-i] Ḳosta Ġunari	ḫāne 27	mücerred 2	bīve 2	aġnām 26

ḥāṣıl 2858

ʿa(n) ispence	ʿöşr-i ḳazz	ʿöşr-i ḥınṭa	ʿöşr-i cev	ʿöşr-i bāġāt	ʿöşr-i meyve	resm-i ḫamr
737	738	900	139	256	8	40

mülk-i
Ṣotoki Ḳaponoloġo der ḳarye-i
meẕkūr
āsiyāb 1 resm 40

ḳarye-i Perisori — ḫāṣṣa-ı Paşa

Miḫal Aḳrati	Dima Beluşi	Andriya Turnari	İstemati İsḳano	İstemati Aryo
İvrato ḫīş-i o	İstemad Fağa	Todoros veled-i o	Niḳola İksipolito	Todoros birāẕer-i o
Miḫal Prezvitereplo	Yorgi İstringiça	Aleksi İstringiça	Todoros dāmād-ı o	Andriya Suḳara
Yorgi veled-i o	İstemad veled-i o	Dimitri Suḳara	Niḳola birāẕer-i o	Miḫal birāẕer-i o
Niḳola Ḳarfi	Dimitri Ḳarfi	Aleksi Ḳarfi	İvrato Siẕeroḳastro	Todoros Patrinos
Dimitri Ġariyo	Todoros Aḳrati	Yorgi birāẕer-i o	Pavlos birāder-i o	Yani Polisḳa
Miḫal birāẕer-i o	Niḳola birāẕer-i o	Ḳosta birāẕer-i o	Miḫal Kârvela	Androni İksanoplo

69

tetimme-i ḳarye-i Perisori el-meẕkūr — ḫāṣṣa-ı Paşa

İstemati [.².]kerma	Yorgi İstringiça	Niḳola birāẕer-i o	Todoros As̲anas	Yani Plis̲aki
Dimitri birāder-i o	Yorgi Pastriḳo	Miḫal Ġavrili	Papatodoros Franḳos	Pavlos veled-i o
Yani veled-i o	Yani Zağranbi	mücerred İstemad Turnari	mücerred Miḫal İksipolito	mücerred Niḳola [P]irezvitereplo
mücerred Yorgi Ya[t]ro[s]	mücerred Yorgi Polisḳa	mücerred Todoros İstringiça	mücerred Andriya As̲anas	mücerred Pavlos Pastriḳo

mücerred Niḳola Ġavrili	mücerred Dimitri veled-i Papatodor Franḳo	bīve Malina	bīve Ḳarfina	ḫāne 47 bīve 2	mücerred 10 ağnām 40

ḥāṣıl 4325

ʿa(n) ispence	ʿöşr-i bāğāt	ʿöşr-i ḳazz	ʿöşr-i ḥınṭa	ʿöşr-i cev	ʿöşr-i meyve selās̲e	resm-i ḫāmr
1437	432	663	1500	230	60	60

ḳarye-i İvlaḫo ez cemāʿat-i Arnavudān — ḫāṣṣa-ı Paşa

Lazaro İskâẕa	Yorgi Vorila	Niḳola birāẕer-i o	Niḳola Zupano	Todoros İskâẕa
Dimitri İskâẕa	Manḳola Maji	Ḳosta Vaşıl	Leḳa Deluşi	mücerred Todoros Vorila

bīve	ḫāne	mücerred	bīve	ağnām
Deluşina	9	1	1	79

ḥāṣıl 449

ʿa(n) ispence	ʿöşr-i ḥınṭa	ʿöşr-i cev	resm-i ḫanāzīr	ʿöşr-i kettān
206	200	31	2	10

ḳarye-i Raḫova — ḫāṣṣa-ı Paşa

Yorgi Franḳos	Yorgi Vari	Dimitri veled-i o	Aleksi veled-i o	Todoros Tefitoplos
Yani veled-i o	Dimitri İstrati	Yorgi birāder-i o	Andriya Ḳondarelo	Todoros birāder-i o
Ḳosta Sarḫani	Todoros veled-i o	Ḳosta Maḳris	Yorgi Plastara	Todoros birāder-i o
Yorgi Maḳri	Miḫal Maḳri	Ḳosta dāmād-ı Seravanye	Dimitri Seravano	Todoros Maḳris
Niḳola birāẕer-i o	Niḳola Maḳris	Yani İstrağaniti	Todoros Riğotis	Papas İstemati İzğoti
Yani Ziğoti	Papaniḳola Ziğoti	Yani Ḳorfiri	Yani İsḳarpeti	Miḫal İsḳarpeti

70

tetimme-i ḳarye-i Raḫova el-meẕkūr — ḫāṣṣa-ı Paşa

Aleksi İsḳarpeti	Dimitri veled-i o	Nikifor İsḳarpeti	Yani İsḳarpeti	Todoros İsḳarpeti
Niḳola Çimina	Yani birāder-i o	Yorgi Çimina	Yani veled-i o	Andriya Simos
Ḳosta Provireti	Yani Provireti	Miḫal birāder-i o	Niḳola birāder-i o	Yani Ḳarẕara
Yorgi Ḳarẕara	Yani Ağuzimos	Yorgi veled-i o	Ḳosta veled-i o	Niḳola Ḳardarya
Miḫal birāder-i o	Yani birāẕer-i o	Dimitri ḫīş-i Ḳardasa	Yorgi Ḳondopoẕi	Ḫaralanbi Rupiya
Papas Manol dāmād-ı o	Dimitri Boliçi	Yorgi birāder-i o	Ḳosta birāder-i o	Niḳola Rupiya
Niḳola İstefanoplo	Yorgi Ḳarderya	mücerred Todoros Franḳos	mücerred Yani Vari	mücerred Ḳosta İskaẕo
mücerred Yani Androniya	mücerred Petros İstrati	mücerred Ḳosta Ḳondarelo	mücerred Niḳola Sarḫani	mücerred Niḳola Aleksi Fağura

mücerred Yani Fağura	mücerred Yorgi birâder-i o	mücerred Dimitri Maḳri	mücerred Yani Maḳris	mücerred Yani Maḳri-i dīğer
mücerred Yani Seravano	mücerred İstemad Maḳris	mücerred Yani Maḳris	mücerred Yorgi Riġotis	mücerred Miḫal İzġoti
mücerred Dimitri Ziġoti	mücerred Miḫal birâder-i o	mücerred Niḳola Ziġoti	mücerred Todoros Ziġoti	mücerred Todoros Ḳorfiri
mücerred Aleksi İsḳarpeti	mücerred Nikifor İsḳarpeti	mücerred Yorgi Çimina	mücerred Niḳola Çimina	mücerred Miḫal Simos
mücerred Dimitri Çanḳari	mücerred Yorgi birāẕer-i o	mücerred Yorgi Ḳardasa	mücerred Niḳola Ḳondopoẕi	mücerred Yani Rupiya
mücerred Niḳola birāẕer-i o	mücerred Yani İstefanaplo	bīve İskâẕu	bīve Androniya	bīve [zen-i] Aleksi Fağura
bīve Seravaniya	bīve Dimitro Maḳri	bīve [zen-i] Yorgo Ziġoti	bīve Miḫaliya Çimyona	bīve Simyosa

bīve [zen-i] Niḳola Çanḳariya	bīve Ḳardasa	bīve Rupiya	ḫāne 62	mücerred 35	bīve 11	agnām 32

ḥāṣıl 9596

ʿa(n) ispence	ʿöşr-i bāġāt	ʿöşr-i ḳazz	ʿöşr-i ḥınṭa	ʿöşr-i cev	ʿöşr-i meyve	resm-i ḫāmr
2491	944	1827	3600	546	8	140

mülk-i
Yani Aġuẕimos der ḳarye-i
meẕkūr
āsiyāb 1 resm 40

71
tetimme-i nāḥiyyet-i Voştiça

ḳarye-i Zaḫoli ḫāṣṣa-ı Paşa

Yani Rakâs	İstemad birāẕer-i o	İsparçi Niḳola	Aleksi Erimoḫori	Todoros Mavroplos
Yani birâder-i o	Niḳola birāẕer-i o	Yani Ḳaryona	İvrato İpsavuẕaki	Todoros Ġavril
Ḳosta Ġurya	Petros Ġurya	Todoros Ġuryas	Manol veled-i o	Yorgi Ġavrili
İsḳalça Ḫartofiliḳa[43]	Miḫal veled-i o	Aleksi veled-i o	As̱anas Ḳuselos	Niḳola birâder-i o
Yani veled-i o	Todoros Ḳorfiri	Miḫal veled-i o	Andriya birâder-i o	Protoyeros Ḳoḫnyoti
Todoros Ḳoḫnyoti	Dimitri veled-i o	Niḳola Ḳoḫnyoti	Aleksi Mamona	Yani Ḳrokiẕa
Todoros Ḳatifora	Niḳola birâder-i o	Manol birâder-i o	Miḫal İpsasinos	Andriya Ġramatiḳoplos
Todoros Ḳılinsos	Yorgi İpsasino	Todoros veled-i o	Yorgi Layiniḳas	Miḫal Ḳuni
Dimitri birâder-i o	Yani Ḳondoplo	Yorgi birâder-i o	Yorgi Rendinos	S̱otoki İsḳarmiköti
Apostolo Maramas̱a	Niḳola birâder-i o	Yani Lusi	Miḫal birâder-i o	Aleksi veled-i o
Papas Ẕikeos	Yani veled-i o	Yorgi Fiẕaki	S̱otoki Amuri	Yorgi veled-i o
Niḳola Monavasyoti	Yorgi birâder-i o	Ḳosta Ḳaḳoġnomo	Yani Manyati	Papas Miḫal Foti
Yani veled-i o	Papas Yani Foti	Yorgi Açiviri	Angelos Açiviris	Yani birâder-i o
S̱otoki Açiviri	Niḳola Açiviri	Niḳola Kliẕaki	Ḳosta Riẕali	Petros veled-i o
Dimitri Ḳrava	S̱otoki İksanomila	Yani birâder-i o	İstemati Ġurya	Dimitri Tomas
Ḳozma Ayiri	Todoros Leftaris	Yorgi birâder-i o	Yani Muzalo	Yorgi İsḳarmiköti
Miḫal İsḳarmiköti	Ẕyaḳos Manyati	İstemati Ġramatiḳoplo	Miḫal Ḫalke	Miḫal Fağrasi

72
tetimme-i ḳarye-i Zaḫoli el-meẕkūr ḫāṣṣa-ı Paşa

Yani Ḳrokiẕa	Yorgi Liġuroplo	Andriya Ḳuni	Andriya Milona	Yorgi İğliġoroplo
Ḳosta Ḳravas	mücerred Yorgi Rakâs	mücerred Yani Ḫarkâs	mücerred Andriya Ḳuşyoti	mücerred Miḫal Ġramatiḳoplo
mücerred Miḫal Fiẕaki	mücerred Yani Amuri	mücerred Manol Liġuroplo	mücerred Miḫal birâder-i o	bīve Mastroaleksiya

bīve	bīve	bīve	bīve	[ḫā]ne	mücerred
Liḳuẕu	Manyatu	Ḳrokiẕa	İsḳarmikö-ti[s]a	91	8
				bīve	aġnām
				5	86

ḥāṣıl 8970

ʿa(n) ispence	ʿöşr-i bāġāt	ʿöşr-i ḳazz	ʿöşr-i ḥınṭa	ʿöşr-i cev	ʿöşr-i meyve	ʿöşr-i zeyt
2505	1408	2052	2300	347	4	4

resm-i ḫāmr	mülk-i Todoros Mavroplos der ḳarye-i meẕkūr	mülk-i İsḳalça Ḫartofilaḳa der ḳarye-i meẕkūr	mülk-i Aṣanas Ḳuselos der ḳarye-i meẕkūr
150	āsiyāb 1 resm 40	āsiyāb 1 resm 80	āsiyāb 1 resm 80

ḳarye-i Yelini — ḫāṣṣa-ı Paşa

Angelos İsḳarmiköti	Manṣos İsḳarmiköti	Todoros Plastara	Yorgi Marḳuri	Petros Ġraveli
Yani Varda	Yorgi Lipsoẕuri	Todoros Lipsoẕuri	Yani İsparçi	Petros Ḳalimani
Aleksi İspartino	Miḫal İspartino	Yani Radosḳlavos	Ḳosta Maẕiñik	Dimitri İsḳarmiköti

ḫāne 15

ḥāṣıl 1360

ʿa(n) ispence	ʿöşr-i bāġāt	ʿöşr-i ḥınṭa	ʿöşr-i cev	ʿöşr-i ḳazz	resm-i ḫāmr
375	192	300	48	180	25

mülk-i Angelos İsḳarmiköti der ḳarye-i meẕkūr	mülk-i Manol İsḳarmiköti Voştiçaʾi	mülk-i Dimo İsḳarmiköti Voştiçaʾi
āsiyāb 1 resm 80	āsiyāb 1 resm 80	āsiyāb 1 resm 80

ḳarye-i Zepandi ez cemāʿat-i Arnavudān — ḫāṣṣa-ı Paşa

Leḳa Zepandi	Yorgi birāder-i o	Todoros Enbuzis	Amrados Enbuzis	İstoyan Servos
Yorgi veled-i o	Yani veled-i o	Dima İvlaḫo	Miḫal birāder-i o	ḫāne 9
				aġnām 200

ḥāṣıl 583

ʿa(n) ispence	ʿöşr-i ḥınṭa	ʿöşr-i cev
180	350	53

mezraʿa-ı Ḳumaniçi Luzi nezd-i ḳarye-i Zepandi el-meẕkūr

ḫāṣṣa-ı Paşa — ḫāliyye

73
tetimme-i nāḥiyyet-i Voştiça

ḳarye-i [S]oḫyana ez cemāʿat-i Arnavudān — ḫāṣṣa-ı Paşa

Dimitri İsḳarmiköti	Niḳola İsḳarmiköti	Yorgi İsḳarmiköti	Yorgi Lapsana	ḫāne 4

ḥāṣıl 292

ʿa(n) ispe[n]ce	ʿöşr-i bāġāt	ʿöşr-i ḳazz	ʿöşr-i ḥınṭa	ʿöşr-i cev
80	72	24	100	16

mezraʿa-ı [Pely]ura nezd-i ḳarye-i meẕkūr — ḫāṣṣa-ı Paşa — ḫāliyye

mezraʿa-ı Mayira nezd-i ḳarye-i meẕkūr ḫāṣṣa-ı Paşa — ḫāliyye

ḳarye-i Revaniça — ḫāṣṣa-ı Paşa

Miḫal İstaniça	Dimitri Suli	Mangişa Suli	Leḳa Nikita	Yani Ḳondepistino

ḫāne 5 — aġnām 85

ḥāṣıl 299

ʿa(n) ispe[n]ce	ʿöşr-i ḥınṭa	ʿöşr-i cev
125	150	24

ḳarye-i Poroviça ki beglik-i ṭuzcılardır — der ḫāṣṣa-ı Paşa

Petros Ẕiplopita	Miḫal veled-i o	Manol veled-i o	Yorgi veled-i o	Yani Namayi
Yani İsḳonco	Yorgi İsḳonco	Yorgi Ẕiplopita	İstemad Ḳromiẕi	Yani Liġuli
Yani Ḳramiẕi	Aleksi Aleksopulyo	Miḫal birāder-i o	Niḳola birāẕer-i o	Ḫıristodulos Ḳalamati
	Niḳola İksano	ḫāne 16	aġnām 90	

ḥāṣıl ġayr ez memlaḥa 936

ʿa(n) ispence	ʿöşr-i bāġāt	ʿöşr-i ḳazz	ʿöşr-i ḥınṭa	ʿöşr-i cev	resm-i ḫāmr
400	128	42	300	46	20

muḳāṭaʿa-ı memlaḥa der ḳarye-i mez̲kūr ki ḫāṣṣa ḫullide mülkühu şüd

ġayr ez maḥṣūlāt-ı ṭuzciyān fī sene sitte ʿaşere elfen ve erbaʿa ve sittūn

74

cemʿan ḫāṣṣhā-<yı> Ḥażret-i Paşa dāme ʿalāhu

ḳurā	mezāriʿ-i ḫāliyye	ḫāne	mücerred	bīve
67	4	1529	265	91

ḥāṣıl ġayr ez memlaḥa ki der bālā z̲ikr reft ve resm-i aġnām

fī sene 160459

aġnām

sitte ālāf ve erbaʿamiʾe ve sitte ve sittūn resā

minhā

resm-i her ḫamsūn resā fī

reʾs miʾe ve tisʿa ve ʿişrūn resā ve naḳd 3

her reʾs fī s̲emāniye elf ve is̲nān ve s̲elās̲ūn

yekūn elf ve ḫamse ve s̲elās̲ūn

el-cümletān 161494

75 blank

76

kendü bürüme	geçim tisʿa	cebelü tisʿūn	günlük 2	çadır maʿa soḳaḳ ve ābrīz	ḫazīne 1	kilar 1	maṭbaḫ 1	serrāc-ḫāne 1

ḫāṣṣhā-<yı> Sinān Beg bin Elvān Beg mīrlivāʾ-ı vilāyet-i Mora

nefs-i Ḫulumiç ḫāṣṣa-ı mīrlivā

mahalle-i Nikifor Ḳavasila[44]

Nikifor el-mez̲kūr	Venyami Filipo	Andriya İksand-[em]ali	Franḳo Ḳoryalisa	Cani Pinaḳa
Z̲anyas Kefalinos	Dimitri Ḳatrava	S̲omas Ḳatrava	Venyami Çanḳareplo	And[o]n As̲uli
Manḳola Andonalo	Yani Velayiti	Dimitri Ḫalvanos	Papas Andriyas	Manol Venaloplo
Niḳola Yaverḳo	Dimitri İksunoroz̲i	Petros Aṣuli	Niḳola Kefalino	Andon Yorġaki
Yorgi Ḫıristiyano	Dimitri Mavroplo	İstemati Pendaḳla	İstas̲i Petrili	Papayorgi Viraḫno
Todoro Ḳalaġri	Andriya Çanḳareplo	Yaḳumelo birāder-i o	Ḳosta Ḳaloviçi	Marḳo S̲emali
Ḳuvara Mazaraki	Yaḳovo Yaleş	Miḫal Eksovunyoti	Yani Eksovunyoti	Andriya Çanḳareplo
Andon S̲arapemeno	Bardi Buryasi	İġliġori Panḳrati	Yani Todoryas	Yani Ḳıremiz̲i
Dimitri Ḳandruço	Yorgi Ḳaliroplo	Yani İsḳlavos	Yani Yohoryari	Ando-nilo
İstematalo Nani	Andon Rinoplo	Miḫal ḫīş-i o	Franceşḳo Mastroḳosto-plo	Manol Mamo[na]
mücerred Manḳolas Ronberto	mücerred Andon Venyami	mücerred Petro Pinaḳa	mücerred S̲oma Pendaḳla	mücerred Petro Mazaraki
mücerred Yani Ḳaliviçi	mücerred Yani Andonilo		ḫāne 50	mücerred 7

mahalle-i Miḫal Yanḳuri

Miḫal el-mez̲kūr	Yani Nikita	S̲oma Delaṣula	Yorgi Pulyaz̲a	Niḳola Papaḳ[o]zma
Dobro Sirvos	Yani La[z]aroplo	Niḳola Aḳsindamali	Yani İpṣomaki	Dimitri Ḳardiḳafti
Aleksi İsḳarcinyoti	Leḳa İşpata	Petro Tolo	Perardo Iştaki	Mastroyorgi Ḫarkâ

77

tetimme-i mahalle-i Miḫal Yanḳuri el-mez̲kūr der nefs-i Ḫulumiç

Manol Kendaḫro[45]	Niḳola Yumurilevi	Vars̲olemyo Vuçanos	Dimitri Ḳaliviça	Ḳosta Ḳaravulḳo
Yorgi Ḳanali	Yorgi Argiroplo	Petro Nikita	Andon Ḳanbaşi	Andriya Petros
Yani Işıḫari	Dimitri İstameni	Yorgi Petro	Todoros Meġaloyani	Yani Orfane
İvrato İsḳura	Petro Manesi	Yorgi Papaz̲at	İstas̲i Furnari	Ḳostandin birāz̲er-i o
Niḳola Mastromesari	Niḳola Pinaḳa	Niḳola Patrino	Kiryaki Kefalino	Dimitri Siriḳari
Dimitri Manyoti	Yani As̲anas	Ḳosta Covanali	Aleksi Mavromati	Yorgi Papaz̲oplo
Yani Ḳaliyor	Yani Maḳri	Yorgi Aramiçyoti	Miḫal Çanburli	Todoros Milonas

Proġono İsḳura	mücerred Yorgi Yanḳuri	mücerred Yorgi Furnari	mücerred Andriya Manyoti	mücerred Petro Çanburli
bīve Ata[46] zen-i Flomoto	bīve Ḳatarina zen-i Velayiti	bīve Ḳatarina zen-i Aleksoplo	bīve Todora zen-i Lanḳaẕitina	bīve Kirana zen-i İzyavol
bīve Marta zen-i Ḳonderata	bīve İstatira zen-i Yaḳumo	bīve Niḳoleta zen-i Andravişan	bīve Anuẕa zen-i İvlaş Mangepe	bīve Tomasa zen-i Ḳatalan
bīve [Ma]riya zen-i Ḳosta	bīve Mariya zen-i Yani	ḫāne 51	mücerred 4	bīve 12

cümletü'l-maḥalleteyni'l-meẕkūreteyn

ḫāne	mücerred	bīve
101	11	12

ḥāṣıl 19404

ʿa(n) ispence 2872	bāġçehā-<yı> türünc-i ḫāṣṣa 3 [resm] 450	muḳāṭaʿa-ı ṭalyan-ı ḫāṣṣa 1 [resm] 750	resm-i ıġrıb-ı māhī gīrān 450	resm-i bāzār ve niyābet 700	resm-i gümrük 1200

ʿöşr-i bāġāt 9350	ʿöşr-i ḥınṭa 2000	ʿöşr-i cev 323	ʿöşr-i meyve 95	ʿöşr-i zeyt 6	resm-i ḫanāzīr 28	resm-i ḫamr 650

ʿöşr-i [penbe] 200	ʿöşr-i kettān 200	mülk-i Yūsuf dizdār-ı ḳalʿa-ı Ḫulumiç āsiyāb 1 resm 40	mülk-i Yūsuf veled-i Şāhīn Dirāz ʿa(n) merdān-ı ḳalʿa-ı meẕkūr āsiyāb 1 resm 40

mülk-i
Ḳuvara Mazaraki
der maḥalle-i Nikifor Ḳavasila
el-meẕkūr
āsiyāb 1 resm 50

78
nāḥiyyet-i Ḫulumiç

ḳarye-i Ġastuni — ḫāṣṣa-ı Mīrlivā

Papas Todoros	Papayani veled-i o	Muriki Platistomo	Dimitri Vaşılopılo	Yani Vaşıl
Niḳola Vaşıl	Andriya Arhani	Yaḳumo Mavroplo	İstaẖi Pranḳari	Yani Pranḳari
Miḫal Mastro	Miḫal S̲erapemeno	Niḳola Argiro	Yani İstovilinos	Yorgi Dabiziva
Yani Mavruli	Dimitri Kendeluri	Yorgi Argiro	Todoro İst[o]yani	Dimitri Mangişa
Yorgi Marcelato	Miḫal Paḫiça	Manol Çorḳanos	Yorgi Liçiri	Dimitri Sinori
Manol Dobro	Todoros Aleksi	İstemad Tirpila	Todoros Maẕiris	Yorgi Ḳalaẕeti
Androni Varano	Yani Dermata	Todoro Marḳo	Todoro Romo	Todoros İbrayimis
Andriya Berdari	Todoros Berdaris	Gin Aleksi	Yani Ḳondos	Yorgi Papaẕato
Nestora Pernardo[47]	Todoros Pernardo[48]	Yani Mavromati	Yorgi Varipatis	Andon Vidos Vundelo
Dimitri Marcelato	Miḫal S̲ofilaḫto	Yorgi Raviẕa	Yorgi Viṣalas	Yorgi Andriçi
İstemad İğliġori	Todoros Filandros	Yani Ẕimitani	Andriya Argiro	Manol S̲ofilaḫto
Miḫal S̲ofilaḫto	Yorgi Filandro	İstemad Filandra	Todoros Filandros	Miḫal Malandari
Yorgi Vilardo	Dimitri Vilardo	Miḫal İksanos	Ḳosta [Ma]rcelato	mücerred Dimitri Miḫal Mastro
mücerred Yani Dabizyo	mücerred Yani Ḳalaẕeti	mücerred Yani Marḳo	mücerred Niḳola Romo	mücerred Niḳola Varipatis
mücerred Dimitri Raviẕa	mücerred Yorgi Malandar	mücerred Niḳola Perdarina	mücerred D[im]itri S[i]norina	bīve Rona zen-i Perdarina

bīve Todora zen-i Sinorina	bīve Mariya zen-i Tirpilina	bīve Evd[o]kiya zen-i [L]iḳuresina	ḫāne 64	mücerred 10	bīve 4

ḥāṣıl 6423

ʿa(n) ispence 1874	bāġāt-ı ḫāṣṣa dönüm 6 [resm] 720	ʿöşr-i penbe 100	ʿöşr-i kettān 200	ʿöşr-i ḥınṭa 3000	ʿöşr-i cev 465	ʿöşr-i bāġāt 32

resm-i ḫanāzīr 25	ʿöşr-i ʿasel 7

79
tetimme-i nāḥiyyet-i Ḫulumiç

mezraʿa-ı Potamya Şarandinu nezd-i ḳarye-i Ġastuni el-meẕkūr ḫāṣṣa-ı Mīrlivā

mezraʿa-ı Kiḫomiro nezd-i ḳarye-i meẕkūr

ḫāliyye ḫāṣṣa-ı Mīrlivā ḫāliyye

ḳarye-i Şavalya ḫāṣṣa-ı Mīrlivā

Yani Finiki	Yani Ḳraya	Miḫal Papaẕato	İlyas İsḳliva	Yorgi Ḳorbiya
Dimitri Ġavrili	Petro Beluşi	Dimitri Miraşoti	Miḫal Bezulḳa	Tonda Arḫondiçi
mücerred İvrato Ḳaliçotina	bīve Todora zen-i İfrati	bīve Mariya zen-i Ḳaliçotina	bīve Todora zen-i Arḫondiçina	ḫāne 10 mücerred 1 bīve selāse

ḥāṣıl 1906

ʿa(n) ispence	bāġāt-ı ḫāṣṣa	ʿöşr-i kettān	ʿöşr-i penbe	ʿöşr-i ḥınṭa	ʿöşr-i cev	resm-i ḫanāzīr
293	dönüm 6 [resm] 720	40	30	700	109	14

mezraʿa-ı İskliva nezd-i ḳarye-i Şavalya el-meẕkūr

ḫāṣṣa-ı Mīrlivā ḫāliyye

ḳarye-i Kelavi ḫāṣṣa-ı Mīrlivā

Miḫal Girḳa	İvlaş Evtuçis	Dima Meliġala	Yorgi Mavroplo	mücerred Yani Pikerna
bīve Skâva zen-i Pikerna			ḫāne 4	mücerred 1 bīve 1

ḥāṣıl 249

ʿa(n) ispence	ʿöşr-i ḥınṭa	ʿöşr-i cev	resm-i ḫanāzīr
131	100	16	2

mezraʿa-ı Sinasi nezd-i ḳarye-i Kelavi el-meẕkūr ḫāṣṣa-ı Mīrlivā

ḫāliyye

ḳarye-i Girḳa Ḳumani ez cemāʿat-i Arnavudān ḫāṣṣa-ı Mīrlivā

Gin Ḳumani	Niḳola Mazaraki	Gin veled-i o	Muriki Ḳumano	Yorgi Argiro
Andriya Burġaki	Yorgi Pilura	mücerred [Yo]rgi Ḳumani	mücerred Yorgi Ha[n]ari	mücerred Diyaleş Pilura

ḫāne 7 mücerred 3

ḥāṣıl 496

ʿa(n) ispence	ʿöşr-i ḥınṭa	ʿöşr-i cev	resm-i ḫanāzīr
200	200	31	65

80
tetimme-i nāḥiyyet-i Ḫulumiç

ḳarye-i Çavuşi ez cemāʿat-i Arnavudān ḫāṣṣa-ı Mīrlivā

Çavuş Majis	Gin Ḳalusi	Nikifor Bezulḳa	Leḳa Ḳalusi	Petro Andruli
Aleksi Zuġras	Gin Maji	bīve Kâna	ḫāne 7	bīve 1

ḥāṣıl 759

ʿa(n) ispence	ʿöşr-i ḥınṭa	ʿöşr-i cev	resm-i ḫanāzīr
146	500	73	40

ḳarye-i Ḳoḳla ez cemāʿat-i Arnavudān ḫāṣṣa-ı Mīrlivā

Gin Ḳoḳla	Gin Proġono	Reçi Proġono	Dimitri Simyoni	Gin Maji
Mengişa Ḳordesi	Yorgi Manḳola		ḫāne 7	

ḥāṣıl 396

ʿa(n) ispence	ʿöşr-i ḥınṭa	ʿöşr-i cev	resm-i ḫanāzīr
140	200	32	24

ḳarye-i Dramşa ez cemāʿat-i Arnavudān ḫāṣṣa-ı Mīrlivā

İstoya Dorja	Gin Dorja	Leḳa Dorja	Pavlos Barça	Todoros Zuġras

Niḳola Dorja	Gön Zuġras	Mengişa Barşi	Ḳondas Zuġras	Yorgi Dramse
Yani Mancoviti	Lazaro Dorja	Domeniḳa Dorja	Miḫal Varniḳa	Yorgi Barça
Niḳola Mamara	Domeniḳa Drapişe	Dimos Voyniḳa	Ḳaznas Proġono	Angelo Frati
		ḫāne 20		

ḥāṣıl 1193

ʿa(n) ispence 400	ʿöşr-i ḥınṭa 600	ʿöşr-i cev 96	resm-i ḫanāzīr 17	ʿöşr-i penbe 50	ʿöşr-i kettān 30

ḳarye-i Polesḳa ez cemāʿat-i Arnavudān ḫāṣṣa-ı Mīrlivā

Miḫa Ḳuçi	Yani Ḳataros	Miḫal Polesḳa	Dima Polesḳa		Marti Ḳoḳla
Aleksi Lulaki	mücerred Yorgi Ḳataros	mücerred Gin Polesḳa	bīve Kirana zen-i [V]odasi	ḫāne 6	mücerred 2
					bīve 1

ḥāṣıl 742

ʿa(n) ispence 166	ʿöşr-i ḥınṭa 500	ʿöşr-i cev 76

81

tetimme-i nāḥiyyet-i Ḫulumiç

ḳarye-i Ḳuçi ez cemāʿat-i Arnavudān ḫāṣṣa-ı Mīrlivā

Petro Ḳuçi	Niḳola Ḳoḳla	Gin Ḳoḳla	Yorgi Ranesi	ḫāne 4

ḥāṣıl 426

ʿa(n) ispence 80	ʿöşr-i ḥınṭa 300	ʿöşr-i cev 46

ḳarye-i Bavasi ez cemāʿat-i Arnavudān ḫāṣṣa-ı Mīrlivā

Yorgi Bavasi	Niḳola Bavasi	Gin Bavasi	Yorgi Ġruzumsa	bīve Martina zen-i Lanbetina

ḫāne 4	bīve 1

ḥāṣıl 318

ʿa(n) ispence 86	ʿöşr-i ḥınṭa 200	ʿöşr-i cev 32

ḳarye-i Ṣarakin ez cemāʿat-i Arnavudān ḫāṣṣa-ı Mīrlivā

Petro Ḳaliça	İştin Ġrapeşi	Gin Ġrapeşi	Todoro Vişa	Gin Şakeşi	
Lazaro Bala	Gön Maji	Andriya Ḫarmesi	bīve Elani zen-i Vişa	ḫāne 8	bīve 1

ḥāṣıl 668

ʿa(n) ispence 166	ʿöşr-i penbe 25	ʿöşr-i kettān 14	ʿöşr-i ḥınṭa 400	ʿöşr-i cev 63

ḳarye-i Zenbeş ez cemāʿat-i Arnavudān ḫāṣṣa-ı Mīrlivā

Andriya Zenbeş	Niḳola Tateşi	Pulimeno Ḳraḳuki	Andriya Mavriki	Leḳa Buzbardi
Lyo Vodila	Leḳa Ḫalanbraza	Laluçi Ḫalanbraza	Leḳa Varbesi	bīve Todora zen-i İsklizina
bīve Martina zen-i Zenbeş	bīve Mañḳa zen-i Buryalisa		ḫāne 9	bīve 3

ḥāṣıl 822

ʿa(n) ispence 198	ʿöşr-i penbe 25	ʿöşr-i kettān 20	ʿöşr-i ḥınṭa 500	ʿöşr-i cev 79

ḳarye-i Orfano ez cemāʿat-i Arnavudān ḫāṣṣa-ı Mīrlivā

Aleksi Orfano	Uzġura Buva	İstefano Barçi	Gin İflamura	Petro Buva
	bīve Giru	ḫāne 5	bīve 1	

ḥāṣıl 499

ʿa(n) ispence 106	ʿöşr-i penbe 25	ʿöşr-i kettān 20	ʿöşr-i ḥınṭa 300	ʿöşr-i cev 48

82

tetimme-i nāḥiyyet-i Ḫulumiç

ḳarye-i Ḳoromiẕi ez cemāʿat-i Arnavudān — ḫāṣṣa-ı Mīrlivā

Leḳa Ḳoromiẕi	Yorgi Sivasto	Yorgi İskâẕa	ḫāne 3

ḥāṣıl 257

ʿa(n) ispence 60	ʿöşr-i penbe 13	ʿöşr-i kettān 10	ʿöşr-i ḥınṭa 150	ʿöşr-i cev 24

yekūn-i ḫāṣṣhā-<yı> Mīrlivā der nāḥiyyet-i Ḫulumiç el-meẕkūr

ḳurā maʿa nefs-i Ḫulumiç 15	mezāriʿ-i ḫāliyye 4	ḫāne 259	mücerred 28	bīve 28

ḥāṣıl 34558

nefs-i Vumero — ḫāṣṣa-ı Mīrlivā

maḥalle-i Todoros Varirvi

Todoros el-meẕkūr	Papaniḳola veled-i o	Papas Livzota	Papayorgi veled-i o	Yani veled-i o
İstefano Marçavila	Yani birāder-i o	Yani Ḳoçiniẕa	Vardo Bastaido	İstemad dāmād-ı o
S̱oma Lisya	Ḳosta veled-i o	Yani Traġuẕi	Lyo birāẕer-i o	Papadimitri Bozan

83

tetimme-i maḥalle-i Todoros Varirvi el-meẕkūr — der nefs-i Vumero

Ḳosta veled-i o	Yorgi Zaviti	Yani Ḳaḳuri	Yorgi Niklöti	Ḳosta Foti
Ḳosta Fameliti	Papayorgi İġliġori	Niḳola Zeskeẕaplo	Dimitri veled-i o	Yani Fameliti
[M]arḳ[o] S̱imibile	Miḫal İstrati	Niḳola Leondoplo	Yani Varẕuvali	Lazar Ḫırisiḳo
Petr[o] birā-der-i o	Yorgi yeñiçe[r]i	Ḳalanci Ḳurto	Petro Siroviç	Ḳozma veled-i o
Yorgi veled-i o	Papas S̱otoki Ḳaḳotar	Papaniḳola Pozoḫtipa	Yani birāder-i o	Yorgi birāder-i o
Todoros birāder-i Īşān	Yani Platindro	Papayani Ḳaravakir	Papayani İstanilo	Papayorgi birāẕer-i o
Vaşıl Papayani	Miḫal Politi	Papas Dimitri	Yani Ḫarkâ	Ẕyaḳo Papaya-noplo
Yorgi birāder-i o	Yorgi Reveliti	Papas Niḳola Paço	Andriya Eraniti	İstefano veled-i o
Yorgi Manyoti	Yani Vumeriti	Miḫal Ḳoçanda	Dimitri birāder-i o	İstemad Ẕroḳadi
Dimitri Mala	Niḳola Renyari	S̱oma ḫīş-i o	Yani Ḳaloyirina	Yorgi Papa-yorġoplo
Niḳola birāder-i o	İstemad birāẕer-i o	Yorgi Varirvi	Ẕyaḳos Varirvi	[Pa]pas Manḳola
veled-i S̱oma Lesina	Yani Politi	Ẕyaḳo Politi	Todoros Lostos	Niḳola Proḳoçila
Andriya İstayḳo	Pasani İksanos	Proġonos Panareti	Yani Ḳaḳotar	Sotiri veled-i o
Yorgi veled-i o	mücerred Miḫal Ḳon-dosfondilo	mücerred Dimitri birāder-i o	mücerred Todoros Ḳaḳuri	mücerred Lazaro Foti
mücerred Yorgi Ḫırisiḳo	mücerred Dimitri Siroviç	mücerred Petros Ḳaḳotar	mücerred Miḫal Pozoḫtipa	mücerred Yani Papayorgi
mücerred Ḳosta Papayanoplo	mücerred Yorgi birāder-i Andriya Eranit	mücerred Yani Anulpisto	mücerred veled-i Yani Traġuẕi	mücerred veled-i Papas Niḳola

ḫāne 81	mücerred 14

84

tetimme-i [nef]s-i Vumero el-meẕkūr — ḫāṣṣa-ı Mīrlivā

maḥalle-i Niḳola Patrino

Niḳola el-meẕkūr	Ḳosta İskâẕaplo	Niḳola Broḳoçilos	Todoro Domano	Yorgi veled-i o
Dimitri Veġazi	Sina Manoloplo	Petro İskâẕeplo	Yani İskâẕeplo	Aleksi veled-i o
Niḳola veled-i o	Lyo Trandafilo	Niḳola İskâẕaplo	Yani veled-i o	Lyo Ḳapsoraḫi
Yani birāder-i o	Manol yeñiçeri	İstemad Pozoḫtipa	Yani Neruli	Todoros birāder-i o
Yorgi ḫīş-i o	Yani Çanḳari	Miḫal birāder-i o	Yorgi Ḳaloġnomo	Niḳola birāẕer-i o

Todoro birāder-i o	İstemad veled-i meẕkūr	Yorgi Likiẕi	Yorgi Eranis	Dimitri birāder-i o
Yani birāẕer-i o	Pavlos Roḳanas	Yani Familet	Todoros Mes̱isti	Yani Farġari
Ḳosta Maṣura	Miḫal Niḳoli	Ḳoḳla Lazari	Dimitri Pinaḳa	Lyo birāẕer-i o
Todoros Dimitri	Papayorgi Kefalino	Papatodoro birāder-i o	Niḳola Doḳsara	Yorgi veled-i o
Yani veled-i o	Pavlo Ḳaliġoplo	Dimitri Litirġo	Ḳosta Litirġo	Yani Papadimitroplo
Miḫal birāder-i o	Ḳaḳur Kiryo	Ḳosta veled-i o	Dimitri ḫīş-i o	Ḳosta Domano
Yani İlyoplo	Yorgi veled-i o	Miḫal veled-i o	Todoro Ḳravaṣa	Proto-papa
Papapavlo veled-i o	Todoro Aleksoplo	Ḳalani Payo	Dimitri İrizomili	Andriya veled-i o
Vars̱alemo veled-i o	Dimitri Mavranci	Niḳola veled-i o	Lazaro veled-i o	mücerred Andriya Domano
mücerred Pavlos Ḳapsoraḫi	mücerred Todoros birāder-i o	mücerred Niḳola Eranas	mücerred Marti Kefalino	mücerred Aleksi Ḳaliġoplo
mücerred Yorgi birāder-i o	mücerred veled-i Yani Familet	bīve Mariya zen-i Ni[ḳo]lla	bīve Mariya zen-i S̱o[m]a[s]	bīve Mariya zen-i Ḳaçanduli
	bīve İstatira zen-i Todoro	[ḫ]āne 6[9]	mü[cerred] 8	bīve 4

85

tetimme-i nefs-i Vumero el-meẕkūr — ḫāṣṣa-ı Mīrlivā

maḫalle-i Yorgi Asani

Yorgi el-meẕkūr	Yani birāder-i o	Yorgi İrizomili	Yorgi İskâẕa	Marti Ḳaloyira
Yani Bersaniti	Petro Papafiliboplo[49]	Todoros birāder-i o	Papatodoro Papaluḳoplo	Yorgi veled-i o
Papayorgi Linofoki	Yani Marmara	İstas̱i Lazaro	S̱otoki Burdari	İstefanos birāẕer-i o
İstemad Ġalatari	Yani birāder-i o	Yorgi birāder-i o	Yorgi Ḳondoyani	Dimitri Muzalo
Yani birāder-i o	Manol Dimitri	Aleksi Kerabnyoti	Papayorgi Roḳano	Todoros veled-i o
Miḫal veled-i o	Dimitri Ḳayiris	Yani veled-i o	Niḳola Kefalino	Yorgi veled-i o
Petro Ḳosti Yaḳo	Niḳola Bozano	Dimitri Damyano	Todoro Paloloġo	Dimitri birāẕer-i o
Yani Flama	Dimitri birāẕer-i o	Manol Ḳoraḳa	Manol-ı dīğer birāder-i o	Yorgi Tiryo
Yani Befani	İlya Tanḳona	Praski Liyoroviti	Aleksi Ḳoçanda	Yaḳumo Miramuro
Niḳola Riḳos	Miḫal veled-i o	Manol veled-i o	Dimitri veled-i o	Andriya Liḳofayiti
S̱otoki Milonoplo	Yorgi Ẕrungiti	Yani birāder-i o	Manol Bozano	Lyo birāẕer-i o
Niḳola Ḳorna	Yorgi Aremuro	Andon Roḳana	Yani veled-i o	Yorgi veled-i o
S̱otoki veled-i o	Yani Yorġa	Andriya Vasḳameno	Todoros veled-i o	Miḫal H̱arara
Dimitri Ayayorgiti	Yani Vasḳameno	Papaniḳola Falaġri	Niḳola Frando	Yorgi veled-i o
Ḳosta İspas̱aris	Papaniḳola Mavruçi	İstefano İskâẕeplo	Niḳola Zonara	Yorgi veled-i o
Dimitri Maġuli	Todoros birāder-i o	Dimitri Himona	Yorgi birāder-i o	Ḳosta İksidya
Yani Himona	Todoro İsḳolari	mücerred Niḳola İrizomili	mücerred Yorgi Burdari	mücerred Yani Ḳondoyani

86

tetimme-i maḫa[ll]e-i Yorgi Asani el-meẕkūr — der nef[s-i V]umero

mücerred Yani Kefalin[o]	mücerred Yorgi Ḳosti Yaḳo	mücerred Yani [M]iramuri	mücerred [Y]ani Him[ona]	mücerred Niḳ[o]lla İk[s]idya
mücerred Niḳola [H]imona	mücerred İstemad birāder-i o	mücerred Todoros birāẕer-i o	bīve Defano zen-i Manol	bīve İ[.².] ḳato zen-i Ernasta

cemāʿat-i çeltükçiyān der nefs-i Vumero el-meẕkūr — ḫāne 4 — mücerred 2

Manol Malano	Yani Ḳaçanduri	Yorgi Varirvi	Papamiḫal birāẕer-i o	mücerred Niḳ[o]la Malano	mücerred Niḳola Ḳaçanduri

ḫāne ma'a çeltükçiyān	mücerred ma'a çeltükçiyān	bīve
86	13	2

yekūn-i nefs-i Vumero

ḫāne	mücerred	bīve	dīnk[50]
236	35	6	2

minhā

ḫāṣṣa	mülk-i Zaġanoz Beg Mīr-livā
1	1

ḥāṣıl ġayr ez çeltük 29679

ʿa(n) ispence 6811	bāġāt-ı ḫāṣṣa dönüm 24 [resm] 2880	eşcār-ı meyve-i ḫāṣṣa ʿaded 200 [resm] 500	āsiyāb-ı ḫāṣṣa 2 [resm] 500	ḳısṭ-ı bāzār ve niyābet 2500

ʿöşr-i penbe	ʿöşr-i kettān	ʿöşr-i bāġāt	ʿöşr-i ḥınṭa	ʿöşr-i cev	ʿöşr-i zeyt
250	300	7548	6500	963	5[7]

ʿöşr-i meyve 53	resm-i ḫamr 640	resm-i ḫanāzīr 2	mülk-i Dimitri ḫīş-i Ḳaḳur Kiryo der maḥalle-i Niḳola Patrino el-mezḳūr āsiyāb 2 resm 80	mülk-i Yūnus nev müslümān āsiyāb-ı ġalle 1 resm 80 āsiyāb-ı peşmīne 1 resm 15

maḥṣul-ı çeltük ki ḫāṣṣa ḫullide mülkühu şüd

fī sene 28500

87

nāḥiyyet-i Vumero

ḳarye-i Ḳonbi Ṣeḳra ez cemāʿat-i Arnavudān — ḫāṣṣa-ı Mīrlivā

Manḳola Ḳonbi Ṣeḳra	Domeniḳa Ḳonb[i] Ṣeḳra	Pelañrin	Yani Mazaraki	Todoro Mazaraki
	Yorgi Ḳonb[i] Ṣeḳra		ḫāne 6	

ḥāṣıl 367

ʿa(n) ispence	ʿöşr-i ḥınṭa	ʿöşr-i cev	resm-i ḫanāzīr
120	200	32	15

ḳarye-i Nasa ez cemāʿat-i Arnavudān — ḫāṣṣa-ı Mīrlivā

Domeniḳa Nasa	Vara Nasa	Dimitri birāder-i o	Miḫal Nasa	Domeniḳa veled-i o
Yan[i] Lu[sa]	Bala Nasa	Yorgi veled-i o		ḫāne 8

ḥāṣıl 571

ʿa(n) ispence	ʿöşr-i ḥınṭa	ʿöşr-i cev	resm-i ḫanāzīr
160	350	53	8

ḳarye-i Ḳaḳusi ez cemāʿat-i Arnavudān — ḫāṣṣa-ı Mīrlivā

Miḫal Laleṣi	Yorgi Ḳaḳusi	İstefano Ḳaḳusi	ḫāne 3

ḥāṣıl 304

ʿa(n) ispence 60	ʿöşr-i ḥınṭa 200	ʿöşr-i cev 31	resm-i ḫanāzīr 13

ḳarye-i Ġurdesi ez cemāʿat-i Arnavudān — ḫāṣṣa-ı Mīrlivā

Marti Ġurdesi	Leḳa Bardi	Andriya birāẕer-i o	ḫāne 3

ḥāṣıl 293

ʿa(n) ispence 60	ʿöşr-i ḥınṭa 200	ʿöşr-i cev 30	resm-i ḫanāzīr 3

ḳarye-i Branca ez cemāʿat-i Arnavudān — ḫāṣṣa-ı Mīrlivā

Todoro Plaşa	Ḳosta Ḳarancuni	ḫāne 2

ḥāṣıl 155

ʿa(n) ispence 40	ʿöşr-i ḥınṭa 100	ʿöşr-i cev 15

ḳarye-i Ṣ[u]rbi ez cemāʿat-i Arnavudān — ḫāṣṣa-ı Mīrlivā

Yorgi Vaşıl Patra	Yorgi Manesi	Todoro Porfiri	Ḳosta Ḳandra[va]	Lazaro Virgi

İl[y]a Ḳuçi	Marti Palunbi	Domeniḳa Proḳoçila	Ḳozma Ruşi	Pavlo Avesi
Yorgi Lukisa	Petro Ḳandrava	Leḳa veled-i o	Niḳola Manesi	Lazaro Ḳosati

88

tetimme-i ḳarye-i Şurbi el-meẕkūr — ḫāṣṣa-ı Mīrlivā

Yorgi Ḳukesi	Yorgi Varda	mücerred Petro Şurbi

cemāʿat-i çeltükçiyān der ḳarye-i meẕkūr — ḫāne 6

Gin Şurbi	Yorgi Buza	Dima Vaşıl Patra	Duḳa Vaşıl Patra	Petro Draji	Gin Ḳalifoni
		ḫāne maʿa çeltükçiyān 23	mücerred 1		

ḥāṣıl 1668

ʿa(n) ispence 480	āsiyāb-ı ḫāṣṣa 1 [resm] 200	ʿöşr-i kettān 30	ʿöşr-i ḥınṭa 800	ʿöşr-i cev 126	ʿöşr-i bāġāt 32

ḳarye-i Lancoy ez cemāʿat-i Arnavudān — ḫāṣṣa-ı Mīrlivā

Pavlo Lancoy	Yorgi birāder-i o	S̱otoki Malaḳas	İstemad birāẕer-i o	İvrato Malaḳas
Varda birāẕer-i o	İstayḳo Lancoy	Yorgi birāder-i o	Manḳola Lancoy	Todoro Malaḳas
Lazaro Ḫoreftira	mücerred Andriya Lancoy	mücerred Domeniḳa Malaḳas	ḫāne 11	mücerred 2

ḥāṣıl 841

ʿa(n) ispence 260	ʿöşr-i penbe 50	ʿöşr-i kettān 55	ʿöşr-i ḥınṭa 400	ʿöşr-i cev 63	resm-i ḫanāzīr 13

ḳarye-i Pratano ez cemāʿat-i Arnavudān — ḫāṣṣa-ı Mīrlivā

Lazaro Lales̱i	Gön birāder-i o	Gin Tanuş	Todoros birāẕer-i o	Niḳola Tanuş
Todoros birāder-i o	Andriya Ḳapareli	İstoyo birāẕer-i o	İstefano Ẕramata	Yorgi birāder-i o
Manḳola Lales̱i	Petros birāẕer-i o	Ḳozma birāder-i o	keşiş[51] Todoros	mücerred Yani Ẕramata
	ḫāne 14		mücerred 1	

ḥāṣıl 1314

ʿa(n) ispence 300	ʿöşr-i penbe 30	ʿöşr-i kettān 40	ʿöşr-i ḥınṭa 500	ʿöşr-i cev 76	ʿöşr-i bāġāt 320	resm-i ḫanāzīr 18
		resm-i ḫamr 25	ʿöşr-i meyve 5			

ḳarye-i Kertiza — ḫāṣṣa-ı Mīrlivā

Niḳola Andriça	Yani veled-i o	Todoro veled-i o	Papaniḳola Ḳaryano	Todoro veled-i o
Todoro Ḳaryano	Protopapa Ḳaryano	Papapavlo veled-i o	Niḳola birāẕer-i meẕkūr	Vaşıl birāẕer-i īşān
Dimitri birāẕer-i īşān	Yorgi Ḳaryano	Todoro veled-i o	Niḳola [İ]ksonoplo	Pavlo birāẕer-i o

89

tetimme-i ḳarye-i Kertiza el-meẕkūr — ḫāṣṣa-ı Mīrlivā

Dimitri Ḳaryano	Miḫal birāder-i o	Vaşıl Ḳaryano	Todoro Andriça	Miḫal Andriça
Ẕyaḳo Andriça	Yani birāẕer-i o	Niḳola Andriça	Miḫal birāder-i o	Yorgi birāder-i o
Dimitri birāder-i işān[52]	S̱otoki Ḳondovaşıl	bīve Dimitro zen-i Andriça	ḫāne 27	bīve 1

ḥāṣıl 3151

ʿa(n) ispence 681	bāġāt-ı ḫāṣṣa dönüm 3 [resm] 720	eşcār-ı meyve-i ḫāṣṣa ʿaded 5 [resm] 15	eşcār-ı tut-ı ḫāṣṣa ʿaded 30 [resm] 150	ʿöşr-i ḥınṭa 800	ʿöşr-i cev 124

ʿöşr-i ḳazz 119	ʿöşr-i bāġāt 384	resm-i ḫanāzīr 5	ʿöşr-i meyve 3	resm-i ḫamr 30	ʿöşr-i kettān 100	mülk-i Todor Andriça der ḳarye-i meẕkūr āsiyāb 1 resm 20

ḳarye-i Loġas̱eti ez cemāʿat-i Arnavudān — ḫāṣṣa-ı Mīrlivā

Gin Loġas̱eti	Andriya birāder-i o	İvlaş Loġas̱eti	Buza Loġas̱eti	Gin Ġulami
Palunbi Loġas̱eti	İvrato Vurġari	Yani birāder-i o	Andriya Ḳravari	Yani birāder-i o
Ḳazneş İşpata	Leḳa veled-i o	Andriya Lata	Proġono Siraḳ	Gin birāder-i o
Petro Vanbaki	Gin birāder-i o	Yorgi Ḳanḳaz̲i	Pavlo birāder-i o	Ḳozma Varponbi
Yorgi veled-i o	Andriya Vanbaḳi	Niḳola veled-i o	Petro Miziya	Yorgi Loġos̱eti
Yorgi Ḳuḳura	Leḳa Çipoplo	Pavlo birāder-i o	Muriki Miziya	Niḳola Plaşa
Yorgi birāder-i o	Gin Miziya	Ḳozma Maz̲iñik	mücerred Yorgi veled-i Petro	mücerred Gön Miziya
bīve Hırisi zen-i Vurġari	bīve Neze zen-i Lazaro	bīve Ḳali zen-i Ġulyamo	ḫāne 33	mücerred 2 bīve 3

ḥāṣıl 2372

ʿa(n) ispence	ʿöşr-i ḥınṭa	ʿöşr-i cev	resm-i ḫanāzīr	ʿöşr-i kettān	mülk-i Gin LoġaMeti der ḳarye-i mez̲kūr
718	1300	198	16	100	āsiyāb 1 resm 20

mülk-i
İvlaş LoġaMeti der ḳarye-i mez̲kūr
āsiyāb 1 resm 20

ḳarye-i Lales̱i ez cemāʿat-i Arnavudān — ḫāṣṣa-ı Mīrlivā

Yorgi Lales̱i	Dimitri birāz̲er-i o	Aġali Lales̱i	İştin birāz̲er-i o	Miḫal Lales̱i
Gin Lales̱i	Lazaro Lales̱i	Petro birāz̲er-i o	Gin Lales̱i-i dīğer	Muriki Ruzupisa

90

[te]timme-i [ḳarye-i] Lales̱i el-mez̲kūr — ḫāṣṣ[a-ı] M[ī]rlivā

[---] Ḳuluri	Gön Ḳalanci	İstefano [---]	[---] [---]	Gö[n] [---]
Bard[i] İşpani	Gin Ḳosta Niḳa		[ḫ]āne 17	

ḥāṣıl 1306

ʿa(n) ispence	ʿöşr-i ḥınṭa	ʿöşr-i cev	ʿö[şr-i] kett[ā]n
340	800	126	40

ḳarye-i Z̲ervini — ḫāṣṣa-ı Mīrlivā

Yani Papaniḳolo- plo	Dimitri birāder-i o	Dimitri Ḳunbari	Todoro Liḳosurati	İstemati Ḫarḳomata
Dimitri birāder-i o	Yani Ḳozma	S̱otoki veled-i o	Andriya veled-i o	To[do]ros veled-i o
İstefano Papayanoplo	Todoros birāder-i o	Yani İstefano	Miḫal Aleksoplo	Yani veled-i o
S̱otoki Mastroniḳola	Yani birāz̲er-i o	Yorgi İsḳolari	Yani İsḳolari	Todoros Papayorġoplos
Yani birāz̲er-i o	Todoros İplaros	Dimitri Yanuli	S̱oto[ki] Mala	İstilyano veled-i o
Yani Aṣpriyano	Yorgi veled-i o	S̱otoki Ḫarkâ	Dimitri veled-i o	Yorgi veled-i o
Niḳola veled-i o	Yani Mala	Miḫal veled-i o	Niḳola veled-i o	Miḫa[l] Ḳoz[m]a
Praski Floḳuni	Drunyoti İsḳolari	Yani İsḳolaroplo	Yani Papas̱ot[o]köplo	Papas Yorgi Papamiḫaloplo
Dimitri birāz̲er-i o	Vaṣıl Papayorgi	Todoro Aleksoplo	İstefano Er[in]os	Pavlos Z̲yaḳoplos
Yan[i] birāder-i o	Yorg[i] Pavlos	Niḳola birāz̲er-i o	Yorg[i] Ġur[---]	Sotiri dāmād-ı o
Vars̱ale[mo] Ḳolfoni	Todo[r]o Viro	Miḫal birāder-i o	Niḳola Aṣpr[iyano]	Yani Malyopl[o]
Yorgi Aṣpriyano	Dimitri birāder-i o	Nikifor birāder-i o	Yani Metaḳsa	Yani dāmād-ı o
Todoro Metaḳsa	Yani Laz̲oplo	Lazaro <A>nastasi	Lazaro İpsomoḳraso	Niḳola İsḳolaro- plo

91

tetimme-i ḳarye-i Z̲ervini el-mez̲kūr — [ḫ]āṣṣa-ı Mīrlivā

Ni[ḳo]la Perdiḳari	Ḫıristofora İsḳolari	Petro Papas̱otoköplo	Dimitri İsḳaviç	Niḳola Papa- yorġoplo

mücerred Miḫal Liḳosurati	mücerred Dimitri birāder-i o	mücerred Petro veled-i Alekso- plo	mücerred Yani İplaros	mücerred Yani birāder-i Dimitri Yanouli
mücerred Ḳosta birāẕer-i Yani	mücerred Yani Aleksoplo	mücerred Niḳola Petro	mücerred Yani birāder-i Niḳola	mücerred Niḳola birāder-i Metaḳsa
mücerred Niḳola Ḳolorda	bīve İstefano Aşpreyano	bīve Zanbali zen-i Papayorgi	bīve Ḳostiya zen-i İsḳolari	bīve Mariya zen-i İstoforo
	ḫāne 70	mücerred 11	bīve 4	

ḥāṣıl 6040

ʿa(n) ispence 2049	eşcār-ı ṭut-ı ḫāṣṣa ʿaded 30 [resm] 120	bāġāt-ı ḫāṣṣa nıṣf dönüm [resm] 84	eşcār-ı meyve-i ḫāṣṣa ʿaded 5 [resm] 15	ʿöşr-i ḥınṭa 2100	ʿöşr-i cev 323

ʿöşr-i ḳazz 264	ʿöşr-i bāġāt 800	ʿöşr-i meyve 36	resm-i ḫanāzīr 4	ʿöşr-i ʿasel 10	ʿöşr-i kettān 100	resm-i ḫamr 65
			resm-i ʿarūsī 70			

mezraʿa-ı Ayo Ḳostandino nezd-i ḳarye-i meẕkūr

ḫāṣṣa-ı Mīrlivā ḫāliyye

ḳarye-i Yir[mo]çani ḫāṣṣa-ı Mīrlivā

Yani Malasi	Yorgi Ḳondyo	Ḳosta Çaronili	İstemad dāmād-ı Yorgi Damyano	Yani Pisali
Andriya Rovari	Miḫal Ḳoraḳa	Niḳola birāder-i o	Ḳosta birāder-i o	İstilyano Ḳoraḳa
Petro Ḳoraḳa	Kiryaki İstavraki	Pavlos veled-i o	Yani Niḫoriti	İstilyano birāẕer-i o
Miḫal İstovraki	Manol Zoġrafo	Papaniḳola dāmād-ı o	Ḳosta Ḳatirva	İlya birāder-i o
Manol birāder-i o	S̱otoki Ḳuḳa	Yani birāder-i o	Yani Ḳatirva	Dimitri Sotos
Yani veled-i o	Papam[a]nol Patrova	Yorgi Papatodoroplo	Yani Vilotoplo	Dimitri Ġa[men]oti
İvlaş Raviti	Miḫal Malasi	Miḫal Ġalani	mücerred Yorgi Damyano	bīve Prasko zen-i Yorgi

92

tetimme-i ḳarye-i Yi[r]moçani el-meẕkūr ḫāṣṣa-ı Mīrlivā

bīve zen-i Pisali	bīve Todora zen-i Ḳoraḳa	bīve Mariya zen-i Papatodoroplo	bīve Sana zen-i Revariya	ḫāne 33	mücerred 1 bīve 5

ḥāṣıl 2673

ʿa(n) ispence 880	ʿöşr-i ḥınṭa 1200	ʿöşr-i cev 188	ʿöşr-i bāġāt 248	ʿöşr-i ḳazz 65	ʿöşr-i meyve 23	resm-i ḫanāzīr 9
		resm-i ḫamr 30		resm-i ʿarūsī 30		

ḳarye-i Poraçiyu ḫāṣṣa-ı Mīrlivā

Papas Andriyas	Ẕyaḳo veled-i o	Yani veled-i o	Andriya Ḳaliva	Yorgi Ḳorna
Todoros Ḫalke	Duḳa İstasino	Petro birāẕer-i o	Mazuli birāẕer-i o	Niḳola Çaḳari
Ḳosta İġliġori	S̱otoki Papayanoplo	Yani Taġari	İstemad Ḳoloḳoni	İstemad Manoloplo
Miḫal Nomiḳoplo	Yorgi Miḫaloplos	Yani Kürya	Miḫal Uzġuroplo	ḫāne 19

ḥāṣıl 1500

ʿa(n) ispence 475	ʿöşr-i ḥınṭa 500	ʿöşr-i cev 78	ʿöşr-i bāġāt 315	ʿöşr-i ḳazz 46	ʿöşr-i meyve 6	resm-i ḫamr 40
			resm-i ʿarūsī 40			

ḳarye-i Hiliẕon ḫāṣṣa-ı Mīrlivā

maḫalle-i Luḳas Loġos̱eti

Luḳas el-meẕkūr	Lazaro İstravo- kefalo	Petro Ḫlorotiri	Yorgi veled-i o	Manol İstilyani

Lazaro Sunotis	Yorgi İstravo- kefalino	İstefano veled-i o	Niḳola veled-i o	Ḳosta Befanoġamro
Yani Ayoliti	Pavlos Papayanoplos	Yorgi Çanḳareruli	Pavlos ḫīş-i o	Yani Vurzuni
Leo birāder-i o	Niḳola Marinaro	Niḳola Ḫarkâ	Todoros birāẕer-i o	Yani Ġurnari
İstemad İsḳaẕeplo	S̱otoki birāẕer-i o	Niḳola Balç[a]	İstefano Ḳaḳ[o]tari	Niḳola birāẕer-i o
İstemad Aspriça	Yaḳumo veled-i o	Yorgi Anbalurġo	Miḫal ḫīş-i o	Laşi Lancaḫo
Yani ḫīş-i o	Petro Ḫarkâ	Ġulyamo birāẕer-i o	Niḳola Manimenas	Ḳozma veled-i o

93

tetimme-i maḫalle-i Luḳas Loġoseti el-meẕkūr der nefs-i Hiliẕon

İstemad İsḳolari	Proḳopi Pelaḳanos	Yani Marinaros	İstemad ḫīş-i o	As̱anas Kipro
Yorgi Pefani	S̱otoki birāẕer-i o	Yani birāder-i o	İstefano Yorgi	Marinos birāder-i o
Yani Menadis	Dimitri İstamiri	Dimitri Ḳoḳalo	İvlaş İvrato	Niḳola İstrati
Dimitri birā- der-i o	Foti İstravoḫiri	Niḳola Panḳali	Andriya Playoti	İkseġu- menoplo
Petro Mavroyanos	Niḳola Vaşama	Yorgi Kiniġos	Dimitri birāder-i o	Papas İstefanos
Ẕyaḳos birāẕer-i o	Andriya Politi	Niḳola İvlito	Petro birāẕer-i o	Yorgi Ḳuçoyani
Andon veled-i o	Yorgi Papaliġuro- plo	Todoros birāẕer-i o	Yani Ḳayi	Yorgi Beli
Aleksi birāẕer-i o	Niḳola İftoḫacis	İstefano birāẕer-i o	Manḳafa birāẕer-i īşān	İstefano İstamiro
Petro veled-i o	Dimitri Uzġuroplo	Yorgi birāder-i o	Yorgi Leġa	Yani veled-i o
Manḳafa Riḳonyoti	Petro İlyoplo	Aleksi veled-i o	Yani Serbaniti	Aleksi birāẕer-i o
Yani Andriyaplo	Todoro Ḳoromali	İvrato Befani	Niḳola Sela	Papas Andriyas
Yorgi dāmād-ı Serbano	Yorgi Vaşıla	Pavlos birāder-i o	Niḳola İvlaşoplo	Yorgi Marḳo
Yorgi ḫīş-i o	Miḫal Ḳumaroyini	Yani birāder-i o	Andriya Arḳadino	Yani Ḳuçoyini

Pelañrin birāẕer-i o	Pelañrin veled-i Petro İlyoplo	mücerred Yani Ḫlorotiri	mücerred İstefano İstilyani	mücerred Todoros birāẕer-i o
mücerred Lazaro İstravo- kefalino	mücerred Yorgi Ayoliti	mücerred Yani Marinaro	mücerred Dimitri birāder-i Ḫarkâ	mücerred Aleksi veled-i Papaandriya
bīve Ḳatarina zen-i Notara	bīve Neze zen-i Miḫal	bīve Frosini zen-i Ġarvoriza	bīve Ḳristyana zen-i Niḳola	bīve Todo[y]i zen-i [M]irito
bīve Kiru zen-i S̱oma	bīve Yanaḳu zen-i Serbano	ḫāne 102	mücerred 8	bīve 7

94

tetimme-i ḳarye-i Hiliẕon ḫāṣṣa-ı Mīrlivā

maḫalle-i İstemati Ḳondovaşıla

İstemad el-meẕkūr	Yorgi veled-i o	Lazaro İstefano	İstemad Monoḳoḳalo	Ḳozma birāder-i o
Manol İstilyariti	Todoro Platis	Yorgi Filipoplo	İstefano Ḫarara	Yani Ḫayḳali
Yani Fesaḳoti	Yorgi Nasis	Yani İsḳaẕe	Marḳo Bufla	Todoros Trandafilo
Niḳola Mandremano	Yani veled-i o	Todoros veled-i o	İstemad İstamiri	Todoros birāder-i o
Niḳola Tanuşi	Papayorgi Androniḳola	Vaşıl Rondaki	Pavlos veled-i o	Yorgi Ḳosti
S̱oma birāder-i o	Niḳola birāẕer-i īşān	Manol Mavroniḳola	İstemati Fenyotis	Todoros birāder-i o
Manol birāder-i o	Dimitri Kipriyanos	Dimitri Março	Ḫıristiyanos Dimitroplos	S̱otoki veled-i o
Yani Dimitroplo	Andriya Dimitroplo	Dimitri birāder-i o	Dimitri Arnaẕi	Niḳola birāẕer-i o
Yorgi Yovani	Yorgi Vurzuni	Varda İstamiri	Marti birāẕer-i o	Yani Varda
Yorgi İsḳorduli	Todoros İsḳorduli	Ḳosta İsḳorduli	Yani veled-i o	Yorgi veled-i o
Angelato Randino	Ḳosta Aşvonikisto	Ḳosta Plaksidi	Marḳo Ḳuri	İstemad Ḳuri
Manol dāmād-ı o	Yani Linoḳuki	Todoros Ḳalyotis	Niḳola veled-i o	Yorgi veled-i o

Yorgi İpşareplo	Yani Ḳoryavlas	Niḳola birāder-i o	Zaḳsas Ḳozma	Papaniḳola Panḳali
Yorgi Raġako	Yorgi Ḳurtoplo	Yorgi Praska	Dimitri Plamaliti	Todoros İstamiri
İstas̱i U[rv]asi	Yani Modonyos	Pavlos [S̱]omas	Ḳosta Şand[.ˀ.]ya	Yorgi veled-i o
Yani veled-i o	Todoros Papayanoplos	İstefanos Mo[.ˀ.]llyos	Papas Niḳolas	Yani Ḳukâs
Miḫal Zirvo	Lazari Plaşa	Manol Argiri	bīve Ana zen-i [İ]stefano	bīve Elani zen-i Andriya
bīve Ḳostini zen-i Platendro	bīve Ḳostana zen-i Zelvuna	bīve Ḫrisi zen-i Vars̱alomo	bīve Mariya zen-i Pavlopulya	bīve Zanbelu zen-i Loġos̱et

95

tetimme-i maḫalle-i İstemati el-meẕkūr — der nefs-i Hiliẕon

bīve İstatira zen-i Yorgi	bīve Yorġu zen-i Celyana	bīve zen-i Yani Ġavriduy	ḫāne 83	bīve 10

cümletü'l-maḫalleteyni'l-meẕkūreteyn

ḫāne 185	mücerred 8	bīve 17

ḥāṣıl 20994

ʿa(n) ispence 4927	āsiyāb-ı ḫāṣṣa 1 [resm] 200	nıṣf-ı āsiyāb-ı ḫāṣṣa 1 [resm] 100	bāġāt-ı ḫāṣṣa dönüm 9 [resm] 2160	eşcār-ı ṭut-ı ḫāṣṣa ʿaded 7 [resm] 25	eşcār-ı zeyt-i ḫāṣṣa ʿaded 10 [resm] 13

eşcār-ı meyve-i ḫāṣṣa ʿaded 9 [resm] 20	ʿöşr-i penbe 120	ʿöşr-i kettān 320	ʿöşr-i bāġāt 5248	ʿöşr-i ḥınṭa 6100	ʿöşr-i cev 936	ʿöşr-i ḳazz 25

ʿöşr-i meyve 154	resm-i ḫanāzīr 16	ʿöşr-i çam saḳızı 10	ʿöşr-i zeyt 34	ʿöşr-i ʿasel 16	resm-i ḫamr 420

mülk-i Loġos̱eti ser-maḫalle der ḳarye-i Hiliẕon el-meẕkūr āsiyāb 1 resm 50

mülk-i İstravokefalo der maḫalle-i Luḳas el-meẕkūr: āsiyāb-ı ġalle 1 resm 25; āsiyāb-ı peşmīne 1 resm 15

mülk-i Martinos birāder-i İstefano der maḫalle-i meẕkūr: āsiyāb-ı ġalle 1 resm 30; āsiyāb-ı peşmīne 1 resm 15

mülk-i Pelañrin veled-i Petro İlyoplo der maḫalle-i o āsiyāb-ı peşmīne 1 resm 15

ḳarye-i Şuli ez cemāʿat-i Arnavudān — ḫāṣṣa-ı Mīrlivā

Petro Şuli	Todoros veled-i o	Petro Manḳafa	Yorgi dāmād-ı o	Seraḳo Manḳafa
Leḳa ḫīş-i o	Yani Graḳa	Mire birāẕer-i o	Ḳuḳa birāẕer-i o	Petro Şuli-i dīğer
Niḳola Şuli	Gin Şuli	Politi ḫīş-i o	Yorgi İflamurari	Dima birāẕer-i o
	Gön Ḳumi		ḫāne 16	

ḥāṣıl 1229

ʿa(n) ispence 320	ʿöşr-i penbe 50	ʿöşr-i kettān 50	ʿöşr-i ḥınṭa 600	ʿöşr-i cev 90	resm-i ḫanāzīr 5	ʿöşr-i bāġāt 64

mülk-i
Petro Manḳafa der ḳarye-i meẕkūr
āsiyāb 1 resm 50

ḳarye-i Ḳuḳura ez cemāʿat-i Arnavudān — ḫāṣṣa-ı Mīrlivā

Petro Ḳuḳura	Niḳola Plaşa	Gin Dramisi	Todoros Ḳondos	İskliro birāẕer-i o
Yorgi İşpata	Niḳola Şurbi	Gön Büs̱oḳuki	Todoro Ḫarara	Petro Ḳunota
Yorgi Doḳsara	Niḳola Ḳatara	Yani Ḳatara	Yorgi Ḫıristodulo	Marti veled-i o
	Yani Ḳovata		ḫāne 16	

96

ḥāṣıl-ı ḳarye-i Ḳuḳura el-meẕkūr 975

ʿa(n) ispence 320	ʿöşr-i penbe 30	ʿöşr-i kettān 30	ʿöşr-i ḥınṭa 500	ʿöşr-i cev 7[6]	resm-i ḫanāzīr 19

ḳarye-i Küraleş ez cemāʿat-i Arnavudān — ḫāṣṣa-ı Mīrlivā

Mangişa Küraleş	Muriki Ḳanaẕo	Petro Ḫotaçi	Niḳola Muşura		Yorgi birāder-i o
Andriya Paliḳano	Petros ḫīş-i o	Yorgi İstayḳo	Yorgi Vaşıl	ḫāne 9	mevżiʿ-i āsiyāb-ı ḫāṣṣa 1

ḥāṣıl 695

ʿa(n) ispence 180	ʿöşr-i penbe 20	ʿöşr-i kettān 20	ʿöşr-i ḥınṭa 400	ʿöşr-i cev 61	resm-i ḫanāzīr 14

ḳarye-i Ḳraḳuki ez cemāʿat-i Arnavudān ḫāṣṣa-ı Mīrlivā

Yani Ḳraḳuki	Gin birāder-i o	İsḳura Ḳraḳuki	Lazaro birāder-i o	Lazaro Lonci
Mengişa Ḳayça	İstoya birāẕer-i o	Gin İsḳura	Todoro birāder-i o	Miḫal Muzaki
Dima birāder-i o	Lazaro Raşi	Domeniḳa dāmād-ı o	Aġali Ḳraḳuki	Vaṣi Ḳraḳuki
Vaṣi-i dīğer Ḳraḳuki		ḫāne 16		

ḥāṣıl 1288

ʿa(n) ispence	ʿöşr-i penbe	ʿöşr-i kettān	ʿöşr-i ḥınṭa	ʿöşr-i cev	resm-i ḫamr	ʿöşr-i ʿasel
360	40	40	700	106	12	5

mülk-i
Yani Ḳraḳuki der ḳarye-i
mezḳūr
āsiyāb 1 resm 25

ḳarye-i Sitara ez cemāʿat-i Arnavudān ḫāṣṣa-ı Mīrlivā

Aleksi Sitara	İvrato Dramesi	Gön veled-i o	Gön Ḳarboçumaẕi	D[o]meniḳa birāẕer-i o
Gön Dramesi	Niḳola birāẕer-i o	Yorgi Sitara	Gön Sitara	ḫāne 9

ḥāṣıl 429

ʿa(n) ispence	ʿöşr-i ḥınṭa	ʿöşr-i cev	resm-i ḫanāzīr	ʿöşr-i kettān
180	200	32	2	15

ḳarye-i Miraḳo ez cemāʿat-i Arnavudān ḫāṣṣa-ı Mīrlivā

Miraḳo Ḳazneş	Gön birāder-i o	Andriya birāder-i o	Miḫal birāder-i o	Biçi birāder-i o
Marti Borşa	Niḳa birāder-i o	Biçi Borşa	Andriya Ḫarma	Todoros birāder-i o
Gön Ḳonbi Ṣeḳra	Miḫa Ḳumi	Yorgi Ḳanaẕo	Andriya Ḳanaẕo	Gön Ḳanaẕo

97

tetimme-i ḳarye-i Miraḳo el-meẕkūr ḫāṣṣ[a-ı] Mīrlivā

Gin Liḳuresi	İstemad birāẕer-i o	Aleksi Ḳaznesi	Gin birāder-i o	Aleksi İşpata
Domeniḳa Varponbi	bīve Mariya zen-i Proġon		ḫāne 21	bīve 1

ḥāṣıl 1326

ʿa(n) ispence	ʿöşr-i penbe	ʿöşr-i kettān	ʿöşr-i ḥınṭa	ʿöşr-i cev	resm-i ḫanāzīr
426	40	50	700	106	4

ḳarye-i İşpata ez cemāʿat-i Arnavudān ḫāṣṣa-ı Mīrlivā

Marti İşpata	İvr<a>tos dāmād-ı o	Miḫayl İşpata	Seraḳo Ḫama	Marti birāẕer-i o
Yorgi Vetaç	Petro Matranḳa	Marti İşpata	Gön birāẕer-i o	Yani Matranḳa
Domeniḳa Buvi		ḫāne 11		

ḥāṣıl 755

ʿa(n) ispence	ʿöşr-i kettān	ʿöşr-i penbe	ʿöşr-i ḥınṭa	ʿöşr-i cev	resm-i ḫanāzīr
220	40	30	400	62	3

ḳarye-i Bruma ez cemāʿat-i Arnavudān ḫāṣṣa-ı Mīrlivā

Andriya Bruma	Yani Bruma	Petros veled-i o	Domeniḳa Bruma	Ḳolimanos birāder-i o
Yorgi Ipṣari	Ḳosta birāẕer-i o	mücerred Pavlos Bruma	ḫāne 7	mücerred 1

ḥāṣıl 663

ʿa(n) ispence	ʿöşr-i kettān	ʿöşr-i ḥınṭa	ʿöşr-i cev	resm-i ḫanāzīr
160	30	400	60	13

ḳarye-i Ḳazani ez cemāʿat-i Arnavudān ḫāṣṣa-ı Mīrlivā

Yani Ḳazani	Yorgi birāder-i o	Lazaro Ḳazani	Yorgi birāder-i o	Todoros birāder-i o
Lazaro-<yı> dīğer Ḳazani	Yorgi birāder-i o	Göḳa Şaleşi	Marti Şaleşi	Yani Şaleşi
İstoya Şaleşi	Ram Buva	Yani birāẕer-i o	Gin birāder-i o	Yorgi Laġopati
	Ḳozma Arosti		ḫāne 16	

ḥāṣıl 961

ʿa(n) ispence 320	ʿöşr-i kettān 40	ʿöşr-i ḥınṭa 500	ʿöşr-i cev 76	mülk-i Yani Ḳazani der ḳarye-i mezḳūr āsiyāb 1 resm 25

98

tetimme-i nāḥiyyet-i Vumero

ḳarye-i Toşkesi ez cemāʿat-i Arnavudān ḫāṣṣa-ı Mīrlivā

Gin Ḳumi	Todoros birāder-i o	Lazaro Toşkesi	Andriya Toşkesi	İş Ari [L]anbeti
Petr[o] birāẕer-i o	Duşa Doşkesi	Yorgi birāder-i o	Leḳa Peta	Lazaro ḫīş-i o
Dima Varponbi	Petro birāder-i o	Niḳola Trandafilo	Niḳola Ġraḳa	Dima Maji
mücerred Yani Peta	mücerred Gin Varponbi	mücerred Yorgi birāder-i Yorgi Drandafilo[53]	ḫāne 15	mücerred 3

ḥāṣıl 1314

ʿa(n) ispence 360	ʿöşr-i ḥınṭa 700	ʿöşr-i cev 107	ʿöşr-i bāġāt 112	resm-i ḫanāzīr 5	ʿöşr-i kettān 30

ḳarye-i Maḳri Poẕi ez cemāʿat-i Arnavudān ḫāṣṣa-ı Mīrlivā

Niḳola Maḳri Poẕi	Miḫal Maḳri Poẕi	Yorgi birāder-i o	Niḳola Belevi	Niḳola Sela
Petro Romyo	Ḳostas Dabos	Yorgi birāder-i o	Manol birāder-i o	Miḫal Maḳri Poẕi
Dimitri Maḳri Poẕi	Ḳosta birāder-i o	Todoros Maḳri Poẕi	Ḳalanduri birāder-i o	Gön Todoros

Nikifor Prundano[54]	Yorgi Prudano[55]	mücerred Gön Belevi	mücerred Leo Maḳri Poẕi	ḫāne 17	mücerred 2

ḥāṣıl 1835

ʿa(n) ispence 380	ʿöşr-i penbe 20	ʿöşr-i kettān 50	ʿöşr-i ḥınṭa 1000	ʿöşr-i cev 152	ʿöşr-i bāġāt 224	resm-i ḫanāzīr 9

mezraʿa-ı Purdanu nezd-i ḳarye el-mezḳūr

ḫāṣṣa-ı Mīrlivā ḫāliyye

mezraʿa-ı Matranḳa nezd-i ḳarye İşpata el-mezḳūr

ḫāṣṣa-ı Mīrlivā ḫāliyye

ḳarye-i Poẕo ez cemāʿat-i Arnavudān ḫāṣṣa-ı Mīrlivā

Andriya Poẕo	Dimitri birāder-i o	Pelaĥris Miḫoyis	Andriya veled-i o	Miḫal Lupo
Miḫal Şuli	Punyas birāẕer-i o	Todoros Matranḳa	Mat-ranḳa Ḳayça	mücerred Yorgi veled-i Pelaĥris el-mezḳūr
	ḫāne 9		mücerred 1	

ḥāṣıl 760

ʿa(n) ispence 200	ʿöşr-i ḥınṭa 450	ʿöşr-i cev 68	resm-i ḫanāzīr 14	ʿöşr-i ʿasel 13	ʿöşr-i kettān 15

99

tetimme-i nāḥiyyet-i Vumero

ḳarye-i Maji ez cemāʿat-i Arnavudān ḫāṣṣa-ı Mīrlivā

Yani Maji	ḫāne 1

ḥāṣıl 78

ʿa(n) ispence 20	ʿöşr-i ḥınṭa 50	ʿöşr-i cev 8

ḳarye-i Sela ez cemāʿat-i Arnavudān — ḫāṣṣa-ı Mīrlivā

Dimitri Franḳoplo	Niḳola veled-i o	Yorgi Franḳoplo	İstefano Manesi	ḫāne 4

ḥāṣıl 340

ʿa(n) ispence 80	ʿöşr-i kettān 20	ʿöşr-i ḥınṭa 200	ʿöşr-i cev 31	resm-i ḫanāzīr 8	ʿöşr-i çam saḳızı 1

ḳarye-i Ẕiminiça — ḫāṣṣa-ı Mīrlivā

Yani Tirsinyoti	Yani Riḫo	Pavlos Mariḳliti	Yorgi Aleksoplo	Todoros Maçuḳa
S̲omoplos Andriyas	Izġurna Dimitra	Andriyas Bratis	bīve Yana zen-i Dermatosa	bīve Yana Murmurane
	ḫāne 8		bīve 2	

ḥāṣıl 2181

ʿa(n) ispence 212	bāġāt-ı ḫāṣṣa dönüm 5 [resm] 600	āsiyāb-ı ḫāṣṣa 1 [resm] 1000	ʿöşr-i ḥınṭa 200	ʿöşr-i cev 32	ʿöşr-i bāġāt 112	resm-i ḫanāzīr 5
	ʿöşr-i kettān 10		resm-i ḫamr 10			

ḳarye-i Ḫayḳal ez cemāʿat-i Arnavudān — ḫāṣṣa-ı Mīrlivā

Petros Ḫayḳal	Todoros Liḳuresi	Gön birāẕer-i o	Yani Ḳaḳuri	Todoros birāder-i o
Dimitri birāder-i o	Manol birāder-i Īşān	Gön Luzi	Yorgi birāder-i o	Todoros Ḳonḳa
Aleksi dāmād-ı o	Petro Zupani	mücerred Petro Luzi	ḫāne 12	mücerred 1

ḥāṣıl 810

ʿa(n) ispence 260	ʿöşr-i kettān 30	ʿöşr-i ḥınṭa 450	ʿöşr-i cev 68	resm-i ḫanāzīr 2

ḳarye-i Ṣarakina ez cemāʿat-i Arnavudān — ḫāṣṣa-ı Mīrlivā

Petrobuva Avriyoni	Lazaro Liḳuryoti	Todoros Buleşi	mücerred Lazaro veled-i o	ḫāne 3	mücerred 1

ḥāṣıl 403

ʿa(n) ispence 80	ʿöşr-i bāġāt 128	ʿöşr-i ḥınṭa 100	ʿöşr-i cev 15	mülk-i Petro Avriyoni der ḳarye-i meẕkūr āsiyāb 1 resm 80

ḳarye-i Plaşa ez cemāʿat-i Arnavudān — ḫāṣṣa-ı Mīrlivā

Yani Plaşa	İştin veled-i o	Petros Pes̲as	Gin veled-i o	Proġonos Ḳazneş

100

tetimme-i ḳarye-i Plaşa el-meẕkūr — ḫāṣṣa-ı Mīrlivā

Petro veled-i o	Şurbi Lopesi	Gin birāder-i o	Ḳosta İvlozima	Yorgi birāder-i o	
Gin Peta	İstefano Argitis	Dimitri İvlaḫo	Petros Provaris	Gin Peta-ı dīğer	
Yani Çingene	Ropanos Çingene birāẕer-i o	Vas̲i Ḳaznes	mücerred Niḳola Peta	mücerred Yorgi Argitis	
mücerred Yani İvlaḫo	mücerred Andriya Provaris	bīve Yana zen-i Ekene	ḫāne 17	mücerred 5	bīve 1

ḥāṣıl 1615

ʿa(n) ispence 446	ʿöşr-i penbe 40	ʿöşr-i kettān 40	ʿöşr-i ḥınṭa 900	ʿöşr-i cev 137	resm-i ḫanāzīr 26	ʿöşr-i ʿasel 26

ḳarye-i Ḳondari ez cemāʿat-i Arnavudān — ḫāṣṣa-ı Mīrlivā

Niḳola Ḳondari	Miḫal veled-i o	Yorgi Ḳondari	Todoros Misopolitis	Lazaro veled-i o

Domeniḳa Ḳondari	Duşa Ḳondari	Niḳola Ḳondari	Niḳaki Pelañrin	Niḳaki Duşa
mücerred Todoros Misopolitis	mücerred Gin Ḳondari	mücerred Miḫal Duşa	ḫāne 10	mücerred 3

ḥāṣıl 806

ʿa(n) ispence	ʿöşr-i penbe	ʿöşr-i kettān	ʿöşr-i ḥınṭa	ʿöşr-i cev	resm-i ḫanāzīr
260	20	30	400	61	35

ḳarye-i Franḳa ez cemāʿat-i Arnavudān — ḫāṣṣa-ı Mīrlivā

Yorgi Franḳa	Roġonos[56] birāẕer-i o	Miḫal birāder-i o	Dima Manesi	Yorgi Zuġras
Dimitri Tiryarhi	Petros Tiryarhi	Niḳola Kirvaniti	İş Ari birāẕer-i o	Niḳola Ḳoḳla
Leḳa Pasanis	mücerred Niḳola Manesi	mücerred Lazaro Zuġra	ḫāne 11	mücerred 2

ḥāṣıl 755

ʿa(n) ispence	ʿöşr-i penbe	ʿöşr-i kettān	ʿöşr-i ḥınṭa	ʿöşr-i cev	resm-i ḫanāzīr
260	20	20	350	55	50

ḳarye-i Lazaro Buva ez cemāʿat-i Arnavudān — ḫāṣṣa-ı Mīrlivā

Lazaro el-meẕkūr	Gön Duḳiza	İştin Duḳiza	İzlatḳa Gire	Gön Ḫarmiya
	Ḳosta Ḳonbi S̱eḳra		ḫāne 6	

ḥāṣıl 434

ʿa(n) ispence	ʿöşr-i ḥınṭa	ʿöşr-i cev	resm-i ḫanāzīr	ʿöşr-i ʿasel
120	250	40	18	6

101
tetimme-i nāḥiyyet-i Vumero

ḳarye-i Liḳuresi ez cemāʿat-i Arnavudān — ḫāṣṣa-ı Mīrlivā

Yani Liḳuresi	Lazaro Liḳuresi	Yani birāder-i o	Yorgi Mano	Yani Mano
Yorgi-i dīğer Mano	Duşa Mano	İstefano birāẕer-i o	Ḳosta Jiva	Niḳola Jiva
Gön Ḳravari	Matranḳa birāder-i o	mücerred Andriya Liḳuresi	ḫāne 12	mücerred 1

ḥāṣıl 1021

ʿa(n) ispence	ʿöşr-i penbe	ʿöşr-i kettān	ʿöşr-i ḥınṭa	ʿöşr-i cev	resm-i ḫanāzīr
260	20	30	600	91	20

ḳarye-i Aranis Ḳuçohyari ez cemāʿat-i Arnavudān — ḫāṣṣa-ı Mīrlivā

Yorgi Aranis	Gin veled-i o	Yani Bala	Gin Bala	Gin Helmesi
	Yani İstratoni	Ḳral Yani	ḫāne 7	

ḥāṣıl 389

ʿa(n) ispence	ʿöşr-i ḥınṭa	ʿöşr-i cev	resm-i ḫanāzīr	ʿöşr-i kettān
140	200	31	8	10

ḳarye-i Aranis Ḳavalari ez cemāʿat-i Arnavudān — ḫāṣṣa-ı Mīrlivā

Yorgi Aranis	Lazaro birāẕer-i o	Yorgi Aranis-i dīğer	Niḳola birāẕer-i o	Leḳa Ḳukesi	
Petro birāẕer-i o	Marḳo Ranesi	Ḳosta Mazaraki	Petro birāẕer-i o	Aleksi Zapandi	
Ġropalati birāder-i o	Mavriçi Yorgi	Todoros birāder-i o	Yorgi Loçi	Dimitri birāder-i o	
Yorgi S̱otoki	mücerred Lazaro veled-i o	bīve Beliye zen-i Vintina	ḫāne 16	mücerred 1	bīve 1

ḥāṣıl 1491

ʿa(n) ispence	ʿöşr-i penbe	ʿöşr-i kettān	ʿöşr-i ḥınṭa	ʿöşr-i cev	resm-i ḫanāzīr
346	30	50	900	136	29

ḳarye-i Romesi ez cemāʿat-i Arnavudān — ḫāṣṣa-ı Mīrlivā

Leḳa Romesi	Duşa Frosina	Yorgi Aḳaromesi	Peta Frosina	Aleksi Yanimita
Marti Romesi	Gön veled-i o	Dima veled-i o	Miḫal Luzi	Niḳola birāẕer-i o

Leḳa birāẕer-i o	Marti Ḳalimani	Dima Romesi	Yorgi Ḳoḳoçomaẕi	Todoros Bafi

102

tetimme-i ḳarye-i Romesi el-meẕkūr ḫāṣṣa-ı Mīrlivā

Andon Şuli	mücerred Yorgi Yanimita	mücerred Gön Frosina	mücerred Loşa Romeşi	mücerred Yorgi Romeşi
mücerred Gin Yinimane		ḫāne 16	mücerred 5	

ḥāṣıl 1073

ʿa(n) ispence 420	ʿöşr-i penbe 20	ʿöşr-i kettān 30	ʿöşr-i ḥınṭa 500	ʿöşr-i cev 77	resm-i ḫanāzīr 6	resm-i ʿarūsī 20

ḳarye-i Vaşıloplos ez cemāʿat-i Arnavudān ḫāṣṣa-ı Mīrlivā

Niḳola Vaşıloplos	Yani Prinos	Niḳola Papayorgi	Dimitri Ḫarara	Yorgi Velçi
	Niḳola birāder-i o		ḫāne 6	

ḥāṣıl 478

ʿa(n) ispence 120	ʿöşr-i penbe 20	ʿöşr-i kettān 30	ʿöşr-i bāġāt 60	ʿöşr-i ḥınṭa 200	ʿöşr-i cev 32	resm-i ḫanāzīr 2
			ʿöşr-i zeyt 4	resm-i ʿarūsī 10		

ḳarye-i Maji ez cemāʿat-i Arnavudān ḫāṣṣa-ı Mīrlivā

Miḫal Pahi	Lyori Beluşi	Manol Kraziya	Gön Gemiri	Ḳosta Podina
Yani Plaşa	Desri Borşa	mücerred Dedese Maẕiñik	ḫāne 7	mücerred 1

ḥāṣıl 510

ʿa(n) ispence 160	ʿöşr-i penbe 20	öşr-i kettān 30	ʿöşr-i ḥınṭa 250	ʿöşr-i cev 40	resm-i ʿarūsī 10

yekūn-i ḫāṣṣhā-<yı> Mīrlivā der nāḥiyyet-i Vumero el-meẕkūr

ḳurā maʿa nefs-i Vumero 43	mezāriʿ-i ḫāliyye 3	ḫāne 988	mücerred 88	bīve 41

ḥāṣıl 97842

103 *blank*

104

nāḥiyyet-i Kirvuḳor

ḳarye-i Artica ḫāṣṣa-ı Mīrlivā

Matyos Ḳosḳos	Yani Ḳosḳo	Yorgi Ḳosḳo	Niḳola Ḳosḳo	Yani Laẕa
Niḳola birāder-i o	Miḫal birāder-i o	Andriya Ġaytano Ḳaligi	Yorgi veled-i o	S̱otoki Ḳurya
Niḳola birāder-i o	Seḫo birāẕer-i o	Miḫal Livani	Ḳosta birāẕer-i o	Niḳolas Livani
Niḳolas Mavropoẕaris	Yani veled-i o	Yorgi veled-i o	Todoros veled-i o	İstemad Mavropoẕaris
Dimitri birāder-i o	S̱otoki Ḳayiri	Yorgi Ḳoköloni	İstemad Coli	Miḫal Çipoliti
Yorgi Hilimiḳo	Niḳola birāder-i o	Lazaro Marino	İstemati Yorgiçoplo	Yorgi Papayorġoplo
Todoros veled-i o	Androniḳo veled-i o	S̱otoki Zaġranos	Papas Niḳolas	Dimitri Vaşılaki
Ḳosta Vaşılaki	Loẕoriti Martini	Niḳola İsḳrivo	Ẕenyamis Ḫıristiyanos	Pavlos veled-i o
Petros veled-i o	Todoros Ḳozomali	Niḳola Ḳozomali	Yani veled-i o	Yani Pepeleş
Todoros birāder-i o	S̱otoki Şuleri	Yorgi Amaẕi	Niḳola Ḳaça	Andriya birāder-i o
Aġapitos Şıpaliẕi	Liġuri Ḳokloni	Niḳola Ḳaryani	Andon ḫīş-i o	Anaġnostis Ravar
Dimitri Bilyardo	Petros Rondaki	Lanteso Rondaki	Miḫal Ḳozyanos	Niḳola Aġapitos
Yorgi Narenca	İstefano Ḳurnoẕori	mücerred Dimitri Ḳosḳo	mücerred S̱otoki Ḳosḳo	mücerred Aleksi Laẕa
mücerred Ḳosta birāder-i o	mücerred Miḫal Ḳurya	mücerred Petro Vaşılaki	mücerred [Y]orgi Pepelaş	mücerred Lazaro İstemati
mücerred Loẕoriti <F>ağurya	mücerred Niḳolas Ġarviça	bīve Mariya zen-i Petra	bīve Ḳatarina zen-i Yorgi	bīve S̱etaḳo zen-i Pavlo

bīve Marġarita zen-i Sarķos	bīve S̱etaķo zen-i Sirvo	bīve zen-i Andro Ruso	bīve [T]odora zen-i Papamiḫalina	bīve İstema[tina] Pra[kina]
bīve S̱etoke zen-i Faġurya		ḫāne 62	mücerred 10	bīve 9

105

ḥāṣıl-ı ķarye-i Artiça el-meẕkūr 8650

ʿa(n) ispence 1854	bāġāt-ı ḫāṣṣa dönüm 1 (?) [resm] 168	öşr-i bāġāt 2250	ʿöşr-i ḥınṭa 3100	ʿöşr-i cev 468	ʿöşr-i ķazz 204

ʿöşr-i meyve 11	mülk-i Yani Ķosķo der ķarye-i meẕkūr āsiyāb 1 resm 80	resm-i ḫanāzīr 5[0]	ʿöşr-i zeyt [5]	resm-i ḫamr 250	ʿöşr-i kettān 100	resm-i ʿarūsī 70

mülk-i
Aġapitos Şıpaliẕi der ķarye-i
meẕkūr
āsiyāb 1 resm 40

ķarye-i Zelaḫova — ḫāṣṣa-ı Mīrlivā

S̱otoki Rasyas	Petros Praski	Yorgi birāder-i o	Todoros birāder-i o	Yani Velçi	
Yani Evẕo[k]i	Todoros Ķostudi	Papas Petros	Yorgi Ķono	Ķozma birāder-i o	
Dimitri E[vẕ]oki	İstilyano Yorġoplo	Yorgi birāder-i o	Ķondoġuno S̱ofilaḫto	Miḫal Ẕiki	
Niķola veled-i o	Niķola Iġlava	S̱oẕosis Ķrokis	S̱otoki birāder-i o	Niķola Buva	
mücerred Yorgi Ḫalaķatava	bīve İrini zen-i Ġulyamina	bīve Anje zen-i İstrazina	ḫāne 20	mücerred 1	bīve 2

ḥāṣıl 2472

ʿa(n) ispence 537	eşcār-ı ṭut-ı ḫāṣṣa· ʿaded 10 [resm] 40	ʿöşr-i ḥınṭa 700	ʿöşr-i cev 108	ʿöşr-i ķazz 69	ʿöşr-i meyve 7
resm-i ḫanāzīr 5	ʿöşr-i kettān 20	öşr-i bāġāt 866	resm-i ḫamr 100	resm-i ʿarūsī 20	

ķarye-i Vervena — ḫāṣṣa-ı Mīrlivā

Ġulimi S̱amona	Todoros veled-i o	Ġulyamo Ķozodramo	Yani birāder-i o	Muriki Ķufoplo	
Vardas Piryoti	Yani Ķ[o]ryamela	Niķola İvlaḫyarniti	Vaşıl veled-i o	Leo Rendeno	
Rados birāder-i o	İstemad Ķutorna	Pavlos Pranovitreplos	Yorgi Ķondoġuni	Yani Randeno	
Yani Şalmeniti	Papas [Yor]gi	Dimitri veled-i o	Niķola Ķaķri	Todoros Paġaris	
Niķola Siryano	Yorgi birāder-i o	S̱oẕoş Ķuliş	Ķosta veled-i o	Yorgi veled-i o	
Yorgi S[oḫa]cis	Vaşıl Piryoti	mücerred Yorgi birāder-i Pavlos	bīve zen-i Yani	bīve Arḫondo zen-i Ķondoyani	
bīve Mariya zen-i Ermoġavliya	bīve Marina zen-i Ķolirya	bīve Ķali zen-i Plumisa	ḫāne 27	mücerred 1	bīve 5

106

ḥāṣıl-ı ķarye-i Vervena el-meẕkūr [4319]

ʿa(n) ispence [680]	bāġāt-ı [ḫā]ṣṣa d[önüm 10] [resm] 1174	ʿöşr-i bāġāt 956	ʿöşr-i ḥınṭa 1000	ʿöşr-i cev 194	ʿöşr-i ķazz 64
ʿöşr-i meyve [26]	resm-i ḫanāzīr 17	ʿöşr-i ʿasel 8	ʿöşr-i kettān 30	resm-i ʿarūsī 30	resm-i ḫamr 100

mülk-i
Ġulimi Şamona der ķarye-i meẕkūr
āsiyāb 1 resm 40

ķarye-i Ķırana — ḫāṣṣa-ı Mīrlivā

Yani Papayanoplo	Papas As̱anas	S̱otoki veled-i o	Dimitri veled-i o	Anastas Ķlukinyoti

Yani Klima	Yorgi Çuki	Dimitri veled-i o	Dimitri Uzġuroniḳola	Terapos Polyomos
Aleksi dāmād-ı o	Niḳola Parzeli	S̱erabinos Ḳapsanbeli	Yani Taġara	Yorgi İkseruni
İlya Ḳapsanbeli	Yorgi Bilis	Yani veled-i o	Yani Puloyimo	Dimitri Puloyimo
Petros Uzġuroniḳola	Yani Paliḳanoplos	Papas Sinapis	Yorgi Ḳaḳavas	Niḳola Ḳlukinyoti
Petros Angeli Sarhi	Todoros Papayanoplos	Nikita Ḳulotina	Niḳola Puloyimo	mücerred Aleksi As̱anas
mücerred Miḫal Ḳlukinyoti	mücerred Yorgi Parzeli	mücerred Vaṣıl İkseruni	bīve Andonina zen-i Izġuroniḳoliya	bīve zen-i Losa Izġuroniḳo-liya
bīve İrini zen-i Ḳarindu		ḫāne 29	mücerred 4	bīve 3

ḥāṣıl 3148

ʿa(n) ispence 843	ʿöşr-i ḥınṭa 1150	ʿöşr-i cev 172	ʿöşr-i ḳazz 86	resm-i ḫanāzīr 14	ʿöşr-i bāġāt 743	ʿöşr-i kettān 30
		resm-i ḫamr 80		resm-i ʿarūsī 30		

ḳarye-i Ḳopaniça ḫāṣṣa-ı Mīrlivā

Miḫal Mavroplo	Ya[ḳ]umo Ḳondo	Petros birāder-i o	Yorgi Damyanos	Franceṣḳo Ma[v]roplo
Dimitri Ma[vrop]llo			ḫāne [6]	

ḥāṣıl 47[0]

ʿa(n) ispence 15[0]	ʿöşr-i bāġ[āt] 1[5]8	ʿöşr-i ḥı[nṭa] [100]	ʿöşr-i cev 16	ʿö[ş]r-i [ḳazz] [9]	ʿöşr-i meyve 1	resm-i ḫanāzīr [1]
		resm-i ḫamr 15	resm-i ʿarūsī 10	ʿöşr-i kettān 10		

107
te[ti]mme-i n[ā]ḥiyyet-i Kirvuḳor

ḳarye-i Velviça ḫāṣṣa-ı Mīrlivā

Yaḳumi Puloyimos	Ḳostandin veled-i o	Yani Ḫarara	[---]ir[---] veled-i o	Todoros veled-i o
Papas Yani Puloyimo	Yaḳumis Ġaloça	Yani Mas̱os	S̱ofilaḫtos Ḫararis	Miḫal Damyano
		ḫāne 10		

ḥāṣıl 1139

ʿa(n) ispence 25[0]	ʿöşr-i bāġāt 248	ʿöşr-i ḥınṭa 500	ʿöşr-i cev 76	ʿöşr-i meyve 3	resm-i ḫanāzīr 7	ʿöşr-i kettān 15	resm-i ḫamr 30
			resm-i ʿarūsī 10				

[ḳa]rye-i Linistena ḫāṣṣa-ı Mīrlivā

Niḳola Zerdo	Petros birāder-i o	Petros Veliġostino	Yorgi Laġafti	Yorgi Andriça	
Dimitri veled-i o	Ḳosta Avrohi	Vaṣıl Saḳukö	Niḳola veled-i o	Yorgi Saḳukö	
S̱otoki İsḳolari	Nikifor Ḫalamiḳo	Yani birāder-i o	mücerred Niḳolas Niḳolaḳoplo	bīve İvrata zen-i Ḳoẕrati	
bīve Marġa-rita zen-i Kitrakiya	bīve Kiryaki zen-i Ḳaḳuçi	bīve Mariya zen-i İsḳolariya	ḫāne 13	mücerred 1	bīve 4

ḥāṣıl 1594

ʿa(n) ispence 374	ʿöşr-i bāġāt 428	ʿöşr-i ḥınṭa 550	ʿöşr-i cev 85	ʿöşr-i ḳazz 28	ʿöşr-i meyve 6	resm-i ḫanāzīr 3
mülk-i Vaṣıl Saḳukö der ḳarye-i meẕkūr āsiyāb 1 resm 40			ʿöşr-i kettān 15	resm-i ʿarūsī 15	resm-i ḫamr 50	

ḳarye-i Ondriçena ḫāṣṣa-ı Mīrlivā

Yani Ḫamaḳo	Todoros Ḫamaḳos	Yorgi Ḫamaḳo	Vaṣıl Ḳuḳoplo	Yorgi veled-i o
[İ]vlaş Laġo	Petro veled-i o	Niḳola Laġos	Yani Laġos	Yani Ḳapsali

Dimitri Ġaloça	S̱otoki Ġaloça	Aleksi Petroplo	Yani [Ġ]aloçi	Leo Maẕro
Yani Ḳaçuli	Vr[..[3].]ris Miḫolos	Dimitri Damaski[n]o[s]	[---]o Damaskino	[Pe]tro bi[r]āder-i o
Yorgi Ḳurya	Dimitri Ḳaloyani	Yani Ḫaltayi	Andriya birāder-i o	Filibos[57] Maẕros

108

tetimme-i ḳarye-i [Ond]riçena el-meẕkūr ḫāṣṣa-ı Mīrlivā

Dimitri Miḫaloplo	Manol Mavra	Ḳosta Mavriya[ni]s	Yani Maẕro	Niḳola Filitinos	
Niḳola Ḫarara	Yani Apoziḫto	Andon Ḳalopeẕarḫis	Yani Doḳ[sa]ra	Andriya Maẕros	
Di[mi]tri Ẕe[r]mato	S̱erapos Maẕros	S̱erapos Maẕros-ı dīğer	Yani Çimeryoti	Yani Ḳalo<p>eẕarhi	
Yorgi Miḫaloplo	Todoros Ġarubiças	mücerred Todoros Maẕros	mücerred Niḳola Miḫaloplo	mücerred Yani Çimeryoti	
mücerred Yani Ġarubiças	mücerred Yerardo Ḳanavaniti	bīve Mariya zen-i Ġalviça	bīve Mariya zen-i Miḫalopulina	bīve Avẕoke zen-i Yanu Madru	
bīve Andona zen-i Papaẕya-mandi	bīve Mariya zen-i Mihelina	bīve İstemati zen-i Ẕyoniya	bīve Beline zen-i Papadya	ḫāne 42	mücerred 5 bīve 7

ḫāṣıl 4187

ʿa(n) ispence 1217	ʿöşr-i bāğāt 945	ʿöşr-i ḫınṭa 1500	ʿöşr-i cev 230	ʿöşr-i ḳazz 94	resm-i ḫanāzīr 6	ʿöşr-i meyve 15
		ʿöşr-i kettān 40	resm-i ʿarūsī 40	resm-i ḫamr 100		

ḳarye-i Ẕolyani ḫāṣṣa-ı Mīrlivā

Miḫal Avroḫi	Martinos Valonç	Yani birāder-i o	Yani Kiraḳo	Yani Vari
Andon birāder-i o	Todoros Pasḳaloplos	Yorgi Hilmiḳo	Ḳosta birāder-i o	Dimitri İstralica
Niḳola Viza	Vaşıl Mavroplo	Papas Andon	Petros veled-i o	Miḫal Leoplo
Niḳola veled-i o	Ḳozma Avrilyoni	mücerred Yani Hilmiḳo	mücerred Miḫal Çoki	ḫāne 17 / mücerred 2

ḫāṣıl 2090

ʿa(n) is[pen]ce 475	ʿöşr-i bāğāt 551	ʿöşr-i ḫınṭa 800	ʿöşr-i cev 122	ʿöş[r-i] ḳazz 37	ʿöşr-i meyv[e] 4	resm-i ḫınzīr 1
		ʿöşr-i kettān 20	resm-i ʿarūsī 20	resm-i ḫamr 60		

ḳarye-i Draġoy ez cemāʿat-i Arnavudān ḫāṣṣa-ı Mīr[livā]

T[odoro]s Dra[ġoy]	[Ya]ni [Draġoy]	Andriy[a] Draġ[o]y	Niḳ[o]la D[raġo]y	Matranḳa D[raġo]y
Yorgi veled-i o	Dimitri [---]	[Yo]rgi [---]	Gi[n] İs[ḳla]va	Leḳa İsḳla[va]

109

tetimme-i ḳarye-i Draġoy el-meẕkūr ḫāṣṣa-ı Mīrlivā

Lazaro Plaşa	Marti Plaşa	Angelos Plaşa	Yani Ḳoli	Gi[n] Ḳoli
Niḳola Ḳoli	Di[m]a Ḳoli	Yorgi Ḳoli	Andriya İskliro	Marti birāder-i o
Gön Küraleşa	Leḳa birāder-i o	Gin Küraleşa	Lazaro veled-i o	Petro Küraleşa
İlya veled-i o	Niḳola Ġazi	Todoros Ġazis	Gin veled-i o	Gin Ḳuliza
Andriya Bura	Gin veled-i o	Marti Mazi	Yorgi Draġoy	mücerred Gin Jiva
mücerred Lazaro İsḳlava	mücerred Şarakin Küraleşa	mücerred Yorgi Ġazis	bīve Vaşa zen-i Mar Draġoy	bīve Ange-lina zen-i İsḳlavina
mücerred Duşa Ġazi	ḫāne 34		mücerred 5	bīve 2

ḥāṣıl 2324

ʿa(n) ispence	ʿöşr-i ḥınṭa	ʿöşr-i cev	resm-i ḫanāzīr	ʿöşr-i ʿasel	ʿöşr-i kettān	resm-i ʿarūsī
792	1200	185	28	59	30	30

ḳarye-i İskâẕa ez cemāʿat-i Arnavudān — ḫāṣṣa-ı Mīrlivā

Yani Ḳulostomanos	Gin İskâẕa	Proġono İskâẕa	Manol İskâẕa	Yorgi birāder-i o	
Manol İskâẕa	Yani İskâẕa	Petros Taç	Ḳosta Taç	Miḫal İskâẕa	
mücerred Dima İskâẕa	mücerred Ḳosta birāder-i o	mücerred Dima veled-i Manol İskâẕa	mücerred Yani Arḫondiçi	ḫāne ʿaşere	mücerred 4

ḥāṣıl 796

ʿa(n) ispence	ʿöşr-i ḥınṭa	ʿöşr-i cev	resm-i ḫanāzīr	ʿöşr-i kettān	resm-i ʿarūsī
280	400	62	29	15	10

ḳarye-i Mazarak ez cemāʿat-i Arnavudān — ḫāṣṣa-ı Mīrlivā

İş Ari Mazarak	Todoros veled-i o	Ḳosta veled-i o	Domeniḳa Boġoryano	İstefano veled-i o
İ[---] veled-i o	Pavlo Ḫırisa	Yorgi veled-i o	Gin Boġoryano	Miḫal Gerbeşi
Petro Gerbesi	Todoros Ḳolosta	Pelañrin birāder-i o	[---]o Ḳolosta	[Y]org[i] ve[led-i] o
Todoros ve[le]d-i o	Niḳola [Ḳ]laẕi	Ḳalenci [Ḳ]laẕi	İvr[a]to Ḳlaẕi	Miḫal Malak

110

tetimme-i ḳarye-i Mazarak el-meẕkūr — ḫāṣṣa-ı Mīrlivā

Yorgi birāder-i o	Gön Mazarak	Niḳol[a] birāder-i o	Dimas birāẕer-i o	Dyaleşi Dramesi
Gön Drame[s]i	Ḳosta Dramesi	Gön Maẕiñik	Yani Ḳolona	Gin birāder-i o
Mataranḳa birāder-i o	Miḫal veled-i Yani Ḳolona	Andriya Gerbesi	Yorgi birāẕer-i o	mücerred Pelañrin Ḳolosta
mücerred Gin Mazarak	mücerred Todoros veled-i Gön Mazarak	mücerred Yorgi birāder-i o	ḫāne 34	mücerred 4

ḥāṣıl 2283

ʿa(n) ispence	ʿöşr-i ḥınṭa	ʿöşr-i cev	resm-i ḫanāzīr	ʿöşr-i meyve	ʿöşr-i kettān	resm-i ʿarūsī
760	1200	185	46	17	45	30

ḳarye-i Mateşi ez cemāʿat-i Arnavudān — ḫāṣṣa-ı Mīrlivā

Ḫarandon Matesi	Yani veled-i o	Proġono Mateşi	Proġono Mateşi-i dīğer	Gin veled-i o
Dimitri Buzbardi	Yorgi Plaşi	Todoro Plaşi	Yani Mateşi	Gin veled-i o
mücerred Miraş Buzbardis		ḫāne 10		mücerred 1

ḥāṣıl 779

ʿa(n) ispence	ʿöşr-i ḥınṭa	ʿöşr-i cev	resm-i ḫanāzīr	ʿöşr-i kettān	resm-i ʿarūsī
220	450	69	15	15	10

ḳarye-i İsfranci ez cemāʿat-i Arnavudān — ḫāṣṣa-ı Mīrlivāʾ

Todoros Francis	Yani Paça	İstemad birāder-i o	Yani Francis	Bramatiḳos Paças
Niḳola veled-i o	mücerred Dimitri veled-i o		ḫāne 6	mücerred 1

ḥāṣıl 439

ʿa(n) ispence	ʿöşr-i ḥı[n]ṭa	ʿöşr-i cev	ʿöşr-i bāğāt	resm-i ḫanāzīr	resm-i ʿarūsī	ʿöşr-i kettān
140	200	31	45	8	5	10

ḳarye-i Mizotoro ez cemāʿat-i Arnavudān — ḫāṣṣa-ı Mīrlivā

Niḳola Mizotoro	Yorg[i] Mizetoro	Yani Mizetoro	Pet[ros] Ari[.[1]]i[.[2].]	Yera[---] A[---]
	[bī]ve Lazarobulina		ḫāne 5	bīve 1

ḥāṣıl 520

ʿa(n) ispence	ʿöşr-i ḥınṭa	ʿöşr-i cev	resm-i ḫanāzīr	ʿöşr-i ʿasel
106	350	54	4	6

111
tetimme-i nāḥiyyet-i Kirvuḳor

ḳarye-i Beluşi ez cemāʿat-i Arnavudān — ḫāṣṣa-ı Mīrlivā

Yorgi Beluşi	Proġonos veled-i o	Yani Beluşi	Miḫal veled-i o	Yorgi birāder-i meẕkūr
Yani Beluşi	Miḫal birāder-i o	Yani Petali	Yorgi Panḳrati	İl[y]a birāder-i o
Petros Panḳrati	Ḳalişa Panḳrati	Ẕyaḳo Pratasa	Marḳo Pranişa	Lazaro Virgi
Gön birāder-i o	Petro Beluşi	mücerred Todoros Beluşi	mücerred Yorgi Panḳrati	mücerred Yani Pranasa
mücerred Marti Pratişa		ḫāne 17		mücerred 4

ḥāṣıl 1048

ʿa(n) ispence	ʿöşr-i ḥınṭa	ʿöşr-i cev	resm-i ḫanāzīr	ʿöşr-i kettān	resm-i ʿarūsī
420	500	78	15	20	15

ḳarye-i Mujak ez cemāʿat-i Arnavudān — ḫāṣṣa-ı Mīrlivā

Leḳa Mujak	Yorgi veled-i o	Aleksi Mujak	Todoros Mujak	Domaniḳa veled-i o
Proġonos veled-i o	Miḫal Mujak	Yorgi veled-i o	Bardi Mujak	Gin Mujak
mücerred Bardi ḫīş-i Proġono		ḫāne 10		mücerred 1

ḥāṣıl 795

ʿa(n) ispence	ʿöşr-i ḥınṭa	ʿöşr-i cev	resm-i ḫanāzīr	ʿöşr-i ʿasel	ʿöşr-i kettān	resm-i ʿarūsī
220	450	68	30	2	15	10

ḳarye-i Ḳanḳaẕi ez cemāʿat-i Arnavudān — ḫāṣṣa-ı Mīrlivā

Yorgi Ḳanḳaẕi	Gön birāder-i o	Petros Parapungi	Lazaro Perleftino	Manḳola Ḳalanci
Ḳozma veled-i o	Gin Ḳalenci	İvrato Ḳavasila	Yorg[i] birāẕer-i o	Uzġuro Ḳanḳaẕi
mücerred Ḳozma Para[p]ungi		ḫāne 10		mücerred 1

ḥāṣıl 854

ʿa(n) ispence	ʿöşr-i ḥınṭa	ʿöşr-i cev	resm-i ḫa[n]āzīr	ʿöşr-i kettān	resm-i ʿarūsī
220	500	76	[33]	15	10

112
[tetimme-i nāḥiyyet-i] Kir[vu]ḳor

ḳarye-i [Ma]zarak Ad[i]po [ez] cemāʿat-i Ar[na]vudān — ḫāṣṣa-ı Mīrlivā

Yorg[i] Mazar[ak]	Petros Şalesi	Domaniḳa birāẕer-i o	Dima Br[a]matiḳa	İştin birāder-i o
Aleksi birāẕer-i o	Andriya Ḳuçi	Gön Ḳuçi	Marti Ḳuçi	Proġono Ḳuçi
Andriya İvlaḫyoti	Ḳozma İvlaḫyoti	Yorgi İvlaḫyoti	Todoros Ḳumis	Dimo Ḳumi
Lazaro Geg	Rayḳa Ḳumi	Todoros veled-i o	İvrato Budina	A[n]driya veled-i o
Andriya Ḳuçi	Gin Parapungi	Yani Şalesi	Domaniḳa Şalesi	Muriki [Şa]lesi
Siryani Şaleşi	Todoro İvlaḫyoti	Andriya İvlaḫyoti	Dima Ġramatiḳo	Yorgi Vuti
Yani birāder-i o	Andriya Ḳumi	Todoros Ḳumi	Yorgi Marḳoplo	Gin Mazarak

Leḳa Ḳuçi	Çingene Ropesi	Çingene Somas	Çingene Ḳosta veled-i o	mücerred Niḳola birāder-i Dima Ġramatiḳo

mücerred Niḳola İvlaḫyoti	mücerred Dima ḫīş-i Ḳumi	mücerred Gön Parabungi[58]	bīve Manḳa zen-i Ḳuçi	bīve Ḫana zen-i İvlaḫyoti
bīve Neje zen-i Ḳumi		ḫāne 39	mücerred 4	bīve 3

ḥāṣıl 3507

ʿa(n) ispence	ʿöşr-i ʿasel	ʿöşr-i kettān	ʿöşr-i ḥınṭa	ʿöşr-i cev	resm-i ḫanāzīr	resm-i ʿarūsī
878	23	100	2050	309	107	40

ḳarye-i Floḳa ez cemāʿat-i Arnavudān — ḫāṣṣa-ı Mīrlivā

Yorgi Floḳa	Petro Floḳa	Niḳola İsratura	Yani birāder-i o	İş Ari Bezulḳa

Lisardo Floḳa	Gön Floḳa	Todoros Mazarak	Ẕonati bir[ād]er-i o	İvrato Burça

ḫāne 10

ḥāṣıl 881

ʿa(n) ispence	ʿöşr-i ḥınṭ[a]	ʿöşr-i ce[v]	resm-i ḫanāzīr	ʿöşr-i kettān	resm-i ʿarūsī
200	550	83	23	15	10

ḳarye-i Jupan ez cemāʿat-i Arnavudān ḫāṣṣa-ı Mīrlivā

İvr[ato] Jupan	Beluşi veled-i o	Dima Zupano	Yani Zupano	Dima Zupano

113

te[ti]mme-i [ḳa]rye-i Jupan[o] el-meẕk[ūr] ḫ[ā]ṣṣa-ı Mīrlivā

Pelañrin [Zu]pa[no]	Niḳola birāder-i o	Andriya birāder-i o	Yor[g]i Mazaraki	Niḳola Mustaki
Ḳosta Meġalyoni	G[i]n [Ḳ]uçi	Marti birāder-i o	Gin Varponbi	Domeniḳa birāẕer-i o
Dara Zupano	Pelañrin Zupano-<yı> dīğer	Lazaro veled-i o	İstefano Floḳa	Lazaro birāder-i o
Floḳa veled-i İste[f]ano	İlya Beṣulḳa	Pelañrin Zupano-<yı> dıger	mücerred Lazaro birāder-i Floḳa	ḫāne 23 mücerred 1

ḥāṣıl 1542

ʿa(n) ispence	ʿöşr-i kettān	ʿöşr-i ḥınṭa	ʿöşr-i cev	resm-i ḫanāzīr	ʿöşr-i ʿasel	resm-i ʿarūsī
480	60	800	120	44	18	20

ḳarye-i Anize ez cemāʿat-i Arnavudān ḫāṣṣa-ı Mīrlivā

Yorgi Anize	Varda Anize	İştin birāder-i o	İstemati Plaşa	Ḫaratin Liveri
Andriya Yela	Ḳaḳuri birāẕer-i o	Domeniḳa Yela	Todoros birāder-i o	Ḳaḳuri Yela
Andriya veled-i o	Yorgi Suḳula	Sirvo birāder-i o	Petros Saḳulas	Yeta Saḳulas

mücerred Yorgi Varda el-meẕkūr	mücerred Gin Yela birāder-i Ḳaḳuri	mücerred Gin Yela-<yı> dīğer	ḫāne 15	mücerred 3

ḥāṣıl 906

ʿa(n) ispence	ʿöşr-i ḥınṭa	ʿöşr-i cev	resm-i ḫanāzīr	ʿöşr-i kettān	resm-i ʿarūsī
360	400	64	52	15	15

ḳarye-i [L]onci ez cemāʿat-i Arnavudān ḫāṣṣa-ı Mīrlivā

Yorgi Lonci	Gön veled-i o	Petros Lonci	Gin Lonci	Marti Ḳuçi
An[d]riya Ḳuçi	Y[o]rgi Ḳuçi	Ḳozma Zotali	Toya Zuġra	Gön Zuġra
Petro Zuġra	Pavlo Zoġr[a]	Ḳral Ḳurtesi	Gin birāder-i o	Oresi birāder-i o
Todoros birāder-i o	Ḳozma Küraleş	Todoros birāder-i o	Petros İsḳlava	Yorgi veled-i o
Marti vele[d-i o]	Lazaro Bala	Andriya birāder-i o	Andriya [Mu]zaki	Gön Ḳriyari
Yorgi İsḳlava	Martin İsḳlava	mücerred Petro Zotali	mücerred Andriya ḫīş-i Ḳral Ḳurtedi	mücerred Niḳola Petros

ḫāne 27 mücerred 3

114

ḥāṣıl-ı ḳarye-i Lonci el-meẕkūr 1704

ʿa(n) ispence	ʿöşr-i ḥınṭa	ʿöşr-i cev	resm-i ḫanāzīr	mülk-i Petros İsḳlava der ḳarye-i meẕkūr āsiyāb 1 resm 80	ʿöşr-i kettān	resm-i ʿarūsī
600	800	123	51		30	20

ḳarye-i Sirvu ez cemāʿat-i Arnavudān ḫāṣṣa-ı Mīrlivā

Yorgi Sirvo	Leḳa birāder-i o	Gin birāder-i o	Yani Dara	Petros Dara
Yorgi birāder-i o	Todoros birāder-i o	Ṣomas Boḳranos	Niḳola birāder-i o	Gin birāder-i o

Marti Dara	Yorgi Klisotis	Leḳa Dara	Yorgi Sirvo	Lazaro Sirvo
Gin birāder-i o	Aġali birāẕer-i o	Sirvo Velyano	Luşi birāẕer-i o	Yorgi Manolato
Sirvo veled-i o	Yorgi Manolato	Niḳola Manolato	Proġono Poġriyano	Yorgi Manolato
Sirvo birāder-i o	Lazaro birāder-i o	mücerred Yorgi Ġavrili	mücerred Leḳa birāder-i o	mücerred Martin Yorgi Manolato
	ḫāne 27		mücerred 3	

ḥāṣıl 1835

ʿa(n) ispence 600	ʿöşr-i kettān 100	ʿöşr-i ḥınṭa 900	ʿöşr-i cev 138	resm-i ḫanāzīr 72	resm-i ʿarūsī 25

ḳarye-i Ranesi ez cemāʿat-i Arnavudān — ḫāṣṣa-ı Mīrlivā

Andriya Ranesi	Yorgi birāder-i o	Petros Ranesi	Vardas birāder-i o	Aleksi Ḳaparalis
Yorgi birāder-i o	Varda Ranesi	Andriya birāder-i o	Yani S̱ana	Gin birāder-i o
Yorgi Mazi	Andriya birāder-i o	Manḳola birāder-i o	Todoros Ranesi	Todoros S̱ana
	mücerred Sirvo birāder-i o	ḫāne 15		mücerred 1

ḥāṣıl 1161

ʿa(n) ispence 320	ʿöşr-i kettān 80	ʿöşr-i ḥınṭa 600	ʿöşr-i cev 91	mülk-i Andriya Ranesi der ḳarye-i meẕkūr āsiyāb 1 resm 40	resm-i ḫanāzīr 15	resm-i ʿarūsī 15

ḳarye-i ez cemāʿat-i Arnavudān — ḫāṣṣa-ı Mīrlivā

Yani Valaḳ	Andriya Floḳa	Petros veled-i o	Gin Riya	Todoros Mavromati
Yorgi Kiraçi	Vaṣıl Maḳri	Yorgi Buva	Proġono Buva	mücerred Gin ḫīş-i Yani Valaḳ

115

tetimme-i ḳarye-i Valaḳ el-meẕkūr — ḫāṣṣa-ı Mīrlivā

mücerred Petro Proġono Buva	bīve Marta Valaḳa	bīve İstatira	ḫāne 9	mücerred 2	bīve 2

ḥāṣıl 653

ʿa(n) ispence 232	ʿöşr-i kettān 40	ʿöşr-i ḥınṭa 300	ʿöşr-i cev 48	resm-i ḫanāzīr 23	resm-i ʿarūsī 10

ḳarye-i Ḳraḳuki ez cemāʿat-i Arnavudān — ḫāṣṣa-ı Mīrlivā

Yorgi Ḳraḳuki	Petro Ḳraḳuki	Aleksi Buḳovi	Gin birāder-i o	Niḳola Ranbiḳa	
Varda Plaşa	Gin birāder-i o	Ġulyamo Plaşa	bīve Babo zen-i Plaşina	ḫāne 8	bīve 1

ḥāṣıl 727

ʿa(n) ispence 166	ʿöşr-i ḥınṭa 450	ʿöşr-i cev 69	resm-i ḫanāzīr 22	ʿöşr-i kettān 10	resm-i ʿarūsī 10

ḳarye-i Peta ez cemāʿat-i Arnavudān — ḫāṣṣa-ı Mīrlivā

Lazaro Peta	Ḳosta Peta	Petro veled-i o	Yorgi veled-i o	Ḳosta Peta
Ḳosta veled-i o	Yorgi Parapungi	Todoros Peta	Lazaro Peta	Gin Parabungi[59]
	bīve Manḳa zen-i Parapunḳina	ḫāne 10		bīve 1

ḥāṣıl 574

ʿa(n) ispence 206	ʿöşr-i kettān 40	ʿöşr-i ḥınṭa 250	ʿöşr-i cev 40	resm-i ḫanāzīr 28	resm-i ʿarūsī 10

ḳarye-i Draġuẕisti ez cemāʿat-i Arnavudān ḫāṣṣa-ı Mīrlivā

Yorgi D[r]aġuẕisti	Lazaro Ḫamaḳo	ḫāne 2

ḥāṣıl 180

ʿa(n) ispence	ʿöşr-i ḥınṭa	ʿöşr-i cev	ʿöşr-i meyve	ʿöşr-i bāġ
40	100	16	2	22

ḳarye-i Drayina ez cemāʿat-i Arnavudān ḫāṣṣa-ı Mīrlivā

Uzġur Drayina	Gin Mustaki	Yorgi Drayina	Gin Drayina	Pavlos Kir[sar]ḫis	
Ḳozma Drayina	Lazaro birāder-i o	Gön Drayina	Gön Drayina-ı dīğer	Yani Klisarhi	
Yorgi Klisarhi	Miḫal Klisarhi	mücerred Gin veled-i Uzġur Drayina	mücerred Gön birāder-i Gin Mustaki	mücerred Niḳola bin Yorgi Drayina	
mücerred Pavlos Drayina	mücerred Todoros veled-i Gön Drayina	mücerred Cingene Yorgi Varinpobi	mücerred Cingene Ḳalanci birāẕer-i o	ḫāne 12	mücerred 7

116

ḥāṣıl-ı ḳarye-i Drayina el-meẕkūr 14[49]

ʿa(n) [ispence]	ʿoşr-i ḥınṭa	ʿöşr-i cev	mülk-i Uzġur Drayina der ḳarye-i meẕkūr āsiyāb 1 resm 80	resm-i ḫanāzī[r]	ʿöşr-i kettān	resm-i ʿarūsī
380	750	109		25	15	10

mülk-i Gön Drayina der ḳarye-i meẕkūr āsiyāb 1 resm 80

ḳarye-i Ḳonbi Ṣeḳra ez cemāʿat-i Arnavudān ḫāṣṣa-ı Mīrlivā

An[.².]se Ḳonbi Ṣeḳra	Ḳanḳaẕi Martino	Gin Ḳanḳaẕi	Ḳozma Ḳonbi Ṣeḳra	Dimitri İstoyanis
Manol İstoyanis	İstemati İstoyanis		ḫāne 7	

ḥāṣıl 522

ʿa(n) ispence	ʿöşr-i ḥınṭa	ʿöşr-i cev	resm-i ḫanāzīr	öşr-i kettān	resm-i ʿarūsī
140	300	46	11	15	10

ḳarye-i İstoya ez cemāʿat-i Arnavudān ḫāṣṣa-ı Mīrlivā

İstoya Maẕi	Marti veled-i o	Gön veled-i o	Marti Maẕi	Yorgi veled-i o	
mücerred Yorgi Maẕi	mücerred Ḳozma Maẕi	bīve Baya zen-i Maẕi	ḫāne 5	mücerred 2	bīve 1

ḥāṣıl 434

ʿa(n) ispence	ʿöşr-i kettān	ʿöşr-i ḥınṭa	ʿöşr-i cev	resm-i ḫanāzīr	öşr-i bāġāt	resm-i ʿarūsī
146	20	200	31	5	22	10

ḳarye-i Lazar Buva ez cemāʿat-i Arnavudān ḫāṣṣa-ı Mīrlivā

Duşi Buva	Yani Graḳa	Yorgi birāder-i o	Dima Ḳusofaki	Proġono birāder-i o	
Ḳalenci Ḳuçi	Gin veled-i o	Gin Mahyara	bīve Frosi zen-i Bura	ḫāne 8	bīve 1

ḥāṣıl 660

ʿa(n) ispence	ʿöşr-i kettān	ʿöşr-i ḥınṭa	ʿöşr-i cev	mülk-i Duşi Buva der ḳarye-i meẕkūr āsiyāb 1 resm 30	öşr-i bāġāt	resm-i ḫanāzīr	resm-i ʿarūsī
166	20	350	54		22	8	[1]0

ḳarye-i Lazaro Kemer ez cemāʿat-i Arnavudān ḫāṣṣa-ı Mīrlivā

Lazaro el-meẕkūr	Marti Kemer	Leḳa Kemeri	Yorgi birāder-i o	Niḳola Kemer

Petro	ḫāne
birāder-i o	6

ḥāṣıl 534

ʿa(n)	ʿöşr-i	ʿöşr-i	ʿöşr-i	resm-i
i[spe]nce	ḥınṭa	cev	bāġāt	ḫanāzīr
120	300	4[5]	44	15
		ʿöşr-i		
		kettān		
		10		

117

tetimme-i [nā]ḥiyyet-i Kirvuḳor

ḳarye-i Ẕunato ez [ce]māʿat-ı Arnavudān — ḫāṣṣa-ı Mīrlivā

Gön	Leḳ[a]	Pulimano	Ḳumani	Andriya
Ẕunato	Z[.ʾ]lcis		Zuġra	Barçi

ḫāne 5

ḥāṣıl 356

ʿa(n)	ʿöşr-i	ʿöşr-i	ʿöşr-i	resm-i
ispence	kettān	ḥınṭa	cev	ḫanāzīr
100	20	200	31	5

ḳarye-i Ḳarvunari ez cemāʿat-i Arnavudān — ḫāṣṣa-ı Mīrlivā

Gin	Yorgi	Niḳola	Dimitri	Dimitri
Ḳarvunari	Ḳarvunari	Sirvo	veled-i o	Ḳumi
Niḳola	Yorgi	Yorgi	Bardi	Yorgi
Buva	Muşura	İşpata	Matranḳa	Floḳa

ḫāne 10

ḥāṣıl 479

ʿa(n)	ʿöşr-i	ʿöşr-i	ʿöşr-i	resm-i	ʿöşr-i	resm-i
ispence	ḥınṭa	cev	bāġāt	ḫanāzīr	kettān	ʿarūsī
200	200	30	22	2	15	10

ḳarye-i Murik Maji ez cemāʿat-i Arnavudān — ḫāṣṣa-ı Mīrlivā

Murik	Yani	Ḳosta	Lazar	Yorgi
Maji	Pravata	birāder-i o	Peta	birāder-i o
el-meẕkūr				
Manol	Miḫal	Proġono	Leḳa	Gön
Velizima	dāmād-ı o	Toya	birāder-i o	Maji
				mücerred
Marti	Gön	Yani	Andriya	Petro
Maji	Maji	Maji	Maji	veled-i o

ḫāne	mücerred
14	1

ḥāṣıl 791

ʿa(n)	ʿöşr-i	ʿöşr-i	ʿöşr-i	mülk-i	resm-i	ʿöşr-i
ispence	kettān	ḥınṭa	cev	Murik Maji	ḫanāzīr	bāġāt
300	20	300	47	der ḳarye-i	57	22
				meẕkūr āsiyāb 1		
				resm 30		

resm-i ʿarūsī 15

ḳarye-i [M]iziḳa ez cemāʿat-i Arnavudān — ḫāṣṣa-ı Mīrlivā

Petros	Yorgi	Yani	Petro	Gön
Miziḳa	Ḳonboti	Rodovano	ḫīş-i o	Maji

ḫāne 5

ḥāṣıl 351

ʿa(n)	ʿöşr-i	ʿöşr-i	ʿöşr-i	resm-i
ispence	kettān	ḥınṭa	cev	ḫanāzīr
100	15	200	30	6

118

tetimme-i [nā]ḥiyyet-i Kirvuḳor

ḳarye-i Ḳuçi ez cemāʿat-i Arnavudān — ḫāṣṣa-ı Mīrlivā

Pr[o]ġono	[Do]meniḳa	Petro	Ḳuçi	[L]ori
Ḳuç[i]	Ḳuçi	Ḳuçi	Domeniḳa	birāder-i o
Gin	Yorgi	Petro	[Ma]rti	Yani
Ḳuçi	Ḳuçi	Ḳuçi-i dīğer	Peta	[Todoros]
Papas			ḫāne	
Miḫal			11	
Protonotari				

ḥāṣıl 677

ʿa(n)	ʿöşr-i	ʿöşr-i	ʿöşr-i	ʿöşr-i	resm-i	resm-i
ispence	kettān	ḥınṭa	cev	bāġāt	ḫanāzīr	ʿarūsī
220	25	300	48	56	18	10

ḳarye-i Ranesi ez cemāʿat-i Arnavudān — ḫāṣṣa-ı Mīrlivā

Rayḳa Ranesi	Yorgi veled-i o	Yani Ranesi	Yorgi Ṣuli	Leḳa birāder-i o
Ḳosta birāder-i o	Lazaro veled-i Yorgi el-meẕkūr	Andriya İspata	Petro Geta	Andriya Ranesi
Lazaro birāder-i o	Marḳo birāder-i o	Sirvo birāder-i o	Leḳa Biçi	Yorgi birāder-i o
Yani Ṣuli	Todoro Tirfila	Dima Ranesi	Yorgi veled-i o	Maji Petro
Yani birāder-i o	Yorgi Ranesi	Petro Ranesi	Lazaro birāder-i o	Yorgi Selyoti
Yorgi İstopas̱i	Ḳosta birāder-i o	Todoros İstopas̱i	Buza birāder-i o	Petro Purnos
Domeniḳa Ranesi	Yorgi birāder-i o	İvretos Ranesi	Yani Ḳaloyoros	mücerred Lazaro İspata
mücerred Yorgi Ṣuli	mücerred Yani Ranesi	mücerred Lazari birāder-i o	mücerred Niḳola Ranesi	mücerred Andriya Ranesi

ḫāne 34 — mücerred 6

ḥāṣıl 2706

ʿa(n) ispence 80[0]	ʿöşr-i kettān [100]	ʿöşr-i ḥınṭa [1]350	ʿöşr-i cev 215	mülk-i Rayḳa Ranesi der ḳarye-i meẕkūr āsiyāb 1 resm 60	ʿöşr-i bāġāt 67

resm-i ḫanāzīr 77	ʿöşr-i meyve 2	resm-i ʿarūsī 35

119

tetimme-i nāḥiyyet-i Kirvuḳor

ḳarye-i Maḳrişa ez cemāʿat-i Arnavudā[n] — ḫāṣṣa-ı Mīrlivā

Yani Maḳrişa	Petro birāder-i o	Yani Dembralis	Gin [bi]rāder-i [o]	Niḳola bir[āde]r-i o
Andriya Ḳostala	Gin Ḳuçi	Yani İstemateplo	Vas̱i birāder-i o	Dima İstema[tep]lo
Niḳola [---]ari	[Ya]ni birāder-i o	Niḳola Ḳuvala	Petro Romo	Yorgi dāmād-ı o
Yorgi [Ḳo]ndo	Petro Ḳondo	Rada Franḳuli	Yani Fila	Petro Ṣuli
Dimitri Ḫoreftara	S̱otoki birāder-i o	Petro Maji	Yani veled-i Papas	Niḳola birāder-i o
Gin Ḳuçi	mücerred Yorgi Romo	mücerred Niḳola Fila	mücerred İvratos Fila	mücerred Yorgi Ṣuli

ḫāne 26 — mücerred 4

ḥāṣıl 1684

ʿa(n) ispence 600	ʿöşr-i kettān 60	ʿöşr-i ḥınṭa 700	ʿöşr-i cev 108	ʿöşr-i bāġāt 78	resm-i ḫanāzīr 63	mülk-i Yani Maḳrişa der ḳarye-i meẕkūr āsiyāb 1 resm 50

resm-i ʿarūsī 25

ḳarye-i Omlo ez cemāʿat-i Arnavudān — ḫāṣṣa-ı Mīrlivā

Leḳa Beluşi	Gön birāder-i o	Todoros birāder-i o	Dima birāder-i o	Pavlos birāder-i o	
Pavlos Argiti	Niḳola Mezaro	Petros Pahistemato	Yani Kipro	Ḳaluşi Vironi	
mücerred Yorgi Beluşi	mücerred Gön Beluşi	mücerred Yorgi Mezaro	mücerred Andrıya Vironi	mücerred Gŏn Flokina	
mücerred Niḳola Ṣuli	bīve Ḳuke zen-i Gön Beluşi	bīve Flokine	ḫāne 10	mücerred 6	bīve 2

ḥāṣıl 734

ʿa(n) ispence 332	ʿöşr-i ḥı[nṭ]a 300	ʿöşr-i cev 45	resm-i ḫanāzīr 22	ʿöşr-i kettān 20	resm-i ʿarūsī 15

ḳarye-i [Bi]zbardi ez cemāʿat-i Arnavudān — ḫāṣṣa-ı Mīrlivā

Gin Bizb[ardi]	Vas̱i Bizbardi	Mangişa Tiryarhi	L[az]aro veled-i o	Yorgi Zervos
Gin Zervos	Marti Franḳına	Gön Zervos	Yorgi Franḳına	İştin birāẕer-i o

120

tetimme-i [Bi]zbar[d]i el-meẕkūr der nā[ḫ]iyyet-i Kirvuḳor ḫāṣṣa-ı Mīrlivā

Yorgi Mayira	Ḳost[a] bi[r]āder-i o	Miḫal Ḳurtesi	To[d]oros veled-i o	Niḳola Ḳurtesi
Todoros veled-i o	T[o]doros Tateza	Todoros Çapoġa	mücerred Todoros Tiryarhi	[müce]rred [To]doros [F]ranḳa
mücerred Yorgi Ḳurtis	mücerred Gin Çapoġa	ḫāne 18		mücerred 4

ḥāṣıl 1187

ʿa(n) ispence	ʿöşr-i ḥınṭa	ʿöşr-i cev	resm-i ḫanāzīr	ʿöşr-i kettān	resm-i ʿarūsī
440	600	91	6	30	20

ḳarye-i Monaḫu ez cemāʿat-i Arnavudān ḫāṣṣa-ı Mīrlivā

Andriya Monaḫo	Gin veled-i o	Todoros veled-i o	Yorgi İzmoliti	Andriya Sirvo
Gin veled-i o	Ḳozma Varponbi	Miḫal veled-i o	Gin veled-i o	Niḳola Manesi
Dimitri Monaḫo	Andriya veled-i o	Yorgi İpṣoma	İvlaşi Monoḫos[60]	Niḳola Ḳuçi
mücerred Ḳosta İpṣoma		ḫāne 15		mücerred 1

ḥāṣıl 886

ʿa(n) ispence	ʿöşr-i kettān	ʿöşr-i ḥınṭa	ʿöşr-i cev	resm-i ḫanāzīr	resm-i ʿarūsī
320	30	400	62	59	15

ḳarye-i Ḳoḳla ez cemāʿat-i Arnavudān ḫāṣṣa-ı Mīrlivā

İvretos Ḳoḳlas	Marti Çapoġa	Petro veled-i o	Andriya Piçi	Gin veled-i o
Bardi Biçi	mücerred Domaniḳa ḫīş-i İvretos el-meẕkūr	mücerred Bardi Çapoġa	ḫāne 6	mücerred 2

ḥāṣıl 413

ʿa(n) ispence	ʿöşr-i ḥınṭa	ʿöşr-i cev	ʿöşr-i ʿasel	resm-i ḫanāzīr	ʿöşr-i kettān
160	200	31	10	2	10

ḳarye-i Kefiñali ez cemāʿat-i Arnavudān ḫāṣṣa-ı Mīrlivā

Ḳozma Kefiñali	[Y]orgi veled-i o	Andriya Kefiñali	Le[ḳa] birāder-i o	Gin ḫīş-i o
	İştin Drameşi[61]		ḫā[n]e 6	

ḥāṣıl 363

ʿa(n) ispence	ʿöşr-i ḥınṭa	ʿöşr-i cev	resm-i ḫanāzīr	ʿöşr-i kettān
120	200	30	3	10

121

tetimme-i nāḫiyyet-i Kirvuḳor

ḳarye-i Ḳopiça e[z cem]āʿa[t-i] Arnavudān ḫāṣṣa-ı Mīrlivā

Muriki Ḳopiça	Ḳazneş veled-i o	İstefano Ḳanota	Andriya Luzi	Andriya Barçi
İştin Küraleş	İştin Floḳa	Petros Floḳa	Gin Floḳa	ḫāne 9

ḥāṣıl 593

ʿa(n) ispence	ʿöşr-i ḥınṭa	ʿöşr-i cev	resm-i ḫanāzīr	ʿöşr-i ʿasel	ʿöşr-i kettān	resm-i ʿarūsī
180	300	46	23	14	20	10

ḳarye-i Barçi ez cemāʿat-i Arnavudān ḫāṣṣa-ı Mīrlivā

Yani Barçi	Girḳa veled-i o	Yorgi Barça	Niḳola Barça	Gin Helmesi
Pavlos veled-i o	Lazaro veled-i o	Pavlos Barça	Çavuşi birā-der-i o	Gön Barça
Yorgi Barçi	Petro veled-i o	Lazaro Ḳuçi	Gin Ranesi	Leḳa Ḳaḳruḳ
Gin Ḳaḳruḳ	Gön Ḳaḳruḳ	Ḳosta Ḳaḳruḳ	Lazaro Debranis	Gin Ḳaḳruḳ-ı dīğer
Ḳosta veled-i o	Niḳola veled-i o	Proġono Barçi	Sin Barçi	Marti Manesi

Andriya Barçi	Yani Panḳrati	Yorgi Praşeri[62]	mücerred Yorgi Panḳrati	ḫāne 28	mücerred 1

ḥāṣıl 1810

ʿa(n) ispence	ʿöşr-i kettān	ʿöşr-i ḥınṭa	ʿöşr-i cev	resm-i ḫanāzīr	ʿöşr-i ʿasel	resm-i ʿarūsī
580	80	900	138	79	8	25

ḳarye-i Maẕi ez cemāʿat-i Arnavudān ḫāṣṣa-ı Mīrlivā

Yorgi Maẕi	Marti veled-i o	Gön veled-i o	İstefano Maẕi	Yorgi Ḳumuzi
		ḫāne 5		

ḥāṣıl 328

ʿa(n) ispence 10[0]	ʿöşr-i ḥınṭa 15[0]	ʿöşr-i cev 23	mülk-i Yorgi Maẕi der ḳarye-i meẕkūr āsiyāb 1 resm 40	ʿöşr-i kettān 15

ḳarye-i Pasḳali ez cemāʿat-i Arnavudān ḫāṣṣa-ı Mīrlivā

Andriya Pasḳali	Dima veled-i o	Yorgi Pasḳali	Yorgi Biḳa	Niḳola birāder-i o
	Gin Maji		ḫāne 6	

122

ḥāṣıl-ı ḳarye-i Pasḳal el-meẕkūr 314

ʿa(n) ispence 120	ʿöşr-i ḥınṭa 150	ʿöşr-i cev 24	ʿöşr-i kettān 10	resm-i ʿarūsī 10

ḳarye-i Ḳukesi ez cemāʿat-i Arnavudān ḫāṣṣa-ı Mīrlivā

Ḳostandin Ḳukesi	Niḳola veled-i o	Yani Ṣarakin	Miḫal Peta	Niḳola veled-i o	
Proġono Beluşi	mücerred Yorgi Ṣarakin	bīve Martina zen-i Niḳola	ḫāne 6	mücerred 1	bīve 1

ḥāṣıl 479

ʿa(n) ispence 146	ʿöşr-i ḥınṭa 250	ʿöşr-i cev 53	resm-i ḫanāzīr 15	ʿöşr-i kettān 15

ḳarye-i Melita ez cemāʿat-i Arnavudān ḫāṣṣa-ı Mīrlivā

Yorgi Melita	Todoros Belutis	Simos Ḳumi	Pelañris veled-i o	ḫāne 4

ḥāṣıl 216

ʿa(n) ispence 80	ʿöşr-i ḥınṭa 100	ʿöşr-i cev 16	resm-i ḫanāzīr 10	ʿöşr-i kettān 10

ḳarye-i Maji ez cemāʿat-i Arnavudān ḫāṣṣa-ı Mīrlivā

Dima Maji	Andriya birāder-i o	Andriya ḫīş-i o	Yorgi Ḫuropalati	Dima birāder-i o
Todoros Rafti	Andriya Maji	Niḳola Maji	Petros Maji	mücerred Gin Bulu[ḳa]
	ḫāne 9		mücerred 1	

ḥāṣıl 654

ʿa(n) ispence 200	ʿöşr-i ḥınṭa 350	ʿöşr-i cev 54	resm-i ḫanāzīr 20	ʿöşr-i kettān 20	resm-i ʿarūsī 10

ḳarye-i Luzi ez cemāʿat-i Arnavudān ḫāṣṣa-ı Mīrlivā

Domeniḳa Luzi	Yorgi Luzi	İvrato Luzi	Yorgi Luzi	mücerred Leḳa Luzi
mücerred Domeniḳa Luzi-i dīğer	mücerred Gin Luzi	ḫāne 4	mücerred 3	

ḥāṣıl 396

ʿa(n) ispence 14[0]	ʿöşr-i ḥınṭa 200	ʿöşr-i cev 31	resm-i ḫanazīr 10	ʿöşr-i kettān 15

ḳarye-i İsḳala ḫāṣṣa-ı Mīrlivā

İ[stem]at[i] Ḳori[t]i	Ḳosta veled-i o	N[i]kita Ḳordo[.^{2}.]ri	Yani Muçi	İlya Ġramatiḳ[o]
			ḫāne 5	

ḥāṣıl

ʿa(n) ispence 125	muḳāṭa[ʿ]a-ı ṭalyan-ı ḫāṣṣa 1 [resm] 250	resm-i sakız-ı çam-ı ḫāṣṣa ʿaded 500 [resm] 90	res[m-i] palām[ū]ṭlu-<yı> ḫāṣṣa ʿaded 200 [resm] 50	eşcār-ı zeyt-i ḫāṣṣa ʿaded 6 [resm] 7	e[ş]cār-ı [me]yve-i ḫ[ā]ṣṣa ʿaded 32 [resm] 60

ʿöşr-i ḥınṭa 200	ʿöşr-i cev 30	ʿöşr-i kettān 15

123
tetimme-i nāḥiyyet-i Kirvuḳor

ḳarye-i Ṣarakin — ḫāṣṣa-ı Mīrlivā

Vaṣi Ṣarakin	Yorgi Ṣarakin	Andon Ṣarakin	İstefano Franḳo	Gin Ḳulami
Muriki Ṣarakin	Aleksi Manol	Gin İsḳarpi	Andriya Ṣarakin	Yorgi Ṣarakin
Lazaro Alaġatora	Miḫal Alaġatora	Petros Ṣarakin	Andriya Ḳandilyoti	Lazaro Ḳandilyoti
Niḳola Ṣarakin	Lazaro Ṣarakin	Gön Ṣarakin	Pavlos Ḫuruso	Gin Ṣarakin
Proġono Ṣarakin	Seraḳo Velize	Gön Ḫalanbraze	bīve Vaṣya	bīve Marta

ḫāne 23 — bīve 2

ḥāṣıl 1257

ʿa(n) ispence	ʿöşr-i ḥınṭa	ʿöşr-i cev	resm-i ḫanāzīr	ʿöşr-i kettān	resm-i ʿarūsī
587	500	80	15	50	25

ḳarye-i Trestena — ḫāṣṣa-ı Mīrlivā

Yani Mavriyano	Manol Porḳopi[63]	Filibos[64] birāder-i o	Yorgi Proḳopi	Niḳola birāẕer-i o
Niḳola Çitroḳos	Petro Çaḳona	Yani Kilifto Kiryaki	Yorgi birāder-i o	Todoros Peliḳanos
Miḫal Laġafti	Todoros birāder-i o	Ṣotoki Çaḳona	İstemad birāẕer-i o	Yani Çaḳona
Ṣotoki birāder-i o	Ṣotoki Panḳari	Andon Ḳartino	Dimitri Pasḳaloplo	bīve Praḳarya

ḫāne 19 — bīve 1

ḥāṣıl 1432

ʿa(n) ispence	ʿöşr-i bāġāt	ʿöşr-i ḥınṭa	ʿöşr-i cev	ʿöşr-i ḳazz	resm-i ḫanāzīr	ʿöşr-i kettān
481	170	600	95	13	3	30

resm-i ḫamr	resm-i ʿarūsī
20	20

ḳarye-i Aḳunba — ḫāṣṣa-ı Mīrlivā

Yorgi Simo	Andriya veled-i o	Dimitri veled-i o	Ṣotoki Ḳalasḳomuzo	İstemati Sarḳomano
[M]iḫal Ġardusi	Petro Ġardusi	[Pa]payani birāẕer-i o	Todoros Ḳaliġa	Yani [ve]led-i o
[M]iḫal Panḳari	Andriya [I]ḳsaftari	Yorgi birāder-i o	Dimitri [Pi]napi	Andriya Ḫarareplo

124
tetimme-i ḳarye-i Aḳunba el-meẕkūr — ḫāṣṣa-ı Mīrlivā

A[nd]riya Ḳaluḳa	[Ni]ḳola Veli Mahiti	Petro Amaṣi	Niḳola Fra[nḳo]	Franḳo Ṣarakineplo
Yani Pavloplo	Niḳola birāẕer-i o	Lazaro Ḳoyoti	Yorgi Filimotomo	Niḳola Ḳardari
Ḳosta Ḳardari	Yorgi Perdiḳari	Filibo[65] birāder-i o	Niḳola Arnoġamro	Yorgi Ḳopti dāmād-ı o
Niḳola Ḳonbosi	Todoros Ḳonbosi	Petro birāder-i o	Ṣotoki Papasinoplo	Miḫal birāder-i o
Yani Miḫaloplo	Yani Velimahiti	Yani Mavriyano	Ḳosta Raft[o]plo	Yorgi birāder-i o
Andon Uzġur	Yani Ḫartulari	Yorgi birāder-i o	Yani Filimotomo	Niḳola veled-i o
Andriya Papayanoplo	Yani birāder-i o	Vaṣıl birāder-i īşān	Todoro Girbenari	Yorgi Mastropano
Niḳola Girbenari	Pavlos Himona	Todoros Mayiros	Dimitri Dobrenbo	Yani veled-i o
Yani Ḳaliġa	Dimitri birāder-i o	Yani Milyari	Yorgi Milyari	Todoros Pasḳal
Yani Pasḳal	İstemad Flasḳomizo	Yani birāder-i o	Niḳola Arni	Aleksi veled-i o
Papamiḫal Ki Taḳiti	Andriya Apergi	Miḫal Çaḳonas	Yani Markâno dāmād-ı o	Vaṣıloplos Lanḳaẕinos
Yorgi Sinapi	Andriya Vaṣelomo[66]	mücerred Yani Sarḳomano	mücerred Yorgi veled-i Todoros Ḳaliġa	mücerred İstefano Perdiḳari
mücerred İstemad Uzġuro	bīve Elani zen-i Girabina	bīve Mavriyani	bīve Zoya zen-i Ġolemoplos	bīve Mariya zen-i [Si]mançe[ḳar]i
bīve Ḳali zen-i Siftarina	ḫāne 72	mücerred 4	bīve 5	mevżiʿ-i āsiy[āb-ı] ḫāṣṣa 1

ḥāṣıl 7245

ʿa(n) ispence 1930	bāġāt-ı ḫāṣṣa dönüm 10 [resm] 1260	ʿöşr-i penbe 50	ʿöşr-i kettān 100	ʿöşr-i bāġ[ā]t 717	ʿöşr-i [ḥın]ṭ[a] 2600	ʿöşr-i cev 395
	ʿöşr-i meyve 1[3]	resm-i ḫanāzīr 10	resm-i ʿarūsī 80	resm-i ḫamr 60		

mülk-i
Petro Amas̱i der ḳarye-i meẕkūr
āsiyāb 1 resm 30

125
tetimme-i nāḥiyyet-i Kirvuḳor

ḳarye-i Maẕi ez cemāʿat-i Arnavudān — ḫāṣṣa-ı Mīrli[v]ā

Marti [Ma]ẕi	İstefano ve[led-i] o	Ḳozma veled-i o	Miḫal veled-i o	Miḫal Maẕi
Marti birāder-i o	Leḳa Maẕi	Miḫal Maẕi	Marti ḫīş-i o	Todoro Maẕi
Marti Maẕi	Lazaro birāder-i o	Ḳozma birāder-i o	Vas̱i Maẕi	Petro birāder-i o
	Niḳola Ḳas̱ari		ḫāne 16	

ḥāṣıl 1020

ʿa(n) ispence 320	[ʿö]şr-i penbe 20	ʿöşr-i kettān 30	ʿöşr-i ḥınṭa 500	ʿöşr-i cev 75	resm-i ḫanāzīr 15	resm-i ʿarūsī 20

mülk-i
Marti Maẕi der ḳarye-i meẕkūr
āsiyāb 1 resm 40

ḳarye-i [Ma]nḳa ez cemāʿat-i Arnavudān — ḫāṣṣa-ı Mīrlivā

[Ḳo]sta [Ma]nḳa	Marti Şuli	Yorgi ḫīş-i o	İlya Lopesi	Gön birāder-i o
Andriya Lo[pesi]	Ḳozma birāder-i o	İstemati Sozos̱i[67]	Yorgi veled-i o	Yorgi Matranḳa
Niḳola İste[f]ano	Yorgi birāder-i o	Petro Ḳuçi	Miḫal Manesi	Manol birāder-i o
mücerred To[do]ros [M]a[nes]i	mücerred Miḫal Matranḳa	ḫāne 15		mücerred 2

ḥāṣıl 1017

ʿa(n) ispence 340	ʿöşr-i penbe 30	ʿöşr-i kettān 50	ʿöşr-i ḥınṭa 500	ʿöşr-i cev 76	resm-i ḫanāzīr 6	resm-i ʿarūsī 15

ḳarye-i Ketesi ez cemāʿat-i Arnavudān — ḫāṣṣa-ı Mīrlivā

Z[ub]an Ketesi	Todoros birāder-i o	Pavlos dāmād-ı o	Miḫal Yirġula	Lala birāẕer-i o
Yorg[i] Yorġula	Dima birāder-i o	İstemad birāẕer-i īşān	Yorgi Şalesi	ḫāne 9

ḥāṣıl 511

ʿa(n) ispence [180]	ʿöşr-i kettān 3[0]	ʿöşr-i ḥınṭa 250	ʿöşr-i cev 38	resm-i ḫanāzīr 3	resm-i ʿarūsī 10

ḳarye-i Mundriza — ḫāṣṣa-ı Mīrlivā

Rardo Ḳaparet[i]	Yani Aġlaçiti	Ḳosta Androni	Dima Viramenos	Franceșḳo veled-i o
Yani Viramenos	Virsteveniti Porfiri	Andon birāder-i o	Niḳola Virsteveniti	Simos Avẕoki
Vaşıl İstilos	Vaşıl Ḳarvali	Niḳola Ḳonbiçi	Yorgi Zalya	Yani birāder-i o

126
tetimme-i ḳarye-i Mundriza el-meẕkūr — ḫāṣṣa-ı Mīrlivā

Ḳosta Ravzolo	Yorgi Virstiyo[t]i	Yani Riziḳari	Simos birāder-i o	Dimitri birāder-i o
Yani Laḫanaḳuki	Manol birāder-i o	Dimitri Himona	Ḳosta İsḳord[a]no	Yani Virstaveniti
Niḳola veled-i o	Niḳola Papayano	Yorgi İsḳlivo	Yani birāder-i o	Yani Vaçi
Petros birāẕer-i o	Yani Zaroni	Andon birāẕer-i o	Todoros Alopoẕari	Yani Bardi
Yani Pranḳo	Niḳola birāder-i o	Filibos[68] Aġlaciti	Franceșḳo Milyano	S̱omas veled-i o
Ḳozma Pirezvitereplo	Manol Aḳoviti	Ḳazomi İspilyoti	Dimitri Raḫarino	Miḫal İstaḫtipa

Niḳola birāder-i o	Yani veled-i o	Aleksi veled-i o	Yorgi Vaştapa	Todoros Vizitreplo
Niḳola Domanos	Yani veled-i o	Gön dāmād-ı o	Niḳola Ḫarkâplo	Ḳostandin Ḳostaplos
Todoros Ḳaḳuçi	mücerred İstemad Virsteveniti	mücerred Dimitri Avẕoki	mücerred İstemad Papayanoplos	mücerred Pavlos Zaroni
mücerred Niḳola Vuẕelos	mücerred Manol Platipoẕi	ḫāne 56	mücerred 6	

ḥāṣıl 5920

ʿa(n) ispence 1550	bāġāt-ı ḫāṣṣa dönüm 5 [resm] 588	ʿöşr-i penbe 50	ʿöşr-i kettān 100	ʿöşr-i bāġāt 1057	ʿöşr-i ḥınṭa 2000	ʿöşr-i cev 308
resm-i ḫanāzīr 40	ʿöşr-i ʿasel 36	ʿöşr-i zeyt 6	ʿöşr-i meyve 5	resm-i ʿarūsī 60	resm-i ḫamr 120	

ḳarye-i Bratiça ez cemāʿat-i Arnavudān ḫāṣṣa-ı Mīrlivā

Ḳoḳas Bratiça	Dimitri veled-i o	Lazaro veled-i o	Petro Bratiça	Yorgi veled-i o
Luḳa Giçi	Lazaro Bratiça	Yorgi veled-i o	Miḫal veled-i o	Leḳa Bratiça
Petros birāder-i o	Todoros birāẕer-i īşān	Yani Niḳo	Leḳa Milyoti	Yorgi birāder-i o
Andriya birāẕer-i o	Lazaro Milyoti	Lazaro Milyoti-i dīğer	Gön veled-i o	Ḳosta Milyoti
Ṭanuş İstilyano	Yorgi birāder-i o	Leḳa birāder-i īşān	İlya birāder-i īşān	Bul[ime]no birāẕer-i īşān
Yorgi Ṣeryanos	Ḳalişa birāẕer-i o	Yorgi Friġani	Lazaro Yeta	Todoros veled-i o

127

tetimme-i ḳarye-i Bratiça el-mezḳūr ḫāṣṣa-ı Mīrlivā

Gön Seryano	Andriya Seryano	Yorgi veled-i o	Gin [Bu]va	Petro Milyo[ti]
Gön Beziḳa	Yorgi Bratiça	Andriya Bratiça	mücerred Dima Milyoti	mücerred Andriya İs[t]ilya[no]

mücerred Dimitri Yeta	mücerred Dima birāder-i o	mücerred Gön Seryano	bīve Mariya [zen-i] Milyoti	ḫāne 38	mücerred [5] bīve 1

ḥāṣıl 2543

ʿa(n) ispence 866	ʿöşr-i kettān 60	ʿöşr-i ḥınṭa 1300	ʿöşr-i cev 198	resm-i ḫanāzīr 79	resm-i ʿarūsī 40

ḳarye-i Papaẕa ez cemāʿat-i Arnavudān ḫāṣṣa-ı Mīrlivā

Ġavrili Papaẕa	Duḳa Papaẕa	Yorgi Papaẕa	Aleksi veled-i o	Lazaro Papaẕa	
Yani Papaẕa	Gin birāder-i o	Gin İvlanduşa	Petro veled-i o	Ẕyaleşi İvlanduşa	
Gin veled-i o	Muriki veled-i o	Petro İvlanduşa	Dimitri İvlanduşa	Marti Bala	
Gin İvlanduşa-ı dīğer	Gön İvlanduşa	Andriya birāẕer-i o	Marti Dorza	Gön Dorza	
Niḳola İstano	Todoros veled-i o	Gön Tana	Petro Ḳuçi	Paloni veled-i o	
Todoros veled-i o	Yorgi veled-i o	Dimitri Ḳuçi	Yani Ḳaçyas	[Pa]vlos veled-i o	
Andriya veled-i o	Niḳola İsḳutara	Gin İsḳutara	Andriya İsḳutara	Gön İstrati	
Dimitri veled-i o	Andriya Rusa	Miḫal Rusa	Papas Dimitri Ḳuçi	mücerred İlya İvlanduşa	
mücerred Varda İvlanduşa	mücerred Niḳola İvlanduşa	mücerred Yorgi Dorza	mücerred İlya Ḳaçyas	mücerred Lazaro Rusa	
mücerred Gin Varda	mücerred Gin İstano	bīve Mariya zen-i Varda	ḫāne 39	mücerred 8	bīve 1

ḥāṣıl 2841

ʿa(n) ispence 946	ʿöşr-i ḥınṭa 1500	ʿöşr-i cev 232	resm-i ḫanāzīr 45	ʿöşr-i ʿasel 18	ʿöşr-i kettān 60	resm-i ʿarūsī 40

ḳarye-i Ġardik ḫāṣṣa-ı Mīrlivā

Yorgi Şarġu[na]	Dimitri birāder-i o	Dimitri İlya	Yani Palḳali	Niḳola Platendro
Ḳosta Akindino	Miḫal birāder-i o	Yani Defteravo-plos	Niḳola Platipoẕi	Luji Platipoẕi

128

tetimme-i Ġardik el-meẕkūr ḫāṣṣa-ı Mīrlivā

Dimitri birāder-i o	Miḫal Rusona	Dimitri birāder-i o	Ḳosta Protoḳo[ta]s	Yorgi Uzġuraki
Lazaro Protoyoris	S̱otoki Ḳunoviça	Ḳosta birāder-i o	Yani İlya	Ẕyaḳos Melisirtos
S̱omas Marḳos	Niḳola İlya	Papas Serakinoplos	Yani birāder-i o	Miḫal Şarakinoplos
Papas Dimitri	Yani Liḳa	Dimitri birāder-i o	Ḳalona Damyanos	Niḳola birāder-i o
Miḫal Androniḳoplo	Yani Zoġuni	Todoros veled-i o	Papas [S̱o]toki	Yorgi Ḳurtali
Ḳalyas Tavulari	Yorgi birāder-i o	Yorgi Ḳalyan	Yani birāder-i o	Yorgi Platendro
Yorgi Liḳa	S̱otoki Liḳa	Yorgi Varila	Niḳola Ḳalya	Dimitri Ḳordalo
Yani veled-i o	Pavlos Rancevi	Pavlos Sarḳona	Pavlos Lopi	Yani mürted
Andriya Gelebas	Yani Ẕyaksenos	Dimitri Platendro	Vaṣıl Pisokeri	Niḳola İprekis
S̱otoki İsḳalina	Vaṣıl Manoti	Yorgi Şayta	Papas Ḫartofilaḳa	mücerred Androniḳo Pronoḳukas
mücerred Dimitri Şarakinoplos	mücerred Aleksi Papadimitri	mücerred Dimitri Varila	bīve Mariya zen-i İsḳufu	bīve Panḳariya
bīve İsḳurake	bīve Kiryaḳo zen-i Rusona	ḫāne 59	mücerred 4	bīve 4

ḥāṣıl 6327

ʿa(n) ispence	bāġāt-ı ḫāṣṣa dönüm 3 [resm] 504	āsiyāb-ı ḫāṣṣa 1 [resm] 300	bostān-ı ḫāṣṣa 1 [resm] 25	ʿöşr-i penbe	ʿöşr-i kettān
1599				50	150

ʿöşr-i bāġāt	ʿöşr-i ḥınṭa	ʿöşr-i cev	resm-i ḫanāzīr	ʿöşr-i meyve	resm-i ʿarūsī
865	2200	342	19	33	60

resm-i ḫamr	mülk-i Ḳalyas Tavulari der ḳarye-i meẕkūr	mülk-i Ḳunoviça der ḳarye-i meẕkūr
100	āsiyāb 1 resm 50	āsiyāb 1 resm 30

ḳarye-i Poḳovina ez cemāʿat-i Arnavudān ḫāṣṣa-ı Mīrlivā

Dimitri Franḳa	Yorgi Ḳusati	Petro Pendeni	Leḳa Mazaraki	Yorgi Mazaraki
Yorgi Ḫarara	Yorgi Fortos	Niḳola Roḫa	Yorgi Graḳa	Pendeni Ḳolosa

129

tetimme-i ḳarye-i Poḳovina el-meẕkūr ḫāṣṣa-ı Mīrlivā

Muriki birāder-i o	Niḳola Pendeni	Gin Ḳalosa	mücerred Gön birāder-i o	ḫāne 13	mücerred 1

ḥāṣıl 842

ʿa(n) ispence	ʿöşr-i kettān	ʿöşr-i ḥınṭa	ʿöşr-i [cev]	resm-i ḫanāzīr	resm-i ʿarūsī
280	20	450	71	6	15

ḳarye-i Zaveti ez cemāʿat-i Arnavudān ḫāṣṣa-ı Mīrli[vā]

Domeniḳa Pendeni	Gön Pendeni	Duşa birāẕer-i o	Yorgi Pendeni	Andon Ḫarara

ḫāne 5

ḥāṣıl 284

ʿa(n) ispence	ʿöşr-i ḥınṭa	ʿöşr-i cev	resm-i ʿarūsī
100	150	24	10

ḳarye-i Virça ḫāṣṣa-ı Mīrlivā

Luḳa Minavi	Miḫal Paḫiyani	Yani Pavlos	Dimitri Zirvo	Yorgi Minavi
Todoros birāder-i o	Yani İksano		ḫāne 7	

ḥāṣıl 502

'a(n) ispence	'öşr-i kettān	'öşr-i ḥınṭa	'öşr-i cev	'öşr-i meyve	resm-i ḫanāzīr	resm-i 'arūsī
175	15	250	40	9	3	10

yekūn-i ḫāṣṣhā-<yı> Mīrlivā der nāḥiyyet-i Kirvuḳor el-meẕkūr

ḳurā	ḫāne	mücerred	bīve
68	1192	136	59

ḥāṣıl 103161

130
nāḥiyyet-i Arḳadya

ḳarye-i Provanda Ayo Yorgi — ḫāṣṣa-ı Mīrlivā

Niḳola Pasḳali	Niḳola Talyara	Yani İksenoẕoḫos	Niḳola İksaroḫto-niẕis	Marina Kipros
Yani Ḳaçiveli	İstefano Leñri	Yani Ḳaçiveli	Yorgi Ġramatiḳo	Melaḫrinos Anaṭoliḳo
İstas̱i Mas̱ye	S̱otoki Ṣamona	Yani Ġulyati	bīve Talyarina	bīve Ḳostandina zen-i Todoros

ḫāne	bīve
13	2

ḥāṣıl 4630

'a(n) ispence	bāġāt-ı ḫāṣṣa	eşcār-ı zeyt-i ḫāṣṣa	ṭāḥūne-i zeyt-i	'öşr-i kettān	'öşr-i bāġāt
337	dönüm 35 [resm] 2588	'aded 301 [resm] 142	ḫāṣṣa 1 [resm] 100	20	1090

'öşr-i ḥınṭa	'öşr-i cev	'öşr-i zeyt	resm-i 'arūsī
250	65	23	15

ḳarye-i Ẕiġanato — ḫāṣṣa-ı Mīrlivā

Anaġnosti İḫtana	Vaṣıl ḫīş-i o	Niḳola Ḫalḳoviçano	Todoros dāmād-ı Miḫalet	Miḫal Ḳolyato
Yani veled-i o	Andon Berleta	Miḫal Tahiti	Niḳola Mondarimos	Yani veled-i o

ḫāne
10

ḥāṣıl ġayr ez memlaḥa 1924

'a(n) ispence	bāġāt-ı ḫāṣṣa	ṭalyan		evvelden üç ḥiṣṣesine Venedik taṣarruf édegelmişdir	eşcār-ı zeyt-i ḫāṣṣa	eşcār-ı meyve-i ḫāṣṣa
250	dönüm 10 [resm] 750	1 [resm] 360 minhā			'aded 152 [resm] 86	'aded 9 [resm] 20
		ḥiṣṣe-i ḫāṣṣa rub' 90	ḥiṣṣe-i beled-i Venedik 270			

'öşr-i kettān	'öşr-i bāġāt	'öşr-i zeyt	'öşr-i meyve	'öşr-i ḥınṭa	'öşr-i cev	'öşr-i penbe	resm-i 'arūsī
30	220	32	14	300	46	20	10

resm-i ḫamr	muḳāṭa'a-ı memlaḥa der ḳarye-i Ẕiġanato el-meẕkūr ki ḫāṣṣa ḫullide mülkühu şüd fī sene mi'e
56	

ḳarye-i Vurçanos — ḫāṣṣa-ı Mīrlivā

As̱anas Ḳuças	Vars̱alemo Ḳuça	Todoros Ḳuças	Niḳola Ṣandaburlo	Papas Anastas
mücerred Manol Ḳuças	mücerred Yani Ḳuça	ḫāne 5		mücerred 2

ḥāṣıl 823

'a(n) ispence	bāġāt-ı ḫāṣṣa	eşcār-ı zeyt-i ḫāṣṣa	eşcār-ı meyve-i ḫāṣṣa	'öşr-i kettān	'öşr-i bāġāt
175	dönüm [2] [resm] 325	'aded 55 [resm] 32	'aded 4 [resm] 10	20	50

'öşr-i ḥınṭa	'öşr-i cev	'öşr-i zeyt	resm-i ḫamr
150	23	33	5

131
tetimme-i nāḥiyyet-i Arḳadya

ḳarye-i Ġırebini — ḫāṣṣa-ı Mīrlivā

[---]uto Yorgiçi	Ḫıristiyano Filas̱ropinos	Yorgi Ẕyavoliçi	Yani Ḫarara	Yorgi Ḫlovaci
Yorgi Anastas	Yani Anastas	S̱ofilaḫto Mavri Poẕi	Yani Luḳa	S̱otoki birāder-i o
Yorgi İsporya	Mandinos İsḳornila	Andriya İsḳornila	Manol İsḳornila	Yani Mamona

S̱otoki veled-i o	S̱ofilaḫto veled-i o	Yani Filimotomo	Miḫal İskilofa	İstemati İsḳotura Yani
Sekelari Papaḳalamatas	Dima İvlaḫo	İstemati Miḫaloplos	Yani Mavrilo	Miḫal veled-i o
Sarḳora Samendi	Vaşıl Çuḳala	Todoros Ḳayça	Petros Paparis	Mastro Dimitri Rafti
Todoros Raḳonyati	Yani Raḳonyati	Vaşıl Raḳonyati	Pavlos veled-i o	Andon veled-i o
Lazaro Ḳaritinos	İvrato Ḳaritinos	İstemati İspora	Yorgi Petroplos	Yani İstasino
Yorgi Ḫaḫali	Andriya Setratili	İlya veled-i o	Kiryaki Simos	Yorgi veled-i o
Niḳola İskilofay	Dimitri Ḳaluna	S̱otoki İskilofa	Yorgi Mantavros	Niḳola Lamari
Yani veled-i o	Todoros Ġalinos	Andriyanos veled-i o	S̱otoki Ḳrasas	Yani Priovolo
Yani Eksosasti	Miḫal Ġalinos	S̱omas veled-i o	Papaniḳola Ġalinos	S̱otoki birāder-i o
Leondariti Protopapaẕaplo	Petros birāder-i o	Yorgi Levoçoviti	Yorgi Yanuloplo	Yani Çuḳala
Yani Ġarvaleviti	Niḳola Anomoẕuri	S̱omas Eklisarḫo	Niḳola Ḳalavuni	Miḫal veled-i o
Yani Ġramatiḳo	S̱otoki Raftoplos	Miḫal Petriyoti	Miḫal Ḳostandinoplos	Yani Simyoni
Yani Bertos	S̱ofilaḫto Ḫaḫali	Dima Ṣamuli	S̱ofilaḫtos Ṣosima	Ṣavatyanos Ṣosima
İstemati Ẕuḳayiti	Yorgi Plimanos	Ḳozma birāẕer-i o	Vaşıl Plimenos	Yorgi Plimenos

132

tetimme-i ḳarye-i Ġırebini el-meẕkūr ḫāṣṣa-ı Mīrlivā

Yani birāder-i o	Todoros Ḳolomeno	Yani birāder-i o	Yorgi birāẕer-i [īşān]	Andriya İsḳlavos
Todoros Ṣosimas	Niḳola Pilemeno	Todoros birāder-i o	Todoros Yorgiçi	Yorgi veled-i o
S̱otoki veled-i o	Andriya Yorgiçi	Yani veled-i o	İstemati Çanḳaroplo	Yani vele[d-i] o
Yorgi veled-i o	Leo veled-i o	Niḳola Ḳaluna	Papas Yani Ḳalamatani	İvlaş Ġramatiḳo
Maryoti Niḳola	mücerred Yorgi Filaṣropinos	mücerred Miḫal Mavropoẕi	mücerred Niḳola İsporya	mücerred [---] Ma[vro]plo

mücerred Aleksi Ḳayça	bīve Ḳutalu	bīve Yorgi zen-i Ḳozma	bīve Papaalekso- pulina	bīve [..[3].]rta [ze]n-i Nikifor

cemāʿat-i Arnavudān der ḳarye-i meẕkūr

Ḳosta Plaşa	Gin Prafti	Todoros Plaşa	Muriki Borşa	Niḳola Borşa
Dima Plaşa	Gin Plaşa	ḫāne maʿa Arnavu- dān 113	mücerred 5	bīve 4

ḥāṣıl ġayr ez çeltük 10315

ʿa(n) ispence maʿa Arnavudān 2939	bāġāt-ı ḫāṣṣa dönüm 8 [resm] 1200	eşcār-ı ṭut-ı ḫāṣṣa ʿaded 50 [resm] 250	eşcār-ı meyve-i ḫāṣṣa ʿaded 32 [resm] 60	ʿöşr-i penbe 100	ʿöşr-i kettān 300

ʿöşr-i bāġāt 1110	ʿöşr-i ḥınṭa 3200	ʿöşr-i cev 489	ʿöşr-i ʿasel 121	resm-i ḫanāzīr 9	ʿöşr-i ḳazz 77	resm-i ʿarūsī 120

resm-i ḫamr 150	mülk-i Yani Anastas der ḳarye-i meẕkūr āsiyāb 1 resm 80	mülk-i Manol İsḳornila der ḳarye-i meẕkūr āsiyāb 1 resm 80	mülk-i Niḳola Anomoẕuri der ḳarye-i meẕkūr āsiyāb 1 resm 30

muḳāṭaʿa-ı çeltük ki ḫāṣṣa ḫullide mülkühu şüd

fī sene ḫamsemıʾe

133

tetimme-i nāḥ[iyyet-i] Arḳad[ya]

[ḳar]ye-i Ar[ḫan]gel[i] ḫāṣṣa-ı Mīrlivā

[cemāʿat-i] Urumiyān[69]

Yani İpsiḫ[ti]ra	[Yo]rgi İsḳarça	Ẕelyos [F]e[n]aropisma	Y[o]rgi Torfos	D[imi]tri R[.[1]]u[.[1]]i
Ki[r]yaki [F]e[n]aropisma	İvra[t]o Berta	İpsiḫtira İstaviti	Todoros İstavraki	ḫāne 9

[cemāʿat-i] Arnavudān

[---] [---]	Yorgi veled-i o	Ḳozma Papari	Niḳola Lopesi	Gön Maliki
[---] Dra[ġoti]	Yorgi Ḳırziya	Milas Ḳırziya	Gin Draġoti	Leḳa Draġoti

[---] Ḳa[znes]	Gin Ḳaznes	Petros Ḳaznes	Yani Drağoti	Niḳola Başta	
Lazaro [Bar]s̱i[mo]	Niḳola Maliki	Andriya Maji	mücerred Petro Drağoti	ḫāne 18	mücerred 1

yekūn-i ḳarye-i Arḫangeli el-meẕkūr

ḫāne	mücerred
27	1

ḥāṣıl 1901

ʿa(n) ispence	ʿöşr-i kettān	ʿöşr-i bāğāt	ʿöşr-i ḥınṭa	ʿöşr-i cev	ʿöşr-i ʿasel	resm-i ḫanāzīr	resm-i ʿarūsī
605	60	80	950	145	13	18	30

ḳarye-i Loyi ḫāṣṣa-ı Mīrlivā

Yani Menca	Yorgi Mihyara	İstefano birāder-i o	Andriya Lağo	Yani Franḳo
Andoni Apanaḫoriti	Petruli Ḳalerñi	Loyizo ·Şarakinoplo	İlya Filimotomo	Yorgi Ḫarara
Z̤yaḳo Ḳursari	Yani Ḳursari	Papas Yani İzmareli	Manol İzmareli	Paraskevo Ḳazani
Papas Yorgi Ḳamaryoti	Vaṣıl Ḳamaryoti	Yani Vizara	Yorgi Maḳri	Todoro Ḳalargi
Papaandriya Rondaki	Yani Rondaki	Todoros Rondaki	Yani Rondaki-i dīğer	Manol birāder-i o
Niḳola Ḳramiz̤ino	Yorgi Petosḳoli	Dimitri Alibora	Andon Lağo	Kiryaki Menca
Leo Menca	Leo Ḳruya	Niḳola Donizo	Todoros Diyasti	Dimitri Metaḳsa

134

tetimme-i ḳarye-i Loyi el-meẕkūr ḫāṣṣa-ı Mīrlivā

Yani Kipro	Miḫal Lales̱i	İstefano Loriḳa	Andriya Paluḳa	İstemati Raftoplo
[Mi]ḫal İskâz̤a	Lazaro Loriḳa	mücerred Vaṣıl Menca	mücerred Yani Lağo	mücerred Pavlos Apanoḫoriti
mücerred Andriya Şarakineplo	mücerred Yorgi Ḳursari	mücerred İstemad Ḳursari	mücerred Yorgi Ḳazani	mücerred Niḳola Ḳamaryoti
mücerred Pavlos Ḳonisari	mücerred Yani Ḳamaryoti	mücerred Petros Vizara	mücerred Dimitri Ḳalargi	mücerred Miḫal Rondaki
mücerred Dimitri Rondaki	mücerred Manol Lağo	mücerred Niḳola Menca	mücerred Yorgi Diyasti	mücerred Vaṣıl Ḳ[ra]miz̤yano
mücerred Yorgi Alipora	bīve İstefaniya zen-i Ḳonisari	bīve Kiryaki zen-i Klimata	bīve Paraskevi zen-i Arḳadini	bīve İstemata zen-i Analita
	bīve Anastasina İskinoplo	ḫāne 42	mücerred 19	bīve 5

ḥāṣıl 5670

ʿa(n) ispence	bāğāt-ı ḫāṣṣa dönüm 7 [resm]	eşcār-ı zeyt-ı ḫāṣṣa ʿaded 153 [resm]	eşcār-ı cevz-i ḫāṣṣa ʿaded 3 [resm]	āsiyāb-ı 1 [resm] 120 minhā	
1555	1050	90	5	ḥiṣṣe-i ḫāṣṣa nıṣf [resm] 100	ḥiṣṣe-i Papa-andriya Rondaki der ḳarye-i meẕkūr nıṣf [resm] 20

ṭāḥūne-i zeyt-i ḫāṣṣa 1 [resm]	ʿöşr-i kettān	ʿöşr-i bāğāt	ʿöşr-i ḥınṭa	ʿöşr-i cev	ʿöşr-i zeyt	resm-i ḫanāzīr
50	100	780	1400	221	60	4

ʿöşr-i ʿasel	resm-i ḫamr	resm-i ʿarūsī	mülk-i Loyizo Şarakinoplo der ḳarye-i meẕkūr āsiyāb 1 resm 50
35	100	50	

ḳarye-i Platana ḫāṣṣa-ı Mīrlivā

Yorgi İsḳura	Niḳola Ḳoryaveli	Pavlos Danbino	Niḳola Ġanbino	Yani Maḳrino
Vaṣıl Ḳamaryoti	Anastas İpsiloplo	Niḳola Ḳoryavelo- plo	Todoros Ḳoḳota	S̱oz̤osi Barbuzi
Todoros Simo	Yorgi Vulḳano	<Pa>payani Vulḳano	mücerred Todoros Ḳoryaveli	mücerred Todoros Ġanbino

mücerred Dimitri Maḳrino	mücerred Yani İpsiloplo	ḫāne 13	mücerred 4

ḥāṣıl ġayr ez memlaḥa 3642

ʿa(n) ispence 425	bāġāt-ı ḫāṣṣa dönüm 14 [resm] 1050	eşcār-ı zeyt-ı ḫāṣṣa ʿaded 375 [resm] 225	ṭalyan-ı ḫāṣṣa 1 [resm] 250	ʿöşr-i bāġāt 820	ʿöşr-i ḥınṭa 400
ʿöşr-i cev 64	ʿöşr-i zeyt 178	ʿöşr-i ḳazz 6	ʿöşr-i meyve 79	resm-i ʿarūsī 15	resm-i ḫamr 100

mülk-i
Niḳola Ḳoryaveli
der ḳarye-i mez̠kūr
āsiyāb 1 resm 30

135
tetimme-i nāḥiyyet-i Arḳadya

muḳāṭaʿa-ı memlaḥa der ḳarye-i Platana el-mez̠kūr ḫāṣṣa ḫullide mülkühu şüd

fī sene 200

ḳarye-i Mili Ḳalivya	ḫāṣṣa-ı Mīrlivā

Niḳola Prasḳa	Miḫal Prasḳa	Miḫal Ḳavlyaḳoti	Niḳola Fotyanos	Yorgi Fotyano
Niḳola Londariti	Yorgi Burdusi	Filibos[70] Milonas	Petro Prasḳa	Leo Prasḳa
Yorgi Yeraki	Lazaro [La]hyoti	Niḳola Zavandri	Yani Yavlyaḳoti	İstefano Mavroġunato
bīve Nikiforina	bīve Astinina	ḫāne 15	bīve 2	mevżiʿ-i āsiyāb-ı ḫāṣṣa 2

ḥāṣıl ġayr ez memlaḥa 5206

ʿa(n) ispence 387	bāġāt-ı ḫāṣṣa dönüm 42 [resm] 3150	eşcār-ı zeyt-ı ḫāṣṣa ʿaded 183 [resm] 124	eşcār-ı meyve-ı ḫāṣṣa ʿaded 22 [resm] 50	āsiyāb-ı ḫāṣṣa 4 [resm] 900	
ʿöşr-i kettān 50	ʿöşr-i ḥınṭa 300	ʿöşr-i cev 48	ʿöşr-i bāġāt 180	ʿöşr-i meyve 2	resm-i ʿarūsī 15

muḳāṭaʿa-ı memlaḥa der ḳarye-i Mili Ḳalivya el-mez̠kūr ki ḫāṣṣa ḫullide mülkühu şüd

fī sene 200

ḳarye-i Palari ez cemāʿat-i Arnavudān	ḫāṣṣa-ı Mīrlivā

Todoros Könsos	Peta Ḳazneş	ḫāne 2

ḥāṣıl 175

ʿa(n) ispence 40	ʿöşr-i kettān 20	ʿöşr-i ḥınṭa 100	ʿöşr-i cev 15

ḳarye-i Platoḳomati	ḫāṣṣa-ı Mīrlivā

Yorgi Valivro	Vaṣıl Ḳurazi	İstemad İspanoplo	Yani Şo[m]a	ḫāne 4

ḥāṣıl 508

ʿa(n) ispence 100	bāġāt-ı ḫāṣṣa dönüm 1 [resm] 150	eşcār-ı zeyt-ı ḫāṣṣa ʿaded 10 [resm] 7	ʿöşr-i bāġāt 120	ʿöşr-i zeyt 8	ʿöşr-i ḥınṭa 100
		ʿöşr-i cev 15	ʿöşr-i meyve 8		

136
tetimme-i [n]āḥiyyet-i [A]rḳadya

mezraʿa-ı Me[ġ]ali[ç]	ḫāli[yye]	ḫaṣṣa-ı M[ī]rlivā
bāġāt-ı ḫ[āṣṣa] dönüm [2] [resm] 150	eşcār-ı zeyt-ı [ḫā]ṣṣa ʿaded [2]0 [resm] 18	ʿöşr-i ġalāt ez ḫāric 1[0]0

yekūn-i ḥāṣıl 268

ḳarye-i [Ma]l[en]a	ḫāṣṣa-ı Mīrlivā

Pavlos Ḳuvaras	S̱ofilaḫtos Panayoti	Paraskevos Şaprokanos	[Ya]ni [---]ni	İvrat[o] Ḳ[---]to

ḫāne
5

ḥāṣıl [76]3

ʿa(n) ispence 125	bāġāt-ı ḫāṣṣa dönüm 1.5 [resm] 225	eşcār-ı zeyt-ı ḫāṣṣa ʿaded 40 [resm] 23	eşcār-ı meyve-ı ḫāṣṣa ʿaded 4 [resm] 10	āsiyāb-ı ḫāṣṣa 1 [resm] 100

ʿöşr-i bāġāt 80	ʿöşr-i zeyt 15	ʿöşr-i ḥınṭa 150	ʿöşr-i cev 23	ʿöşr-i meyve 2	resm-i ʿarūsī 10

ḳarye-i Ḳalazoni ḫāṣṣa-ı Mīrlivā

Niḳola Ḫosto	İstemati İsḳarmikâno	Niḳola Braḳo	Yani Sivastos	Yorg[i] Pren[---]	
Todoros dāmād-ı Sivasto	Yani Noyiti	bīve Voẕamatina	bīve Voyẕomati	ḫāne 7	bīve 2

ḥāṣıl 708

ʿa(n) ispence 187	bāġāt-ı ḫāṣṣa dönüm 3 [resm] 225	eşcār-ı zeyt-ı ḫāṣṣa ʿaded 20 [resm] 12	ʿöşr-i bāġāt 102	ʿöşr-i ḥınṭa 143	ʿöşr-i [cev] 24
		ʿöşr-i zeyt 5	resm-i ʿarūsī 10		

mezraʿa-ı Ḳozomuli ḫāliyye ḫāṣṣa-ı Mīrlivā

bāġāt-ı ḫāṣṣa dönüm 3 [resm] 225	eşcār-ı zeyt-ı ḫāṣṣa ʿaded 30 [resm] 18	ʿöşr-i ġalāt ez ḫāric 100	ʿöşr-i kettān ez ḫāric 20

yekūn-i ḥāṣıl 363

cemʿan ḫāṣṣhā-<yı> Mīrlivā der nāḥiyyet-i Arḳadya

ḳurā 12	mezraʿa-ı ḫāliyye 2	ḫāne 256	mücerred 31	bīve 15

ḥāṣıl 36896

137

nefs-i Londar ḫāṣṣa-ı Mīrlivā

maḥalle-i Niḳola Ṣalamono

Niḳola el-meẕkūr	Leo Virs[t]eni	Dimitri Anapl[yo]ti	Va[şıl] Roḫoḳl[.^{2}.]	Yani Ruṣala
Dimitri Ġalya[nos]	Andriya Çiḫi	Miḫal Marti	Yani Doḳsamanol	Domaniḳa Pulimeánñi
[---] [---]e	[---]nos [İsta]vraki	Dimitri Raftoplo	Yorgi Eglazo	Ni[ḳ]ola Zirama[ni]
[Ḳo]sta [---]ari	Dimitri Ḳo[r]limo	Niḳola Çuḳala	İstemad Bufla	Manṣos Ṣapuna
Ni[ḳo]la [M]oskâ[n]o	Yorgi Ḫalḳomata	Andriya Fameliti	Dimitri Fameliti	Sivastos Moskino
Mi[ḫa]l [Ḳa]lab[ri]	Yorgi Zġuvorvi	Todoros İstanota	Niḳola Yelinani	Manṣos Yelinani
A[---]s B[---]i	Leo Yorgüçoplo	Yorgi Nikliçi	Ṣotoki Çaḳona	Dimitri İsfandona
Miḫal İstanota	Yani İstanota	Todoros İpṣomuri	Yorgi Yiri	Yorgi Yorgiçoplo
Yani Ḳulopana	Yani ʿulūfcı[71]	Ġumenos İsḳolari	Niḳola Pr<a>pa	Yorgi İstanota
Ṣotoki Lakeẕemoniti	Yani Ḫamilo	Niḳola İstraliça	Manol Ḳaçarapi	Dimitri Ḳaçarapi
Dimitri Prapa	Yorgi Ḳaçarapi	Dimitri Ḳaçarapi-i dīğer	Niḳola Franḳo	Todoro Franḳo
Yani İstanota	Dimitri Ḳoliẕa	Todoro Musino	Todoro Hilyasto	Yani Çanḳaruli
Yorgi Ḳaloniḳola	Dimitri Foro	Leo Ḳaravokiẕi	Dimitri Peramonari	Manṣos Papaṣeoġnostu
Niḳola Ḫorsimo	Yani Miḫalic	Yani Ḳroki	Manṣos Vuçara	Yani Vuçara
Papamiḫano	Todoros Çaruḫya	Yorgi Paniḳa	Yani Buni[ḳa]	Todoros Ḳolofakiẕi
Yorgi Proḳopi	Yani Ḳalamisto	Dimitri Ṣavalaveryoti	Dimitri Rondaki	Miḫal Miçuni

138

tetimme-i maḥalle-i Niḳola el-meẕkūr der nefs-i Londar

Ḳosta Ṣalasino	Leo Petrokili	Yani Ġat[---]	Milengi[t] C[---] müsellem zīrā āhenger-i ḳalʿa-ı Londar şüd	Petros C[---]
Leo Ruḳuna	Ḫartofilaḳa Rasa	Niḳola Pan[ḳ]alo	Andon Zemeniti	Yani Proḳopi
İstemati İstravovaşılı	Niḳola Zemeniti	Miḫal Ḳornyaniti	Dimitri İsḳlavo	Yani Ḳumaniçi
Ḳosta Ḳuḳo	İstemati İsfriza	Yorgi İsfriẕa	Yorgi Zemerġo	Vaṣi Lala
Dimitri Ġalyardo	Papas Filitinos	Yorgi Digini	İstemati Ḫusari	Todoros Triḳalo

Niḳola Aleksoplo	Dimitri Yelinati	İstayḳo Sirvo	Andriya Foḳa	Todoros Foḳas
Todoros Ranbari	Andriya Duḳoplo	Yorgi Perdiḳari	Todoros Ḳorḳondilo	mücerred Yani veled-i Ḫartofilaḳa
bīve Yanu zen-i Mano	bīve Franḳa zen-i Todoro	bīve Yorgu zen-i Marḳopulina	bīve Kirana zen-i Niḳola Man- tariya	

ḫāne maʿa müsellem 114 — mücerred 1 — bīve 4

mahalle-i Todoros Ḳraçi

Todoros el-mezḳūr	Niḳola Papakiryaḳoplo	Yani Ḳurupya	Dimitri Ġramatiḳo	Sotoki Paḫisomato
Miḫal Ḳoronyaniti	Manso Fuski	Sotoki Fuski	İstemati Rosa	Sotoki Fuski
Sotoki Renbiti	Niḳola Ḫordoliva	Yorgi Ḳapsari	Pavlos Trandafilos	Sotoki Niromali
Yorgi Ġoraniti	Zyaḳo Papaargisa	Miḫal Fuski	Manol Ḳavasila	S[i]mo Ḳo[tur]mo
Miḫal Draḳoplo	İstemati Nomiḳo	Sotoki Araksa	Ḫıristofor[o] Ḳanbano	Miḫal Çarnuḫlu
Miḫal Çuḳala	Niḳola Protimo	Vasıl Ḳrasna	Yani Papayanoplo	Papas Todoros
Todoros Todoroplo	Manol Todoroplo	Yorgi Ḳopri	Yani Zirvo	Dimitri Zeraza
Yani İstimeni	Niḳola Perdiḳari	Yorgi Ḳarfi	Miḫal R[odi]no	Niḳola Punḳa
Andon Tavularoplo	Yorgi Pramonari	Dimitri İspano	Yorgi Ḳayani	Todoros Papayanoplo

139

tetimme-i Todoros el-mezḳūr

der nefs-i Londar

Yorgi Perdiḳari [D]amitiḳo	Andriya [H]ila	Y[a]ni Çaḳona	Sotoki Ġavra	Yani Muselino
Manol Tartari	Sotoki Boḫa	Yani Maġula	Yani İstavraki	Nikifor Rupani
Leo Ġurmo- yiri	Mano[l] dāmād-ı Papayano- plo	Yorgi Mavroyorgi	Niḳola Ḳoryamela	Miḫal Prasopisa
Ya[ni] Rondaki	Yorgi Ġavra	Leo Proḳono	Ḳosta İstanota	Niḳola Panḳalo
Sofilaḫto Arasa	Yani Ḳaryoti	Niḳola Popri	Niḳola Ġulyamo	Dimitri Mavroyani
Pavlos Papakiryaḳoplos	Aleksi İsparto- yini	bīve Yanimato	bīve Forana	bīve Ḳalivoḳavo
bīve Ḳoyisa	bīve İsḳarpina	bīve Avramina	bīve Ḳofteri	bīve Ḳapsariya
bīve Ḫasomanuru	bīve Ḫalkisa	bīve Mariya zen-i Zemerġu	bīve Luḳu	bīve Ḳromizya
	bīve Ġalini	ḫāne 72	bīve 14	

yekūn-i nefs-i Londar

ḫāne maʿa müsellem 186	mücerred 1	bīve 18

ḥāṣıl ġayr ez müsellem 31542

ʿa(n) ispence 4[7]58	bāġāt-ı ḫāṣṣa dönüm 40 [resm] 3600	ʿöşr-i kettān 325	muḳāṭaʿa-ı niyābet ve bāzār 3500	ʿöşr-i bāġāt 14768

resm-i ḫāmr 1200	ʿöşr-i ḥınṭa 2600	ʿöşr-i cev 393	resm-i ḫanāzīr 18	mülk-i Zaġanoz Beg ki p<ī>ş ez <ī>n Mīılivāʾ-ı vilāyct-i Mora būd āsiyāb 2 resm 100

mülk-i ʿAbdu'[l-l]āh dizdār-ı ḳalʿ[a]-ı Londar āsiyāb 4 resm 180	mülk-i Muṣṭafā tīmār eri Fenarī āsiyāb 1 resm 50	mülk-i Todoro Ḳomita āsiyāb 1 resm 50

mescid-i
cem[āʿat-i Londa]r
1
ammā fi'l-aṣl manastır
būd

vaẓīfe-i
Mevlānā-ı Muḥyi'd-dīn ḳāḍī-ı Londar
ki i[m]āmet-i mescid-i mezḳūr
fī yevm
5
bu iliñ ḫarācından ḥavāle olunmuşdur her yıl ḫarācı vėrüb tecdīd-i ḥükm ve pervāne ṭaleb ėtmeye deyü berātında ḳaydolunmuşdur

140

nāḥiyyet-i Londar

[ḳarye-i] Maji ez cemāʿat-i Arnavudān — [ḫāṣṣa-ı Mīr]l[iv]ā

[Yor]g[i] [M]a[ji]	Todoros veled-i o	D[ome]n[iḳa] Ma[ji]	D[---] Maj[i]	Niḳola Ḳo[---]
Niḳ[o]la Aznati	[Y]ani Ḳatrava	Ḳozma İzġuri	Yorgi İ[z]ġ[u]ri	ḫāne [9]

ḥāṣıl [6]25

ʿa(n) ispence	ʿöşr-i ḥınṭa	ʿöşr-i cev	res[m-i] ḫ[anāzīr]	[ʿöşr-i] kettān
180	300	45	85	15

ḳarye-i Aya Yorgi — [ḫā]ṣṣa-ı Mīrlivā

maḥalle-i Todoros Simyos

Todoros el-meẕkūr	Yani Panḳalo	Dimitri İksano	Pavlos Ananos	Yorgi [---]i
Yani İpşomuri	Todoros Palḳas	Niḳola Makeẕo	Niḳola Ḳloniti	[Yor]gi Vela[---]
Todoros Ḳalonas	Miḫal Barçelos	Yorgi İpsilo	Yani Çimlaḳo	[Yor]g[i] [---]
Yani Aḳriḳondilo	Yorgi Ḳuzmanis	Dimitri İsḳutara	Yani İsḳutara	Niḳ[o]la İs[ḳutare]
Niḳola Siranyoti	Yorgi veled-i o	İstemad Aploḫyiri	S̱otoki birāder-i o	S̱otoki Çemandro
Niḳola İzviri	Dimitri Laġomati	Andriya Androplo	Yorgi veled-i o	Yan[i] veled-i o
İstemad Makeẕo	Yorgi Maḳri	Apostolos Çonḳorina	Yorgi Yanuloplo	[Yor]g[i] Ḫar[a]r[e]
S̱otoki veled-i o	Dimitri birāẕer-i o	Todoros Ḫandrinos	Leo birāẕer-i o	Niḳola Todor[o]
[---] Çervoya[n]i	Yani Polyaniti	Yorgi Lanḳazyoti	S̱otok[i] [---]	A[ndr]iya As̱a[nas]
[Yo]rg[i] Ḫandri[no]	İ[s]temat[i] Ḫandrino	Niḳola Ça[re]toplo	İstemati [ve]le[d-i] o	S̱otoki İrg[---]i
İstemati Liḳ[o]ta	Denremari İk[s]a[na]s	Andron İz[d]iri	Niḳola Ber[---]lo	Niḳola Anemo[---]i
Leo Ḳozma	Yani Surseti	S̱otoki İksano	Dimitri Ḳalibas	Todoros Ġorġos

141

tetimme-i maḥalle-i Todoros el-meẕkūr — der nefs-i Aya Yorgi

Niḳola [Ze]razi	[Y]ani Maẕro	Todoros Laġos	Dimitri veled-i o	Dimitri Ḳurti
Yani Ḳurti	[Dimit]ri Melaçi	Todoros Laḳasa	İstemati Yopa	Yani Ça[.2.] neplo
S̱otoki Ġorġo	Yani Ġorġo	Yorgi Iḳraḳuki	Niḳola Maẕro	Papas Yani Maẕros
Leo Turnas	Yan[i] Mar[---]	S̱otoki İsḳortina	Papas Rumenimos	İvratos Zirvos
[T]odoro Ḳardamiçi	Petros Ḳala[---]as	Yorgi Papaandroplo	Leo veled-i o	Yani Aḳovunyati
Ni[ḳo]la Ḳalpa	Niḳola Ḳoçarato	Yorgi Surseti	As̱anas Vuçara	Yorgi Malesini
[Yor]g[i] Ḫarara	Angelos Ġazi	Todoros Ḫomenos	Todoros Aninos	Niḳola Lepsuta
[Yo]rgi [---]voġri[t]i	Miḫal Simyos	Niḳola Lanḳuḳo	Yani Simos	S̱otoki Simos
Niki[foro]s [---]s	Niḳola Surġoplo	Yorgi Surġoplo	Eksarḫo Murmuro	Niḳola veled-i o
Papas [---]sodoto [.2.]ta[---]	Todoros birāder-i o	Niḳola Beluçi	Yani Marḳoplo	Sakelari Yotis
Miḫal Maẕrero	Todoros Ḳardamiçi	S̱otoki veled-i o	Niḳola Radinos	Papas Ḳotrifas
Yorgi Vuçara	Todoros Siranyoti	Leo veled-i o	Niḳola Argiroḳastriti	Yani Zirvos
Miḫal Zirv[o]s	Yorgi Zirvos	Lazaro İstruza	Niḳola Arḫiyoplo	mücerred Yorgi İsḳutara

ḫāne 124 — mücerred 1

maḥalle-i Yorgi Simos

Yorgi el-meẕkūr	[---] [---]ro	Niḳola Ḳapsari	Yani Papaandro- plo	Protopapas A[---]zmas
[---]s Nuyaras	Yani Radinos	Papas Marti	Miḫalis Ḳotomis	Ẕyaḳos Muselyoti
Yorgi Varilas	[Y]ani [Ḳoḳ]oriça	Niḳola Mavriyanos	Lazaro Androniḳa	Lepṣuta Ḫartofilaḳa
Niḳola birāẕer-i o	Yani Arḫiyoplo	Yorgi veled-i o	Todoros Arḫiyoplo	Yorgi Ḳoliẕa

142

tetimme-i maḥalle-i Yorgi el-meẕkūr — der ḳarye-i Aya Yorgi

Dimitri [M]anoti	Niḳola Ḳalaẕa	Todoros veled-i o	Dimitri veled-i o	Niḳola Zirvos
Todoros İsḳornila	İstemad Aḳorḳongelo	Vaşıl veled-i o	S̱otoki Ḳutala	Yorgi Ḳonbiçi
Andriya Ḳoçonyoti	Yorgi Ḳoçonyoti	Yani Ḳoçonyoti	S̱otoki Ḳoçonyoti	Dimitri Ḳoçoriẕi
Niḳola veled-i o	Gin Ḳayi	Dimitri Ḳayi	Rodoġatora dāmād-ı o	Yorgi Ḳayi
Argiri Ḳuḳli	Yorgi Punḳayiti	Niḳola Punḳayiti	Andron Viryoti	Todoros veled-i o
Ḳosta Başta	Vaşıl Viryoti	Ġayẕo-rufti	Petruça Yorgi	Yorgi Ḳo[.^{2}.]sma
Yorgi Manoloplo	S̱otoki Ḳurtesi	Todoros Selenberdis	Yani Ḳayati	Androniḳo Ḳotomano
Yani Çuḳala	Vaşıl Pramehyiri	Dimitri Kipriyano	Yani Pramehyiri	Yani Çuḳala
Vaşıl Selenberḳa	Niḳola Ġramatiḳo	Vaşıl Pramehyiri	İstilyano Çuḳala	Todoros Çuḳala
Argiro Ahilos	Niḳola veled-i o	İstemati Ahilos	İstilyano veled-i o	Manol Ahilos
S̱oloġos Franboviti	Yorgi Varinbi	S̱otoki Selenberda	İstemati Ḳurtesi	Andon Manesi
Miḫal Ḳayani	Yorgi Maḳriniḳola	Miḫal birāder-i o	İstemati İstematinos	İstemati Yazinos
Todoros İzviri	Papas Uġrandos	İstemati Maḳari	Niḳola İsḳolari	Petros Muşura
Mangişa Manesi	Pavlos Arvaniti	Yorgi Muşura	Todoros Aḳorḳongelo	İstemati birāẕer-i o
Ḳosta Iḳr<a>ḳuki	Vaşıl Punḳayiti	Miḫal Simos	Vaşıl Surseti	Leḳa Miġalyoti
[Ḳa]lḳuli Miġalyoti	Yorgi Aḳroḳuki	Ḳaluẕi Aḳroḳuki	Midrepolid Maḳaryos	Ḳalyoros Malahiyas
Ḳaloyiros Ġuzaris	Aleksi Iġlava	mücerred Niḳola Andraplo	mücerred Todoros Ḳos-tandinoplos	mücerred Dimitri Firuni
mücerred İstemati Miġzalime[n]os	mücerred Niḳola Zirvos	mücerred İstemati Ḳurtesi	mücerred Yorgi Surseti	mücerred Yorgi Ḳalonas

143

tetimme-i maḥalle-i Yorgi el-meẕkūr — der ḳarye-i Aya Yorgi

mücerred Dimitri Arḳana	mücerred Dimitri Mavriyano	mücerred İstefano Arkâniti	mücerred Miḫal İsḳaryano	mücerred Manol Ḳlada
mücerred Ḳoḳoriç	mücerred Niḳola Ḳuparato	mücerred Vaşıl Surseti	mücerred Yorgi Moskino	mücerred Miġalyoti
mücerred Manol Selenberda	mücerred Yani Ġazi	mücerred Yani Sirinyoti	mücerred S̱otoki Ḫartofilaḳ[a]	mücerred S̱otoki Berçilo
mücerred Yani Ḳuçun[yo]ti	mücerred Todoros Punḳayiti	mücerred Todoros Ġramatiḳos	mücerred Miḫal Çuḳala	mücerred Dimitri Çuḳala
mücerred İstemati Ḫandro	mücerred Pavlos Ḳardamiti	mücerred Yorgi Ḳuşomiti	mücerred Miḫal Androniḳo	mücerred Yorgi Liḳovunyati
mücerred [Dimi]t[r]i Sḳutara	mücerred Andriya Ḳaloyiri	mücerred Todoros Ḫandrinos	mücerred Dimitri Zosimas	mücerred Mans̱os Serġoplos
mücerred Leo Çaḳonoplo	mücerred Yani Marti	bīve Çivikina	bīve Ḳoru	bīve Ḳurtasina
bīve İskâvo zen-i Flakiya	bīve Bulyanitisa	bīve Zosimina	bīve Yanu zen-i Ẕoḳsara	bīve Ḳoliẕo
bīve Anamoyanina	bīve Lizimo	bīve Pozoḫtipina	bīve Ḫarkisa	bīve Yirina
bīve Filikini	bīve Ḫomenu	bīve İpsila	ḫāne 102 / mücerred 40	bīve 16

yekūn-i ḳarye-i Aya Yorgi el-meẕkūr

ḫāne 226	mücerred 41	bīve 16	manastır-ı ḫāṣṣa 1

ḥāṣıl 31427

ʿa(n) ispence 6771	bāġāt-ı ḫāṣṣa dönüm 68 [resm] 5280	eşcār-ı ṭut-ı ḫāṣṣa ʿaded 217 [resm] 1050	eşcār-ı zeyt-i ḫāṣṣa ʿaded 8 [resm] 9	eşcār-ı meyve-ı ḫāṣṣa ʿaded 8 [resm] 15

āsiyāb-ı ḫāṣṣa 2 [resm] 800	ʿöşr-i kettān 200	ʿöşr-i bā[ġ]āt 7680	resm-i ḫamr 960	ʿöşr-i ḥınṭa 6900	ʿöşr-i cev 1035

ʿöşr-i ḳazz 178	ʿöşr-i meyve 14	resm-i ḫanāzīr 73	ʿöşr-i ʿasel 52	mülk-i Todoros Ḳorḳondilo ki der nefs-i Londar mī şeved āsiyāb 1 resm [5]0
mülk-i Yorgi İpsilo der ḳarye-i meẕkūr āsiyāb 1 resm 30	mülk-i Yorgi Ḫarara der ḳarye-i meẕkūr āsiyāb 1 resm 30	mülk-i Todoros Ḫandri-nos der ḳarye-i meẕkūr āsiyāb 1 resm 30	mülk-i Yani Polyaniti der ḳarye-i meẕkūr āsiyāb 1 resm 80	
mülk-i Yorgi Ḫandro der ḳarye-i meẕkūr āsiyāb 1 resm 30	mülk-i Niḳola Lanḳuḳo der ḳarye-i meẕkūr āsiyāb 1 resm 50	mülk-i Niḳola Ḳlaẓa der ḳarye-i meẕkūr āsiyāb 1 resm 50	mülk-i Niḳola Zirvos der ḳarye-i meẕkūr āsiyāb 1 resm 30	

mülk-i
İstemad Aḳorḳongelo der ḳarye-i meẕkūr
āsiyāb 1 resm 30

144

tetimme-i nāḥiyyet-i Londar

ḳarye-i Lonḳanik — ḫāṣṣa-ı Mīrliv[ā]

Maṣos Uzġuromali	Yorgi Anaġn[o]s Kefala	Dimitri Ġa[v]ala	Yorgi Polyaniti	Niḳola P[o]lyaniti
Yani Zamoro	Niḳola İsḳolari	Ṣotoki Ḳurtesi	Ṣotoki Faköli	Leo [Ne]m[y]amata
Yorgi Anifandi	Miliġos Ḫartofilaḳa	Papas Yani Ḳatomeriti	Papavaṣ[ıl] Polyaniti	Dim[itri] veled-i [o]
Dimitri Polyaniti	Andriya İpşaltiri	Yani Papa-yorġoplo	Todoros birāder-i [o]	Ṣotoki Miliġos
Dimitri Miliġos	Vaşıl Ġarpişo	Miḫal Dimitroplo	Dimitri Kefalas	Yani Polondaya
Yani Ṣalasino	Andronis Kirinos	Yani Kirinos	Yani Variyorġa	Yorgi Plaḳas
Dimitri Pol-yaniti Ḳuluri	Miḫal Polyaniti	Yorgi Sakâloroplos	Niḳola Kefalas	Miḫal Ḳalandriya
Dimitri Kefalas	Todoros Peliḳas	Yorgi Ḳalandriya	Yorgi Nikiforo	Niḳola Miliġo
Ḳosta Ḳurtesi	Dimitri Romoyeni	Ṣotoki Ropoli	Todoros Ḫarkâplos	Yani Ropoli
Yorgi Zanḳrabeşa	İstratiḳo Polyaniti	Yani Ḳondopetri	Dimitri Ḳaloẓraḳo	Nikit Pulo
Yani Kefala	Niḳola Aḳrasi	Yorgi Polondaya	Niḳola Ḳastriti	İstratiḳo Suḳara
Niḳola Miliġos	Yani Serġoplo	Yorgi Ḫaros	Dimitri Kefala	Yani Kefala
Todoros Kefala	Vaşıl Zamoro	Miḫal Ḳofina	İstratiḳo Porfiri	Ḫıristodulos Farḳos
Todoros Kefalas-ı dīğer	Yani İsaltiri[72]	Leo Ḳuluris	Yani Avriyoni	Anastas Miliġos
Yorgi İskrazi	İstemati Franḳoplo	Papayorgi Kefala	Dimitri [P]eli	Dimitri Peliḳas
Todoros Faköli	İstemati İskrazi	Yani Porfiri	mücerred Todoros Ḳofina	mücerred Yorgi Dimitroplo
mücerred Yorgi Kirinos	mücerred Todoros Miḫanos	bīve Dimitro Polyanitisa	bīve Dimitro P[o]rfiru	bīve Ḳoçiro-pula

145

tetimme-i ḳarye-i Lonḳanik el-meẕkūr — ḫāṣṣa-ı Mīrlivā

bīve Franḳopu-lina	bīve İstratiki Peliḳasu	bīve Yorġu Peliḳasu	ḫāne 78	mücerred 4	bīve 6

ḥāṣıl 7220

ʿa(n) ispence [2]086	bāġāt-ı ḫāṣṣa dönüm 3 [resm] 360	eşcār-ı zeyt-i ḫāṣṣa ʿaded 12 [resm] 6	ʿöşr-i bāġāt 2672	ʿöşr-i ḥınṭa 1600	ʿöşr-i cev 240
resm-i [ḫan]āzīr 2[9]	ʿöşr-i zeyt 2[1]	ʿöşr-i ḳazz 26	ʿöşr-i kettān 150	resm-i ḫamr 330	mülk-i Dimitri Polyaniti der ḳarye-i meẕkūr āsiyāb 1 resm 50

eşcār-ı ṭut-ı ḫāṣṣa ʿa[de]d 10 [resm] 50	mülk-i Yani Ṣalasino der ḳarye-i mezḳūr āsiyāb 1 resm 50	mülk-i Ḳosta Ḳurtesi der ḳarye-i mezḳūr āsiyāb 1 resm 50

ḳarye-i Ġurenas — ḫāṣṣa-ı Mīrlivā

Miḫal Rosa	Dimitri Rosa	Papas Sakeliyos	Niḳola Asani	Yorgi Zifo
Miḫal Rosa	Niḳola Rosa	Yorgi Ḳalomiyo	Niḳola Ḳuçohyiri	Miḫal Ḳostila
Yani Çermomi	Dima Rosa	İstemati Yorgiçi	Papas Evẓikos	Yani Rosa
Todoros Ḫarkâs	Todoros Ġaġriyas	Todoros Miḫanos	Todoros Ḳoskina	Vaṣıl Varvari
Niḳola Çermomi	Ẓyaḳos Papayani	Yorgi Peliḳas	Dimitri Peliḳas	Drosino Faköli
Petros Fakölis	Misiriġo	Yorgi Paroni	Çironḳasti	bīve Papaẓya Miḫalina

bīve Ḳuçohyiro	ḫāne 29	bīve 2

ḥāṣıl 3222

ʿa(n) ispence 737	bāġāt-ı ḫāṣṣa dönüm 6 [resm] 540	eşcār-ı ṭut-ı ḫāṣṣa ʿaded 50 [resm] 250	eşcār-ı zeyt-i ḫāṣṣa ʿaded 60 [resm] 34	eşcār-ı cevz-i ḫāṣṣa ʿaded 11 [resm] 20

ʿöşr-i bāġāt 832	ʿöşr-i zeyt 8	ʿöşr-i ḳazz 37	ʿöşr-i meyve 9	resm-i ḫamr 100	ʿöşr-i kettān 80	ʿöşr-i ḥınṭa 500	ʿöşr-i cev 75

ḳarye-i Ḳoçiça — ḫāṣṣa-ı Mīrlivā

Niḳola Ḫordiya	Vaṣıl Ḫordiya	Papaandriya Ḫartofilaḳa	İstemati Ḫordiya	Yorgi Faköli
Dimitri Niḳoli	Vaṣıl Niḳoli	Niḳola Niḳoli	Niḳola Zefiri	Yorgi Dimitroplo
Yani Manesi	Todoros Demestiḳa	Ṣotoki Ḳaçiyiro	İstefanos İksanos	Ṣotoki Suḳara

146

tetimme-i ḳarye-i Ḳoçiça el-mezḳūr — ḫāṣṣa-ı Mīrlivā

Niḳola Ḳaçiro	Ṣotoki Mandi	Ẓyaḳo Viryoti	Papavaṣıl İskâvofilaḳa	Todoros Niḳoli
Yorgi Niḳoli	mücerred Todoros Ḳaçiyiro	mücerred Niḳola Mandi	bīve Dimitro Suḳaro	bīve Ġarġaro
	bīve Bazeni	ḫāne 21	mücerred 2	bīve 3

ḥāṣıl 2747

ʿa(n) ispence 593	bāġāt-ı ḫāṣṣa dönüm 4 [resm] 480	eşcār-ı ṭut-ı ḫāṣṣa ʿaded 20 [resm] 100	eşcār-ı zeyt-i ḫāṣṣa ʿaded 10 [resm] 6	ʿöşr-i bāġāt 752

ʿöşr-i ḳazz 61	ʿöşr-i ḥınṭa 500	ʿöşr-i cev 75	ʿöşr-i zeyt 10	ʿöşr-i kettān 50	resm-i ḫamr 90	mülk-i Todoros Demestiḳa der ḳarye-i mezḳūr āsiyāb 1 resm 30

ḳarye-i İksifya ez cemāʿat-i Arnavudān — ḫāṣṣa-ı Mīrlivā

Todoro İksifya	Yorgi İksifya	Andriya İksifya	Petro İksifya	Andriya Lata	
Niḳola Lata	Ḳozma Ipṣari	İvlaş Ipṣari	Andriya Ḳopuço- maẓi	Niḳola İksifya	
bīve Leḳa	bīve mana İpsari	bīve māder-i Andriya	bīve Andriya Barça	ḫāne 10	bīve 4

ḥāṣıl 506

ʿa(n) ispence 224	ʿöşr-i ḥınṭa 200	ʿöşr-i cev 32	ʿöşr-i kettān 50

ḳarye-i Yani Ẓyavoliçi ez cemāʿat-i Arnavudān — ḫāṣṣa-ı Mīrlivā

Yani el-mezḳūr	Yani Pikerni	Yorgi Pikerni	Gin Pikerni	Yorgi Pikerni-i dīğer
Niḳola Pikerni	Todoro Helmesi	Dimitri Helmesi	Andriya Ẓyavoliçi	Niḳola Ẓyavoliçi

mücerred Dima Pikerni	mücerred Gin Helmesi	mücerred Andriya Floḳa	bīve Zupanina	bīve Floḳa
	ḫāne 10	mücerred 3	bīve 2	

ḥāṣıl 640

[ʿa](n) ispence 272	ʿöşr-i ḥınṭa 300	ʿöşr-i cev 48	ʿöşr-i kettān 20

ḳarye-i Marti Helmi ez cemāʿat-i Arnavudān ḫāṣṣa-ı Mīrlivā

Marti el-mezḳūr	Pavlos Helmi	Yani Helmi	Todoros Helmi	Aleksi Sinaki
Petro Maji	Lazaro Maji	Marti Hilmi	Petro Hilmi	Aleksi Plaşa

147

tetimme-i ḳarye-i Marti Helmi el-mezḳūr ḫāṣṣa-ı Mīrlivā

Pavlo Maji	mücerred Yani Helmi	bīve Lula	ḫāne 11	mücerred 1	bīve 1

ḥāṣıl 528

ʿa(n) ispence 246	ʿöşr-i ḥınṭa 200	ʿöşr-i cev 32	ʿöşr-i kettān 50

ḳarye-i Yani Evzenati ez cemāʿat-i Arnavudān ḫāṣṣa-ı Mīrlivā

Yani el-mezḳūr	Pavlos Evzenati	İstefa Misr Domeniḳa	Yani Misr Domeniḳa	İstemati Evzenati
Niḳola Ḳ[ok]la	Todoro Evzenati	mücerred Leḳa Evzenati	mücerred Proġono Evzenati	bīve Marta
	bīve Manḳa	ḫāne 7	mücerred 2	bīve 2

ḥāṣıl 458

ʿa(n) ispence 192	ʿöşr-i ḥınṭa 200	ʿöşr-i cev 31	resm-i ḫanāzīr 20	ʿöşr-i kettān 15

ḳarye-i Aleksi Manesi ez cemāʿat-i Arnavudān ḫāṣṣa-ı Mīrlivā

Aleksi el-mezḳūr	Todoro Manesi	Yorgi Manesi	Domeniḳa Manesi	Domeniḳa Plaşa
Lazaro Lukisa	Yani Lukisa	Yani İzlatḳa	Gin Voniḳa	Domeniḳa Voniḳa
Domeniḳa Ġavra	Aleksi Zupata	Yani Zupata	Yani Manesi	Yani Voniḳa
Petro İzlatḳa	Andriya Zupata	mücerred Ḳosta Voniḳa	bīve Yorgi Manesi	ḫāne 17 mücerred 1 bīve 1

ḥāṣıl 857

ʿa(n) ispence 366	ʿöşr-i ḥınṭa 400	ʿöşr-i cev 61	ʿöşr-i kettān 30

ḳarye-i Yorgi Maji ez cemāʿat-i Arnavudān ḫāṣṣa-ı Mīrlivā

Yorgi el-mezḳūr	Andriya Maji	Androniḳo Maji	Yorgi Maji	Todoro Ġramşa
Yorgi Maji	İvlaş Mazi	Yorgi Mazi	Ḳondo Mazi	Petro Maji
mücerred Yani Maji	mücerred Niḳola Maji	mücerred Yorgi Ġramşa	bīve Martina	ḫāne 10 mücerred 3 bīve 1

ḥāṣıl 691

ʿa(n) ispence 266	ʿöşr-i ḥınṭa 300	ʿöşr-i cev 45	resm-i ḫanāzīr 60	ʿöşr-i kettān 20

148

tetimme-i nāḥiyyet-i Londar

ḳarye-i Yani Lata ez cemāʿat-i Arnavudān ḫāṣṣa-ı Mīrlivā

Yani el-mezḳūr	Dima Masḳaluri	Yani Ḳalanci	Niḳola Lata	Todoro Ḳonbi
Niḳola Lata-ı [di]ğ[er]	Todoro Lata-ı dīğer	Lala Lata	Yorgi Lata	Yani Lata
Andriya Lata	Yorgi Lata	Marti İspolata	Leḳa Plaşa	Andriya Ḳaznes
Pavlos Plaşa	Petro Lata	Demastiḳa	Niḳola Masḳaluri	Yani Pendeni

Niḳola Lata	Yani Sana	İş Ari Sana	Aleksi Mazaraki	mücerred Todoro Lata
mücerred Varda Lata	mücerred Yorgi Lata	mücerred İştin Lata	mücerred Niḳola Lata	mücerred Gin Lata
mücerred Marti Lata	mücerred Petro Ḳaznes	mücerred Yorgi Masḳaluri	mücerred Lazaro Lata	bīve Petru Lata
bīve Aposkepina	bīve Latina	bīve duḫter-i Ḳalanci	bīve Mara Ḳunba	ḫāne 24 · mücerred 10 · bīve 5

ḥāṣıl 1418

ʿa(n) ispence	ʿöşr-i ḥınṭa	ʿöşr-i cev	resm-i ḫanāzīr	ʿöşr-i kettān
710	550	85	33	40

ḳarye-i Niḳola Maḳrişa ez cemāʿat-i Arnavudān — ḫāṣṣa-ı Mīrlivā

Niḳola el-meẕkūr	Dimitri Maḳrişa	Lazaro Maḳrişa	Domeniḳa Maḳrişa	Yorgi İstopaniti
Palunbi Maḳrişa	Yani Maḳrişa	Yani Maḳrişa-ı dīğer	Lazaro Maḳrişa	Dimitri Maḳrişa
	mücerred Yani Maḳrişa	ḫāne 10		mücerred 1

ḥāṣıl 534

ʿa(n) ispence	ʿöşr-i ḥınṭa	ʿöşr-i cev	resm-i ḫanāzīr	ʿöşr-i kettān
220	250	40	9	15

ḳarye-i Marti Plaşa ez cemāʿat-i Arnavudān — ḫāṣṣa-ı Mīrlivā

Marti el-meẕkūr	Kâleşi Plaşa	Domeniḳa Plaşa	Andriya Plaşa	Yani Plaşa	
Kâleşi Plaşa-ı dīğer	Duḳa Plaşa	Yorgi Plaşa	bīve mana māder-i Andriya Plaşa	ḫāne 8	bīve 1

ḥāṣıl 428

ʿa(n) ispence	ʿöşr-i ḥınṭa	ʿöşr-i cev	resm-i ḫanāzīr	ʿöşr-i kettān
166	200	32	20	10

149

tetimme-i nāḥiyyet-i Londar

ḳarye-i Domaniḳa Beluşi ez cemāʿat-i Arnavudān — ḫāṣṣa-ı Mīrlivā

Domaniḳa el-meẕkūr	Yorgi Beluşi	Pavlo Beluşi	Gön Beluşi	Yani Beluşi	
mücerred Yani Cancali	mücerred Yorgi Domeniḳa	bīve Cancalina	ḫāne 5	mücerred 2	bīve 1

ḥāṣıl 284

ʿa(n) ispence	ʿöşr-i ḥınṭa	ʿöşr-i cev	resm-i ḫanāzīr	ʿöşr-i kettān
146	100	16	12	10

ḳarye-i Dimitri Maçuki ez cemāʿat-i Arnavudān — ḫāṣṣa-ı Mīrlivā

Dimitri el-meẕkūr	Yani Maçuki	Petro Maçuki	Marti Dyaleşi	Ḳosta Buzbardi
mücerred Aleksi veled-i Yani Maçuki	bīve Trifilina	ḫāne 5	mücerred 1	bīve 1

ḥāṣıl 256

ʿa(n) ispence	ʿöşr-i ḥınṭa	ʿöşr-i cev	ʿöşr-i kettān
126	100	15	15

ḳarye-i Duḳa Plaşa ez cemāʿat-i Arnavudān — ḫāṣṣa-ı Mīrlivā

Duḳa el-meẕkūr	Ḳozma Plaşa	Yorgi Plaşa	Petro Jupano	mücerred veled-i o
	bīve māẕer-i[73] Duḳa	ḫāne 4	mücerred 1	bīve 1

ḥāṣıl 240

ʿa(n) ispence	ʿöşr-i ḥınṭa	ʿöşr-i cev	resm-i ḫanāzīr	ʿöşr-i kettān
106	100	16	8	10

ḳarye-i Miḫal Manesi ez cemāʿat-i Arnavudān — ḫāṣṣa-ı Mīrlivā

Miḫal el-meẕkūr	Petro Manesi	İlya Manesi	Yani Manesi	Aleksi Manesi

Valaḳa Manesi	Merti[74] Manesi	Yani Manesi	Yorgi Manesi	Yani Manesi
	Yani Ġolemi		ḫāne 11	

ḥāṣıl 475

ʿa(n) ispence	ʿöşr-i ḥınṭa	ʿöşr-i cev	resm-i ḫanāzīr	ʿöşr-i kettān
220	200	32	3	20

ḳarye-i Miḫal Zora ez cemāʿat-i Arnavudān ḫāṣṣa-ı Mīrlivā

Miḫal [el-mez̲]kūr	Niḳola Zora	Yani Zora	Aleksi Zora	Lazaro Maji
Yani Dara	Zora Buḳuyi	Todoro Zora	Aleksi Zora	Yani Dara

150

tetimme-i ḳarye-i Miḫal Zora el-mez̲kūr ḫāṣṣa-ı Mīrlivā

mücerred Niḳola Zora	bīve Çernota	ḫāne 10	mücerred 1	bīve 1

ḥāṣıl 523

ʿa(n) ispence	ʿöşr-i ḥınṭa	ʿöşr-i cev	resm-i ḫanāzīr	ʿöşr-i kettān
226	200	32	45	20

ḳarye-i Pavlo Doçi ez cemāʿat-i Arnavudān ḫāṣṣa-ı Mīrlivā

Pavlo el-mez̲kūr	Andriya Doşkesi	Todoro Doskesi	Marti Doşkesi	bīve Barda
	ḫāne 4		bīve 1	

ḥāṣıl 238

ʿa(n) ispence	ʿöşr-i ḥınṭa	ʿöşr-i cev	resm-i ḫanāzīr	ʿöşr-i kettān
86	100	16	16	20

ḳarye-i Mangişa Burlaşa ez cemāʿat-i Arnavudān ʿan ḫāṣṣa-ı o

Mangişa el-mez̲kūr	Niḳola Burlaşa	Yani Burlaşa	İstefano Burlaşa	Yani Çernota
Ḳozma Dorza	Yorgi Dorza	İstefano Dorza	Niḳola Lonca	İstefano Buvasi
Petro Burlaşa	mücerred Niḳola Dorza	bīve Buvasina	ḫāne 11	mücerred 1 / bīve 1

ḥāṣıl 528

ʿa(n) ispence	ʿöşr-i ḥınṭa	ʿöşr-i cev	resm-i ḫanāzīr	ʿöşr-i kettān
246	200	32	30	20

ḳarye-i Yorgi Muzaki ez cemāʿat-i Arnavudān ḫāṣṣa-ı Mīrlivā

Yorgi el-mez̲kūr	İstefano Muzaki	Yorgi Muzaki	Miḳra Muzaki	Yani Muzaki
Andriya Muzaki	Todoro Muzaki		ḫāne 7	

ḥāṣıl 284

ʿa(n) ispence	ʿöşr-i ḥınṭa	ʿöşr-i cev	resm-i ḫanāzīr	ʿöşr-i kettān
140	100	16	13	15

ḳarye-i Ġulyamu Argiroplu ez cemāʿat-i Arnavudān ḫāṣṣa-ı Mīrlivā

Ġulyamo el-mez̲kūr	Yani Argiroplo	Yorgi Argiroplo	Pavlos Doşkesi	Todoros Doskesi
Petro Doskesi	Lazaro Doskesi	Todoro Doskesi-i dīğer	Yani Doskesi	Andriya Doskesi
Marḳo Doskesi	Yani Argiroplos	mücerred Marti Argiroplo	bīve Argiropulina	ḫāne 12 / mücerred 1 / bīve 1

ḥāṣıl 658

ʿa(n) ispence	ʿöşr-i ḥınṭa	ʿöşr-i cev	resm-i ḫanāzīr	ʿöşr-i kettān
266	300	48	24	20

151

tetimme-i nāḥiyyet-i Londar

ḳarye-i Todoro Zupata ez cemāʿat-i Arnavudān ḫāṣṣa-ı Mīrlivā

Todoros el-mez̲kūr	Andriya Zupata	Ġazi Zupata	Yani Zupata	Yani Zupata-ı dīğer
Yorgi Zupata	Andon Zupata	bīve Alekso	ḫāne 7	bīve 1

ḥāṣıl 340

ʿa(n) ispence	ʿöşr-i ḥınṭa	ʿöşr-i cev	ʿöşr-i kettān
146	150	24	20

ḳarye-i İlya Maji ez cemāʿat-i Arnavudān ḫāṣṣa-ı Mīrlivā

İlya el-mezkūr	Yani Maji	Yani Maji-i dīğer	Petro Ranesi	bīve Andro Majina

ḫāne 4 bīve 1

ḥāṣıl 214

ʿa(n) ispence	ʿöşr-i ḥınṭa	ʿöşr-i cev	resm-i ḫanāzīr	ʿöşr-i kettān
86	100	16	2	10

ḳarye-i Lazaro Zupata ez cemāʿat-i Arnavudān ḫāṣṣa-ı Mīrlivā

Lazaro el-mezkūr	Yorgi Zupata	Aleksi Zupata	İş Ari Zupata	Zupan Zupata
Varda Zupata	Yani Zupata			

ḫāne 7

ḥāṣıl 334

ʿa(n) ispence	ʿöşr-i ḥınṭa	ʿöşr-i cev	ʿöşr-ı kettān
140	150	24	20

ḳarye-i Petro Dorza ez cemāʿat-i Arnavudān ḫāṣṣa-ı Mīrlivā

Petro el-mezkūr	Yani Dorza	Niḳola Dorza	Niḳola Dorza-ı dīğer	Ḳosta Buza
Yani Dorza-ı dīğer	Yani Dorza-ı dīğer	Mila Dorza	Andriya Dorza	Marti Dorza
İlya Ḳurtesi	Miḫal Dorza	Yani İvlaḫyoti	Niḳola Dorza	Yorgi Dorza
İstefano Maçuki	Ġarḳa Yani	Niḳola Ġarḳa	Petro Papazoplo	bīve Ḳanḳazina
	bīve Nikolo			

ḫāne 19 bīve 2

ḥāṣıl 770

ʿa(n) ispence	ʿöşr-i ḥınṭa	ʿöşr-i cev	ʿöşr-i kettān
392	300	48	30

ḳarye-i Lala Ẕyavoliçi ez cemāʿat-i Arnavudān ḫāṣṣa-ı Mīrlivā

Lala el-mezkūr	Gin Ezenati	Yani Hilmi	Todoros Hilmi	Mangişa Lonci

152

tetimme-i ḳarye-i Ẕyavol[içi] el-mezkūr ḫāṣṣa-ı Mīrlivā

Niḳola Ẕyavoliçi	Andriya Plaşa	mücerred Petro Senati	mücerred Gin Senati	bīve Mahiro

ḫāne 7 mücerred 2 bīve 1

ḥāṣıl 577

ʿa(n) ispence	ʿöşr-i ḥınṭa	ʿöşr-i cev	resm-i ḫanāzī[r]	ʿöşr-i kettān
186	300	46	[25]	20

ḳarye-i Ẕupano Buryalişa ez cemāʿat-i Arnavudān ḫāṣṣa-ı Mīrlivā

Zupano el-mezkūr	Niḳola Ḳalamatyano	Yani Ḳalamatyano	[Yorg]i [Ḳalama]tyano	Yorgi Peli[ḳan]o
Niḳola Peliḳano	Niḳola Mortato	Andriya Ḳalamatyano		

ḫāne 8

ḥāṣıl 558

ʿa(n) ispence	ʿöşr-i ḥınṭa	ʿöşr-i cev	resm-i ḫanāzīr	ʿöşr-i kettān
160	300	46	42	10

ḳarye-i Yani Jura ez cemāʿat-i Arnavudān ḫā[ṣṣa-ı Mīr]livā

Yani el-mezkūr	Boğovi Zora	Miḫal Zora	Aleksi Zora	Manol Zora

ḫāne 5

ḥāṣıl 226

ʿa(n) ispence 100	ʿöşr-i ḥınṭa 100	ʿöşr-i cev 16	ʿöşr-i kettān 10

ḳarye-i Todoro Doşkesi ez cemāʿat-i Arnavudān ḫāṣṣa-ı Mīrlivā

Todoro el-mezḳūr	Petro Doşkesi	Dimitri Doşkesi	ḫāne 3

ḥāṣıl 186

ʿa(n) ispence 60	ʿöşr-i ḥınṭa 100	ʿöşr-i cev 16	ʿöşr-i kettān 10

ḳarye-i İstoya Volomiri ez cemāʿat-i Arnavudān ḫā[ṣṣa-ı] Mīrlivā

İstoya el-mezḳūr	Petro Volimiri	Andriya Volimiri	ḫāne 3

ḥāṣıl 175

ʿa(n) ispence 60	ʿöşr-i ḥınṭa 100	ʿöşr-i cev 15

ḳarye-i Yani Mazaraki ez cemāʿat-i Arnavudān ḫāṣṣa-ı Mīrlivā

Yani el-mezḳūr	Merti[75] Mazaraki	Pavlo Mazaraki	Lazaro [Ma]zarak[i]	Yani Pla[şa]	
Andriya Plaşa	Varda Mazaraki	Miḫal Mazaraki	mücerred Miḫ[a] Plaşa	ḫāne 8	mücerred 1

ḥāṣıl 511

ʿa(n) ispence 180	ʿöşr-i ḥınṭa 200	ʿöşr-i cev 31	resm-i ḫanāzīr [8]0	ʿöşr-i kettān 20

153
[tetimme-i] nāḥiyyet-i Londar

ḳarye-i Niḳola Sirgi ez cemāʿat-i Arnavudān ḫāṣṣa-ı Mīrlivā

Niḳola el-mezḳūr	Ḳozma [Si]rgi	Yorgi Plaşa	İstefano Simyos	Bardi Dara	
Marḳo Dara	Niḳola Ḳaluta	Yani Sonda	Andriya Sirgi	Marti Sirgi	
[Yani] Buv[a]	Y[or]g[i] D[a]ra	Martin Şonda	mücerred Niḳola Dara	mücerred Yani Dara	
mücerred Yani Ḳaluta	mücerred Yorgi Sirgi	mücerred Aleksi Buva	ḫāne 13	mücerred 5	

ḥāṣıl 854

ʿa(n) ispence 38[0]	ʿöşr-i ḥınṭa 300	ʿöşr-i cev 48	resm-i ḫanāzīr 96	ʿöşr-i kettān 30

ḳarye-i Lazar Palunbi ez cemāʿat-i Arnavudān ḫāṣṣa-ı Mīrlivā

Lazaro el-mezḳūr	Andriya Lukisa	Yani Lukisa	Lumi Lukisa	Dimitri Lopesi		
Yani Lopesi	Todoro Lopesi	Domeniḳa Ḳuki	Niḳola Ḳuki	İş Ari Ḳlaẕo		
Yani Ḳlaẕa	Andriya Ġropa	Bardi Ġropa	Miḫal Ġropa	Andriya Zenişa		
Todoro L[o]pe[s]i	Yani Lopesi	mücerred Lazaro Ġropa	mücerred Petro Ġropa	mücerred Pavlo Ġropa		
bīve Anje	bīve Anje-i dīğer	bīve Mara	bīve Pavlo Pirmikir[76]	ḫāne 17	mücerred 4	bīve 3

ḥāṣıl 1087

ʿa(n) ispence 438	ʿöşr-i ḥınṭa 500	ʿöşr-i cev 80	resm-i ḫanāzīr 19	ʿöşr-i kettān 50

ḳarye-i Yorgi Mujaki ez cemāʿat-i Arnavudān ḫāṣṣa-ı Mīrlivā

Yorgi el-mezbūr	Dimitri Muzaki	Yorgi Mujaki-i dīğer	Varda Muzaki	Yani Muzaki	
Petro Muzaki	Yorgi İvlaḫo	bīve Ḳuke	bīve Mara	ḫāne 7	bīve 2

ḥāṣıl 412

ʿa(n) ispence 152	ʿöşr-i ḥınṭa 200	ʿöşr-i cev 31	resm-i ḫanāzīr 9	ʿöşr-i kettān 20

ḳarye-i Andriya Pupuḳa ez cemāʿat-i Arnavudān ḫāṣṣa-ı Mīrlivā

Andriy[a] el-mezḳūr	Yani Bubuḳa	Ḳozma Badra	Gin Bubuḳa	[ḫā]ne 4

ḥā[ṣı]l [2]17

ʿa(n) ispence	ʿöşr-i ḥınṭa	ʿöşr-i cev	resm-i ḫanāzīr	ʿöşr-i kettān
80	100	16	11	10

154
tetimme-i nāḥiyyet-i Londar

ḳarye-i Yani Ḳanḳazi ez cemāʿat-i Arnavudān ḫāṣṣa-ı Mīrlivā

Yani el-mezḳūr	Andriya Ḳanḳazi	Petro Ḳanḳazi	Pavlo Ḳanḳazi	Aleksi Ḳanḳazi
Yani Ḳanḳazi	Yorgi Ḳanḳazi	Petro Ḳanḳazi-i dīğer	Todoro Vorila	Angelo Ḳanḳazi
Lazaro Başta	Dimitri Başta	Niḳola Başta	Petro Kle[s]ura	ḫāne 14

ḥāṣıl 1270

ʿa(n) ispence	ʿöşr-i ḥınṭa	ʿöşr-i cev	resm-i ḫanāzīr	ʿöşr-i kettān
280	800	120	10	60

ḳarye-i Lazaro Klesura ez cemāʿat-i Arnavudān ḫāṣṣa-ı Mīrlivā

Lazaro el-mezḳūr	Yani Klesura	Niḳola Klesura	Petro Klesura	İstefano Vuti[77]
Yani Doskesi	mücerred Aleksi Ḳanḳazi	mücerred Yani Ḳanḳazi	mücerred Yani veled-i Aleksi	mücerred Andriya birāder-i o
mücerred Petro birāder-i o	mücerred Andriya Buḳa	mücerred Petro Ḳanḳazi	mücerred Lazaro Ḳanḳazi	mücerred Andriya Başta
mücerred Gön Başta	mücerred Yorgi Klesura	mücerred Lazaro Vuti[78]	mücerred Yorgi Doskesi	mücerred veled-i Todora
bīve Todora	ḫāne 6	mücerred 14	bīve 1	

ḥāṣıl 707

ʿa(n) ispence	ʿöşr-i ḥınṭa	ʿöşr-i cev	resm-i ḫanāzīr	ʿöşr-i kettān
406	200	31	20	50

ḳarye-i Marti Çaşi ez cemāʿat-i Arnavudān ḫāṣṣa-ı Mīrlivā

Marti el-mezḳūr	Yani Çaşi	Yorgi Çaşi	Niḳola Çaşi	Yorgi Çaşi-i dīğer
Runcari Çaşi	Todoro Çaşi	Lonca Lala	bīve Marti Çaşi	bīve Yani Çaşi
	ḫāne 8		bīve 2	

ḥāṣıl 371

ʿa(n) ispence	ʿöşr-i ḥınṭa	ʿöşr-i cev	resm-i ḫanāzīr	ʿöşr-i kettān
172	150	24	5	20

ḳarye-i Ḳokino Marti ez cemāʿat-i Arnavudān ḫāṣṣa-ı Mīrlivā

Ḳokino el-mezḳūr	Niḳola Ḳuke	Yani birāder-i Ḳokino el-mezḳūr	Aleksi Manesi	Yani Manesi
Marti Maḳri	İlya Mavromati	Yorgi Mavromati	Yani Mavromati	Pavlo Manesi
İlya Manesi	Yorgi İvlaḫo	Merti[79] Manesi	Yani Ḳuçi	Niḳola Ḳuçi
bīve Burşina	bīve Sirgina	bīve İlya Manesi	bīve Manesina	ḫāne 15 bīve 4

155
ḥāṣıl-ı ḳarye-i Ḳokino el-masṭūr 717

ʿa(n) ispence	ʿöşr-i ḥınṭa	ʿöşr-i cev	resm-i ḫanāzīr	ʿöşr-i kettān
324	300	47	16	30

ḳarye-i Barbuçi ez cemāʿat-i Arnavudān ḫāṣṣa-ı Mīrlivā

Petro Barbuçi	Dimitri Barbuçi	Yani Barbuçi	Dimitri Barbuçi-i dīğer	ḫāne 4

ḥāṣıl 216

ʿa(n) ispence	ʿöşr-i ḥınṭa	ʿöşr-i cev	resm-i ḫanāzīr	ʿöşr-i kettān
80	100	15	11	10

ḳarye-i Ḫırisoviryi Ḳozma ez cemāʿat-i Arnavudān ḫāṣṣa-ı Mīrlivā

Ḫıriso-viryi el-mezḳūr	Yani Zenişa	Loşa Ḫırisoviryi	Yorgi Ḫırisoviryi	mücerred Todoros veled-i Loşa
	ḫāne 4		mücerred 1	

ḥāṣıl 234

ʿa(n) ispence	ʿöşr-i ḥınṭa	ʿöşr-i cev	resm-i ḫanāzīr	ʿöşr-i kettān
100	100	16	8	10

ḳarye-i Trima İşpata ez cemāʿat-i Arnavudān ḫāṣṣa-ı Mīrlivā

Trima el-meẕkūr	Miḫal İşpata	Todoro İşpata	Dimitri İşpata	Yorgi Badra
Ḳozma Badra	Yani Ḳanḳadi	Todoro Bojik	Duḳa İşpata	ḫāne 9

ḥāṣıl 439

ʿa(n) ispence	ʿöşr-i ḥınṭa	ʿöşr-i cev	resm-i ḫanāzīr	ʿöşr-i kettān
180	200	31	8	20

ḳarye-i Ẕima Rala ez cemāʿat-i Arnavudān ḫāṣṣa-ı Mīrlivā

Dima el-meẕkūr	Dimitri Manesi	Nikifor İvlaḫo	ḫāne 3

ḥāṣıl 196

ʿa(n) ispence	ʿöşr-i ḥınṭa	ʿöşr-i cev	resm-i ḫanāzīr
60	100	16	20

ḳarye-i Yani Dara ez cemāʿat-i Arnavudān ḫāṣṣa-ı Mīrlivā

Yani el-meẕkūr	Pelaññrin Dara	Aleksi Dara	Yani Simyo	Loşa Ḫayḳal
Lazaro Ḫayḳal	Lala İpsari	Yorgi İpsari	Yorgi Ḫayḳal	Andriya Dar[a]
Yani Ḫayḳal	Yorgi Dara	mücerred Ḳumani Ḫayḳal	mücerred Muriki	mücerred Miḫo
bīve Ḳumaniya	bīve Iḳrorizina	ḫāne 12	mücerred 3	bīve 2

ḥāṣıl [6]87

ʿa(n) ispence	ʿöşr-i ḥınṭa	ʿöşr-i cev	resm-i ḫanāzīr	ʿöşr-i kettān
312	250	40	55	30

156

tetimme-i nāḥiyyet-i Londar

ḳarye-i Yorgi Manesi ez cemāʿat-i Arnavudān ḫāṣṣa-ı Mīrlivā

Yorgi el-meẕkūr	Dima Manesi	bīve Yani Manesi	bīve Niḳola Manesi	bīve Niḳola Manesi-i dīğer
	ḫāne 2	bīve 3		

ḥāṣıl 126

ʿa(n) ispence	ʿöşr-i ḥınṭa	ʿöşr-i cev	ʿöşr-i kettān
58	50	8	10

ḳarye-i Gin Ḳondostavlo Manesi ez cemāʿat-i Arnavudān ḫāṣṣa-ı Mīrlivā

Gin el-meẕkūr	Gin Çaşi	Gin Yiroçaşi	Loşa Manesi	Andriya Ḳondostavlo
Ẕyaleşi Manesi	Yorgi Manesi	Yorgi Manesi-i dīğer	Andriya Manesi	Ẕyaleşi Manesi
Yani Manesi	Ḳondo Manesi	Gin Leḳa	ḫāne 13	

ḥāṣıl 836

ʿa(n) ispence	ʿöşr-i ḥınṭa	ʿöşr-i cev	resm-i ḫanāzīr	ʿöşr-i kettān
260	450	72	4	50

ḳarye-i Lazaro Ḳuveli ez cemāʿat-i Arnavudān ḫāṣṣa-ı Mīrlivā

Lazaro el-meẕkūr	Yani Ḳuveli	Yorgi Ḳuveli	Yorgi Ḳostomanesi	Ḳosta Manesi
Yorgi Aġuridi	Yorgi Çaşi	Yorgi Nikifor İvlaḫo	Palunbi	Lazaro birāẕer-i o
Laluḳas	Ḳosta Yatrinas	bīve İvlaḫo	ḫāne 12	bīve 1

ḥāṣıl 683

ʿa(n) ispence	ʿöşr-i ḥınṭa	ʿöşr-i cev	resm-i ḫanāzīr	ʿöşr-i kettān
246	350	54	3	30

ḳarye-i Velize ez cemāʿat-i Arnavudān ḫāṣṣa-ı Mīrlivā

şu Velize Primikir	Petro Velize	Niḳola veled-i o	Yorgi Muriki	Andriya Muriki

Lazaro Ḫalanbraza	Mangişa Ḫalanbraza	Leḳa Ḫalanbraza	Yorgi Ḫalanbraza	Aġabito
Gön Şalesi	Petro veled-i o	Andriya Ṣameri	Petro Ṣameri	Yorgi Ṣameri
Dima Franḳo	Atarodima Franḳo	Gön Franḳa	Yani Ḫalanbriza	Martin veled-i o
	bīve Buja zen-i Ṣameri		ḫāne 20	bīve 1

ḥāṣıl 1065

ʿa(n) ispence	ʿöşr-i ḥınṭa	ʿöşr-i cev	resm-i ḫanāzīr	ʿöşr-i kettān
406	500	80	29	50

157
tetimme-i nāḥiyyet-i Londar

ḳarye-i Maḳrisa Ustruza ez cemāʿat-i Arnavudān — ḫāṣṣa-ı Mīrlivā

Maḳrisa el-mezḳūr	Yani veled-i o	Pulimenos Maḳrisa	Ḳozma veled-i o	İlya Pendeni
Lazaro Ḳonbi Seḳra	Todoros Ḳonbi Seḳra	Lazaro Tuçi	Petro Tuçi	Todoros Ġavras
Yorgi veled-i o	Lala Ġavra	Yani Ġavra	İlya Ġrubya	Yani Ḳosta Niḳa
	Pavlo Ġavra		ḫāne 16	

ḥāṣıl 705

ʿa(n) ispence	ʿöşr-i ḥınṭa	ʿöşr-i cev	resm-i ḫanāzīr	ʿöşr-i kettān
320	300	48	7	30

ḳarye-i Zimiçana — ḫāṣṣa-ı Mīrlivā

Papadimitri Papandroplo	Yorgi birāder-i o	Muriki Papandroplo	Yorgi birāder-i o	Niḳola Krevavos
Yorgi birāder-i o	Sotoki birāder-i o	Pavlos Krevavos	Niḳola Rondaya	Todoros Rondaya
Yani birāder-i o	Manol Praski	İstemati Floḳyaniti	Yorgi Ḳordoro	Yani veled-i o
Yani Papaandro- plo	Dimitri birāder-i o	Yorgi veled-i o	Sotoki İş Avro	Todoros Ḳavuras
Yani İlyoplo	Niḳola veled-i o	Petro İlyoplo	Manol Benato	Todoro veled-i o
Manol Plastara	İstemad birāẕer-i o	Yorgi Plastara	Yorgi Benato	Miḫal Nomiḳo
Yorgi Ḳuḳli	Niḳola Ḳaçura	Ḫıristofora veled-i o	Dimitri İstefanoplo	Manol birāder-i o
Sotoki Vuçara	Miḫal Ḳavra	Ḳosta birāder-i o	Anaġnos Nomiḳos	Nikifor Nomiḳo
Yorgi Androplo	Vaṣıl Malaviti	Ḳondostavla Manesi	Yani Manesi	Sotoki veled-i o
Petros Benato	Yani Vuçara	Manol Protonotari	Sotoki Nomiḳo	Anaġnosti Ḳaraḳala
Yani Ḳondoyani	Petros Ḳrovavos	Todoros Ḳarḳala	Yani birāder-i o	Miḫal Notara
Manol veled-i o	Vaṣıl Seniẕura	Niḳola birāẕer-i o	Todoros Nomiḳos	Manol Ḳataḫorinos

158
[tetimme-i] ḳary[e-i Zim]iç[a]na el-mezḳūr — [ḫāṣṣa-ı Mīr]livā

[Yan]i [---]co	[Ni]ḳola [.^{1}]lik[iy]o	[---]i [bi]r[ā]der-i o	[Dimi]tri [---]plo	Manol [---]
[Yo]rgi [---]tu[---]	Niḳola birāder-i o	[M]anol P[..^{3}.]ota	Miḫal [Ma]vroya[ni]	Ya[ni] P[---]
Niḳola birāder-i o	Ḳosta Ġavriloplo	Yorgi Ġavriloplo	Yorgi Mu[s]to	Todor[os] [---]a[---]
Dimitri Somoplo	Sotoki veled-i o	Petro veled-i o	Vaṣıl Ḳav[---]i	[---] Ḳa[---]
Yani Ḳaritino	Vaṣıl Ġavriloplo	Aleksi Ġavriloplo	Vaṣıl Ġavriloplo	Miḫal Ġavriloplo
Dimitri Ġavriloplo	Yani Muso	Niḳola Platendro	Yani Ḳaḳoliri	Todoros Ḳacas
Miḫal Malusalis	Niḳola Ḳruki	İstemati Zirvo	Aleksi İstrongilo	Todoros İs[k]a[.^{2}.]
Yorgi Armonġavli	Papas Zirvo	Todoros veled-i o	Anaġnos Siriza	Leo Zirvo
Todoros Simyoni	Yorgi Simyoni	Yani birāẕer-i o	Yani Simyoni	Yani Ranbari
Todoros Asanas	Yani veled-i o	Leo Meġalyoti	Niḳola Ġavriloplo	Niḳola Biryoti
Yorgi İstasila	Dimitri İvlasi	Yorgi İvlasi	Dimitri Lonbardoplo	Niḳola Ġavra
Manol veled-i o	Yorgi veled-i o	Yani veled-i o	Todoro İstefanoplo	So[t]ok[i] birāder-i o

Miḫal Lanbardoplo	Miḫal Ẕiminoyani	S̱otoki Ḳalavuni	Ẕyaḳumi Mandila	Miḫal [Ḳ]aḳoliri
Pavlo Meġalyoti	Miḫal As̱anas	Yani Armonġavli	Todoros Meġalyoti	Yani Ḳalusi
Dimitri Ẕimonoyani	Leo ḫīş-i o	Todoros Ḳurtoplos	Manol ḫīş-i o	Yani ḫīş-i o
Androniḳo Ẕimon[oy]an[i]	Niḳola Notara	Niḳola Ḳarvavo	Yorgi Ḳuḳli	Yorgi Niḳoli
L[---] Mano[lo]plo	Niḳola [---]	mücerred Ya[ni] Papaandr[oplo]	mücerred An[d]riya [---]plo	mücerred Yani Lastara
mücerred Yani Ḳavra	mücerred Miḫal Nomiḳo	mücerred Leo Manesi	mücerred İstemati Benato	mücerred Yorgi Vuçara

159

tetimme-i ḳarye-i Ẕ[imi]çana el-mezbūr ḫāṣṣa-ı Mīrlivā

mücerred Le[o] Ḳataḫorinos	mücerred [Pav]los Pavlota	mücerred S̱otoki Armonġavli	mücerred S̱otoki Ḳaça	mücerred Miḫal [.².]aẕis
[mücerre]d [---]os [K]a[ḳ]olir[i]	mücerred [Ya]ni Ḳaritino	mücerred [Var]s̱alemo [Ġ]avriloplo	mücerred Niḳola Ġavriloplo	mücerred Yani [Ġ]avr[ilo]plo
[mücerred] Ḳosta Ḳuli	mücerred Miḫal Platendro	mücerred Leo Ḳaḳoliri	mücerred Niḳola Malusalis	mücerred Todoros Ḳroki
[mücerred] Dimitri İstrongilo	mücerred Yorgi Simyoni	mücerred S̱otoki Simyoni	mücerred Yorgi Meġalyoti	mücerred Niḳola Armonġavli
mücerred [M]iḫal Biryoti	mücerred [S]uvani Piryoti	mücerred Dimitri Ḳondoyani	bīve Yani Ḳarḳala	bīve Ḫartofilaḳa
bīve İstratu Beẕar[---]	bīve S̱omayi zen-i Lasḳari	bīve Liḳovunyo-tisa	bīve Ziruna	bīve Siridya
[bī]ve Manişa	bīve Nomiki zen-i S̱otoḳu	bīve Dimitri Nomiḳo	bīve Manol Nomiḳo	bīve Todoro Malesiya
	bīve Faḳrasi Protonotari	ḫāne 142	mücerred 31	bīve 13

ḥāṣıl 10447

ʿa(n) ispence 45[28]	ʿöşr-i bāġāt 1120	ʿöşr-i ḥınṭa 3500	ʿöşr-i cev 548	ʿöşr-i ḳazz 82	ʿöşr-i meyve 15
resm-i ḫanāzīr 4	resm-i ḫamr 150	ʿöşr-i kettān 200	mülk-i Papadimitri Papa-androplo der ḳarye-i meẕkūr āsiyāb 1 resm 50		

mülk-i Yorgi Ḳordoro der ḳarye-i meẕkūr āsiyāb 1 resm 50

mülk-i Yani Papaandroplo der ḳarye-i meẕkūr āsiyāb 1 resm 50	mülk-i Ḳondostavla Manesi der ḳarye-i meẕkūr āsiyāb 1 resm 50	mülk-i bīve S̱omayi zen-i Lasḳari der ḳarye-i meẕkūr āsiyāb 1 resm 50

mülk-i Todoros Ḳurtoplos der ḳarye-i meẕkūr āsiyāb 1 resm 50

ḳarye-i Ḳoḳova ḫāṣṣa-ı Mīrlivā

Ṣarandi Protoyoros	Marḳos Niḳolas	Papaniḳola Ḫarḳomata	İstefano Matrofina	Niḳola Ṣarandi
İlya Brati	Yorgi Lukişa	Duḳa veled-i o	Niḳola veled-i o	b[īve] [T]aġarin[a]

ḫāne 9 bīve 1

ḥāṣıl 881

ʿa(n) ispence 186	ʿöşr-i b[āġā]t 1[00]	bāġ[ā]t-ı [ḫāṣṣa] d[önüm] 1 [resm] 150	ʿöşr-i ḥınṭa 350	ʿöşr-i cev 5[3]	ʿöşr-i meyve 2	resm-i ḫı[nzī]r [10]
		resm-i ḫamr [10]	ʿöşr-i kettān 20			

160

tetimme-i nāḥiyyet-i Londar

ḳarye-i Çarnuḫlu ḫāṣṣa-ı Mīrlivā

Niḳola Ġaziri	Miḫal Manciri	Yorgi Mavroplo	Andriya Buva	Mangişa Traḫya

Andriya İsḳandali	Yorgi İzlatḳa	Petros Bezulḳa	Duşa Sirvos	Gin Ḫayḳal
mücerred Miḫal Mavroplo	mücerred Dima Bezulḳa	mücerred Leḳa Sirvos	ḫāne 10	mücerred s̱elās̱e

mevżiʿ-i āsiyāb-ı ḫāṣṣa 1

ḥāṣıl 787

ʿa(n) ispence 325	eşcār-ı ṭut-ı ḫāṣṣa ʿaded 4 [resm] 20	ʿöşr-i bāġāt 56	ʿöşr-i ḥınṭa 300	ʿöşr-i cev 48	ʿöşr-i ḳazz 7	ʿöşr-i meyve 6

resm-i ʿarūsī 10	ʿöşr-i kettān 15

mezraʿa-ı İvrato Ḳuçi Ḳonbi S̱eḳra nezd-i ḳarye-i Çarnuḫlu el-meẕkūr

ḫāṣṣa-ı Mīrlivā ḫāliyye

yekūn-i ḫāṣṣhā-<yı> Mīrlivā der nāḥiyyet-i Londar

ḳurā maʿa nefs-i Londar 55	mezraʿa-ı ḫāliyye 1	ḫāne 1136	mücerred 140	bīve 107

ḥāṣıl 113647

161

nefs-i Ḳoris̱os ḫāṣṣa-ı Mīrlivā

maḥalle-i Pavlos Lanbo

Pavlos el-meẕkūr	Yani Anbala	Niḳola Praski	Todoro Lazaro	Niḳola Siripali
Miḫal Vurva	Niḳola Ḳanafaġa	Dimitri Fivo	Miḫal Plafano	Petros Armani
Marḳo Anbala	Dimitri Arḫimandriti	Yani Bresti	Niḳola Ġalya	Paraskavos İksanos
İstemati Velivasta	Yorgi Lupos	Yani Mamora	İstefano Selaniti	Dimitri İstavraki
Yani Plati	Niḳola İstamina	Todoros dāmād-ı Ġalara	Yorgi Aleksoplo	İstas̱i Yaḫşi
Ḳostandin Bukâniş	Yani Serġalo	Miḫal Azraḫta	Niḳola Ḳono	Yani Maġo
Manol Kerama	Yani İsḳapiçi	Yorgi Ẕomoliti	Yani Maki	Yani Senaḫyiri
[Ḳo]standin Sindirvina	Todoros İsḳlavos	Yani Saġo	Yani Anbelaki	Yani Ḳamaryoti
Dimitri Pisoḫaravo	Niḳola Ḫomari	Dimitri Liḳuḳa	Papas Pinaḳa	Yorgi Ḳonomosoli
Dimitri Atomano	Niḳola [D]oḳsapatri	Dimitri Peristari	Dimitri Turḳo	Niḳola Ṣaloniti
Ḳostandin Maḳriyeni	Yani Maḳriyeni	Niḳola Ḳalandra	Niḳola Ḳurtesi	Yorgi Ġuryaras
Ḳostandin Todoros	Niḳola Pandala	Yorgi Brato	Anaġnosti Ḳormoli	Yorgi Ḳatiḳora
Yani Piro	Ḳostandin Ṣarakino	Yorgi Mali	Paloloġos Aleksoplos	İstemati Ḳormoli
Iġlava Melisino	Yani Ḳutruli	[Y]orgi Ḫono	Niḳola Limozi	mücerred Dimitri Vurva
mücerred Yani Pelaḳano	mücerred Dimitri İsḳayçi	mücerred Yani İsḳlavos	mücerred Yani Pungina	mücerred Dimitri Sakerna
mücerred Yorgi Maḳriyeni	mücerred Niḳola Mali	bīve Manda-tina zen-i Ẕyaḳonisa	bīve Siriparo	bīve Aḳratina
bīve Maḳriyanu	bīve Peristarina	bīve Ḳaliçina	bīve Serġalo	bīve Saḳonina

162

tetimme-i maḥalle-i Pavlos el-meẕkūr der nefs-i Ḳoris̱os

bīve Azraḫtu	bīve Bratina	bīve Vlanusa	bīve Makina	bīve Alġorina
bīve Petro Moskina	bīve Elani İksekilo-ḳati	bīve Aġapi	bīve Punkina	bīve Sinaḫyirina
bīve Sakerina	bīve İpsoḫrava	bīve Ġulamina	bīve Tatomano	bīve Proġoplo
bīve Ḳurtasina	bīve İksenoẕoḫisa	bīve Mamatina	bīve İksaniya	bīve Parorotisa
	ḫāne 69	mücerred 8	bīve 28	

maḥalle-i Yani Meliġari

Yani el-meẕkūr	Dimitri Amiraliẕi	Dimitri Ḳalargi	Miḥal Balasi	Yani Marino
Niḳola Perdiḳari	S̱oma Meġariti	Yorgi İsḳanci	Yorgi As̱inos	Niḳola Milona
Yorgi İzvolo	Dimitri Riços	Yorgi Dara	Niḳola Ḳondulo	Dimitri Apostolo
Vaşıl İstrati	Vaşıl Peristari	Manol Peristari	Yani Traġuẕaki	Yani İstamena
Niḳola Peristari	Yani Doḳsapatri	Yani Ḳavlora	Yani Ġavra	Manol Ġalari
Yorgi Rayḳos	Manol Kerama	Andon Kerama	Yani Ḳono	Niḳola Alupotrupi
Todoros Aḥlaẕi	Miḥal Tirva	Dimitri Maġo	Yorgi Plasi	Dimitri dāmād-ı Aġas̱oni
Yani Ġalati	Dimitri İksano	Yorgi Marġaliç	Miḥal Ḳormoli	İstefano Ḳormolis
İstefano Armani	İstemati Perḳardo	Yorgi Lavoni	Yorgi Ḳamuzos	Manol İstaveni
Yani Ḳoryalos	Yorgi Ḳazos	Manol İpsara	Niḳola Mavromati	Yorgi İstratiri
Yorgi Senelyati	Yani Ḳuḳas	Ḳostandin Rafti	Apostolos Şelinati	Dimitri Tavri
Andriya dāmād-ı Gin	Damyanos Ġulyamos	Yani Veliveça	Dimitri Proḳopi	Miḥal [Te]mandi
Manol Plangi	Andon Saḳovalo	Ḳostandin Lanbaẕari	Damyanos Ḳalotovis	As̱anas Trapeẕandos

163

tetimme-i maḥalle-i Yani Meliġari el-meẕkūr der nefs-i Ḳoris̱os

İstemad Sumlos	Marti Zepandi	İstefano İsḳuliḳa	Manol Kâlari	Yani Lapsana
İstemad Draġos	Yani Matos[80]	Vas̱i Ranesi	Petros S̱omas	Miḥal Poniros
Dimitri Prafti	Yani Kerama	Yani Amiraliẕi	Yani Ḳarçivelo	Miḥal Ḳozmo
Dimitri dāmād-ı Ḳarçivelo	Dimitri Aḥlaẕi	mücerred Miḥal Pulya Lavri	mücerred Yorgi Ḳarçivelo	bīve Ḳaterġaro

bīve Parorotisa	bīve Ḳondolevo	bīve Yirgo İksiloḳaki	bīve Miḥalu Maġu	bīve Şaloniti
bīve Kiryaḳo	bīve Melisini	bīve Ḳıniso	bīve Ġardinaro	bīve Dimitri İksandalipa
bīve Şomelina	bīve Vaftizmano	bīve Prilepo	bīve İstemati Amiraliẕi	bīve Çaperno
	ḫāne 82	mücerred 2	bīve 16	

maḥalle-i Ḳondostavlos Alyotos

Ḳondos-tavlos el-meẕkūr	İstemati Royani	Manol Ḳanbova	Manol İpsoḥalaz-meno	Niḳola Ḳaliḳa
Yorgi Şurbi	Niḳola Manḳola	İstemati Ḥamaloni	Yorgi Şamandi	Dimitri Marmara
Manol Şerpa	Dimitri Azapi	Yorgi Ravis̱a	Pavlos Ranbaḳa	Ḳostanco Rafti
Miḥal Zaḥoli	Yani Protopapa	Yorgi Doḳsapatri	Kiryaḳos Danili	Niḳola Ḳondoyani
Todoros A[.2.]ris	İstemati Aski	Niḳola Eḥmalotos	[T]odoros Perdiki	Dimitri Ḥarkâs
İstematos Berardos	Dimitri As̱inos	Yani Mos̱onos	Dimitri Ḥırisinos	Yani Ġatinari
Niḳola Ḳoskina	Yorgi Selaniḳös	Dimitri Ġuveviya	Yorgi Hitos	Niḳola Ḳalana
Dimitri Mastro-mesaro	Niḳola Ḳater[ġ]ari	Niḳola Savos	Ḳomninos Çimanduri	Ḥıristaḳo Aspyoti
[D]imitri Birsti	[D]imitri Ḳo[.2.]os	Yorgi Rayḳos	Miḥal İpsara	Dimitri Praski
Yorgi Saḳovalo	Yorgi [Ba]rdano	Manol İġliġoras	İspilyoti Ḳ[a]lopoto	Todoros Ḳoroyan[o]

164

tetimme-i maḥalle-i Ḳondostavlos el-meẕkūr der nefs-i Ḳoris̱os

[D]imitri Ḳumis	Todoros Ḳumi	Dimitri Las[ḳ]alos	Yani Pla[n]gi	Yorgi [---]
Yorgi Ġoẕolos	Ḥıristoẕulos Meġariti	Niḳola Çaprinos	Niḳola Perdiki	Proḳos Ḥırisinos

Yorgi Duḳa	Miḫal Mavropa	Dimitri Ḳondolos	Andon Doḳsapatri	Yani Ḳoryolesi
Yani veled-i Miḫal Ḳormoli	Miḫal Papaẕoplos	Niḳola Sinaḫyiris	Yani Simuli	Yani Aḫlaẕa
Yorgi Ḳomori	Yani Peraroti	Niḳola Luḳaniḳa	Niḳola Pirpiri	Dimitri Çanḳari
Niḳola Zatuni	Yaḳumis Limoyani	Todoros Luḳas	Yorgi Aḳrati	Dimitri Filimotomo
Duḳa Tarḫanyoti	Yorgi Ḳolato	Ḳosta Izġuroplos	Miḫal Izġuroplos	Niḳola Ranḳavas
Niḳola Ġavevi	Miḫal Lanbaẕari	Yani İstavraki	Niḳola İzvolo	Todoros İzvolos
mücerred Anakiro Meġariti	mücerred Yorgi Çaprinos	mücerred Niḳola Lasḳari	bīve Papadya Aḳokirina	bīve Ḳalotirkiri
bīve Ḳalos̱itina	bīve Pulumano	bīve Ġulinina	bīve Ḳartalo	bīve Yorgi A[m]iraliẕi
bīve Papadya Sinedriyo	bīve Ḳalostefano	bīve Porto- papaẕya[81] Plangi	bīve Yorgi Miḫalyoti	bīve Yani Mali
bīve Darulya	bīve Ḳostanda	ḫāne 90	mücerred 3	bīve 14

maḫalle-i Niḳola Luzi

Niḳola el-meẕkūr	Niḳola Ḳartelya	Niḳola Ḳolato	Dimitri Perato	Yorgi Rali
Yorgi Raġuço	Dimitri Raġuços	Niḳola Duḳa	Andriya Ḫırisayiti	Yorgi Nisyoti
Aleksi Rafti	Dimitri Ḳastelyano	Yani Melati	Leḳa Ḳanavuri	Yani Birsti
Yani İstrati	Niḳola İstrati	Andon Pepano	Yani Ḳolato	İstas̱i veled-i Papayani
Ḳostandin Maki	Niḳola Paroriti	İstemati Marino	Niḳola Yani İstamna	Yani Ḳanavuri
Apostolos Vosḳos	Todoros Ġramatiḳos	Dimitri birāder-i o	Yorgi birāder-i o	Ḳostandin birāẕer-i o

165

tetimme-i maḫalle-i Niḳola el-meẕkūr

Yorgi Ġrama[tiḳ]os	Dimitri İspartino	Niḳola İstanişa	Yani Ḳorẕoni	Andon Rusavos

Niḳola Ḳaḳoyani	Dimitri Maġos	Yorgi Saḳuli	Anargiro Aġas̱uli	Yani Mayiẕos
Andon Riços	Pisḳopos Niḳokiri	Papas Borfali	Papas Ravis̱a	Papas İksanos
Ẕyaḳos Amiraliẕi	Papas Ġolovas	Papas Ḳolato	Papas Romenos	Papas Ġalari
Papas Maġos	Papas Poniros	Papas Niḳokiri	müsellem zīrā bennāʾ-ı ḳalʿa-ı Ḳoris̱os şüd Yani Mikâli	müsellem zīrā neccār-ı ḳalʿa-ı Ḳoris̱os şüd İstemati Ḫirisinos
Yorgi Ḫırisinos	Mastro- todoros	Todoros Ḳaluẕi	Dimitri Andriya	Ḳostandin Ḳarçivelo
Yorgi Ṣari	Miḫal İstavniköti	Piros Fanġo	Miḫal birāẕer-i o	Yani Moskinos
Niḳola Iḫyami	Vaşıl Filimotomo	Todoros Runbiḳa	Yorgi Runbiḳa	Andriya Runbiḳa
Yani Ḳastelano	Aleksi Muzalo	Yani Ḫolova	Gin Plaşa	Dimitri Ḫalkâ Lipsoẕuri
Vaşıl Ḳanıḳlı	İstas̱i Ḳanıḳlı	Niḳola dāmād-ı Ḳanıḳlı	Yani Ḳalanba	Yani Poẕopana
müsellem zīrā āhenger-ı ḳalʿa-ı Ḳoris̱os şüd Mastro- toma Cingene	Mastro- miḫal Cingene	Ranesi dāmād-ı o	Kiryaki birāder-i Miḫal el-meẕkūr	mücerred Dimitri Lanbaẕari
mücerred Franceşko[82] Niḳokiri	mücerred Yani Şari	mücerred Manol birāder-i o	mücerred Todoros Praski	mücerred Manol Loġaryasti
mücerred Ḳostandin Velivaça	mücerred Yorgi Plati	mücerred Yorgi Maġo	mücerred Dimitri Kerama	mücerred İspilyoti Aġapi
mücerred İstas̱i Pandela	mücerred Niḳola Mali	mücerred Yorgi Ḳalotoẕi	mücerred Niḳola Sumelo	mücerred Yorgi Ḳariḳa

mücerred Dimitri Ḳanena	mücerred Z̲yaḳovi Ḳatatomari	mücerred Yani Amiraliz̲i	mücerred Manol Saḳovelo	mücerred Anargiro Meġariti
mücerred Pavlos Simuli	mücerred Manol Tarḫanyoti	mücerred Yani Maġo	mücerred Andon Maġo	mücerred Yani Broḳali
mücerred İstemati İksano	mücerred Miḫal Ḳolato	mücerred Niḳola Mastrotodor	mücerred Dimitri İstrati	mücerred Yani Ḳanıḳlı
mücerred Yorgi Atomano	bīve Andon Marġota	bīve Yanulya	bīve Liḳomatina	bīve Argiropulina

166

tetimme-i maḥalle-i Niḳola el-mez̲kūr der nefs-i Ḳoris̲os

bīve Biçina	bīve Sivasto

cemāʿat-i Yahūd ki der nefs-i Ḳoris̲os mī-şevend

İbrahīm[83] Pepano	Yūsuf veled-i Mūsā	İlyaḫu Peto

ḫāne maʿa müsellemān ve Yahūd 87	mücerred 32	bīve 6

mez̲kūr Ḳoris̲os cemāʿatiniñ ellerinde ḥükümleri vardır ki ḫarācdan ve ispenceden ve mecmūʿ-ı ʿavārıż ve tekālīf-i dīvāniyyeden muʿāf ve müsellem olalar ve dizdār dėdügi vaḳt ḥiṣārda nevbet bekliyeler deyü ammā defter ʿarż olundugı vaḳt hemān ispenceleri muʿāf olundı ḫarācları ve ġayri muʿāf olunmadı

yekūn-i nefs-i Ḳoris̲os

ḫāne 328	mücerred 45	bīve 64

ḥāṣıl ġayr ez ispence ve memlaḥa ve müsellemān 27151

bāġāt-ı ḫāṣṣa dönüm 12 [resm] 720	muḳāṭaʿa-ı bāzār ve gümrük ve maʿber der nefs-i Ḳoris̲os 3000	resm-i niyābet-i vilāyet-i mez̲kūr 2000	eşcār-ı saḳız-ı çam-ı ḫāṣṣa ʿaded taḫmīnen 1000 [resm] 500	ʿöşr-i besātīn 200

ʿöşr-i penbe 200	ʿöşr-i kettān 380	ʿöşr-i bāġāt 7191	ʿöşr-i ḥınṭa 10400	ʿöşr-i cev 1592	ʿöşr-i ʿasel 28

resm-i ḫamr 740	mülk-i Ḥāccī Ḳaraca dizdār-ı ḳalʿa-ı Ḳoris̲os āsiyāb 1 resm 40	mülk-i Dimitri Peristari der maḥalle-i Pavlos el-mez̲kūr āsiyāb 1 resm 80	mülk-i Dimitri İksano der maḥalle-i Yani el-mezbūr āsiyāb 1 resm 80

cemʿ-i ḳażā der taṣarruf-ı Mevlānā Muḥyi'd-dīn ḳāḍī-ı Ḳoris̲os ġayr ez ʿöşr
fī sene 375

bāġāt dönüm 6 [resm] 360	eşcār-ı meyve ʿaded 30 [resm] 15	mezraʿa-ı ḫāliyye 1	mescid-i cāmiʿ der Ḳoris̲os 1

ammā z̲ikr olan bāġāt ve eşcār-ı meyve ve mezraʿa aṣılda cāmiʿ olan kenīsānıñ[84] imiş şoñra cihet-i ḳażā olunmuş mez̲kūr ḳāḍīnıñ elinde bulundugı sebebden üzerine yazıldı

ammā fi'l-aṣl manastır būd

vaz̲īfe-ḫorān-ı cāmiʿ-i mez̲kūr

Mevlānā Muḥyi'd-dīn ḳāḍī-ı Ḳoris̲os ki imāmet ve ḫiṭābet fī yevm 6	ʿAlī el-müʾez̲z̲in fī yevm 2	şeyḫ ḳayyım fī yevm 2	bahā-<yı> pīh ve ḥaṣīr 1

yekūn fī yevm
11

meẕkūrler ki ḥükümlerinde ḳayd olunmuşdur ki istifā ḫarācından her yıl ḫarāc vėrüb tecdīd-i ḥükm ve pervāne ṭaleb etmeye deyü

mukāṭaʿa-ı memlaḥa ki ḫāṣṣa ḫullide mülküḥu şüd

fī sene mīʾe ve ʿişrun

167

nāḥiyyet-i Ḳoriṣos

ḳarye-i Vaṣılıḳa ḫāṣṣa-ı Mīrlivā

İstemad Ḳaḳotari	Niḳola Aġori	Dimitri Doḫali	Yani Ḳaḳotari	Andon Laḳasa
Papas Niḳola Musara	Todoros Şarvano	Yanul İsḳutari	Dimitri Zestos	İstemati Zestos
Niḳola Ḳoḫanyoti	Andriya Şarvano	Papas Ḫıristodulos	Yani Vaṣıl	Miḫal Lipsoẕuri
Papayani Playani	Niḳola Yanuli	Yani Ḳarofila	Ḳozma Ḳaṣoliḳari	Aleksi Plataniti
Miḫal Londiçi	Yani Famozo	Petros Boḫatis	Papatodoros Tetraẕi	Niḳola Paḫyani
Todoros Ḳoḫanyoti	Filibos[85] Varilo	Yorgi Ḳativa	Yani Ḳativa	Yorgi Aryoḳosta
Yani Ḳuvuki	Dimitri Ḳalofila	Yani Virgi	S̱otoki Danili	Niḳola Aryoḳosta
İṣtasi[86] Tetraẕi	Yani Maṣya	Yani Aleksi	Dimitri Tetraẕi	Yorgi Panayoti
Yani Varilo	Yorgi Marḳuli	Todoros S̱odosi	Yani İstanilo	Dimitri Ḳolyostomo
Dimitri Ḳalanyoti	S̱oẕosi Lanḳaẕinos	Papas Anastas	Todoros İstanila	İlya Aryoḳosta
Papas Niḳola İsḳutali	Dimitri veled-i o	Yani Remondo	Dimitri Palapanbiẕi	Yani Ḫarkâ
Yani Rupakyoti	Yani Ḳaramuẕi	Yorgi Pelaḳano	Yani Şarakino	Miḫal Kipros
Niḳola Bardos	Yani Ḳaṣoliḳari	Niḳola Ġaryo	Papayorgi Ḳoḫanyoti	Yani Mandilya
Yorgi Kipro	Todoros Platyas	S̱omas Keẕoḳlas	İstilyano Pelaḳano	Petro Apato
Yani Yanota	Dimitri Velona	Ḳoloḳari İksanos	Ḳordosi İksanos	Andriya İlyoplos
Tarḫanyoti İk[s]anos	Petro Ḳronbiya	Ḳonda Dara	S̱odoro Dara	Niḳola Ḳaçiḳani
Niḳola Papaẕaplo	Niḳola Ḳurtesa	Dimitri Ḳaçiḳani	mücerred Niḳola Ḳoḫnyoti	mücerred Ḫıristodulo Lupo

168

tetimme-i ḳarye-i Vaṣılıḳa el-meẕkūr ḫāṣṣa-ı Mīrlivā

mücerred Dimitri Musari	mücerred Yani İstanilo	mücerred Miḫal Mesargi	mücerred Yani Palapanbi	mücerred İstefano Ḳalanyoti
bīve Paras-kevi zen-i As̱anasiya	bīve Bi[ḫ]omato	bīve Ma[m]oḳulo	bīve Papadya zen-i Laletina	bīve Andilavina
bīve Andronu	bīve Marġarita Maṣyusa	bīve Vukösa	bīve Mariya Restina	bīve Şaravano

ḫāne 83 mücerred 7 bīve 10

ḥāṣıl ġayr ez memlaḥa 10749

ʿa(n) ispence	bāġāt-ı ḫāṣṣa dönüm 3	mukāṭaʿa-ı bāġçe-i türünc-i ḫāṣṣa 1	ʿöşr-i bāġāt	ʿöşr-i ḥınṭa	ʿöşr-i cev
2310	[resm] 360	[resm] 450	1888	4000	620

ʿöşr-i meyve	ʿöşr-i ʿasel	resm-i ḫamr	ʿöşr-i kettān	ʿöşr-i penbe	resm-i ʿarūsī
339	22	240	100	200	100

mülk-i Andriya Şarvano der ḳarye-i meẕkūr āsiyāb 1 resm 80

mülk-i bīve Mamoḳulo der ḳarye-i meẕkūr āsiyāb 1 resm 40

mukāṭaʿa-ı memlaḥa ki ḫāṣṣa ḫullide mülküḥu şüd der ḳarye-i Vaṣılıḳa el-mezbū[r]

fī sene miʾetān

mezraʿa-ı Ḳuvara nezd-i ḳarye-i Vaṣılıḳa el-meẕkūr ḫāṣṣa-ı Mīrlivā

ḫāliyye

ḳarye-i Ayo Vaṣıl ve nām-ı dīğer Çağıl Ḥiṣārı ḫāṣṣa-ı Mīrlivā

Dimitri Ḫali	Yorgi veled-i o	Yani veled-i o	Todoros Ḫali	Yorgi Ġorġo
Yorgi İşpata	Yani veled-i o	Dimitri İstaṣi	Proḳopi birāẕer-i o	Papayani Filivari
İstemati Foḳa	Kiryaḳo Ḳaliḳa	İstemati Virveti	Niḳola Andoni	İstefano Andoni

169

tetimme-i ḳarye-i Ayo Vaṣıl el-meẕkūr ḫāṣṣa-ı Mīrlivā

Niḳola Rokâti	İstefano Ḳulostomalo	Yorgi Ḳoromiẕi	Yani veled-i o	Anargiro Paroriti
Niḳola Paroriti	Yorgi Papalo	Dimitri Ḳulomardo	Yorgi Ḳulosomalo	Todoros veled-i o
Luḳa Ḳokiro	Yani Pararoti	İstaṣi Paroriti	Yani veled-i o	Dimitri Ḳulostomalo
Ṣotoki Virveti	İstavroforo Ḳariẕa	Yorgi veled-i o	Niḳola Ḳotriki	Miḫal İskina
İstemati Pavlo	Ṣimos veled-i o	Papayani Lanḳaẕiti	Yani Ẕamyano	Niḳola Ẕamyano
Ḳokino Ḳonboṣo	Yani birāder-i o	Dimitri Çanḳaroplo	Yani Velçina	İstaṣi Ḳulomardo
İstefano Famelyari	Dimitri Virvati	Mari Norisa	Yani İsḳalçiya	Pavlos Petrukö
Yani Çanḳari	Yani Ṣaravali	Yorgi Ṣaravali	Yorgi İstaṣo	Panayoti İskina
İspilyoti Vilona	Yani Aḳriẕa	Yani Vevara	Yorgi Petrukö	Yorgi Ḳanboso
Yani Akriẕa	Papaniḳola Ḳondoḫyini	Vaṣıl veled-i o	Vaṣıl Peḫaviti	Pavlos Peḫaviti
Panayoti Zuma	Niḳola Yoti	Yani Ḳuropalati	Niḳola Vevara	Miḫal Kimina
Yorgi Ḫonino	Yorgi Ḳaçuli	Niḳola Ḳuti	Niḳola Turlunbi	Papaniḳola Ḳondoḫyini
Pavlos Paḫaviti	Gin Ṣalesi	Dimitri Zaḫarya	Niḳola Ḫalḳomata	Papavaṣıl İskliro
mücerred Manol Ġorġo	mücerred İstemati Ḳulostemalo	mücerred Dimitri Ḳoromiẕi	mücerred Panayoti birāder-i Yorgi Papalo	mücerred Dimitri Ḳokiri
mücerred İstefano Peraroti	mücerred Yorgi Ḳulostemalo	mücerred Ḫıristoforo Ẕamyano	mücerred Yorgi Aḳriẕa	mücerred Andon Ṣaravali
mücerred Ṣoẕosi [Ḳon]doḫyini	mücerred Yani İvlaşi	bīve Ṣaravalo	bīve Anifando Ḳulina	bīve Filivaro
	bīve Niḳola Aḳriẕa	ḫāne 80	mücerred 12	bīve 4

170

ḥāṣıl-ı ḳarye-i Ayo Vaṣıl el-meẕkūr 8544

ʿa(n) ispence 2324	bāğāt-ı ḫāṣṣa dönüm 4 [resm] 480	eşcār-ı meyve-i ḫāṣṣa ʿaded 23 [resm] 50	ʿöşr-i bāğāt 2014 ʿa(n) istafide [5]50 ʿa(n) şīre 1464

ʿöşr-i [ḫın]ṭa 25[0]0	ʿöşr-i cev 387	ʿöşr-i meyve 91	resm-i ḫanāzīr 8	ʿöşr-i ʿasel 60	resm-i ḫamr 200	resm-i ʿarūsī 100

ʿöşr-i kettān 200	ʿöşr-i penbe 50	mülk-i Papaniḳola Ḳondoḫyini der ḳarye-i meẕkūr āsiyāb 1 resm 40	mülk-i Todoros Ḫıristodulos Ḳoriṣosī āsiyāb 1 resm 40

mezraʿa-ı Petro Ḫayḳal nezd-i ḳarye-i meẕkūr	mezraʿa-ı Manesi nezd-i ḳarye-i mezbūr
ḫāṣṣa-ı Mīrlivā ḫāliyye	ḫāṣṣa-ı Mīrlivā ḫāliyye
mezraʿa-ı Sermorini nezd-i ḳarye-i masṭūr	mezraʿa-ı Ḳalo İstemati nezd-i ḳarye-i mesfūr
ḫāṣṣa-ı Mīrlivā ḫāliyye	ḫāṣṣa-ı Mīrlivā ḫāliyye

ḳarye-i Pulimeno Ḳondostavlo ez cemāʿat-i Arnavudān ḫāṣṣa-ı Mīrlivā

Miro Piça	Yorgi veled-i o	Leḳa Filovari	Pulimeno İvrato	Yani Romyo
Mangişa veled-i o	Miḫal veled-i o	Andriya Filovari	İstefano Filovari	Mangişa Lala
Manḳolas Minas	Yani Filovari	Miḫal Filovari	Yorgi Proġono	Todoros Peşkâṣeni
	mücerred İvrato Filovari	ḫāne 15		mücerred 1

ḥāṣıl 835

ʿa(n) ispence	ʿöşr-i ḥınṭa	ʿöşr-i cev	ʿöşr-i bāġāt	resm-i ʿarūsī	ʿöşr-i kettān
320	400	64	16	15	20

mezraʿa-ı Piça nezd-i ḳarye-i Pulimeno el-mezḳūr

ḫāṣṣa-ı Mīrlivā ḫāliyye

ḳarye-i Buzbardi ez cemāʿat-i Arnavudān ḫāṣṣa-ı Mīrlivā

Leḳa Buzbardi	Bardi birāder-i o	Gin Maji	Miḫal Manesi	Yani Klişa
Gin Miru[ş]li	Gön birāder-i o	mücerred İştin Buzbardi	ḫāne 7	mücerred 1

171

ḥāṣıl-ı ḳarye-i Buzbardi el-mezḳūr 402

ʿa(n) ispence	ʿöşr-i ḥınṭa	ʿöşr-i cev	resm-i ʿarūsī
160	200	32	10

ḳarye-i Ḫarkâ ez cemāʿat-i Arnavudān ḫāṣṣa-ı Mīrliv[ā]

Yorgi Ḫarkâ	Ḳosta veled-i o	Yani Ḫarkâ	İvrato Ḫarkâ	Yani Ḫarkâ-<yı> dıġer
Niḳola Ḫarkâ	Yorgi veled-i o	Niḳola İvrato	Dima birāder-i o	bīve Mariya

ḫāne 9 bīve 1

ḥāṣıl 658

ʿa(n) ispence	ʿöşr-i ḥınṭa	ʿöşr-i cev	resm-i ʿarūsī
186	400	62	10

ḳarye-i Ḳutala ez cemāʿat-i Arnavudān ḫāṣṣa-ı Mīrlivā

Yorgi Ḳutala ḫāne 1

ḥāṣıl 78

ʿa(n) ispence	ʿöşr-i ḥınṭa	ʿöşr-i cev
20	50	8

ḳarye-i Ayonori ḫāṣṣa-ı Mīrlivā

Miḫal Amirali	Yani Aleksandro	Todoros Luḳaniḳa	Ḳosta veled-i o	Miḫal Roḳana
Sotoki Ḳalonari	Yani Biftaki	Marḳo Tamyata	Miḫal birāder-i o	Papas Muli
Sotoki İstasino	Manol İstasino	Niḳola Filoḳsano	Todoros birāder-i o	Papas Ḳusonizi
Somas birāder-i o	Yani birāder-i o	Niḳola Çanḳaroplo	Dimitri Çanḳaroplo	Papaniḳola Rodova
Dimitri Ḳoromizi	Sotoki birāẕer-i o	Miḫal Şolomo	Niḳola Lavoni	Papas Lavoni
İlya İstroḫili	Panayoti birāder-i o	Yorgi İstroḫili	Manol birāder-i o	Dimitri Ḳavasa
Marino Maġuli	Yani Lupo	Marino Peftaki	Todoros Muli	Sotoki birāder-i o
Niḳola Muli	Ḳostandin Ḳaterġari	Yani Ḳasimo	Yorgi İġliġori	Yani Maġuli
mücerred [M]iḫal [Filo]ḳsano	mücerred Miḫal Niḳola Rodova	mücerred Dimitri Lavoni	mücerred İstasi [La]voni	mücerred Dimitri İstroḫyili
mücerred Soma Maġuli	mücerred Yorgi Ḳusonizi	bīve Luḳaniḳu	bīve Sunbulina	bīve Ḳondarina

172

tetimme-i ḳarye-i Ayonori el-mezḳūr ḫāṣṣa-ı Mīrlivā

bīve İstemata	ḫāne 40	mücerred 7	bīve 4

ḥāṣıl 4132

ʿa(n) ispence	ʿöşr-i bāġāt	ʿöşr-i ḥınṭa	ʿöşr-i cev	ʿöşr-i meyve	ʿöşr-i ʿasel
1199	676 ʿa(n) şīre 656 ʿa(n) istafide 20	1700	26[7]	15	25

resm-i ḫamr	ʿöşr-i kettān
100	150

mezraʿa-ı İksaroḳastalya nezd-i ḳarye-i Ayonori el-mezḳūr

ḫāṣṣa-ı Mīrlivā ḫāliyye

ḳarye-i Liḳuresi ez cemāʿat-i Arnavudān ḫāṣṣa-ı Mīrlivā

Todoros Liḳuresi	Ḳozma Şalesi	Lazaro Ḳalanci	İlya Sivasto	[---]o Dr[..⁴..]o[.¹]i
Gin Doyḳa	Pavlos Liḳuresi	ḫāne 7		

ḥāṣıl 276

ʿa(n) ispence	ʿöşr-i ḥınṭa	ʿöşr-i cev	resm-i ʿarūsī
140	100	16	20

ḳarye-i Ḳlimandi ez cemāʿat-i Arnavudān ḫāṣṣa-ı Mīrlivā

Soki İẕyavoliçi	Gön Marġariti	Bardi birāder-i o	Yorgi Toskesi	Gin Toskesi
Gön Boġdano	Leḳa Petralifi	Niḳola Zalo	Vaşıl Budya	Yorgi Ḳalanci
Seraḳo Ḳals̱aniki	Gön Luzi	Gin Luzi	ḫāne 13	

ḥāṣıl 1013

ʿa(n) ispence	bāġāt-ı ḫāṣṣa	ʿöşr-i ḥınṭa	ʿöşr-i cev	ʿöşr-i meyve	ʿöşr-i ḳazz
260	dönüm 2 [resm] 240	300	48	3	15

ʿöşr-i bāġāt	resm-i ḫamr	ʿöşr-i kettān
112	15	20

ḳarye-i Pulimeno Soyḳa ez cemāʿat-i Arnavudān ḫāṣṣa-ı Mīrli[v]ā

Ḳaratula Soyḳa	Petro Soyḳa	Pavlos veled-i o	Soyḳa veled-i Pavli	Niḳola birāder-i o
Petros Soyḳa-ı dīğer	Pavlos Soyḳa	Todoros veled-i o	Yani Soyḳa	Pulimeno Soyḳa
Andriya Soyḳa	Niḳa Soyḳa	Todoros Borşa	Dima Maji	ḫāne 14

173

ḥāṣıl-ı ḳarye-i Pulimeno el-meẕkūr 880

ʿa(n) ispence	ʿöşr-i ḥınṭa	ʿöşr-i cev	ʿöşr-i kettān
[2]80	500	80	20

ḳarye-i Fenari ḫāṣṣa-ı Mīrlivā

Yorgi Mala[ḳ]so	Yorgi Ḳumunduri	Dimitri Ḳalaẕuri	Manol Ḳalaẕuri	Yani Vurvu[n]i
Papas Defteros	Dimitri Ġoniti	Yani Ḫalḳotovi	Niḳola Ḳarvuni	Dimitri Ḫartofilaḳa
Todoros Ḫartofilaḳa	Yani [P]iro	Yani Poẕara	Yorgi Ḳalaẕuri	Niḳola Ḳunduri
Dimitri Ḳunduri	Ḳozma Ġoniti	Todoros Ḳolokis̱a	Yani Argiti	Yani Ḫartofilaḳa
Papas Nomiḳos	Todoros Arvaniti		ḫāne 22	

ḥāṣıl 1819

ʿa(n) ispence	ʿöşr-i ḥınṭa	ʿöşr-i cev	ʿöşr-i bāġāt	ʿöşr-i ʿasel	ʿöşr-i meyve	ʿöşr-i kettān
550	800	127	96	139	7	50

resm-i ḫamr	mülk-i Manol Ḳalaẕuri der ḳarye-i meẕkūr āsiyāb 1 resm 40
10	

ḳarye-i Bardi ez cemāʿat-i Arnavudān ḫāṣṣa-ı Mīrlivā

Lala Bardi	Todoro Bardi	Andriya veled-i o	Petro Bardi	Yorgi Ḳramasto
[B]ardi Zuġra	Yorgi Zuġra	Miḫal İstavari	Dima Peta	mücerred Sarakin Peta
	ḫāne 9		mücerred 1	

ḥāṣıl 490

ʿa(n) ispence	ʿöşr-i ḥınṭa	ʿöşr-i cev	ʿöşr-i ʿasel	resm-i ḫanāzīr	ʿöşr-i kettān
2[0]0	200	32	35	8	15

ḳarye-i Ḳunbaki ez cemāʿat-i Arnavudān ḫāṣṣa-ı Mīrlivā

İstefano Ḳunbaki	Pavlos Ḳunbaki	Yorgi Ḳuçi	Gön Ḳuçi	Niḳola Plaşa	
Miḫal Plaşa	Sina Mamala	Sina Loġotira	Domaniḳa Başta	Miyaḳra Başta	
Ḳosta [Lo]ġos̱eti	Andriya Ḳuçoḫyiri	mücerred Ḳoşta Başta	mücerred Miḫal Loġos̱eti	ḫāne 12	mücerred 2

ḥāṣıl [7]85

ʿa(n) ispence	ʿöşr-i ḥınṭa	ʿöşr-i cev	resm-i ḫanāzīr	ʿöşr-i ʿasel	ʿöşr-i kettān
280	400	64	6	15	20

174

tetimme-i nāḥiyyet-i Ḳoriṣos

ḳarye-i Biçi [ez ce]māʿat-i Arnavudān — ḫāṣṣa-ı Mīrlivā

Lazaro Biçi	Gön Biçi	Gin Biçi	Todoros Biçi	Niḳola Peşkâ[l]i
		ḫāne 5		

ḥāṣıl 346

ʿa(n) ispence	ʿöşr-i ḥınṭa	ʿöşr-i cev	ʿöşr-i ʿasel	resm-i ḫanāzīr	ʿöşr-i kettān
100	200	32	3	1	10

ḳarye-i Ṣarakin ez cemāʿat-i Arnavudān — ḫāṣṣa-ı Mīrlivā

Miroti Ḳuçi	Lazaro Dara	Miḫal Ḳuçi	Yorgi Ḳuçi	Yorgi Ḳuçi-i dīğer	
Yorgi Lata	mücerred Niḳola Ḳuçi	bīve Buja	ḫāne 6	mücerred 1	bīve 1

ḥāṣıl 455

ʿa(n) ispence	ʿöşr-i ḥınṭa	ʿöşr-i cev	ʿöşr-i ʿasel	resm-i ḫanāzīr	ʿöşr-i kettān
146	250	40	6	3	10

ḳarye-i Luḳa ez cemāʿat-i Arnavudān — ḫāṣṣa-ı Mīrlivā

Sina Maji	Yorgi Ḳumi	Gin Maji	Ḳozma Maji	Ṣarakin Ḳanḳaẕi
Ḳosta Luḳa	İstefano Luḳa	Yorgi Luḳa	Ḳozma Uğur	Leḳ[a] Ġrape[ta]
		ḫāne 10		

ḥāṣıl 511

ʿa(n) ispence	ʿöşr-i ḥınṭa	ʿöşr-i cev	resm-i ḫanāzīr	ʿöşr-i kettān
200	250	40	1	20

ḳarye-i Laluḳa ez cemāʿat-i Arnavudān — ḫāṣṣa-ı Mīrlivā

Yorgi Laluḳa	Gin Laluḳa	Gön Ḳuçi	Miras Zuğra	Gin Zuğra
		ḫāne 5		

ḥāṣıl 407

ʿa(n) ispence	ʿöşr-i ḥınṭa	ʿöşr-i cev	resm-i ḫanāzīr	ʿöşr-i kettān
100	250	40	7	10

ḳarye-i Frati ez cemāʿat-i Arnavudān — ḫāṣṣa-ı [Mī]rlivā

Miḫal Frati	İvlaşi Frati	Niḳola Frati	Marti Frati	ḫāne 4

ḥāṣıl 218

ʿa(n) ispence	ʿöşr-i ḥınṭa	ʿöşr-i cev	resm-i ḫanāzīr
80	100	16	[22]

175

tetimme-i nāḥiyyet-i Ḳoriṣos

ḳarye-i Pisratu ez cemāʿat-i Arnavudān — ḫā[ṣṣa-ı Mīr]livā

Y[or]gi Pisrato	Yani Pisrato	Andriya Pisrato	Proġono [B]içi	Andriya Maji
	mücerred Marti Pisra[t]o	ḫāne 5		mücerred 1

ḥāṣıl 307

ʿa(n) ispence	ʿöşr-i ḥınṭa	ʿöşr-i cev	resm-i ḫanāzīr	ʿöşr-i kettān
120	150	24	3	10

ḳarye-i Frosina ez cemāʿat-i Arnavudān — ḫāṣṣa-ı Mīrlivā

Petro Frosina	Gin Frosina	Todoro Frosina	Gin Frosina	Leḳa Frosina
Niḳola Buva	Petro Varirvi	Andriya Ḳaḳaruḳ	Niḳola Ḳaḳaruḳ	Dimitri Ḳaḳaruḳ
Proġono Frosina	Niḳa Mila	Ninos Frosina	Miḫal veled-i o	Yorgi veled-i o

Tonda Başi	Yani veled-i o	Miḫal Başi	Yorgi Domeniḳa	Ḳosta Domeniḳa
Dima Domeniḳa	Niḳola birāder-i o	Dima Domeniḳa-ı dīğer	Ḳosta Domeniḳa	Niḳola Ḳaprali
Yorgi Parbamari	Niḳola Parbamari	Niḳola İskâẕa	Petro Ḳancali	Todoros Ḳancali
Yani Ḳancali	İvrato Ḥacali	mücerred Petro Domeniḳa	mücerred Marti Domeniḳa	mücerred Niḳola Varirvi
mücerred Domeniḳa Frosina	mücerred Ḳosta Praẕamari	ḫāne 32		mücerred 5

ḥāṣıl 2450

ʿa(n) ispence 740	ʿöşr-i ḥınṭa 1300	ʿöşr-i cev 203	resm-i ḫanāzīr 22	resm-i ʿarūsī 35

mülk-i Meġa Ẕuḳa ki p<ī>ş ez <ī>n der ḳarye-i meẕkūr tīmār eri būd āsiyāb 1 resm 50	mülk-i Niḳola Buva der ḳarye-i meẕkūr āsiyāb 1 resm 50	mülk-i Todoro Frosin[a] der ḳarye-i meẕkūr āsiyāb 1 resm 50

yekūn-i ḫāṣṣhā-<yı> Mīrlivā der nāḥiyyet-i Ḳoriẕos el-meẕkūr

ḳurā	mezāriʿ-i	ḫāne	mücerred	bīve
maʿa nefs-i Ḳoriẕos 21	ḫāliyye 7	707	83	84

ḥāṣıl 62506

176

ḫāṣṣhā-<yı> Mīrlivāʾ-ı vilāyet-i Mora

ḳurā	mezāriʿ-i	ḫāne	mücerred	bīve
maʿa şehir 214	ḫāliyye 17	4538	502	334

ḥāṣıl 448610

177 *blank*

178

nāḥiyyet-i Balya Badra

kendü	geçim	cebelü	günlük	çadır	tenktür
bürüme	1	13	1	1	1

ḫāṣṣhā-<yı> Murād Beg veled-i Timurtaş s[ubaş]ı-ı Balya Badra

ḳarye-i Lala Vizi ez cemāʿat-i Arnavudān — ḫāṣṣa-ı zaʿīm

Gin Lala	Şava Ḳarteniki	Ḳozma Lopeşi	Manḳola Şavas	Pavlo İsḳordala
Niḳolas Ḫarkâ	İvlaḫo Paruca	Gin Çapoġa	Marti İsḳordala	ḫāne 9

ḥāṣıl 581

ʿa(n) ispence 180	ʿöşr-i bāġāt 21	ʿöşr-i ḳazz 5	ʿöşr-i ḥınṭa 325	ʿöşr-i cev 50

ḳarye-i Ḳoşta Ḫāṣṣ ez cemāʿat-i Arnavudān — ḫāṣṣa-ı zaʿīm

Aleksi Muzaki	Niḳola Plameno	Niḳola Muraki[87]	Gin Ḳanca	ḫāne 4

ḥāṣıl 311

ʿa(n) ispence 80	ʿöşr-i ḥınṭa 200	ʿöşr-i cev 31

ḳarye-i Ranesi ez cemāʿat-i Arnavudān — ḫāṣṣa-ı zaʿīm

Petro Ranesi	mücerred Gin Ranesi	mücerred Gön Ranesi	ḫāne 1	mücerred 2

ḥāṣıl 175

ʿa(n) ispence 60	ʿöşr-i ḥınṭa 100	ʿöşr-i cev 15

ḳarye-i Siẕereḳastro — ḫāṣṣa-ı zaʿīm

Ḳozma Varoplo	İstefanos Papamanoloplos	Yani Ḳondostavlepulo	Yorgi veled-i o	Yani Ḳutruli
Niḳola Ḳrovili	Papayorgi Pavloplo	Miḫal Ẕaẕaki	Yani Yaḳumi	Aleksi Ḳaliṣi
İstasino Zatali	Yorgi İskineplo	Niḳola Ġaytani	Andriya Kiropoẕi	Yani Ġal Vuni
Niḳola Petrosḳufi	Papamiḫal Yaḳumis	İstemad Ġalvica	Yani Plavatomo	Andriya Papamanoloplo
Yorgi Livari	Yorgi Varoplo	Todoros Varirvi	İvrato Ẕenbroto	Ṣoma İlyoplo

Yani Ṣarakinoplo	Papayorgi Zoytos	İstilyano Zoytos	Manol Zoytos	Yani Rinoplo
Todoros İvlas	Andriya Varoplo	Dimitri Niḳoluço	Todora Baliḳura	Andon Ġaẕuryari
Miḫal Ḳorovyari	Yorgi Ġayduryari	Yani birāder-i o	Yorgi Paralito	Yorgi S̱omoplo
İvrato Ḳostandinoplo	Miḫal Ḫalanos	Yani Kirepos̱i	Todoro Kiloni	Dima Maji

179

tetimme-i ḳarye-i Siẕereḳastro el-meẕk[ū]r — ḫāṣṣa-ı zaʿīm

mücerred Yorgi Papa-manoloplos	mücerred Petro Ḳutruli	mücerred [Pe]t[ro] birāẕer-i o	mücerred Yorgi Plava-to[m]o	mücerred Yani Ḳruyi
mücerred Niḳola İlyoplo	mücerred Niḳola Facupi	mücerred Marḳo Ġa[y]ẕuryari	bīve Ḳatarina zen-i İsḳalçu-niya	

ḫāne 45 — mücerred 8 — bīve 1

ḥāṣıl 5528

ʿa(n) ispence 1331	eşcār-ı zeyt-i ḫāṣṣa ʿaded 102 [resm] 135	eşcār-ı ṭut-ı ḫāṣṣa ʿaded 170 [resm] 375	eşcār-ı meyve-i ḫāṣṣa ʿaded 140 [resm] 70	ʿöşr-i bāġāt 1823	resm-i ḫamr 194
ʿöşr-i zeyt 43	ʿöşr-i meyve 9	ʿöşr-i ḥınṭa 1300	ʿöşr-i cev 195	ʿöşr-i ḳazz 3	ʿöşr-i penbe 50

ḳarye-i Petro Ḳarava Klesura ez cemāʿat-i Arnavudān — ḫāṣṣa-ı zaʿīm

Petro el-meẕkūr	Ḳozma Marti	Dimitri İsḳura	ḫāne 3

ḥāṣıl 265

ʿa(n) ispence 60	ʿöşr-i bāġāt 90	ʿöşr-i ḥınṭa 100	ʿöşr-i cev 15

ḳarye-i A[yo] Ẕimitri Liḳo Anbali ez cemāʿat-i Arnavudān — ḫāṣṣa-ı zaʿīm

Andriya Ḳosta	Dima Luḳa	Gin Lonḳa	Niḳola Lonḳa	ḫāne 4

ḥāṣıl 312

ʿa(n) ispence 80	ʿöşr-i ḥınṭa 200	ʿöşr-i cev 32

ḳarye-i Dardesi ez cemāʿat-i Arnavudān — ḫāṣṣa-ı zaʿīm

İvrato Geg	Niḳola Maji	ḫāne 2	ḥāṣıl ʿa(n) ispence 40

ḳarye-i Klesura ez cemāʿat-i Arnavudān — ḫāṣṣa-ı zaʿīm

Yani Baytani	Yani Ḫalka	Todoros Lukişa	Miḫal Bicyoti	Manḳola Lukişa
Poniros İksanos	Todoros Ḫarkâ	Miḫal Ḫarkâ	Dima Ḫarkâ	Dima Piçyoti
Yorgi Kraspa	Yani Melita		ḫāne 12	

ḥāṣıl 797

ʿa(n) ispence 240	ʿöşr-i ḥınṭa 450	ʿöşr-i cev 72	resm-i ʿarūsī 15	ʿöşr-i kettān 20

ḳarye-i Pavloḳastro — ḫāṣṣa-ı zaʿīm

Andon Lanboẕi	Niḳola İẕyasiro	Yani Ḫarareplo	Yorgi Ḫarareplo	Andriya Ẕyasiro
Niḳola Lanboẕi	Niḳola Pirzvitereplo	Dimitri İsḳaryano	Petro Poliḳarpo	Andriya Pirzvitereplo

180

tetimme-i ḳary[e-i P]avloḳastro el-meẕkūr — ḫāṣṣa-ı zaʿīm

Dan[i]li birā[der-i o]	Dim[itr]i İst[a]ḫtiya	Andriya La[.².]ki	Niḳola Damyano	D[---] İ[---]
İstemad Zamerya	Todoros Kefalino	Niḳola Damaskino	Yani Moloni	Yorgi Fr[---]p[lo]
Ḳostandin İsḳura	Filibos[88] As̱inyos	Aleksi Uzġuroplo	Dimitri Ḳo[n]idi	Petro İvlaşoplo
Dimitri İsḳulariḳa	Todoros Vumeriti	Ḳostandin Papaandriya	Andriya Ḳorfiri	Yani İs[ḳu]ra

Andon Şapuna	Meksa-ķoplo	Pavlo İksafini	Manol Mavriya	Petro Ķoryani
Andriya Zervoplo	Yorgi Zervoplo	İstemad Mavriya	Papamiḫal İstoyano	Miḫal Şapuna
Yorgi Triķoķali	Niķola Valandi	İstefanos Fireparis	Dimitri Zopoça	Yani Şapu[na]
İstemad Orfano-yani	Niķola Yiroķosto-plos	İstefanos Domali	Yani Filiboplo[89]	Pa[pa-andriya] Orfano[yanis]
mücerred Ķosta Ḫarareplo	mücerred Niķola Poliķarpo	mücerred Pavlo Damyano	mücerred Yani İsķotomen	mücerred Andriya İsķura
mücerred Todoros Ķorfiris	mücerred Dimitri veled-i Anastasiya	mücerred Andriya Valandi	bīve Mariya zen-i Delyarhina	bīve Anastasiya zen-i Ceponi
bīve Mariya zen-i Aporiḫtina	bīve Niķolatisa zen-i Pavlu	bīve Ķali zen-i İvratina	bīve Marġarita zen-i İvranu	bīve Anaza zen-i İstematikina

bīve Ķata-rina zen-i Papatodoros	bīve Anasta-siya zen-i Eksindaevġa	bīve Cana zen-i Mavriya	ḫāne 50	mücerred 8	bīve 10

ḥāṣıl 6149

ʿa(n) ispence 1510	eşcār-ı zeyt-i ḫāṣṣa ʿaded 296 [resm] 338	eşcār-ı ṭut-ı ḫāṣṣa ʿaded 3 [resm] 4	eşcār-ı meyve-i ḫāṣṣa ʿaded 136 [resm] 45	bostān-ı ḫāṣṣa 1 [resm] 20	ʿöşr-i penbe 125

ʿöşr-i kettān 200	ʿöşr-i bāġāt 2633	ʿöşr-i zeyt 87	ʿöşr-i ḥınṭa 725	ʿöşr-i bostān 10	ʿöşr-i meyve 6	ʿöşr-i cev 110
			resm-i ḫamr 336			

ķarye-i Vola ez cemāʿat-i Arnavudān ḫāṣṣa-ı zaʿīm

Todoro Dim[o]	Yani [bi]rāder-i o	Niķa birāder-i o	Ķosta Ẓima	Todoros Yirodimas
Bardi veled-i o	Niķola [P]ra[t]ino	Miḫal birāẕer-i o	Yani Ķo[n]b[o]ti	ḫāne 9

ḥāṣıl 670

ʿa(n) ispence 180	ʿöşr-i bāġāt 90	ʿöşr-i ḥınṭa 350	ʿöşr-i cev 50

mezraʿa-ı Patura nezd-i ķarye-i Pavloķastro el-meẕkūr

ḫāṣṣa-ı zaʿīm ḫāliyye

181

tetimme-i nāḥiyyet-i Balya Badra

ķarye-i İstefano Mazaraki ez cemāʿat-i Arnavudān ḫāṣṣa-ı zaʿīm

[Ġulya]mo Mazaraki	[---] Mazaraki	Andr[iya] Pilura	Gö[n] veled-i [o]	Lo[---] [---]p[---]
[---] [---]	[---] [Ṣ]a[ra]	Ķozma Şara	Yorgi Pilura	mücerred Mangişa Mazar[aki]
	mücerred Pavlo Pilura	ḫāne 9	mücerred 2	

ḥāṣıl 813

ʿa(n) ispence 220	ʿöşr-i [pe]nbe 30	ʿöşr-i kettān 15	ʿöşr-i ḥınṭa 400	ʿöşr-i cev 60	resm-i ḫanāzīr 8

mülk-i Ġulyamo Mazaraki der ķarye-i meẕkūr āsiyāb 1 resm 80

[ķar]ye-i Ķamaniça ḫāṣṣa-ı zaʿīm

Pavlo Ç[alardi]	Yani Runcari	İstemad Yeraki	Martin Servo	Ķostandin Ķafariẓi
Yani ve[le]d-i o	Dimitri Ẓyaķoplo	Yani Ġaytani	Todoros Vaşıl İsķamiç	İstaşi Ķalyoroplo
Filibos[90] M[a]rinos	Yani veled-i o	Yani Gerbesi	Niķola Ķaloṣetos	Ġulyamo Çalardi
Ķostandin Ḫar[a]r[e]plo	Ġulyamo birāder-i o	Papayorgi birāder-i o	Gin Orfano	Papaandriya Mandula
Yorgi veled-i o	Todoro Ġarẓisyoti	Niķola Ṭarsos	Yani Prostondoġos	İstemad Aķaṣaķoṣos
Petruço İksiromeriti	Dimitri Şava	Dimitri Şava-ı dīğer	Niķola Çavala	Papas Dimitrula

Ḳosta Palopoliti	Dimitri Ḫaliki	İstefano Çalardi	İstilyano Hiromandra	Dimitri Aranid
Mavrongele	Dimitri İvlaḫo	Yorgi Pinaḳa	Ḳosta Mavrangelo	Yani İstanis̱eplo
Proġono Lanbano	Petro veled-i o	Yani Palaẕino	Ḳozma Lamyano	Ḳondaki Muzaki
Gön İştranb[i]	Gön İştranbi-i dīğer	Gin İştranbi	Gön Manesi	Petro Longişti
Yani Miseriti	Yani Servoplo	Yorgi Draġos	Yani Rupaki	Lula[ḳo]s Lazari
Yorgi Fiḳulo	Marti Tizo[ve]la	Dimitri Furlaro	Niḳola Ḳostaliva	Papadimitri Ḳoçiḳari
Ḳosta Mavrasi	Miḫal Bo[no]suri	Gön Muzaki	Gin Ḫayḳal	Yorgi Ḳondeyorgi
mücerred Gön Mavrongele	mücerred Dimitri Ġaytani	mücerred Niḳola Marinos	mücerred Yani Ḳaçiri	mücerred Ḳamyo Ġardişyoti

182

tetimme-i ḳarye-i Ḳamaniça el-meẕkūr ḫāṣṣa-ı zaʿīm

bīve İrini zen-i Miḫal Yeraki	bīve Ḳatarina zen-i Vurlya	bīve Marġaro zen-i Yirovaşıla	bīve Alişafi zen-i Nikifor	bīve Elani zen-i Kiryaḳoplo	
bīve Matofanya zen-i Yorgi	bīve İstematiki zen-i Andriya	bīve Marġa- rita zen-i Palandina	bīve Anastasiya zen-i Ḳalu	bīve Revi zen-i Anamos- kaẕina	
bīve zen-i Mucana	bīve İstemata zen-i Menci	bīve Anuda zen-i İstravaplo	ḫāne 65	mücerred 5	bīve 13

ḥāṣıl ġayr ez memlaḥa 8125

ʿa(n) ispence 1828	bāġāt-ı ḫāṣṣa dönüm 3 [resm] 508	eşcār-ı zeyt-i ḫāṣṣa ʿaded 25 [resm] 90	eşcār-ı meyve-i ḫāṣṣa ʿaded 20 [resm] 20	ʿöşr-i [bā]ġāt 1812	ʿöşr-i zeyt 29

ʿöşr-i meyve 26	ʿöşr-i ḥınṭa 2225	resm-i ḫanāzīr 19	resm-i ḫamr 270	ʿöşr-i cev 338	mülk-i Yūsuf veled-i İsmaʿīl[91] merdüm-i İbrahīm[92] Beg bin Süle Beg āsiyāb 1 resm 80

ʿöşr-i penbe 600	ʿöşr-i kettān 200	mülk-i Meliġala Balya Badraʾi der maḥalle-i Yani Maḳaroni āsiyāb 1 resm 80	muḳāṭaʿa-ı memlaḥa der ḳarye-i Ḳamaniça el-meẕkūr ki ḫāṣṣa ḫullide mülkühu şüd fī sene sebʿa ālāf

ḳarye-i S̱eryanu ez cemāʿat-i Arnavudān ḫāṣṣa-ı zaʿīm

İstemad S̱eryano	Miḫal S̱eryano	Niḳola S̱eryano	İvrato S̱eryano	Yorgi S̱eryano
Todoro Avriyoni	Miḫal Avriyoni	Duşa Ḳonboti	mücerred Yorgi Avriyoni	Gön birāder-i o
		ḫāne 9	mücerred 1	

ḥāṣıl 705

ʿa(n) ispence 200	ʿöşr-i bāġāt 45	ʿöşr-i ḥınṭa 400	ʿöşr-i cev 60

ḳarye-i Runbaḳa ez cemāʿat-i Arnavudān ḫāṣṣa-ı zaʿīm

Petro Ḳonboti	Yorgi İstavraki	mücerred Duḳa Mazaraki	ḫāne 2	mücerred 1

ḥāṣıl 208

ʿa(n) ispence 60	ʿöşr-i bāġāt 33	ʿöşr-i ḥınṭa 100	ʿöşr-i cev 15

ḳarye-i İzlatḳa ez cemāʿat-i Arnavudān ḫāṣṣa-ı zaʿīm

Gin İzlatḳa	Lalas İzlatḳa	Andriya İzlatḳa	Petros İzlatḳa	Andriya İzlatḳa-ı dīğer
Dima Doşkesi	Gön Geg	Reyḳos İzlatḳa	Niḳola Gön Taçi Matranḳa	Ḳosta Bambyoti
Gön Mazaraki	Todoros Alaman	Reyḳos İzlatḳa-ı dīğer	Gön Taçi	Petro veled-i o
Andriya Taçi	Gin Ḳulumbi	Gin Ḳuc	Miḫal Ḳumani	İvrato Ḳuçi
Simo Franḳo	Yorgi Soyḳa	Petro Valima	mücerred Petro İzlatḳa	bīve Elani zen-i Yorgi

ḫāne	mücerred	bīve
23	1	1

183

ḥāṣıl-ı ḳarye-i İzlatḳa el-meẕkūr 1525

ʿa(n) ispence 486	ʿöşr-i ḥınṭa 918	resm-i ḫanāzīr 11	ʿöşr-i cev 110

ḳarye-i Çuḳala ḫāṣṣa-ı zaʿīm

Yorgi Çuḳala	Yorgi Varvaro	Petro Varvaro	Pavlos Varvaro	Yani Ḳolyandro
Niḳola Ḳolyandro	İştin Ḳolyandro		ḫāne 7	

ḥāṣıl 533

ʿa(n) ispence 175	ʿöşr-i bāġāt 68	ʿöşr-i ḥınṭa 250	ʿöşr-i cev 40

ḳarye-i Ribesi ez cemāʿat-i Arnavudān ḫāṣṣa-ı zaʿīm

Mangişa Peta	Mastro- miḫal	bīve Ḳali zen-i Ḳrazina	bīve Martina zen-i Ḳozma	ḫāne 2	bīve 2

ḥāṣıl 147

ʿa(n) ispence 52	ʿöşr-i ḥınṭa 65	ʿöşr-i cev 30

mezraʿa-ı Meliġala nezd-i ḳarye-i Ḳamaniça

ḫāṣṣa-ı zaʿīm ḫāliyye

mezraʿa-ı Liḳuresi nezd-i ḳarye-i o

ḫāṣṣa-ı zaʿīm ḫāliyye

mezraʿa-ı Draġoti nezd-i ḳarye-i o

ḫāṣṣa-ı zaʿīm ḫāliyye

mezraʿa-ı İksenoẕoḫiyo nezd-i ḳarye-i o

ḫāṣṣa-ı zaʿīm ḫāliyye

mezraʿa-ı Ḳomi tābiʿ-i ḳarye-i o ḫāṣṣa-ı zaʿīm

ḫāliyye

ḳarye-i Ḳastriçi ḫāṣṣa-ı zaʿīm

Yani Ṣaloniti	Miḫal veled-i o	Dimitri Tirpiẕi	Andriya Zanbuça	Yani veled-i o
Ḳosta Zanbuça	Filibos[93] Petros	Ḳostandin İpsomaki	Yani Hiliyarḫo	Yani Franḳa
Niḳola Avriyoni	Petro Ṣaloniti	Miḫal Ḳuloḳurdi	Ḳostandin Ḳuloḳurdi	Yorgi Ḳuloḳurdi
Yani Broro	Niḳola Çanḳaraplo	Yani Metaḳsa	Niḳola Tomas	Niḳola Ġramatiḳoplo
Todoro Ġramatiḳo- plo	Yorgi Kiryaḳoplo	Ġulyama Mordomusi	Petra As̱uli	Yorgi Vunyo
Filarato Vunyo	Aşpiyoti Petroplo	Ḳosta Fanasi	Niḳola Ye[.ʾ]a[.ʾ]a	Andriya Visanco
Andriya Froġos	Petro Lesalya	Yorgi Provata	Miḫal Provata	Niḳola Froġo

184

tetimme-i ḳarye-i Ḳastriçi el-meẕkūr ḫāṣṣa-ı zaʿīm

Yani Froġo	Ḳosta Froġo	Andriya Leḫ[y]aniti	Ḳostandin Andriva	Yorgi Mazaraki
Ḳostandin Mordomusi	Ḳos[t]andinos Marinos	Ḳ[a]stri Ḳuri	Todoro Vunyoti	mücerred Miḫal Tirpi[ẕ]i
mücerred Manol Zanbuça	mücerred Ḳostandin Filarato	mücerred Yorgi birāder-i o	mücerred Yani Visanco	mücerred Yani V[u]nyoti
bīve Ḳolomandilina	bīve Papadya zen-i İstefaniya	bīve İstemato zen-i Tomas	bīve Anize zen-i Pravata[94]	bīve Para[skev]i zen-i [Pa]paandro
bīve Anuẕa zen-i Mordomusi	bīve Morofiya zen-i Çanḳarina	ḫāne 44	mücerred 6	bīve 7

ḥāṣıl 5471

ʿa(n) ispence 1292	eşcār-ı ṭut-ı ḫāṣṣa ʿaded 70 [resm] 250	eşcār-ı meyve-i ḫāṣṣa ʿaded 50 [resm] 100	āsiyāb-ı ḫāṣṣa 1 [resm] 300	ʿöşr-i penbe 50	ʿöşr-i kettān 15

ʿöşr-i bāġāt 1238	ʿöşr-i ḳazz 164	ʿöşr-i meyve 41	ʿöşr-i ḥınṭa 1510	ʿöşr-i cev 230	ʿöşr-i zeyt 28	ʿöşr-i ṭut 13

resm-i ḫamr 160	mülk-i Ḳastri Ḳuri der ḳarye-i mezḳūr āsiyāb 1 resm 80

ḳarye-i Lihyana maʿa cemāʿat-i İpsari — ḫāṣṣa-ı zaʿīm

Papas Ḳostandinos	Ḳostandin Ḳrupi	Miḫal Linbiẕi	Petro veled-i o	Ḳosta Linbiẕi
Andriya Linbiẕi	Ḳosta Çanḳaraplo	Todoros Dimitruli	İstemad Ḳondoyani	İste[mad] Ḳord[---]
İstefano Çira	Yani Aġranca	Dimitri Çira	Petro Mazaraki	Yani Mazaraki
Niḳola Buryalişa	mücerred Ḳosta Çipra	bīve Marġaro zen-i Yiromiḫal	bīve Ḳatarina zen-i Andon Çipra	ḫāne 16
mücerred 1	bīve 2			

ḥāṣıl 2204

ʿa(n) ispence 437	eşcār-ı ṭut-ı ḫāṣṣa ʿaded 50 [resm] 210	eşcār-ı meyve-i ḫāṣṣa ʿaded 30 [resm] 10	ʿöşr-i penbe 100	ʿöşr-i kettān 40	ʿöşr-i bāġāt 293
ʿöşr-i zeyt 26	ʿöşr-i ḳazz 23	ʿöşr-i meyve 8	ʿöşr-i ḥınṭa 750	resm-i ḫamr 194	ʿöşr-i cev 113

bu köyde olan Bāle ḥiṣṣesi Salmenik dizdārı Ayas'a tīmār olunub defterde üzerine yazıldı

ʿa(n) ḳarye-i Vundeni — ḫāṣṣa-ı zaʿīm

Yani Mandala	Papamiḫal Mandala	Aleksi Ḳavasila	Ḳostandin Ḳanaluzo	İvlaşi Defteri
bīve Ḳatarina zen-i Ḳavasila		ḫāne 5	bīve 1	mevżiʿ-i āsiyāb-ı ḫāṣṣa 1

ḥāṣıl 3[16]

ʿa(n) ispence 1[3]1	eşcār-ı zeyt-i ḫāṣṣa ʿaded 5 [resm] 9	eşcār-ı meyve-i ḫāṣṣa ʿaded 7 [resm] 15	eşcār-ı ṭut-ı ḫāṣṣa ʿaded 15 [resm] 40	ʿöşr-i bāġāt 90
ʿöşr-i ḳazz 12	ʿöşr-i meyve 4	ʿöşr-i zeyt 3	resm-i ḫamr 12	

185

tetimme-i nāḥiyyet-i Balya Badra

[ḳar]ye-i Ṣofyana — ḫāṣṣa-ı zaʿīm

cemāʿat-i Rūmiyān

Petro Manoliçi	Miḫal Ḳatici	Dimitri Ḳolokiṣa	Dimitri Ẕyonisi	Yorgi Seryano
Dim[itr]i Naranca	Niḳola Rafti	Yorgi Petroplo	Niḳola Kliẕi	İlya Papadimitri
mücerred A[---] [R]aft[i]	bīve [---]it[e] zen-i Mini	bīve Mariya zen-i Çanbuya	bīve Ḳatarina zen-i İskâẕa	ḫāne 10
mücerred 1	bīve 3			

cemāʿat-i Arnavudān

Petro Manesi	Andriya Manesi	Gin Ġanbesi	Ẕima Ḳanci	Niḳola Ḳanci
Ḳosta Plaşa	Gön Plaşa	Gön Manesi	Bardo Manesi	Brayila Ḳanḳaẕi
Lazaro Ḳuçi	Muzak Ori	Ori birāder-i o	İstefano Çapoġa	İvrato Lonci
Gön İş Ari	İş Ari Borşi	Marḳo Ḳosati	Piyater Mincirıḳ	Vuġa Şuli
Yani Fusḳari	İş Ari Maji	Ḳosta Manesi	mücerred Mirti Manesi	mücerred Bratis Manesi
mücerred Petro Maloyoplo	mücerred Ḳozma Muzaki	mücerred Gin Çapoġa	ḫāne 23	mücerred 5

yekūn-i ḳarye-i Ṣofyana el-mezḳūr

ḫāne 33	mücerred 6	bīve 3

ḥāṣıl 4053

ʿa(n) ispence 85[3]	eşcār-ı zeyt-i ḫāṣṣa ʿaded 40 [resm] 63	eşcār-ı ṭut-ı ḫāṣṣa ʿaded 21 [resm] 44	eşcār-ı meyve-i ḫāṣṣa ʿaded 30 [resm] 60	nıṣf-ı āsiyāb-ı ḫāṣṣa 1 [resm] 800	ʿöşr-i penbe 100

ʿöşr-i kettān 30	ʿöşr-i bāġāt 529	ʿöşr-i zeyt 11	ʿöşr-i ḳazz 15	ʿöşr-i meyve 22	ʿöşr-i ḥınṭa 1033	ʿöşr-i cev 158	resm-i ḫamr 215

mülk-i İbrahīm[95] Beg ki p<ī>ş ez <ī>n sipāhī-i Balya Badra būd āsiyāb 1 resm 80	mülk-i Niḳola Piromayiri Balya Badraʾi āsiyāb 1 resm 40

ḳarye-i Raḫova ḫāṣṣa-ı zaʿīm

Manol İḫtisti Veneti | Papadimitri İstavraki | Papaistemati veled-i o | Yani Avroyorgi | Dimitri Kefalino

Andriya Mengibiti | Yorgi Sirvo | Yani Ḳaçuli | Dimitri Pafla | mücerred Todoros veled-i Manol el-mezḳūr

bīve Ḳali zen-i Todoro | ḫāne 9 | mücerred 1 | bīve 1

ḥāṣıl 1395

ʿa(n) ispence 256 | eşcār-ı t[u]t-ı [ḫāṣṣ]a ʿaded 48 [resm] 170 | eşcār-ı meyve-i ḫāṣṣa ʿaded 10 [resm] 20 | ʿöşr-i penbe 40 | ʿöşr-i kettān 10 | ʿöşr-i bāġāt 293 | ʿöşr-i ḳazz 14

ʿöşr-i meyve 8 | ʿöşr-i ḥınṭa 400 | ʿöşr-i cev 60 | ʿöşr-i zeyt 8 | resm-i ḫamr 36 | mülk-i Manol İ[ḫt]isti Veneti der ḳarye-i mezḳūr āsiyāb 1 resm 80

186

tetimme-i nāḥiyyet-i Balya Badra

ḳarye-i Buryalisa ez cemāʿat-i Arnavudān ḫāṣṣa-ı zaʿīm

Pavlo Laġatora | Lazar Peta | Beleşi Lonci | ḫāne 3

ḥāṣıl 1062

ʿa(n) ispence 60 | eşcār-ı balamutlu-<yı>[96] ḫāṣṣa ʿaded taḫmīnen 1500 [resm] 1000 | resm-i ḫanāzīr 2

mezraʿa-ı Çernota nezd-i ḳarye-i Buryalisa el-mezḳūr

ḫāṣṣa-ı zaʿīm ḫāliyye

ḳarye-i İsḳura ez cemāʿat-i Arnavudān ḫāṣṣa-ı zaʿīm

Gin İsḳura | Pavlo Maji | Niḳola Zuḳor | Marti Ranesi | Andra Mire

Domaniḳa İsḳura | ḫāne 6

ḥāṣıl 820

ʿa(n) ispence 120 | āsiyāb-ı ḫāṣṣa 1 [resm] 300 | ʿöşr-i ḥınṭa 350 | ʿöşr-i cev 50

ḳarye-i Ḳurnaroḳastro ḫāṣṣa-ı zaʿīm

Miḫal Ḳoḳla | Andriya İstrato | Andriya Ḳaçuli | Yorgi Vaşıloplo | Andriya veled-i o

Todoros Vaşıloplos | Niḳola Lanbiri | Varṣolomo Aḫtanistos | Dimitri Ḫamenaẓa | Yorgi Zoma

Petro Ḳrokiẓa | Yani Yaḳova | Petros Zomas | Andriya Zomas | Nikifor Romo

Yorgi Morasi | Ḳosta İskâẓa | Niḳoli Draġoni | Niḳola Linbiẓi | Yani Lonḳos

Miḫal Tirġani | İstemad İvlaşi | Bojik İstratiri | Dimitri Vari | Miḫal Draġo

Todoro Bojik | Dimitri Nikifor | Niḳola Ḳondoḳosta | Petros Şalmeniḳo | Ḳurnos Mazarak

Lazaro Maçuki | mücerred Yani İstrato | mücerred Yorgi Ḳaçuli | mücerred Miḫal Lanbiri | mücerred Dimitri Lanbiri

mücerred Gin veled-i Nikifor | mücerred İstefano birāder-i o | mücerred Dimitri Lonḳos | mücerred Ḳosta birāder-i o | mücerred Yani İvlaşi

bīve Reviya [ze]n-i Mordari | bīve Elani zen-i İstrati | bīve zen-i Silu | bīve Ḳali zen-i Dimitri | ḫāne 31 | mücerred 9 | bīve 4

ḥāṣıl 4420

ʿa(n) ispence 1024 | bāġāt-ı ḫāṣṣa dönüm 12 [resm] 900 | eşcār-ı ṭut-ı ḫāṣṣa ʿaded 150 [resm] 200 | āsiyāb-ı peşmīne-i ḫāṣṣa 2 [resm] 100 | ʿöşr-i penbe 100 | ʿöşr-i bāġāt 590 | resm-i ḫamr 64

ʿöşr-i meyve 18 | ʿöşr-i ḳazz 15 | ʿöşr-i ḥınṭa 685 | ʿöşr-i cev 100 | āsiyāb-ı ḫāṣṣa 1 [resm] 450 | resm-i ʿarūsī 30 | mülk-i Yorgi Vaşıloplo der ḳarye-i mezḳūr āsiyāb 1 resm 80

ʿöşr-i kettān 64

187

tetimme-i nāḥiyyet-i Balya Badra

mezraʿa-ı Zastupa nezd-i ḳarye-i Ḳurnaroḳastro

el-meẕkūr ḫāṣṣa-ı zaʿīm

ḫāliyye

ḳarye-i Suli ez cemāʿat-i Arnavudān ḫāṣṣa-ı zaʿīm

Dima Suli	Yorgi Suli	Todoro Suli	Martin Suli	Yorgi Suli-i dīğer
Gin Suli	Gin Suli-i dīğer	Ḳosta Ṣofos	Todoro Bojik	Niḳola Manesi
Yorgi Suli İspano	Y[o]rgi Tatina	Petro Suli	Gin Pavlo	mücerred Gön Suli

ḫāne 14 mücerred 1

ḥāṣıl 773

ʿa(n) ispence	resm-i ḫanāzīr	ʿöşr-i ḥınṭa	ʿöşr-i cev	resm-i ʿarūsī
300	3	400	60	10

ḳarye-i Topolova ez cemāʿat-i Arnavudān ḫāṣṣa-ı zaʿīm

Domaniḳa Rapesi	Gön Ḫronberi	Petros Ḳrato	Maji Tomro	Gin Beluşi
Maji Reçi	Gön Reçi	Gin birāder-i o	Petro Maji	Brati Maji
Petro veled-i o	Filibos[97] Bardi	Niḳola Borşi	Petros birāẕer-i o	Gön Ḳaparali
Leḳa Küğa	Yorgi İştarbi	Aleksi Masḳulori	Yorgi birāder-i o	Duḳa Ḫronberi
Gin Şalesi	Seni birāder-i o	Filibos[98] İksanos	Domeniḳa birāẕer-i o	Papas Dimitri
Niḳola Ḳaraḫulḳa	Gin Ḫronberi	Todoros Muzaki	Petro Ḳarpeşi	Niḳola Mujaki
Mangişa Masḳulori	Papadimitri Ḳuçi	mücerred İstefano Ḫronberi	mücerred Yorgi Bardi	bīve Buḳurina

ḫāne 32 mücerred 2 bīve 1

ḥāṣıl 2174

ʿa(n) ispence	ʿöşr-i ḥınṭa	ʿöşr-i cev	resm-i ḫanāzīr	resm-i ʿarūsī	ʿöşr-i kettān
686	1200	188	15	35	50

ḳarye-i Bardoḳosta ez cemāʿat-i Arnavudān ḫāṣṣa-ı zaʿīm

Gin Iğlava	Andriya Seraḳo	Yorgi Seraḳo	Proğono Lukişa	Andriya Lukişa
Gön Lukişa	Gin Lukişa	Yorgi Lonḳa	Leḳa Manḳa	Reçi Bu[b]a

ḫāne 10

188

ḥāṣıl-ı ḳarye-i Bardoḳosta el-meẕkūr 578

ʿa(n) ispence	ʿöşr-i ḥınṭa	ʿöşr-i cev	resm-i ʿarūsī	ʿöşr-i kettān
200	300	48	10	20

cemʿan ḫāṣṣhā-<yı> subaşı-ı Balya Badra el-meẕkūr

ḳurā maʿa ḥiṣṣe	ḫāne	mücerred	bīve	mezraʿa-ı ḫāliyye
28	459	54	46	8

ḥāṣıl 50150

ENDNOTES

1 شيغونى (Şiğuni) corr.: سيغونى (Siğuni).
2 براذر (birāẕer) variant of برادر (birāder) (*Pers. n.* brother).
3 Cf. Zepandi, 11.
4 فلپوس (Filipos) corr.: فلبوس (Filibos).
5 كشيش (keşīş) corr.: كشش (keşiş).
6 Cf. Zapandi, 4.
7 زپاندى (Zepandi) corr.: رپاندى (Repandi).
8 پلاكرين (Pelañrin) corr.: پلاكرى (Pelañri).
9 پاپاذيه (Papaẕya) corr.: پاپاويه (Papavya).
10 فلپوس (Filipos) corr.: فلبوس (Filibos).
11 ازلتقو (İzletḳo) vel ازلاتقو (İzlatḳo) corr.: ازليقه (İzliḳa).
12 پالونبى (Palunbi) corr.: پولنبى (Pulunbi).
13 مارتى (Marti) corr.: مرتى (Merti).
14 قوسته (Ḳosta) corr.: قوشته (Ḳoşta).
15 خراختنو (Ḫaraḫtino) vel خراقتنو (Ḫaraḳtino) corr.: خرامتنو (Ḫaramtino).
16 مارتى (Marti) corr.: مرتى (Merti).
17 ابراهيم vel ابرٰهم (İbrāhīm) corr.: ابرهيم (İbrahīm).
18 بنّاء (bennāʾ) corr.: بنّا (bennā).
19 ابراهيم vel ابرٰهم (İbrāhīm) corr.: ابرهيم (İbrahīm).
20 ابراهيم vel ابرٰهم (İbrāhīm) corr.: ابرهيم (İbrahīm).
21 قاليوروس (Ḳalyoros) corr.: قاليروس (Ḳaliros).
22 قاليوروس (Ḳalyoros) corr.: قاليروس (Ḳaliros).
23 قاليوروس (Ḳalyoros) corr.: قاليروس (Ḳaliros).
24 قاليوروس (Ḳalyoros) corr.: قاليروس (Ḳaliros).
25 قاليوروس (Ḳalyoros) corr.: قاليروس (Ḳaliros).
26 قاليوروس (Ḳalyoros) corr.: قاليروس (Ḳaliros).
27 قاليوروس (Ḳalyoros) corr.: قاليروس (Ḳaliros).
28 قاليوروس (Ḳalyoros) corr.: قاليروس (Ḳaliros).
29 قاليوروس (Ḳalyoros) corr.: قاليروس (Ḳaliros).
30 قاليوروس (Ḳalyoros) corr.: قاليروس (Ḳaliros).
31 قاليوروس (Ḳalyoros) corr.: قاليروس (Ḳaliros).
32 قاليوروس (Ḳalyoros) corr.: قاليروس (Ḳaliros).
33 پاپاسلرنك (papaslarınıñ) corr.: باباسلرينك (babaslarınıñ).
34 قاليوروس (Ḳalyoros) corr.: قاليروس (Ḳaliros).
35 پاپاسان (papasān) corr.: باباسان (babasān).
36 اشتنى (İştini) corr.: استنى (İstini).
37 فلپو (Filipo) corr.: فلبو (Filibo).
38 فلپو (Filipo) corr.: فلبو (Filibo).
39 اسقازيه (İsḳaziya) corr.: اسفازيه (İsfaziya).
40 اسقازه (İsḳaze) corr.: اسفازه (İsfaze).
41 رادوسقلاوس (Radosḳlavos) corr.: رودقسلاوس (Rodoḳslavos).
42 اشتنى (İştini) corr.: استنى (İstini).
43 خارتوفيلقه (Ḫartofilaḳa) corr.: خارتوفليقه (Ḫartofiliḳa).
44 Cf. 1/14662, 49.
45 كندارخو (Kendarḫo) corr.: كنداخرو (Kendaḫro).

46 آنا (Ana) corr.: آتا (Ata).
47 برناردو (Bernardo) corr.: پرناردو (Pernardo).
48 برناردو (Bernardo) corr.: پرناردو (Pernardo).
49 پاپافلیپوپلو (Papafilipoplo) corr.: پاپافلبوپلو (Papafiliboplo).
50 دنك (ding) corr.: دینك (dīnk); دنك (ding) (*Pers. n.* wooden instrument with iron teeth used in separating rice from the chaff; machine for making powder; oil press): Steingass 1892, 538; Vullers 1962, I 913-914; Pakalin 1946, 'Dinkhane', I 452. For the similar term دبك (dibek) see Kołodziejczyk 2004, I 511. Beldiceanu and Beldiceanu-Steinherr translated *dink* as rice mill: Beldiceanu–Beldiceanu-Steinherr 1978, 25. This fits our case, since a rice-cultivator community is mentioned in Vumero.
51 کشیش (keşīş) corr.: کشش (keşiş).
52 ایشان (īşān) corr.: اشان (işān).
53 تراندافلو (Trandafilo) corr.: دراندآفلو (Drandafilo).
54 پوردانو (Purdano) corr.: پروندانو (Prundano).
55 پوردانو (Purdano) corr.: پرودانو (Prudano).
56 پروغنوس (Proġonos) corr.: روغنوس (Roġonos).
57 فلپوس (Filipos) corr.: فلبوس (Filibos).
58 پراپونکی (Parapungi) corr.: پرابونکی (Parabungi).
59 پراپونکی (Parapungi) corr.: پرابونکی (Parabungi).
60 موناخوس (Monaḫos) corr.: مونوخوس (Monoḫos).
61 درامسی (Dramesi) corr.: درامشی (Drameşi).
62 فراشری (Fraşeri) corr.: پراشری (Praşeri).
63 پروقوپی (Proḳopi) corr.: پورقوپی (Porḳopi).
64 فلپوس (Filipos) corr.: فلبوس (Filibos).
65 فلپو (Filipo) corr.: فلبو (Filibo).
66 ورثه‌لومو (Vars̱elomo) corr.: وثه‌لومو (Vas̱elomo).
67 ثوذوسی (S̱ozosi) corr.: سوذوثی (Sozos̱i).
68 فلپوس (Filipos) corr.: فلبوس (Filibos).
69 اوروميان (Ūrūmiyān) corr.: ارميان (Urumiyān), (*Pers. n. pl.* Byzantines, Greeks, members of the Greek Orthodox Church). The Medieval Islamic world used to call the inhabitants of the Byzantine Empire Rūm < Ῥωμαῖος (*Byz. Gr. n.* Byzantine, Greek). For the use of the term among the Turks see Savvides 1984-5.
70 فلپوس (Filipos) corr.: فلبوس (Filibos).
71 علوفه جی (ʿulūfeci) corr.: علوفجی (ʿulufcı).
72 ایپسالتیری (İpsaltiri) corr.: ایسالتیری (İsaltiri).
73 ماذر (māẕer) variant of مادر (māder) (*Pers. n.* mother).
74 مارتی (Marti) corr.: مرتی (Merti).
75 مارتی (Marti) corr.: مرتی (Merti).
76 پریمکیر (Primikir) corr.: پیرمکیر (Pirmikir) < πριμικήριος (*Gr. n.*) < primicerius (*Lat. n.*); Kazhdan 1991, 'primikerios', III 1719-1720. In Walachia the term پرمکور (pirmikür) was attributed to the chieftain of the village, see the *ḳānūnnāme* of Semendire Eflaḳları, AH 833 (AD 1429-1430): MS Istanbul, BOA, TT16, 10_{14} in Akgündüz 1990, I 528, 530.
77 ووثی (Vus̱i) corr.: ووتی (Vuti).
78 ووثی (Vus̱i) corr.: ووتی (Vuti).
79 مارتی (Marti) corr.: مرتی (Merti).
80 ماثوس (Mas̱os) corr.: ماتوس (Matos).
81 پروتوپاپاذیه (Protopapaẕya) corr.: پورتوپاپاذیه (Portopapaẕya).
82 فرانجسقو (Francesḳo) corr.: فرانجشقو (Franceşḳo).
83 إبراهيم vel ابرٰهم (İbrāhīm) corr.: ابرهيم (İbrahīm).
84 کنیسه‌نك (kenīseniñ vel kenīsanıñ) corr.: کنیسانك (kenīsānıñ).
85 فلپوس (Filipos) corr.: فلبوس (Filibos).
86 استاثی (İstas̱i) corr.: اثتاسی (İs̱tasi).
87 موزاکی (Muzaki) corr.: موراکی (Muraki).

88 فلپوس (Filipos) corr.: فلبوس (Filibos).
89 فلپوپلو (Filipoplo) corr.: فلبوپلو (Filiboplo).
90 فلپوس (Filipos) corr.: فلبوس (Filibos).
91 اسماعيل vel اسمٰعيل (İsmāʿīl) corr.: اسمعيل (İsmaʿīl).
92 ابراهيم vel ابرٰهِم (İbrāhīm) corr.: ابرهيم (İbrahīm).
93 فلپوس (Filipos) corr.: فلبوس (Filibos).
94 پرووواته (Provata) corr.: پراواته (Pravata).
95 ابراهيم vel ابرٰهِم (İbrāhīm) corr.: ابرهيم (İbrahīm).
96 پلاموتلو (palamutlu) corr.: بلامتلو (balamutlu).
97 فلپوس (Filipos) corr.: فلبوس (Filibos).
98 فلپوس (Filipos) corr.: فلبوس (Filibos).

Appendix II

***Editio Princeps* of 1/14662**

(Sts Cyril & Methodius National Library of Bulgaria, Sofia)

1 blank
2 blank
3 blank

4

kendü bürüme	cebelü	çadır	tenktür
	5	1	1

ze'āmet-i Ḳalandriça za'īmeş Evrenos veled-i Ya'ḳūb Beg bin İştin

nefs-i Ḳalandriça ḫāṣṣa-ı za'īm

maḥalle-i Niḳola Mavropoẕi

Niḳola el-meẕkūr	Yani Saḳomanos	Dimitri Papapetrop- los	Andonis Deloliva	Lonberda Ḳuḳuki
Niḳola veled-i o	Yani Ḳordaḳoli	Niḳola Ḳordaḳoli	Yani Ḳuzuḫo	Yani Mermingi
İstefano Mermingi	Yorgi Ḳalavros	Gön Pavlo	Aleksi İskina	Yorgi Ḳaloviça
Yani Ḳuḳuçi	Papaniḳola Yaniçi	Andon Ḳalavritino	Miḫal Ḳapsal	Petro Ḳatunari
Miḫal Luras	Papaniḳola Ḳroḳa	İvratos Renbas	Zaḫaryos Ḳapsaris	Papayani Ṣolomos
Dimitri Civas	Yorgi İstratiġo- plos	Miḫal Kertona	Dimitri Ḫoloroplos	Miḫal Ḳunadi
Ḳostandin Ḳondoniḳola	Papaandriya Ḳorḳa	Niḳola İstivaḳati	Miḫal Liġura	Yorgi Ḳutula
Andriya Nikiforos	Yani Ḳuçomuli	Andriya birāder-i o	Ḳostandin Ḫarareplo	Dimitri Paliġura
Yani Nitola	Yani Mali	Dimitri İstaridi	Yani Jurpo	Yani Serḳura
Rinas Romanos	Yorgi Romanos	Yani Mavriyor	Niḳola Mavriyor	Petros mürted
Niḳola mürted	Yani Gegiẕi	Yani Tirfero	Dimitri Farinos	Yorgi İsḳanbos
Ḳostandin İsḳanbos	Yani Valandi	Miḫal Ṣarakinoplos	Yani Petroplos	mücerred Filyano Ḳalavros
mücerred Franḳo veled-i bīve Marġari	mücerred Dimitri veled-i Aleksi	mücerred Yorgi Luras	mücerred Yorgi Ṣolomos	mücerred Yani Ḳorḳas
mücerred Yorgi Ḳorḳas	mücerred Miḫal Ḳuçomuli	mücerred Petro birāder-i o	mücerred İstefanos Nitolas	bīve Franḳa zen-i Bufo
bīve Marġari zen-i Yani	bīve Andulina zen-i Papa-yorġoplos			

ḫāne	mücerred	bīve
58	11	3

5

tetimme-i nefs-i Ḳalandriça el-meẕkūr ḫāṣṣa-ı za'īm

maḥalle-i Matyos Mamuẕa

Matyos el-meẕkūr	Yorgi Ġramatiḳos	Yorgi Yanuli	Papayani Pulos	Yani Ẕanili
Andriya Ẕanili	Franḳo Tiroplo	Papayani Perpatis	Dimitri Valandi	Yani Voġdan
Yani Zino	Ḳaloyiros Yaniçis	İstemati Ḳlaftomuni	Petros Domaniḳos	Andriya Ṣavas
[M]iḫal Asanas	Yani İḫtenya	Yani İskâẕeplo	Andriya Ḳavurelis	Asani Malis
Todoros A<r>giros	Dimitri Ḳotara	Yorgi Troyila	Dimitri Tusunas	Yanuça İksavros
Niḳola Ġato	Andon Filipeplo	Yani Petroḳosta	Yorgi Çalardi	Miḫal Reçinyos
Andon Lamri	Andruça Ḳalisos	Manol Armaġaẕo- yinos	Benos Ẕokimos	Niḳola İksenoplo
İstemad İksenoplo	Papas Niḳoluços	Niḳola Ḳalaẕo	Niḳola Ḳofina	Ḳocos Todoros
Niḳola Faryari	Ḳostandin Yani	Petros Mazaraki	Ḳostandin Pisaski	Yani Ḳondo
Ẕomeniḳa Manḳulo	Yani İġliġora	Dimitri İġliġora	Miḫal Ḳuroyani	Todoros Bojik
Yani veled-i o	Yorgi Ḫarkâ	Yani Taravija	Yorgi Taraviza	Pavlos Maṣrifos
Gin Gerḳas	Gön biraẕer-i o	Niḳola Morfana	mücerred Yorgi Mamuẕa	mücerred Niḳola Pulos
[mü]cerred İstemad Perpatis	mücerred Dimitri Ġato	mücerred Petros Yiroḳosta	mücerred Yorgi Lamri	mücerred Yani Ḳalistos
mücerred Dimitri Pratar	mücerred Yani Petroplo	mücerred Dimitri Pojik	mücerred Todoros Gerḳas	bīve Morfiya zen-i Ḫararepulya
bīve Elani zen-i Likina	bīve İvr<a>ti zen-i Menalẕina	bīve İstematiki zen-i Lazar	bīve [M]aro zen-i Ḳanavina	bīve Zanyato zen-i Varṣalemo

bīve Plişa zen-i Filib[1]	bīve Zuba zen-i Yorgi	bīve İvrato zen-i Papapetrop- ulya	bīve Mariya zen-i Niḳola Ḳaluẕi	bīve Todor zen-i Nikita
bīve Ḳali zen-i Papadya		ḫāne 58	mücerred 11	bīve 12

6
cemʿan nefs-i Ḳalandriça el-[me]ẕkūr

ḫāne 116	[müce]rred 22	bīve 15	mevżiʿ-i āsiyāb-ı ḫāṣṣa 2

ḥāṣıl 18439

ʿa(n) is[pe]nce 3540	eşcār-ı zeyt-i ḫāṣṣa ʿaded 15 [resm] 563	bāġāt-ı ḫāṣṣa dönüm 20 [resm] 1500	eşcār-ı ṭut-ı ḫāṣṣa ʿaded 410 [resm] 2000	[re]sm-i [bā]zār ve niyābet 500
āsiyāb-ı ḫāṣṣa 1 [resm] 160	bostān-ı ḫāṣṣa 1 [resm] 180	eşcār-ı meyve-i ḫāṣṣa ʿaded 56 [resm] 100	ʿöşr-i penbe 750	ʿöşr-i kettān 150
ʿöşr-i bāġāt 3668	ʿöşr-i ḥınṭa 3390	ʿöşr-i cev 476	ʿöşr-i zeyt 335	ʿöşr-i meyve 72
ʿöşr-i ḳazz 359	resm-i ḫamr 456	mülk-i Papaandriya Ḳorḳa der maḥalle-i Niḳola Mavropoẕi el-meẕkūr āsiyāb 1 resm 80		

mülk-i
Yani Ḳuçomuli der maḥalle-i
meẕkūr
āsiyāb 1 resm 80

mülk-i
Ḳostandin Pisaski der
maḥalle-i Matyos Mamuẕa
el-meẕkūr
āsiyāb 1 resm 80

7
nāḥiyyet-i Ḳalandriça

kendü cebelü	oġla[n][2] 1

tīmār-ı ġarīb yiğitlerden İbrahīm[3] Zerd

ḳarye-i Ḳazneş ez cemāʿat-i Arnavudān — tīmār-ı İbrahīm[4] el-meẕk[ū]r

Şoki Ḳazneş	Lazar Buva	Vaṣi Muriki	Todoros Muriki	Niḳola Maji	[Ya]ni [T]irfa	Petros Ṣomas	mücerred Gin Ḳazneş	Dimitri İvlasoplo	ḫāne 8

mücerred
1

ḥāṣıl 525

ʿa(n) ispence 180	ʿöşr-i ḥınṭa 300	ʿöşr-i cev 45

ḳarye-i Ḳuçi ez cemāʿat-i Arnavudān — tīmār-ı İbrahīm[5] el-mezbūr

Dima Ḳuçi	Andriya Ḳuçi	Niḳola Ḳuçi	ḫāne 3

ḥāṣıl 118

ʿa(n) ispence 60	ʿöşr-i ḥınṭa 50	ʿöşr-i cev 8

ḳarye-i Maji ez cemāʿat-i Arnavudān — tīmār-ı İbrahīm[6] el-mesfūr

Lazari Maji	İstiyafer Maji	Mates Maji	ḫāne 3

ḥāṣıl 176

ʿa(n) ispence 60	ʿöşr-i ḥınṭa 100	ʿöşr-i cev 16

ḳarye-i Ġolemi ez cemāʿat-i Arnavudān — tīmār-ı İbrahīm[7] el-masṭūr

Todor Ġolemi	Gin Ġolemi	ḫāne 2

ḥāṣıl 156

ʿa(n) ispence 40	ʿöşr-i ḥınṭa 100	ʿöşr-i cev 16

ḳarye-i Rapsomati ez cemāʿat-i Arnavudān — tīmār-ı İbrahīm[8] el-meẕkūr

Andriya Rapsomati	Niḳola Meġaṣi	Ḳozma Rapsomati	Andriya Tirifa	Marḳ Peratino
Yani Rapsomati	Papas Ṣotoki		ḫāne 7	

ḥāṣıl 430

ʿa(n) ispence 140	ʿöşr-i ḥınṭa 250	ʿöşr-i cev 40

8
tetimme-i nāḥiyyet-i Ḳalandriça

ḳarye-i Lisarya ez cemāʿat-i Arnavudān — tīmār-ı İbrahīm[9] el-mezbūr

S̱oma Buva	Dimenik Buva	Lazaro Ḳonboti	Gin Ḳrapesi	Piyater veled-i o	
Gergi Draġoti	Eştir Draġoti	Gin Ḳozma	Gergi Siliḳa	Andriya Şuvaldi	
Yani birāder-i o	Andriya Zapend	Niḳola Ḳulam	Zes Luvri	mücerred Gerg Ḳrapesi	
mücerred Pal Draġoti	mücerred Gin Siliḳa	bīve Todora zen-i Çapoġa	ḫāne 14	mücerred 3	bīve 1

ḥāṣıl 943

ʿa(n) ispence	ʿöşr-i ḥınṭa	ʿöşr-i cev	resm-i ḫanāzīr
346	500	79	18

cemʿan tīmār-ı İbrahīm[10] el-masṭūr

ḳurā	ḫāne	mücerred	bīve
6	37	4	1

ḥāṣıl 2348

kendü cebelü	ġulām
	1

tīmār-ı ġarīb yiğitlerden Ḥaccī Kürd

ḳarye-i Bala ez cemāʿat-i Arnavudān — tīmār-ı Ḥāccī el-mezḳūr

Gin Bala	Petros S̱omas	Gerg S̱omas	Leḳa Muştaki	Petro Runcari
Niḳola Runcari	bīve Mariya zen-i Votaça	ḫāne 6		bīve 1

ḥāṣıl 529

ʿa(n) ispence	ʿöşr-i ḥınṭa	ʿöşr-i cev
126	350	53

9
tetimme-i nāḥiyyet-i Ḳalandriça

ḳarye-i İş Ari ez cemāʿat-i Arnavudān — tīmār-ı Ḥāccī el-mezḳūr

Brayla İş Ari	Gin İşpata	Gin Çapoġa	Tanuş Çapoġa	S̱otoki A[---]o	
Martin birāẕer-i o	Manḳola Maṭranḳa	Miḫal Çapoġa	Petro Buḳraçi	İş Ari İşpata	
Yorgi İşpata	Leḳa Çapoġa	Dimitri Çapoġa	mücerred Yorgi Brayila	mücerred İvrato Çapoġa	
mücerred Dimitri Çapoġa	mücerred Niḳola Ḳosati	Yorgi İşpata	Tanuş Çapoġa	Yorgi Çapoġa	
Petro İşpata	Todoros İşpata	bīve Mariya zen-i Buva	ḫāne 18	mücerred 4	bīve 1

ḥāṣıl 1394

ʿa(n) ispence	ʿöşr-i ḥınṭa	ʿöşr-i cev	resm-i ḫanāzīr
446	800	124	24

ḳarye-i Mazaraki ez cemāʿat-i Arnavudān — tīmār-ı Ḥaccī el-mezḳūr

Yorgi Mazaraki	Petro Mazaraki	Todoros Mazaraki	Gin Lonci	Ḳosta Panariti	
Ḳosta Ḳonboti	İstemad İstavraki	Todoros Manesi	bīve Göna zen-i Deliza	ḫāne 8	bīve 1

ḥāṣıl 553

ʿa(n) ispence	ʿöşr-i ḥınṭa	ʿöşr-i cev	mülk-i Yorgi Mazaraki der ḳarye-i mezḳūr āsiyāb 1 resm 40
166	300	47	

cemʿan tīmār-ı Ḥaccī Kürd el-mezḳūr

ḳurā	ḫāne	mücerred	bīve
3	32	4	3

ḥāṣıl 2476

10
tetimme-i nāḥiyyet-i Ḳalandriça

kendü bürüme	cebelü	tenktür
	1	1

tīmār-ı ġarīb yiğitlerden Seyyidī ʿAlī

ḳarye-i Ḳral ez cemāʿat-i Arnavudān — tīmār-ı mezkūr

Lazar Ḳral	Proġono Ḳral	Pavlo Ḳral	Andriya Peta	Pavlos Peta
Petro Peta	S̲omas Latas	Niḳola Lata	İstefanos İzyav[o]litis	Toz̲oros İzyavolitis
Gön Pilura	İvlaş Gireḳuki	Reçi Romanos	Petro Ḳuliza	ḫāne 14

ḥāṣıl 576

ʿa(n) ispence	ʿöşr-i ḥınṭa	ʿöşr-i cev	resm-i ḫanāzīr
280	250	39	7

ḳarye-i Zoġa ez cemāʿat-i Arnavudān — tīmār-ı Seyyidī el-mez̲kūr

İvrato Peşkafti	İlya Zoġa	Pavlo Zoġa	Klüş Aġali	Gin Braçi
	Dimitri Taçi	ḫāne 6		

ḥāṣıl 525

ʿa(n) ispence	ʿöşr-i ḥınṭa	ʿöşr-i cev
120	350	55

ḳarye-i Laluş ez cemāʿat-i Arnavudān — tīmār-ı Seyyidī el-mez̲kūr

Laluş Buryaşa	Domeniḳa Buva	Leḳa Bedeni	Andriya Bedeni	Dimas Felas
Miḫas Bedanis	Pulun<b>i Vaġali	Tora Ḳarteroris	Ḳosta Zemara	Yani Ḳalfoni
Dima Ḳırman	Tanuş Buva	Mengişa birāz̲er-i o	Petro Manesi	bīve Kâne zen-i Muriki

ḫāne	bīve
14	1

ḥāṣıl 988

ʿa(n) ispence	ʿöşr-i bāġāt	ʿöşr-i ḥınṭa	ʿöşr-i cev	resm-i ḫanāzīr
286	113	500	79	10

ḳarye-i Virzaḫo ez cemāʿat-i Arnavudān — tīmār-ı Seyyidī el-mez̲kūr

Ḳozma Mirali	Gön Mirali	Yorgi Mirali	Yorgi İzmolda	Todoros Aḳritis
Dimitri İksaneplo	Miḫal İksaneplo	Truşa Buḳa	Yorgi Ġranca	Pavlos Maḳroḳukis
Aleksi Vala	Miḫal Vala	Andriya Vala	mücerred Miḫal İzmolda	mücerred Yani İzmolda

11

tetimme-i ḳarye-i Virzaḫo el-mez̲kūr — tīmār-ı Seyyidī el-mezbūr

mücerred Yani Aḳritis	mücerred Yani İksaneplo	ḫāne 13	mücerred 4

ḥāṣıl 953

ʿa(n) ispence	ʿöşr-i ḥınṭa	ʿöşr-i cev	resm-i ḫanāzīr
340	500	76	37

cemʿan tīmār-ı tīmār-ı Seyyidī ʿAlī el-mezbūr

ḳurā	ḫāne	mücerred	bīve
4	47	4	1

ḥāṣıl 3042

12 blank
13 blank

14

kendü bürüme	cebelü	çadır	tenktür
	6	1	1

zeʿāmet-i Şandamiri zaʿīmeş İbrahīm[11] veled-i ʿĪsā Beg bin Pavlo Kurtik

nefs-i Şandamiri — ḫāṣṣa-ı zaʿīm

Aporiḫto Manoloplo	Yani Çanḳaruli	Dimitri Şurunbi	Dimitri Flada	To[do]ros Rusalos
Ḳosta Rusanos	Filibe Malaluġa	Ḳostandin İvlaşoplo	Yorgi Mavri Papa	Dimitri Ġramatiḳo
Leḳuz̲i Papayani	Todoros S̲ozosis	Yani Marnavelo	Niḳola Panzi	Yani Ḳoleçi
Niḳola Mancavi	Rados Pasḳali	Yorgi İvlasoplo	İvlaş birāder-i o	Niḳola Vaşıloplo
Dimitri Ḳocayorgi	Yorgi Ḫarareplo	Dimitri Androni	Yorgi İlyoplo	Lyo Çivrili
İstematiḳo Vilona	Yorgi birāder-i o	Yani Duşa	Petro Ḳalanbura	Gin Floḳa
İlya Şarakin	Mirşekle Buva	İstilyano Zatuni	Niḳola Mermere	Ḳosta Papayorġoplo
Marġariti Ḳordoni	As̲anas Ḳavaḳi	Papa İstafenos Vaşılaḳaris	Niḳola birāz̲er-i o	Niḳola Ḳolyati

Todoros İstamiris	Dimitri Iḳsapoliti	İstemad Tulupi	Miḫal Uzġuroplo	İstemati Yiruli
Papavaşıl Ḳunbuli	Ḳozma Ḳuri	Paraski Ġumeriti	İstefanos Ġurniḳas	Dima Arvaniti
Miḫal Şandamiri	Bonufaço Ḳalçöti	Dimitri Vurnera	Yani Popri	Todoros Piġaẕyoti
Dimitri İsḳotomen	Yorgi Mastro İstemati	Yani Ḳaslo	S̠otoki İvlaşoplo	Ḳaloyiros Panci
Miḫal Apostoli	Papas Petros	Yorgi Anamoyani	Yorgi Valuḫa	Niḳola Zoġrafo
Niḳola Ḳuvara	Niḳola Filibos[12]	Miḫa Yorgi	İvretos Miḫoys	Petros Viruni
Lazari Miḫoys	Yorgi İvlaşoplo	Yani İvlaşoplo	Dimitri Panzi	Benatos Paskali
Yani Vaşıloplo	Yorgi Tulupi	Papamanol Balçoti	İstemati veled-i o	Niḳola Mastro İstemati
mücerred Ḳozma Ḳotuli	mücerred Lös Andriyaplos	mücerred Todoros Ḳuvaki	bīve İrini zen-i Niḳola Beratiḳo	bīve Sotirḫiya
bīve Andulina zen-i İstemati	bīve zen-i Arastina	bīve Yorya zen-i Runcari	bīve Elani zen-i Papalyosa	bīve Yorgâ zen-i Vaşıl Porġona[13]
	ḫāne 80	mücerred 3	bīve 7	

15

ḥāṣıl-ı nefs-i Şandamir el-meẕkūr 12655

ʿa(n) ispence 2117	bāġāt-i ḫāṣṣa dönüm 42 [resm] 2912	eşcār-ı zeyt-i ḫāṣṣa ʿaded 100 [resm] 225	eşcār-ı meyve-i ḫāṣṣa ʿaded 43 [resm] 100	ʿöşr-i ḥınṭa 2500

[ʿöşr-i] cev 500	ʿöşr-i bāġāt 3510	ʿöşr-i meyve 29	ʿöşr-i zeyt 84	resm-i ḫanāzīr 8	resm-i ḫamr 350	resm-i ʿarūsī 80	resm-i niyābet 200

mülk-i Yani Ḳaslo der nefs-i Şandamir el-mezbūr āsiyāb 1 resm 40

nāḥiyyet-i Şandamiri

ḳarye-i Porta ḫāṣṣa-ı zaʿīm

Papavaşıl Andrena	Niḳola veled-i o	Dimitri Pandimo	Papas Niḳolas	Todoros veled-i o
Yani veled-i o	Yorgi veled-i o	Papavaşıl Maḳroplo	Dimitri Lizi	Yorgi Ḳuli
Yani Ġulimoplo	Papayorgi Promoyini	Işlav Yani	Varto-lomyo	Yani Penduli
Todoros Penduli	Niḳola Ḳunupoẕi	Yani veled-i o	Yorgi veled-i o	Yani Ḫarkâ
Yani Çani	Pavlos Papa-yanoplos	Yorgi Ḳoçato	Todoros İġliġori	Miḫal İġliġori
Andon Veluḫa	Yani Aġrilo	Çimara Marġariti	Yorgi Kirlesaḳo	Aleksi Niromali
Yorgi Klimano	Andon veled-i o	Niḳola İġliġori	Papas Lyos	Papayorgi İġ[liġ]ori
Dimitri Niromali	Ġulyamo Papas̠otoki	S̠otoki İstefanoplo	Yorgi Ḳuri	Yani İstratiḳo
İstemati Maçuḳa	Yorgi Maçuḳa	Dimitri Andoplo	Yorgi veled-i o	Yani Andoni

16

tetimme-i ḳarye-i Porta el-meẕkūr ḫāṣṣa-ı zaʿīm

Dimitri Kendarḫo	Petro Nikiforoplo	Niḳola bi[r]āẕer-i o	S̠oma Arsini	Miraş Ḫarkâ
Mavro Yani	Yani Nikiforoplo	Dimitri birāder-i Pavlo	Yorgi İlyoplo	S̠omas Liz[yo]s
Petros Papaandriya	Andriya Lizyo	Yani birāder-i o	Dimitri Pavlos	Petros Ḫıyara
Yorgi Perso	Miḫal Kilomeno	Miḫal Ġolemi	Vaşıl Ḳunupoẕi	Yani Varselamyo
İstemad Ḳunupoẕi	mücerred Apostoli Ġulimoplo	mücerred Dimitri Liziri	mücerred Dimitri birāẕer-i Ḫarkâ	mücerred Petro Papavaşıl
mücerred Miḫal Papaniḳola	mücerred Niḳola Kirlesaḳo	mücerred Ġulyamo Maçuḳa	mücerred Miḫal Angelomano	mücerred Andriya İġliġori
mücerred Niḳola Ġulyamo	mücerred Andriya Lizopo	bīve Filyoni zen-i İlyoplo	bīve Todora zen-i İstematiḳo	bīve Mariya zen-i İvlaşoplo
bīve Andriyusa zen-i Çuḳalo	bīve Ḳoçatina	ḫāne 66	mücerred 11	bīve 5

ḥāṣıl 8146

ʿa(n) ispence 1955	āsiyāb-ı ḫāṣṣa 2 [resm] 1200	bāġāt-i ḫāṣṣa dönüm 4 [resm] 630	eşcār-ı zeyt-i ḫāṣṣa ʿaded 15 [resm] 34	eşcār-ı emrūd-ı ḫāṣṣa ʿadedān [resm] 5

ʿöşr-i penbe 50	ʿöşr-i kettān 100	ʿöşr-i bāġāt 1102	ʿöşr-i ḥınṭa 2200	ʿöşr-i cev 336	ʿöşr-i meyve 8	ʿöşr-i zeyt 34

resm-i ḫanāzīr 2	resm-i ḫamr 110	resm-i ʿarūsī 60	mülk-i Ḳāsım İzdinī tīmār eri āsiyāb 2 resm 160

mülk-i Yorgi Ḳuli der ḳarye-i meẕkūr āsiyāb 1 resm 80	mülk-i bīve Todora zen-i İstematiḳo der ḳarye-i meẕkūr āsiyāb 1 resm 80

ḳarye-i Maẕiñik ez cemāʿat-i Arnavudān — ḫāṣṣa-ı zaʿīm

Gin Maẕiñik	Andriya veled-i o	Aleksi veled-i o	Lazari Maẕiñik	Lulaki İstoyan
Todoros birāder-i o	Martin birāder-i o	Niḳola birāder-i işān[14]	İlya Manduḳa	Gön veled-i o
Miḫal Repe[s]i	Leḳa Manduḳa	Ḳosta Manduḳa	Leḳa-ı dīğer Manduḳa	Peta Ḳana
Todoros Gönesi	Yorgi Lavẕa	Andriya [bir]āder-i o	Niḳola birāẕer-i o	Andriya Seriḳal
Gin [---]	Gön İzḳuri	Dimitri birāder-i o	Gön Manḳola	Todoros Manḳola
Todoros mürted	Andriya Barçi	Gin Barçi	Niḳola Barçi	Bardi Şalesi

17

tetimme-i ḳarye-i Maẕiñik el-meẕkūr — ḫāṣṣa-ı zaʿīm el-mezbūr

Marti Şaleşi	Yani As̱anas	Yani Aġabito[15]	Nikita Pulimene	Yorgi Mazaraki	
Yorgi Ḫarkâ	bīve Sina zen-i Ḳraḳuki	bīve Ḳuke zen-i Barşena	bīve Zora	ḫāne 36	bīve 3

ḥāṣıl 2151

ʿa(n) ispence 738	ʿöşr-i kettān 100	ʿöşr-i ḥınṭa 1150	ʿöşr-i cev 124	resm-i ḫanāzīr 9	resm-i ʿarūsī 30

cemʿan tīmār-ı subaşı-ı Şandamir el-meẕkūr

ḳurā maʿa nefs-i Şandamir 3	ḫāne 182	mücerred 14	bīve 15

ḥāṣıl 22952

kendü bürüme	cebelü 1	ġulām 1	tenktür 1

tīmār-ı ġarīb yiğitlerden Burhān Aġa

ḳarye-i İksanya ez cemāʿat-i Arnavudān — tīmār-ı Burhān el-meẕkūr

Todoro Mazaraki	Yani Mazaraki	Andriya Simopula	Taruşi Zeze	Pavlo Ḳuvara	
Yorgi Ḳuçoḫyari	Lazar Frati	Manol Avrami	Dimitri birāder-i o	Brat Maji	
Ḳo[zma] birāder-i o	Todoros Filibos[16]	Pa[v]los Gerbesi	Aleksi Mavrangelos	[Yo]rgi Papadato	
Tonda Yorgi	Tonda İstefano	Rimnita Ropota	M[u]riki Muzaki	İvlaş Ḳondoyorgi	
mücerred Miḫal Gerbesi	mücerred Miḫal Ḳondoyorgi	bīve Mari zen-i Ḳalivesila	ḫāne 20	mücerred 2	bīve 1

18

ḥāṣıl-ı ḳarye-i İksanya el-meẕkūr 1108

ʿa(n) ispence 446	ʿöşr-i kettān 50	ʿöşr-i ḥınṭa 500	ʿöşr-i cev 80	resm-i ḫanāzīr 12	resm-i ʿarūsī 20

ḳarye-i Mirati ez cemāʿat-i Arnavudān — tīmār-ı Burhān el-meẕkūr

Birat Mirati	Gön Mertiş	Petro Lopesi	Gön veled-i o	Ḳalusi Mirati
Gin birāder-i o	Miḫal Mirati	Pavlos Başta	Yorgi Mirati	Ḳosta Martini
		ḫāne 10		

ḥāṣıl 467

ʿa(n) ispence 200	ʿöşr-i kettān 25	ʿöşr-i ḥınṭa 200	ʿöşr-i cev 32	resm-i ʿarūsī 10

ḳarye-i Platistomo ez cemāʿat-i Arnavudān   tīmār-ı Burhān el-meẕkūr

Yorgi Platistomo	İstemad veled-i o	Todoros Ġramatiḳo	Yorgi veled-i o	Niḳola Gerbesi
Gin birāder-i o	Todoro Loşa	Gin Loşa	İstaṡi Sila	Gin Ḳasṭamoniti
Yorgi Ḳrumşa	Gön birāder-i o	Yorgi Yirġoplo	Miḫal Platistomo	mücerred İstaṡi Platistomo

ḫāne	mücerred
14	1

ḥāṣıl 996

ʿa(n) ispence	ʿöşr-i kettān	ʿöşr-i ḥınṭa	ʿöşr-i cev	resm-i ḫanāzīr	resm-i ʿarūsī
300	38	550	85	8	15

ḳarye-i Valmi ez cemāʿat-i Arnavudān   tīmār-ı Burhān el-mezbūr

Vaşıl Valmi	Andriya Ḳuliza	İstaṡi Ġulyamo	Aleksi veled-i o	ḫāne 4

ḥāṣıl 323

ʿa(n) ispence	ʿöşr-i ḥınṭa	ʿöşr-i cev	resm-i ḫanāzīr	ʿöşr-i kettān
80	200	31	2	10

mezraʿa-ı Orfano nezd-i ḳarye-i Porta   tīmār-ı Burhān el-mezbūr

ḫāliyye

ḳarye-i Ġarnaze ez cemāʿat-i Arnavudān   nezd-i nefs-i Şandamir   tīmār-ı mezḳūr

Mangişa Mavromati	Todoros Mavromati	Dima Tunari	Miḫal veled-i o	ḫāne 4

ḥāṣıl 311

ʿa(n) ispence	ʿöşr-i ḥınṭa	ʿöşr-i cev
80	200	31

19
tetimme-i nāḥiyyet-i Şandamiri

ḳarye-i Puliça ez cemāʿat-i Arnavudān nezd-i o   tīmār-ı Burhān el-mezbūr

Martin Loġoṡeti	Yorgi Piluşa	ḫāne 2

ḥāṣıl 155

ʿa(n) ispence	ʿöşr-i ḥınṭa	ʿöşr-i cev
40	100	15

mezraʿa-ı Lukişta nezd-i o tīmār-ı mezḳūr   mezraʿa-ı Gin Floḳa nezd-i o tīmār-ı mezḳūr

ḫāliyye   ḫāliyye

mezraʿa-ı Mariçi nezd-i o   tīmār-ı mezḳūr

ḫāliyye

ḳarye-i Ẕervini ez cemāʿat-i Arnavudān nezd-i o   tīmār-ı Burhān el-mezḳūr

Domeniḳa Ḳozomato	Pavlos İşpata	Dima Turnari	Mavro-mati	birāẕer-i mezḳūr

ḫāne 5

ḥāṣıl 216

ʿa(n) ispence	ʿöşr-i ḥınṭa	ʿöşr-i cev
100	100	16

cemʿan tīmār-ı tīmār-ı Burhān el-mezḳūr

ḳurā	mezāriʿ-i ḫāliyye	ḫāne	mücerred	bīve
7	4	59	3	1

ḥāṣıl 3576

20 blank

21
tetimme-i nāḥiyyet-i Girbene

kendü	cebelü	tenktür
bürüme	1	1

tīmār-ı Zaġanos Arnavud Timurḥiṣārī

ḳarye-i Motista   tīmār-ı Zaġanos el-mezḳūr

Yani Aṡanas	Yorgi veled-i o	Miḫal Urdusi[17]	Dimitri veled-i o	Niḳola Panaris
Todoros birāder-i o	Ḳovondi Ḳaloyeros	Ḳosta veled-i o	Todoros Vayaniti	Yani Vayaniti
İstemad Vayaniti	Miḫal veled-i o	Ḳosta Ḳovondi	Dimitri Ḳovondi	Petro birāẕer-i o

Todoros Vardusi	Yani Papasaki	Yani Perdiki	Todoros Perdiki	Todoros Vurdusi
Yani Meġalomati	Manol Meġalomati	Ḳosta Manyoti	Yani Vardusi	Dimitri A<u>s</u>anas
Yorgi birā<u>z</u>er-i Papasaki	İstefano Vayaniti	Leḳa İskâ<u>z</u>oplo	mücerred Todoros veled-i Ḳaloyeros	bīve Dyala zen-i Ḳovondi
bīve Mariya zen-i Patrata	bīve Anaza zen-i Ḳovondi	ḫāne 28	mücerred 1	bīve 3

ḥāṣıl 1736

ʿa(n) ispence	ʿöşr-i ḥınṭa	ʿöşr-i cev	ʿöşr-i bāġāt	ʿöşr-i meyve
743	850	130	12	1

ḳarye-i Gin Manesi ez cemāʿat-i Arnavudān tīmār-ı Zaġanos el-mezbūr

Gin el-me<u>z</u>kūr	Dimitri birāder-i o	Yorgi Maji	Yorgi Burşa	Gin Ḳapsa
Gön veled-i o	Todoros Fratis	Yorgi Fratis	Gin Fratis	Ḳosta Fratis
Gin Ḳapsa	İvratos Mazarakis	bīve Dyala zen-i Andriya	ḫāne 12	bīve 1

ḥāṣıl 1136

ʿa(n) ispence	ʿöşr-i bāġāt	ʿöşr-i ḥınṭa	ʿöşr-i cev	resm-i ḫanāzīr	resm-i ḫamr
246	68	700	106	7	9

cümletü'l-ḳaryeteyni'l-me<u>z</u>kūreteyn

ḫāne	mücerred	bīve
40	1	4

ḥāṣıl 2872

22
tetimme-i nāḥiyyet-i Girbene

ken[dü] bürü[m]e	cebelü	tenktür
	1	1

tīmār-ı Ḳar<a>göz Arnavu[d] birāder-i Çāşnigir[18] İsḥāḳ Paşa

ḳarye-i İsfardina tīmār-ı Ḳar<a>göz el-me<u>z</u>kūr

Todoros Ruḳaças	Yani veled-i o	Andriya veled-i o	Lazaro Serḳov[a]	Yani veled-i o
Ḳosta Filipeplo	Dimitri veled-i o	Yorgi veled-i o	Yani Filibeplo[19]	Todoros İpsomoḳrasi
Aleksi Livari	Yorgi Livari	Todoros Livari	Yani Misoḳa<u>s</u>aro	Yani Miḫaloplo
Yani Beradiḳo	Dimitri Varsame	Niḳola İskâ<u>z</u>eplo	İstilyano İsḳalyoti	Yorgi birāder-i o
Yani İskâ<u>z</u>eplo	Andriya Trikâfelo	İstemati Livari	Pavlos Filibeplos[20]	Zaḫaryas İsḳalyoti

ḫāne 25

ḥāṣıl 1793

ʿa(n) ispence	ʿöşr-i bāġāt	ʿöşr-i ḥınṭa	ʿöşr-i cev	ʿöşr-i ḳazz	ʿöşr-i meyve	ʿöşr-i zey[t]
625	224	750	94	10	3	15

resm-i ḫanāzīr	resm-i ḫamr	resm-i ʿarūsī
17	35	20

ḳarye-i Avrami ez cemāʿat-i Arnavudān tīmār-ı Ḳar<a>göz el-mezbūr

Andriya Ḳoḳla	Dimitri veled-i o	Yorgi veled-i o	Lazar Ḳoḳla	Gin Liḳ[u]resi
Todoros Niḳos	Muriki Avram	Yorgi Başi	Todoros Damija	Petro Avram
Andriya Ḳoḳla	Miḫal Ḳoḳla	Gin Ḳoḳla	Andriya Ḳoḳla-ı dīğer	Niḳola Ḳoḳla
Niḳola Plaşa	Yorgi Plaşa	Marḳo Ḳaravaçi	Dimitri Jupano	ḫāne 19

ḥāṣıl 1068

ʿa(n) ispence	ʿöşr-i ḥınṭa	ʿöşr-i cev	ʿöşr-i bāġāt	resm-i ʿarūsī
380	550	95	23	20

cümletü'l-ḳaryeteyni'l-me<u>z</u>kūreteyn

ḫāne	ḥāṣıl
44	2861

23
tetimme-i nāḥiyyet-i Girbene

kendü bürüme	cebelü	tenktür
	1	1

tīmār-ı Ḥamza Derbendci ġulām-ı mīr

ḳarye-i Lazaryo ez cemāʿat-i Arnavudān — tīmār-ı Ḥamza el-mezḳūr

Yorgi Meziye	Yani İstas̱i	Andriya Ḳaratula	Ḳozma Ḳaratula	Andriya Las̱a
Niḳola Buḳura	Dima Bos̱ito[21]	Pavlo Ḳaratula	İstemati Ḫarareplo	Lazaro Sivasto
Andriya Punḳa	Niḳola Ḳaratula	Niḳola Proġono	Pavlo Ḫarareplo	Dima Proġono
Filibo[22] Martino	Yani Ḳaẕondi	Niḳola birāder-i o	Petro İstematoplo	Pavlo İstas̱i
Ḳ[o]sta İstirpi	Ḳosta Manesi	Niḳola Pilura	Andriya birāder-i o	Petro Proġono
Lazaro birāder-i o	Gin Biça	Miḫal Praski	Peta Fameliti	Niḳola Pos̱ito
Yorgi birāder-i o	Leḳa Ḳaratula	bīve Marina zen-i Pavlo	bīve Ḳali zen-i Niḳola	bīve Beliya zen-i Ḳaratula

ḫāne 32 — bīve 3

ḥāṣıl 2996

ʿa(n) ispence	ʿöşr-i bāğāt	ʿöşr-i ḥınṭa	ʿöşr-i cev	resm-i ḫanāzīr	ʿöşr-i zeyt
658	338	1650	257	15	2

ʿöşr-i meyve	resm-i ḫamr	mülk-i Filibo[23] Martino der ḳarye-i mezḳūr āsiyāb 1 resm
1	45	30

ḳarye-i Papaẕato ez cemāʿat-i Arnavudān — tīmār-ı Ḥamza el-mezḳūr

Yorgi Papaẕato	Yani Maji	Domeniḳa Papaẕato	Dimitri Papaẕato	Dimitri-i dīğer Papaẕato
Gin Marḳosa	bīve Papa zen-i Lopesi	bīve Ḳali zen-i Ḳurpazi	ḫāne 6	bīve 2

ḥāṣıl 608

ʿa(n) ispence	ʿöşr-i ḥınṭa	ʿöşr-i cev	ʿöşr-i bāğāt	resm-i ḫınzīr
132	400	63	12	1

cümletü'l-ḳaryeteyni'l-mezḳūreteyn

ḫāne 38 — bīve 5

ḥāṣıl 3604

24

tetimme-i nāḥiyyet-i Girbene

kendü	cebelü	ġulām	tenktür
bürüme	1	1	1

tīmār-ı Meḥmed veled-i Ḥāccī Bāyezīd Yeñişehirī

ḳarye-i Ḳavalari Trusa ez cemāʿat-i Arnavudān — tīmār-ı Meḥmed el-mezḳūr

Miḫal Trusa	Angel veled-i o	Mengişa veled-i o	Dima Muriki	Gin birāder-i o
Niḳa Trusa	Yorgi Kesari	Bardi Vanara	Leḳa Vanara	Angelos Buzis
Martin birāder-i o	Miraş birāẕer-i o	Niḳola İştarpi	Trusa Ḳaḳusi	Pilura
Todoros Pandimos	Trusa Lumi	Martin birāder-i o	Dimitri Muriki	Gön Muriki
Ḳosta Lopesi	Yorgi Lopesi	Gin Kesari	mücerred Dima Ḳaḳusi	bīve Buza zen-i Mengişa

ḫāne 23 — mücerred 1 — bīve 1

ḥāṣıl 1140

ʿa(n) ispence	ʿöşr-i ḥınṭa	ʿöşr-i cev	resm-i ḫanāzīr
486	550	86	18

ḳarye-i Bardi Zuġra ez cemāʿat-i Arnavudān — tīmār-ı Meḥmed el-mezḳūr

Bardi el-mezḳūr	Pyater Mursi	Dima Valosi	Yani Armani	İvrato Tunba
Yorgi Alavriça	Niḳola Vuluḳsi		ḫāne 7	

ḥāṣıl 495

ʿa(n) ispence	ʿöşr-i bāğāt	ʿöşr-i ḥınṭa	ʿöşr-i cev	resm-i ḫanāzīr	resm-i ḫamr
140	57	250	38	5	5

ḳarye-i Ayo Yani ez cemāʿat-i Arnavudān — tīmār-ı Meḥmed el-mezbūr

Dimitri Borşi	Vars̱i Borşi	Leḳa Borşi	İştin Ḳraḳuki	Miḫa Borşi
Andriya Sinova	Gön Borşi	Gin Borşi	Ḳosta Borşi	Gön Lopesi

Lazaro Ḳraḳuki	Yani Damyan	Dima Sinova	Todoros Suli	Andriya Suli

ḫāne 15

ḥāṣıl 715

ʿa(n) ispence	ʿöşr-i ḥınṭa	ʿöşr-i cev	resm-i ḫanāzīr
300	350	56	9

25
tetimme-i tīmār-ı Meḥmed el-meẕkūr

ḳarye-i Vesini tābiʿ-i Ḳalavrita — tīmār-ı Meḥmed el-meẕkūr

Papas Akindinos	Praski Niḳoliçi	Vaşıl Loro	Dimitri Loro	Dimitri Leondoplo
Miḫal Potamiti	Yani [Ḥ]alandrino	S̱oẕosi Ẕurami	Yani Çipyaniti	Ḳosta Mavra
Todoros Mavra	Yani Loro	Yani Ẕurami	ḫāne 13	

ḥāṣıl 1042

ʿa(n) ispence	ʿöşr-i bāġāt	ʿöşr-i ḥınṭa	ʿöşr-i cev	ʿöşr-i ḳazz	ʿöşr-i meyve
355	128	400	64	36	4

resm-i ʿarūsī	resm-i ḫamr	ʿöşr-i kettān
15	20	20

ḳarye-i Ḳaratula ez cemāʿat-i Arnavudān tābiʿ-i o — tīmār-ı Meḥmed el-meẕkūr

Manḳola Ḳaratula	Niḳola Ḳaratula	Gön Ḳaratula	Andriya Ḳaratula	Niḳola Ḳaratula-<yı> dīğer
Dima Bondya	Manol Ḳaratula	Andriya Frati		ḫāne 8

ḥāṣıl 422

ʿa(n) ispence	ʿöşr-i ḥınṭa	ʿöşr-i cev	resm-i ʿarūsī	ʿöşr-i kettān
160	200	32	10	20

ḳarye-i Sumaki ez cemāʿat-i Arnavudān tābiʿ-i o — tīmār-ı Meḥmed el-mezbūr

Ḳosta Biçi	Andriya Sumaki	Yorgi Lonci	Lazaro Liḳuresi	Pavlo Liḳuresi
Niḳola Ḫayḳal			ḫāne 6	

ḥāṣıl 304

ʿa(n) ispence	ʿöşr-i ḥınṭa	ʿöşr-i cev	resm-i ʿarūsī
120	150	24	10

mezraʿa-ı Liḳuresi nezd-i ḳarye-i Sumaki el-meẕkūr — tābiʿ-i o

tīmār-ı Meḥmed el-mesfūr — ḫāliyye

cemʿan tīmār-ı Meḥmed el-masṭūr

ḳurā	mezraʿa-ı ḫāliyye	ḫāne	mücerred	bīve
6	1	72	1	1

ḥāṣıl 4118

26
tetimme-i nāḥiyyet-i Girbene

kendü bürü[me]	[cebe]l[ü]	tenktür
	[1]	1

tīmār-ı Ḫıżır veled-i Şavcı Sirozī

ḳarye-i Ḳavalari ez cemāʿat-i Arnavudān — tīmār-ı [Ḫıżır] el-meẕkūr

Me[n]geşe Ḳavalari	Yorgi Ḳavalari	Vlaḳa Ġulumi	Y[or]gi Ġu[lu]mi	Ḳosta [Ġulumi]
Gin Malandrinos	Gön Taçi	Niḳola Muşura	Proġono Plaşa	Gin [veled-i o]
Lazaros Zuġras	Miḫal Zuġras	İştin Çapoġa	Gin Zuġras	Bardi Çapoġa
Todoros Trimas	Gön Piluras	Mengişa İsḳanḳaẕi	Leḳa Şuli	Yani [Şu]li
Dimitri Ḫaraḫtinos	Pavlos Şulis	Yorgi Plaşa	Gin Plaşa	Ḳosta Ḳraḳuki
Ḳosta Ġramatiḳo	İstefano birāẕer-i o	Gön Ḫayḳal	Leḳa Plaşa	Niḳola Ḳoḳla
Petri Ḳardiçi	Ḳosta Şanaris	Gön veled-i o	Dimo Anaza	Gön Vuzula
Gin Maji	Gin Ġulami	Petros Muzakis	Gön Çavuşi	mücerred Mengişa Şuli
mücerred Yorgi Vorila		ḫāne 39	mücerred 2	

ḥāṣıl 3416

ʿa(n) ispence 820	ʿöşr-i bāġāt 360	ʿöşr-i ḥınṭa 1850	ʿöşr-i cev 288	resm-i ḫanāzīr 13	resm-i ḫamr 45

mülk-i
Mengişa Ḳavalari der ḳarye-i
mezḳūr
āsiyāb 1 resm 40

kendü bürüme	cebelü 1	tenktür 1

tīmār-ı ġarīb yiğitlerden Kürd Şeyḫ Ḥasan

ḳarye-i Asfalaḫto tīmār-ı mezḳūr

Dimitri Sḳali	İstemad Ḳapsaloni	Pavlo Ḳapsaloni	Aleksi Bufoplo	mücerred Niḳola Ḳapsaloni

ḫāne 3	mücerred 1

ḥāṣıl 3355

ʿa(n) ispence 125	bāġāt-ı ḫāṣṣa dönüm 5 [resm] 394	muḳāṭaʿa-ı ṭalyan-ı ḫāṣṣa 1 [resm] 2500	ʿöşr-i bāġāt 220	ʿöşr-i ḥınṭa 100	ʿöşr-i cev 16

27
tetimme-i nāḥiyyet-i Girbene

kendü cebelü

tīmār-ı Rus Ormanı

[ḳarye-i] [---]şta ez cemāʿat-i Arnavudān tīmār-ı Rus el-mezḳūr

[---] [---]	[---] [---]ri	Gin birāder-i o	Niḳola birāẕer-i o	Yani Mancaro

[Y]orgi Rovyaniti	mücerred Todoros Mancaro	mücerred Aleksi Rovyaniti	mücerred İstemad birāẕer-i o	ḫāne 6	mücerred 3

ḥāṣıl 570

[ʿa(n) ispen]ce 1[80]	ʿöş[r-i] ḥınṭa 300	ʿöşr-i cev 46	ʿöşr-i bāġāt 22	resm-i ḫanāzīr 7	ʿöşr-i kettān 15

ḳarye-i Divye ez cemāʿat-i Arnavudān tīmār-ı Rus el-mezbūr

G[i]n [D]ivye	İlya Floḳa	Gin Votani	Todoros veled-i o	Gön veled-i o
Gin Ḳalobiçari	İvratos Maliki	Todoros Ḳalobiçari	Pavlos birāder-i o	mücerred Todoros veled-i İvrato el-mezbūr
bīve Mariya zen-i Maḳrosḳol				

ḫāne 9	mücerred 1	bīve 1

ḥāṣıl 696

ʿa(n) ispence 206	ʿöşr-i ḥınṭa 400	ʿöşr-i cev 62	resm-i ḫanāzīr 8	ʿöşr-i kettān 20

mezraʿa-ı Viriça nezd-i ḳarye-i mezḳūr tīmār-ı Rus el-mezbūr

ḫāliyye

cemʿan tīmār-ı Rus el-masṭūr

ḳurā 2	mezraʿa-ı ḫāliyye 1	ḫāne 15	mücerred 4	bīve 1

ḥāṣıl 1266

28
tetimme-i nāḥiyyet-i Girbene

kendü bürüme	cebelü 1	ġulām 1	tenktür 1

tīmār-ı Muḥyi'd-dīn Yaninaʾi

ʿa(n) ḳarye-i Arula

ḥiṣṣ[e]

Gön Ḫruso	Todoros Vanbaki	Yorgi Kiryaki	Todoros Kiryaki	[---] Ayo[menbi]
Andon birāẕer-i o	Yani birāder-i īşān	Dimitri Ḳondova	Todoros Mancaris	Dimitri Farmaki
Yani Farmaki	Ẕyaḳos Varsalemos	İstemad İsḳardonḳori	Yorgi Prasaniti	İstilyano İsḳardonḳori
Pandos Miseḳordos	Yani Leondariti	Petro birāẕer-i o	Yorgi Marnavros	Petros İstumnos
Pavlos Maḳrimalis	İstefanos İsḳordonḳori	Marġariti İskâẓa	Niḳola Ḫarkâplos	Todoros İvlaḫyoti

İstasi Mastro | Nikola Kondovaşılı | Dimitri Malasi | Dimitri İvlaho | Mihal Peratiko
Yani Dimitrula | Yani Kiryakoplo | Kostandin Polikastra | İstilyano Molohis | Sotoki veled-i o
Yorgi Mermingi | Yani Halandrisyanos | mücerred Nikola Vanbaki | mücerred Yorgi Peratiko | mücerred Nikola birāzer-i o
bīve Mariya zen-i Papa İstilyano | bīve Mariya zen-i Mancar | bīve Avzoke zen-i Kondovyos | bīve Andisa zen-i Andriya

hāne 37 | mücerred 3 | bīve 4

hāṣıl 4842

ʿa(n) ispence 1024 | bāğāt-ı hāṣṣa dönüm 6 [resm] 868 | eşcār-ı meyve-i hāṣṣa ʿaded 8 [resm] 20 | bostān-ı hāṣṣa 1 [resm] 100 | ʿöşr-i hınṭa 1150 | ʿöşr-i cev 192
ʿöşr-i bāğāt 112[5] | ʿöşr-i zeyt 21 | resm-i ʿarūsī 40 | resm-i hamr 80 | ʿöşr-i penbe 150
ʿöşr-i kettān 80 | resm-i hanāzīr 2

29
tetimme-i nāhiyyet-i Girbene

kendü cebelü | oğlan 1

tīmār-ı Ķāsım veled-i Muhyi'd-dīn Yaninaʾi el-mezkūr

ʿa(n) ķarye-i Arula el-mezkūr

hiṣṣe

Kosta Ru[p]lati | Vaşıl Kutruça | Dimitri Aleksi | Malesini Rupato | Yani Eftakamito
Yani Holyano | Marko Şabori | Andriya Ğaryos | Yorgi Kurti | Protopapa Yani
Dimitri veled-i o | Nikola Sotiri | Todoros Tirsenyotis | Apostoli Turmayiri | Yani Horeftira
İstil[y]ano Manasiryotis | Yorgi Kalorozi | mücerred Yorgi Rupati | mücerred Yorgi Kutruça | mücerred Petro Rupato

[mü]cerred Mihal birāder-i o | mücerred Andriya Tirsinyotis | bīve Poşiti zen-i Papadya | bīve Komnini zen-i Turmayirin | bīve Elani zen-i Kaliça

hāne 17 | mücerred 5 | bīve 3

hāṣıl 2538

ʿa(n) ispence 568 | āsiyāb-ı hāṣṣa 1 [resm] 200 | ʿöşr-i hınṭa 850 | ʿöşr-i cev 132 | ʿöşr-i penbe 50 | ʿöşr-i kettān 50 | ʿöşr-i bāğāt 585
ʿöşr-i zeyt 13 | resm-i ʿarūsī 20 | resm-i hamr 70

kendü cebelü | oğlan 1

tīmār-ı Yūsuf Arnavud

ķarye-i Trahya Manesi ez cemāʿat-i Arnavudān | tīmār-ı Yūsuf el-mezbūr

Trahya el-mezkūr | Mihal Malişaziti | Gin Ğramatikoplo | Todor Melyoti | Gerg Dramesi
Todoros Mazarakis | Marko Varbobi | Muzak veled-i o | Petro veled-i o | Mihal veled-i o

30
tetimme-i ķarye-i Trahya el-mezkūr | tīmār-ı Yūsuf el-mezbū[r]

Y[o]rgi Ğramatiko | Yani veled-i o | Gön Ara[ni]ti | Todoros Araniti | Gön Ma[m]osi
Lek[a] Karusi | Andriya Araniti | Dar Diko | Leka Mila | Petro Şiko
İştin Frati | bīve Kañire zen-i Gön Manesi | bīve Babe zen | hāne 21 | b[īve] 2

hāṣıl 1622

ʿa(n) ispence 432 | ʿöşr-i bāğāt 45 | ʿöşr-i hınṭa 950 | ʿöşr-i cev 148 | resm-i hınzīr 1 | res[m-i] [hamr] 6

mülk-i
Trahya Manesi der ķarye-i mezkūr
āsiyāb 1 resm 40

ḳarye-i Trusa ez cemāʿat-i Arnavudān — tīmār-ı Yūsuf el-mez̲kūr

Duḳa Trusa	Poloni veled-i o	Aleksi Trusa	Gerg Ḳonbes̲eḳr	Marino Trusa
Petro Başi	İvlaş Jirava	Leḳa Dozra[24]	Andriya dāmād-ı Mavriyati	Mileş H̱alke
Lazar Kesar	mücerred Petro Trusa	mücerred Ḳozma Mazaraki	mücerred Todoros H̱ayḳali	bīve Anuz̲a zen-i Ḳozma
bīve Marġaruta	ẖāne 11	mücerred 3	bīve 2	

ḥāṣıl 932

ʿa(n) ispence 292	ʿöşr-i ḥınṭa 550	ʿöşr-i cev 86	resm-i ẖanāzīr 4

cümletü'l-ḳaryeteyni'l-mez̲kūreteyn

ẖāne 32	mücerred 3	bīve 4	ḥāṣıl 2554

kendü bürüme	cebelü 2	çadır 1

tīmār-ı ʿAlī veled-i Ḳulaġuz ve İskender veled-i ʿAlī el-mez̲kūr müşterek be-nevbet

ḳarye-i Fostana — tīmār-ı mez̲kūrān

Yani Simoplos	Andriya Biçi Ḳar[d]i	Todoros Ziyoti	Yorgi Simoplo	Andriya Ḳaloyiros

31

tetimme-i [ḳa]r[y]e-i Fostana el-mez̲kūr — tīmār-ı mez̲kūrān

Pa[ni] Ṣarandi	Yorgi Uranyo	Kiryaḳoplo A[r]as	İstilyanos Maḳris	Dimitri [Ḳ]al[oy]ir
[Yor]g[i] [---]	Papas Andriy[a]	Yani Çaḳoniti	bīve Ḳatarina zen-i Niḳola	bīve Mariya zen-i İsḳotomeni
bīve Morfiya [ze]n-i İstilyano	bīve Mariya zen-i Maḳriya		ẖāne 13	bīve 4

ḥāṣıl 2991

ʿa(n) i[spence]e [3]49	bāġāt-ı ẖāṣṣa dönüm 6 [resm] 472	eşcār-ı zeyt-i ẖāṣṣa ʿaded 10 [resm] 45	bostān-ı ẖāṣṣa 1 [resm] 200	āsiyāb-ı ẖāṣṣa 1 [resm] 500	eşcār-ı meyve-i ẖāṣṣa ʿaded 6 [resm] 15

ʿöşr-i penbe 150	ʿöşr-i kettān 60	ʿöşr-i bāġāt 450	ʿöşr-i ḥınṭa 600	ʿöşr-i cev 93	ʿöşr-i zeyt 12	ʿöşr-i meyve 5
		resm-i ẖamr 30	resm-i ʿarūsī 10			

ḳarye-i Ayo Niḳolas ez cemāʿat-i Arnavudān — tīmār-ı mez̲kūrān

Gin Pavloplo	Ḳosta Pavloplo	İvrato Ḳanḳaz̲i	Gin veled-i o	Gön Ḳrozepsa
İstefano Ḳanḳaz̲i	Andriya İpṣari	mücerred Gin Promovini	ẖāne 7	mücerred 1

ḥāṣıl 605

ʿa(n) ispence 160	bāġçe-i ẖāṣṣa 1 [resm] 50	ʿöşr-i ḥınṭa 200	ʿöşr-i cev 32	ʿöşr-i zeyt 8	ʿöşr-i bāġāt 135	ʿöşr-i kettān 10
			resm-i ʿarūsī 10			

ḳarye-i Oṣiya Mariya ez cemāʿat-i Arnavudān — tīmār-ı mez̲kūrān

Yorgi S̱ana	ẖāne 1	ḥāṣıl 150

ʿa(n) ispence 20	ʿöşr-i bāġāt 67	ʿöşr-i zeyt 2	ʿöşr-i meyve 3	ʿöşr-i ḥınṭa 50	ʿöşr-i cev 8

ḳarye-i Ayo Lisyo ez cemāʿat-i Arnavudān — tīmār-ı mez̲kūrān

Leḳa Maji	ẖāne 1	ḥāṣıl 124

ʿa(n) ispence 20	ʿöşr-i bāġāt 45	ʿöşr-i ḥınṭa 50	ʿöşr-i cev 8	ʿöşr-i meyve 1

ḳarye-i Venetiḳa ez cemāʿat-i Arnavudān — tīmār-ı meẕkūrān

Andriya Beṣulḳa	İvrato Beṣulḳa	Ḳosta Beṣulḳa	Gin Beṣulḳa	Yaḳumo Beṣulḳa

ḫāne 5

ḥāṣıl 515

ʿa(n) ispence	ʿöşr-i bāġāt	ʿöşr-i ḥınṭa	ʿöşr-i cev	resm-i ḫanāzīr	ʿöşr-i kettān
100	45	300	46	14	10

32

tetimme-i nāḥiyyet-i Girbene

ḳarye-i Lenḳoni ez cemāʿat-i Arnavudān — tīmār-ı meẕkūrān

Gin İflamura	Niḳola İflamura	Miḫal Ṣamri	ḫāne 3

ḥāṣıl 342

ʿa(n) ispence	eşcār-ı zeyt-i ḫāṣṣa	eşcār-ı meyve-i ḫāṣṣa	ʿöşr-i ḥınṭa	ʿöşr-i cev
60	ʿaded 30 [resm] 67	ʿaded 44 [resm] 100	100	15

mezraʿa-ı Besulḳa[25] nezd-i ḳarye-i meẕkūr — tīmār-ı mezbūrān — ḫāliyye

mezraʿa-ı Ayo Yorgi nezd-i ḳarye-i o — tīmār-ı meẕkūrān — ḫāliyye

ḳarye-i Balçi ez cemāʿat-i Arnavudān — tīmār-ı meẕkūrān

Niḳola Baẕa	Yorgi Baẕa	Gin Baẕa	Dimitri Manḳola	ḫāne 4

ḥāṣıl 278

ʿa(n) ispence	ʿöşr-i bāġāt	ʿöşr-i zeyt	ʿöşr-i ḥınṭa	ʿöşr-i cev	ʿöşr-i kettān
80	67	5	100	16	10

ḳarye-i Sirveliça ez cemāʿat-i Arnavudān — tīmār-ı meẕkūrān

Dimitri Ḳandrava	Yorgi Muṣura	Ḳozma Ḳuza	Andriya Andriçoplo	mücerred Ḳozma Peta

ḫāne	mücerred
4	1

ḥāṣıl 249

ʿa(n) ispence	ʿöşr-i ḥınṭa	ʿöşr-i cev	ʿöşr-i bāġāt	ʿöşr-i meyve	ʿöşr-i zeyt	ʿöşr-i kettān
100	100	15	22	1	1	10

ḳarye-i Palopirġo ez cemāʿat-i Arnavudān — tīmār-ı meẕkūrān

Petro Buḳura	Yorgi Evyanos	Andriya Bejan	Niḳola Pasḳal	ḫāne 4

ḥāṣıl 275

ʿa(n) ispence	ʿöşr-i ḥınṭa	ʿöşr-i cev	ʿöşr-i bāġāt	ʿöşr-i meyve	ʿöşr-i zeyt	ʿöşr-i kettān
80	100	15	67	1	2	10

ḳarye-i Yirano ez cemāʿat-i Arnavudān — tīmār-ı meẕkūrān

Todoro Loġoṣeti	Dimitri Loġoṣeti	Bardi Ṣurbi	mücerred Yani Loġoṣeti	ḫāne 3	mücerred 1

ḥāṣıl 218

ʿa(n) ispence	ʿöşr-i bāġāt	ʿöşr-i ḥınṭa	ʿöşr-i cev
80	22	100	16

ḳarye-i Petroviṣta ez cemāʿat-i Arnavudān — tīmār-ı meẕkūrān

Niḳola Draġoliş	Yorgi Draġoliş	mücerred Petro Draġoliş	ḫāne 2	mücerred 1

ḥāṣıl 197

ʿa(n) ispence	ʿöşr-i ḥınṭa	ʿöşr-i cev	ʿöşr-i bāġāt
60	100	15	22

33

tetimme-i nāḥiyyet-i Girbene

mezraʿa-ı Serḳofayi nezd-i ḳarye-i Petroviṣta el-meẕkūr — tīmār-ı mezbūrān — ḫāliyye

mezraʿa-ı Ṣurbi nezd-i ḳarye-i meẕkūr — tīmār-ı mezbūrān — ḫāliyye

cemʿan tīmār-ı ʿAlī ve veledeş İskender el-meẕkūr

ḳurā	mezāriʿ-i ḫāliyye	ḫāne	mücerred	bīve
11	4	47	4	1

ḥāṣıl 5944

kendü cebelü	ġulām 1

tīmār-ı Mūsā Siyāh Livadya'i

ḳarye-i Miḫoy ez cemā'at-i Arnavudān — tīmār-ı Mūsā el-meẕkūr

Niḳola Miḫoy	Pavlos Buva	Şeni Maji	Pavlo Maji	Gin Dramesi
Yani Dramesi		ḫāne 6		

ḥāṣıl 352

'a(n) ispence 120	'öşr-i ḥınṭa 200	'öşr-i cev 32

ḳarye-i Ḳazneş ez cemā'at-i Arnavudān — tīmār-ı Mūsā el-mezbūr

Andriya Ḳazneş	Leḳa birāẕer-i o	Manol Ḳuçi	Gön birāder-i o	Todoro Ḳrapesi
Yorgi Ḳazneş			ḫāne 6	

ḥāṣıl 366

'a(n) ispence 120	'öşr-i ḥınṭa 200	'öşr-i cev 30	'öşr-i kettān 10	resm-i 'arūsī 6

ḳarye-i Maliki ez cemā'at-i Arnavudān — tīmār-ı Mūsā el-[me]ẕkūr

Yorgi Maliki	Andriya Maliki	Andriya Maliki-i dīğer	Petro Maliki	Martin birāẕer-i o

34

tetimme-i ḳarye-i Maliki el-meẕkūr — tīmār-ı Mūsā el-mezbūr

Petro Floḳa	Niḳola Lonci	Yorgi birāder-i o	Gin Çarn[o]ta	Niḳola Luvro
Bardi Peta	bīve S̱oẕo zen-i Frati		ḫāne 11	bī[ve] 1

ḥāṣıl 695

'a(n) ispence 226	'öşr-i ḥınṭa 350	'öşr-i cev 54	'öşr-i kettān 15	resm-i 'arūsī 10	mülk-i Yorgi Maliki der ḳarye-i meẕkūr āsiyāb 1 resm 40

ḳarye-i Ḳonbi S̱eḳra ez cemā'at-i Arnavudān — tīmār-ı Mūsā el-me[ẕ]k[ūr]

Niḳola Ḳonbi S̱eḳra	Yorgi Ḳonbi S̱eḳra	Andriya birāẕer-i o	Gin Ḳonbi S̱eḳra	Dimitri birāẕer-i o
Leḳa Helmesi	Leḳa Anavati	Lazaro Siryi	Petro Mangliça	İvrato Maji
Gön Zula	bīve Manḳo zen-i Malḳas	bīve S̱oẕo zen-i İvlaş	ḫāne 11	bīve 2

ḥāṣıl 597

'a(n) ispence 232	'öşr-i ḥınṭa 300	'öşr-i cev 48	resm-i ḫanāzīr 2	'öşr-i kettān 15

ḳarye-i Gerbesi ez cemā'at-i Arnavudān — tīmār-ı Mūsā el-mezbūr

Ẕermata Gerbesi	ḫāne 1

ḥāṣıl 93

'a(n) ispence 20	eşcār-ı zeyt-i ḫāṣṣa 'aded 15 [resm] 33	mülk-i Ẕermata Gerbesi el-meẕkūr āsiyāb 1 resm 40

cem'an tīmār-ı Mūsā el-meẕkūr

ḳurā 5	ḫāne 35	bīve 3

ḥāṣıl 2103

35

tetimme-i nāḥiyyet-i Girbene

kendü bürüme	cebelü 1	ġulām 1	tenktür 1

tīmār-ı Mevlānā 'Abdu['l-l]āh ḳāḍī-ı Balya Badra

ḳarye-i Mitepoli — tīmār-ı ḳāḍī el-meẕkūr

Runcari Durf[is]	Ronbeto Bayizi	Yani Vuki	Niḳola Kiryaḳoplo	Yorgi Kiryaḳoplo
[Y]ani birāder-i o	Yorgi İsḳuri	İstemad birāẕer-i o	Niḳola Ḫıristodulos	Papayorgi Paġoyani
Niḳ[o]la Ḫı[r]p[.l]s	Yorgi Ḳoftiris	Andon İksanoplo	Andriya Aleksi	Yorgi Zoḫo
Yani Ḫıristodulo	Andon Ḫıristodulos	Yani Petroplo	Riḳos Çifoni	Niḳola birāẕer-i o

Yorgi Kiryaḳoplo	Yani Manida	Todoros Avramis	Yani Franḳo	mücerred Ḳostandin Runcari
mücerred Todoros Miranbaki	mücerred Yani İksanoplo	bīve Yana zen-i Pariçan	bīve İstefaniya zen-i Ruḫya	bīve Manḳa zen-i Ḫıristodulya
	bīve İrini zen-i Kiryaḳoplo	ḫāne 24	mücerred 3	bīve 4

ḥāṣıl 2643

ʿa(n) ispence 699	bāġāt-ı ḫāṣṣa dönüm 6 [resm] 472	eşcār-ı zeyt-i ḫāṣṣa ʿaded 40 [resm] 45	eşcār-ı ṭut-ı ḫāṣṣa ʿaded 30 [resm] 160	ʿöşr-i penbe 50	ʿöşr-i kettān 50

ʿöşr-i bāġāt 563	ʿöşr-i zeyt 36	ʿöşr-i ḥınṭa 350	ʿöşr-i cev 56	ʿöşr-i ḳazz 56	resm-i ḫanāzīr 5	resm-i ḫamr 61

mülk-i
Yani Vuki der ḳarye-i mezḳūr
āsiyāb 1 resm 40

ḳarye-i Yatopa ez cemāʿat-i Arnavudān — tīmār-ı ḳāḍī el-mezbūr

Niḳola Toskesi	Gön veled-i o	Gin Taçi	Ḳozma Toskesi	Lazaro Liḳuresi
Gön Taçi		ḫāne 6		

ḥāṣıl 393

ʿa(n) ispence 120	ʿöşr-i ḥınṭa 150	ʿöşr-i cev 23	resm-i ḫanāzīr 5	mülk-i Niḳola Toskesi der ḳarye-i mezḳūr

āsiyāb-ı ġalle 1 resm 80	āsiyāb-ı peşmīne 1 resm 15

ḳarye-i Melitena ez cemāʿat-i Arnavudān — tīmār-ı ḳāḍī el-mezḳūr

Gön Asteri	Yani Vaşıl	Lazaro Ḳaloplo	Yani Posito	Marti Maḳros
Petros Asteri	Yorgi veled-i Vaşıl	Gön Maziñik	Soma İksanos	Maḳros İksanos

36

tetimme-i ḳarye-i Melitena el-mezḳūr — tīmār-ı ḳāḍī el-mezbūr

Yani Ḳapapazuḳa	Marti dāmād-ı Lazaro	ḫāne 12

ḥāṣıl 575

ʿa(n) ispence 240	ʿöşr-i bāġāt 42	ʿöşr-i ḥınṭa 250	ʿöşr-i cev 40	resm-i ḫanāzīr 3

ḳarye-i Malesina ez cemāʿat-i Arnavudān — tīmār-ı ḳāḍī el-mezbūr

Andriya Maji	Dimitri Todoro	Niḳola Murati	Gön Maji	Gön Ḳlazi
Ḳozma Novaḳo	Petros Çurḳas	Niḳola Çurḳa	Gön İsḳordo	ḫāne 9

ḥāṣıl 354

ʿa(n) ispence 180	ʿöşr-i ḥınṭa 150	ʿöşr-i cev 24

ḳarye-i Eksoriya ez cemāʿat-i Arnavudān — tīmār-ı ḳāḍī el-mezbūr

Domeniḳa Ḳumi	Miḫa Ḳumi	Yorgi Lukisa	Gön Rali	ḫāne 4

ḥāṣıl 336

ʿa(n) ispence 80	ʿöşr-i bāġāt 21	ʿöşr-i ḥınṭa 200	ʿöşr-i cev 31	ʿöşr-i ḳazz 4

ḳarye-i Şalesi ez cemāʿat-i Arnavudān — tīmār-ı ḳāḍī el-mezbūr

Andriya Dardesi	Ḳozma Rus	Ḳosta Vari	İlya Nikiforo	Niḳola Lumi
		Leḳa Buniḳa	ḫāne 6	

ḥāṣıl 296

ʿa(n) ispence 120	ʿöşr-i ḥınṭa 150	ʿöşr-i cev 24	resm-i ḫanāzīr 2

ḳarye-i Tiristena — tābiʿ-i Balya Badra — tīmār-ı ḳāḍī el-mezbūr

Niḳola Paturi	Muriki Paturi	Pavlo Paturi	Yani İstavraki	Yani Marḳuca
	Niḳola Ḫarara		ḫāne 6	

ḥāṣıl 422

ʿa(n) ispence	eşcār-ı meyve-i ḫāṣṣa	ʿöşr-i ḥınṭa	ʿöşr-i cev
150	ʿaded 20 [resm] 40	200	32

cemʿan tīmār-ı ḳāḍī el-meẕkūr

ḳurā	ḫāne	mücerred	bīve
7	67	3	4

ḥāṣıl 5019

37

tetimme-i nāḥiyyet-i Girbene

kendü	cebelü	ġulām	çadır
bürüme	2	1	1

tīmār-ı Ḫoca ʿAlī

ḳarye-i Mazarak ez cemāʿat-i Arnavudān — tīmār-ı ʿAlī el-meẕkūr

Ḳaleşa Mazaraki	Leḳa Mazaraki	Gön veled-i o	Leḳa İpṣari	Niḳola birāder-i o
Gö[n] Baştı[r]a	Miḫal Bondaya	Andriya birāder-i o	Yani Miḫali	Domeniḳa birāẕer-i o
İksano Baştira	Tonda birāder-i o	Leḳa Baştira	Andriya Baştira	Lazaro Ḳaparali
Gin Ḳaparali	Gön Mazaraki	İstefano Liḳuresi	Yorgi birāẕer-i o	bīve Mazarakina
bīve Mariya Ḳaparelina			ḫāne 19	bīve 2

ḥāṣıl 1361

ʿa(n) ispence	ʿöşr-i ḥınṭa	ʿöşr-i cev	ʿöşr-i ḳazz	resm-i ḫanāzīr	resm-i ʿarūsī
392	800	124	2	23	20

ḳarye-i Junbata ez cemāʿat-i Arnavudān — tīmār-ı meẕkūr

Gin Junbata	Trimi Junbata	Lazaro Junbata	Lazaro-<yı> dīğer Junbata	ḫāne 4

ḥāṣıl 230

ʿa(n) ispence	ʿöşr-i ḥınṭa	ʿöşr-i cev	ʿöşr-i meyve
80	100	16	4

mülk-i Gin Junbata der ḳarye-i meẕkūr
āsiyāb 1 resm 30

ḳarye-i Milyas ez cemāʿat-i Arnavudān — tīmār-ı meẕkūr

Ral Privoy	Dimitri İpṣari	Gön Tatḳo	Miḫal İpsari	ḫāne 4

ḥāṣıl 253

ʿa(n) ispence	ʿöşr-i ḥınṭa	ʿöşr-i cev
80	150	23

ḳarye-i Frat[i] ez [ce]māʿat-i Arnavudān — tīmār-ı meẕkūr

Yorgi Frati	Niḳola Frati	Petros birāẕer-i o	Andriya Frati	Ginizi Frati
Petros Frati		ḫāne 6		

ḥāṣıl 384

ʿa(n) ispence	ʿöşr-i ḥınṭa	ʿöşr-i cev	ʿöşr-i bāġāt	ʿöşr-i kettān
120	200	32	22	10

38

tetimme-i nāḥiyyet-i Girbene

ḳarye-i İstoyan ez cemāʿat-i Arnavudān — tīmār-ı ʿAlī el-meẕkūr

Yani İstoyan	Gin İstoyan	Petros veled-i o	Miḫal İstoyan	Ḳ[o]sta K[ini]ġo
Petros veled-i o	İstefano Kiniġo	Petros Orfano	Domeniḳa Ẕuḳa	Gön İp[s]ari
Martin Peta		ḫāne 11		

ḥāṣıl 800

ʿa(n) ispence	ʿöşr-i ḥınṭa	ʿöşr-i cev	ʿöşr-i bāġāt	ʿöşr-i ḳazz	ʿöşr-i meyve	resm-i ḫanāzī[r]	resm-i ʿarūsī
220	350	56	77	2	9	16	15

mülk-i
Gin İstoyan der ḳarye-i meẕkūr

āsiyāb-ı ġalle 1	āsiyāb-ı peşmīne 1
resm 40	resm 15

ḳarye-i Ġurzumişa ez cemāʿat-i Arnavudān — tīmār-ı meẕkūr

Balvini Ġurzumişa	Gin Ġurzumişa	Gin Ġurzumişa-ı dīğer	Kenazi Ġurzumişa	G[ö]n Ġurzumişa
Gin Maji	Mengişa Taçi	Leḳa Vergi	Yorgi veled-i o	Petros İstanḳos

Yorgi Taçi	Domenika Ġurzumişa	Miḥal Ġurzumişa	Leḳa birāẓer-i o	Marti Ġurzumişa
Bardi birāẓer-i o	Andriya Ġurzumişa	Yani birāder-i o	Bardi Ġurzumişa	Leḳa Ġurzumişa

ḫāne 20

ḥāṣıl 1349

ʿa(n) ispence 400	ʿöşr-i ḥınṭa 750	ʿöşr-i cev 119	ʿöşr-i kettān 20	resm-i ʿarūsī 20	mülk-i Gin Maji der ḳarye-i meẕkūr āsiyāb 1 resm 40

ḳarye-i Buza ez cemāʿat-i Arnavudān   tīmār-ı meẕkūr

Petro Buza	İvrato Leki	Gin Maḳras	Pavlo İvlaḥyoti	Niḳola İvlaḥyoti
Yorgi İvlaḥyoti	İstemati İvlaḥyoti	Dimitri İvlaḥyoti	Dimitri Mavrota	Dimitri İvlaḥyoti
Gin Maḳriş	mücerred Petro İvlaḥyoti		ḫāne 11	mücerred 1

ḥāṣıl 848

ʿa(n) ispence 240	eşcār-ı zeyt-i ḫāṣṣa ʿaded 4 [resm] 10	ʿöşr-i ḥınṭa 500	ʿöşr-i cev 79	resm-i ḫanāzīr 4
		ʿöşr-i kettān 15		

39

tetimme-i nāḥiyyet-i Girbene

ḳarye-i Duḳati ez cemāʿat-i Arnavudān   tīmār-ı meẕkūr

To[do]ros Duḳas	Tonda Ġurzumişa	Petro veled-i o	Gin Ġurzumişa	Gin İşpata
Artik[i] Melaḥrino	Gin Şuli	Miḥal Zaġarino	Tonda Şuli	Gin Zaġarino
Gerka Zaġarino	Gin Ġulami	Todoros Ġulami	Pavlo Beşulḳa	Duḳa Ḳoḳla
Duḳa Ḳoḳla-ı dīğer	Todoros Ḳ[o]ḳla	Dima Ḳoḳla	Yorgi Şameri	Ḳozma Miloti

ḫāne 20

ḥāṣıl 1121

ʿa(n) ispence 400	ʿöşr-i ḥınṭa 600	ʿöşr-i cev 96	resm-i ḫanāzīr 5	resm-i ʿarūsī 20

ḳarye-i Gi[n] Bodya ez cemāʿat-i Arnavudān   tīmār-ı meẕkūr

Gin el-meẕkūr	Bardi veled-i o	Yorgi Klasira	Leḳa Ġurzumişa	Leḳa Burlaşa
mücerred Gin Usnato			ḫāne 5	mücerred 1

ḥāṣıl 397

ʿa(n) ispence 120	ʿöşr-i ḥınṭa 200	ʿöşr-i cev 32	resm-i ḫanāzīr 5	mülk-i Gin Bodya der ḳarye-i meẕkūr āsiyāb 1 resm 40

ḳarye-i Şergi ez cemāʿat-i Arnavudān   tīmār-ı meẕkūr

Yorgi Şergi	Lazaro Şergi	İvlaş Posito	Yorgi veled-i o	Todoros Maḥtata
Zonato Ḳanḳazi	Yorgi Pilura	Gin Maḥtata	Lazaro veled-i o	Zonato Sergi[26]
mücerred Yorgi Ḳanḳazi	mücerred Gin Pilura		ḫāne 10	mücerred 2

ḥāṣıl 617

[ʿa(n)] ispence 240	ʿöşr-i bāġāt 113	ʿöşr-i ḥınṭa 200	ʿöşr-i cev 31	resm-i ḫanāzīr 23	resm-i ʿarūsī 10

cemʿan tīmār-ı Ḫoca ʿAlī el- meẕkūr

ḳurā	ḫāne	mücerred	bīve
10	110	4	2

ḥāṣıl 7360

40/42

nāḥiyyet-i Ḫulumiç

kendü bürüme	cebelü 2	çadır 1

tīmār-ı Ḫıżır serʿasker-i Ḫulumiç ve Ayo İlya ve Ġardicḳo

ḳarye-i Ḳarẓiyoḳafti ez cemāʿat-i Arnavudān   tīmār-ı Ḫıżır el-meẕkūr

Todoros Ḳarẕoḳafti | Dimitri Ḳarẕoḳafti | Todoros-ı dīğer Ḳarẕoḳafti | Niḳola Ḳurtik | Ḳosta Vuya

ḫāne 5

ḥāṣıl 364

ʿa(n) ispence 100 | ʿöşr-i ḥınṭa 200 | ʿöşr-i cev 32 | ʿöşr-i bāġāt 32

ḳarye-i Jujli Palamiẕi — tīmār-ı Ḫıżır el-mezbūr

Niḳola Ḳonda | Yani Uzġuro | İstemati Uzġuro | ḫāne 3

ḥāṣıl 176

ʿa(n) ispence 60 | ʿöşr-i ḥınṭa 100 | ʿöşr-i cev 16

ḳarye-i Ḫavaro Protopapa ez cemāʿat-i Arnavudān — tīmār-ı Ḫıżır el-mesfūr

Papayorgi Ḫavaro | Niḳola Ḫavaro | Miḫal Ḫavaro | Yorgi Kriyaḳuki | Andriya Ḳuḳura

bīve zen-i Aleksi | ḫāne 5 | bīve 1

ḥāṣıl 497

ʿa(n) ispence 106 | ʿöşr-i bāġāt 96 | ʿöşr-i ḥınṭa 250 | ʿöşr-i cev 40 | resm-i ḫanāzīr 5

ḳarye-i Ḳoḳla Marġariti ez cemāʿat-i Arnavudān — tīmār-ı Ḫıżır el-masṭūr

İstefano Marġariti | Andriya Ġurzumişa | Gön Ḳonbi Ṣeḳra | ḫāne 3

ḥāṣıl 175

ʿa(n) ispence 60 | ʿöşr-i ḥınṭa 100 | ʿöşr-i cev 15

mezraʿa-ı Potamya Ṣarandinu nezd-i ḳarye-i mezḳūr tīmār-ı mezbūr ḫāliyye

ḳarye-i Añloniça tābiʿ-i Vumero — tīmār-ı Ḫıżır el-meẕkūr

Miḫal İsḳardi | Miḫal Mavromati | Todoro Taşa | ḫāne 3

ḥāṣıl 4805

ʿa(n) ispence 75 | ʿöşr-i ḥınṭa 200 | ʿöşr-i cev 30 | muḳāṭaʿa-ı ṭalyan maʿa maʿber-i ḫāṣṣa 4500

cemʿan tīmār-ı Ḫıżır el-mezbūr

ḳurā 5 | mezraʿa-ı ḫāliyye 1 | ḫāne 19 | bīve 1

ḥāṣıl 6017

43
tetimme-i nāḥiyyet-i Ḫulumiç

kendü cebelü | ġulām 1

tīmār-ı ġarīb yiğitlerden Elvānoġlı Maḥmūd

ḳarye-i Niḫor — tīmār-ı Maḥmūd el-meẕkūr

Niḳola Aroni | Yani Çernari | Andriya Doḳsamanol | Yani Pulya Efendi | Todoro Liẕoriti

İstefano Metaḳsomati | Yani Yaço | Andriya Ḳaloyir | Todoro Triẕemona | Todoro Mardari

Marḳoplo Andriya | Ġulyamo İstilyano | Mileş Aġabito[27] | mücerred Miḫal Monaḫinos | mücerred Miḫal Çernari

mücerred Lazaro Metaḳsomati | ḫāne 13 | mücerred 3

ḥāṣıl 1117

ʿa(n) ispence 400 | ʿöşr-i bāġāt 224 | ʿöşr-i ḥınṭa 400 | ʿöşr-i cev 63 | ʿöşr-i meyve 2 | resm-i ḫanāzīr 2 | resm-i ḫamr 16

resm-i ʿarūsī 10

ḳarye-i Şuli ez cemāʿat-i Arnavudān — tīmār-ı Maḥmūd el-mezḳūr

Gin Matranḳa	Todoros Şuli	Praḳopi Ġrapsomati	Gin Ḳurtesi	Ḳosta Ḳonbi S̱eḳra
Gön Matranḳa	Miḫal İvlaḫyoti	Andriya Lonci	Martin Malen	Yorgi Paliḫoric
mücerred Gön Matranḳa-ı dīğer	bīve Loron			

ḫāne	mücerred	bīve
10	1	1

ḥāṣıl 815

ʿa(n) ispence	ʿöşr-i ḥınṭa	ʿöşr-i cev	resm-i ʿarūsī
226	500	79	10

ḳarye-i Manesi ez cemāʿat-i Arnavudān — tīmār-ı Maḥmūd el-mezḳūr

Manol Manesi	Gön Manesi	Miḫal Manoliçi

ḫāne 3

ḥāṣıl 290

ʿa(n) ispence	ʿöşr-i ḥınṭa	ʿöşr-i cev
60	200	30

cemʿan tīmār-ı Maḥmūd el-mezḳūr

ḳurā	ḫāne	mücerred	bīve
3	[2]6	4	1

ḥāṣıl 2222

44

tetimme-i nāḥiyyet-i Ḫulumiç

kendü bürüme	cebelü	tenktür
	1	1

tīmār-ı Balaban Yaninaʾi

ḳarye-i Andraviza — tīmār-ı Balaban el-mezḳūr

Gin Ḳaluẕi	Niḳola Ḳaluẕi	Muriki Floḳa	Duḳa Rosa	Miḫal Yorġula
Tiḫo Miros	Dimitri Yirġulas	Ḳosta Ḫartulari	Yani Varda	Yorgi Burdari
Andon Maniki	Ḳosta Manesi	Todoro Navos	Yorgi Mavroplo	Yorgi Maniki
İstemati Sinori	Yorgi Vaşılato	Yani İskâẕeplo	Dimitri Ḳaṣaromandri	Miḫal Mavroplo
Ḳomnino İsḳurulya	Dimitri Braniḳaris	Gön Artiki	İstasino Ḳanava	Todoro Şarandi
Petro Virgi	Pavlos Ayyas	Peta Ḳazneş	Miḫal Romano	İstanilo Dyaḳo
Papayani Mavroplo	Miḫal Turḳos	mücerred Niḳola Turḳos	mücerred Yorgi birāder-i o	bīve İrini zen-i Ġurġuri
bīve Mariya zen-i Ḫandakötina				

ḫāne	mücerred	bīve
32	2	2

ḥāṣıl 3085

ʿa(n) ispence	ʿöşr-i ḥınṭa	ʿöşr-i cev	resm-i ʿarūsī
862	1900	293	30

mezraʿa-ı Foloḳobuva — nezd-i ḳarye-i mezḳūr

tīmār-ı mezbūr — ḫāliyye

kendü cebelü	ġulām
	1

tīmār-ı Ḫalīl Siyāh Tırḫalaʾi

ḳarye-i İzlatḳa ez cemāʿat-i Arnavudān — tīmār-ı Ḫalīl el-mezḳūr

Yorgi İzlatḳa	Gön veled-i o	Gin İzlatḳa	Yorgi-i dīğer İzlatḳa	Leḳa Ḳalimeni
Ḳosta İvlaḫyoti	Leḳa Buzbardo	Yani Serbano	Miḫal İvlaḫyoti	Leḳa Prifti

45

tetimme-i ḳarye-i İzlatḳa el-mezḳūr — tīmār-ı Ḫalīl el-mezbūr

Lazaro Prifti	Misḳas Varis	Niḳola Ġurġura	Dimitri Ġurġura	Niḳa Gerbesi
mücerred Miḫal İzlato	mücerred Gön Ḳalimani	mücerred Gön İvlaḫyoti	mücerred Gön Varis	mücerred Dimitri Ġurġura
	bīve Ḳali zen-i İvlaḫyoti			

ḫāne	mücerred	bīve
15	5	1

ḥāṣıl 1028

ʿa(n) ispence	ʿöşr-i ḥınṭa	ʿöşr-i cev	resm-i ḫanāẕīr	resm-i ʿarūsī	mülk-i Yorgi İzlatḳa der ḳarye-i mezḳūr āsiyāb 1 resm 20
406	500	79	8	15	

ḳarye-i Ḳanḳazi ez cemāʿat-i Arnavudān | tīmār-ı Ḫalīl el-mezbūr

Gin Ḳanḳazi	Buʿa Plaşa	Dimo Plaşa	Pavlos Plaşa	Yorgi İpṣari
Andriya İpṣari	Ḳazneş Ḳordas	Manḳola Ḳordas	İştin Ḳanḳazi	Ḳozma İpṣari
Aleksi Mamula	Yorgi Beluşi	Mengişa Ḳoryazi	Gön Plaşi	Todoro Çapoġa
İvrato Zula	Gin Soḫorvuro	Bardi Jula	Muriki Bedeni	mücerred Todor Plaşa
	bīve Manḳa zen-i Plaşa			

ḫāne	mücerred	bīve
19	1	1

ḥāṣıl 1011

ʿa(n) ispence	ʿöşr-i ḥınṭa	ʿöşr-i cev	resm-i ḫanāzīr	resm-i ʿarūsī
406	500	80	5	20

cümletü'l-ḳaryeteyni'l-meẕkūreteyn

ḫāne	mücerred	bīve
34	6	2

ḥāṣıl 2039

kendü cebelü	ġulām
	1

tīmār-ı ʿĪsā birāder-i İlyās Siyāh

ḳarye-i Marḳoplo ez cemāʿat-i Arnavudān | tīmār-ı ʿĪsā el-mezbūr

Mengişa Alaman	Niḳola Lopesi	Duḳa L[o]pesi	Sirma İpṣari	Gin İpṣari
Ḳosta Ḳuẕunato	Gin Buvaşi	Yorgi Bedeni	Gön Bedeni	Yorgi Yaniçi

46

tetimme-i ḳarye-i Marḳoplu el-meẕkūr | tīmār-ı ʿĪsā el-mezbūr

Todoros Ġuşati	Andriya Maji	Niḳola Maji	Todoros Maḳriyanis	Andriya Floḳa
Gön Gönce	bīve Baba zen-i Lenger			

ḫāne	bīve
16	1

ḥāṣıl 975

ʿa(n) ispence	ʿöşr-i ḥınṭa	ʿöşr-i cev	resm-i ḫanāzīr	resm-i ʿarūsī	mülk-i Niḳola Lopesi [der] ḳarye-i meẕkūr āsiyāb 1 resm 50
326	500	80	4	15	

mezraʿa-ı Ḳanbiziya | nezd-i ḳarye-i meẕkūr | tīmār-ı ʿĪsā el-mezbūr

ḫāliyye

ḳarye-i İvlanduşa ez cemāʿat-i Arnavudān | tīmār-ı ʿĪsā el-meẕkūr

Martin İvlanduşa	Marḳo Simiza	Leḳa Ḳuçi	Ḳalani Mazarak	Niḳola Arvaniti
İvrato Ḳabaşi	Petro İvlanduşa	Todoro Ḳalanci	Ġulyamo Ḫavari	mücerred Yorgi İvlanduşa
mücerred Petro Simiza	bīve Baba zen-i Mazarakina			

ḫāne	mücerred	bīve
9	2	1

ḥāṣıl 764

ʿa(n) ispence	ʿöşr-i ḥınṭa	ʿöşr-i cev	resm-i ḫanāzīr	resm-i ʿarūsī
226	450	69	9	10

ḳarye-i Ḳavasila ez cemāʿat-i Arnavudān | tīmār-ı ʿĪsā el-mezbūr

Andriya Ḳavasila	Niḳola Manḳola	Ḳomnino Ḳavasila	Pavlos Liḳudi	Yorgi Graḳo
Yani birāder-i o	Yorgi Liḳuẕi	Yorgi Lanbuẕi	Niḳola birāder-i o	Dimitri Vurġari
Yani Tetraġoniti	Dimitri birāder-i o	bīve İstemata zen-i Vurġari	bīve Baba zen-i Melito	

ḫāne	bīve
12	2

ḥāṣıl 734

ʿa(n) ispence	ʿöşr-i ḥınṭa	ʿöşr-i cev	resm-i ḫanāzīr	resm-i ʿarūsī
252	400	63	4	15

cemʿan tīmār-ı ʿĪsā el-masṭūr

ḳurā	mezraʿa-ı ḫāliyye	ḫāne	mücerred	bīve
3	1	37	2	4

ḥāṣıl 2473

47

tetimme-i nāḥiyyet-i Ḫulumiç

kendü	cebelü	ġulām	tenktür
bürüme	1	1	1

tīmār-ı Ḳasṭamonlu Pīr Ḥasanoğlı Aḥmed

ḳarye-i Lihyana tīmār-ı Aḥmed el-meẕkūr

Andon İstematina	İştin Buḳomad	Yorgi Tuçi	Yorgi Ḳondoma	İstayḳo Vuya
[M]iḫal [Ser]yamos	Yorgi Kefalino	Niḳola Ḳaḳuri	Yani Sinasi	Yorgi Boğdan
Yani Boğdan	Niḳola Ḳuvara	Niḳa Ḳunḳuli	Leḳa Ḳunḳuli	Andriya Maḳriyolyoti
Yani Ġonoparḳo	İstemad Ḳapura	Marti İskliva	Dima Ḳunḳuli	İstemad Evlivis
Manol Cingene	Yani Ḳaḳuri	Todoro Silota	Yorgi birāder-i o	Yorgi Dermi
	mücerred Petro Ḳaḳuri	bīve Alaksandra zen-i Liḳoẕun	ḫāne 25	mücerred 1

bīve 1

ḥāṣıl ġayr ez memlaḥa 2174

ʿa(n) ispence	ʿöşr-i ḥınṭa	ʿöşr-i cev	ʿöşr-i bāġāt	resm-i ḫamr	resm-i ʿarūsī
656	600	77	784	32	25

muḳāṭaʿa-ı memlaḥa der ḳarye-i meẕkūr ki ḫāṣṣa ḫullide mülkühu şüd

fī sene 9000

ḳarye-i Muzak Mengişa ez cemāʿat-i Arnavudān tābiʿ-i Arḳadya tīmār-ı o

Petro Muzak	Ḳalanci Muzak	Andriya Mumba	Ḳosta Mumba	Gin Mumba
Yorgi Parapungi	Todoro Buva	Gin Tuç	Gön Buva	mücerred Marti Muzaki
mücerred Gin Mumba	mücerred Gin Buva		ḫāne 9	mücerred 3

ḥāṣıl 588

ʿa(n) ispence	ʿöşr-i ḥınṭa	ʿöşr-i cev
240	300	48

ḳarye-i Gerbesi ez cemāʿat-i Arnavudān tābiʿ-i Arḳadya tīmār-ı o

T[odo]ros Gerbesi	Pavlos Gerbesi	Gin Siraḳ	Yorgi Ḳrapeşa	Vaġali Buzbardi
Pavlo Bafi	Gin Bafi	Pavlos Bafi-i dīğer	Ḳumi Lalos	Yanul birāder-i o

48

tetimme-i ḳarye-i Gerbesi el-meẕkūr tīmār-ı Aḥmed el-mezbūr

M[iḫ]al R[o]manos	Yani İstarġari	[La]zaro Mukita	Andriya Ro[m]anos	Todoro Buryalisa
Petro Dramesi	Niḳola Bafi	Mangişa Lata	Yorgi Başta	Gin Mayiri
Ḳosta Ġramişa	mücerred Dima İstarġari	mücerred Ḳosta Buryalisa	mücerred Ḳozma Ġramişa	bīve Ḳuke zen-i Mar[ti]n

bīve Mariya zen-i Gerbesi	bīve Manḳa zen-i Ḳomo	ḫāne 21	mücerred 3	bīve 3

ḥāṣıl 1278

ʿa(n) ispence	ʿöşr-i penbe	ʿöşr-i kettān	ʿöşr-i ḥınṭa	ʿöşr-i cev	resm-i ḫanāzīr
498	30	40	600	96	1[4]

cemʿan tīmār-ı Aḥmed el-masṭūr

ḳurā	ḫāne	mücerred	bīve
3	55	7	4

ḥāṣıl 4040

kendü cebelü

tīmār-ı Manol Mahtar

ḳarye-i İpsari ez cemāʿat-i Arnavudān tīmār-ı meẕkūr

Runcar İpsari	Mangişa İpsari	Gin Ḳavalaris	Şeni Plaşa	Gön Şurbi
Proġono Ġuzeri	Gön İstasino	Miḫal Miyaḳo	Zonato Ġuruzi	Andriya Sergi
Yorgi Lonḳa	Ḳozma İvlaşoplo	bīve İskava zen-i Palunbi	bīve Manḳa zen-i İpsari	ḫāne 12

bīve 2

ḥāṣıl 994

ʿa(n) ispence	ʿöşr-i ḥınṭa	ʿöşr-i cev	resm-i ḫanāzīr	resm-i ʿarūsī	mülk-i Runcar İpsari der ḳarye-i mezḳūr āsiyāb 1 resm 30
252	600	94	8	10	

mezraʿa-ı Pendani nezd-i ḳarye-i mezḳūr tīmār-ı o

ḫāliyye

mevḳūf mevḳūf

mezraʿa-ı Lonci nezd-i ḳarye-i İpsari el-mezḳūr

ḫāliyye

mezraʿa-ı Başta nezd-i ḳa[rye-i] o

ḫāliyye

mevḳūf mevḳūf

mezraʿa-ı Tunba nezd-i ḳarye-i o

ḫāliyye

mezraʿa-ı [Ḳ]apaleto nez[d-i] ḳarye-i o

ḫāliyye

49

tetimme-i nāḥiyyet-i Ḫulumiç

kendü eşer

tīmār-ı Nikifor Ḳavasila[28]

ḳarye-i Aya Baraskevi[29] tīmār-ı mezḳūr

İstema[d] Po[m]yola	Todoro Çancali	Yorgi veled-i o	Miḫal Varsalomyo-plos	Muriki Leoplos
Niḳola Ḫu[l]yani	Yorgi Meliġala	Nikifor Matinyoti	ḫāne 8	

ḥāṣıl 739

ʿa(n) is[pence]	ʿöşr-i ḥınṭa	ʿöşr-i cev	ʿöşr-i bāġāt	resm-i ḫanāzīr	ʿöşr-i kettān	resm-i ʿarūsī
200	250	39	186	4	50	10

kendü eşer

tīmār-ı Leḳa İzmolda

ḳarye-i Ġramatiḳo tīmār-ı o

Murik Franḳuli	Uzġos Yani	Gön Siraḳ	ḫāne 3

ḥāṣıl 378

ʿa(n) ispence	ʿöşr-i ḥınṭa	ʿöşr-i cev	resm-i ḫanāzīr	ʿöşr-i kettān
75	250	38	5	10

50

kendü bürüme	geçim	cebelü	günlük	çadır	tenktür
	2	17	1	2	2

zeʿāmet-i Ayo İlya zaʿīmeş Paşa Yiğit veled-i Ḳar<a>göz Beg bin Yuvan

nefs-i Ayo İlya ḫāṣṣa-ı zaʿīm

Yani Kiryaḳoplo	Ġulumi birāder-i o	Papadimitri Ḫıristodulos	Uranya İsḳortino	Mastroyani Papaan-drinoplo
Mastromiḫal Zarḫani	Yani Vidara	İstasi Yiro	Dimitri Zarḫani	İstefano Zarḫani
Niḳola Zarḫani	Todoro Filevotomo	Yani Ḫarkâ	Dimitri Burdunba	Todoro Tirsenyoti
Yani Tirsenyoti	Niḳola Befani	Yani Ḳosoliva	Franḳo dāmād-ı o	Ḳosta Ḳaçuli
Todoro Burdunba	Niḳola Burdunba	Niḳola Aloġoklefti	İstemati Aloġoklefti	Yani Aloġoklefti
Yani Papa-asanasoplo	Andriya Ḳanbos	Papaluḳa Papayorgi	Yani birāder-i o	Yani Ḳrokidi
Niḳola Ḳrokizi	İvrato Ḳoriso	Yani Ḳoriso	Vaşıl Kiryaḳoplo	Dimitri Ġatro yiros
Dimitri Ġatro-<yı> dīğer	Niḳola Sodosi	Yani Mastroniḳolo-plo	Niḳola birāder-i o	Papadimitri Filarato
Yani Marmara	Ḳosta Marmara	Todoro Perastasi	Petro Ḳalasa	Yani Ḳorisos
İvlaş veled-i o	İstefano Aroni	Todoro Vari	Niḳola Ḳapsokili	Aleksi Fraġos
Yorgi Maroti	İvrato Maroti	Yani Maroti	Niḳola Zakita	Andriya Avram
Niḳola Manoloplo	Dimitri birāder-i o	Todoro Pravata	Soma Arsani	Yani Ṣarandino
Yani Draġaşi	Mihil İskliro	Andron veled-i o	Vaşıl Marmara	Dimitri Marmara

Vaşıl S̲alasino	Yorgi Bedeni	Niḳola Ḳasopi	Petro Ḳayani	Miḫal Mavroçi
Anastas Lefteri	Yorgi Siroviça	Andon İsḳufi	İstemad İsḳufi	Ḳosta Miḫaluçi
Petro veled-i o	Manol veled-i o	Pavlos Ġulami	Niḳola Ẓiyaksenos	Andriya Aranis
Petro İstamiriti	Yuvan Servo	Yani Marḳoplo	Filibo[30] Cincarlo	Ḳosta Avrami
Yorgi Marġariti	Mastro- todor Maġuli	S̲oma veled-i o	Gin Mayiro	İştin Ṣuli

51

tetimme-i nefs-i Ayo İlya el-mez̲kūr — ḫāṣṣa-ı zaʿīm

Yorgi Filibos[31]	Petro Manoloplo	Marti Ḳalavriy[o]	Miḫal Lisareti	Yorgi Praski
Yani Mastroniḳolo- plo	Niḳola İsḳurḳo	Petro Lisareti	Dimitri Mastroniḳolo- plo	Dimitri Perastati
Ḳosta Polesḳa	Todoro İsariti	İstefano birāz̲er-i İsḳurḳo	Todoro Ḫarkâ	Niḳola Ṣandameriti
Andron Zarḫani	Manol Ḳaçuli	Yorgi İvlaḫaçi	Sotiri Ġastro	İvlaş Ḳoris̲o
Yorgi Miḫaliç	İstefano Ḳolokis̲a	Yani As̲anas̲i	Niḳola Filimotomo	mücerred Niḳola Kiryaḳoplo
mücerred Niḳola İsḳortino	mücerred Ḳori Videra	mücerred Dimitri Tirsenyoti	mücerred Petro Aloġoklefti	mücerred Aleksi Mastroniḳolo- plo
mücerred Yani Filareto	mücerred Yorgi Marmara	mücerred İstematiḳo Ḳalas̲a	mücerred Yorgi birāder-i Yani Ḳoris̲o	mücerred Niḳola İskliro
mücerred Loyizo Simos	mücerred Loyzo-<yı> dīğer Simos	mücerred Yorgi S̲alasino	mücerred Niḳola Rayḳo	mücerred Dimitri Luḳoplo
bīve Ḳali zen-i Papaaleksi	bīve Todora zen-i Papas Flari	bīve Ranbalu zen-i Ḫıristyano	bīve Ṣofya zen-i Uzġur	bīve Andanyusa

bīve Covanela zen-i Mavromati	bīve Maġdalini zen-i Ḳorikiz̲a	bīve Aġas̲i zen-i Burdunya	bīve Simolina

ḫāne	mücerred	bīve	manastır-ı ḫāṣṣa
114	16	9	1

ḥāṣıl 20659

ʿa(n) ispence 3304	bāġāt-ı ḫāṣṣa dönüm 53 [resm] 7200	eşcār-ı meyve-i ḫāṣṣa ʿaded 42 [resm] 100	eşcār-ı zeyt-i ḫāṣṣa ʿaded 9 [resm] 23	āsiyābhā-<yı> ḫāṣṣa 4 [resm] 1800

bostān-ı ḫāṣṣa 1 [resm] 80	ʿöşr-i penbe 200	ʿöşr-i kettān 250	ʿöşr-i bāġāt 2656	ʿöşr-i ḥınṭa 3500	ʿöşr-i cev 545
ʿöşr-i meyve 50	ʿöşr-i ʿasel 6	resm-i ḫanāzīr 15	resm-i ʿarūsī 150	resm-i ḫamr 250	resm-i niyābet 500

mülk-i
Niḳola Zakita der nefs-i
Ayo İlya el-mez̲kūr
āsiyāb 1 resm 30

52

nāḥiyyet-i Ayo İlya

ḳarye-i Muzak ez cemāʿat-i Arnavudān — ḫāṣṣa-ı zaʿīm

Muzak Pilura	İvlado birāder-i o	Caha veled-i o	Petro Lukişa	Gin Lukişa
Niḳola Lukişa	Yorgi Lukişa	Ḳozma Rinbari	Mengişa Maji	Dimitri Papaz̲ato
Gin Graḳa	Yorgi Lata	Gön Liḳolic	Gin Orfano	Yorgi Rinbari
mücerred Gin Lata	bīve İskâva	bīve Dyala zen-i Gergil	bīve Ḳukö zen-i Gürḳo	bīve İ[s]kâva zen-i Lukisa[32]
	bīve Vaşa zen-i Miḫal			

ḫāne	mücerred	bīve
15	1	5

ḥāṣıl 1253

ʿa(n) ispence 350	ʿöşr-i kettān 50	ʿöşr-i ḥınṭa 700	ʿöşr-i cev 108	resm-i ḫanāzīr 25	resm-i ʿarūsī 20

ḳarye-i İşpata ez cemāʿat-i Arnavudān — ḫāṣṣa-ı zaʿīm

Andriya İşpata	Leḳa İşpata	Leḳa-ı dīğer İşpata	Niḳola Ḳumno	İvlaş Pavlo Maji	
mücerred Niḳola İşpata	bīve Todora zen-i Pavlo Maji	bīve Todora zen-i Andriyaplo	ḫāne 5	mücerred 1	bīve 2

ḥāṣıl 522

ʿa(n) ispence	ʿöşr-i kettān	ʿöşr-i ḥınṭa	ʿöşr-i cev	resm-i ḫanāzīr	resm-i ʿarūsī
132	20	300	46	14	10

ḳarye-i Ḳozma Greḳa ez cemāʿat-i Arnavudān — ḫāṣṣa-ı zaʿīm

Andriya Greḳa	Andriya-ı dīğer Greḳa	Yorgi Ṣuli	Gin Liḳuresi	Duma Maranci	
Pelaħri Ḫayḳal	İvrato Aġali	Ḳozma İstaşi	mücerred Leḳa Liḳuresi	mücerred Niḳola Ṣulima	
	bīve İsklâva		ḫāne 8	mücerred 2	bīve 1

ḥāṣıl 1000

ʿa(n) ispence	ʿöşr-i kettān	ʿöşr-i ḥınṭa	ʿöşr-i cev	resm-i ḫanāzīr	resm-i ʿarūsī
206	30	650	100	4	10

ḳarye-i Simiza ez cemāʿat-i Arnavudān — ḫāṣṣa-ı zaʿīm

Leḳa Simiza	Yorgi veled-i o	Dima Simiza	Lazar Barça	Miḫal Barça
	bīve Mariya zen-i Dima	ḫāne 5	bīve 1	

ḥāṣıl 353

ʿa(n) ispence	ʿöşr-i kettān	ʿöşr-i ḥınṭa	ʿöşr-i cev	resm-i ʿarūsī
150	20	150	23	10

53
tetimme-i nāḥiyyet-i Ayo İlya

ḳarye-i Ayo Vaşıl ez cemāʿat-i Arnavudān — ḫāṣṣa-ı zaʿīm

Ẕiyaluşi Manesi	Miloş veled-i o	Petro Asani	keşiş[33] Asani	Yorgi Maḳrosḳuli
Y[or]gi Ḳonbos̱eḳra	Dima Sirvos		ḫāne 7	

ḥāṣıl 286

ʿa(n) ispence	ʿöşr-i kettān	ʿöşr-i ḥınṭa	ʿöşr-i cev	resm-i ʿarūsī
140	20	100	16	10

ḳarye-i Romyo ez cemāʿat-i Arnavudān — ḫāṣṣa-ı zaʿīm

Todoros Romyos	Miḫal birāẕer-i o	Todoros Filimotomo	Niḳola Romyo	Gin dāmād-ı o
Yani Ḳurtesi	Yani Romiyo	Ḳozma Liğero	Luḳa Romyo	ḫāne 9

ḥāṣıl 448

ʿa(n) ispence	ʿöşr-i kettān	ʿöşr-i ḥınṭa	ʿöşr-i cev	resm-i ḫanāzīr	resm-i ʿarūsī
180	28	200	31	2	10

ḳarye-i İştopans̱i Lopesi ez cemāʿat-i Arnavudān — ḫāṣṣa-ı zaʿīm

Dimitri Papayanoplo	Petro veled-i o	Niḳola Papayanoplo	Lala Maji	Bardi Maji
Yorgi Tunba	İştopans̱i Yorondo	Gin veled-i o	Gön veled- i Papayanoplo	mücerred Lazaro Papayanoplo
mücerred Niḳola Maji	mücerred Proġono Tunba		ḫāne 9	mücerred 3

ḥāṣıl 509

ʿa(n) ispence	ʿöşr-i kettān	ʿöşr-i ḥınṭa	ʿöşr-i cev	resm-i ḫanāzīr	ʿöşr-i ʿasel	resm-i ʿarūsī
240	10	200	31	7	11	10

ḳarye-i Ġolomi ez cemāʿat-i Arnavudān — ḫāṣṣa-ı zaʿīm

Miḫal Ġolomi	Gin Ġolomi	Yorgi Miziḳa	Ḳozma birāder-i o	Yorgi Pavlos
Andriya birāder-i o	Andriya Ṣurbi	Lazaro birāẕer-i o	Gin Purno	Proġono Ḳuçi
Ḳozma Orfano	Todoros Sulani	Bardi Buçi	mücerred Todoros Ġolomi	mücerred Niḳola Pavlos
mücerred Şeni Purno	mücerred Gin Ḳuçi		ḫāne 13	mücerred 4

ḫāṣıl 980

ʿa(n) ispence 340	ʿöşr-i ḫınṭa 500	ʿöşr-i cev 77	ʿöşr-i ʿasel 7	resm-i ḫanāzīr 6	ʿöşr-i kettān 30
		resm-i ʿarūsī 20			

54

tetimme-i nāḫiyye[t-i] Ayo İlya

ḳarye-i Arvano Ḳastro — ḫāṣṣa-ı zaʿīm

Pavlo Ḳuçi	Niḳola Ḳuçi	Papaniḳola Eksoẕondi	Pavlos veled-i o	İlya Çuḳala
Todoros Çuḳala	Vaṣıl Ḳavaki	Yorgi Pikilo	Todoros Eksovunyoti	Yani Uzġur
Andon Uzġur	Gön Zenbeş	Lal İskeliti	Yani Raviti	Aleksi Damyanos
Dimitri Damyanos	Niḳola Piroplo	Yani Piroplo	Yorgi Riġato	Petro Turḳoplo
Todoros Canis	Yani Ḫarkâ	Todoros Ḫarkâ	Yani İskâẕe	Niḳola İstilyano
Manol İstilyano	İstemad Ḳosarin	Dimitri Ḳavaki	Yorgi Ẕerḳaẕi	Ḳondostovla[34] Çaḳumi
Todoros Ḳaloyoroplos	Andon Ẕirvaẕyoti	Niḳola Ḳomnino	Todoro Zematomati	Yani Lazaroplo
Todoro Mastrangi	Dimitri Ġadro	Niḳola Plaksiẕi	Yani İsḳufi	Yani Tirvala
Miḫal Ḳaçandori	Yani Metaḳsomati	Dimitri Muḫriç	Ḳosta Raviṣa	Yani Maroti
İstoya Yuẕa	Petros Porisas	Niḳola Ḳalamatyani	Yani Ḳoloni	Dimitri Fevata
Andon Ṣarandino	mücerred Yani Eksovunyoti	mücerred Yorgi Ẕamyanos	mücerred Todoros Riġato	mücerred Todoros Ḳavaki
mücerred Miḫal birāder-i Todoros Ḳaloyiro-plos	bīve Todora zen-i Varvara	bīve Aneza zen-i Pinaḳa	bīve zen-i Ḫıristovulo	bīve ḫira Pungi

ḫāne 51	mücerred 5	bīve 4

ḫāṣıl 5190

ʿa(n) ispence 1424	bāġāt-ı ḫāṣṣa dönüm 4 [resm] 720	āsiyāb-ı ḫāṣṣa 1 [resm] 100	eşcār-ı zeyt-i ḫāṣṣa ʿaded 6 [resm] 13	eşcār-ı meyve-i ḫāṣṣa ʿaded 10 [resm] 20

eşcār-ı saḳız-ı çam-ı ḫāṣṣa ʿaded 300 [resm] 50	ʿöşr-i kettān 200	ʿöşr-i penbe 30	ʿöşr-i bāġāt 910	ʿöşr-i ḫınṭa 1300	ʿöşr-i cev 200

ʿöşr-i meyve 8	ʿöşr-i zeyt 19	resm-i ḫanāzīr 4	ʿöşr-i ʿasel 22	resm-i ʿarūsī 50
		resm-i ḫamr 120		

55

tetimme-i nāḫiyyet-i Ayo İlya

ḳarye-i Sirvu ez cemāʿat-i Arnavudān — ḫāṣṣa-ı zaʿīm

Yani Sirvo	Todoros birāder-i o	mücerred Yani birāẕer-i īşān	ḫāne 2	mücerred 1

ḫāṣıl 175

ʿa(n) ispence 60	ʿöşr-i ḫınṭa 100	ʿöşr-i cev 15

ḳarye-i Bavasi ez cemāʿat-i Arnavudān — ḫāṣṣa-ı zaʿīm

İstefano Bavasi	Gin Liḳuresi	Andriya Bavasi	bīve Ḳali zen-i Yorgi Bavasi	ḫāne 3	bīve 1

ḫāṣıl 299

ʿa(n) ispence 66	ʿöşr-i ḫınṭa 200	ʿöşr-i cev 30	resm-i ḫanāzīr 3

ḳarye-i Ḳastel İksovuni — ḫāṣṣa-ı zaʿīm

Aleksi Ḳrokiẕa	Ḳosta veled-i o	Todoros Ḫandruli	Petros birāẕer-i o	Dimitri Ḫandruli
Yani birāder-i o	Niḳola Ḫarkâ	Yani S̱oma	Niḳola Todoriç	Yorgi veled-i o
Todoros Todoriç	S̱otoki birāder-i o	Pavlos Rafti	Andriya Anastas	İstemati Ḳaḳotari

Ḳosta İstratili	Todoros birāder-i o	Yani Alupi	Todoros İstratili	Ḳosta Alupi
İlyo İpsarovaşıli	İstemad birāẕer-i o	Niḳola Lonberdo	Miḫal birāder-i o	Yani Ḫandruli
Miḫal [bi]rāder-i o	Yorgi As̱anas	Yani birāder-i o	Niḳola Niḳoluti	Dimitri Ḫandruli
Ḳosta veled-i o	Ovindiyos Piros	Miḫal birāder-i o	Yani Ovindiyos	Papayorgi Praġando
Papaniḳola veled-i o	Yani Ḫandruli	Dimitri İstrati	Yani birāder-i o	Yani Pilomata
Niḳola Azarya	Niḳola Todoriç	Dimitri Rayi	Yani Niḳola	Niḳola Ẕrosilo
Petro Ẕrosilo	Yani veled-i o	Todoros Martin	Niḳola Furtuno	Yorgi birāder-i o
Romanos Barbuzas	Yorgi birāder-i o	Miḫal Piri	Todoros Vuryas	Yani Orfano
Papayani Rayi	Ḳosta birāder-i o	Papas Andriya	S̱otoki veled-i o	Dimitri veled-i o
Vaşıl veled-i o	Miḫal veled-i o	Ḳosta Zadoni	Yani birāẕer-i o	Aleksi Ḳuromali

56

tetimme-i ḳarye-i Ḳastel İksovuni el-meẕkūr ḫāṣṣa-ı zaʿīm

Yorgi Mencili	Yani Todoriç	Yani Ḳrokiẕa	Miḫal Todoriç	Yani S̱eryano
Niḳola S̱eryano	Niḳola Ḫarḳomati	Niḳola Ḳarçikâneplo	Yani Lepşuta	Niḳola Ḫandruli
Yani İksuri	Yorgi Praġuli	Yani Vura	Dimitri Randonas	Vaşıl veled-i Rafti
Yani Lonbardo	Miḫal birāder-i Dimitri Tavlaviya	Yani Niḳoluti	Yorgi Ḫandruli	S̱otoki Perġando
Niḳola veled-i Yani Ḫandruli	Yani Azariya	Todoros birāder-i Todoriç	Miḫal Ẕrosilo	Andriya veled-i Petro Ẕrosilo
Dimitri Furtuno	S̱otoki Lonberdo	S̱omas Vuras	Niḳola Lepşuta	Ḳosta Draġovit
Niḳola Lazaro	Niḳola veled-i Yani Todoriç	Yorgi Papaandriya	Papaniḳola Ḳalavokiri[35]	Yorgi Argiris

Niḳola Ḳanado	Petros Martin	Niḳola Ḳondro	Dimitri birāẕer-i İstratili	Manol Tavlari
Yani Tavlari	Yani Ḳırçikâno	Yorgi Piri birāẕer-i İspano	Manol Platindro	Todoros Platindro
Yani Aleksi Ḳurupa	Yani Drosilo	İstemati birāder-i Praġuli	Yani Ḫıristiyano	Ḳosta Rayi
Yani veled-i o	Dimitri Iḳsuri	Yani Lonberdo	Dimitri Vura	Dimitri Lolopi
Niḳola Ḳostiyaḳo	Yorgi veled-i Petro Drosilo	Dimitri Ḳaḳotari	Andron Niḳola Drosilo	Dimitri Lanberdoplo
Papas Bicanos	Niḳola Bicanos	mücerred Yorgi İspano	mücerred S̱otoki Malaki	mücerred Yani Ḳaḳotari
mücerred Dimitri Tavlarya	mücerred Yorgi veled-i Yani Ḫandruli	mücerred Miḫal S̱eryano	mücerred Miḫal birāẕer-i S̱oma	mücerred Yani birāder-i Yorgi Todoriç
mücerred Niḳola Ḳorokis̱a	mücerred Yorgi Ḫandruli	mücerred Andon birāder-i o	mücerred Yorgi birāder-i Dimitri Ḫandruli	mücerred Manol birāder-i o
mücerred Yorgi birāder-i Ḫarkâ	mücerred Yani birāẕer-i Malaki	mücerred Yani veled-i Rafti	mücerred Yorgi Anastas	mücerred Yorgi Alupi
mücerred Miḫal Alupi	mücerred Andriya birāẕer-i Lös	mücerred Ḳosta Lonbardo	mücerred Yorgi Lonbardo	mücerred Yani [bi]rāder-i Todoriç
mücerred Yorgi veled-i Petro Drosila	mücerred Niḳola veled-i Papaandriya	mücerred Pavlos birāẕer-i Ḳarçikâneplo	mücerred Dimitri İstematili	mücerred Yani veled-i Siluriya
mücerred Andriya Ḳaravokiri	mücerred Dimitri birāẕer-i o	bīve zen-i Miḫal Ḫarkâ	bīve Mariya zen-i Ḫarkâ	bīve Ḳali zen-i Malaki

57

tetimme-i ḳarye-i Ḳastel İksovuni el-meẕḳūr — ḫāṣṣa-ı zaʿīm

bīve İrini zen-i Ḳorvaşıla	bīve Mariya zen-i Toma	bīve Elani zen-i Tavlariya	bīve İḫtano	bīve Todora zen-i Azar[o]
bīve Mariya zen-i Yovaliya	bīve Paraskevi zen-i Franḳoyani	bīve Yana zen-i Yani Ḫarḳomata	bīve İrini zen-i İḫtana	bīve zen-i İstematiki
bīve zen-i Dokimena	bīve zen-i Silyorina			

ḫāne	mücerred	bīve
127	30	15

ḫāṣıl 11301

ʿa(n) ispence 4015	bāġāt-ı ḫāṣṣa dönüm 5 [resm] 1125	eşcār-ı ṭut-ı ḫāṣṣa ʿaded 14 [resm] 60	āsiyāb-ı ḫāṣṣa 1 [resm] 250	ʿöşr-i bāġāt 1200	
ʿöşr-i ḫınṭa 3[6]50	ʿöşr-i cev 450	ʿöşr-i ḳazz 6	resm-i ʿarūsī 150	ʿöşr-i kettān 200	resm-i ḫamr 120

mülk-i
Niḳola Lonberdo
der ḳarye-i meẕḳūr

mülk-i
Miḫal Piri der ḳarye-i
meẕḳūr
āsiyāb 1 resm 30

āsiyāb-ı ġalle 1 resm 30	āsiyāb-ı peşmīne 1 resm 15

ḳarye-i Poliça — ḫāṣṣa-ı zaʿīm

Ḳosta Ḳondeniḳola	Niḳola birāẕer-i o	Ḳosta Piri	Nıḳola Ḳulukinyoti	Yorgi Ḳostyaḳo
Dimitri veled-i o	Todoro Ḳostyaḳo	Yorgi Ḳostyaḳo	Yani veled-i o	Niḳola Foraẕa
Yani Foraẕa	Yorgi veled-i o	<A>nastas Ḳondoniḳola	Yani Ḳostyaḳo	mücerred Miḫal Ḳondeniḳola
	mücerred Yani Ḳostyaḳo			

ḫāne	mücerred
14	2

ḫāṣıl 1229

ʿa(n) ispence 400	ʿöşr-i bāġāt 210	ʿöşr-i ḫınṭa 450	ʿöşr-i cev 72	resm-i ḫanāzīr 10	ʿöşr-i meyve 2
resm-i ʿarūsī 15	ʿöşr-i kettān 30	resm-i ḫamr 10			

mülk-i
Niḳola Ḳulukinyoti
der ḳarye-i meẕḳūr
āsiyāb 1 resm 30

ḳarye-i Zorila ez cemāʿat-i Arnavudān — ḫāṣṣa-ı zaʿīm

Yani Zorila	Dima İvlaḫyoti	Gin veled-i o	Leḳa veled-i o	Miḫal veled-i o
Niḳola İvlaḫy[o]ti	Dima Zorila	Niḳola birāẕer-i o	Pelañrin birāder-i o	Niḳola Masḳari
Leḳa Manali	Yorgi birāẕer-i o	Ḳozma Toskesi	Evato Masḳari	Yani Ẕimiçaniti
Dima Maji	Gön Manesi	Gin Toskesi	veled-i İsḳliva birāder-i İlya	Todoros Pasḳali

58

tetimme-i ḳarye-i Zorila el-meẕḳūr — [ḫā]ṣṣa-ı zaʿīm

Gön İvladuşa	mücerred Yani Masḳari	mücerred Yorgi birāẕer-i o	mücerred Mano T[o]skesi	bīve Zoġa zen-i Maḳrisa
	bīve Mariya zen-i Yorgi			

ḫāne	mücerred	bīve
21	3	2

ḫāṣıl 1368

ʿa(n) ispence 492	ʿöşr-i ḫınṭa 700	ʿöşr-i cev 108	resm-i ḫanāzīr 23	resm-i ʿarūsī 25	ʿöşr-i kettān 20

ḳarye-i Miġali Ẕivri — ḫāṣṣa-ı zaʿīm

Dimitri Perdikari	Yani Perdiḳari	Vaşıl Perdiḳari	Todoro Çirina	S̱otoki Per[di]ḳari
Yani Perdiḳari	Dimitri Biçiḳulo	Niḳola Perdiḳari	Yani Çirina	Yani Ḳu[r]i
Manol Vaşılaki	Yani Mavroplo	Dimitri birāder-i o	Papayani Mavroplo	Yorgi Ġumeno
Miḫal İstatiḳoplo	Akindinos Mavriyanis	Papaandriya Ḳuruşta	Yorgi Doni	Dimitri Doni
As̱anas Dimitriçi	Ḳosta Şulima	Niḳola birāẕer-i o	Ḳozma Luçito	Yani Randona
Niḳola birāẕer-i o	Yorgi Ḳaryana	S̱otoki Petroplo	Yani Fusḳari	Yani Simiẕula
Todoros veled-i o	Miḫal Rafti	Dimitri Zaḳsoplo	Dimitri Falça	Yani Eksarḫoplo
Yani Androplo	Miḫal Ḫarkâ	Yani veled-i o	Yani Monaġriza	Dimitri birāder-i o

Yani Lazaro	Yorgi Lazaro	Yani birāder-i o	Ḳosta İstrazi	Niḳola birāẕer-i o
S̱otoki Andreplo	Yani Lazaro	Niḳola birāẕer-i o	Vaşıl birāẕer-i o	Aleksi birāẕer-i īşān
Vaşıl Şulima	Dimitri Anastas	Miḫal Ḳaloyira	Todoros Yorġoplo	Yani Yorġoplo
Niḳola Yorġoplo	İstemad Papayorġoplo	Yorgi Ḳaloyira	Todoro Ḳaloyira	Yorgi Draġoviti
Niḳola Miḫalic	Dimitri birāder-i o	Vaşıl Draġoviti	Miḫal A̱sanasaplo	Yani A̱sanasaplo
İstemad A̱sanasaplo	Yorgi Pavlo	Yorgi Protopapaẕaplo	Todoro [Pe]risteriçi	Andriya Nomiḳoplo
Ḳosta Monaġriẕa	Mastroyani Monaġriẕa	Ḳosta Protopapa	Yani A̱sanasaplo	Manol Ḳaloyira

59

tetimme-i ḳarye-i Miġali Ẕivri el-meẕkūr — ḫāṣṣa-ı zaʿīm

To[do]ro Simiẕulo	Yani Suġli	Niḳola Patra	Todoros ḫirāẕer-i o	İstemad Eksarḫoplo
Niḳola Platindro	Yani Ḳaḳuçi	Ḳosta Ḳaçipoẕi	Niḳola Randona	Dimitri birāder-i o
Niḳ[o]la Protoẕiḳoplo	Andron A̱sanas	Yani Yimnosofisti	Papadimitri Monaġrida	Vaşıl İstrazi
Miḫal veled-i o	Ḳozma Loncino	Yani Randona	Niḳola birāẕer-i o	İstas̱i Metaḳsa
Dimitri Papasimoplo	Yani Ḫarara	Ḫartofilaḳa Merḳuri	Ẕyaḳo Çavya	Todoros Ġavrili
Todoros Petroplos	mücerred Todoros Perdiḳari	mücerred Ḳosta Ḳaryana	mücerred Petro Petroplo	mücerred Todoros Zaḳsoplos
mücerred S̱otoki Falca	mücerred Menol[36] Monaġriẕa	mücerred Dimitri Lazaro	mücerred Dimitri birāẕer-i Yorgi Lazaro	mücerred Dimitri Niḳola
mücerred İstas̱i Papasimoplo	mücerred İstemad Yorġoplo	mücerred Niḳola Ḳaloyira	mücerred Todoros Monaġriẕa	mücerred Ḳosta A̱sanasaplo
mücerred Yorgi Tirozumi	mücerred Todoro Ḳaḳatira	mücerred Yani Ayiri	mücerred Niḳola Poẕoḫtipo	bīve Todora zen-i Niḳola

bīve Andro zen-i İsḳolarya	ḫāne 101	mücerred 18	bīve 2

ḥāṣıl 10787

ʿa(n) ispence 2987	bāġāt-ı ḫāṣṣa dönüm 3 [resm] 720	eşcār-ı ṭut-ı ḫāṣṣa ʿaded 115 [resm] 350	eşcār-ı meyve-i ḫāṣṣa ʿaded 15 [resm] 30	ʿöşr-i bāġāt 1980

ʿöşr-i ḥınṭa 3000	ʿöşr-i cev 458	ʿöşr-i ḳazz 644	ʿöşr-i meyve 58	resm-i ʿarūsī 100	resm-i ḫamr 170	ʿöşr-i kettān 200

mülk-i Papayorġoplo der ḳarye-i meẕkūr āsiyāb 1 resm 30	mülk-i Ḳosta Ḳaçipoẕi der ḳarye-i meẕkūr āsiyāb 1 resm 30	mülk-i Papadimitri der ḳarye-i meẕkūr āsiyāb 1 resm 30

ḳarye-i Vunarġo — ḫāṣṣa-ı zaʿīm

Yani Loġos̱e[t]i	Petro Ḳavuriçi	Yorgi Ḳapandriti	Ayoto İvlandiḳa	Manol A̱sanas	
Andriya Befani	Cingene Mastromiḫal	mücerred Yani Draġo	mücerred S̱oma birāder-i o	mücerred Dimitri Ḳavuriçi	
mücerred Dimitri A̱sanas	bīve Mariya zen-i ʿazab	ḫāne 7	mücerred 4	bīve 1	mevẕiʿ-i āsiyāb-ı ḫāṣṣa 1

60

ḥāṣıl-ı ḳarye-i Vunarġo el-meẕkūr 3629

ʿa(n) ispence 281	bāġāt-ı ḫāṣṣa dönüm 20 [resm] 2400	eşcār-ı zeyt-i ḫāṣṣa ʿaded 100 [resm] 203	eşcār-ı meyve-i ḫāṣṣa ʿaded 46 [resm] 100	ʿöşr-i penbe 30

ʿöşr-i kettān 40	ʿöşr-i bāġāt 210	ʿöşr-i ḥınṭa 300	ʿöşr-i cev 48	ʿöşr-i zeyt 7	resm-i ʿarūsī 10

ḳarye-i Mihili ez cemāʿat-i Arnavudān — ḫāṣṣa-ı zaʿīm

Yani Mihili	Ġulamo birāder-i o	Petro Şalesi	Ḳosta Ḳuçi	Yorgi Nikifor
İstefano Nikifor	mücerred Angelos Şalesi	mücerred Andriya Şalesi	mücerred Niḳola Ḫarkâ	mücerred Niḳola Mihili

ḫāne 6	mücerred 4

ḥāṣıl 560

ʿa(n) ispence	ʿöşr-i penbe	ʿöşr-i kettān	ʿöşr-i ḥınṭa	ʿöşr-i cev	resm-i ʿarūsī
200	20	40	250	40	10

ḳarye-i İryolo ḫāṣṣa-ı zaʿīm

Gin Maẕiñik	Dimitri Ḳapsoloni	Yorgi Ḳapsoloni	Todoro Maẕiñik	Peta Mazaraki
Andriya Ḳonbi Ṣeḳra	Yorgi Dramesi	Niḳola Çaḳani	Niḳola Malya	Yani Uzġuro
Gin Ḫarma	Andriya Floḳali	Yorgi Piça	Petro Çimri	Miḫal Pandimo
Yani Ḳapsoloni	Ḫarma Drameşi[37]	İlya Maliya	bīve Mariya zen-i Ermiḫorita	bīve Mariya zen-i İstematina

ḫāne	bīve
18	2

ḥāṣıl 4517

ʿa(n) ispence	bāġāt-ı ḫāṣṣa	eşcār-ı zeyt-i ḫāṣṣa	āsiyāb-ı ḫāṣṣa 1	eşcār-ı meyve-i ḫāṣṣa	ḳısṭ-ı ṭalyan-ı ḫāṣṣa 1
462	dönüm 20 [resm] 1920	ʿaded 200 [resm] 270	[resm] 250	ʿaded 31 [resm] 50	[resm] 160

ʿöşr-i penbe	ʿöşr-i kettān	ʿöşr-i bāġāt	ʿöşr-i ḥınṭa	ʿöşr-i cev	ʿöşr-i zeyt	ʿöşr-i meyve	resm-i ḫamr
62	48	660	500	77	4	4	30

resm-i ʿarūsī
20

ḳarye-i Prifti ez cemāʿat-i Arnavudān ḫāṣṣa-ı zaʿīm

Asanas Prifti	Dima Prifti	Dimitri Ḳuḳulo	Todoro Prifti	Dimitri Prifti
Yorgi Varḳopo	Todoros Prifti	mücerred Todoros Prifti-i dīğer	ḫāne 7	mücerred 1

ḥāṣıl 636

ʿa(n) ispence	ʿöşr-i ḥınṭa	ʿöşr-i cev	resm-i ḫanāzīr	resm-i ʿarūsī
160	400	63	5	8

61
tetimme-i nāḥiyyet-i Ayo İlya

ḳarye-i Ḳarta[zori] ez cemāʿat-i Arnavudān ḫāṣṣa-ı zaʿīm

T[o]doros [Ḳartazori]	Petro Ḳaḳusi	Martin İşpata	Gön Şamroy	Yani Ḳure[s]
Yorgi Purno	Niḳola Ḳaḳusi	Niḳola Çirnota	ḫāne 8	

ḥāṣıl 519

ʿa(n) ispence	ʿöşr-i ḥınṭa	ʿöşr-i cev	resm-i ḫanāzīr	resm-i ʿarūsī
160	300	47	4	8

ḳarye-i Mayira ez cemāʿat-i Arnavudān ḫāṣṣa-ı zaʿīm

Todoro Mayira	Petro İvlando	Yorgi Maḳri Şuli	Andriya Ḳrapesi	ḫāne 4

ḥāṣıl 195

ʿa(n) ispence	ʿöşr-i ḥınṭa	ʿöşr-i cev
80	100	15

mezraʿa-ı Ayiya nezd-i ḳarye-i İryolo el-mezkūr	mezraʿa-ı Fenaromeni nezd-i ḳarye-i mezkūr
ḫāṣṣa-ı zaʿīm ḫāliyye	ḫāṣṣa-ı zaʿīm ḫāliyye

cemʿan ḫāṣṣhā-<yı> subaşı-ı Ayo İlya

ḳurā maʿa nefs-i Ayo İlya	mezāriʿ-i ḫāliyye	ḫāne	mücerred	bīve
22	2	554	95	45

ḥāṣıl 66411

mevḳūf

mezraʿa-ı Şamuna nezd-i ḳarye-i Vunarġo el-mezkūr

ḫāliyye

62
tetimme-i nāḥiyyet-i Ayo İlya

kendü bürüme	cebelü	ġulām	çadır
	2	1	1

tīmār-ı İbrahīm[38] Dīvāne ġulām-ı mīr ki ez merdān-ı ḳalʿa-ı Balya Badra būd ḳarye-i Franḳa Vila   tīmār-ı İbrahīm[39] el-meẕkūr

Miḫal İsḳutari	Todoros Pirezvitereplo	Ḳosta Pirezvitereplo	Niḳola Maniki	Petro İstaşi
Niḳa Nikifor	Yorgi Nikifor	İstefano Lafteri	Pavlo Ḳurtik	Yorgi Şamari
Yani Ḳurtik	Yorgi Velḳaşin	Yorgi Servo	Niḳola Pirezvitereplo	bīve Pelañrin zen-i Ḳurtik

ḫāne	bīve	ḫāṣṣa-ı kenīse-i Ayo Niḳola
14	1	1

ḥāṣıl 4256

ʿa(n) ispence 356	bāġāt-ı ḫāṣṣa dönüm 19 [resm] 2280	eşcār-ı zeyt-i ḫāṣṣa ʿaded 6 [resm] 14	eşcār-ı meyve-i ḫāṣṣa ʿaded 15 [resm] 15	bāġçe-i ḫāṣṣa 1 [resm] 150

āsiyāb-ı ḫāṣṣa 2 [resm] 700	ʿöşr-i penbe 25	ʿöşr-i kettān 60	ʿöşr-i ḥınṭa 400	ʿöşr-i cev 63	ʿöşr-i bāġāt 144	resm-i ḫanāzīr 34
			resm-i ʿarūsī 15			

ḳarye-i Rovyata maʿa cemāʿat-i Niḳola Buva ve Plaşa ez cemāʿat-i Arnavudān

tīmār-ı İbrahīm[40] el-meẕkūr

Andriya İvlaḫyoti	Gin Ḳurtesi	Mirşekle Viloşi	Aḳrati Vloşi	Todoro Peliḳana
Ḳosta Muzaki	Yorgi Liḳuresi	Yorgi Ẓravoliti	Bardi Deş	Yorgi Ḳurti
Ḳosta Muzaki-i dīğer	Mirşekle Bala	Yorgi Peliḳano	Miḫal İsḳutira	Gin Bardi
Vanşi Liḳomati	Gön Saḳula	İstemati İsḳutira	Lazaro Plaş	Yorgi Muzaki
Gön Pilura	Luzi Muzaki	Yani Dravoleti	Yorgi Vendara	Tanus[41] Muzaki
Ḳineta [---]	Duşa Liḳuresi	Gin Muzaki	Todoro Maḳrişa	Domeniḳa İksano
Muriki Parapungi	Dimitri Ḳunḳuli	Yorgi Şurbi	Mesara İksanos	mücerred Gin Paliḳanos
mücerred Dima Peliḳano				

ḫāne	mücerred
34	2

63

ḥāṣıl-ı ḳarye-i Rovyata el-meẕkūr 2427

ʿa(n) ispence	ʿöşr-i penbe	ʿöşr-i kettān	ʿöşr-i ḥınṭa	ʿöşr-i cev	resm-i ḫanāzīr	resm-i ʿarūsī
720	125	80	1200	186	76	40

mezraʿa-ı Rado nezd-i ḳarye-i Rovyata el-meẕkūr   mezraʿa-ı Barçi nezd-i ḳarye-i meẕkūr

tīmār-ı İbrahīm[42] el-meẕkūr	ḫāliyye	tīmār-ı mezbūr	ḫāliyye

cemʿan tīmār-ı İbrahīm[43] el-meẕkūr

ḳurā	mezāriʿ	ḫāne	mücerred	bīve
[2]	2	48	2	1

ḥāṣıl 6683

kendü cebelü ġulām
1

tīmār-ı ʿAlī Tekkelü

ḳarye-i Ḳrapeşi ez cemāʿat-i Arnavudān   tīmār-ı ʿAlī el-meẕkūr

Duḳa Ḳrapeşi	Petro Gürḳa	Niḳola Baltavi	Miḫal Ġavri	Ḳozma Ḳuḳulo
	Proġono İşpati		ḫāne 6	

ḥāṣıl 406

ʿa(n) ispence	ʿöşr-i kettān	ʿöşr-i ḥınṭa	ʿöşr-i cev	resm-i ḫanāzīr	resm-i ʿarūsī
120	20	200	48	8	10

ḳarye-i Androniḳa ez cemāʿat-i Arnavudān   tīmār-ı ʿAlī el-mezbūr

Gön Androniḳa	Niḳola Androniḳa	Dima Androniḳa	Petro İsḳutari	Gin İsḳutari
Y[o]rg[i] İsḳutari	Niḳola İsḳutari	Niḳola Rafti	[Yo]rgi Rafti	Miḫal Papayanoplo
	To[do]ros Papayanoplo	Yani İsḳutari	ḫāne 12	

64

ḥāṣıl-ı ḳarye-i Androniḳa el-meẕkūr 1197

ʿa(n) ispence	bāġāt-ı ḫāṣṣa dönüm 1 [resm]	ʿöşr-i kettān	ʿöşr-i ḥınṭa	ʿöşr-i cev	resm-i ḫanāzīr	ʿöşr-i bāġāt
240	240	40	500	79	19	64

resm-i
ʿarūsī
15

ḳarye-i Niḳola Ḳumi ez cemāʿat-i Arnavudān tīmār-ı ʿAlī el-mezbūr

Niḳola el-meẕkūr	Yorgi Peta	Ġolomi Pulimano	Miḫal Ġurya	Domeniḳa Ḳravari
İstemad Çenḳaruli	Lazaro Penati	Angelo İstrovini		

ḫāne 8

ḥāṣıl 936

ʿa(n) ispence	ʿöşr-i kettān	ʿöşr-i ḥınṭa	ʿöşr-i cev	resm-i ḫanāzīr	resm-i ʿarūsī
160	30	600	91	45	10

cemʿan tīmār-ı ʿAlī Tekkelü el-meẕkūr

ḳurā 3 ḫāne 26

ḥāṣıl 2539

kendü eşer

tīmār-ı Andriya Fenarī maʿa birāẕereş Yorgi müşterek be-nevbet

ḳarye-i Pendeni maʿa cemāʿat-i Palunbi İpşari ez cemāʿat-i Arnavudān

Gön Ḳarlaremi	Dima Ḳarlaremi	Domeniḳa Ḳalifoni	Serakin	Yorgi Ḳatalani

ḫāne 5

ḥāṣıl 283

ʿa(n) ispence	ʿöşr-i ḥınṭa	ʿöşr-i cev	resm-i ʿarūsī
100	150	23	10

65 blank

66

kendü	geçim	cebelü	çadır	tenktür
bürüme	1	10	1	1

zeʿāmet-i Ġardicḳo zaʿīmeş Sinān Ġaşır Beg veled-i Süleymān Beg bin Ẕū'l-ḳādir

nefs-i Ġardicḳo ḫāṣṣa-ı zaʿīm

Miḫal Evorondino	Yani Proḳas̱imeno	Yorgi veled-i o	Manol Proḳas̱imenos	Yani veled-i o
Duḳa Ḳamuna	Protopapa Kiryaniti	Miḫal Nomiḳos	S̱oma birāẕer-i o	Dimitri birāẕer-i o
S̱otoki Ẕerḳaẕi	Yorgi Mala	Yani Akindino	Ḳosta Proḳas̱imeno	Dimitri veled-i o
İstefano Ḳordonis	Yorgi Ḳandruli	Yani veled-i o	Niḳola veled-i o	Todoros Proḳas̱imenos
Todoros Ḳavuçi	Dimitri veled-i o	Yani veled-i o	Sirvo Rafti	Ḳosta Ḳaltizaniti
Andon Ḳondro	Manol Ḫandruli	Yorgi Martin	Ḳosta Ḳaloyira	Dimitri Covani
Dimitri Foti	Vars̱alemos Piros	Yani birāder-i o	Aleksi Papayanoplo	Ḳosta Ḳosovya
Yani birāder-i o	Yani Kefala	Niḳola Patari	Yani İvrato	Todoros Momos
Niḳola Aġraẕyoti	Dimitri Ḳoḳoviça	Todoros Germocaniti	S̱otoki Moloḫi	Yorgi Moloḫi
Petro [M]anoloplo	Niḳola Çeponi	Todoros Ḳavuçi	Yorgi Ḳaḳomanol	Yani veled-i o
Todoros Ḫarkâs	Niḳolas Ḫarkâs	Petro birāẕer-i o	Yani Niḳoloplo	Manol Ḳaḳomanol
Marti Liḳo	Ḳosta birāder-i o	Manol Avriyoni	Todoros Armiros	Yorgi Monaġriẕa
Dimitri Ḳaryano	S̱otoki Mirali	S̱otoki Suḳara	Miḫal Ṣarando	Niḳola birāẕer-i o
Yani Ḳaloyira	İstas̱i Papayanoplo	Manol Pavlo	Yorgi veled-i o	Andon İspanoplo
Yani birāẕer-i o	Niḳola Prastetoplo	İstilyano Papaẕato	Miḫal Covani	Niḳola Ravis̱i
Ḳosta Petriti	Lazaros Ḳandrolis	Yorgi Foti	Niḳola Tiryo	Andon Ḳaliva
Yorgi Ḳaloyira	Yani Ẕiyaksenos	Ḳosta Peratiḳos	Andriya Manoloplo	Yani Ḳutruli

67

tetimme-i nefs-i Ġardicḳo el-meẕkūr ḫāṣṣa-ı zaʿīm

Yani Plaḳas	İstemad Trikâfelo	Todoros İsḳaryanos	Yani Robi	Yorgi Ḳamuna
Gin Nomiḳo	Ḳosta veled-i Martin	Ḳosta Peri	keşiş[44] Nofitos Ḳaloyiros	Dimitri Ḳoraḳa
Dimitri Mayndos	İstemad Kefalino	Andriya Vuçara	Dimitri Marmara	Dimitri Ḳaçulis

Yorgi Yerardo	Petro Zonara	Manol S̱alali	Todoros Vuçara	Ḳosta Moloḫi
Dimitri Pasenoviti	Yorgi Papaẕato	Niḳola Moloḫi	Dimitri Baştardo	Andon Ḳapardi
Yorgi Ḳaçari	Dimitri Randona	Niḳola Liḳuẕi	Ḳosta Randona	Papayani Zoġrafo
Aleksi Pavlos	Miḫal Trikâfelo	Niḳola Ḫarara	Todoro Yafra	Yani Zerḳadi
Miḫal birāder-i o	Ḳosta Lora	Niḳola Covani	Dimitri İskina	Yani Aẕyani
Reçi ki nezd-i Aresti mī-şeved	Yani Ḳoḳali	Todoro Ḫırisiḳo	Papas Nomiḳos	Todoros Ḫaleli
Niḳola Maẕiḳo	Yorgi Pateri	İstematiḳo İslaviçi	Andon Martin	S̱otoki Kipriyano
Dimitri Ḳaḳomanol	Vaşıl Ḳaḳomanol	Todoros Onbrali	Dimitri Ḳamana	Manol Ḳosti
S̱otoki Poliğiri	Niḳola Çeponi	Yorgi Paştardo Evorondino	İstemad Miḫaliç	Yani Peliḳani
Yadriḳo Miziṣra'i	Yorgi Todoros	Niḳola Ḳaloyoro	Manol İskavriya	Dimitri veled-i S̱otoki Onbrali
S̱oẕos	mücerred Dimitri Evorondino	mücerred Miḫal birāder-i o	mücerred Niḳola birāẕer-i o	mücerred Yorgi Ḳamuna
mücerred Yani Ẕerḳaẕi	mücerred Yorgi Proḳaṣimeno	mücerred Yani Ḳordonis	mücerred S̱otoki birāder-i o	mücerred Dimitri Martin
mücerred Yorgi Foti	mücerred Manol Moloḫi	mücerred Niḳola birāẕer-i Ḫarkâ	mücerred Dimitri Mirali	mücerred Dimitri Suḳara
mücerred Andriya Ḳ[o]ro[n]i	mücerred Yorgi birāẕer-i o	mücerred Manol Evorondino	mücerred Yani besleme-i Evorondino	bīve Ḳatarina zen-i Ḳaletranitisa

68

tetimme-i nefs-i Ġardicḳo el-meẕkūr — ḫāṣṣa-ı zaʿīm

bīve Yorġo zen-i Ḳavurya	bīve Elani zen-i Marula	bīve Papayanopulya	bīve [zen-i] Manol Ḳaçuli	bīve Çeponina
bīve Runbina	bīve [zen-i] Vaşıl Ḳapardi	bīve zen-i Dimitri	bīve zen-i Yorgi	bīve Ḫırisikina

bīve Monaġriẕya — ḫāne 151 — mücerred 18 — bīve 12

ḫāṣıl 21828

ʿa(n) ispence 4297	bāġāt-ı ḫāṣṣa dönüm 21 [resm] 3960	eşcār-ı ṭut-ı ḫāṣṣa ʿaded 125 [resm] 300	eşcār-ı meyve-i ḫāṣṣa ʿaded 36 [resm] 70	āsiyāb-ı ḫāṣṣa 1 [resm] 300

ʿöşr-i bāġāt 5376	ʿöşr-i ḥınṭa 6000	ʿöşr-i cev 918	ʿöşr-i ḳazz 97	ʿöşr-i zeyt 8	ʿöşr-i meyve 40	resm-i ḫanāzīr 32

resm-i niyābet 220	mülk-i Niḳola birāẕer-i Dimitri Evorondino der ḳarye-i meẕkūr āsiyāb-ı ġalle 1 resm 80 āsiyāb-ı peşmīne 2 resm 30	mülk-i Yani Proḳaṣimeno der ḳarye-i meẕkūr āsiyāb 1 resm 80	mülk-i Ḳozma kemḫācı[45] der ḳarye-i meẕkūr āsiyāb-ı peşmīne 1 resm 20

nāḥiyyet-i Ġardicḳo

ḳarye-i İvlanduşa ez cemāʿat-i Arnavudān — ḫāṣṣa-ı zaʿīm

Ḳozma İvlanduşa	Gin İvlanduşa	Dimo İvlanduşa	Ḳozma-ı dīğer İvlanduşa	Miraş İvlanduşa

ḫāne 5

ḫāṣıl 284

ʿa(n) ispence 100	öşr-i ḥınṭa 150	ʿöşr-i cev 24	resm-i ʿarūsī 10

ḳarye-i Ranesi ez cemāʿat-i Arnavudān — ḫāṣṣa-ı zaʿīm

Niḳola Ranesi	Ḳuvara birāder-i o	Gin Bami	Gön birāder-i o	İştin Canata
Gön birāder-i o	Gön Ranesi	Yorgi Geta	Gön veled-i o	Marti veled-i o
Andriya Ġamra	Gön veled-i o	Todoros veled-i o	Leḳa Barça	Todoros birāẕer-i o

69

tetimme-i ḳarye-i Ranesi el-meẕkūr — ḫāṣṣa-ı zaʿīm

Ḳozma Yuvani	Gin birāder-i o	Petro İstratira	Yorgi birāder-i o	Niḳola Yuvani

Miḫal Süleġati	Ḳozma Süleġati	Miḫal birāder-i o	Yorgi Geta	Gön veled-i o
Leḳa Barçi	Pavlo Ranesi	Yorgi veled-i o	Gön Muṣura	Ḳosta Ranesi
Yorgi Maj[i]	Martes Alaġatori	Pavlos Ḳalusi	Niḳola Barçi	Todoros Orfanos
Petro Liẕiḳa	Ḳosta Yuvani	Pavlos Ġamras	Todoros veled-i Gön Ranesi	Pavlos Ḳoza
Vas̱is birāder-i Ḳozma Livan	Niḳola anebsosti Niḳola Livan	Lazaro birāẕer-i Ankinita	Niḳola Orfano	Palunbi Ẕokâno
Pavlos birāder-i Palunbi	Marti anebsosti Ḳosta Ranesi	Yorgi Ġamra	Niḳola anebsosti Barçi	Ḳosta Lukişta
Petro Lukişta	Miḫal Orfano	Gin veled-i Pavlo Ranesi	Gin Narenca	Domeniḳa ḫīş-i Yani
Gin ḫīş-i Ġamra	Miḫa Livani	Martin veled-i Leḳa	Petros ḫīş-i Yani	mücerred Todoros Barçi
mücerred Pavlos Ḳavalari	bīve Neranca zen-i Palunbi	bīve [zen-i] Leḳa Ranesi	bīve Ḳavalarina	bīve Ẕokâna

ḫāne	mücerred	bīve
59	2	4

ḥāṣıl 3448

ʿa(n) ispence	ʿöşr-i ḥınṭa	ʿöşr-i cev	resm-i ḫanāzīr	ʿöşr-i bāġāt	resm-i ʿarūsī	ʿöşr-i kettān
1244	1600	248	9	192	55	100

ḳarye-i Ġomosto ez cemāʿat-i Arnavudān — ḫāṣṣa-ı zaʿīm

Yorgi Ġomosto	Dimitri veled-i o	İstemad veled-i o	Niḳola Yemişto	S̱otoki dāmād-ı o
Petro Yemişto	Manol Yemişto	Niḳola Yemişto	İstemad birāẕer-i o	Ḳozma Rado
Lazaro Ġomosto	Miḫal Ġomosto	Andriza dāmād-ı Manol	Domeniḳa veled-i Menol[46]	Yorgi veled-i Niḳola Ġomosto
Miḫal İstoyan	Todoros veled-i Yorgi Ġomosto		ḫāne 17	

ḥāṣıl 999

ʿa(n) ispence	ʿöşr-i ḥınṭa	ʿöşr-i cev	ʿöşr-i bāġāt	resm-i ʿarūsī	ʿöşr-i kettān
340	500	77	32	20	30

70
tetimme-i nāḥiyyet-i Ġardicḳo

ḳarye-i [Ṣ]uli ez cemāʿat-i Arnavudān — ḫāṣṣa-ı zaʿīm

Todoro Ṣuli	Ḳosta veled-i o	Mangişa Rapesi	Gin Orfano	Dima Ṣ[u]li
Gin Ḫayḳal	Ḫondro Miḫal	Gön Başi	Gin-i dīğer Orfano	Ḳosta-ı d[ī]ğer Ṣ[u]li
mücerred Dimo Rapesi	mücerred Yani Ḫondromiḫal		ḫāne 10	mücerred 2

ḥāṣıl 723

ʿa(n) ispence	ʿöşr-i ḥınṭa	ʿöşr-i cev	resm-i ḫanāzīr	resm-i ʿarūsī
240	400	63	10	10

ḳarye-i Gön Lopesi ez cemāʿat-i Arnavudān — ḫāṣṣa-ı zaʿīm

Gön el-meẕkūr	Todoros veled-i o	Andriya Lopesi	Yorgi Lopesi	Leḳa Lopesi
İştin veled-i Yorgi Lopesi	Ḳozma Barşi	Mila Suli	Ḳozma veled-i Ḫondromiḫal	Reçi Lopesi
		ḫāne 10		

ḥāṣıl 561

ʿa(n) ispence	ʿöşr-i ḥınṭa	ʿöşr-i cev	resm-i ḫanāzīr	resm-i ʿarūsī
200	300	48	3	10

ḳarye-i Çapoġa ez cemāʿat-i Arnavudān — ḫāṣṣa-ı zaʿīm

Matesi Çapoġa	Dima birāẕer-i o	Petro Malayoti	Seni birāẕer-i o	S̱oma Çapoġa
Niḳola Biçi	Gin birāẕer-i o	Yorgi Peçali	Dima Peta	İstefano birāẕer-i o
Andriya Ḳuralisa	Gin Çapoġa	Gin Ḳoryazi	Gin Biç	Yani Lopesi
Gin Briḫti	Gön Biçi	Yorgi Malayoti	Yorgi Virviri	Todoros proġonostu Andra

Muriki Ḳonduta	Niḳola Peta	Papas Andra	Manol veled-i o	Niḳola Lopesi
Meşili Çapoġa	Dima birāder-i Manesi Çapoġa	mücerred Niḳola Virviri	bīve Ḳali zen-i Virvira	bīve Buja zen-i Küraleş

ḫāne	mücerred	bīve
27	1	2

ḥāṣıl 1806

ʿa(n) ispence	ʿöşr-i ḥınṭa	ʿöşr-i cev	ʿöşr-i bāġāt	resm-i ḫanāzīr	resm-i ʿarūsī	ʿöşr-i ke[tt]ān
572	800	128	160	26	30	50

mülk-i
Matesi Çapoġa der ḳarye-i meẕkūr
āsiyāb 1 resm 40

71
tetimme-i nāḥiyyet-i Ġardicḳo

ḳarye-i İvlaḫo ez cemāʿat-i Arnavudān — ḫāṣṣa-ı zaʿīm

Manol S̱eryano	Niḳola Pernebe	Niḳola Todoras	S̱oma Franḳa	Aleksi veled-i o
Yani Pernardo	S̱eryanos İksanos	Yorgi veled-i Berba	Dimitri veled-i S̱oma İvlaḫo	Palunbi birāẕer-i o
Yorgi Ḳalanci	Gin Ḳozma	Miḫal Vardusi	Petro S̱eryano	Ḳozma Rado

ḫāne 15

ḥāṣıl 866

ʿa(n) ispence	ʿöşr-i ḥınṭa	ʿöşr-i cev	resm-i ʿarūsī	ʿöşr-i kettān
300	450	71	15	30

ḳarye-i Maji ez cemāʿat-i Arnavudān — ḫāṣṣa-ı zaʿīm

Uzġur Maji	Gin Maji	Andriya Maji	Niḳola birāẕer-i o	Todoro Çimiri
Gin veled-i o	Andriya Zapandi	Ḳosta birāder-i o	Yorgi Livari	Niḳola Dimitriçi
Todoro Ġato	Gön Maji	Ḳozma Maji	Yorgi İstatoplo[47]	Ḳosta Zapandi
Miḫal Plaşa	Niḳola İstas̱oplo	Yorgi İstas̱oplo	Dimitriçi dāmād-ı Maji	Leḳa Maji

Andriya proġonostu Liveri	Dimitri Çimiri	Manol Ġato	Dimitri Turnari	ḫāne 24

ḥāṣıl 1600

ʿa(n) ispence	ʿöşr-i bāġāt	ʿöşr-i ḥınṭa	ʿöşr-i cev	resm-i ʿarūsī	ʿöşr-i kettān
480	160	750	115	25	30

mülk-i
Uzġur Maji
der ḳarye-i meẕkūr
āsiyāb 1 resm 40

ḳarye-i Mastro Andoni ez cemāʿat-i Arnavudān — ḫāṣṣa-ı zaʿīm

Gön Mastroandon	Pavlo Turnari	Yorgi Bicano	Gin İşpata	Yorgi Mastroandon
Gön İstilyano	Gin Vodino	Andon Mastroandon	Yani Turnari	Gin Ḳuraleş
Dima Voẕinos	Niḳola Turnari	Todoros Bejani	Andriya Turnari	Niḳola İşpata
Pavlos Kriyobardis	Miḫa İşpata	Niḳola Mastroandon	Yorgi Ḳaloyoro	Uzġur Mastroandon

bīve Yara Nerena

ḫāne	bīve
20	1

ḥāṣıl 1192

ʿa(n) ispence	ʿöşr-i bāġāt	ʿöşr-i ḥınṭa	ʿöşr-i cev	resm-i ʿarūsī
406	128	550	84	24

72
tetimme-i nāḥiyyet-i Ġardicḳo

ḳarye-i Barbuc ez cemāʿat-i Arnavudān — ḫāṣṣa-ı zaʿīm

Pavlo Barbuc	Andriya veled-i o	Yorgi veled-i o	Yorgi Barbuc	Pavlos veled-i o
Niḳola Ḳlaẕi	Yorgi Ḳanburi	Pavlos-ı dīğer Barbuc	Yorgi Iġrasiça	Gön Barbuc
Petro Ġrasiça	Boḫali birāẕer-i o	Yorgi Iġrasiça	Duḳa veled-i Manḳolena	Gin birāder-i Ḳlaẕi
Ḳosta veled-i Yorgi Barbuc	Yorgi Ġulami	Domeniḳa Orfano	Todoros veled-i Yorgi Ḳanburi	Niḳola Vlasi
Mangişa Ḳrasiça	Yorgi Zoġa	Domeniḳa Ḳrasiça	Gön Barbuc	Dimitri Zoġa

Todoros Duḳa	Gin Zoġa	mücerred Gürḳa Barbuc	bīve Manḳolena	Marti Ḳrasiça		
Dima veled-i o	Duḳa Ḳrasiça	Marḳo Ḳrasiça	Todoro Ḳrasiça	ḫāne 32	mücerred 1	bīve 1

ḥāṣıl 1911

ʿa(n) ispence 666	ʿöşr-i ḥınṭa 1000	ʿöşr-i cev 155	resm-i ʿarūsī 40	ʿöşr-i kettān 50

ḳarye-i S̱opiya ez cemāʿat-i Arnavudān ḫāṣṣa-ı zaʿīm

Pavlo S̱opiya	Gin Ranesi	Yorgi birāẕer-i o	Gin S̱opiya	Andriya Ranesi	
Yorgi Zoġa	Rado veled-i o	Ẕiyaleşi birāẕer-i Ranesi	bīve Ranasina	ḫāne 8	bīve 1

ḥāṣıl 462

ʿa(n) ispence 166	ʿöşr-i ḥınṭa 250	ʿöşr-i cev 38	resm-i ʿarūsī 8

ḳarye-i Lopesi ez cemāʿat-i Arnavudān ḫāṣṣa-ı zaʿīm

Mangişa Buvaşi	Domeniḳa Ḳuço	Muriki veled-i o	Leḳa veled-i o	Yani Jupano
Todoro Lata	Gin birāder-i o	Niḳola Ḫarara	Andriya As̱anas	Dimitri Ḳuvara
Eksa- zaḫtulos[48]	Muriki Mavromati	Trusa Tirbesi	Marti Şalesi	mücerred Dimitri Gerbesi
	bīve Manḳa zen-i Gerbesi	ḫāne 14	mücerred 1	bīve 1

ḥāṣıl 929

ʿa(n) ispence 306	ʿöşr-i ḥınṭa 500	ʿöşr-i cev 80	resm-i ḫanāzīr 8	resm-i ʿarūsī 15	ʿöşr-i kettān 20

73
tetimme-i nāḥiyyet-i Ġardicḳo

ḳarye-i Simoplu ez cemāʿat-i Arnavudān ḫāṣṣa-ı zaʿīm

Todoro Dramesi	Petro Zuġra	Yorgi Todoroplo	Yorgi Ḳataḳalo	Niḳola İsbe<ni>ca
Dimitri Draġona	Ḳuḳo Vuyvundo	Yorgi Dramesi	Mangişa Zuġra	Niḳola Todoroplo
[Ḳur]tesi dāmād-ı Simolena	Pavlos birāẕer-i İspaniça	bīve Simolena	bīve Zoġrafo	bīve Ḳozma Ẕiyaleşi
bīve Dramena		ḫāne 12	bīve 4	

ḥāṣıl 766

ʿa(n) ispence 264	ʿöşr-i kettān 20	ʿöşr-i ḥınṭa 400	ʿöşr-i cev 64	resm-i ḫanāzīr 3	resm-i ʿarūsī 15

ḳarye-i Ḳalanci ez cemāʿat-i Arnavudān ḫāṣṣa-ı zaʿīm

Gin Ḳalanci	Asani Ḳalanci	Rapi Demiri	Andriya Ḳalanci	Ḳalanci Ẕiyaleşi
Laluḳa Ḳalanci	Dimitri Ḳalanci		ḫāne 7	

ḥāṣıl 442

ʿa(n) ispence 140	ʿöşr-i ḥınṭa 250	ʿöşr-i cev 40	resm-i ḫanāzīr 2	resm-i ʿarūsī 10

ḳarye-i İsliva ez cemāʿat-i Arnavudān ḫāṣṣa-ı zaʿīm

Yorgi İsliva	Gin Ḳumi	Gön İsliva	Todoro Leoplo	Leḳa Bala
Yorgi Peta	Gön Peta	Niḳola Lopesi	İstefano Lonc	Gön İsliva-ı dīğer
Andriya Plaşa	Ḳosta İsliva	Gön Ḳumi	Petro Gönec	Niḳola İsliva
Duşa İsliva	Todoros Leoplo	bīve Panya zen-i İsliva	ḫāne 17	bīve 1

ḥāṣıl 1102

ʿa(n) ispence 346	ʿöşr-i kettān 25	ʿöşr-i ḥınṭa 600	ʿöşr-i cev 94	resm-i ḫanāzīr 17	resm-i ʿarūsī 20

ḳarye-i Şaleşi ez cemāʿat-i Arnavudān ḫāṣṣa-ı zaʿīm

Andriya Şaleşi	Gin Glaşira	Petro Şaleşi	Gön Şalesi	Petro Şalesi
İşt[in] Glasira	ḫāne 6			

ḥāṣıl 361

ʿa(n) ispence 120	ʿöşr-i ḥınṭa 200	ʿöşr-i cev 31	resm-i ʿarūsī 10

74
tetimme-i nāḥiyyet-i Ġ[ardi]cḳo

ḳarye-i Lala ez cemāʿat-i Arnavudān — ḫāṣṣa-ı zaʿīm

Gin Ḳaḳruḳa	Domeniḳa İsḳupa	Dima İsḳupa	Niḳola Lata	Petros Ranesi
Gön birāder-i o	Gin İstruza	Ḳozma Ḳuçi	ḫāne 8	

ḥāṣıl 453

ʿa(n) ispence 160	ʿöşr-i ḥınṭa 250	ʿöşr-i cev 43

ḳarye-i Gerbeşi[49] ez cemāʿat-i Arnavudān — ḫāṣṣa-ı zaʿīm

Martin Şalesi	Yorgi Ḫaraḳtino	Trusa İksano	Niḳola Lopesi	Mangişa Burleşa
Todoro Jupano	Yorgi proġonostu Domeniḳa	Dimitri proġonostu Domeniḳa	Miḫal Ḫaraḳtino	ḫāne 9

ḥāṣıl 538

ʿa(n) ispence 180	ʿöşr-i ḥınṭa 300	ʿöşr-i cev 48	resm-i ʿarūsī 10

ḳarye-i İsturġova — ḫāṣṣa-ı zaʿīm

Petro İstrongilo	Todoros Ḳolotiri	Vaşıl Maṣa	Miḫal Ġaralanbo	Aleksi Muyi
Yani veled-i Martin	mücerred Yani Ġaralanbo	mücerred Palunbi Ġaralanbo	ḫāne 6	mücerred 2

ḥāṣıl 768

ʿa(n) ispence 200	bāġāt-ı ḫāṣṣa dönüm 1 [resm] 112	eşcār-ı meyve-i ḫāṣṣa ʿaded 44 [resm] 100	eşcār-ı ṭut-ı ḫāṣṣa ʿaded 81 [resm] 120	ʿöşr-i ḥınṭa 100	ʿöşr-i cev 15
	ʿöşr-i meyve 58	ʿöşr-i ḳazz 63			

mezraʿa-ı Rozinotiḫo tābiʿ-i Ġardicḳo el-mezḳūr — ḫāṣṣa-ı zaʿīm

ḫāliyye

mezraʿa-ı Ḳumi tābiʿ-i o ḫāṣṣa-ı zaʿīm

ḫāliyye

mezraʿa-ı İsliva-ı dīğer tābiʿ-i o ḫāṣṣa-ı zaʿīm

ḫāliyye

cemʿan ḫāṣṣhā-<yı> subaşı-ı Ġardicḳo el-mezḳūr

ḳurā maʿa nefs-i Ġardicḳo	mezāriʿ-i ḫāliyye	ḫāne	mücerred	bīve
20	3	457	27	27

ḥāṣıl 41039

75
tetimme-i nāḥiyyet-i Ġardicḳo

kendüler bürüme	ġulām	tenktür
	1	1

tīmār-ı ġarīb yiğitlerden Aḥmed Simġārī ve Ḳaraca Aġa ki müşterek yiyüb ikisi bile eşer

ḳarye-i İstamiro — tīmār-ı mezḳūrān

Niḳola Mastro-manoplo	Todoros birāder-i o	Andriya Paromariti	Domeniḳa birāder-i o	Ḳosta Maṣulino
Leo birāẕer-i o	Dimitri İstematiḳo	Yani Mavruçi	Yani Rina	Niḳola Raviṣi
İstemad Rujo	Niḳola Ḳoruḳo	Angelo Ḳapudan	Miḫal Şaluri	Yani-i dīğer Mavruçi
Yorgi Çivra	Yorgi Flasḳonburo	Yorgi Lanco	Niḳola Ḳratiḳo	Yani Ẓuḳata
Yorgi Ẓuḳata	Manol Petritari	Petros Petritari	Andriya Petritari	Petros Petritari
mücerred Manṣos Raviṣi	mücerred İstefano Varpongi	bīve Mariça zen-i Valṣemo	bīve Elani zen-i Makiẕina	

cemāʿat-i çeltükciyān der ḳarye-i mezḳūr — ḫāne 15

Muriki Kiziḳuma	Andriya Varsama	Ḳosta Çivra	Yani veled-i o	Yani Çivra
Ḳosta birāder-i o	Papaniḳola Varirvi	Ḳosta veled-i o	Ḳosta Marti	Yani veled-i o
Gön Vaşıl	Niḳola Vari	Vaşıl Şupaki	Dimitri Varipongi	İstefano veled-i o
	ḫāne maʿa çeltükciyān 40	mücerred 2	bīve 2	

ḥāṣıl 5172

ʿa(n) ispence 1062	āsiyāb-ı ḫāṣṣa 1 [resm] 250	nıṣf-ı āsiyāb-ı ḫāṣṣa 1 [resm] 125	bāġāt-ı ḫāṣṣa dönüm 6 [resm] 720	eşcār-ı zeyt-i ḫāṣṣa ʿaded 12 [resm] 23

ʿöşr-i penbe 40	bostān-ı ḫāṣṣa 1 [resm] 100	ʿöşr-i kettān 100	ʿöşr-i bāġāt 778	ʿöşr-i ḥınṭa 1550	ʿöşr-i cev 236	ʿöşr-i zeyt 33
		ʿöşr-i meyve 5	resm-i ḫamr 100	resm-i ʿarūsī 50		

76
tetimme-i nā[ḥ]iyyet-i Ġardicḳ[o]

kendü bürüme	cebelü 1	ġulām 1	tenktür 1

tīmār-ı ġarīb yiğitlerden Ṭāhir veled-i Seyf

ḳarye-i Mazarak maʿa cemāʿat-i Ḳuçi ez cemāʿat-i Arnavudān tīmār-ı Ṭāhir el-meẕkūr

Gin Mazarak	İstefano Mazarak	Muriki veled-i o	Gin Mazarak-i dīğer	Marti Mazarak	
Andriya Mazarak	Ḳaḳusi	Yorgi Ḳuça	Todoros İştopanṣi	Yorgi Şulani	
Petros Ḳumis	Petro Ḳumi-i dīğer	Ḳaratula Mazarak	Andriya Suleni	Aleksi S[ulen]i	
Biçi Ḳumi	Andriya Zapandi	Todoros Zapandi	Niḳola Ḫarara	Mastr[o]-miḫa[l] Ḫarara	
bīve Manḳa zen-i Mazaraki	bīve zen-i Leo	bīve Luḳa zen-i Ḳuçi	bīve Güra Petrena	ḫāne 20	bīve 4

ḥāṣıl 1135

ʿa(n) ispence 424	ʿöşr-i ḥınṭa 600	ʿöşr-i cev 94	resm-i ḫanāzīr 2	resm-i ʿarūsī 15

ḳarye-i Manesi ez cemāʿat-i Arnavudān tīmār-ı Ṭāhir el-meẕkūr

Yorgi Manesi	Gin birāder-i o	Gin Manesi	Niḳola Manesi	Aġali Manesi
Dima Manesi	Aġali Ḳuçi	Gin Ḳuçi	Leḳa Rafti	Yorgi Lata
Lazaro Lata	Petro birāẕer-i o	Niḳola Lata	Dima Laḳa	Lazaro Lata-ı dīğer
Gin birāder-i Nayib	Yorgi Lata	Lazaro birāẕer-i Yorgi Lata	Gin birāder-i o	ḫāne 19

ḥāṣıl 1092

ʿa(n) ispence 380	ʿöşr-i ḥınṭa 600	ʿöşr-i cev 92	resm-i ʿarūsī 20

ḳarye-i Ẕirmi ez cemāʿat-i Arnavudān tīmār-ı Ṭāhir el-mezbūr

Andriya Ẕirmi	Muriki Zula	Yorgi Petroplos	Ḳozma Maji	Yorgi Anamiçi	
Marti Frati	Yorgi Ḫarkâ	Yorgi Ḫarkâ-<yı> dīğer	Lazaro Frati	[M]a[r]ti Fra[ti-i] [dī]ğer	
Petro Plaşa	Dimos Zula	Yani Ḫıristiyani	bīve [Pe]tropulya	ḫāne 1[3]	bīve 1

ḥāṣıl 851

ʿa(n) ispence 266	ʿöşr-i ḥı[n]ṭa 450	ʿöşr-i cev 70	resm-i ḫanāzīr 10	resm-i ʿarūsī 15	mülk-i Andriya Ẕirmi der ḳarye-i meẕkūr āsiyāb 1 resm 40

77
tetimme-i nāḥiyyet-i Ġardicḳo

ḳarye-i Ḫarkâ ez cemāʿat-i Arnavudān tīmār-ı Ṭāhir el-meẕkūr

Mastro Y[or]gi	Lazaro veled-i o	Perdano veled-i o	Niḳola Ḫarkâ	Lazaro Biçi
Man[o]l Biç[i]	Pilura Ḳuçi	Proġonos	Leḳa Biçi	ḫāne 9

ḥāṣıl 480

ʿa(n) ispence 180	ʿöşr-i ḥınṭa 250	ʿöşr-i cev 40	resm-i ʿarūsī 10

ḳarye-i [Mihi]li ez cemāʿat-i Arnavudān tābiʿ-i Vumero tīmār-ı Ṭāhir el-mezbūr

Andriya [---]ya	Todoros Polotira	Palunbi İẕini	İstefano İstrati	Niḳola Politi
Pavlos Ṣotoki	mücerred İştini Polotira	mücerred Petro Borşa	ḫāne 6	mücerred 2

ḥāṣıl 452

ʿa(n) ispence	ʿöşr-i penbe	ʿöşr-i kettān	ʿöşr-i ḥınṭa	ʿöşr-i cev	resm-i ʿarūsī
160	20	30	200	32	10

cemʿan tīmār-ı Ṭāhir el-meẕkūr

ḳurā	ḫāne	mücerred	bīve
5	67	2	5

ḥāṣıl 4010

kendü cebelü	ġulām
	1

tīmār-ı ġarīb yiğitlerden Meḥmed veled-i Alagöz

ḳarye-i Maẕiñik ez cemāʿat-i Arnavudān — tīmār-ı Meḥmed el-meẕkūr

Yan[i] İ[---]ti	Dima Ḳaluta	Todor Avrana	Gin Maẕiñik	Martin Ḳaluta
	Ṣotoki Marḳuçi	Yorgi Maẕiñik	mücerred Marḳuçi	bīve Todora zen-i Yavirna

cemāʿat-i çeltü[kciyān] der ḳarye-i meẕkūr — [ḫ]āne 4

Miḫal [Ḳ]oças	Ṣotoki birāder-i [o]	Yani Ḳal[a] mira	Yorgi Ḳurtiḳ[a]

ḫāne maʿa çeltükciyān	mücerred	bīve
11	1	1

78

ḥāṣıl-ı ḳarye-i Maẕiñik el-meẕkūr 604

ʿa(n) ispence	ʿöş[r-i] ḥınṭ[a]	ʿöşr-i cev	resm-i ʿarūsī
246	300	48	10

ḳarye-i Ranbiyaḳa ez cemāʿat-i Arnavudān — tīmār-ı Meḥmed [el-meẕkūr]

Domeniḳa Ranbiyaḳa	Dima Dorza	Petro İflamurari	Gön Ranbiyaḳa	[Yani] İ[---]
Bardi Ḳumi	Dimitri Mamula	Ḳalifoni	Perinos İksanos	bīve Ç[---]

ḫāne	bīve
9	1

ḥāṣıl 701

ʿa(n) ispence	ʿöşr-i ḥınṭa	ʿöşr-i cev	resm-i ḫanāzīr	resm-i ʿarūsī	mülk-i Domeniḳa Ranbiya[ḳa] der ḳarye-i meẕ[kūr] āsiyāb 1 resm 40
186	400	63	2	10	

ḳarye-i Liḳuresi maʿa cemāʿat-i Bura ez cemāʿat-i Arnavudān — tīmār-ı Meḥmed el-mezbūr

İvrato Ḳaloyiri	Gön Maji	Petro Dorza	Niḳola Naja	Ḳalanca Liḳuresi
Yorgi Mavri	Dima birāder-i o	Ḳosta Ranesi	Yorgi Ranesi	Ḳosta veled-i o
Duḳa Ranesi	Lazaro Liḳuresi	Petro Bura	Dima Ranesi	Gön Bura
Pelañrin Matesi	Niḳola Draġa	Yorgi Manḳola		ḫāne 18

ḥāṣıl 1053

ʿa(n) ispence	ʿöşr-i ḥınṭa	ʿöşr-i cev	resm-i ḫanāzīr	ʿöşr-i bāġāt	resm-i ʿarūsī
360	550	83	10	35	15

mezraʿa-ı Ranesi nezd-i ḳarye-i meẕkūr — tīmār-ı Meḥmed el-mezbūr

ḫāliyye

cemʿan tīmār-ı Meḥmed el-masṭūr

ḳurā	mezraʿa-ı ḫāliyye	ḫāne	mücerred	bīve
3	1	38	1	2

ḥāṣıl 2358

79

tetimme-i nāḥiyyet-i Ġardicḳo

kendü cebelü	ġulām
	1

tīmār-ı ġarīb yiğitlerden Umūr veled-i Devlet Paşa

ḳarye-i Fil Adrofinos maʿa cemāʿat-i Muzak ez cemāʿat-i Arnavudān — tīmār-ı meẕkūr

Gön Fil Adrofino	Gön Franḳa	Yorgi veled-i o	Plaşa veled-i o	Domeniḳa Ġosti
Andriya Vestriti	Petro birāẕer-i o	Martin Damija	Andriya Franḳa	Lazaro Pendeni

Dima Muzaki	Aleksi Muzaki	Aleksi-i dīğer Muzaki	Petro Muzaki	Petro Ḳuşuti
Gin Fil Adrofino	Yorgi Fil Adrofino	Ġlava İstasino	Yani Plaşa	mücerred Ġlava Fil Adrofino
Yani Plaşa	bīve Petropulya	ḫāne 20	mücerred 1	bīve 1

ḥāṣıl 1195

ʿa(n) ispence 426	ʿöşr-i ḥınṭa 600	ʿöşr-i cev 93	resm-i ḫanāzīr 16	resm-i ʿarūsī 20	mülk-i Fil Adrofino der ḳarye-i mez̠kūr āsiyāb 1 resm 40

ḳarye-i Malaḳas ez cemāʿat-i Arnavudān tīmār-ı Umūr el-mez̠kūr

Yorgi Malaḳas	Niḳola Malaḳas	Suya Malaḳas	Gin Meliti	Dimitri Meliti
Martin Şara	Gön Malaḳas		ḫāne 7	

ḥāṣıl 495

ʿa(n) ispence 140	ʿöşr-i ḥınṭa 300	ʿöşr-i cev 45	resm-i ʿarūsī 10

ḳarye-i Andon ez cemāʿat-i Arnavudān tīmār-ı Umūr el-mezbūr

Miḫal Andoni	Niḳola Andoni	Todoros Dimaris	Yorgi Prifti	Gön Prifti
Leo Vanbaḳas	Gön Ḳazneş	Bardi veled-i o	Gön Andoni	Miḫal Prifti
			ḫāne 10	

ḥāṣıl 441

ʿa(n) ispence 200	ʿöşr-i ḥınṭa 200	ʿöşr-i cev 31	resm-i ʿarūsī 10

cemʿan tīmār-ı Umūr el-mesfūr

ḳurā 3	ḫāne 37	mücerred 1	bīve 1

ḥāṣıl 2131

80

tetimme-i nāḥiyyet-i Ġardicḳo

kendü	ġulām
cebelü	1

tīmār-ı Tırḫallü Timur Ḫanoğlı Muḥammed

ḳarye-i Manesi ez cemāʿat-i Arnavudān tīmār-ı Muḥammed el-mezbūr

Yorgi Manesi	Yorgi Ḳandrava	Yorgi Manesi-i dīğer	Niḳola Manesi	Yorgi Mazarak
Gin Mazarak	Gön Mazarak		ḫāne 7	

ḥāṣıl 602

ʿa(n) ispence 140	nıṣf-ı āsiyāb-ı ḫāṣṣa 1 resm 200	ʿöşr-i ḥınṭa 200	ʿöşr-i cev 32	resm-i ʿarūsī 10	ʿöşr-i kettān 20

ḳarye-i Murik Buva ez cemāʿat-i Arnavudān tīmār-ı Muḥammed el-mezbūr

Orfano Murik Buva	İstefano Vloşi	Gin Manesi	Yorgi Menaki	Todoro veled-i o
Gön veled-i o	Yorgi Pavloplo	Andriya Patyani	İvlaş Kiz̠iḳuma	Ḳosta Ḳanḳaz̠i
Niḳola Dadiz̠o	çeltükci Gön Bafi	bīve Mariya zen-i Hiliz̠on	ḫāne maʿa çeltükci 12	bīve 1

ḥāṣıl 809

ʿa(n) ispence 246	ʿöşr-i bāğāt 64	ʿöşr-i ḥınṭa 400	ʿöşr-ı cev 64	ʿöşr-i zeyt 5	ʿoşr-i meyve 2	resm-i ḫanāzīr 13

resm-i
ʿarūsī
15

ḳarye-i Niḳola Buva ez cemāʿat-i Arnavudān tīmār-ı Muḥammed el-masṭūr

Niḳola el-mez̠kūr	Todoro Yatro	Miḫal Manesi	Niḳola Çaresi	Gön veled-i o
Petro Manesi	Gin Yatro	İvrato Yalca	Ḳosta Buva	ḫāne 9

ḥāṣıl 542

ʿa(n) ispence 180	ʿöşr-i ḥınṭa 300	ʿöşr-i cev 47	resm-i ḫanāzīr 5	resm-i ʿarūsī 10

ḳarye-i Duranḳorgi ez cemāʿat-i Arnavudān tīmār-ı Muḥammed el-meẕkūr

İştin Duranḳorgi	Gön Duranḳorgi	Niḳola Duranḳorgi	mücerred Duḳa birāẕer-i o	ḫāne 3	mücerred 1

ḥāṣıl 184

ʿa(n) ispence	ʿöşr-i ḥınṭa	ʿöşr-i cev	resm-i ḫanāzīr
66	100	16	2

cemʿan tīmār-ı Muḥammed el-masṭūr

ḳurā	ḫāne	mücerred	bīve
4	31	1	1

ḥāṣıl 2137

81
tetimme-i Ġardicḳo

mevḳūf

mezraʿa-ı Kiẕiḳuma ḫāliyye

82 blank
83 blank
84
nāḥiyyet-i Vumero

kendü	cebelü	çadır
bürüme	1	1

tīmār-ı İbrahīm[50] Engürüs ʿa(n) cemāʿat-i mehterān-ı ḫayme-i serʿasker-i Vumero ve Kirvuḳor

ḳarye-i Ṭarpun tābiʿ-i Londar tīmār-ı İbrahīm[51] el-meẕkūr

Yorgiçi Portoyoro[52]	İstemati Ḳondiva	İvlaşi Ṣotoki	Niḳola Ḳumari	Yorgi Ḳumari
Ṣotoki Ḳumari	Petros Ḳumari	Niḳola Ḳatoviti	Dimitri Ḳazavana	Todoros Monoliḳofos
Ṣotoki İzvalyano	Yani İzvalyano	Ṣotoki Manyati	mücerred Yani Ṣotoki	mücerred Mi[ḫ]al Ḳumari
mücerred Varda Ḳumari	bīve Eksarḫo-pulina			

ḫāne	mücerred	bīve
13	3	1

ḥāṣıl 1477

ʿa(n) ispence	bāġāt-ı ḫāṣṣa	eşcār-ı ṭut-ı ḫāṣṣa	ʿöşr-i bāġāt	ʿöşr-i ḥınṭa	ʿöşr-i cev
406	dönüm 3 [resm] 180	ʿaded 6 [resm] 30	224	500	75

ʿöşr-i ḳazz	resm-i ʿarūsī	resm-i ḫamr
17	15	30

ḳarye-i Amuri tābiʿ-i Londar tīmār-ı İbrahīm[53] el-mezbūr

Pavlos Ḳofina	Pulimenos Mertinos	Yorgi Varṣalemo	mücerred Aleksi Ḳofina

ḫāne	mücerred
selāṣe	1

ḥāṣıl 359

ʿa(n) ispence	ʿöşr-i bāġāt	ʿöşr-i ḥınṭa	ʿöşr-i cev
100	144	100	15

mezraʿa-ı Veliġosti nezd-i nefs-i Londar tīmār-ı İbrahīm[54] el-mezbūr

ḫāliyye

ḥāṣıl ez ḫāric 280

ʿöşr-i ḥınṭa	ʿöşr-i cev	ʿöşr-i bostān
200	30	50

mezraʿa-ı Aya Niḳola nezd-i ḳarye-i Amuri el-meẕkūr

tīmār-ı İbrahīm[55] el-mezbūr ḫāliyye

85
tetimme-i nāḥiyyet-i Vumero

ḳarye-i Pavla tābiʿ-i Londar tīmār-ı İbrahīm[56] el-mezbūr

Niḳola Maḳriyani	İstemad veled-i o	Yorgi Maḳriyani	Yani Maḳriyani	Niḳola Ḳayẓo
Dimitri Petruli	Yorgi Maḳri	Angelos Ḳoramilas	Yorgi İspati	Yani İstrati
İstemad Petruli	mücerred Dimitri Maḳriyani	mücerred Ṣotoki Ḳuruno	mücerred Niḳola birāder-i o	mücerred Niḳola İstrati

mücerred Yani Niḳola Maḳriyani	mücerred Dimitri Yorgi Maḳriyani	mücerred Todoros veled-i İspani	mücerred Dimitri Rafteplo	mücerred Todoros veled-i Petruli

ḫāne	mücerred
11	9

ḥāṣıl 2609

ʿa(n) ispence 500	bāġāt-ı ḫāṣṣa dönüm 11 [resm] 660	eşcār-ı meyve-i ḫāṣṣa ʿaded 100 [resm] 200	ʿöşr-i bāġāt 584	ʿöşr-i ḥınṭa 450	ʿöşr-i cev 70

ʿöşr-i meyve 40	resm-i ḫanāzīr 5	resm-i ʿarūsī 10	resm-i ḫamr 70	ʿöşr-i kettān 20

ḳarye-i Murji tābiʿ-i Ḫulumiç tīmār-ı İbrahīm[57] el-mezbūr

Pavlos İvratos	Petro Vlaşi	Mangişa Murji	Yorgi İstari	Andriya Variprati
Marti Klasira	Todoro İspartino	İstas̱i İspartino	Dimitri İspartino	Ḳosta Mavromati
Leḳa Prifti	Proġono İsḳura	İstefano Rafti	Petro Lata	Marti Kiriçi
Gön birāder-i o	İlya Paliḳuri	Proġono Paliḳuri	bīve Todora zen-i Toskesina	ḫāne 18 / bīve 1

ḥāṣıl 1367

ʿa(n) ispence 456	ʿöşr-i ḥınṭa 700	ʿöşr-i cev 109	resm-i ḫanāzīr 52	ʿöşr-i kettān 20	resm-i penbe 30

cemʿan tīmār-ı İbrahīm[58] el-meẕkūr

ḳurā	mezāriʿ-i ḫāliyye	ḫāne	mücerred	bīve
4	2	45	13	2

ḥāṣıl 6092

86
tetimme-i nāḥiyyet-i Vu[me]ro

kendü bürüme	cebelü	çadır
	2	1

tīmār-ı Ḥamza ġulām-ı mīr ki ez merdān-ı ḳalʿa-ı Balya Badra būd

ḳarye-i Sipyani tīmār-ı Ḥamza el-meẕkūr

Niḳola Petraki	İvrato Petroplos	Niḳola Manoloplo	Todoro veled-i o	Papas Yorgi Tul[u]pi
Ḳosta birāder-i o	Todoro birāder-i o	İstemad ḫīş-i o	Yani Papa- istefanaplo	Yani Tulupi
İstemad Tirḳarda	Yorgi birāder-i o	Yorgi Anaġnostos	Yorgi Ḳomoyani	Dimitri Aspraki
Todoros birāder-i o	Vaşıl Polugiro	Niḳola veled-i o	Dimitri veled-i o	Yani Aspraki
S̱otoki birāder-i o	Dimitri Aspraki	Ḳosta birāder-i o	Yani Papa- andraplo	Aleksi Çağrıpa
Yani Çağrıpa	Andriya Marġazi	Dimitri İsḳoniçina	mücerred Yani Manoloplo	mücerred Yorgi birāder-i o
mücerred İstemad Ḳomoyani	mücerred Yorgi Todoriç	mücerred Ḳosta birāẕer-i o	mücerred Miḫal Aspraki	mücerred Andriya Çağrıpa
	bīve İsḳoniçina	ḫāne 28	mücerred 7	bīve 1

ḥāṣıl 3080

ʿa(n) ispence 881	ʿöşr-i bāġāt 512	ʿöşr-i ḥınṭa 1250	ʿöşr-i cev 193	ʿöşr-i ḳazz 164	resm-i ḫanāzīr 7

ʿöşr-i meyve 18	resm-i ʿarūsī 30	mülk-i Papas Yorgi Tulupi der ḳarye-i meẕkūr āsiyāb 1 resm 25

ḳarye-i Mangişa Ḳumani ez cemāʿat-i Arnavudān tīmār-ı Ḥamza el-mezbūr

Gin Ḳumani	Ḳoma veled-i o	Laluş Ḳuḳula	Gin Ḳoḳla	Yorgi birāder-i o
Ġulami Loncas	Yorgi Dara	Yorgi Mita	Andriya Ḳuraleşa	Bardi İşpata
Sina Maḳrişi	Mangişa veled-i o	Miḫal Ḳumano	Dimitri birāẕer-i o	Niḳola Muşura
İvrato Ḳoḳla	Marti Ḳoḳla	Mangişa Ḳaratula	Gön veled-i o	Todoro Mita
Mangişa Ḳaratula-<yı> dīğer	Dimitri birāder-i o	Ḳumani birāẕer-i o	Yorgi Ġunari	Aleksi Maḳriça

87

tetimme-i ḳarye-i Mangişa el-meẕkūr tīmār-ı Ḥamza el-mezbūr

Gin Buva	Gin Peta	Gön birāder-i o	Domeniḳa Muşura	Manḳola Ḳumani
mücerred Al[eksi] Ḳoḳla	mücerred Todoros Loncas	mücerred Andriya Ḳumano	mücerred Miḫal Ḳaratula	mücerred Andriya Ḳumani-i dīğer
mücerred Ale[ks]i Buzi	bīve Manḳa zen-i Küraleş	bīve Todora zen-i Dama		

hāne	mücerred	bīve
30	6	2

ḥāṣıl 2340

ʿa(n) ispence	ʿöşr-i ḥınṭa	ʿöşr-i cev	ʿöşr-i bāġāt	resm-i ḫanāzīr	resm-i ʿarūsī
732	1200	188	128	62	30

cümletü'l-ḳaryeteyni'l-meẕkūreteyn

hāne	mücerred	bīve
58	13	3

ḥāṣıl 5420

kendü	cebelü	tenktür
bürüme	1	1

tīmār-ı ʿAlī Ṣūfī İzdinī merdüm-i Balaban Aġa

ḳarye-i İspani ez cemāʿat-i Arnavudān tīmār-ı ʿAlī el-meẕkūr

Pavlo İspani	Mangişa İspani	Niḳola İspani	Todoro Ḳrapeşi	Domeniḳa İspani
Gin İspani	mücerred Gön İspani	mücerred Yorgi İşpata	bīve Anaza zen-i İspana	bīve Babe zen-i Yani İspana

hāne	mücerred	bīve
6	2	2

ḥāṣıl 497

ʿa(n) ispence	ʿöşr-i kettān	ʿöşr-i ḥınṭa	ʿöşr-i cev	resm-i ḫanāzīr	resm-i ʿarūsī
172	20	250	42	3	10

mezraʿa-ı İspani-i dīğer nezd-i ḳarye-i İspani el-meẕkūr

tīmār-ı mezbūr ḫāliyye

mezraʿa-ı Persena nezd-i ḳarye-i meẕkūr tīmār-ı ʿAlī el-mezbūr ḫāliyye

88

tetimme-i nāḥiyyet-i Vumero

ḳarye-i Ḳuçi ez cemāʿat-i Arnavudān tīmār-ı ʿAlī el-meẕkūr

Yorgi Ḳuçi	Andriya Ḳuçi	Gin Lata	Gön Dorja[59]	Ḳondo Yorgi
bīve Kirana zen-i Klasira				

hāne	bīve
5	1

ḥāṣıl 415

ʿa(n) ispence	ʿöşr-i ḥınṭa	ʿöşr-i cev	resm-i ḫanāzīr	mülk-i Yorgi Ḳuçi [der ḳarye-i] meẕkūr
106	250	40	4	āsiyāb-ı peşmīne 1 resm 15

ḳarye-i Yirmena tīmār-ı ʿAlī el-mezbūr

Niḳola Ḳondovaşıl	Ḳosta veled-i o	Yani Aṣanas	Todoro İflama	Ḳosta veled-i o

hāne
5

ḥāṣıl 755

ʿa(n) ispence	āsiyāb-ı ḫāṣṣa 1 [resm]	ʿöşr-i bāġāt	ʿöşr-i meyve	ʿöşr-i ḥınṭa	ʿöşr-i cev	resm-i ʿarūsī
125	300	90	5	200	25	10

ḳarye-i Ḳaçaru ez cemāʿat-i Arnavudān tīmār-ı ʿAlī el-masṭūr

Gön Buva	Lazaro Buva	İstefano Muzaki	Ḳosta Bedeni	Andriya Ḳaçaro
Gin Ẓramesi	İzmoldi Domeniḳa	Ḳosta Mazaraki	Yorgi Ḳuḳuçomaẕi[60]	Gön Buza
Gin Tarusi	Loşa Bura	mücerred Vaġali Bura	mücerred Dima İstasino	mücerred Petros Ḳuçomaẕi

ḫāne	mücerred
12	3

ḥāṣıl 1214

ʿa(n) ispence	ʿöşr-i ḥınṭa	ʿöşr-i cev	ʿöşr-i bāġāt	resm-i ḫanāzīr	resm-i ʿarūsī	mülk-i Gön Bura der ḳarye-i mezḳūr āsiyāb 1 resm 30
300	650	102	75	42	15	

cemʿan tīmār-ı ʿAlī Ṣūfī el-mezḳūr

ḳurā	mezāriʿ-i ḫāliyye	ḫāne	mücerred	bīve
4	2	28	5	3

ḥāṣıl 2881

89

tetimme-i nāḥiyyet-i Vumero

kendü bürüme	cebelü	ġulām	çadır
	2	1	1

tīmār-ı Ḳāsım ġulām-ı mīr ki ez merdān-ı ḳalʿa-ı Balya Badra būd

ḳarye-i Dumeña — tīmār-ı Ḳāsım el-mezḳūr

Niḳola Çiyani	Dyaḳo Maroplo	Niḳola Pavlo	Miḫal Murmuro	Ḳosta Draġavliti
Yorgı Andoni	Ḳosta Murmuro	Vaşıl Pavlo	Niḳola Ḳaloyira	Dimitri Luçinos
Miḫal Maġuli	Niḳola Ḳostaplo	Yani Mazarak	Aleksi Pavlos	Niḳola birāder-i o
Todoros Pavlos	Petro Zervuni	Andriya birāder-i o	Yani Ẕelvuni	Niḳola birāder-i o
Yani Ḫarkâ	Yorgi veled-i o	Ṡotoki veled-i o	İstefano Ḫarkâ	Yani Ḳalapüş̱
Ṡotoki Porotopapaẕo-plo	Maġuli Yorgi	Todoros Ḳaravokiri	Yani Divya	Niḳola birāẕer-i o
Yani Ḳomoyani	mücerred Niḳola Draġavliti	mücerred Mayiro Dimitri	mücerred Yani Andoni	mücerred Niḳola Pavlo
mücerred Yorgi Mazarak	mücerred Yorgi Ḳalapüş̱	mücerred Ḳosta veled-i Yani Ḫarkâ	mücerred Todoros veled-i Maġuli Yorgi	mücerred Ṡotoki Ḳaravokiri

bīve Ṡotoke zen-i Platindra	bīve Ṡotoke zen-i Pavlana	ḫāne	mücerred	bīve	mevżiʿ-i āsiyāb-ı ḫāṣṣa
		31	9	2	1

ḥāṣıl 4879

ʿa(n) ispence	bāġāt-ı ḫāṣṣa dönüm 8 [resm] 880	eşcār-ı meyve-i ḫāṣṣa ʿaded 4 [resm] 10	ʿöşr-i bāġāt	ʿöşr-i ḥınṭa	ʿöşr-i cev
1012			1320	1200	188

resm-i ḫanāzīr	ʿöşr-i meyve	resm-i ʿarūsī	ʿöşr-i kettān	resm-i ḫamr	mülk-i Ṡotoki Protopapaẕoplo der ḳarye-i mezḳūr āsiyāb 1 resm 50
4	10	35	50	120	

ḳarye-i İsḳlaviça tābiʿ-i Girbene — tīmār-ı Ḳāsım el-mezḳūr

Papas Yaḳumos	Yorgi Pasḳali	Yani Pasḳali	Yorgi Ḳaçiḳo	Dimitri Malya
Todoros Bulyaşa	Yorgi Roḳoça	Papayani Mavruçi	Yani Yeraḳar	Filibos[61] Hiliẕonis
İstemad Rupato	Yani Traġodi	İstilyano Ḳaḳuçi	İstemad Liçardo	bīve Alişafi zen-i Potamya
bīve Elani zen-i Ḳozmana	bīve Mariya Ḳondeyano		ḫāne 14	bīve 3

90

ḥāṣıl-ı ḳarye-i İsḳlaviça el-mezḳūr 2078

ʿa(n) ispence	bāġāt-ı ḫāṣṣa dönüm 5 [resm] 528	eşcār-ı zey[t-i] ḫāṣṣa ʿaded 100 [resm] 225	eşcār-ı meyve-i ḫāṣṣa ʿaded 17 [resm] 40	ʿöşr-i bāġāt
368				371

ʿöşr-i ḥınṭa	ʿöşr-i cev	ʿöşr-i zeyt	ʿöşr-i meyve	ʿöşr-i kettān	resm-i ḫamr	resm-i ʿarūsī
300	48	30	18	20	35	15

mülk-i Papas Yaḳumis der ḳarye-i mezḳūr āsiyāb 1 resm 40	mülk-i Todoros Bulyaşa der ḳarye-i mezḳūr āsiyāb 1 resm 40

cümletü'l-ḳaryeteyni'l-mezḳūreteyn

ḫāne	mücerred	bīve
45	9	5

ḥāṣıl 6957

tetimme-i nāḥiyyet-i Girbene

kendü cebelü	ġulām 1

tīmār-ı Fīrūz veled-i ʿĪsā Ḳaraviryevī

ḳarye-i Ḳariza tīmār-ı Fīrūz el-mezḳūr

Miḫal Ḳariza	Gin Ḳarida	Petros Ḳariza	Dimitri Ḳarida	Yorgi veled-i o
Andriya Başta	mücerred İvrato Ḳarida	mücerred Yani Ḳarida	ḫāne 6	mücerred 2

ḥāṣıl 554

ʿa(n) ispence 200	ʿöşr-i bāġāt 90	ʿöşr-i ḥınṭa 200	ʿöşr-i cev 32	resm-i ḫanāzīr 2	resm-i ʿarūsī 10	ʿöşr-i kettān 20

ḳarye-i Lali ez cemāʿat-i Arnavudān tīmār-ı Fīrūz el-mezḳūr

Andriya Kiniġo	Miḫal veled-i o	Manḳola veled-i o	Miḫal Lala	Andriya veled-i o
Gin veled-i o	Niḳola Muşura	Andriya veled-i o	Miḫal veled-i o	Manḳola veled-i o
Mangişa Muşula	İştin Muşura	Ḳosta Ḫarkâplo	İş Ari Peta	Gin Peta
Ḳozma Lonci	Mangişa Dayçi	Ḳosta Kiniġo	Ġulami Dayça	ḫāne 19

91

ḥāṣıl-ı ḳarye-i Lali el-mezḳūr 1461

ʿa(n) ispence 380	ʿöşr-i ḥınṭa 900	ʿöşr-i cev 138	resm-i ḫanāzīr 23	resm-i ʿarūsī 20

cümletü'l-ḳaryeteyni'l-mezḳūreteyn

ḫāne 25	mücerred 2	ḥāṣıl 2015

kendü bürüme cebelü	ġulām	tenktür
1	1	1

tīmār-ı İlyās ġulām-ı mīr ki ez merdān-ı ḳalʿa-ı Miḫlu būd

ḳarye-i Coya tīmār-ı İlyās el-mezḳūr

Andriya Lonberto	Yani Ḳarlato	Andon Papamiḫalo	Dimitri Amreni	Andriya Mastroandoni
Andon Ġramatiḳos	Artavas dāmād-ı Primikir	mücerred Todoros Andriya Lonberto	mücerred Aleksi Amerimni	mücerred Todoros Filipo
bīve Mariya zen-i Ġavril	bīve Asanasiya zen-i Sirġoviti	bīve Mariya zen-i Manoli	bīve zen-i İvrato	bīve Yorya zen-i Ḳarlatisa

bīve Mariya zen-i Ġavrila	bīve Mariya zen-i Iġliḳoma	bīve zen-i Yavatina	bīve Yanina zen-i Biçi	ḫāne 7	mücerred 3 bīve 9

ḥāṣıl 1999

ʿa(n) ispence 304	bāġāt-ı ḫāṣṣa dönüm 3 [resm] 720	eşcār-ı meyve-i ḫāṣṣa ʿaded 20 [resm] 52	bāġçe-i ḫāṣṣa 1 [resm] 100	ʿöşr-i penbe 30	ʿöşr-i kettān 40
ʿöşr-i bāġāt 360	ʿöşr-i ḥınṭa 300	ʿöşr-i cev 48	ʿöşr-i meyve 5	resm-i ʿarūsī 10	resm-i ḫamr 30

mezraʿa-ı Velizi nezd-i ḳarye-i mezḳūr tīmār-ı mezbūr

ḫāliyye

ḳarye-i Lanbeti ez cemāʿat-i Arnavudān tīmār-ı İlyās el-mezḳūr

Todoro Lanbeti	Yorgi Miḫala	Gin veled-i o	Niḳola Kefalino	Gin birāder-i o
İlya birāder-i o	Petro birāder-i o	Ḳonda Niḳola	Ḳonda Yorgi	İstasino Sofilaḫto
Petro İstasino	Niḳola Ḳosoni	Yani Ḳosoni	Yani İksanoplo	Papas Dimitri

92

tetimme-i ḳarye-i Lanbeti el-mezḳūr tīmār-ı İlyās el-mezbūr

Miḫal Mancaviti	Mastro- yani	Ḳondo Ḳalanci	Yorgi Meliġala	İstefano Varava
Yorgi Ḳosoni	Niḳola Vuḳolo	Todoros İskliva	Yorgi Mancaviti	Lazar Fila
mücerred İvrato Lanbeti	mücerred Yorgi Lanbeti	mücerred Niḳola Papazato	bīve Mariya zen-i Ḳonda İstefano	bīve İrini zen-i Papazato

bīve Ḳatarina zen-i Yani Papaẕato	ḫāne 25	mücerred 3	bīve 3

ḥāṣıl 1544

ʿa(n) ispence 578	ʿöşr-i penbe 30	ʿöşr-i kettān 40	ʿöşr-i bāġāt 60	ʿöşr-i ḥınṭa 700	ʿöşr-i cev 108	resm-i ḫanāzīr 3
			resm-i ʿarūsī 25			

ḳarye-i Ḳuçi ez cemāʿat-i Arnavudān — tīmār-ı İlyās el-mezbūr

Gin Ḳuçi	Ḳozma İpşari	Yorgi Lopesi	Lazaro Ḳuçi	Vaṣi Liḳuresi
Gön Ḳuçi	Andriya Ḳuçi	Yorgi Bulyari	Yorgi Ḳuçi	İstoya Ḳaparali
Gön Bulyari	İş Ari Şalesi	Andriya Demestiḳa	Gin Demestiḳa	Yorgi Nanḳaro
Gön İpşari	mücerred Niḳola Lopesi	mücerred Todoro Ḳuçi	mücerred Seraḳo Bulyari	mücerred Todoro Ḳuçi
mücerred Andriya Ġulyamo	bīve İskava zen-i Gön	bīve Belya zen-i Todor Ḳuçi	bīve Gâne zen-i Bulyarina	

ḫāne 16	mücerred 5
bīve 3	

ḥāṣıl 1574

ʿa(n) ispence 438	ʿöşr-i kettān 30	ʿöşr-i penbe 30	ʿöşr-i ḥınṭa 700	ʿöşr-i bāġāt 240	resm-i ḫanāzīr 8	resm-i ʿarūsī 20
			ʿöşr-i cev 108			

cemʿan tīmār-ı İlyās el-meẕkūr

ḳurā 3	mezraʿa-ı ḫāliyye 1	ḫāne 48	mücerred 11	bīve 15

ḥāṣıl 5117

93

tetimme-i nāḥiyyet-i Vumero

kendü bürüme	cebelü 1	tenktür 1

tīmār-ı Ġarb birāẕer-i Süleymān

ḳarye-i Ḳondomiḫal ez cemāʿat-i Arnavudān — tīmār-ı Ġarb el-meẕkūr

Yorgi Ḳondomiḫal	Yani veled-i o	Petro Ḳolovo	Niḳola Ratonda	Dima Maji
Dimitri Laġoçi	Niḳola Oroẕoḳron	Andriya Çaşi	Yorgi Orfano	Todoros Ḳondomiḫali
mücerred Pavlos Ḳondomiḫal	mücerred İstefano Ḳolovo	mücerred Todoros Majis	mücerred Yorgi Laġoçi	mücerred Dimitri Ratendos
bīve Ḳali zen-i Maji	bīve Mariya Çasa[62]	ḫāne 10	mücerred 5	bīve 2

ḥāṣıl 948

ʿa(n) ispence 312	ʿöşr-i penbe 40	ʿöşr-i kettān 50	ʿöşr-i bāġāt 60	ʿöşr-i ḥınṭa 400	ʿöşr-i cev 64	resm-i ḫanāzīr 12
			resm-i ʿarūsī 10			

ḳarye-i Ratendu ez cemāʿat-i Arnavudān — tīmār-ı Ġarb el-meẕkūr

Loẕoret Ratendo	Yorgi Beluşi	Marti veled-i o	Todoros Ratendos	Petro Ruyi
Manol Vozayiti	Yorgi Ḳraḳa	Yani Vaçi	mücerred Lala Beluşi	mücerred Andon Rayi

ḫāne 8	mücerred 2

ḥāṣıl 687

ʿa(n) ispence 200	ʿöşr-i penbe 30	ʿöşr-i kettān 40	ʿöşr-i ḥınṭa 300	ʿöşr-i cev 47	ʿöşr-i bāġāt 60	resm-i ʿarūsī 10

ḳarye-i Ḳosta Lanca ez cemāʿat-i Arnavudān — tīmār-ı Ġarb el-meẕkūr

Ḳosta el-meẕkūr	Gön Buzbardi	Yorgi Maji	Gin Şurbi	Lazaro Iḳlosa
Petro Iġlava	Bardi Ḳazneş	Lazaro Arḳuda	Dimo Dimoryari	Proġono İstratik

Sotoki İstratik	mücerred Mihal Buzbardi	mücerred Mihal Şurbi	mücerred Dima Dorza	mücerred Petro Ḳazneş
mücerred Petro Dorza	mücerred Gin Ḳuçi		ḫāne 11	mücerred 6

ḥāṣıl 1168

ʿa(n) ispence	ʿöşr-i penbe	ʿöşr-i kettān	ʿöşr-i bāġāt	ʿöşr-i ḥınṭa	ʿöşr-i cev	resm-i ḫanāzīr
320	30	40	135	500	78	5

resm-i ʿarūsī 10

mülk-i Ḳosta Lanci der ḳarye-i mezkūr āsiyāb 1 resm 30

94

tetimme-i nāḥiyyet-i Vumero

ḳarye-i Nikifor ez cemāʿat-i Arnavudān — tīmār-ı Ġarb el-mezkūr

Gin Nikifor	Todoros Nikifor	Gin Ḳonbosekra	ḫāne 3

ḥāṣıl 176

ʿa(n) ispence	ʿöşr-i ḥınṭa	ʿöşr-i cev
60	100	16

cemʿan tīmār-ı Ġarb el-mezkūr

ḳurā	ḫāne	mücerred	bīve
4	32	13	2

ḥāṣıl 2979

kendü	cebelü	çadır
bürüme	3	1

tīmār-ı Nuṣret veled-i Celāl Ḳasṭamonī ve İlyās veled-i Nuṣret el-mezkūr ki müşterek be-nevbet dāde şüd

ḳarye-i Olana — tīmār-ı mezkūrān

Todoros İstilyano	Niḳola birāzer-i o	Papamihal Papadimitri	Dimitri veled-i o	Andriya Revi
Yorgi Ḳokino	Andriya Ḳoçanda	Todoros birāzer-i o	Yorgi İpsasa[63]	Ḳosta Ḳoçanda
İstasino Tetrazi	Yani İstematiḳoplo	Yorgi birāzer-i o	Andon birāzer-i o	Yorgi Tetrazi
Domeniḳa birāzer-i o	Petro birāder-i o	Yani Çavala	Mihal Ḳlapesi	Vaşıl Leonizi
Andriya İvlaho	Mihal Protopapazaplo	Yorgi birāder-i o	Yani Simyaplo	Yorgi Simyaplo
Yani Ḳalimara	Yorgi Ḳalimara	Pavlos birāder-i o	Petro Lata	Dimitri birāzer-i o
Lazaro Marnari	Sotoki Aşfonikisto	Ḳosta Parasḳavoplo	Niḳola birāder-i o	Lazaro Argiro

95

tetimme-i ḳarye-i Olana el-mezkūr — tīmār-ı mezbūrān

Niḳola Halḳomata	Dimitri Şarakinos	Yani veled-i o	Yani Parasḳavoplo	Andon İkselazinos
Domeniḳa İspani	Mastro-yorgi İskâze	Andriya birāder-i o	Yani Ḳanava	Mastro-manol İskâze
İstemad Arna	Yorgi veled-i o	Yani Şaranda	Papas Mansos	Filibos[64] Sinadinos
İstemad Ḳomerki	mücerred Angelos Revi	mücerred Todoros Leonizi	mücerred Todoros Simyeplo	mücerred İstemad Halḳomata
bīve Todora zen-i Yartusa	bīve Ḳali zen-i Ḳapsura	bīve Marġaro zen-i Merḳuriya	ḫāne 51 / mücerred 4	bīve 3

ḥāṣıl 5807

ʿa(n) ispence 1393	bāġāt-ı ḫāṣṣa dönüm 5 [resm] 600	eşcār-ı zeyt-i ḫāṣṣa ʿaded 20 [resm] 22	āsiyāb-ı ḫāṣṣa 1 [resm] 250	eşcār-ı saḳız-ı çam-ı ḫāṣṣa ʿaded 300 [resm] 80

ʿöşr-i penbe	ʿöşr-i kettān	ʿöşr-i bāġāt	ʿöşr-i ḥınṭa	ʿöşr-i cev	ʿöşr-i meyve	ʿöşr-i zeyt
200	100	1080	1600	250	50	10

resm-i ḫanāzīr	ʿöşr-i ʿasel	resm-i ʿarūsī	resm-i ḫamr
12	10	50	100

ḳarye-i Iġlava ez cemāʿat-i Arnavudān — tīmār-ı mezkūrān

Nikifor Iġlava	Andriya veled-i o	Yani Iġlava	Niḳola Lavda	Pavlos Iġlava
Marti birāzer-i o	Leḳa Muzaki	Marti veled-i o	Niḳola Braçi	Gön Tatezas
Dimitri Bulyari	Lazaro Peta	bīve Ḳali zen-i Dima Iġlava	bīve Sina zen-i Dima Purdan	ḫāne 12 / bīve 2

ḥāṣıl 845

ʿa(n) ispence 252	ʿöşr-i kettān 40	ʿöşr-i penbe 30	ʿöşr-i ḥınṭa 300	ʿöşr-i cev 48	ʿöşr-i bāġāt 150	resm-i ḫanāzīr 10
			resm-i ʿarūsī 15			

ḳarye-i Şopi ez cemāʿat-i Arnavudān — tīmār-ı mezḳūrān

Yorgi Şopi	Dimitri birāder-i o	Manol Yorgi Şopi	Yani Riḳa	İvlaş veled-i o
Andriya Ḳoḳla	Todoro Kenanci	Dima Papayanoplo	Gin Lavẕa	bīve Ḳal[i] zen-i Ḳoḳla

ḫāne 9 — bīve 1

ḥāṣıl 720

ʿa(n) ispence 186	ʿöşr-i penbe 20	ʿöşr-i kettān 30	ʿöşr-i ḥınṭa 400	ʿöşr-i cev 64	resm-i ḫanāzīr 10	resm-i ʿarūsī 10

96
tetimme-i nāḥiyyet-i Vumero

ḳarye-i Dorza ez cemāʿat-i Arnavudān — tīmār-ı mezḳūrān

Leḳa Dorza	Andriya Dorza	bīve Neja zen-i Dorza	ḫāne 2	bīve 1

ḥāṣıl 200

ʿa(n) ispence 46	ʿöşr-i penbe 15	ʿöşr-i kettān 20	ʿöşr-i ḥınṭa 100	ʿöşr-i cev 16	resm-i ḫanāzīr 3

ḳarye-i Ḳonbi Ṣeḳra ez cemāʿat-i Arnavudān — tīmār-ı mezḳūrān

Yani İspeca	Dima Manesi	Domeniḳa Ḳonbi Ṣeḳra	Petros Ḳonbi Ṣeḳra	Marti Ḳonbi Ṣeḳra
	Yorgi Plaşa		ḫāne 6	

ḥāṣıl 427

ʿa(n) ispence 120	ʿöşr-i penbe 15	ʿöşr-i kettān 20	ʿöşr-i ḥınṭa 200	ʿöşr-i cev 32	resm-i ʿarūsī 10	mülk-i Petros Ḳonbi Ṣeḳra āsiyāb 1 resm 30

ḳarye-i Ḳoḳla ez cemāʿat-i Arnavudān — tīmār-ı mezḳūrān

İstefanos Ḳoḳlas	Gin birāder-i o	Lazaro Ḳoḳla	Dima birāẕer-i o	Gin Ḳoḳla
		ḫāne 5		

ḥāṣıl 249

ʿa(n) ispence 100	ʿöşr-i penbe 10	ʿöşr-i kettān 20	ʿöşr-i ḥınṭa 100	ʿöşr-i cev 16	resm-i ḫanāzīr 3

ḳarye-i Ḳaratula ez cemāʿat-i Arnavudān — tīmār-ı mezḳūrān

Ḳosta Ḳaratula	Dima birāder-i o	Marti Lavẕa	Todoros birāder-i o	Yorgi Ḳaratula	
Manḳola veled-i o	Lazaro veled-i o	Andriya veled-i o	mücerred Floḳa Diẕmari	ḫāne 8	mücerred 1

ḥāṣıl 580

ʿa(n) ispence 180	ʿöşr-i bāġāt 80	ʿöşr-i ḥınṭa 250	ʿöşr-i cev 40	ʿöşr-i kettān 20	resm-i ʿarūsī 10

cemʿan tīmār-ı Nuṣret maʿa veledeş el-meẕkūr

ḳurā 7	ḫāne 93	mücerred 5	bīve 7

ḥāṣıl 8828

97
tetimme-i nāḥiyyet-i Vumero

kendü bürüme	cebelü 1	tenktür 1

tīmār-ı Süleymān birāder-i Ġarb

ḳarye-i Pondiḳo — tīmār-ı Süleymān el-meẕkūr

Yani Maṣyas	Miḫal Ḳosovya	Yorgi İskliva	Andriya Mengeli	Niḳola Klasira	
Ġulyamo tu-Maṣya	Yorgi İskâẕe	Yani Marḳata	Lazaro Ḳuçoḫyiri	Petros Salivara	
L[a]zaro Klaşira	Yani Salivara	Yani Ḳoloni	İstemad Maṣyo	Yaḳumo birāẕer-i Maṣya	
mücerred İstefano Ḫarara	mücerred İlya Kipro	bīve zen-i Ḳuluḳa	ḫāne 15	mücerred 2	bīve 1
			manastır-ı ḫāṣṣa 1	mevżiʿ-i āsiyāb-ı ḫāṣṣa 1	

ḥāṣıl ġayr ez memlaḥa 1853

ʿa(n) ispence 431	bāġāt-ı ḫāṣṣa dönüm 6 [resm] 720	eşcār-ı zeyt-i ḫāṣṣa ʿaded 10 [resm] 14	eşcār-ı meyve-i ḫāṣṣa ʿaded 9 [resm] 15	ʿöşr-i penbe 30

ʿöşr-i kettān 50	resm-i ʿarūsī 15	ʿöşr-i ḥınṭa 500	ʿöşr-i cev 74	resm-i ḫanāzīr 4

muḳāṭaʿa-ı memlaḥa der ḳarye-i mez̲ḳūr ki ḫāṣṣa ḫullide mülkühu şüd

fī sene 7000

ḳarye-i Mavromati ez cemāʿat-i Arnavudān — tīmār-ı Süleymān el-mez̲ḳūr

Yorgi Mavromati	Mangişa ḫīş-i o	Marti Mavromati	Niḳola Şalesi	Yani Yorgi
İstefano Çihyorini	Ḳral Lukişa	Miḫal Graḳa	Leḳa Dorza	Yani Ḳuḳura
Andriya Raġuli	Niḳola Romo	Lazaro Maçuki	Niḳola Iġliġori	mücerred İvrato Şalesi
mücerred Gön ḫīş-i Ḳral el-mez̲ḳūr	mücerred Gön Graḳa		ḫāne 14	mücerred 3

ḥāṣıl 1032

ʿa(n) ispence 340	ʿöşr-i penbe 40	ʿöşr-i kettān 50	ʿöşr-i ḥınṭa 500	ʿöşr-i cev 77	resm-i ḫanāzīr 10	resm-i ʿarūsī 15

cümletü'l-ḳaryeteyni'l-mez̲kūreteyn

ḫāne 29	mücerred 5	bīve 1	ḥāṣıl 2885

98

tetimme-i nāḥiyyet-i Vumero

kendü bürüme	cebelü 1	tenktür 1

tīmār-ı Mezīd nev müslümān

ḳarye-i Livarzi — tīmār-ı Mezīd el-mez̲kūr

S̲otoki Zuli	Niḳola Papayorġo-plo	Andon Popriçi	Miḫal Papayorġoplo	Yani İspano
Yani Mavroplo	Vaşıl Ḳaliva	Yorgi Ḳaçimiġas	Ḫartofilaḳa Ḳaçimiġas	Papayani Ḳoḳoviti
İstemad Niḫoriti	Papaniḳola Popriti	Papamiḫal Punca	İstefano birāz̲er-i o	İvrato Nerozumi
Befani Brasupa	Yani Punḳali	Niḳola Ḳaḳuri	Todoros Ḳalivas	Kiryaki Ḳoraḳa
Yani İvlaḫos	Todoros Siviçi	Yorgi Matrilo	Filipos Papayanoplos	mücerred Todoros Androni
mücerred Pavlos Ḳaçimiġas	mücerred Yani Nomiti	mücerred Yorgi veled-i Filibos[65] el-mez̲ḳūr	ḫāne 24	mücerred 4

ḥāṣıl 2447

ʿa(n) ispence 700	ʿöşr-i bāġāt 480	ʿöşr-i ḥınṭa 800	ʿöşr-i cev 124	ʿöşr-i ḳazz 172	ʿöşr-i meyve 14	resm-i ḫanāzīr 2

resm-i ʿarūsī 25	resm-i ḫamr 40	mülk-i Andon Popriçi der ḳarye-i mez̲ḳūr āsiyāb 1 resm 60	mülk-i Todoros Ḳalivas der ḳarye-i mez̲ḳūr āsiyāb 1 resm 30

ḳarye-i Keraşova — tīmār-ı Mezīd el-mez̲ḳūr

Dimitri Lupis	Papas Manol Ḫaraç	Aleksi Ḫaraç	Yorgi Valḳaçi	Yani Ḳokalinos
Todoros Matrilo	Yorgi Sotiri	mücerred Ḳosta birāder-i Papas Manol el-mez̲ḳūr	mücerred Dimitri Matrilo	mücerred Niḳola Parḳari

ḫāne 7	mücerred 3

ḥāṣıl 1168

ʿa(n) ispence 250	ʿöşr-i bāġāt 420	ʿöşr-i ḥınṭa 300	ʿöşr-i cev 48	ʿöşr-i ḳazz 68	ʿöşr-i meyve 7	resm-i ḫamr 35

mülk-i Papas Manol Ḫaraç der ḳarye-i mez̲ḳūr āsiyāb 1 resm 30	resm-i ʿarūsī 10

cümletü'l-ḳaryeteyni'l-mez̲kūreteyn

ḫāne 31	mücerred 7	ḥāṣıl 3615

ENDNOTES

1 فلپ (Filip) corr.: فلب (Filib).
2 اوغلان (oğlan) corr.: اغلان (oğlan).
3 ابراهيم vel ابرٰهم (İbrāhīm) corr.: ابرهيم (İbrahīm).
4 ابراهيم vel ابرٰهم (İbrāhīm) corr.: ابرهيم (İbrahīm).
5 ابراهيم vel ابرٰهم (İbrāhīm) corr.: ابرهيم (İbrahīm).
6 ابراهيم vel ابرٰهم (İbrāhīm) corr.: ابرهيم (İbrahīm).
7 ابراهيم vel ابرٰهم (İbrāhīm) corr.: ابرهيم (İbrahīm).
8 ابراهيم vel ابرٰهم (İbrāhīm) corr.: ابرهيم (İbrahīm).
9 ابراهيم vel ابرٰهم (İbrāhīm) corr.: ابرهيم (İbrahīm).
10 ابراهيم vel ابرٰهم (İbrāhīm) corr.: ابرهيم (İbrahīm).
11 ابراهيم vel ابرٰهم (İbrāhīm) corr.: ابرهيم (İbrahīm).
12 فلپوس (Filipos) corr.: فلبوس (Filibos).
13 پروغونه (Proġona) corr.: پورغونه (Porġona).
14 ايشان (īşān) corr.: اشان (işān).
15 اغاپتو (Aġapito) corr.: اغابتو (Aġabito).
16 فلپوس (Filipos) corr.: فلبوس (Filibos).
17 واردسى (Vardusi) vel ووردسى (Vurdusi) corr.: اوردسى (Urdusi).
18 چاشنيگير (Çāşnīgīr) cor.: چاشنگر (Çāşnigir).
19 فلپهپلو (Filipeplo) corr.: فلبهپلو (Filibeplo).
20 فلپهپلوس (Filipeplos) corr.: فلبهپلوس (Filibeplos).
21 پوثتو (Pos̱ito) corr.: بوثتو (Bos̱ito).
22 فلپو (Filipo) corr.: فلبو (Filibo).
23 فلپو (Filipo) corr.: فلبو (Filibo).
24 دورزه (Dorza) corr.: دوزره (Dozra).
25 بثولقه (Bes̱ulḳa) corr.: بسولقه (Besulḳa).
26 شركى (Şergi) corr.: سركى (Sergi).
27 اغاپتو (Aġapito) corr.: اغابنو (Aġabito).
28 Cf. TT10, 76.
29 پراسكوى (Paraskevi) corr.: براسكوى (Baraskevi).
30 فلپو (Filipo) corr.: فلبو (Filibo).
31 فلپوس (Filipos) corr.: فلبوس (Filibos).
32 لوكشه (Lukişa) corr.: لوكسه (Lukisa).
33 كشيش (keşīş) corr.: كشش (keşiş).
34 قوندستاولو (Ḳondostavlo) corr.: قوندستوولا (Ḳondostovla).
35 قاراووكيرى (Ḳaravokiri) corr.: قالاووكيرى (Ḳalavokiri).
36 مانول (Manol) corr.: منول (Menol).
37 درامسى (Dramesi) corr.: درامشى (Drameşi).
38 ابراهيم vel ابرٰهم (İbrāhīm) corr.: ابرهيم (İbrahīm).
39 ابراهيم vel ابرٰهم (İbrāhīm) corr.: ابرهيم (İbrahīm).
40 ابراهيم vel ابرٰهم (İbrāhīm) corr.: ابرهيم (İbrahīm).
41 تانوش (Tanuş) corr.: تانوس (Tanus).
42 ابراهيم vel ابرٰهم (İbrāhīm) corr.: ابرهيم (İbrahīm).
43 ابراهيم vel ابرٰهم (İbrāhīm) corr.: ابرهيم (İbrahīm).
44 كشيش (keşīş) corr.: كشش (keşiş).
45 كمخاجى (kemḫācı) corr.: كمحاجى (kemḥācı).

46 مانول (Manol) corr.: منول (Menol).
47 استاثوپلو (İstas̱oplo) corr.: استاتوپلو (İstatoplo).
48 اکساذاختیلوس (Eksaẕaḫtilos) corr.: اکساذاختولوس (Eksaẕaḫtulos).
49 کربسی (Gerbesi) corr.: کربشی (Gerbeşi).
50 ابراهیم vel ابرٰهِم (İbrāhīm) corr.: ابرهیم (İbrahīm).
51 ابراهیم vel ابرٰهِم (İbrāhīm) corr.: ابرهیم (İbrahīm).
52 پروتویرو (Protoyero) corr.: پورتویورو (Portoyoro).
53 ابراهیم vel ابرٰهِم (İbrāhīm) corr.: ابرهیم (İbrahīm).
54 ابراهیم vel ابرٰهِم (İbrāhīm) corr.: ابرهیم (İbrahīm).
55 ابراهیم vel ابرٰهِم (İbrāhīm) corr.: ابرهیم (İbrahīm).
56 ابراهیم vel ابرٰهِم (İbrāhīm) corr.: ابرهیم (İbrahīm).
57 ابراهیم vel ابرٰهِم (İbrāhīm) corr.: ابرهیم (İbrahīm).
58 ابراهیم vel ابرٰهِم (İbrāhīm) corr.: ابرهیم (İbrahīm).
59 دورزه (Dorza) corr.: دورژه (Dorja).
60 قوچوماذی (Ḳuçomaẕi) corr.: قوقوچوماذی (Ḳuḳuçomaẕi).
61 فلپوس (Filipos) corr.: فلبوس (Filibos).
62 چاشه (Çaşa) corr.: چاسه (Çasa).
63 اپساثه (İpsas̱a) corr.: اپثاسه (İps̱asa).
64 فلپوس (Filipos) corr.: فلبوس (Filibos).
65 فلپوس (Filipos) corr.: فلبوس (Filibos).

Bibliography and Abbreviations

I. MANUSCRIPTS

1/14662 Sts Cyril and Methodius National Library of Bulgaria, Sofia

Anonymous–BNF Anonymous, *Tevārīḫ-i Āl-i ʿOs̱mān*, Suppl. Turc No. 1047, Bibliothèque Nationale de France, Paris

Anonymous–İKK Anonim, *Tevārīḫ-i Āl-i ʿOs̱mān (II. Bayezid Devrine Kadar)*, No. A-1465, İzzet Koyunoğlu Kütüphanesi, Konya

TT10 Tapu Tahrir 10, Başbakanlık Osmanlı Arşivi, Istanbul

TT80 Tapu Tahrir 80, Başbakanlık Osmanlı Arşivi, Istanbul

II. PRINTED WORKS

A. DICTIONARIES

Atanassova et al. 1980 T. Atanassova, M. Rankova, R. Roussev, D. Spassov, Vl. Phillipov, G. Chakalov, *Bulgarian–English Dictionary, Българско–Английски Речник* (Sofia, 1980[?])

Bambiniotis 2002 Giorgos Bambiniotis, *Λεξικό της νέας ελληνικής γλώσσας* (Athens, 2002[2])

Benson 1978 Morton Benson, *Serbocroatian–English Dictionary – Srpskohrvatsko–Engleski Rečnik* (Beograd, 1978)

Benson 1992 Morton Benson, *Dictionary of Russian Personal Names with a Revised Guide to Stress and Morphology* (Cambridge, 1992)

Botsaris 1993 Markos Botsaris, *Lexicon*, ed. Titos P. Jochalas, *Μάρκου Μπότσαρη Λεξικὸν τῆς Ῥωμαϊκῆς καὶ Ἀρβανιτικῆς ἁπλῆς, φιλολογικὴ ἔκδοσις τοῦ αὐτογράφου* (Athens, 1980,[1] 1993[2])

Briquet 1968 Charles-Moïse Briquet, *Les filigranes. Dictionnaire historique des marques du papier dès leur apparition vers 1282 jusqu'en 1600*, ed. J.S.G. Simmons, 4 vols (Amsterdam, 1907,[1] 1968[2])

Buda 1985 Aleks Buda, ed.-in-chief, *Fjalori enciklopedik shqiptar* (Tirana, 1985)

Çabej 1976- Eqrem Çabej, *Studime etimologjike në fushë të shqipes*, 6 vols (Tirana, 1976–)

Dilgin 1983	Cem Dilgin, *Yeni Tarama Sözlüğü* (Ankara, 1983)
Du Cange 1688	Carolus Du Fresne Du Cange, *Glossarium ad scriptores mediæ at infimæ græcitatis*, 2 vols (Lugdunum, 1688)
Gelasius 1942a	Gelasius (Nikollë Gazulli), 'Fjalor toponomastik. Êmna vendesh', *Hylli i Dritës* 18/1–2 (January–February 1942), 40–45.
Gelasius 1942b	Gelasius (Nikollë Gazulli), 'Fjalor toponomastik. Êmna vendesh', *Hylli i Dritës* 18/5–10 (May–November 1942), 269–274.
Ginis 1998	Nikos H. Ginis, *Αλβανο-Ελληνικό λεξικό – Fjalor Shqip-Greqisht* (Ioannina, 1998)
Giordano 1963	Emanuele Giordano, *Fjalor i Arbëreshvet t'Italisë – Dizionario degli Albanesi d'Italia* (Bari, 1963)
GLET 1998	Hellenic Military Geographical Service, *Γεωγραφικό Λεξικό Ελληνικών Τοπωνυμίων*, 3 vols (Athens, 1998)
Gülensoy 1995	Tuncer Gülensoy, *Türkçe Yer Adları Kılavuzu* (Ankara, 1995)
Hloros 1899–1900	Ioannis Hloros, *Λεξικὸν Τουρκο-Ἑλληνικὸν – Ḳāmūs-ı ʿOs̱mānī Türkçe-Rūmca*, 2 vols (Constantinople, 1899–1900)
Hristoforidis 1904	Konstantinos Hristoforidis, *Λεξικὸν τῆς Ἀλβανικῆς γλώσσης* (Athens, 1904)
Kadri 1927–45	Hüseyin Kâzim Kadri, *Türk Lûgatı. Türk Dillerinin İştikakı ve Edebi Lûgatları*, 4 vols (İstanbul, 1927–1945)
Kahane–Tietze 1958	Henry and Renée Kahane, Andreas Tietze, *The Lingua Franca in the Levant. Turkish Nautical Terms of Italian and Greek Origin* (Urbana, 1958)
Kamsi 2000	Kolë Kamsi, *Fjalor arbërisht-shqip: me rreth 8500 fjalë dhe shënime gramatikore* (Shkodër, 2000)
Kazhdan 1991	Alexander P. Kazhdan, ed.-in-chief, *The Oxford Dictionary of Byzantium*, 3 vols (New York-Oxford, 1991)
Kostallari 1981	Androkli Kostallari, ed.-in-chief, *Fjalor i gjuhës së sotme shqipe*, 2 vols (Prishtinë, 1981)
Kostallari 1984	Androkli Kostallari, ed.-in-chief, *Fjalor i shqipes së sotme* (Tirana, 1984)
Kriaras 1969–	Emmanuel Kriaras, *Λεξικὸ τῆς μεσαιωνικῆς ἑλληνικῆς δημώδους γραμματείας: 1100–1669*, 19 vols (Thessaloniki, 1969–)
Mann 1948	Stuart E. Mann, *An Historical Albanian–English Dictionary* (London, 1948)
Meyer 1982	Gustav Meyer, *Etymologisches Wörterbuch der albanesischen Sprache* (Strassburg, 1891,[1] Leipzig, 1982[2])
Newmark 1998	Leonard Newmark, *Albanian–English Dictionary* (Oxford, 1998)
Nezeritis 1998	Angelos Th. Nezeritis, *Λεξικόν της βυζαντινής Πελοποννήσου* (Athens, 1998)
Niermeyer–van de Kieft 2002	Jan Frederik Niermeyer, Co van de Kieft, *Mediae latinitatis lexicon minus. Lexique latin médiévale – Medieval Latin Dictionary – Mittellateinisches Wörterbuch*, rev. J.W.J Burgers, 2 vols (Leiden-Boston, 2002)

Nişanyan 2010 — Sevan Nişanyan, *Sözlerin Soyağacı. Çağdaş Türkçenin Etimolojik Sözlüğü* (İstanbul, 2002,[1] 2010[5])

Orel 1998 — Vladimir Orel, *Albanian Etymological Dictionary* (Leiden, 1998)

Pakalin 1946–56 — Mehmet Zeki Pakalin, *Osmanlı Tarih Deyimleri ve Terimleri Sözlüğü*, 3 vols (İstanbul, 1946–1956)

Pikoulas 2001a — Yanis A. Pikoulas, *Λεξικό των οικισμών της Πελοποννήσου. Παλαιά και νέα τοπωνύμια* (Athens, 2001)

Preobrazhensky 1951 — Aleksandr Grigor'evitch Preobrazhensky, *Etymological Dictionary of the Russian Language* (New York, 1951)

Redhouse 1992 — Sir James W. Redhouse, *A Turkish and English Lexicon* (İstanbul, 1992[2])

Rhsj 1880–1976 — *Rječnik Hrvatskoga ili Srpskoga Jezika*, 23 vols (Zagreb, 1880–1976)

Seremetakis–Dimitriou 2005 — Theodoros Seremetakis, Maria Dimitriou, *Τα νεοελληνικά κύρια ονόματα. Αλφαβητική παρουσίαση* (Athens, 2005)

Skok 1971–74 — Petar Skok, *Etimologijski Rječnik Hrvatskoga ili Srpskoga Jezika*, 4 vols (Zagreb, 1971–1974)

Stamatelatos–Vamva-Stamatelatou 2001 — Michael Stamatelatos, Foteini Vamva-Stamatelatou, *Επίτομο γεωγραφικό λεξικό της Ελλάδος* (Athens, 2001)

Steingass 1892 — Francis Joseph Steingass, *A Comprehensive Persian–English Dictionary* (London, 1892)

Symeonidis 2010 — Haralambos P. Symeonidis, *Ετυμολογικό λεξικό των νεοελληνικών οικωνυμίων*, 2 vols (Nicosia-Thessaloniki, 2010)

Tmyk 1946–47 — T.C. İçişleri Bakanliği, *Türkiye'de Meskûn Yerler Kılavuzu*, 2 vols (Ankara, 1946–1947)

Triantafyllou 1995 — Kostas N. Triantafyllou, *Ἱστορικὸν λεξικὸν τῶν Πατρῶν. Ἱστορία τῆς πόλεως καὶ ἐπαρχίας Πατρῶν ἀπὸ τῆς ἀρχαιότητος ἕως σήμερον κατὰ ἀλφαβητικὴν εἰδολογικὴν κατάταξιν* (Patra, 1959,[1] 1995[3])

Vullers 1962 — Ioannes Augustus Vullers, *Lexicon Persico-Latinum etymologicum: cum linguis maxime cognatis Sanscrita et Zendica et Pehlevica comparatum, e lexicis Persice scriptis Borhâni Qâtiu, Haft Qulzum et Bahâri agam et Persico-Turcico Farhangi-Shuûrî confectum, adhibitis etiam Castelli, Meninski, Richardson et aliorum operibus et auctoritate scriptorum Persicorum adauctum*, 2 vols (Bonnae ad Rhenum, 1855–1864,[1] Graz, 1962[2])

Zoto 2005 — Vladimir Zoto, *Fjalor emrash* (Tirana, 2005)

B. PRIMARY SOURCES

Acropolites 1978 — Georgius Acropolites, *Opera*, ed. August Heisenberg, *Bibliotheca Scriptorum Graecorum et Romanorum Teubneriana*, 2 vols (Stuttgart, 1978)

Akgündüz 1990–96 — Ahmet Akgündüz, *Osmanlı Kanunnâmeleri ve Hukukî Tahlilleri*, 9 vols (İstanbul, 1990–1996)

ALEXANDER 1985	JOHN CHRISTOS ALEXANDER, *Toward a History of Post-Byzantine Greece. The Ottoman Kanunnames for the Greek Lands, circa 1500–circa 1600* (Ph.D. thesis, Columbia University; repr. Athens, 1985)
ANONYMOUS– ÖZTÜRK 2000	ANONYMOUS, *Tevārīḫ-i Āl-i ʿOs̱mān*, ed. Necdet Öztürk, *Osmanlı Kroniği (1299–1512)* (İstanbul, 2000)
ANONYMOUS–GIESE 1922–25	ANONYMOUS, *Tevārīḫ-i Āl-i ʿOs̱mān*, ed. Friedrich Giese, *Die altosmanischen anonymen Chroniken* تواريخ آل عثمان *in Text und Übersetzung*, 2 vols (Breslau, 1922–1925)
ʿĀŞIḲPAŞAZĀDE 1913	ʿĀŞIḲPAŞAZĀDE, *Tevārīḫ-i Āl-i ʿOs̱mān*, ed. ʿĀlī Beg, *Tevārīḫ-i Āl-i ʿOs̱mān'dan ʿĀşıḳpaşazāde Tārīḫi* [İstanbul, AH 1332 (AD 1913)]
ʿĀŞIḲPAŞAZĀDE 1929	ʿĀŞIḲPAŞAZĀDE, *Tevārīḫ-i Āl-i ʿOs̱mān*, ed. Friedrich Giese, *Die altosmanische Chronik des ʿĀšıḳpašazāde* (Leipzig, 1929; repr. Osnabrück, 1972)
ASSENOVA–STOJKOV–KACORI 1977	PETIA ASSENOVA, ROUSSI STOJKOV, THOMA KACORI, 'Селищни, лични и фамилни имена от Северозападен Пелопонес през средата на XV век', *Годишник на Софийския Университет, Факултет по Славянски Филологии* 68/3 (1977), 213–297.
ATTALEIATES 1853	MICHAEL ATTALEIATES, *Historia*, ed. Immanuel Bekker, Corpus Scriptorum Historiae Byzantinae (Bonn, 1853)
ATTALEIATES 2002	MICHAEL ATTALEIATES, *Historia*, ed. Inmaculada Pérez Martín, Nueva Roma (Madrid, 2002)
BALTA 1989	EVANGELIA BALTA, *L'Eubée à la fin du XVe siècle. Économie et population, les registres de l'année 1474* (Athens, 1989)
BALTA 1990–91	EVANGELIA BALTA, 'Rural and Urban Population in the Sancak of Euripos in the Early 16th Century', *Αρχείο Ευβοϊκών Μελετών* 29 (1990–1991), 55–185.
BALTA 1993	EVANGELIA BALTA, 'Οι κανουνναμέδες του Μοριά', *Ίστωρ* 6 (1993), 29–70.
BEES 1956	NIKOS A. BEES, 'Χαρτία τοῦ Κλαβαζοῦ', *Πελοποννησιακὰ* 1 (1956), 441–453.
BELDICEANU 1960–64	NICOARĂ BELDICEANU, *Les actes des premiers sultans conservés dans les manuscrits turcs de la bibliothèque nationale à Paris. Tome I, Actes de Mehmed II et de Bayezid II du ms. fonds turc ancien 39. Tome II, Règlements miniers 1390–1512* (Paris-La Haye, 1960–1964)
BELDICEANU 1967	NICOARĂ BELDICEANU, *Code de lois coutumières de Meḥmed II. Kitāb-i qavānīn-i ʿörfiyye-i ʿosmānī* (Wiesbaden, 1967)
BENJAMIN OF TUDELA 1907	BENJAMIN OF TUDELA, *The Itinerary of Benjamin of Tudela*, ed. Marcus Nathan Adler (London, 1907)
BENJAMIN OF TUDELA 1995	BENJAMIN OF TUDELA, *The World of Benjamin of Tudela. A Medieval Mediterranean Travelogue*, ed. Sandra Benjamin (Madison-Teaneck, 1995)
BORY DE SAINT-VINCENT 1834	JEAN BAPTISTE GENEVIÈVE MARCELLIN BORY DE SAINT-VINCENT, *Expédition scientifique de Morée; section des sciences physiques; tome II–1re partie, Géographie* (Paris, 1834)
BUCHON 1843a	JEAN ALEXANDRE C. BUCHON, *La Grèce continentale et la Morée. Voyage, séjour et études historiques en 1840 et 1841* (Paris, 1843)

Cantacuzenus 1828–32 — Ioannes Cantacuzenus, *Historiarum libri IV*, ed. Ludovicus Schopen, Corpus Scriptorum Historiae Byzantinae, 3 vols (Bonn, 1828–1832)

Chalcocondyles 1922–23 — Laonicus Chalcocondyles, *Historiarum demonstrationes*, ed. Eugenius Darkó, Editiones Criticæ Scriptorum Græcorum et Romanorum, 2 vols (Budapest, 1922–1923)

Chrysostomides 1995 — Julian Chrysostomides, *Monumenta Peloponnesiaca. Documents for the History of the Peloponnese in the 14th and 15th Centuries* (Camberley, 1995)

Comnena 2001 — Anna Comnena, *Alexias*, eds Diether R. Reinsch, Athanasios Kambylis, Corpus Fontium Historiae Byzantinae (Berlin-New York, 2001)

Critobulus 1983 — Critobulus Imbriotes, *Historiae*, ed. Diether Roderich Reinsch, Corpus Fontium Historiae Byzantinae (Berlin, New York, 1983)

Delilbaşi–Arikan 2001 — Melek Delilbaşi, Muzaffer Arikan, *Hicrî 859 Tarihli Sûret-i Defter-i Sancak-ı Tırhala*, 2 vols (Ankara, 2001)

Dodwell 1819 — Edward Dodwell, *A Classical and Topographical Tour through Greece during the Years 1801, 1805, and 1806*, 2 vols (London, 1819)

Dokos 1971–74 — Konstantinos Dokos, 'Ἡ ἐν Πελοποννήσῳ ἐκκλησιαστ. περιουσία κατὰ τὴν περίοδον τῆς β΄ ἐνετοκρατίας. Ἀνέκδοτα ἔγγραφα ἐκ τῶν ἀρχείων Ἐνετίας', *Byzantinisch-neugriechische Jahrbücher* 21 (1971–1974), 43–168.

Dokos 1977–84 — Konstantinos Dokos, 'Ἡ ἐν Πελοποννήσῳ ἐκκλησιαστ. περιουσία κατὰ τὴν περίοδον τῆς β΄ ἐνετοκρατίας. Ἀνέκδοτα ἔγγραφα ἐκ τῶν ἀρχείων Ἐνετίας', *Byzantinisch-neugriechische Jahrbücher* 22 (1977–1984), 285–374.

Dokos 1993 — Konstantinos Dokos, 'Breve descrittione del Regno di Morea. Αφηγηματική ιστορική πηγή ή επίσημο βενετικό έγγραφο της Β΄ Βενετοκρατίας στην Πελοπόννησο', *Ἑῴα καὶ Ἑσπέρια* 1 (1993), 81–131.

Dokos–Panagopoulos 1993 — Konstantinos Dokos, Georgios Panagopoulos, *Το βενετικό κτηματολόγιο της Βοστίτσας* (Athens, 1993)

Ducas 1834 — Michael Ducas, *Historia Byzantina*, ed. Immanuel Bekker, Corpus Scriptorum Historiae Byzantinae (Bonn, 1834)

Fatio 1885 — Morel Fatio, ed., *Libro de los fechos et conquistas del Principado de la Morea. Compilado por comandamiento de Don Fray Johan Ferrandez de Heredia, maetsro de Hospital de S. Johan de Jerusalem* (Genève, 1885)

Gell 1817 — Sir William Gell, *Itinerary of the Morea: Being a Description of the Routes of that Peninsula* (London, 1817)

Ḥadīdī 1991 — Hadîdî, *Tevârih-i Âl-i Osman (1299–1523)*, ed. Necdet Öztürk (İstanbul, 1991)

Hopf 1873 — Charles Hopf, *Chroniques gréco-romanes inédits ou peu connues* (Berlin, 1873)

İbn Kemāl 1954–57 — İbn Kemal, *Tevârih-i Âl-i Osman, VII. Defter*, ed. Şerafettin Turan, 2 vols (Ankara, 1954–1957)

İnalcik 1954a — Halil İnalcik, *Hicrî 835 Tarihli Sûret-i Defter-i Sancak-i Arvanid* (Ankara, 1954; repr. 1987)

Kalonaros 1989 — Petros P. Kalonaros, *Τὸ Χρονικὸν τοῦ Μορέως. Το ἑλληνικὸν κείμενον κατὰ τὸν Κώδικα τῆς Κοπεγχάγης μετὰ συμπληρώσεων καὶ παραλλαγῶν ἐκ τοῦ Παρισινοῦ* (Athens, 1989[3])

KOŁODZIEJCZYK 2004	DARIUSZ KOŁODZIEJCZYK, *The Ottoman Survey Register of Podolia (ca. 1681). Defter-i Mufassal-i Eyalet-i Kamaniçe*, 2 vols (Cambridge MA-Kyiv, 2004)
KOLOKOTRONIS 1981	THEODOROS KOLOKOTRONIS, *Διήγησις συμβάντων τῆς ἑλληνικῆς φυλῆς ἀπὸ τὰ 1770 ἕως τὰ 1836*, ed. Tasos Ath. Gritsopoulos, *Θεοδώρου Κ. Κολοκοτρώνη Διήγησις συμβάντων τῆς ἑλληνικῆς φυλῆς ἀπὸ τὰ 1770 ἕως τὰ 1836. Φωτομηχανικὴ ἐπανέκδοσις (ἐκ τῆς α΄ ἐκδόσεως)* (Athens, 1981)
KRAELITZ-GREIFENHORST 1921–22	FRIEDRICH KRAELITZ-GREIFENHORST, 'Ḳānūnnāme Sultan Meḥmeds des Eroberers. Die ältesten osmanischen Straf- und Finanzgesetze', *Mitteilungen zur Osmanischen Geschichte* 1 (1921–1922), 13–48.
LAMBROS 1880	SPYRIDON P. LAMBROS, *Collection de romans Grecs en langue vulgaire et en vers publiés pour la première fois d'après les manuscrits de Leyde et d'Oxford* (Paris, 1880)
LAMBROS 1884	SPYRIDON P. LAMBROS, 'Τὰ ἀρχεῖα τῆς Βενετίας καὶ ἡ περὶ Πελοποννήσου ἔκθεσις τοῦ Μαρίνου Μικιέλ', in *Ἱστορικὰ μελετήματα* (Athens, 1884), 173–220.
LAMBROS 1900	SPYRIDON P. LAMBROS, 'Ἐκθέσεις τῶν Βενετῶν προνοητῶν τῆς Πελοποννήσου ἐκ τῶν ἐν Βενετίᾳ ἀρχείων ἐκδιδόμεναι', *Δελτίον τῆς Ἱστορικῆς καὶ Ἐθνολογικῆς Ἑταιρείας τῆς Ἑλλάδος* 5 (1900), 605–823.
LAMBROS 1924	SPYRIDON P. LAMBROS, 'Κτηματολόγια Πελοποννήσου', *Νέος Ἑλληνομνήμων* 18 (1924), 223–238.
LAMBROS 1926	SPYRIDON LAMBROS, 'Ἀνωνύμου Πανηγυρικὸς εἰς Μανουὴλ καὶ Ἰωάννην Η΄ τοὺς Παλαιολόγους', in *Παλαιολόγεια καὶ Πελοποννησιακά*, vol. 3 (Athens, 1926), 132–199.
LEAKE 1830	WILLIAM MARTIN LEAKE, *Travels in the Morea. With a Map and Plans*, 3 vols (London, 1830)
LEAKE 1846	WILLIAM MARTIN LEAKE, *Peloponnesiaca. Supplement to Travels on the Moréa* (London, 1846)
LONGNON–TOPPING 1969	JEAN LONGNON, PETER TOPPING, *Documents sur le régime des terres dans la Principauté de Morée au XIVe siècle* (Paris-La Haye, 1969)
LUṬFĪ PAŞA 1910	LUṬFÎ PASCHA, *Das Aṣafnâme des Luṭfî Pascha nach den Handschriften zu Wien, Dresden und Konstantinopel*, ed., trans. Rudolf Tschudi (Berlin, 1910)
MAZARIS 1975	MAZARIS, *Journey to Hades or Interviews with Dead Men about Certain Officials of the Imperial Court*, Seminar Classics 609, State University of New York (Buffalo, 1975)
MEḤMED ŞÜREYYĀ 1996	MEHMED SÜREYYA, *Sicill-i Osmanî*, eds Nuri Akbayar, Seyit Ali Kahraman, Yücel Demirel, 6 vols (İstanbul, 1996)
MÜNECCİMBAŞI 1995	MÜNECCİMBAŞI AHMED B. LÜTFULLAH, *Câmiü'd-düvel. Osmanlı Tarihi (1299–1481)*, ed. Ahmet Ağırakça (İstanbul, 1995)
NEŞRĪ 1995	MEHMED NEŞRİ, *Kitâb-ı Cihan-nümâ. Neşri Tarihi*, eds Faik Reşit Unat, Mehmed A. Köymen, 2 vols (Ankara, 1995)
OĞUZ–BALTA 1998	MUSTAFA OĞUZ, EVANGELIA BALTA, 'Le *kanunnâme* de l'Euripe (milieu du XVIe siècle)', *Osmanlı Araştırmaları* 18 (1998), 9–45.
OIKONOMIDÈS 1968	NICOLAS OIKONOMIDÈS, ed., *Actes de Dionysiou, Texte* (Paris, 1968)

Oikonomidès 1984	Nicolas Oikonomidès, ed., *Actes de Docheiariou, Texte* (Paris, 1984)
Oruc 1925	Oruc, *Tevārīḫ-i Āl-i ʿOsmān*, ed. Franz Babinger, *Die frühosmanischen Jahrbücher des Urudsch* (Hannover, 1925)
Özkılınç–Coşkun–Sivridağ–Yüzbaşıoğlu 2007	*367 Numaralı Muhâsebe-i Vilâyet-i Rûm-İli Defteri ile 114, 390 ve 101 Numaralı İcmâl Defterleri (920–937/1514–1530). Karlı-ili, Agrıboz, Mora, Rodos ve Tırhala Livâları Dizin ve Tıpkıbasım*, eds Ahmet Özkılınç, Ali Coşkun, Abdullah Sivridağ, Murat Yüzbaşıoğlu, T.C. Başbakanlık Devlet Arşivleri Genel Müdürlüğü, Osmanlı Arşivi Daire Başkanlığı, 2 vols (Ankara, 2007)
Pacifico 1700	D. Pier'Antonio Pacifico, *Breve descrizzione corografica del Peloponneso ò Morea. Con l'Origine de primi habitanti, Serie de Prencipi, Titolo di ciascheduna Prouincia, Possessori di quelle, Natura de Paesi, Costumi de Popoli, Principio, e fine d'ogni loro auenimento sino aldì presente, con suoi testi latini, con Geroglifici, Imprese, Medaglie, & Armi gentilitie d'ogni Prouincia* (Venetia, 1700[1])
Pacifico 1704	D. Pier'Antonio Pacifico, *Breve descrizzione corografica del Peloponneso ò Morea. Con l'Origine de primi habitanti, Serie de Prencipi, Titolo di ciascheduna Provincia, Possessori di quelle, Natura de Paesi, Costumi de Popoli, Principio, e fine d'ogni loro avvenimento, con suoi testi latini, con Geroglifici, Imprese, Medaglie, & Armi gentilitie d'ogni Provincia* (Venetia, 1704[2])
Palaeologus 1985	Manuel Palaeologus, *Funeral Oration on his Brother Theodore*, ed. Julian Chrysostomides, Corpus Fontium Historiae Byzantinae (Thessaloniki, 1985)
Pausanias 1960	Pausanias, *Description of Greece with an English Translation by W.H.S. Jones and H.A. Ormerod*, The Loeb Classical Library, 4 vols (London-Cambridge Massachusetts, 1960)
Philo Alexandrinus 1970	Philo Alexandrinus, *Legatio ad Gaium*, ed. E. Mary Smallwood (Leiden, 1970[2])
Pouqueville 1826–27	François Charles Hugues Laurent Pouqueville, *Voyage de la Grèce*, 6 vols (Paris, 1826–1827)
Procopius 1838	Procopius, *De Aedificiis*, ed. Guilielmus Dindorf, *Procopius*, Corpus Scriptorum Historiae Byzantinae, vol. 3 (Bonn, 1838)
Pulaha 1974	Selami Pulaha, *Defteri i regjistrimit të sanxhakut të Shkodrës i vitit 1485*, 2 vols (Tirana, 1974)
Sanudo 1940	Marino Sanudo, *Letters*, ed. Aldo Cerlini, 'Nuove lettere di Marino Sanudo il vecchio', *La Bibliofilia, Rivista di storia del libro e delle arti grafiche di bibliografia ed erudizione* 42/11–12 (1940), 321–359.
Sathas 1867	Konstantinos N. Sathas, *Ἑλληνικὰ ἀνέκδοτα. Περισυναχθέντα καὶ ἐκδιδόμενα κατ' ἔγκρισιν τῆς Βουλῆς ἐθνικῇ δαπάνῃ*, 2 vols (Athens, 1867; repr. 1982–84)
Sathas 1880–90	Constantine N. Sathas, *Documents inédits relatifs à l'histoire de la Grèce au Moyen Âge publiés sous les auspices de la Chambre des députés de Grèce*, 9 vols (Paris, 1880–1890)
Schreiner 1975–79	Peter Schreiner, *Die byzantinischen Kleinchroniken*, 3 vols (Wien, 1975–1979)
Spandounes 1997	Theodore Spandounes, *On the Origin of the Ottoman Emperors*, trans. Donald M. Nicol (Cambridge, 1997)

SPHRANTZES 1990 — GEORGIUS SPHRANTZES, *Chronicon*, ed. Riccardo Maisano, Corpus Fontium Historiae Byzantinae (Roma, 1990)

SVORONOS 1959 — NIKOS G. SVORONOS, 'Recherches sur le cadastre byzantin et la fiscalité aux XIe et XIIe siècles: le cadastre de Thèbes', *Bulletin de Correspondance Hellénique* 83 (1959), 1–166.

TOPPING 1949 — PETER W. TOPPING, *Feudal Institutions as Revealed in the Assizes of Romania, the Law Code of Frankish Greece. Translation of the Text of the Assizes with a Commentary on Feudal Institutions in Greece and in Medieval Europe* (Philadelphia, 1949)

TSELIKAS 1982–84 — AGAMEMNON TSELIKAS, 'Μεταφράσεις βενετικών εκθέσεων περί Πελοποννήσου', *Πελοποννησιακά* 15 (1982–1984), 127–152.

TSELIKAS 1987–88 — AGAMEMNON TSELIKAS, 'Μεταφράσεις βενετικών εκθέσεων περί Πελοποννήσου Β΄', *Πελοποννησιακά* 17 (1987–1988), 141–171.

TSELIKAS 1995 — AGAMEMNON TSELIKAS, 'Μεταφράσεις βενετικών εκθέσεων περί Πελοποννήσου Γ΄', *Πελοποννησιακά* 21 (1995), 33–53.

TSELIKAS 1996–97 — AGAMEMNON TSELIKAS, 'Μεταφράσεις βενετικών εκθέσεων περί Πελοποννήσου Δ΄', *Πελοποννησιακά* 22 (1996–1997), 58–80.

ṬURSUN BEG 1977 — TURSUN BEY, *Târîh-i Ebü'l-Feth*, ed. Mertol Tulum (İstanbul, 1977)

ṬURSUN BEG 1978 — TURSUN BEG, *Tārīḫ-i Ebü'l-Feth*, eds Halil İnalcık, Rhoads Murphey, *The History of Mehmed the Conqueror* (Minneapolis-Chicago, 1978)

VRANOUSSI 1998 — ERA L. VRANOUSSI, 'Deux documents byzantins inédits sur la présence des Albanais dans le Péloponnèse au XVe siècle', in *Οι Αλβανοί στο Μεσαίωνα*, ed. Charalambos Gasparis (Athens, 1998), 293–305.

VRANOUSSIS 1967 — LEANDROS VRANOUSSIS, *Τὰ χειρόγραφα τῶν Μετεώρων. Κατάλογος περιγραφικὸς τῶν χειρογράφων κωδίκων τῶν ἀποκειμένων εἰς τὰς μονὰς τῶν Μετεώρων ἐκδιδόμενος ἐκ τῶν καταλοίπων Νίκου Ἀ. Βέη*, vol. 1 (Athens, 1967)

ZARINEBAF–BENNET–DAVIS 2005 — Fariba Zarinebaf, John Bennet, Jack L. Davis, *A Historical and Economic Geography of Ottoman Greece. The Southwestern Morea in the 18th Century* (Athens, 2005)

C. SECONDARY STUDIES

AKDAĞ 1999 — MUSTAFA AKDAĞ, *Türkiye'nin İktisadî ve İçtimaî Tarihi. 1 (1243–1453). 2 (1453–1559)* 2 vols (Ankara, 1959–71,[1] 1999[5])

AKTAŞ–KAHRAMAN 1994 — NECATİ AKTAŞ, SEYİT ALİ KAHRAMAN, *Bulgaristan'daki Osmanlı Evrakı*, T.C. Başbakanlık Devlet Arşivleri Genel Müdürlüğü, Osmanlı Arşivi Daire Başkanlığı (Ankara, 1994)

AKTEPE 1950 — MÜNİR M. AKTEPE, 'Osmanlı'ların Rumeli'de İlk Fethettikleri Çimbi Kal'ası', *İstanbul Üniversitesi Edebiyat Fakültesi Tarih Dergisi* 2 (1950), 283–306.

Alexakis 1994 — Eleftherios P. Alexakis, ‘Αμφιγραμμικές ομάδες καταγωγής και γαμήλια στρατηγική στους αλβανόφωνους της ΝΑ. Αττικής-Λαυρεωτικής (1850–1940)’, in *Ε΄ Επιστημονική Συνάντηση Νοτιοανατολικής Αττικής (Παιανία, 5–8 Δεκεμβρίου 1991)*, eds Lefteris Vekris, Evanthia Syrmou (Paiania, 1994), 145–224.

Alexander 1999 — John C. Alexander, ‘Counting the Grains: Conceptual and Methodological Issues in Reading the Ottoman *Mufassal Tahrir Defters*’, *Arab Historical Review for Ottoman Studies* 19–20 (Oct. 1999), 55–70.

Alexandropoulos 1978 — Ioannis H. Alexandropoulos (Alexander), ‘Δύο ὀθωμανικὰ κατάστιχα τοῦ Μοριᾶ (1460–1463) (Εἰδήσεις γιὰ τὸ nahiye τῆς Ἀρκαδιᾶς: πρόδρομη ἀνακοίνωση)’, in *Πρακτικὰ τοῦ Α΄ Συνεδρίου Μεσσηνιακῶν Σπουδῶν (Καλαμάτα, 2–4 Δεκεμβρίου 1977), Πελοποννησιακὰ Παράρτημα 5* (Athens, 1978), 398–407.

Altay 2017 — Ahmet Altay, ‘A Migration Story from İstanbul to Sofia: The Ottoman Archival Records in Bulgarian St Cyril and Methodius National Library’, *Journal of Balkan Libraries Union* 5/2 (2017), 34–37.

Anastopoulos 1994 — Nikos V. Anastopoulos, *Η Δίβρη – Ηλείας στο διάβα των αιώνων* (Piraeus, 1994)

Andrews 2006 — Kevin Andrews, *Castles of the Morea* (Princeton, 2006²)

Androulakakis 2000 — Nikos Androulakakis, *Εισαγωγή στο ArcView* (Athens, 2000)

Antoniadi 1966 — Sofia L. Antoniadi, ‘Συμβολὴ στὴν ἱστορία τῆς Πελοποννήσου κατὰ τὸν 17ον αἰώνα, τὸ ἀρχεῖον Grimani’, in *Χαριστήριον εἰς Ἀναστάσιον Κ. Ὀρλάνδον*, vol. 3 (Athens, 1966), 153–165.

Antoniadis-Bibicou 1965 — Hélène Antoniadis-Bibicou, ‘Villages désertés en Grèce: un bilan provisoire’, in *Villages désertés et histoire économique, XIe–XVIIIe siècles*, École Pratique des Hautes Études, VIe section (Paris, 1965), 343–417.

Antonios 1961 — Mitropolitis pr. Ileias Antonios, ‘Ἡ Δίβρη’, *Πελοποννησιακὴ Πρωτοχρονιὰ* 5 (1961), 29–42.

Asdrachas 1988 — Spyros I. Asdrachas, *Οικονομία και νοοτροπίες* (Athens, 1988)

Asdrachas 1999 — Spyros Asdrachas, *Μηχανισμοί της αγροτικής οικονομίας στην τουρκοκρατία (ΙΕ΄–ΙΣΤ΄ αιώνας)* (Athens, 1978,¹ 1999²)

Asdrachas 2003a — Spyros I. Asdrachas, ‘Η αγροτική οικονομία’, in Spyros I. Asdrachas, Nikos E. Karapidakis, Olga Katsiardi-Hering, Eftyhia D. Liata, Anna Matthaiou, Michel Sivignon, Traian Stoianovich, *Ελληνική οικονομική ιστορία, ΙΕ΄-ΙΘ΄ αιώνας*, vol. 1 (Athens, 2003), 289–356.

Asdrachas 2003b — Spyros I. Asdrachas, ‘Η διακίνηση των ανθρώπων και των αγαθών: μία τυπολογία των μετακινήσεων. 1. Οι γενικοί χαρακτήρες’, in Spyros I. Asdrachas, Nikos E. Karapidakis, Olga Katsiardi-Hering, Eftyhia D. Liata, Anna Matthaiou, Michel Sivignon, Traian Stoianovich, *Ελληνική οικονομική ιστορία, ΙΕ΄-ΙΘ΄ αιώνας*, vol. 1 (Athens, 2003), 219–236.

Asdrachas 2003c — Spyros I. Asdrachas, ‘Η δομή του πληθυσμού’, in Spyros I. Asdrachas, Nikos E. Karapidakis, Olga Katsiardi-Hering, Eftyhia D. Liata, Anna Matthaiou, Michel Sivignon, Traian Stoianovich, *Ελληνική οικονομική ιστορία, ΙΕ΄-ΙΘ΄ αιώνας*, vol. 1 (Athens, 2003), 118–136.

Assenova–Kacori–Stojkov 1974 — Petia Assenova, Thoma Kacori, Roussi Stojkov, ‘Oikonymes et anthroponymes de Péloponnèse vers la moitié du XVe siècle’, in *Actes du XIe Congrès International des Sciences Onomastiques (Sofia, 28.VI–4.VII.1972)*, eds V.I. Georgiev, I.V. Duridanov, J.D. Zaimov, vol. 1 (Sofia, 1974), 69–72.

Asvesta 2012	Aliki Asvesta, 'Η βορειοδυτική Πελοπόννησος: περιηγητικές ανιχνεύσεις και αφηγήσεις', in *Πρακτικά Συνεδρίου Δύμη Φραγκοκρατία – Βενετοκρατία – Α΄ Τουρκοκρατία*, ed. Eleni G. Saranti (Patra, 2012), 297–315.
Atsuyuki 2004	Okabe Atsuyuki, 'Introducing Geographical Information Systems in Islamic Area Studies', in *Islamic Area Studies with Geographical Information Systems*, ed. Okabe Atsuyuki (London-New York, 2004), 1–18.
Avramea 1974	Anna Avramea, 'Ὁ «Τζάσις τῶν Μεληγγῶν». Νέα ἀνάγνωσις ἐπιγραφῶν ἐξ Οἰτύλου', *Παρνασσὸς* 16 (1974), 288–300.
Aykut 2002	Şevki Nezihi Aykut, 'Osmanlı Sikkeleri', in *Türkler*, eds Hasan Celâl, Kemal Çiçek, Salim Koca, vol. 10 (Ankara, 2002), 823–842.
Bailey–Gatrell 1995	Trevor C. Bailey, Anthony C. Gatrell, *Interactive Spatial Data Analysis* (Harlow, 1995)
Ballas 1995	A.I. Ballas, 'Τα μεσαιωνικά κάστρα του Μαινάλου', *Πελοποννησιακά* 21 (1995), 129–192.
Ballas 2001–2	A. Ballas, 'Κάστρα της Κυνουρίας, επισκόπηση των μεσαιωνικών κάστρων της Τσακωνιάς', *Πελοποννησιακά* 26 (2001–2002), 193–227.
Balta 2007	Evangelia Balta, 'Η ελαιοκαλλιέργεια στον τουρκοκρατούμενο Μοριά', in *«Ο δε τόπος... ελαιοφόρος». Η παρουσία της ελιάς στην Πελοπόννησο*, ed. Eleni Benaki (Athens, 2007), 91–105.
Barkan 1943	Ömer Lûtfi Barkan, *XV ve XVIıncı Asırlarda Osmanlı İmparatorluğunda Ziraî Ekonominin Hukukî ve Malî Esasları. 1. cilt, Kanunlar* (İstanbul, 1943)
Barkan 1953	Ömer Lûtfi Barkan, '«Tarihî Demografi» Araştırmaları ve Osmanlı Tarihi', *Türkiyat Mecmuası* 10 (1953), 1–26.
Barkan 1958	Ömer Lutfi Barkan, 'Essai sur les données statistiques des registres de recensement dans l'Empire ottoman aux XVe et XVIe siècles', *Journal of the Economic and Social History of the Orient* 1 (1958), 9–36.
Barkan 1964	Ömer Barkan, 'Edirne ve Civarındaki Bazı İmâret Tesislerinin Yıllık Muhasebe Bilânçoları', *Belgeler* 1/2 (1964), 235–377.
Barkan, *Timar*	Ömer Lûtfi Barkan, 'Timar', *İslâm Ansiklopedisi*, vol. 12/1 (İstanbul: Millî Eğitim Bakanlığı), 286–333.
Bees 1908	Nikos A. Bees, 'Μνεῖαι τοῦ Ἄστρους κατὰ τοὺς μέσους αἰώνας καὶ τὰ παρ' αὐτῷ κάστρα. Τὸ τοπωνυμικὸν «Ἄρια»', *Byzantinische Zeitschrift* 17 (1908), 92–107.
Bees, *Mora*	Nikos. A. Bees, 'Mora', *İslâm Ansiklopedisi*, vol. 8 (İstanbul: Millî Eğitim Bakanlığı), 413–427.
Beldiceanu 1965	Nicoară Beldiceanu, 'Recherches sur la réform foncière de Mehmed II', *Acta Historica* 4 (1965), 25–39.
Beldiceanu 1980	Nicoară Beldiceanu, *Le timar dans l'État ottoman (début XIVe–début XVIe siècle)* (Wiesbaden, 1980)
Beldiceanu 1985	Nicoară Beldiceanu, 'Timariotes chrétiens en Thessalie (1454/55)', *Südost-Forschungen* 44 (1985), 45–81.
Beldiceanu–Beldiceanu-Steinherr 1978	Nicoară Beldiceanu, Irène Beldiceanu-Steinherr, 'Riziculture dans l'Empire ottoman (XIVe–XVe siècle)', *Turcica* 9/2–10 (1978), 9–28.

Beldiceanu–Beldiceanu-Steinherr 1980	Nicoară Beldiceanu, Irène Beldiceanu-Steinherr, 'Recherches sur la Morée (1461–1512)', *Südost-Forschungen* 39 (1980), 17–74.
Beldiceanu–Beldiceanu-Steinherr 1986	Nicoară Beldiceanu, Irène Beldiceanu-Steinherr, 'Corinthe et sa région en 1461 d'après le registre TT10', *Südost-Forschungen* 45 (1986), 37–53.
Beldiceanu–Năsturel 1983	Nicoară Beldiceanu, Petre Ş. Năsturel, 'La Thessalie entre 1454/55 et 1506', *Byzantion* 53/1 (1983), 104–156.
Beldiceanu-Steinherr–Beldiceanu 1978	Irène Beldiceanu-Steinherr, Nicoară Beldiceanu, 'Règlement ottoman concernant le recensement (première moitié du XVIe siècle)', *Südost-Forschungen* 37 (1978), 1–40.
Bellusci 1994	Antonio Bellusci, *Ricerche e studi tra gli Arberori dell'Ellade. Kërkime dhe studime ndër Arbëroret e Helladhes. Έρευνες και μελέτες επί των Αρβανιτών της Ελλάδας* (Cosenza, 1994)
Biris 1998	Kostas I. Biris, *Ἀρβανῖτες, οἱ Δωριεῖς τοῦ νεώτερου ἑλληνισμοῦ. Ἱστορία τῶν Ἑλλήνων Ἀρβανιτῶν* (Athens, 1960,[1] 1998[4])
Bojanić-Lukač 1976	Dušanka Bojanić-Lukač, 'De la nature et de l'origine de l'ispendje', *Wiener Zeitschrift für die Kunde des Morgenlandes* 68 (1976), 9–30.
Bon 1967	Antoine Bon, 'Τὰ σύνορα τῶν Ἑνετικῶν κτήσεων ἐν Μεσσηνίᾳ, ἀπὸ τοῦ 13ου ἕως τοῦ 15ου αἰῶνος', *Μεσσηνιακὰ Γράμματα* 2 (1967), 20–31.
Bon 1969	Antoine Bon, *La Morée franque. Recherches historiques, topographiques et archéologiques sur la principauté d'Achaïe (1205–1430)*, vol. 1 (Paris, 1969)
Bowman 1985	Steven B. Bowman, *The Jews of Byzantium 1204–1453* (Alabama, 1985)
Braudel 1972–73	Fernand Braudel, *The Mediterranean and the Mediterranean World in the Age of Philip II*, trans. Siân Reynolds, 2 vols (London, 1972–1973)
Buchon 1843b	Jean Alexandre C. Buchon, *Nouvelles recherches historiques de la principauté française de Morée et ses baronnies*, 2 vols (Paris, 1843)
Burrough–McDonnell 1998	Peter A. Burrough, Rachael A. McDonnell, *Principles of Geographical Information Systems* (Oxford, 1998)
Cahen 1953	Claude Cahen, 'L'évolution de l'iqtâʿ du IXe au XIIIe siècle: Contribution à une histoire comparée des sociétés médiévales', *Annales Économies – Sociétés – Civilisations* 8 (1953), 25–52.
Cahen, *Iḳṭāʿ*	Claude Cahen, 'Iḳṭāʿ', *The Encyclopaedia of Islam²*, vol. 3 (Leiden: E.J. Brill), 1088–1091.
Cahen–İnalcik–Hardy, *Djizya*	Claude Cahen, Halil İnalcik, P. Hardy, 'Djizya', *The Encyclopaedia of Islam²*, vol. 2 (Leiden: E.J. Brill), 559–567.
Carile 1970	Antonio Carile, 'Una lista toponomastica di Morea del 1469', *Studi Veneziani* 12 (1970), 394–404.

CHEYNET 2006 — JEAN-CLAUDE CHEYNET, 'The Byzantine Aristocracy (8th–13th Centuries)', in *The Byzantine Aristocracy and Its Military Function* (Aldershot, 2006), I, 1–43.

CHRYSOSTOMIDES 1975 — JULIAN CHRYSOSTOMIDES, 'Corinth 1392–1397: Some New Facts', *Βυζαντινὰ* 7 (1975), 81–110.

CHRYSOSTOMIDES 1992–93 — JULIAN CHRYSOSTOMIDES, 'Merchant versus Nobles: A Sensational Court Case in the Peloponnese (1391–1404)', in *Πρακτικά του Δ΄ Διεθνούς Συνεδρίου Πελοποννησιακών Σπουδών (Κόρινθος, 9–16 Σεπτεμβρίου 1990), Πελοποννησιακά Παράρτημα 19*, vol. 2 (Athens, 1992–1993), 116–134.

CHRYSOSTOMIDES 2003 — JULIAN CHRYSOSTOMIDES, 'Symbiosis in the Peloponnese in the Aftermath of the Fourth Crusade', in *Byzantium. State and Society. In Memory of Nikos Oikonomides*, eds Anna Avramea, Angeliki Laiou, Evangelos Chrysos (Athens, 2003), 155–167.

COHEN–LEWIS 1978 — AMNON COHEN, BERNARD LEWIS, *Population and Revenue in the Towns of Palestine in the Sixteenth Century* (Princeton, 1978)

COOK 1972 — MICHAEL ALLAN COOK, *Population Pressure in Rural Anatolia, 1450–1600* (London, 1972)

CVETKOVA 1958 — BISTRA A. CVETKOVA, 'Новые данные о христианах-спахиях на Балканском полуострове в период турецкого господства', *Византийский Временник* 13 (1958), 184–197.

CVETKOVA 1962 — BISTRA CVETKOVA, 'Influence exercée par certaines institutions de Byzance et des Balkans du moyen âge sur le système féodal ottoman', *Byzantinobulgarica* 1 (1962), 237–267.

CVETKOVA 1983 — BISTRA CVETKOVA, 'Early Ottoman *Tahrir Defters* as a Source for Studies on the History of Bulgaria and the Balkans', *Archivum Ottomanicum* 8 (1983), 133–213.

ÇAĞATAY 1947 — NEŞET ÇAĞATAY, 'Osmanlı İmparatorluğunda Reayadan Alınan Vergi ve Resimler', *Ankara Üniversitesi Dil ve Tarih-Coğrafya Fakültesi Dergisi* 5 (1947), 483–511.

DAKA 1988 — PALOK DAKA, 'Toponimia e fshatit Damës', *Studime Gjeografike* 3 (1988), 249–256.

DANİŞMEND 1947–72 — İSMAİL HÂMİ DANİŞMEND, *İzahlı Osmanlı Tarihi Kronolojisi*, 6 vols (İstanbul, 1947–1972)

DARLING 1996 — LINDA T. DARLING, *Revenue-Raising and Legitimacy. Tax Collection and Finance Administration in the Ottoman Empire 1560–1660* (Leiden-New York-Köln, 1996)

DÁVID 1977 — GÉZA DÁVID, 'The Age of Unmarried Male Children in the *Taḥrīr-Defter*s (Notes on the Coefficient)', *Acta Orientalia Academiae Scientiarum Hungaricae* 31 (1977), 347–357.

DAVIES 1996 — SIRIOL ANNE DAVIES, *The Fiscal System of the Venetian Peloponnese. The Province of Romania 1688–1715* (unpublished Ph.D. thesis, University of Birmingham, 1996)

DELİLBAŞI 2005 — MELEK DELİLBAŞI, 'Christian *Sipahi*s in the Tırhala Taxation Registers (Fifteenth and Sixteenth Centuries)', in *Provincial Elites in the Ottoman Empire. Halcyon Days in Crete V, A Symposium Held in Rethymno, 10–12 January 2003*, ed. Antonis Anastasopoulos (Rethymno, 2005), 87–114.

DETORAKIS 1976–78 — THEOHARIS E. DETORAKIS, ''Ενθυμητικαὶ καὶ ἱστορικαὶ μαρτυρίαι περὶ ἐπιδημιῶν πανώλους εἰς Πελοπόννησον', in *Πρακτικὰ τοῦ Α΄ Διεθνοῦς Συνεδρίου Πελοποννησιακῶν Σπουδῶν (Σπάρτη, 7–14 Σεπτεμβρίου 1975), Πελοποννησιακὰ Παράρτημα 6*, vol. 3 (Athens, 1976–1978), 15–21.

DILO 1969 — TIMO DILO, 'Les luttes des Albanais du Péloponnèse contre les Turcs au XVe siècle', in *Deuxième conférence des études albanologiques à l'occasion du 5e centenaire de la mort de Georges Kastriote-Skanderbeg (Tirana, 12–18 Janvier 1968)*, ed. Androkli Kostallari, vol. 1 (Tirana, 1969), 251–260.

DOKOS 1975 — KONSTANTINOS DOKOS, *Ἡ Στερεὰ Ἑλλὰς κατὰ τὸν Ἐνετοτουρκικὸν πόλεμον (1684–1699) καὶ ὁ Σαλώνων Φιλόθεος* (Athens, 1975; repr. 1985)

DRAGOUMIS 1921 — STEFANOS N. DRAGOUMIS, *Χρονικῶν Μορέως τοπωνυμικά-τοπογραφικά-ἱστορικὰ* (Athens, 1921; repr. 2006)

DRAKAKIS–KOUNDOUROS 1939–40 — ALEXIOS TH. DRAKAKIS, STYLIANOS I. KOUNDOUROS, *Ἀρχεῖα περὶ συστάσεως καὶ ἐξελίξεως τῶν δήμων καὶ κοινοτήτων 1836–1939 καὶ τῆς διοικητικῆς διαιρέσεως τοῦ κράτους*, 2 vols (Athens, 1939–1940)

DUCELLIER 1968a — ALAIN DUCELLIER, 'L'Arbanon et les albanais au XIe siècle', *Travaux et Mémoires* 3 (1968), 353–368.

DUCELLIER 1968b — ALAIN DUCELLIER, 'Les Albanais dans les colonies vénitiennes au XVe siècle', *Studi Veneziani* 10 (1968), 47–64.

DUCELLIER 1979 — ALAIN DUCELLIER, 'Les Albanais du XIe au XIIIe siècle: nomades ou sédentaires?', *Byzantinische Forschungen* 7 (1979), 23–36.

DUCELLIER 1994 — ALAIN DUCELLIER, *Οι Αλβανοί στην Ελλάδα (13ος–15ος αι.). Η μετανάστευση μιας κοινότητας* (Athens, 1994)

DUCELLIER 1998 — ALAIN DUCELLIER, 'Les Albanais dans l'Empire byzantin: de la communauté à l'expansion', in *Οι Αλβανοί στο Μεσαίωνα*, ed. Charalambos Gasparis (Athens, 1998), 17–45.

EGRO 2005 — DRITAN EGRO, 'The Place of Albanian Lands in the Balkan Geopolitics during the Ottoman Invasion (the 14th–15th centuries)', *Studia Albanica* 1 (2005), 79–91.

ELDEM 1916 — ḪALĪL EDHEM ELDEM, *Müze-i Hümāyūn, Meskūkāt-ı Ḳadīme-i İslāmiyye Ḳataloğu. Meskūkāt-ı ʿOs̱māniyye*, vol. 1 [Ḳosṭanṭiniyye, AH 1334 (AD 1916)]

ELEFTHERIOU 2004 — EVANGELIA P. ELEFTHERIOU, *Το Μουχλί της Αρκαδίας. Συμβολή στην ιστορία και αρχαιολογία της πόλης* (unpublished MA dissertation, University of Athens, 2004)

ERDER 1975 — LEILA ERDER, 'The Measurement of Preindustrial Population Changes: the Ottoman Empire from the 15th to the 17th Century', *Middle Eastern Studies* 11 (1975), 284–301.

FAROQHI 1983 — SURAIYA FAROQHI, 'The Peasants of Saideli in the Late Sixteenth Century', *Archivum Ottomanicum* 8 (1983), 215–250.

FAROQHI 1999 — SURAIYA FAROQHI, *Approaching Ottoman History. An Introduction to the Sources* (Cambridge, 1999)

FEKETE 1955 — LAJOS FEKETE, *Die Siyāqat-schrift in der türkischen Finanzverwaltung*, 2 vols (Budapest, 1955)

FERLUGA 1975 — JADRAN FERLUGA, 'Le clisure bizantine in Asia Minore', *Zbornik Radova Vizantološkog Instituta* 16 (1975), 9–23.

FOTOPOULOS 1982 — ATHANASIOS TH. FOTOPOULOS, *Ιστορικά και λαογραφικά της ανατολικής περιοχής Αιγιαλείας και Καλαβρύτων, ήτοι των τ. δήμων Ακράτας – Αιγείρας – Κράθιδος – Φελλόης και Νωνάκριδος*, 2 vols (Athens, 1982)

FOURIKIS 1922 — PETROS FOURIKIS, 'Πόθεν τὸ ὄνομα Σοῦλι', in *Ἡμερολόγιον τῆς Μεγάλης Ἑλλάδος*, ed. Georgios Drosinis, vol. 1 (Athens, 1922), 404–420.

Fourikis 1929	Petros Fourikis, 'Συμβολαὶ εἰς τὸ τοπωνυμικὸν τῆς Ἀττικῆς', *Ἀθηνᾶ* 41 (1929), 27–178.
Fourikis 1931	Petros A. Fourikis, 'Πόθεν τὸ ἐθνικὸν *Ἀρβανίτης*', *Ἀθηνᾶ* 43 (1931), 3–37.
Fourikis 1933	Petros A. Fourikis, 'Ἡ ἐν Ἀττικῇ ἑλληναλβανικὴ διάλεκτος', *Ἀθηνᾶ* 45 (1933), 4–181.
Frashëri 1969	Kristo Frashëri, 'Le pays des Albanais au XVe siècle', in *Deuxième conférence des études albanologiques à l'occasion du 5e centenaire de la mort de Georges Kastriote-Skanderbeg (Tirana, 12–18 Janvier 1968)*, ed. Androkli Kostallari, vol. 1 (Tirana, 1969), 127–141.
Georgacas 1938	Dimitrios I. Georgacas, 'Συμβολὴ εἰς τὴν τοπωνυμικὴν ἔρευναν', *Ἀθηνᾶ* 48 (1938), 15–76.
Georgacas 1938–48	Dimitrios I. Georgacas, 'Τοπωνυμικά', *Λαογραφία* 12 (1938–1948), 62–78, 177–194.
Georgacas 1941	Demetrius J. Georgacas, 'Beiträge zur Deutung als Slavisch erklärter Ortsnamen', *Byzantinische Zeitschrift* 41 (1941), 351–358.
Georgacas 1956	Dimitrios Georgacas, 'Μερικοὶ σλαβικοὶ ὅροι καὶ τοπωνύμια στὴν Πελοπόννησο', *Πελοποννησιακὰ* 1 (1956), 385–408.
Georgacas 1965	Dimitrios I. Georgacas, 'Τὰ τοπωνύμια τῆς Ἀργολίδος καὶ τῶν Μυκηνῶν καὶ ἡ ἱστορία τοῦ τόπου', *Πελοποννησιακὴ Πρωτοχρονιὰ* 9 (1965), 159–167.
Georgacas–McDonald 1968	Demetrius J. Georgacas, William A. McDonald, *Place Names of Southwest Peloponnesus. Register and Indexes* (Athens, 1967); repr. *Πελοποννησιακὰ* 6 (1968, Suppl.), 1–403.
Gerber, *Muḳāṭaʿa*	Haim Gerber, 'Muḳāṭaʿa', *The Encyclopaedia of Islam*[2], vol. 7 (Leiden: E.J. Brill), 508.
Gerland 1903	Ernst Gerland, *Neue Quellen zur Geschichte des lateinischen Erzbistums Patras* (Leipzig, 1903)
Giannakopoulos 1994	Theodoros D. Giannakopoulos, 'Επισκόπησις της ιστορικής τοπογραφίας της Ηλείας', in *Πρακτικά του Ηλειακού Πνευματικού Συμποσίου 1993 (Πύργος-Γαστούνη 26–28 Νοεμβρίου 1993), Πελοποννησιακά Παράρτημα 21* (Athens, 1994), 355–454.
Giannaropoulou 1979	Ioanna Giannaropoulou, 'Κατάλογοι κωμοπόλεων καὶ χωριῶν τῶν ἐπαρχιῶν Ναυπλίας καὶ Κάτω Ναχαγιέ', in *Πρακτικὰ τοῦ Α΄ Συνεδρίου Ἀργολικῶν Σπουδῶν (Ναύπλιον, 4–6 Δεκεμβρίου 1976), Πελοποννησιακὰ Παράρτημα 4* (Athens, 1979), 121–128.
Giannopoulou 2007	Mimika Giannopoulou, 'Τα ελαιοτριβεία στην Πελοπόννησο από τον 19[ο] έως και τα μέσα του 20[ού] αιώνα', in *«Ο δε τόπος... ελαιοφόρος». Η παρουσία της ελιάς στην Πελοπόννησο*, ed. Eleni Benaki (Athens, 2007), 107–119.
Ginosatis 1988	Panagiotis A. Ginosatis, 'Απ' το τοπωνυμικό του Σπάτα', *Onomata Revue Onomastique* 12 (1988), 126–131.
Ginosatis 1994	Panagiotis A. Ginosatis, 'Ονοματολογικά Πικερμίου', in *Ε΄ Επιστημονική Συνάντηση Νοτιοανατολικής Αττικής (Παιανία, 5–8 Δεκεμβρίου 1991)*, eds Lefteris Vekris, Evanthia Syrmou (Paiania, 1994), 225–230.
Glykatzi-Ahrweiler 1960	Hélène Glykatzi-Ahrweiler, 'Recherches sur l'administration de l'Empire iscale aux IXe–XIe siècles', *Bulletin de Correspondance hellénique* 84 (1960), 1–109.

Gökbilgin 1952 — M. Tayyib Gökbilgin, *XV–XVI. Asırlarda Edirne ve Paşa Livâsı Vakıflar – Mülkler – Mukataalar* (İstanbul, 1952)

Göyünç 1969 — Nejat Göyünç, *XVI. Yüzyılda Mardin Sancağı* (İstanbul, 1969)

Göyünç 1979 — Nejat Göyünç, '«H̱âne» Deyimi Hakkında', *Tarih Dergisi* 32 (1979), 331–348.

Göyünç–Hütteroth 1997 — Nejat Göyünç, Wolf-Dieter Hütteroth, *Land an der Grenze. Osmanische Verwaltung im heutigen türkisch-syrisch-irakischen Grenzgebiet im 16. Jahrhundert* (İstanbul, 1997)

Grigoriou-Ioannidou 1989 — Martha Grigoriou-Ioannidou, 'Οι βυζαντινές κλεισούρες και κλεισουραρχίες', *Βυζαντιακά* 9 (1989), 180–202.

Gritsopoulos 1960 — Tasos Ath. Gritsopoulos, *Μονὴ Φιλοσόφου* (Athens, 1960)

Gritsopoulos 1971 — Tasos Ath. Gritsopoulos, 'Στατιστικαὶ εἰδήσεις περὶ Πελοποννήσου', *Πελοποννησιακὰ* 8 (1971), 411–459.

Gritsopoulos 1972 — Tasos Gritsopoulos, 'Σύμμεικτα Ἀρκαδικά', *Γορτυνιακὰ* 1 (1972), 143–290.

Gritsopoulos 1987–88 — Tasos Ath. Gritsopoulos, 'Ιστορική παράδοσις τοπωνυμίων περιοχής Δημητσάνας', in *Πρακτικά του Γ′ Διεθνούς Συνεδρίου Πελοποννησιακών Σπουδών (Καλαμάτα, 8–15 Σεπτεμβρίου 1985), Πελοποννησιακά Παράρτημα 13*, vol. 3 (Athens, 1987–1988), 407–459.

Guilland 1967 — Rodolphe Guilland, *Recherches sur les institutions byzantines*, 2 vols (Berlin-Amsterdam, 1967)

Güçer 1964 — Lütfi Güçer, *XVI–XVII. Asırlarda Osmanlı İmparatorluğunda Hububat Meselesi ve Hububattan Alınan Vergiler* (İstanbul, 1964)

Hahn 1854 — Johann Georg von Hahn, *Albanesische Studien*, 3 vols (Jena, 1854)

Haldon 1999 — John Haldon, *Warfare, State and Society in the Byzantine World, 565–1204* (London, 1999)

Hammer-Purgstall 1815 — Joseph Freiherr von Hammer-Purgstall, *Des osmanischen Reichs Staatsverfassung und Staatsverwaltung. Dargestellt aus den Quellen seiner Grundgesetze*, 2 vols (Wien, 1815)

Hatzisotiriou 1988 — Georgios D. Hatzisotiriou, 'Μερικά ξενόγλωσσα τοπωνύμια της Ν.Α. Αττικής. Η ετυμολογία τους', *Onomata Revue Onomastique* 12 (1988), 626–639.

Hendrickx 1970 — Benjamin Hendrickx, *Οἱ πολιτικοὶ καὶ στρατιωτικοὶ θεσμοὶ τῆς Λατινικῆς Αὐτοκρατορίας τῆς Κωνσταντινουπόλεως κατὰ τοὺς πρώτους χρόνους τῆς ὑπάρξεώς της* (Thessaloniki, 1970)

Hendrickx 1992 — Benjamin Hendrickx, 'Allagion, tzaousios et prôtallagatôr dans le contexte moréote : quelques remarques', *Revue des Études Byzantines* 50 (1992), 207–217.

Heywood 1988 — Colin Heywood, 'Between Historical Myth and 'Mythohistory': The Limits of Ottoman History', *Byzantine and Modern Greek Studies* 12 (1988), 315–345.

Hinz 1955 — Walther Hinz, *Islamische Masse und Gewichte umgerechnet ins metrische System* (Leiden, 1955)

Hodgetts 1983 — Christine Hodgetts, 'Land Problems in Coron 1298–1347: A Contribution on Venetian Colonial Rule', *Βυζαντινά* 12 (1983), 135–157.

Houliarakis 1973 — Michael Houliarakis, *Γεωγραφική, διοικητική καὶ πληθυσμιακὴ ἐξέλιξις τῆς Ἑλλάδος, 1821–1971*, vol. 1a (Athens, 1973)

Houliarakis 1974 — Michael Houliarakis, *Γεωγραφική, διοικητική καὶ πληθυσμιακὴ ἐξέλιξις τῆς Ἑλλάδος, 1821–1971. Πραγματικὸς πληθυσμὸς τῶν ἀπογραφῶν 1848–1911*, vol. 1b (Athens, 1974)

Hütteroth 1968 — Wolf-Dieter Hütteroth, *Ländliche Siedlungen im südlichen Inneranatolien in den letzten vierhundert Jahren* (Göttingen, 1968)

Hütteroth–Abdulfattah 1977 — Wolf-Dieter Hütteroth, Kamal Abdulfattah, *Historical Geography of Palestine, Transjordan and Southern Syria in the Late 16th Century* (Erlangen, 1977)

IEE 1974 — *Ἱστορία τοῦ Ἑλληνικοῦ Ἔθνους. Ὁ ἑλληνισμὸς ὑπὸ ξένη κυριαρχία (περίοδος 1453–1669), τουρκοκρατία-λατινοκρατία*, vol. 10 (Athens, 1974)

Ilieva 1991 — Aneta Ilieva, *Frankish Morea (1205–1262). Socio-cultural Interaction between the Franks and the Local Population* (Athens, 1991)

Iliopoulos 1948 — Konstantinos N. Iliopoulos, 'Τὸ τοπωνυμικὸν τῆς Ἠλείας', *Ἀθηνᾶ* 52 (1948), 145–216.

Imber 1997 — Colin Imber, *Ebu's-su'ud. The Islamic Legal Tradition* (Edinburgh, 1997)

İnal 2011 — Onur İnal, 'Environmental History as an Emerging Field in Ottoman Studies: An Historiographical Overview', *Osmanlı Araştırmaları* 38 (2011), 1–25.

İnalcık 1951 — Halil İnalcık, 'Timariotes chrétiens en Albanie au XV. Siècle d'après un registre de timars ottoman', *Mitteilungen des Österreichischen Staatsarchivs* 4 (1951), 118–138.

İnalcık 1953 — Halil İnalcık, 'Stefan Duşan'dan Osmanlı İmparatorluğuna. XV. Asırda Rumeli'de Hıristiyan Sipahiler ve Menşeleri', in *60. Doğum Yılı Münasebetiyle Fuad Köprülü Armağanı. Mélanges Fuad Köprülü* (İstanbul, 1953), 207–248.

İnalcık 1954b — Halil İnalcık, 'Ottoman Methods of Conquest', *Studia Islamica* 3 (1954), 103–129.

İnalcık 1956 — Halil İnalcık, 'The Land Surveys in the Ottoman Empire as a Source of Place-Names', *Belleten* 20/78 (1956), 228–230.

İnalcık 1959 — Halil İnalcık, 'Osmanlılar'da Raiyyet Rüsûmu', *Belleten* 23 (1959), 575–610.

İnalcık 1960 — Halil İnalcık, 'The Problem of the Relationship between Byzantine and Ottoman Taxation', in *Akten des XI. Internationalen Byzantinisten-Kongresses 1958*, eds Franz Dölger, Hans-Georg Beck (München, 1960), 237–242; repr. In *The Ottoman Empire. Conquest, Organization and Economy* (London, 1978)

İnalcık 1980a — Halil İnalcık, 'Military and Fiscal Transformation in the Ottoman Empire', *Archivum Ottomanicum* 6 (1980), 283–337

İnalcık 1980b — Halil İnalcık, 'Osmanlı Bürokrasisinde Aklâm ve Muâmelât', *Osmanlı Araştırmaları* 1 (1980), 1–14.

İNALCIK 1982 — HALİL İNALCIK, 'Rice Cultivation and the *Çeltükci-Reʿâyâ* System in the Ottoman Empire', *Turcica* 14 (1982), 69–141.

İNALCIK 1983 — HALİL İNALCIK, 'Introduction to Ottoman Metrology', *Turcica* 15 (1983), 311–348.

İNALCIK 1992 — HALİL İNALCIK, 'Islamization of Ottoman Laws on Land and Land Tax', in *Festgabe an Josef Matuz. Osmanistik-Turkologie-Diplomatik*, eds, Christa Fragner, Klaus Schwarz (Berlin, 1992), 101–118.

İNALCIK 1994 — HALİL İNALCIK, 'The Ottoman State: Economy and Society, 1300–1600', in *An Economic and Social History of the Ottoman Empire*, eds Halil İnalcık, Donald Quataert vol. 1 (Cambridge, 1994)

İNALCIK 1997 — HALİL İNALCIK, *The Ottoman Empire. The Classical Age 1300–1600* (London, 1997[3])

İNALCIK, *Čift-Resmi* — HALİL İNALCIK, 'Čift-Resmi', *The Encyclopaedia of Islam*[2], vol. 2 (Leiden: E.J. Brill), 32.

İNALCIK, *Ispendje* — HALİL İNALCIK, 'Ispendje', *The Encyclopaedia of Islam*[2], vol. 4 (Leiden: E.J. Brill), 211.

İNALCIK, *Tīmār* — HALİL İNALCIK, 'Tīmār', *The Encyclopaedia of Islam*[2], vol. 10 (Leiden: E.J. Brill), 502–507.

JACOBY 1973 — DAVID JACOBY, 'The Encounter of Two Societies: Western Conquerors and Byzantines in the Peloponnesus after the Fourth Crusade', *The American Historical Review* 78/4 (October 1973), 873–906.

JARAUSCH–HARDY 1991 — KONRAD H. JARAUSCH – KENNETH A. HARDY, *Quantitative Methods for Historians. A Guide to Research, Data and Statistics* (Chapel Hill-London, 1991)

JEM SULTAN 1977 — JEM SULTAN (BILL HOLBERTON), *Coins of the Ottoman Empire and the Turkish Republic. A Detailed Catalogue of the Jem Sultan Collection*, 2 vols (Thousand Oaks, 1977)

JOCHALAS 1971 — TITOS JOCHALAS, 'Über die Einwanderung der Albaner in Griechenland (Eine zusammenfassende Betrachtung)', in *Dissertationes Albanicae in honorem Josephi Valentini et Ernesti Koliqi septuagenariorum*, eds Peter Bartl, Martin Camaj, Gerhard Grimm (München, 1971), 89–106

JOCHALAS 1976 — TITOS P. JOCHALAS, 'Considerazioni sull'onomastica e toponomastica albanese in Grecia', *Balkan Studies* 17/2 (1976), 313–329.

JOCHALAS 2002 — TITOS JOCHALAS, *Εύβοια. Τα Αρβανίτικα* (Athens, 2002)

JOCHALAS 2006 — TITOS JOCHALAS, *Ύδρα. Λησμονημένη γλώσσα*, 2 vols (Athens, 2006)

JOCHALAS 2011 — TITOS JOCHALAS, *Η αρβανιτιά στο Μοριά. Χρονικά πορείας*, 2 vols (Athens, 2011)

KÁLDY-NAGY 1968 — GYULA KÁLDY-NAGY, 'The Administration of the Ṣanǰāq Registrations in Hungary', *Acta Orientalia Hungarica* 21 (1968), 181–223.

KALICIN 1983 — MARIA KALICIN, 'L'homme dans l'œuvre de Neşri "Tarih-i Al-i Osman"', *Études Balkaniques* 2 (1983), 64–82.

KALLIVRETAKIS 2003 LEONIDAS F. KALLIVRETAKIS, 'Νέα Πικέρνη Δήμου Βουπρασίων: το χρονικό του οικισμού της Πελοποννήσου τον 19ο αιώνα (και η περιπέτεια του πληθυσμού)', in *Πληθυσμοί και οικισμοί του ελληνικού χώρου. Ιστορικά Μελετήματα, KNE/EIE Τετράδια Εργασίας 18* (Athens, 2003), 221–242.

KATRIVANOS 1960 THEODOROS KATRIVANOS, 'Βελιγοστή-Λεοντάρι, μεσαιωνικὰ κάστρα', *Πελοποννησιακὴ Πρωτοχρονιὰ* 4 (1960), 344–349.

KATSAROS 2014 VASILIS KATSAROS, 'Οικογενειακά ονόματα Αγιονορίου, Αγίου Βασιλείου και γειτονικών οικισμών στο μεταίχμιο της τουρκικής κατάκτησης', *Ιστορικογεωγραφικά* 13–15 (2014), 207–223.

KATSIARDI-HERING 2018 OLGA KATSIARDI-HERING, ed., *Βενετικοί χάρτες της Πελοποννήσου, τέλη 17ου – αρχές 18ου αιώνα. Από τη συλλογή του Πολεμικού Αρχείου της Αυστρίας* (Athens, 2018)

KATSOULEAS 1978 STAVROS G. KATSOULEAS, 'Ἀρχαιοπινῆ τοπωνύμια Μεσσηνίας', in *Πρακτικὰ τοῦ Α΄ Συνεδρίου Μεσσηνιακῶν Σπουδῶν (Καλαμάτα, 2–4 Δεκεμβρίου 1977), Πελοποννησιακὰ Παράρτημα 5* (Athens, 1978), 348–358.

KATSOULEAS 1979 STAVROS G. KATSOULEAS, 'Ἀπὸ τὸ τοπωνυμικὸ τῆς Ἀργολίδας', in *Πρακτικὰ τοῦ Α΄ Συνεδρίου Ἀργολικῶν Σπουδῶν (Ναύπλιον, 4–6 Δεκεμβρίου 1976), Πελοποννησιακὰ Παράρτημα 4* (Athens, 1979), 87–99.

KAVVADIA-SPONDYLI 2002 ARISTEA KAVVADIA-SPONDYLI, 'Πρωτοβυζαντινή Πυλία', in *Πρωτοβυζαντινή Μεσσήνη και Ολυμπία. Αστικός και αγροτικός χώρος στη Δυτική Πελοπόννησο. Πρακτικά του Διεθνούς Συμποσίου (Αθήνα, 29–30 Μαΐου 1998)*, eds Petros G. Themelis – Voula Konti (Athens, 2002), 219–228.

KAYAPINAR 1999 LEVENT KAYAPINAR, *Osmanlı Klasik Dönemi Mora Tarihi* (unpublished Ph.D. thesis, Ankara University, 1999)

KAYAPINAR 2005a LEVENT KAYAPINAR, 'Δημογραφική Σύνθεση της Δημητσάνας με βάση τα Οθωμανικά Αρχεία', in *Α΄Παγκόσμιο Διαδικτυακό Παναρκαδικό Συνέδριο*, http://conference.arcadians.gr/ (2005)

KAYAPINAR 2005b LEVENT KAYAPINAR, 'Δημογραφική Σύνθεση του Λεονταρίου Αρκαδίας με βάση τα Οθωμανικά Αρχεία', in *Α΄ Παγκόσμιο Διαδικτυακό Παναρκαδικό Συνέδριο*, http://conference.arcadians.gr/ (2005)

KIEL 1996 MACHIEL KIEL, 'Das türkische Thessalien. Etabliertes Geschichtsbild versus osmanische Quellen. Ein Beitrag zur Entmythologisierung der Geschichte Griechenlands', in *Die Kultur Griechenlands in Mittelalter und Neuzeit. Bericht über das Kolloquium der Südosteuropa-Kommission 28–31 Oktober 1992*, eds Reinhard Lauer, Peter Schreiner (Göttingen, 1996)

KIEL 2007 MACHIEL KIEL, 'The Smaller Aegean Islands in the 16th–18th Centuries according to Ottoman Administrative Documents', in *Between Venice and Istanbul. Colonial Landscapes in Early Modern Greece*, eds Siriol Davis, Jack L. Davis (Athens, 2007), 35–54.

KLADOS 1837 A.I. KLADOS, *Ἐφετηρὶς (Almanach) τοῦ Βασιλείου τῆς Ἑλλάδος, διὰ τὸ ἔτος 1837* (Athens, 1837)

KODER 1978 JOHANNES KODER, 'Zur Frage der slavischen Siedlungsgebiete im mittelalterlichen Griechenland', *Byzantinische Zeitschrift* 71 (1978), 315–331.

KOKKAS 1996 PANAGIOTIS G. KOKKAS, 'Για το οθωμανικό νομισματοκοπείο των Σερρών', *Νομισματικά Χρονικά* 15 (1996), 77–100.

KOLLEKA 1982 GIANNA KOLLEKA, 'Αλβανικά επώνυμα Ελλήνων', *Onomata Revue Onomastique* 7 (1982), 28–32.

Kolleka 1983 — Gianna Kolleka, 'Αλβανικά επώνυμα Ελλήνων', *Onomata Revue Onomastique* 8 (1983), 10–31.

Kolleka 1987 — Gianna Kolleka, 'Οικογενειακά ονόματα σε -ούσης', *Onomata Revue Onomastique* 11 (1987), 83–89.

Kolovos 2012 — Ilias Kolovos, 'Πίσω στα *τεφτέρια*; Οικονομικά μεγέθη και κοινωνική δομή στην Άνδρο του 17ου αιώνα με βάση το οθωμανικό κτηματολόγιο: τρόποι ανάλυσης, μεθοδολογικά προβλήματα και ιστοριογραφικά ζητήματα', *Θεωρητικές αναζητήσεις και εμπειρικές έρευνες. Πρακτικά Διεθνούς Συνεδρίου Οικονομικής και Κοινωνικής Ιστορίας (Ρέθυμνο, 10–13.12.2008)*, eds Sokratis Petmezas, Tzelina Harlafti, Andreas Lymberatos, Katerina Papakonstantinou (Athens, 2012), 69–94.

Kolovos–Kotzageorgis 2015 — Elias Kolovos, Phokion Kotzageorgis, 'Halkidiki in the Early Modern Period: Towards an Environmental History', in *Mines, Olives and Monasteries. Aspects of Halkidiki's Environmetal History*, ed. Basil C. Gounaris (Thessaloniki, 2015), 123–161.

Komborozos 1962 — Fotis A. Komborozos, 'Τοπωνυμικὰ τῆς Ὀλυμπίας', *Πελοποννησιακὴ Πρωτοχρονιὰ* 6 (1962), 341–346.

Komborozos 1967 — Fotis A. Komborozos, 'Μεσσηνιακὰ τοπωνύμια (βυζαντινὰ καὶ μεταβυζαντινά)', *Μεσσηνιακὰ Γράμματα* 2 (1967), 356–382.

Konti 1983 — Voula Konti, 'Συμβολή στην ιστορική γεωγραφία του νομού Αργολίδας', *Σύμμεικτα* 5 (1983), 169–202.

Konti 1985 — Voula Konti, 'Συμβολή στην ιστορική γεωγραφία της Αρκαδίας, 395-1209', *Σύμμεικτα* 6 (1985), 91–124.

Kordosis 1981a — Michael S. Kordosis, 'Η σλαβική εποίκηση στην Πελοπόννησο με βάση τα σλαβικά τοπωνύμια', *Δωδώνη* 10 (1981), 381–444.

Kordosis 1981b — Michael S. Kordosis, *Συμβολή στην ιστορία και τοπογραφία της περιοχής Κορίνθου στους μέσους χρόνους* (Athens, 1981)

Kordosis 1984 — Michael S. Kordosis, 'Ιστορικά-τοπογραφικά Μορέως κατά την πρώτην εκστρατεία του Μεχμέτ Β΄', *Πελοποννησιακά* 15 (1984), 153–160.

Kordosis 1986a — Michael S. Kordosis, 'Η κατάκτηση της νότιας Ελλάδας από τους Φράγκους, ιστορικά και τοπογραφικά προβλήματα', *Ιστορικογεωγραφικά* 1 (1986), 53–194.

Kordosis 1986b — Michael S. Kordosis, 'Κόρινθος και Άγιος Γεώργιος (Νεμέα), σχέσεις φρουρίου και κάτω πόλεως (από Δ΄-ΙΗ΄ αι.)', in *Πρακτικά του Β΄ Τοπικού Συνεδρίου Κορινθιακών Ερευνών (Λουτράκι, 25–27 Νοεμβρίου 1984), Πελοποννησιακά Παράρτημα 12* (Athens, 1986), 49–56.

Kordosis 1986c — Michael S. Kordosis, 'Το βυζαντινό Νίκλι', *Ιστορικογεωγραφικά* 1 (1986), 197–198.

Kordosis 1988 — Michael S. Kordosis, 'Συλλογή τοπογραφικού υλικού από την προφορική παράδοση: Αγιονόρι (Αϊνόρι) Κορινθίας', *Ιστορικογεωγραφικά* 2 (1988), 293.

Kordosis 1989 — Michael S. Kordosis, 'Ταύτιση του βυζαντινού κάστρου Αράκλοβον (Άλβαινα Ηλείας)', *Δωδώνη* 18/1 (1989), 63–91.

KORDOSIS 1992–93 MICHAEL S. KORDOSIS, 'Χαρακτηριστικά γνωρίσματα του κάστρου Αράκλοβο ως ενιαίου οικιστικού συνόλου', in *Πρακτικά του Δ΄ Διεθνούς Συνεδρίου Πελοποννησιακών Σπουδών (Κόρινθος, 9–16 Σεπτεμβρίου 1990), Πελοποννησιακά Παράρτημα 19*, vol. 2 (Athens, 1992–1993), 7–10.

KORDOSIS 1999 MICHAEL S. KORDOSIS, 'Αρχαία Τενέα μεσαιωνική και νεώτερη Κλένια', in *Πρακτικά του Γ΄ Τοπικού Συνεδρίου Κορινθιακών Ερευνών (Κόρινθος, 28–30 Νοεμβρίου 1997), Πελοποννησιακά Παράρτημα 23* (Athens, 1999), 137–144.

KOSTOPOULOS 1989 ANDREAS V. KOSTOPOULOS, 'Τοπωνύμια Ερυμανθείας Πατρών', *Πελοποννησιακά* 17 (1989), 184–185.

KOTSONIS 1990 KONSTANTINOS L. KOTSONIS, 'Οικισμοί και δημογέροντες Καρυταίνης-Φαναρίου', in *Πρακτικά του Β΄ Τοπικού Συνεδρίου Αρκαδικών Σπουδών (Τεγέα-Τρίπολις, 11–14 Νοεμβρίου 1988), Πελοποννησιακά Παράρτημα 17* (Athens, 1990), 193–208.

KOTZAGEORGIS 2018 PHOKION KOTZAGEORGIS, 'Ottoman Tax Registers and Geo-history', *Ιστορικογεωγραφικά* 16–17 (2018), 17–29.

KOUKOULES 1948 FAIDON I. KOUKOULES, 'Ἐκ τοῦ ἁλιευτικοῦ βίου τῶν Βυζαντινῶν', *Ἐπετηρὶς τῆς Ἑταιρείας Βυζαντινῶν Σπουδῶν* 18 (1948), 28–41.

KOUKOULES 1948–55 FAIDON I. KOUKOULES, *Βυζαντινῶν βίος καὶ πολιτισμός*, 6 vols (Athens, 1948–1955)

KOUMOUSI 2007 ANASTASIA KOUMOUSI, 'Το φραγκικό κάστρο Παυλόκαστρο Πατρών', in *Πρακτικά του Ζ΄ Διεθνούς Συνεδρίου Πελοποννησιακών Σπουδών (Πύργος-Γαστούνη-Αμαλιάδα, 11–17 Σεπτεμβρίου 2005), Πελοποννησιακά Παράρτημα 27*, vol. 4 (Athens, 2007), 323–336.

KOURELIS 2003 KONSTANTINOS KOURELIS, *Monuments of Rural Archaeology. Medieval Settlements in the Northwestern Peloponnese* (unpublished Ph.D. thesis, University of Pennsylvania, 2003)

KÖPRÜLÜZADE 1931 MEHMET FUAT KÖPRÜLÜZADE, 'Bizans Müesseselerinin Osmanlı Müesseselerine Te'siri Hakkında Bâzı Mülâhazalar', *Türk Hukuk ve İktisat Tarihi Mecmuası* 1 (1931), 165–313.

KREKOUKIAS 1955 DIMITRIOS A. KREKOUKIAS, *Τριφυλίων βαπτιστικά, ἐπωνυμίαι, παρωνύμια* (Athens, 1955)

KYRIAKIDIS 1926 STILPON KYRIAKIDIS, *Ὁδηγίαι διὰ τὴν μετονομασίαν κοινοτήτων καὶ συνοικισμῶν ἐχόντων τουρκικὸν ἢ σλαβικὸν ὄνομα* (Athens, 1926)

KYRIAKIDIS 1947 STILPON P. KYRIAKIDIS, *Βυζαντιναὶ Μελέται VI. Οἱ Σλάβοι ἐν Πελοποννήσῳ: i) Κωνσταντῖνος ὁ Πορφυρογέννητος ii) Πατριάρχης Νικόλαος iii) Χρονικὸν τῆς Μονεμβασίας. Ἀρέθας* (Thessaloniki, 1947)

LAIOU-THOMADAKIS 1977 ANGELIKI E. LAIOU-THOMADAKIS, *Peasant Society in the Late Byzantine Empire. A Social and Demographic Study* (Princeton, 1977)

LAMBROPOULOU 1995 ANNA LAMBROPOULOU, 'Η εβραϊκή παρουσία στην Πελοπόννησο κατά τη βυζαντινή περίοδο', in *Οι Εβραίοι στον ελληνικό χώρο. Ζητήματα ιστορίας στη μακρά διάρκεια. Πρακτικά του Α΄ Συμπόσιου Ιστορίας (Θεσσαλονίκη, 23–24 Νοεμβρίου 1991)* (Athens, 1995), 45–61.

LAMBROPOULOU 1999 ANNA LAMBROPOULOU, 'Οι Εβραίοι στην Πελοπόννησο κατά την υστεροβυζαντινή περίοδο', in *Ο ελληνικός εβραϊσμός. Επιστημονικό συμπόσιο. Εταιρεία Σπουδών Νεοελληνικού Πολιτισμού και Γενικής Παιδείας (3 και 4 Απριλίου 1998)* (Athens, 1999), 33–63.

LAMBROS 1896 — SPYRIDON P. LAMBROS, 'Ἡ ὀνοματολογία τῆς Ἀττικῆς καὶ ἡ εἰς τὴν χώραν ἐποίκησις τῶν Ἀλβανῶν', *Ἐπετηρὶς Φιλολογικοῦ Συλλόγου «Παρνασσὸς»* 1 (1896), 156–192.

LEMERLE 1979 — PAUL LEMERLE, *The Agrarian History of Byzantium from the Origins to the Twelfth Century. The Sources and Problems*, trans. Gearóid Mac Niocaill (Galway, 1979)

LEWIS–PELLAT–SCHACHT, *Bālig͟h* — B. LEWIS, CH. PELLAT, J. SCHACHT, 'Bālig͟h', *The Encyclopaedia of Islam*², vol. 1 (Leiden: E.J. Brill), 993.

LIAKOPOULOS 2009 — GEORGIOS C. LIAKOPOULOS, 'Η αμπελοκαλλιέργεια και η οινοπαραγωγή στην πρώιμη οθωμανική Πελοπόννησο, βάσει του κατάστιχου TT10-1/14662', in *Οἶνον ἱστορῶ IX Πολυστάφυλος Πελοπόννησος*, ed. Yanis A. Pikoulas (Athens 2009), 197–222.

LIATA 1996 — EFTYHIA D. LIATA, *Φλωρία δεκατέσσερα στένουν γρόσια σαράντα. Η κυκλοφορία των νομισμάτων στον ελληνικό χώρο, 15ος–19ος αι.* (Athens, 1996)

LOENERTZ 1943 — RAYMOND-JOSEPH LOENERTZ, 'Pour l'histoire du Péloponèse au XIVe siècle (1382–1404)', *Études Byzantines* 1 (1943), 152–196.

LOENERTZ 1970 — RAYMOND-JOSEPH LOENERTZ, *Byzantina et Franco-Graeca. Articles parus de 1935 à 1966* (Roma, 1970), 227–265.

LONGNON 1949 — JEAN LONGNON, *L'empire latin de Constantinople et la principauté de Morée* (Paris, 1949)

LOWRY 1990 — HEATH LOWRY, 'The Role of Byzantine Provincial Officials Following the Ottoman Conquests of their Lands', in *IIIrd Congress on the Social and Economic History of Turkey, Princeton University 24–26 August 1983*, eds Heath Lowry, Ralph S. Hattox (Istanbul-Washington-Paris, 1990), 261–267.

LOWRY 1992 — HEATH W. JR. LOWRY, 'The Ottoman *Tahrîr Defterleri* as a Source for Social and Economic History: Pitfalls and Limitations', in *Studies in Defterology. Ottoman Society in the Fifteenth and Sixteenth Centuries* (Istanbul, 1992), 3–18.

LUKA 1984 — KOLË LUKA, 'Evidence of the Antiquity and Extension of the Ethnic Name Arbën/Arbër', in *Problems of the Formation of the Albanian People, their Language and Culture* (Tirana, 1984), 258–273.

MALINGOUDIS 1981 — PHAEDON MALINGOUDIS, *Studien zu den slavischen Ortsnamen Griechenlands. 1. Slavische Flurnamen aus der messenischen Mani mit 7 Karten* (Mainz Wiesbaden, 1981)

MALINGOUDIS 1983 — PHAEDON MALINGOUDIS, 'Toponymy and History. Observations Concerning the Slavonic Toponymy of the Peloponnese', *Cyrillomethodianum* 7 (1983), 99–111.

MALLIARIS 2008 — ALEXIS MALLIARIS, *Η Πάτρα κατά τη βενετική περίοδο (1687–1715). Γη, πληθυσμοί, κοινωνία στη Β.Δ. Πελοπόννησο* (Venice, 2008)

MANIATI-KOKKINI 1990 — TRIANTAFYLLITSA MANIATI-KOKKINI, *Ο βυζαντινός θεσμός της* πρόνοιας. *Συμβολή στη μελέτη του χαρακτήρα του* (unpublished Ph.D. thesis, Aristotle University of Thessaloniki, 1990)

MARKL 1966 — OTTO MARKL, *Ortsnamen Griechenlands in 'fränkischer' Zeit* (Graz, 1966)

McGowan 1969 — Bruce McGowan, 'Food Supply and Taxation on the Middle Danube (1568–1579)', *Archivum Ottomanicum* 1 (1969), 139–196.

McGowan 1981 — Bruce McGowan, *Economic Life in Ottoman Europe. Taxation, Trade and the Struggle for Land, 1600–1800* (Cambridge, 1981)

Melas 2006 — Viktor Th. Melas, ed., *Η Πελοπόννησος. Χαρτογραφία και Ιστορία, 16ος–18ος αιώνας* (Athens: 2006)

Ménage 1964 — Victor Louis Ménage, *Neshrī's History of the Ottomans. The Sources and the Development of the Text* (London, 1964)

Mercati 1926 — Giovanni Mercati, *Scritti d'Isidoro il cardinale Ruteno e codici a lui appartenuti che si conservano nella Biblioteca Apostolica Vaticana*, Studi e Testi 46 (Roma, 1926)

Meyer 1957 — Ernst Meyer, *Neue peloponnesische Wanderungen* (Bern, 1957)

Miliarakis 1886 — Antonios Miliarakis, *Γεωγραφία νέα καὶ ἀρχαία τοῦ νομοῦ Ἀργολίδος καὶ Κορινθίας μετὰ γεωγραφικοῦ πίνακος τοῦ νομοῦ* (Athens, 1886; repr. 1997)

Moutafchieva 1988 — Vera P. Moutafchieva, *Agrarian Relations in the Ottoman Empire in the 15th and 16th Centuries* (New York, 1988)

Moutoulas 2007 — Pantelis Moutoulas, 'Η ελαιοκαλλιέργεια στην Πελοπόννησο κατά τον μεσοπόλεμο. Οικονομία, θεσμοί', in *«Ο δε τόπος… ελαιοφόρος». Η παρουσία της ελιάς στην Πελοπόννησο*, ed. Eleni Benaki (Athens, 2007), 147–159.

Moutzali 1994 — Afendra G. Moutzali, 'Τοπογραφικά της μεσαιωνικής Πάτρας', in *Αντίφωνον, Αφιέρωμα στον καθηγητή Ν.Β. Δρανδάκη*, ed. Vasilis Katsaros (Thessaloniki, 1994), 132–157.

Murphey 1988 — Rhoads Murphey, 'Provisioning Istanbul: The State and Subsistence in the Early Modern Middle East', *Food and Foodways* 2 (1988), 217–263; repr. In *Studies on Ottoman Society and Culture, 16th–18th Centuries* (Aldershot, 2007)

Nanetti 2011 — Andrea Nanetti, *Atlante della Messenia Veneziana. Corone, Modone, Pilos e le loro isole. Atlas of Venetian Messenia. Coron, Modon, Pylos and their Islands. Άτλας της Ενετικής Μεσσηνίας. Κορώνη, Μεθώνη, Πύλος και τα νησιά τους (1207–1500 & 1685–1715)* (Imola, 2011)

Nomikos 1997a — Stefanos Nomikos, *Η υδροκίνηση στην προβιομηχανική Ελλάδα* (Athens, 1997)

Nomikos 1997b — Stefanos Nomikos, 'Ο νερόμυλος και η νεροτριβή,' in *Υπαίθριο μουσείο υδροκίνησης, συνοπτικός οδηγός* (Athens, 1997), 10–20.

Nomikos 1999 — Stefanos Nomikos, 'Ο ρόλος της υδρενέργειας στην προβιομηχανική τεχνολογία και τα έργα υποδομής για τη λειτουργία των υδροκίνητων εγκαταστάσεων', in ΥΠ.ΠΟ, Μουσείο Ελληνικής Λαϊκής Τέχνης, *Το νερό, πηγή ζωής, κίνησης, καθαρμού. Πρακτικά Επιστημονικής Συνάντησης (12–14 Δεκεμβρίου 1997, Αίθουσα Παλαιάς Βουλής)* (Athens, 1999), 77–80.

Nouhakis 1901 — Ioannis Emm. Nouhakis, *Ἑλληνικὴ χωρογραφία. Γεωγραφία, ἱστορία, στατιστικὴ πληθυσμοῦ καὶ ἀποστάσεων συνταχθεῖσα καὶ ἐκδοθεῖσα ἐγκρίσει τῆς Α.Β.Υ. τοῦ Διαδόχου Γενικοῦ Διοικητοῦ τοῦ Στρατοῦ, τοῦ Ὑπουργείου τῶν Στρατιωτικῶν, ἀναγνωρισθεῖσα δὲ παρὰ τοῦ Ὑπουργείου τῶν Ἐσωτερικῶν*, 2 vols (Athens, 1901[3])

24 Nāḥiyyet-i Balya Badra (Patra)
Economic Distribution

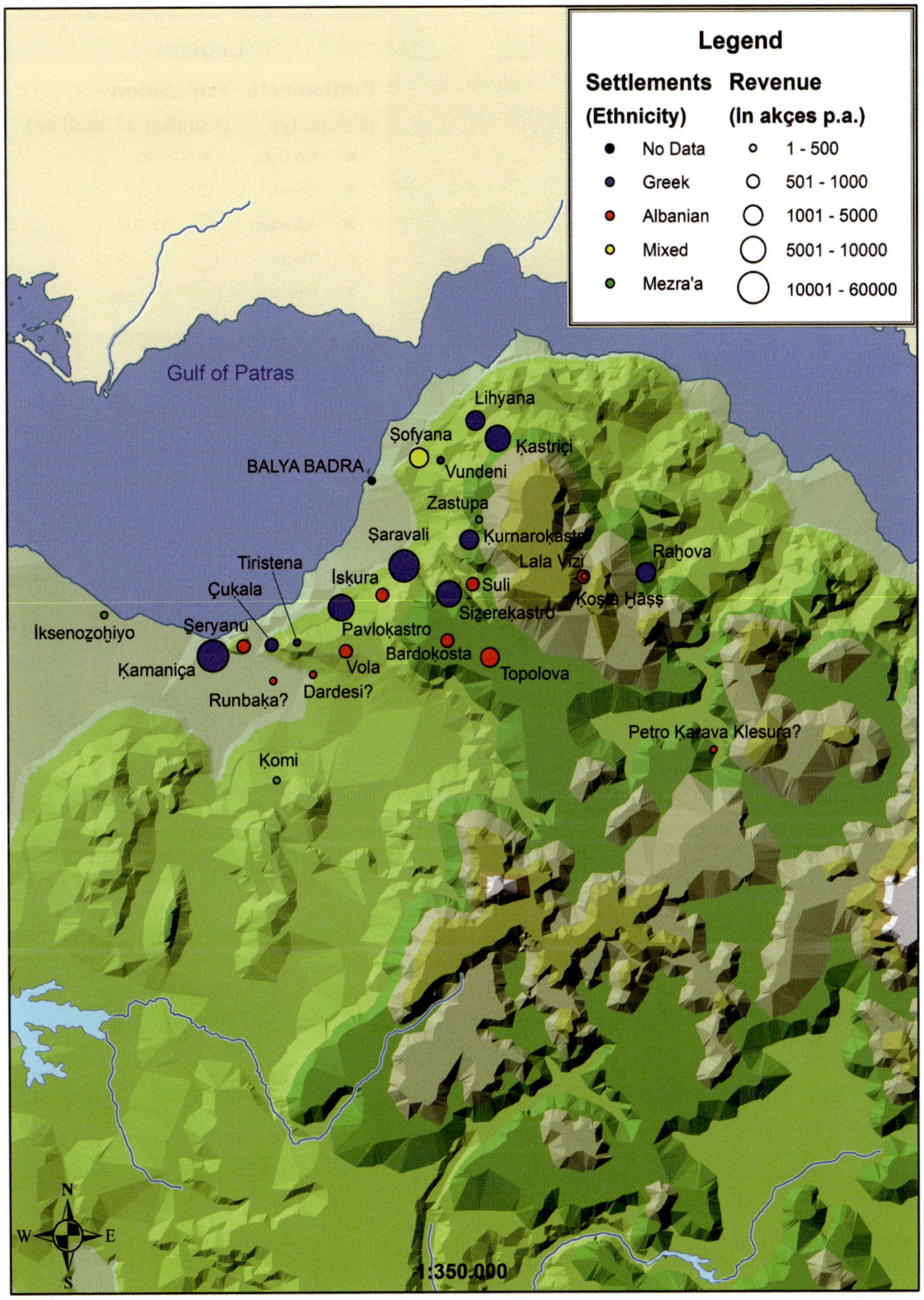

Designed by G.C. Liakopoulos

25 Nāḥiyyet-i Ḳalandriça (Halandritsa)
Demographic Distribution

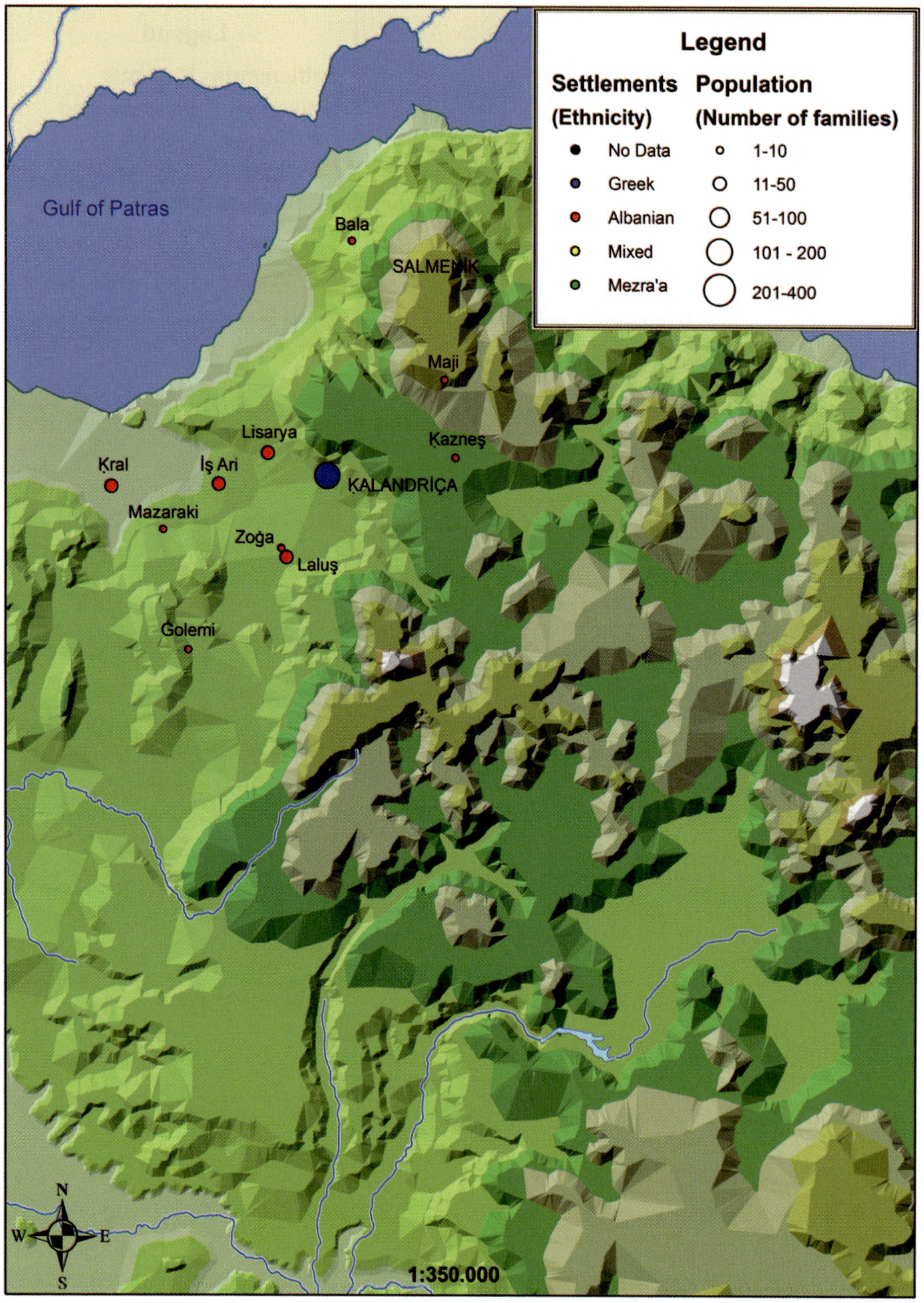

Designed by G.C. Liakopoulos

26 Nāḥiyyet-i Ḳalandriça (Halandritsa)
Economic Distribution

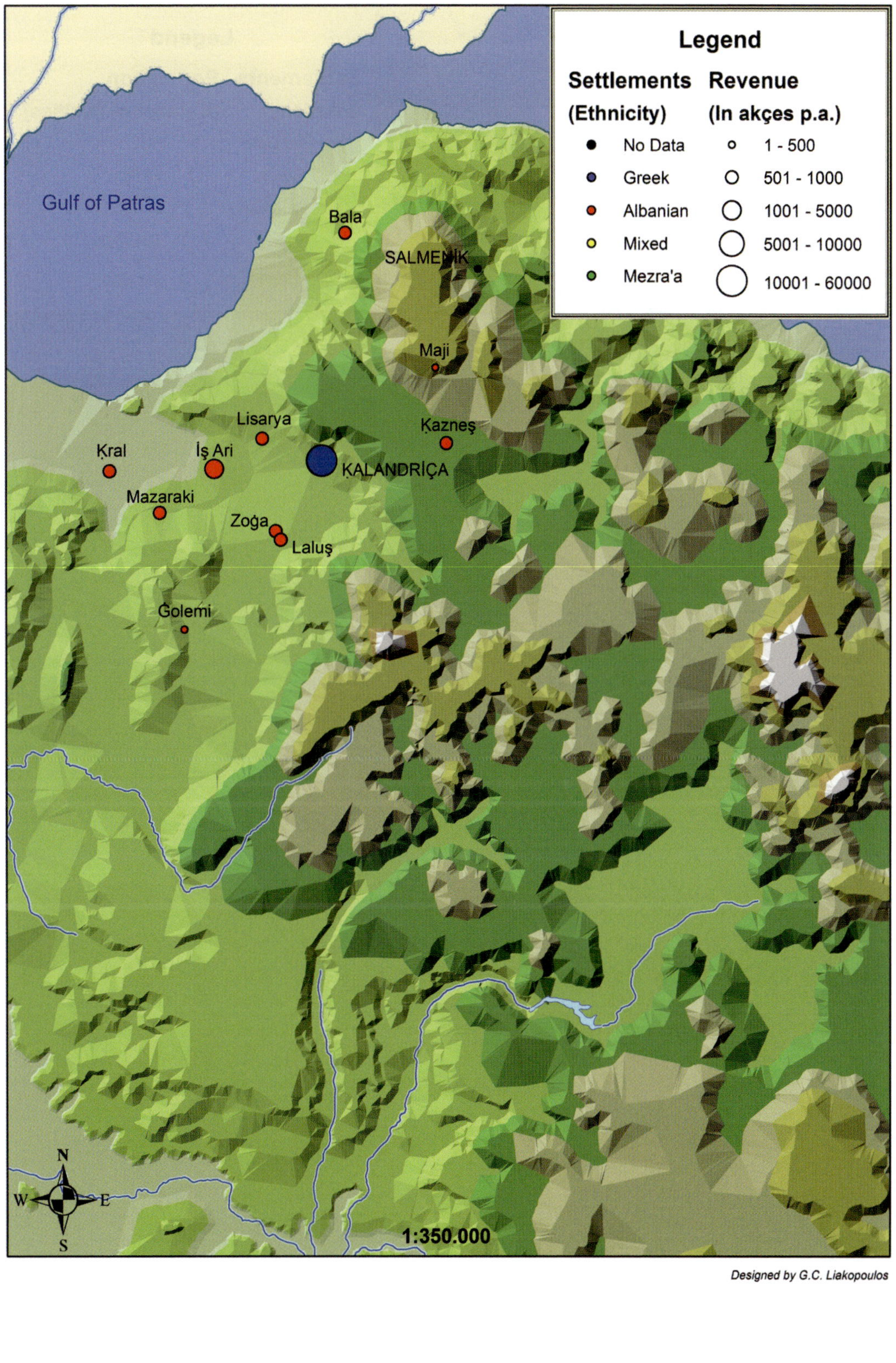

Designed by G.C. Liakopoulos

27 Nāḥiyyet-i Şandamiri (Santomeri)
Demographic Distribution

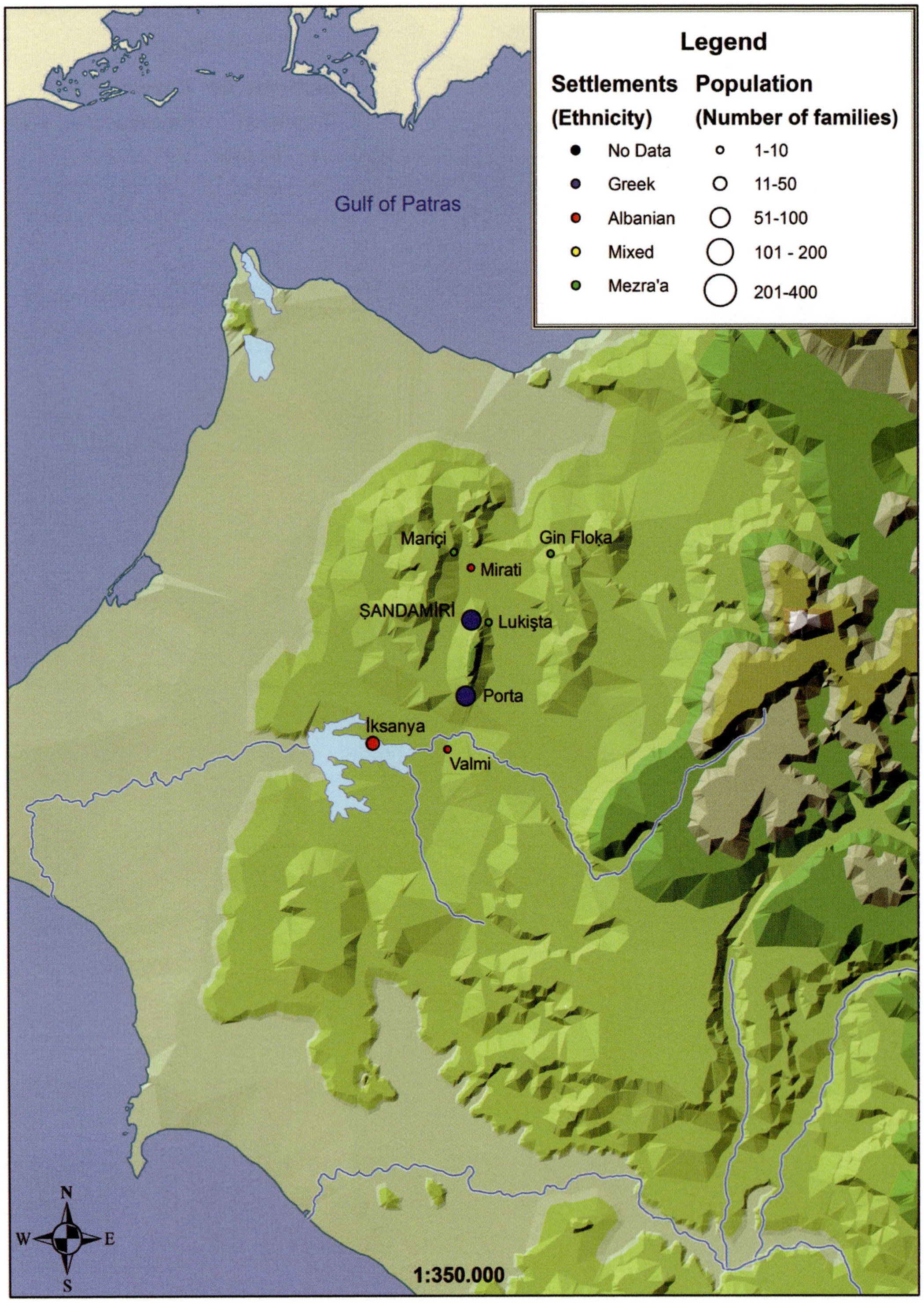

Designed by G.C. Liakopoulos

28 Nāḥiyyet-i Ṣandamiri (Santomeri)
Economic Distribution

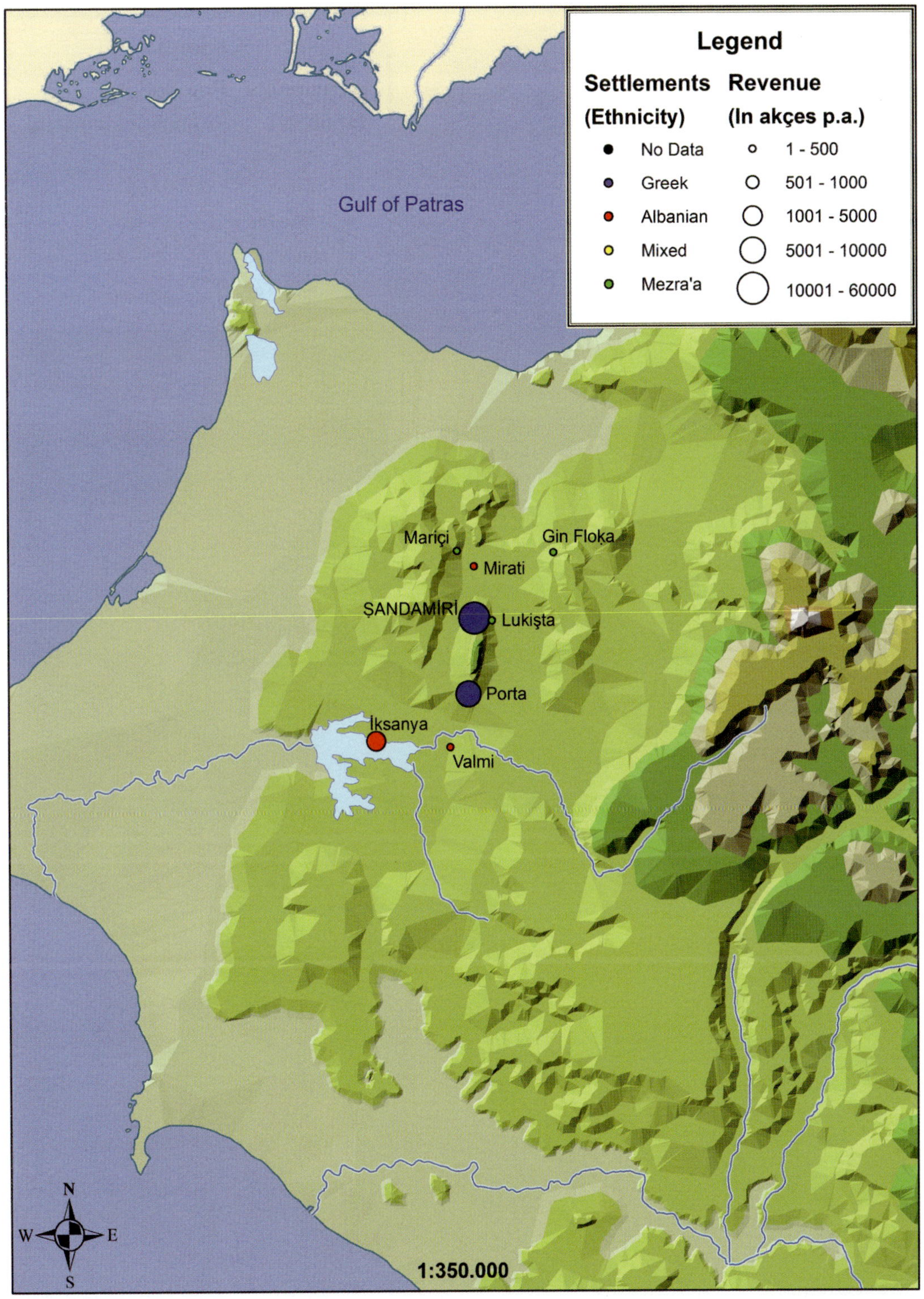

Designed by G.C. Liakopoulos

29 Nāḥiyyet-i Girbene (Spartia) Demographic Distribution

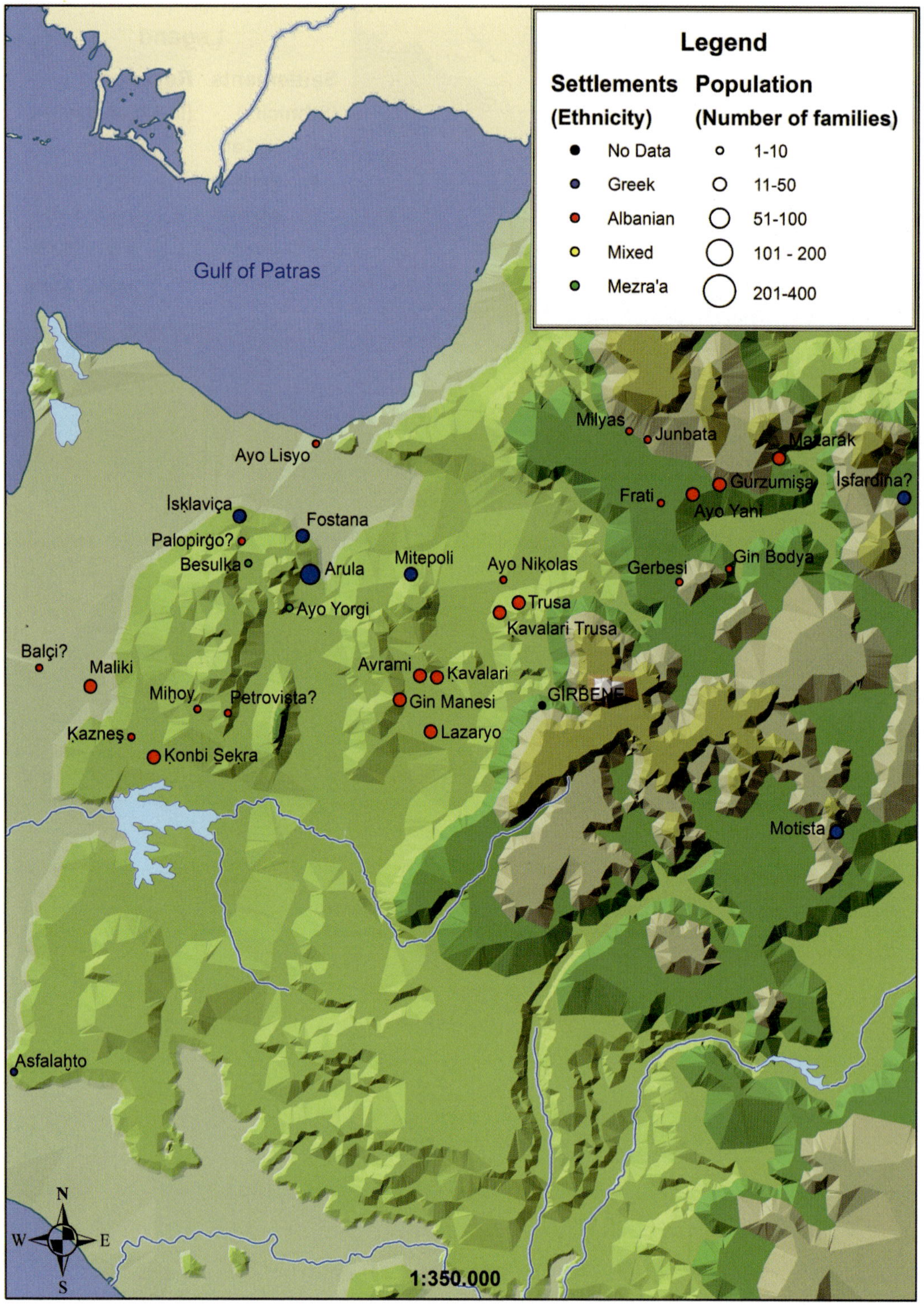

Designed by G.C. Liakopoulos

30 Nāḫiyyet-i Girbene (Spartia)
Economic Distribution

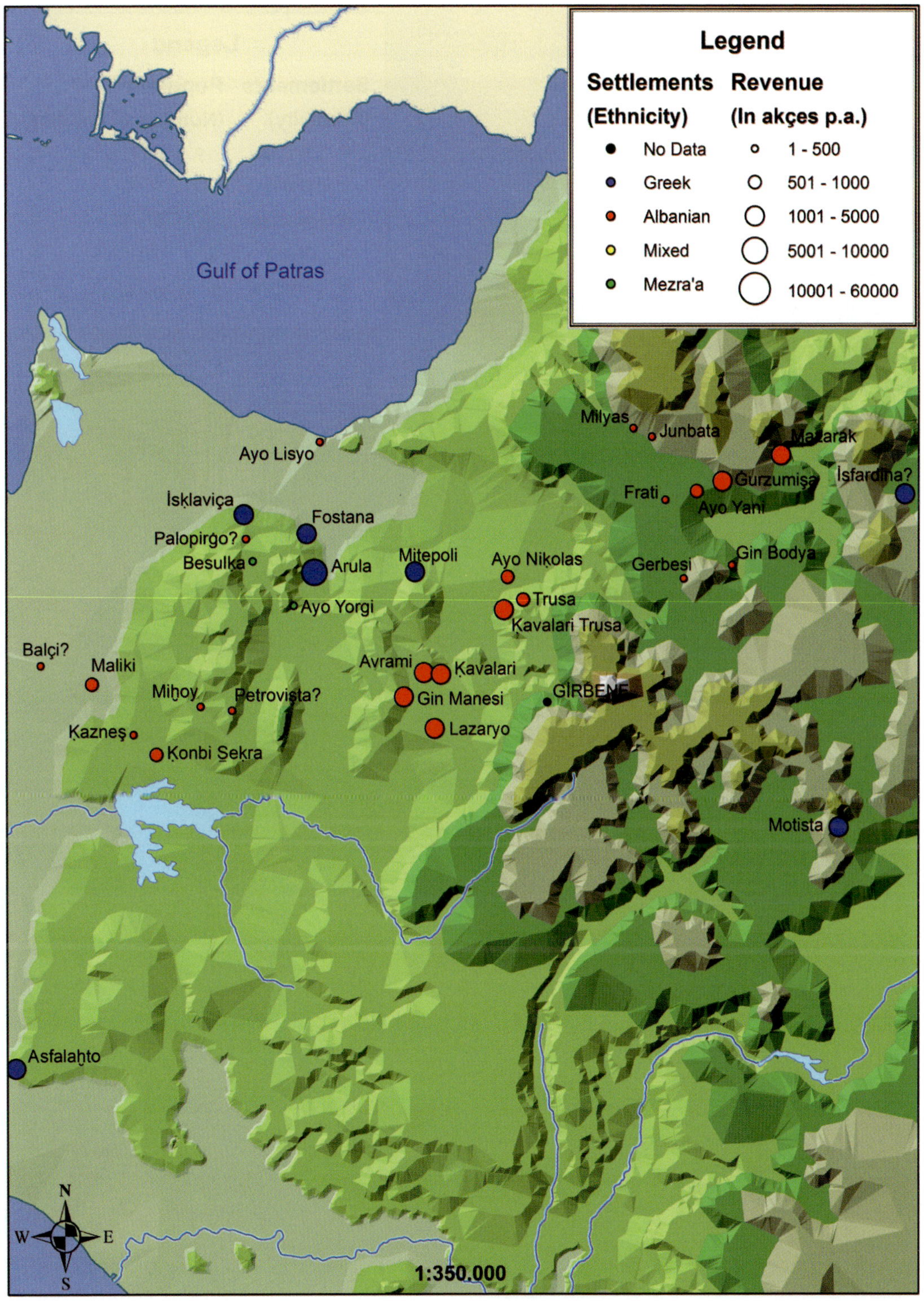

Designed by G.C. Liakopoulos

31 Nāḥiyyet-i Ayo İlya (Agios Ilias)
Demographic Distribution

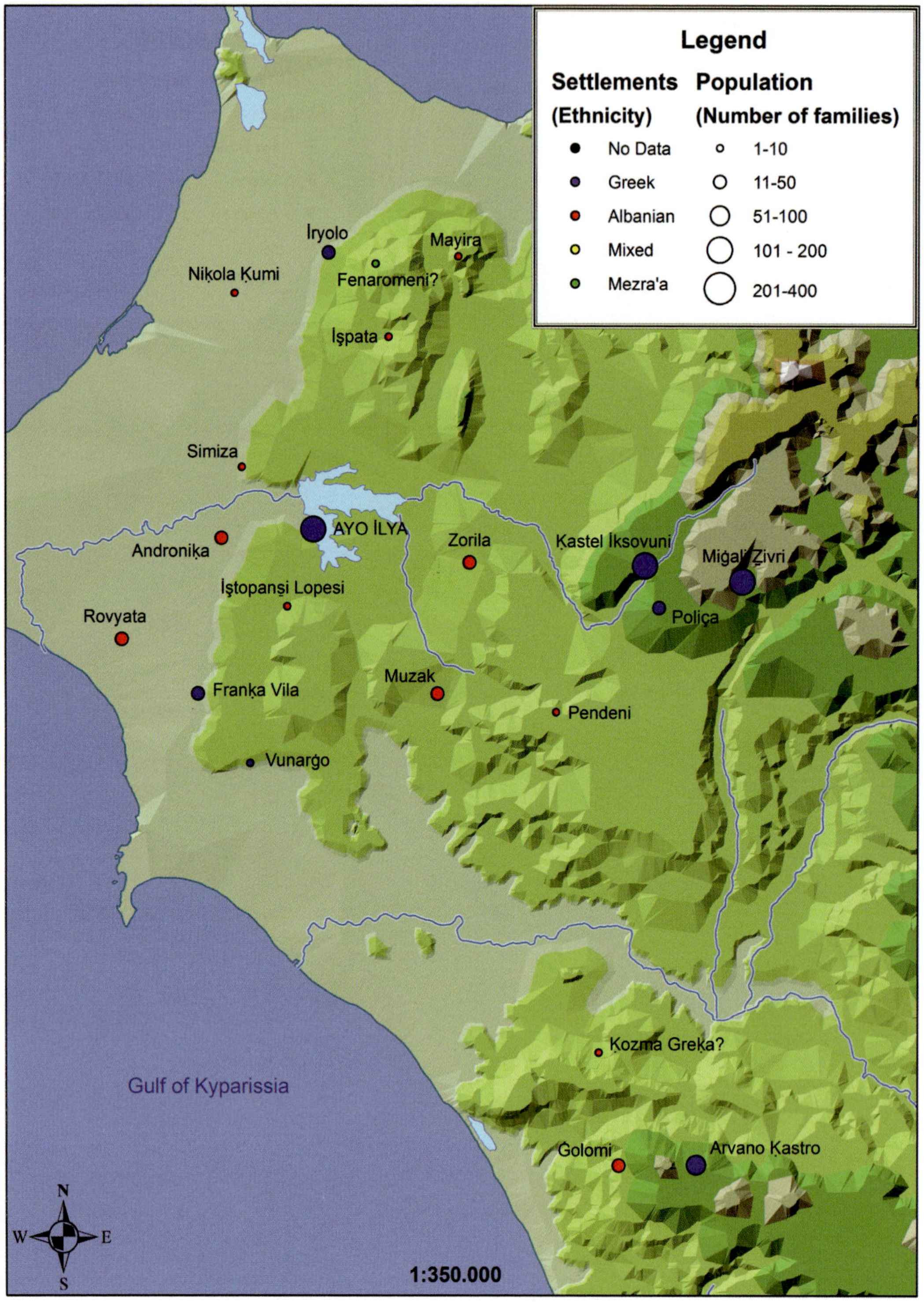

Designed by G.C. Liakopoulos

32 Nāḥiyyet-i Ayo İlya (Agios Ilias)
Economic Distribution

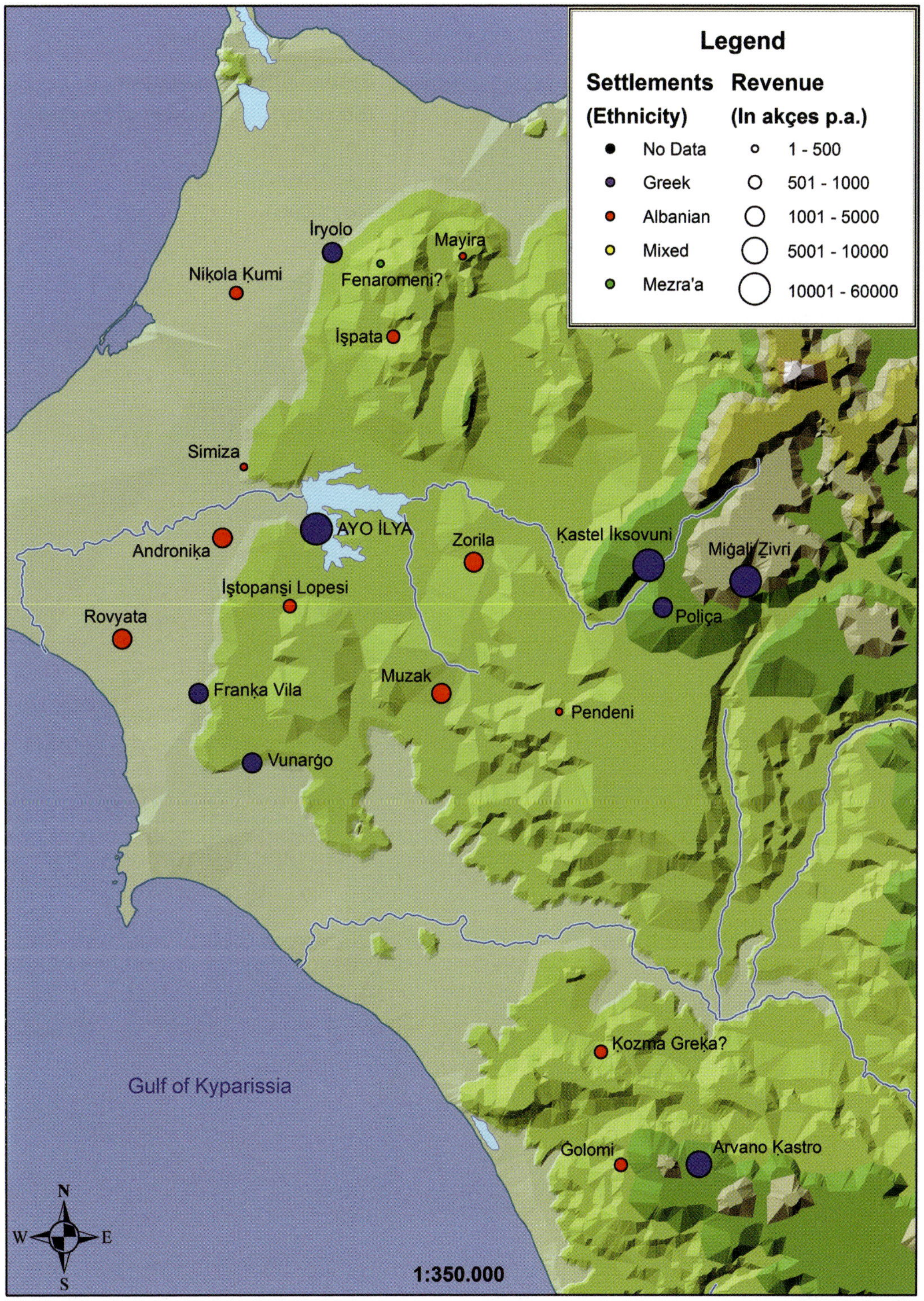

Designed by G.C. Liakopoulos

33 Nāḫiyyet-i Ġardicḳo (Gatsiko)
Demographic Distribution

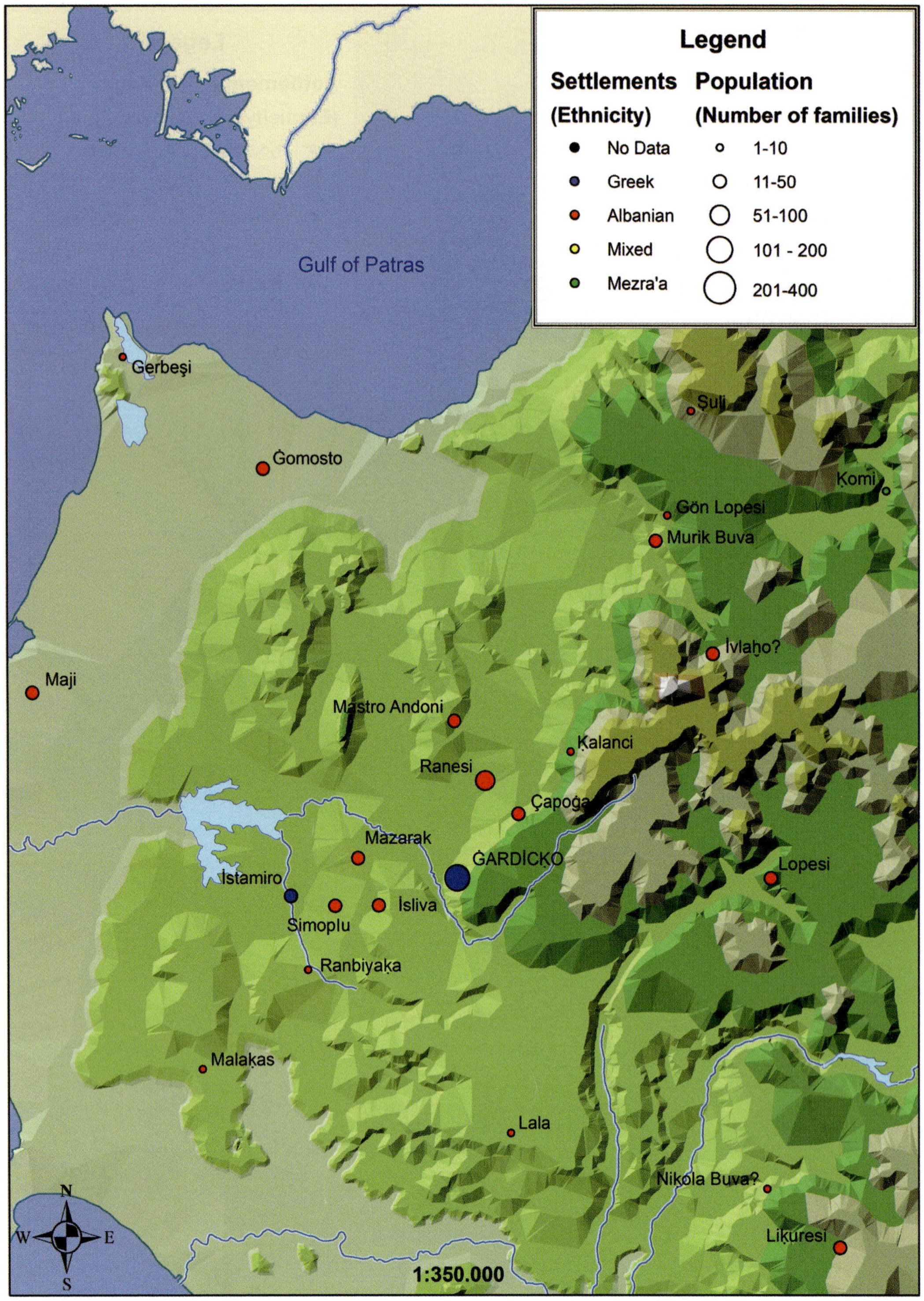

Designed by G.C. Liakopoulos

34 Nāḥiyyet-i Ġardicḳo (Gatsiko)
Economic Distribution

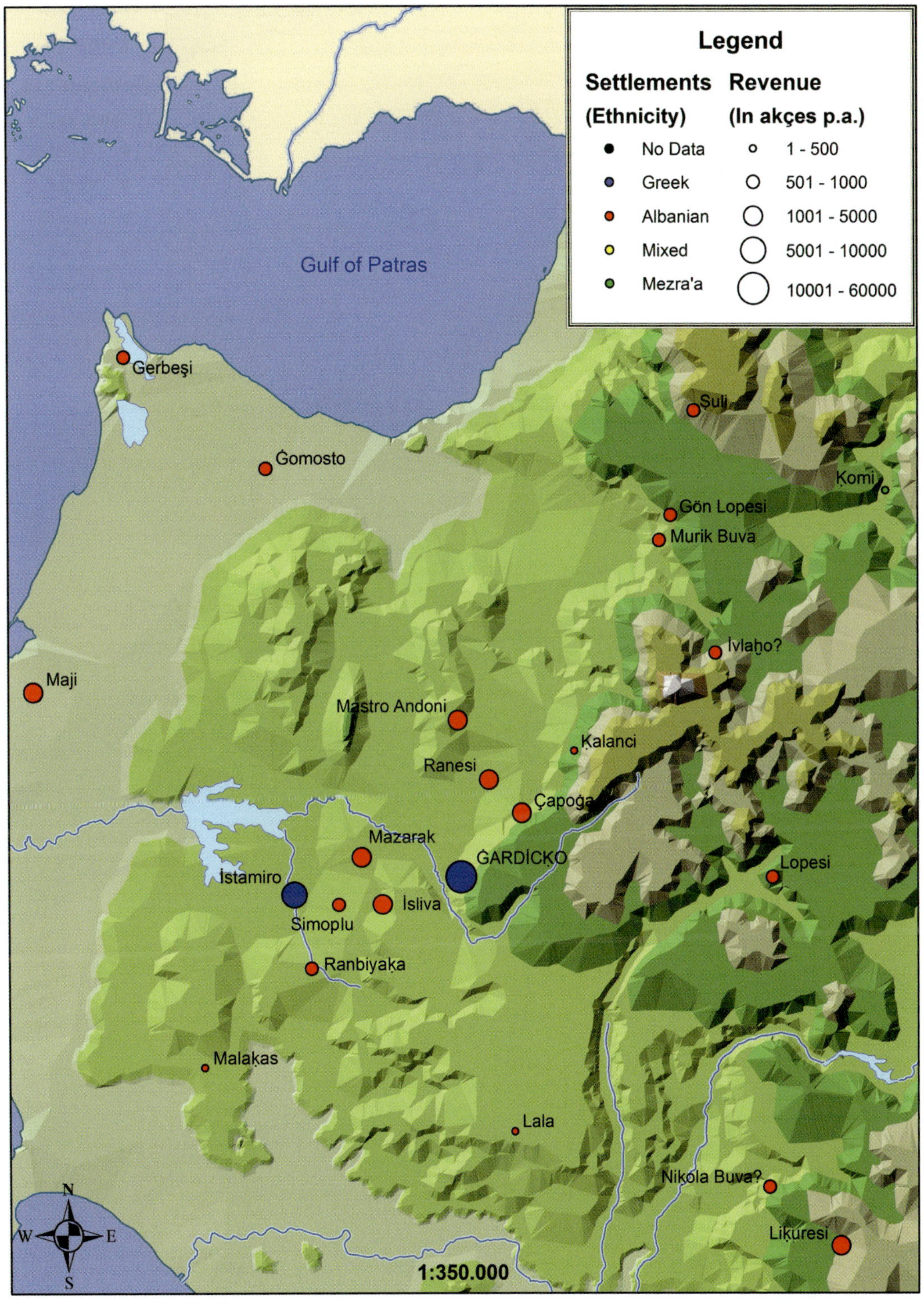

Designed by G.C. Liakopoulos

35 Livā'-ı Mora (The Peloponnese)
Ethnic Composition

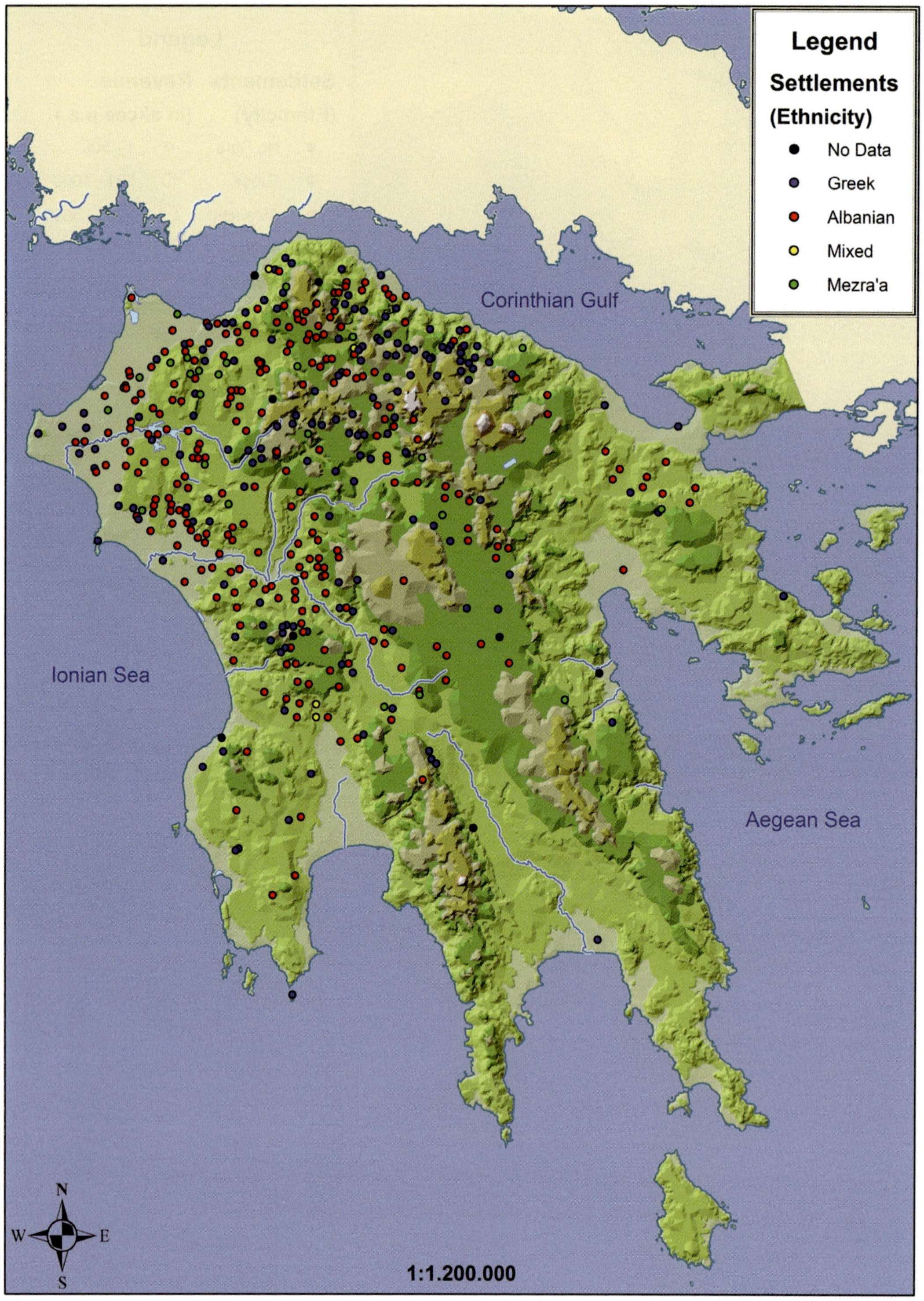

Designed by G.C. Liakopoulos

36 Livā'-ı Mora (The Peloponnese)
Demographic Distribution

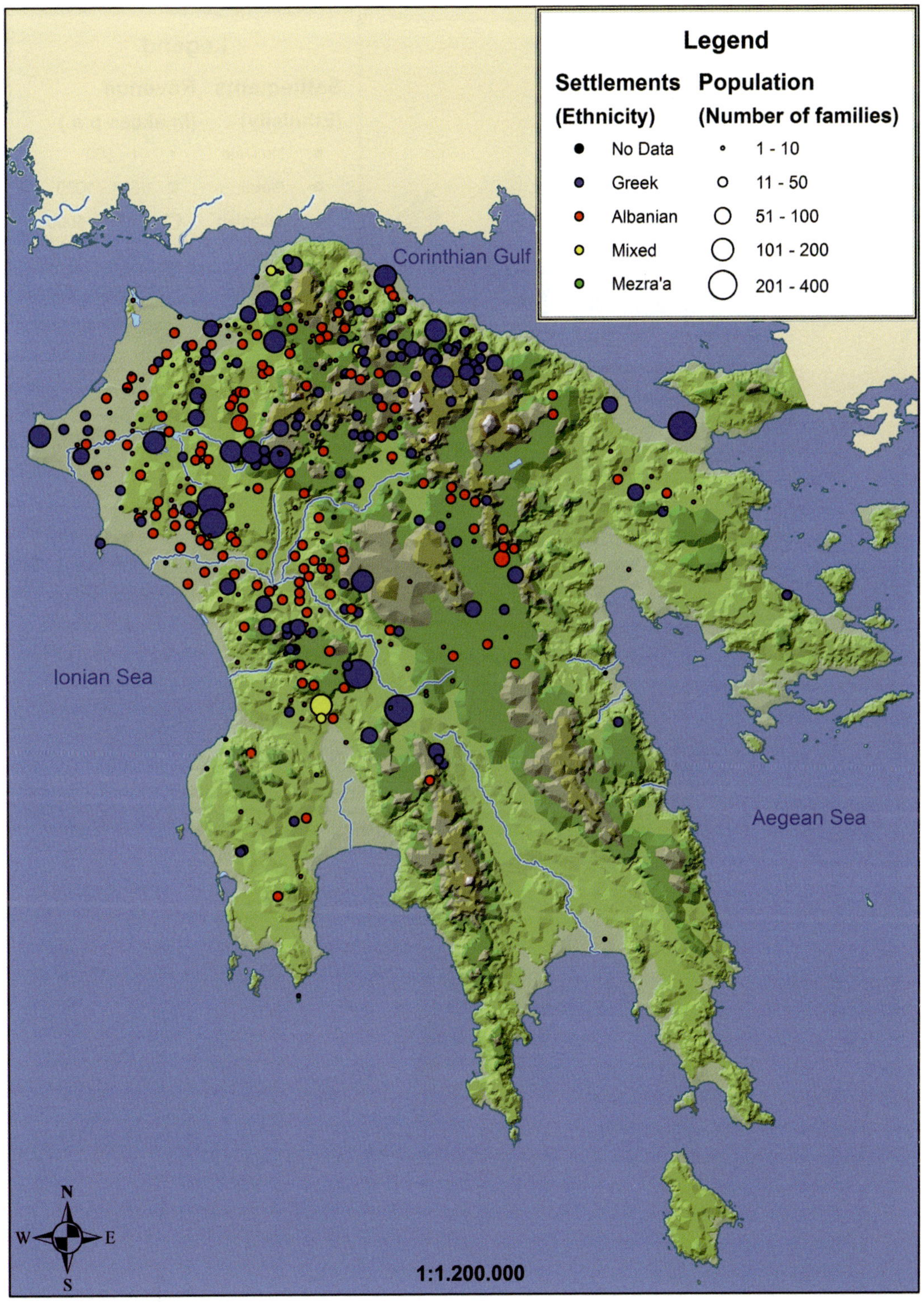

Designed by G.C. Liakopoulos

37 Livā'-ı Mora (The Peloponnese)
Economic Distribution

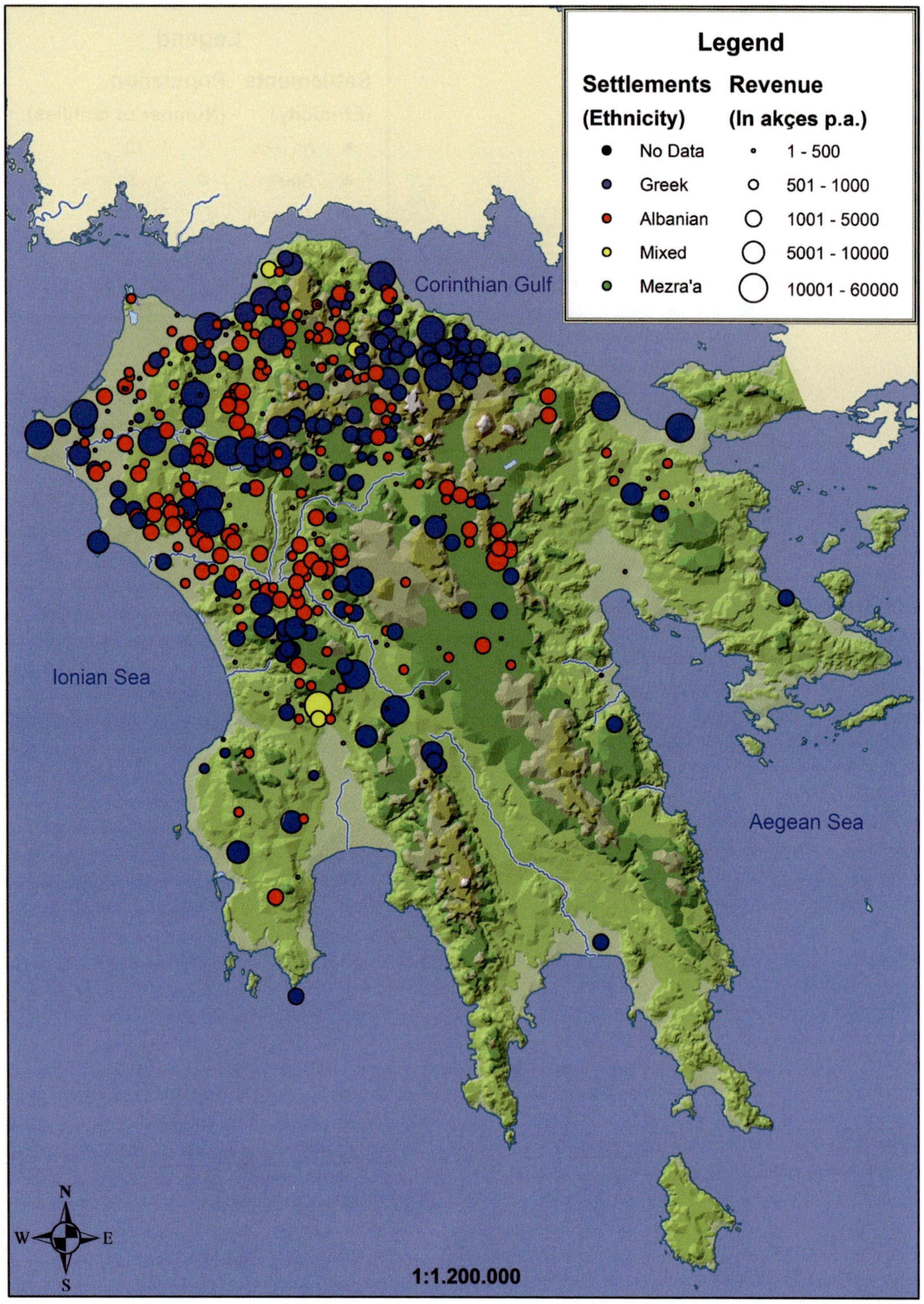

Designed by G.C. Liakopoulos

38 Livā'-ı Mora (The Peloponnese)
Demographic / Ethnic Distribution

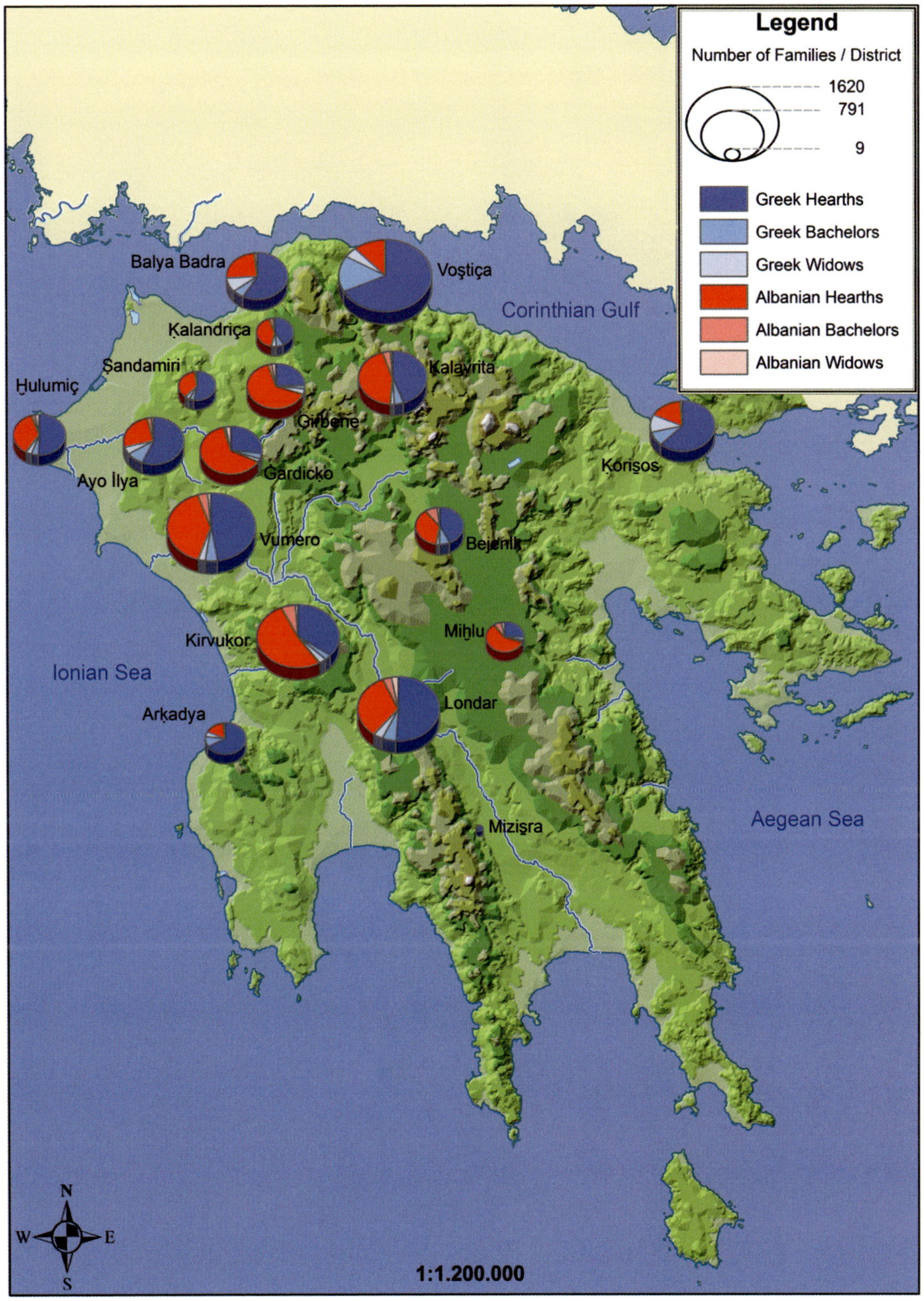

Designed by G.C. Liakopoulos

NSID 1917 — Great Britain Naval Staff Intelligence Division, *An Index of Place-Names in Bulgaria Shown in the Austrian Map and War Office Map* (London, 1917)

Oğuz–Balta 1999 — Mustafa Oğuz, Evangelia Balta, 'Le *kanunname* du sandjak d'Eğriboz (milieu du XVIe siècle)', in Evangelia Balta, *Peuple et production. Pour une interprétation des sources ottomanes* (Istanbul, 1999), 147–177.

Oikonomides 1969 — Nicolas Oikonomides, 'Le haradj dans l'Empire byzantine du XVe siècle', in *Actes du premier congrès international des études balkaniques et sud-est européennes (Sofia, 26 août – 1 septembre 1966)*, eds V. Georgiev, N. Todorov, V. Tăpkova-Zaïmova, vol. 3 (Sofia, 1969), 681–688.

Oikonomidès 1996 — Nicolas Oikonomidès, *Fiscalité et exemption iscal à Byzance (IXe–XIe s.)* (Athens, 1996)

Oikonomidou–Skambalis 2006 — Foteini Oikonomidou, Zisis Skambalis, *Στους μύλους της Μακεδονίας και της Θράκης. At the Mills of Macedonia and Thrace* (Thessaloniki, 2006[2])

Oikonomou 1988 — Konstantinos Ev. Oikonomou, 'Συμβολή στο τοπωνυμικό Κορινθίας, τα τοπωνυμικά του Αγιονορίου', *Ιστορικογεωγραφικά* 2 (1988), 271–289.

Oikonomou 1999 — Andromahi Oikonomou, 'Νεροτριβές: η λειτουργία και η χρήση τους στον ελλαδικό χώρο', in ΥΠ.ΠΟ, Μουσείο Ελληνικής Λαϊκής Τέχνης, *Το νερό, πηγή ζωής, κίνησης, καθαρμού. Πρακτικά Επιστημονικής Συνάντησης (12–14 Δεκεμβρίου 1997, Αίθουσα Παλαιάς Βουλής)* (Athens, 1999), 93–98.

Orhonlu 1990 — Cengiz Orhonlu, *Osmanlı İmparatorluğu'nda Derbend Teşkilâtı* (İstanbul, 1967,[1] 1990[2])

Öztürk 1996 — Said Öztürk, *Osmanlı Arşiv Belgelerinde Siyakat Yazısı ve Tarihî Gelişimi* (İstanbul, 1996)

Palla-Hronopoulou 2003 — Evi Palla-Hronopoulou, 'Οικισμοί και τοπωνύμια στην Αμαλιάδα', in *Πρακτικά του Έκτακτου Ηλειακού Συμποσίου 2001 (Αμαλιάδα, 7–9 Δεκεμβρίου 2001), Πελοποννησιακά Παράρτημα 25* (Athens, 2003), 241–271.

Pamuk 2000 — Şevket Pamuk, *A Monetary History of the Ottoman Empire* (Cambridge, 2000)

Pamuk 2004 — Şevket Pamuk, 'Money in the Ottoman Empire, 1326–1914', in *An Economic and Social History of the Ottoman Empire*, eds Halil İnalcık, Donald Quataert, vol. 2 (Cambridge, 2004), 945–980.

Panagiotopoulos 1976–78 — Vasilis Panagiotopoulos, 'Ἡ βενετικὴ απογραφὴ τῆς Πελοποννήσου τοῦ 1700', in *Πρακτικὰ τοῦ Α΄ Διεθνοῦς Συνεδρίου Πελοποννησιακῶν Σπουδῶν (Σπάρτη, 7–14 Σεπτεμβρίου 1975), Πελοποννησιακὰ Παράρτημα 6*, vol. 3 (Athens, 1976–1978), 203–216.

Panagiotopoulos 1987 — Vasilis Panagiotopoulos, *Πληθυσμός και οικισμοί της Πελοποννήσου, 13^ος^–18^ος^ αιώνας* (Athens, 1987)

Panagiotopoulos 2007 — Anastasios Ath. Panagiotopoulos, *Μεσαιωνικής Μεσσηνίας ιστορικογεωγραφικά και Κοντοβουνίων οικιστικά* (Athens, 2007)

Panitsas–Papagiannopoulos 2012 — Konstantinos G. Panitsas, Konstantinos V. Papagiannopoulos, 'Η διαμόρφωση του φεουδαρχικού συστήματος στην επαρχία Πατρών κατά τη Φραγκοκρατία', in *Πρακτικά Συνεδρίου Δύμη Φραγκοκρατία – Βενετοκρατία – Α΄ Τουρκοκρατία*, ed. Eleni G. Saranti (Patra, 2012), 61–85.

Panitsas–Papatheodorou 2003 — Panagiotis Panitsas, Panagiotis Papatheodorou, *Ο Όσιος Λεόντιος και η Μονή Ταξιαρχών Αιγιαλείας* (Aigio, 2003)

Panopoulou 1987–88 — Angeliki Panopoulou, 'Αλυκές και παραγωγή αλατιού στην Πελοπόννησο με βάση το αρχείο Grimani (1698–1700)', in *Πρακτικά του Γ΄ Διεθνούς Συνεδρίου Πελοποννησιακών Σπουδών (Καλαμάτα, 8–15 Σεπτεμβρίου 1985), Πελοποννησιακά Παράρτημα 13*, vol. 3 (Athens, 1987–88), 305–329.

Panopoulou 2003 — Angeliki Panopoulou, 'Παραγωγή και εμπόριο αλατιού στην Πελοπόννησο (13ος–16ος αι.)', in *Χρήμα και αγορά στην εποχή των Παλαιολόγων*, ed. Nikolaos G. Moschonas (Athens, 2003), 157–179.

Panopoulou 2007 — Angeliki Panopoulou, 'Από το trapetum στη macina d'oglio. Ελαιώνες, λάδι και ελαιοτριβεία στη νοτιοδυτική Πελοπόννησο', in *«Ο δε τόπος... ελαιοφόρος». Η παρουσία της ελιάς στην Πελοπόννησο*, ed. Eleni Benaki (Athens, 2007), 75–89.

Panopoulou 2012 — Angeliki Panopoulou, 'Ένα παράδειγμα εκμετάλλευσης των θαλάσσιων πόρων: οι αλυκές της Καμενίτσας (17ος–18ος αι.)', in *Πρακτικά Συνεδρίου Δύμη Φραγκοκρατία – Βενετοκρατία – Α΄ Τουρκοκρατία*, ed. Eleni G. Saranti (Patra, 2012), 269–277.

Pantelidis 2001a — Nikolaos Pantelidis, 'Πελοποννησιακός ιδιωματικός λόγος και κοινή νεοελληνική', in *Μελέτες για την Ελληνική Γλώσσα. Πρακτικά της 21ης ετήσιας συνάντησης του Τομέα Γλωσσολογίας της Φιλοσοφικής Σχολής του Αριστοτελείου Πανεπιστημίου Θεσσαλονίκης (12–14 Μαΐου 2000)* (Thessaloniki, 2001), 550–561.

Pantelidis 2001b — Nikolaos Pantelidis, 'Φωνητικές παρατηρήσεις σε ένα μεσσηνιακό ιδίωμα', in *Ελληνική Γλωσσολογία '99. Πρακτικά 4ου Διεθνούς Συνεδρίου Ελληνικής Γλωσσολογίας (Λευκωσία, 17–19 Σεπτεμβρίου 1999)*, eds Amalia Arvaniti, Georgia Aggouraki, Dionysis Goutsos (Thessaloniki, 2001), 480–486.

Papadopoulos-Papargyriadis 1986 — Panos D. Papadopoulos-Papargyriadis, 'Τα χάσια των Καλαβρύτων', in *Πρακτικά του Β΄ Τοπικού Συνεδρίου Αχαϊκών Σπουδών (Καλάβρυτα, 24–27 Ιουνίου 1983), Πελοποννησιακά Παράρτημα 11* (Athens, 1986), 156–160.

Papageorgiou 1975 — Georgios Th. Papageorgiou, *Τὸ Διακοπτὸν διὰ μέσου τῶν αἰώνων. Μὲ ἐπιλογὴν ἀνεκδότων ἐγγράφων. Συμβολὴ εἰς τὴν ἱστορίαν τῆς Αἰγιαλείας* (Athens, 1975)

Papandreou 1924 — Georgios Papandreou, *Ἡ Ἠλεία διὰ μέσου τῶν αἰώνων. Πρωτότυπον σύγγραμμα ἐξετάζον τὴν Ἠλείαν ἀπὸ τῶν ἀρχαιοτάτων μέχρι τῶν καθ' ἡμᾶς χρόνων ἀπὸ πάσης ἀπόψεως μετὰ καὶ τῶν σχετικῶν χαρτῶν καὶ εἰκόνων* (Athens, 1924; repr. Lehaina, 1991)

Papandreou 2011 — Georgios Papandreou, *Ἱστορία τῶν Καλαβρύτων*, ed. Dimitris S. Arvanitis (Kalavryta, 1927,[1] 2011[2])

Papantoniou 1964 — Kostas D. Papantoniou, *Τὸ χωριό μας Δάρα-Ἀρκαδίας. Ἱστορία-Λαογραφία* (Athens, 1964)

Parveva 2001 — Stefka Parveva, *The Sofia Oriental Archives. History, Structure and Organisation, Catalogues, and Publication of Documents*, Islamic Area Studies Working Paper Series No. 21 (Tokyo, 2001)

Parveva 2003 — Stefka Parveva, 'Agrarian Land and Harvest in South-West Peloponnese in the Early 18th Century', *Études Balkaniques* 39/1 (2003), 83–123.

Pikoulas 1988 — Yanis A. Pikoulas, *Η νότια Μεγαλοπολιτική χώρα από τον 8ο π.Χ. ως τον 4ο μ.Χ. αιώνα [συμβολή στην τοπογραφία της]. Διδακτορική διατριβή* (Athens, 1988)

PIKOULAS 2001b YANIS A. PIKOULAS 'Οι αλυκές στο Τηγάνι της Μάνης', in *Το ελληνικό αλάτι. Η΄ τριήμερο εργασίας (Μυτιλήνη, 6–8 Νοεμβρίου 1998)* (Athens, 2001), 295–302.

POLITIS 1912–13 NIKOLAOS POLITIS, 'Τοπωνυμικά', *Λαογραφία* 4 (1912–1913), 12–21, 572–600.

POLITIS 1915 NIKOLAOS POLITIS, 'Τοπωνυμικά', *Λαογραφία* 5 (1915), 249–308, 522–552.

POLITIS 1920a NIKOLAOS POLITIS, *Γνωμοδοτήσεις περὶ μετονομασίας συνοικισμῶν καὶ κοινοτήτων ἐκδιδόμεναι ἀποφάσει τοῦ Ὑπουργείου τῶν Ἐσωτερικῶν* (Athens, 1920)

POLITIS 1920b NIKOLAOS POLITIS, 'Τὰ ὀνόματα τῶν δήμων', in *Λαογραφικὰ Σύμμεικτα*, vol. 1 (Athens, 1920), 148–170

POULOS 1950 IOANNIS H. POULOS, ''Η ἐποίκησις τῶν Ἀλβανῶν εἰς Κορινθίαν', *Ἐπετηρὶς τοῦ Μεσαιωνικοῦ Ἀρχείου* 3 (1950), 31–105.

PULAHA 1976 SELAMI PULAHA, 'Formation des régions de selfgovernment dans les Malessies du Sandjak de Shkodër au XV–XVIIe siècles', *Studia Albanica* 13/2 (1976), 173–179.

RANGAVIS 1853–54 IAKOVOS R. RANGAVIS, *Τὰ ἑλληνικά, ἤτοι περιγραφὴ γεωγραφική, ἱστορική, ἀρχαιολογικὴ καὶ στατιστικὴ τῆς ἀρχαίας καὶ νέας Ἑλλάδος*, 3 vols (Athens, 1853–1854)

REPPAS 2008–9 HRISTOS K. REPPAS, 'Απογραφή (1828) οικισμών, οικογενειών και δημογερόντων του τμήματος Άνω Μεσσηνίας', *Μεσσηνιακά Χρονικά* 4 (2008–2009), 511–528.

ROMAIOS 1957 KOSTAS A. ROMAIOS, 'Τοπογραφικὰ τῆς Φραγκοκρατίας', *Πελοποννησιακὰ* 2 (1957), 1–26.

RUSSELL 1960 JOSIAH C. RUSSELL, 'Late Medieval Balkan and Asia Minor Population', *Journal of the Economic and Social History of the Orient* 3 (1960), 265–274.

SAKELLARIOU 1939 MICHAEL V. SAKELLARIOU, *Ἡ Πελοπόννησος κατὰ τὴν δευτέραν τουρκοκρατίαν (1715–1821)* (Athens, 1939; repr. 2000)

SARIGIANNIS 1981 GEORGIOS M. SARIGIANNIS, *Η δημιουργία, η εξέλιξη και η συγκρότηση της Σουλιώτικης Ομοσπονδίας (16[ος]–18[ος] αι.)* (Ioannina, 1981)

SARRIS 1928 IOANNIS SARRIS, 'Τὰ τοπωνύμια τῆς Ἀττικῆς', *Ἀθηνᾶ* 40 (1928), 117–160.

SARRIS 1934–5 IOANNIS S. SARRIS, 'Τὰ «κάστρα τῶν Σκόρτων» Ἀράκλοβον και Ἅγιος Γεώργιος', *Ἀρχαιολογικὴ Ἐφημερὶς* (1934–1935), 57–84.

SAUERWEIN 1969 FRIEDRICH SAUERWEIN, 'Das Siedlungsbild der Peloponnes um das Jahr 1700', *Erdkunde* 23 (1969), 237–244.

SAVVIDES 1984–85 ALEXIS G.C. SAVVIDES, 'A Note on the Terms *Rûm* and *Anatolia* in Seljuk and Early Ottoman Times', *Δελτίο Κέντρου Μικρασιατικών Σπουδών* 5 (1984–1985), 95–102.

SAVVIDES 1995 ALEXIS SAVVIDES, 'Τα προβλήματα για την οθωμανική κατάληψη και την εξάπλωση των κατακτητών στο Θεσσαλικό χώρο', *Θεσσαλικό Ημερολόγιο* 28 (1995), 33–64.

SCHILBACH 1970 ERICH SCHILBACH, *Byzantinische Metrologie* (München, 1970)

SCHWARZ 1916 P. SCHWARZ, 'Die Herkunft von arabisch *ḫarāğ*, (Grund-)Steuer', *Der Islam* 6 (1916), 97–99.

Setton 1976–78 — Kenneth M. Setton, *The Papacy and the Levant (1204–1571)*, 2 vols (Philadelphia, 1976–1978; repr. 1997)

Sfikopoulos 1987 — Ioannis Th. Sfikopoulos, *Τὰ μεσαιωνικὰ κάστρα τοῦ Μορηᾶ* (Athens, 1968,[1] 1987[2])

Sharf 1971 — Andrew Sharf, *Byzantine Jewry. From Justinian to the Fourth Crusade* (London, 1971)

Shariat-Panahi 2015 — Seyyed Mohammad Taghi Shariat-Panahi, 'Demography, Economy and Settlements: The Life of the Common People in Ottoman Corinthia', in *Ottoman Corinthia*, ed. Seyyed Mohammad Taghi Shariat-Panahi (Kiato, 2015), 21–98.

Skiadas 1993 — Eleftherios G. Skiadas, *Ιστορικό διάγραμμα των δήμων της Ελλάδος. Σχηματισμός, σύσταση, εξέλιξη, πληθυσμός, εμβλήματα* (Athens, 1993)

Smyrnis 1989 — Stavros Smyrnis, 'Τοπωνυμίαι Λινίσταινας Ολυμπίας', *Πελοποννησιακά* 17 (1989), 179–183.

Souhleris 2000 — Leonidas Souhleris, 'Κοτίτζα, η αρχόντισσα της ΒΔ Λακεδαίμονος', *Λακωνικά* 198 (2000), 29–32.

Souhleris 2001–2 — Leonidas Souhleris, 'Υστεροβυζαντινή κώμη Λογκανίκου Λακωνίας. Νεώτερα αρχαιολογικά ευρήματα', in *Πρακτικά του Στ΄ Διεθνούς Συνεδρίου Πελοποννησιακών Σπουδών (Τρίπολις, 24–29 Σεπτεμβρίου 2000), Πελοποννησιακά Παράρτημα 24*, vol. 1 (Athens, 2001–2002), 355–385.

Srećković 2000– — Slobodan Srećković, *Akches*, 5 vols (Belgrade, 2000–)

Stadtmüller 1942 — Georg Stadtmüller, *Forschungen zur albanischen Frühgeschichte* (Budapest, 1942)

Star–Estes 1990 — Jeffrey Star, John Estes, *Geographic Information Systems. An Introduction* (Englewood Cliffs, NJ, 1990)

Stavropoulos 1988 — Vasilis Styl. Stavropoulos, 'Τοπωνύμια και τοπωνυμικά του χωριού Μάλθη (Μποντιά) επαρχίας Τριφυλίας νομού Μεσσηνίας', *Onomata Revue Onomastique* 12 (1988), 541–560.

Stavroulakis–DeVinney 1992 — Nicholas P. Stavroulakis, Timothy J. DeVinney, *Jewish Sites and Synagogues of Greece* (Athens, 1992)

Sümer, *Kayı* — Faruk Sümer, 'Kayı', *İslâm Ansiklopedisi*, vol. 6 (İstanbul: Millî Eğitim Bakanlığı), 459–462.

Tabak 2008 — Faruk Tabak, *The Waning of the Mediterranean 1550–1870. A Geohistorical Approach* (Baltimore, 2008)

Thanopoulos 1988 — Georgios I. Thanopoulos, 'Το τοπωνύμιο *Σαρακήνι* της Αρκαδίας', *Onomata Revue Onomastique* 12 (1988) 196–198.

Thiriet 1959 — Freddy Thiriet, *La Romanie vénitienne au moyen âge. Le développement et l'exploitation du domaine colonial vénitien (XIIe–XVe siècles)* (Paris, 1959)

Thiriet 1976–78 — Freddy Thiriet, 'La Messénie meridionale dans le système colonial des Vénitiens en Romanie', in *Πρακτικὰ τοῦ Α΄ Διεθνοῦς Συνεδρίου Πελοποννησιακῶν Σπουδῶν (Σπάρτη, 7–14 Σεπτεμβρίου 1975), Πελοποννησιακὰ Παράρτημα 6*, vol. 1 (Athens, 1976–1978), 86–98.

Thomopoulos 1950 — Stefanos N. Thomopoulos, *Ἱστορία τῆς πόλεως Πατρῶν. Ἀπὸ ἀρχαιοτάτων χρόνων μέχρι τοῦ 1821* (Athens, 1888,[1] Patra, 1950[2])

Topping 1976 — Peter Topping, 'Co-existence of Greeks and Latins in Frankish Morea and Venetian Crete', in *XVe congrès international d'études byzantines. Rapports et co-rapports. I. Histoire. 3. La symbiose dans les États Latins formés sur les territoires byzantins : phénomènes sociaux, économiques, religieux et culturels* (Athens, 1976), 3–23.

Topping 1980 — Peter Topping, 'Albanian Settlements in Medieval Greece: Some Venetian Testimonies', in *Charanis Studies. Essays in Honor of Peter Charanis*, ed. Angeliki E. Laiou-Thomadakis (New Brunswick, 1980), 261–271.

Triantafyllou 1974 — Kostas N. Triantafyllou, 'Τὰ τοπωνύμια Καλάβρυτα-Καλάβριτο, Νεζερόν-Νεζερά', in *Πρακτικὰ τοῦ Α΄ ἐν Πάτραις Συνεδρίου Ἀχαϊκῶν Σπουδῶν, Πελοποννησιακὰ Παράρτημα 1* (Athens, 1974), 61–65.

Trojanos 1969 — Spyridon Trojanos, 'Καστροκτισία: Einige Bemerkungen über die finanziellen Grundlagen des Festungsbaues im byzantinischen Reich', *Βυζαντινὰ* 1 (1969), 39–57.

Tsamboukou 1988 — Ourania Tsamboukou, 'Κάστρο Ηλείας', *Ιστορικογεωγραφικά* 2 (1988), 294–295.

Tsiknakis 1995 — Kostas G. Tsiknakis, 'Η Μονή Ταξιαρχών του Αιγίου στα τέλη του 16ου αι.', *Πελοποννησιακά* 21 (1995), 54–72.

Tsopanakis 1958–59 — Agapitos G. Tsopanakis, 'Βέρβενα', *Πελοποννησιακὰ* 3–4 (1958–59), 396–400.

Tsotsoros 1986 — Stathis N. Tsotsoros, *Οικονομικοί και κοινωνικοί μηχανισμοί στον ορεινό χώρο. Γορτυνία (1715–1828)* (Athens, 1986)

Uzunçarşili 1947–62 — İsmaİl Hakki Uzunçarşili, *Osmanlı Tarihi*, vols 1–4, İ.H. Uzunçarşili, Enver Zİya Karal, vols 5–8 (Ankara, 1947–1962)

Uzunçarşili 1988 — İsmaİl Hakki Uzunçarşili, *Kapukulu Ocakları*, 2 vols (Ankara, 1943–1944[1], 1988[3])

Vagenas 1986 — Thanos K. Vagenas, *Ιστορικά της Κανδύλας* (Athens, 1986)

Vagiakakos 1962 — Dikaios V. Vagiakakos, 'Σχεδίασμα περὶ τῶν τοπωνυμικῶν καὶ ἀνθρωπωνυμικῶν σπουδῶν ἐν Ἑλλάδι 1833–1962', *Ἀθηνᾶ* 66 (1962), 301–424.

Vagiakakos 1963–64 — Dikaios V. Vagiakakos, 'Σχεδίασμα περὶ τῶν τοπωνυμικῶν καὶ ἀνθρωπωνυμικῶν σπουδῶν ἐν Ἑλλάδι 1833–1962', *Ἀθηνᾶ* 67 (1963–1964), 145–369.

Vagiakakos 1975 — Dikaios V. Vagiakakos, 'Γλωσσικαί-λαογραφικαί-τοπωνυμικαὶ ἔρευναι περὶ Κορινθίας', in *Πρακτικὰ τοῦ Α΄ Τοπικοῦ Συνεδρίου Κορινθιακῶν Ἐρευνῶν (Κόρινθος, 27–28 Ἀπριλίου 1974), Πελοποννησιακὰ Παράρτημα 2* (Athens, 1975), 47–91.

Vagiakakos 1987 — Dikaios V. Vagiakakos, 'Κυπαρισσίας ονοματολογικά', in *Πρακτικά του Β΄ Τοπικού Συνεδρίου Μεσσηνιακών Σπουδών (Κυπαρισσία, 27–29 Νοεμβρίου 1982), Πελοποννησιακά Παράρτημα 12* (Athens, 1987), 269–289.

Vagiakakos 1991 — Dikaios V. Vagiakakos, 'Συμβολή εις την μελέτην του τοπωνυμικού της Καλαμάτας και της πέριξ αυτής περιοχής', in *Πρακτικά του Γ΄ Τοπικού Συνεδρίου Μεσσηνιακών Σπουδών (Φιλιατρά-Γαργαλιάνοι, 24–26 Νοεμβρίου 1989), Πελοποννησιακά Παράρτημα 18* (Athens, 1991), 431–550.

Vakalopoulos 1974–82 — Apostolos, E. Vakalopoulos, *Ἱστορία τοῦ Νέου Ἑλληνισμοῦ*, 6 vols (Thessaloniki, 1974–1982[2])

VASILIKOPOULOU 1990 AGNI VASILIKOPOULOU, 'Το κάστρο του Νικλή και η επισκοπή Αμυκλών', in *Πρακτικά του Β΄ Τοπικού Συνεδρίου Αρκαδικών Σπουδών (Τεγέα-Τρίπολις, 11–14 Νοεμβρίου 1988), Πελοποννησιακά Παράρτημα 17* (Athens, 1990), 497–504.

VASMER 1941 MAX VASMER, *Die Slaven in Griechenland* (Berlin, 1941)

VEIS 1957 KOSTAS VEIS, 'Μέθοδοι ἀποξηράνσεως τῆς σταφίδος ἀπὸ τῆς ἀρχαιότητος μέχρι σήμερον', *Πελοποννησιακὴ Πρωτοχρονιὰ* 1 (1957), 10–14.

VELISSARIOU 1984 PANAGIOTIS VELISSARIOU, 'Ο ποταμός Γαθεάτας-Βελιγοστή', *Πελοποννησιακά* 15 (1984), 119–126.

VERTSETIS 1991 ATHANASIOS V. VERTSETIS, 'Από το σύγχρονο τοπωνυμικό της Άνω Μεσσηνίας (Μελιγαλά-Ζευγολατειό-Τσορωτά)', in *Πρακτικά του Γ΄ Τοπικού Συνεδρίου Μεσσηνιακών Σπουδών (Φιλιατρά-Γαργαλιάνοι, 24–26 Νοεμβρίου 1989), Πελοποννησιακά Παράρτημα 18* (Athens, 1991), 113–124.

VRANOUSSI 1970 ERA L. VRANOUSSI, 'Οἱ ὅροι «Ἀλβανοὶ» καὶ «Ἀρβανῖται» καὶ ἡ πρώτη μνεία τοῦ ὁμωνύμου λαοῦ τῆς Βαλκανικῆς εἰς τὰς πηγὰς τοῦ ΙΑ΄ αἰώνος', *Σύμμεικτα* 2 (1970), 207–254.

VRYONIS 1969–70 SPEROS VRYONIS JR., 'Byzantine Legacy and Ottoman Forms', *Dumbarton Oaks Papers* 23–24 (1969–1970), 251–308.

VUCINICH 1975 WAYNE S. VUCINICH, *A Study in Social Survival. Katun in the Bileća Rudine*, Monograph Series in World Affairs, University of Denver, vol. 13/1, Studies in Honor of Josef Korbel (Denver, 1975)

WAGSTAFF 1978 J. MALCOLM WAGSTAFF, 'War and Settlement Desertion in the Morea, 1685–1830', *Transactions of the Institute of British Geographers, Settlement and Conflict in the Mediterranean World* 3/3 (1978), 295–308.

WAGSTAFF–SLOANE–CHRYSOCHOOU 2002 MALCOLM WAGSTAFF, LESLEY SLOANE, STELLA CHRYSOCHOOU, 'The Town of Vostizza in AD 1700', *Πελοποννησιακά* 26 (2001–2002), 35–48.

WHITE 2011 SAM WHITE, *The Climate of Rebellion in The Early Modern Ottoman Empire* (New York, 2011)

WITTEK 1935 PAUL WITTEK, 'Von der byzantinischen zur türkischen Toponymie', *Byzantion* 10 (1935), 11–64.

WITTEK 1938 PAUL WITTEK, 'Les archives de Turquie', *Byzantion* 13 (1938), 691–699.

WITTEK 1955 PAUL WITTEK, 'Devshirme and Sharīʿa', *Bulletin of the School of Oriental and African Studies* 17/2 (1955), 271–278.

WRIGHT ET AL. 1990 JAMES C. WRIGHT, JOHN F. CHERRY, JACK L. DAVIS, ELENI MANTZOURANI, SUSAN B. SUTTON, ROBERT F. SUTTON JR., 'The Nemea Valley Archaeological Project: A Preliminary Report', *Hesperia* 59/4 (October–December 1990), 579–659.

YAZIR 1974 MAHMUD YAZIR, *Eski Yazıları Okuma Anahtarı* (İstanbul, 1942,[1] 1974[2])

ZACHARIADOU 1983 ELIZABETH A. ZACHARIADOU, *Trade and Crusade. Venetian Crete and the Emirates of Menteshe and Aydin (1300–1415)*, Library of the Hellenic Institute of Byzantine and Post-Byzantine Studies 11 (Venice, 1983)

ZAKYTHINOS 1944 DIONYSIOS ZAKYTHINOS, 'Οἱ Σλάβοι ἐν Ἑλλάδι καὶ αἱ σλαβικαὶ τοπωνυμίαι', *Νέα Ἑστία* 35 (1944), 485–490.

ZAKYTHINOS 1949a — DENIS A. ZAKYTHINOS, 'La population de la Morée byzantine', *L'Hellénisme contemporain* 3/1 (January–February 1949), 7–25.

ZAKYTHINOS 1949b — DENIS A. ZAKYTHINOS, 'La population de la Morée byzantine', *L'Hellénisme contemporain* 3/2 (March–April 1949), 107–132.

ZAKYTHINOS 1953 — DENIS A. ZAKYTHINOS, *Le Despotat grec de Morée. Vie et institutions*, vol. 2 (Paris-Athènes, 1953)

ZAKYTHINOS 1975 — DENIS A. ZAKYTHINOS, *Le Despotat grec de Morée. Histoire politique*, ed. Chryssa Maltezou, vol. 1 (London, 1975)

ZERLENTOS 1922 — PERIKLIS G. ZERLENTOS, *Μηλιγγοὶ καὶ Ἐζερῖται Σλάβοι ἐν Πελοποννήσῳ* (Ermoupolis, 1922; repr. Athens, 2000)

D. MAPS

ANAVASI 2009 — ANAVASI, *Πελοπόννησος: οδικός και περιηγητικός άτλας. Peloponnese: Road and Touring Atlas. (1:50,000)* (Athens, 2009)

EXPÉDITION 1832 — *Carte de la Morée rédigée et gravée au Dépôt Général de la Guerre, d'après la triangulation et les levés exécutés en 1829, 1830 et 1831 par les officiers d'état-major attachés au Corps d'occupation, par ordre de M. le Maréchal Duc de Dalmatie Ministre de la Guerre, sous la direction de M. le Lieutenant Général Pelet (1:200,000)* (Paris, 1832)

GSGS 1944 — GEOGRAPHICAL SECTION, GENERAL STAFF, *Greece (1:100,000)* (War Office, No. 4439, 1944)

HMGS 1977–79 — HELLENIC MILITARY GEOGRAPHICAL SERVICE, *(1:100,000)* (Athens, 1977–1979)

LUFTWAFFE 1943 — GENERALSTAB DER LUFTWAFFE, *Deutsche Heereskarte. Südost-Europa (1:200,000)* (1943)

PHILIPPSON 1890 — ALFRED PHILIPPSON, *Ethnographische Karte des Peloponnes (1:1,000,000)* (Gotha, 1890)

General Index

A

Acarnania, 212–13
Acciaiuoli, Neri, 163, 213, 219
Achaia regional unit
  Amuri, 20
  Anastasova, 30
  Arfara, 65
  Arula, 180
  Avrami, 177
  Ayo İvlaşi, 28
  Ayo Ḳostandino, *mezraʿa* in the vicinity of Ẕervini, 84–85
  Ayo Lisyo, 181–82
  Ayo Niḳolas, 181
  Ayo Paraskevi, 50
  Ayo Yani, 48, 178–79
  Ayo Yorgi, 62
  Ayo Yorgi, *mezraʿa* in the vicinity of Lenḳoni, 182–83
  Bala, 170
  Balya Badra, 156
  Bardoḳosta, 167
  Beçaḳus, 54–55
  Besulḳa, *mezraʿa* in the vicinity of Lenḳoni, 182
  Buḫuşta, 47
  Burlaşa, 54
  Çapoġa, 201
  Çarnota, 42
  Çarnuḫlu, 145–46
  Cilardi, 63–64
  Çimlo, 60
  Çuḳala, 161
  Dardesi, 158–59
  Droġolavoş, 30–31
  Epano Ḳurnofita, 21
  Epanolaġo, 53
  Fenaromeni, *mezraʿa* in the vicinity of İryolo, 197
  Fila, 27–28
  Fostana, 181
  Franḳo, 51
  Frati, 188
  Ġardena, 47–48
  Ġardicḳo, nefs-i, 199–200
  Gerbesi, 186
  Gerbeşi, 205
  Gin Bodya, 189–90
  Gin Floḳa, *mezraʿa* in the vicinity of Puliça, 175
  Gin Manesi, 177
  Girbene, 176
  Ġolemi, 25, 169
  Ġomosto, 200
  Gön Lopesi, 201
  Graḳa, 52–53
  Ġumaniça, 55
  Ġurzumişa, 189
  Ḫamaḳu, 19
  Ḫaraḳtinu, 20
  İflamurari, 27
  İksenoẕoḫiyo, *mezraʿa* in the vicinity of Ḳamaniça, 162
  İryolo, 196
  İş Ari, 170
  İsfardina, 177
  İsḳlaviça, 190
  İsḳura, 165
  İşpata, 191
  İstavriya/İstavrina, 59
  İstilivena, 60–61
  İştin Bondaya, 29
  İstrazova, 32–33
  İvlaḫo Ḳalanas, *mezraʿa* in the vicinity of Ṣavanus, 31
  İvlaḫo, 201–2
  Junbata, 187–88
  Ḳaḳoḫoryo, 50
  Ḳalanci, 204
  Ḳalandriça, nefs-i, 167–68
  Ḳalavrita, 17
  Ḳamaniça, 160
  Ḳani, 22–23
  Ḳanḳaẕi, 77
  Ḳastel, 32
  Ḳastriçi, 163
  Ḳastriya, 21
  Ḳato Ḳurnofita, 24–25
  Ḳavalari Trusa, 178
  Ḳavalari, 179
  Ḳazneş, 32, 168
  Keraşova, 101
  Kerpini, 57
  Ḳılapaçuna, 58–59
  Kiriçova, 55
  Ḳoḳova, 145
  Ḳomi, *mezraʿa* dependent on Ġardicḳo, 205
  Ḳomi, *mezraʿa* in the vicinity of Ḳamaniça, 162
  Ḳoşta Ḫāṣṣ, 157
  Ḳral, 171
  Ḳroḳova, 48
  Ḳulukina, 61
  Ḳurnaroḳastro, 165
  Lala Vizi, 157
  Laluş, 171–72
  Lapata, 24
  Lazaryo, 178
  Lihyana including the community of İpsari, 163

Li̇kuresi, *mezra'a* in the vicinity of Sumaki, 34
Lisarya, 169
Listirna, 52
Livarzi, 101
Loğaseti, 83–84
Lopesi, 50, 203
Lovoḳa, 63
Luḳa İfrati, 49
Lukişta, *mezra'a* in the vicinity of Puliça, 175
Maji, 55–56, 168–69
Maḳriyeni Çamanda, 25
Manastır-ı Meġaspilyo Aya Ḳori, 17–18
Manastır-ı S̱otoḳos, 47
Manastır-ı Yirondos der Taḳsiyarḫi, 46
Mariçi, *mezra'a* in the vicinity of Puliça, 175
Martina der Noḳastro, 53
Mastro Andoni, 202
Mayira, 196–97
Mazarak, 187
Miḫoy, 184–85
Milyas, 188
Mirati, 173–74
Mitepoli, 186
Motista, 176–77
Murik Buva, 208–9
Muriki, 29
Niḳola Manesi, 27
Orfano, *mezra'a* in the vicinity of Porta, 174
Palopirġo, 183
Pavloḳastro, 159
Peris̱ori, 66
Petro Ḳarava Klesura, 158
Petrovişta, 184
Plaşa, 64–65
Poraçyu, 85
Poroviça, 69
Porta, 172–73
Potamya, 60
Raḫova, 66–67, 164
Ranesi, 200
Rayḳu, 56
Revaniça, 69
Rolo, 58
Roẕa, 48–49
Runbaḳa, 160–61
Salmenik, 209–10
Ṣandamiri, nefs-i, 172
Ṣaravali, 156–57
Ṣavanus, 30
Seliça, 31
Selyana, 66
S̱eryanu, 160
Şiġuni, 19
Sinoviro, 64
Siyiniski, 62
Siẕereḳastro, 157–58
Ṣofyana, 164
Sotira, 54
Sudana, 18
Suli, 166
Ṣuli, 200–201
Tireḫlista, 28
Tiristena, 167
Topolova, 166–67
Trusa, 180
Tumena, 57–58
Valimi, 62
Valḳu, 53–54
Vela, 64
Velimiri, 22
Verġuviça, 65
Vesini, 33
Virastova, 63
Visoḳa, 56–57
Vola, 159
Vorstena, 21–22
Voştiça, nefs-i, 46
Vundeni, 163–64
Yaḳoḫto, 59
Yirmoçani, 85
Zaḫlori, 57
Ẕaruḫla, 61
Zastupa, *mezra'a* in the vicinity of Ḳurnaroḳastro, 166
Ẕilivina, 58
Ẕiminiça, 90
Ẕiyaleş Tunba, 49
Zoġa, 171
Zuġra, 19–20
Açiḫolos, 44
'aded (unit), 240
Adrianople, 5, 249
Aetolia, 213
Aetolia-Acarnania, 212
Aġali, 40–41
age of puberty, 212
Agia Kyriaki (Αγία Κυριακή), 83
Agia Marina (Αγία Μαρίνα), 185
Agia Paraskevi (Αγία Παρασκευή), 80, 107, 166–67
Agias Marinis Maritsis Monastery (I.M. Αγίας Μαρίνης Μαρίτσης), 175
Agioi Theodoroi (Άγιοι Θεόδωροι), 79–80, 203
Agionori (Αγιονόρι), 152
Agios Georgios (Άγιος Γεώργιος), 62, 125–26, 182–83
Agios Ilias (Άγιος Ηλίας), 190–91
Agios Ioannis (Άγιος Ιωάννης), 48, 154, 178–79
Agios Ioannis/Kastro Orias (Άγιος Ιωάννης/Κάστρο Ωριάς), 36
Agios Konstantinos (Άγιος Κωνσταντίνος), 84–85
Agios Nikolaos (Άγιος Νικόλαος), 147,

171, 181, 191
Agios Vasileios (Άγιος Βασίλειος), 149, 192
Agios Vlasios (Άγιος Βλάσιος), 28
Agoriani (Αγόριανη), 132
Agrambela (Αγράμπελα), 85
Agrapidokambos (Αγραπιδόκαμπος), 158–59
Agrippa, 219
āhenger (blacksmith), 243
Aḥmed III (1703–1730), 242
Aigeira municipal unit
  Arfara, 65
  Aya İğliġori, 52
  Ayo Paraskevi, 50
  Cilardi, 63–64
  Lovoḳa, 63
  Periṣori, 66
  Raḫova, 66–67
  Selyana, 66
  Sinoviro, 64
  Vela, 64
  Verġuviça, 65
  Virastova, 63
Aiges (Αιγές), 63
Aigialeia municipality
  Arfara, 65
  Ayo Yani, 48
  Ayo Yorgi, 62
  Buḫuşta, 47
  Cilardi, 63–64
  Çimlo, 60
  Ġardena, 47–48
  Graḳa, 52–53
  İstavriya/İstavrina, 59
  İstilivena, 60–61
  Ḳaḳoḫoryo, 50
  Ḳoşta Ḫāṣṣ, 157
  Ḳroḳova, 48
  Ḳulukina, 61
  Lala Vizi, 157
  Listirna, 52
  Lopesi, 50
  Lovoḳa, 63
  Luḳa İfrati, 49
  Manastır-ı Ṣotoḳos, 47
  Manastır-ı Yirondos der Taḳsiyarḫi, 46
  Periṣori, 66
  Plaşa, 64–65
  Poroviça, 69
  Potamya, 60
  Raḫova, 66–67, 164
  Revaniça, 69
  Roẕa, 48–49
  Salmenik, 209–10
  Seliça, 31
  Selyana, 66
  Sinoviro, 64
  Siyiniski, 62
  Sotira, 54
  Valimi, 62
  Valḳu, 53–54
  Vela, 64
  Verġuviça, 65
  Virastova, 63
  Voştiça, nefs-i, 46
  Yaḳoḫto, 59
  Ẕaruḫla, 61
  Ẕiyaleş Tunba, 49
Aiginio, 243
Aigio (Αίγιο), 46
Aigio municipal unit
  Ayo Paraskevi, 50
  Buḫuşta, 47
  Ḳaḳoḫoryo, 50
  Ḳroḳova, 48
  Luḳa İfrati, 49
  Manastır-ı Ṣotoḳos, 47
  Manastır-ı Yirondos der Taḳsiyarḫi, 46
  Seliça, 31
  Sotira, 54
  Voştiça, nefs-i, 46
Ainos (Enez), 5
akçe (*ἄσπρον*, *asper*), 242
Akrata municipal unit
  Ayo Yorgi, 62
  Çimlo, 60
  İstilivena, 60–61
  Ḳulukina, 61
  Plaşa, 64–65
  Poroviça, 69
  Potamya, 60
  Siyiniski, 62
  Valimi, 62
  Valḳu, 53–54
  Ẕaruḫla, 61
Aḳunba, 121
Albania cadastre (1431), 2, 7
Albania, 1–2, 13, 19, 21, 23, 25, 29, 32, 36–37, 40, 42–43, 45, 68, 73, 77, 79, 81, 86–87, 92, 97, 99, 107, 111, 119, 124, 130–31, 140–41, 153, 159, 162, 165, 170, 178, 185, 187, 189, 195–96, 198, 206–8, 212–13, 217, 221, 237, 241
Albanian immigrants, 213–14
Albanian inhabitants in Greek settlements, 214–16
Albanian settlements, place names, 13
Alea municipal unit, Frosina, 156
Aleksi Manesi, 133–34
Alemanni, 220
Alexandropoulos (Alexander), John, 1, 3, 7, 238
Alifeira municipal unit
  Drayina, 112
  Jupan/Jupano, 109
  Ḳırana, 103
  Vervena, 103
  Zelaḫova, 102–3

alphabet used in the taxation cadastre, 11
Amaliada municipal unit
  Andronika, 198
  Ayo İlya, nefs-i, 190–91
  Çavuşi, 72
  Franka Vila, 197
  Havaro Protopapa, 75
  İştopansi Lopesi, 193
  Kokla Marğariti, 75
  Mizika, 115
  Ranesi, 116
  Rovyata including the communities of Nikola Buva and Plaşa, 197–98
  Şarakin, 73–74
  Şavalya, 71
Ambelaki (Αμπελάκι), 142
Ambelokipoi (Αμπελόκηποι), 65
Ambelonas (Αμπελώνας), 92
Ambelos (Άμπελος), 53–54
Amfithea (Αμφιθέα), 140–41
ʿāmil (imperial appointee), 241
Amouri (Αμούρι), 20
Amuri, 20, 146–47
Amygdalies (Αμυγδαλιές), 102–3
Anastasi (Ανάσταση), 30
Anastasova, 30
Anaziri (Αναζήρι), 109
Andania municipal unit
  Ġırebini, 127
  Yani Zyavoliçi, 133
Andon, 208
Andravida (Ανδραβίδα), 76
Andravida municipal unit, Andraviza, 76
Andravida-Kyllini municipality
  Andraviza, 76
  Aya Baraskevi, 80
  Balçi, 183
  Başta, *mezraʿa* in the vicinity of İpsari, 79–80
  Hulumiç, nefs-i, 70
  İzlatka, 77
  Kapaleto, *mezraʿa* in the vicinity of İpsari, 80
  Kazneş, 185
  Konbi Şekra, 185–86
  Koromizi, 74
  Lihyana, 78-79
  Maji, 202
  Maliki, 185
  Nihor, 75–76
  Nikola Kumi, 199
  Pendani, *mezraʿa* in the vicinity of İpsari, 79
  Simiza, 192
Andraviza, 76
Andritsaina (Ανδρίτσαινα), 105
Andritsaina municipal unit
  Artica, 102
  Barçi, 118–19
  Beluşi, 107
  Draġoy, 105–6
  İsfranci, 107
  İskâza, 106
  Kirvukor, 101–2
  Kuçi, 115
  Linistena, 104–5
  Mateşi, 106–7
  Ondriçena, 105
  Paskali/Paskal, 119
  Zolyani, 105
Andritsaina-Krestena municipality
  Akunba, 121
  Artica, 102
  Barçi, 118–19
  Beluşi, 107
  Bizbardi, 117
  Draġoy, 105–6
  Drayina, 112
  Floka, 108–9
  İsfranci, 107
  İskâza, 106
  İstoya, 112–13
  Jupan/Jupano, 109
  Kankazi, 108
  Kırana, 103
  Kirvukor, 101–2
  Kozma Greka, 192
  Kuçi, 115
  Linistena, 104–5
  Makrişa, 116
  Mateşi, 106–7
  Mazi, 122
  Monahu, 117
  Mundriza, 122–23
  Omlo, 116–17
  Ondriçena, 105
  Paskali/Paskal, 119
  Vervena, 103
  Zelahova, 102–3
  Zolyani, 105
Andriya Pupuka, 140
Andronicus III Palaeologus (1328–1341), 212
Andronika (Ανδρόνικα), 198
Andronika, 198
anebsosti (nephew), 211
Anemodouri (Ανεμοδούρι), 146–47
anġarya (corvée), 238
Angelo Emo, 227
Aniza, 109
Ankara, battle of, 3
Añloniça, 93
Ano & Kato Loussoi (Άνω & Κάτω Λούσσοι), 18
Ano & Kato Potamia (Άνω & Κάτω Ποταμιά), 60
Ano & Kato Zahlorou (Άνω & Κάτω Ζαχλωρού), 57
Ano Diakopto/Diakofto (Άνω Διακοπτό/Διακοφτό), 59

Ano Fanari (Άνω Φανάρι), 153
Ano Franga (Άνω Φράγκα), 51
Ano Kastritsi (Άνω Καστρίτσι), 163
Ano Kleitoria (Άνω Κλειτορία), 32
Ano Kourtesi/Kourtesis (Άνω Κούρτεσι/ Κουρτέσης), 202
Ano Mazaraki (Άνω Μαζαράκι), 187
Ano Salmeniko (Άνω Σαλμενίκο), 209–10
Ano Souli (Άνω Σούλι), 200–201
Ano Starohori (Άνω Σταροχώρι), 171–72
Antoni (Αντώνη), 208
apiculture, 249
Aranis Ḳavalari, 92
Aranis Ḳuçohyari, 92
Arbanon, 212
Arcadia regional unit
- Açiḫolos, 44
- Aġali, 40–41
- Aleksi Manesi, 133–34
- Amuri, 146–47
- Andon, 208
- Aniza, 109
- Astriçi, 35–36
- Astro, *mezraʿa* in the vicinity of Astriçi, 36
- Aya Niḳola, *mezraʿa* in the vicinity of Amuri, 147
- Aya Yorgi, 131–32
- Barbuçi, 142
- Bejenik, nefs-i, 39
- Bendeni/Pendeni, 41
- Bondaya, 41–42
- Brasna Sanḳa, 37
- Bratiça, 123
- Çipyana, 38
- Dara, 25–26
- Domaniḳa Beluşi, 134–35
- Dorza, 99
- Doşkesi, 43
- Draġuẕisti, 111–12
- Ġardik, 123–24
- Ḫırisoviryi Ḳozma, 142
- İskiliç, 44
- Ḳameniça, 40
- Ḳandila, 42–43
- Ḳaratula, 33
- Ḳarvunari, 114
- Kerbova, 45
- Ḳokino Marti, 141–42
- Ḳoḳla, 118
- Ḳoraḳovuni, 43
- Lazar Palunbi, 139–40
- Leviẕi, 39–40
- Liḳuresi including the community of Bura, 207
- Lonci, 109–10
- Londar, nefs-i, 131
- Lopesi, 40
- Maḳrisa Ustruza, 144–45
- Marti Çaşi, 141
- Mazarak Adipo, 108
- Miḫal Manesi, 135
- Miḫlu, 35
- Mujaki, 44–45
- Murik Maji, 114–15
- Naşi, 37
- Niḳola Buva, 209
- Niḳola Maḳrişa, 134
- Papaẕa, 123
- Pavla, 148
- Periṣori, 38
- Perṣor, 43–44
- Peta, 111
- Petro Dorza, 137
- Pikerni, 36–37
- Plaşa, *mezraʿa* in the vicinity of Bejenik, 39
- Poḳovina, 124
- Ranesi, 110
- Ṣarakin, 120–21
- Ṣarakina, 90
- Sina, 42
- Sirvu, 110
- Ṭarpun, 146
- Trestena, 121
- Ustruza/İstruza Potamya, 45
- Valaḳ, 110–11
- Veliġosti, *mezraʿa* in the vicinity of Londar, 147
- Virça, 125
- Yani Mazaraki, 139
- Zaveti, 124
- Ẕimiçana, 145
- Ẕunato, 114

ArcGIS 9, 17, 311
aʿrec (lame), 211
Arfara, 65
Argolis regional unit
- Frosina, 156
- Laluḳa, 155

Argos municipal unit, Laluḳa, 155
Argos, 4–5, 213, 221
Argos-Mykines municipality
- Frosina, 156
- Laluḳa, 155

Arhaia Olympia municipal unit
- Ayo Vaşıl, 192
- Bruma, 88
- Hiliẕon, 86
- Kefiñali, 118
- Ḳraḳuki, 87
- Liḳuresi, 91–92
- Maḳri Poẕi, 88–89
- Miraḳo, 87
- Pratano, 83
- Velize, 144

Arhaia Olympia municipality
- Bruma, 88
- Hiliẕon, 86

Ḳastel İksovuni, 194
Kefiñali, 118
Ḳraḳuki, 87
Lazar Buva, 113
Lazaro Kemer, 113
Liḳuresi, 91–92
Maḳri Poẓi, 88–89
Mangişa Ḳumani, 94
Miġali Ẓivri, 195
Miraḳo, 87
Persena, *mezraʿa* in the vicinity of İspani, 95
Poliça, 194
Pratano, 83
Sipyani, 94
Velize, 144
Yirmena, 95
Ẓervini, 84
Arhaia Pisa (Αρχαία Πίσα), 87
Arhaies Kleones (Αρχαίες Κλεωνές), 150
Arḫangeli, 127–28
Aristomenis municipal unit
Gin Ḳondostavlo Manesi, 143
Loyi, 128
ʿāriyye/*ʿāriyyet* (lease), 229
Arḳadya (Kyparissia), district of
Arḫangeli, 127–28
Arḳadya, 125
average taxes, *226t9*
demographic statistics, *221t4*
Gerbesi, 131
Ġırebini, 127
identified and unidentified localities, *12t2*
Ḳalazoni, 130
Ḳozomuli, *mezraʿa*, *15t3*, 130
Loyi, 128
Malena, 129–30
Meġaliç, *mezraʿa*, *15t3*, 129
Mili Ḳalivya, 128–29
Muzak Mengişa, 130
Palari, 129
Platana, 128
Platoḳomati, 129
Provanda Aya Yorgi, 125–26
tax analysis, *272–73t19*
tax revenues of, 246
taxes from wheat and barley, *309t29*
viticulture yield, *310t31*
Vurçanos, 126–27
Ẓiġanato, 126
Arḳadya, 125
Arla (Άρλα), 180
Aroania municipal unit
Anastasova, 30
Ayo Ḳostandino, *mezraʿa* in the vicinity of Ẓervini, 84–85
Droġolavoş, 30
Keraşova, 101
Livarzi, 101
Lopesi, 203
Poraçyu, 85
Yirmoçani, 85
Ẓiminiça, 90
Arravonitsa (Αρραβωνίτσα), 69
Arta, 69, 212–13
Artemida (Αρτέμιδα), 112
Artica, 102
Arula, 180
Arulia, 9
Arvano Ḳastro, 193–94
Arvanokastro (Αρβανόκαστρο), 193–94
Asan, Matthew, 4
Asdrachas, Spyros, 212, 248–49
Asfalaḫto, 179
Asfalakto (Ασφάλακτο), 179
Asia Minor, 4, 234
ʿĀşıḳpaşazāde, 4, 8
ʿaskerī class, 229
Assenova, Petia, 1–2
Asteri (Αστέρι), 34–35
Astriçi, 35–36
Astrizi, 9
Astro, 9
Astro, *mezraʿa* in the vicinity of Astriçi, *14t3*, 36
Astros (Άστρος), 35–36
Athens, Duchy of, 4
Atsiholos (Ατσίχολος), 44
Attaleiates, Michael, 212
auxiliary soldiers and accessories, of timariot, 235
ʿavārıż (extraordinary taxes), 244
Avlonas municipal unit, Ẓima Rala, 142–43
Avolanizza, 9
Avrami (Αβράμι), 177
Avrami, 177
Aya Baraskevi, 80
Aya İġliġori, 52
Aya Niḳola, *mezraʿa* in the vicinity of Amuri, *15t3*, 147
Aya Yorgi, 131–32, *225t8*
Ayiya, *mezraʿa* in the vicinity of İryolo, *16t3*, 197
Ayo İlya (Agios Ilias), district of
Androniḳa, 198
Arvano Ḳastro, 193–94
average taxes, *226t9*
Ayiya, *mezraʿa* in the vicinity of İryolo, *16t3*, 197
Ayo İlya, nefs-i, 190–91
Ayo Vaşıl, 192
Barçi, *mezraʿa* in the vicinity of Rovyata, *16t3*, 198
Bavasi, 194
demographic statistics, *221t4*
Fenaromeni, *mezraʿa* in the vicinity of İryolo, *16t3*, 197

Franḳa Vila, 197
Ġolomi, 193
identified and unidentified localities, 12t2
İryolo, 196
İşpata, 191
İştopansi Lopesi, 193
Ḳartazori, 196
Ḳastel İksovuni, 194
Ḳozma Greḳa, 192
Ḳrapeşi, 198
Mayira, 196–97
Miġali Ẕivri, 195
Mihili, 196
Muzak, 191
Niḳola Ḳumi, 199
Pendeni including the community of Palunbi Ipşari, 199
Poliça, 194
Prifti, 196
Rado, *mezraʿa* in the vicinity of Rovyata, *16t3*, 198
Romyo, 192
Rovyata including the communities of Niḳola Buva and Plaşa, 197–98
Şamuna, *mezraʿa* in the vicinity of Vunarġo, *16t3*, 197
Simiza, 192
Sirvu, 194
tax analysis, *294–96t26*
tax revenues of, 247
taxes from wheat and barley, 309t29
viticulture yield, 310t31
Vunarġo, 195–96
Zorila, 195
Ayo İlya, nefs-i, 190–91
Ayo İvlaşi, 28
Ayo Ḳostandino, *mezraʿa* in the vicinity of Ẕervini, *15t3*, 84–85
Ayo Lisyo, 181–82
Ayo Niḳolas, 181
Ayo Paraskevi, 50
Ayo Vaşıl, 192
Ayo Vaşıl/Çağıl Ḥiṣārı, 149
Ayo Yani, 48, 178–79
Ayo Yorgi, 62
Ayo Yorgi, *mezraʿa* in the vicinity of Lenḳoni, *16t3*, 182–83
Ayo Ẕimitri Liḳo Anbali, 158
Ayonori, 152
ʿazab (soldier), 211

B

bahā (value), 242
Bala, 170
Balas (Μπάλας), 170
Balçi, 183
Baliza (Μπάλιζα), 97
Balkan/Balkans, 1, 3, 5, 217–18, 234, 240, 311
Baltzes (Μπάλτζες), 183
Balya Badra (Patra), district of
average taxes, 226t9
Ayo Ẕimitri Liḳo Anbali, 158
Balya Badra, 156
Bardoḳosta, 167
Buryalisa, 165
Çernota, *mezraʿa* in the vicinity of Buryalisa, *16t3*, 165
Çuḳala, 161
Dardesi, 158–59
demographic statistics, 221t4
Draġoti, *mezraʿa* in the vicinity of Ḳamaniça, *16t3*, 162
identified and unidentified localities, 12t2
İksenoẕoḫiyo, *mezraʿa* in the vicinity of Ḳamaniça, *16t3*, 162
İsḳura, 165
İstefano Mazaraki, 160
İzlatḳa, 161
Ḳamaniça, 160
Ḳastriçi, 163
Klesura, 159
Ḳomi, *mezraʿa* in the vicinity of Ḳamaniça, *16t3*, 162
Ḳoşta Ḫāṣṣ, 157
Ḳurnaroḳastro, 165
Lala Vizi, 157
Lihyana including the community of İpsari, 163
Liḳuresi, *mezraʿa* in the vicinity of Ḳamaniça, *16t3*, 161
Meliġala, *mezraʿa* in the vicinity of Ḳamaniça, *16t3*, 161
Patura, *mezraʿa* in the vicinity of Pavloḳastro, *16t3*, 159
Pavloḳastro, 159
Petro Ḳarava Klesura, 158
Raḫova, 164
Ranesi, 157
Ribesi, 161
Runbaḳa, 160–61
Şaravali, 156–57
Şeryanu, 160
Siẕereḳastro, 157–58
Şofyana, 164
Suli, 166
tax analysis, *282–84t22*
tax revenues of, 246
taxes from wheat and barley, 309t29
Tiristena, 167
Topolova, 166–67
viticulture yield, 310t31
Vola, 159
Vundeni, 163–64
Zastupa, *mezraʿa* in the vicinity of Ḳurnaroḳastro, *16t3*, 166
Balya Badra, 156
Barbuc, 203

Barbuçi, 142
Barçi, 23, 118–19
Barçi, *mezraʿa* in the vicinity of
Rovyata, *16t3*, 198
bardaḳ (cup), 240
Bardi Zuġra, 178
Bardi, 154
Bardoḳosta, 167
Barkan, Ömer Lûtfi, 2
Barkan-Braudelian School, 2
barley, cultivation of, 247–48
Başta, *mezraʿa* in the vicinity of İpsari,
15t3, 79–80
Bavasi, 73, 194
Bāyezīd I (1389–1402), 3–4
Beçaḳus, 54–55
Bejenik (Vlaherna), district of
Açiḫolos, 44
Aġali, 40–41
average taxes, 226t9
Bejenik, nefs-i, 39
Bendeni/Pendeni, 41
Bondaya, 41–42
Çarnota, 42
demographic statistics, 221t4
Doşkesi, 43
Ḥayḳal, 43
*identified and unidentified localities,
12t2*
İskiliç, 44
İvlaḫo Filito, *mezraʿa* in the vicinity
of İstruza Potamya, *14t3*, 46
Ḳameniça, 40
Ḳandila, 42–43
Kerbova, 45
Ḳoraḳovuni, 43
Leviẕi, 39–40
Lopesi, 40
Mujaki, 44–45
Perṣor, 43–44
Plaşa, *mezraʿa* in the vicinity of
Bejenik, *14t3*, 39
Sina, 42
tax analysis, *254t14*
tax revenues of, 245
taxes from wheat and barley, 309t29
Ustruza/İstruza Potamya, 45
viticulture yield, 310t31
Vuzyas, *mezraʿa* in the vicinity of
Bejenik, *14t3*, 39
Bejenik, nefs-i, 39
Beldiceanu, Nicoară, 2–3
Beldiceanu-Steinherr, Irène, 2–3
Belousia (Μπελούσια), 134–35
Beluşi, 19, 107
Belveder, 9
Bendeni/Pendeni, 41
Benjamin of Tudela, 219
bennāʾ (builder), 242
ber vech-i maḳṭūʿ (estimated in a lump
sum), 241
Besulḳa, *mezraʿa* in the vicinity of
Lenḳoni, 182
beytüʾl-māl (public treasury), 229
Biçi, 154
birāder (brother), 211–12
bīve (widow), 211–12, 221, 223, *224t7*,
234, 238
Bizbardi, 117
Bocenico, 9
Bondaya, 41–42
Bosnia & Herzegovina, 31, 45, 51, 69,
111, 123, 131, 146, 184, 195
Boufouskia/Bofonokia (Μπουφούσκια/
Μποφονόκια), 47
Boumboukas (Μπούμπουκας), 140
Bourlesia (Μπουρλέσια), 54
Bouzia (Μπούζια), 189
Branca, 82
Brasna Sanḳa, 37
Bratiça, 123
Braudel's 'eternal trinity', 249
Bruma, 88
Buḫuşta, 47
Bulgaria, 5, 19, 31, 33, 35, 38, 54, 65,
69, 90, 104–5, 116, 123, 167, 171, 175,
180, 185
Bulgarians, 216–17
Bura, community included in Liḳuresi,
207
Burlaşa, 54
bürüme (breastplated soldier), 235–36
Buryalisa, 165
Buza, 189
Buzbardi, 151
Byzantine Peloponnese, 1–3

C

çadır (tent), 235–36
çadır maʿa soḳaḳ ve ābrīz (tent with
curtains), 235
Calaurata vel Calavita, 9
Calendrizzo, 9
Camenizza vel Camomenizza, 9
Camero Castro vel Cumero Castro, 9
Cantacuzenus, John VI (1347–1354),
212
Cantacuzenus, Manuel (1348–1380), 213
Çapoġa, 201
Carlo Tocco, 3, 213
Çarnota, 42
Çarnuḫlu, 145–46
çāşnīgīrbaşı (chief butler), 35
castles occupied by Venetians, 9
Catalans, 219
Catherine, 4
Çavuşi, 72
cebelü (armoured soldier), 235–36
census, regional, 234
Centurione Zaccaria (1404–1432), 4

Cephalonia, 3, 213
Çernota, *mezra'a* in the vicinity of Buryalisa, *16t3*, 165
Cevdet, Muallim (İnançalp), 5
Chalcocondyles, 4–5, 8
Chilidoni vel Clidoni, 9
Cilardi, 63–64
Çimlo, 60
Çingene/Cingene (Gypsy), 216, 219, 243
Çipyana, 38
cizye (capitation), 243
coefficient, 3, 212
commercialisation of crop surpluses, 249
Commission for the Toponyms of Greece (*Ἐπιτροπεία τῶν τοπωνυμίων τῆς Ἑλλάδος*), 12
complementarity of agrarian production, 249
Constantine Palaeologus, 4
Constantinople, 3–4, 143
Corinthia regional unit
  Ayo Vaşıl/Çağıl Ḥiṣārı, 149
  Ayonori, 152
  Bardi, 154
  Buzbardi, 151
  Ḫarkâ, 151
  İksaroḳastalya, *mezra'a* in the vicinity of Ayonori, 152
  İvlanduşa, 51
  Ḳlimandi, 152–53
  Ḳorisos, nefs-i, 148
  Ḳumaniçi Luzi, *mezra'a* in the vicinity of Zepandi, 68
  Ḳutala, 151
  Luḳa, 154–55
  Pisratu, 155
  Pulimeno Ḳondostavlo, 150
  Pulimeno Soyḳa, 153
  Şarakin, 154
  Ṣoḫyana, 68
  Vaşılıḳa, 148–49
  Yelini, 67
  Zaḫoli, 67
Coron, 4–5, 10, 14
cotton, cultivation of, 248
Coya, 96–97
Critobulus, 5, 8
Croatia, 45, 51, 104, 111, 121, 132, 138, 167, 190, 195
crop surpluses, 249
crops, taxes on, 238–39. *see also* taxes
Çuḳala, 161
Cumans, 220
Cüneyd, 4
Cvetkova, Bistra, 1
Czech Republic, 18, 39, 105, 124, 146, 172, 177

D

Dafnes (Δάφνες), 50
Dafni (Δάφνη), 32–33, 185–86
Dafniotissa (Δαφνιώτισσα), 115
Dafnoula (Δαφνούλα), 118–19
dāmād (son-in-law), 211–12
Dara, 25–26
Daras (Δάρας), 25–26, 143
Dardesi, 158–59
Debrani, 29
defterology, 2, 312
delineation of districts, 307
Demetrius Palaeologus, 4–5, 243
Demetrius Raoul, 213
Demir Hisar, 218
demographic figures
  Albanian settlements, 224–25
  by division of families, households-bachelors-widows, 223–24
  locations, by size and population, 220–21
Demographic statistics of the Peloponnese, *221t4*
derbend (mountainous pass, *kleisoura*), 244
Dervini (Δερβίνι), 176
Despotate of Mystras, 4
Diakopi (Διακόπι), 41
Diakopto municipal unit
  Ayo Yani, 48
  Ġardena, 47–48
  İstavriya/İstavrina, 59
  Roẕa, 48–49
  Yaḳoḫto, 59
Diavolitsi (Διαβολίτσι), 133
dīğer (other), 211
Dima Plaşa, 21
Dimitri Maçuki, 135
Dimitsana (Δημητσάνα), 145
Dimitsana municipal unit
  Maḳrisa Ustruza, 144–45
  Trestena, 121
  Ẕimiçana, 145
Dimizana vel Dimiza, 9
Diodia (Διόδια), 128
Divye, 180
dizdār (castle warden), 244
Domaniḳa Beluşi, 134–35
dönüm, 240, 248
Dorio municipal unit
  Lazaro Klesura, 140–41
  Lazaro Ḳuveli, 144
  Lazaro Zupata, 137
  Provanda Aya Yorgi, 125–26
  Todoro Zupata, 136
Doriza (Δόριζα), 99
Dorizas (Δόριζας), 137
Dorza, 99
Doşkesi, 43
Doumena (Δουμενά), 57–58
Dragogi (Δραγώγι), 105–6

Draġoti, *mezra'a* in the vicinity of
Ḳamaniça, *16t3*, 162
Draġoy, 105–6
Draġuẕisti, 111–12
Drakakis, Alexios, 14
Dramesi (Δράμεσι), 73
Dramşa, 73
Drayina, 112
Droġolavoş, 30–31
Drosato (Δροσάτο), 55
Drovolovo (Δροβολοβό), 30–31
Drymos (Δρυμός), 176–77
ducat, Venetian, 242
Duchy of Athens, 4
Duḳa Plaşa, 135
Duḳati, 189
Dumeña, 96
Duranḳorgi, 209
Duşa Dara, *mezra'a* in the vicinity of
Astriçi, *14t3*, 36
Dušan, Stefan, 212, 237
Dymi municipal unit
Ayo Lisyo, 181–82
Besulḳa, *mezra'a* in the vicinity of
Lenḳoni, 182
İksenoẕoḫiyo, *mezra'a* in the vicinity
of Ḳamaniça, 162
İsḳlaviça, 190
Ḳamaniça, 160
Loġaṣeti, 83–84
Palopirġo, 183
Dytiki Ahaïa municipality
Arula, 180
Ayo Lisyo, 181–82
Ayo Yorgi, *mezra'a* in the vicinity of
Lenḳoni, 182–83
Besulḳa, *mezra'a* in the vicinity of
Lenḳoni, 182
Fenaromeni, *mezra'a* in the vicinity of
İryolo, 197
Fostana, 181
Franḳa, 91
Gerbeşi, 205
Gin Floḳa, *mezra'a* in the vicinity of
Puliça, 175
Ġomosto, 200
İksenoẕoḫiyo, *mezra'a* in the vicinity
of Ḳamaniça, 162
İryolo, 196
İsḳlaviça, 190
İşpata, 191
Ḳamaniça, 160
Ḳanḳaẕi, 77
Ḳomi, *mezra'a* in the vicinity of
Ḳamaniça, 162
Ḳral, 171
Loġaṣeti, 83–84
Lukişta, *mezra'a* in the vicinity of
Puliça, 175
Mariçi, *mezra'a* in the vicinity of
Puliça, 175
Mayira, 196–97
Mazaraki, 170–71
Miḫoy, 184–85
Mirati, 173–74
Mitepoli, 186
Palopirġo, 183
Petrovişta, 184
Porta, 172–73
Runbaḳa, 160–61
Ṣandamiri, nefs-i, 172

E

Ebū's-su'ūd, Meḥmed, 229
editio princeps of 1/14662, 455–506
editio princeps of TT10, 339–454
Eira municipal unit
Miḫal Zora, 135–36
Niḳola Sirgi, 139
Eksoriya, 187
Elaionas (Ελαιώνας), 208
Elatofyto (Ελατόφυτο), 55–56
Elatos (Έλατος), 40–41
Elena vel Alona, 9
Elis regional unit
Aḳunba, 121
Andraviza, 76–77
Androniḳa, 198–99
Añloniça, 93
Aranis Ḳuçohyari, 92
Artica, 102
Arvano Ḳastro, 193–94
Asfalaḫto, 179
Aya Baraskevi, 80
Ayo İlya, nefs-i, 190–91
Ayo Vaṣıl, 192
Balçi, 183
Barçi, 118–19
Başta, *mezra'a* in the vicinity of
İpsari, 79–80
Beluşi, 107
Bizbardi, 117
Bruma, 88
Buza, 189
Çavuşi, 72
Coya, 96–97
Draġoy, 105–6
Dramşa, 73
Drayina, 112
Floḳa, 108–9
Franḳa Vila, 197
Ġastuni, 70
Ġolomi, 193
Ġramatiḳo, 81
Ḫavaro Protopapa, 75
Hiliẕon, 86
Ḫulumiç, nefs-i, 70
İksanya, 173
İpsari, 79
İsfranci, 107

İsḳala, 120
İskâẕa, 106
İsliva, 204
İstamiro, 206
İştopanṣi Lopesi, 193
İstoya Volomiri, 138
İstoya, 112–13
İzlatḳa, 77
Jupan/Jupano, 109
Ḳaçaru, 95–96
Ḳanḳaẕi, 108
Ḳapaleto, *mezraʿa* in the vicinity of İpsari, 80
Ḳaratula, 100
Ḳarẕiyoḳafti, 74
Ḳastel İksovuni, 194
Ḳavasila, 78
Ḳazneş, 185
Kefiñali, 118
Kelavi, 71
Kertiza, 83
Ḳırana, 103
Kirvuḳor, 101–2
Ḳoḳla Marġariti, 75
Ḳoḳla, 72
Ḳonbi Ṣeḳra, 112, 185–86
Ḳopaniça, 103–4
Ḳoromiẕi, 74
Ḳozma Greḳa, 192
Ḳraḳuki, 87
Ḳuçi, 115
Ḳuḳura, 86
Lala, 204–5
Laleṣi, 84
Lali, 96
Lanbeti, 97
Lancoy, 82–83
Lazar Buva, 113
Lazaro Kemer, 113
Lihyana, 78–79
Liḳuresi, 91–92
Linistena, 104–5
Luzi, 120
Maji, 93, 202
Maḳri Poẕi, 88–89
Maḳrişa, 116
Malaḳas, 208
Maliki, 185
Mangişa Ḳumani, 94
Marḳoplu, 77–78
Mateşi, 106–7
Mavromati, 100–101
Mazarak including the community of Ḳuçi, 206
Maẕi, 122
Melita, 119–20
Miġali Ẕivri, 195
Mihili, 93–94
Miraḳo, 87
Miziḳa, 115
Monaḫu, 117
Mundriza, 122–23
Muzak, 191
Nasa, 82
Niḫor, 75–76
Niḳola Ḳumi, 199
Olana, 98–99
Omlo, 116–17
Ondriçena, 105
Pasḳali/Pasḳal, 119
Pendani, *mezraʿa* in the vicinity of İpsari, 79
Pendeni including the community of Palunbi Ipṣari, 199
Persena, *mezraʿa* in the vicinity of İspani, 95
Poliça, 194
Pondiḳo, 100
Poṣo, 89
Potamya Ṣarandinu, *mezraʿa* in the vicinity of Ġastuni, 70–71
Pratano, 83
Purdanu, *mezraʿa* in the vicinity of Maḳri Poẕi, 89
Ranbiyaḳa, 207
Ranesi, 116
Ratendu, 98
Romesi, 92
Rovyata including the communities of Niḳola Buva and Plaşa, 197–98
Ṣarakin, 73–74
Ṣavalya, 71
Simiza, 192
Simoplu, 203
Sipyani, 94
Ṣopi, 99
Ṣuli, 76
Valmi, 174
Velize, 144
Veliẓi, *mezraʿa* in the vicinity of Coya, 97
Velviça, 104
Vervena, 103
Vumero, nefs-i, 81
Vunarġo, 195–96
Yirmena, 95
Zelaḫova, 102–3
Ẕervini, 84, 176
Ẕolyani, 105
Zorila, 195
Elliniko (Ελληνικό), 68
Elos municipal unit, Priniḳos, 34–35
Elvān Beg, 8
Elvān Beg-oġlı, Sinān Beg, 8
emīn (dignitary), 234
emīn/mübāşir (governmental agent), 241
Emo, Angelo, 227
environmental history, 312
Epano Ḳurnofita, 21
Epanolaġo, 53

Epirus, 212
Epitalio (Επιτάλιο), 93
Ereipia Maziou (Ερείπια Μαζίου), 168–69
Erineos municipal unit
  Ḳoşta Ḫāṣṣ, 157
  Lala Vizi, 157
  Revaniça, 69
  Salmenik, 209–10
Erymanthos municipality
  Avrami, 177
  Ayo Niḳolas, 181
  Ayo Yani, 178–79
  Çapoġa, 201
  Dardesi, 158–59
  Franḳo, 51
  Frati, 188
  Ġardicḳo, nefs-i, 199–200
  Gin Manesi, 177
  Girbene, 176
  Ġolemi, 25, 169
  Gön Lopesi, 201
  Ġurzumişa, 189
  İş Ari, 170
  İvlaḫo Ḳalanas, 31
  İvlaḫo, 201–2
  Ḳalanci, 204
  Ḳalandriça, nefs-i, 167–68
  Ḳavalari Trusa, 178
  Ḳavalari, 179
  Ḳazneş, 168
  Laluş, 171–72
  Lazaryo, 178
  Lisarya, 169
  Mastro Andoni, 202
  Mazarak, 187
  Murik Buva, 208–9
  Ranesi, 200
  Trusa, 180
  Zoġa, 171
ESRI, 17
ethnic groups, recorded in TT10–1/14662, 214–20
Euboea cadastre (1474), 214, 238
Evrenos Beg, Ġāzī, 3–4
Evrostina (Εβροστίνα), 67
Evrostini municipal unit
  Ḳumaniçi Luzi, *mezraʿa* in the vicinity of Zepandi, 68
  Zaḫoli, 67
Evrotas municipality, Priniḳos, 34–35
Exohi (Εξοχή), 66–67
Expédition scientifique de Morée, 15

F

Falaisia municipal unit
  Amuri, 146–47
  Aya Niḳola, *mezraʿa* in the vicinity of Amuri, 147
  Londar, nefs-i, 131
  Miḫal Manesi, 135
  Ustruza/İstruza Potamya, 45
  Veliġosti, *mezraʿa* in the vicinity of Londar, 147
family size/structure, 212, 221–24
Fanari (Φανάρι), 102
Farres municipal unit
  Ayo Niḳolas, 181
  Dardesi, 158–59
  Gön Lopesi, 201
  İş Ari, 170
  İvlaḫo Ḳalanas, *mezraʿa* in the vicinity of Şavanus, 31
  İvlaḫo, 201–2
  Ḳalandriça, nefs-i, 167–68
  Ḳavalari Trusa, 178
  Laluş, 171–72
  Lisarya, 169
  Murik Buva, 208–9
  Trusa, 180
  Zoġa, 171
Fenari, 153
Fenaromeni, *mezraʿa* in the vicinity of İryolo, *16t3*, 197
Figaleia municipal unit
  İstoya Volomiri, 138
  Ḳopaniça, 103–4
  Velviça, 104
Fil Adrofinos including the community of Muzak, 207
Fila, 27–28
Filia (Φίλια), 27–28
Filiatra municipal unit, Ḳalazoni, 130
1st Panarcadic Internet Conference (2006), 2
fiscal units, 12–17
Flamboura (Φλάμπουρα), 27
flax, cultivation of, 248
Floḳa, 108–9
Flokas (Φλόκας), 108–9, 175
flora, 13
Focena vel Phonea, 9
Foloï (Φολόη), 95
Foloï municipal unit
  Lala, 204–5
  Mangişa Ḳumani, 94
  Persena, *mezraʿa* in the vicinity of İspani, 95
  Poṣo, 89
  Yirmena, 95
Foloḳobuva, *mezraʿa* in the vicinity of Andraviza, *14t3*, 77
Fostaina (Φώσταινα), 181
Fostana, 181
Francavilla, 9
Franga (Φράγκα), 91
Frangavilas Monastery (I.M. Φραγκαβίλας), 197
Franḳa Vila, 197
Franḳa, 91

Franḳo, 51
Frati (Φράτι), 188
Frati, 155, 188
free landowners (*πάροικοι*; *villani*), 312
Frosina, 156
Frousiouna (Φρουσιούνα), 156
fruit trees, cultivation of, 248
Funeral Oration on his Brother Theodore (1407) (Manuel II Palaeologus), 213

G

Gaius, 219
Gallipoli, *hyparch* of, 8
Ġardena, 47–48
Ġardicḳo (Gatsiko), district of
  Andon, 208
  average taxes, 226t9
  Barbuc, 203
  Çapoġa, 201
  demographic statistics, 221t4
  Duranḳorgi, 209
  Fil Adrofinos including the community of Muzak, 207
  Ġardicḳo, nefs-i, 199–200
  Gerbeşi, 205
  Ġomosto, 200
  Gön Lopesi, 201
  Ḫarkâ, 207
  identified and unidentified localities, 12t2
  İsliva, 204
  İsliva-ı dīğer, *mezraʿa* dependent on Ġardicḳo, *16t3*, 206
  İstamiro, 206
  İsturġova, 205
  İvlaḫo, 201–2
  İvlanduşa, 200
  Ḳalanci, 204
  Kiẕiḳuma, *mezraʿa*, *16t3*, 209
  Ḳomi, *mezraʿa* dependent on Ġardicḳo, *16t3*, 205
  Lala, 204–5
  Liḳuresi including the community of Bura, 207
  Lopesi, 203
  Maji, 202
  Malaḳas, 208
  Manesi, 206, 208
  Mastro Andoni, 202
  Mazarak including the community of Ḳuçi, 206
  Maẕiñik, 207
  Murik Buva, 208–9
  Niḳola Buva, 209
  Ranbiyaḳa, 207
  Ranesi, 200
  Ranesi, *mezraʿa* in the vicinity of Liḳuresi, *16t3*, 207
  Roẕinotiḫo, *mezraʿa* dependent on Ġardicḳo, *16t3*, 205
  Şaleşi, 204
  Simoplu, 203
  Ṣopiya, 203
  Ṣuli, 200–201
  tax analysis, *297–99t27*
  tax revenues of, 247
  taxes from wheat and barley, 309t29
  viticulture yield, 310t31
  Ẕirmi, 206
Ġardicḳo, nefs-i, 199–200
Ġardik, 123–24
Gardiki-Amfeia (Γαρδίκι-Άμφεια), 123–24
Gardisco vel Cradici, 9
Gargalianoi municipal unit, Muzak Mengişa, 130
ġarīb yiğit (soldier of non-Turkish or non-Muslim origin), 218
Ġarnaze, 174
Gastouni (Γαστούνη), 70
Gastouni municipal unit
  Dramşa, 73
  Ġastuni, 70
  Ḳarẕiyoḳafti, 74
  Ḳavasila, 78
  Kelavi, 71
  Potamya Şarandinu, *mezraʿa* in the vicinity of Ġastuni, 70–71
Ġastuni, 70
Gatsiko (Γάτσικο), 199–200
Gazetteer of the Greek Toponyms, 13
geçim (armour for a soldier and his horse), 235
Gelini (Γελήνη/Γελήνι), 67
Generalstab der Luftwaffe, 15
Geographical Information Systems, 17
geographical phenomenon, 17
Geographical Section, General Staff, 15
geohistory, 312
Georgacas, Demetrius, 14
George Maniakes, 212
Gerbesi, 131, 186
Gerbeşi, 205
Gerontos Osiou Leontiou Monastery (I.M. Γέροντος Οσίου Λεοντίου), 46
GGRS87 (*Greek Geodetic Reference System 1987*), 16
Gin Bodya, 189–90
Gin Floḳa, *mezraʿa* in the vicinity of Puliça, *16t3*, 175
Gin Ḳondostavlo Manesi, 143
Gin Manesi, 177
Girbene (Spartia), district of
  Arula, 180
  Asfalaḫto, 179
  average taxes, 226t9
  Avrami, 177
  Ayo Lisyo, 181–82
  Ayo Niḳolas, 181

240, 242–43
Gribani vel Grebani, 9
Grigoris (Γρηγόρης), 52
Grimani census, 2, 14
Gryllos (Γρύλλος), 122–23
ġulām (military servant), 235–36
Ġulyamu Argiroplu, 136
Ġumaniça, 55
günlük (tent), 235
Ġurdesi, 82
Ġurenas, 132
Gurenes, 9
Ġurġa, 29
Ġurzumişa, 189

H

Ḥadīdī, 8
Hahn, Johan Georg von, 224
Hakkı, İbrahim (Koyalı), 5
Halandritsa (Χαλανδρίτσα), 167–68
Halazoni (Χαλαζόνι), 130
Halkeio (Χαλκείο), 151
Ḫamaḳu, 19
Ḥamza Beg, 8
ḫāne (household/hearth), 211–12, 221, *224t7*, 234, 237, 244
ḫarāc (capitation, poll-tax), 243
ḫarāc-ı muḳāseme (proportional levy), 229, 243
ḫarāc-ı muvaẓẓaf (fixed levy), 243
Haraktinou (Χαρακτινού), 20
Ḫaraḳtinu, 20
Ḫarkâ, 151, 207
ḥaṣīr (mat), 244
ḫāṣṣ (land grand), 12, 157, 229, 234, 237
Hatzi (Χατζί), 206
Ḫavaro Protopapa, 75
Ḫayḳal, 43, 90
ḫazīne (treasury tent), 235
Heimadio (Χειμαδιό), 98
Helidoni (Χελιδόνι), 86, 115
Hellenic Military Geographical Service, 13, 15
Hexamilion, 4, 8
Heywood, Colin, 2
Hiliẕon, 86, *225t8*
Ḫırisoviryi Ḳozma, 142
ḫīş (relative), 211
ḥiṣār yapması (castle-building, *kastroktisia*), 243
ḥiṣṣe (income; share), 229
Hlemoutsi/Kastro (Χλεμούτσι/Κάστρο), 70
Ḫoloropoẕi, 21
Ḫotoġosti, 62
Houliarakis, Michael, 14
households–bachelors–widows, 224t7
Hrysanthi (Χρυσάνθι), 63
Hrysohori (Χρυσοχώρι), 110–11
ḥükm (decree), 243
Ḫulumiç (Hlemoutsi), district of
Andraviza, 76
average taxes, 226t9
Aya Baraskevi, 80
Başta, *mezraʿa* in the vicinity of İpsari, *15t3*, 79–80
Bavasi, 73
Çavuşi, 72
demographic statistics, 221t4
Dramşa, 73
Foloḳobuva, *mezraʿa* in the vicinity of Andraviza, *14t3*, 77
Ġastuni, 70
Girḳa Ḳumani, 72
Ġramatiḳo, 81
Ḫavaro Protopapa, 75
Ḫulumiç, nefs-i, 70
identified and unidentified localities, 12t2
İpsari, 79
İskliva, *mezraʿa* in the vicinity of Şavalya, *14t3*, 71
İvlanduşa, 78
İzlatḳa, 77
Jujli Palamiẕi, 75
Ḳanbiziya, *mezraʿa* in the vicinity of Marḳoplu, *14t3*, 78
Ḳanḳaẕi, 77
Ḳapaleto, *mezraʿa* in the vicinity of İpsari, *15t3*, 80
Ḳarẕiyoḳafti, 74
Ḳavasila, 78
Kelavi, 71
Kiḫomiro, *mezraʿa* in the vicinity of Ġastuni, *14t3*, 71
Ḳoḳla Marġariti, 75
Ḳoḳla, 72
Ḳoromiẕi, 74
Ḳuçi, 73
Lihyana, 78–79
Lonci, *mezraʿa* in the vicinity of İpsari, *15t3*, 79
Manesi, 76
Marḳoplu, 77–78
Murji, 81
Niḫor, 75–76
Orfano, 74
Pendani, *mezraʿa* in the vicinity of İpsari, *14t3*, 79
Poleşḳa, 73
Potamya Şarandinu, *mezraʿa* in the vicinity of Ġastuni, *14t3*, 70–71
Potamya Şarandinu, *mezraʿa* in the vicinity of Ḳoḳla Marġariti, *14t3*, 75
Şarakin, 73–74
Şavalya, 71
Sinasi, *mezraʿa* in the vicinity of Kelavi, *14t3*, 72
Şuli, 76
tax analysis, *259–61t16*

tax revenues of, 245
taxes from wheat and barley, 309t29
Tunba, *mezraʿa* in the vicinity of İpsari, *15t3*, 80
viticulture yield, 310t31
Zenbeş, 74
Ḫulumiç, nefs-i, 70, *225t8*
Hungarians, 218–19
ḫutbe (sermon), 244

I

Iardanos municipal unit
Asfalaḫto, 179
Coya, 96–97
Ḳaçaru, 95–96
Lali, 96
Velizi, *mezraʿa* in the vicinity of Coya, 97
Vunarġo, 195–96
İbn Kemāl, 8
İflamurari, 27
Iġlava, 99
İksanya, 173
İksaroḳastalya, *mezraʿa* in the vicinity of Ayonori, *15t3*, 152
İksenozoḫiyo, *mezraʿa* in the vicinity of Ḳamaniça, *16t3*, 162
İksifya, 133
iḳṭāʿ, 234
Ilida municipality
Androniḳa, 198
Ayo İlya, nefs-i, 190–91
Buza, 189
Çavuşi, 72
Franḳa Vila, 197
Ḫavaro Protopapa, 75
İksanya, 173
İsliva, 204
İstamiro, 206
İştopanṣi Lopesi, 193
Ḳoḳla Marġariti, 75
Maji, 93
Mazarak including the community of Ḳuçi, 206
Miziḳa, 115
Purdanu, *mezraʿa* in the vicinity of Maḳri Pozi, 89
Ranesi, 116
Rovyata including the communities of Niḳola Buva and Plaşa, 197–98
Ṣarakin, 73–74
Ṣavalya, 71
Simoplu, 203
Ṣuli, 76
Valmi, 174
Zervini, 176
Zorila, 195
iltizām (tax farming), 241
İlya Maji, 137
imām (prayer leader), 244
Imber, Colin, 229
Imbros, 5
immigrants, Albanian, 213–14
İnalcık, Halil, 2–3, 234, 237
İnönü, İsmet, 5
Ioannina, 218
İpsari, 79
İpsari, community included in Lihyana, 163
Iraia municipal unit
Aniza, 109
Bratiça, 123
Draġuzisti, 111–12
Ḫırisoviryi Ḳozma, 142
Lazar Palunbi, 139–40
Liḳuresi including the community of Bura, 207
Lonci, 109–10
Papaza, 123
Ṣarakina, 90
Sirvu, 110
Valaḳ, 110–11
Irakleia (Ηράκλεια), 88
İryolo, 196
İş Ari, 170
İsfardina, 177
İsfranci, 107
İsḳala, 120
İskâza, 106
İskiliç, 44
İsḳlaviça, 190
İskliva, *mezraʿa* in the vicinity of Niḳola Manesi, *14t3*, 27
İskliva, *mezraʿa* in the vicinity of Ṣavalya, *14t3*, 71
İsḳura, 165
Islam, 217–18, 235
İsliva, 204
İsliva-ı dīğer, *mezraʿa* dependent on Ġardicḳo, *16t3*, 206
İsmet İnönü, 5
Isoma (Ἴσωμα), 170
İspani, 94
İspani-i dīğer, *mezraʿa* in the vicinity of İspani, *15t3*, 94
İşpata, 88, 191
ispence (non-Muslims taxation), 211, 214, 237–38, 248. *see also* taxes
İstamiro, 206
İstanbul Evrak Hazinesi (Istanbul Treasury Office), 5
İstavriya/İstavrina, 59
İstefano Mazaraki, 160
İstemati Ḳondovaşıl, quarter of Hilizon, *225t8*
Isthmus, 4, 213
İstilivena, 60–61
İstilyano Ḳuzuni, quarter of Ṣaravali, *225t8*
İştin Bondaya, 29

İştopanṡi Lopesi, 193
İştopanṡi, community included in Ḳaçana, 23
İstoya Volomiri, 138
İstoya, 112–13
İstoyan, 188
İstrazova, 32–33
İsturġova, 205
Italy, 138, 212
Ithomi municipal unit, Vurçanos, 126–27
İvlaḫo Filito, *mezraʿa* in the vicinity of İstruza Potamya, *14t3*, 46
İvlaḫo Ḳalanas, *mezraʿa* in the vicinity of Ṣavanus, *14t3*, 31
İvlaḫo Yalya, *mezraʿa* in the vicinity of Ṣavanus, *14t3*, 32
İvlaḫo, 66, 201–2
İvlanduşa, 51, 78, 200
İvraḫni, 18
İvrato Ḳuçi Ḳonbi Ṣeḳra, *mezraʿa* in the vicinity of Çarnuḫlu, *15t3*, 146
İzlatḳa, 77, 161

J
Jewish community in Corinth, 219
John VI Cantacuzenus (1347–1354), 212
John VIII Palaeologus, 4
Jujli Palamiẕi, 75
Junbata, 187–88
Jupan/Jupano, 109

K
Ḳaçana including the community of İştopanṡi, 23–24
Ḳaçaru, 95–96
Kaçori, Thoma, 1–2
ḳāḍī (judge), 231, 243–44
Kafkonia (Καυκωνία), 118
Ḳaḳoḫoryo, 50
Ḳaḳusi, 82
Ḳalanci, 204
Ḳalandriça (Halandritsa), district of
average taxes, 226t9
Bala, 170
demographic statistics, 221t4
Ġolemi, 169
identified and unidentified localities, 12t2
İş Ari, 170
Ḳalandriça, nefs-i, 167–68
Ḳazneş, 168
Ḳral, 171
Ḳuçi, 168
Laluş, 171–72
Lisarya, 169
Maji, 168–69
Rapsomati, 169
tax analysis, *285–86t23*
tax revenues of, 247
taxes from wheat and barley, 309t29
Virzaḫo, 172
viticulture yield, 310t31
Zoġa, 171
Ḳalandriça, nefs-i, 167–68, *225t8*
Kalanos (Κάλανος), 31
Ḳalavrita (Kalavryta), district of
Amuri, 20
Anastasova, 30
average taxes, 226t9
Ayo İvlaşi, 28
Barçi, 23
Beluşi, 19
Dara, 25–26
Debrani, 29
demographic statistics, 221t4
Dima Plaşa, 21
Droġolavoş, 30–31
Epano Ḳurnofita, 21
Fila, 27–28
Ġolemi, 25
Ġurġa, 29
Ḫamaḳu, 19
Ḫaraḳtinu, 20
Ḫoloropoẕi, 21
identified and unidentified localities, 12t2
İflamurari, 27
İskliva, *mezraʿa* in the vicinity of Niḳola Manesi, *14t3*, 27
İştin Bondaya, 29
İstrazova, 32–33
İvlaḫo Ḳalanas, *mezraʿa* in the vicinity of Ṣavanus, *14t3*, 31
İvlaḫo Yalya, *mezraʿa* in the vicinity of Ṣavanus, *14t3*, 32
İvraḫni, 18
Ḳaçana including the community of İştopanṡi, 23–24
Ḳalavrita, nefs-i, 17
Ḳani, 22–23
Ḳaratula, 33
Ḳaratula-ı dīğer, *mezraʿa* in the vicinity of Ḳaçana, *14t3*, 24
Ḳastel, 32
Ḳastriya, 21
Ḳato Ḳurnofita, 24–25
Ḳazneş, 32
Ḳrastiki, 26
Lapata, 24
Liḳuresi, *mezraʿa* in the vicinity of Sumaki, *14t3*, 34
Maḳriyeni Çamanda, 25
Manastır-ı Meġaspilyo Aya Ḳori, 17–18
Marti Plaşa, 23
Mavromati, 31
Muriki, 29
Niḳola Manesi, 27
Palunbi Ranesi, 28
Peryale, 26

Petros Ḳaratula, 23
Petrovuni, *mezraʿa* in the vicinity of Amuri, *14t3*, 20
Puloti, *mezraʿa* in the vicinity of Dara, *14t3*, 26
Ṣavanus, 30
Seliça, 31
Şiġuni, 19
Sudana, 18
Suli, 26
Sumaki, 34
Taşi, 22
tax analysis, *250–52t11*
tax revenues of, 245
taxes from wheat and barley, 309t29
Tireẖlista, 28
Todoro Manesi, 23
Todoroplu, 23
Velimiri, 22
Vesini, 33
viticulture yield, 310t31
Vorstena, 21–22
Zepandi, 26
Zuġra, 19–20
Zuġra-ı dīğer, 20
Ḳalavrita, nefs-i, 17
Kalavryta (Καλάβρυτα), 17
Kalavryta municipal unit
Amuri, 20
Beçaḳus, 54–55
Burlaşa, 54
Droġolavoş, 30–31
Epanolaġo, 53
Gerbesi, 186
Gin Bodya, 189–90
Ġumaniça, 55
Ḫamaḳu, 19
Ḫaraḳtinu, 20
İflamurari, 27
İsfardina, 177
İştin Bondaya, 29
İvraẖni, 18
Ḳalavrita, nefs-i, 17
Kerpini, 57
Ḳılapaçuna, 58–59
Kiriçova, 55
Ḳomi, *mezraʿa* dependent on Ġardicḳo, 205
Ḳrastiki, 26
Lapata, 24
Maḳriyeni Çamanda, 25
Manastır-ı Meġaspilyo Aya Ḳori, 17–18
Martina der Noḳastro, 53
Muriki, 29
Niḳola Manesi, 27
Petro Ḳarava Klesura, 158
Rayḳu, 56
Rolo, 58
Ṣavanus, 30
Şiġuni, 19
Sudana, 18
Tireẖlista, 28
Tumena, 57–58
Visoḳa, 56–57
Zaẖlori, 57
Ẕilivina, 58
Zuġra, 19–20
Kalavryta municipality
Amuri, 20
Anastasova, 30
Ayo İvlaşi, 28
Ayo Ḳostandino, *mezraʿa* in the vicinity of Ẕervini, 84–85
Beçaḳus, 54–55
Burlaşa, 54
Çarnota, 42
Çarnuẖlu, 145–46
Droġolavoş, 30–31
Epano Ḳurnofita, 21
Epanolaġo, 53
Fila, 27–28
Gerbesi, 186
Gin Bodya, 189–90
Ġumaniça, 55
Ḫamaḳu, 19
Ḫaraḳtinu, 20
İflamurari, 27
İsfardina, 177
İştin Bondaya, 29
İstrazova, 32–33
İvraẖni, 18
Ḳalavrita, nefs-i, 17
Ḳani, 22–23
Ḳastel, 32
Ḳastriya, 21
Ḳato Ḳurnofita, 24–25
Ḳazneş, 32
Keraṣova, 101
Kerpini, 57
Ḳılapaçuna, 58–59
Kiriçova, 55
Ḳoḳova, 145
Ḳomi, *mezraʿa* dependent on Ġardicḳo, 205
Ḳrastiki, 26
Lapata, 24
Liḳuresi, *mezraʿa* in the vicinity of Sumaki, 34
Livarzi, 101
Lopesi, 203
Maji, 55–56
Maḳriyeni Çamanda, 25
Manastır-ı Meġaspilyo Aya Ḳori, 17–18
Martina der Noḳastro, 53
Motista, 176–77
Muriki, 29
Niḳola Manesi, 27
Petro Ḳarava Klesura, 158

Poraçyu, 85
Rayḳu, 56
Rolo, 58
Ṣavanus, 30
Şiġuni, 19
Sudana, 18
Tireẖlista, 28
Tumena, 57–58
Velimiri, 22
Vesini, 33
Visoḳa, 56–57
Vorstena, 21–22
Yirmoçani, 85
Zaẖlori, 57
Z̲ilivina, 58
Z̲iminiça, 90
Zuġra, 19–20
Ḳalazoni, 130
Kalentzi (Καλέντζι), 204
Kalentzi municipal unit
Avrami, 177
Ḳalanci, 204
Ḳavalari, 179
Lazaryo, 178
Kallifoni (Καλλιφώνι), 30
Kallithea (Καλλιθέα), 22–23
Ḳalo İstemati, *mezraʿa* in the vicinity of Ayo Vaṣıl, *15t3*, 150
Kalyvia Laliokosta (Καλύβια Λαλιοκώστα), 157
Ḳamaniça, 160
Ḳameniça, 40
Kamenitsa (Καμενίτσα), 40, 160
Ḳanbiziya, *mezraʿa* in the vicinity of Marḳoplu, *14t3*, 78
Kandila (Κανδήλα), 42–43
Ḳandila, 42–43
Kangadi (Καγκάδη), 140
Kangadi (Καγκάδι), 77, 108
Ḳani, 22–23
Ḳanḳaz̲i, 77, 108
ḳānūnnāme (law code), 214, 234, 238–39, 241–43, 453
Kapaleto (Καπαλέτο), 80
Ḳapaleto, *mezraʿa* in the vicinity of İpsari, *15t3*, 80
Ḳapareli, *mezraʿa* in the vicinity of Maji, *14t3*, 56
Karatoula (Καράτουλα), 33
Karatoulas (Καράτουλας), 100
Ḳaratula, 33, 100
Ḳaratula-ı dīğer, *mezraʿa* in the vicinity of Ḳaçana, *14t3*, 24
Karava rahi (Καραβά ράχη), 158
Kardiakafti (Καρδιακαύτι), 74
Ḳariza, 96
Ḳartazori, 196
Karvounaris (Καρβουνάρης), 114
Ḳarvunari, 114
ḳarye (village), 12
Ḳarz̲iyoḳafti, 74
Kastanohori (Καστανοχώρι), 45
Ḳastel İksovuni, 194
Ḳastel, 32
Kastelli (Καστέλλι), 32
Kastraki (Καστράκι), 110
Kastria (Καστρία), 21
Ḳastriçi, 163
Ḳastriya, 21
Kastro (Κάστρο), 90
Kastro-Kyllini municipal unit
H̱ulumiç, nefs-i, 70
Niẖor, 75–76
Katakolo (Κατάκολο), 100
Katarraktis (Καταρράκτης), 201
kātib (scribe), 234
Kato Fanari/Dryopi (Κάτω Φανάρι/Δρυόπη), 153
Ḳato Ḳurnofita, 24–25
Kato Makrysi (Κάτω Μακρύσι), 134
Kato Mazaraki (Κάτω Μαζαράκι), 170–71
Kato Melpeia (Κάτω Μέλπεια), 127
Kato Pteri (Κάτω Πτέρη), 31
Katsaïtaiika (Κατσαϊταίικα), 168
Katsaros (Κατσαρός), 95–96
katund (small Albanian settlement), 221–22
Kavalari (Καβαλάρη), 179
Ḳavalari Trusa, 178
Ḳavalari, 179
Ḳavasila, 78
Kavasilas (Καβάσιλας), 78
Kayapınar, Levent, 2, 5, 7
ḳayyım (caretaker), 244
Ḳazani, 88
Ḳazneş, 32, 168, 185
kebe değirmenleri (fulling mills), 240
Kefiñali, 118
Kelavi, 71
Kenderova, Stoyanka, 7
Kentro (Κέντρο), 72
Kerasia (Κερασιά), 101
Keraṣova, 101
Kerbova, 45
Kerpini (Κερπινή), 57
Kerpini, 57
Keryneia (Κερύνεια), 47–48
keşīş (monk), 211
Ketesi, 122
keylciyān (official assayers), 242
Kiẖomiro, *mezraʿa* in the vicinity of Ġastuni, *14t3*, 71
Ḳılapaçuna, 58–59
kilar (provisions tent), 235
ḳılıç (*tīmār* nucleus), 229
ḳılıç yeri, *ẖāṣṣa çiftliği* (*tīmār* demesne), 229
Ḳırana, 103
Kiriçova, 55

Kirvuḳor (Palaiokastro/Koufoplaiiko Kastro), district of
Aḳunba, 121
Aniza, 109
Artica, 102
average taxes, 226t9
Barçi, 118–19
Beluşi, 107
Bizbardi, 117
Bratiça, 123
demographic statistics, 221t4
Dragoy, 105–6
Draġuzisti, 111–12
Drayina, 112
Floḳa, 108–9
Ġardik, 123–24
identified and unidentified localities, 12t2
İsfranci, 107
İsḳala, 120
İskâza, 106
İstoya, 112–13
Jupan/Jupano, 109
Ḳanḳaẕi, 108
Ḳarvunari, 114
Kefiñali, 118
Ketesi, 122
Ḳırana, 103
Kirvuḳor, 101–2
Ḳoḳla, 118
Ḳonbi Ṣeḳra, 112
Ḳopaniça, 103–4
Ḳopiça, 118
Ḳraḳuki, 111
Ḳuçi, 115
Ḳukesi, 119
Lazar Buva, 113
Lazaro Kemer, 113
Linistena, 104–5
Lonci, 109–10
Luzi, 120
Maji, 120
Maḳrişa, 116
Manḳa, 122
Mateşi, 106–7
Mazarak Adipo, 108
Mazarak, 106
Maẕi, 119, 122
Melita, 119–20
Miziḳa, 115
Mizotoro, 107
Monaḫu, 117
Mujak, 108
Mundriza, 122–23
Murik Maji, 114–15
Omlo, 116–17
Ondriçena, 105
Papaẕa, 123
Pasḳali/Pasḳal, 119
Peta, 111
Poḳovina, 124
Ranesi, 110, 116
Ṣarakin, 120–21
Sirvu, 110
tax analysis, *268–72t18*
tax revenues of, 246
taxes from wheat and barley, 309t29
Trestena, 121
Valaḳ, 110–11
Velviça, 104
Vervena, 103
Virça, 125
viticulture yield, 310t31
Zaveti, 124
Zelaḫova, 102–3
Ẕolyani, 105
Ẕunato, 114
Kirvuḳor, 101–2
Kitros, 243
Kiẕiḳuma, *mezraʿa*, *16t3*, 209
Klados, A.I., 14
Ḳlaẕi, 52
Kleitoras municipal unit
Ḳaratula, 33
Kleitoria municipal unit
Ayo İvlaşi, 28
Çarnota, 42
Epano Ḳurnofita, 21
Fila, 27–28
Ḳani, 22
Ḳaratula, 33
Ḳastel, 32
Ḳastriya, 21
Ḳato Ḳurnofita, 24–25
Ḳazneş, 32
Liḳuresi, *mezraʿa* in the vicinity of Sumaki, 34
Maji, 55–56
Motista, 176–77
Velimiri, 22
Vorstena, 21–22
Klesura, 159
Ḳlimandi, 152–53
Klimenti (Κλημέντι), 152–53
Kloukines/Kloukinohoria (Κλουκίνες/Κλουκινοχώρια), 61
Knjaževo, 5
Ḳoçiça, 132–33
Koder, Johannes, 13
kodikes, 3
Ḳokino Marti, 141–42
Kokkaliara (Κοκκαλιάρα), 105
Kokkino Diaselo (Κόκκινο Διάσελο), 141–42
Kokkinorrahi (Κοκκινορράχη), 209
Kokla (Κόκλα), 118
Ḳoḳla Marġariti, 75
Ḳoḳla, 72, 100, 118
Koklaki (Κοκλάκι), 75
Ḳoḳova, 145

Kolokotronis, Theodore, 15
Komi (Κώμη), 162, 199, 205
Ḳomi, *mezraʿa* dependent on Ġardicḳo, *16t3*, 205
Ḳomi, *mezraʿa* in the vicinity of Ḳamaniça, *16t3*, 162
Ḳonbi Ṣeḳra, 81, 100, 112, 185–86
Ḳondari, 91
Ḳondomiḫal, 98
Ḳondorafti, 49
Ḳondostavlos Alyotos, quarter of Ḳoriṣos, *225t8*
Kontovazaina municipal unit
  Peta, 111
  Poḳovina, 124
Ḳopaniça, 103–4
Ḳopiça, 118
Ḳoraḳovuni, 43
Kordosis, Michael, 13
Korfes (Κορφές), 55
Korinthos (Κόρινθος), 148
Korinthos municipal unit
  Ḳoriṣos, nefs-i, 148
  Luḳa, 154–55
Korinthos municipality
  Ayo Vaṣıl/Çağıl Ḥiṣārı, 149
  Ayonori, 152
  Bardi, 154
  İksaroḳastalya, *mezraʿa* in the vicinity of Ayonori, 152
  Ḳoriṣos, nefs-i, 148
  Ḳutala, 151
  Luḳa, 154–55
  Pisratu, 155
  Pulimeno Soyḳa, 153
  Ṣarakin, 154
Ḳoriṣos (Korinthos), district of
  average taxes, 226t9
  Ayo Vaṣıl/Çağıl Ḥiṣārı, 149
  Ayonori, 152
  Bardi, 154
  Biçi, 154
  Buzbardi, 151
  demographic statistics, 221t4
  Fenari, 153
  Frati, 155
  Frosina, 156
  Ḫarkâ, 151
  identified and unidentified localities, 12t2
  İksaroḳastalya, *mezraʿa* in the vicinity of Ayonori, *15t3*, 152
  Ḳalo İstemati, *mezraʿa* in the vicinity of Ayo Vaṣıl, *15t3*, 150
  Ḳlimandi, 152–53
  Ḳoriṣos, nefs-i, 148
  Ḳunbaki, 154
  Ḳutala, 151
  Ḳuvara, *mezraʿa* in the vicinity of Vaṣılıḳa, *15t3*, 149
  Laluḳa, 155
  Liḳuresi, 152
  Luḳa, 154–55
  Manesi, *mezraʿa* in the vicinity of Ayo Vaṣıl, *15t3*, 149
  Petro Ḫayḳal, *mezraʿa* in the vicinity of Ayo Vaṣıl, *15t3*, 149
  Piça, *mezraʿa* in the vicinity of Pulimeno Ḳondostavlo, *15t3*, 150
  Pisratu, 155
  Pulimeno Ḳondostavlo, 150
  Pulimeno Soyḳa, 153
  Ṣarakin, 154
  Sermorini, *mezraʿa* in the vicinity of Ayo Vaṣıl, *15t3*, 150
  tax analysis, *279–81t21*
  tax revenues of, 246
  taxes from wheat and barley, 309t29
  Vaṣılıḳa, 148–49
  viticulture yield, 310t31
Ḳoriṣos, nefs-i, 148, *225t8*
Koroivos (Κόροιβος), 71
Ḳoromiẕi, 74
Koroni municipal unit, Ẕiġanato, 126
Korythio municipal unit, Periṣori, 38
Kosma (Κοσμά), 142
Kosovo, 40
Ḳoṣta Ḫāṣṣ, 157
Ḳosta Lanca, 98
Ḳostenec, 5
Kotitsa (Κοτίτσα), 132–33
Koumanis (Κουμάνης), 94
Koundouros, Stylianos, 14
Koutalas (Κουταλάς), 151
Koutsohera (Κουτσοχέρα), 92
Kouvelas (Κούβελας), 144
Ḳozma Greḳa, 192
Ḳozomuli, *mezraʿa, 15t3*, 130
Ḳraḳuki, 87, 111
Ḳral, 171
Krana (Κράνα), 103
Ḳrapeşi, 198
Ḳrastiki, 26
Krastikoi (Κραστικοί), 26
Kremmydi (Κρεμμύδι), 74
Krini (Κρήνη), 164
Krinofyta (Κρινόφυτα), 21, 24–25
Ḳroḳova, 48
Kryoneri (Κρυονέρι), 103–4
Kryonero (Κρυόνερο), 193
Kryovrysi (Κρυόβρυση), 84
Krystallovrysi (Κρυσταλλόβρυση), 167
Ḳuçi, 73, 95, 97, 115, 168
Ḳuçi, community included in Mazarak, 206
küçük oğlan (young boy), 211
Ḳukesi, 119
Ḳuḳura, 86
Ḳulukina, 61
Ḳumaniçi Luzi, *mezraʿa* in the vicinity

of Zepandi, *14t3*, 68
Ḳunbaki, 154
Küraleş, 86
Ḳurnaroḳastro, 165
Kurtik, mediaeval Albanian family, 217–18
Ḳutala, 151
Ḳuvara, *mezraʿa* in the vicinity of Vaşılıḳa, 149
Kydonies (Κυδωνίες), 169
Kyparissia (Κυπαρισσία), 125
Kyparissia municipal unit
 Arḳadya, 125
 Malena, 129–30

L

Laconia regional unit
 Ġurenas, 132
 Ḳoçiça, 132–33
 Lonḳanik, 132
 Miziṣra, 34
 Priniḳos, 34–35
laftero (tax exempt), 243
Lala Vizi, 157
Lala Ẕyavoliçi, 137
Lala, 204–5
Lalas (Λάλας), 204–5
Laleṣi, 84
Lali, 96
Laloi (Λαλοί), 96
Laloukas (Λάλουκας), 155
Laluḳa, 155
Laluş, 171–72
Lambeia (Λάμπεια), 195
Lambeia municipal unit
 Lazar Buva, 113
 Lazaro Kemer, 113
 Miġali Ẕivri, 195
Lambeti/Anthopyrgos (Λαμπέτη/Ανθόπυργος), 97
Lamia, 218
Lanbeti, 97
Lancoy, 82–83
land parcels (*στάσεις*; *stasia*), 312
Lanthi (Λάνθι), 84
Lapanagoi (Λαπαναγοί), 53
Lapata, 24
Lapatheia (Λαπάθεια), 24
Larissa, 183, 218
Larissa, acropolis of Argos, 221
Larissos municipal unit
 Fenaromeni, *mezraʿa* in the vicinity of İryolo, 197
 Gerbeşi, 205
 İryolo, 196
 İşpata, 191
 Ḳanḳaẕi, 77
 Miḫoy, 184–85
 Petrovişta, 184
Lasionas municipal unit
 Ḳastel İksovuni, 194
 Kertiza, 83
 Poliça, 194
 Sipyani, 94
 Ẕervini, 84
Lastrana vel Listrenu, 9
Latzoï (Λατζόι), 82–83
Lazar Buva, 113
Lazar Palunbi, 139–40
Lazarades/Gynaikohori (Λαζαράδες/Γυναικοχώρι), 113
Lazargio/Bantsaiika (Λαζαργιό/Μπαντσαίικα), 178
Lazaro Buva, 91
Lazaro Kemer, 113
Lazaro Klesura, 140–41
Lazaro Ḳuveli, 144
Lazaro Zupata, 137
Lazaro-Bouga (Λαζαρο-Μπούγα), 91
Lazaryo, 178
Leake, William Martin, 14
Lebourd de Saint Supéran, Pierre, 213
Lefka (Λεύκα), 154–55
Lefkasio (Λευκάσιο), 42
legumes, cultivation of, 311
Lehaina (Λεχαινά), 78–79, 163
Lehaina municipal unit
 Aya Baraskevi, 80
 Başta, *mezraʿa* in the vicinity of İpsari, 79–80
 Lihyana, 78–79
 Simiza, 192
Lemnos, 5
Lendari, 9
Lenḳoni, 182
Leontari (Λεοντάρι), 131
Leontio (Λεόντιο), 189
Leontio municipal unit
 Ayo Yani, 178–79
 Franḳo, 51
 Frati, 188
 Ġolemi, 25
 Ġurzumişa, 189
 Ḳazneş, 168
 Mazarak, 187
Levidi (Λεβίδι), 39–40
Levidi municipal unit
 Aġali, 40–41
 Bejenik, nefs-i, 39
 Bendeni/Pendeni, 41
 Bondaya, 41–42
 Dara, 25–26
 Doşkesi, 43
 Ḳandila, 42–43
 Leviẕi, 39–40
 Lopesi, 40
 Plaşa, *mezraʿa* in the vicinity of Bejenik, 39
 Sina, 42
Leviẕi, 39–40

Libanovo (Aiginio), 243
Lihyana including the community of İpsari, 163
Lihyana, 78–79
Liḳuresi including the community of Bura, 207
Liḳuresi, 91–92, 152
Liḳuresi, *mezraʿa* in the vicinity of Ḳamaniça, *16t3*, 161
Liḳuresi, *mezraʿa* in the vicinity of Sumaki, *14t3*, 34
Linistaina (Λινίσταινα), 104–5
Linistena, 104–5
Lisarya, 169
Listirna, 52
Listraina/Listrena/Listrina (Λίστραινα/Λίστρενα/Λίστρινα), 52
Livadeia, 214, 218
Livartzi (Λιβάρτζι), 101
Livarzi, 101
livestock, taxes on, 249. *see also* taxes
localities, identified and unidentified, 12t2
Loġaṣeti, 83–84
Logothetis (Λογοθέτης), 83–84
Lonci, 19–10
Lonci, *mezraʿa* in the vicinity of İpsari, *15t3*, 79
Londar (Leontari), district of
  Aleksi Manesi, 133–34
  Amuri, 146–47
  Andriya Pupuḳa, 140
  average taxes, 226t9
  Aya Niḳola, *mezraʿa* in the vicinity of Amuri, *15t3*, 147
  Aya Yorgi, 131–32
  Barbuçi, 142
  Çarnuẖlu, 145–46
  demographic statistics, 221t4
  Dimitri Maçuki, 135
  Domaniḳa Beluşi, 134–35
  Duḳa Plaşa, 135
  Gin Ḳondostavlo Manesi, 143
  Ġulyamu Argiroplu, 136
  Ġurenas, 132
  Ḫırisoviryi Ḳozma, 142
  identified and unidentified localities, 12t2
  İksifya, 133
  İlya Maji, 137
  İstoya Volomiri, 138
  İvrato Ḳuçi Ḳonbi Ṣeḳra, *mezraʿa* in the vicinity of Çarnuẖlu, *15t3*, 146
  Ḳoçiça, 132–33
  Ḳokino Marti, 141–42
  Ḳoḳova, 145
  Lala Ẕyavoliçi, 137
  Lazar Palunbi, 139–40
  Lazaro Klesura, 140–41
  Lazaro Ḳuveli, 144
  Lazaro Zupata, 137
  Londar, nefs-i, 131
  Lonḳanik, 132
  Maji, 131
  Maḳrisa Ustruza, 144–45
  Mangişa Burlaşa, 136
  Marti Çaşi, 141
  Marti Helmi, 133
  Marti Plaşa, 134
  Miẖal Manesi, 135
  Miẖal Zora, 135–36
  Niḳola Maḳrişa, 134
  Niḳola Sirgi, 139
  Pavla, 148
  Pavlo Doçi, 136
  Petro Dorza, 137
  Ṭarpun, 146
  tax analysis, *274–78t20*
  tax revenues of, 246
  taxes from wheat and barley, 309t29
  Todoro Doşkesi, 138
  Todoro Zupata, 136
  Trima İşpata, 142
  Veliġosti, *mezraʿa* in the vicinity of Londar, *15t3*, 147
  Velize, 144
  viticulture yield, 310t31
  Yani Dara, 143
  Yani Evzenati, 133
  Yani Jura, 138
  Yani Ḳanḳaẕi, 140
  Yani Lata, 134
  Yani Mazaraki, 139
  Yani Ẕyavoliçi, 133
  Yorgi Maji, 134
  Yorgi Manesi, 143
  Yorgi Mujaki, 140
  Yorgi Muzaki, 136
  Ẕima Rala, 142–43
  Ẕimiçana, 145
  Ẕupano Buryalişa, 138
Londar, nefs-i, 131, *225t8*
Longanikos (Λογκανίκος), 132
Longonico, 9
longue durée, 312
Lonḳanik, 132
Lopesi (Λόπεσι), 40, 50
Lopesi, 40, 50, 203
Lotis (Λώτης), 109–10
Loukistra (Λουκίστρα), 175
Lousiko (Λουσικό), 19
Lovoḳa, 63
Lowry, Heath, 2, 311
Loyi, 128
Luḳa İfrati, 49
Luḳa, 154–55
Luḳas Loġoṣeti, quarter of Hiliẕon, *225t8*
Lukişta, *mezraʿa* in the vicinity of Puliça, *16t3*, 175

Luvari, *mezraʿa* in the vicinity of Astriçi, *14t3*, 36
Luzi, 120
Lykaio (Λύκαιο), 146
Lykosoura (Λυκόσουρα), 131–32
Lykouresis (Λυκούρεσης), 207
Lykouria (Λυκουρία), 34

M

macro-economy, 312
Magera (Μάγερα), 196–97
Magno, Stefano, 9
maḥalle (quarter, neighbourhood), 12, 224, *225t8*
Maḥmūd Paşa, 8, *230t10*, 233
Maji, 55–56, 89, 93, 120, 131, 168–69, 202
Maḳri Poẓi, 88–89
Maḳrisa Ustruza, 144–45
Maḳrişa, 116
Makrisia (Μακρίσια), 116
Maḳriyeni Çamanda, 25
Makrypodi (Μακρυπόδι), 88–89
Malaḳas, 208
Malena, 129–30
Malesina, 187
Maliki, 185
Maliye Vekâleti (Ministry of Finance), 5
Manastır-ı Meġaspilyo Aya Ḳori, 17–18
Manastır-ı Ṣotoḳos, 47
Manastır-ı Yirondos der Taḳsiyarḫi, 46
Manesi (Μάνεσι), 27, 135, 177
Maneşi, 65
Manesi, 76, 206, 208
Manesi, *mezraʿa* in the vicinity of Ayo Vaṣıl, *15t3*, 149
Manesis (Μάνεσης), 143
Mangişa Burlaşa, 136
Mangişa Ḳumani, 94
Maniakes, George, 212
Manḳa, 122
Mantineia municipal unit
  Brasna Sanḳa, 37
  Çipyana, 38
  Miḫlu, 35
  Naşi, 37
  Pikerni, 36–37
Manuel Cantacuzenus (1348–1380), 213
Manuel II Palaeologus (1391–1425), 3–4, 213
Mariçi, *mezraʿa* in the vicinity of Puliça, *16t3*, 175
Marḳoplu, 77–78, 190
Markopoulo (Μαρκόπουλο), 77–78
Marti Çaşi, 141
Marti Helmi, 133
Marti Plaşa, 23, 134
Martina (Μαρτίνα), 53
Martina der Noḳastro, 53
Mastrantonis (Μαστραντώνης), 202
Mastro Andoni, 202
maṭbaḫ (kitchen tent), 235
Matesi (Μάτεσι), 106–7
Mateşi, 106–7
Matranḳa, *mezraʿa* in the vicinity of İşpata, *15t3*, 89
Matthew Asan, 4
Matyos Mamuẓa, quarter of Ḳalandriça, *225t8*
Mavromati (Μαυρομάτη), 100–101
Mavromati, 31, 100–101
Mavrommati (Μαυρομμάτι), 126–27
Mayira, 196–97
Mayira, *mezraʿa* in the vicinity of Ṣoḫyana, *14t3*, 69
Mazarak Adipo, 108
Mazarak including the community of Ḳuçi, 206
Mazarak, 106, 187
Mazaraki (Μαζαράκι), 108, 139, 206
Mazaraki, 170–71
Mazi (Μάζι), 93
Maẓi, 119, 122
Maẓiñik, 173, 207
McDonald, William, 14
Meġaliç, *mezraʿa*, *15t3*, 129
Megalopoli municipality
  Açiḫolos, 44
  Amuri, 146–47
  Andon, 208
  Aya Niḳola, *mezraʿa* in the vicinity of Amuri, 147
  Aya Yorgi, 131–32
  Ġardik, 123–24
  Ḳarvunari, 114
  Kerbova, 45
  Ḳokino Marti, 141–42
  Londar, nefs-i, 131
  Marti Çaşi, 141
  Miḫal Manesi, 135
  Murik Maji, 114–15
  Niḳola Maḳrişa, 134
  Ṣarakin, 120–21
  Ṭarpun, 146
  Ustruza/İstruza Potamya, 46
  Veliġosti, *mezraʿa* in the vicinity of Londar, 147
  Ẓunato, 114
Megalopoli municipal unit
  Aya Yorgi, 131–32
  Ġardik, 123–24
  Kerbova, 45
  Ḳokino Marti, 141–42
  Marti Çaşi, 141
  Niḳola Maḳrişa, 134
  Ṭarpun, 146
Megalou Spilaiou Monastery (I.M. Μεγάλου Σπηλαίου), 17–18
Megas Pontias (Μέγας Ποντιάς), 29
Meḥmed Ebū's-suʿūd, 229

Meḥmed I (1413–1421), 8
Meḥmed II (1444–1446, 1451–1481), 4–5, 8, 235, 238–39
Meligala municipal unit, Arḫangeli, 127–28
Meliğala, *mezra'a* in the vicinity of Ḳamaniça, *16t3*, 161
Melingoi/Milingoi, 220
Melissopetra (Μελισσόπετρα), 121
Melita (Μελιτά), 119–20
Melita, 119–20
Melitena, 187
Messatida municipal unit
  Bardoḳosta, 167
  İsḳura, 165
  Pavloḳastro, 159
  Ṣaravali, 156–57
  Sizereḳastro, 157–58
  Topolova, 166–67
  Vola, 159
Messenia regional unit
  Andriya Pupuḳa, 140
  Arḫangeli, 127–28
  Arḳadya, 125
  Gin Ḳondostavlo Manesi, 143
  Ġırebini, 127
  Ḳalazoni, 130
  Lazaro Klesura, 140–41
  Lazaro Ḳuveli, 144
  Lazaro Zupata, 137
  Loyi, 128
  Malena, 129–30
  Miḫal Zora, 135–36
  Mili Ḳalivya, 128–29
  Muzak Mengişa, 130
  Niḳola Sirgi, 139
  Palari, 129
  Platana, 128
  Provanda Aya Yorgi, 125–26
  Todoro Doşkesi, 138
  Todoro Zupata, 136
  Vurçanos, 126–27
  Yani Dara, 143
  Yani Ḳanḳazi, 140
  Yani Ẕyavoliçi, 133
  Ẕiğanato, 126
  Ẕima Rala, 142–43
Messini municipality
  Andriya Pupuḳa, 140
  Gin Ḳondostavlo Manesi, 143
  Loyi, 128
  Vurçanos, 126–27
  Yani Ḳanḳazi, 140
mezra'a (arable land with no settlement), 12
mezra'as, list of, *14–16t3*
mezra'as, place names, 13
Michael Attaleiates, 212
micro-economy, 312
microtoponymy, 312
Miğali Ẕivri, 195
Miḫal Manesi, 135
Miḫal Yanḳuri, quarter of Ḫulumiç, *225t8*
Miḫal Zora, 135–36
Mihalos (Μίχαλος), 93–94
Mihili, 93–94, 196
Miḫlu (Mouhli), district of
  Astriçi, 35–36
  Astro, *mezra'a* in the vicinity of Astriçi, *14t3*, 36
  average taxes, *226t9*
  Brasna Sanḳa, 37
  Çipyana, 38
  demographic statistics, *221t4*
  Duşa Dara, *mezra'a* in the vicinity of Astriçi, *14t3*, 36
  identified and unidentified localities, *12t2*
  Luvari, *mezra'a* in the vicinity of Astriçi, *14t3*, 36
  Miḫlu, 35
  Naşi, 37
  Perisori, 38
  Pikerni, 36–37
  Plaşa, *mezra'a* in the vicinity of Astriçi, *14t3*, 36
  Plaşa, *mezra'a* in the vicinity of Raḫova, *14t3*, 38
  Raḫova, 38
  tax analysis, *253t13*
  tax revenues of, 245
  taxes from wheat and barley, *309t29*
  viticulture yield, *310t31*
Miḫlu, 35
Mihoïo (Μιχόιο), 184–85
Miḫoy, 184–85
Mikros Pontias (Μικρός Ποντιάς), 189–90
Mili Ḳalivya, 128–29
Milyas, 188
Miraḳo, 87
Mirati, 173–74
mīrlivā'-ı vilāyet-i Mora (governor of the Peloponnese/Morea), 7–8, 10, 218, 234, 245–46
Mitepoli, 186
Mitopoli (Μιτόπολη), 186
Miziḳa, 115
Mizisra (Mystras), district of
  average taxes, *226t9*
  demographic statistics, *221t4*
  identified and unidentified localities, *12t2*
  Mizisra, 34
  Priniḳos, 34–35
  tax analysis, *252t12*
  tax revenues of, 245
  taxes from wheat and barley, *309t29*
  viticulture yield, *310t31*

Mizis̱ra, 34
Mizotoro, 107
Moira (Μοίρα), 188
Modon, 4–5, 10, 14
Monahou (Μοναχού), 117
Monaẖu, 117
Monastiri (Μοναστήρι), 65
Mondrusa vel Mondrizza, 9
Monemvasia, 5
Montenegro, 31, 66, 105, 171, 180, 195, 205
Montepoli, 9
Mora (the Peloponnese), province of
  tax analysis, *300–308t28*
  tax revenues of, 247–49
Morea, 3–4, 8, 10, 13–14, 213, 224, 227, 234, 238–39, 241, 247–48
mosques (Leontari and Corinth), 219, 244
Motista, 176–77
Mouhli (Μούχλι/Μουχλί), 35
Mouriki (Μουρίκι), 29, 114–15
Mouzaki (Μουζάκι), 130, 191
Movri municipal unit
  Franḳa, 91
  Ġomosto, 200
mu ʿāf ve müsellem (tax-exempt group), 243
mücerred (bachelor/single adult man), 211–12, 221, 223, *224t7*, 234, 244
müdd-i Edrene (Adrianople *müdd*), 242, 247
mü ʾez̠z̠in (muezzin), 244
Mujak, 108
Mujaki, 44–45
*muḳāṭa ʿa*s, 241–42, 249. *see also* taxes
mulberry trees, cultivation of, 248
Mundriza, 122–23
Murād I (1362–1389), 3
Murād II (1421–1451), 4
Murik Buva, 208–9
Murik Maji, 114–15
Muriki, 29
Murji, 81
mürted (apostate), 211
müsellem (tax-exempt individual), 242–43
Muslim community, 219
Muslim/Turkish element (by references to timariots), 217–18
Muslim/Turkish population (authorities and garrisons), 218
Musṭafā, 4
Muzak Mengişa, 130
Muzak, 191
Muzak, community included in Fil Adrofinos, 207
müzevvec (male married adult), 234
Mystras (Μυστράς), 34
Mystras municipal unit, Mizis̱ra, 34

N

nāḥiyyet (district), 12
Namuni, 59
Nasa (Νάσα), 82
Nasa, 82
Naşi, 37
Nasia (Νάσια), 37
Nauplion, 5
Navarrese Military Company, 3, 213
Neapoli (Νεάπολη), 79
neccār (carpenter), 242
nefs (local centre), 12
Nemea municipal unit
  Buzbardi, 151
  Pulimeno Ḳondostavlo, 150
Nemea municipality
  Buzbardi, 151
  Pulimeno Ḳondostavlo, 150
Neohori (Νεοχώρι), 75–76
Neri Acciaiuoli, 163, 213, 219
Neromylos (Νερόμυλος), 77
nesiẖ script, 7
Neşrī, 8
Nestani (Νεστάνη), 38
Niẖor, 75–76
Nikifor Ḳavasila, quarter of Ḫulumiç, 7, *225t8*
Nikifor, 98
Niḳola Buva, 209
Niḳola Ḳumi, 199
Niḳola Luzi, quarter of Ḳoris̱os, *225t8*
Niḳola Maḳrişa, 134
Niḳola Manesi, 27
Niḳola Mavropoz̠i, quarter of Ḳalandriça, *225t8*
Niḳola Patrino, quarter of Vumero, *225t8*
Niḳola Ṣalamono, quarter of Londar, *225t8*
Niḳola Sirgi, 139
Nisi (Νησί), 185
North Macedonia, 18, 29, 33, 105, 147, 195, 218
Nouhakis, Ioannis, 14

O

oğlan (military servant), 235
Oihalia municipal unit
  Palari, 129
  Todoro Doşkesi, 138
Oihalia municipality
  Arẖangeli, 127–28
  Ġırebini, 127
  Lazaro Klesura, 140–41
  Lazaro Ḳuveli, 144
  Lazaro Zupata, 137
  Miẖal Zora, 135–36
  Niḳola Sirgi, 139
  Palari, 129
  Provanda Aya Yorgi, 125–26

Todoro Doşkesi, 138
Todoro Zupata, 136
Yani Ẕyavoliçi, 133
Olana, 98–99
Oleni (Ωλένη), 98–99
Oleni municipal unit
Aranis Ḳuçohyari, 92
Ġramatiḳo, 81
Ḳaratula, 100
Laleṣi, 84
Lancoy, 82–83
Mavromati, 100–101
Mihili, 93–94
Muzak, 191
Olana, 98–99
Pendeni including the community of Palunbi Ipṣari, 199
Ranbiyaḳa, 207
Ratendu, 98
Ṣopi, 99
Vumero, nefs-i, 81
Olenia municipal unit
Arula, 180
Ayo Yorgi, *mezra'a* in the vicinity of Lenḳoni, 182–83
Fostana, 181
Gin Floḳa, *mezra'a* in the vicinity of Puliça, 175
Ḳomi, *mezra'a* in the vicinity of Ḳamaniça, 162
Ḳral, 171
Lukişta, *mezra'a* in the vicinity of Puliça, 175
Mariçi, *mezra'a* in the vicinity of Puliça, 175
Mayira, 196–97
Mazaraki, 170–71
Mirati, 173–74
Mitepoli, 186
Porta, 172–73
Runbaḳa, 160–61
Ṣandamiri, nefs-i, 172
olive trees, cultivation of, 248–49
Ombras (Ομπράς), 116–17
'Ömer Beg, 4, 8
Omlo, 116–17
Ondriçena, 105
onomatopoeia, 13
Oreino Korakovouni (Ορεινό Κορακοβούνι), 43
Orfano (Ορφανό), 174
Orfano, 74
Orfano, *mezra'a* in the vicinity of Porta, *16t3*, 174
Oṣiya Mariya, 181
Ottoman interregnum (1402–1413), 4
Ottomanisation, 244
Ottoman–Venetian war (1463), 1, 8–10

P

Pacifico, Pier' Antonio, 14
Païoi municipal unit
Çarnuḫlu, 145–46
İstrazova, 32–33
Ḳoḳova, 145
Vesini, 33
Palaeologus, Andronicus III (1328–1341), 212
Palaeologus, Constantine, 4
Palaeologus, Demetrius, 4–5, 243
Palaeologus, John VIII, 4
Palaeologus, Manuel II (1391–1425), 3–4, 213
Palaeologus, Theodore I (1384–1407), 3–4, 213
Palaeologus, Theodore II (1407–1443), 4
Palaeologus, Thomas, 4–5, 8
Palaiokastro/Koufoplaiiko Kastro (Παλαιόκαστρο/Κουφοπλαίικο Κάστρο), 101–2
Palaiomonastiro (Παλαιομονάστηρο), 46
Palaiopyrgos (Παλαιόπυργος), 41–42, 128–29
Palari, 129
Paleo Castro vel Paolo Castro, 9
Paliakoumba Platianas (Παλιάκουμπα Πλατιάνας), 121
Paliarovouni (Παλιαροβούνι), 129
Paliolena (Παλιόλενα), 98–99
Palioloukas (Παλιολουκάς), 49
Palopirġo, 183
Paloumba (Παλούμπα), 139–40
Palunbi Ipṣari, community included in Pendeni, 199
Palunbi Ranesi, 28
Panagias Filokaliotissas Monastery (I.M. Παναγίας Φιλοκαλιώτισσας), 197
Panagias Pepelenitsis Monastery (I.M. Παναγίας Πεπελενίτσης), 47
Panagiotopoulos, Vasilis, 2, 14, 213, 225
Papaẕa, 123
Papaẕato, 178
Pappadas (Παππαδάς), 123
Paralia Niforaiikon (Παραλία Νιφοραϊικων), 162
Paralimni (Παραλίμνη), 205
Paraskevi (Παρασκευή), 50
Parnassos (Παρνασσός), 123
Parori (Παρόρι), 38
Paschalinou t' aloni (Πασχαλινού τ' αλώνι), 119
Pasḳali/Pasḳal, 119
Patra (Πάτρα), 156
Patra municipal unit
Bala, 170
Balya Badra, 156
Junbata, 187–88
Ḳurnaroḳastro, 165
Maji, 168–69
Milyas, 188

Ṣofyana, 164
Suli, 166
Ṣuli, 200–201
Vundeni, 163–64
Zastupa, *mezraʿa* in the vicinity of Ḳurnaroḳastro, 166
Patra municipality
Bala, 170
Balya Badra, 156
Bardoḳosta, 167
Çuḳala, 161
İsḳura, 165
Junbata, 187–88
Ḳastriçi, 163
Ḳurnaroḳastro, 165
Lihyana including the community of İpsari, 163
Maji, 168–69
Milyas, 188
Pavloḳastro, 159
Ṣaravali, 156–57
Ṣeryanu, 160
Sizereḳastro, 157–58
Ṣofyana, 164
Suli, 166
Ṣuli, 200–201
Tiristena, 167
Topolova, 166–67
Vola, 159
Vundeni, 163–64
Zastupa, *mezraʿa* in the vicinity of Ḳurnaroḳastro, 166
Patura, *mezraʿa* in the vicinity of Pavloḳastro, *16t3*, 159
Pavla, 148
Pavlia (Παύλια), 148
Pavlo Doçi, 136
Pavlokastro (Παυλόκαστρο), 159
Pavloḳastro, 159
Pavlos Lanbo, quarter of Ḳorisos, *225t8*
Pax Ottomana, 2
Pefkes (Πεύκες), 144
Pefki (Πεύκη), 199
Pefki (Πευκί), 112
Pefko (Πεύκο), 145–46
Peleki (Πελέκι), 124
Pellana municipal unit
Ġurenas, 132
Ḳoçiça, 132–33
Lonḳanik, 132
Pelopio (Πελόπιο), 87
Pelyura, *mezraʿa* in the vicinity of Ṣoḫyana, *14t3*, 68
Pendani, *mezraʿa* in the vicinity of İpsari, *14t3*, 79
Pendeni including the community of Palunbi Ipṣari, 199
per capita taxes, 237–38. *see also* taxes
Perisori, 38, 66
Perithori (Περιθώρι), 66
Perpataris (Περπατάρης), 44–45
Persaina (Πέρσαινα), 95
Persena, *mezraʿa* in the vicinity of İspani, *15t3*, 95
personal holdings (*ḫāṣṣa*), revenues from, 240–41. *see also* taxes
Persor, 43–44
Perthori (Περθώρι), 43–44
Peryale, 26
Peta, 111
Petalidi municipal unit
Andriya Pupuḳa, 140
Yani Ḳanḳazi, 140
Petas (Πέτας), 111
Petralona (Πετράλωνα), 104
Petro Dorza, 137
Petro Ḫayḳal, *mezraʿa* in the vicinity of Ayo Vaṣıl, *15t3*, 149
Petro Ḳarava Klesura, 158
Petro Tunba, 51
Petros Ḳaratula, 23
Petroviṣta, 184
Petrovithia (Πετροβίθια), 184
Petrovuni, *mezraʿa* in the vicinity of Amuri, *14t3*, 20
Petsakoi (Πετσάκοι), 54–55
Phlious, 213
Piça, *mezraʿa* in the vicinity of Pulimeno Ḳondostavlo, *15t3*, 150
Pier' Antonio Pacifico, 14
Pierre Lebourd de Saint Supéran, 213
Pigadi (Πηγάδι), 72
Pigi (Πηγή), 187–88
pīh (lamp oil), 244
Pikerni, 36–37
Pikernis (Πικέρνης), 36–37
Pikoulas, Yanis, 13
Pineia municipal unit
İksanya, 173
İsliva, 204
İstamiro, 206
Maji, 93
Mazarak including the community of Ḳuçi, 206
Purdanu, *mezraʿa* in the vicinity of Maḳri Pozi, 89
Simoplu, 203
Ṣuli, 76
Valmi, 174
Zorila, 195
Pineios municipality
Dramṣa, 73
Ġastuni, 70
Ḳarziyoḳafti, 74
Ḳavasila, 78
Kelavi, 71
Ḳoḳla, 72
Marḳoplu, 77–78
Potamya Ṣarandinu, *mezraʿa* in the

vicinity of Ġastuni, 70–71
Piraeus (Nisoi) regional unit, Fenari, 153
Pisratu, 155
Pistratou (Πιστρατού), 155
place names, identification of, 12–17
Plaşa, 64–65, 91
Plaşa, *mezra'a* in the vicinity of Astriçi, *14t3*, 36
Plaşa, *mezra'a* in the vicinity of Bejenik, *14t3*, 39
Plaşa, *mezra'a* in the vicinity of Raḫova, 10, *14t3*, 38
Platana, 128
Plataniotissa (Πλατανιώτισσα), 58–59
Platanitsa (Πλατανίτσα), 85
Platanos (Πλάτανος), 83, 128
Platistomo, 174
Platoḳomati, 129
Ples(i)a [Πλέσ(ι)α], 39
Plessa (Πλέσσα), 64–65
Ploutohori (Πλουτοχώρι), 112–13
Poḳovina, 124
Poland, 39, 103–4, 124, 132, 144, 172, 210
Poleska, 73
Poliça, 194
Polihni (Πολίχνη), 127–28
Politis, Nikolaos, 12
Politsa (Πολίτσα), 194
poll-tax (*ḫarāc*), paid by non-Muslim subjects, 243
Polylofo (Πολύλοφο), 173–74
Pondiḳo, 100
population (families), distribution of, 223t6
Poraçyu, 85
Poroviça, 69
Porovitsa (Ποροβίτσα), 69
Porsos vel Pertes, 9
Porta, 172–73
Portes (Πόρτες), 172–73
Poso, 89
Potamia (Ποταμιά), 45
Potamya Şarandinu, *mezra'a* in the vicinity of Ġastuni, *14t3*, 70–71
Potamya Şarandinu, *mezra'a* in the vicinity of Ḳoḳla Marġariti, *14t3*, 75
Potamya, 60
Pothos (Πόθος), 89
Poulos, Ioannis, 213
Pouqueville, François C.H.L., 15
Pournarokastro (Πουρναρόκαστρο), 165
praktika, 3
Prasino (Πράσινο), 96–97
Pratano, 83
Prifti, 196
Prime Ministry Ottoman Archives, 1, 5
Priniḳos, 34–35
private property (*mülk*), taxes on, 240. *see also* taxes
Profitis Elissaios (Προφήτης Ελισσαίος), 181–82
Profitis Ilias (Προφήτης Ηλίας), 186
proġonostu (stepson), 211
pronoia, 234
Provanda Aya Yorgi, 125–26
Psari (Ψάρι), 79
Psili Vrysi (Ψηλή Βρύση), 133–34
Pteri (Πτέρη), 201
Puliça, 174
Pulimeno Ḳondostavlo, 150
Pulimeno Soyḳa, 153
Puloti, *mezra'a* in the vicinity of Dara, *14t3*, 26
Purdanu, *mezra'a* in the vicinity of Maḳri Pozi, *15t3*, 89
Pylos municipal unit
Mili Ḳalivya, 128–29
Platana, 128
Pylos-Nestoras municipality
Mili Ḳalivya, 128–29
Platana, 128
Ẓiġanato, 126
Pyrgaki (Πυργάκι), 183
Pyrgos municipal unit
Ḳuḳura, 86
Lanbeti, 97
Malaḳas, 208
Pondiḳo, 100
Romesi, 92
Pyrgos municipality
Añloniça, 93
Aranis Ḳuçohyari, 92
Asfalaḫto, 179
Coya, 96–97
Ġramatiḳo, 81
Ḳaçaru, 95–96
Ḳaratula, 100
Ḳuḳura, 86
Lalesi, 84
Lali, 96
Lanbeti, 97
Lancoy, 82–83
Malaḳas, 208
Mavromati, 100–101
Mihili, 93–94
Muzak, 191
Olana, 98–99
Pendeni including the community of Palunbi Ipşari, 199
Pondiḳo, 100
Ranbiyaḳa, 207
Ratendu, 98
Romesi, 92
Şopi, 99
Velizi, *mezra'a* in the vicinity of Coya, 97
Vumero, nefs-i, 81
Vunarġo, 195–96

şerīʿat (Islamic law), 8, 240
Serḳofayi, *mezraʿa* in the vicinity of Petrovişta, *16t3*, 184
Sermorini, *mezraʿa* in the vicinity of Ayo Vaṣıl, *15t3*, 150
serrācḫāne (saddlery tent), 235
Serres, 218, 242
Servos (Σέρβος), 110
Ṣeryanu, 160
settlement patterns, 1, 227
settlements according to their size, distribution of, 222t5
settlements, division into Greek and Albanian, 212
settler, 13
Sfikopoulos, Ioannis, 14
Sicily, 212
Sidero Castro, 9
Sidirokastro (Σιδηρόκαστρο), 157–58
Siginiskes (Σιγίνισκες), 62
Sigouni (Σιγούνι), 19
Şiġuni, 19
Sikyona (Σικυώνα), 148–49
Sikyona municipal unit
  Ḳlimandi, 152–53
  Vaṣılıḳa, 148–49
Sikyona municipality
  Ḳlimandi, 152–53
  Vaṣılıḳa, 148–49
silk industry, 248
Simiza (Σιμίζα), 192
Simiza, 192
Simoplu, 203
Simopoulo (Σιμόπουλο), 203
Sina, 42
Sinān Beg bin Elvān Beg, 7–8
Sinān Beg, 8, 10
Sinas (Σίνας), 42
Sinasi, *mezraʿa* in the vicinity of Kelavi, *14t3*, 72
Sinevro (Σινεβρό), 64
Sinoviro, 64
Sipyani, 94
Sirveliça, 183
Sirvu, 110, 194
Sitara, 87
siyāḳat script, 7
Siyiniski, 62
Sizereḳastro, 157–58
Skala (Σκάλα), 120
Skepasto (Σκεπαστό), 56–57
Skiadas (Σκιαδάς), 106
Skiadas, Eleftherios, 14
Skillountas municipal unit
  Aḳunba, 121
  Bizbardi, 117
  Floḳa, 108–9
  İstoya, 112–13
  Ḳanḳazi, 108
  Ḳozma Greḳa, 192
  Maḳrişa, 116
  Mazi, 122
  Monaḫu, 117
  Mundriza, 122–23
  Omlo, 116–17
Skillountia (Σκιλλουντία), 122
Skioessa (Σκιόεσσα), 163–64
Sklavoutsa (Σκλάβουτσα), 190
Skliva (Σκλίβα), 204
Skotani (Σκοτάνη), 145
Skoura (Σκούρα), 165
Skyliki (Σκυλίκη), 44
Slavic element (Slavic names), 216–17
Slavic toponyms, 13
Slavs, 13, 216–17
Slovakia, 18, 104, 121, 124
Slovenia, 18, 38, 45, 52, 68, 132, 167, 171, 177, 210
Sofiana (Σοφιανά), 68
Ṣofyana, 164
Ṣoḫyana, 68
Soïka/Skopia (Σόικα/Σκοπιά), 153
Son Posta, 5
Sopi (Σόπι), 99
Ṣopi, 99
Ṣopiya, 203
Sotira, 54
Sotiras (Σωτήρας), 54
Souli (Σούλι), 76, 166
Sparti municipality
  Ġurenas, 132
  Ḳoçiça, 132–33
  Lonḳanik, 132
  Mizisra, 34
Spartia (Σπαρτιά), 176
Spartinou (Σπαρτινού), 177
Stamatelatos, Michael, 13–14
Stamero vel Stamiro, 9
Stavria (Σταυριά), 59
Stavros (Σταυρός), 167
Stefan Dušan, 212, 237
Stefano Magno, 9
stock-rearing, taxes on, 239. *see also* taxes
Stojkov, Roussi, 1–2
Sts Cyril and Methodius National Library of Bulgaria, 1, 5
Stylia (Στύλια), 51
subsistence minimum, 248
Sudana, 18
Suli, 26, 166
Ṣuli, 76, 86, 200–201
sülüs script, 7
Sumaki, 34
Şurbi, 82
Şurbi, *mezraʿa* in the vicinity of Petrovişta, *16t3*, 184
sustainability, 249
Syhaina (Συχαινά), 164
Sykies (Συκιές), 107

Sylivaina (Συλίβαινα), 60–61
Sympoliteia municipal unit
  Aya İğliğori, 52
  Graḳa, 52–53
  Listirna, 52
  Lopesi, 50
  Raḫova, 164
  Ẓiyaleş Tunba, 49
Synoikismos Havariou/Palaio Havari (Συνοικισμός Χαβαρίου/Παλαιό Χάβαρι), 75
Syrrizo (Σύρριζο), 139

T

taḥrīr defteri
  icmāl (abridged), 229
  inaccuracies of, 236–37
  mufaṣṣal (detailed), 229
*taḥrīr defter*s
  alphabet used in the taxation cadastre, 11
  drawbacks of, 311
  limitations and reliability of, 2–3
  purpose of, 211
  TT10–1/14662 history and description of, 5–10. *see also* Tapu Tahrir Defteri no. 10 (TT10)
Tapu Tahrir Defteri no. 10 (TT10)
  codicological description of, 5–7
  date of compilation, 7–10
  pagination, *6t1*
Ṭarpun, 146
Taşi, 22
Tavia/Davia, 4
taxes
  āsiyāb, *āsiyāb-ı ġalle* (tax on water-powered gristmills), 240
  āsiyāb-ı ḫāṣṣa (revenue from water-powered gristmills in personal holding), 240
  āsiyāb-ı peşmīne (tax on water-powered fulling mills), 240
  āsiyāb-ı peşmīne-i ḫāṣṣa (revenue from water-powered fulling mills in personal holding), 240
  average taxes, *226t9*
  bāġāt-ı ḫāṣṣa (revenue from vineyards in personal holding), 240, *310t31*
  bāġçe-i ḫāṣṣa (revenue from gardens in personal holding), 240
  bāġçe-i, bāġçehā-yı türünc-i ḫāṣṣa (revenue from bitter orange groves in personal holding), 240
  bostān-ı ḫāṣṣa (revenue from kitchen gardens in personal holding), 240
  eşcār-ı balamutlu-yı ḫāṣṣa (revenue from oak trees in personal holding), 240
  eşcār-ı cevz-i ḫāṣṣa (revenue from walnut trees in personal holding), 240
  eşcār-ı emrūd-ı ḫāṣṣa (revenue from pear trees in personal holding), 240
  eşcār-ı enār-ı ḫāṣṣa (revenue from pomegranate trees in personal holding), 240
  eşcār-ı meyve-i ḫāṣṣa (revenue from fruit trees in personal holding), 240
  eşcār-ı saḳız-ı çam-ı ḫāṣṣa (revenue from resin trees in personal holding), 241
  eşcār-ı ṭut-ı ḫāṣṣa (revenue from mulberry trees in personal holding), 241
  eşcār-ı zeyt-i ḫāṣṣa (revenue from olive trees in personal holding), 241
  ḫāṣṣa (revenue from personal holdings), 240–41
  ispence (capital tax), 237–38
  istafide, *ʿöşr ʿan* (tithe on dry raisins), 238. *see also ʿöşr-i bāġāt*
  muḳāṭaʿa-ı bāġçe-i türünc-i ḫāṣṣa (tax on bitter orange groves in *tīmār*), 241
  muḳāṭaʿa-ı bāzār (market tax), 241
  muḳāṭaʿa-ı çeltük (tax on rice fields in imperial demesne), 241
  muḳāṭaʿa-ı gümrük (customs dues), 241
  muḳāṭaʿa-ı maʿber (transit duty), 241
  muḳāṭaʿa-ı memlaḥa (tax on salt-pans in imperial demesne), 241
  muḳāṭaʿa-ı niyābet (tax on criminals), 242
  muḳāṭaʿa-ı ṭāḥūne-i zeyt-i ḫāṣṣa (tax on oil presses), 242
  muḳāṭaʿa-ı ṭalyan (tax on fish-farms), 242
  *muḳāṭaʿa*s, 241–42, 249
  mülk (tax on private property), 240
  niyābet (tax on criminals), 238
  ʿöşr (tithe), 238–239, *310t30*
  ʿöşr-i ʿasel (tithe on honey), 239
  ʿöşr-i āsiyāb (tithe on water-powered gristmills), 239
  ʿöşr-i bāġāt, *ʿöşr-i bāġ* (tithe on vineyards), 238
  ʿöşr-i bostān, *ʿöşr-i besātīn* (tithe on kitchen gardens), 239
  ʿöşr-i çam saḳızı (tithe on resin), 239
  ʿöşr-i cev, *ʿöşr-i şaʿīr* (tithe on barley), 238, *305t29*
  ʿöşr-i ḥınṭa, *ʿöşr-i gendüm* (tithe on wheat), 238, *305t29*
  ʿöşr-i ḳazz (tithe on raw silk), 239
  ʿöşr-i kettān (tithe on flax), 239
  ʿöşr-i meyve (tithe on fruit), 239
  ʿöşr-i penbe (tithe on cotton), 239
  ʿöşr-i ṭut (tithe on mulberries), 239
  ʿöşr-i zeyt (tithe on olive oil), 239
  per capita taxes, 237–38

resm-i aġnām (tax on sheep), 239
resm-i ʿarūsī (tax on marriage), 238
resm-i bāzār (market tax), 242
resm-i gümrük (custom dues), 242
resm-i ḫamr (tax on wine), 239
resm-i ḫanāzīr, *resm-i ḫınzīr* (tax on swine), 239
resm-i ıġrıb-ı māhī gīrān (tax on drag seine fishing), 242
resm-i maʿber (transit duty), 242
ṣīre, *ʿöşr ʿan* (tithe on grape-must), 238. *see also ʿöşr-i bāġāt*
ṭāḥūne-i zeyt-i ḫāṣṣa (revenue from oil presses in personal holding), 241
ṭalyan-ı ḫāṣṣa, *ḳısṭ-ı ṭalyan-ı ḫāṣṣa* (revenue from fish-farms in personal holding), 241
taxpayer identification and registration, 211–12
Tegea municipal unit, Aleksi Manesi, 133–34
tekālif-i dīvāniyye (customary impositions), 244
Tenea municipal unit
Ayo Vaṣıl/Çağıl Ḥiṣārı, 149
Ayonori, 152
İksaroḳastalya, *mezraʿa* in the vicinity of Ayonori, 152
Ḳutala, 151
Pisratu, 155
Pulimeno Soyḳa, 153
tenktür (tent), 235–36
tevḳīʿ script, 7
Thasos, 5
Thebes, 3, 214
Theodore I Palaeologus (1384–1407), 3–4, 213
Theodore II Palaeologus (1407–1443), 4
Theriano (Θεριανό), 160
Thessaloniki, capture of, 3
Thessaly, 4, 8, 11, 212–13, 218
Thomas Palaeologus, 4–5, 8
Thrace, 3, 5, 238
tīmār (land grant), 12, 217–18, 229, 234–37, 240–41, 243, 246–47
tīmār holder
responsibilities of, 235–36
rights of, 229–34
tīmār revenue, 3, 229, 234–35, 243
tīmār system, 1, 3, 234, 236, 311
timariots, list of, 230–34t10
Aḥmed Simġārī, 218, *232t10*, 234, 236
ʿAlī son of Cāyim, *230t10*, 233, 245
ʿAlī son of Ḳulaġuz, *231t10*, 233, 236
ʿAlī Ṣūfī İzdinī man of Balaban Aġa, 218, *232t10*, 234, 236
ʿAlī Tekkelü, *232t10*, 234
Andriya Fenārī, *232t10*, 234
Balaban Yaninaʾi, 218, *231t10*, 233, 236
Burhān Aġa, 218, *230t10*, 233
Elvānoġlı Maḥmūd, 218, *231t10*, 233
Evrenos son of Yaʿḳūb Beg bin İştin, 217, *230t10*, 233, 236
Fīrūz son of ʿĪsā Ḳaraviryevī, 218, *232t10*, 234
Ġarb brother of Süleymān, *232t10*, 234, 236
Ḥāccī Kürd, 218, *230t10*, 233
Ḫalīl Siyāh Tırḫalaʾi, 218, *231t10*, 233
Ḥamza Derbendci, *231t10*, 233, 236
Ḥamza new Muslim, *230t10*, 233, 235–36
Ḥamza, *232t10*, 234, 236
Ḫıżır son of Ṣavcı Sirozī, 218, *231t10*, 233, 236
Ḫıżır, *231t10*, 233, 236
Ḫoca ʿAlī, *231t10*, 233, 236
İbrāhīm Beg, *230t10*, 233, 236–37
İbrāhīm Dīvāne, *231t10*, 234, 236
İbrāhīm Engürüs, 218, *232t10*, 234, 236
İbrāhīm son of ʿĪsā Beg bin Pavlo Kurtik, 217–18, *230t10*, 233, 237
İbrāhīm Zerd, 218, *230t10*, 233
İlyās son of Nuṣret, *232t10*, 234
İlyās, *232t10*, 234
ʿĪsā brother of İlyās Siyāh, *231t10*, 233
İskender son of ʿAlī, *231t10*, 233, 236
Ḳaraca Aġa, 218, *232t10*, 234, 236
Ḳaragöz Arnavud brother of Çāşnīgīr İsḥāḳ Paşa, 218, *230t10*, 233, 236
Ḳāsım son of Muḥyi'd-dīn Yaninaʾi, 218, *231t10*, 233
Ḳāsım, *232t10*, 234, 236
Ḳasṭamonlu Pīr Ḥasanoġlı Aḥmed, *231t10*, 233
Kürd Şeyḫ Ḥasan, 218, *231t10*, 233, 236
Leḳa İzmolda, *231t10*, 233–34
Maḥmūd Paşa, Ḥażret-i, 8, *230t10*, 233
Manol Mahtar, *231t10*, 234
Meḥmed new Muslim, *230t10*, 233, 235–36
Meḥmed son of Alagöz, 218, *232t10*, 234
Meḥmed son of Ḥāccī Bāyezīd Yeñişehirī, 218, *231t10*, 233
Mevlānā ʿAbdu'l-lāh, *231t10*, 233
Mezīd new Muslim, *232t10*, 234–36
Mübārek, *230t10*, 233, 244
Muḥyi'd-dīn Yaninaʾi, 218, *231t10*, 233
Murād Beg son of Timurtaş, *230t10*, 233
Mūsā Siyāh Livadyaʾi, 218, *231t10*, 233

Müstaḳdim, *230t10*, 233
Nikifor Ḳavasila, 7, *231t10*, 233–34
Nuṣret son of Celāl Ḳasṭamonī, *232t10*, 234
ʿÖmer Beg son of Ezmir, *230t10*, 233, 237
Paşa Yiğit son of Ḳaragöz Beg bin Yuvan, 218, *231t10*, 233, 237
Rus Ormanı, *231t10*, 233
Seyyidī ʿAlī, 218, *230t10*, 233, 236
Sinān Beg bin Elvān Beg, 7–8, 10, *230t10*, 233–34, 246
Sinān Ġaṣır Beg son of Süleymān Beg bin Ẕū'l-ḳādir, *232t10*, 234, 237
Süleymān brother of Ġarb, *232t10*, 234, 236
Ṭāhir son of Seyf, 218, *232t10*, 234
Tırḫallü Timur Ḫānoğlı Muḥammed, 218, *232t10*, 234
Umūr son of Devlet Paşa, 218, *232t10*, 234
Yaʿḳūb new Muslim, 218, *230t10*, 233, 235
Yorgi Fenārī, *232t10*, 234
Yūsuf Arnavud, 218, *231t10*, 233
Yūsuf new Muslim, 218, *230t10*, 233, 235
Yūsuf, *230t10*, 233, 236
Zaġanos Arnavud Timurḥiṣārī, 217–18, *230t10*, 233, 236
tīmārlı sipāhī (cavalryman), 218, 229
tithe (*ʿöşr*), 229, 234, 237–39, *310t30*. *see also* taxes
Tireḫlista, 28
Tiristena, 167
Tocco, Carlo, 3, 213
Todoro Doşkesi, 138
Todoro Manesi, 23
Todoro Zupata, 136
Todoroplu, 23
Todoros Ḳraçi, quarter of Londar, *225t8*
Todoros Simyos, quarter of Aya Yorgi, *225t8*
Todoros Varirvi, quarter of Vumero, *225t8*
Topolova, 166–67
Toskesi (Τόσκεσι), 138
Toşkesi, 88
Toskesi/Doskesi (Τόσκεσι/Ντόσκεσι), 43
Toumba (Τούμπα), 49
Towns and their quarters, *225t8*
Tragano municipal unit
Ḳoḳla, 72
Marḳoplu, 77–78
Tragoudisti (Τραγουδιστή), 111–12
Traḫya Manesi, 180
Trani Louza (Τρανή Λούζα), 120
Trehlo (Τρεχλό), 28
Trestena, 121
Trifylia municipality
Arḳadya, 125
Ḳalazoni, 130
Malena, 129–30
Muzak Mengişa, 130
Yani Dara, 143
Ẕima Rala, 142–43
Trikala cadastre (1454/5), 7, 11, 214, 218
Trikolona municipal unit
İskiliç, 44
Pavla, 148
Trima İşpata, 142
Tripoli municipal unit
Mujaki, 44–45
Perṣor, 43–44
Tripoli municipality
Aġali, 40–41
Aleksi Manesi, 133–34
Barbuçi, 142
Bejenik, nefs-i, 39
Bendeni/Pendeni, 41
Bondaya, 41–42
Brasna Sanḳa, 37
Çipyana, 38
Dara, 25–26
Domaniḳa Beluşi, 134–35
Doşkesi, 43
Ḳandila, 42–43
Leviẕi, 39–40
Lopesi, 40
Miḫlu, 35
Mujaki, 44–45
Naşi, 37
Periṣori, 38
Perṣor, 43–44
Petro Dorza, 137
Pikerni, 36–37
Plaşa, *mezraʿa* in the vicinity of Bejenik, 39
Sina, 42
Tripotama (Τριπόταμα), 90
Tripotama vel Trisetenia, 9
Tripyla municipal unit, Yani Dara, 143
Tritaia municipal unit
Çapoġa, 201
Ġardicḳo, nefs-i, 199–200
Gin Manesi, 177
Girbene, 176
Ġolemi, 169
Mastro Andoni, 202
Ranesi, 200
Troizina municipal unit, Fenari, 153
Troizinia municipality, Fenari, 153
Tropaia (Τρόπαια), 125
Tropaia municipal unit
Ḳoḳla, 118
Mazarak Adipo, 108
Niḳola Buva, 209
Ranesi, 110
Virça, 125
Zaveti, 124

Trousaki (Τρουσάκι), 180
Trousas (Τρούσας), 178
Trusa, 180
Trypiti (Τρυπητή), 117
Tsamanta (Τσαμαντά), 25
Tsasi (Τσάση), 141
Tsilardi (Τσιλάρδι/Τσιλαρδί), 63–64
Tsipiana (Τσιπιανά), 94
Tsivlos (Τσιβλός), 60
Tsoukala (Τσουκαλά), 161
TT10–1/14662 cadastre. *see also taḥrīr defteri*
  Albanian immigrants, 213–14
  alphabet used in the taxation cadastre, 11
  demographic figures, 220–21
  division of settlements into Greek and Albanian, 212
  family size/structure, 221–24
  Muslim/Turkish element (by references to timariots), 217–18
  scripts of, 7
  Slavic element (Slavic ethnic names), 216–17
  tax exemptions, 242–44
  taxes mentioned, 237–44
  timariots listed, *230–34t10*, 234–35
Tumena, 57–58
Tunba, *mezraʿa* in the vicinity of İpsari, *15t3*, 80
Turaḫan Beg, 4, 8
Turkey, 149
Ṭursun Beg, 8
Tzympi, 3

U
Ukraine, 3, 124, 242
ʿulūfeci (paid cavalryman), 211
Umūr Beg of Aydın (1334–1348), 3
underexploitation of earth, 249
units of measurement, 242
Ustruza/İstruza Potamya, 45
Uzunçarşılı, İsmail Hakkı, 8

V
vaḳf (pious endowment), 240
*vaḳf defter*s (pious endowment registers), 244, 311
Valaḳ, 110–11
Valimi (Βαλιμή), 62
Valimi, 62
Valḳu, 53–54
Valmi (Βάλμη), 174
Valmi, 174
Valtetsi municipal unit
  Barbuçi, 142
  Domaniḳa Beluşi, 134–35
  Petro Dorza, 137
Vamva-Stamatelatou, Foteini, 13–14
Vasilaki (Βασιλάκι), 91–92
Vasilica sivè Valica, 9
Vaṣıliḳa, 148–49
Vaṣıloplos, 92
Vasmer, Max, 13
Vela (Βελά), 64
Vela, 64
Velanidies (Βελανιδιές), 151
veled (son), 211–212
Veligosti (Βελιγοστή), 147
Veligosti area, 213
Veliġosti, *mezraʿa* in the vicinity of Londar, *15t3*, 147
Velimiri (Βελιμίρι), 22
Velimiri, 22
Velize, 144
Velizi, *mezraʿa* in the vicinity of Coya, *15t3*, 97
Velo-Voha municipality, Ḫarkâ, 151
Velviça, 104
Venetian Grimani census (1700), 2, 14
Venetiḳa, 182
Venetiko/Tigani Island (Νήσος Βενέτικο/Τηγάνι), 126
Venice, 10, 14
Verġuviça, 65
Veroia, 218
Vervena (Βέρβενα), 103
Vervena, 103
Vesini (Βεσίνι), 33
Vesini, 33
Vilivina (Βιλιβίνα), 58
villains (*δημοσιάριοι πάροικοι, κληροπάροικοι; villani communis, villani ecclesie*), 312
villains bound to the soil (*δουλοπάροικοι; villani serve conditionis*), 312
Virastova, 63
Virça, 125
Viriça, *mezraʿa* in the vicinity of Divye, *16t3*, 180
Virzaḫo, 172
Visoḳa, 56–57
viticulture, 237–38, 248–49, *310t31*, 311
Vlaherna (Βλαχέρνα), 39
Vlahoi (Βλάχοι), 201–2
Voha municipal unit, Ḫarkâ, 151
Vola (Βόλα), 159
Vola, 159
Volakas municipal unit, Añloniça, 93
Voliria/Volirіes (Βολιριά/Βολιριές), 138
Voreia Kynouria municipal unit
  Astriçi, 35–36
  Astro, *mezraʿa* in the vicinity of Astriçi, 36
  Ḳoraḳovuni, 43
Voreia Kynouria municipality
  Astriçi, 35–36
  Astro, *mezraʿa* in the vicinity of Astriçi, 36

Ḳoraḳovuni, 43
Vorstena, 21–22
Voştiça (Aigio), district of
Arfara, 65
average taxes, 226t9
Aya İğliġori, 52
Ayo Paraskevi, 50
Ayo Yani, 48
Ayo Yorgi, 62
Beçaḳus, 54–55
Buḫuşta, 47
Burlaşa, 54
Cilardi, 63–64
Çimlo, 60
demographic statistics, 221t4
Epanolaġo, 53
Franḳo, 51
Ġardena, 47–48
Graḳa, 52–53
Ġumaniça, 55
Ḫotoġosti, 62
identified and unidentified localities, 12t2
İstavriya/İstavrina, 59
İstilivena, 60–61
İvlaḫo, 66
İvlanduşa, 51
Ḳaḳoḫoryo, 50
Ḳapareli, *mezraʿa* in the vicinity of Maji, *14t3*, 56
Kerpini, 57
Ḳılapaçuna, 58–59
Kiriçova, 55
Ḳlaẕi, 52
Ḳondorafti, 49
Ḳroḳova, 48
Ḳulukina, 61
Ḳumaniçi Luzi, *mezraʿa* in the vicinity of Zepandi, *14t3*, 68
Listirna, 52
Lopesi, 50
Lovoḳa, 63
Luḳa İfrati, 49
Maji, 55–56
Manastır-ı Ṣotoḳos, 47
Manastır-ı Yirondos der Taḳsiyarḫi, 46
Maneşi, 65
Martina der Noḳastro, 53
Mayira, *mezraʿa* in the vicinity of Ṣoḫyana, *14t3*, 69
Namuni, 59
Pelyura, *mezraʿa* in the vicinity of Ṣoḫyana, *14t3*, 68
Periẕori, 66
Petro Tunba, 51
Plaşa, 64–65
Poroviça, 69
Potamya, 60
Raḫova, 66–67
Rayḳu, 56
Revaniça, 69
Rolo, 58
Roẕa, 48–49
Selyana, 66
Sinoviro, 64
Siyiniski, 62
Ṣoḫyana, 68
Sotira, 54
tax analysis, *255–58t15*
tax revenues of, 245
taxes from wheat and barley, 309t29
Tumena, 57–58
Valimi, 62
Valḳu, 53–54
Vela, 64
Verġuviça, 65
Virastova, 63
Visoḳa, 56–57
viticulture yield, 310t31
Voştiça, nefs-i, 46
Yaḳoḫto, 59
Yelini, 67
Zaḫlori, 57
Zaḫoli, 67
Ẕaruḫla, 61
Zepandi, 68
Ẕilivina, 58
Ẕiyaleş Tunba, 49
Voştiça, nefs-i, 46
Vostizza vel Vistizza, 9
Vouliagmeni (Βουλιαγμένη), 89
Vounargo (Βούναργο), 195–96
Vouprasia municipal unit
Balçi, 183
İpsari, 79
İzlatḳa, 77
Ḳapaleto, *mezraʿa* in the vicinity of İpsari, 80
Ḳazneş, 185
Ḳonbi Ṣeḳra, 185–86
Ḳoromiẕi, 74
Maji, 202
Maliki, 185
Niḳola Ḳumi, 199
Pendani, *mezraʿa* in the vicinity of İpsari, 79
Vrahnaiika municipal unit
Çuḳala, 161
Ṣeryanu, 160
Tiristena, 167
Vrahni (Βράχνι), 18
Vumeri, 9
Vumero (Goumero), district of
Añloniça, 93
Aranis Ḳavalari, 92
Aranis Ḳuçohyari, 92
average taxes, 226t9
Ayo Ḳostandino, *mezraʿa* in the vicinity of Ẕervini, *15t3*, 84–85
Branca, 82

Bruma, 88
Coya, 96–97
demographic statistics, 221t4
Dorza, 99
Dumeña, 96
Franḳa, 91
Ġurdesi, 82
Ḫayḳal, 90
Hiliẕon, 86
identified and unidentified localities, 12t2
Iğlava, 99
İspani, 94
İspani-i dīğer, *mezraʿa* in the vicinity of İspani, *15t3*, 94
İşpata, 88
Ḳaçaru, 95–96
Ḳaḳusi, 82
Ḳaratula, 100
Ḳariza, 96
Ḳazani, 88
Keraṣova, 101
Kertiza, 83
Ḳoḳla, 100
Ḳonbi Ṣeḳra, 81, 100
Ḳondari, 91
Ḳondomiḫal, 98
Ḳosta Lanca, 98
Ḳraḳuki, 87
Ḳuçi, 95, 97
Ḳuḳura, 86
Küraleş, 86
Laleṣi, 84
Lali, 96
Lanbeti, 97
Lancoy, 82–83
Lazaro Buva, 91
Liḳuresi, 91–92
Livarzi, 101
Loġaṣeti, 83–84
Maji, 89, 93
Maḳri Poẕi, 88–89
Mangişa Ḳumani, 94
Matranḳa, *mezraʿa* in the vicinity of İşpata, *15t3*, 89
Mavromati, 100–101
Mihili, 93–94
Miraḳo, 87
Nasa, 82
Nikifor, 98
Olana, 98–99
Persena, *mezraʿa* in the vicinity of İspani, *15t3*, 95
Plaşa, 91
Pondiḳo, 100
Poraçyu, 85
Poṣo, 89
Pratano, 83
Purdanu, *mezraʿa* in the vicinity of Maḳri Poẕi, *15t3*, 89
Ratendu, 98
Romesi, 92
Ṣarakina, 90
Sela, 90
Sipyani, 94
Sitara, 87
Ṣopi, 99
Ṣuli, 86
Şurbi, 82
tax analysis, *262–67t17*
tax revenues of, 246
taxes from wheat and barley, 309t29
Toşkesi, 88
Vaşıloplos, 92
Velizi, *mezraʿa* in the vicinity of Coya, *15t3*, 97
viticulture yield, 310t31
Vumero, nefs-i, 81
Yirmena, 95
Yirmoçani, 85
Ẕervini, 84
Ẕiminiça, 90
Vumero, nefs-i, 81, *225t8*
Vunarġo, 195–96
Vundeni, 163–64
Vunengo vel Vunango, 9
Vurçanos, 126–27
Vuzyas, *mezraʿa* in the vicinity of Bejenik, *14t3*, 39
Vythoulkas (Βυθούλκας), 182
Vytina municipal unit
Ḳameniça, 40
Yani Mazaraki, 139

W

wheat, cultivation of, 247–49
wine production, 249

X

Xenies (Ξενιές), 173
Xerokastellia (Ξεροκαστελλιά), 152
XIe Congrès International des Sciences Onomastiques (Sofia, 1974), 1
Xirohori (Ξηροχώρι), 200
Xirokambos (Ξηρόκαμπος), 129–30
Xylokastro municipal unit
İvlanduşa, 51
Ṣoḫyana, 68
Yelini, 67
Xylokastro-Evrostini municipality
İvlanduşa, 51
Ḳumaniçi Luzi, *mezraʿa* in the vicinity of Zepandi, 68
Ṣoḫyana, 68
Yelini, 67
Zaḫoli, 67
Xyvouni/Xivouni (Ξυβούνι/Ξίβουνι), 194

Y

Yaḳoḫto, 59
Ya'ḳūb Paşa, 4
Yani Dara, 143
Yani Evzenati, 133
Yani Jura, 138
Yani Ḳaḳosimani, quarter of Ṣaravali, *225t8*
Yani Ḳanḳaẕi, 140
Yani Lata, 134
Yani Mazaraki, 139
Yani Meliġari, quarter of Ḳoriṣos, *225t8*
Yani Ẕyavoliçi, 133
Yatopa, 186
Yelini, 67
yeñiçeri (janissary), 211
Yirano, 184
Yirmena, 95
Yirmoçani, 85
yiros (elderly man), 211
Yorgi Asani, quarter of Vumero, *225t8*
Yorgi Maji, 134
Yorgi Manesi, 143
Yorgi Mujaki, 140
Yorgi Muzaki, 136
Yorgi Peliḳanos, quarter of Ṣaravali, *225t8*
Yorgi Simos, quarter of Aya Yorgi, *225t8*

Z

Zaccaria, Centurione (1404–1432), 4
Zaġanos Paşa, 4, 8
Zaġanoz Beg, 8
Zaharo municipal unit
  Arvano Ḳastro, 193–94
  Ġolomi, 193
  İsḳala, 120
  Ḳonbi Ṣeḳra, 112
  Luzi, 120
  Melita, 119–20
Zaharo municipality
  Arvano Ḳastro, 193–94
  Ġolomi, 193
  İsḳala, 120
  İstoya Volomiri, 138
  Ḳonbi Ṣeḳra, 112
  Ḳopaniça, 103–4
  Luzi, 120
  Melita, 119–20
  Velviça, 104
Zaḫlori, 57
Zaḫoli, 67
Zakythinos, Dionysios (Denis), 213
Zarouhla (Ζαρούχλα), 61
Ẕaruḫla, 61
Zastova (Ζάστοβα), 166
Zastupa, *mezra'a* in the vicinity of Ḳurnaroḳastro, *16t3*, 166
Zaveti (Ζάβετη), 124
Zaveti, 124
ze'āmet (land grand), 12, 229, 234, 236–37
Zelaḫova, 102–3
Zenbeş, 74
Zepandi, 26, 68
Ẕervini, 84, 176
zeyt yağı değirmenleri (oil presses), 241
Ẕiġanato, 126
Ẕilivina, 58
Ẕima Rala, 142–43
Ẕimiçana, 145
Ẕiminiça, 90
Zioupani (Ζιουπάνη), 109
Ẕirmi, 206
Ẕiyaleş Tunba, 49
Zoġa, 171
Zogas (Ζώγας), 171
Zoia, 9
Ẕolyani, 105
Zoni (Ζώνη), 114
Zoria (Ζοριά), 135–36
Zorila, 195
Zorlia (Ζορλιά), 195
Zougras (Ζούγρας), 19–20
Zoumbata (Ζουμπάτα), 136
Zoumbatiza, (Ζουμπάτιζα), 137
Zuġra, 19–20
Zuġra-ı dīğer, 20
Ẕunato, 114
Ẕupano Buryalişa, 138

Facsimile of TT10

(Prime Ministry Ottoman Archives, Istanbul)

KOD:	SIRA NU:	ORİJİNAL NU:
T.T.	**0010**	

TAPU TAHRİR DEFTERİ

BAŞLANGIÇ TARİHİ :	BİTİŞ TARİHİ :
ŞEKLİ: **Ciltli** X **Ciltsiz** **Ebrulu** **Ebrusuz** X	EBADI: **37 X 14**
NUMARALAMA USULÜ: **Varak** **Sayfa** X	TOPLAM SAYFA SAYISI: **Numaralı 192**

BOŞ SAYFALARI :

Numaralı boş sayfalar: **192**

Numaralandırılmamış boş sayfalar: -

AÇIKLAMALAR:

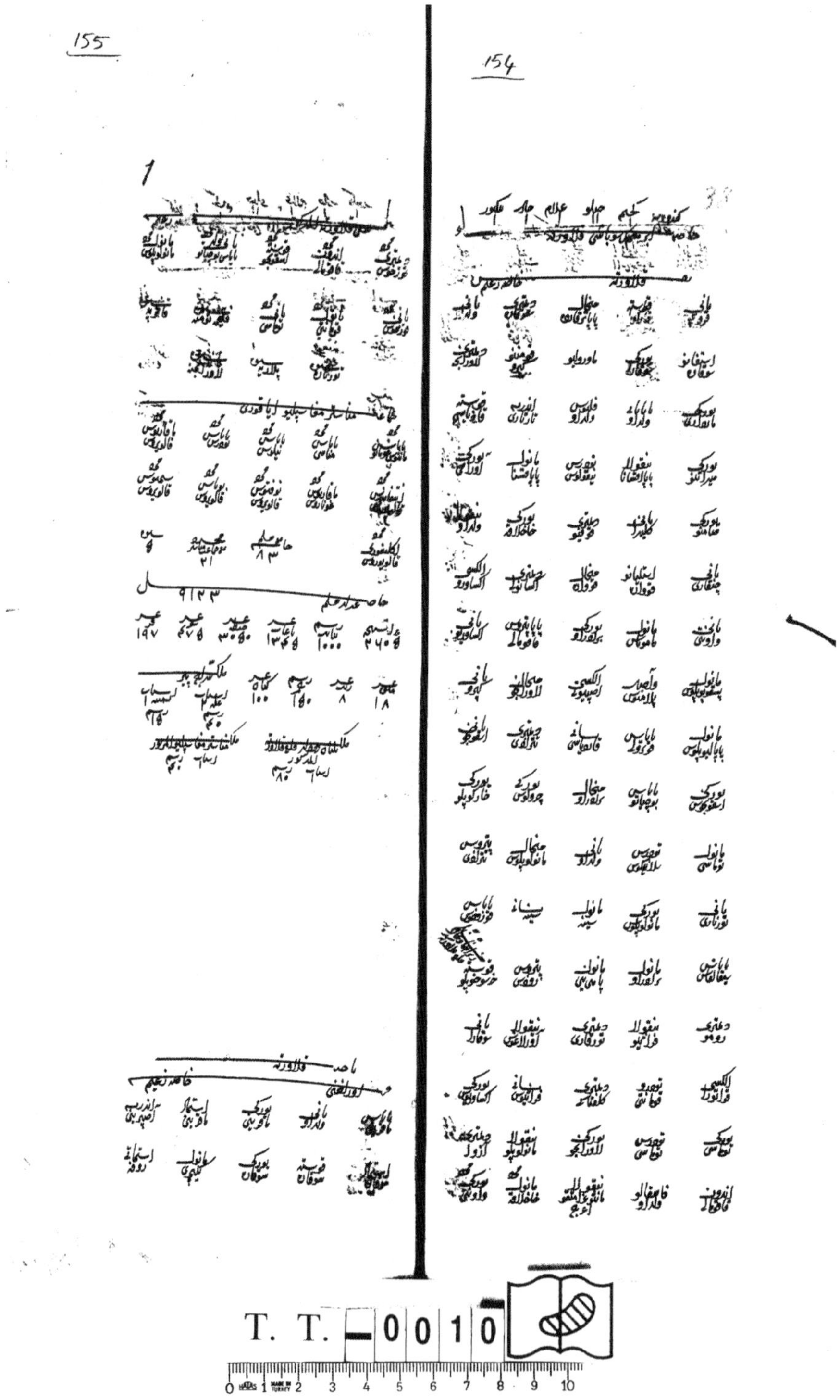

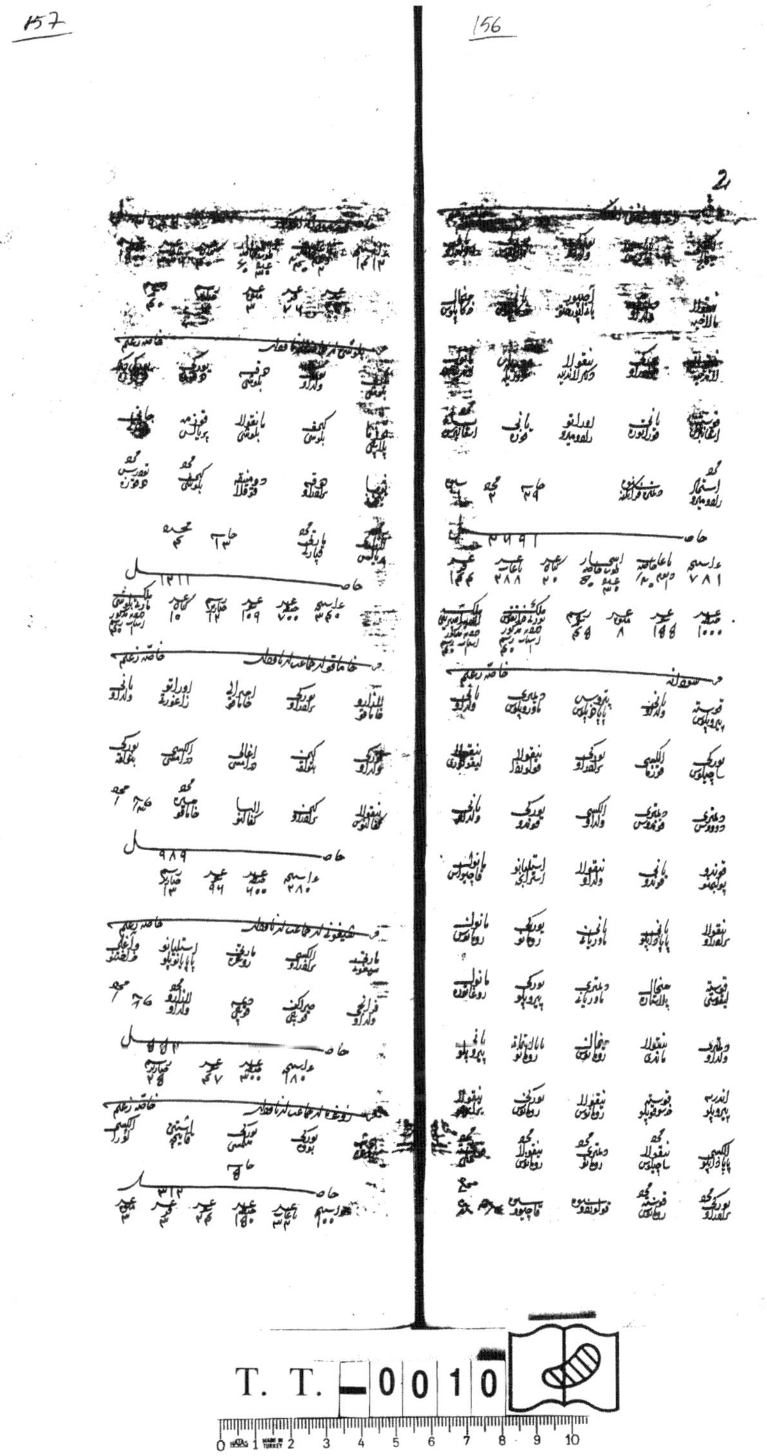
157
156
T. T. 0010

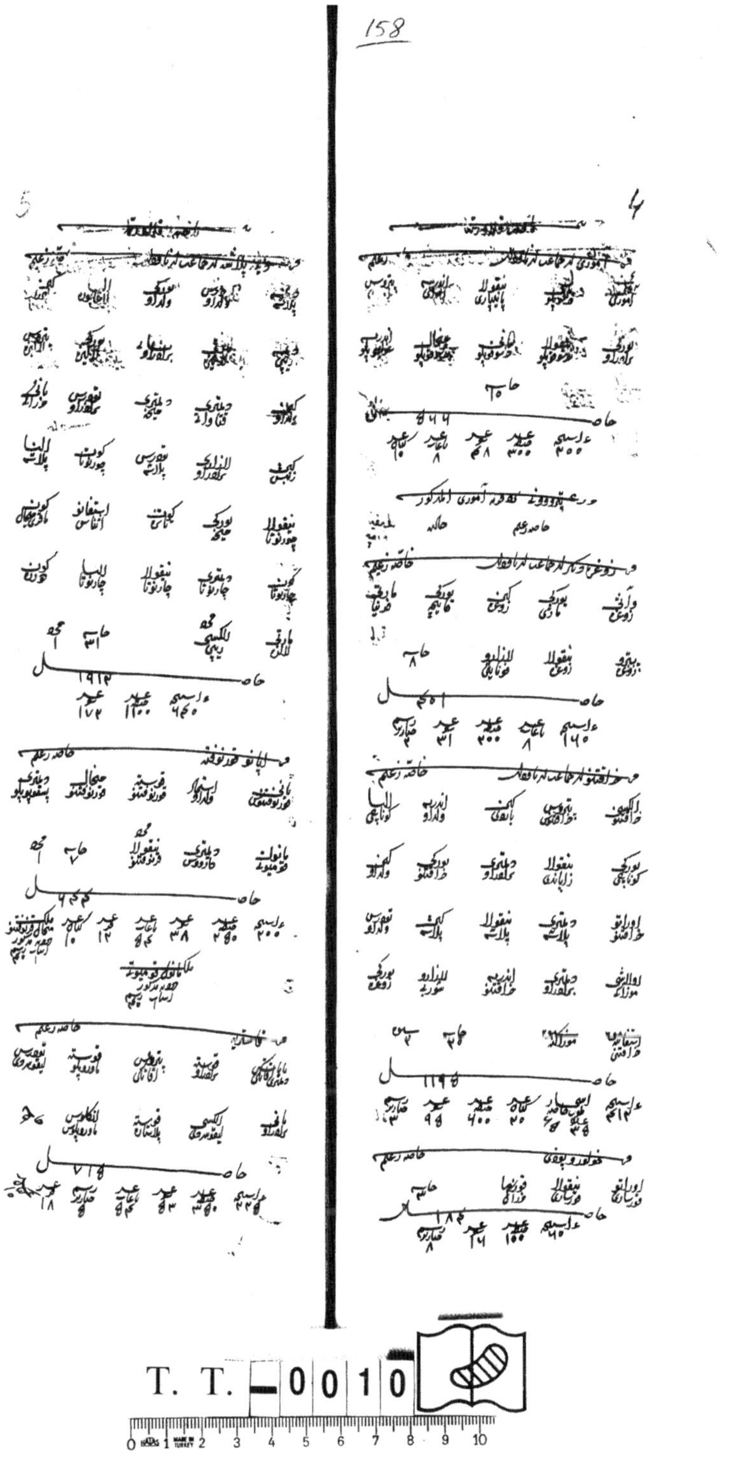
159
158
T. T. 0010

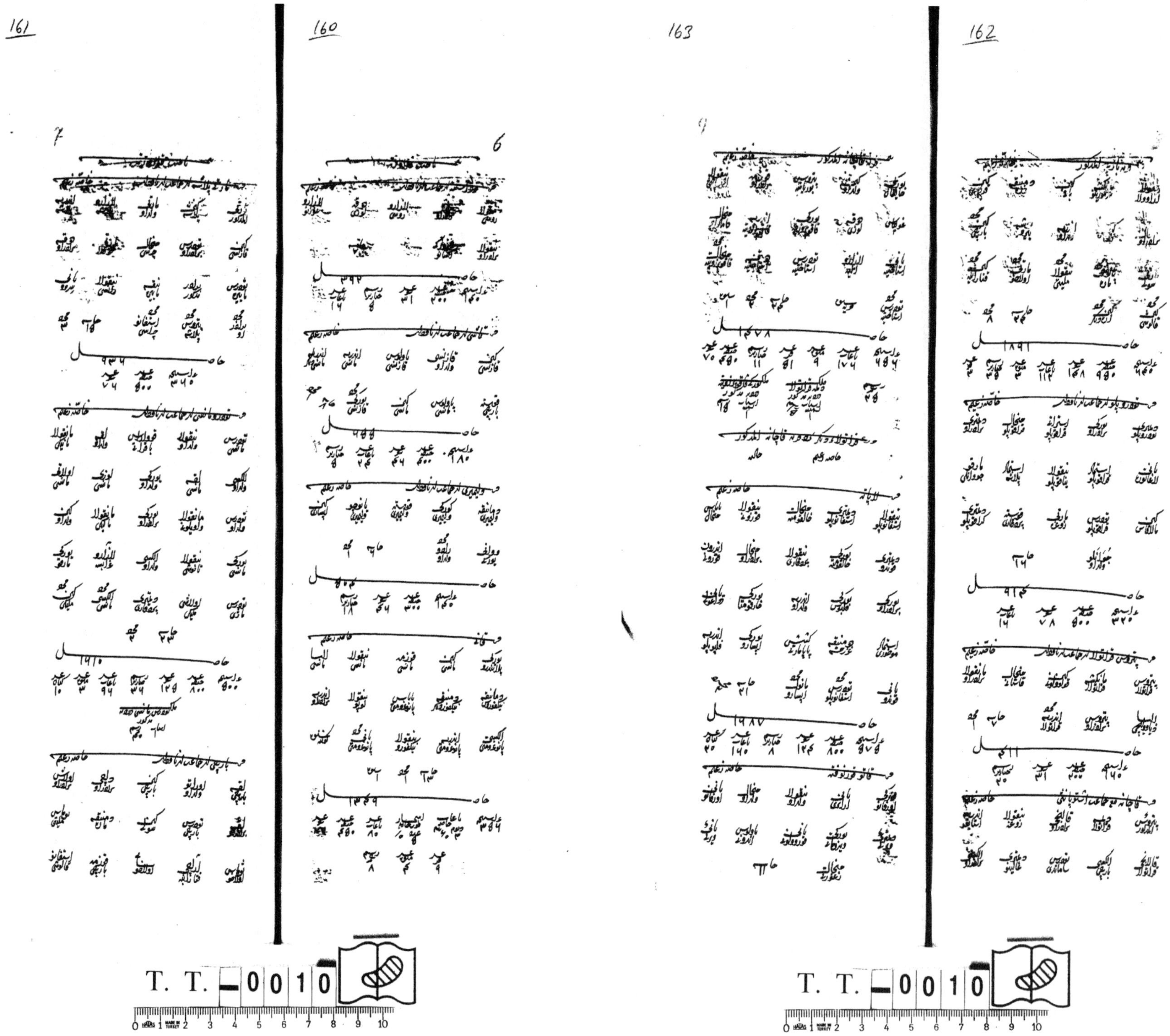

165
164
T. T. - 0010

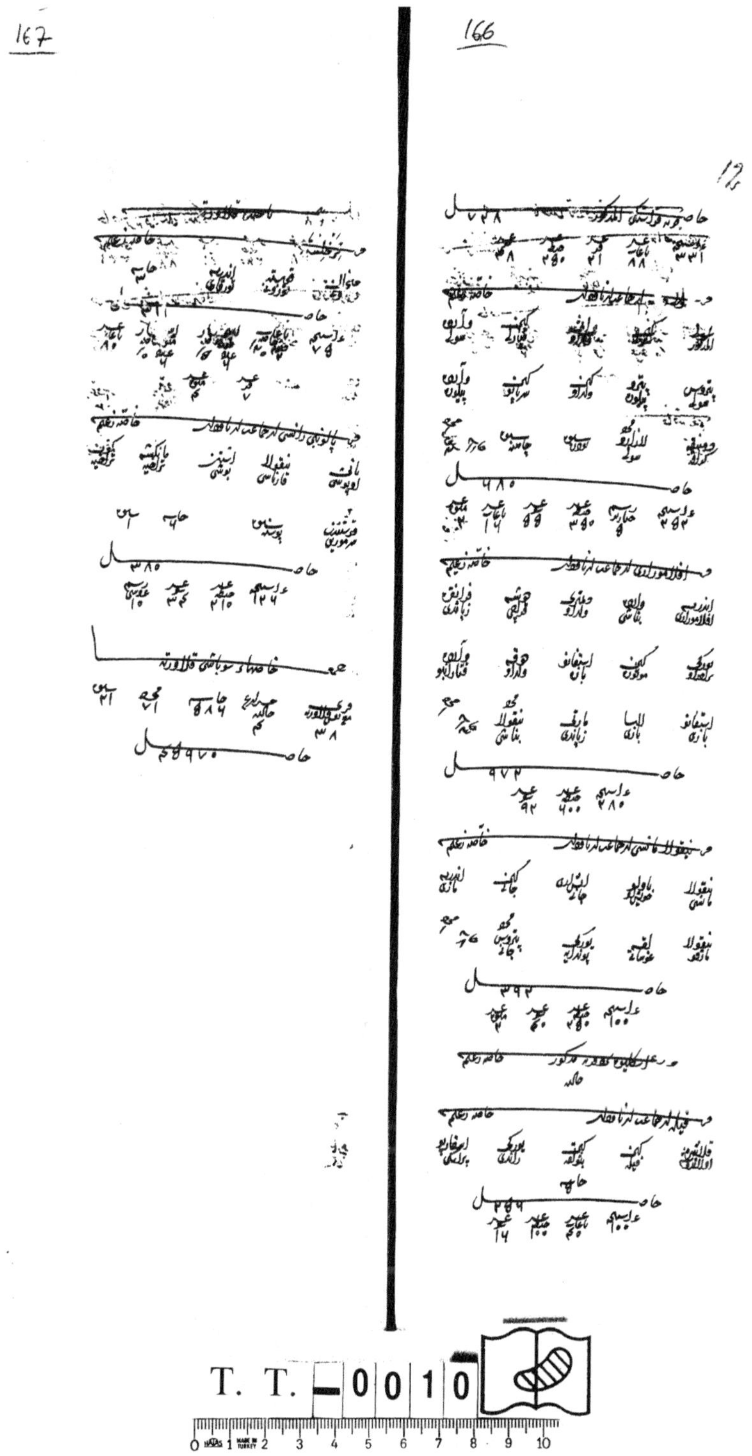
167
166
T. T. - 0010

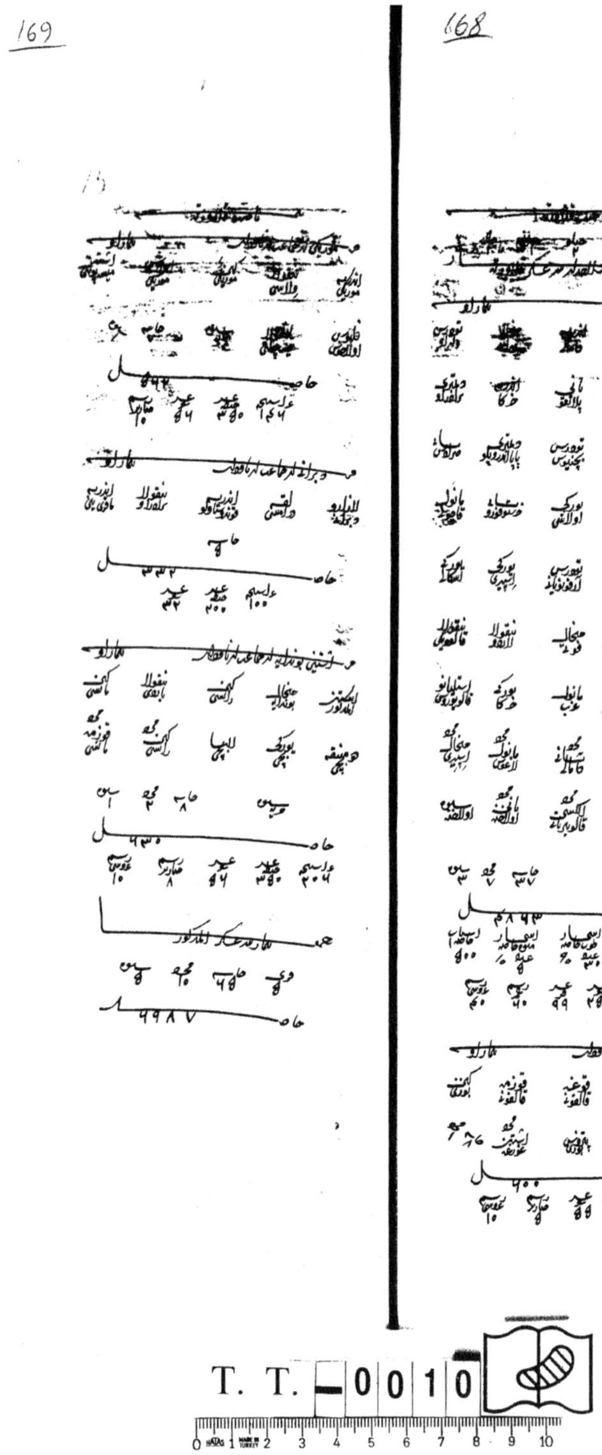
169
168
T. T. 0010

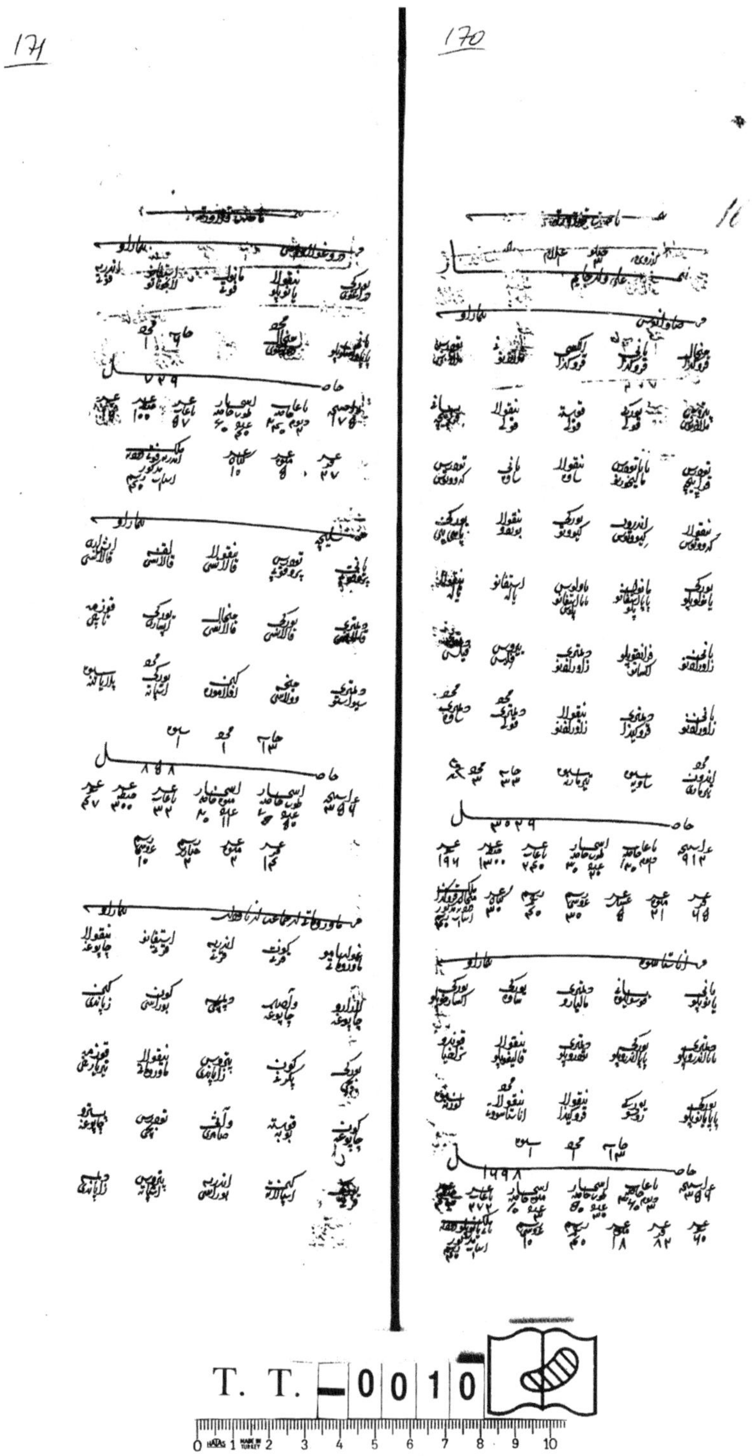
171
170
T. T. 0010

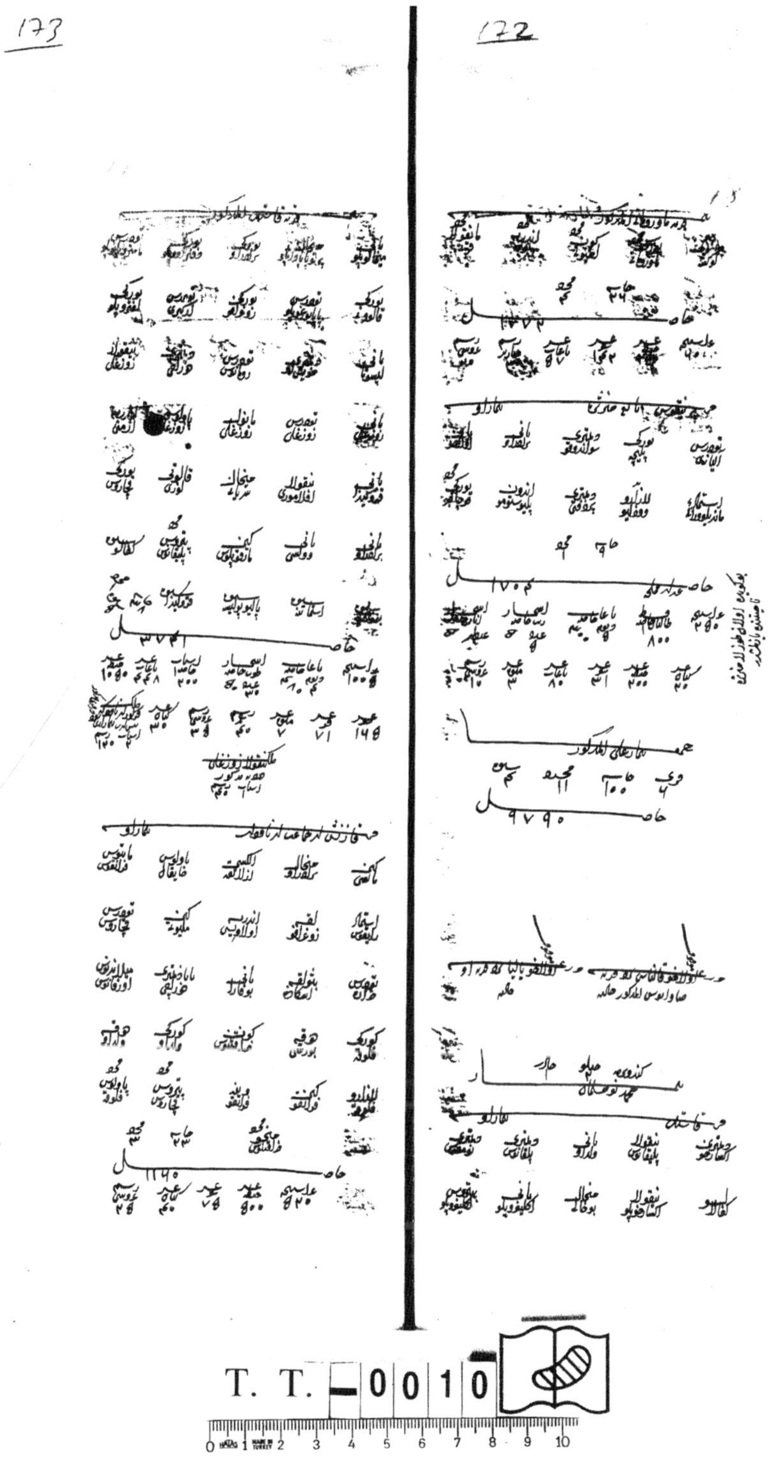
173
172
T. T. 0010

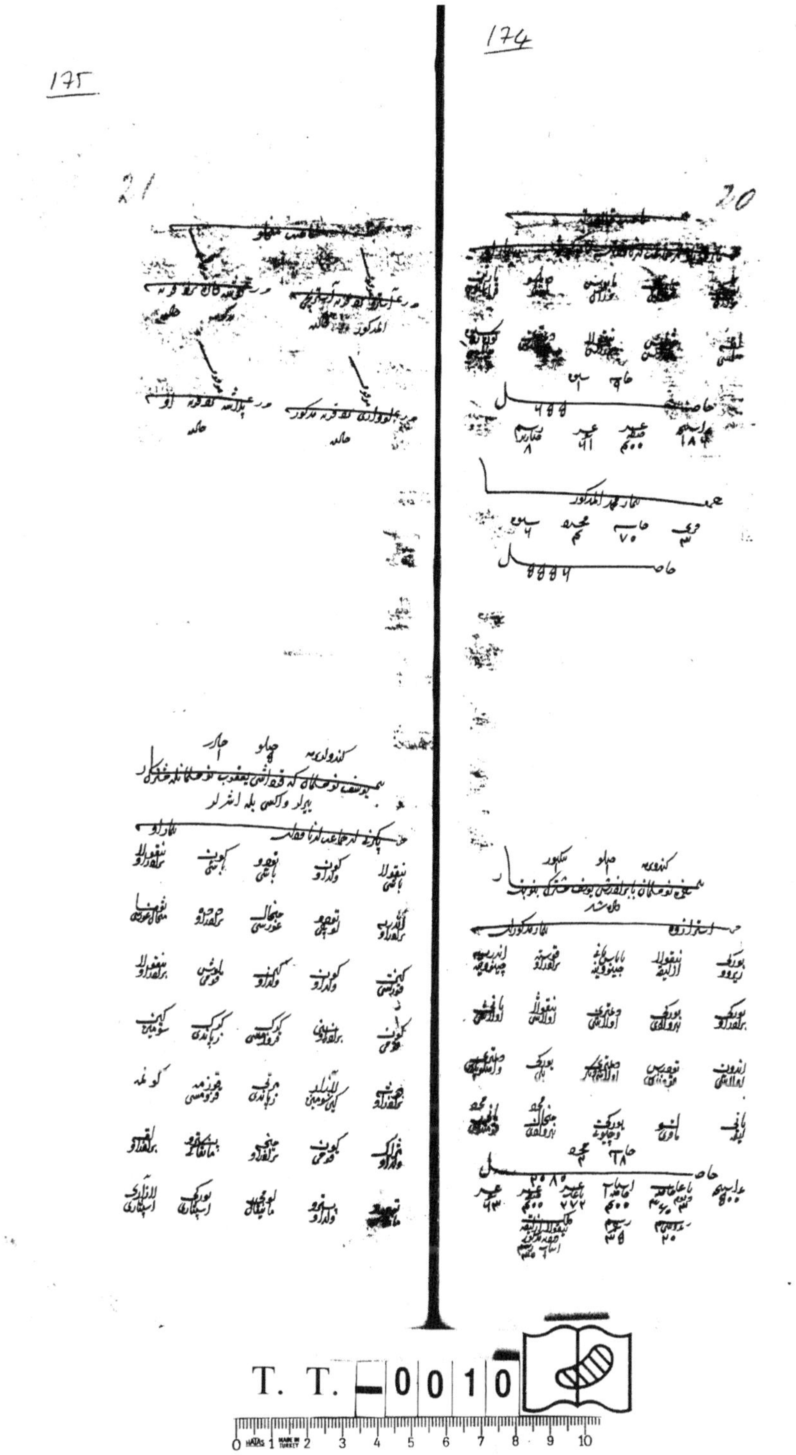
175
174
T. T. 0010

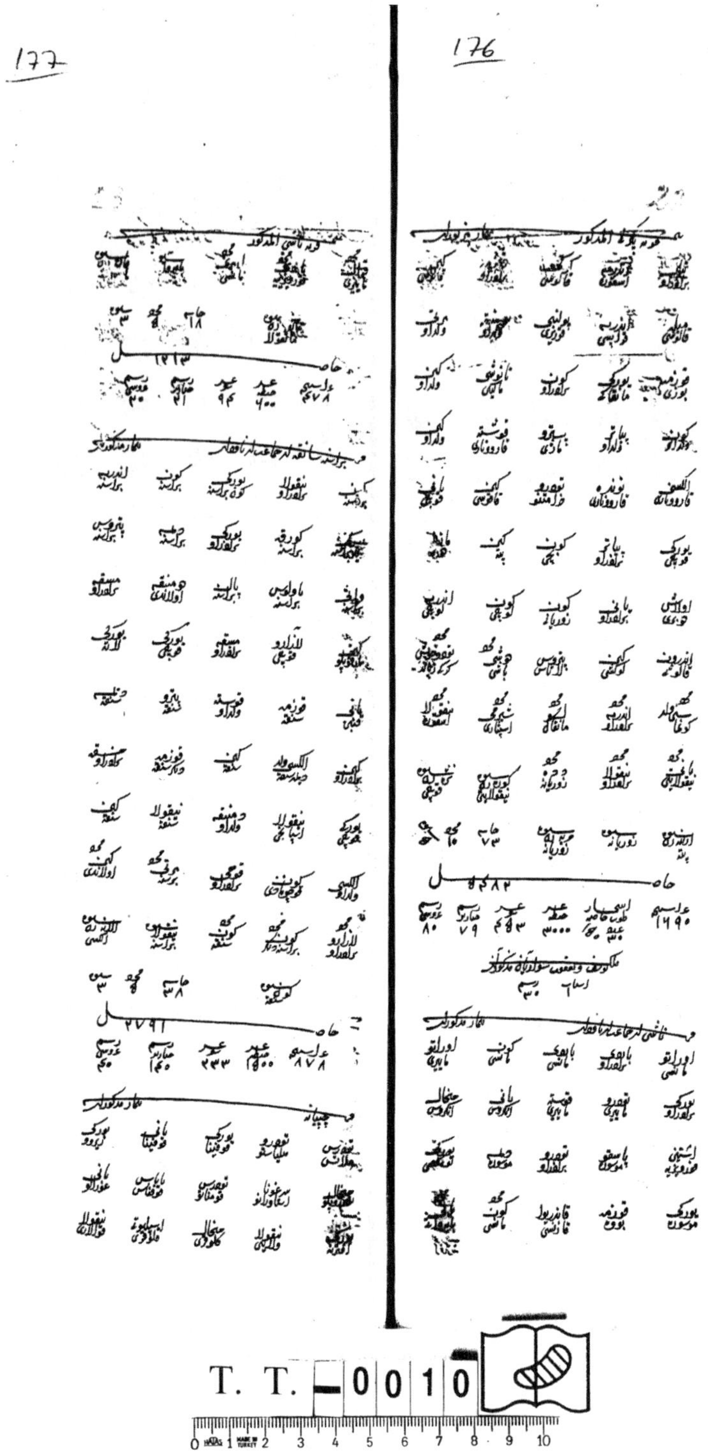
177
176
T. T. 0010

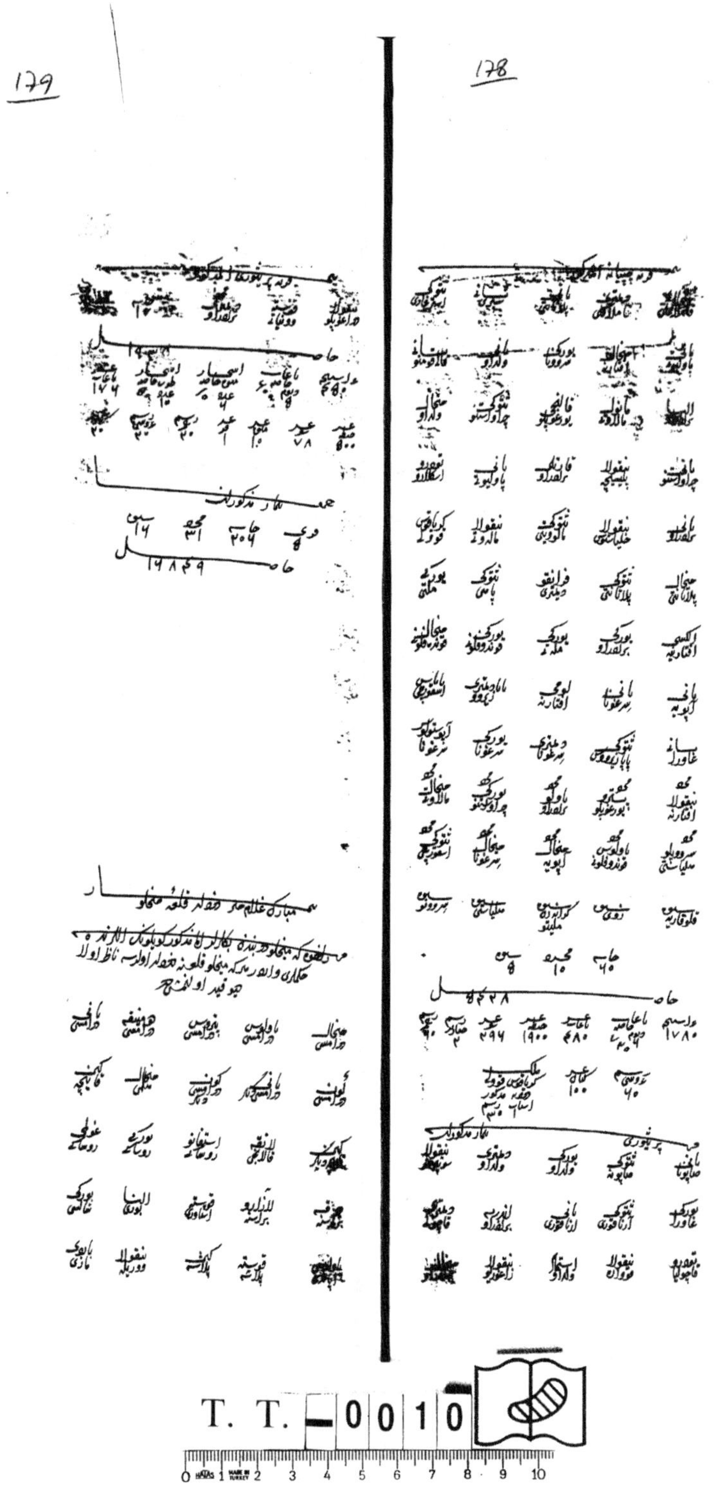
179
178
T. T. 0010

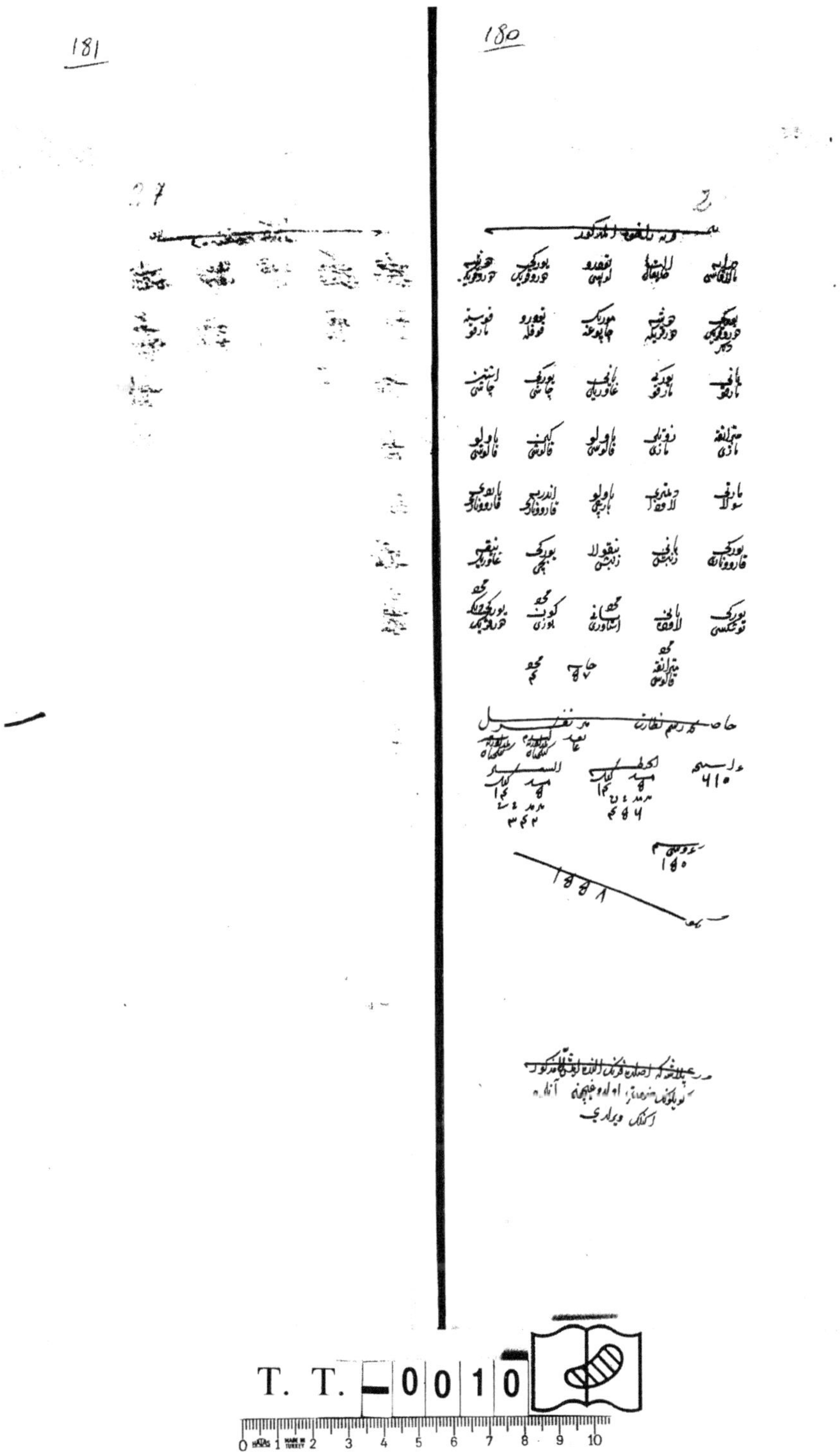
181
180
T. T. 0010

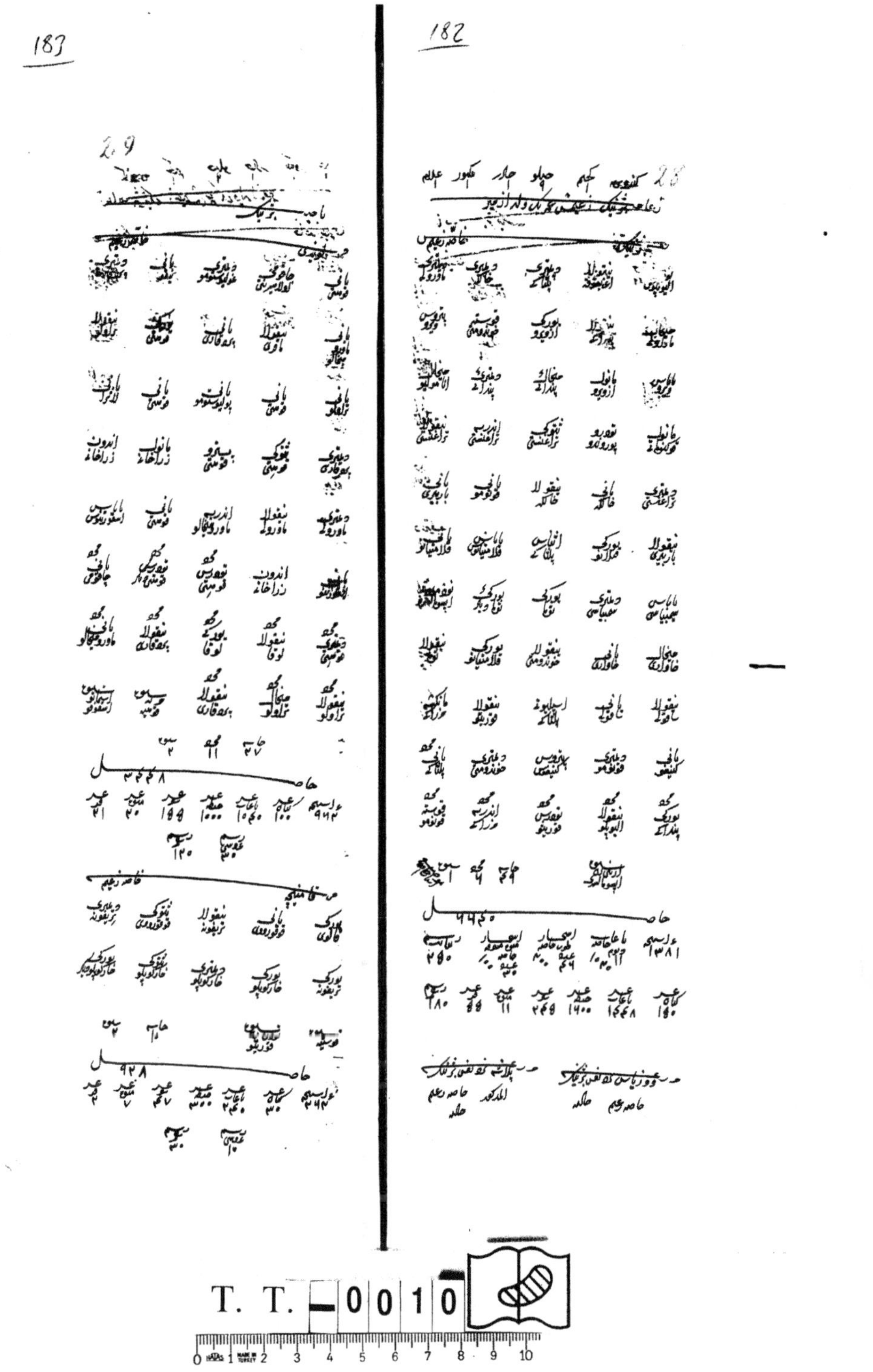
183
182
T. T. 0010

185
184
T. T. 0010

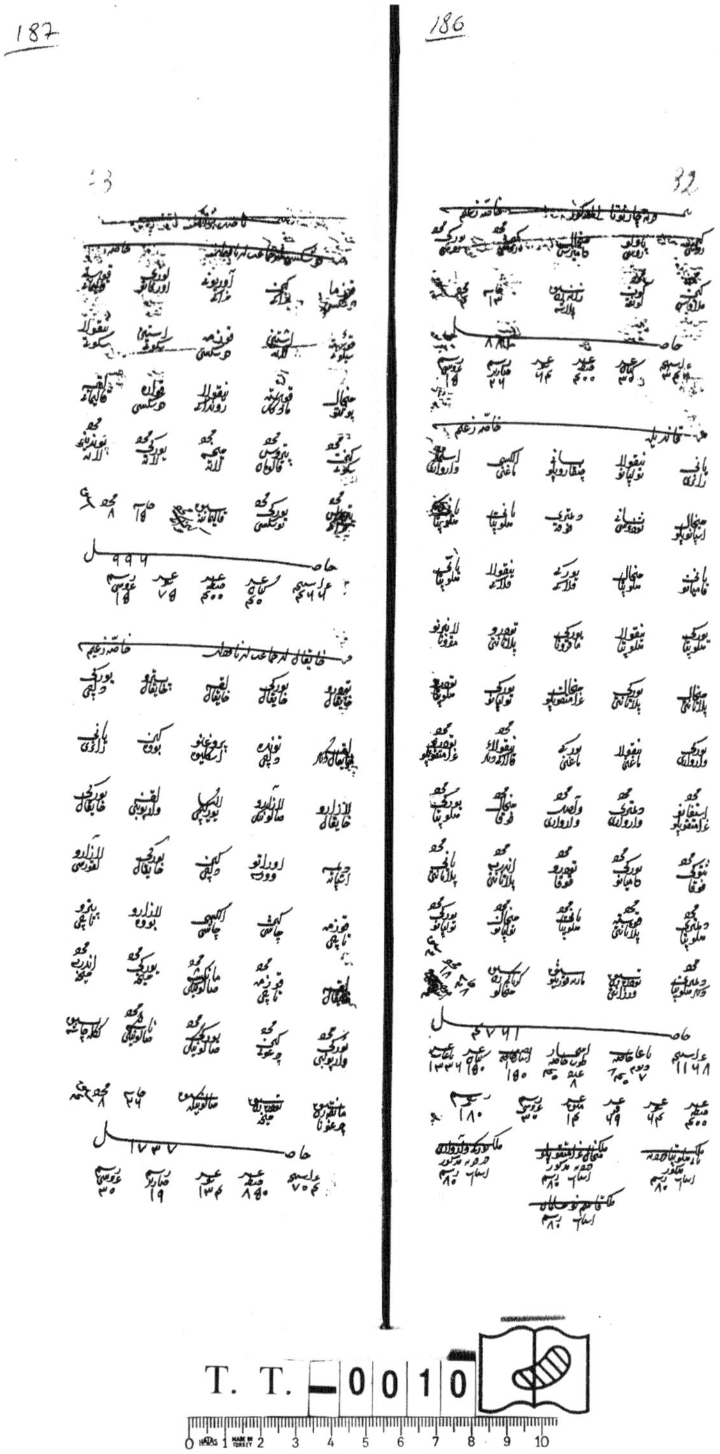
187
186
T. T. 0010

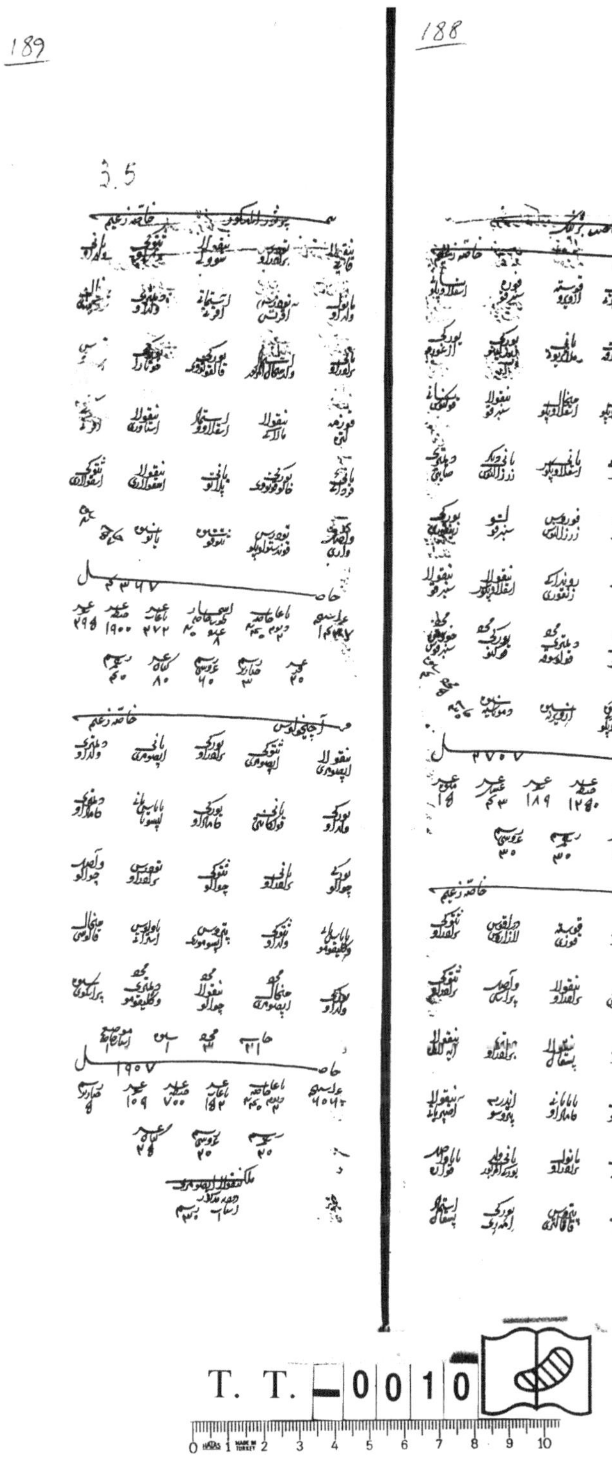
189
188
35
36
T. T. 0010

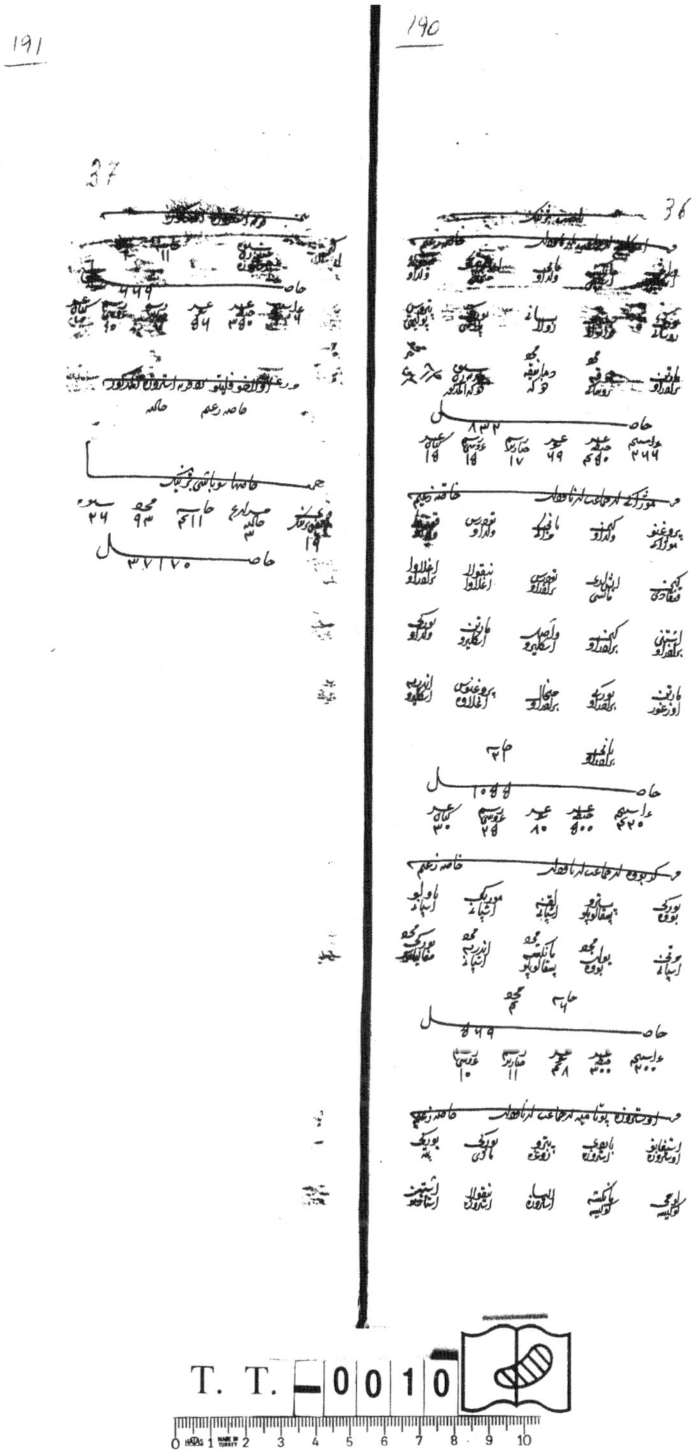
191
190
37
36
T. T. 0010

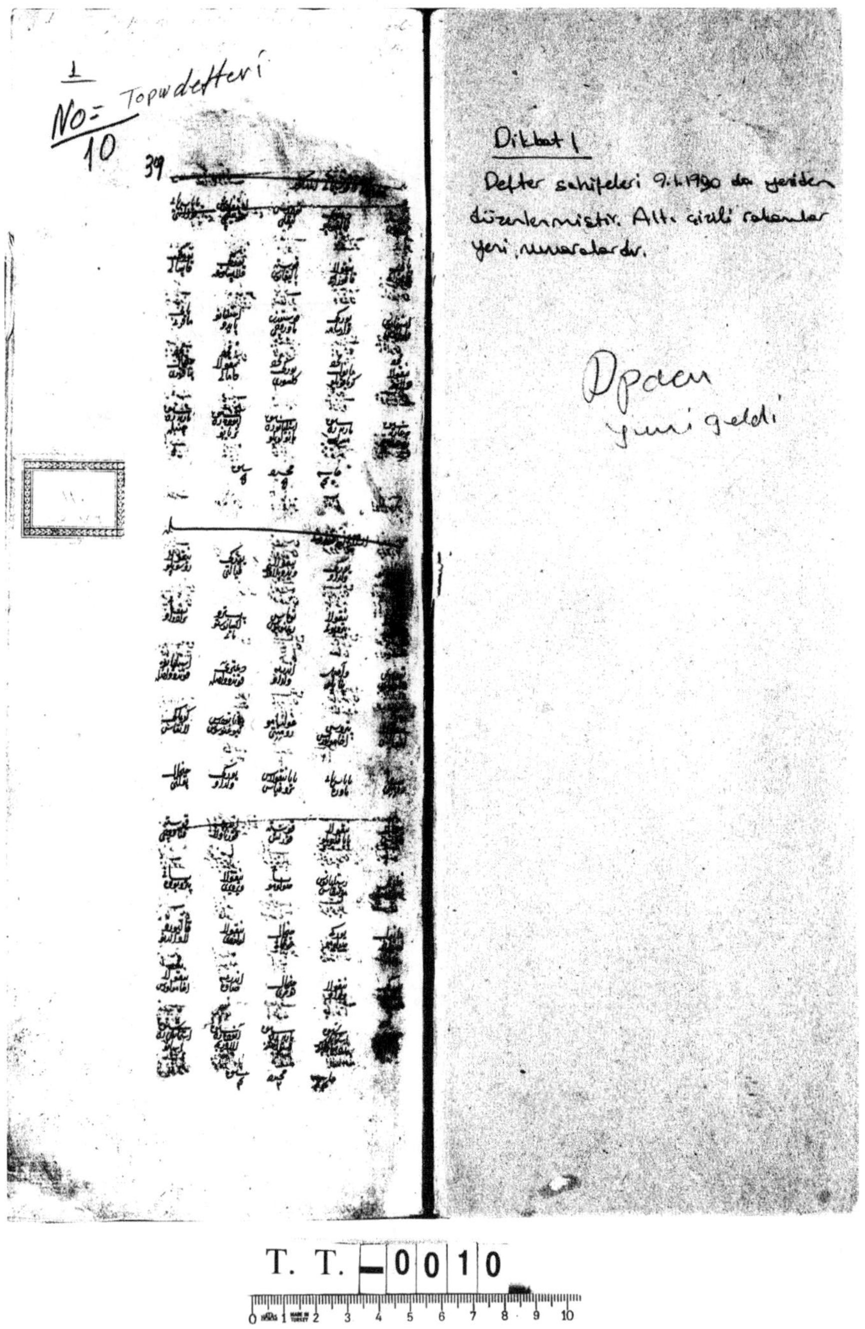
Dikkat!
Defter sahifeleri 9.1.1990 da yeniden düzenlenmiştir. Altı çizili rakamlar yeni numaralardır.
T. T. 0010

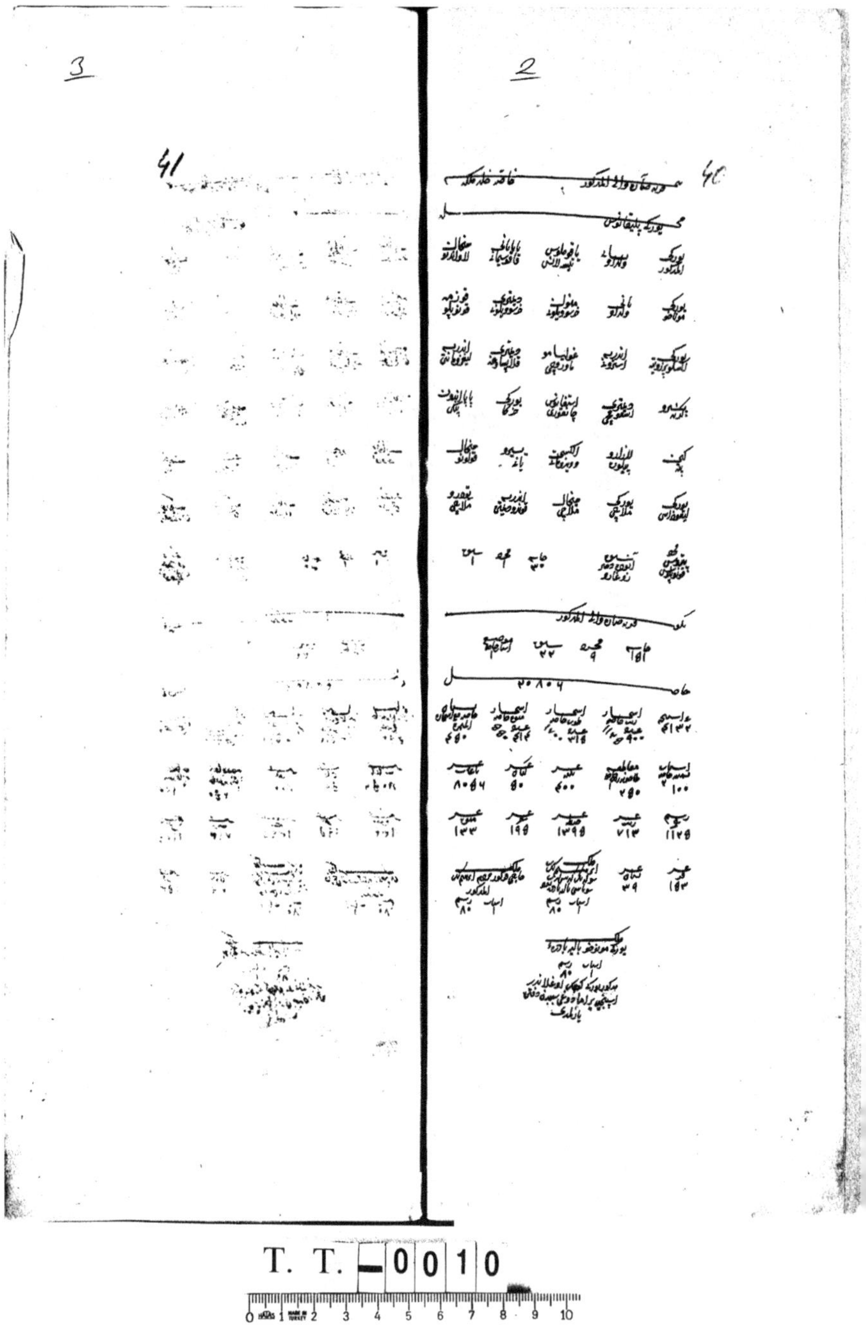
T. T. 0010

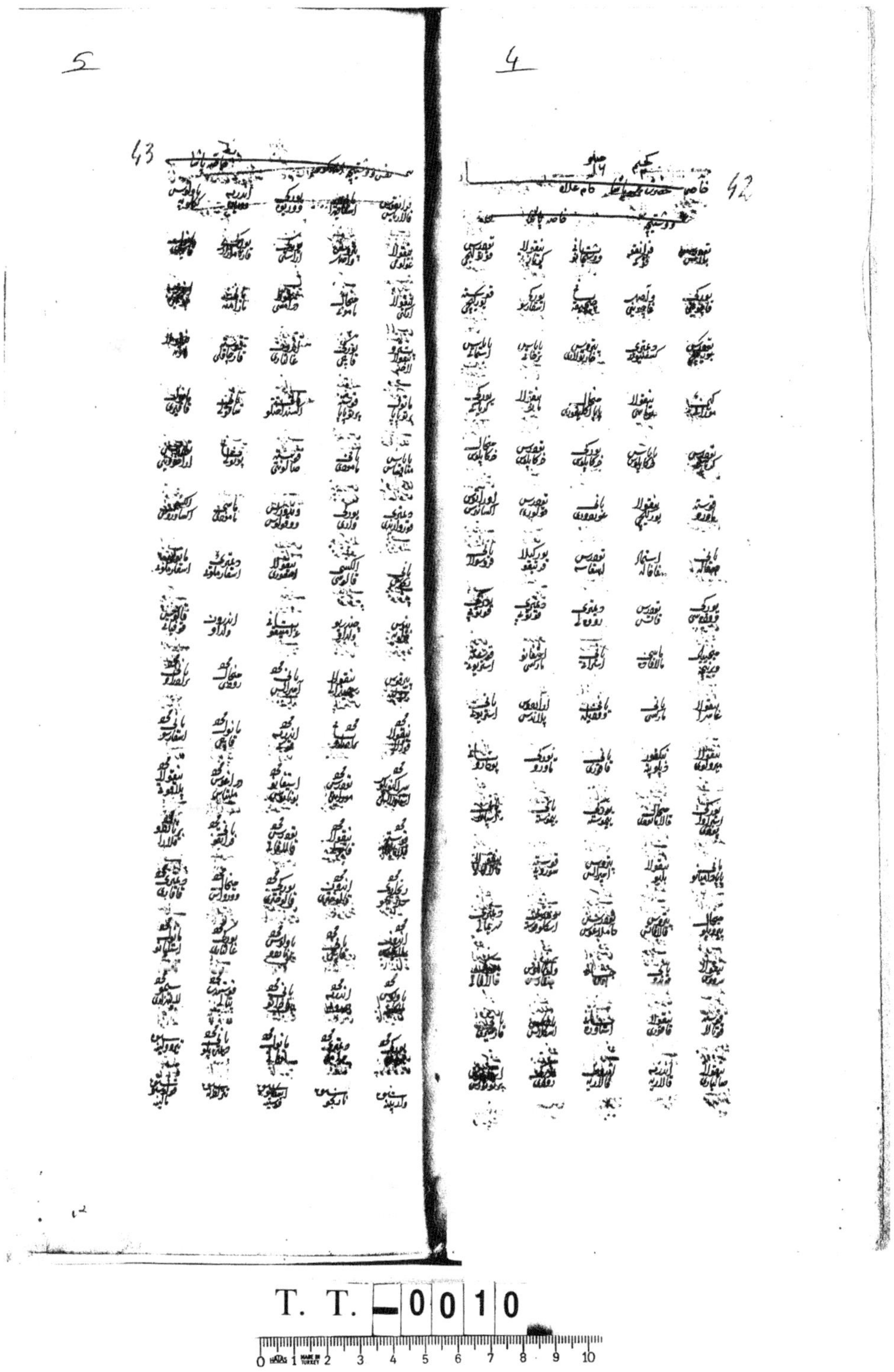
5
4
T. T. 0010

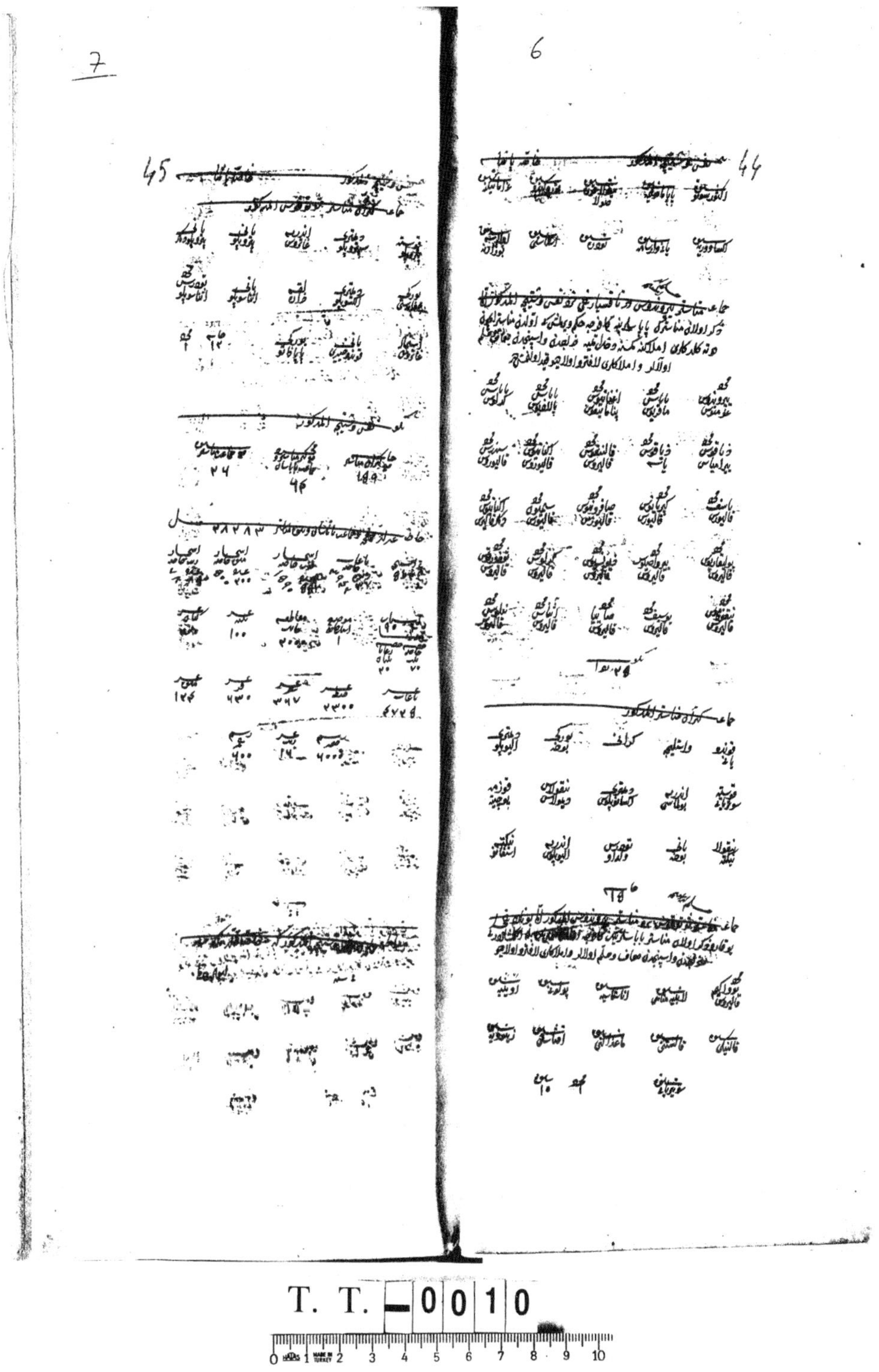
7
6
T. T. 0010

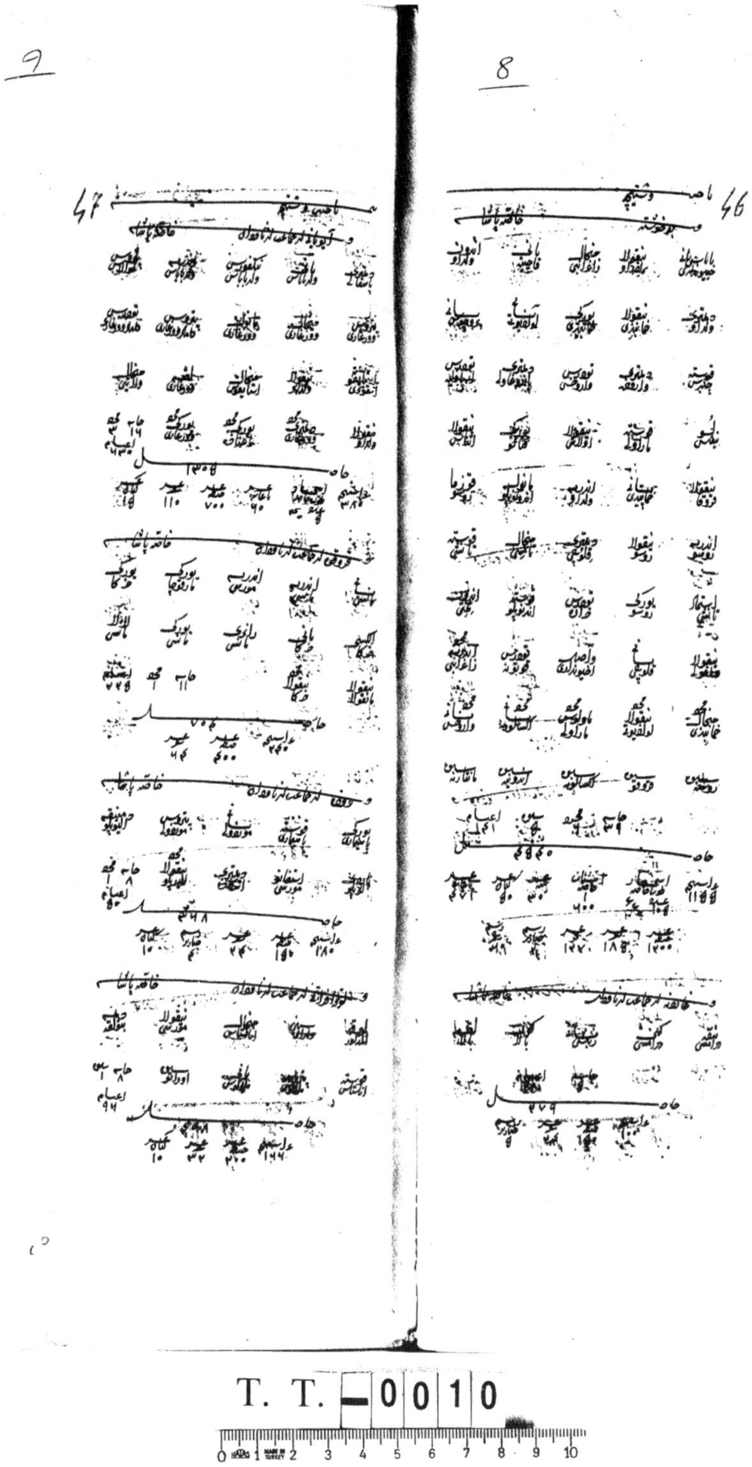
9
8
47
46
T. T. 0010

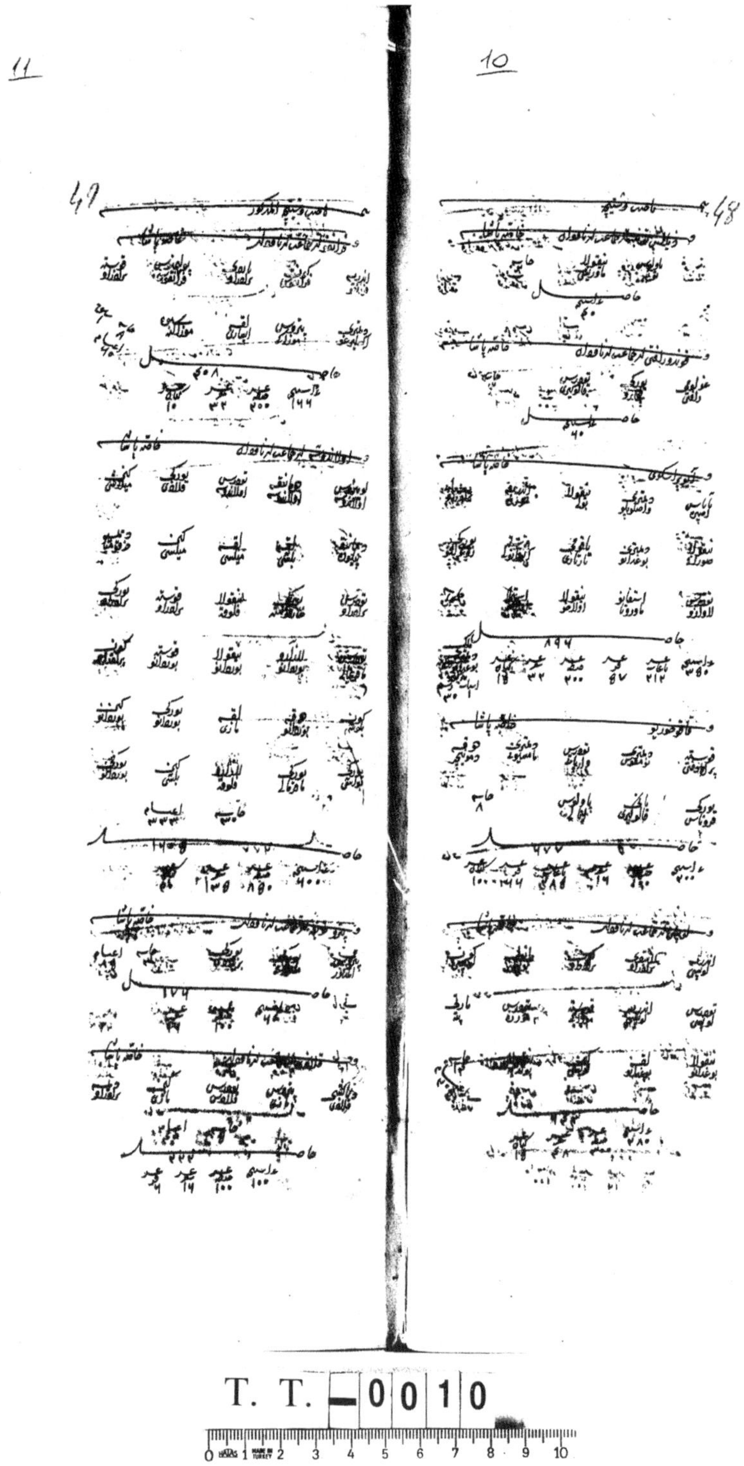
11
10
49
48
T. T. 0010

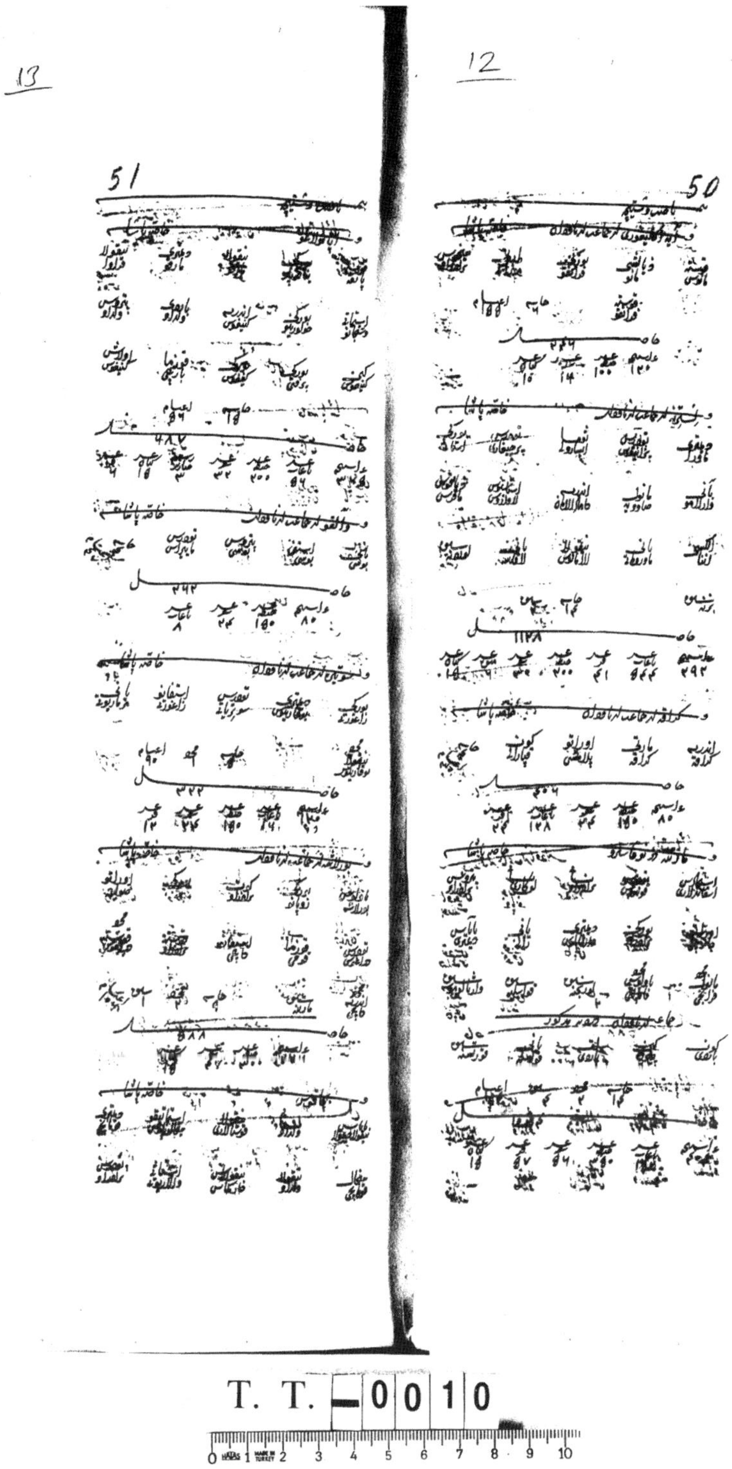

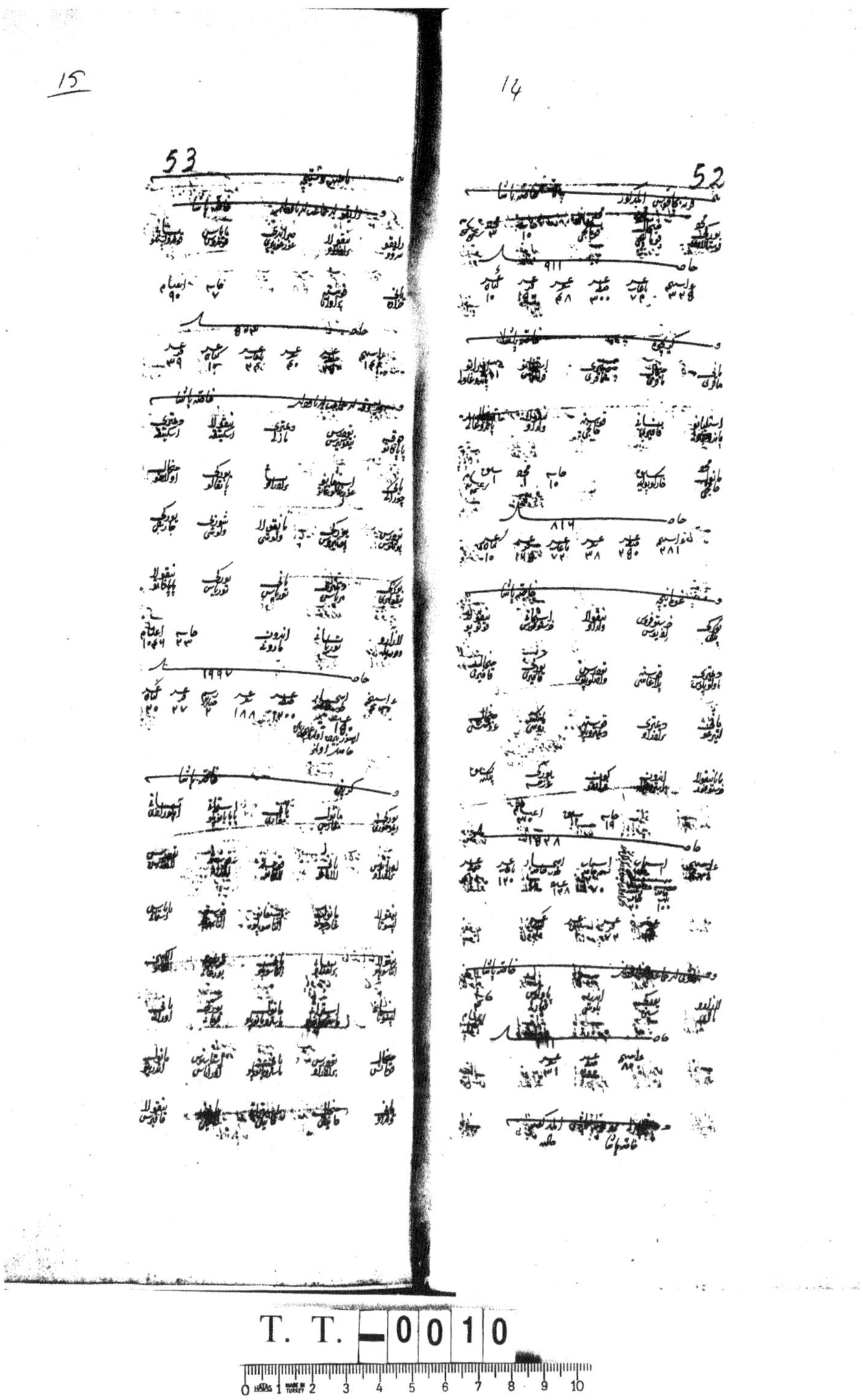

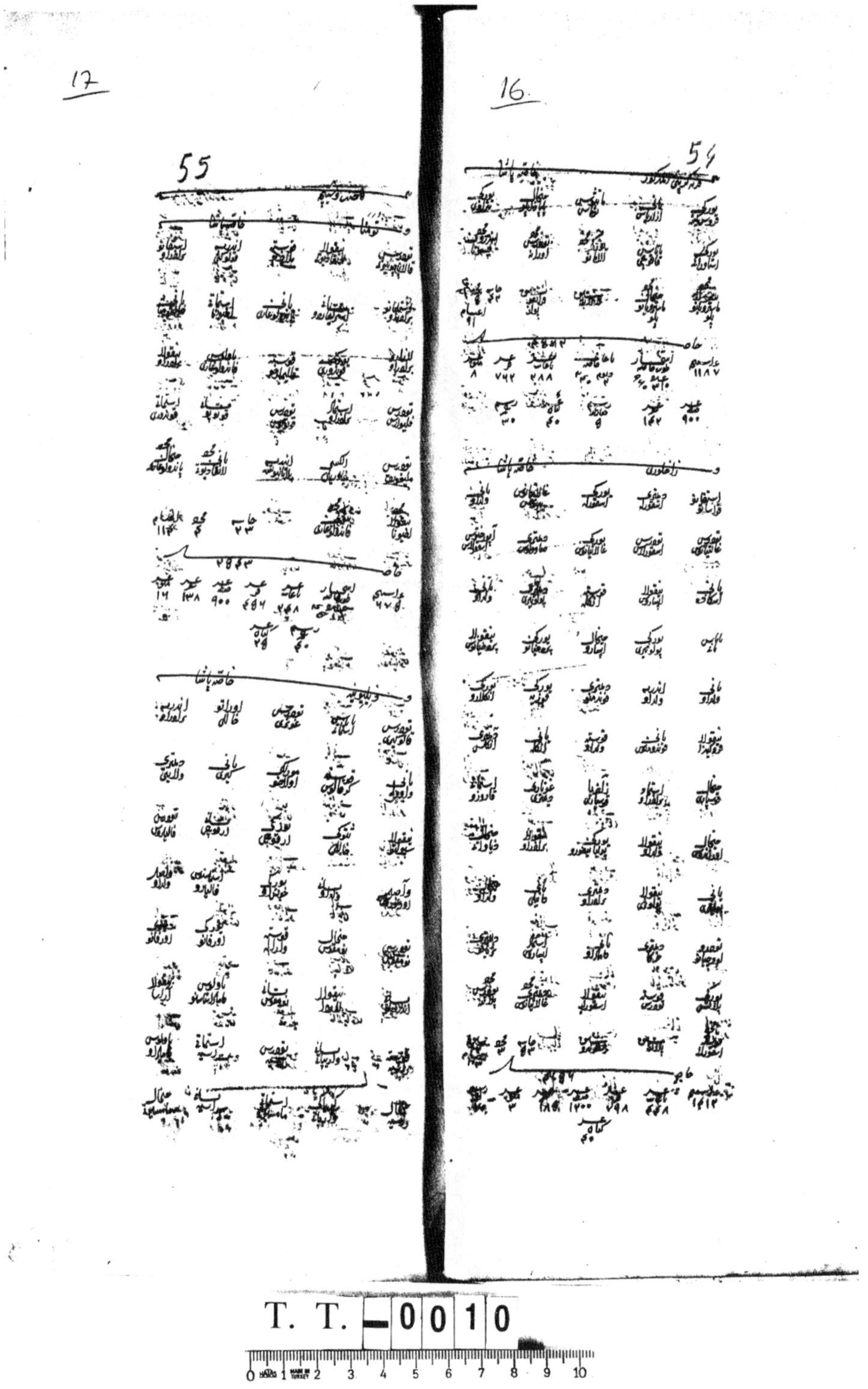
17
16
T. T. 0010

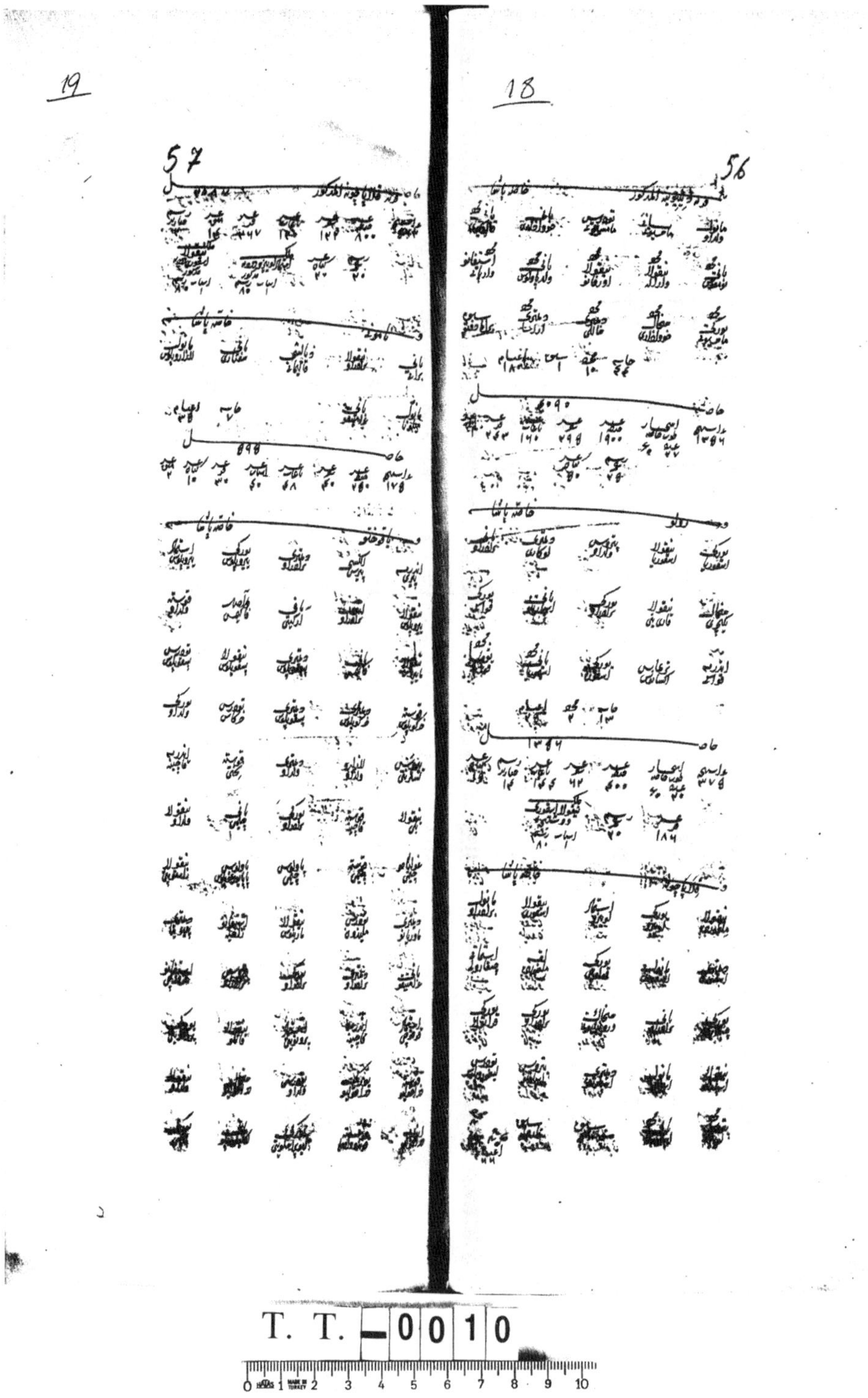
19
18
T. T. 0010

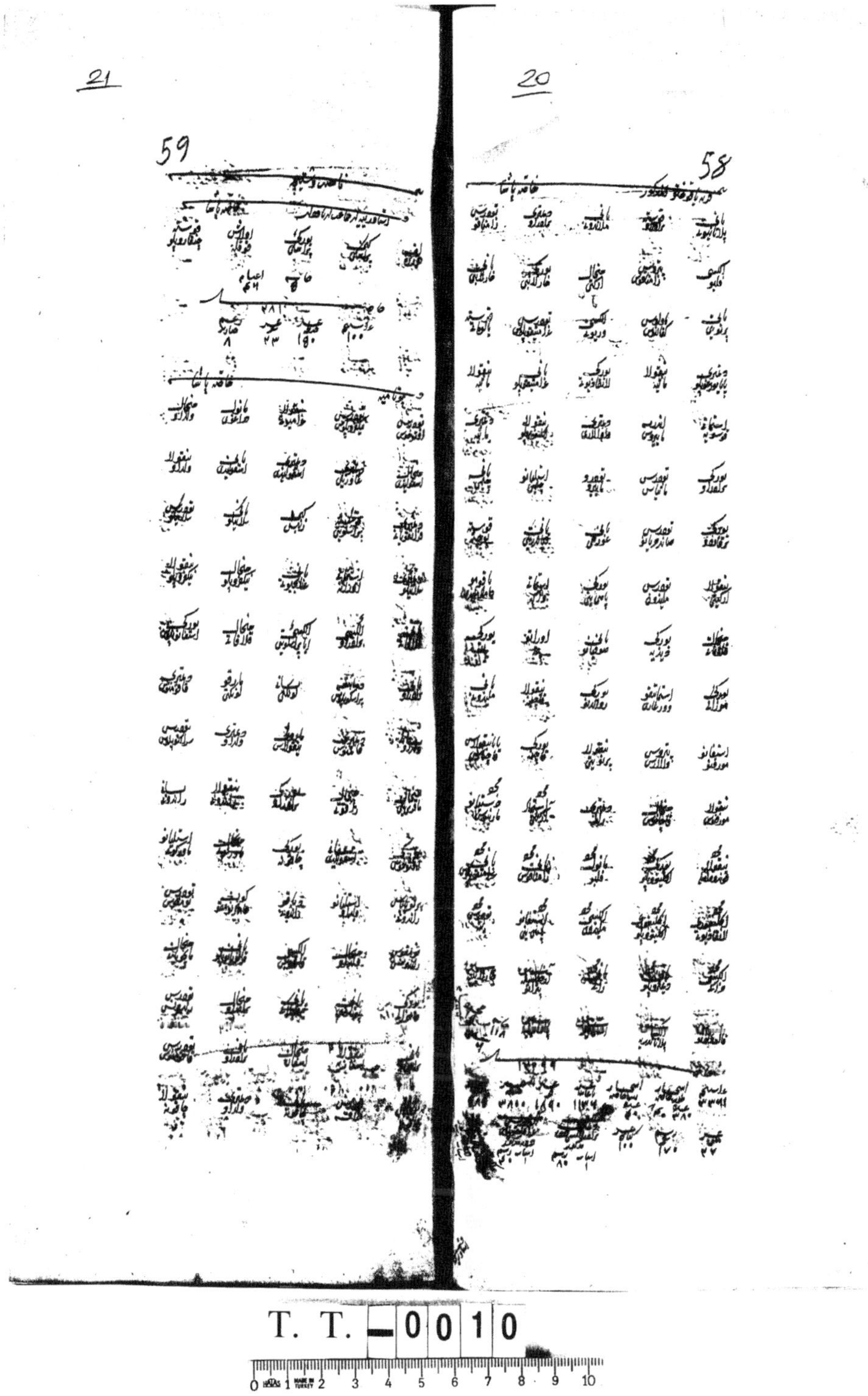
21
20
59
58
T. T. -0010

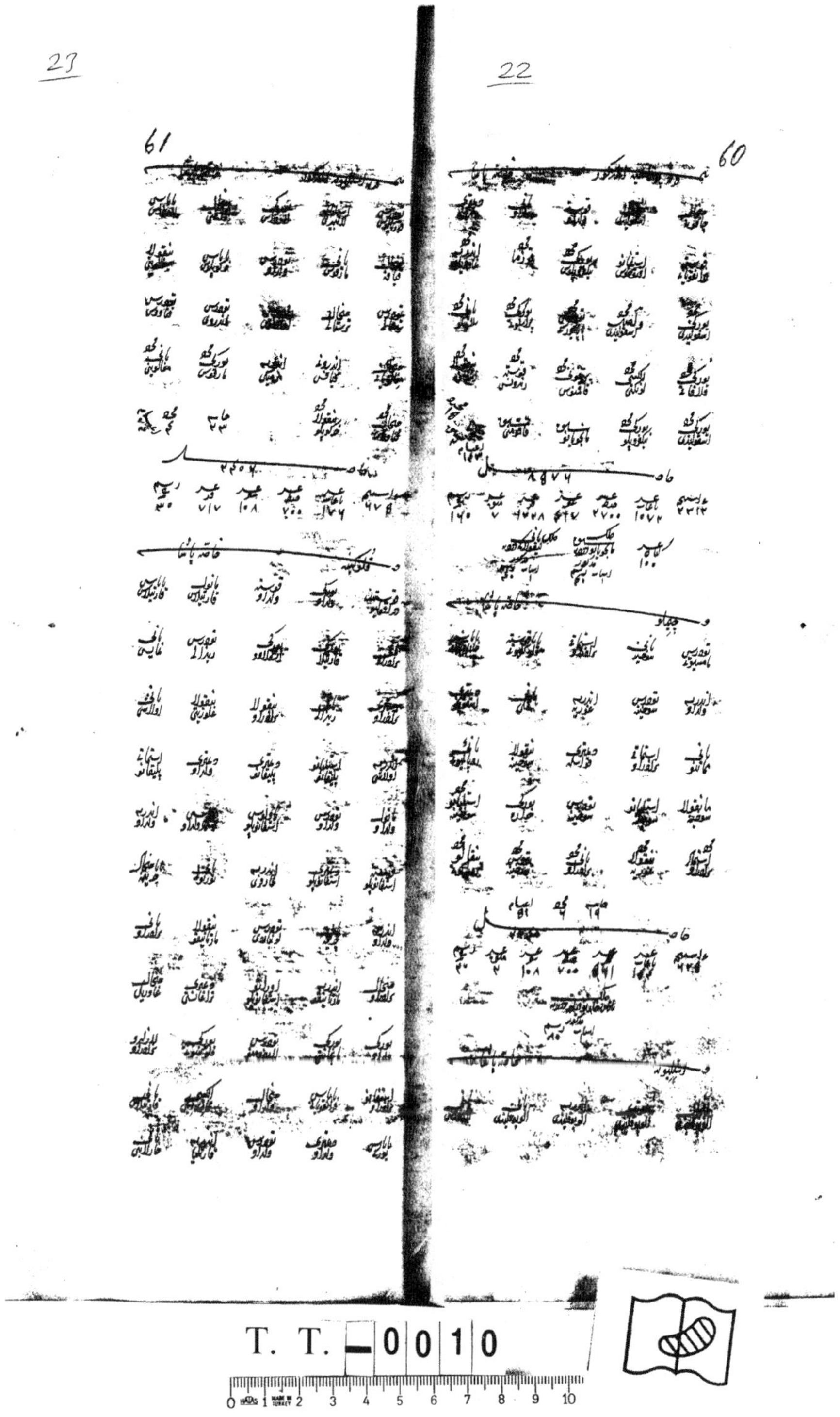
23
22
61
60
T. T. -0010

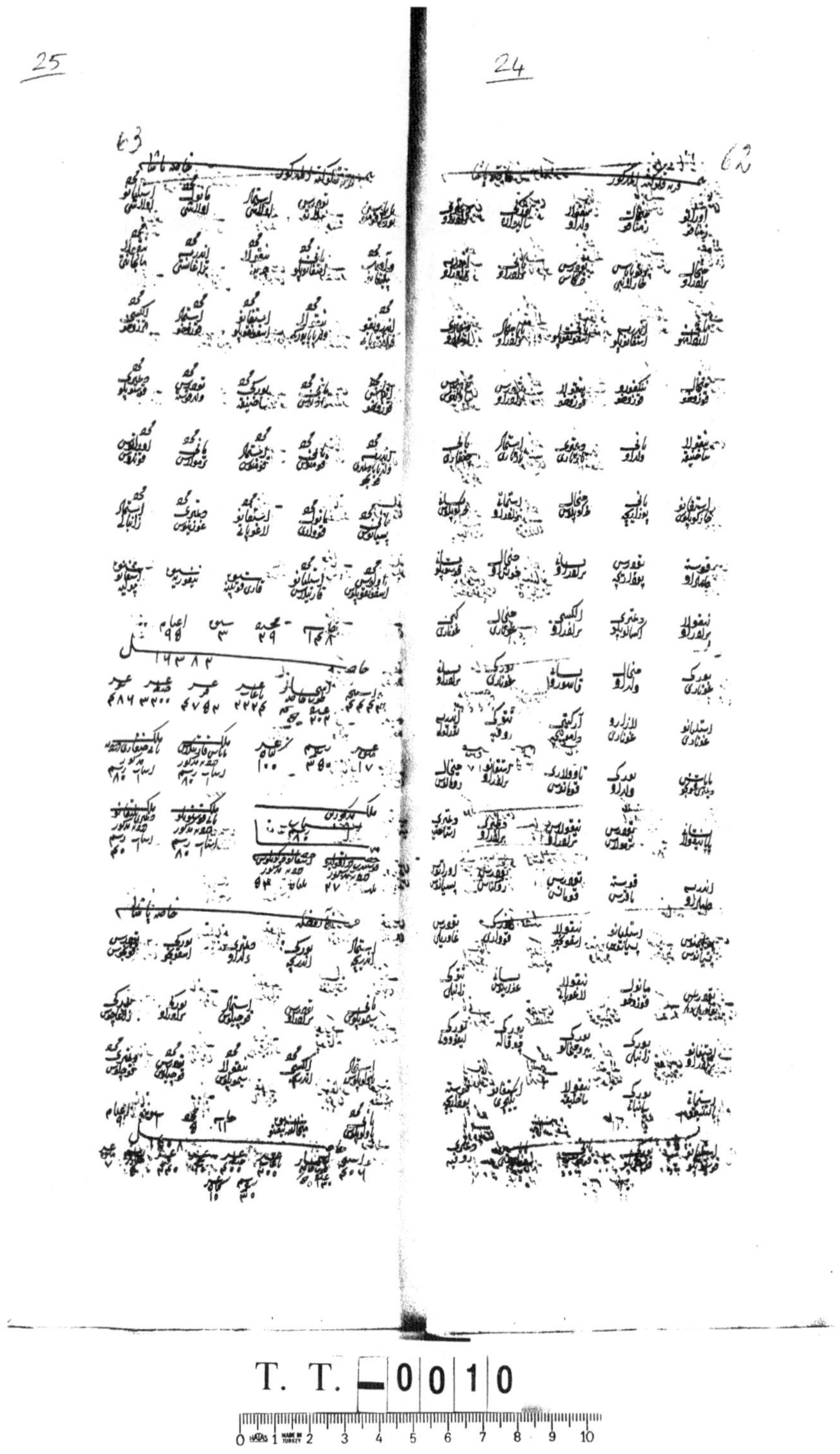
25
24
63
62
T. T. 0010

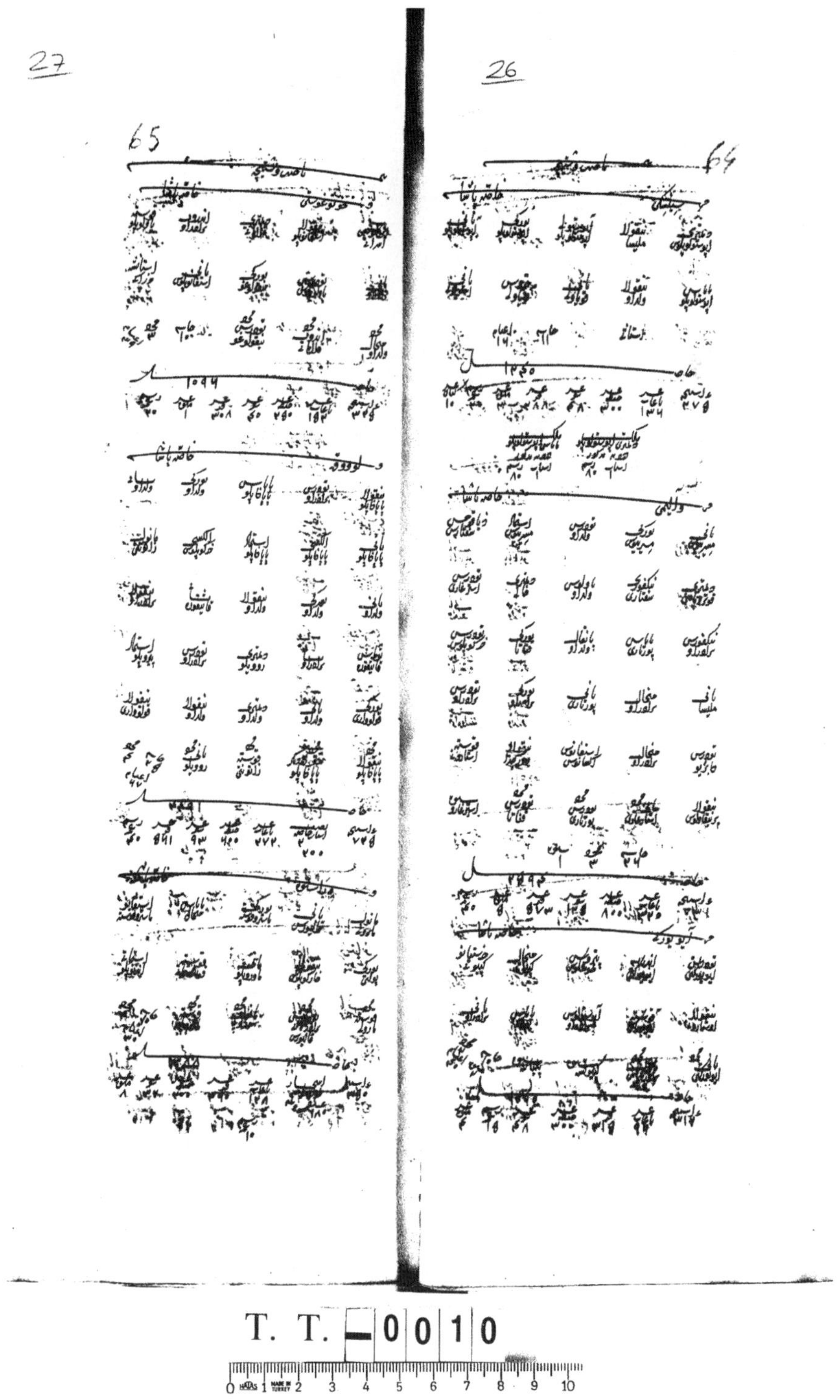
27
26
65
64
T. T. 0010

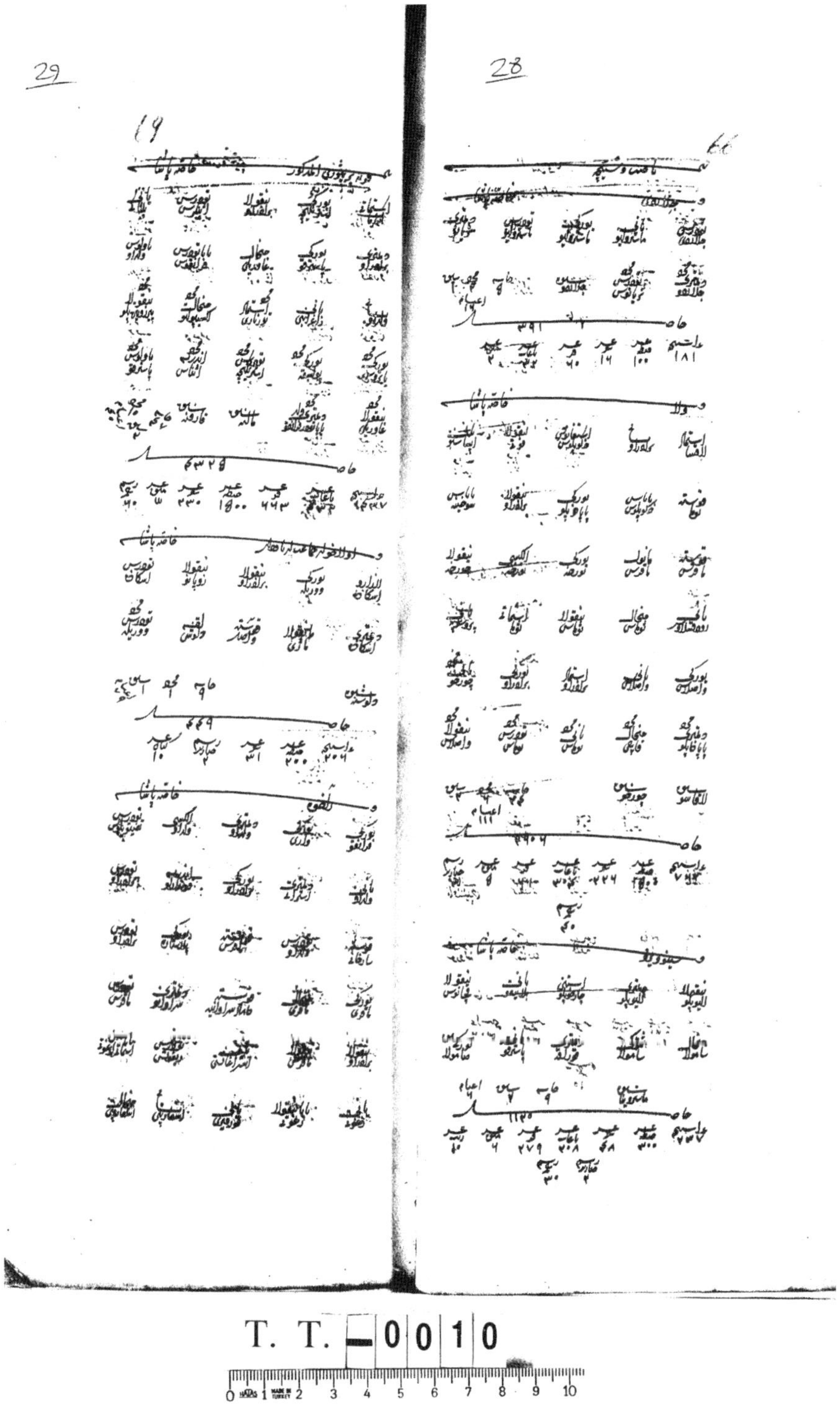
T. T. 0010

T. T. 0010

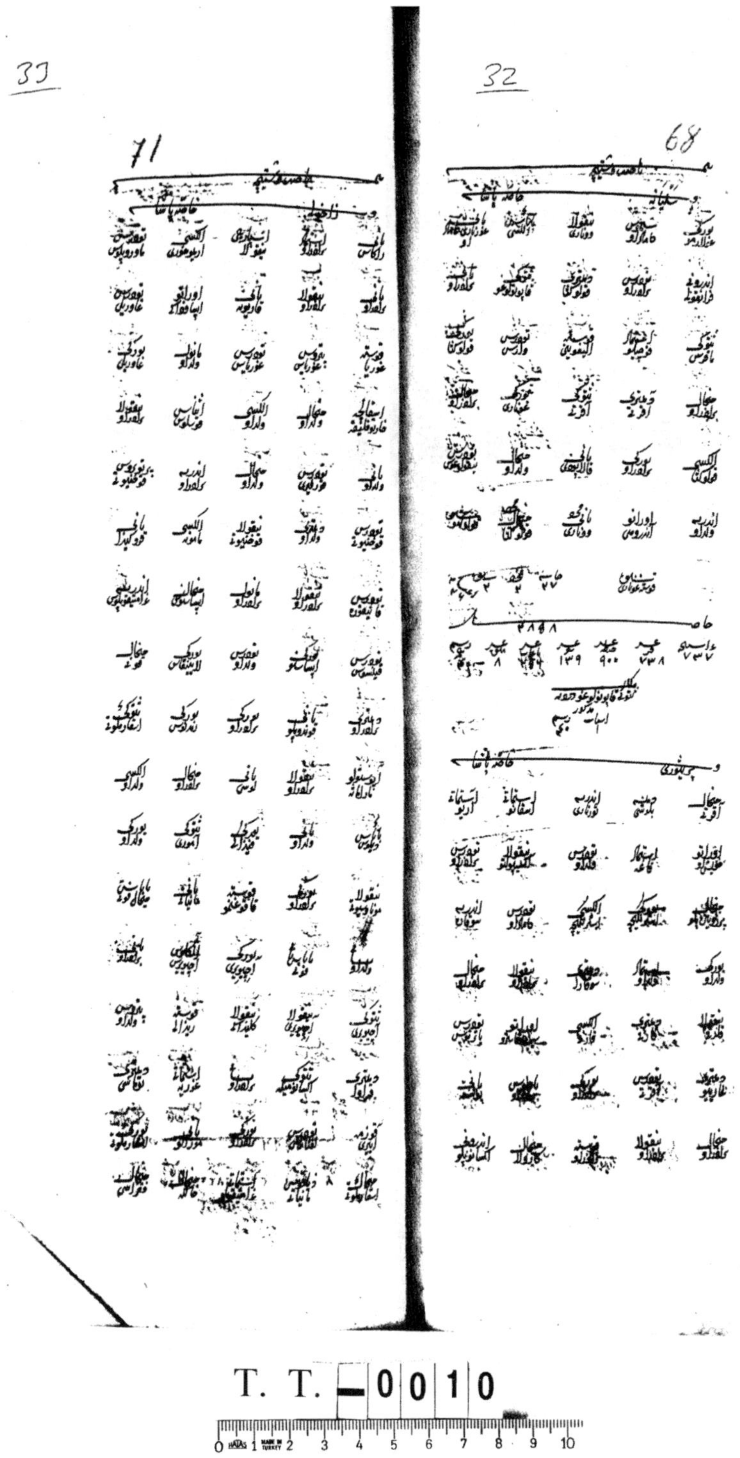

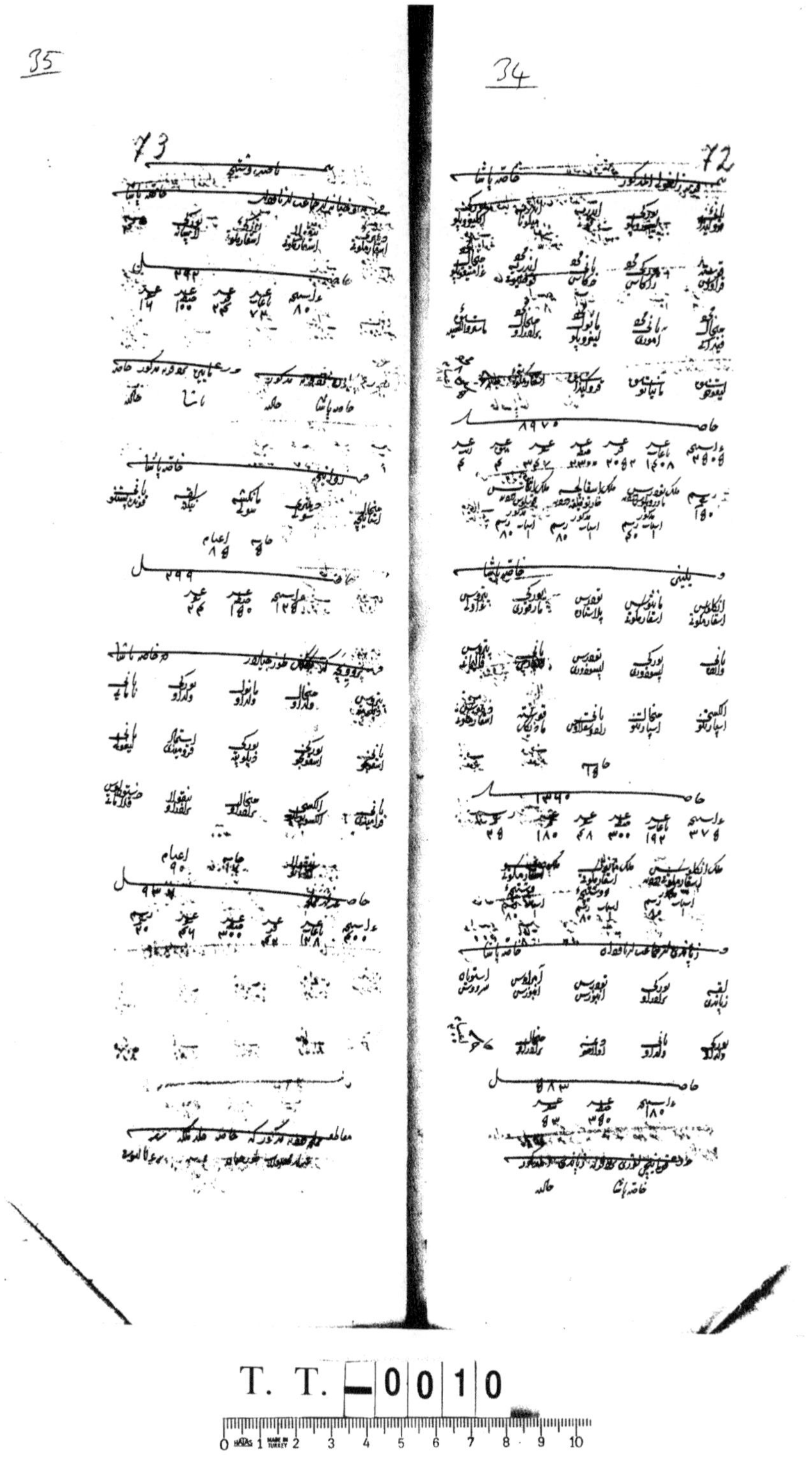

37
36
75
74
T. T. 0010

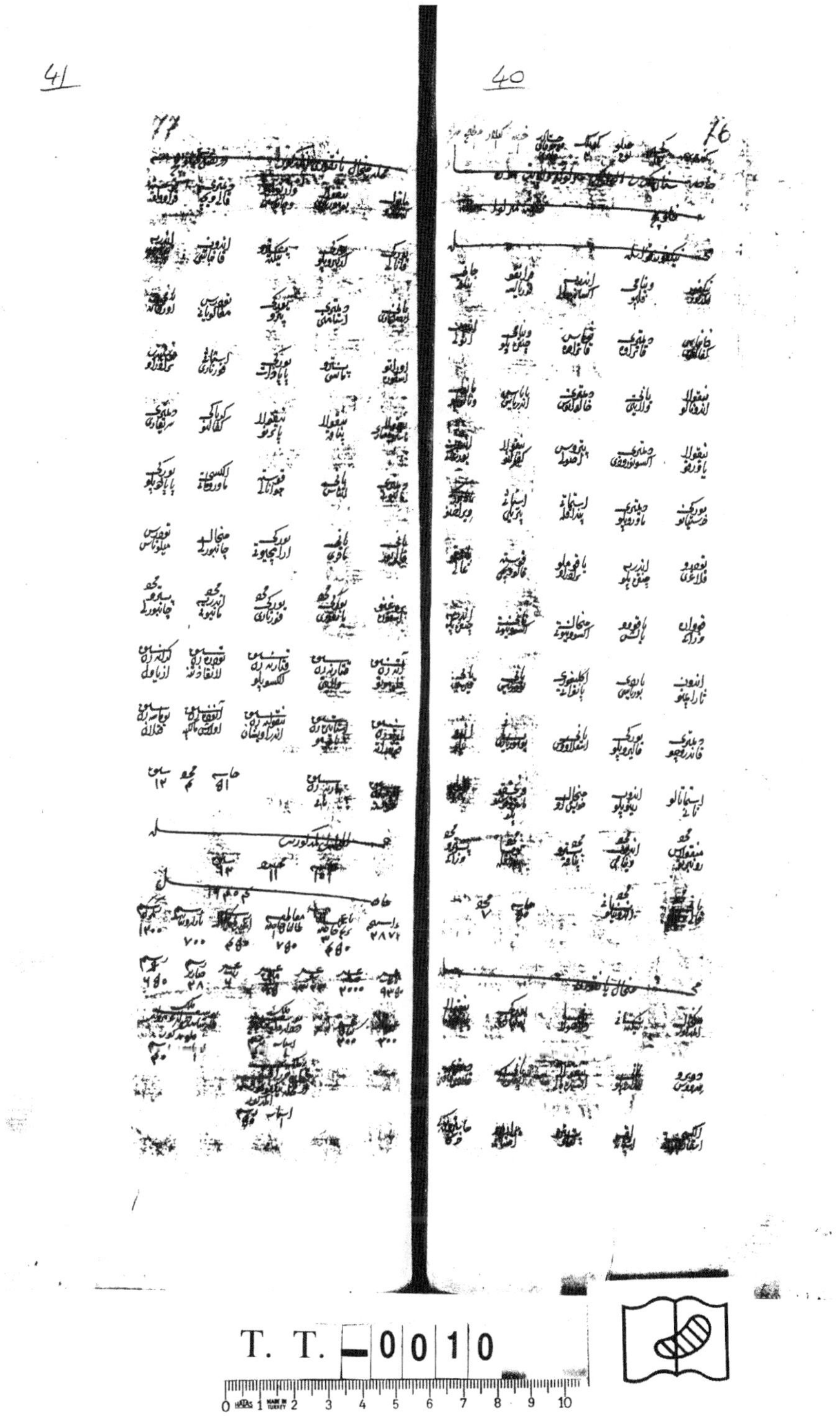
41
40
77
76
T. T. 0010

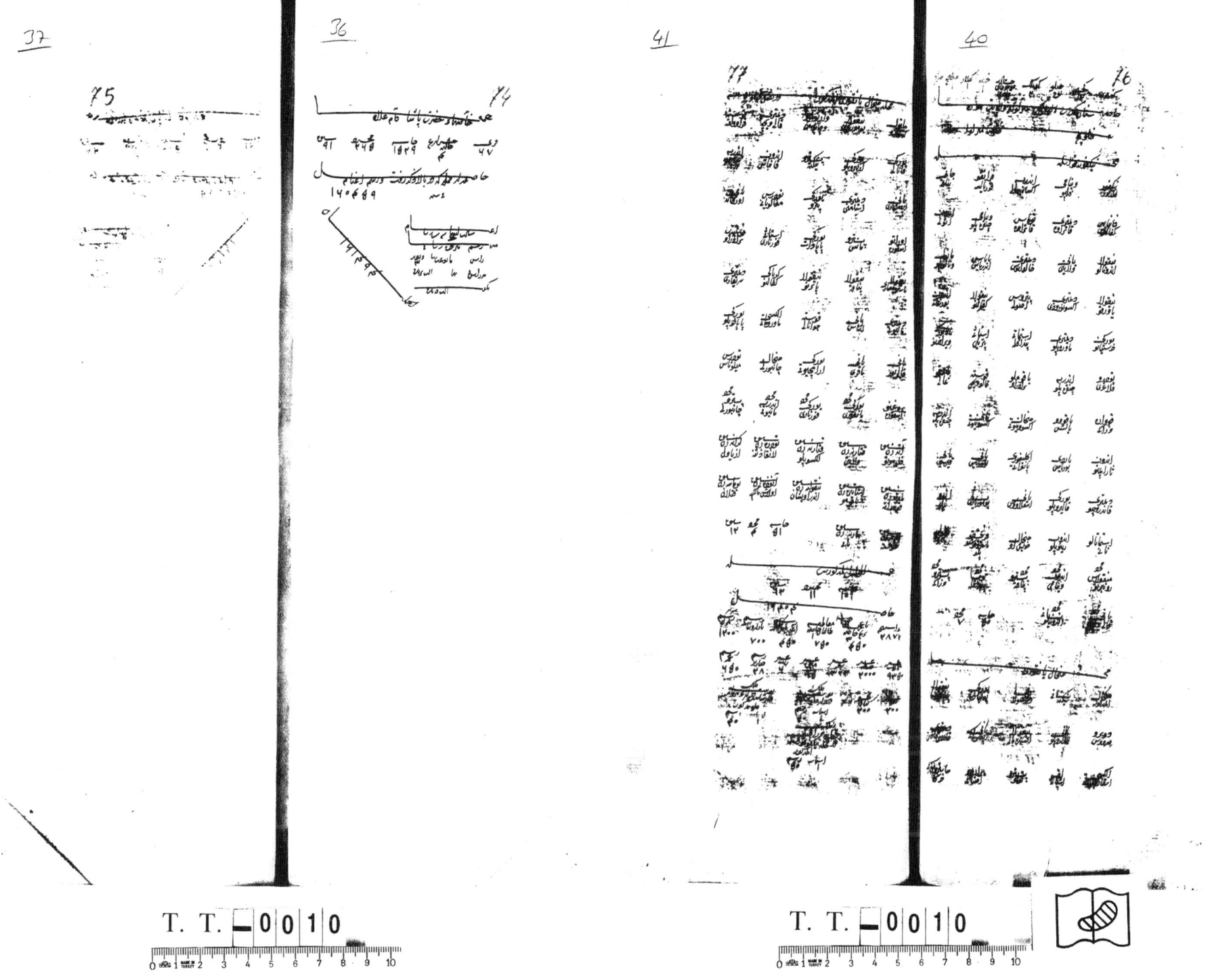

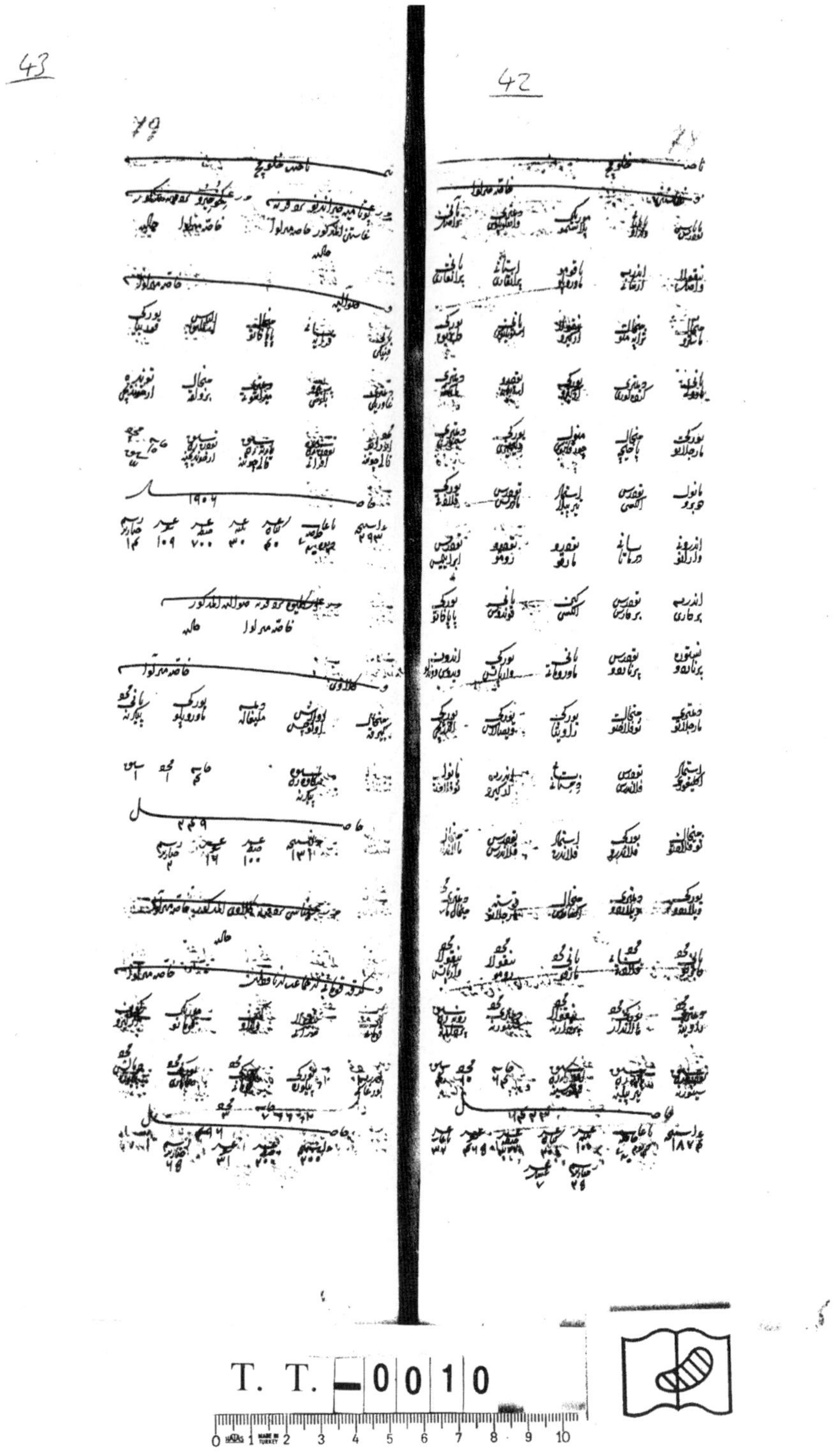

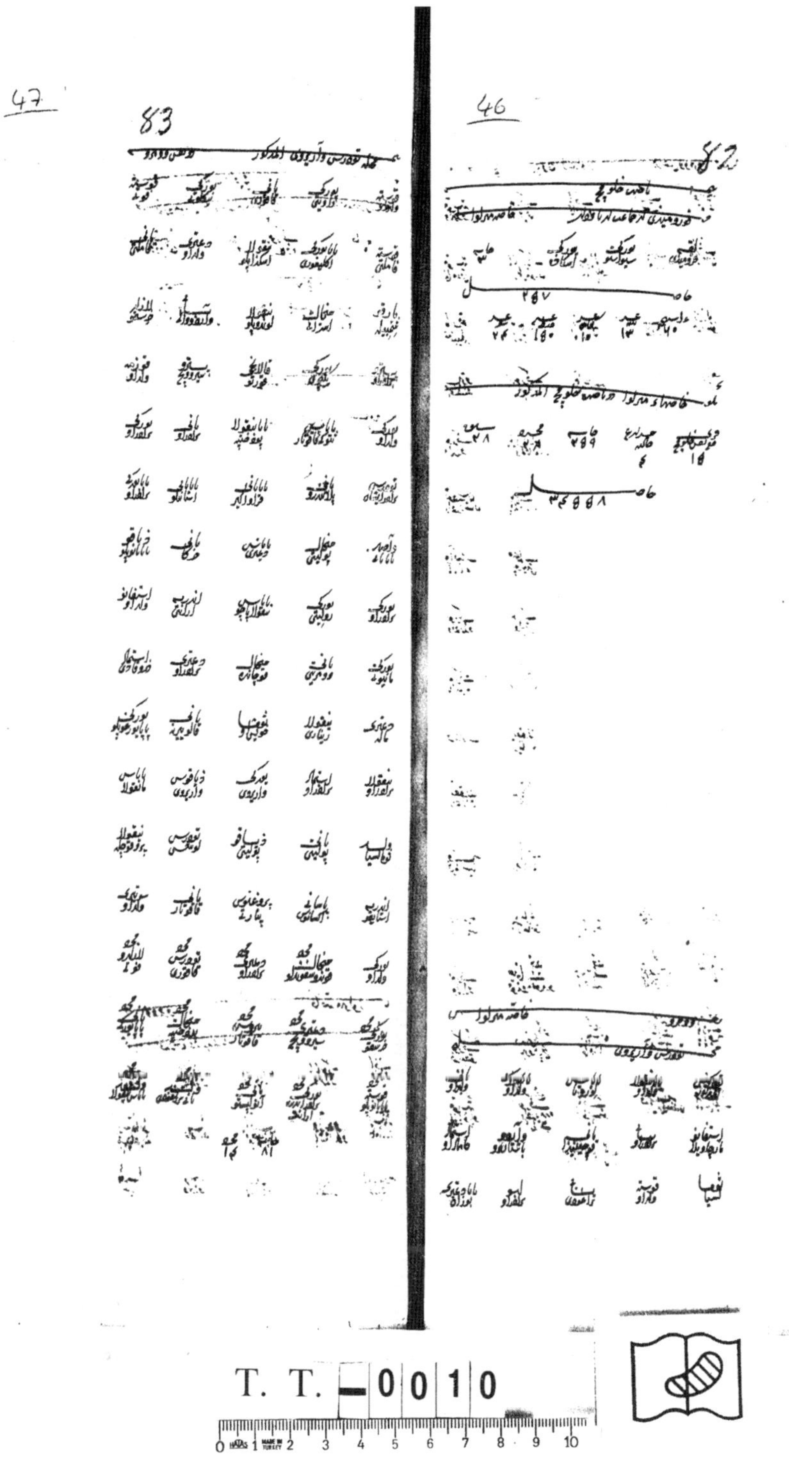
47
83
46
82
T. T. 0010

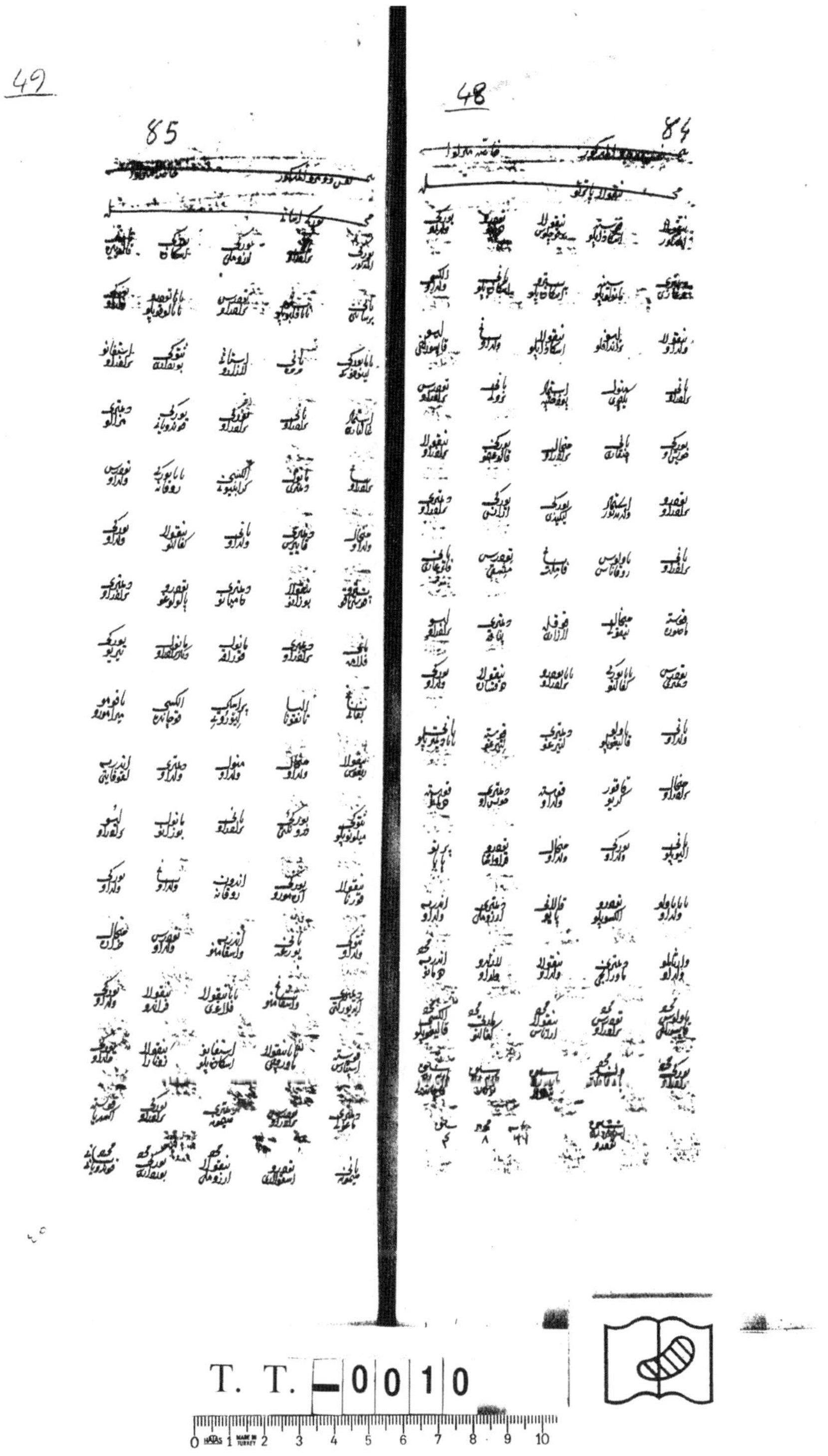
49
85
48
84
T. T. 0010

51
50
T. T. 0010

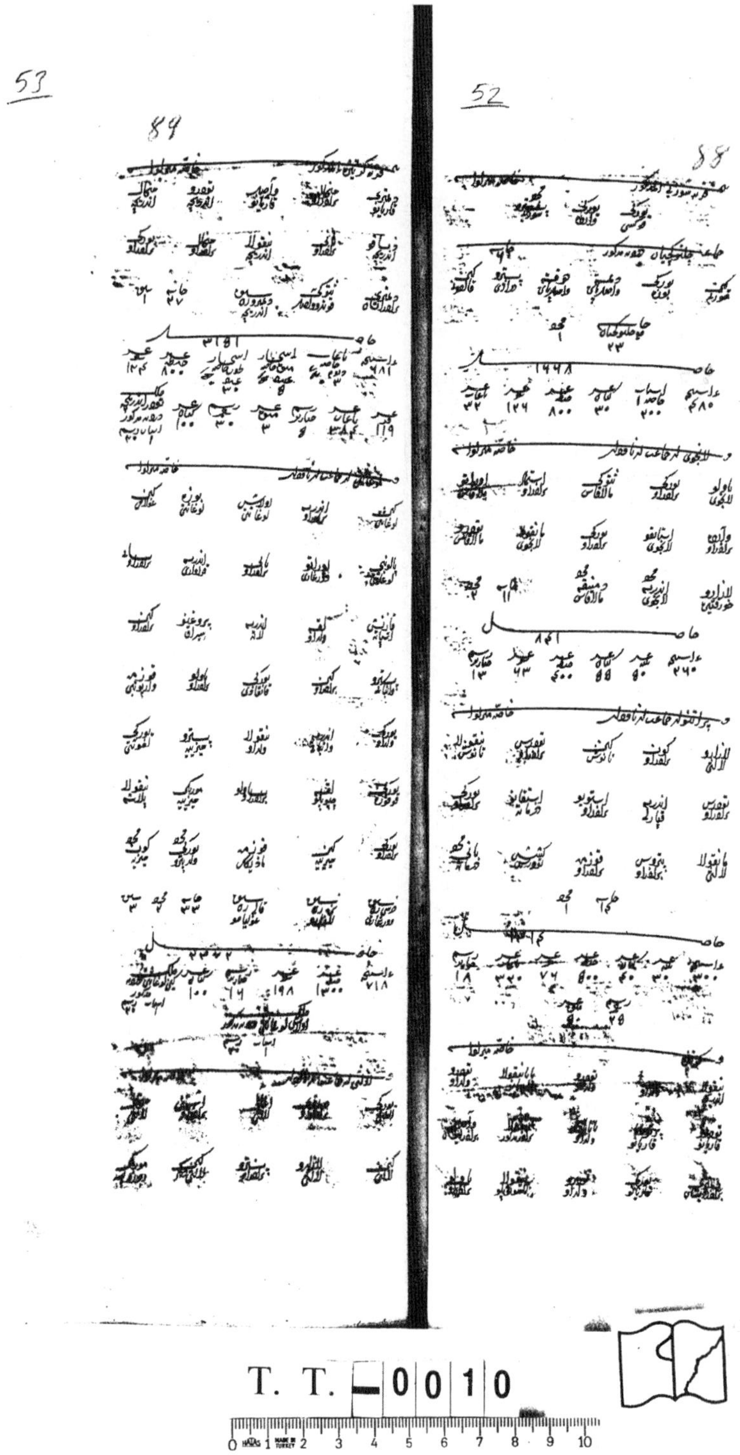
53
52
T. T. 0010

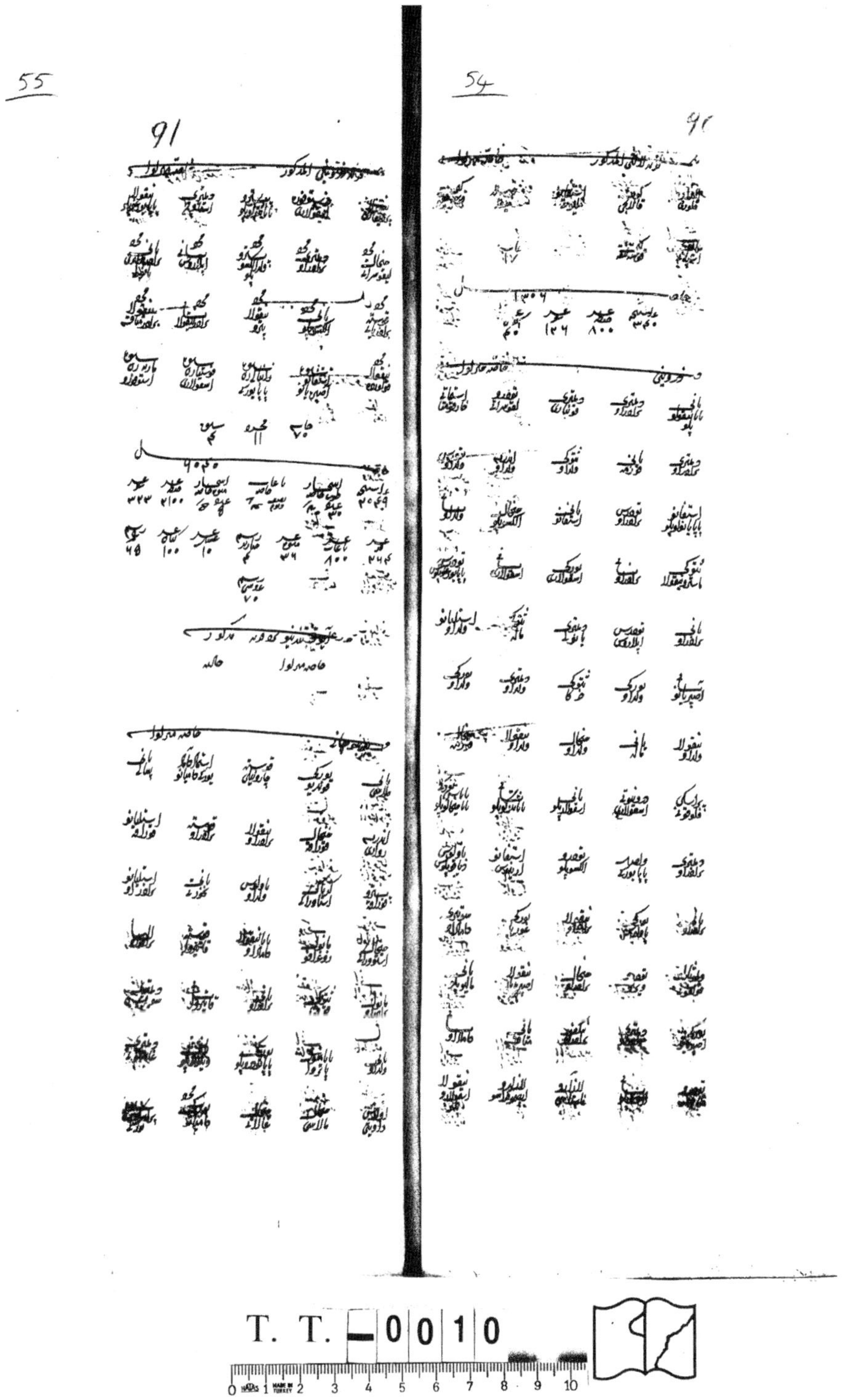
55
54
91
T. T. 0010

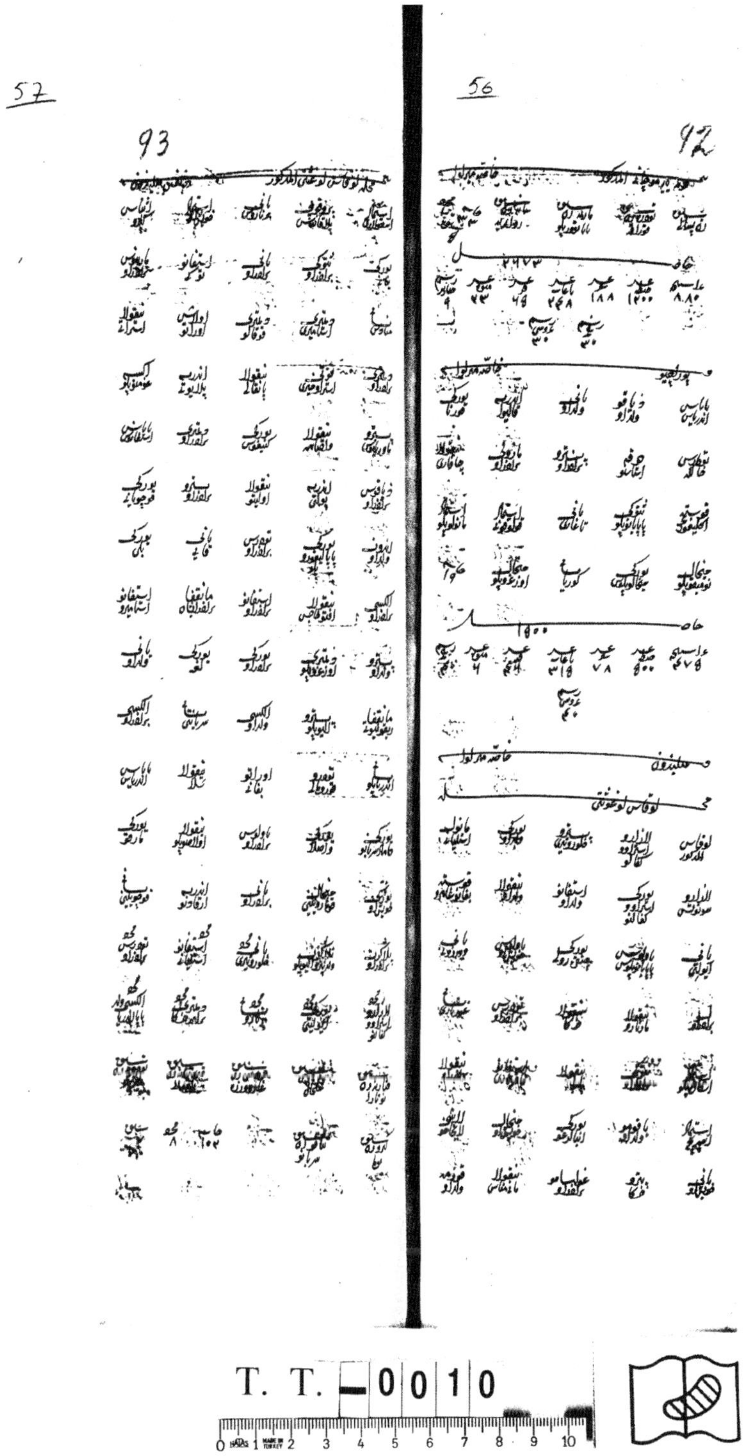
57
56
93
92
T. T. 0010

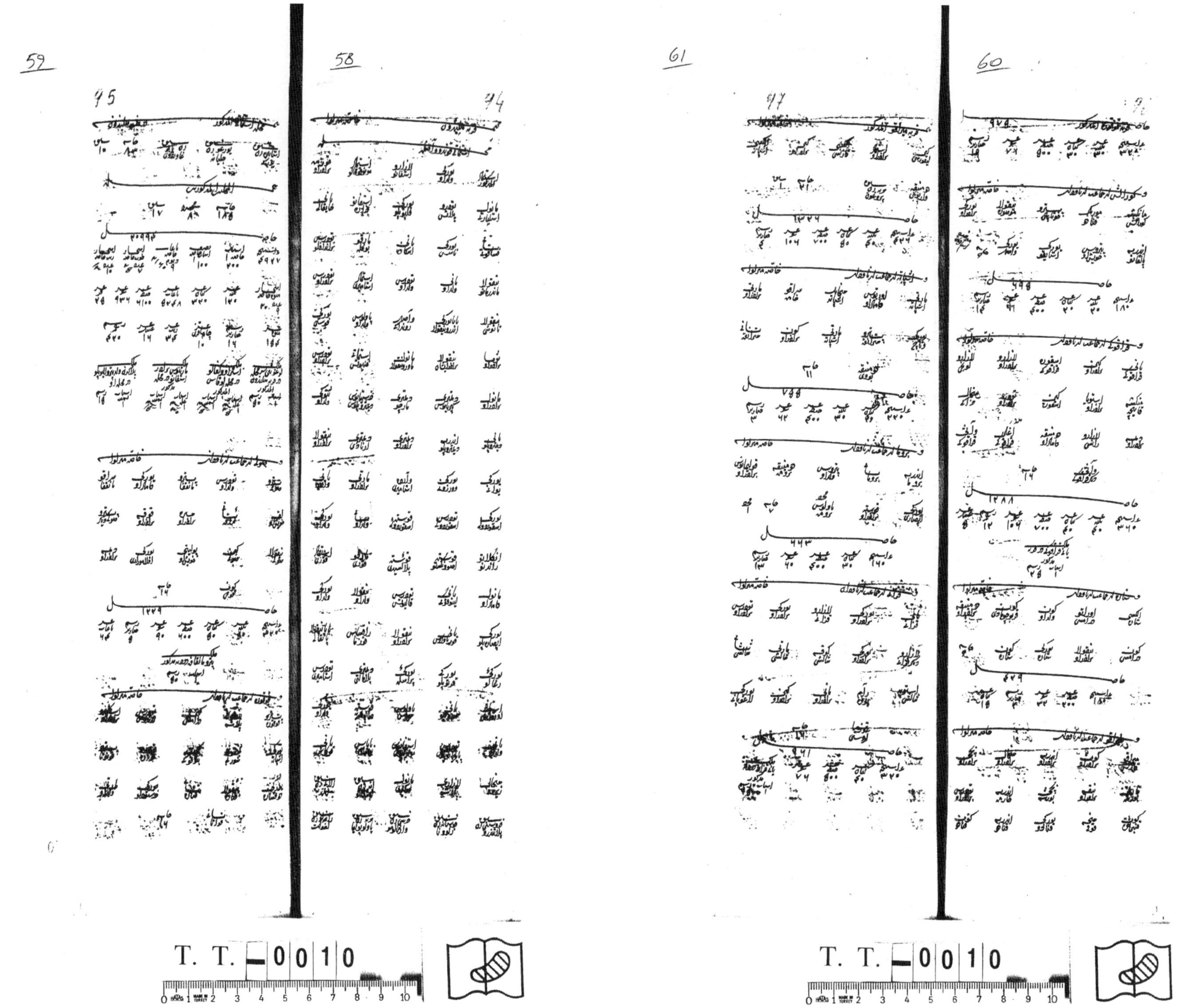
59
58
61
60
T. T. 0010
T. T. 0010

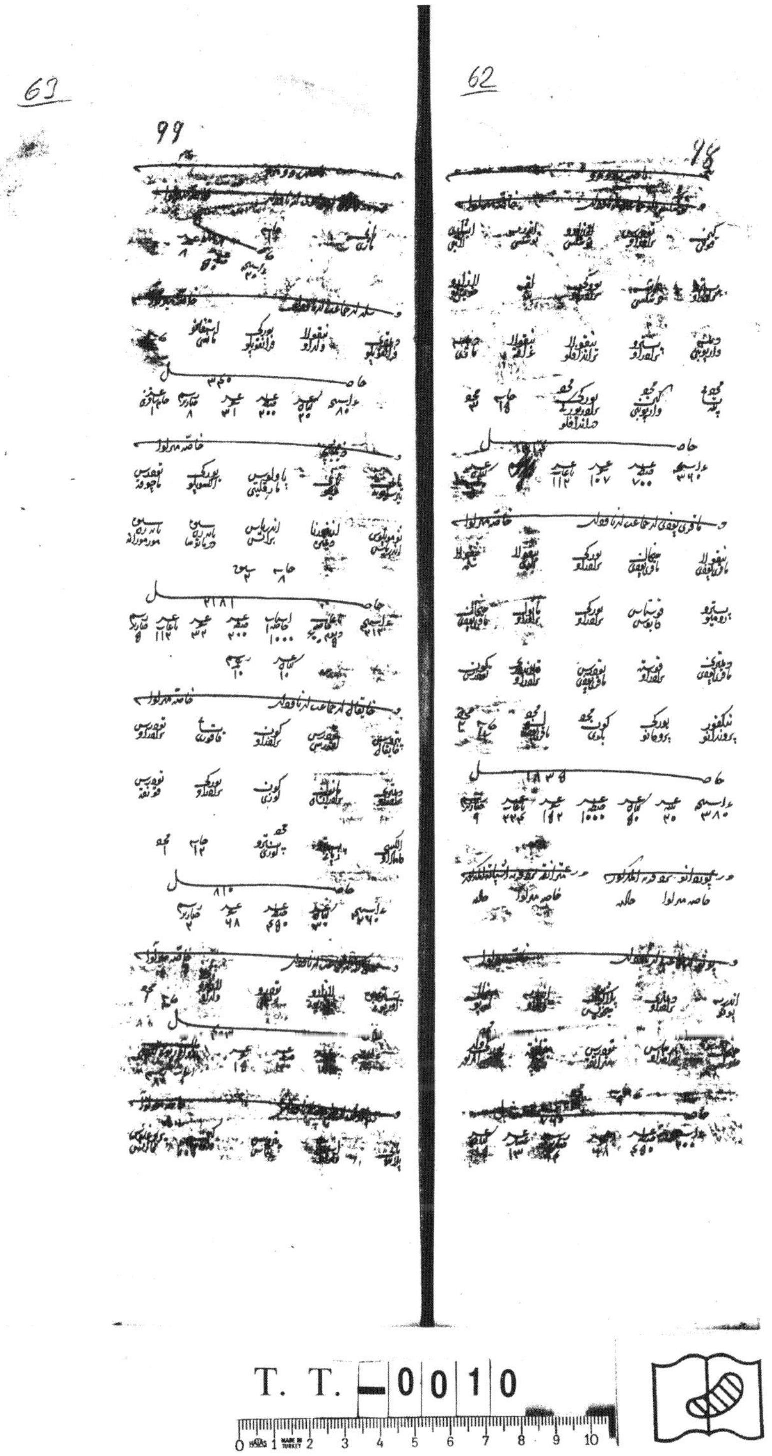
63
62
99
98
T. T. 0010

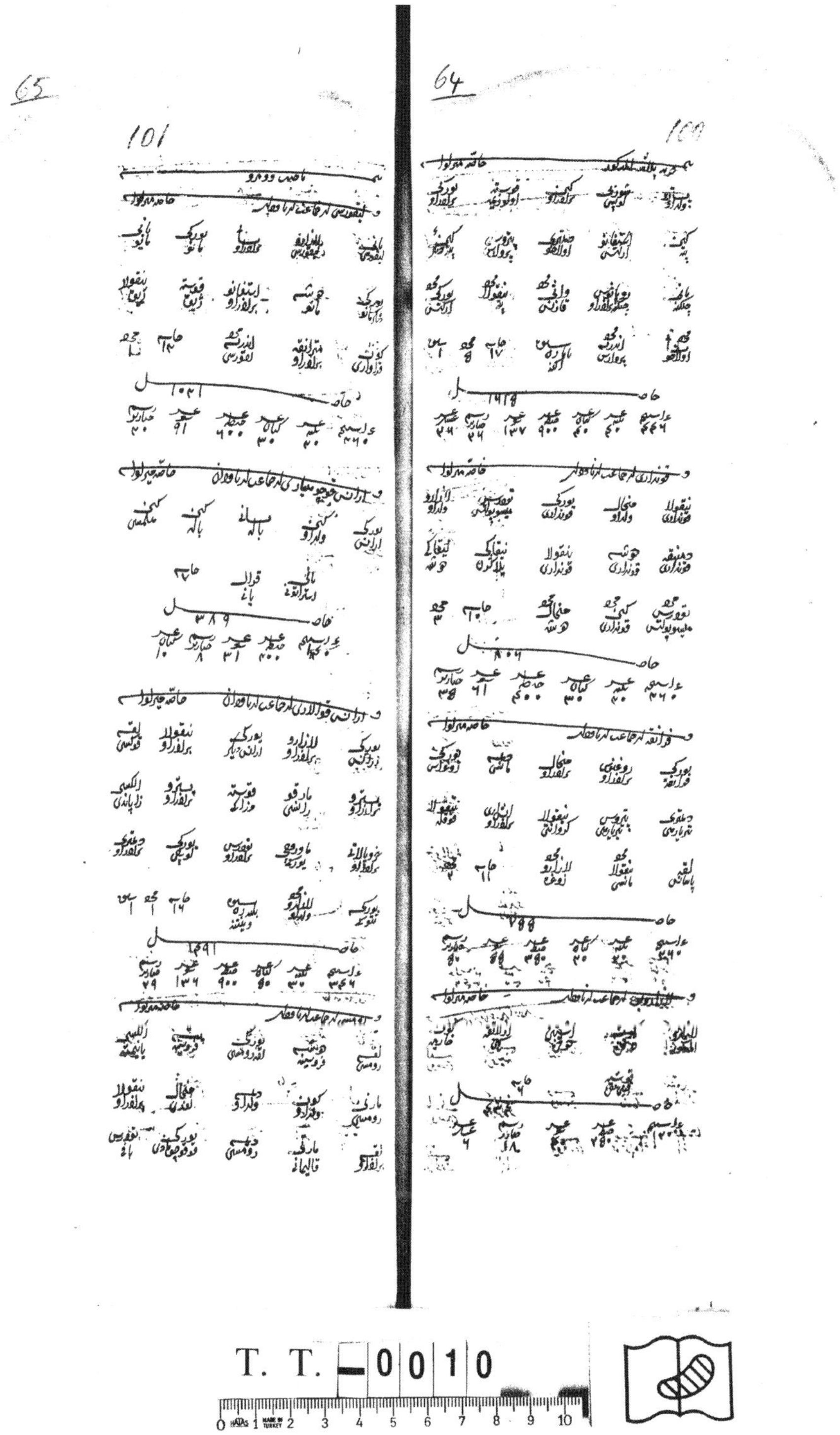
65
64
101
100
T. T. 0010

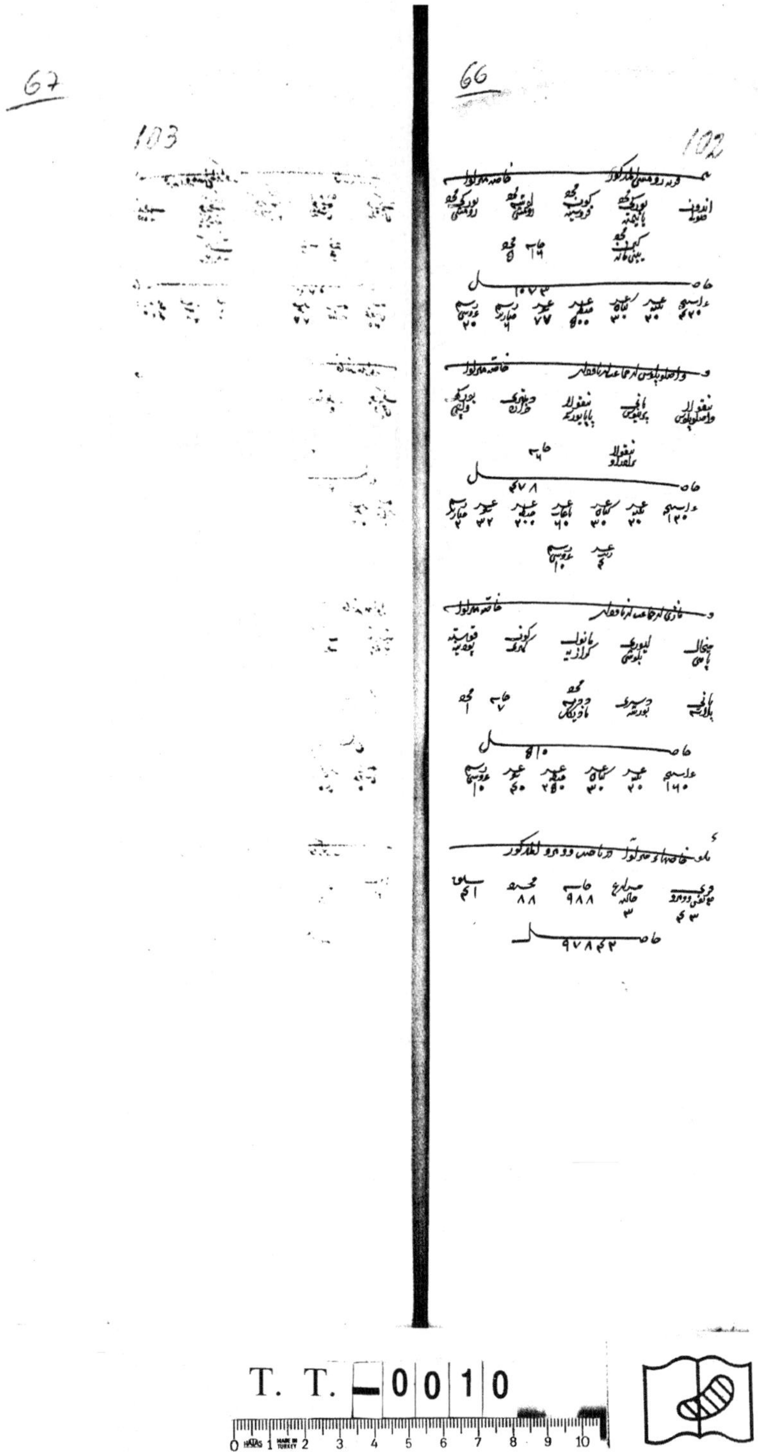
67
66
103
102
T. T. 0010

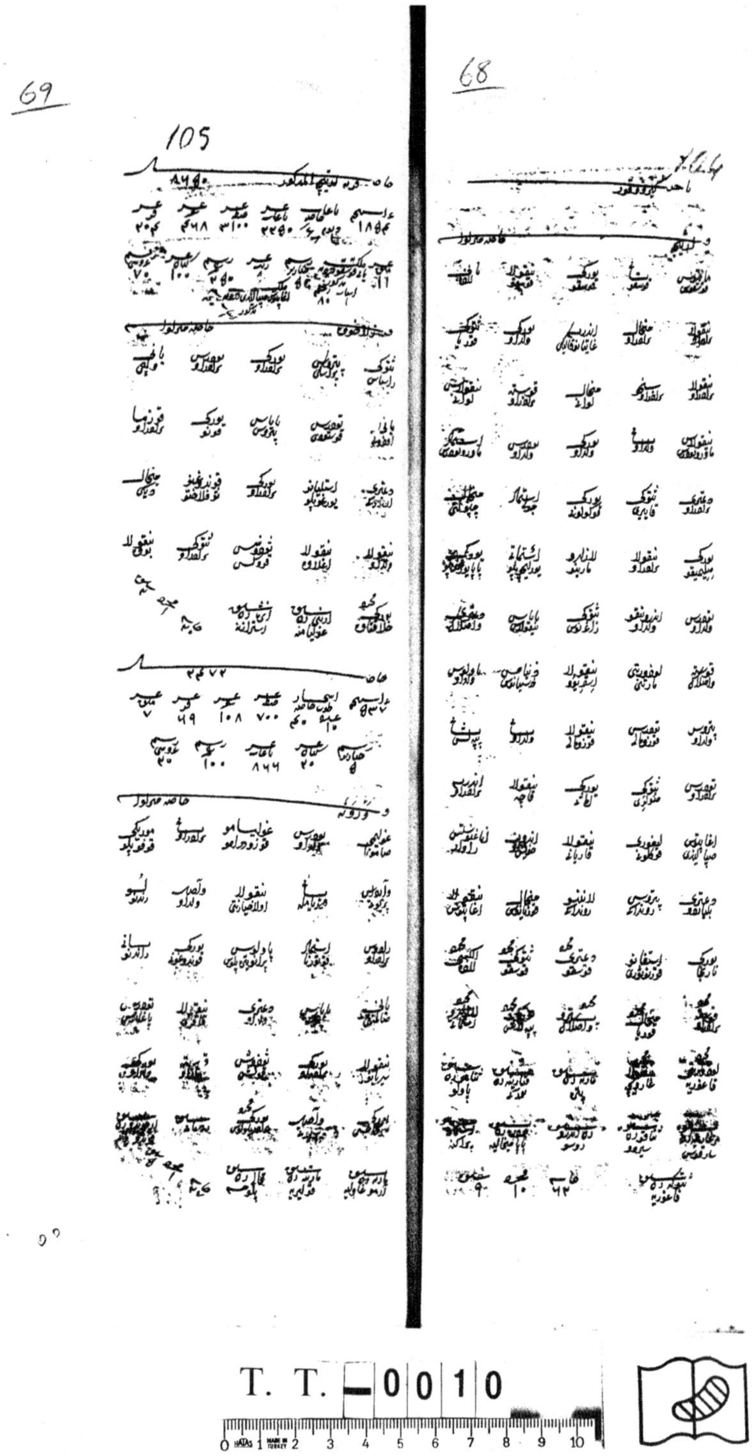
69
68
105
T. T. 0010

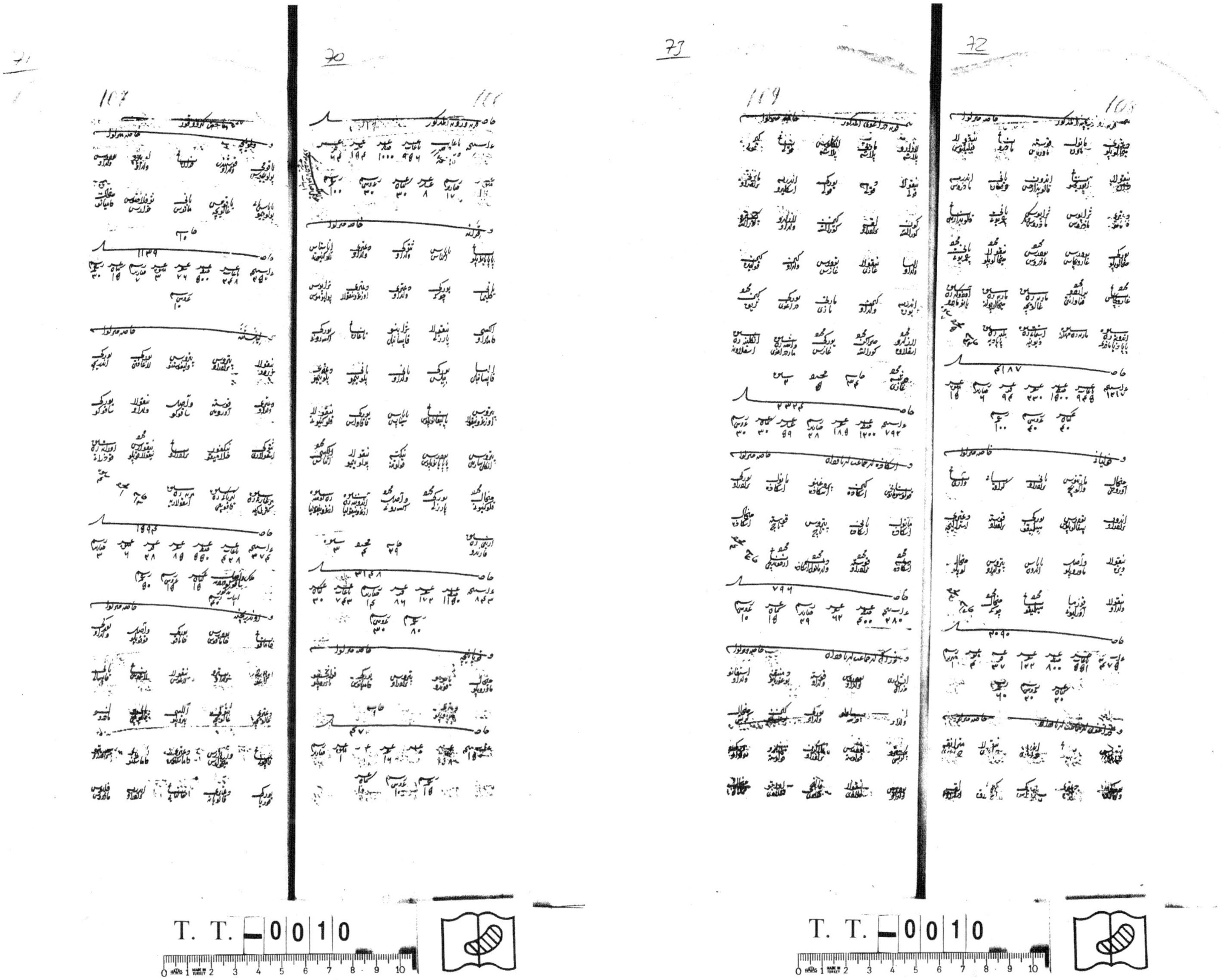
T. T. 0010
T. T. 0010

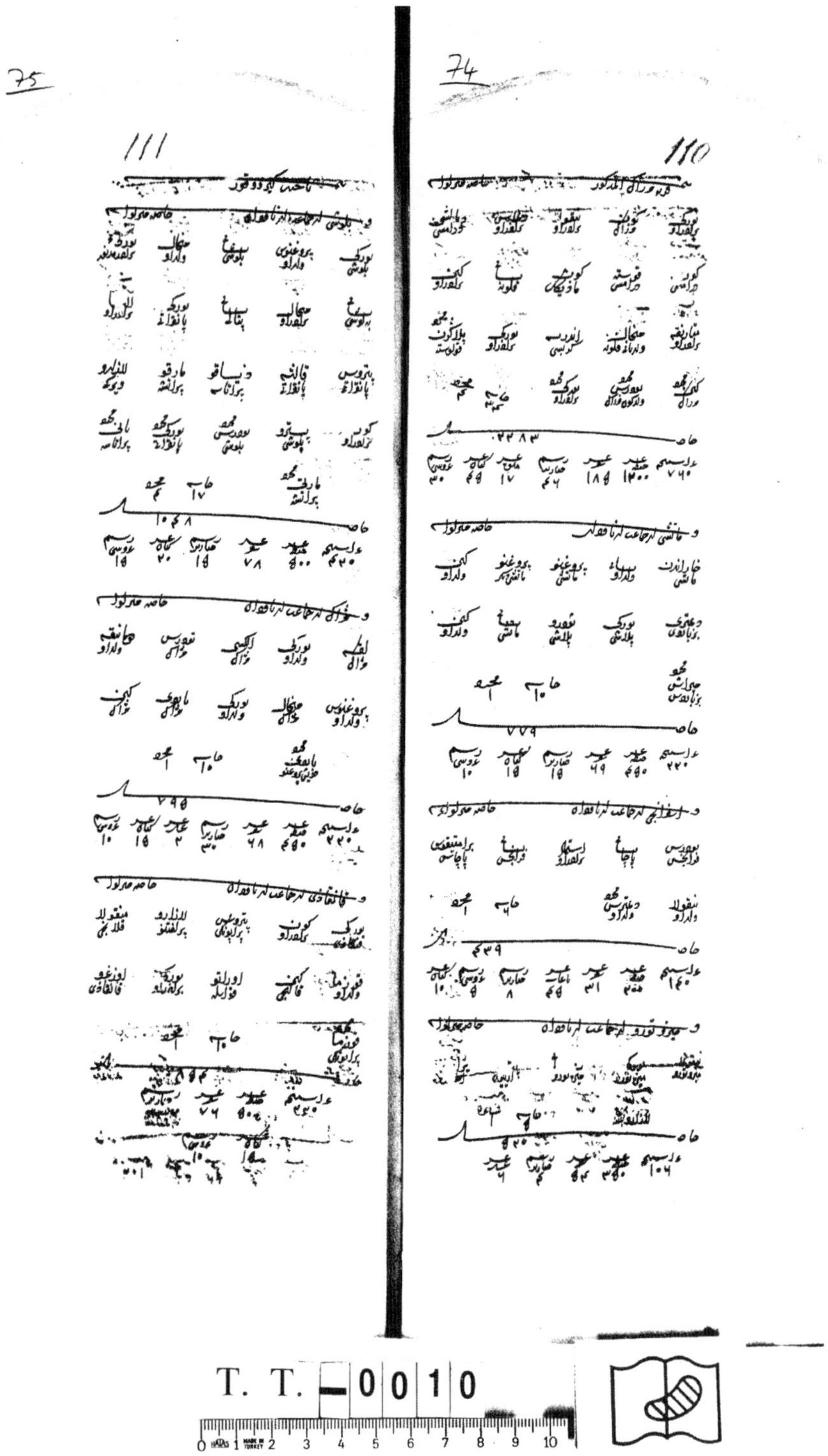
75
74
111
110
T. T. 0010

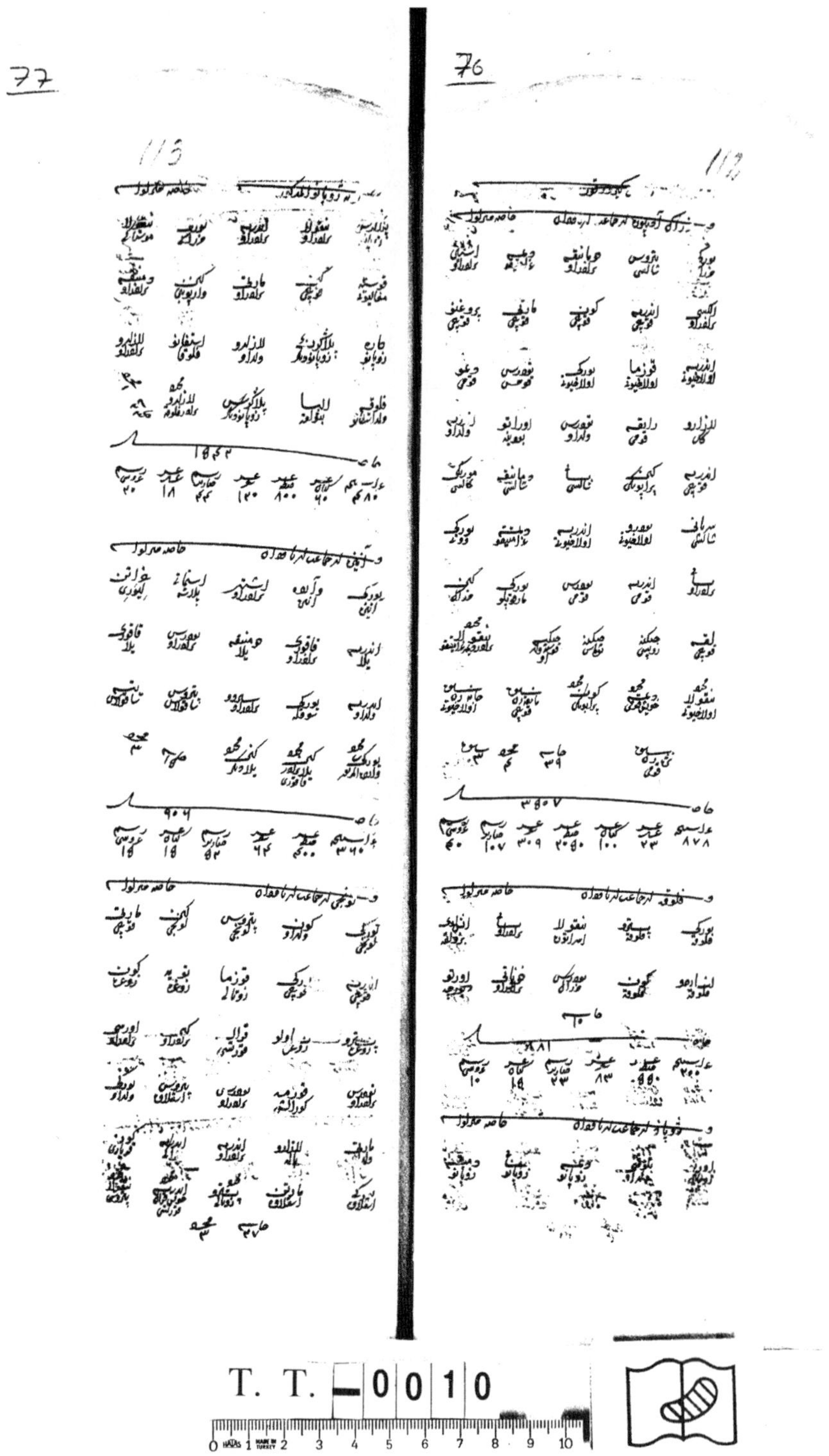
77
76
113
112
T. T. 0010

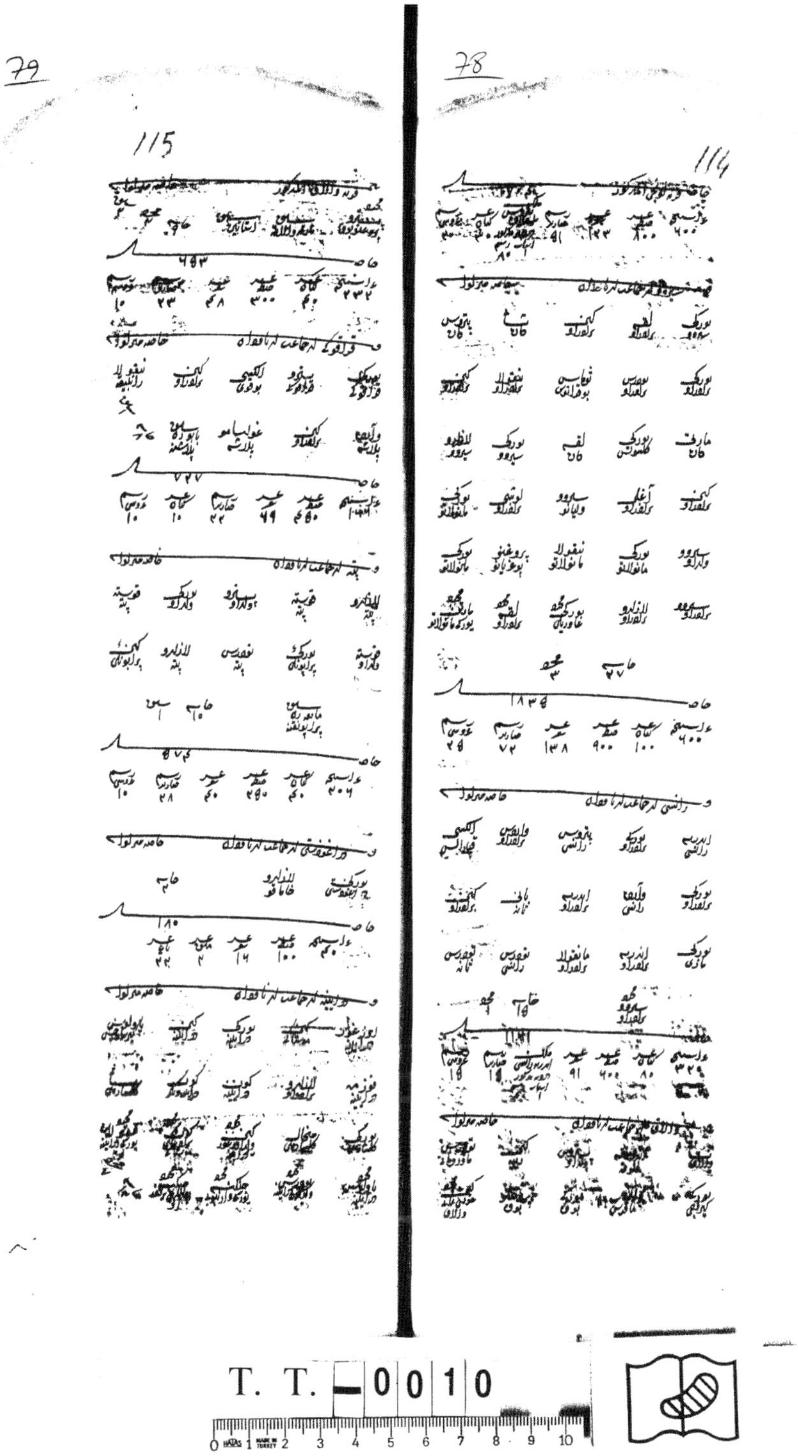
79
78
115
114
T. T. 0010

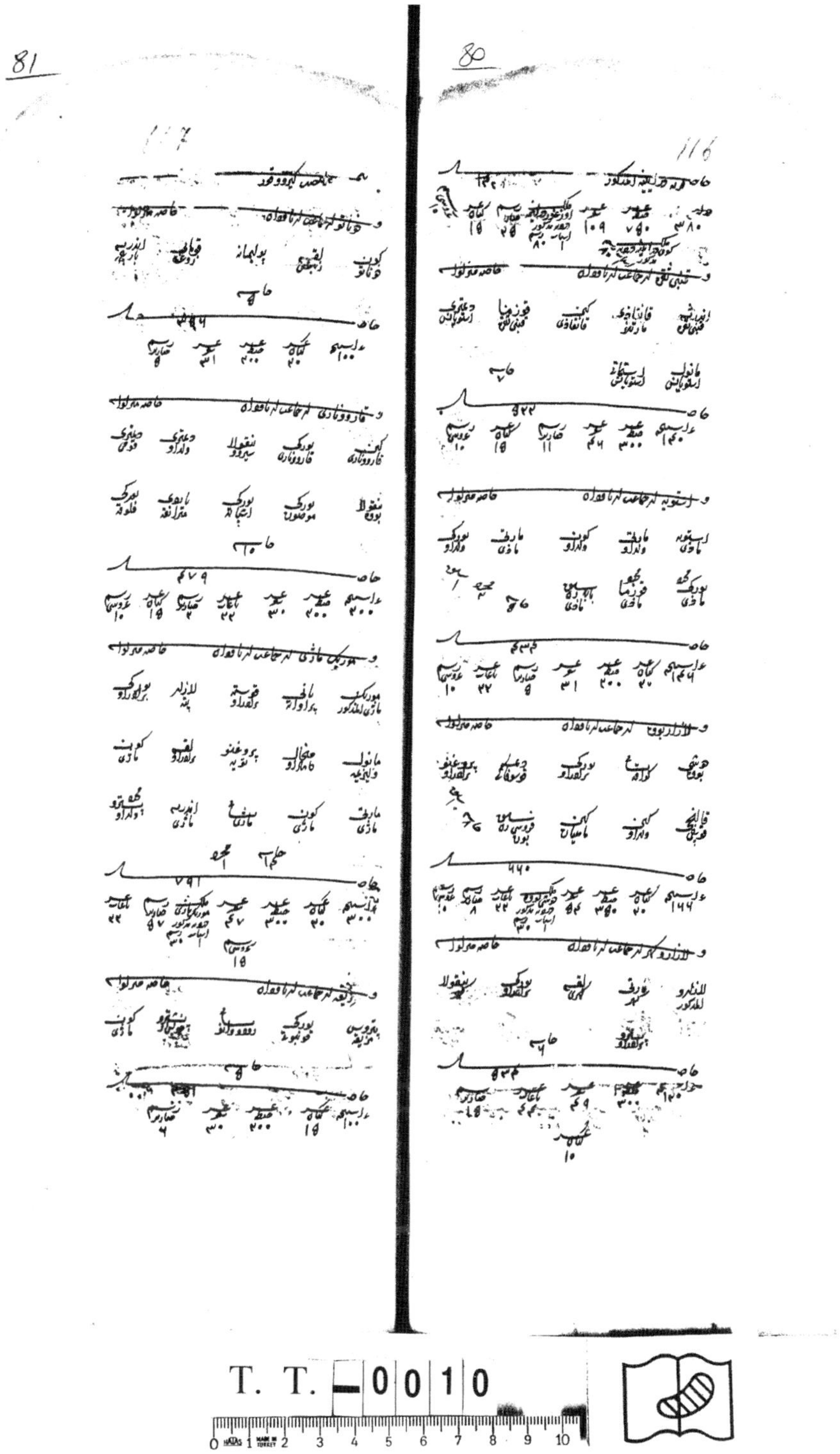
81
80
116
T. T. 0010

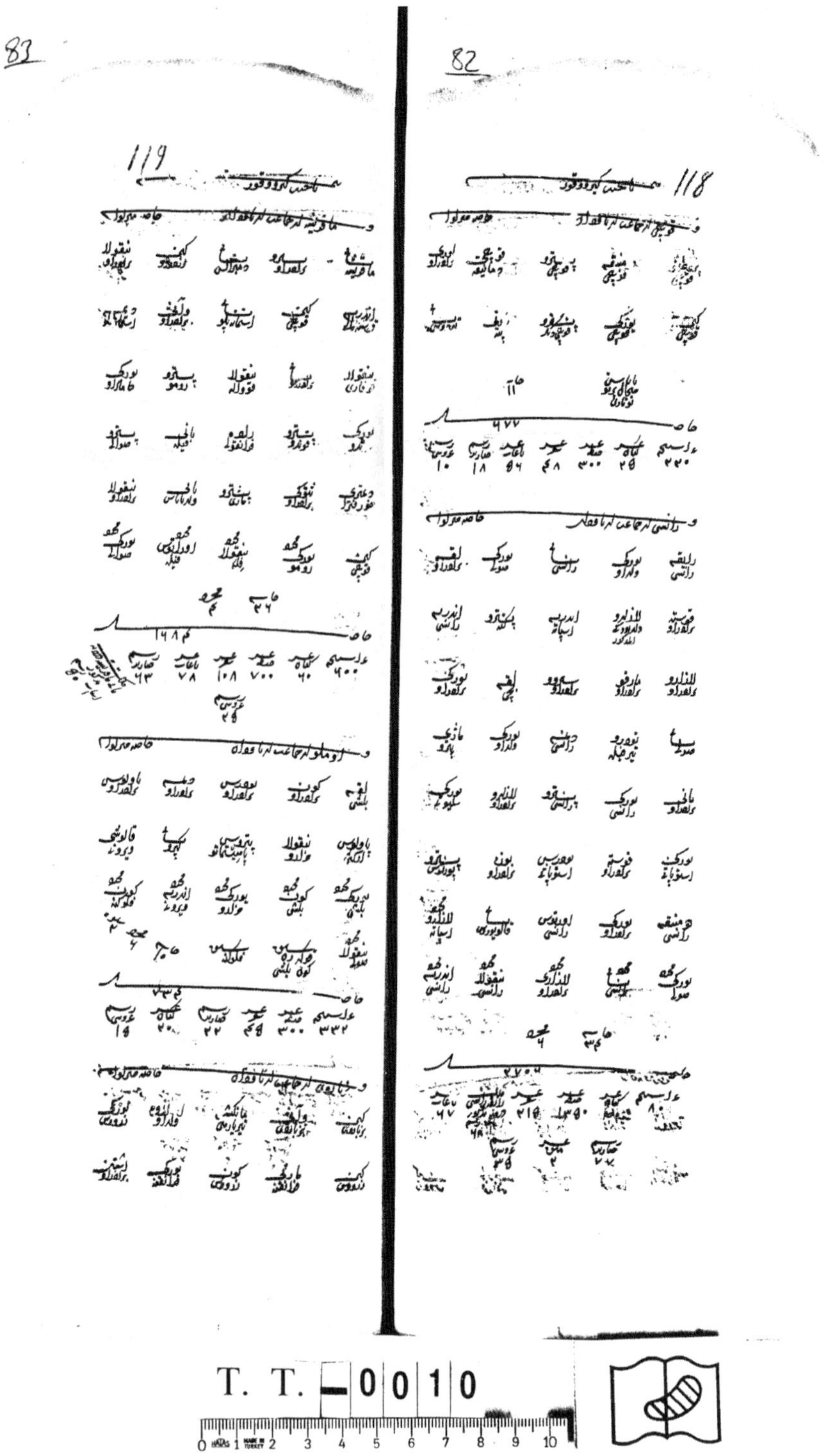
83
82
119
118
T. T. 0010

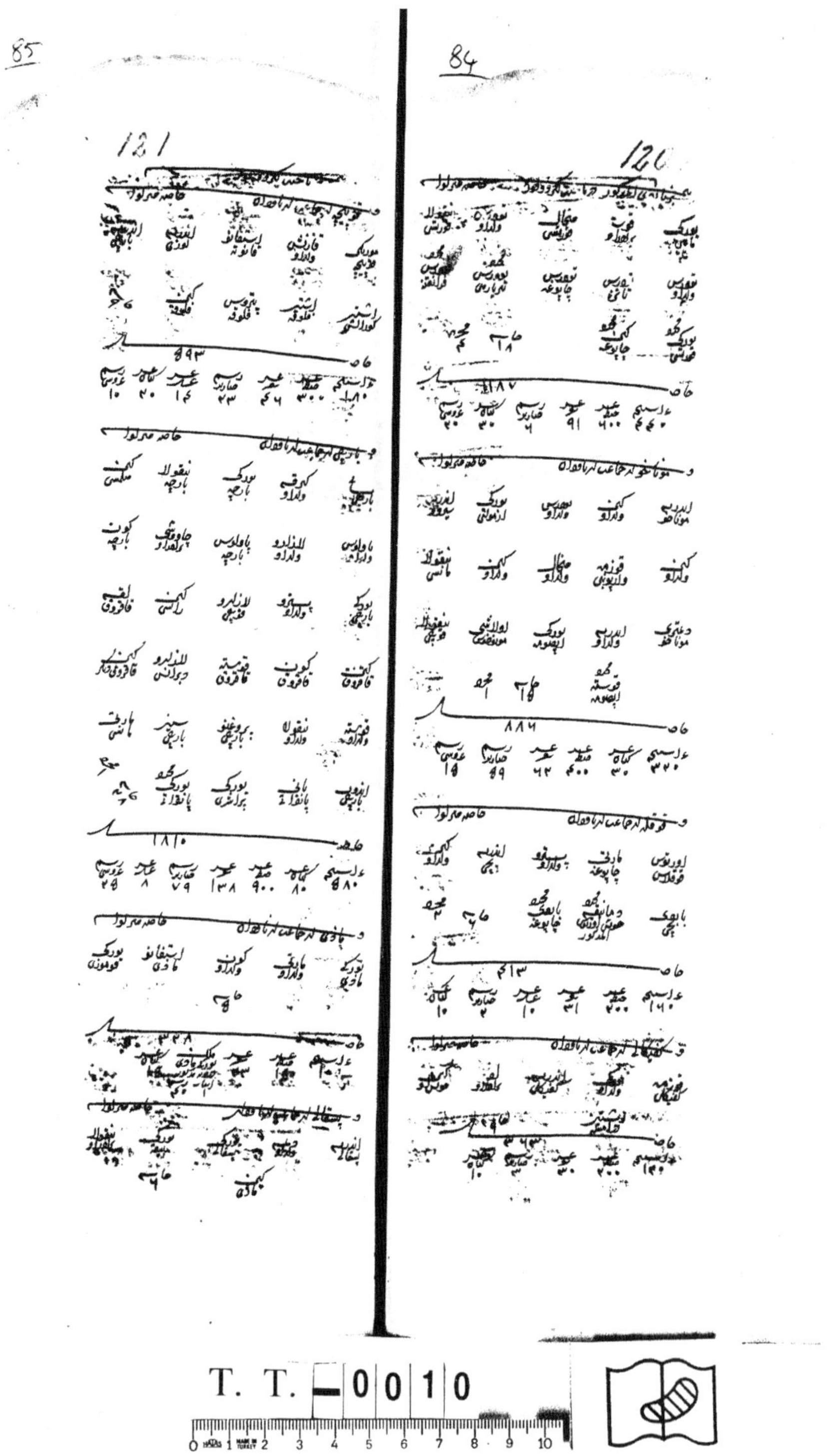
85
84
121
120
T. T. 0010

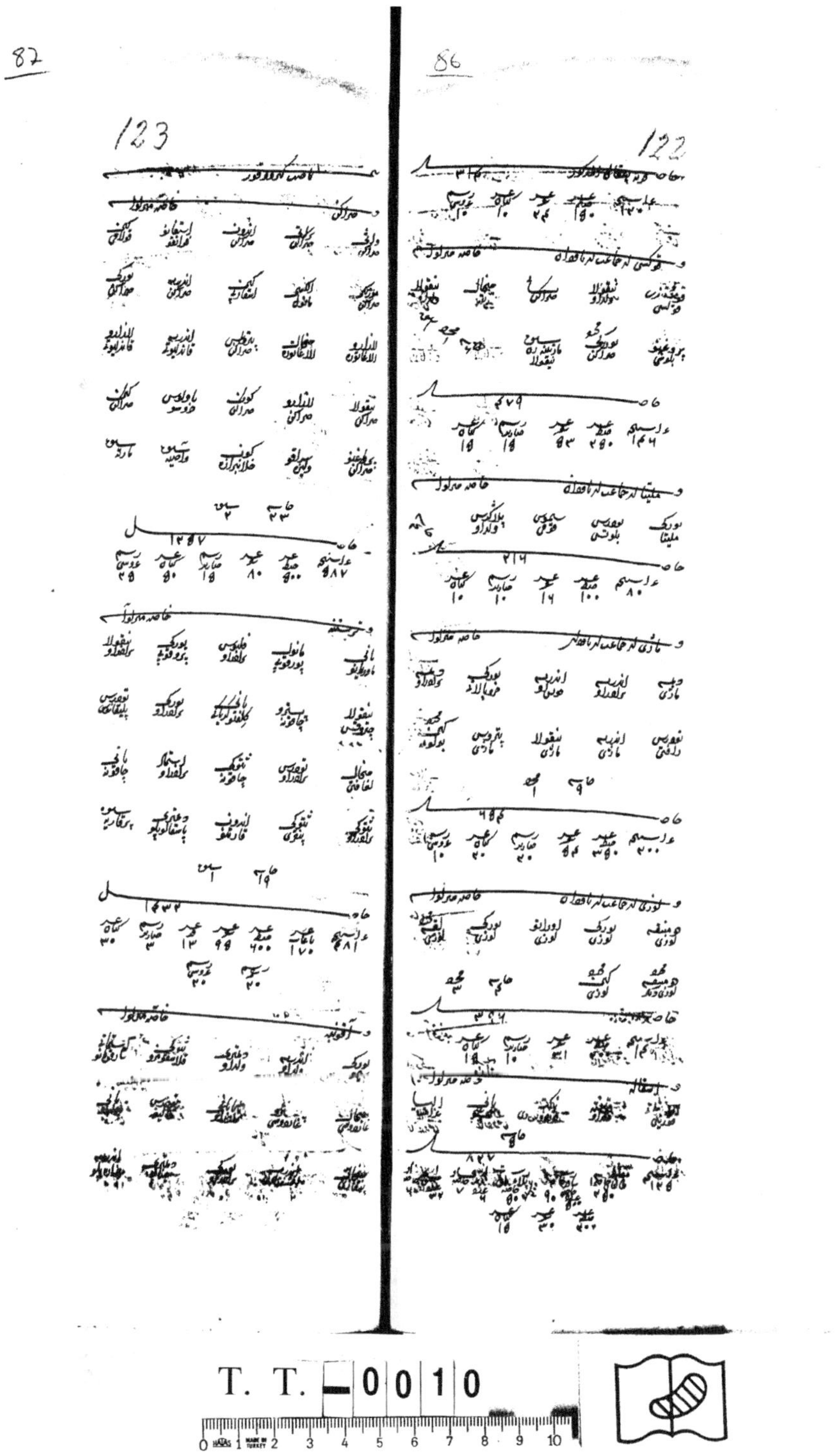
87
86
123
122
T. T. 0010

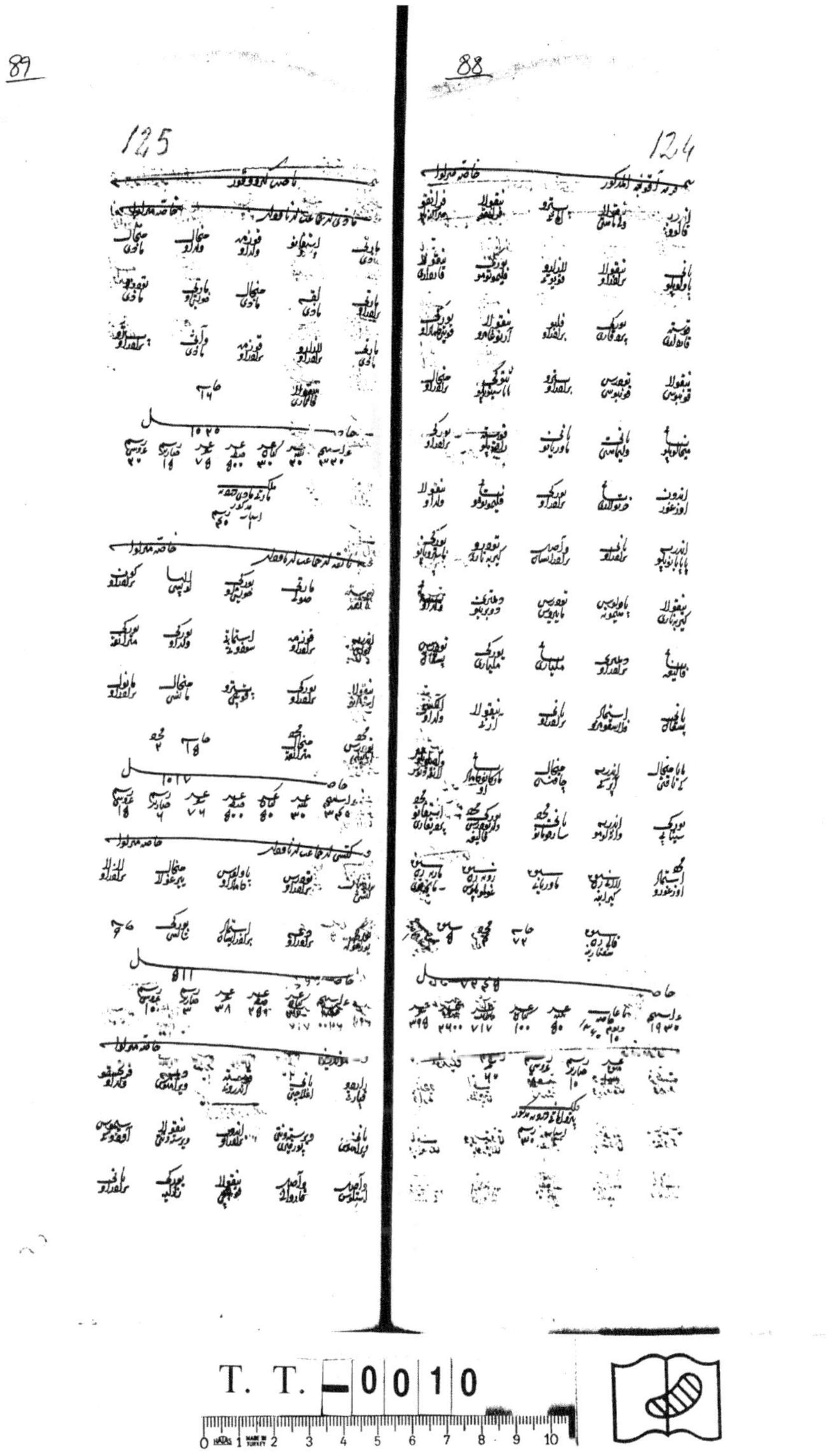
89
88
125
124
T. T. 0010

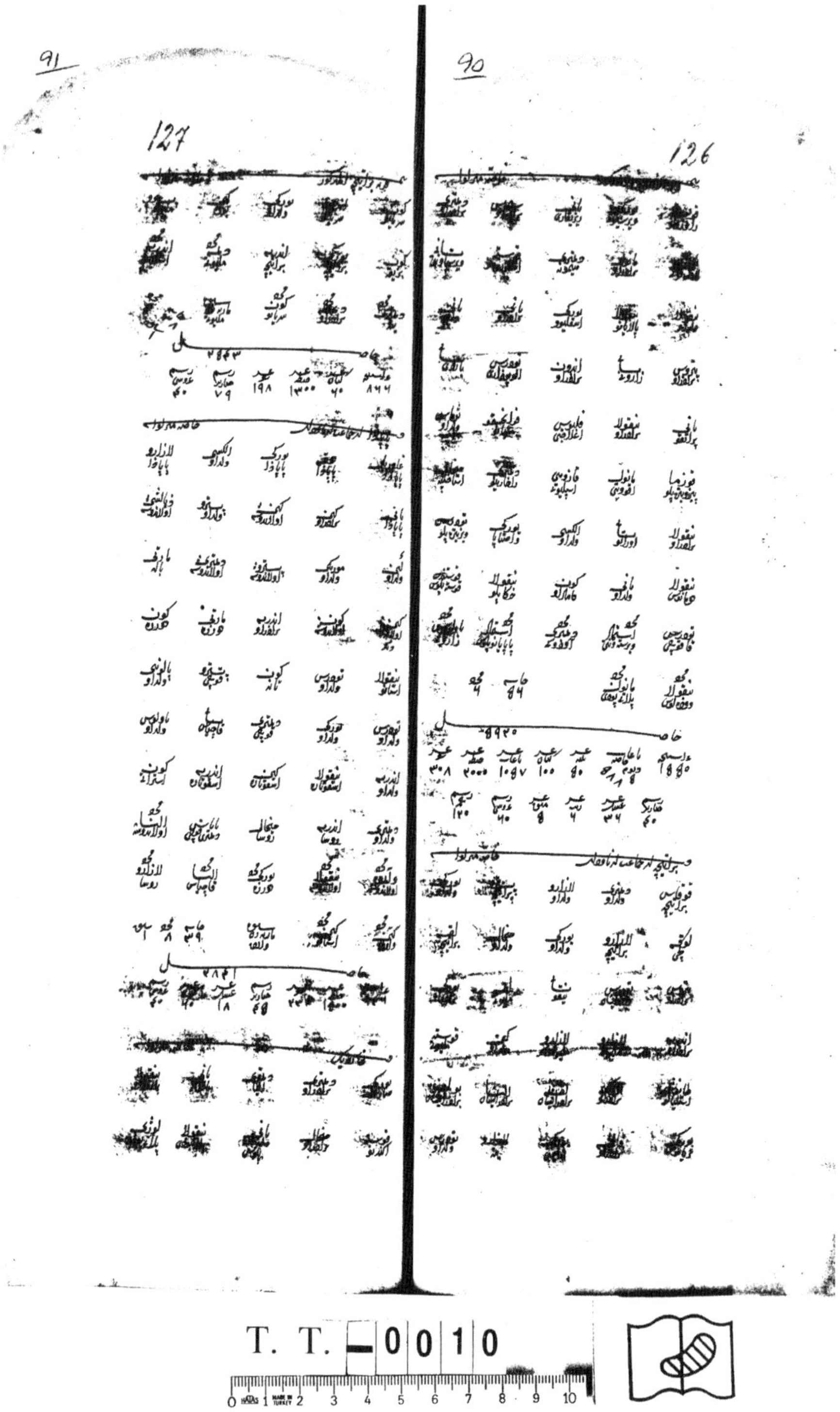
T. T. 0010

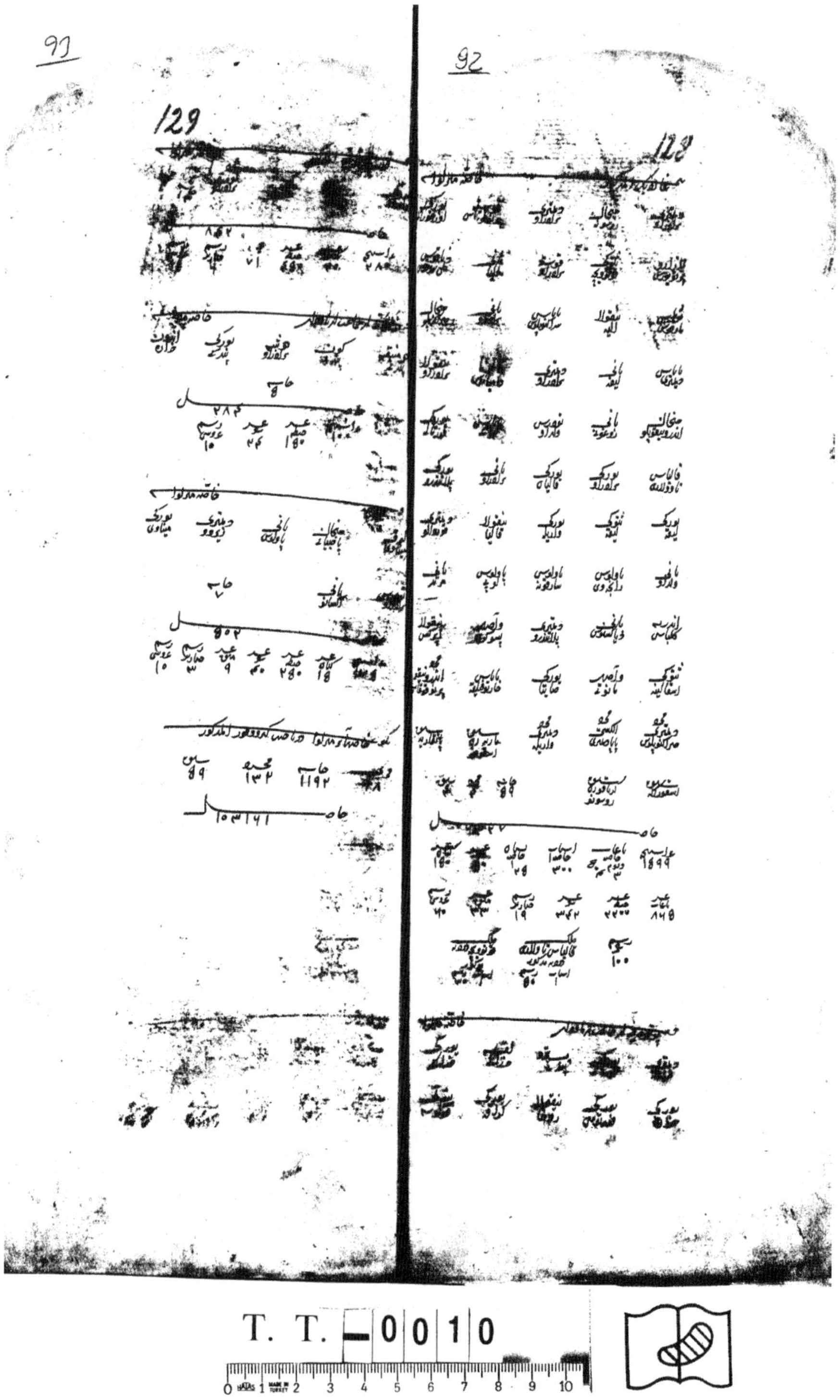
T. T. 0010

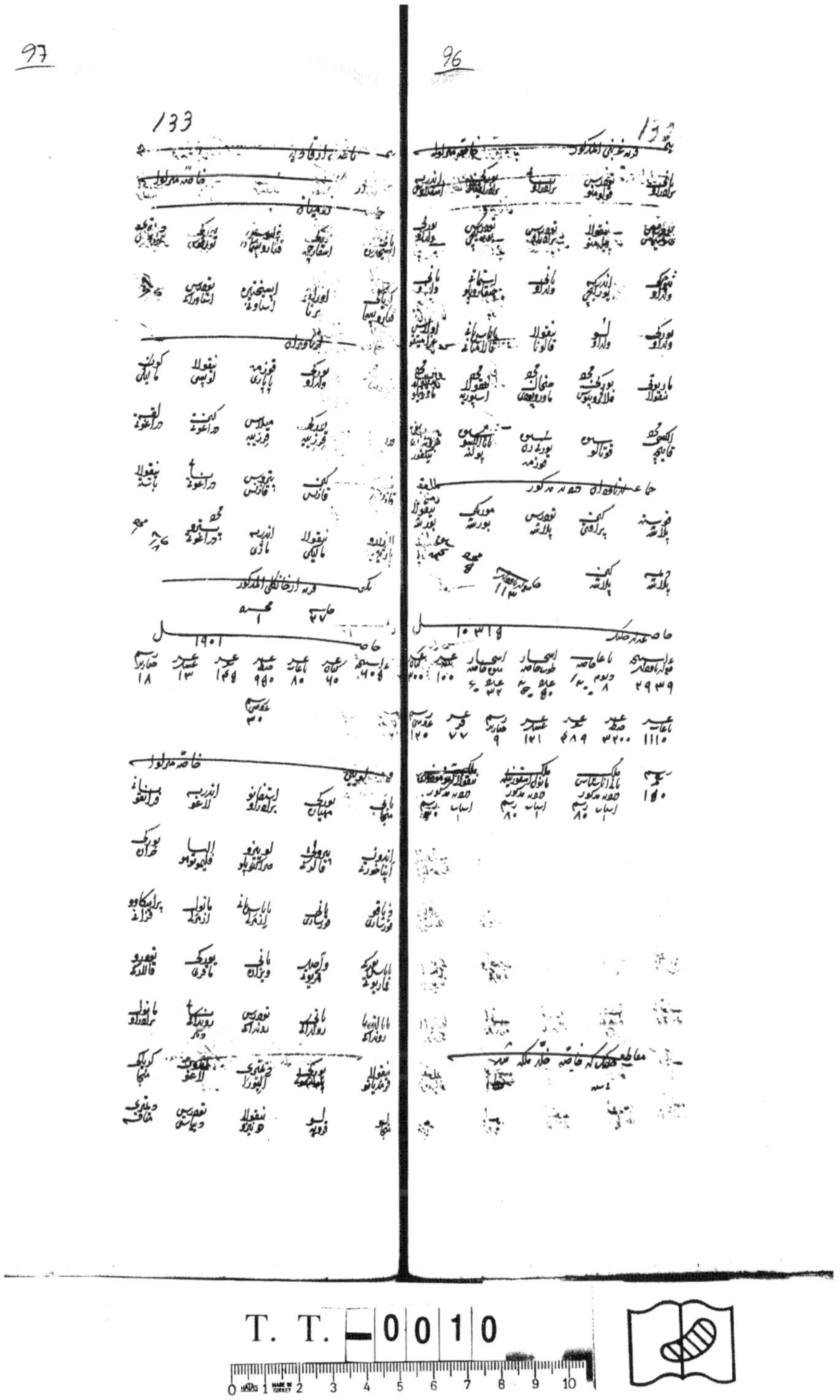

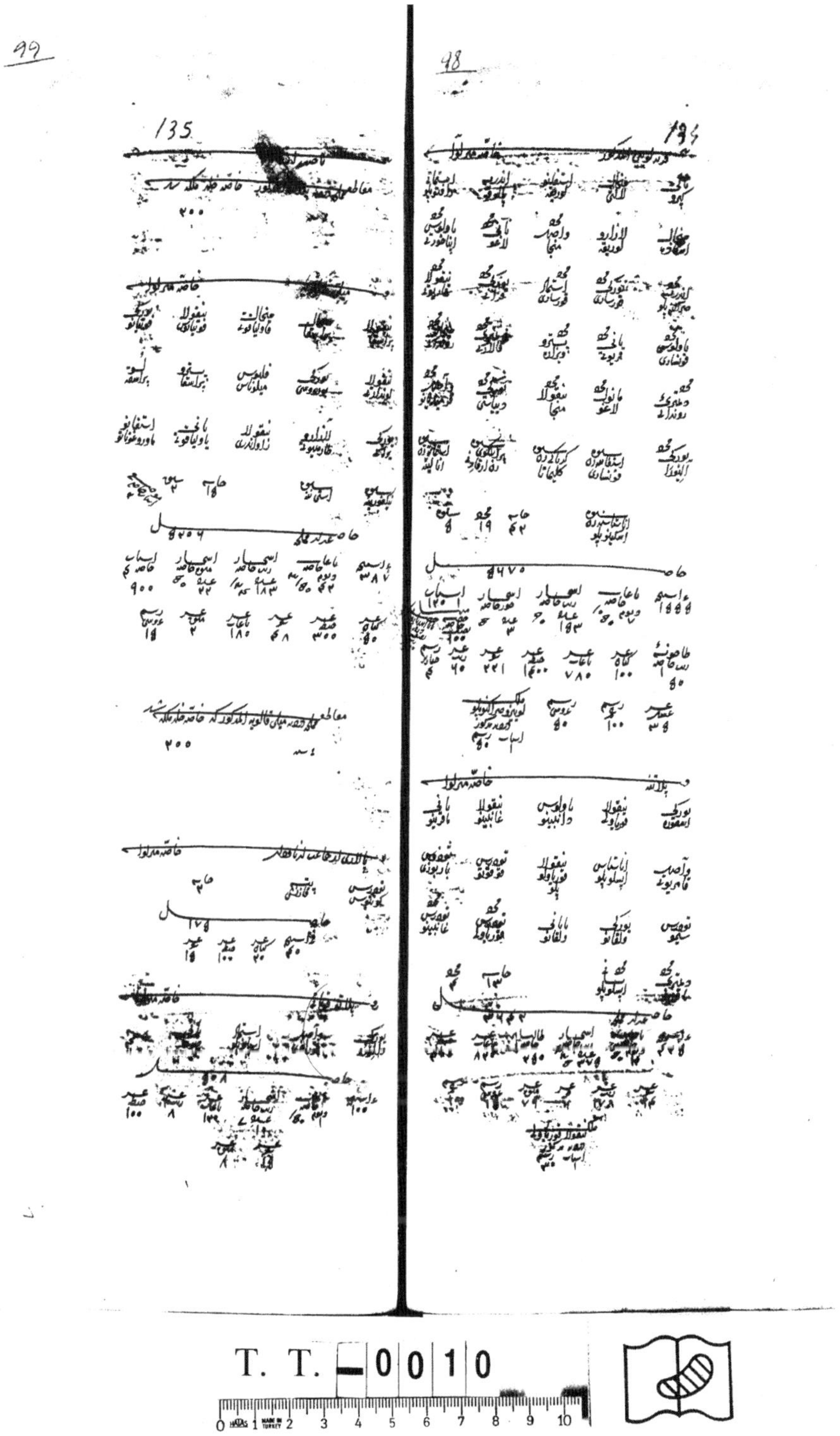

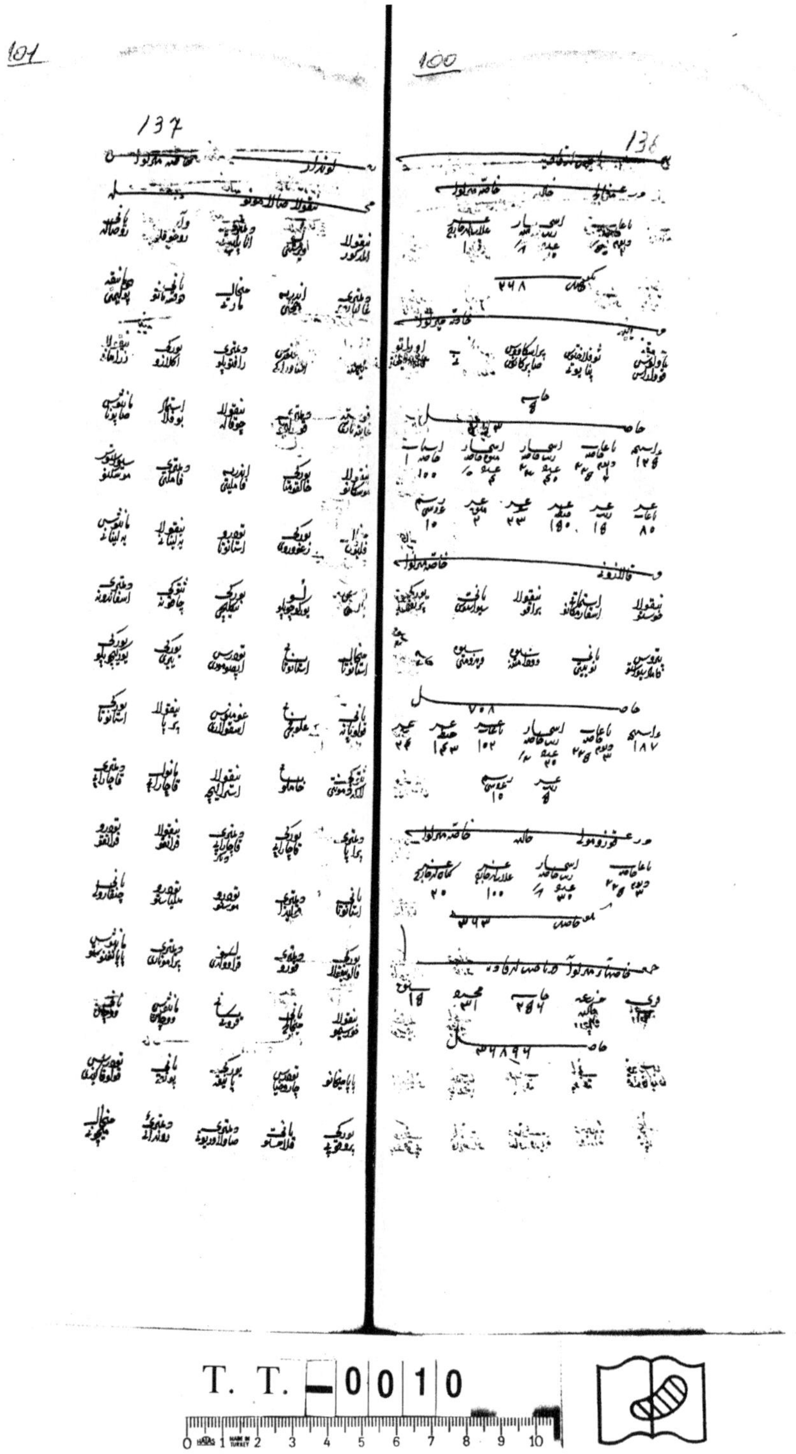
101
100
137
136
T. T. 0010

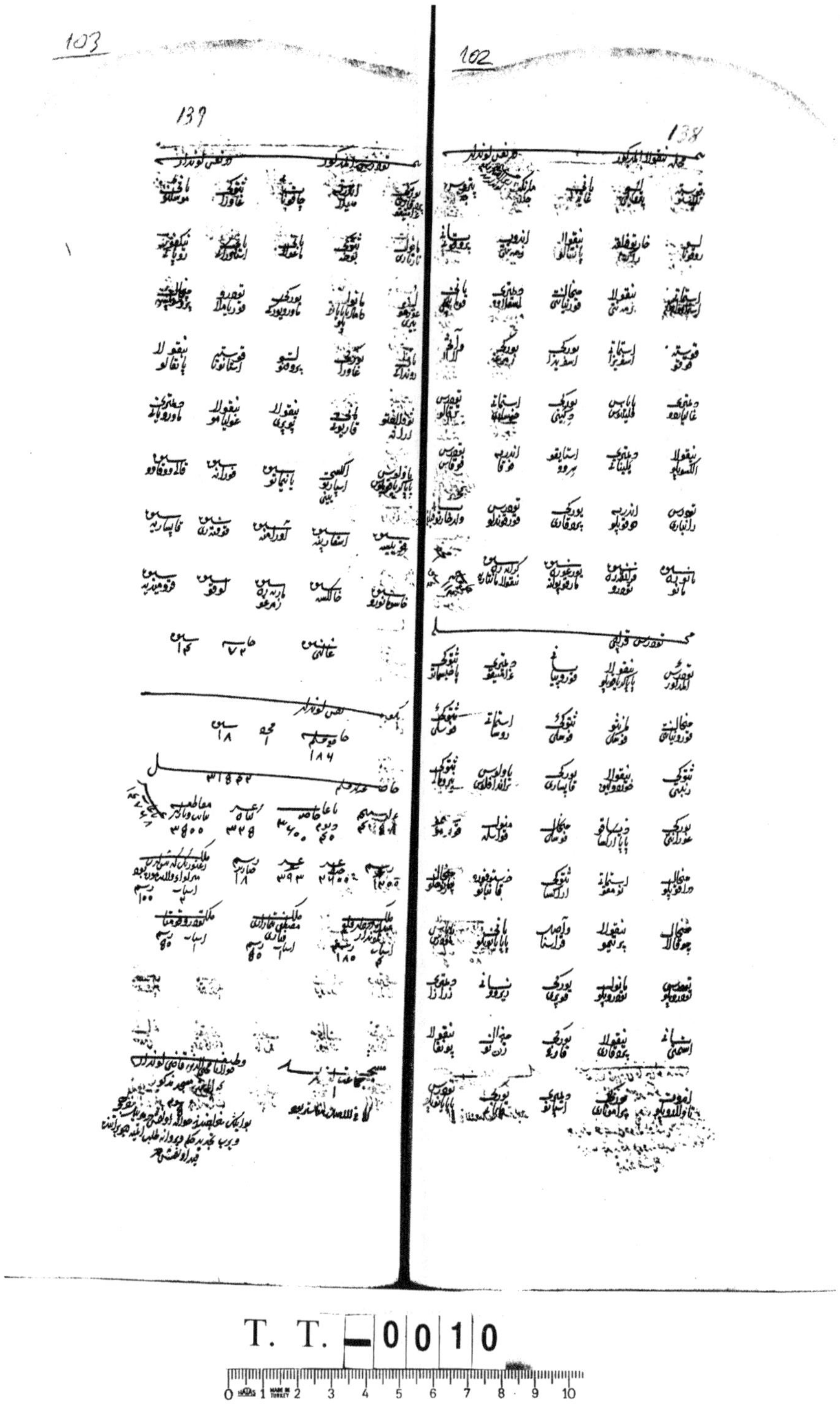
103
102
139
138
T. T. 0010

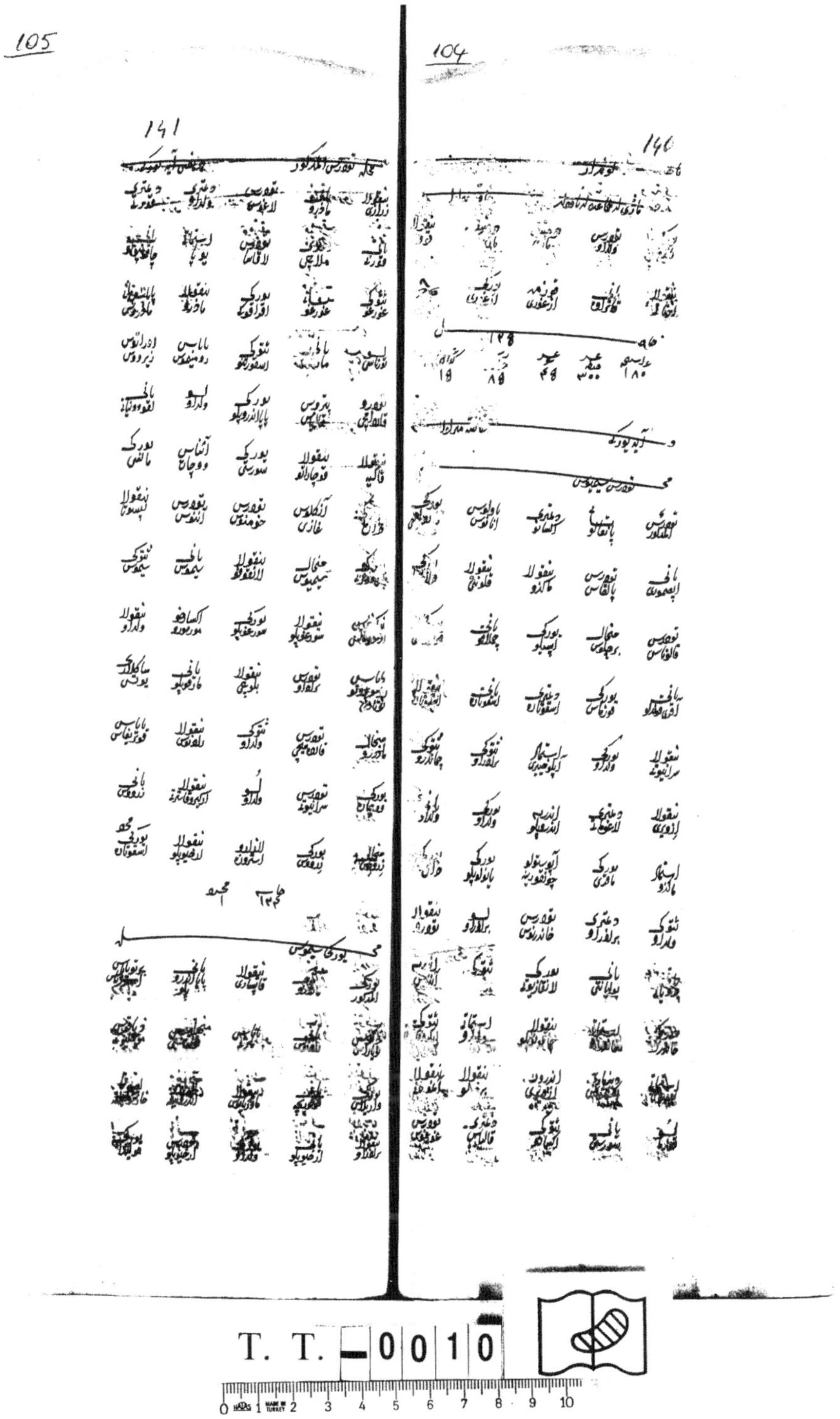
T. T. 0010

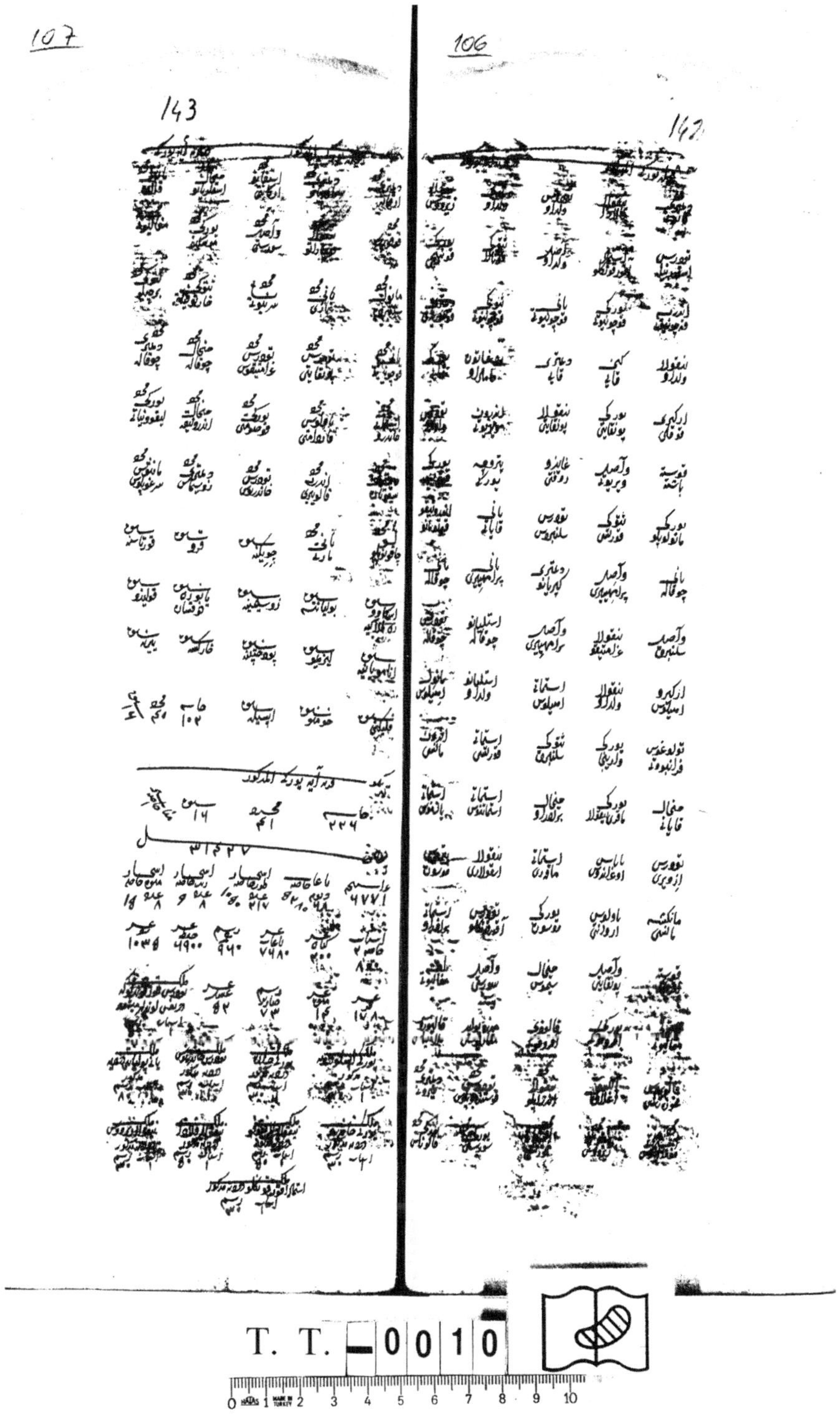
T. T. 0010

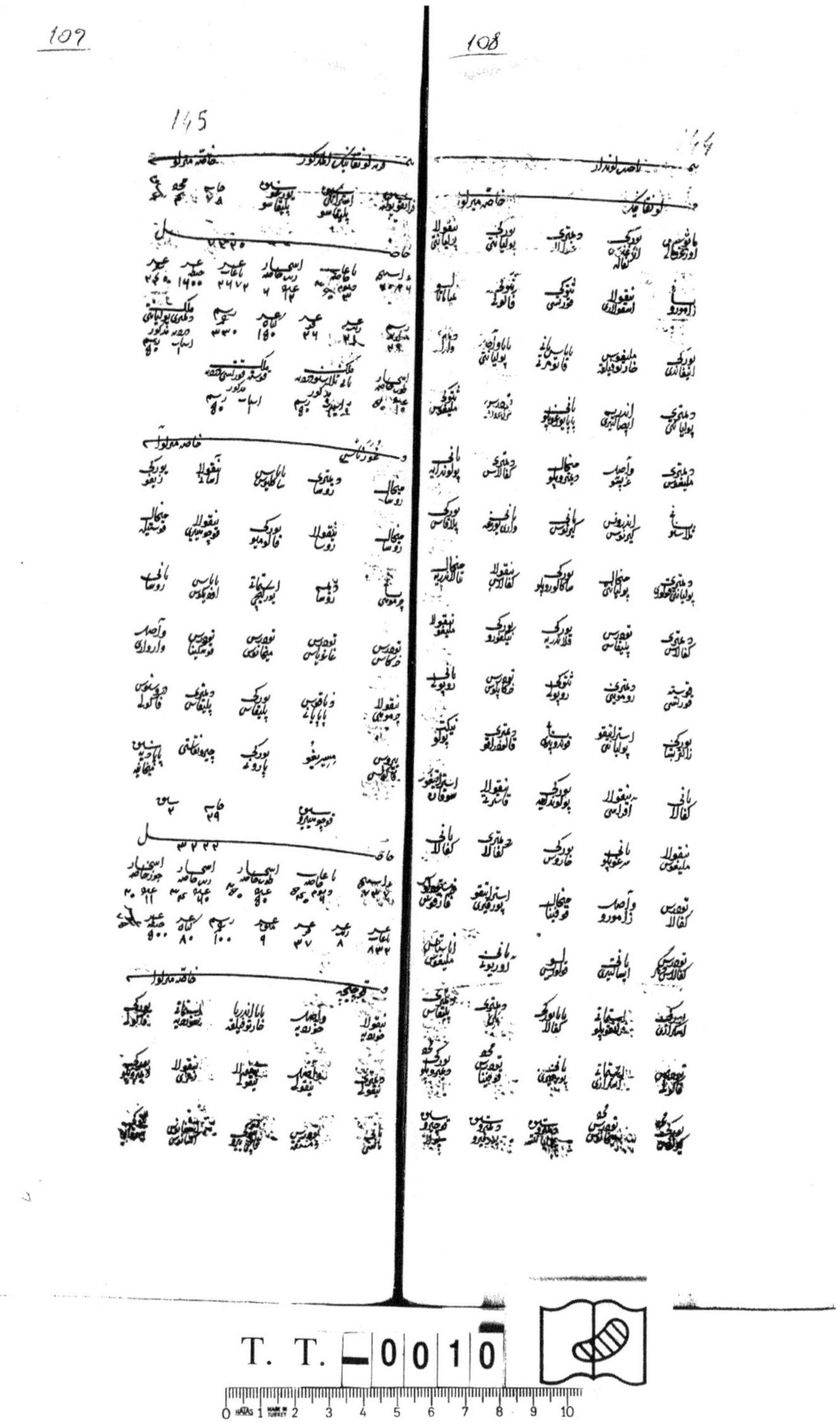
107 108 145 144

T. T. 0010

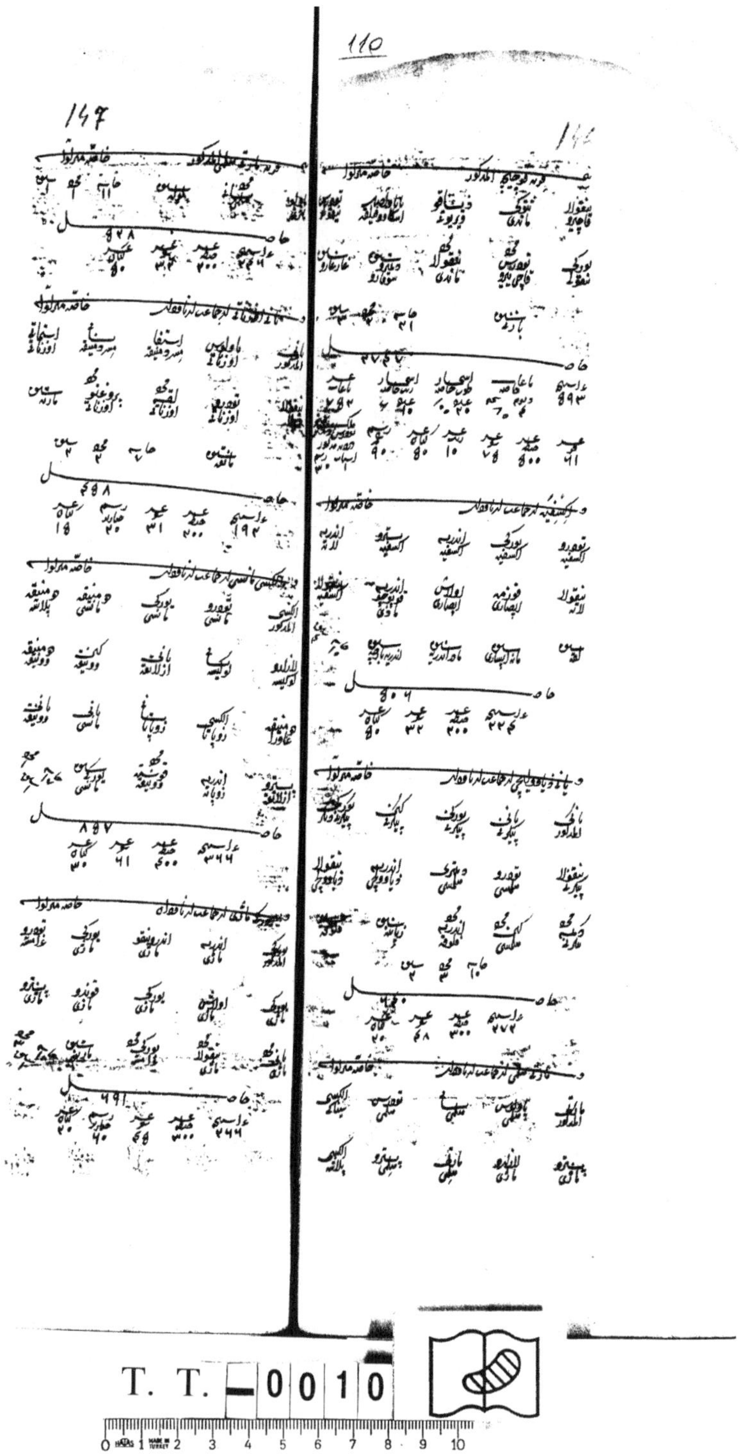
111 110 147 146

T. T. 0010

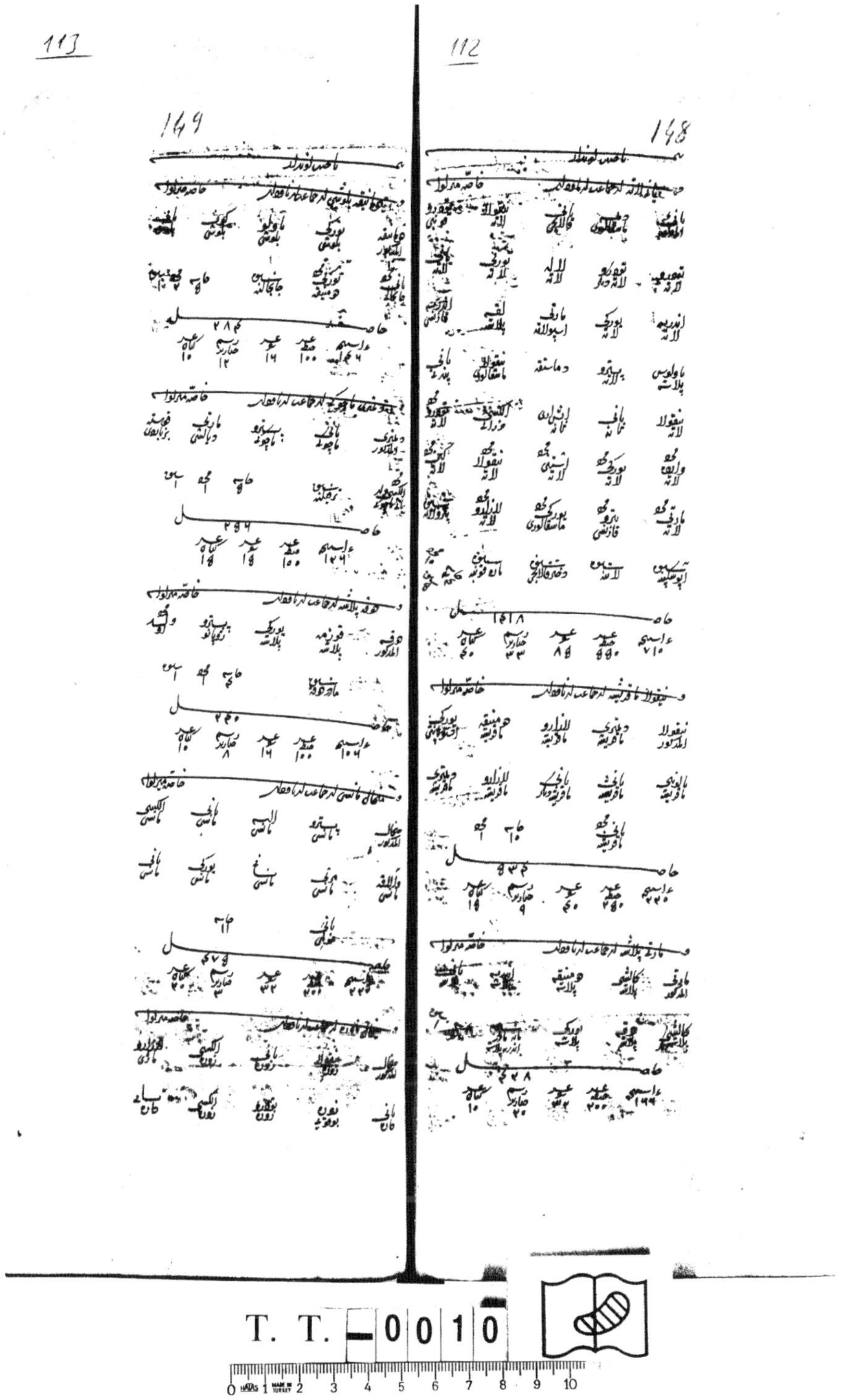
113
112
149
148
T. T. 0010

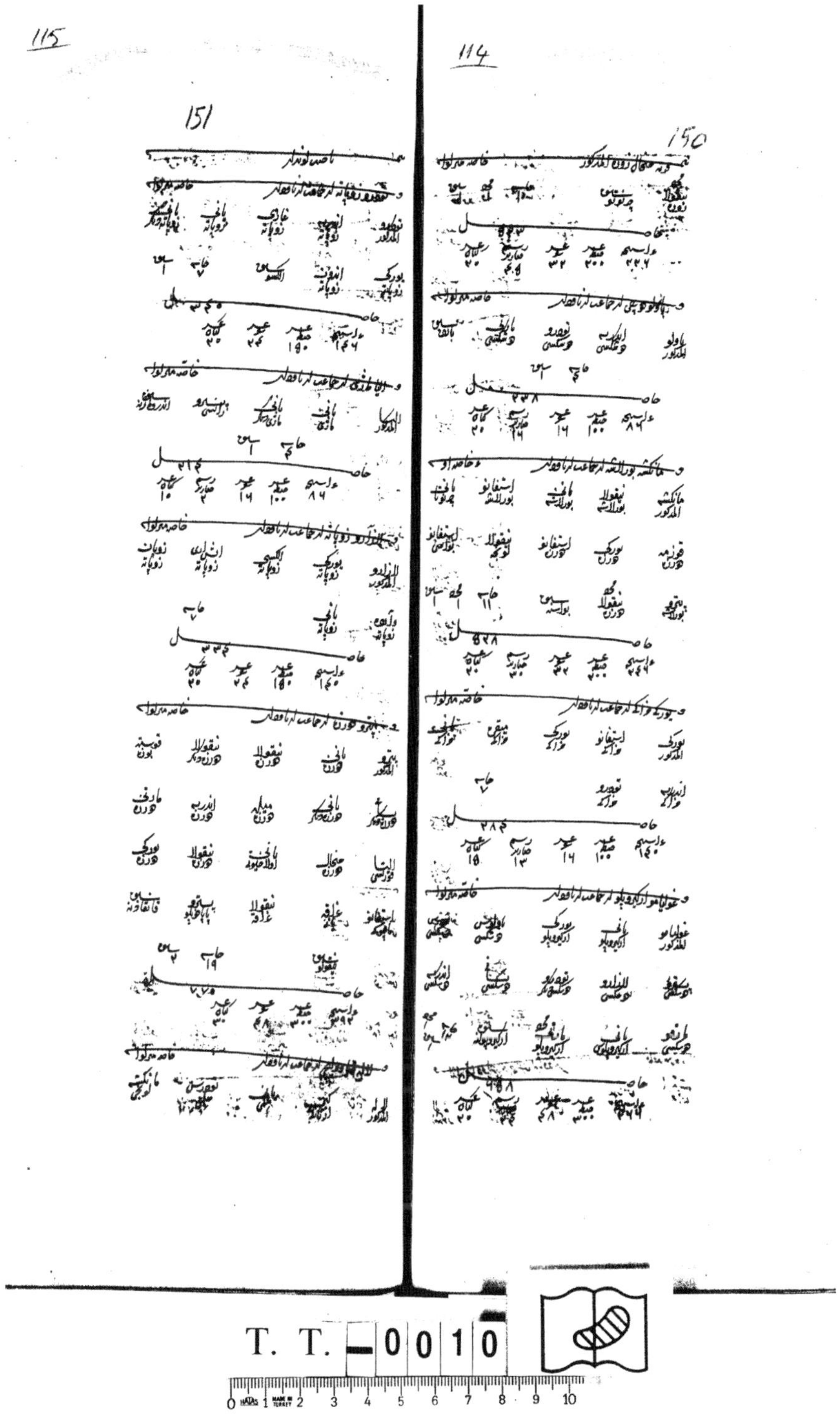
115
114
151
150
T. T. 0010

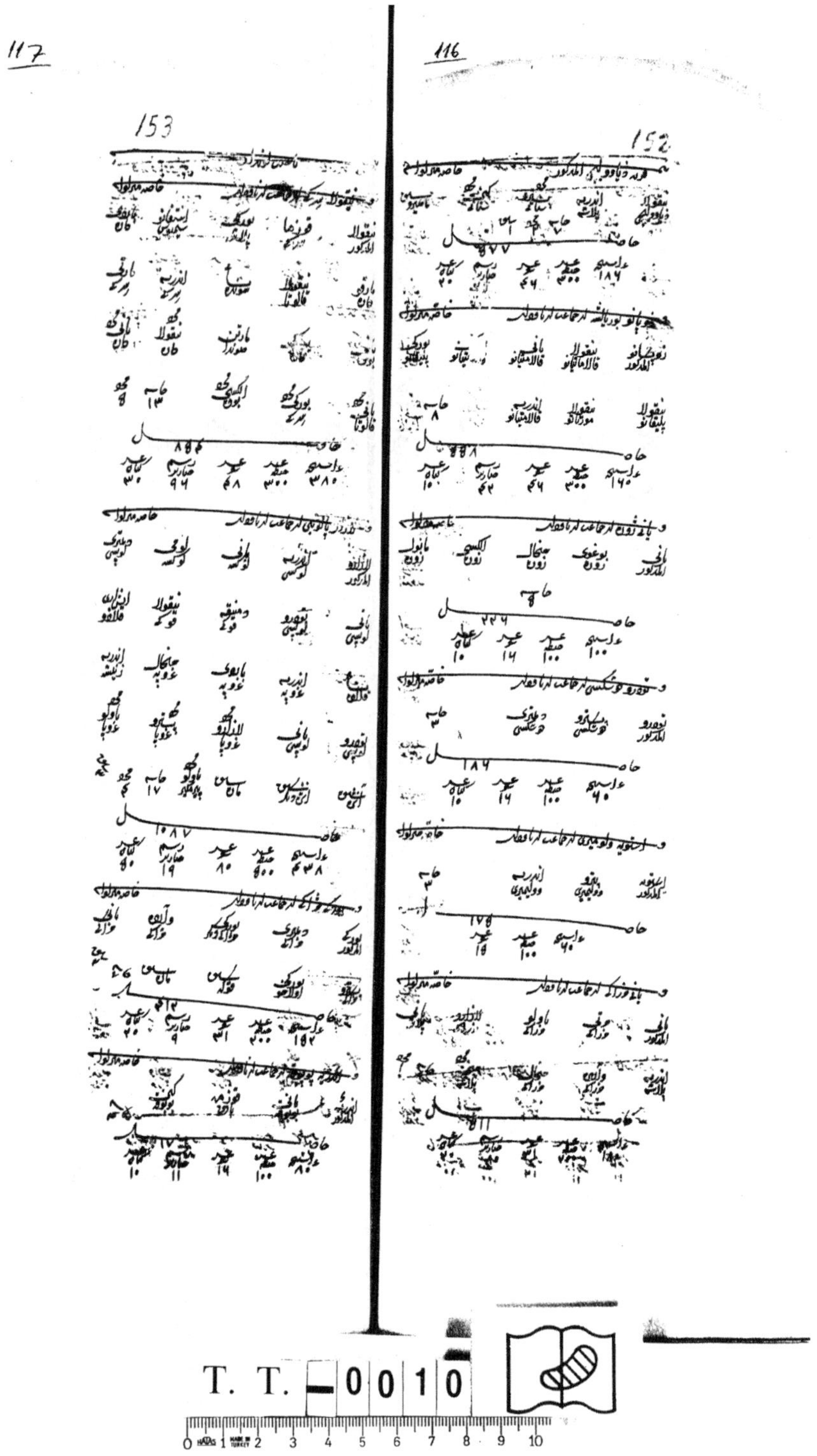
117
116
153
152
T. T. 0010

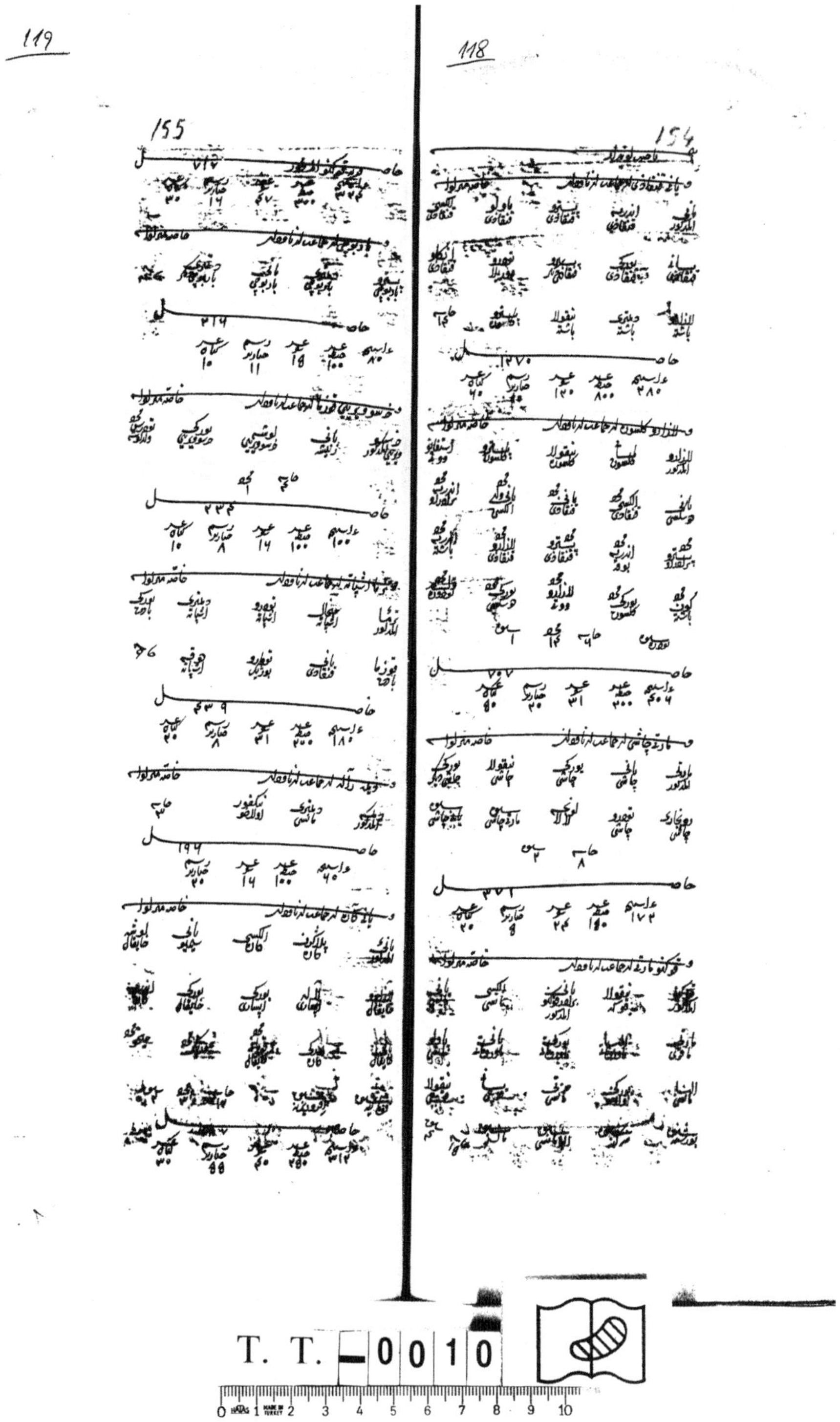
119
118
155
154
T. T. 0010

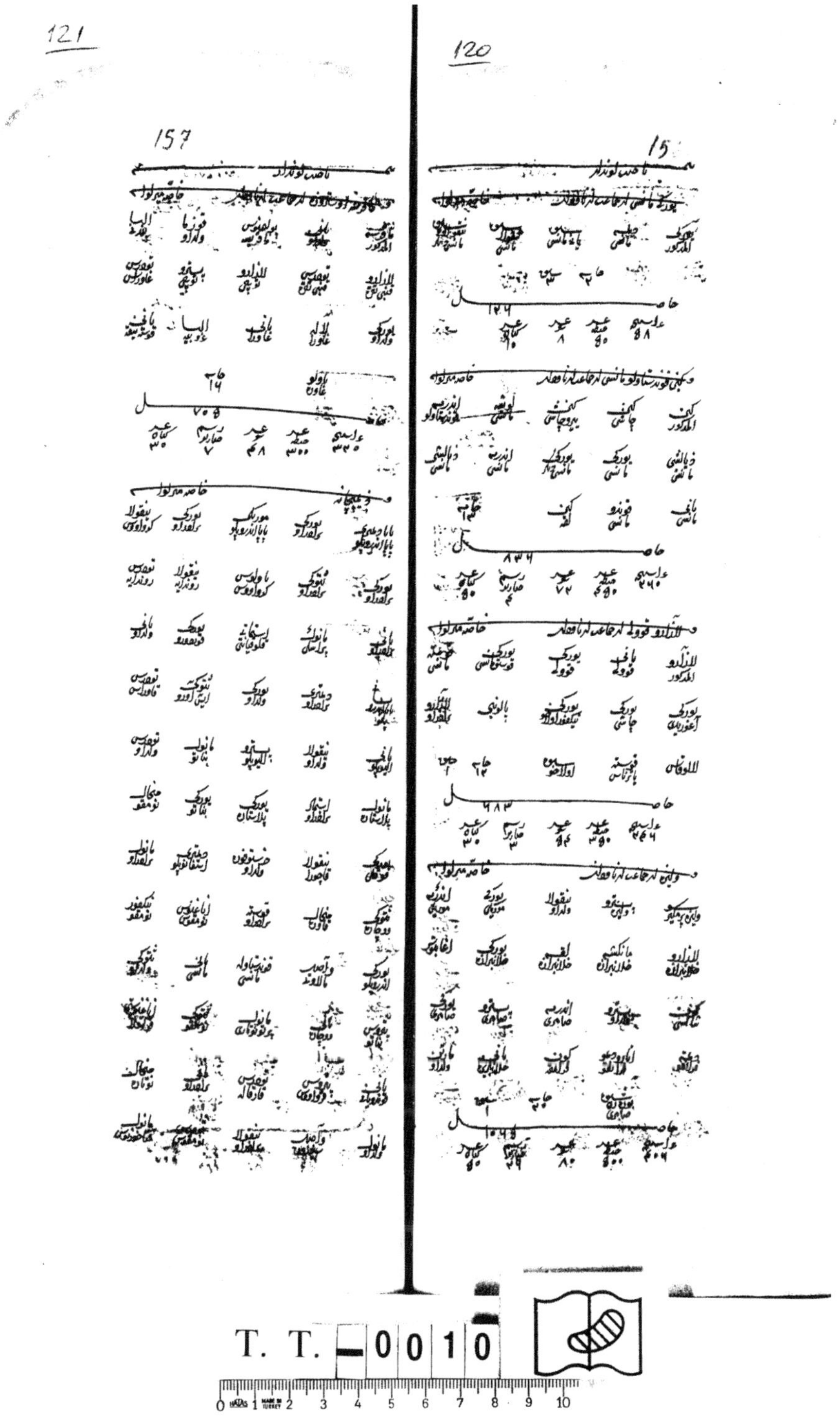
121
120
157
T. T. 0010

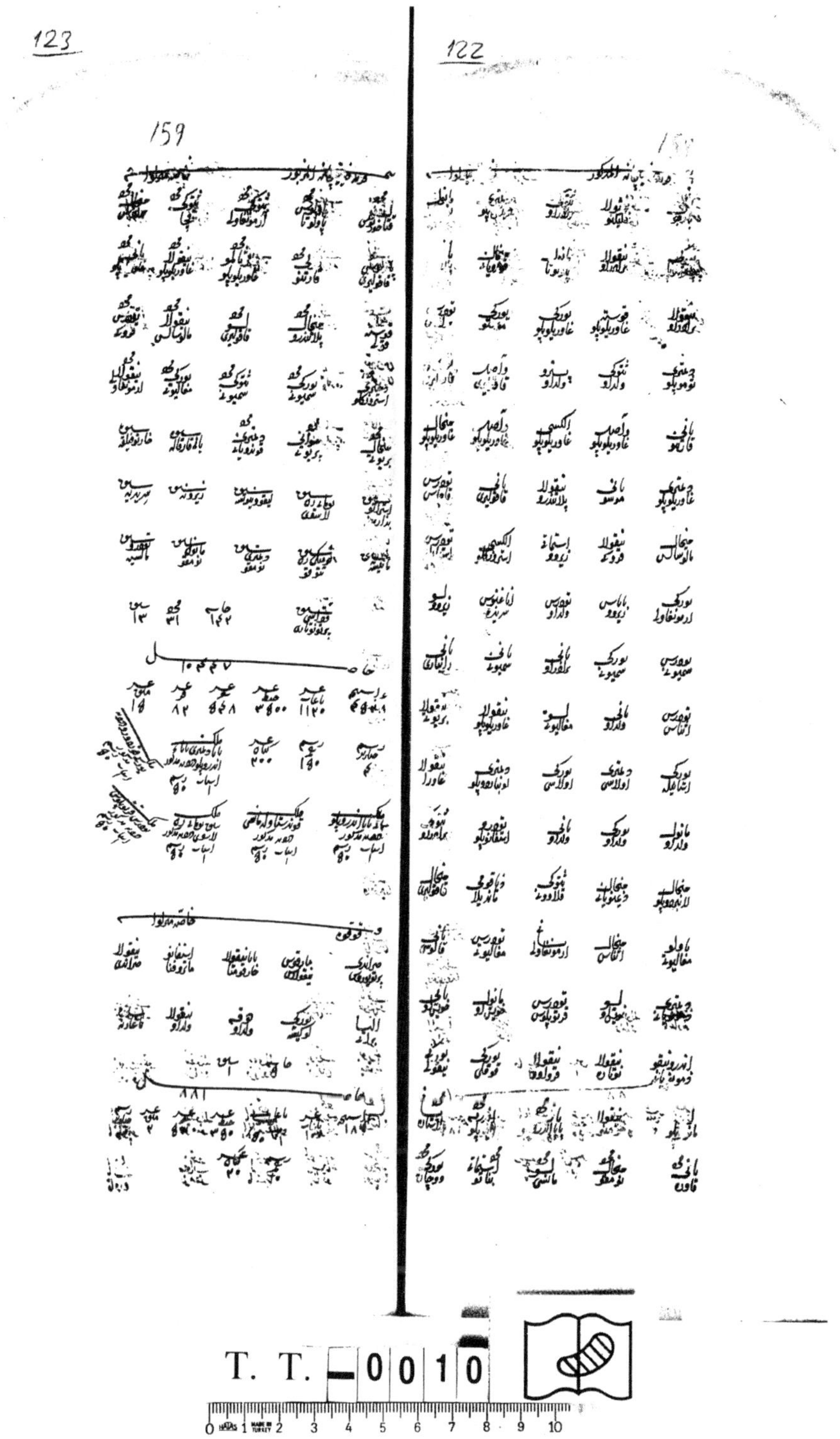
123
122
159
T. T. 0010

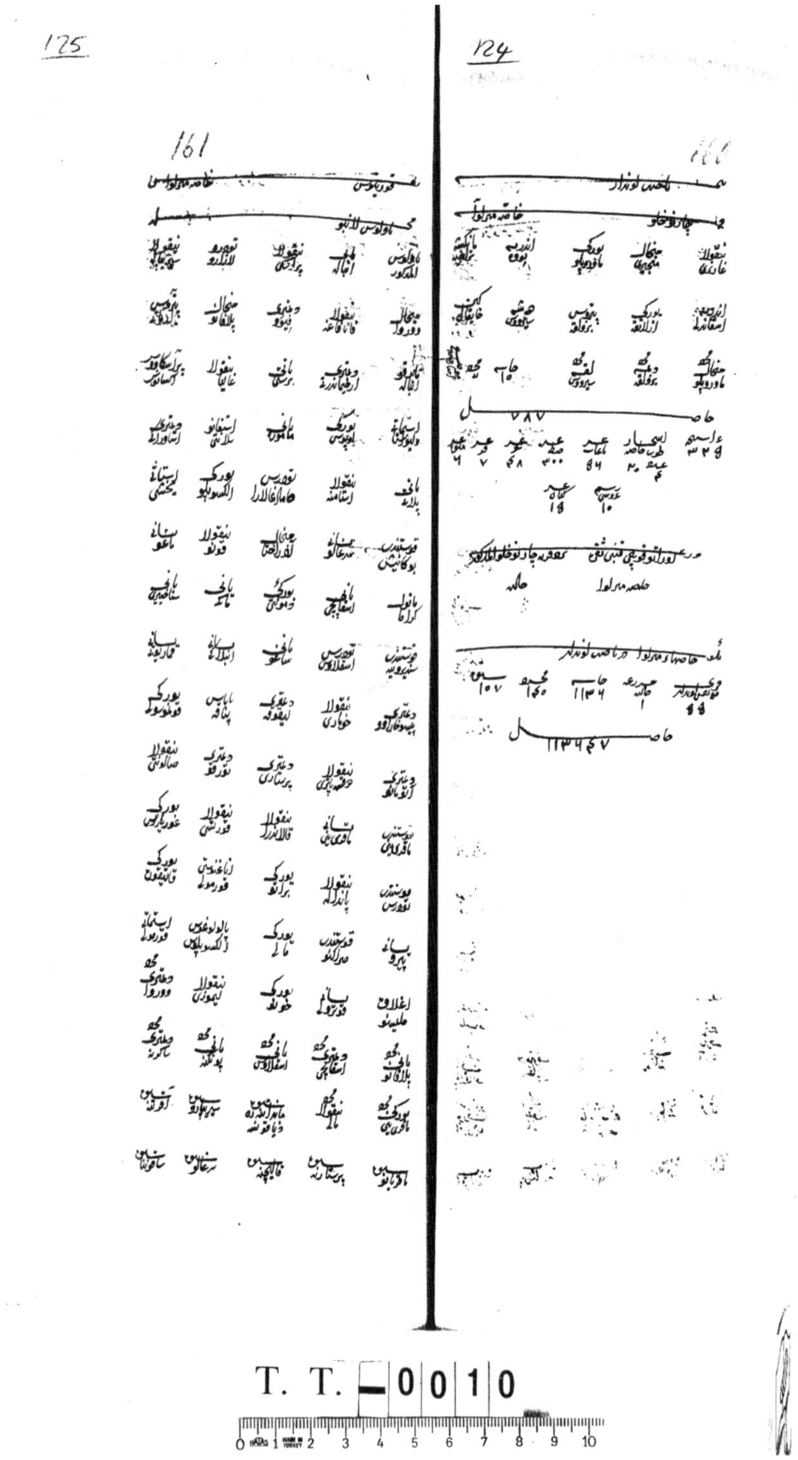
125
124
161
T. T. 0010

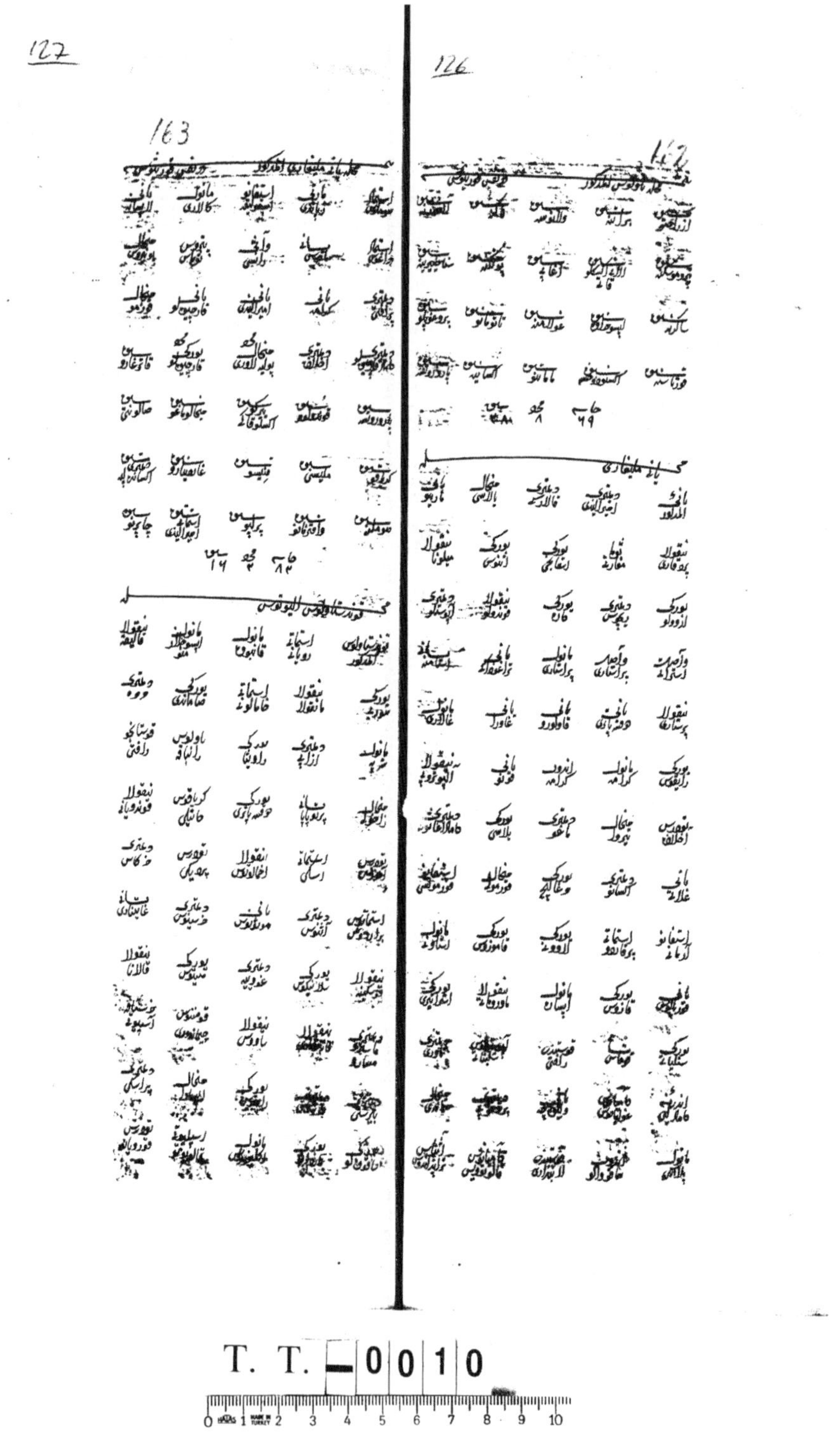
127
126
163
T. T. 0010

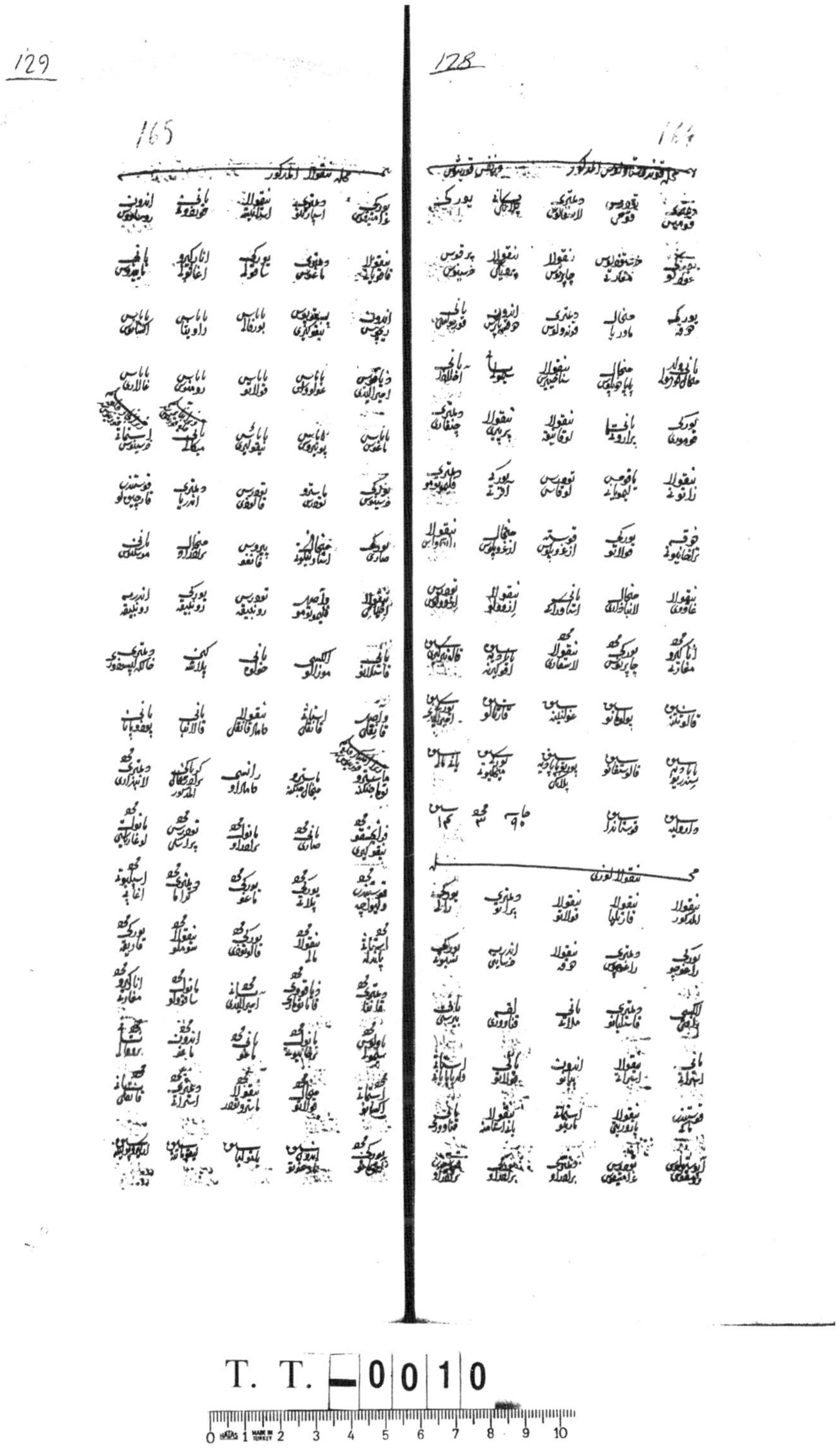
129
128
165
164
T. T. 0010

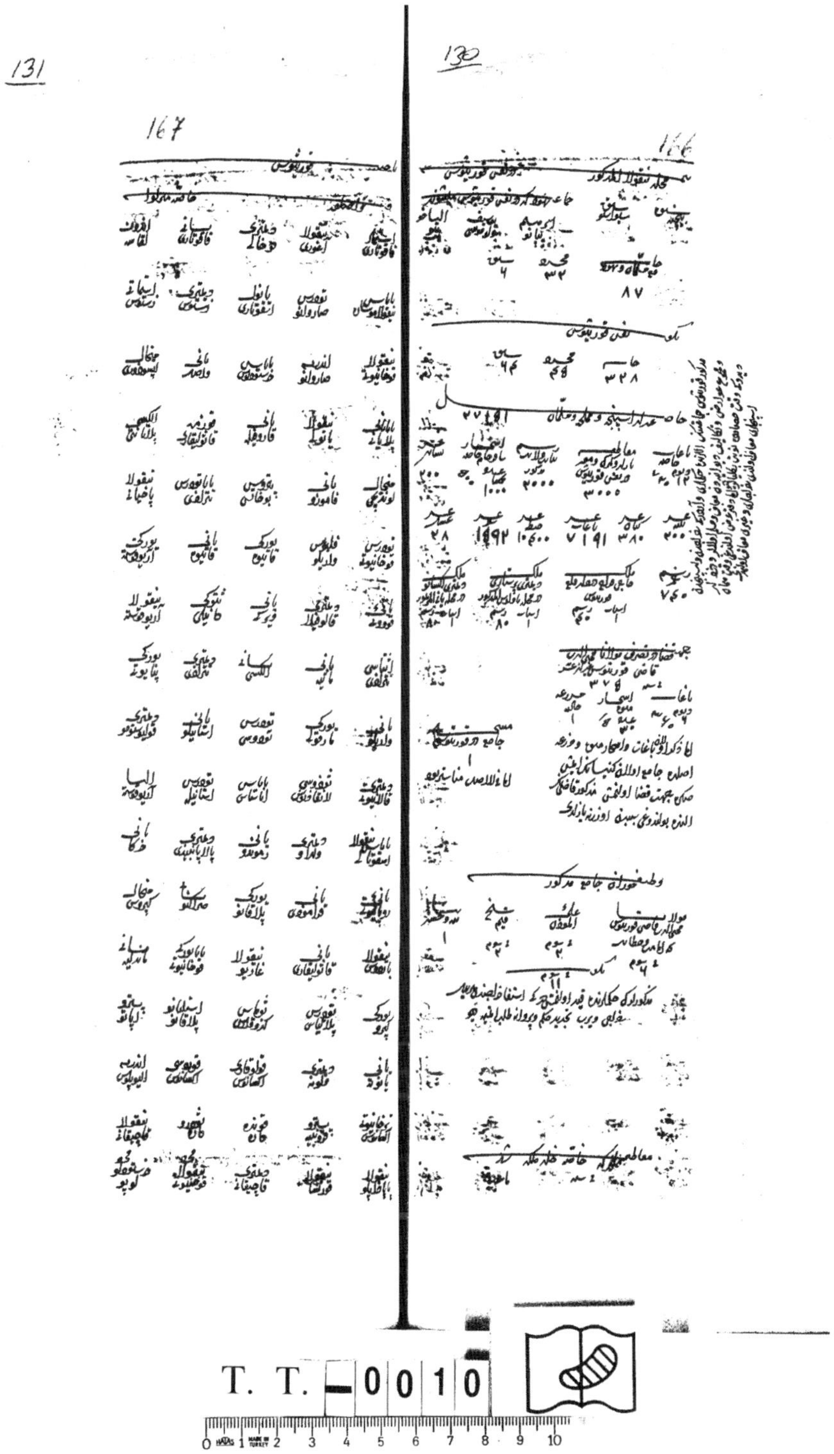
131
130
167
166
T. T. 0010

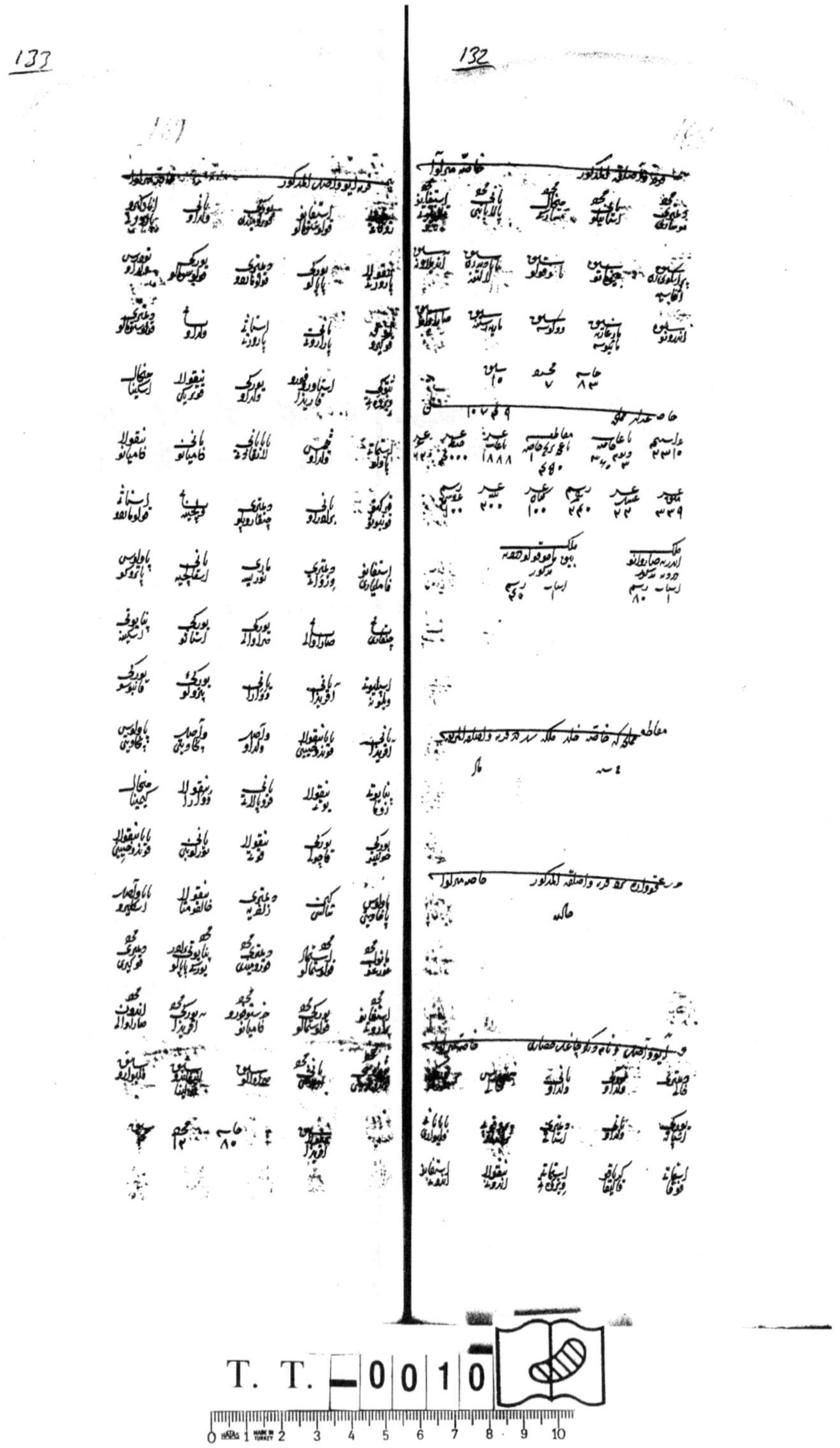
133
132
T. T. 0010

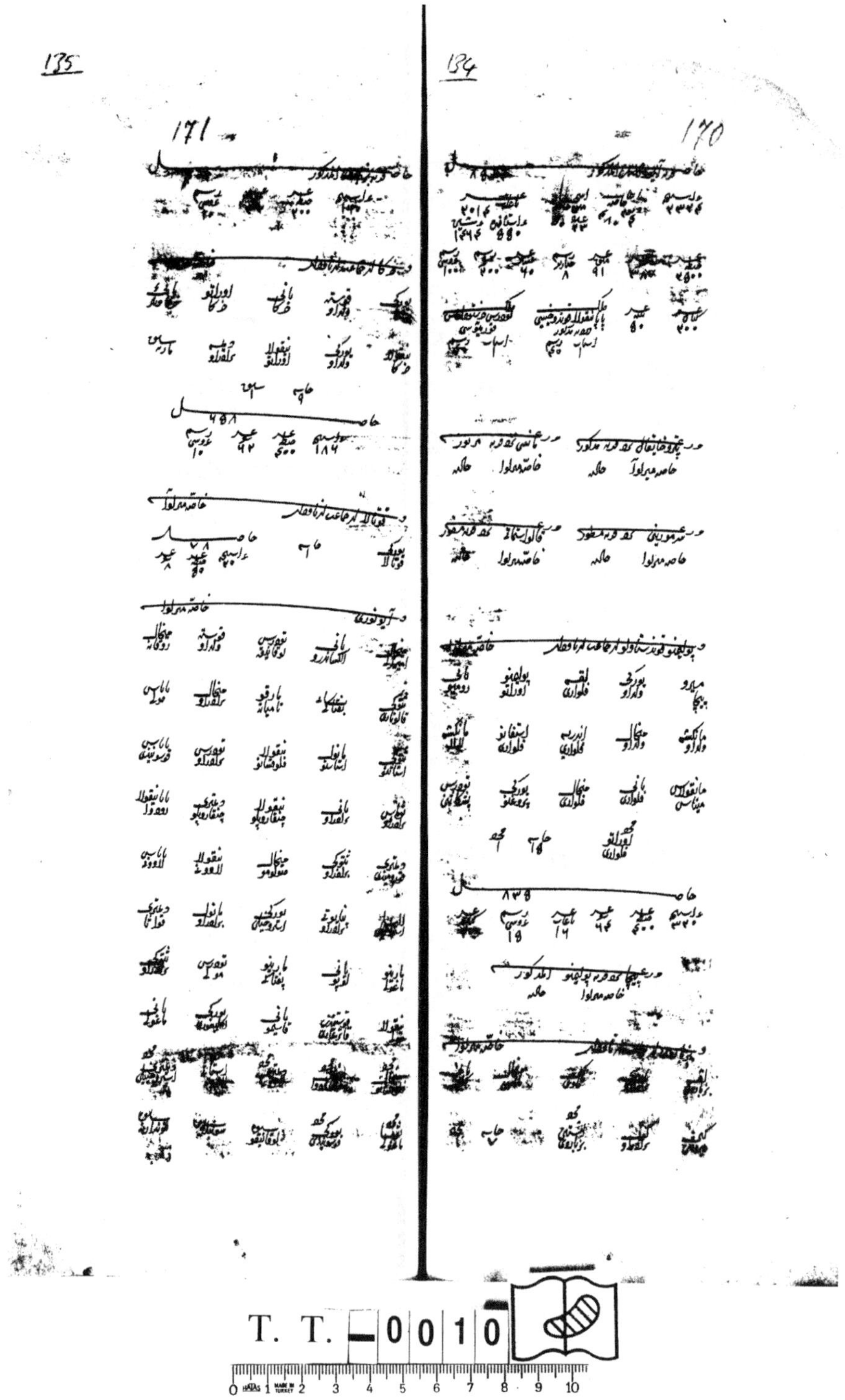
135
134
171
170
T. T. 0010

T. T. 0010

T. T. 0010

T. T. 0010

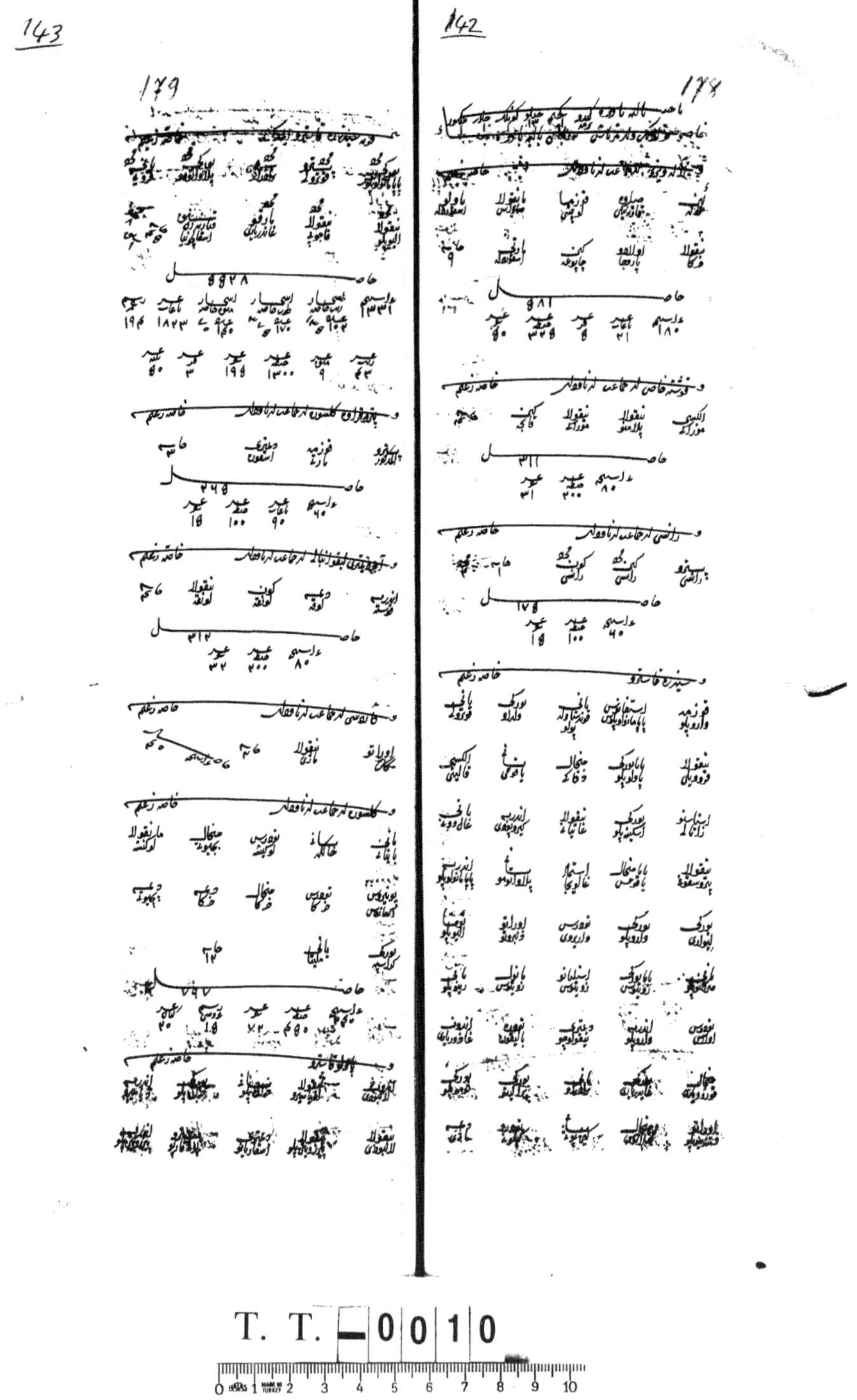
T. T. 0010

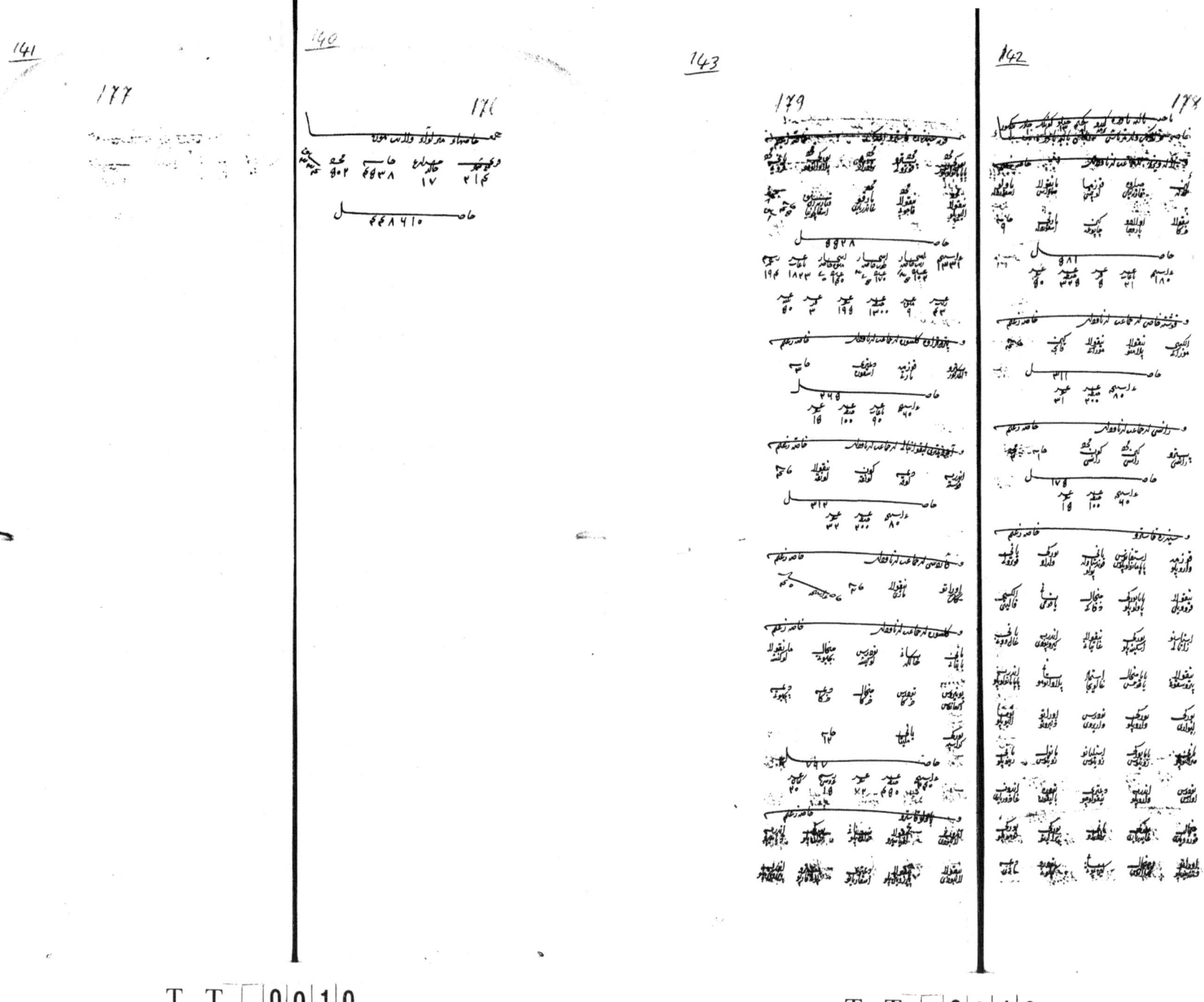

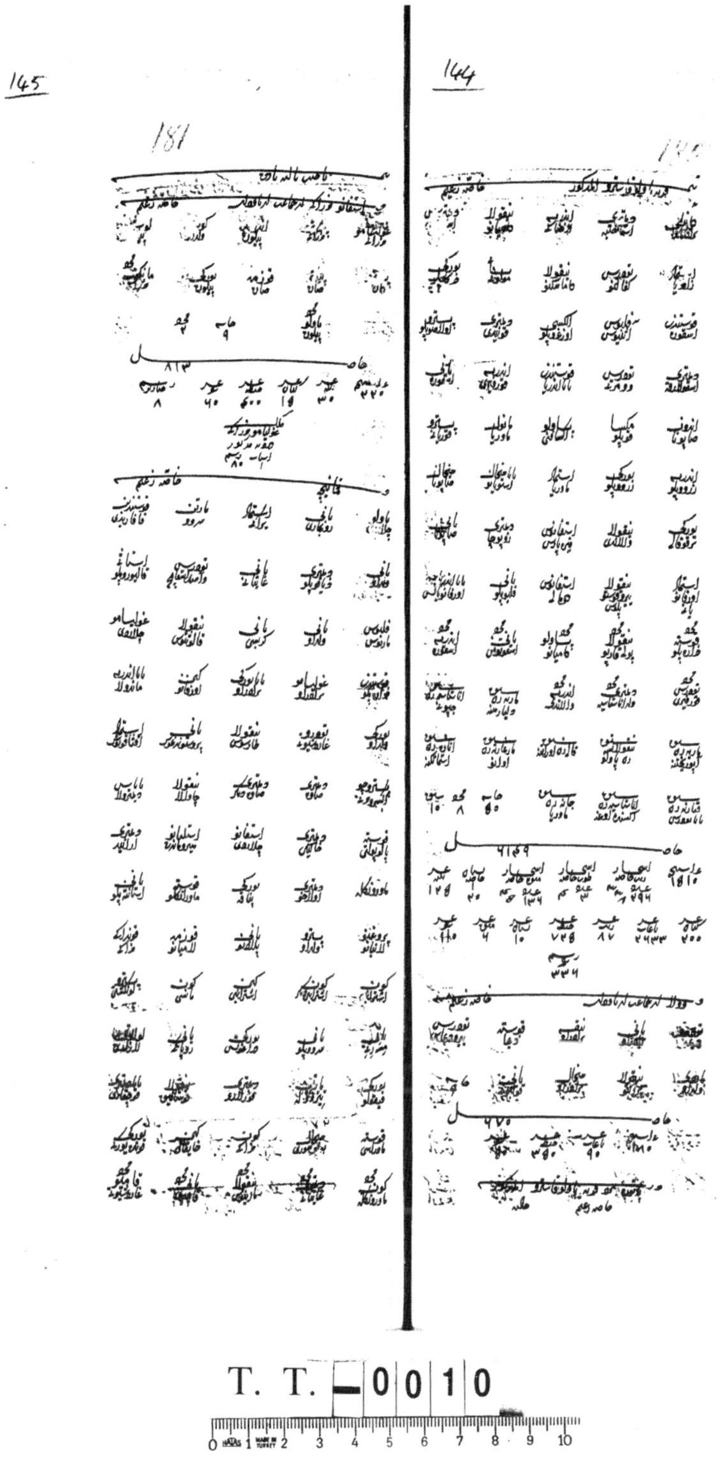
145
144
T. T. 0010

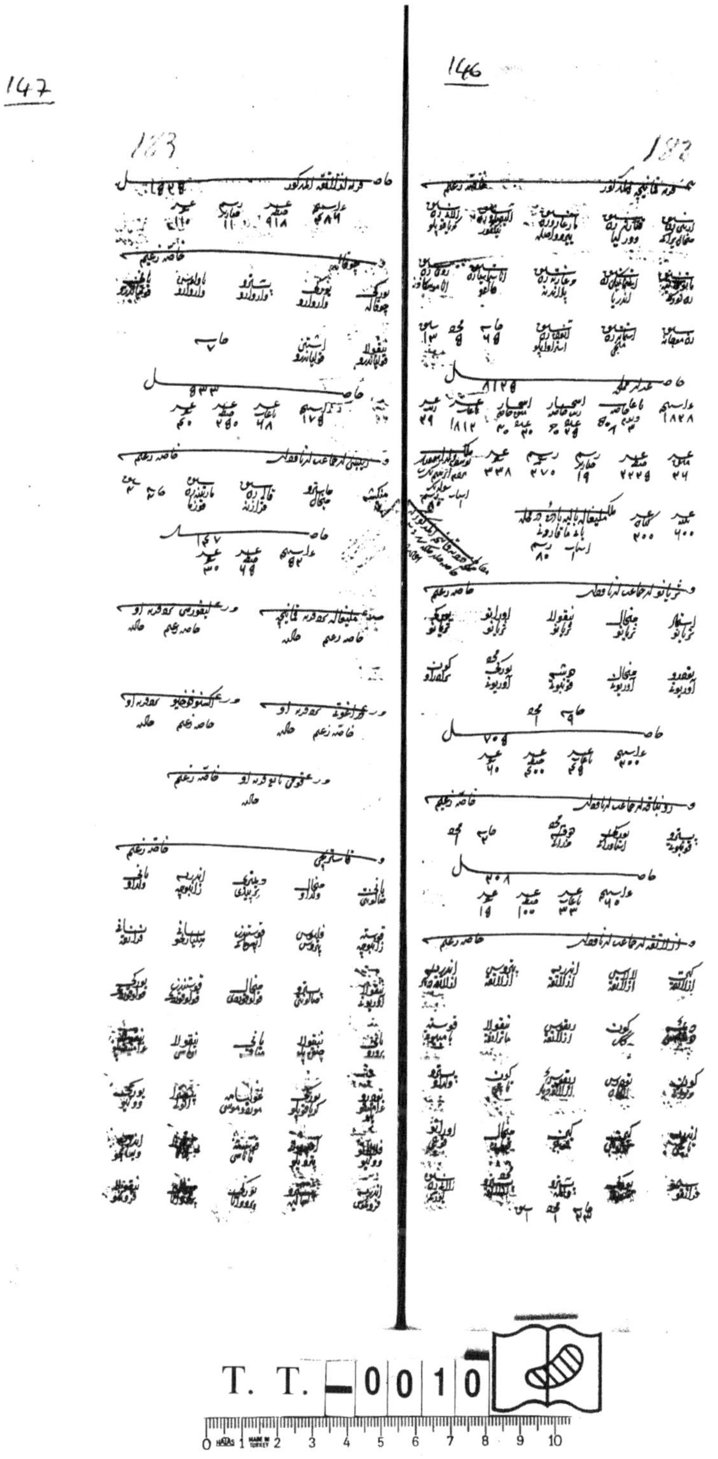
147
146
T. T. 0010

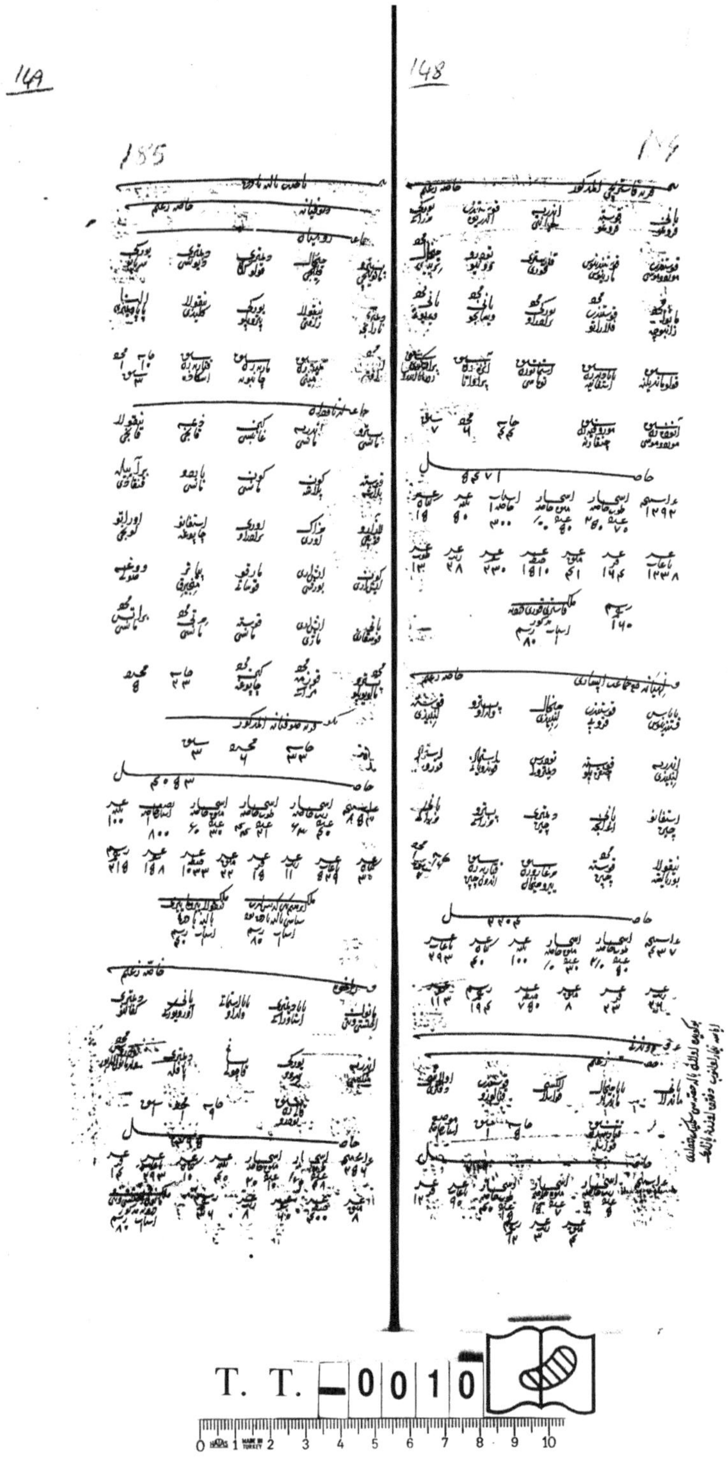
T. T. 0010

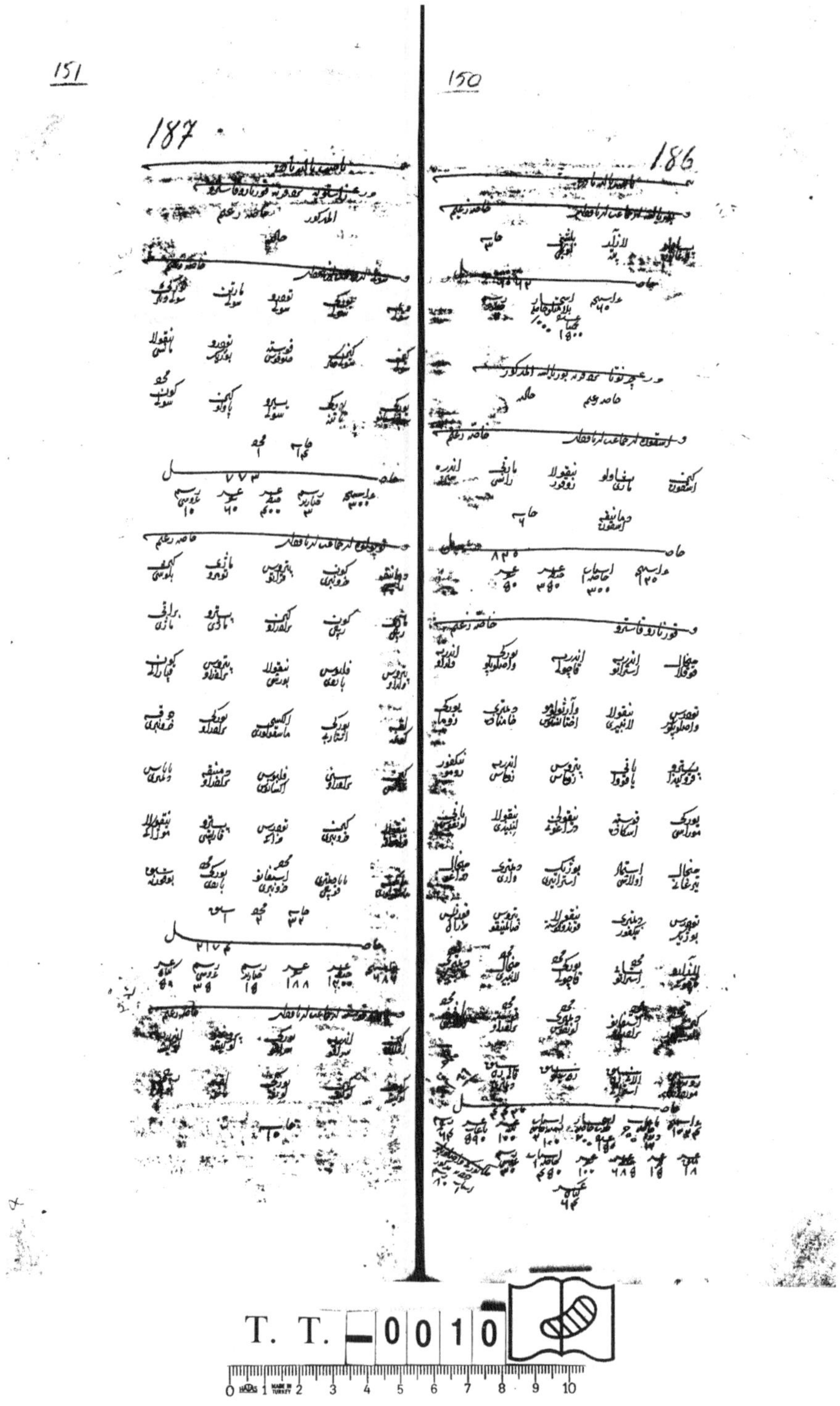
T. T. 0010

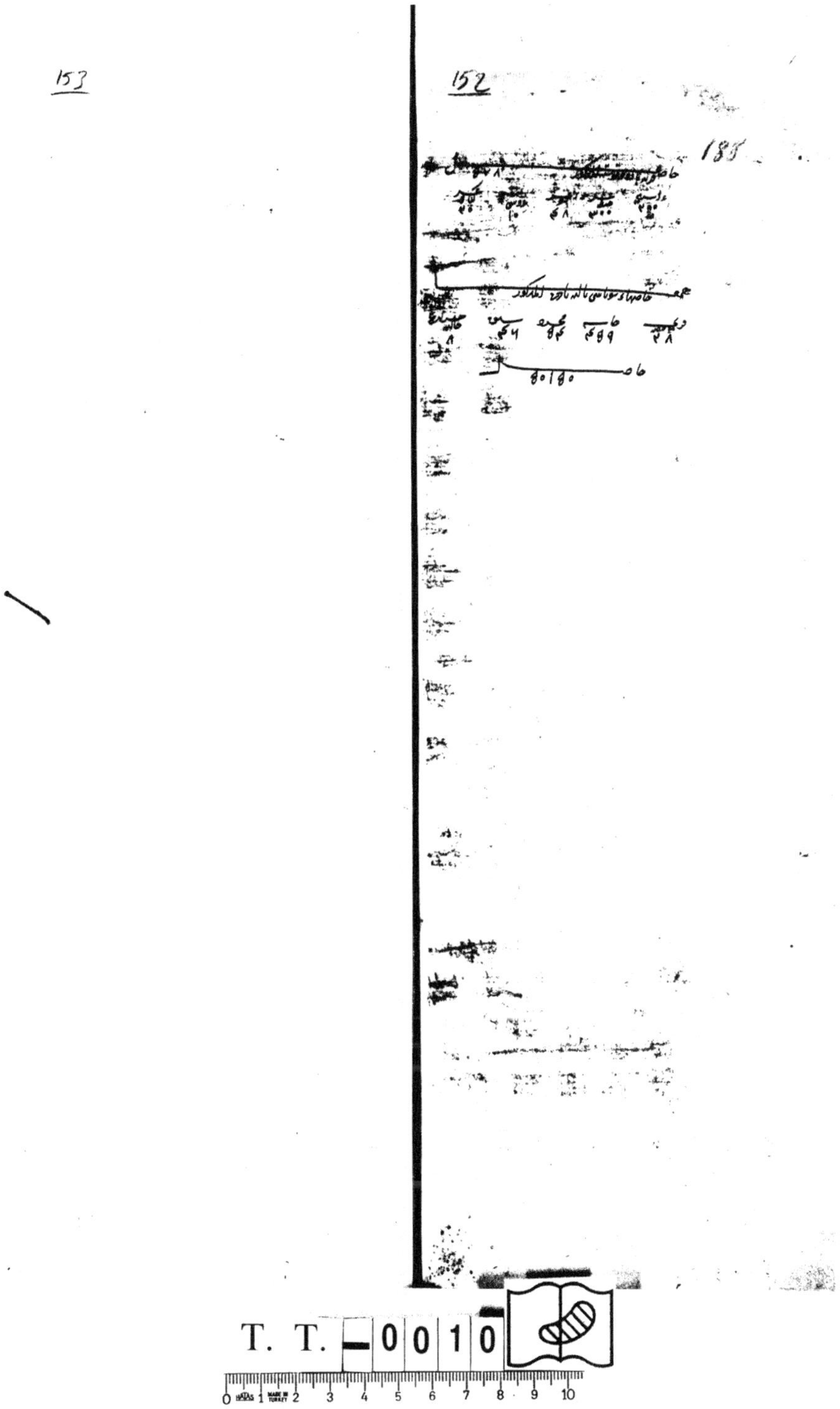
153
152
188
T. T. 0010

Facsimile of 1/14662

(Sts Cyril & Methodius National Library of Bulgaria, Sofia)

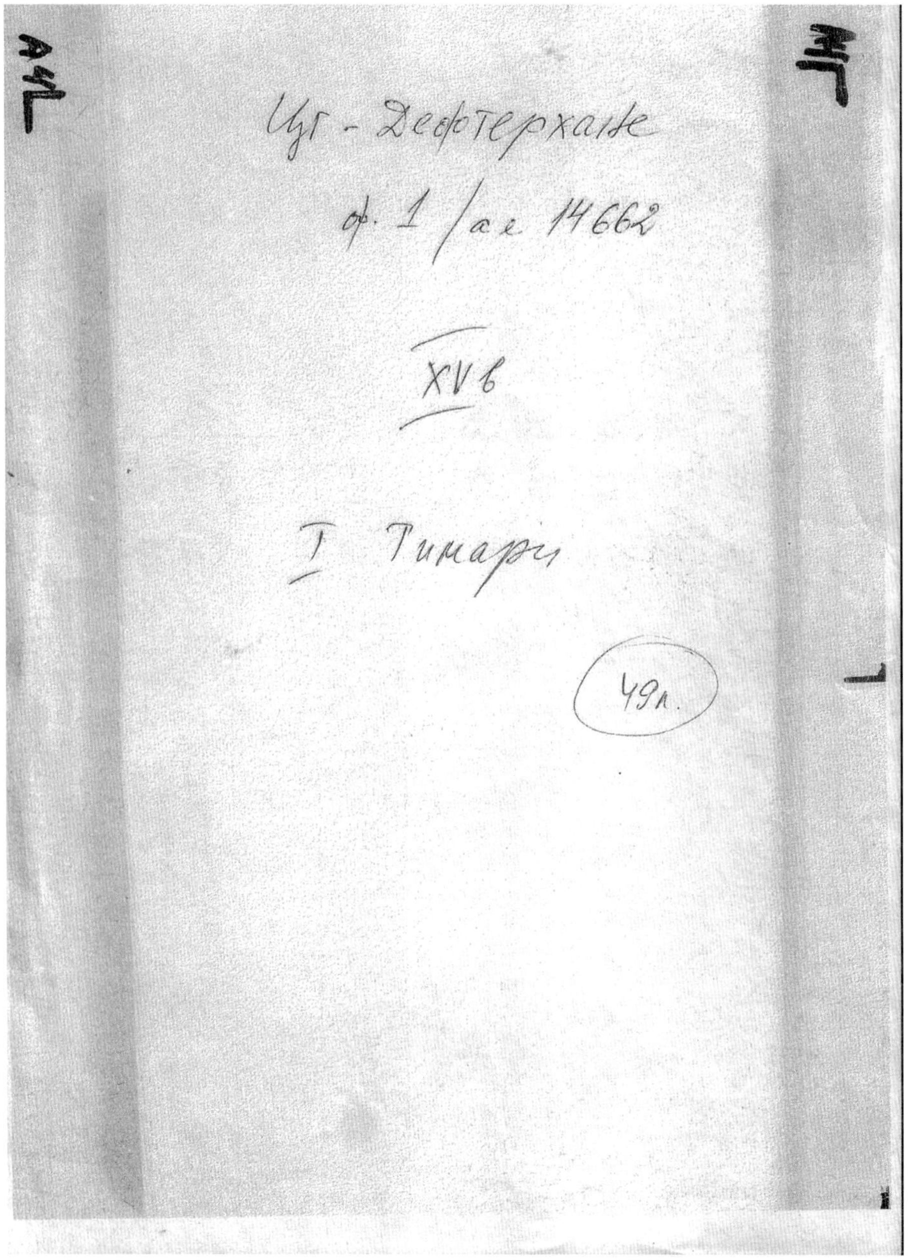
Ицг - Дефтерхане
ф. 1 / ае 14662
XVв
I Тимари
49л.

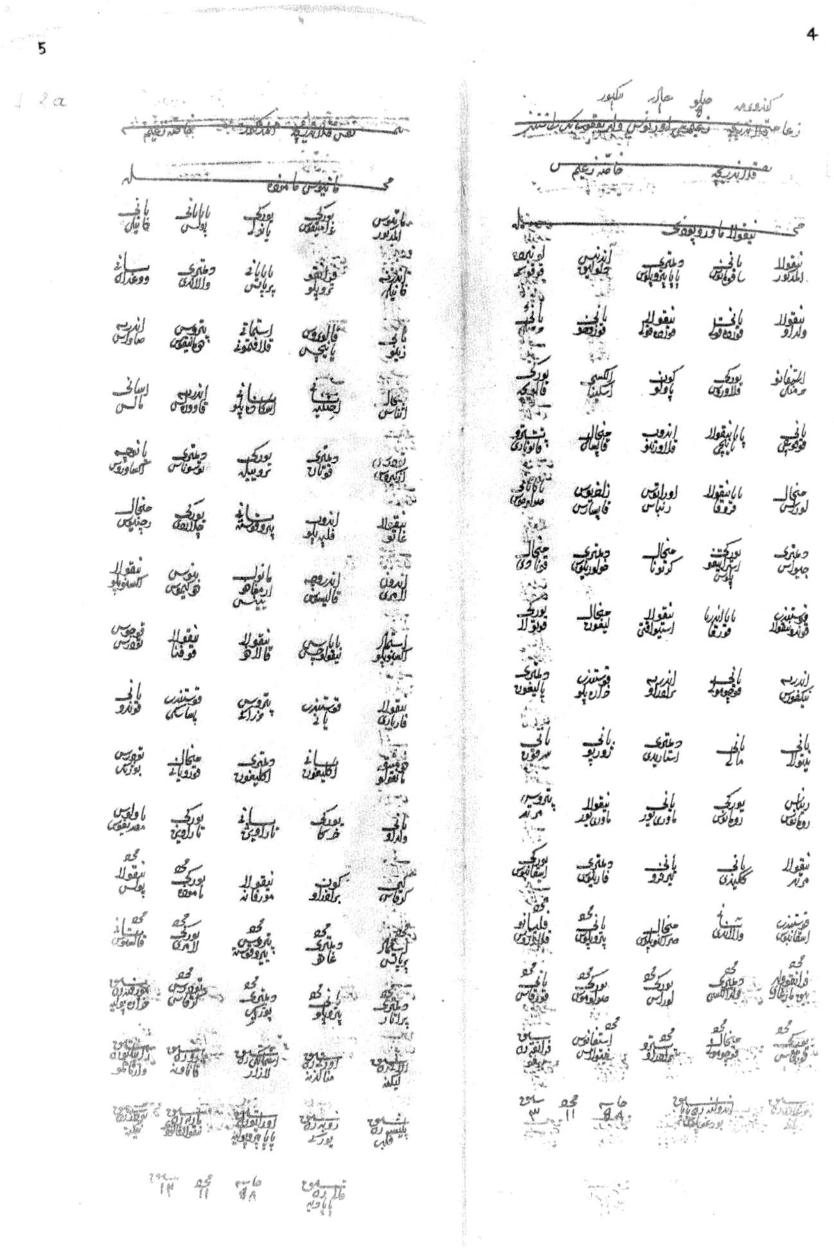
5
4

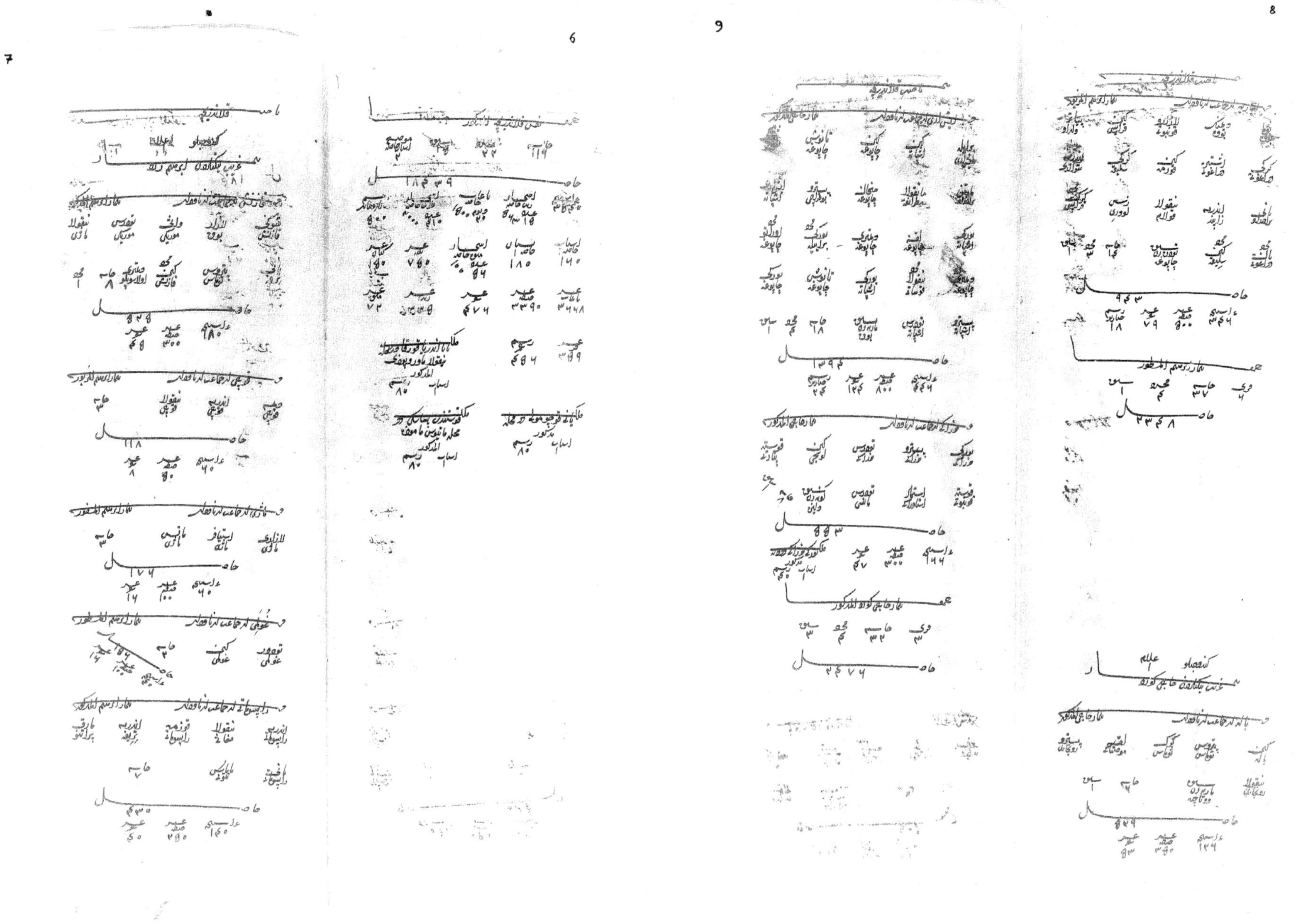

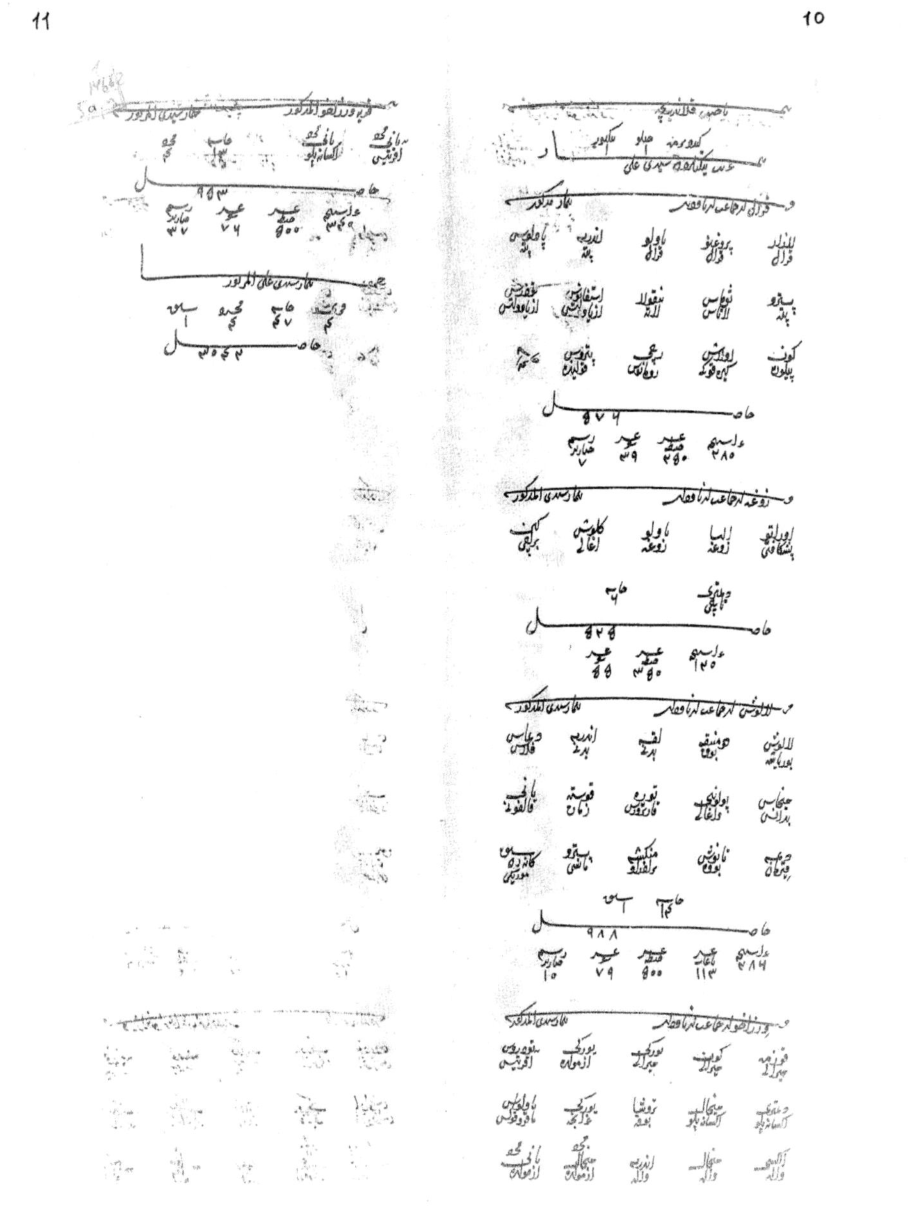
11
10

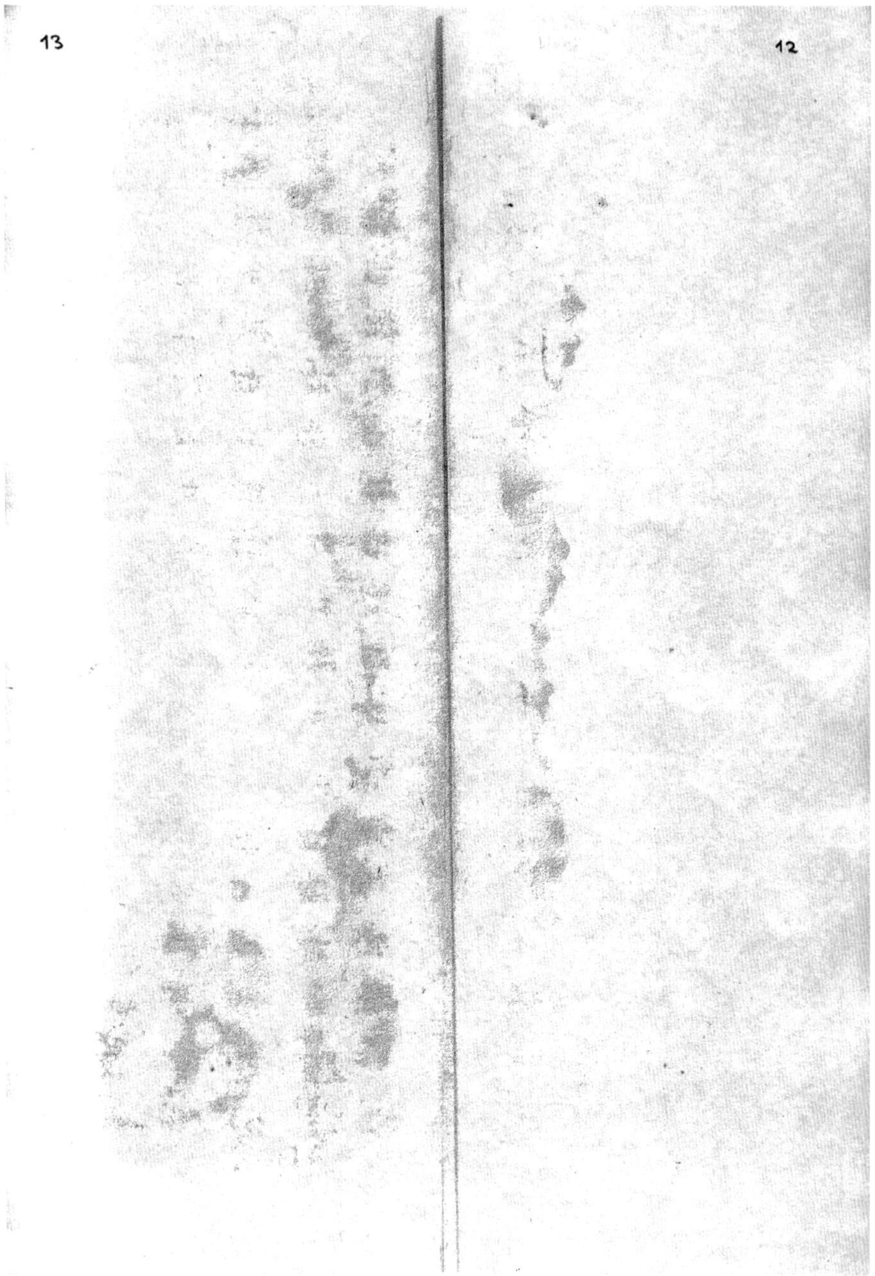
13
12

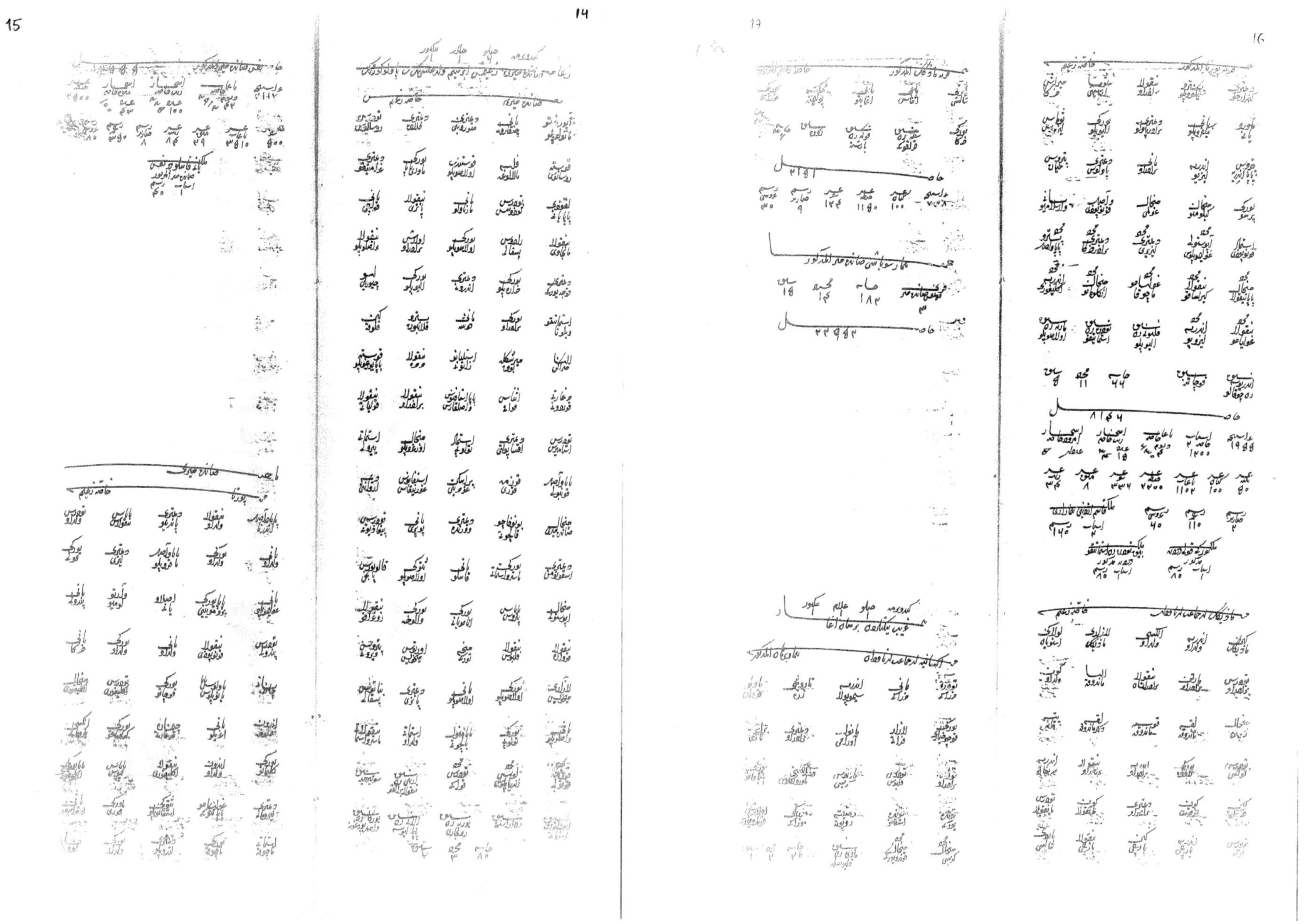

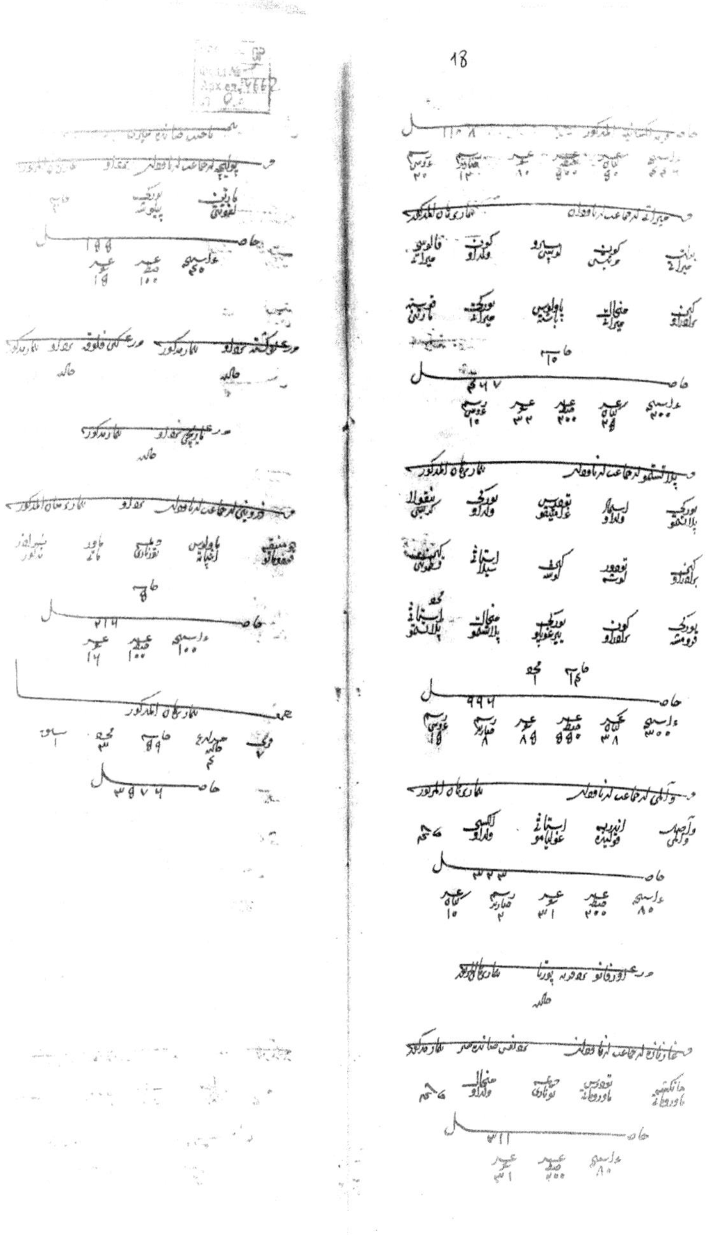

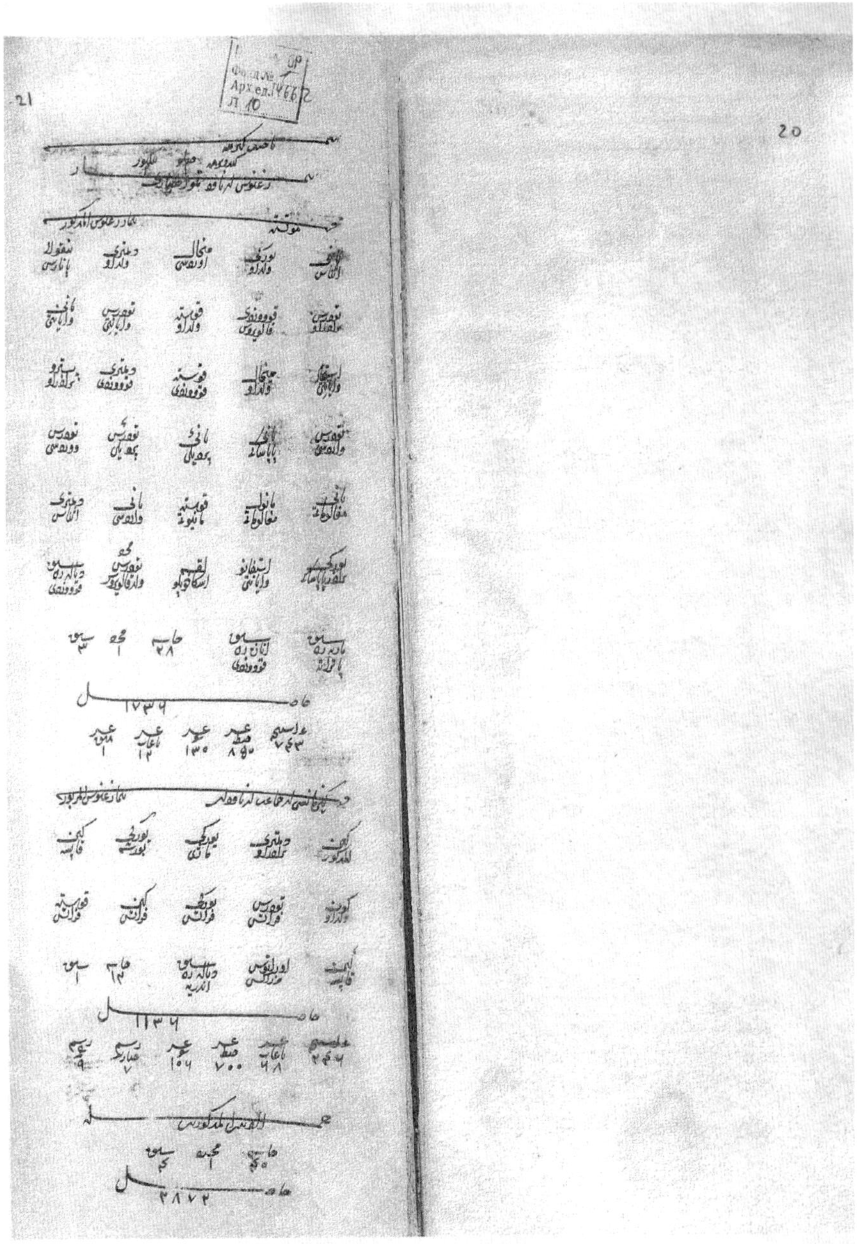

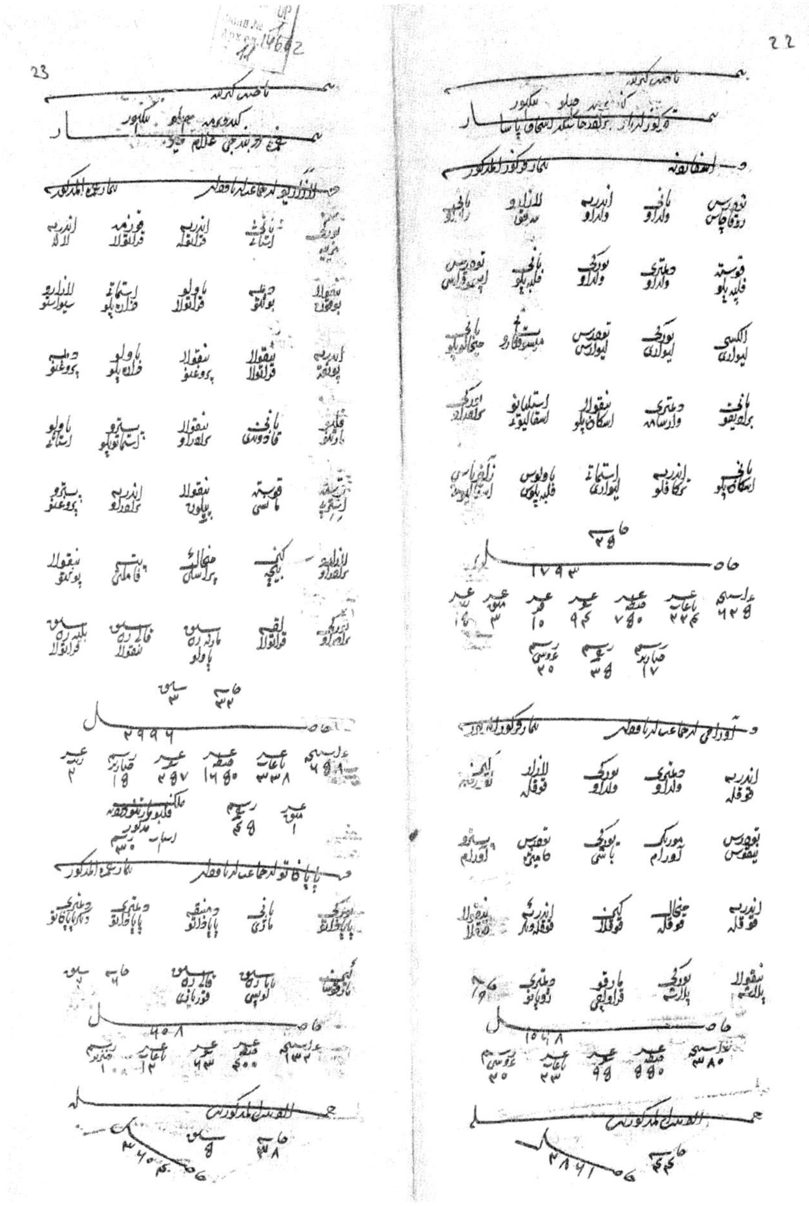
14662
23
22

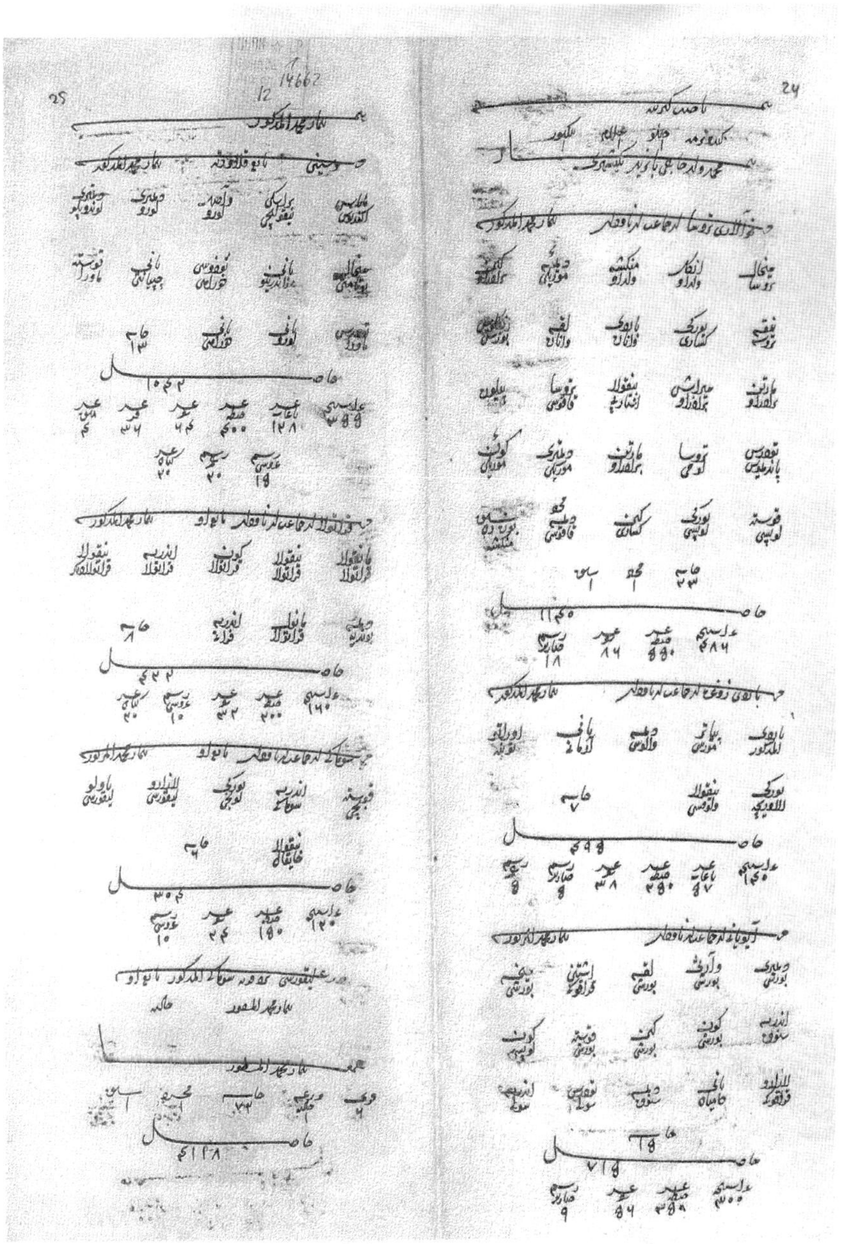
25
12
14662
24

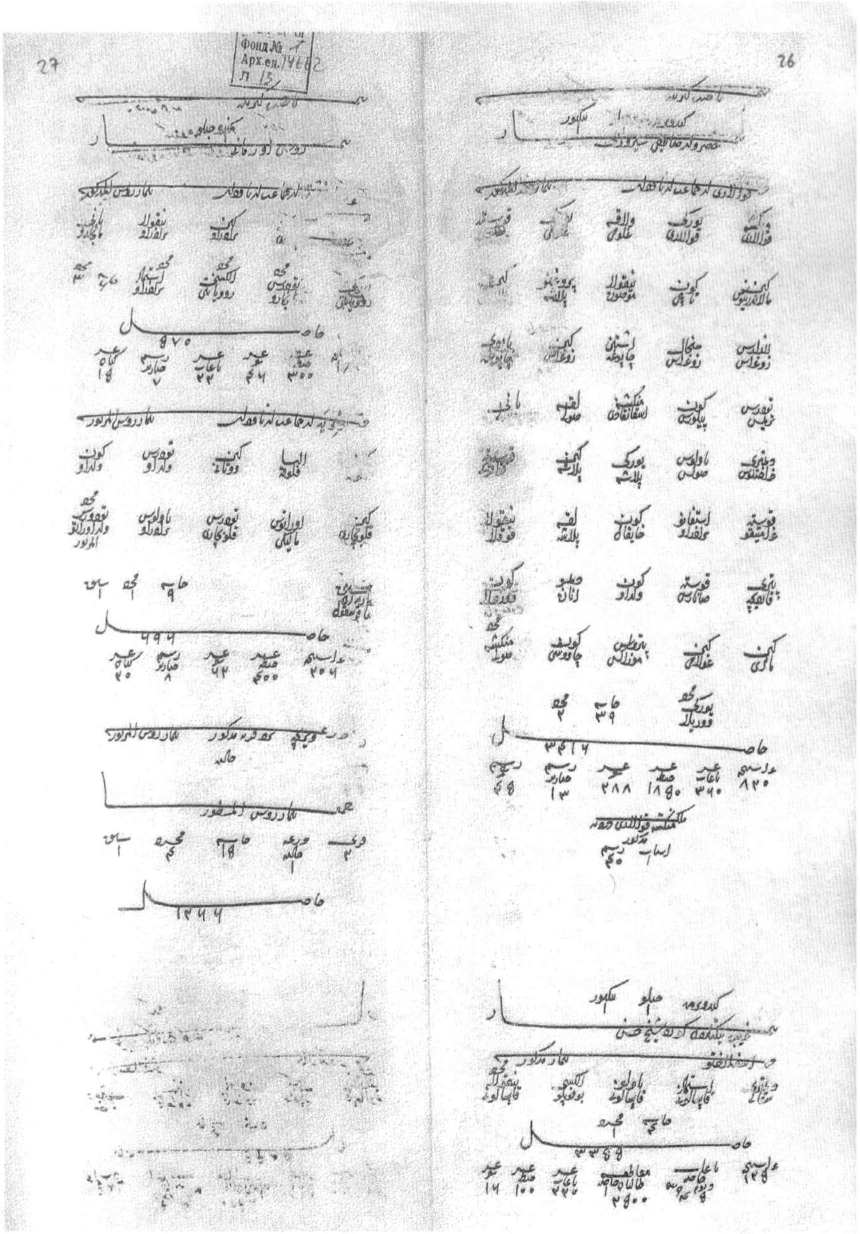

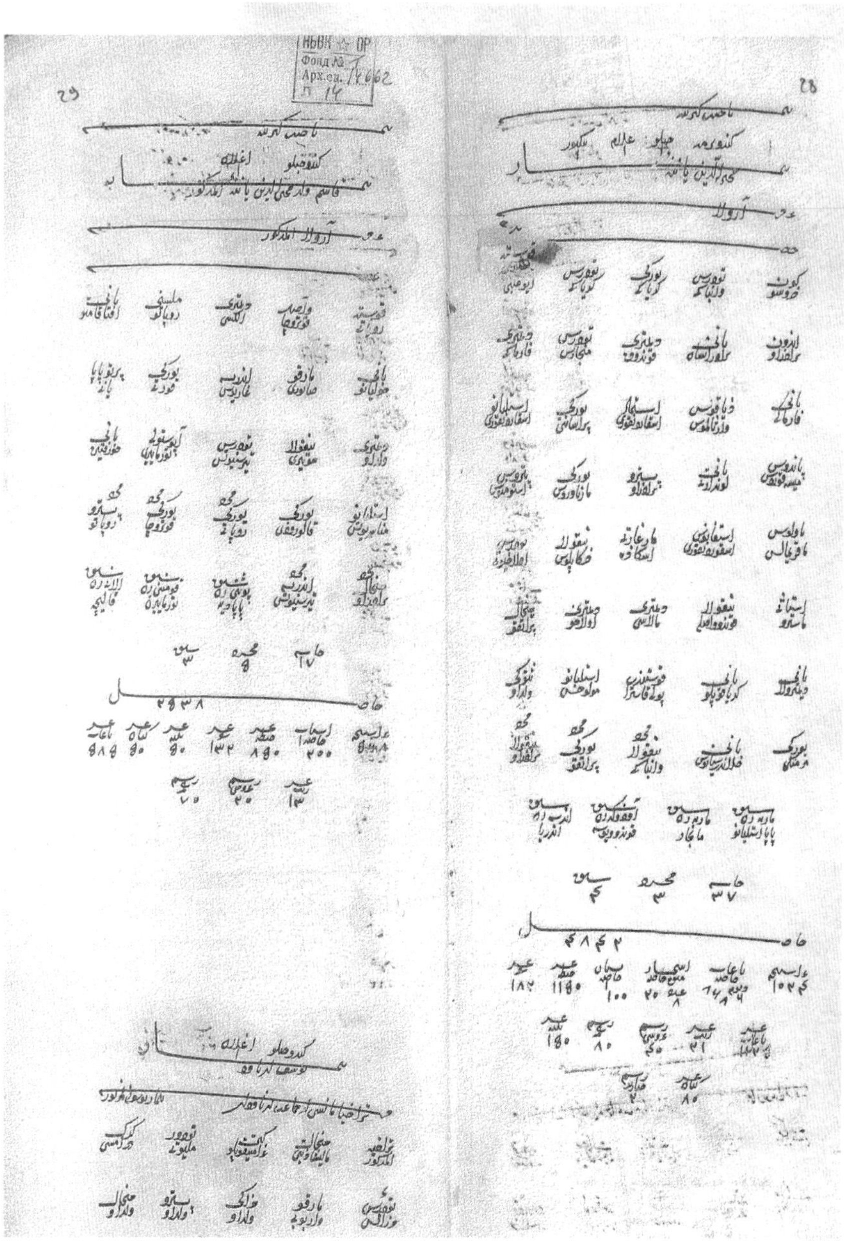

Фонд №
Арх.ед. 14662
Фонд №
Арх.ед. 14662

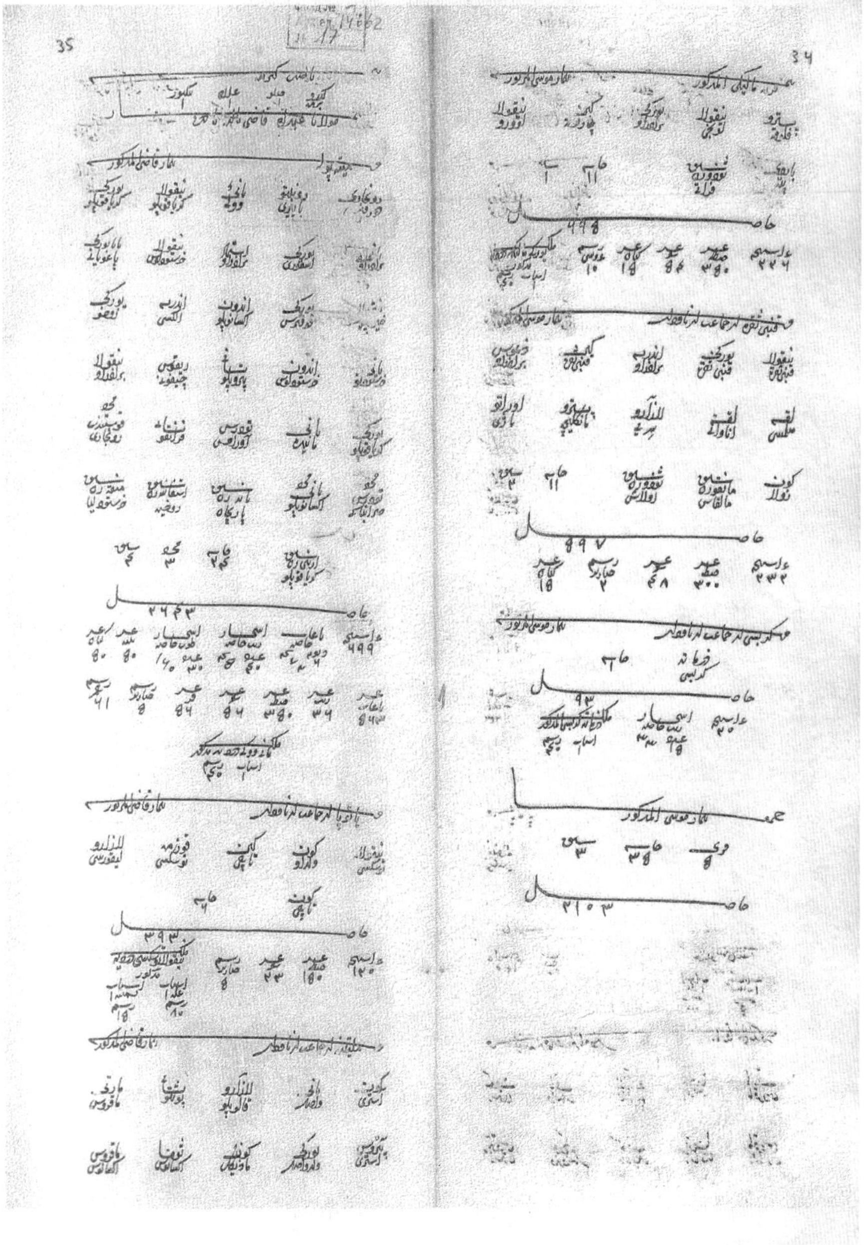

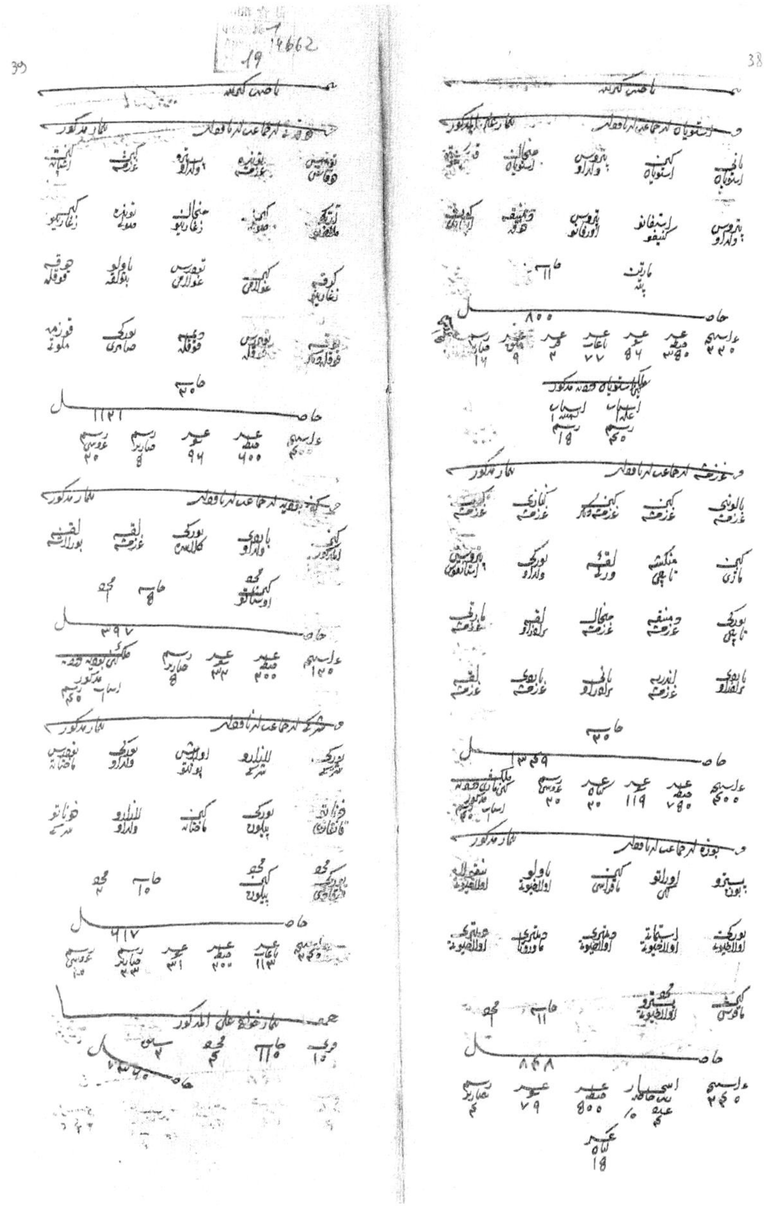

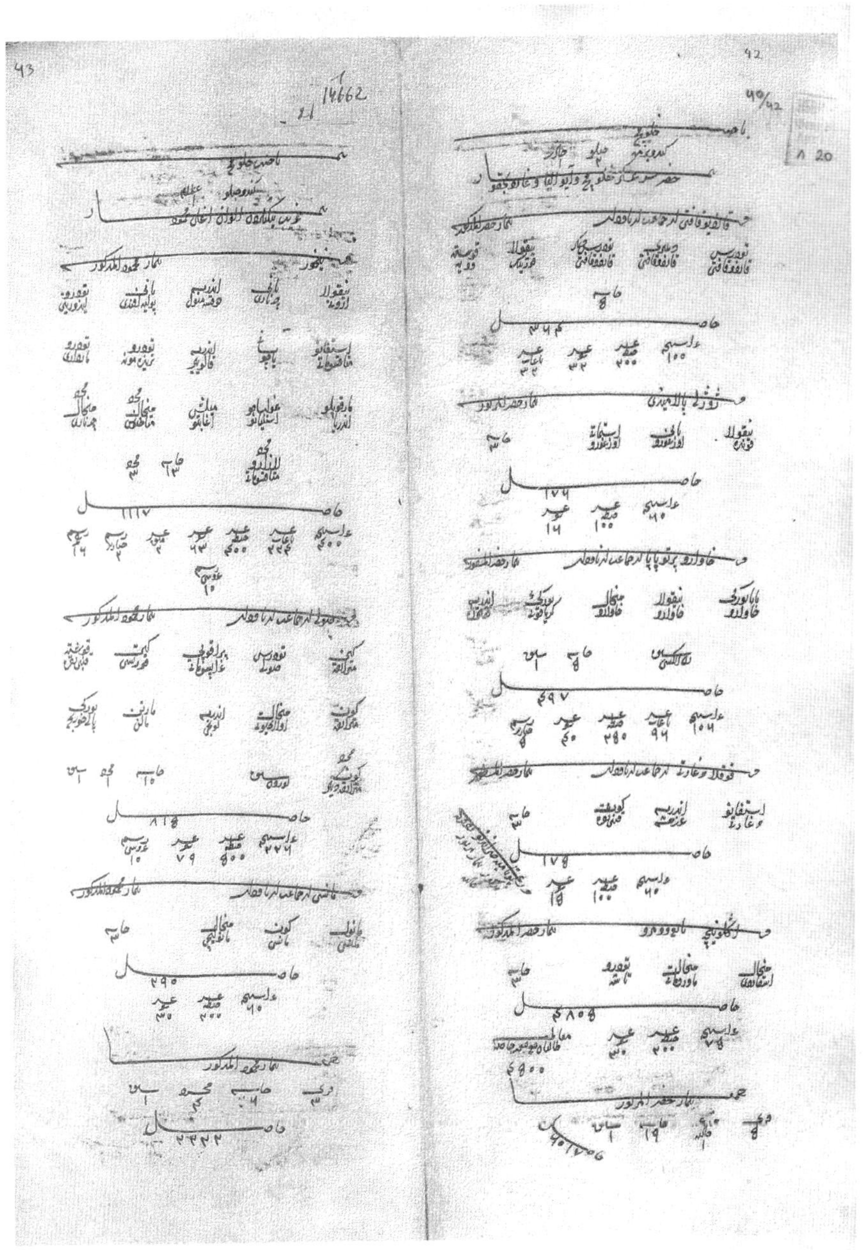

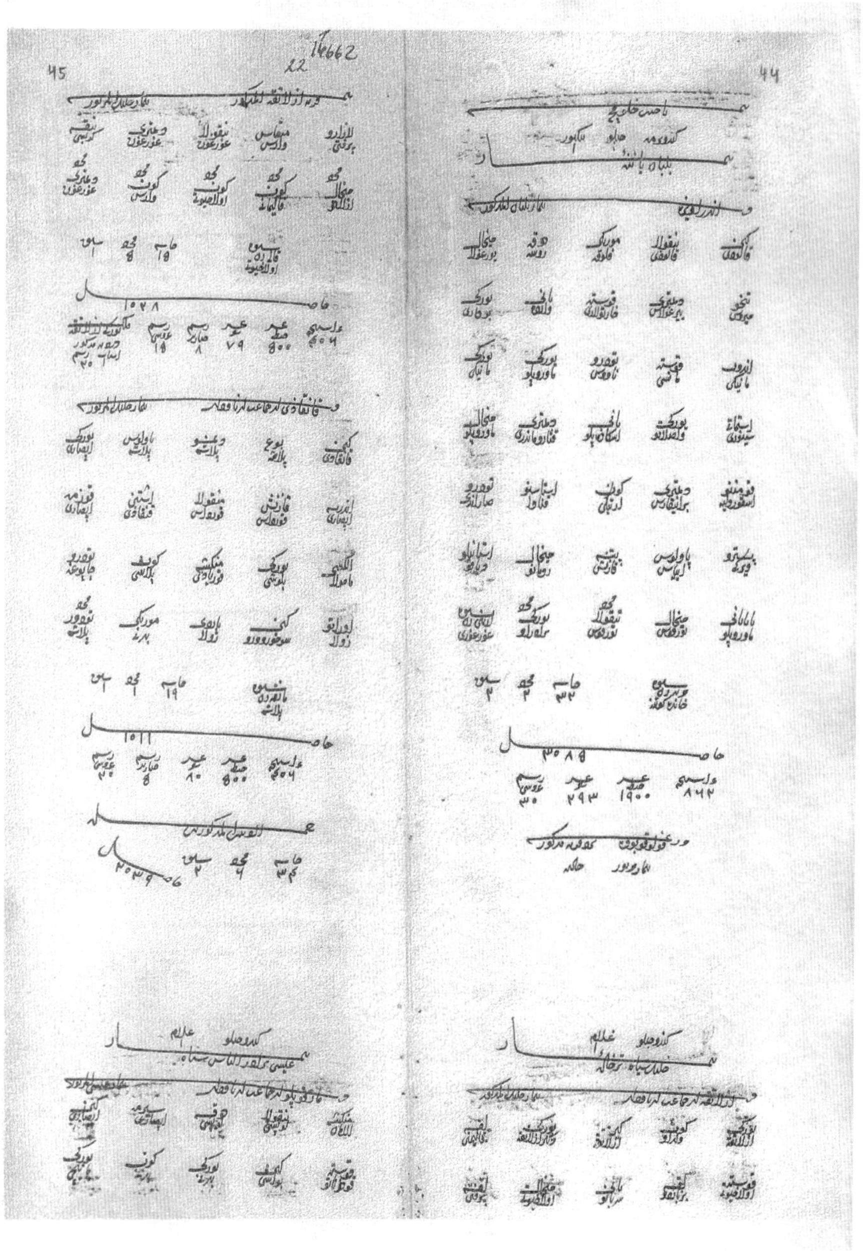

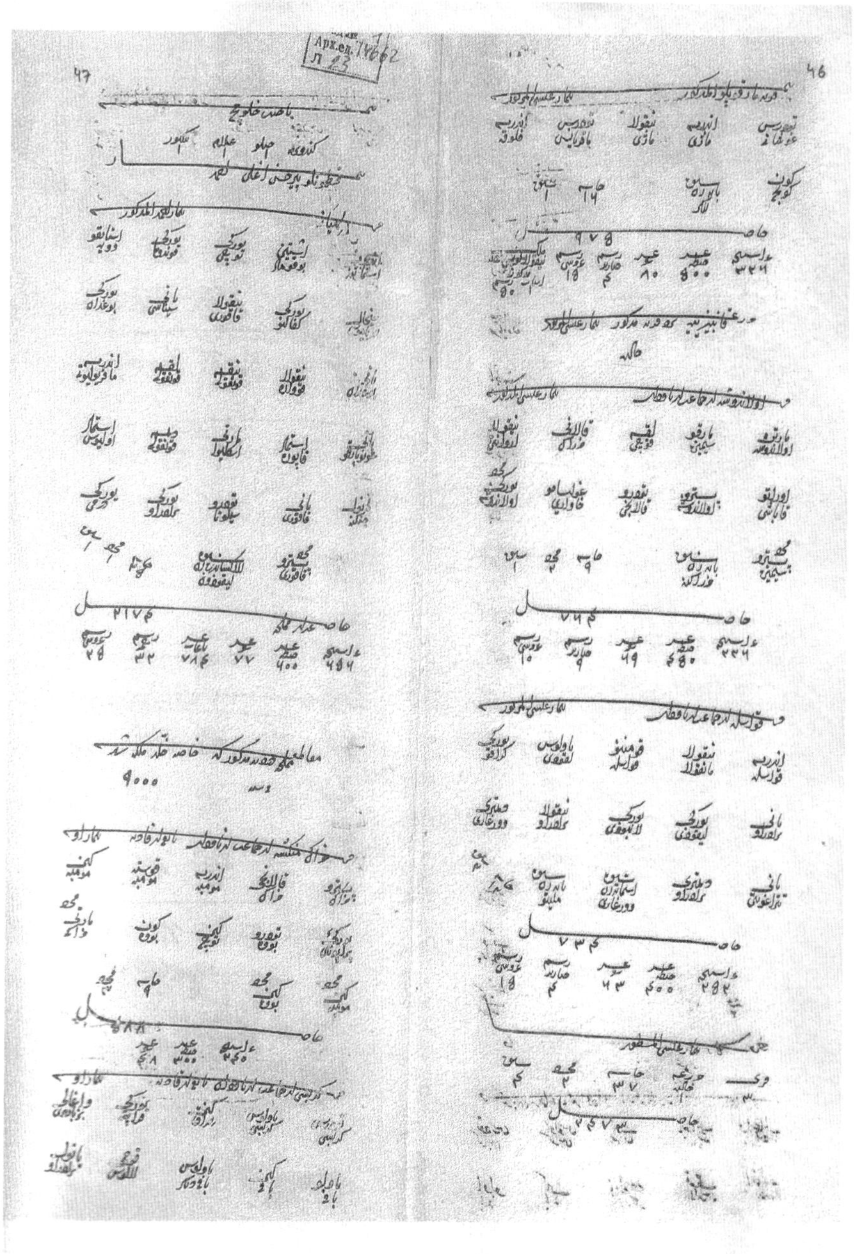

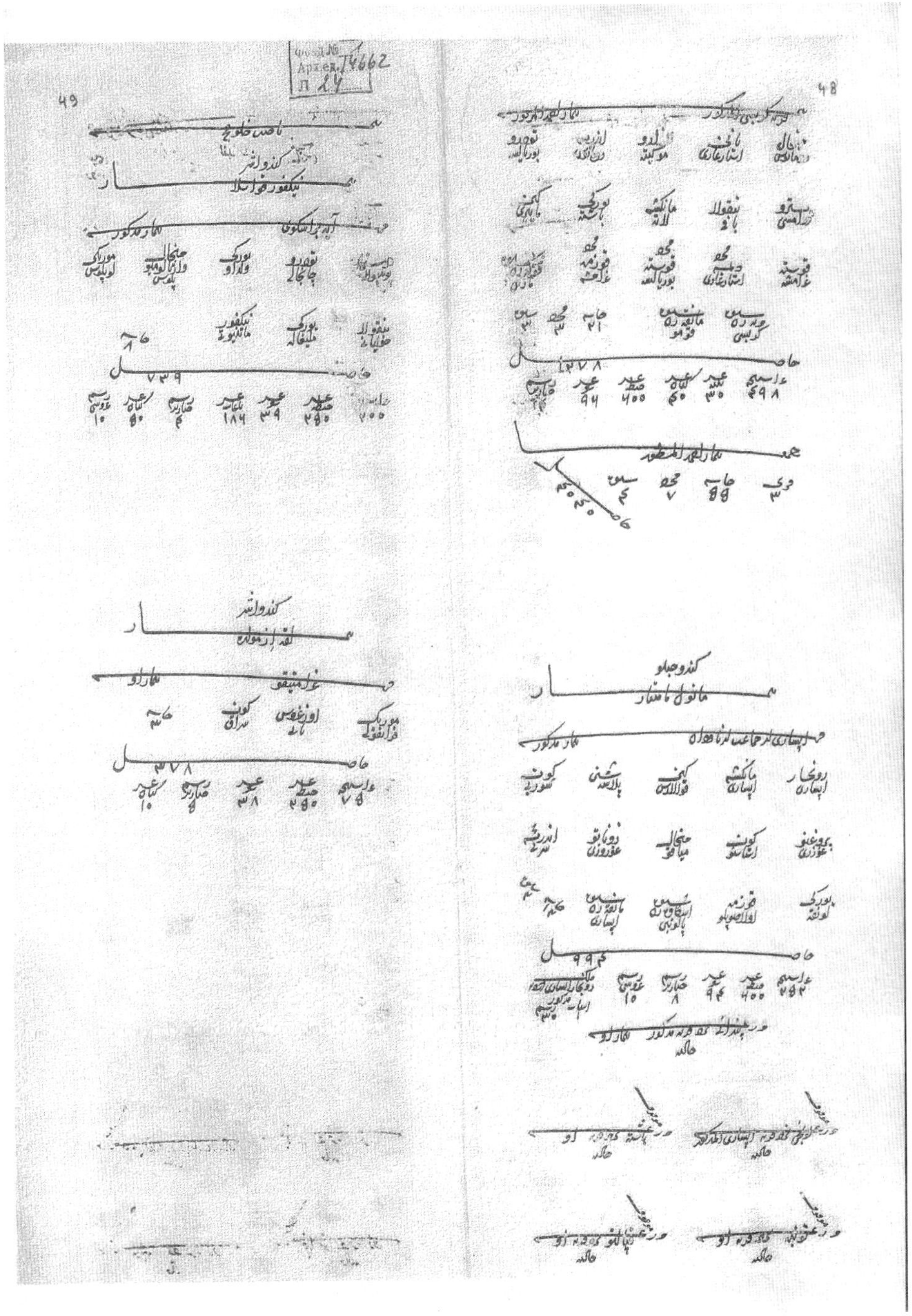

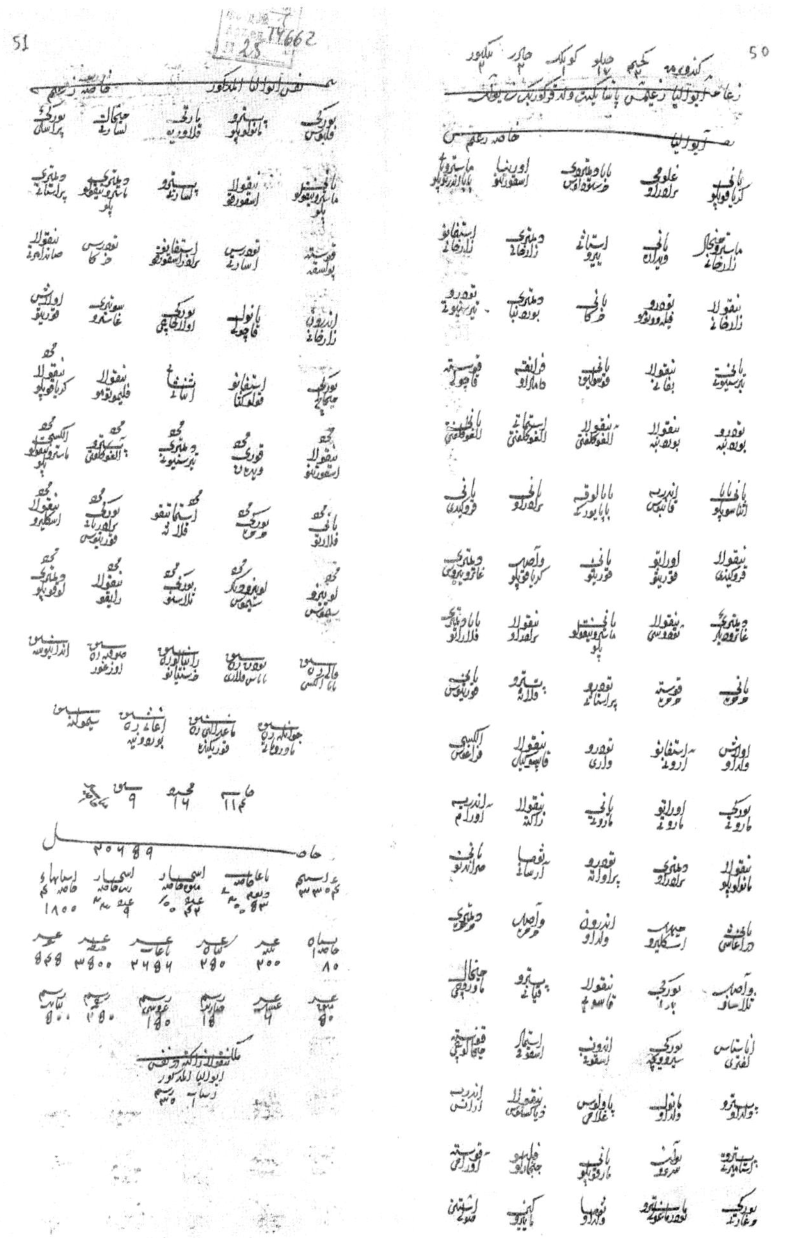

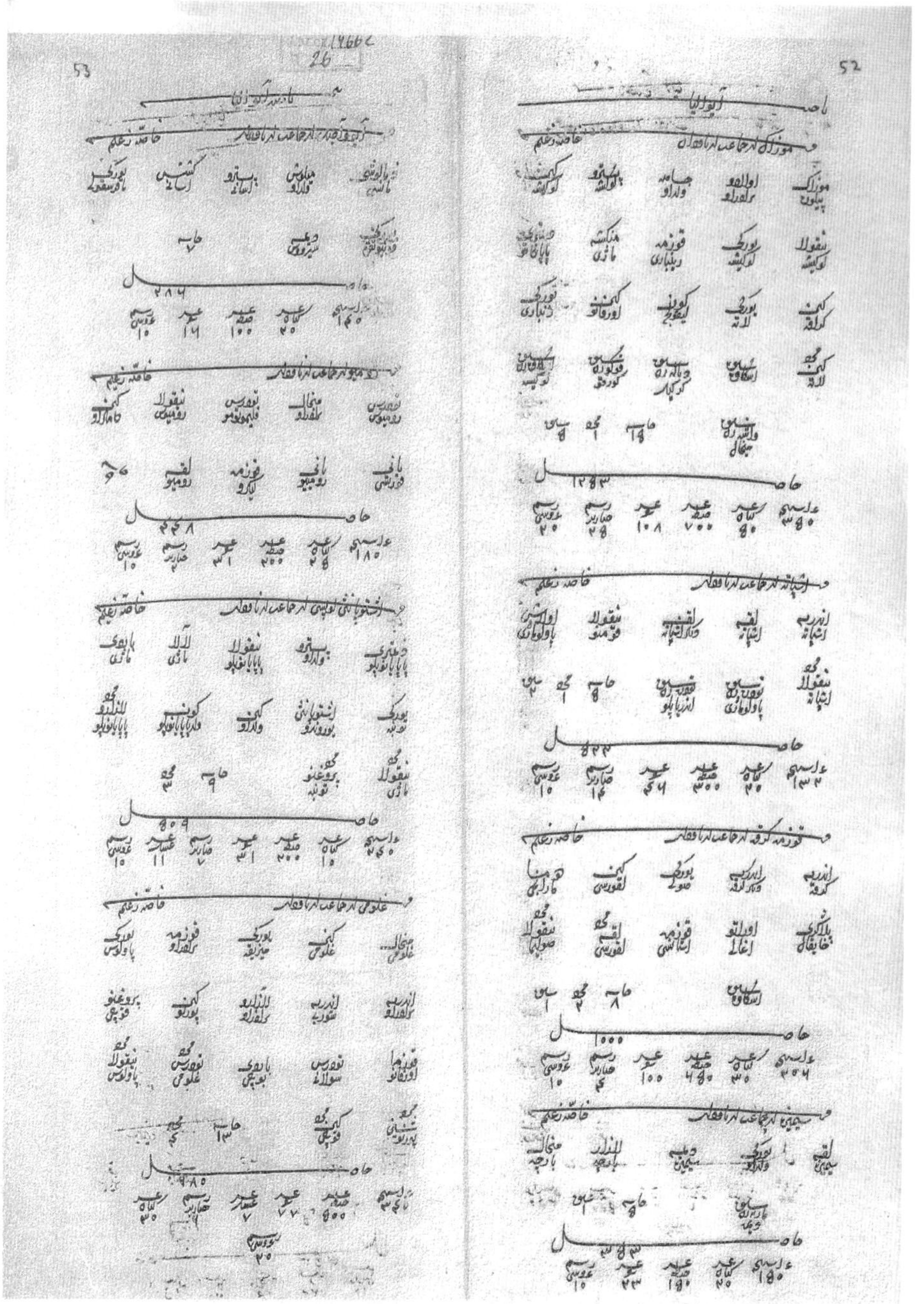

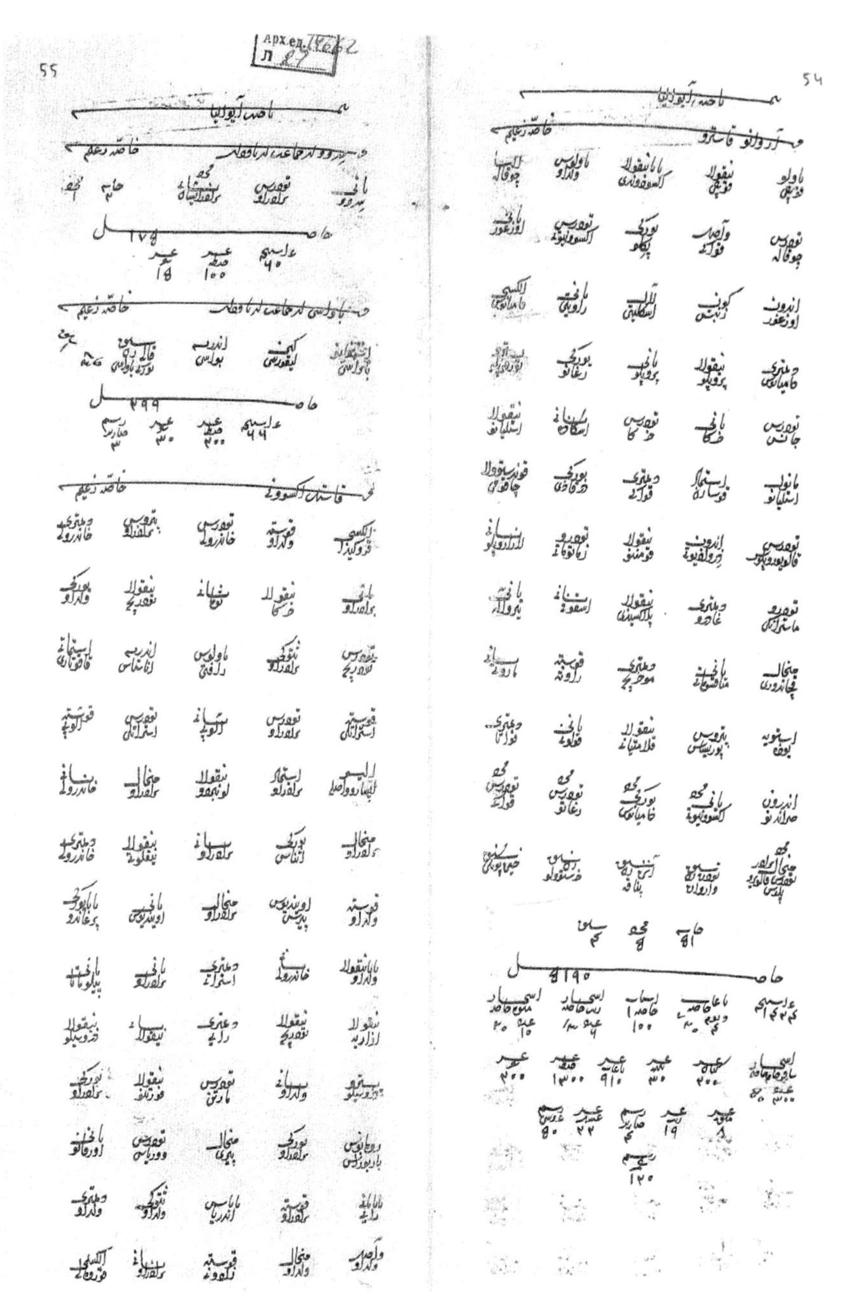

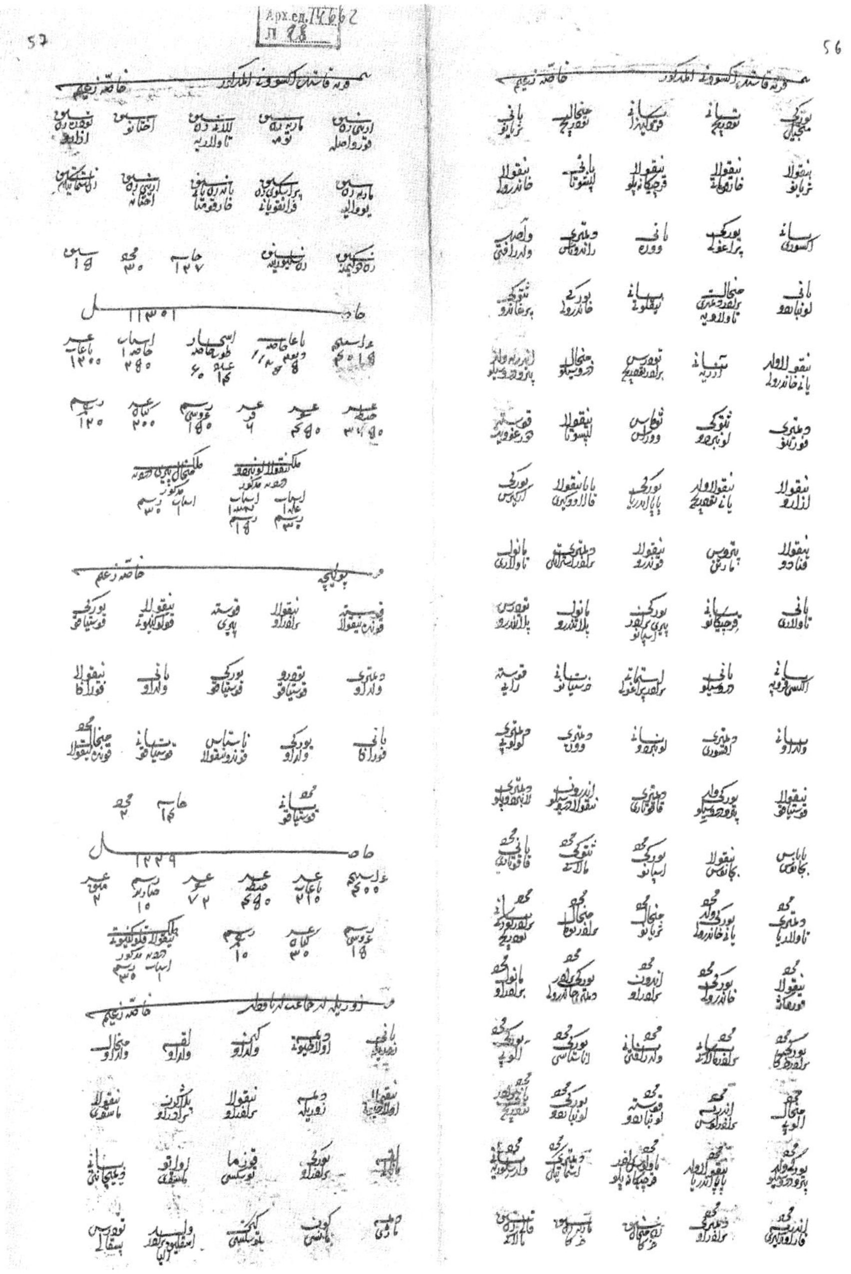

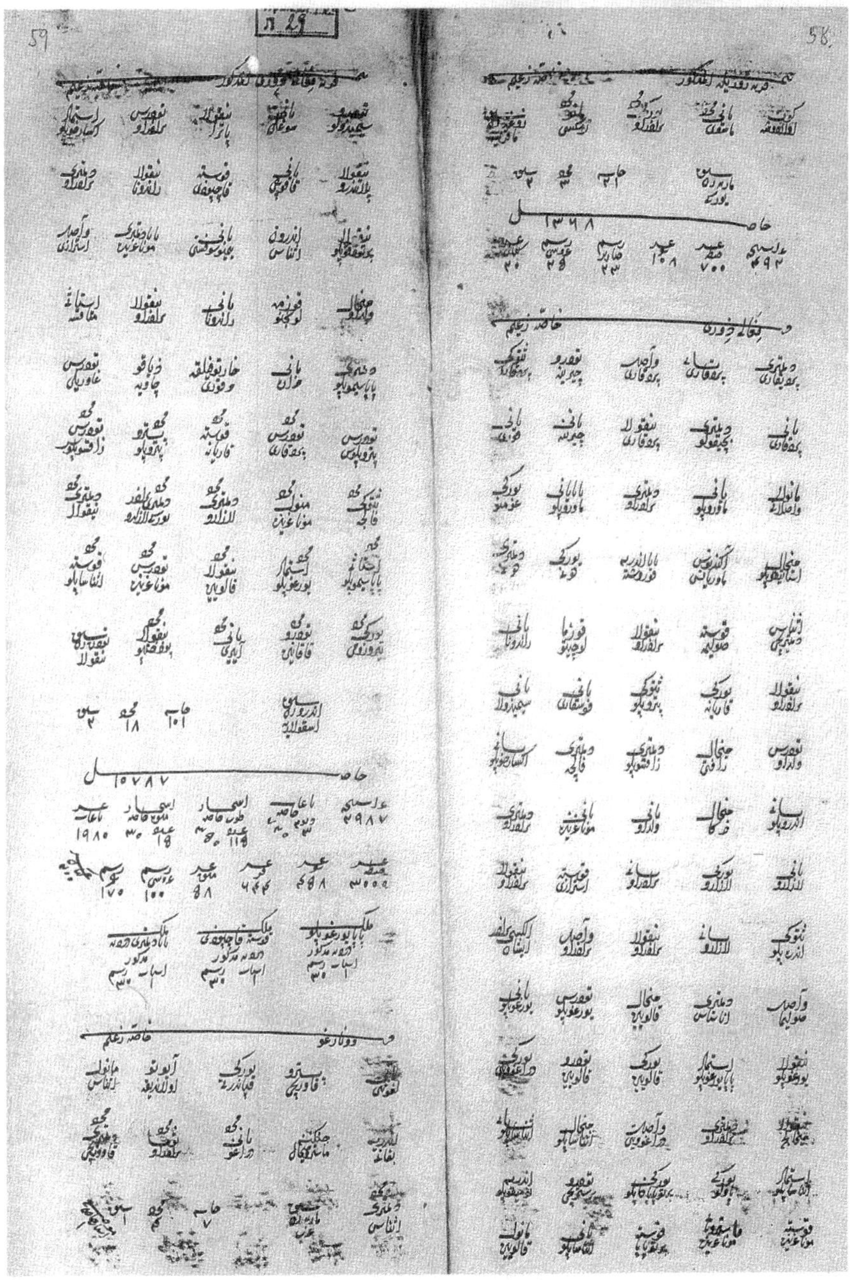

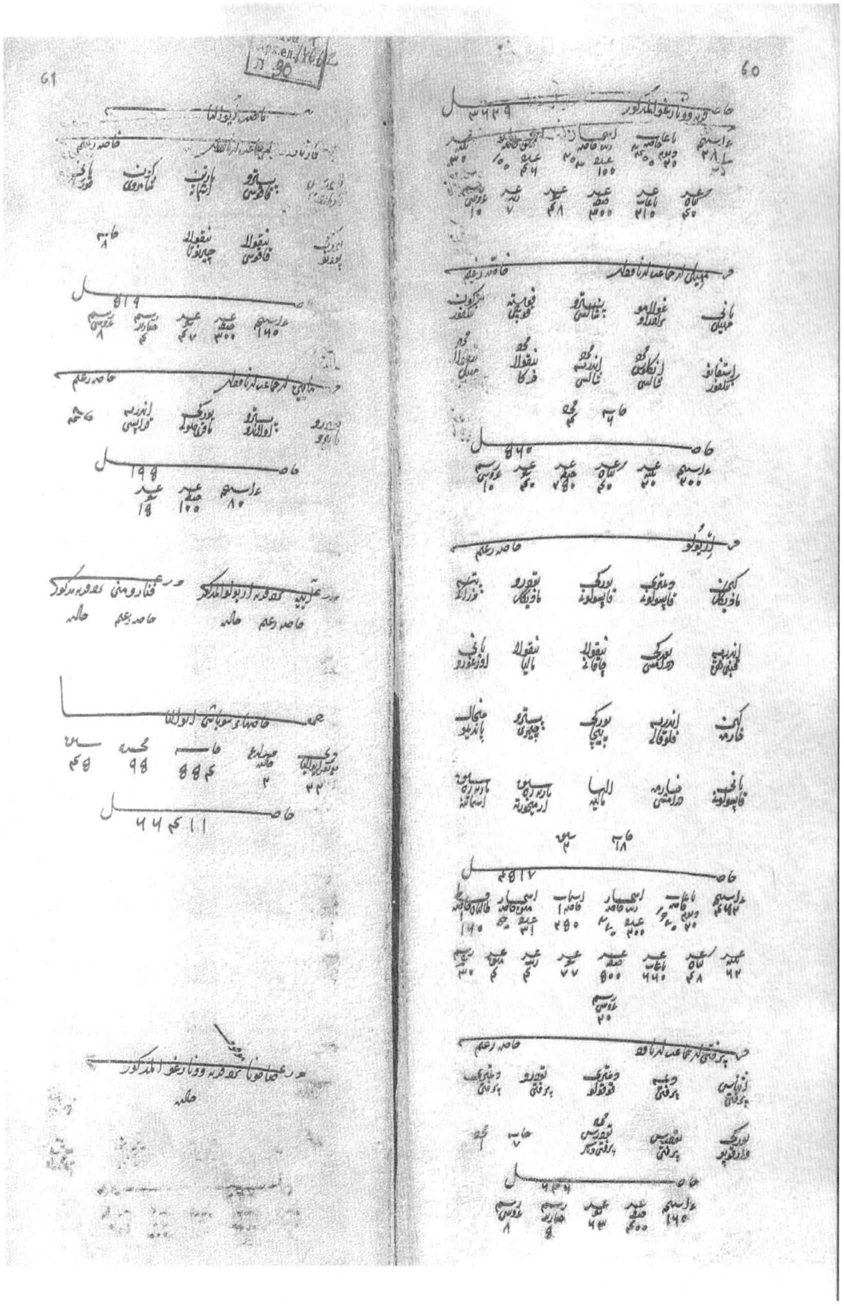

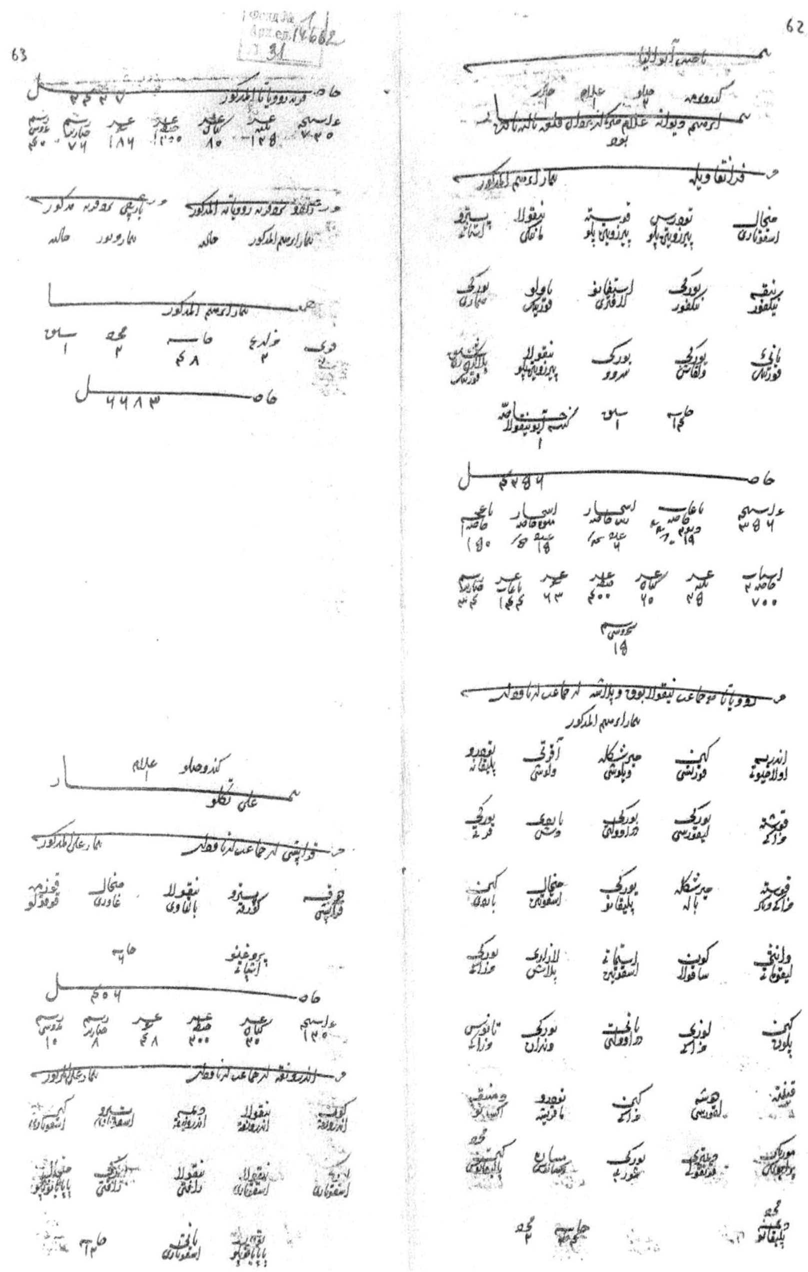

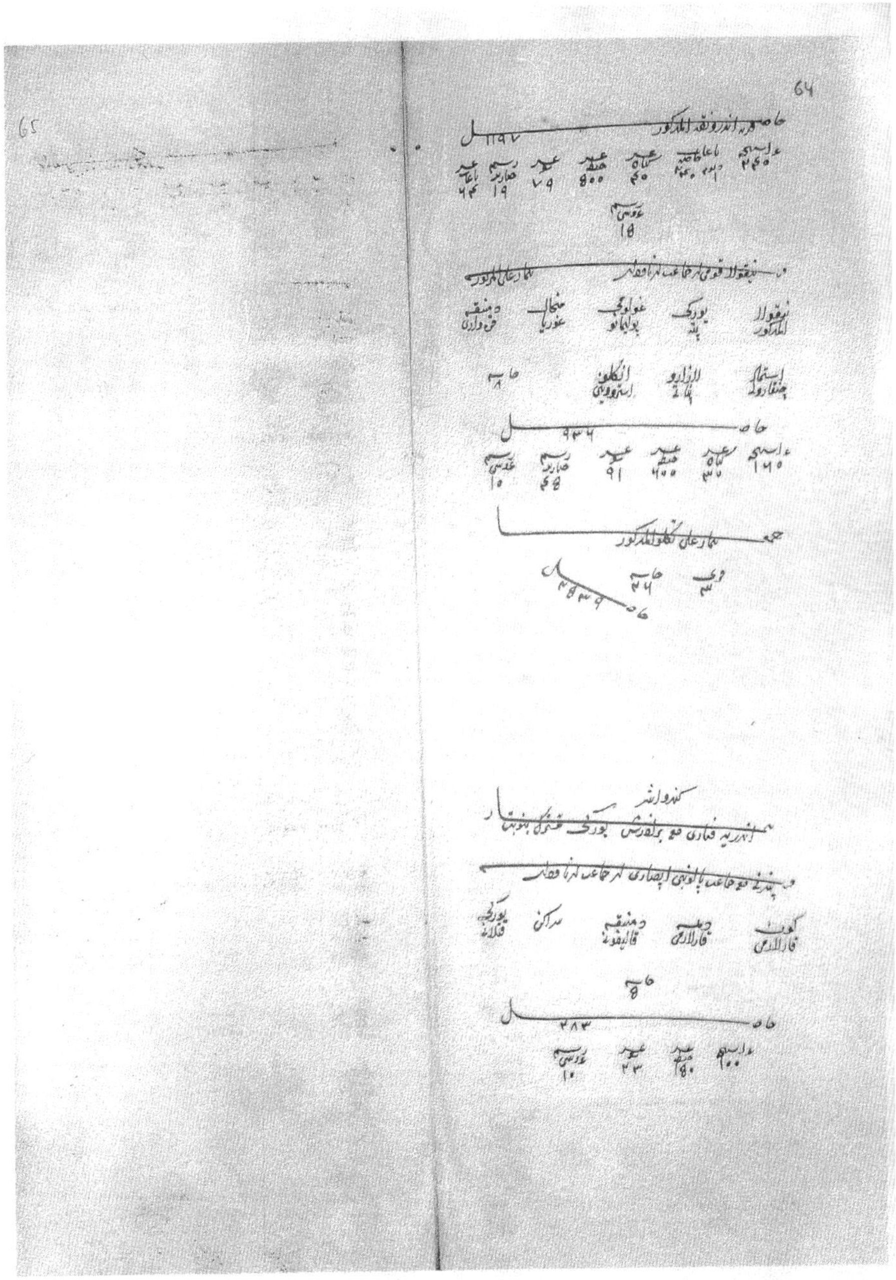

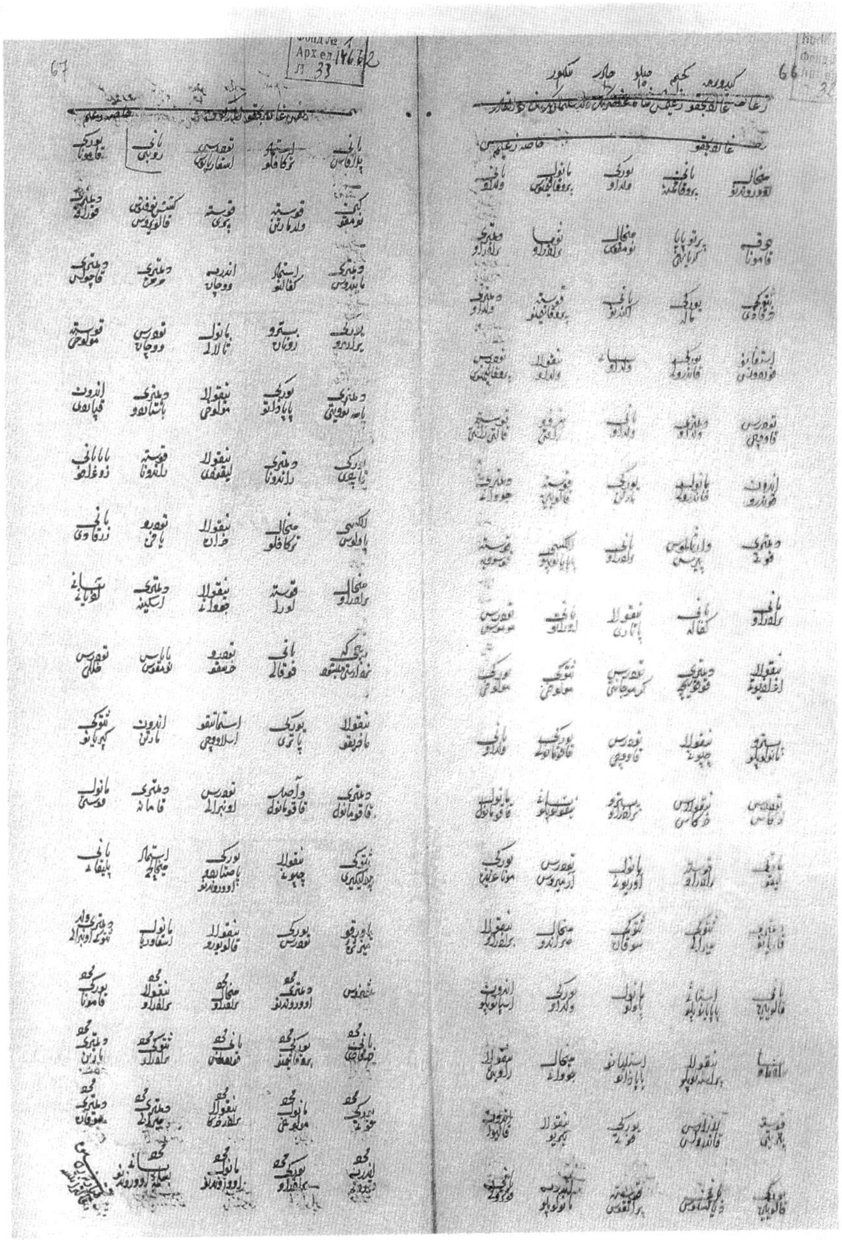

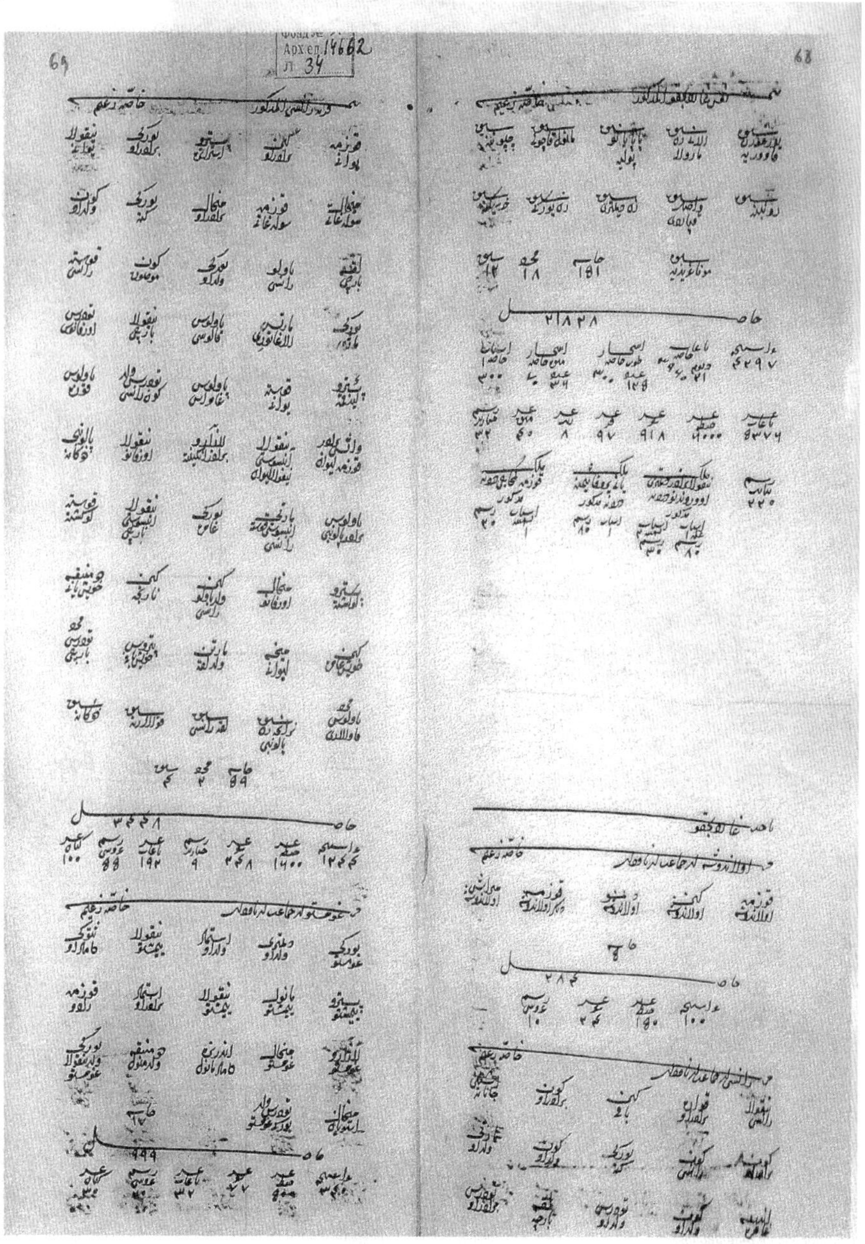

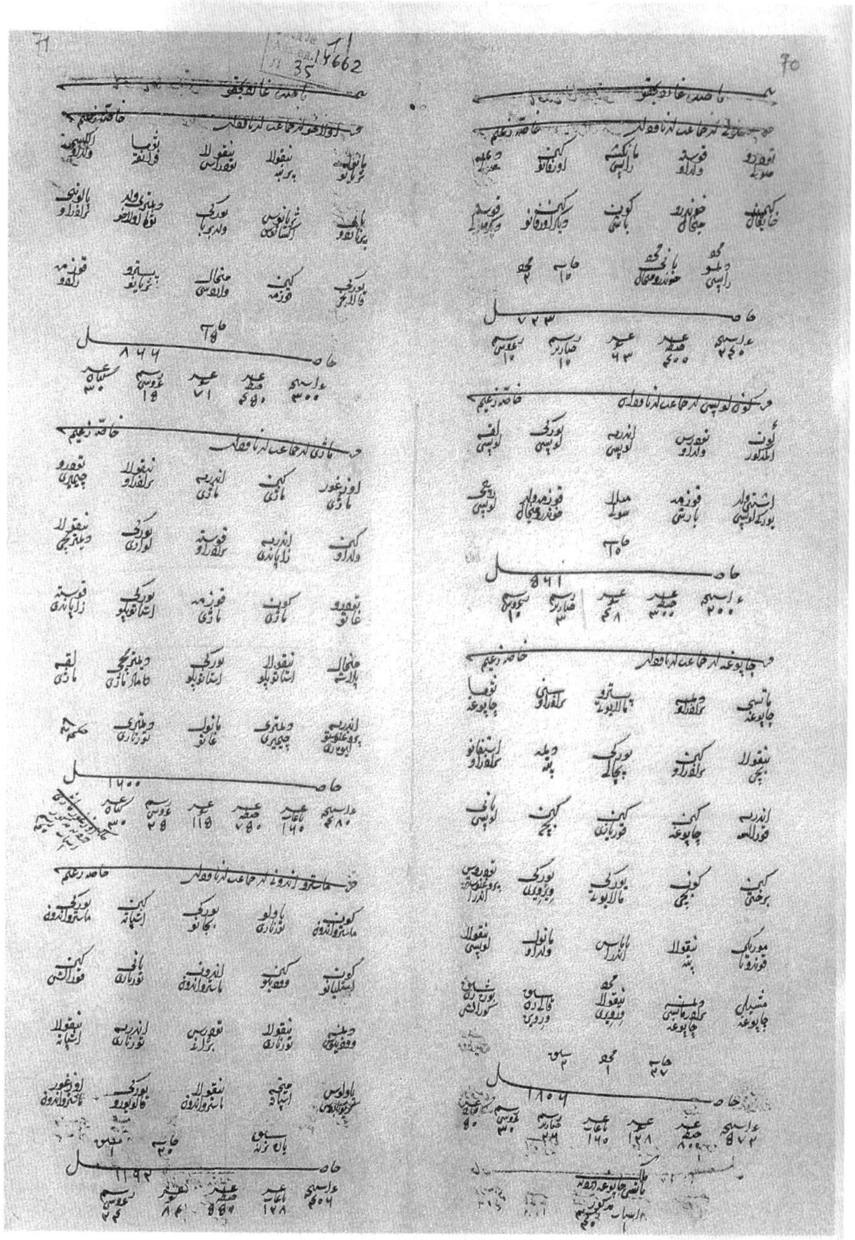

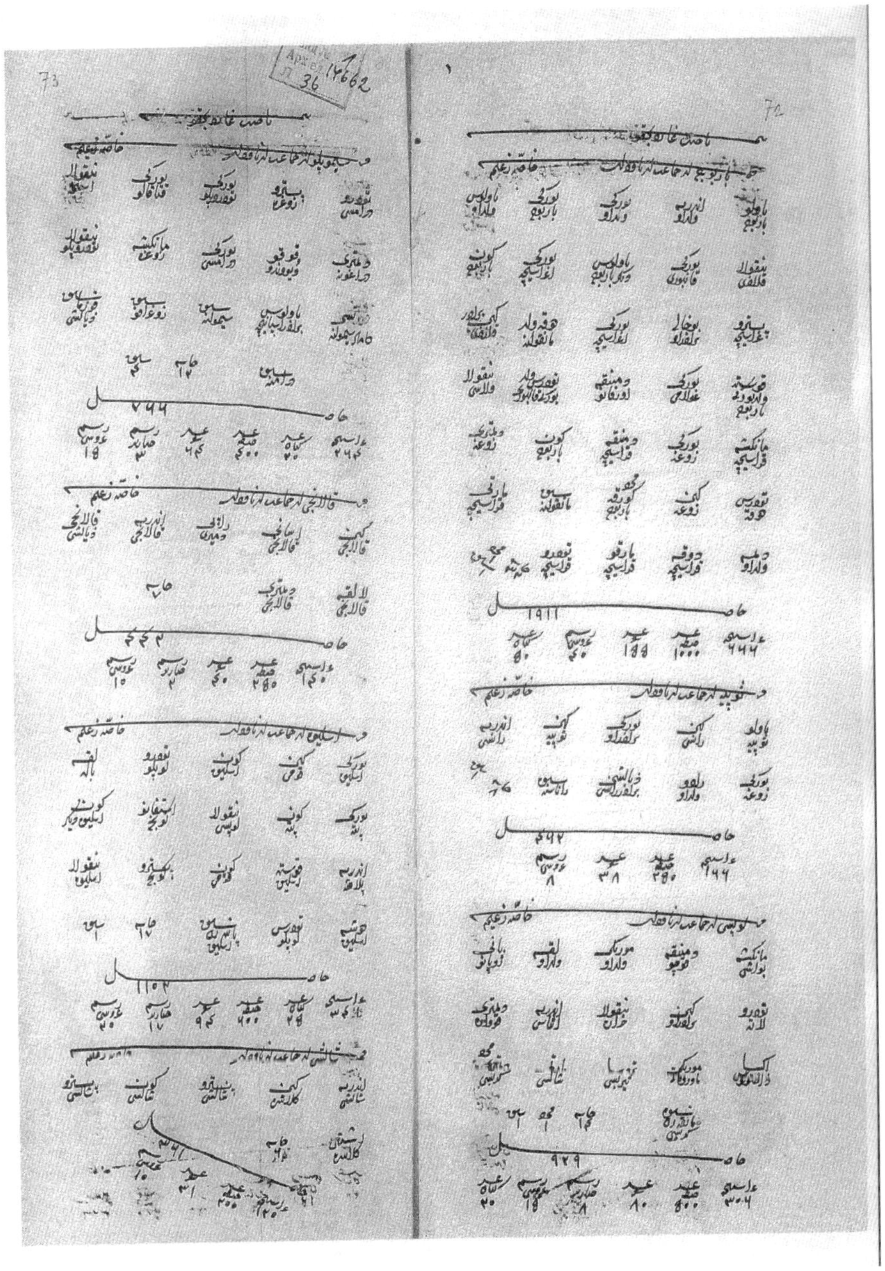
Арх.ед. 14662
Л 36

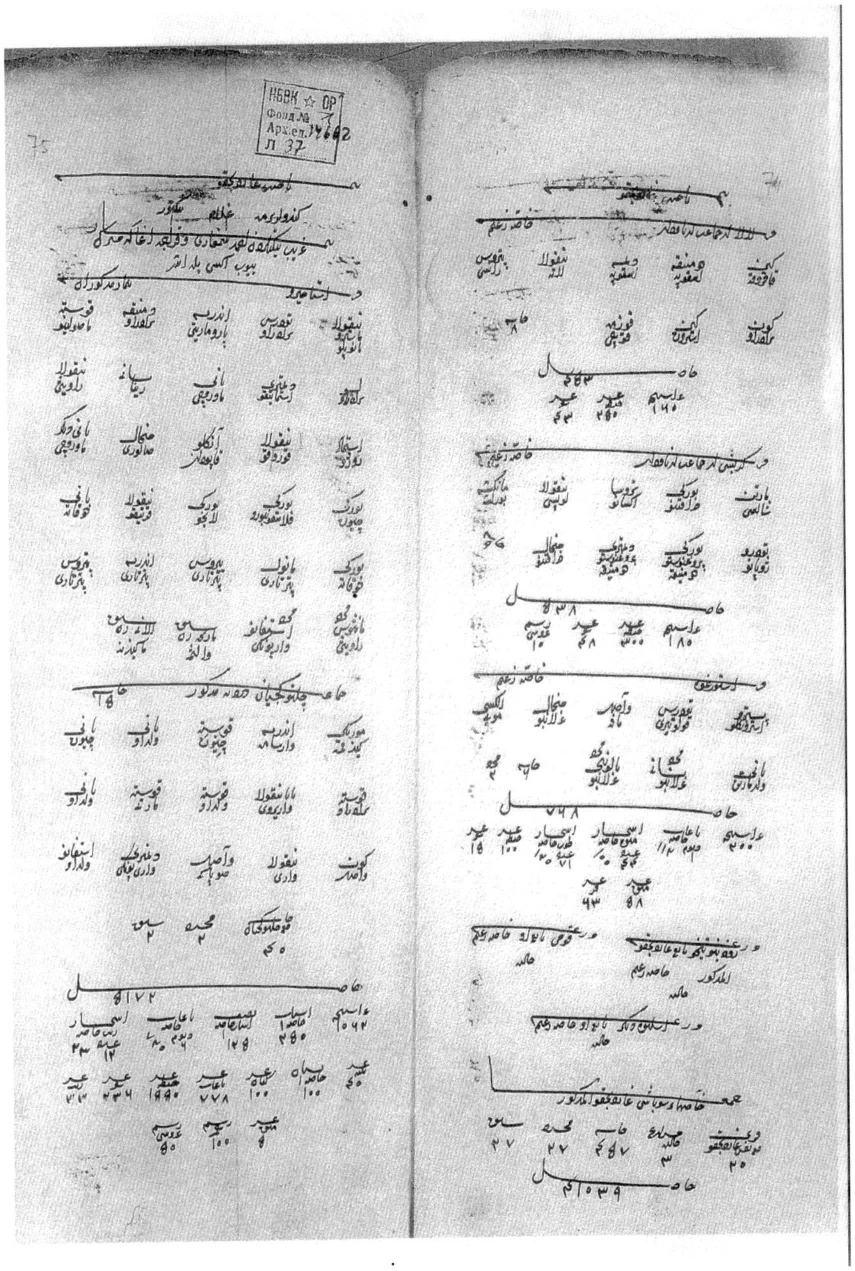
НБВК ☆ ОР
Фонд №
Арх.ед. 14662
Л 37

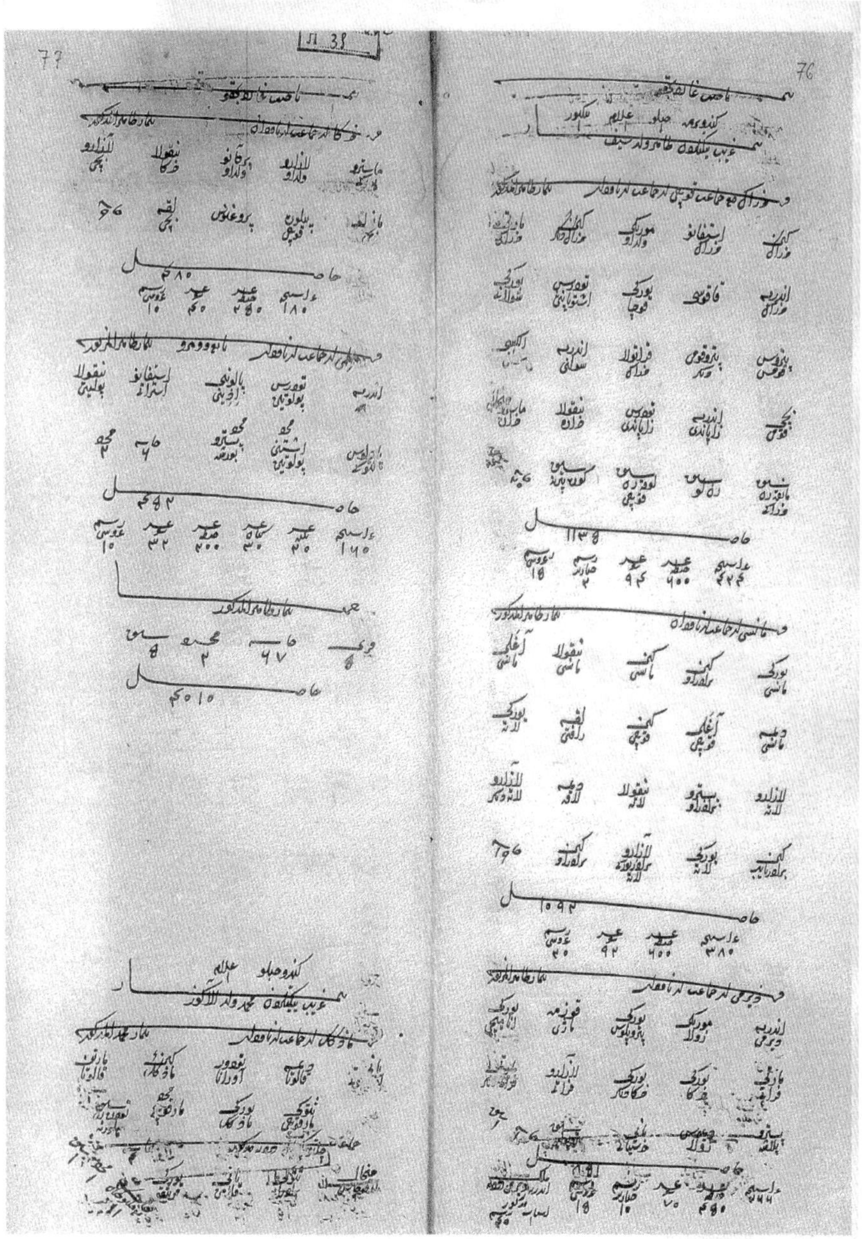

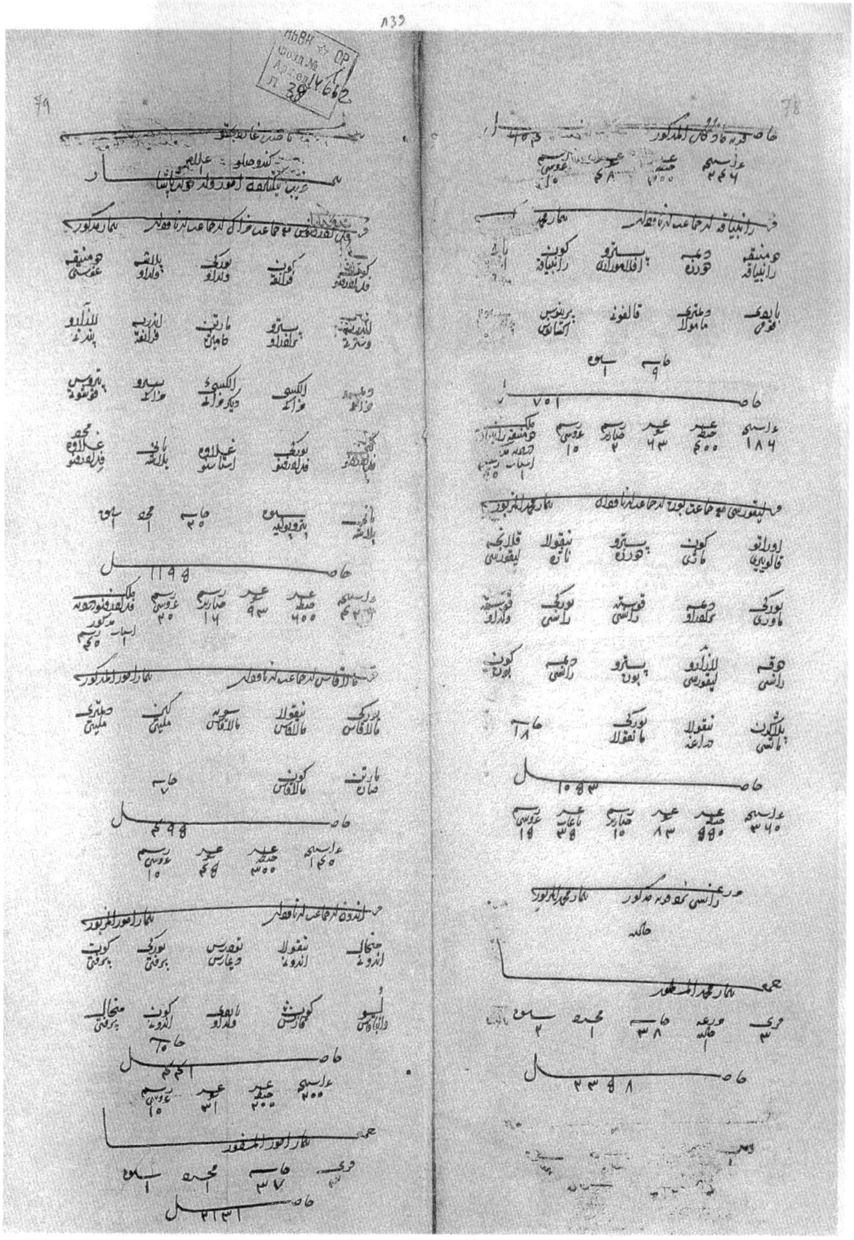

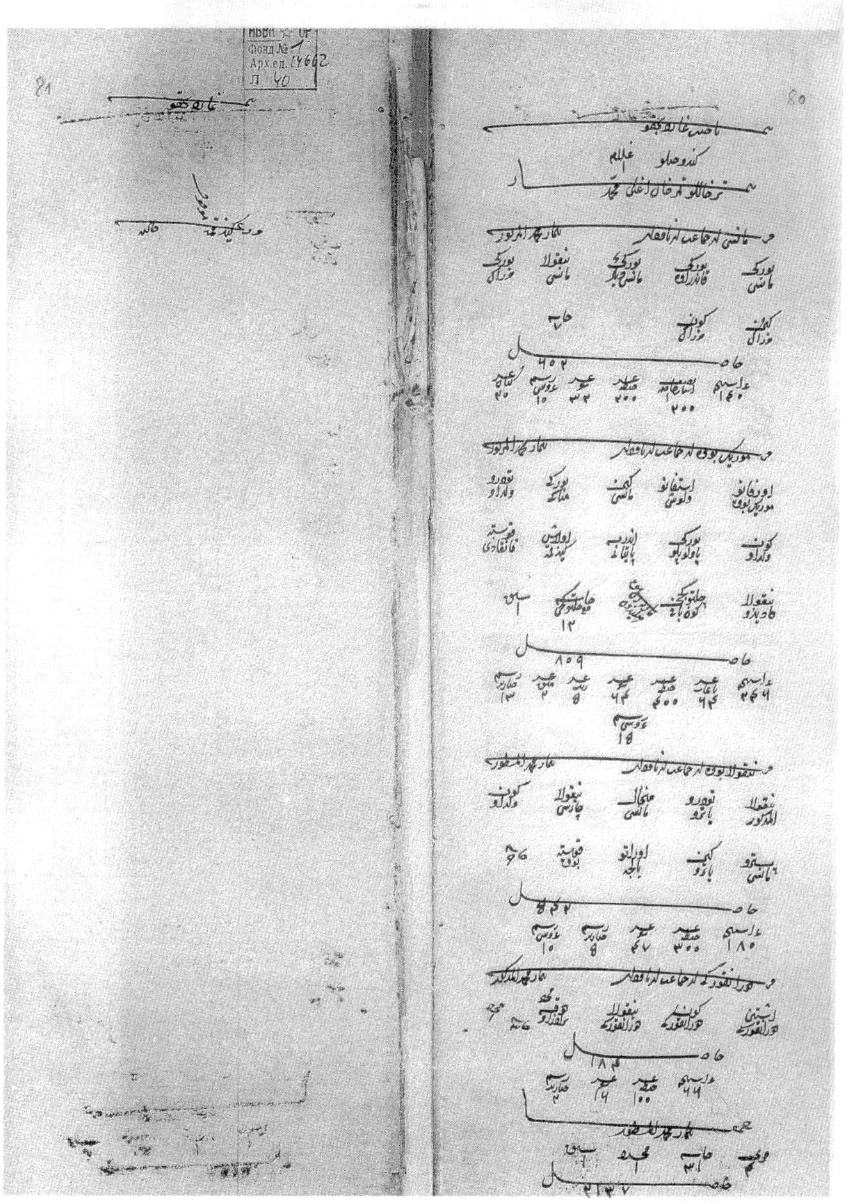

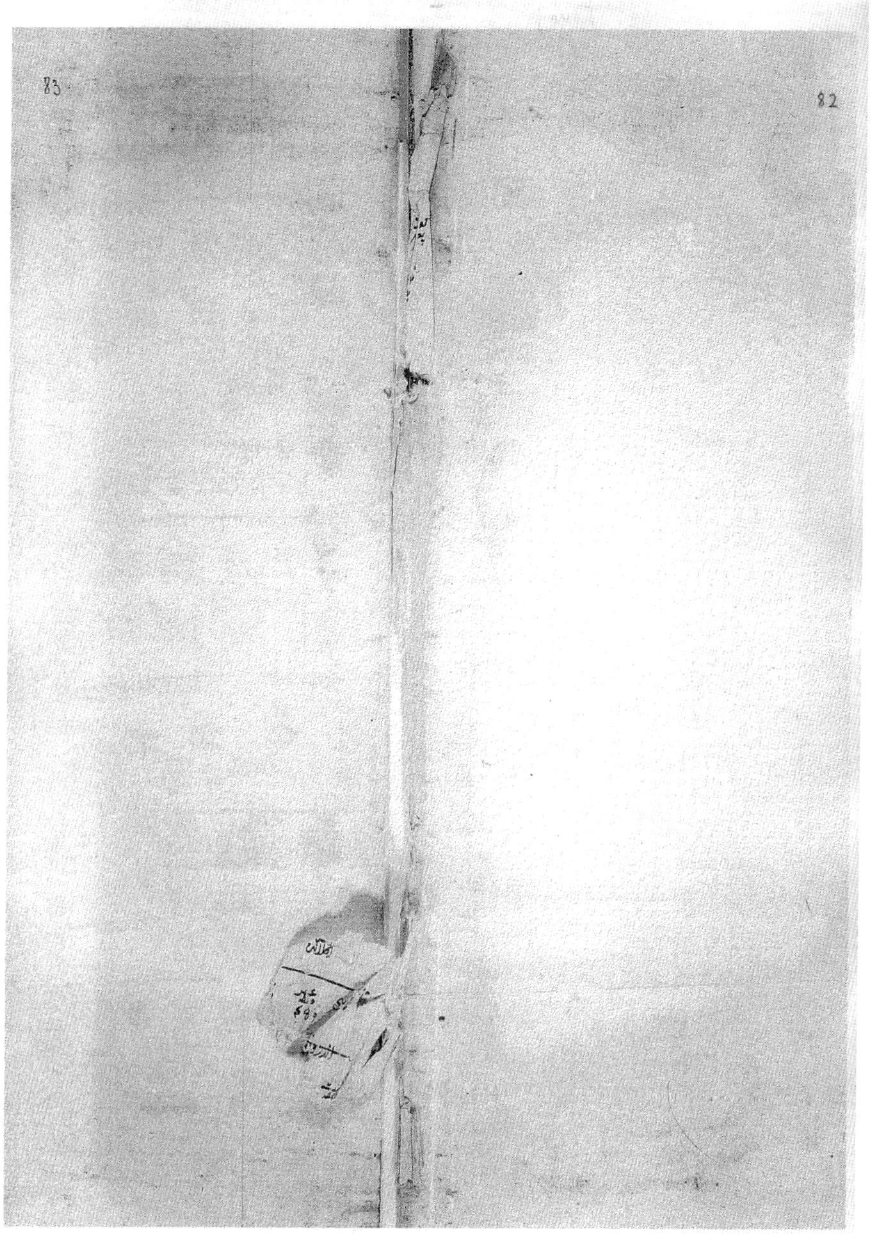

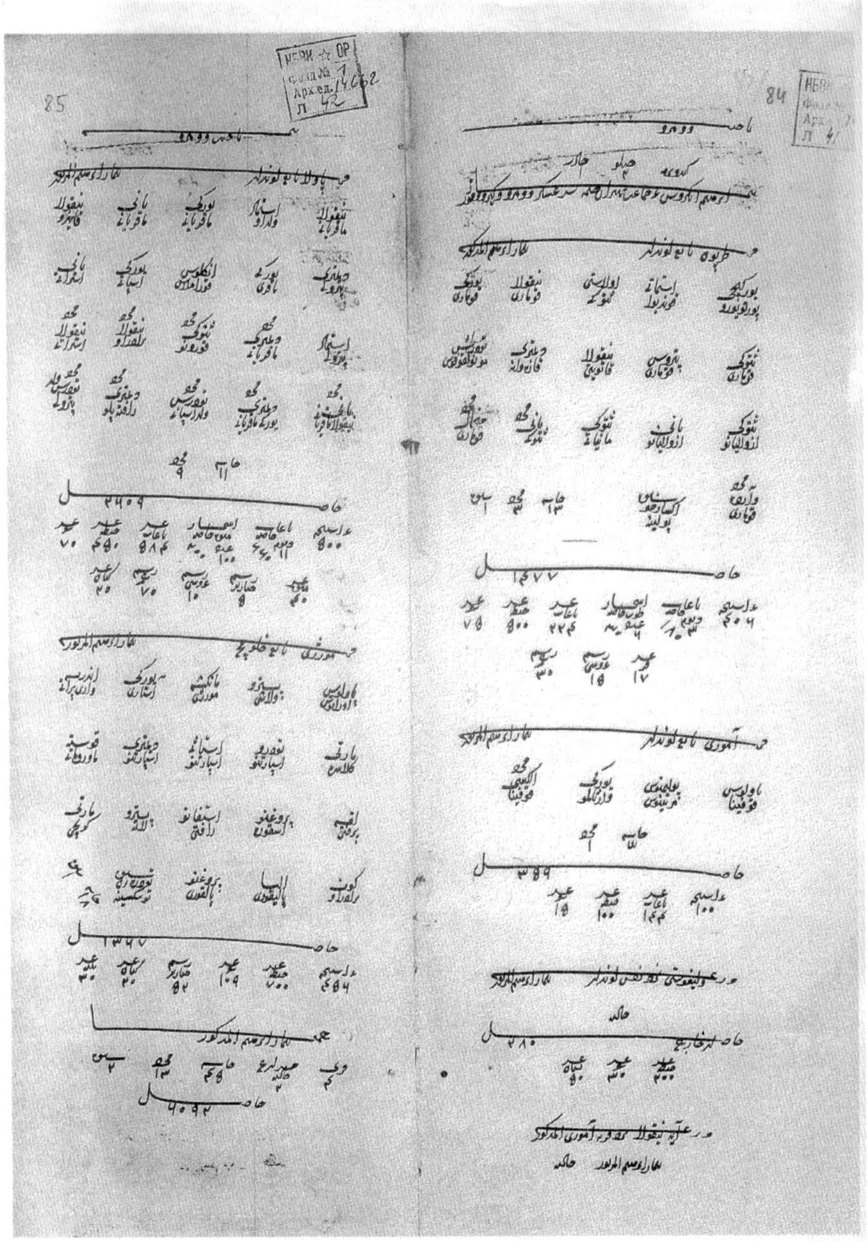

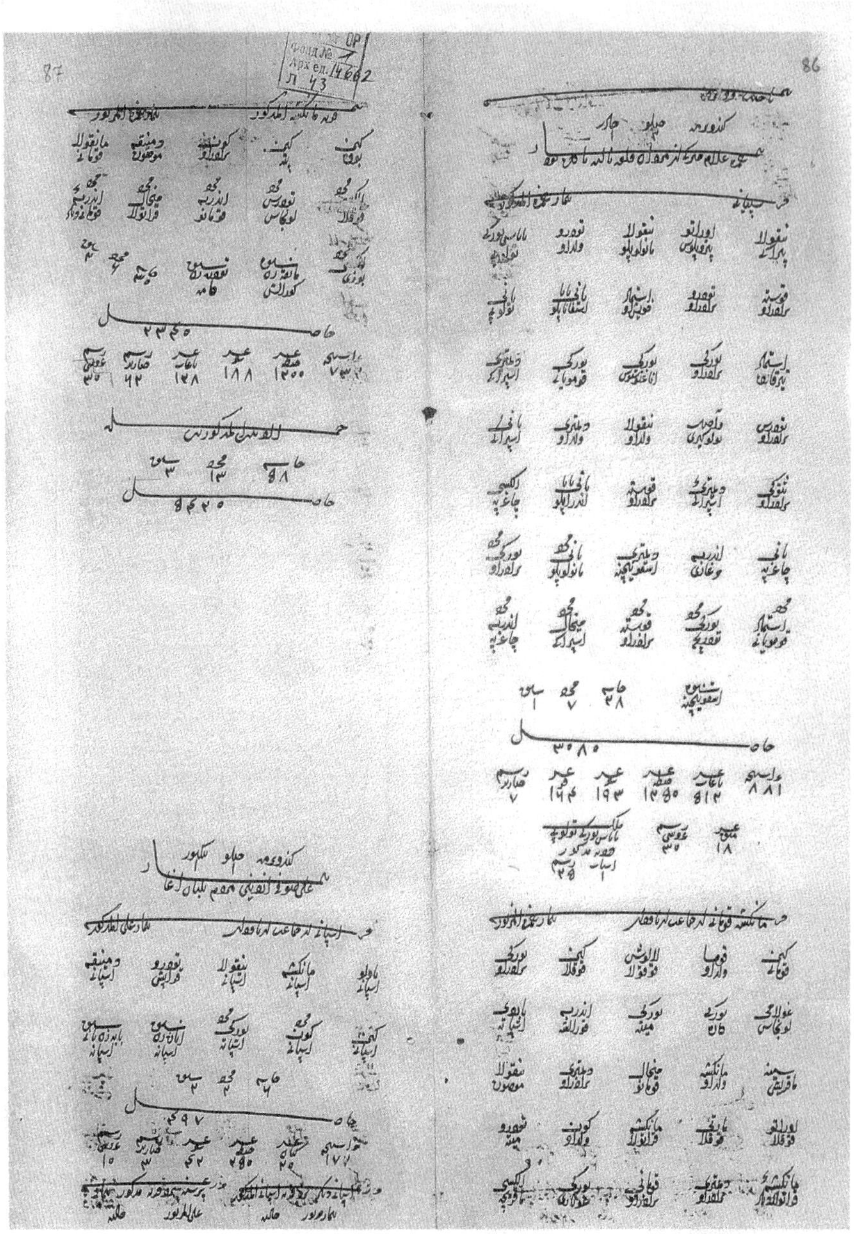

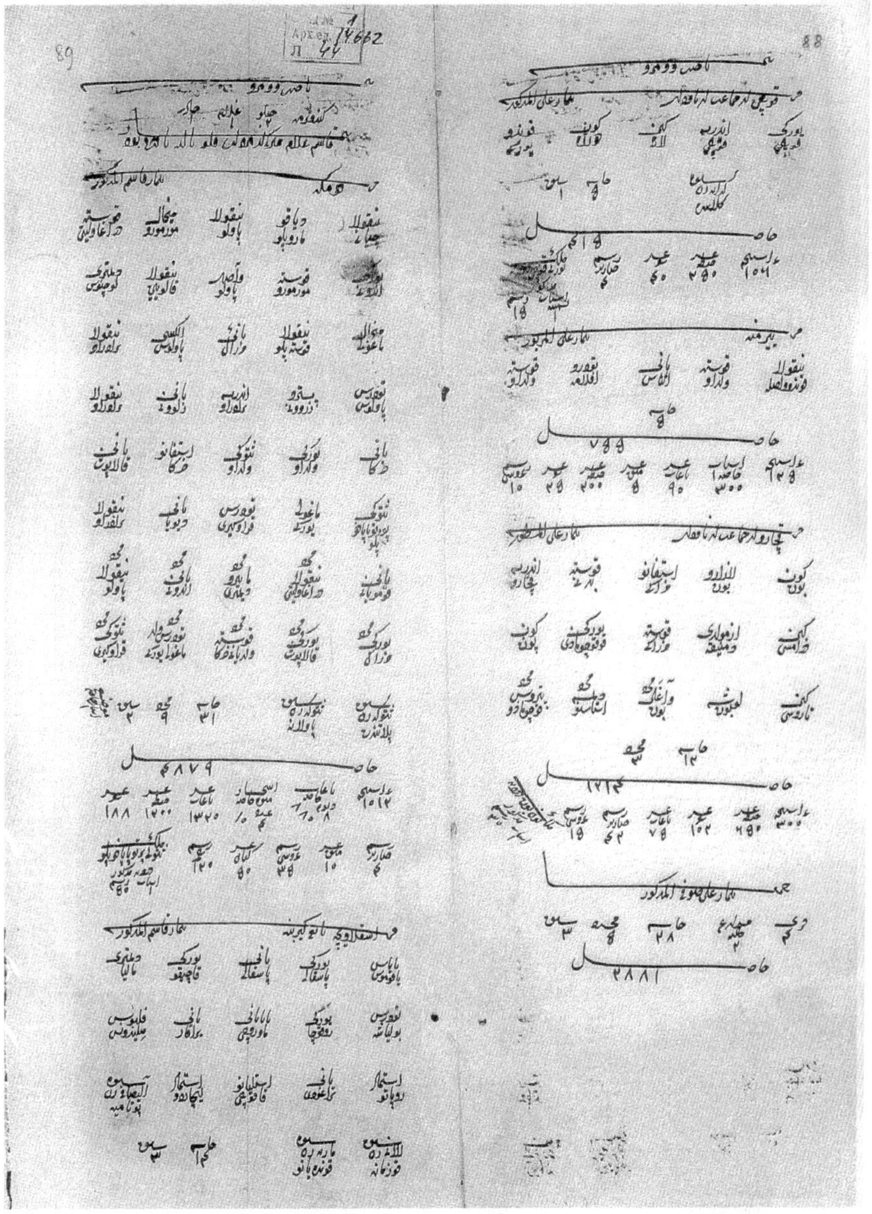

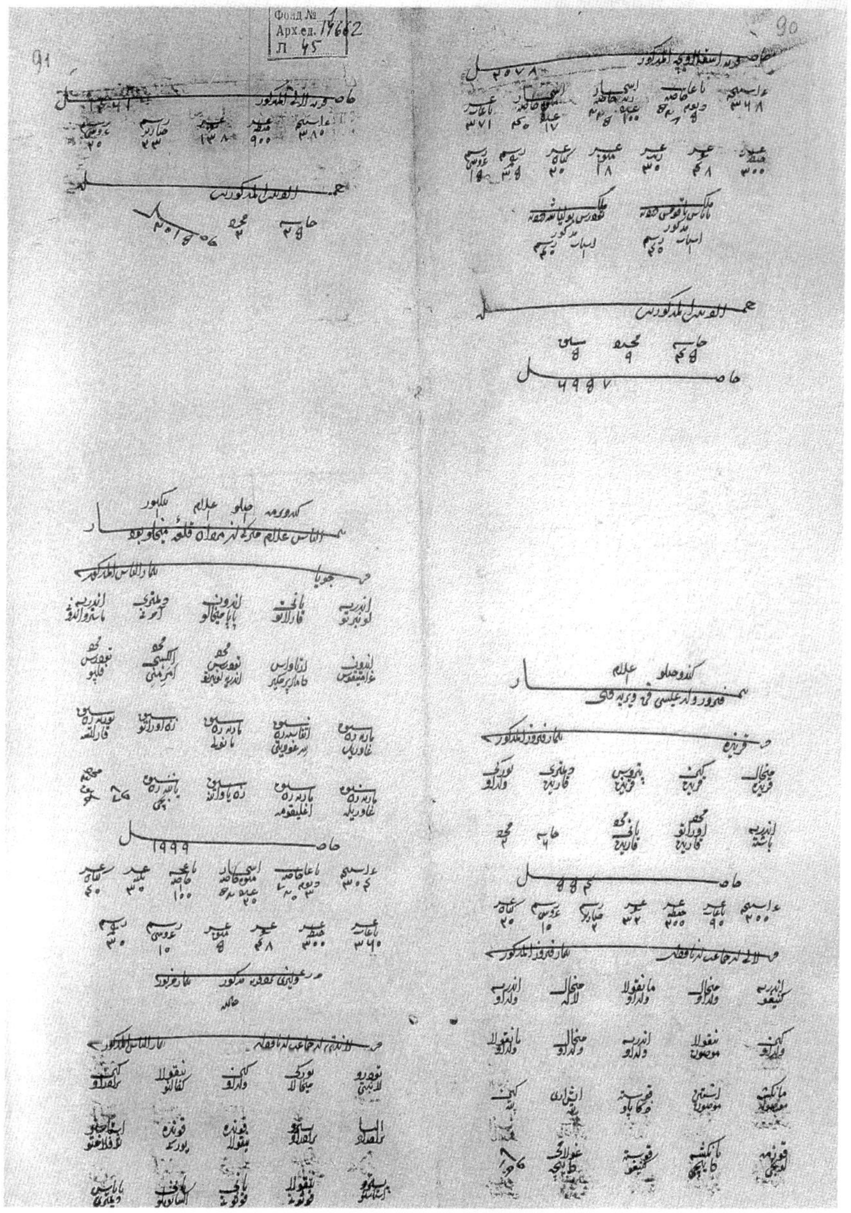

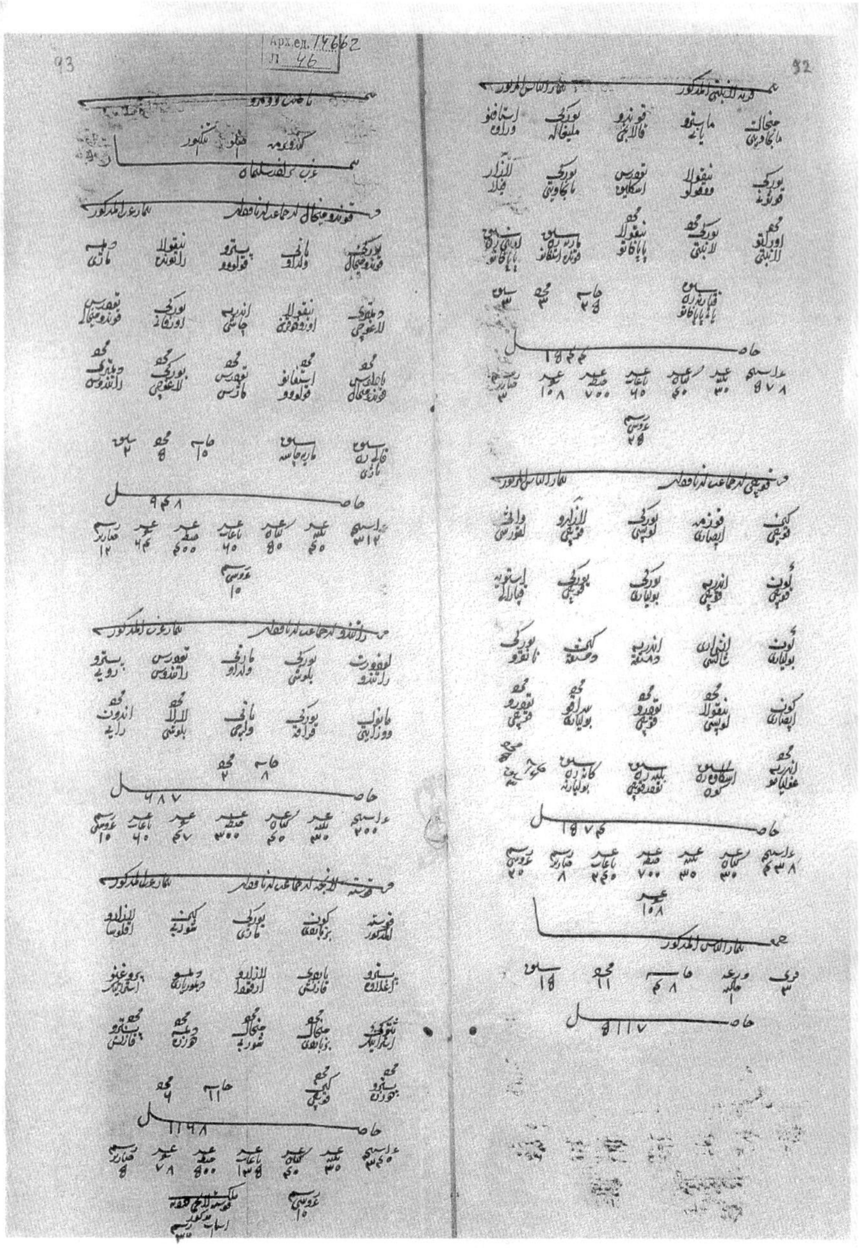
Арх.ед. 14662
п 46

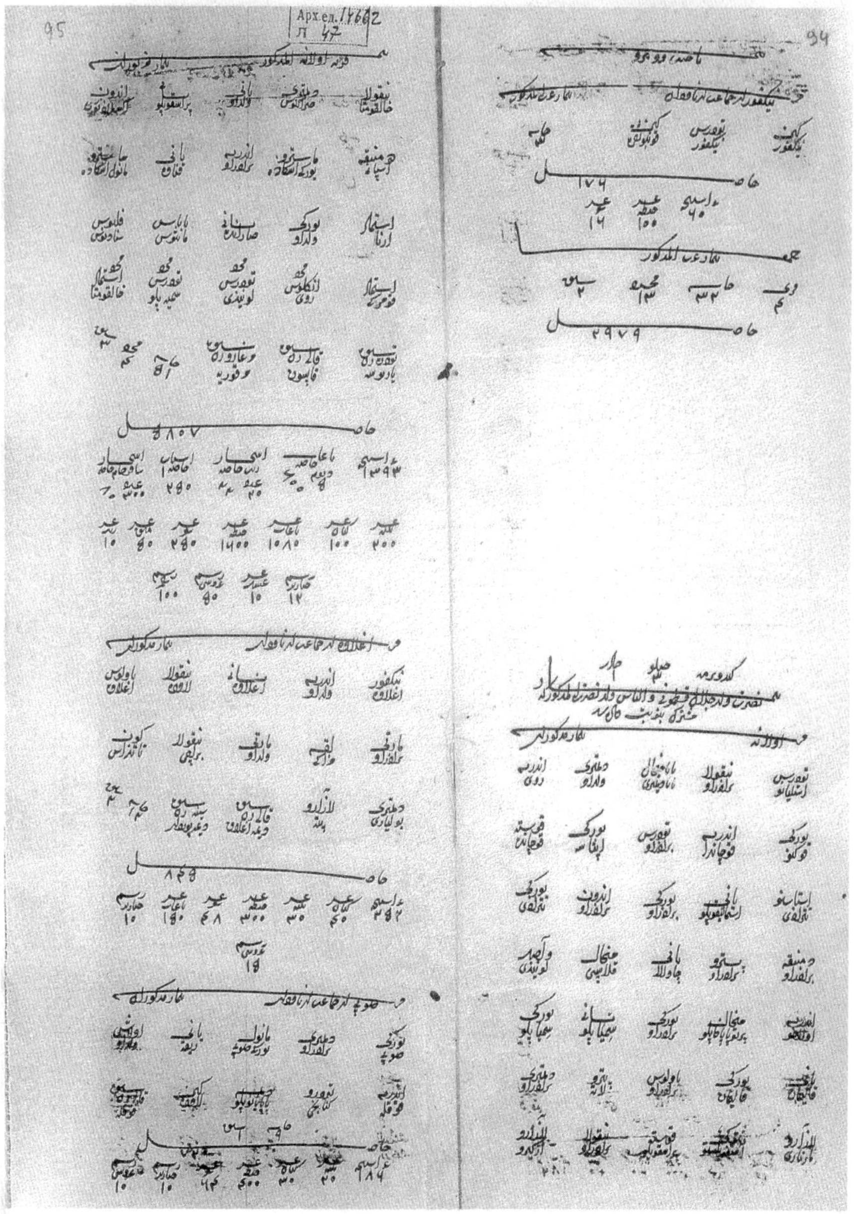
Арх.ед. 14662
п 47

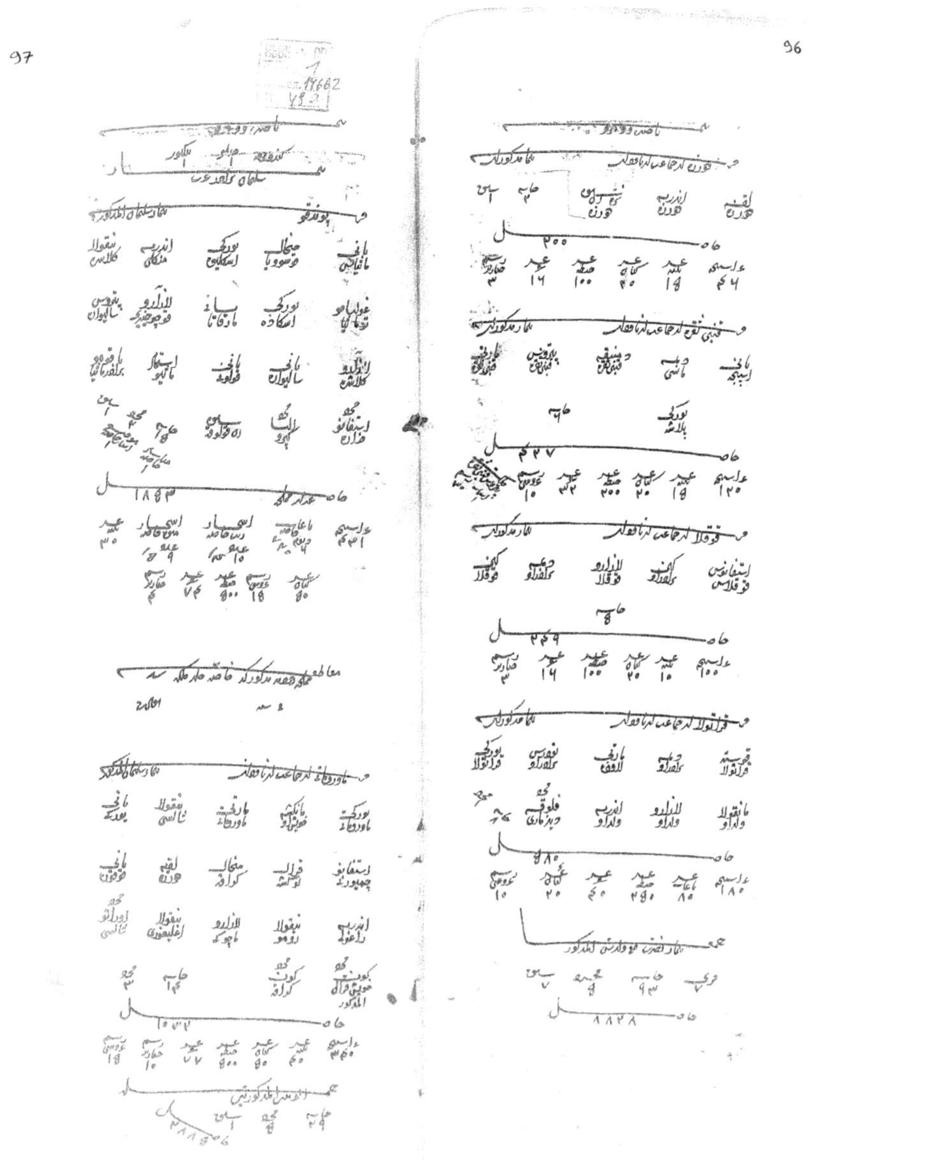

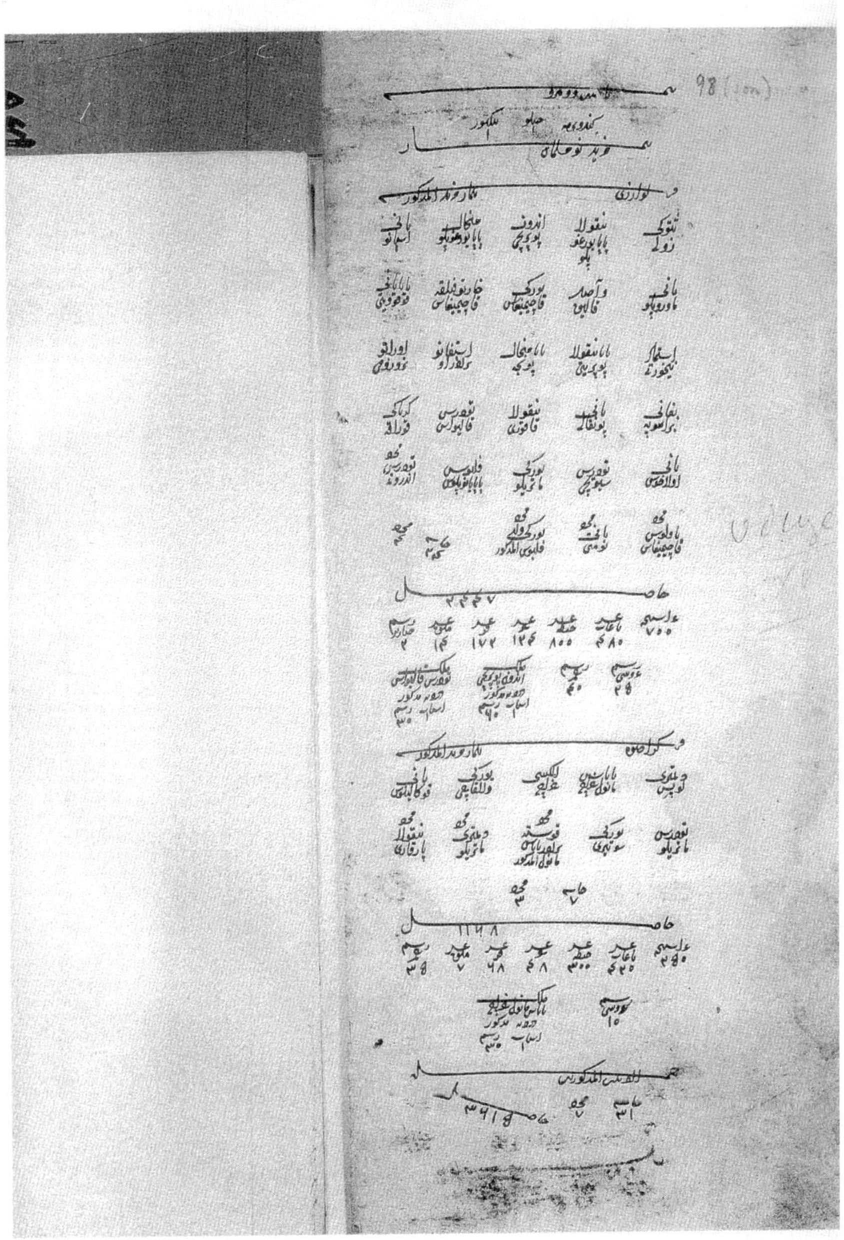